ENCYCLOPEDIA OF WORLD DRESS AND FASHION

Volume 3

The United States and Canada

ENCYCLOPEDIA WORLD

OF
DRESS
AND FASHION

Volume 3

The United States and Canada

Edited by Phyllis G. Tortora

OXFORD
UNIVERSITY PRESS

2010

Oxford University Press, Inc., publishes works that further
Oxford University's objective of excellence
in research, scholarship, and education.

Oxford   New York
Auckland   Cape Town   Dar es Salaam   Hong Kong   Karachi
Kuala Lumpur   Madrid   Melbourne   Mexico City   Nairobi
New Delhi   Shanghai   Taipei   Toronto

With offices in
Argentina   Austria   Brazil   Chile   Czech Republic   France   Greece
Guatemala   Hungary   Italy   Japan   Poland   Portugal   Singapore
South Korea   Switzerland   Thailand   Turkey   Ukraine   Vietnam

© Berg Publishers 2010

Published by Oxford University Press, Inc.
198 Madison Avenue, New York, NY 10016
http://www.oup.com/us/

Oxford is a registered trademark of Oxford University Press

Published simultaneously outside North America by Berg Publishers.

The Library of Congress Cataloging-in-Publication Data

Encyclopedia of world dress and fashion.

v. cm.

"Published simultaneously outside North America by Berg Publishers"–V. 1, t.p. verso.

"Available online as part of the Berg Fashion Library"–V. 1, t.p. verso.

Includes bibliographical references.

Contents: v. 1. Africa / editors, Joanne B. Eicher, Doran H. Ross – v. 2. Latin America and the Caribbean /
editor, Margot Blum Schevill ; consulting editor, Blenda Femenías – v. 3. The United States and Canada /
editor, Phyllis Tortora ; consultant, Joseph D. Horse Capture – v. 4. South Asia and Southeast Asia /
editor, Jasleen Dhamija – v. 5. Central and Southwest Asia / editor, Gillian Vogelsang-Eastwood –
v. 6. East Asia / editor, John Vollmer – v. 7. Australia, New Zealand, and the Pacific Islands /
editor, Margaret Maynard – v. 8. West Europe / editor, Lise Skov ; consulting editor, Valerie Cumming –
v. 9. East Europe, Russia, and the Caucasus / editor, Djurdja Bartlett ; assistant editor, Pamela Smith –
v. 10. Global perspectives / editor, Joanne B. Eicher ; assistant editor, Phyllis Tortora.

ISBN 978-0-19-537733-0 (hbk.)

1. Clothing and dress–Encyclopedias.   I. Eicher, Joanne Bubolz.   II. Oxford University Press.

GT507.E54   2010
391.003—dc22   2010008843

ISBN 978-0-19-975728-2 (vol. 1)
ISBN 978-0-19-975729-9 (vol. 2)
ISBN 978-0-19-975730-5 (vol. 3)
ISBN 978-0-19-975731-2 (vol. 4)
ISBN 978-0-19-975732-9 (vol. 5)
ISBN 978-0-19-975733-6 (vol. 6)
ISBN 978-0-19-975734-3 (vol. 7)
ISBN 978-0-19-975735-0 (vol. 8)
ISBN 978-0-19-975736-7 (vol. 9)
ISBN 978-0-19-975737-4 (vol. 10)

1   3   5   7   9   8   6   4   2

This Encyclopedia is available online as part of the Berg Fashion Library.
For further information see www.bergfashionlibrary.com.

Typeset by Apex CoVantage, Madison, WI.
Printed in the USA by Courier Companies Inc., Westford, MA.

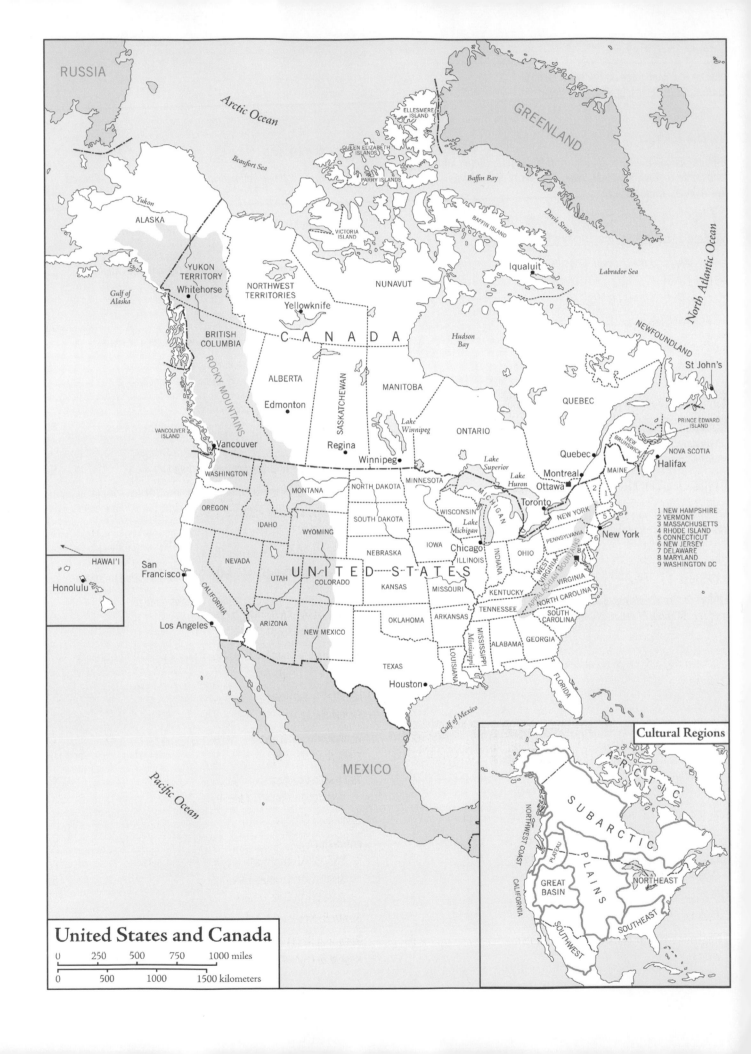

RUSSIA

Arctic Ocean

GREENLAND

Beaufort Sea

ELLESMERE
ISLAND

QUEEN ELIZABETH
ISLANDS

Baffin Bay

Yukon

ALASKA

PARRY ISLANDS

VICTORIA
ISLAND

BAFFIN ISLAND

Davis Strait

YUKON
TERRITORY

Whitehorse

NORTHWEST
TERRITORIES

Yellowknife

C A N A D A

Labrador Sea

Iqaluit

*Hudson
Bay*

NEWFOUNDLAND

North Atlantic Ocean

*Gulf of
Alaska*

BRITISH
COLUMBIA

ROCKY MOUNTAINS

ALBERTA

Edmonton

SASKATCHEWAN

MANITOBA

*Lake
Winnipeg*

ONTARIO

QUEBEC

St John's

PRINCE EDWARD
ISLAND

VANCOUVER
ISLAND

Vancouver

WASHINGTON

Regina

Winnipeg

NORTH DAKOTA

*Lake
Superior*

*Lake
Huron*

MINNESOTA

MICHIGAN

NEW
BRUNSWICK

Quebec

Montreal

Ottawa

Toronto

NOVA SCOTIA

Halifax

MAINE

2

1

OREGON

IDAHO

MONTANA

SOUTH DAKOTA

WISCONSIN

*Lake
Michigan*

IOWA

NEW YORK

PENNSYLVANIA

3

5

New York

1 NEW HAMPSHIRE
2 VERMONT
3 MASSACHUSETTS
4 RHODE ISLAND
5 CONNECTICUT
6 NEW JERSEY
7 DELAWARE
8 MARYLAND
9 WASHINGTON DC

WYOMING

NEBRASKA

Chicago

ILLINOIS

INDIANA

OHIO

WEST
VIRGINIA

APPALACHIAN MOUNTAINS

6

8

9

HAWAI'I

San
Francisco

Honolulu

NEVADA

UTAH

COLORADO

KANSAS

MISSOURI

KENTUCKY

VIRGINIA

CALIFORNIA

UNITED STATES

NORTH CAROLINA

ARIZONA

NEW MEXICO

OKLAHOMA

ARKANSAS

TENNESSEE

SOUTH
CAROLINA

Los Angeles

MISSISSIPPI

ALABAMA

GEORGIA

TEXAS

LOUISIANA

Houston

FLORIDA

Gulf of Mexico

MEXICO

Pacific Ocean

Cultural Regions

A R C T I C

S U B A R C T I C

NORTHWEST COAST

PLATEAU

P L A I N S

NORTHEAST

CALIFORNIA

GREAT
BASIN

SOUTHEAST

SOUTHWEST

United States and Canada

| 0 | 250 | 500 | 750 | 1000 miles |

| 0 | 500 | 1000 | 1500 kilometers |

Contents

Contributors

Thomas S. Abler, *University of Waterloo, Canada*

Cynthia Amnéus, *Cincinnati Art Museum, United States*

Pamela C. Baker, *Touch of Culture, Canada*

Christina Bates, *Canadian Museum of Civilization, Canada*

José Blanco F., *University of Georgia, United States*

Linda Boynton Arthur, *Washington State University, United States*

Nancy O. Bryant, *Oregon State University, United States*

Sandra Stansbery Buckland, *University of Akron, United States*

Kathryn B. Bunn-Marcuse, *University of Washington, United States*

Usha Chowdhary, *Central Michigan University, United States*

Cynthia Cooper, *McCord Museum of Canadian History, Canada*

Patricia A. Cunningham, *The Ohio State University, United States*

Kitty Dickerson, *University of Missouri, United States*

Carol Anne Dickson, *University of Hawai'i, United States*

Jean L. Druesedow, *Kent State University Museum, United States*

Angela Durante, *York University, Canada*

Jenny Ellison, *York University, Canada*

Mary H. Farahnakian, *Brigham Young University, United States*

Jane Farrell-Beck, *Iowa State University, United States*

Judy Zaccagnini Flynn, *Framingham State College, United States*

Helen Bradley Foster, *Independent Scholar, United States*

Catherine S. Fowler, *University of Nevada, Reno, United States*

Colleen Gau, *Independent Scholar, United States*

Beverly Gordon, *University of Wisconsin–Madison, United States*

Steven L. Grafe, *Maryhill Museum of Art, United States*

Adriana Greci Green, *Northern Michigan University, United States*

Jana M. Hawley, *Kansas State University, United States*

Michèle Hayeur Smith, *Rhode Island School of Design, United States*

Jason Baird Jackson, *Indiana University, United States*

Sara J. Kadolph, *Iowa State University, United States*

Susan B. Kaiser, *University of California, Davis, United States*

Martha Ladly, *Ontario College of Art and Design, Canada*

Ryan Looysen, *University of California, Davis, United States*

Elizabeth D. Lowe, *Queens College, City University of New York, United States*

Annette Lynch, *University of Northern Iowa, United States*

Nora M. MacDonald, *West Virginia University, United States*

Sara B. Marcketti, *Iowa State University, United States*

Susan O. Michelman, *University of Kentucky, United States*

Kimberly Miller-Spillman, *University of Kentucky, United States*

Josephine M. Moreno, *University of California, Berkeley, United States*

Nan H. Mutnick, *Marymount College–Tarrytown, United States*

Gwendolyn S. O'Neal, *University of North California at Greensboro, United States*

Jo Paoletti, *University of Maryland, United States*

Nancy J. Parezo, *University of Arizona, United States*

Jean L. Parsons, *Iowa State University, United States*

Birgit Pauksztat, *Rijksuniversiteit Groningen, Netherlands*

Sandra Price, *Freelance Writer, Curator and Textile Artist, Canada*

Andy Reilly, *Northern Illinois University, United States*

David W. Rickman, *Consultant and Independent Scholar, United States*

Rob Schorman, *Miami University, United States*

Elizabeth Semmelhack, *Bata Shoe Museum, Canada*

Eric K. Silverman, *Wheelock College, United States and Brandeis University, United States*

Susan L. Sokolowski, *Nike, Inc., United States*

Jo Ann C. Stabb, *University of California, Davis, United States*

Celia Stall-Meadows, *Oklahoma State University–Tulsa, United States*

Mitchell D. Strauss, *University of Northern Iowa, United States*

Joyce M. Szabo, *University of New Mexico, United States*

Jenna Tedrick Kuttruff, *Louisiana State University, United States*

Judy Thompson, *Canadian Museum of Civilization, Canada*

Phyllis G. Tortora, *Queens College, City University of New York, United States*

Heather Van Wormer, *Grand Valley State University, United States*

Patricia Campbell Warner, *University of Massachusetts, United States*

Susan M. Watkins, *Cornell University, United States*

Linda Welters, *University of Rhode Island, United States*

Laurel Wilson, *University of Missouri, United States*

Therèsa M. Winge, *Indiana University, United States*

Encyclopedia Preface

The *Encyclopedia of World Dress and Fashion* covers a fundamental and universal human activity relating to personal and social identity—the vast topic of how more than six billion people dress across the globe. To accomplish this, the first nine volumes are organized geographically, and the tenth addresses global issues. The approach throughout is both cross-cultural and multidisciplinary and allows readers to appreciate the richness and complexity of dress in all its manifestations. However, even a ten-volume encyclopedia must limit itself in either time or geography in order to provide in-depth scholarship. The focus is therefore on the nineteenth to the early twenty-first centuries, although overview materials covering the long history of dress have been included to provide essential context, as is appropriate in so ambitious a scholarly undertaking.

Many disciplines have developed an interest in dress studies, underscoring the need for a major reference work with a broad scope. The range of interpretations will help readers develop a critical understanding of cultural practices. The intended audience for the *Encyclopedia* is broad and encompasses general and curious readers as well as students and teachers in the humanities and social sciences, in short, anyone interested in the full spectrum of issues relating to dress in a given time and place. More specialized researchers in anthropology, apparel design, art and cultural history, cinema, cultural studies, dance and drama, fashion, folklore, history, and sociology will also find the *Encyclopedia* an invaluable reference.

Dress, costume, and *fashion* are often used interchangeably in common parlance, but this work makes crucial distinctions between them because terminology is important. The aim of this preface is to clarify for readers the distinctions that have been drawn throughout this particular project by the editors and contributors, in order to achieve scholarly consistency across the work. Contributors were asked to define *dress* as any supplement or modification to the body, the purpose of which is either to cover or to adorn. Dress is a broad category that includes costume and fashion, with the term *costume* defined as a specific type of dress that is worn for theatrical, dance, or masquerade performances. *Costume* is frequently used by many distinguished museum curators and scholars in connection with both the historical study and the display of clothing in a general way. In contrast to dress, which ordinarily expresses a wearer's identity, costume hides or conceals it in various degrees. *Fashion* is defined as changes relating to body modifications and supplements, usually easily perceived and tracked, often within short periods of time.

While fashions may have permanent consequences with respect to an individual (as in the case of tattooing, for example), most are characterized by impermanence within the larger socioeconomic or fashion system (a complex process by which changing fashions in dress spread through formal and/or informal channels of design, manufacture, merchandising, and communication).

Supplements to the body include conventional attire such as clothing, jewelry, and items typically called *accessories,* such as hats, shoes, handbags, and canes. Modifications include cosmetics, hair care (cutting, combing, and styling), scarification, tattooing, tooth filing, piercings, and gentle molding of the human skull or binding of feet (the latter two usually done during infancy). Thus, in many cultures where people display these modifications alone, a person can be unclothed but still dressed. In addition to visually oriented practices, the definition of *dress* acknowledges that all senses may be incorporated, not just the visual. Therefore, sound (for example, rustling or jingling), odor (perfumes or incense), touch (such as tight or loose, silky or rough), and even taste when applicable (some cosmetics, breath fresheners, and tobacco products) frequently feature in discussions.

Being dressed is a normative act because human beings are taught what is right and wrong in concealing and revealing the body and keeping it clean and attractive. Contributors to this encyclopedia primarily describe dress and explain how it is worn within specific cultural contexts, although, where it is likely to be helpful, they have been encouraged to embrace and explain theoretical approaches to the interpretation of dress (for example, postmodernism, psychoanalytic theory, semiotics, and queer theory). The geographic organization provides overviews by country. An attempt has been made to focus on all countries, but in some cases, qualified authors could not be found and an entry was regretfully omitted. Readers may, however, find references to a country in the volume and section introductions and in the index. Supplementing country essays are articles on types or categories of dress along with select articles on influential or particularly well-known ethnic groups. Shorter "snapshots" on specific topics serve as sidebars to longer articles. Volume 10 addresses issues of global interest relating to the first nine volumes and is divided into five main sections: Overview of Global Perspectives; Forms of Dress Worldwide; Dress and the Arts Worldwide; Fashion Worldwide; and Dress and Fashion Resources Worldwide. Inclusion of a timeline on the development of dress and related technologies is a special feature.

At the end of each article, a list of references and suggestions for further reading has been included. Where possible, cross-references to other relevant articles in the *Encyclopedia* have also been inserted. Each volume has its own index, and readers will find a cumulative index to the entire set in volume 10. Volumes 1 to 9 also each feature a regional map.

While it is tempting when writing on the body and dress to focus on the most spectacular or visually engaging examples of dress from a given culture, authors have been asked to balance their discussions between the ordinary dress of daily life and the extraordinary dress of special occasions. In both instances this includes protective clothing of various sorts as well as general distinctions between genders, among age groups and various vocations, and within other realms of social status, as defined by religion, wealth, and political position. Along with prehistoric and historical traditions of dress, authors have been charged with addressing contemporary fashions in their own areas of interest, as well as traditional dress forms. An important aim of the *Encyclopedia* is to show the full range and transformative power of dress in cultural exchanges that occur all over the world, of which the influence of Western fashion on other parts of the world is only one example.

The editor in chief recruited scholars with particular expertise in dress, textiles, and fashion in their geographic areas and a scholarly network to edit specific volumes, develop tables of contents, draft a descriptive scope for articles requested, and contact and commission contributors. (Some experts were not available to participate in contributing articles.) The ten volumes include 854 articles written by 585 authors residing in over 60 different countries. Authors had freedom to develop their articles but always with a general reader in mind. Scholarship around the world and in different disciplines has many approaches; this presents daunting challenges for authors, who were asked to employ a relatively broad but consistent definition of dress. As a result of a rigorous review and revision process, their work has resulted in a comprehensive compilation of material not found before in a reference work of this type. Their efforts allow readers to find the excitement, variety, sensuality, and complexity of dress presented in clear descriptions, reinforced by historical and cultural context. As much as possible, entries have been written by experts from within the culture being discussed. Each was assigned a certain number of words, determined by the volume editor and editor in chief in the context of the desired depth and balance of the *Encyclopedia* as a whole, and each followed instructions and guidelines developed by the editorial board and publisher. The structure of each volume also varies according to the editor's perspective, the constraints of the historical, political, and social configuration of the geographic area, and the research known to be available.

A variety of images have been included, from museum photographs that show detail, to anthropological photographs that show dress in action and context, to fashion and artistic images that help to convey attitudes and ideals. Many of these have come from the contributors' own fieldwork. The goal is that the variety of approaches and interpretations presented within the *Encyclopedia*'s architecture combine to create a worldwide presentation of dress that is more varied, less biased, and more complete than any heretofore published. Articles are extensively illustrated with 2,300 images—many seen here for the first time.

The process of conceiving of and completing the *Encyclopedia* took place over a number of years and involved much scholarly consultation among editors, contributors, and staff. The common goal demanded a flexible approach within a set framework, and such a balancing act presented a range of challenges. Doubtless some decisions could be argued at further length, but hopefully readers will find most were sensible, bearing in mind the daunting ambitions of the work. Specific terms for items of dress vary throughout the world, and such variation often also reflects regional differences in the item of dress itself. Where possible, the editors have worked with contributors and translators to preserve the closest regional spelling of the indigenous term for the area under discussion, bearing in mind also the necessity to translate or transliterate such terms into English, the language of publication. While the *Encyclopedia* cannot be perfectly complete and consistent, the goal has been to produce a landmark achievement for its scholarly standards and impressive scope. The editorial team has endeavored to present authoritative treatments of the subject, with the particular hope that readers will find in the *Encyclopedia*'s pages a measure of the excitement, fun, and fascination that characterize dress across time and cultures. Browsing or reading in depth, volume to volume, will provide readers with many examples of what people wear, whether mundane or marvelous, uniform or unique, commonplace or rare. The encyclopedia will continue to grow as articles on recent developments, new information, and research add to knowledge on dress and fashion in the online Berg Fashion Library.

The volume editors and contributors are gratefully acknowledged and thanked for their enthusiasm for and dedication to the enormous task that has culminated in this encyclopedia. Many thanks also go to the publisher and project management team, who have valiantly seen the project to its successful completion.

Joanne B. Eicher

Preface to the United States and Canada

This volume of the *Encyclopedia of World Dress and Fashion* encompasses the geographic region that is occupied by the United States and Canada in 2010. *Dress* is defined in this work, following Joanne B. Eicher and Mary Ellen Roach-Higgins, as "the assemblage of body modifications and body supplements displayed by a person and worn at the particular moment in time" (quoted from Eicher's *The Visible Self*). As used here, *fashion* is a strong preference shared by a large group of people for a relatively short period of time that is quickly replaced by a new preference. Fashion is an essential part of life in most of the United States and Canada in the twenty-first century. Fashion is evident not only in dress but also in other objects from the material culture and in some aspects of behavior. As expressed in the dress of West Europeans and North Americans, its major distinguishing feature is rapid change, or what some authors have called *fashion racing*. Many articles in this volume focus on fashionable dress. But there are also situations in which tradition mandates or subtly imposes requirements on the fashionable dress worn by individuals. Therefore, some articles will address traditional elements within dress that persist beyond or override fashion cycles.

The articles in this volume are organized to provide a smooth flow of content from one topic to another. At the same time, each article stands alone in its treatment of some specific facet of dress and/or fashion. The organization of the articles into five parts is intended to develop the material in a logical sequence, beginning with information about the region and identification of existing evidence on dress in North America that serves as the basis of knowledge about dress, past and present. Only two countries are included in this volume, and those countries have much in common. Part 1 introduces readers to the geographic and cultural region. Conflicts in current theories about how this part of North America was first reached by human inhabitants are acknowledged. Subsequent immigrations and patterns of settlement are noted where relevant, as well as the impact of geography, climate, and natural resources on dress. Fashion, which is a strong factor in the dress of both nations, can then be explored in depth in part 2. Part 3 examines influences that are not solely an outgrowth of fashion, and parts 4 and 5 examine dress as shaped by culture.

The people who populate the territory occupied by the United States and Canada in the early twenty-first century trace their ancestry to all parts of the globe, including the Americas. Terminology used to refer to indigenous people, and those non-native people arriving before, in, and after 1492, is problematic. After careful consideration of current usage in such diverse fields as archaeology, anthropology, and history, as well as preferences expressed by descendants of the people living in these countries before 1492, the editors have settled on the following vocabulary and definitions. Individual authors may, however, choose to use different terms, based on current usage in their specialized disciplines.

The origin of the name assigned to the indigenous people of North and South America, *Indians*, originated from the mistake made by European explorers in believing they had reached lands called India. This mistake was reinforced by the explorers' observation that some people they encountered wore elements of dress made of cotton. A species of cotton is indigenous to South America, but the Europeans knew this fabric as a trade item from the Indian Subcontinent, where a different species of cotton grows.

In recent years, some writers have substituted the term *Native American* for *Indian* in the United States, but this usage has not been universally accepted. As the Smithsonian Institution has noted, the term *Native American* has not been accepted by many of the people to whom it was assigned, who continue to call themselves *Indians* or may prefer a tribal-language term. Canadians prefer to use the term *First Nations* instead of *Indians*. This volume will, when speaking of the Indians of the United States and Canada collectively, follow the usage in the Smithsonian *Handbook of the North American Indians* and use the terms *North American Indians* and *First Nations Peoples* or, sometimes, the names of tribal groups. Joe D. Horse Capture, Associate Curator, African, Oceanic, and Native American Art, The Minneapolis Institute of Arts, guided us toward the selection of appropriate authors for the articles dealing with dress in the ten North American Indian/First Nations regions. His review of the table of contents and the scope of the articles in part 4 made sure these sections were as comprehensive as space limitations allowed.

When speaking of U.S. and Canadian residents who clearly identify with the countries or regions where their families originate, the name of the country of origin will be used with the word *American* or, sometimes, *Canadian*, as, for example, *Asian American*. The term *people of color* is not used because it is less specific.

Part 1 introduces readers to archaeological and other data supporting the study of dress in the United States and Canada. Articles explore the kind of research that serves as a foundation for what is known about the history of dress and current practices related to dress and fashion. The identification of important publications and museum collections in both the United States and Canada shows how knowledge in the field is shared and how and where actual artifacts of dress are being preserved and can be seen.

Part 2 examines many aspects of fashionable dress. Articles range from an exploration of the differences between traditional and fashionable dress to the history of the textile and fashion industries in the United States and Canada. They include the relationship between the body and dress. In part 3, "Demographic and Social Influences on Dress," following a general introduction, the first two articles consider how age may impact dress. Other articles examine such diverse areas as gender, class, health, and leisure and dress, and how music, the arts, film, television, or occupations influence what people wear.

Parts 4 and 5 recognize that some traditions and practices that might be called unique exist within some identifiable groups living in the United States and Canada. Part 4 looks at aspects of the dress of North American Indians/First Nations Peoples, dividing them by region. Part 5 identifies and examines practices within other groups living in the broader societies. Some of these groups are ethnically based; others are self-identified subcultures within the broader society. Articles also explore the varied experiences with dress of the indigenous peoples, settlers, immigrants, and residents who live in the United States and Canada. It should be noted here that dress in Hawai'i is examined in this volume from the date of its annexation to the United States in 1898. Readers wishing to find articles on the earlier history of dress on this island should refer to volume 7 of this encyclopedia.

A work of this scope can be completed only with contributions from many individuals. It is not possible to acknowledge all those who provided assistance to the editor and contributors, but the contributions of some stand out. Joanne B. Eicher, editor in chief of the *Berg Encyclopedia of World Dress and Fashion*, who originated the idea for this work and who tended it so carefully and ensured its survival, has been a source of inspiration. Publishing staff have responded to a blizzard of e-mails, always having the right answers and providing superb guidance for contributors and the editor.

Consulting editors have played a large and special role in this volume. Sylvia K. Miller, a consultant, was part of the project at its beginnings, taught us the ins and outs of making an encyclopedia, and was an outstanding source of ideas. Once again we recognize the contributions of Joe D. Horse Capture, Associate Curator, African, Oceanic, and Native American Art, The Minneapolis Institute of Arts, in his role as a consultant for part 4 of this volume.

Several of the authors of articles in this volume should be acknowledged for special assistance they provided beyond the articles they wrote. The volume editor is from the United States, and there were a number of times when Cynthia Cooper, Curator, Costume and Textiles, McCord Museum of Canadian History, helped resolve issues such as terminology differences between Canadian and U.S. usage. She reviewed the table of contents to assure its inclusion of Canadian topics was adequate. She was also very helpful in identifying appropriate Canadian authors. We offer her our sincere appreciation. Patricia Warner, Professor Emerita, University of Massachusetts Amherst, who was born and raised in Canada and later lived and worked in the United States, was also helpful in providing insight into questions relating to differences between U.S. and Canadian fashion-related topics, and the balance between Canadian and U.S. material.

Early in the development of the table of contents, scholar and author Betty Kobayashi Issenman provided insight into the development of content related to North American Indians. Although other commitments prevented her from writing for the publication, her comments are much valued and appreciated.

And, finally, thanks to all of the authors who labored so diligently to make this volume comprehensive, accurate, and insightful. Their contributions are the bedrock of this work, and they deserve my sincere gratitude for a job well done.

Phyllis G. Tortora

PART 1

Overview of Dress and Fashion in the United States and Canada

The Geographic and Cultural Region

The geography of the region occupied by any nation will be a major factor in the establishment of climate zones. Not only the latitudes at which a country lies but also the elevations, proximity to seas, and patterns of wind and rainfall will affect the climate. The relationship between dress and climate is strong. Climate is directly related to the kind of raw materials available for constructing elements of dress. One of the major functions of dress is to assist humans to adapt to climate, and another is to protect the body from hazardous materials in the environment.

Both Canada and the United States cover vast regions. Canada is the second largest country in the world, after Russia; however, due to the proportion of the nation that lies far to the north and has a much less hospitable climate, the bulk of the population has tended to settle in the southernmost portions of the country. The United States, by contrast, has a far more moderate climate and is far more densely settled in all but a few areas, such as northern Alaska. When one contemplates the geographic areas occupied by these countries, one can easily understand that needs related to dress may differ substantially from one area to another.

Situated in the northern portion of the Western Hemisphere, the lands that the United States and Canada occupy are bounded to the north by the Arctic Ocean, to the east by the Atlantic Ocean, to the west by the Bering Straits and the Pacific Ocean, and to the southeast by the Gulf of Mexico. At the south, Canada shares a border with the United States that stretches from east to west for some 5,525 miles (8,892 kilometers). To the south, the United States shares a border with Mexico. One state of the fifty United States, Hawai'i, lies west of the mainland in the mid-Pacific Ocean and another, Alaska, borders Canada on the northwest.

Most of the boundary between the United States and Canada does not result from divisions based on features of physical geography. The border runs east and west. Many of the physiographic features of the landscape, such as mountain ranges, that create logical geographic regions run north and south. In both countries there are eight distinct regions, and some of these zones cross the political borders. The diversity of these requires residents to adapt to a wide range of climate zones.

DRESS AND CLIMATE

Dress, as used in this encyclopedia, includes anything that in any way modifies the human body (body modifications) or is added to the body (body supplements). Body modifications can be temporary or permanent and might include such actions as purposeful weight gain or loss, ornamentation of the skin, binding of a portion of the body to alter its shape, wearing deodorant, or having a cosmetic surgery procedure. Body supplements, also either temporary or permanent, can include clothing, which encloses the body in various kinds of materials that are either preshaped or wrapped, suspended, or some combination of these processes. Body supplements may be attached to the body in various ways. Examples include hair transplants or jewelry attached by piercing the skin, or objects such as fans, parasols, or umbrellas that can be held in the hand. In elaborating on this conceptualization of dress, Joanne Eicher and Mary Ellen Roach-Higgins have described the properties of body modifications and body supplements as color, volume and proportion, shape and structure, surface design, texture, odors and scents, sound, and taste.

When faced with extremes of climate, either cold or heat, humans will choose forms of dress that either conserve body heat or allow it to dissipate. As noted previously, one can choose among body enclosures that are wrapped, suspended, or preshaped. Where climate is hot, dress that is suspended or loosely wrapped will allow greater air flow and as a result will feel cooler. When climate is cold, garments that are preshaped to fit close to the body will serve to conserve body heat and thereby keep the wearer warmer. In any review of the kinds of clothing worn in different parts of the world, one can see that traditional dress in warmer areas tends to be draped or suspended, whereas in arctic areas, such as those in northern Canada and Alaska, clothing is generally tailored and preshaped to fit the body closely.

Dress is also related to other aspects of climate and environment. These include preference for materials that are better insulators against cold, or materials that allow the passage of air or absorption of perspiration when temperatures climb. Light colors that reflect the sun are more comfortable in hot weather, whereas dark colors that absorb sunlight feel warmer. In a damp, cold climate, nonabsorbent materials and those that are waterproof are preferred. Where undergrowth is dense and sharp and where spiny plants abound, an impenetrable material, such as leather, is desirable. Eye shields against the bright sunlight of the Arctic help to ward off snow blindness.

In contemporary United States and Canada, the development of climate control within buildings, such as air conditioning and central heating, has made occupation of regions with extremes of weather easier, and using dress as a means of adapting to climate is less important than it was in the past. No longer are people dependent on local resources; national and international trade networks allow distribution of products to all provinces and states.

SETTLEMENT OF THE REGIONS OCCUPIED BY THE UNITED STATES AND CANADA

Those studying the prehistory of North America had generally accepted the view that the first people to reach the region traveled from Asia to Alaska about twenty thousand years ago across a land bridge formed during the last Ice Age. However, recent theories and the results of some archaeological excavations have raised questions about how and when the first people arrived, and these debates remain unresolved. Moreover, North American Indian and First Nations peoples have their own views expressed in creation stories that set their origins in this hemisphere.

No matter when or how the first people arrived in North America, at times those people moved into lands that were new to them. They had to satisfy their basic needs for food, shelter, and dress through the use of the resources that were available.

The primary motivations leading people to dress themselves have been identified as protection (against both physical and spiritual threats), decoration of the body, demonstration of status, and conforming to standards of modesty. In any environment the raw materials available are animal, vegetable, or mineral. In a new environment, some types of raw materials may have been unfamiliar to new arrivals, and they needed to learn how to exploit them.

The end of the last Ice Age about ten thousand years ago gradually opened up areas for human occupation. What resources would have been available to use for dress? Throughout human history animal skins are likely to have been among the earliest materials used for clothing. Furs and leather would have been a useful by-product of the harvesting of animals for food. Furs would provide protection against cold weather. After tanning, skins could be cut and sewn into variously shaped garments and accessories. It is uncertain exactly when weaving or other fabric construction techniques developed in North America, but various animal hair fibers such as weasel and bison have been identified in prehistoric bags made by twining spun yarns. Blankets, worn as cloaks, were made from mountain goat hair and dog hair. Not only was animal hair and skin exploited, but grease rendered from animal fat was used in cosmetics and to protect against insects.

Plant materials were processed and used in fabric construction and as dyestuffs. Archaeologists have found footwear made of plant leaves that date to about eight thousand years ago. One of the plants most commonly used for textiles was dogbane (*Apocynum cannabinum*). Strong fibers were obtained from the stems of this plant, and European settlers used the fibers, which they called "Indian hemp," to make string and twine.

The desire to decorate the body, either because it makes the person more beautiful and more desirable or as a demonstration of status, is thought to be the most compelling reason for humans to dress themselves. Evidence for this view can be seen in the vast distances that raw materials for decorative objects traveled. It is clear from the artifacts found in archaeological sites that trading networks were well established in North America. Copper from deposits in the Lake Superior region of the Great Lakes is found as far east as New York and as far south as Texas. Shells, turquoise, jade, and other ornamental materials have been associated with sites half a continent away from their point of origin.

The societies that developed over the thousands of years preceding the first contacts with Europeans and Asians have a history that is largely unknown today. The arrival of Europeans,

Girl in parka in Nome, Alaska, early twentieth century. In the Arctic regions of North America, garments made of fur were developed for protection against the cold. Library of Congress Prints and Photographs Division, LC-DIG-ppmsc-02369.

first on the Atlantic coasts and slightly later on the Pacific shores, disrupted the lives of the earliest Americans, forcing many North American Indian and First Nation people to move from the homelands they had occupied to other places. Tribal regions occupied were in no way based on the present national boundaries of these two countries, and today native peoples may identify with a tribe or Indian nation that lives on both sides of the border.

Although there are still debates about when and why the first Europeans reached North America, it is known that Norse people established a settlement about 1000 C.E. at a site called L'Anse aux Meadows in northern Newfoundland. The settlement did not thrive, due to internal discord and conflicts with local natives, and was apparently abandoned after about two or three years.

It is likely that these Norse men and women, or Basque fishermen, or Portuguese or Asian sailors were actually the first nonnative people to set foot on some of the lands that now make up the countries of Canada and the United States; however, because historians lack specific documentary evidence of earlier arrivals, the men sailing under the Spanish flag have been called "the discoverers of America." And it is at this point more information about the dress of Americans, both native and immigrant, becomes available through written records and depictions by artists.

Western dress, the dress of people in Western Europe and their descendants who now live in other parts of the world, is much influenced by fashion. *Fashion* is a social phenomenon that can be defined as a taste shared by many for a relatively short period of time. Although it is possible to identify fashion in some aspects of dress in regions other than those influenced by Europe, there are few places in which fashion change permeates dress to the same extent. Costume historians generally see fashionable dress as first appearing in Medieval Europe. By the fifteenth century, the time of the voyages of discovery, styles were changing about every thirty to forty years. The dress of explorers and the settlers who followed them was shaped to a great extent by the fashions of the countries that they represented.

EUROPEAN COLONIZATION OF NORTH AMERICA

The Spanish, French, British, Swedish, and Dutch each claimed parts of northeastern America. Spain sponsored the first permanent settlement in St. Augustine, Florida, in 1565. In 1607, France founded Quebec, and in 1642, Montreal. The British sent settlers to Jamestown in 1607 and to New England in 1620. New Amsterdam, about 1624–1625, was the focal point for Dutch colonization.

Spanish explorers visited the California region of the far west of North America in the sixteenth century but began colonization only after the 1770s. The British had visited the shores of the Pacific Coast in 1579 when Sir Francis Drake circumnavigated the globe. The Inuit of the Arctic regions encountered whalers and explorers from the sixteenth century on. British explorers Captain James Cook and George Vancouver made voyages in 1778 and 1793, respectively, that followed the western coast far to the north. The Russians had been to Alaska as early as 1732. By the early 1800s, they had established trading posts and hunted sea otters almost to extinction to obtain pelts to sell to the Chinese. J.C.H. King has neatly summed up the role of dress as a primary factor in European settlement of North America when he says, "If Southeastern United States was colonized so that Europeans could use deerskin gloves and breeches, and the Sub-arctic so people could wear felted beaver hats, then the Northwest Coast succumbed to satisfy the Chinese taste in sea otter furs."

From the earliest of these settlements until both countries stretched from sea to sea, those settlers moving into new areas attempted to dress in styles they considered up-to-date and fashionable. However, practical adaptations sometimes had to be made. As a result, some differences can be seen in separate regions of each country.

What regional style differences existed and continue to exist can arise from many factors. Climate is one obvious factor, and the native and immigrant populations of the far northern regions of both the United States and Canada adopted and wore the hooded jacket called a *parka* long before it spread continent-wide as a basic winter garment. Occupation is another factor, which can be seen in the adoption by male farmers of straw hats and by their wives of sunbonnets to protect against sunburn.

Fashion consciousness itself can be a factor in regional dress. Observers have noted that Canadians from Montreal are "more fashionable" than those from other large cities such as Toronto. In the United States, New York has been considered the major site for high-end fashion, while Los Angeles has a reputation for outstanding design in sportswear.

The first wave of settlers in any area had to rely on what they had brought with them. But once a settlement had been established, supplies arrived regularly, and items such as fabrics, wigs, hair powder, fans, and sewing supplies could be purchased. Depending on the region and climate, settlers could cultivate flax and hemp and raise sheep and use their wool. When it suited the economic policies of Britain, colonies were either encouraged to produce textiles, or local manufacture was banned and colonists had to import them. But whether made by local production or imported, the textiles were available.

Information about current fashions was in demand. European goods arrived by ship, therefore fashions tended to lag somewhat behind those of Europe. But circulation of fashion plates, available from the eighteenth century on; fashion babies, that is, dolls dressed in current fashions; and import of actual fashionable garments kept men and women informed about current styles.

The contacts between Europeans and native people contributed to changes in the dress of both groups. One of the trade items most highly prized by Indians was glass beads. Although European traders scoffed at the willingness of Indians and First Nations people to trade valuable furs for cheap colorful glass beads, each partner in the trade was obtaining materials that they prized in return for something that in their view was of little use. The glass beads became an important element in highly decorative, prized garments for the North American Indians, and the furs were used to produce luxury items for Europeans across the Atlantic.

In many areas of North America, dress of the First Nations and Indian people had developed as an adaptation to climate and terrain. Where it was practical, explorers adopted elements of North American Indian dress. Moccasins were quickly accepted as much more comfortable and durable in the undeveloped regions than the stiff, heavy boots of European dress. Leggings of deerskin were preferable to the knee breeches of urban centers. At the same time, probably as a marker of status, the cut of the European coat was imitated in skin garments by Indian men.

Throughout the history of the United States and Canada, technology has played a role in increasing the availability of raw materials and tools that create the elements of dress. By 1800, a large part of the eastern seaboard of the United States and Canada had been settled. A thriving textile industry was developing in the United States. In Canada, still a British colony, manufacturing was not encouraged. The British preferred to take raw materials from Canada and sell finished products to their colonists.

European trade with India had brought delicate cotton fabrics to consumers. These fabrics were costly and used for luxury products. When entrepreneurs realized that the southern region of North America was ideal for growing cotton, many plantations were established. The use of water power for weaving and advances in cotton spinning made production of cotton fabric more efficient and less expensive. Demand for cotton goods increased. There was, however, one drawback. Separating the cotton seeds from the fibers was very slow and labor intensive. The invention

This hand-colored French fashion plate, reproduced in the Philadelphia-based *Graham's Magazine* in 1851, illustrates the latest styles from Paris. Information about European fashion was in demand in post-Colonial North America. Courtesy of Phyllis Tortora.

of the cotton gin in 1793 solved this problem, and still more cotton was planted. Cotton planting, growing, and picking was still labor intensive; the answer for the growers was slave labor. The rapid growth in the slave trade was the result.

Textile technology continually improved. In the mid-nineteenth century synthetic dyestuffs were created that produced a wider range of colors with better durability. By the twentieth century, technology made it possible to create new fibers either by regenerating materials such as wood chips into fibers or by creating fibers through chemical synthesis. Medical science, too, made its contribution to dress as techniques for safe cosmetic surgery allowed for permanent body modifications.

CULTURAL CONTEXTS FOR DRESS

Residents of Canada and the United States probably have more similarities than differences in most aspects of their dress. The overwhelming majority of the original settlers in both countries came from Great Britain and France. After the War of Independence fought between Britain and its thirteen colonies, many loyalists relocated to Canada because it had not rebelled against the mother country. In the mid-1800s, many French Canadians left Canada for the United States, and during the Vietnam War in the 1970s, U.S. protesters fled to Canada. These exchanges of populations between the two countries have not been unusual and have contributed to maintaining the many similarities between the two countries.

Probably the most important shared context that relates to dress is an emphasis on fashionable dress. Participation in the fashion process was common to most European countries of origin of early settlers. Until after the first part of the nineteenth century, immigrants to both countries were largely from western Europe. European fashionable dress practices were, therefore, firmly established. When, by the late nineteenth and the twentieth centuries, larger numbers of immigrants to both countries began arriving from central and southern Europe and from Asia, they entered countries that stretched from coast to coast and had well established, fairly homogeneous cultures. The new arrivals were expected to conform.

By the twenty-first century, however, some differences had developed in the attitudes expressed toward immigrants. In the United States, people spoke of the melting pot. Immigrants were expected to become Americans first, and their country of origin was secondary. Canada, however, encouraged a population mosaic. Maintenance of tradition was not discouraged. The federal government in Canada actively promoted multiculturalism and, in 1988, enacted the Canadian Multicultural Act.

Both countries also shared and have continued to share common sources of information about dress. Not only did residents in both countries look to the same European sources for fashion leadership, but they also shared other sources of information more directly in such media as film, television, the Internet, and magazines. By the twenty-first century, merchandisers such as Wal-Mart and Gap from the United States had moved into Canada. Common attitudes and values can also be seen in shared ideals of beauty and grooming. Wearing deodorant, for example, is almost obligatory, and attitudes toward obesity seem to be similar.

In any discussion of factors that influence dress in the region included in this volume, one must acknowledge that there are those within the population who are unwilling or unable to make choices about dress, and discussions of fashion do not pertain to them. There were, for example, the enslaved who had little or no choice in how they would dress. For the poverty stricken, keeping up with fashion was an economic impossibility, and simply finding clothing for daily needs was often difficult. Some groups who held unique religious or sociopolitical beliefs wore only what was prescribed for them. But the large majority of individuals living in both of these countries could and did make choices about their dress. These choices were subject to other influences that could lead to differences in dress.

As noted earlier, climate can lead to differences in dress from one region to another. Thanks to interior-space climate control mechanisms the need to adapt to climatic differences diminished, but it did not entirely disappear. Those living in northern Canada are likely to have more flannel shirts and parkas in their wardrobes than residents of Miami, Florida.

Differences can also be seen in urban and rural dress. These differences arise from the kinds of employment available in the city and the country, conventions about dress as appropriate for city and country wear, and availability of opportunities to shop for clothing. These differences were particularly pronounced in the eighteenth, nineteenth, and early twentieth centuries when men and women in rural areas were more likely to be engaged in agricultural labor, were living on the frontier, or were part of the westward migration. For example, the *bloomer dress* was a style promoted by feminists around 1850 that consisted of a dress with a skirt of about knee length that was worn over trousers. The style was ridiculed by many and was never widely adopted, but in *Dressed for the Photographer*, author Joan Severa has included a number of photographs of women in frontier and rural settings who obviously wear the style because it is far more practical than the wide, floor-length skirts of that period. But the bloomer-clad woman of the frontier would not have worn her bloomer dress to church. She would have made a dress to serve as her "best" dress that was as close to the current fashion as she could determine, perhaps by looking at a fashion magazine such as *Godey's Ladies Book*.

Small rural communities had general stores, but from the 1870s on, cities had department stores. After the first mail order catalogs were available beginning in 1872, it was possible for rural residents to purchase many items used for dress.

The invention and widespread adoption of the automobile had much to do with mitigating the sharp differences between cities and rural areas in the twentieth century. After World War II, people found it easy to commute by bus and rail to jobs in the cities, and suburbs grew up around the major cities. For life in the suburbs, a different kind of dress was needed. Suburban homes usually had large yards. Suburban families spent more time outdoors involved in sports or caring for yards and gardens. Casual styles, now known as sportswear, became the appropriate dress for leisure time. Women wore slacks and shorts instead of *housedresses*, which were inexpensive cotton dresses worn by housewives in the 1930s that could be laundered easily.

The acceptance of casual dress in the suburbs gradually caused alterations in attitudes about appropriate dress. Before the 1960s, few women would appear in downtown areas of cities in slacks or shorts. For any formal daytime social event a woman was expected to wear a hat and gloves. College dormitories required co-eds to wear skirts when entering their lobbies. A businessman was not

Moccasin with glass beads, Eastern Woodlands, ca. 1845–1855. After the arrival of Europeans in America, glass beads became a trade item, prized among North American Indians for their decorative qualities. McCord Museum ME982X.479.1-2. http://www.mccord-museum.qc.ca/en/

properly dressed if he did not wear a hat when outdoors and a necktie with his suit. Over the next few decades all this changed. And by the turn of the millennium, many businesses had established "casual Fridays" or done away with restrictions on dress altogether.

AMERICAN INFLUENCES ON DRESS IN THE REST OF THE WORLD

Until World War II, those living in North America who wanted to follow fashion generally looked to Paris to decide what styles to wear. American designers, such as Adrian and Irene, had become influential as a result of work in films. But when Paris was occupied and news about the French haute couture was halted during World War II, American designers flourished. Their newly won place as fashion innovators was not lost after the war.

The ready-to-wear industry emerged in the United States in the early twentieth century. Mass production of clothing did not spread to other parts of the globe until after World War II. The importance of the ready-to-wear concept increased to such an extent by the 1960s that Paris began to host showings of *prêt-à-porter*, or ready-to-wear, designs by well-known designers. This American innovation in design and manufacture has been a major contribution to present-day world fashion. Consumers in North America began to make purchases on the basis of fashion trademarks. Sometimes these trademarks carried the names of

designers, but often they were named for the company manufacturing the fashions.

One can find many examples of dress fashions that have had their origins in North America. These include blue jeans and sneakers, which originated as styles associated with youth. Although still sold in their original form, they are also seen in adaptations far different from the prototypes. Sneakers can be made of gold lamé fabric decorated with sequins, and the blue denim characteristic of jeans has been made into glamorous evening gowns. Foundation makeup invented by Max Factor for Hollywood stars and marketed to the public and the practice of using Botox injections to maintain a youthful appearance are fashions that started in the United States and have spread worldwide.

How and why do such developments spread across national boundaries? American movies and other media are seen around the world; American music is heard everywhere, and the singers are depicted on posters or seen on television. Internet fashion sites are globally accessible. The young are often the first adopters of new styles, and the adoption of both sneakers and blue jeans was first associated with youth in other countries. American affluence is envied by the less affluent. Could it be that owning these items conveys a sense of status?

Some American style markers are not flattering. Residents of other countries claim to be able to spot American tourists immediately. The caricature of the older American male traveler focuses

EDUCATION AND RESEARCH RELATED TO DRESS

Postsecondary education in both the United States and Canada offers undergraduate and postgraduate studies that prepare students for careers in industries related to dress or provide them with the knowledge and skills that enable them to teach and carry out research about dress. Because dress can be studied from so many perspectives, these studies may be carried out in programs that can be part of the sciences (chemistry, technology, physics, biology), the social sciences (archaeology, anthropology, history, sociology, family and consumer studies, psychology), the arts (fashion, textile, and interior design; art history; museum studies), and business (merchandising, management, journalism). As a result, published research and writing about dress can touch on any of these areas and more. The bibliographical references at the end of each essay will provide readers with some sense of the enormous variety of approaches authors may take to this always fascinating area.

SOURCES OF INFORMATION

Readers may be interested in looking beyond this volume at the study of aspects of dress in the United States and Canada. A number of national and international organizations report on and publish the results of research. Several are listed below. This list includes only a few that focus on scholarly material related to dress. In addition to this brief list, there are many trade associations or organizations for practitioners of textile crafts and professional associations in academic areas that may include research on dress.

- American Association of Textile Chemists and Colorists (AATCC), PO Box 12215, Research Triangle Park, NC 27709
- Costume Society of America, 203 Towne Centre Drive, Hillsborough, NJ 08844
- International Textile and Apparel Association (ITAA), 6060 Sunrise Vista Dr., Suite 1300, Citrus Heights, CA 95610
- Textile Society of America, P.O. Box 193, Middletown, DE 19709

There are also a number of scholarly journals that include material about dress in the United States and Canada. These include:

- *AATCC Journal.* Journal of the American Association of Textile Chemists and Colorists.
- *Clothing and Textiles Research Journal.* Journal of the International Textile and Apparel Association.
- *Dress.* Journal of the Costume Society of America.
- *Fashion Theory: The Journal of Dress, Body & Culture.* Berg Publishers.
- *Textile: The Journal of Cloth & Culture.* Berg Publishers.

The Hawaiian shirt. Because it is made from fabrics comfortable in a tropical climate and is cut with short sleeves and a loose fit, the Hawaiian shirt is the preferred dress for Hawaiian residents. Courtesy of Phyllis Tortora.

on dress, often showing him in Hawaiian shirt and shorts, and his overweight wife in shorts and a straw hat. Younger travelers usually blend in better, possibly because fashions worn by the young have become virtually international.

INDUSTRIES RELATED TO DRESS

Dress has had a substantial impact on the economies of both the United States and Canada from their beginnings. Two of the earliest examples are furs obtained through trade with Indians or First Nations people and the cultivating and processing of cotton from fiber to finished fabric. The synthesis of high-technology fibers used in clothing for space exploration and athletic competitions is a more recent example. Once fabric is imported or made domestically, the garment industry takes over from the textile industry. When the garment or accessory is complete (it could be made in the home country or abroad), the retail sales industry enters the distribution chain and sells it to consumers. Another industry provides the means for cleaning and laundering either in the home or elsewhere. A substantial amount of media attention, both print and electronic, is devoted to dress. With the globalization of industries, manufacturers and retailers of textiles and apparel of all kinds find themselves working and organizing beyond the boundaries of their home countries.

References and Further Reading

Eicher, Joanne B., and Mary Ellen Roach-Higgins. "A System of Classifying and Defining." In *Dress and Gender: Making and Meaning in Cultural Context*, edited by R. Barnes and J. B. Eicher, 8–28. Oxford/Washington, DC: Berg, 1992. (Reprinted in paperback, 1993.)

Eicher, Joanne B., Sandra Lee Evenson, and Hazel A. Lutz. *The Visible Self*. New York: Fairchild Publications, 2000.

Kidwell, Claudia, and Margaret Christman. *Suiting Everyone: The Democratization of Clothing in America*. Washington, DC: Smithsonian Institution Press, 1974.

King, J.C.H. *First Peoples First Contacts*. Cambridge, MA: Harvard University Press, 1999.

Kuttruff, Jenna Tedrick. "Mississippian Period Status Differentiation through Textile Analysis: A Caddoan Example." *American Antiquity* 58, no. 1 (1993): 125–145.

Mitchell, Robert D., and Paul A. Graves. *North America: The Historical Geography of a Changing Continent*. Totowa, NJ: Rowman & Littlefield, 1987.

Severa, Joan. *Dressed for the Photographer: Ordinary Americans and Fashion 1840–1900*. Kent, OH: Kent State University Press, 1995.

Phyllis G. Tortora

See also Regional Differences in Dress and Fashion; Shared and Unique Traditions and Practices.

Evidence about Dress of Indigenous People: United States Territory

- Types and Limitations of Archaeological Evidence
- Records of Early Contacts
- Preservation of Information and Traditional Dress Artifacts
- Dress in the Prehistoric Southwest
- Snapshot: Prehistoric Moccasins

American archaeology focuses, as does archaeology in other parts of the world, on the study of the human past by excavating and analyzing the material remains and monuments of past cultures and the contexts in which they are found. Archaeological findings and interpretations can be combined with information found in historical accounts to enhance the study of dress of North American Indian peoples not only at the times of early European contact but also prehistorically. Archaeology has provided evidence of North American Indian cultures that are well over ten thousand years old. Over this extensive time period and across the varied geography of what is now the United States, dress has been extremely varied and has undergone tremendous change. Because throughout most of America perishable items (e.g., garments) and other aspects of dress (e.g., body painting, tattoos, or hair styles) are not preserved in the archaeological record, what is known about the dress of prehistoric indigenous peoples is sparse and incomplete. Archaeology provides glimpses of the past that is no longer directly visible.

Preservation in the archaeological record of organic artifacts is highly dependent upon the physical environment of those remains. Special circumstances allow for the preservation of perishable artifacts, such as textiles or leather for clothing and other items of adornment. In America, perishable artifacts are most commonly preserved in dry areas, such as deserts, caves, or rock shelters, but frozen and wet sites increasingly are being recognized as potential locations for recovery. In open sites, textiles are most often preserved through charring or contact with metals. Because preservation is made possible in the arid climate of the desert Southwest, this area has provided the greatest amount of data concerning dress of prehistoric North American Indians. Bog conditions, such as those found at the Windover Site in Florida, also have preserved human remains and organic artifacts, some of which are related to dress from 6,000 years ago. Special burial circumstances, for example, the impervious clay matrix within the Great Mound at the Spiro Site in Oklahoma, which preserved numerous garments and other textiles from approximately one thousand years ago, can provide additional evidence of dress.

TYPES AND LIMITATIONS OF ARCHAEOLOGICAL EVIDENCE

Even though the study of dress is very culturally revealing, when compared with other aspects of prehistoric peoples of North America, little is known about the way they dressed. Beyond their functional aspects, dress artifacts are very personal items that reflect not only individual preferences but also those that are regionally, culturally, and temporally based. Dress evidence in the form of naturally perishable artifacts and aspects of dress are, of course, the most elusive in the archaeological record. However, other types of artifacts can provide additional information. Many aspects of dress have been represented in various art forms over the millennia, including statuary, carvings, pottery, paintings, and engravings, and not all dress artifacts are made of perishable materials. Stone, clay, bone, shell, and metal beads and pendants are examples of such artifacts that were commonly used by North American Indians to adorn the body. Impressions of textiles in previously plastic materials are sometimes recovered and have been found in dried or fired mud, pottery, and even the desiccated skin of mummies.

Many organic prehistoric specimens, including artifacts related to dress, that are currently in museum collections have not been radiocarbon dated, and it is not always possible to assign a cultural period based on archaeological context alone. The use of accelerator mass spectrometry, or AMS dating, has provided much-needed information for researchers. This technique is more expensive than conventional radiocarbon dating, but the recommended amount of organic sample needed for dating is 50 milligrams for AMS as compared to 100 grams for conventional dates. AMS dates therefore require 2,000 times less than that needed for conventional dates and can be obtained using as little as 10 milligrams. Because these analytical processes are destructive, the small sample size needed for AMS dating means that an entire specimen would not need to be destroyed in order to know how old it is as is often the case with conventional dating methods.

A complete picture of the varied dress of prehistoric North American Indians will never be known because the randomly preserved evidence is sparse and frequently fragmentary and degraded in nature. In the past, some textile evidence was not recognized by archaeologists or may not have been considered important to someone who was accustomed to working with the more "solid" evidence of stone and clay. Poor handling of fragile artifacts and lack of proper conservation measures has also led to the loss of important evidence of dress. These incidents are much less likely to occur today than in the past because of increased awareness on the part of the archaeological community and improvements in excavation and conservation techniques, but they still can be a factor.

In 1990, the North American Indian Graves Protection and Repatriation Act (NAGPRA) was passed. This U.S. federal law requires federal agencies and museums that receive federal funding to return North American Indian cultural items to their respective peoples. The Smithsonian Institution is exempt from this act, but it does fall under the National Museum of the American Indian Act that was passed in 1989. NAGPRA allows archaeological teams a short time for analysis before the remains must be returned. Cultural items include funerary objects, sacred objects, and objects of cultural patrimony. Consequently, this legislation applies to many North American Indian artifacts, especially

This hide shirt with scalp locks and woodpecker feathers belonged to Chief Ta-Sunko-Wirko (Crazy Horse, 1842–1877). It is an iconic item in the collection of the National Museum of the American Indian—a primary resource for evidence about North American Indian dress. Courtesy, National Museum of the American Indian, Smithsonian Institution.

burial items and religious artifacts. Evidence of North American Indian dress that has been recovered is frequently associated with human burials, and thus, information associated with dress artifacts is affected. The law has necessitated massive cataloging of the North American Indian collections in many museums in order to associate archaeological remains and artifacts with their living heirs and culturally affiliated Indian tribes and organizations. Analysis of previously unanalyzed collections has taken place in many instances before the artifacts were repatriated, and this may have provided some information on dress that was not previously available. However, any repatriated artifacts that have been reburied are no longer available for future research.

One of the primary resources for evidence about North American Indian dress is the National Museum of the American Indian. The cornerstone of this Smithsonian Institution museum is the collection of the former Museum of the American Indian, Heye Foundation, which was assembled at the turn of the twentieth century by George Gustav Heye. The current collections include both archaeological and ethnographic materials from the varied geographic regions of the United States and many other regions and cultures of North and South America. Exhibition galleries are located on the National Mall in Washington, D.C., and the collections are housed at the Cultural Resources Center in Suitland, Maryland. During the move of the Heye collection artifacts from

New York, which began in 1999, inventory and condition assessment was completed, and a comprehensive database with basic information and digitized images was developed. The Smithsonian Institution Libraries are also a valuable resource for written documents, publications, and images. The archaeological materials are located in the Anthropology collection of the library.

For those individuals who are interested in dress from a specific geographic region, most archaeological materials, including those relating to indigenous dress, are housed within regional, state, and university museums located across the country. Museums in the Southwest generally have more specimens in their collections because of the enhanced preservation of organic remains. However, many museums do have specimens that were either a part of or depict prehistoric indigenous dress. More and more museums across the country are developing databases of their collections, and many examples are now accessible via the Internet.

Sixteenth- and seventeenth-century documents and reports from European exploration and colonization of the United States are the best resources for descriptions of North American Indian dress in the Early Contact period, and some of these include illustrations of people. When these documents are consulted, the knowledge of the person doing both the verbal and visual recording, accuracy of the recording, and ethnocentrism all come into play and must be taken into consideration by researchers. Some drawings were based on the verbal descriptions of explorers that were given to European artists who had never been to the New World. Early reports were written in a variety of languages, including English, French, Spanish, and Russian. Many have been reprinted or translated. John R. Swanton, an ethnologist and ethnohistorian who worked in the early twentieth century for the Smithsonian Institution, has published works on the indigenous peoples of the Southeast and the Pacific Northwest. In some of his publications he integrated and organized information from Contact period publications and ethnographic accounts according to cultural group and topic. He provides numerous descriptions of dress that includes garments, ornaments, hairstyles, and body modifications.

RECORDS OF EARLY CONTACTS

One of the important examples of early European depictions of indigenous North American Indians at the time of early colonization on the East Coast of America are those produced by John White, who sailed with Sir Richard Grenville in 1585 as an artist-illustrator and returned with Sir Francis Drake in 1586. During this journey he made numerous famous sketches of the landscape and native peoples encountered near Roanoke Island, then a part of Virginia but now located in North Carolina. These extremely significant, original watercolor works were quickly reproduced in etchings that were then printed and widely circulated. White's illustrations predate the body of "discovery voyage art" created by artists in the late eighteenth century.

British Captain James Cook is regarded as one of the most ambitious explorers of all time. His three expeditions between 1776 and 1779 accomplished an impressive list of firsts, including the first European sighting of Hawai'i. His exploration of the coast of Alaska in 1778 added an enormous amount of information to the blank spots on the maps of the Northwest Coast of North America. Vitus Bering, who sailed for Russia, had reached Alaska in 1741, and the Spanish sent exploration parties north from California to Alaska in 1774 and 1775. The draftsman and watercolorist John Webber, who accompanied Cook on his last voyage, produced numerous drawings from this voyage that illustrate basic aspects of dress from both Hawai'i and Alaska.

In the early sixteenth century, a series of books on European explorations to the Americas were published. Starting in 1590, Theodor De Bry, a Flemish engraver, and his two sons gathered up every available picture and description from the new voyages. By 1634, the family had used them to create thirty books filled with hundreds of stunning and exotic copper-plate illustrations. The De Brys redrew pictures and expanded the stories that went with them. They made North American Indians look Graeco-Roman and mixed up cultural details, such as putting Indians from opposite hemispheres in the same picture. Still, their reports are among the most detailed of the sixteenth-century Americas. The De Brys were Protestants who had no knowledge of North American Indians and had no love for their Catholic invaders. Some of the results might be considered appalling, as the De Brys illustrate cannibalism and slaughter, such as Indians killing and eating Spaniards and Spaniards killing Indians. When they were finished working their way through the data and recasting it, they had created some of the first European iconography of the American Indian and unwittingly bent their historical record as they did so. Because many details were changed in republication, it is best to glean visual information from the works of the original artists rather than from the often more readily available De Bry etchings.

Journals left by individuals who participated in many of these New World explorations provide the primary historical sources.

Hernando De Soto's expedition through Florida and a large portion of the southern United States (1538–1543) is described in journals left by the Spaniards, including de Soto's own secretary. René Robert Cavelier, Sieur de La Salle's French expedition to Texas (1684–1687), has also been described in Henri Joutel's classic account. Many of these early accounts are discussed and interpreted in scholarly works such as Jerald Milanich and Susan Milbrath's *First Encounters, Spanish Exploration in the Caribbean and the United States, 1492–1570* (1989) and William Foster's *Spanish Expeditions into Texas, 1689–1768* (1995). Emma Fundaburk has compiled a catalog of pictures of North American Indians from 1564 to 1860 in her *Southeastern Indians Life Portraits* (1958), which provides a good resource for studying their dress.

PRESERVATION OF INFORMATION AND TRADITIONAL DRESS ARTIFACTS

The conservation and preservation of archaeological artifacts has long been an important function of museums across the United States; however, when physical facilities, staff, and funding are limited, this job becomes difficult. The care of organic materials is more complex than that of inorganic materials, and the combination of different materials into a single dress artifact makes conservation and preservation even more challenging. The availability of the archaeological data necessary for proper interpretation of production technology and cultural significance of dress in prehistoric societies is dependent primarily upon the archaeologists

Sixteenth-century engraving by Theodor De Bry intended to depict North American Indian men and women dancing around three women in a circle defined by posts with carved faces. De Bry and his sons reworked original pictures, in this case a watercolor by John White, and in the process introduced distortions. Here the figures show Graeco-Roman influences. Library of Congress Rare Book and Special Collections Division, LC-USZ62-40055.

who recover the remains and the specialists who analyze the specimens. However, museum and collection curators responsible for the maintenance, protection, and accessibility of artifacts to researchers also play an important role in this process. Because of their fragile nature, organic remains require extreme care and special handling on the part of all who work with them to protect the valuable information contained within them.

Jenna Kuttruff and Mary Strickland-Olsen (2000) have addressed the importance of proper handling techniques of fragile organic remains such as textiles in both the field and the laboratory. In the past, some archaeologists in the United States paid little attention to textile remains, and some textile evidence was purposefully destroyed in order to enhance the visual appearance of other artifacts considered to be more important or prestigious. Textile *pseudomorphs*, which are mineralized replacements of organic textile structures, were sometimes removed from copper artifacts such as those recovered from Hopewellian and Mississippian sites in eastern North America. Although their presence may have been noted, most often no attempt was made to analyze and record the textile data. The few known examples of such happenings leave one to wonder how much evidence was destroyed without archaeologists either being aware of, or concerned about, its existence. Although this is much less likely to occur today, it unfortunately still can happen when individual curators or researchers act according to their own biases on the importance of various types of archaeological artifacts and data.

The monumental work of the Smithsonian's National Museum of the American Indian to evaluate their collections, create a database, and provide safe and easily accessible storage for their artifacts, many of which relate to dress of North American Indians, is a prime example of steps that are being taken in the United States for the long-term preservation of information and artifacts. Other museums across the country are using federal, state, and private funding to preserve their collections.

DRESS IN THE PREHISTORIC SOUTHWEST

The archaeology of the American Southwest has yielded information about prehistoric dress based on perishable remains, which include textile remains from wearing apparel, utilitarian articles, and ceremonial paraphernalia. Both Kate Peck Kent (1983) and Lynn S. Teague (1998) have published books on the topic of prehistoric textiles in the Southwest, but Kent has specifically addressed their use in North American Indian dress. She states that it is possible to reconstruct the dress of the Basketmaker and Early Mogollon cultures (ca. 200 B.C.E. to 700 C.E.) with some degree of accuracy. According to Kent, they wore fur yarn robes, fringed aprons for females, and breechcloths for males. Yucca and apocynum fiber blankets may have been worn, and skin clothing supplemented textiles to some extent. (*Apocynaceae* is a family of plants, some of which can be processed to obtain fibers.) They also wore a variety of sandals and skin moccasins as well as headbands and perhaps looped or netted head coverings.

With the development of the loom weaving of cotton during the period between 1000 and 1400 C.E., skirts, shirts, socks, and leggings were added to the repertoire of clothing. Hides and furs appear to have been used largely as untailored shoulder robes. Types and styles of clothing worn by the different cultures in the Southwest did vary during this period. Blanket or robe styles included those made of feather fabrics and plain-weave cotton

Full-length, front and back portraits of a sixteenth-century North American Indian chief, with bow and arrow, in Virginia. Engraving by Theodor De Bry after a watercolor by John White. White accompanied both Sir Richard Grenville and Sir Francis Drake on their voyages to the East Coast of America in the 1580s. Library of Congress Rare Book and Special Collections Division, LC-USZ62-53338.

fabrics. The woven blankets were often solid colored (white, red, brown, or black), plaid, or checked plain weaves or twills with weft stripes. Some plain-weave fabrics were elaborately decorated with painted patterns or were tie-dyed. One blanket in a diamond twill tapestry has been recovered, and Hohokam robes may have been embellished with openwork, brocade, or embroidery. Sleeved shirts and sleeveless tunics were important upper-body garments, and white lacelike fabrics along with painted fabrics were evidently in vogue. Tassels and pompoms decorated the corners of some shirts. Shirts of a variety of styles and patterns are depicted on Mimbres pottery that dates from circa 1200 C.E. Skirts, often referred to in the literature as *kilts*, were long rectangular cloths folded around the hips that reached from the waist to the knee or slightly above. Kilts were a standard part of the dress of male participants in ceremonials and are depicted on prehistoric pottery and murals, some with painted or embroidered lower borders or all-over patterning by tie-dyeing, painting, tapestry weave, or openwork. The men's breechcloths were made of a narrow strip of material with one end folded to make a doubled front section. A belt was run through the fold to hold the garment in place against the body. The other end, which was sometimes fringed, was passed between the legs and fastened to the belt behind. Women wore aprons and skirts with narrow woven waistbands and free-hanging fringe. Both men and women wore breech coverings made of bundles of string or fiber pads that were passed between the legs and fastened in the front and the back.

Pueblo period peoples in all parts of the Southwest wore sandals. Socks and sandal uppers were also fashioned in simple looping with human hair yarn, feather-wrapped yarn, and yucca or cotton cord with animal hair pile. Southwestern dress incorporated narrow fabrics used as belts, hair ties, garters, and sashes. These were woven in many techniques that were temporally and regionally differentiated. Other than the use of hair ties, examples of headgear are rare. A possible skull cap, yarn turban, and twill-weave cotton hat suggest that headgear was not unknown prehistorically, but it apparently was not common. Some of the bags produced prehistorically may have been worn or carried by individuals and thus may be considered as a part of their dress. Many bags were made from fragments torn from larger fabrics that may

have been too worn to serve their original purposes. Cloth bags vary considerably in size according to their intended usage. They frequently held ceremonial objects, but seeds and knives have also been found in bags. Bags were used as quivers to hold arrows that were then worn or carried by individuals. Gourd canteens were also carried in string or netlike coverings.

Although individual examples of prehistoric dress artifacts can be described in detail, the general descriptions provided for dress over time in the Southwest are among the most complete information known for the United States. This is due to the preservation of many organic remains in the Southwest, which also provide a suggestion of the variety of dress artifacts that no longer exist in other areas. However, chance survival of dress artifacts from across the continent is vital to the piecing together of information that can make it possible to describe the dress of prehistoric North American Indians over the extended period of time before exploration and the subsequent settlement by Europeans.

Snapshot: Prehistoric Moccasins

Footwear is one class of perishable prehistoric artifacts that is often easily identifiable as to end use. Shoes serve as attire or clothing for human feet and provide protection from rough terrain and temperature extremes. In addition to their functional aspects, footwear reflects individually, regionally, culturally, and temporally based preferences.

Because the fibrous materials and leather used in construction of prehistoric footwear are perishable, they are seldom preserved in the archaeological record. Neither prehistoric nor European representations, and few European descriptions, provide much technical information on native North American footwear. Therefore, the fortuitous preservation of archaeological examples is the best source for this information and provides the primary resource for the study of prehistoric footwear. Many specimens currently in museum collections have not been radiocarbon dated, and often it is not possible to assign a cultural period based on archaeological context. The use of AMS dating has provided much needed information for researchers.

Extant footwear from Missouri and Arkansas include examples made from both fibrous plant materials and leather. The dates obtained on specimens from Arnold Research Cave in Missouri indicated a change over time from fiber to leather, but additional footwear dates from Arkansas reveal that the use of fibrous footwear did not disappear after the introduction of leather moccasins. Jenna Kuttruff has obtained AMS dates for a total of fourteen specimens ranging in date from approximately 6375 B.C.E. to 1430 C.E. The examination of the remains of prehistoric leather moccasins that were recovered from these sites has revealed many interesting practices relating to their use, wear, and reuse. Details of the design and construction of leather footwear in this region are evident in these specimens.

The leather in the moccasins has not been identified. Deer, buffalo, elk, and bear have all been mentioned as being used for moccasins in eastern North America in early historic accounts and in the ethnographic literature. Because the leather used in the specimens in this study was relatively thin, it is thought to be deer. C. Johnson has examined primary and selected secondary sources for information relating to moccasins and states that elk skins were much thicker and tougher than deer skins, which were easier to sew but wore out more quickly. Moccasins tended to wear out quickly, and a deerhide moccasin might last only one or two days when traveling. Repairing moccasins took place nearly every night on the trail, and the necessary tools and materials were carried with them. Most Eastern Woodlands moccasins were soft soled, rather than hard soled, as was more common in the American West.

A cache of leather moccasins was recovered from a bluff shelter in northwest Arkansas that contained the remains of nine moccasins plus seven additional pieces of leather with lacing holes. A small leather sample from one specimen was radiocarbon dated to 630 to 710 C.E. The cache itself appears to have been used as a source of pieces of leather for moccasin repair. By patching holes in the soles of worn moccasins, the use-life of the footwear could be extended. A replication of a moccasin was made of tanned deerskin based on a composite drawing produced from the information gleaned from this cache.

Two leather footwear specimens were recovered from a Missouri River bluff shelter. Cordage from one of the two similar specimens was AMS dated to 990 to 1170 C.E. This specimen was the latest of the seven footwear specimens dated from this cave. The better-preserved example is smaller in size and appears to have been made for a subadult. Another moccasin of this style was recovered in Arkansas. These leather specimens

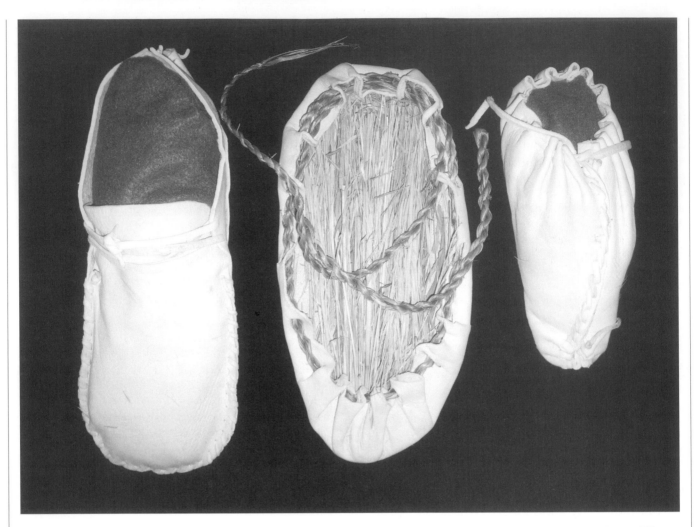

Deerskin replications of three prehistoric leather moccasins from Missouri and Arkansas: (left) two-piece moccasin from Arkansas cache, ca. 670 B.C.E.; (center) one-piece moccasin with big bluestem padding from Missouri, ca. 1080 C.E.; (right) one-piece moccasin with vamp seam from Arkansas, ca. 1365 C.E. Photograph by Jenna Tedrick Kuttruff.

were each made from a single piece of leather that had been drawn up and around the foot by running a drawstring through holes made around the outer edges of an oval piece of leather. During replication of this moccasin, the tanned deerskin was dampened to facilitate stretching of the lacing holes and shaping the shoe.

The moccasin with the latest date, 1300 to 1430 C.E., is from Arkansas and of one-piece construction with a vamp seam. (The vamp is the area of the shoe between the toes and the ankle.) Two additional undated specimens that are similar in style have been recovered from other Arkansas shelters. The pattern for this moccasin is somewhat fan shaped. The edges of the seam over the instep were brought together and stitched with a backstitch so that the stitching is on the outside of the moccasin and runs along the top of the foot. The toe is gathered with running stitches, and the narrow leather lacing is knotted with an overhand knot to secure both ends.

Some information on indigenous North American footwear can be found in early European accounts. However, descriptions of North American Indian dress were often superficial, and many times the natives were described simply as "naked."

When descriptions of footwear were omitted in early accounts, it may be questionable as to whether footwear was not present or simply not described or illustrated. M. Du Pratz, in his account originally published in 1774, has described the attire of the natives of Louisiana and provided a description and illustrations of a man, woman, and young girl wearing moccasins. However, he stated that they seldom wore shoes except when they traveled. The moccasins in the illustrations are taller but otherwise appear to be similar in construction to the one-piece moccasins with a vamp seam like those recovered from Arkansas.

Replication of these leather moccasins as well as selected examples of fibrous footwear reported by Kuttruff and colleagues in 2004 has led to a greater understanding of the characteristics of prehistoric footwear from this region and has helped to answer questions that would be difficult to answer from technical analysis alone. It is now possible to answer questions concerning materials, tools, construction techniques, and labor input, and important knowledge has been gained about the skill and human effort that went into their construction. Replications make it possible to identify the probable steps required to produce such artifacts and have helped to clarify specific or detailed aspects of their construction processes. Also, some of the thought and decision-making processes required to design and construct these artifacts became more apparent to the researchers. This new knowledge increases our understanding of attendant lifestyles in prehistoric eastern North America.

REFERENCES AND FURTHER READING

Du Pratz, M. Le Page. *The History of Louisiana, or of the Western Parts of Virginia and Carolina.* Translated by T. Becket. Baton Rouge, LA: Claitor's Publishing Division, 1972. (Originally published in 1774.)

Johnson, C. *Walk Softly, Moccasins in the Primary Documents.* Excelsior Springs, MO: Graphics/Fine Arts Press, 1996.

Kuttruff, J. T., S. G. DeHart, and M. J. O'Brien. "7500 Years of Prehistoric Footwear from Arnold Research Cave, Missouri." *Science* 281, no. 5373 (1998): 72–75.

Kuttruff, J. T., M. S. Standifer, and S. G. DeHart. "Replication of Prehistoric Footwear and Bags." *Louisiana Agriculture* 47, no. 1 (2004): 20–22.

References and Further Reading

Adair, James. *History of the American Indians.* Edited by Samuel C. Williams. New York: Promontory Press, 1930. (Originally published in 1775.)

Charlevoux, Pierre de. *Journal of a Voyage to North-America.* 2 vols. New York: Readex Microprint, 1966. (Originally published in 1744; first English translation published in 1761.)

Foster, William C. *Spanish Expeditions into Texas, 1689–1768.* Austin: University of Texas Press, 1995.

Fundaburk, Emma Lila, ed. *Southeastern Indians Life Portraits, A Catalogue of Pictures 1564–1860.* Tallahassee, FL: Rose Printing Company, Inc., 1958; reprint, 1996.

Joppien, Rüdiger, and Bernard Smith. *The Art of Captain Cook's Voyages, Volume Three Text and Volume Three Catalogue, The Voyage of the Resolution and Discovery 1776–1780.* New Haven, CT: Yale University Press, 1988.

Kent, Kate Peck. *Prehistoric Textiles of the Southwest.* Santa Fe, NM: School of American Research, 1983.

Kuttruff, Jenna Tedrick, and Mary Strickland-Olsen. "Handling Archaeological Textile Remains in the Field and Laboratory." In *Beyond Cloth and Cordage: Current Approaches to Archaeological Textile Research in the Americas,* edited by Penelope Drooker and Laurie Webster, 25–50. Salt Lake City: University of Utah Press, 2000.

Milanich, Jerald T., and Susan Milbrath, eds. *First Encounters, Spanish Exploration in the Caribbean and the United States, 1492–1570.* Gainesville: University of Florida Press, 1989.

Phillips, Phillip, and James A. Brown. *Pre-Columbian Shell Engravings from the Craig Mound at Spiro, Oklahoma.* 6 vols. Cambridge, MA: Peabody Museum of Archaeology and Ethnology, 1975–1982.

Swanton, John R. *The Indians of the Southeastern United States.* Bureau of American Ethnology, Bulletin 173. Washington, DC: Smithsonian Institution Press, 1979. (Originally published in 1946.)

Teague, Lynn S. *Textiles in Southwestern Prehistory.* Albuquerque: University of New Mexico Press, 1998.

Jenna Tedrick Kuttruff

See also Introduction to North American Indian/First Nation Peoples.

Evidence about Dress of Indigenous People: Canadian Territory

Cordage from the Kilii Gwaay site, Ellen Island, in southern Haida Gwaii. This piece of braided string was made using two strands of split spruce root and one strand of a monocot (flowering plant). The string dates to circa 9,450 radiocarbon years ago (10,700 calendar years ago) and demonstrates knowledge of weaving technology. Photograph by Daryl Fedje.

Studying dress archaeologically poses unique challenges. Preservation is a primary concern because elements of dress involving hair, skin, and most fibers are usually absent. These limitations can be overcome through reference to other sources of dress-related data: written accounts, imagery, and ethnographic comparisons. However, for many periods these analogies may be inappropriate, and archaeological data, alone, provide clues to missing elements.

Some types of sites are better suited than others for preserving archaeological information relevant to the study of dress. Mortuary sites tend to be more revealing than settlement sites, because elements of dress are frequently disposed in their normal mode on the bodies of the deceased. However, the analysis of mortuary sites requires a great degree of cultural sensitivity. For most native North American cultures the exhumation or examination of the dead and their grave goods is considered problematic and disrespectful.

While laws such as the Native American Graves Protection and Repatriation Act (NAGPRA) protect these beliefs in the United States, no such laws exist in Canada, though certain museums have their own rules regarding what may or may not be examined, photographed, or published by researchers. If museums provide no guidelines, consulting aboriginal communities directly is advised. Most Canadian aboriginal communities maintain cultural centers to deal with questions of cultural heritage and their past, and they may also hold collections and archival resources. More information on cultural property issues can be found in the Canadian Archaeological Association's "Statement of Principles for Ethical Conduct Pertaining to Aboriginal Peoples," and the Aboriginal Canada Portal provides information and links to First Nations, Inuit, and Métis communities.

The preservation of information on traditional dress artifacts through archaeological collections in Canada is done largely by museums and archival centers. Except for the work of Marc Laberge, Karlis Karklins, and Michèle Hayeur Smith, relatively little research is being done to expand information on traditional dress based on these collections. As a result, the literature on the archaeology of dress of First Nations is deeply embedded in general archaeological literature and is descriptive. The symbolic analysis of dress in archaeological contexts owes much of its vigor to postprocessual theory, a postmodernist perspective, more completely developed in European than North American archaeology.

THE PALEOINDIAN PERIOD

Humans arrived in the Americas from Siberia at least twelve thousand years ago. The earliest colonizing communities south of the Pleistocene ice sheets are known as the *Paleoindian cultures*. Their descendants, generally referred to as the *Plano cultures*, spread northward into northern Ontario, Quebec, Labrador, the Plains, and the Subarctic regions as the Laurentide ice sheet melted, eight to ten thousand years ago.

Hunters and gatherers colonizing newly exposed land south of the ice mass hunted both extinct and still extant animals and gathered wild plant resources that may have provided raw materials for clothing and dress. Population density appears to have been low, groups were highly mobile, and their archaeological record is, therefore, limited. A few sites from this period have revealed components of dress that indicate that it was considered more than functional and carried symbolic overtones as in subsequent periods.

On-Your-Knees Cave, British Columbia (8300 B.C.E.) produced one bone awl, or punch used for the working of hides, and at the site of Kilii Gwaay (7500 B.C.E.) a piece of three-strand braided cordage was found. Although cordage does not imply its use in clothing manufacture, it demonstrates knowledge of weaving technology. At Charlie Lake Cave, in the Peace River region of British Columbia, a stone bead was uncovered in strata dating to 8770 B.C.E. Similar beads have been recovered at other Paleoindian sites.

The absence of preserved bone on most Paleoindian sites limits inferences regarding dress-related implements, such as tattooing needles, jewelry made of bone, and so forth. Paleoindian culture formed the groundwork for subsequent cultures to follow. In the East, they evolved into the Archaic periods, while in the West, the Plano culture continued.

THE NORTHEAST: DRESS FOR THE PRE-COLUMBIAN PERIOD

The Northeast includes parts of New England in the United States, as well as the Canadian Maritime Provinces (Nova Scotia, New Brunswick, Prince Edward Island), Newfoundland and Labrador, Quebec, the Gulf of the Saint Lawrence, and southern Ontario. During the Archaic period (8000–1000 B.C.E.) dress artifacts appear with increasing diversity and frequency, particularly during the Middle to Late Archaic (6000 to 2000 B.C.E.).

The eastern seaboard from Labrador to the Gulf of the Saint Lawrence was home to Maritime Archaic cultures founded on the exploitation of maritime resources. Dress-related artifacts of the Maritime Archaic period include objects of native copper, shell, and red ochre. Red ochre was widely used in prehistoric and historic contexts for ritual activity and was frequently incorporated into burials or smudged on ritual objects, items of dress, and on the deceased. For many First Nations people, red was a socially ambivalent color, expressing both animate and emotive aspects of life. Anthropology and archaeology scholar George Hamell has noted that it was "socially positive when connoting life in contrast to death or it was antisocial when connoting hostility in contrast to harmony."

At Port-au-Choix, Newfoundland, fifty-three burials were discovered in 1968. Along with stone tools and hunting equipment, the people of Port-aux-Choix were buried with bone and antler combs, hairpins, bone tubes, whistles, sewing needles, and pendants. Shell beads and pendants as well as the teeth, feet, and beaks of diverse birds, including loon, gulls, ducks, and the now-extinct great auk, were present. Graves containing the remains of some birds also held effigy combs depicting the same birds.

A mound dated 5000 to 5500 B.C.E. at l'Anse-d'Amour, Labrador, covered the burial of a child twelve or thirteen years of age. The child had been covered with red ochre and was buried with red ochre nodules, graphite, and other colored stones, as well as a bone implement used for grinding pigments. In front of his face lay a walrus tusk and under his neck, an engraved bone pendant.

Approximately four thousand years ago, a deteriorating climate in the maritime region made it less habitable for Maritime Archaic hunter-gatherers, and shortly thereafter the Paleo-Eskimo populations entered the regions from the Arctic. Eventually the descendants of Maritime Archaic people became the Beothuk, occupying Newfoundland's coastal region and Labrador.

In southern Quebec, parts of the Gulf and southern Ontario, Laurentian Archaic communities developed after 4000 B.C.E. These communities were intimately adapted to the resources of the hardwood forests of the interior. Red ochre and bright green clay were both used to dress their dead and were probably also used for body coloration. Native copper objects also appear in Laurentian burials in the form of utilitarian implements or as emblems of identity. Ornaments such as beads and pendants, ear spools, and pan pipes were also known and became more abundant in the later Archaic. Copper artifacts from the Lake Superior region, as well as beads, pendants, and gorgets (large

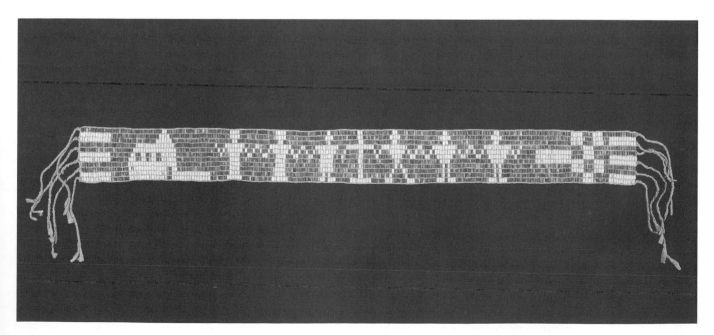

Wampum belt made from hide, shell, and beads ca. 1650–1780, Eastern Woodlands, (?)Huron-Wendat. The appearance of wampum beads on Iroquoian garments during the seventeenth century reflects expanded interaction with Algonquian cultures of the New England coast. McCord M1905. http://www.mccord-museum.qc.ca/en/

pendants) made from shells originating in the Gulf of Mexico and Atlantic seaboard, document long-distance trade networks across northeastern North America in the Late Archaic.

Pre-Contact dress artifacts in the Northeast consist of natural materials, because the technology of smelting metals was unknown to native people of Canada. Metals that were used predating European contact were usually meteoric or native copper.

The Woodland period in the Northeast is marked by changes in technology, notably the introduction of ceramics and agriculture followed by population explosion and palisaded villages in some areas. The adoption of pottery marks the beginning of a new era for archaeologists, but not all areas of the Northeast adopted pottery simultaneously, and agriculture arrived late or was never adopted in many parts.

The Augustine Mound in New Brunswick is affiliated with the Early Woodland Adena culture (800–200 B.C.E.) of the Ohio Valley. Multiple caches interred along with human remains within the mound contained tools and dress-related artifacts such as polished stones, smoking pipes, copper beads, and shell pendants. Textiles were also found partially preserved by proximity to copper artifacts. Their complex weaving techniques suggest that the people of this period were equipped with rugs, baskets, complex fiber clothing, and bags. Analyses of the textiles revealed that the fibers used included deer, beaver, dog, and wolf fur as well as plant fibers.

The Middle Woodland of southern Quebec and Ontario (ca. 200 B.C.E. to 1000 C.E.) witnessed an increase in burial goods and items of dress as well as mound burial ceremonialism, thought to have originated in the Hopewellian cultures of the Ohio Valley. Dress-related artifacts of this period include large undecorated stone gorgets, shell beads from the Gulf of Mexico and the Atlantic seaboards; copper ear spools; stone platform pipes; copper and silver pan pipes, worked bear and wolf skull parts probably used in headdresses; and red ochre, limonite, and graphite possibly used as body-painting pigments.

THE NORTHEAST: PRE- AND POST-EUROPEAN CONTACT

During the Late Woodland phase, the ancestral cultures of the historic Iroquois (including the Saint Lawrence Iroquois, the Huron, Petun, Neutral, Erie, Wenro, Seneca, Cayuga, Oneida, Onondaga, and the Mohawk) developed in Quebec, Ontario, and adjacent parts of New York State. Algonquian-speaking people (probably ancestors of the contemporary Ojibwa, Cree, Algonquin Montagnais, Naskapi or Labrador, Malecite, Micmac, and the now-extinct Beothuk) were found through the Canadian Maritime provinces and much of Ontario and Quebec.

Among the early historic Iroquoians, dress-related artifacts began to reflect specific cultural affiliation, with dress increasing in elaboration westward through a territory extending from the north shore of the Saint Lawrence to southeastern Ontario and into New York State. Items most commonly recovered on Saint Lawrence Iroquoian archaeological sites included bear, deer, and beaver teeth pendants, plain clay beads; stone beads; and freshwater and marine shell beads. Iroquoian effigy pipes document the role of tattooing, facial painting, and elaborate hairstyles.

Although historical descriptions attest that Iroquoians wore skin garments, none survive archaeologically. Perforated deer phalange "tinklers" seem likely counterparts to the copper or tin tinkling cones sewn onto garments after European contact. Gorgets made from human parietal bones were also greatly valued by the Saint Lawrence Iroquois and neighboring Iroquoians.

After European contact, trade items such as glass beads, tinkling cones, and copper cauldrons cut and modified into items of dress were integrated into regional Iroquoian and Algonquian

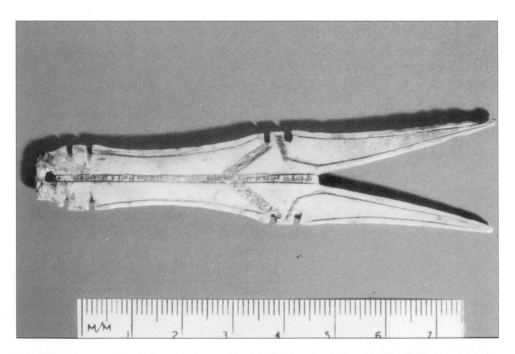

This intricately carved Beothuk pendant was found in Newfoundland, Canada. The Beothuk people were descendants of the Maritime Archaic hunter-gatherers who populated the region about four thousand years ago. © Canadian Museum of Civilization, artifact VIII-A102, image S78-1213. http://www.civilization.ca/

dress. Indigenous trade in shells expanded at the same time. Among the Neutral, large shell ear spools and massive shell gorgets document intensifying trade networks with cultures of the Mississippi Valley and the Gulf of Mexico, while the appearance of whelk and quahog wampum beads during the seventeenth century reflects expanded interaction with Algonquian cultures of the New England coast. Certain Iroquoians are described in European accounts as being fully tattooed from head to toe while others, such as the Petun, adorned themselves with different materials such as red catlinite and slate.

Northern Algonquian bands maintained independent identities as nomadic hunters and gatherers through the Contact period. In Ontario they also established friendly relationships with the Iroquoian Huron and Petun, trading resources for meat.

The archaeological record of these prehistoric Algonquian bands is poorly known. Sites yield evidence for isolated fragments of native copper jewelry and stone pendants. Documentary records preserved in the Jesuit Relations indicate that at the time of European contact the Northern Algonquians employed a well-established tradition of painted garments. This tradition later developed into the famous painted coats worn by the Naskapi and Montagnais of the Historic period.

THE SUBARCTIC: DRESS OF THE PRE-COLUMBIAN PERIOD

Canada's Subarctic region is conventionally divided into three main areas: the Eastern, North-Central, and Western Subarctic. These are occupied by two main cultural-linguistic groups: Algonquian cultures in the Eastern and Athapaskans in North-Central and Western regions. The Eastern Subarctic was occupied in the Archaic period after the area was freed by the melting of the Laurentide Ice Sheet. The Shield archaic was found throughout northern Ontario, Manitoba, Quebec, and interior Labrador. With low population density and acidic soil, few sites are known and few organic artifacts remain today, though the recovery of bone snowshoe netting needles implied adaptation to deep winter conditions and knowledge of sewing technologies. With the addition of pottery to the Shield Archaic traditions, ca. 1000 B.C.E. in Manitoba, East-Central Saskatchewan, Ontario, and extreme Western Quebec, regional traditions developed that are now known as the Laurel culture. Laurel artifacts related to dress include snowshoeing netting needles, tubular copper beads, bangles, and abundant quantities of red ochre.

Western Subarctic Paleo-Eskimo groups briefly occupied the barren lands west of Hudson's Bay 4,200 years ago, and by 2,600 years ago they had retreated northward. Another Subarctic group, the Taltheilei culture, ancestral to later Athapaskans, migrated into land formerly occupied by the Paleo-Eskimo in northern Alberta and the Northwest Territories. Flaked tablets, called *chithos*, found in Taltheilei sites were used for scraping of hides.

Northern Archaic cultures occupied the Yukon and Northwest Territories, as well as northern British Columbia and Alberta, from 8000 B.C.E. to 700 C.E., and by 700 C.E. the area was populated by early Athapaskans. Dress-related artifacts are rare on these sites and first appear in significant numbers after 700 C.E., when there is an increase in tools used for making garments and tanning hides. A fourteen-hundred-year-old moccasin, recently recovered from a melting ice field in the mountains of the southern Yukon, was ankle-high and tied by a drawstring. It may have been part of summer wear for an ancient hunter.

THE SUBARCTIC: PRE- AND POST-EUROPEAN CONTACT

The Beothuk of Labrador and Newfoundland were the first native Canadian peoples encountered by Europeans. Splendid examples of dress-related artifacts have been found on Beothuk sites, including a moccasin from Dark Tickle, in Notre-Dame Bay, Newfoundland, found on a mummified child. Wonderfully carved bone clothing ornaments or pendants are prolific, as are bone combs and small humanoid carvings.

THE ARCTIC: DRESS OF THE PRE-COLUMBIAN PERIOD

The Canadian Arctic was populated in a sequence of waves from Siberia. The earliest pioneers, known as the Paleo-Eskimos, arrived roughly four thousand years ago. Their descendants, known archaeologically as Pre-Dorset and Dorset cultures, occupied the Canadian Arctic for nearly thirty-three hundred years. Early Paleo-Eskimo hunted muskoxen and used their furs and skins to construct tents and blankets. Women prepared skins using caribou and muskox hides for clothing and sealskins for footwear; they used sinew from caribou for thread. Abundant small bone needles and needle fragments found on High Arctic sites testify to this lifestyle.

Dress-related artifacts are abundant on permanently frozen Dorset sites. Most are bone pendant amulets and small items carried on the body. Approximately one thousand of these small ivory carvings have been recovered and are believed to be amulets worn for their talismanic powers in hunting or other types of magic. Most represent humans or animals, such as polar bears, walrus, caribou (often depicted as a hoof), seals, and birds. Humanoid representations include miniature masks, some with elaborate markings depicting tattoo motifs similar to those worn by later men and women of the Arctic.

A set of carved animal teeth with large canines, dated to 500–1000 C.E., are thought to have been used during shamanistic ceremonies to give the shaman the appearance of a wolf, bear, or predator. The Dundas Island site in the High Arctic produced a number of these small amulets along with a wooden human figure and a small pair of ivory sunglasses. Another figure from Devon Island represents a man dressed in traditional Dorset clothing: parka, trousers, and *kamiks* (boots) along with a hoodless high-collared coat. A wooden shaman's mask, found eroding from a sea beach in the High Arctic, testifies to Dorset skills as master carvers and includes a labret-like spur above the upper lip of the mask.

THE ARCTIC: PRE- AND POST-EUROPEAN CONTACT

A few centuries prior to 1000 C.E. the climate of the Arctic underwent a warming phase, and for Dorset hunters, who had thrived in colder environments, the sudden change must have brought on unexpected challenges. The end of the Dorset cultures, by 1350 C.E., remains a mystery, although this warming period also witnessed the introduction of a new people: the Thule ancestors of the present-day Inuit. The Thule were proficient open-water sea hunters who

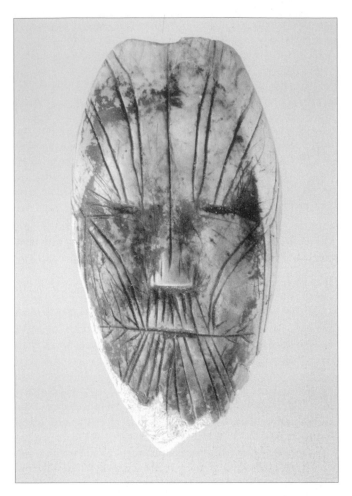

Mask with markings that may represent tattoos, 1700 B.C.E., Canadian Arctic. © Canadian Museum of Civilization, artifact QkHn-13:489, image S90-4013. http://www.civilization.ca/

spread rapidly across Canada and into Greenland. Thule items of dress include amulets, ivory sculptural pendants, and snow goggles as well as knives and portable items carried on the body.

Thule and later Inuit women have been described as the most skilled seamstresses of native Canada. Decorative ivory needle cases and thimble holders testify to their talents. Evidence of their sewing abilities can also be observed on clothing recovered from a site at Qilakitsoq, Western Greenland, and areas settled by the Inuit of Labrador and the adjacent Canadian shores. Around 1475 C.E., six women and two children were buried at Qilakitsoq under a rock shelter, where they mummified naturally. Each individual was fully clothed in tailored parkas, trousers, and kamiks made from skins. The mummification process preserved facial tattoos, a common practice across the Eastern and Central Arctic and frequently consisting of vertical lines drawn on women's chins to mark major life events. Male facial tattooing was practiced in the Western Arctic, where it was linked to the whale hunt, and in the Labrador region among the Copper Inuit.

THE PLAINS: DRESS OF THE PRE-COLUMBIAN PERIOD

The Plains extend southward from the short-grass prairies of the Saskatchewan River into south-central United States, with the Canadian portion occupying southern Manitoba, Saskatchewan, Alberta, and the southern Subarctic boreal forests.

Plains Archaic people were nomadic, surviving predominantly by hunting buffalo or bison from which they made clothing, bags, moccasins, and skin tent covers. Similar subsistence patterns continued into the Historic period. On Middle period sites (ca. 6000–2000 B.C.E.), scrapers frequently outnumber projectile points, stressing the importance of tanning and treating hides for all manner of dress and portable containers used in a nomadic lifestyle.

Bone artifacts are not abundant. A bone needle used in the manufacture of clothing was found at the Stampede site, and the Whitemouth falls site in Manitoba yielded an adult female burial covered in red ochre with an ochre-filled clam shell near her head.

Evidence for long-distance trade is apparent on Oxbow complex sites (2000 B.C.E.) with copper from the Great Lakes region and marine shell beads from the Atlantic coast. Bone was used to make beads and gorgets, and a copper crescent pendant found at Castor Creek, Alberta, most likely originated in the Great Lakes. Eagle talons were also found in burials from the Gray site in Saskatchewan; whether they had amuletic purposes or were worn as items of dress is unclear. Ammonite fossils, called Buffalo stones, were considered personally owned effigies of bison by the later Blackfoot and have been found in Alberta, and dentalia shells, obtained through trade with Pacific coast societies, were uncovered at the Crown site in Saskatchewan.

The Late period on the Plains (2000 B.C.E. to 1750 C.E.) saw the introduction of pottery, an intensification of bison hunting, and the introduction of the bow and arrow. Burials also changed during the Pelican Lake phase (1000 B.C.E.). Pelican Lake people, like earlier Plains cultures, obtained exotic goods from across North America, including olivella and dentalium shells used in dress. Bone and animal teeth that had been perforated and worn as pendants were found at the Highwood River site in Alberta.

A highly successful bison-hunting culture, the Besant Series (first century C.E.), produced mound burials in the southeastern Canadian Plains. These burials were equipped with a myriad of grave goods, including ceramic pipes; pendants of shell, tooth, and bone; beads of bone, shell, and rolled copper; and red and green pigments.

The carved and painted petroglyphs of Alberta's badlands also provide information on early Plains dress. The Writing-on-Stone site preserves rock carvings with images of war, hunting, and ceremonial activities, suggesting that the area was visited for its sacred character for three thousand years. One figure, a rider on horseback wearing a feathered headdress, clearly dates to the period after horses were reintroduced to North America from the Spanish colonies. Other scenes depicting men with large circular shields decorated with fringe and heraldic designs are probably of far greater antiquity.

THE PLAINS: PRE- AND POST-EUROPEAN CONTACT

As elsewhere in Canada, greater diversity and abundance of dress-related artifacts is noted from approximately 1000 C.E. to the Contact period. The Devil's Lake–Soursiford burial complex of southwestern Manitoba, southeastern Saskatchewan, and northeastern North Dakota provides evidence for a rapid intensification in the diversity and frequency of dress items, including: marine shell (whelk) gorgets, pendants, columella beads, and trapezoidal shell pendants; bone anklets, bracelets, collars, and wrist guards; bird bone beads; and headbands. Shell continued to dominate the dress attachments in the protohistoric phase (called the Mortlach aggregate) with buffalo-tooth necklaces appearing by the sixteenth century.

European contact introduced new materials to the Plains cultures. Items collected in the eighteenth, nineteenth, and twentieth centuries document a wealth of dress practices that are invisible in the archaeological record. Garments were painted, decorated with beadwork, and overlaid with porcupine-quill embroidery probably originating in an ancient tradition that archaeology cannot document.

THE NORTHWEST COAST: DRESS OF THE PRE-COLUMBIAN PERIOD

The Northwest Coast cultural region extends from Oregon to British Columbia and southern Alaska; its villages and tribes cluster between the Pacific Coast and high coastal mountain ranges.

The terms *Paleoindian*, *Archaic*, and *Woodland*, which are encountered in other parts of Canada, are not applicable to the Northwest Coast. The area is culturally and environmentally diverse, with long and continuous records of hunting, fishing, and gathering cultures of considerable complexity. Archaeologists working in this region divided its cultural record into the Lithic stage and Early, Middle, and Late Developmental stages. The Lithic stage is contemporary with the Paleoindian period, described previously.

The Developmental stage (4000 B.C.E. to Contact period) is marked by increased artifact diversification, the appearance of specialized fishing and sea mammal hunting, large houses, complex woodworking, larger populations, and art and durable objects that were worn to mark wealth and status. Labrets—bone, wood, or stone plugs worn below the lower lip—appear during the Early Developmental phase ca. 4000–1000 B.C.E. Small pin-shaped labrets made of soft stone were recovered from Late Charles Mayne phase (4000 B.C.E.) deposits at the Helen Point site. Another Early Developmental phase site, Glenrose Cannery, produced a small antler carving revealing extraordinary details about dress practices, with pendulous ear lobes, a flared hairdo, and a pointed chin interpreted as a beard.

The Middle Developmental phase (1000 B.C.E. to 500 C.E.) is marked by an intensification of woodworking technology, an increase in art objects, and craft specialization. Dress artifacts, some incorporating exotic materials, indicate concerns with status display and social complexity that are also apparent in burial practices. Labrets proliferate and are joined by ear spools and beads of varied type, size, and shape. Stone sculptures offer supplementary details on dress practices of the period. A seated human-figure bowl was represented with a pierced nasal septum, while stone sculptures and bowls dating to this period were used as mortars for mixing pigments and grease, perhaps for face and body painting.

Waterlogged sites offer evidence of the richness of Northwest Coast perishable technologies with basketry and cordage demonstrating knowledge of weaving techniques that may imply non-preserved textiles similar to those of the Historic period. Exotic raw materials, such as amber, appear in Middle Developmental phase burials. Copper from the Copper River region of Alaska

was made into bracelets, pendants, and tubular beads by people living at Prince Rupert Harbor. Cranial modification, found among skeletal remains from the southern portions of the Northwest Coast, suggests that it was used as a marker of ranking.

Late Developmental stage sites (500 C.E. to the Contact period) were occupied by the ancestors of Historic period Northwest Coast tribes. Artifact types such as hair pins, combs, and slate "mirrors" in early northern Tsimshian sites appear for the first time. Although the function of these latter objects has been a topic of debate, the slate surface, when wet, is reflective, supporting the mirror hypothesis.

The arts of this period clearly resemble later Historic period Northwest Coast artistic expressions. Weaving appears to assume new importance, particularly among the Salishan peoples of the southern Northwest Coasts, who produced an expanded range of decorated wood, bone, and antler spindle whorls along with blanket pins. Blankets were apparently woven from mountain goat and dog hair, along with cedar bark, and were worn as shawls, not unlike the chilkat blankets of Tlingit in late nineteenth century.

THE NORTHWEST COAST: PRE- AND POST-EUROPEAN CONTACT

Although labrets ceased to be worn on most of the Northwest Coast after the first century C.E., they were readopted by the Tlingit, Haida, and Tsimshian after 500 C.E. These ornaments

Salish spindle whorl, British Columbia, typical of the Late Developmental stage, ca. 500 C.E. This would have been used as a weight placed on a spindle. The spinner drops and twists the spindle while continually feeding additional fiber to be twisted into the yarn. The weight of the whorl maintains the momentum, allowing the twisting motion to continue for the maximum length of time. © Canadian Museum of Civilization, artifact VIII-G-6, image S82-268. http://www.civilization.ca/

were frequently described by early European travelers and were inserted into an incision cut below women's lower lips at the onset of puberty to advertise their marriageability. After marriage and the birth of children, the piercings were enlarged with more prominent labrets of precious materials (copper or abalone shell inlay) used to mark the status of elite women.

Other significant items of dress recorded at European contact included copper neck rings made of heavy twisted rods and copper shields found among the Historic period Tlingit, Haida, Tsimshian, Bella Coola, and Kwakiutl.

Copper shields were given names and were thought to represent the ancestors of their owners. Although larger shields were neither worn nor carried into battle, smaller copper shields two to three inches (five to eight centimeters) in length were sewn onto garments or worn as earrings by the wealthy. The larger shields were displayed at potlatch ceremonies, rites of succession for chiefs, and at elite marriages.

Masks were also produced and worn throughout the Northwest Coast. According to Madonna Moss (1999), masks evoked the spirits and were the most important elements of Tlingit shamans' dress. Masks facilitated shamans' abilities to take on the spirits' speech and dance; labrets denoted female spirits.

RECORDS OF EARLY CONTACTS

The written records of early explorers, missionaries, and captives provide the earliest comprehensive descriptions of durable and perishable dress-related items. While relatively few offer detailed accounts of dress, most contain useful anecdotes. Not without their own problems, including observers' biases and variable skills of observation, these historic records provide valuable European eyewitness accounts about Aboriginal dress. Descriptions of tattooed or painted facial and bodily decoration, hairstyles, headdresses, the construction of clothing, and practices relating to the body offer information inaccessible through archaeological material alone.

A vast corpus of historical texts exists for the Northeast. The most renowned are the Jesuit Relations, of which several editions exist. An English translation by Reuben Gold Thwaites (1896–1901) is available online. Other critical documents exist in French with English translations: Jacques Cartier, Samuel de Champlain, Marc Lescarbot, Gabriel Sagard, Baron de Lahontan (1709), François-Joseph Lafitau (1724), among others. Marc Laberge (1998) has provided a good overview of early historical sources relating to dress practices in the Northeast, while Marius Barbeau's (1950) "Indian Captivities" summarizes the literature regarding Indian captivities. Some of these are also available online at Early Canadiana Online.

A valuable account of the eastern Canadian Subarctic is Baqueville de la Potherie (1722), volume 1. More westerly regions of the Subarctic have been described by employees of the Hudson's Bay Company, notably Samuel Hearne (1768 voyage) and Sir Alexander Mackenzie (1789 voyage), who also ventured across the Rockies into British Columbia.

The early Contact period Canadian Arctic has been best described by Franz Boas (1885, 1888), Kund Rasmussen (1999), and Diamond Jenness (1928). Valuable early accounts of the Plains cultures have also been recorded by employees of the Hudson's Bay Company who explored the region with Henry Kelsey (1684 voyage). Pierre Gaultier de Varennes, sieur de La Vérendrye (1685–1749), a soldier and explorer who reached the mouth of the Saskatchewan River in 1741, has also recorded informative details.

Carol F. Jopling (1989) has provided an extensive description and bibliography of Russian, British, and Spanish explorers to the Northwest Coast who described dress-related practices and the use of copper. Among the earliest accounts are from the voyages of Juan Perez, who in 1774 explored the coasts of British Columbia, the Queen Charlotte Islands, Prince of Wales Island, Vancouver Island, and the coasts of Washington and Oregon. One of his chaplains, Juan Crespi (1774), described the Haida. On another voyage, Captain Cook (1778) offered details about the Nootka. Many more documentary sources exist and can be accessed through the Handbook of North American Indians, a twenty-volume encyclopedia summarizing knowledge about all native peoples north of Mesoamerica.

MUSEUMS AND ARCHIVAL COLLECTIONS

A number of museums and archival centers across Canada house collections of archaeological and ethnographic materials. Those with collections primarily of archaeological materials include the Laboratoires et réserve d'archéologie du Québec; the Newfoundland Museum: The Rooms, with a collection of Beothuk archaeological material; the Huronia Museum and Huron Ouandat Village in Midland, Ontario, which has archaeological collections of the Huron Petun and Ojibwa; and the Museum of Ontario Archaeology in London, Ontario, with Iroquoian material. This collection is located on the Lawson Late Prehistoric village site. Other collections of note are found at the Royal Saskatchewan Museum in Regina, which holds archaeological collections from Saskatchewan and Plains prehistory, and the Royal British Columbia Museum in Victoria, with archaeological collections for the Northwest Coast.

Other museums with useful collections include the Nova Scotia Museum in Halifax, Nova Scotia, with archaeological and ethnographic collections for the Micmac; the McCord Museum of Canadian History in Montreal, Quebec province, with ethnographic material and minimal archaeological collections of the Saint Lawrence Iroquois (Dawson site); and the Royal Ontario Museum, Toronto, Ontario, which holds ethnographic collections from across Canada and archaeological collections from Ontario. The Canadian Museum of Civilization, Quebec province, has archaeological and ethnographic collections for all of Canada that are accessible online. The Manitoba Museum of Man and Nature is home to the Winnipeg Hudson's Bay Company and contains mostly ethnographic collections from Plains, Subarctic, and Northwest Coast peoples. The Glenbow Foundation, Calgary, Alberta, has ethnographic holdings of Plains, Inuit, Northwest Coast, and Métis people, as well as some Subarctic, Iroquoian, and Micmac, and it also has an accessible Web site. The Museum of Anthropology at the University of British Columbia, Vancouver, holds ethnographic and archaeological material from the Northwest Coast, and the Simon Fraser University Museum in Burnaby, British Columbia, houses archaeological and ethnographic collections of Northwest Coast material.

In addition to museum collections, a number of archives hold material relating to First Nations peoples. These include some that can be reached on the Internet: Library and Archives Canada in Ottawa, Ontario, contains all forms of historical documentation.

Some items in the image library are available online. John Carter Brown Library, Brown University, Providence, Rhode Island, has information related to Colonial America, substantial information on native peoples of New France and the Northeast, and an online image library. Archives Canada France is another source for documentary evidence. Other possible alternatives include consulting French archives such as the Archives d'Outre mer, Colonial archives Aix-en-Provence, France. Not available by Internet are the Hudson's Bay Company archives in the Archives of Manitoba in Winnipeg, which include the Northeast, Subarctic, and Plains; and the British Columbia Archives, Victoria, British Columbia, where documents, maps, and images from the Pacific Northwest Coast are housed.

The Virtual Museums of Canada is a useful Internet source. It has online exhibits about First Nations as well as artifact catalogs uploaded from museums across Canada.

References and Further Reading

Ammitzbøl, T., M. Bencard, J. Bodenhoff, Rolf Gilberg, A. Johansson, J. Medlgaard, G. Møller, R. Møller, E. Svejgaard, and L. Vanggaard. "Clothing." In *The Greenland Mummies*. Published for the Trustees of the British Museum. London: British Museum Publications, 1985.

Bacqueville de la Potherie, Claude-Charles. *Histoire de l'Amerique Septentrionale: Divisée en quatre tomes. Tome premier. Contenant le voyage du fort de Nelson, dans la baye d'Hudson, à l'extrémité de l'Amerique. Le premier établissement des François dans ce vaste païs, la prise dudit fort de Nelson, la description du fleuve de Saint Laurent, le gouvernement de Quebec, des trois rivieres & de Montreal, depuis 1534. jusqu'à 1701. / Par Mr. de Bacqueville de la Potherie, né à la Guadaloupe, dans l'Amerique Meridionale, aide major de ladite isle.* Paris: Chez Jean-Luc Nion, au premier pavillon des quatre nations, à Ste. Monique. Et François Didot à l'entrée du quai des Augustins, à la Bible d'or, 1722.

Barbeau, Marius. "Indian Captivities." *Proceedings of the American Philosophical Society* 94, no. 6 (Dec 22nd 1950): 522–548.

Beaglehole, J. C., ed. *Journal of Captain James Cook on His Voyage of Discovery, the Voyage of the Resolution and Discovery 1776–1780.* Vol. 4. Cambridge: Cambridge University Press for Hakuyt Society, 1967.

Boas, Franz. "The Eskimo of Baffin Land." *Transactions of the Anthropological Society of Washington* 3 (1885): 95–102.

Boas, Franz. *The Central Eskimo. Sixth Annual Report of the Bureau of American Ethnology for the Years 1884–1885.* Washington, DC: Bureau of American Ethnology, 1888.

Canadian Archaeological Association. "Statement of Principles for Ethical Conduct Pertaining to Aboriginal Peoples." http://www.canadian archaeology.com/ethical.lasso (accessed 10 May 2008).

Cartier, Jacques. *Discours du Voyage fait par le Capitaine Iaques Cartier aux Terres-neufues de Canada, Norembergue, Hochelaga, Labrador, & pays adiacens, dite nouuelle France,: auec particulieres mœurs, langage, & ceremonies des habitants d'icelle.* Rouen: Imp Raphaël du Petit Val, 1598.

Cartier, Jacques. *Bref récit et succinte narration de la navigation faite en MDXXXV et MDXXXVI par le Capitain Jacques Catier aux îles de Canada, Hochelaga, Saguenay, et autres.* Paris: Lib. Tross, 1863.

Champlain, Samuel de. *Les voyages du Sieur de Champlain Xaintongeois, capitaine ordinaire pour le roy, en la marine.* Paris: Jean Berjon, 1613.

Chapdelaine, Claude. *Le Site Mandeville à Tracy Variabilité culturelle des Iroquoiens du Saint-Laurent.* Montreal: Recherches amérindiennes au Québec, 1989.

Clark, Donald W. *Western Subarctic Prehistory.* Hull, QC: Canadian Museum of Civilization, 1991.

Crespi, Fray Juan. "Journal of Fray Juan Crespi, Kept during the Same Voyage 1774." In *California Coast*, edited by D. C. Cutter, 207–274. Norman: University of Oklahoma Press, 1969.

Dyck, Ian, and Richard E. Morlan. "Hunting and Gathering Tradition: Canadian Plains." In *Handbook of North American Indians, Plains*, vol. 13, part 1 of 2, edited by William C. Sturtevant, 115–130. Washington, DC: Smithsonian Institution, 2001.

Early Canadiana Online. http://www.canadiana.org/eco.php?page= ItemRecord&id=92ef49c25bd608a9 (accessed 10 May 2008).

Englebrecht, William. *Iroquoia: The Development of a Native World.* Syracuse, NY: Syracuse University Press, 2003.

Fedje, Daryl. "Ancient Landscapes and Archaeology in Haida Gwaii and Hecate Strait." In *Archaeology of Coastal B.C.*, edited by R. L. Carlson, 29–38. Burnaby: Archaeology Press, Simon Fraser University, 2003.

Fladmark, Knut R. "An Introduction to the Prehistory of British Columbia." *Canadian Journal of Archaeology* 6 (1982): 95–156.

Hammel, George. "The Iroquois and the World's Rim: Speculations on Color, Culture, and Contact." *American Indian Quarterly* 16, no. 4, Special Issue: Shamans and Preachers, Color Symbolism and Commercial Evangelism: Reflections on Early Mid-Atlantic Religious Encounter in Light of the Columbian Quincentennial (Autumn, 1992): 451–469.

Hayeur Smith, Michèle. "Hides, Clay, Beads and Bear Teeth: Iroquoian Fashions." In *The St Lawrence Iroquois, Corn People.* Montreal: Musée d'archéologie Pointe-à-Callières en collaboration les Éditions de l'Homme, 2006.

Hearne, Samuel. *Journals of Samuel Hearne and Philip Turnor between the Years 1774 and 1792,* edited by J. B. Tyrell. Toronto: Publications of the Champlain Society, 1934.

Jenness, Diamond. *The People of the Twilight.* New York: Macmillan, 1928.

Jopling, C. F. "The Copper of the Northwest Coast Indians: Their Origin, Development, and Possible Antecedents." *Transactions for the American Philosophical Society*, New Ser. 79, no. 1 (1989): i–xii, 164.

Kapel, H., N. Kroman, F. Mikkelsen, and E. Løytved Rosenløv. "Tattooing." In *The Greenland Mummies*. Published for the Trustees of the British Museum. London: British Museum Publications, 1985.

Karklins, Karlis. *Trade Ornament Usage among the Native Peoples of Canada. Studies in Archaeology.* Ottawa: Architecture and History National Parks Service, Environment Canada, 1992.

Kelsey, Henry. *The Kelsey Papers,* edited by A. C. Doughty and C. Martin. Ottawa: King's Printer, 1929.

Laberge, Marc. *Affiquets matachias et vermillon, éthnographie illustrée des Algonquiens du nord-est de l'amérique aux XVIe, XVIIe et XVIIIe siècles.* Montreal: Recherches amérindiennes au Québec, 1998.

Lafitau, François-Joseph. *Moeurs des sauvages ameriquain, comparés aux moeurs des premiers temps.* Paris, 1724.

Lahontan Louis, Armand de Lom d'Arc, Baron de. *Nouveaux Voyages de mr le baron de Lahontan, dans l'Amérique Septentrionale.*, Vol. 2. La Haye: Les frères L'honoré, 1709.

Lescarbot, Marc. *Histoire de la Nouvelle-France.* Paris: Jean Millot, 1611.

La Vérendrye, Sieur de. "Pierre Gauthier de Varennes." In *Journals and Letters of Pierre Gaultier de Varennes de La Vérendrye and His Sons: With Correspondence between the Governors of Canada and the French Court, Touching the Search for the Western Sea,* edited by Lawrence J. Burpee. Toronto: Champlain Society, 1927.

Mackenzie, Sir, Alexander. *Exploring the Northwest Territory: Sir Alexander Mackenzie's Journal of a Voyage by Bark Canoe from Lake*

Athabasca to the Pacific Ocean in the Summer of 1789, edited by T. H. McDonald. Norman: University of Oklahoma Press, 1966.

Maurault, Joseph Pierre, Anselme. *Histoire des Abénakis depuis 1605 jusqu'à nos jours*. Sorel: Gazette de Sorel, 1866.

McGhee, Robert. *La sépulture de L'Anse-Amour*. Ottawa: Commission archéologique du Canada, Musée national de l'Homme, 1979.

McGhee, Robert. *Ancient Canada*. Ottawa: Canadian Museum of Civilization, 1989.

McGhee, Robert. *Ancient People of the Arctic*. Hull, QC: Canadian Museum of Civilization, 1996.

Moss, Madonna L. "George Catlin among the Nayas: Understanding the Practise of Labret Wearing on the Northwest Coast." *Ethnohistory* 46, no. 1 (Winter, 1999): 31–65.

Neusius, Sarah W., and G. Timothy Gross. *Seeking Our Past, an Introduction to North American Archaeology*. New York: Oxford University Press, 2007.

Pendergast, James F., and Bruce G. Trigger. *Cartier's Hochelaga and the Dawson Site*. Montreal: McGill, Queen's University Press, 1972.

Rasmussen, Kund. *Across Arctic America: Narrative of the Fifth Thule Expedition*. Fairbanks: University of Alaska Press, 1999.

Relations des Jésuites. *Relations des Jésuites: contenant ce qui s',est passé de plus remarquable dans les missions des pères de la Compagnie de Jésus dans la Nouvelle-France*. Vols. 1–3. Quebec: Augustin Coté, 1858.

Sagard, Gabriel. *Le Grand Voyage au Pays des Hurons*. Quebec: Bibiothèque québecoise, 1990.

Sutherland, Patricia. "Shamanism and the Iconography of Paleo-Eskimo Art." In *The Archaeology of Shamanism*, edited by N. Price. London: Routledge, 2001.

Thwaites, G. R., ed. *The Jesuit Relations and Allied Documents: Travels and Explorations of the Jesuit Missionaries in New France 1610–1791*. Vol. 38. Cleveland: Burrows Brothers, 1896–1901.

Tuck, James. "An Archaic Cemetary at Port -aux- Choix, Newfoundland." *American Antiquity* 36, no. 3 (July, 1971): 343–358.

Tuck, James. *La préhistoire des provinces maritimes*. Commission archéologique du Canada. Ottawa: Musée national de l'homme, 1985.

Wintemberg, W. J. *Roebuck Prehistoric Village Site, Grenville County, Ontario*. Bulletin No. 83, Anthropological Series No. 19, Facsimile Edition 1972. Ottawa: Ontario National Museums of Canada, 1972.

Wright, James V. *Ontario Prehistory an Eleven-thousand Year Archaeological Outline*. Ottawa: Archaeological Survey of Canada, National Museum of Man, 1972.

Michèle Hayeur Smith

See also Evidence about Dress of Indigenous People: United States Territory; Introduction to North American Indian/First Nation Peoples.

Evidence about Dress in the United States

- Evidence from Primary Sources
- Evaluation of Evidence
- Evidence from Extant Garments
- Evidence from Documents and Visual Sources
- Evidence from Theater, Film, and Television
- Evidence from Dress Scholarship

Dress is one of the most informative aspects of any culture. In the United States as well as across the globe, dress can reveal the personal aesthetic of the wearer in response to specific times, places, and events. Through dress one can often ascertain the age, sex, occupation, socioeconomic status, and religion of the wearer. One can investigate life rituals, family relationships, and cross-cultural and regional attitudes. Politics, war, and morality can be reflected in clothing choices. A great deal can be learned about popular and material culture. American clothing speaks about the fashion industry in the United States, the range of a designer's work, and about the customer's personal taste, standard of attractiveness, and access to wearing apparel. U.S. technological change, trade, and manufacturing all can be explored through dress. For all that can be learned from clothing, however, there are dangers in making unwarranted assumptions. It is of the utmost importance that scholars of dress be cognizant of the limits to what can be established factually and of the enormous range of possibilities that exist in how any one garment may have been worn or used. It is rare to be able to know why an individual chose a specific garment to wear. Beyond describing the characteristics of a particular piece of clothing, what one most often can describe is how that garment resembles others of a similar kind and how, taken together, these like garments fit into the broader spectrum of dress studies. Modes of dress have been of interest at least since Vecellio published *Habiti antichi et moderni* in Venice in 1598. In the study of dress in the United States, from exploration and early settlement, through the Colonial period, and up to the present day, many different kinds of evidence are available to be evaluated. The relative economic and political stability in the United States have made the preservation of that evidence possible. Modern media and the Internet have increased access to information about dress exponentially.

EVIDENCE FROM PRIMARY SOURCES

There are a number of primary sources to choose from when researching information about the history of dress. Each scholar must determine an approach appropriate to the questions that direct a specific study; therefore, different types of evidence are emphasized in different studies. Records from early exploration companies, extant garments, oral histories, letters, diaries, scrapbooks, paintings, fashion illustrations, photographs, store catalogs, popular literature, magazines, film and video, Web sites, and blogs all may contribute to knowledge depending on the nature of the study. In each case, however, the scholar must remain skeptical and evaluate the evidence carefully because no single source will reveal the whole story.

For example, the earliest explorers of what is now the continental United States were European and wore the current dress of their country of origin. It is possible to form some idea of the garments worn from the records of these voyages of discovery, such as the contracts that established the companies that undertook the explorations, from diaries and journals and from existing portraits of the explorers and early settlers painted from life. By extension, one can make some assumptions about the dress in early settlements by studying import and export records, the modes of dress customary in the settlers' country of origin, as well as shopkeepers' accounts. Generally colonists in the seventeenth and eighteenth centuries were aware of the fashions current in London and followed them as word reached the New World. Elisabeth McClellan, in her *History of American Costume, 1607–1870*, has listed the articles of dress each immigrant to Virginia was advised by the Virginia Company to take with him from London: "a Monmouth cap, three shirts, one suit of canvas, one pair of garters, four pairs of shoes, three falling bands [a large, flat collar], one waistcoat, one suit of frieze [a heavy fabric], one suit of broadcloth, three pairs of silk stockings, one dozen pairs of points [laces with metal tips at either end that were used to hold parts of garments closed or together]" (p. 46). In this list there seems to be little acknowledgment of the wilderness in which these "gentlemen adventurers" would find themselves, but everything necessary for a stylish English gentleman of the early 1600s. The most significant differences in the dress of the colonists and that of Londoners resulted from accommodation to differences in climate. The arrival of European settlers brought the possibility of cultural authentication, a process whereby elements of dress of one culture are incorporated into that of another, and over time both the native North Americans and the Europeans experienced these cross-cultural influences, sometimes borne of necessity.

Evidence about dress can be found in garments preserved in institutions such as museums and historical societies. If garments are used as evidence, the scholar must take into consideration the fact that most extant garments made before the mid-nineteenth century are unique and made for or by an individual. Depending on the purposes of the study, a garment might be examined on purely aesthetic grounds, in terms of how it relates to other arts contemporary with it, or the study might require that the garment be placed in a social context. If it is to be placed within a social context, the evidence the garment provides must be interpreted in light of other kinds of historical documents contemporary with the piece being studied, such as historical records, diaries, or fashion periodicals.

EVALUATION OF EVIDENCE

Just as there is no single source of evidence for costume, there is no single method of evaluating evidence of dress. It is, however, essential to establish both the authenticity and credibility of all sources, whether extant garments or written or visual documents. For example, the pristine state of any garment must be

On the left is an illustration from *Les Modes Parisiennes*, 27 July 1872. On the right is a plate from *Peterson's Magazine*, April 1873, that combines images from the French publication shown in several issues of the previous year. American periodicals in the nineteenth century often copied fashion illustrations from European publications. Kent State University Museum. www.kent.edu/museum

established. If a garment has been altered, it is important to attempt to ascertain the original configuration or to determine how or why it was altered and at what point in its history. As an example, an eighteenth-century dress of imported saffron-yellow Chinese silk, hand-painted with a scattered stenciled floral pattern, is in the Costume Institute of the Metropolitan Museum of Art, New York (1970.87ab). The dress is said to have belonged to the family of Jonathan Belcher, the colonial governor of New Jersey from 1747 to 1757. When the dress arrived at the museum, it had been altered, apparently during the nineteenth century. Through careful study of the shapes of the pieces making up the dress, and existing evidence of the dress having been draped in a style with an overskirt called *à la Polonaise*, the dress was restored to a configuration appropriate to the date of the textile and that style of draping popular in the 1770s. The existence of this particular dress in colonial New Jersey reveals additional information about the relative wealth of the family. English trade legislation prohibited any imports or exports to the colonies except through England on English ships. Thus, duty would have been paid at least twice on a Chinese silk—first upon its arrival in England, and next on its export to New Jersey—making it especially costly.

Likewise, any textual source must be in its original, unedited form, however fragmentary, and any edited version or interpretative commentary on that text must be identified as such. If working solely from an edited version of a text, the biases or interests of the editor need to be identified and understood. This would be especially important with early texts, for example, those of Captain John Smith relating to the settlement of Jamestown, Virginia, or those of William Bradford concerning Plymouth, Massachusetts. Newspaper advertisements can be especially valuable sources of information about seventeenth- and eighteenth-century

dress. One of the most persistent problems in dress history is the changing definition of a single term depending on both time and place. The word *costume* is an example. Historically derived from the French in the sense of "custom" or "habit," and referring to clothing, the word costume is used by historians and curators of dress collections to mean apparel worn by real people in real times and places. The common general usage of the word, however, implies something worn in a theatrical production or film, for fancy dress, or on Halloween. For this reason, the editorial staff of this encyclopedia have chosen to use the word *dress* to indicate what people wear from their own wardrobes for everyday or special occasion, and *costume* for theater, film, fancy dress, and masquerade. With written sources, a careful analysis of the literal meaning of words at the time of their use is required, especially because the vocabulary of fashion is often ambiguous, using foreign words and phrases, archaic or technical terms that may not be generally familiar or may not carry the same meaning over a period of time. Thus, the terminology used to describe dress is often confusing. Words describing dress may carry meanings that imply topical, historical, political, or popular ideas, sometimes seemingly unrelated to the object itself. The cuirass worn by the Spanish Conquistadores in the sixteenth century, as they explored the southwestern part of the American continent, was close-fitting metal chest armor while the cuirass bodice of the 1880s referred to a fashionable fabric bodice that was closely fitted over a corseted shape.

In another example, the American Periodical Series Online 1740–1900 includes an entry for the Philadelphia periodical *Atkinson's Casket* of March 1835, where in an article entitled "The Present London Fashions," the third of three descriptions refers to a fashion plate and reads as follows: "A white satin robe, short sabot sleeves and drapery á la enfant, gathered full round the corsage. Coiffure á la Grisi, parted in front with giraffe bows and braids upon each temple" (p. 121). This is typical of nineteenth-century descriptions and requires some investigation to discover that a *robe* is a dress; that *sabot*, French for "clog or hoof," refers to the shape of the puffed sleeve; and that *corsage* means bodice; thus, the "child-like" drapery *á la enfant* must enhance the description of a full, gathered bodice. The hairstyle refers to the Italian opera star Giulia Grisi, a soprano who had made her London debut in 1834 in the Rossini opera *The Thieving Magpie*. In mid-1830s portraits of Grisi, her hair is shown drawn back from her face with a center part but no adornment. As for "giraffe bows and braids upon each temple," the reference may be a fanciful description applied to the elaborate hairstyles fashionable at the time or a misprinting or interpretation of a form of the French verb *agrafer*, meaning "to fasten." Beyond vocabulary, the description is even less clear when the periodical itself

is studied, because none of the descriptions match the adjacent fashion illustration where only two garments are shown. This is yet another typical and frustrating problem for the researcher using nineteenth-century U.S. fashion periodicals and indicates that the descriptions and the plates were most probably taken, out of sequence, from an English publication such as *The Court Magazine and Belle Assemblée*. Fashion periodicals in the United States in the nineteenth century regularly pirated both plates and descriptions, publishing them sometimes months after their original appearance in France or England. Fashion journalists draw analogies that are specific to a given time, place, and readership and often invent descriptive terms. Fashion publicists may invent biographical information about designers or exaggerate or "spin" facts to enhance the status of their clients. Some designers themselves adjust their birth dates or personal histories. It is important to glean information from more than one source and to establish the credibility of each.

Suit by the American designer Gilbert Adrian, ca. 1940, exhibited twice at the Kent State University Museum, United States. Depending on the style and purpose of an exhibition, a garment can be presented in various ways to convey different information. In one exhibition, the suit was fully accessorized to convey its social context; in another, it was very simply mounted to emphasize the cut of the jacket and skirt and the economy of detail typical of restrictions on fabric and decoration during World War II. Kent State University Museum. www.kent.edu/museum

EVIDENCE FROM EXTANT GARMENTS

Extant examples of sixteenth- and seventeenth-century European dress worn in the United States during the period of exploration and early settlement are extremely rare, with only a few examples known. Archaeological evidence from early settlements remains scarce as well. There are considerably more eighteenth-century examples extant in major collections and historical societies, although condition and provenance are often problematic. Actual examples of nineteenth- through twenty-first-century dress are plentiful and constitute important sources for dress research. Many historic sites seek to costume their interpreters in historically correct garments, and many use museum collections as well as documentary evidence to study garments from the period. Such re-creations are only as successful as the research and fabrication are accurate. Usually it is possible to request an appointment to study objects in museum and historical society collections, but arrangements must be made well in advance. These collections contain apparel selected and worn by an individual in a certain time and place. In the best case, the garment is well documented with the following information available: who made the piece, where and when it was made, if it was worn, who wore it, when and where it was worn, how it was acquired, why it was selected, and how much it cost. For garments made after 1840, there may be a photograph of the original owner wearing it. The instances where all of this information is available are few and are determined by the circumstances of collection. The criteria for dress collected by historical societies differ from those of fine arts museums. A historical society collects only what was worn or used in the area covered by its mission statement and can be expected to record the significance of the donor or the wearer of the garment to the history of that area. It is more common to find garments representing various economic levels in a historical society because those institutions often attempt to represent the range of lifestyles in a specific community. Fine arts institutions with dress departments often collect for the aesthetic expressed in the garment's style or silhouette, for the textiles used, the trimmings applied, the inherent craftsmanship, for the designer or country of origin, and whether Western or non-Western, fashionable dress or regional traditional dress. Most often garments collected by fine arts institutions reflect the highest socioeconomic levels, where luxury textiles and superb dressmaking and tailoring were available to the wearer and where there was enough affluence that the garments were not worn out or used up. Such examples are often purchased at auction, in antique shops, or from art dealers, so little of the desired documentation will exist. The visual presentation of dress in exhibitions offers yet another way to assess evidence of dress history through the garments themselves. When exhibitions take place in museums and historical societies, the gallery displays and the techniques of dressing and accessorizing mannequins impact what the gallery visitors see and understand about particular garments. Questions must be asked about the purpose and intent behind the exhibition, the authority of the curator, the care taken in establishing the correct silhouette, the accuracy of the gallery labels, and the legitimacy of the way the garments are represented in the context of the exhibition. If the exhibition seeks to represent the historic look of the garment, comparisons with documents or illustrations from the period of the garment are very important in establishing the correct presentation, as is an understanding of the underlayers of

Phyllis Primrose Peckham (a society belle of Cleveland, Ohio) was photographed wearing this dress about 1922. There is a sketch of this design, by Jeanne Lanvin, in the November 1922 issue of *Harper's Bazaar*, described as ivory-white taffeta edged with narrow black lace mounted on white net. Miss Peckham's dress, however, is of pale peach taffeta and bears a store label, Quinn-Maahs, Inc./Cleveland. The actual dress is in the collection of the Western Reserve Historical Society in Cleveland, Ohio. This photograph, at the Kent State University Museum, is overpainted in oil that looks white. It is possible that the overpainting may have faded or that Miss Peckham may have wanted a white dress after all. Kent State University Museum. www.kent.edu/museum

supporting devices such as corsets and hoops, and the construction of the garment. Many who dress mannequins have difficulty differentiating their own contemporary fashionable ideal from that of a historical period.

Many garments survive through serendipitous accident and cannot be assumed to reflect "what everyone wore." Surviving garments are often those that could not be remodeled or reused, or had such a strong sentimental attachment for the wearer that they were kept. Everyday garments from households of average or below average income were usually worn out and sold as rags, leaving few extant examples. When a garment is given to a collection, there is an opportunity to acquire related documentation from the donor. Donor information, however, unless supported by documentary evidence in the form of dated photographs or bills of sale, for example, may be unreliable. A note pinned to a dress in an unknown hand indicating that the piece is "Grandmother's wedding dress" cannot be taken at face value. The collector must probe to determine when "Grandmother" was born, when she married, whether the dress was passed down from generation to generation, and whether the garment in question reflects similar usage, time, and place when compared with other like examples. It is important to determine if the garment is in its original state or if it has been altered, and how many times, as well as how close it comes to the fashionable ideal of the period.

Tools for evaluating the aesthetic evidence in a garment begin with an understanding of the silhouette, or line, of the piece, and with its materials and construction. As in dressing mannequins for exhibition, it is important to have knowledge of those garments that serve as the understructure supporting the volumes of the silhouette and the construction of the piece itself. The use of color is often an indicator of a specific period and involves knowledge of scientific advances in dye technology as well as the color choices common or available in a given time and place. The textures of the materials used can help to determine the aesthetic qualities of a piece. The contrast between flat and shiny or rough and smooth surfaces and the proportion of each is an important consideration. As the silhouette is evaluated, the volumes of the various components of the garment, such as the sleeves or the skirt, and the overall mass can indicate how closely the garment comes to the fashionable ideal as represented in published illustrations. Although difficult to ascertain when not on a person, an analysis of how a garment was intended to move is another tool that can be used to judge how well the piece in question expresses the aesthetic of its moment of creation. Although it may be impossible to know if the original wearer was conservative or avant garde in taste, a comparative aesthetic analysis of line, color, texture, volume, and movement can help to determine how a garment fits into the continuum of dress history. Likewise, to determine how a style evolves and, therefore, where a given piece belongs in fashion's evolutionary process, it is helpful to look at the areas most frequently affected by fashion changes: the volume of the hat and hairstyle; the placement of the neckline and waistline; the configuration of the bodice; the nature and placement of the skirt fullness and hemline; the sleeve shape and fullness; the nature and placement of applied decoration; the jacket and trouser shape, length, and fullness; and the shoe shape and heel height. Many of these details are subtle and require careful observation to determine. In men's clothing this is especially important because the spacing of the buttonholes or the width of a lapel may change by a fraction of an inch to indicate a change in style. The bespoke suit for men and the made-to-order garment for women may not follow the style of the moment exactly because there is more opportunity for personal taste to be expressed when a garment is custom made.

EVIDENCE FROM DOCUMENTS AND VISUAL SOURCES

Other types of evidence also present a need for careful evaluation as indicated by the previous discussion of *Atkinson's Casket*. The researcher must assess the competence and self-interest of the observer as a witness recording impressions in autobiographical accounts, letters, diaries, and scrapbooks. For example, the extensive correspondence between Josephine du Pont and her friend Margaret Manigault, preserved in the Eleutherian Mills Historical

This U.S. family portrait was taken around 1900. Dating this image is problematic because of the varying styles seen on the women's bodices. The older women appear to be wearing earlier sleeve and bodice styles, while the younger ones seem to have chosen later styles. The family is lower middle class and is represented wearing their best clothing rather than fashionable dress. Note the photographer's elaborate backdrop that lends an air of elegance to the family pictured. Courtesy of Jean Druesedow.

Library in Greenville, Delaware, spans the years 1798–1824 with many references to fashion. Because of the prominence of both families, the extensive archive of objects at Winterthur, the du Pont estate, as well as written documents, the competencies of both women as observers of their milieu can be evaluated more fully. Oral histories can be invaluable sources of fashion information, but they may reflect selective memory. When taking oral histories, it is important to conduct a series of interviews, if possible, and approach topics from several directions, thus breaking down memory patterns that result from the retelling of a story or event time after time. Once the oral history is recorded, the researcher must determine if the person interviewed was actually in a position to know or observe what was described, was aware of the significance of what was described, and knew what should have been known and did not claim knowledge that could not have been known. Further, the researcher must assess the possible prejudices or personal interests of the person interviewed and find other evidence to support the observations. These cautions are also applicable to other kinds of documents.

Visual evidence of dress presents different problems in evaluation. Some of the only evidence of those who settled in Jamestown or Plymouth is portraiture, not all done from life. Portraiture may flatter the sitter or may record a garment not owned by the sitter at all. Detailed rendering of fabrics and trimmings may or may not be present. Society portraits, which often contain important details of fashionable dress, are vulnerable to the desires of the sitter taking precedence over verisimilitude. In a photograph dating from about 1922 of a society belle of Cleveland, Ohio, Miss Phyllis Primrose Peckham (1903–1999), the young woman is shown wearing a dress by Jeanne Lanvin sketched in the *Harper's Bazaar* of November of that year and described as being made of ivory-

white taffeta edged with narrow black lace mounted on white net. Miss Peckham later gave her dress to the Western Reserve Historical Society in Cleveland. The photograph is at the Kent State University Museum in Kent, Ohio. The dress has rows of pale peach-pink silk taffeta ruffles trimmed with white silk tulle, black machine embroidery and black machine-made lace. It is certainly the same model as the Lanvin sketched in *Harper's Bazaar*. However, it is labeled "Quinn-Maahs, Inc., Cleveland," a specialty store that imported French models. Furthermore, the photograph has been over-painted in oil and shows the dress as white rather than pink, more like the magazine description. There are several questions to be asked at this point: first, is the dress from Lanvin in Paris or is it an American copy? Did Quinn-Maahs simply substitute a store label for the designer's label in an imported dress as was frequently done? Did Miss Peckham ask the photographer to over-paint the photograph in white rather than pink, or has the pink in the over-painting faded, leaving the image white? The wishes of the sitter, artistic license, and the social and artistic conventions of a certain time and place influence a finished photograph as they do a finished painting. Photographers may use studio props, including clothing and accessories, or may shoot from an angle that distorts reality. Illustrations and photographs for fashion publications seek to idealize the human figure through exaggeration, often elongating the body to achieve a long, lean silhouette. Editorial direction influences the final appearance of an image in a fashion magazine in terms of layout as well as the combination of garments on a single model. Fashion advertising usually seeks to sell the designer's persona or the branding of the label and sometimes does so at the expense of a clear image of the garment. The availability of fashion shows on television and the Internet brings another source of information. The fashion

This fashion illustration from *Godey's Lady's Book and Magazine* (April, 1860) is useful for comparing the illustration of an accessory with an extant example. The illustration of the green dress on the left is described as a "dress of apple green taffeta, shaded with black, a spray of leaves broché in black, at regular intervals; corsage plain and high; sleeve demi long, and of a narrow pagoda shape, trimmed with flat bows of apple green ribbon, as are the skirt and corsage, in a continuous line. Bonnet of peach blossom crape, with a fall of blonde. Rich lace shawl, lined with black marcelline." On the right is a mannequin dressed with a similar shawl from the Kent State University Museum collection, Ohio, USA. Kent State University Museum. www.kent.edu/museum

runway presents the designer's selection and choice of accessories on professional models, and insofar as possible, shows the garments as the designer intended them to look. When a given clothing product reaches the consumer in a range of sizes and colors, there is likely to be little relationship between the look on the runway or in a fashion illustration and the appearance of the garment on the street.

EVIDENCE FROM THEATER, FILM, AND TELEVISION

Costume for theater, film, and television is designed in accordance with a script in keeping with the artistic concept of the director and producer and the financial and time constraints of production. No matter whether the setting calls for period or contemporary dress, whether the clothes are purchased or made to order, a professional costume designer plans the wardrobe carefully in order to reveal character. With the possible exception of documentaries and newsreels, the costumes in film and television cannot be assumed to be the same as garments worn by anyone other than the actors or actresses in the specific production. However, costumes worn in performance may influence subsequent fashion on the street. For example, Valentina, a fashion designer working in New York in the 1930s, dressed actresses such as Lynn Fontanne, Katharine Hepburn, and Katharine Cornell for the stage. People would go to the theater to see what these leading ladies were wearing and then attempt to imitate the styles, or visit Valentina in her shop. When Gilbert Adrian designed the film costumes for Joan Crawford as "Letty Lynton" in 1932, the style of the costumes caught the public imagination. The style was copied on New York's Seventh Avenue and became a best seller in the ready-to-wear market. Most individuals wearing "Letty Lynton" dresses had little idea that Adrian had designed the ruffled sleeves and slightly raised waistline to mask Joan Crawford's wide shoulders and exceptionally long waist and thus give her figure a better proportion for the silver screen. The costumes used for the U.S. television series *Dallas*, which started its thirteen-year run in 1978, resulted in the development of a line of clothing marketed under the series name, while the clothing worn by Sarah Jessica Parker in *Sex and the City* between 1998 and 2004 created additional demand for products selected by the costume designer to be used on the show. A fashion icon or celebrity often has a stylist or advisor who uses clothing to reinforce a specific personal image, and this personal style, covered by the media, may then influence the clothing choices of the more general population. Hip-hop fashions and clothing lines created and marketed by hip-hop artists, and the public fascination with "red carpet" events, such as the Hollywood Academy Awards, with the media coverage of the fashions worn by celebrities attending, are examples.

EVIDENCE FROM DRESS SCHOLARSHIP

Dress scholarship in the United States began in earnest in 1890 with a series of books by Alice Morse Earle (1851–1911) on Colonial dress that culminated with the 1903 publication of her *Two Centuries of Costume in America*. Elisabeth McClellan (1851–1920) first published *History of American Costume 1607–1870* in 1904. M.D.C. Crawford (1882–1949), a design and research editor for *Women's Wear Daily*, was also a research associate at the American Museum of Natural History in New York City. He was in many ways responsible for encouraging the New York fashion design community to use museum collections for research, and he was instrumental in the establishment of study rooms in both the American Museum of Natural History and the Brooklyn Museum for this purpose by 1918. His published books and articles emphasized a variety of ethnographic design resources. The researcher tracing influences on U.S. fashion in the aftermath of World War I may need to take into consideration the influence of the ethnographic textiles championed by M.D.C. Crawford. In 1919, Crawford did an exhibition at the American Museum of Natural History titled "Industrial Art in Textiles and Costumes." This kind of activity in the early twentieth century did a great deal to stimulate research in dress. The establishment of The Museum of Costume Art, Costume Institute, Inc., conceived in 1928 but incorporated in 1937, supported by Irene Lewisohn, Alice Lewisohn Crowley, M.D.C. Crawford, and the theatrical designers Lee Simonson and Aline Bernstein was of great importance in raising the profile of the study of dress. The Costume Institute's influence expanded when it became a curatorial department of the Metropolitan Museum of Art in 1944. The theatrical costume designer Millia Davenport (1896–1992) published her two-volume *History of Costume* in 1948, a landmark in its use of photographs of visual sources rather than the typical redrawing of works of art so prone to misinterpretation. Much impetus for the study of historic dress in the United States resulted from the research needs of theater and film designers doing period costumes. The establishment of the Costume Society of America in 1973, with annual symposia and the publication of the society's journal *Dress*, beginning in 1975, has encouraged scholarship in American dress. Since 1976, influenced by the Bicentennial celebrations, a wider segment of the population has become interested in dress history through reenacting historical events. Costumed interpreters at historic sites also have spurred interest. The last quarter of the twentieth century saw a significant increase in the publication of scholarly books, articles, and exhibition catalogs covering a wide range of dress studies, including dress theory. Many of these publications have expanded the field and, through new research, have challenged earlier assumptions. Subject to critical evaluation, these publications serve as important evidence about dress in the United States over more than four hundred years.

References and Further Reading

Baumgarten, Linda. *What Clothes Reveal*. Williamsburg, VA: The Colonial Williamsburg Foundation, 2002.

Bradley, Barry W., Jean L. Druesedow, and Shirley Teresa Wajda. "Phyllis Primrose Peckham: Dressed for Posterity." *Dress, the Journal of the Costume Society of America* 29 (2002): 59–74.

Cunningham, Patricia A. *Reforming Women's Fashion, 1850–1920, Politics, Health and Art*. Kent, OH: The Kent State University Press, 2003.

Earle, Alice Morse. *Two Centuries of Costume in America*. New York: Dover Publications, 1970.

Foster, Helen Bradley. "New Raiments of Self." *African American Clothing in the Antebellum South*. Oxford: Berg, 1997.

Kent State University Museum Web site. http://www.kent.edu/museum (accessed 13 March 2007).

McClellan, Elisabeth. *History of American Costume, 1607–1870*. New York: Arno Press, 1977.

Milbank, Caroline Rennolds. *New York Fashion, the Evolution of American Style.* New York: Harry N. Abrams, Inc., 1989.

Rexford, Nancy, Patricia Cunningham, Robert Kaufmann, and Patricia Trautman. "Forum: Research and Publication." *Dress, the Journal of the Costume Society of America* 14 (1988): 68–82.

Severa, Joan L. *Dressed for the Photographer, Ordinary Americans and Fashion 1840–1900.* Kent, OH: The Kent State University Press, 1995.

Severa, Joan L. *My Likeness Taken, Daguerreian Portraits in America.* Kent, OH: The Kent State University Press, 2005.

Taylor, Lou. *The Study of Dress History.* Manchester, UK: Manchester University Press, 2002.

Warner, Patricia Campbell. *When the Girls Came Out to Play.* Amherst and Boston: University of Massachusetts Press, 2006.

Jean L. Druesedow

See also Evidence about Dress of Indigenous People: United States Territory; Evidence about Dress of Indigenous People: Canadian Territory; Evidence about Dress in Canada.

Evidence about Dress in Canada

- French Canada
- English Canada
- Organizations of Dress and Fashion
- Significant Museum Collections of Dress
- Significant University Collections of Dress
- Significant Archival Collections Relating to Dress

Dress in Canada is a complex topic. First, there is the geography, from maritime to prairie to Pacific temperate to the frozen North. Second, there is timeframe, from seventeenth-century New France, to the settling of the West in the late nineteenth century, to the growing multicultural cities of the twenty-first century. Third, Canada is a land of immigrants, from the founding nations of France and England to the waves of European and now Asian immigration. Fourth, there is the strong influence of England on the Commonwealth nation, and of the United States, its mighty neighbor. The study of dress is spread across Canada, although unevenly, engaging academics, museum curators, public historians, and people from many other disciplines and interests, often working independently.

Our understanding of the development of the study of dress in Canada is greatly facilitated by two bibliographies of written works on Canadian dress from the early twentieth century to 1991. Compiled by Jacqueline Beaudoin-Ross, former curator of costume and textiles at the McCord Museum of Canadian History, Montreal, and Pamela Blackstock, former curator of costumes, Parks Canada, these excellent annotated bibliographies include entries in both French and English and so bring together the two trajectories of French- and English-language dress research in Canada.

FRENCH CANADA

It is important to note that the approach to dress in French-speaking Quebec is quite different from that in other parts of Canada. In Quebec, the study of dress is subsumed under the discipline of folklore, which is now more widely called *ethnology*. It focuses on the description and interpretation of cultural traditions based on fieldwork, material culture, and theory.

The study of dress in Canada originated in Quebec in the early twentieth century as part of the documentation of French Canadian folk culture. Marius Barbeau, a pioneer in the field of anthropology and folklore, began this field of research by focusing in particular on the *ceinture fléchée*, Quebec's colorful finger-woven sash. Indeed, more has been written about this iconic sash than about any other garment in Canada. Two of Barbeau's contemporaries, archivists Edouard-Zotique Massicotte and Pierre-Georges Roy, documented Quebec traditional garments such as the *botte sauvage*, or tall moccasin, through the clothing and textiles inventoried in Quebec marriage contracts and estate notarial records.

Study of traditional dress in Quebec continued through the 1970s and 1980s, with examination of Acadian dress, wedding dress, hatmaking, and another Canadian icon, the *capote*, or blanket-coat. In the Quebec literature, the combination of the capote belted with the ceinture fléchée and worn with the botte sauvage during the cold Quebec winters forms the "holy trinity" of traditional Quebec clothing. Written material on Quebec dress from the seventeenth to eighteenth centuries and its survival as traditional dress can be found in the Beaudoin-Ross and Blackstock bibliographies, including articles in English by Beaudoin-Ross and Francis Back. In her article in *Fashion: A Canadian Perspective*, Eileen Stack has updated the capote as a symbol of identity appropriated by English Canadians through to the twentieth century.

Intense interest in the rural culture of Quebec has led to the founding of numerous centers of folklore studies. Ethnologist Robert-Lionel Seguin has collected some 35,000 artifacts and a huge archive housed at the Musée québecois de culture populaire in Trois Rivières, Quebec, while Madeleine Doyon-Ferland has left a vast folklore archive at Laval University, Quebec, now part of the Centre d'études sur la langue, les arts et les traditions populaires des francophones en Amérique du Nord (CELAT).

Colonel and Mrs. Wolseley are photographed here wearing the *capote*, belted with the *ceinture fléchée*. Montreal, Canada, 1868. McCord Museum I-30223. http://www.mccord-museum.qc.ca/en/

By the 1980s, Quebec ethnologists turned to the twentieth century, thereby moving from traditional culture to popular culture. For example, Jocelyn Mathieu and Christine Godin used oral history in their study of Montreal milliners, designers, and department stores. Suzanne Marchand examined the desire for fashion and its critics in conservative Quebec society of the 1920s and 1930s. Several writers at this time began to tackle the relationship between traditional dress and mainstream fashion, bridging tradition and modernity. Two journals have each devoted a volume to the topic of dress, and in particular, Quebec dress, in 1988: *Cap-aux-diamants*, a popular history French-only journal, and the bilingual *Canadian Folklore canadien*, an academic journal (now called *Ethnologies*). Articles—mostly in French—in these journals and by the authors mentioned are referenced in the Beaudoin-Ross and Blackstock bibliographies. In addition, ethnologist Gérald Baril has spotlighted Quebec fashion from 1900 to 2004 in his volume containing biographies of designers, retailers, fashion schools, and journals.

ENGLISH CANADA

By contrast, research on dress in English Canada was conceived not in an academic setting but rather in the museum. Research was based not on fieldwork but on museum collections and exhibitions, centered mainly in Ontario and initially with curators at the Royal Ontario Museum (ROM), Toronto, where the costume and textile collections encompass world dress but also have considerable Canadian content. It all began in 1967, Canada's centennial year, when Katherine Brett curated *Modesty to Mod*, an exhibition and catalog at the ROM, which sparked an interest in Canadian dress. She and other Ontario-based curators produced the first overviews, although brief, of Canadian fashion based on museum collections. Their aim was to set standards for the identification, description, and details of cut and construction of dress in central Canada. Unlike Quebec studies that focused on the sartorial expression within Quebec itself, the Toronto curators attempted to place Canadian dress within British and European fashion trends.

This flurry of activity was followed by a few landmark studies in the 1990s. The most comprehensive overview of Canadian fashion for the twentieth century was Caroline Routh's 1993 *In Style: 100 Years of Canadian Women's Fashion*, based on the collection she curated at Seneca College, Toronto, and on other collections across Canada. *In Style* surveys the forces that have influenced Canadian fashion and social life decade by decade and is illustrated with the author's drawings of actual garments. In 1992, Jacqueline Beaudoin-Ross curated an exhibition and book, *Form and Fashion*, at the McCord Museum, profiling sixteen nineteenth-century Montreal dresses, each with detailed provenance, description, and comparison with period photographs. The book includes insightful essays on Canadian fashion evolution and dissemination.

The most concentrated attempt to bring serious attention to Canadian fashion is the work of Alexandra Palmer, curator of costume and textiles at the ROM. Her 1997 exhibition, Au Courant: Contemporary Canadian Fashion, featuring the work of forty designers, was a first crack at raising public awareness of the diversity of Canadian fashion. Palmer's 2002 exhibition Elite Elegance presented exclusive garments worn by Toronto socialites and explored the relationship between Toronto and Paris,

London and New York fashion, a topic much expanded in her book *Couture and Commerce: The Transatlantic Fashion Trade in the 1950s*. The 2004 volume she edited, *Fashion: A Canadian Perspective*, was the first of its kind to bring together a multidisciplinary group of curators, designers, fashion writers, historians, and artists to explore the fashion trade, merchandising, and journalism in Canada.

Another branch of the study of dress in Canada has emanated from social and material history. Several articles on dress have been published in the journal *Material History Review*, which was launched in 1976 by the National Museum of Man (now the Canadian Museum of Civilization), whose aim was to "encourage the use of three-dimensional evidence in understanding historical change and continuity." As part of the "new social history" movement, these and articles in other venues were less concerned with fashion and more with everyday people and society. The authors were primarily museum curators within the discipline of history who contextualized dress within a specific period and social setting—for example, how urban middle-class Ontarians dressed their children to enhance their social status. Two volumes of *Material History Review* have been devoted to clothing (51, Spring 2000, and 56, Fall 2002); unlike the earlier volumes, the essays are mostly ethnographic in approach and not all relate to Canada.

A revealing microcosm of the Canadian social milieu of the late nineteenth century is Cynthia Cooper's study of the viceregal fancy dress balls, where Victorian imperialism, imagination, and sexuality were played out on the ballroom floor. Sociologist Kathryn Church's project to exhibit twenty-five wedding dresses made by her mother in small-town Alberta is a profound reflection on rural society, family, and gender described in her chapter in *Fashion: A Canadian Perspective*.

Labor history has contributed to our understanding of the crucial role of garment manufacturing to the Canadian economy and society. Historian Gerald Tulchinsky points out that in 1871 the clothing industry was the largest employer in Toronto. The book and film, *Les ouvrières de Dominion Corset à Québec, 1886–1988*, based on interviews with twenty factory workers, is an inside look at a major Canadian manufacturer. Moving away from central Canada, there are good histories of garment manufacturing in western Canada, specifically Edmonton and Winnipeg, and two solid essays in *Fashion: A Canadian Perspective* on the industry in Saint John, New Brunswick, and Halifax, Nova Scotia. Because a large proportion of the garment industry was staffed by female labor, feminist historians have turned their focus on the trade. While most labor studies include scant discussion of the actual garments produced, Christina Bates's chapter on the millinery trade in *Fashion: A Canadian Perspective* includes an analysis of a collection of 500 hats from one millinery shop.

Alexandra Palmer has asked, "What is Canadian dress?" This question has been explored in detail in French-speaking Quebec, where there is a strong sense of cultural identity—although the relationship between traditional and mainstream apparel has been problematic. But the study of dress in English Canada remains marginal in the university, in museums, and other public institutions. There are only two departments of human ecology with graduate science programs in clothing and textiles, and none for apparel design or history. There are only two human history museums with curators of dress. There is no national organization such as, for example, the Costume Society of Great Britain.

This dress was made in the early 1890s by Glover, Fry and Company, a Quebec City dry goods and millinery firm founded in 1842. It is now held in the McCord Museum of Canadian History in Montreal, Canada. McCord Museum M968.2.1.1-3. http://www.mccord-museum.qc.ca/en/

Yet regional organizations and passionate dress researchers continue to explore the field. Canada has been described as a mosaic, where multiple cultures and views coexist, as opposed to the U.S. melting pot. The variety of approaches to dress in Canada could be viewed as a mosaic, where there is no need for a national identity. But critics of the idea of the Canadian mosaic claim that it tends to marginalize people, which in some ways is analogous to the disparate, isolated, and often overlooked nature of dress study in Canada. Palmer has pointed out that Canadians do not claim as their own international businesses with connections to Canada, such as Club Monaco, Roots, and MAC, thus raising the "complex issue of internationalism and the globalization of fashion and Canada's role in this matrix." Yet all across Canada are people who have started to add to the picture of Canadian dress and fashion. Much more remains to be done, and there is no scarcity of resources in Canada, as the next section will show.

ORGANIZATIONS OF DRESS AND FASHION

While there is no cross-Canada organization of those working in the field of dress and fashion, three provinces have their own costume society, and each maintains a Web site. The oldest and

A nurse's uniform from the Western Hospital, Montreal, Canada, 1916–1920. Photograph by Harry Foster. Courtesy of the Canadian Nursing History Collection, Canadian Museum of Civilization.

strongest is the Costume Society of Ontario (CSO), founded in 1970. CSO is based in Toronto, although its approximately two hundred members live throughout Ontario and eastern Quebec. Its dual mission is to promote education and interest in dress and to encourage the preservation of historic dress. Three times a year it publishes the *Costume Journal*, which contains a calendar of events, resources listings, research essays, book and exhibition reviews, and member profiles. Events include lectures, behind-the-scenes tours of museums and performing arts costume studios, field trips, and workshops.

The Costume Society of Nova Scotia, on Canada's East Coast, was founded in 1981 and has approximately sixty members in Halifax and throughout the province. Its quarterly newsletter, *The Clothes Press*, includes book and exhibition reviews and brief articles. Moving to the other side of the country, the Canadiana Costume Society of British Columbia and Western Canada, established in 1976, mounts exhibitions and historical fashion shows, mostly in Vancouver and environs.

While these costume societies occasionally feature programs and publish on current fashion, their focus is usually historic dress. Information on contemporary Canadian fashion designers is found in Canada's two fashion centers, Toronto and Montreal. In an effort to brand Canadian fashion domestically and internationally, the Fashion Design Council of Canada sponsors a Fashion Week in Toronto and maintains an online database of Canadian designers. Its counterpart in Quebec is the Liaison Mode Montréal, the organizer of the Montreal Fashion week.

SIGNIFICANT MUSEUM COLLECTIONS OF DRESS

Most museums in Canada, large and small, are funded fully or in part by federal, provincial, or municipal governments. Most cities and many smaller communities have local history museums that have garments, related photographs, and archives that uniquely express the people of their region past and present. In some museums, the clothing collection will be well cataloged and exhibited, but in others textile objects languish in boxes. Most collections are rich in women's dress but lacking in men's and children's clothes. Most have plenty of christening gowns and wedding dresses, but few have significant work or everyday garments. An integrated searchable access to Canadian collections, including dress, of over 1,025 heritage organizations is the Canadian Heritage Information Network's Web site, Artifacts Canada. Its gateway project, The Virtual Museum of Canada, presents virtual exhibits, education materials, images, and records of museum treasures.

Canada has a museum dedicated exclusively to dress: the Costume Museum of Canada (CMC), which began as a collection of clothing and documents representing a small rural community. It is now located in Winnipeg, the gateway to the western prairies and capital of the province of Manitoba. The CMC is home to thirty-five thousand articles of dress spanning four hundred years, although the majority of its collection is twentieth century. While it has some haute couture apparel, the collection mainly represents what everyday Canadians made and wore, although not all of their collection is well documented as to provenance. The CMC also holds the Family Photography Collection of over four thousand portraits and related images.

Two museums in Canada are devoted to textiles, and while their focus is on the production and significance of textiles from around the world, part of their collection consists of Canadian garments. The Musée du costume et du textile du Québec in St. Lambert near Montreal explores dress, textiles, and fiber across cultures, from the past through today. The collection of approximately four thousand objects dates from the nineteenth and twentieth centuries. The Textile Museum of Canada in Toronto has twelve thousand textiles that span almost two thousand years and two hundred world regions. The collection reflects the ethnographic, cultural, and aesthetic significance that cloth has held over the centuries. Their Web site includes a searchable database.

Another unique museum related to one aspect of dress is the Bata Shoe Museum (BSM), founded by Sonja Bata and managed by a foundation. Housed in a purpose-built museum in downtown Toronto, its collection of over ten thousand shoes from four thousand five hundred years of history includes important ethnographic objects from North America and around the world, as well as twentieth-century international designer and celebrity shoes. The BSM Web site's "All about Shoes" features stories and artifacts related to Canada's aboriginal peoples and multicultural communities.

A few general human history museums have outstanding collections of dress that have been used extensively in publications and exhibitions. The McCord Museum of Canadian History in Montreal, founded in 1921, has an important holding, encompassing over sixteen thousand textile and clothing objects, well documented as being made or used by Canadians, especially by Montrealers, over the last three hundred years, including a few important eighteenth-century garments. Reflecting Montreal as the fashion center of Canada, the collection excels in superb examples of nineteenth-century fashionable female dress, as well as garments from leading twentieth-century Montreal designers, boutiques, and department stores. The McCord Museum has a costume and textiles curator and frequently mounts exhibitions. Examples of dress are used in most of their other thematic exhibitions. The museum's excellent Web site includes a searchable database of 125,000 images of artifacts, photographs, and related material. The Web site has several well-researched thematic presentations that draw upon the dress collection.

The Royal Ontario Museum (ROM) houses the largest textile and dress collection in Canada. Opened in downtown Toronto in 1914, the ROM has had an active research program in human history and the natural sciences. The dress and textile collection numbers fifty thousand objects from cultures around the world, ranging from archaeological finds to contemporary designs, with an outstanding selection of eighteenth-century garments, although not all Canadian. The Patricia Harris Gallery is devoted to the exhibition of dress collections organized by the ROM curator of costume and textiles. While the scope of the clothing collection is worldwide, the ROM has a fine collection of garments made or worn in Canada from the eighteenth century to the present, including Canadian couture. The ROM's Web site has a visual database of a small selection of its collections.

The Canadian Museum of Civilization (CMC) is Canada's national human history institution located in Gatineau, Quebec. It holds about five thousand textile and clothing objects in its renowned ethnographic collection of native artifacts, about three thousand articles of folk or ethnic dress, and eight thousand garments and accessories in its history collection. Documentation of the history holding is spotty, but the majority of the garments were worn by everyday Canadians from the mid-nineteenth century to the 1940s. Much of this collection is organized by region, so it is possible to do cross-regional analyses. It includes a small collection related to occupational dress in Canada, including nurses' uniforms, clothing worn by workers in primary industries in the 1980s, and millinery trade tools, as well as a few garments worn by Canadian politicians and other public figures. The CMC's Web site has a searchable database to a large percentage of its collections, including dress.

Moving to the East Coast, the New Brunswick Museum in Saint John documents the human and natural history of the province and has had a mandate to acquire dress and accessories since 1842. The clothing collection comprises 4,400 well-documented objects made, worn, or collected by New Brunswickers from the early eighteenth to the late twentieth century. Selections from the collection are rotated within the permanent exhibitions of the decorative arts and in special feature exhibitions. Their Web site has no searchable database, but it does describe the decorative arts collection and includes the online exhibition Vanity and Virtue: Women's Dress from 19th Century New Brunswick.

SIGNIFICANT UNIVERSITY COLLECTIONS OF DRESS

The Queen's University collection of dress in Kingston, Ontario, started as a resource for the Drama Department in the 1930s, but the historical importance of the collection was soon recognized when many long-established Kingston families began to donate clothing that had belonged to former generations. The collection consists of approximately two thousand well-documented items, the majority from the nineteenth and early twentieth centuries. The collection has had a checkered career, but now it has a permanent home and curator. An outstanding exhibition of clothing worn by Kingston women from 1810 to 1930 was mounted in 2007–2008 at the Agnes Etherington Art Centre on campus, with an insightful catalog by guest curator M. Elaine MacKay.

Ryerson University in Toronto has a Fashion Research Collection consisting of more than three thousand articles of dress, dating from the 1830s to the present. The purpose of the collection is to provide hands-on exploration of clothing for its school of fashion and to encourage faculty and student research. Because it is conceived as a general design collection, only some of the garments are documented as made or worn in Canada.

The Fashion Resource Centre at Seneca College, Toronto, houses ten thousand articles of clothing and accessories that span the years 1840 to the present. Some of the clothing is well documented as having been made or worn by Canadians, including several Canadian designers. About 85 percent of the collection is twentieth century. The collection is used by students in fashion design and visual and fashion merchandising.

Moving west, the University of Alberta Clothing and Textiles Collection in Edmonton has nearly seventeen thousand artifacts spanning two hundred and fifty years. While some parts of the clothing collection are documented as Canadian, many have no known provenance or are from other parts of the world. Maintained by the Department of Human Ecology, the collection provides insights into clothing and accessories design and construction, as well as historical and material culture. Exhibitions based on the collection are mounted on campus and across Alberta. Several theses related to dress from this department are listed in

A page from Eaton's mail order catalog, Fall and Winter Winnipeg issue, Canada, 1918–1919. Reproduced with the permission of Sears Canada Inc.

the Beaudoin-Ross and Blackstock bibliography. Although there is no online searchable database to the collection, their Web site does include a panoramic tour of their storage facilities and detailed information about selections from the collection.

SIGNIFICANT ARCHIVAL COLLECTIONS RELATING TO DRESS

As historians of dress know, photographs are invaluable. Canada has a few outstanding photography collections, the most important of which is the renowned Notman Photographic Archives at the McCord Museum, comprising over 1,250,000 photographs by numerous Canadian photographers. The major strength of the archives is the series of 450,000 photographs taken by the prolific Notman studio during its 78 years from 1840 to 1935. Notman operated seven studios in Canada and thirteen in the United States, but most of the photographs at the McCord relate to his Montreal business. About 80 percent of the Notman collection is portraiture, and as each photograph is numbered and identified as to sitter or subject, the collection provides a virtual parade of the changing fashions of (mainly English) Montrealers over time. A large selection of this collection can be viewed on the Web site's searchable database.

Similarly, the Topley Studio collection at Library Archives Canada comprises 150,000 mainly studio portrait photographs

taken in Ottawa in the period 1868–1924, including portraits of governors general, prime ministers and other politicians, civil servants, and residents of Ottawa. Library Archives Canada also sponsors the online Portrait Gallery of Canada, which displays a selection of images of Canadians great and small.

Another major source for dress historians is the mail order catalog, and Canada has a rich and accessible collection. The records of the T. Eaton Company, the founder of a major Canadian department store and mail order catalog, is at the Archives of Ontario in Toronto. The holdings include a full run of Eaton's Toronto catalogs from 1884 to 1976, Montreal catalogs from 1928 to 1942, and Winnipeg catalogs from 1905 to 1976. The catalogs are also available on microfilm. In addition, the Eaton company records have ninety thousand photographs, including images of merchandise, store interiors, garment manufacturing, advertising art, and fashion shows.

Library Archives Canada sponsors an online searchable database to selected issues of nine Canadian mail order catalogs—including Eatons and Simpsons of Toronto, Legaré and Dupuis Frères in Montreal, and Army and Navy in the west—from the 1880s to the 1970s. The Canadian Museum of Civilization has an excellent interactive Web site *Before E-commerce: A History of Canadian Mail-order Catalogues*, which includes a searchable database to hundreds of catalogs, as well as histories of mail order companies and essays such as "Custom-made to Ready-made: Women's Clothing in the Eaton's Catalogue, 1884 to 1930," "Catalogues and Women's Fashion," and "Dress Reform and Mail-Order."

Fashion journalism in Canada includes contemporary magazines such as *Flare*, *Elle*, and *Fashion Magazine*. Two long-lasting and important journals housed at the Thomas Fisher Rare Books Library at the University of Toronto are the *Dry Goods Review*, which started as a trade journal in 1891 and, in 1946, changed its name to *Style* (to 1981); and *Chatelaine*, the influential women's magazine of health, food, decor, style, and beauty from 1928 to 1994 (current issues are housed at many public libraries). Most issues of these journals are available in microform.

References and Further Reading

Baril, Gérard. *Dicomode, Dictionnaire de la mode au Québec de 1900 à nos jours*. Montreal: Éditions Fidès, 2004.

Bates, Christina. "How to Dress the Children? A Comparison of Prescription and Practice in Late-Nineteenth Century North America." *Dress* 24 (1997): 43–54.

Bates, Christina. "Creative Abilities and Business Sense: The Millinery Trade in Ontario." In *Framing Our Past: Canadian Women's History in the Twentieth Century*, edited by Sharon Anne Cook, Lorna R. McLean, and Kate O'Rourke, 348–358. Montreal and Kingston: McGill-Queens University Press, 2001.

Beaudoin-Ross, Jacqueline. "*A la Canadienne*: Some Aspects of 19th Century Habitant Dress." *Dress* 5 (1980): 71–82.

Beaudoin-Ross, Jacqueline. "'*A la Canadienne*' Once More: Some Insights into Quebec Rural Female Dress." *Dress* 7 (1981): 69–81.

Beaudoin-Ross, Jacqueline. *Form and Fashion: Nineteenth-Century Montreal Dress*. Montreal: McCord Museum of Canadian History, 1992.

Beaudoin-Ross, Jacqueline, and Pamela Blackstock. "Costume in Canada: An Annotated Bibliography." *Material History Bulletin* 19 (Spring, 1984): 59–92.

Beaudoin-Ross, Jacqueline, and Pamela Blackstock. "Costume in Canada: The Sequel." *Material History Review* 34 (Fall, 1991): 42–67.

Brett, Katharine B. *Modesty to Mod: Dress and Undress in Canada, 1780–1967.* Toronto: Royal Ontario Museum/University of Toronto Press, 1967.

Cooper, Cynthia. *Magnificent Entertainments: Fancy Dress Balls of Canada's Governors General, 1876–1898.* Fredericton and Hull: Goose Lane Editions and the Canadian Museum of Civilization, 1997.

Du Berger, Jean, and Jacques Mathieu, eds. *Les ouvrières de Dominion Corset à Québec, 1886–1988.* Sainte-Foy: Les presses de l'Université Laval, 1993.

MacKay, M. Elaine. *Beyond the Silhouette: Fashion and the Women of Historic Kingston.* Kingston, ON: Agnes Etherington Art Centre, 2007.

Palmer, Alexandra. *Couture and Commerce: The Transatlantic Fashion Trade in the 1950s.* Vancouver: University of British Columbia Press, 2001.

Palmer, Alexandra, ed. *Fashion: A Canadian Perspective.* Toronto: University of Toronto Press, 2004.

Routh, Caroline. *In Style. 100 Years of Canadian Women's Fashion.* Toronto: Stoddart, 1993.

Christina Bates

See also Evidence about Dress of Indigenous People: Canadian Territory; Regional Differences in Dress and Fashion; The Garment Industry and Retailing in Canada; Music and Dress in Canada.

PART 2

Fashion in the United States and Canada

Introduction to Fashion

- Ideals of Beauty
- Technology and Fashion
- Economic Developments
- Fashion as a Reflection of Its Times

The word *fashion* implies transience, mutability, and variability. Acceptance by a large number of people is also part of fashion, but adoption by many people alone does not make an item fashionable. Dress traditions can and do persist for centuries with little change. Fashion, by contrast, comes and goes. Fashion has been a feature of Western dress since the Middle Ages.

Clear evidence of fashion change appears by the fourteenth century, when styles of dress can be seen to have altered every thirty to forty years. Century by century these changes came more frequently until by the end of the twentieth century, fashion designer Karl Lagerfeld saw major fashion changes coming as often as every five to seven years.

Many people believe that the modern fashion industry imposes fashion change on consumers. But the fashion industry came into being only in the latter part of the nineteenth century in the United States, and fashion change had been a feature of Western dress for more than five centuries. Although this industry does not "cause" fashion change, it does manipulate styles to some extent. The garment industry in the United States and Canada is a business built on fashion, a sociocultural phenomenon that is an integral part of Western societies. While fashion is an easily identifiable aspect of dress, it is also a factor in other consumer products and in many aspects of life. There are fashions in automobiles, architecture, popularity of certain foods, styles of writing, electronic gear, and the like. The United States and Canada satisfy the conditions necessary for fashion, which are as follows: some degree of social mobility, sufficient affluence to participate in fashionable behavior, and means of communicating information about fashion to a broad audience.

Fashion trends are established in many ways. Until the late twentieth century, many social scientists subscribed to what has been called the "trickle-down theory of fashion," in which new styles were seen to originate at the highest socioeconomic or status levels and were then copied by those at lower status levels. By the time a fashion reached the lowest income levels, those at the highest levels changed their preferred styles in order to separate themselves from the less affluent. Once the fashion industry had been established, fashion designers created apparel for the elite that satisfied the demand for new styles. As the fashion industry broadened to include more innovation at lower price levels, designers looked for new sources of design ideas. One source was called "street style," or styles of young people from the counterculture or from diverse ethnic groups. These styles were said to "percolate up" because they often served as an inspiration for haute couture (the highest fashion) designs.

As more and more clothing production moved out of the home or away from seamstresses and tailors and into factories during the twentieth century, fashion racing accelerated and

designers were expected to produce innovations more often. As a result, many sources ranging from film (Dr. Zhivago coats in the 1970s) to social protest movements (hippie-inspired clothes) and political figures (Jackie Kennedy in the 1960s) or military actions (camouflage prints after 2000) were mined for design ideas.

IDEALS OF BEAUTY

Although the words *fashion* and *dress* are often used interchangeably, *fashion* is often used to mean women's styles, especially the garments called dresses and their accessories. But fashion in dress goes well beyond garments. There are fashions in women's body shapes. In the seventeenth century, the preferred body shape can be seen in paintings by Rubens. He painted women with full figures who would be considered overweight by modern standards. In the early nineteenth century, women with exceptionally full bosoms were the preferred ideal of feminine beauty. A boyish shape was seen as the correct figure in the 1920s, but in the 1930s a more womanly figure was preferred. Magazine advertisements, haute couture models, and actresses of the early twenty-first century portray the fashionable body for women as thin, almost to the point of emaciation. Interestingly, this is also a time when more and more women (and men) are regarded as obese, more than exceeding the appropriate health standards for ideal body weight. It is also a time when fitness is said to be important and health clubs abound. One fashion inspired by working out is the running suit, a combination of a loose-fitting jacket and drawstring pants of simple design. And the ironic result seems to be that oversized men and women often adopt this garment because it is so comfortable!

Achieving the current fashionable ideal of beauty for men or women in a particular time period usually requires some efforts in addition to the selection of fashionable body coverings and accessories. Body shape can be manipulated through diet and exercise or through physical alterations by cosmetic surgical enhancements. Temporary changes in body shape can be made with undergarments that support or compress areas of the body, by choosing garments that follow the preferred shape, or a combination of both. Skin color can be enhanced by applying cosmetics or using chemical treatments to tan or bleach skin. Hair can be colored, cut, curled, or removed. Contact lenses can be used to change eye color. Surgery to correct vision is used to eliminate the need to wear eyeglasses.

TECHNOLOGY AND FASHION

Technology contributed to the birth of the fashion industry. In the earliest years that Europeans lived in the United States and Canada, items of dress were either imported from abroad or made in the home or by dressmakers or tailors. Dressmakers were paid to make clothes for women, and tailors generally made men's clothing. The Industrial Revolution helped to make mechanization acceptable as a way of producing many products. The invention of the sewing machine in the first half of the nineteenth century, its use for mass production of uniforms for soldiers fighting the U.S. Civil War, and its subsequent acceptance for making garments in the home were some of the factors leading to the development

This illustration, ca. 1860, shows how North American fashion can alter body shape through the addition of corsetry and undergarments such as bustles. Courtesy of Phyllis Tortora.

of the U.S. garment industry. Other inventions contributed. Ebeneezer Butterick's sized paper patterns (patented in 1863) made standardized sizing possible. A cutting machine that could cut multiple layers of fabric facilitated mass production. By the early twentieth century, some fashionable apparel was being produced in factories, and by the end of that century, the U.S. mass production system was imitated all over the globe.

Fashion trends sometimes came about as indirect results of other technological changes. It is likely that the widespread use of automobiles in the early 1900s had some impact on encouraging women, who were by then driving cars, to wear shorter skirts. Prior to about 1915 women's skirts reached close to the ground. In the 1920s, women's daytime dresses shortened and could end at the knee. Although skirt lengths have fluctuated, it has been rare for women to wear daytime garments in lengths that might impede driving. Automobiles were also responsible for the disappearance of the parasol from women's wardrobes. Parasols were used to keep the sun from ladies riding in carriages. Cars without roofs moved far too rapidly to allow a delicate parasol to survive, and a car with a roof provided protection from the sun. Advances in textile technology also affected fashion trends. As manufactured stretch fibers, such as spandex, improved, they were incorporated into more and more fabrics so that by the turn of the

millennium, they contributed to a preference for stretch fabrics in garments as diverse as clothes for bicycling and cocktail dresses.

ECONOMIC DEVELOPMENTS

Those settlers and immigrants who came to the Northern Hemisphere and remained to become citizens participated in growing economies. They tended to consider themselves members of the middle class. Often they gained affluence and had disposable income far beyond anything they experienced in the countries they had left. They soon became consumers of a wide variety of goods. Then as now, increased demand by consumers with disposable income led to development of new industries to provide desired products, and demand for those products could be stimulated by media presentations.

From the seventeenth century to the nineteenth century, dress was a major factor in the Canadian and U.S. economies. Although the Canadians had initially harvested fish in great quantities and had established the first settlements because they had to dry the fish they were shipping back to Europe, the focus of trade soon became fur. French Canadian fur traders traveled to the interior of what was to become Canada to secure pelts from First Nations people who were pleased to get highly desirable products in

Women sewing by hand the clothing sold at A. T. Stewart's Department Store in New York City. In addition to ready-to-wear clothing, the store sold fabrics and other supplies for making garments at home. (Drawing from *Frank Leslie's Weekly*, 24 April 1875.) Courtesy of Phyllis Tortora.

return. Many of these products were not practical tools but rather ornamental materials such as beads and colorful woven fabrics. A fashion in Europe for beaver hats, made from felt constructed in part with the soft underlayer of the fur of beaver pelts, stimulated the fur trade and the establishment of trading post settlements. In the early seventeenth century, historians report that an estimated eighty thousand Europe-bound beaver pelts intended for use in fashionable men's fashionable hats passed through New Amsterdam (later to become New York). These status symbols were extraordinarily expensive, costing, as author Russell Shorto has pointed out, "about three months wages for an average worker." When the fashion for beaver hats waned in the early 1800s, other areas of economic development were found.

The southernmost region of what was to become the United States also flourished because of dress-related products. Cotton was first imported to Europe from India, and its scarcity made it very expensive. Southern farmers soon found that cotton thrived in this region. The combination of greater speed in preparing cotton for spinning that came as a result of the invention of the cotton gin and of mechanized spinning and weaving that were early manifestations of the Industrial Revolution made cotton production enormously profitable. It also stimulated the slave trade and undoubtedly prolonged the period during which slavery was practiced in the United States because more and more workers were needed to pick the cotton.

Sudden economic changes may result in sudden changes in dress. This is particularly evident at times when two distinctly different cultures come into contact for the first time and begin to trade. As a result of trade, glass beads quickly became an important ornamentation for many elements of North American Indian and First Nations dress. Gradual economic changes can

also have a profound effect on dress. As clothing manufacture moved out of the home and into factories, these new businesses needed to make a profit. Mass production required employees with the requisite skills. Fortunately, around the turn of the nineteenth century, a huge influx of immigrants included many women who could sew. But if the items being made were too complex, the cost of production would make the final product too expensive for a mass market, and profits would be realized only by attracting as large a market as possible. One result was a tendency to simplify the design of garments so they could be made quickly and economically. The unique development of the U.S. garment industry was a system of manufacture called *piecework*, in which one operator made only one part of a garment, for example, the sleeve, then passed the garment along to the next operator who added the next section, and so on until the assembly was complete.

As more women entered the job market after the turn of the nineteenth century, fewer women sewed clothing at home and, consequently, demand for ready-to-wear clothing increased. The change from home-based production to production outside the home meant that items of dress had to be purchased, which required the establishment of retail outlets. Retailing, too, evolved to handle these products, and in cities, one saw the growth of department stores that sold all kinds of clothing for men, women, and children; specialty stores that dealt with merchandise only for men or for women or for children; and mail order catalogs that could supply people in rural areas. The well-to-do were still likely to have their clothing made by dressmakers or by tailors who made clothing to order. In ready-to-wear clothing, price and quality levels were established. The department store that one patronized could be a status symbol.

Boys' clothing, United States, ca. 1940. Here the youngest boys wear knickers with knee socks; a slightly older boy and the three eldest have graduated to long pants. Photographer unknown. Courtesy of Phyllis Tortora.

Many modifications in manufacturing and retailing practices took place in the last quarter of the twentieth century. These reflected economic changes such as the globalization of the fashion industry and the movement of a large portion of manufacturing from North America to lower wage countries all over the world. Retail stores continued to occupy an important place in the supply chain. Many store chains that had developed in the United States opened branches in Canada. By 1998, seven of the top retail outlets in Canada were U.S.-based firms.

Other types of merchandising attracted consumers. Promotion of products through mail order catalogs has grown in both countries, with many of the same companies selling by mail order on both sides of the border. Television marketing began with one channel in the late 1980s, and the positive response led several other companies to sell fashion-related products. Internet sales have grown steadily, and it is the rare major retailer (whether that retailer began as a store, mail order business, or television marketer) that does not have a Web site where orders can be placed.

FASHION AS A REFLECTION OF ITS TIMES

Fashion is often said to mirror social change. These connections can be quite obvious or more subtle. Several examples may serve to make the point. Sociologists George Bush and Perry London have described the relationships between changes in the societal expectations of prepubescent boys in the late 1930s to 1940 and concurrent changes in the garments they customarily wore. They describe children's clothing practices of the 1920s and 1930s as follows. Boys under the age of five or six were usually dressed in short pants, and boys from about age seven to puberty wore knickers, a garment that reached to below the knee, where it was gathered into a fitted cuff. Once they reached puberty or began to take on adult work, adolescent boys switched to full-length trousers. In the late 1930s this changed. No longer was the dress of boys determined by their age. By 1940, knickers were rarely seen. At the same time, ideas were changing about stages of childhood, when they began and ended, and expectations about the social roles young boys should play were unclear. Why the end of knickers? To paraphrase the theory that Bush and London have illustrated, the stability of the accepted pattern of dressing gave way to greater variability when the place in society of these preadolescent boys became more uncertain.

Another example of how variations in dress norms can be a visual manifestation of changes in expectations about social roles can be seen when, about forty years ago, many women who were members of Roman Catholic religious orders abandoned the dress prescribed by their religious orders. Instead of the traditional habit, many nuns adopted either ordinary street dress or radically modified habits. These changes took place at a time when those within these religious orders were questioning the roles that had been assigned to them or were exchanging more passive lives for greater activism outside the convent walls.

For most of the 1800s and 1900s up to the late 1960s, men were expected to wear clothing of relatively conservative cut and subdued colors. Their hair was usually cut short, in contrast to longer hair for women. Jewelry for men was limited to conservative watches, cuff links, and rings. Over this time period, the roles of men and women in society were fairly well defined. With the revival of feminism in the post–World War II period, those definitions began to seem less rigid. And as these role expectations changed, men's clothing changed. By the 1970s, men could buy vividly colored clothing; they grew their hair longer, some long enough for ponytails; and many wore earrings and necklaces.

Fashion can also reflect other aspects of its time. Military actions frequently have an echo in dress. During the U.S. Civil War, one of the most popular items of dress was the Zouave jacket. This collarless jacket decorated with braid was an imitation of the uniform of one army unit of the Northern states called the Zouaves. The omnipresent camouflage prints of the years after 2000 appeared in clothing ranging from T-shirts to high-priced fashions.

Dress can often be seen to have lines and decorative motifs that are similar to those in contemporary fine and applied art forms. During the 1920s, the lines of the skyscrapers rising in New York City were straight and vertical. So, too, were the lines of women's dresses. Art historians call the design motifs that appeared in architecture art deco, and jewelry and textile fabrics employed these same motifs. When artists of the 1960s created optical effects in the style known as op art, textile fabrics used for dress soon incorporated the same kinds of visual effects.

References and Further Reading

Bush, George, and Perry London. "On the Disappearance of Knickers." *Journal of Social Psychology* 51 (May 1960): 359–366.

Evans, W., and P. Barbiero. "Foreign Retailers in Canada: Survey Results, Including a Special Feature on Wal-Mart International." Toronto, Canada: Ryerson University, Centre for the Study of Commercial Activity, 1999. http://www.csca.ryerson.ca/Publications/1999-11.html (accessed 8 April 2008).

Martin, Richard, and Harold Koda. *Jocks and Nerds: Men's Style in the Twentieth Century.* New York: Rizzoli, 1989.

Schorman, Rob. *Selling Style: Clothing and Social Change at the Turn of the Century.* Philadelphia: University of Pennsylvania Press, 2003.

Shorto, Russell. *The Island at the Center of the World.* New York: Doubleday, 2004.

Tortora, Phyllis, and Keith Eubank. *Survey of Historic Costume.* New York: Fairchild Publications, 2005.

Zakim, M. *Ready-made Democracy: History of Men's Dress in the American Republic: 1760–1860.* Chicago: University of Chicago Press, 2003.

Phyllis G. Tortora

See also Tradition in Fashion; Types and Properties of Fashionable Dress; The Pattern Industry; The Garment Industry and Retailing in the United States; The Garment Industry and Retailing in Canada; Fashion Designers, Seamstresses and Tailors; Gender; Class; Influence of the Arts.

Tradition and Fashion

One might think that because Canada and the United States are countries that can be considered technologically advanced and would be characterized as thoroughly modern societies, the role of fashion in the lives of these countries' residents would be strong and the place of tradition would be minimal. But to understand where and how tradition and fashion contrast, complement, and intersect in these modern Western societies, it is necessary to begin by exploring the meaning of these concepts.

On the face of it, tradition, which could be summed up as "We have always done it this way," would seem to be at war with both technological progress and fashion. When tradition permeates all corners of society, can fashion even exist? Tradition and fashion would seem to be perfect opposites. After all, fashion is *expected* to change, whereas tradition is not. What drives fashion is the power of novelty; the new seems better than the old. For tradition, it is just the reverse; the old is better than the new. In addition, fashion is at its core individualistic, whereas tradition celebrates group solidarity. But in actuality, the relationship is not so simple.

It is common to see tradition and fashion as inhabiting different portions of the same continuum. All social interaction evolves over time, but the rate of change varies considerably between fads, fashions, customs, and traditions. Fads and fashions change much more quickly than customs and traditions. Also, customs and traditions are far more deeply embedded in culture than are the fleeting styles associated with fads and fashions. While the connotations may be slightly different, anthropologist Edward Sapir has argued that words such as *custom, convention, tradition,* and *mores* are more or less interchangeable.

Fads are short-lived fashions that often contain an element of the bizarre. A fad that lasts more than two years is on borrowed time. Swallowing live goldfish (1920s); youth stuffing themselves into telephone booths (1960s); wearing mood rings, Afro hairstyles, or streaking (1970s); and putting up inflatable lawn decorations for a variety of occasions (2000s) are all examples of fads. The fascination with women's handbags the size of small suitcases may be a contemporary fad.

Fashions are generally defined as what the majority of people are wearing at a particular time and place. By that definition, Mao suits (loose pants worn with a matching, front-buttoned shirt with a stand-up collar in drab colors) were the fashions worn by most Chinese for years after the Cultural Revolution. By that definition, all dress becomes fashion. But clothing changes by political fiat are not what are meant by changes due to participation in the fashion process. Mao suits were not expected to be replaced in a few years by something different; they were the dawning of a new tradition.

Clothing subject to the fashion process is expected to change quickly and incessantly. One style replaces another, not because it is better but simply because it seems better—people like new styles and enjoy change. As Shakespeare put it in the sixteenth century, "Fashion wears out more clothes than the man." Better examples of fashion than Mao suits would be knee-length skirts in the early 1960s giving way to miniskirts in the late 1960s or the tailored, knee-length suits inspired by military uniforms worn by women in the United States and Canada during World War II giving way to the more feminine, flared, mid-calf-length skirts of Dior's New Look in 1947.

As sociologist Fred Davis has noted, fashion is fueled by cultural ambivalence; it involves those elements of culture about which no solution seems right. Long skirts may initially feel elegant and dignified, but all too soon they seem cumbersome and frumpy; so, too, with short skirts. Likewise, padded shoulders can seem assertive and bold at one time, only to appear too masculine and ridiculous in a few years. All fashion solutions are temporary ones because no optimum solution exists.

African American infant wearing a traditional christening gown, Georgia, United States, ca. 1900. Library of Congress Prints and Photographs Division, LC-USZ62-124810.

While it is true that even traditions change, the change is slow and gradual, thereby preserving continuity. A good analogy can be made with an individual's body. Over a period of about seven years, most cells in the body die and are replaced, yet the person is still the same person. Dress scholars George Sproles and Leslie Burns have divided traditions into formal and informal. Formal traditions are customs and behaviors so deeply embedded in a culture that they are passed along from one generation to the next with very little questioning. And they are explicit and usually strictly enforced, either with actual laws or through extreme social pressure. In the United States and Canada there is a strong, formal tradition that adults must wear clothes when they move about outside of their own homes, and there are indecent exposure laws to deal with individuals who do not comply. Clothing customs often revolve around rituals that are themselves deeply rooted in tradition and so change very slowly. For example, rites of passage are associated with a change in an individual's status. A white lace gown, longer than the baby, is the traditional christening outfit in North America. A mortarboard and gown have been worn at graduations for centuries. They may be made out of polyester today, where once they were wool, but the style of the gown is remarkably unchanged.

In contrast to formal traditions, Sproles and Burns have described informal traditions as more implicit than explicit, "as behaviors learned by imitating models within a society." Who those models are varies over time. As an example, the feminine ideal body shape in Canada and the United States has gone through many versions in the past one hundred years. In the early twentieth century, a full-breasted woman with a narrow waist would have filled out the monobosom dresses of the day. By the 1920s, the ideal feminine form was the flat-breasted, slender form of the flapper. Skipping ahead to the 1950s, the ideal was manifested in curvy actresses such as Marilyn Monroe, Jayne Mansfield, and Gina Lollobrigida. In the 1960s, the almost anorexic-looking model, Twiggy, became the new ideal. Now, in the twenty-first century, a well-toned, thin, but not anorexic-looking body is the ideal.

Another informal set of rituals are what dress scholar Susan Kaiser has called "rituals of intensification." They are community-based rituals that may keep traditions alive. There are numerous community festivals, street fairs, and parades in Canada and the United States each year that involve dressing up in clothes of another culture or of bygone days. In New York City, the Puerto Rican Day parade is an opportunity for people of Puerto Rican descent to dress in more traditional clothing than they would ordinarily wear to work. Similar celebrations occur for many other ethnicities in the United States. For Chinese New Year, Chinatown comes alive with paper dragons and people in traditional Chinese outfits. In Quebec City, seventeenth- and eighteenth-century music, dance, clothing, and entertainment are featured at the SAQ New France Festival each year. In the Yukon, the Tr'ondëk Hwëch'in First Nation hosts a day of cultural celebrations.

FASHION WITHIN TRADITION

While the ever-changing face of fashion would seem to work against the glacial pace of tradition, fashion actually works within the confines of tradition. An example of this is the strongly held belief that there should be a distinction between the appearances of the sexes. Throughout most of the history of Canada and the United States, the sexes could be distinguished simply by looking at the lower half of the body. Men wore pants and women wore skirts. This distinction was especially helpful in the seventeenth century, when the upper part of the body was clothed in remarkably similar form for men and women. Namely, among the upper classes at least, there was a profusion of lace worn with long locks, a rather feminine look by twenty-first-century standards. By the nineteenth century, there was a stark contrast between the sexes,

A Chinese New Year parade in Chinatown, Los Angeles, United States, 2008, in which traditional Chinese outfits are worn. Copyright Jose Gil, 2007. Used under license from Shutterstock.com

with men wearing rather undecorated suits and women wearing highly decorated dresses.

Attempts at dress reform began in the mid-nineteenth century in the United States. At that time, Elizabeth Smith designed an outfit that she thought would liberate women from the yards of fabric and hoop undergarments popular at that time. It had a modest bodice combined with a full skirt, cut off at the knees, and harem pants peeking out below the hem. This outfit became known as the *bloomer*, named after Mrs. Amelia Jenks Bloomer, who tried to promote its use in the feminist publication she edited, *The Lily*. Although the look was quite modest by twenty-first-century standards, it was thought to be fairly scandalous because it let the world know that women had two legs. Not only was it calling into question the tradition of men being the wearers of pants, but it was not at all fashionable. All but a few women rejected it outright. The bloomer outfit was not even on the Canadian woman's radar because she was still looking to England for fashion direction and the English thought that the bloomer was totally ridiculous. Canadian women mounted their own dress reform movement about twenty-five years later when Clara Graham wrote to the editor of *Public Health Magazine* extolling the virtues of her new, nonconfining underwear and recommending that women read a book called *Dress and Health*, which mainly criticized the wearing of tightly laced corsets because of health issues.

True dress reform did not arrive until the twentieth century, when women gave up their corsets and raised the hems of their skirts, allowing greater physical mobility in the 1910s. With greater mobility and getting the vote (ca. 1920), U.S. and Canadian women were moving into the world outside of the home. The way was primed for a real change in tradition, namely, the gradual, growing acceptance of seeing women in pants. Marlene Dietrich and Katharine Hepburn, two U.S. actresses, were often photographed wearing pants in the 1930s, but wearing pants on the streets was just not done. When the United States and Canada joined World War II, women went to work in factories, often wearing their husband's civilian pants in order to save their rations for other clothes. Women got used to seeing women in pants during this time, but after the war, most women went back to wearing skirts. In the 1960s, André Courrèges included long pants as a fashion item in his collection and ushered in the era of the pantsuit and designer jeans. What Mrs. Bloomer tried to introduce overnight actually took about a century to reach real acceptance. In the twenty-first century, North American women are accepted in pants or skirts. The tradition of women only wearing skirts had changed. The same cannot be said for men. Despite periodic attempts to show skirts for men in the twentieth century, this practice has never caught on in Canada or the United States. It is ironic that women, traditionally thought of as "the weaker sex," now have greater freedom to wear what they want. Perhaps because of the fact that skirts symbolized women's subservient position in society for so long, it is understandable that men would think that putting on skirts would devalue them. For women, on the other hand, putting on pants empowers them.

Attempts to develop unisex clothing in the 1970s had about as much success as the bloomer did in the 1850s. Even though women had adopted pants, they did not want to dress the same as men. Sexual distinctions remained even when a woman borrowed her husband's shirt. It was not supposed to look the same on the woman. So it seems that the tradition of distinguishing the sexes through their clothing remains intact today.

Another example of fashion working within tradition can be found in the distinction between work and home. As men went to work in factories in the nineteenth century, a clear distinction was made between clothing for work and clothing for the home. The workplace was competitive, rational, and male dominated. The home was compassionate, sentimental, and female dominated. The clothes of men and women took completely different trajectories; "irrational fashion" became the prerogative of females.

Men wore somber, dark suits to work, but they relaxed in more casual attire at home. This distinction was intensified with the advent of sportswear for men in the 1920s and 1930s. But as women moved into the workforce in record numbers in the 1970s, there began to be a blurring of the differences between work and home. Employers became aware of the need for cooperation and teamwork. Today, companies pay for their employees to go on retreats, encourage them to form baseball teams, or even have them cook a meal together, all in the name of building community. With this emphasis on team building has come a loosening of the tradition of formal work clothes. Dress-down or casual Fridays began in the 1990s and provided legitimacy for more casual dress one day a week. At the beginning of the twenty-first century, business attire is much more casual everyday, for all but a few occupations.

There are some occupations that have resisted the trend toward more casual dress in the workplace. Military and police uniforms come to mind. Because individuals in these occupations are meant to preserve order and society, it is not surprising that their uniforms would be consistent and slow to change. These occupations are marked by hierarchy and authority. Few would fail to recognize or question the authority of the Royal Canadian Mounted Police in their distinctive red jackets, black pants and boots, and brimmed hats. Three other occupations also are characterized by hierarchy, authority, and a need to project stability: judges, bankers, and the clergy. In contrast, people in the entertainment industry are supposed to be creative. Seeing a favorite rock star performing in a three-piece suit would be just as jarring as seeing a banker in hip-hop fashions or a judge in dreadlocks and sneakers.

IMMIGRATION

Both the United States and Canada are countries that have been built on immigrants who brought with them their own traditions, including their own dress styles. As a result, North American traditions have taken on a different character than European ones. The original European settlers came primarily from England and France in Canada and the United States. As they came ashore and explored westward, they encountered the earlier settlers, various North American Indian tribes (now known in Canada as First Nations) who are thought to have come to North America thousands of years before on a land bridge from Asia across the Bering Strait. Later waves of immigrants included Germans, Irish, Italians, Poles, and Jews from Europe; Chinese and Japanese from Asia; and Mexicans, Puerto Ricans, and other Spanish speakers from other parts of the Americas. Today there are immigrants from every corner of the world in both countries.

Settlers came to the New World wearing whatever they had worn in their country of origin. Most of the earliest immigrants were young men from the lower ranks of society, so their clothing did not reflect the most fashionable clothing of their day. While it is impossible to pick a particular date after which the colonists

An example of a bloomer outfit, New York, ca. 1851. This garment was created by Elizabeth Smith, who wanted to liberate women from the yards of fabric and hoop undergarments popular at that time. It had a modest bodice combined with a full skirt, cut off at the knees, and harem pants underneath. Library of Congress, Prints and Photographs Division, cph 3b49861.

participated in the fashion process, it is safe to say that it occurred after the colonists were established enough to be past survival mode and the sex ratio became more balanced, probably at least a couple of generations after the first disastrous attempt to establish a colony at Jamestown in 1607.

Certainly by the end of the seventeenth century, as the settlers' wealth increased and many became established landowners, they began to get caught up in European fashion. Diaries and letters sent to relatives "back home" often listed items of clothing or cloth and accessories that the wealthy in the colonies wished to order from Europe. Fashion dolls (dolls dressed in the latest fashions from their underwear on up to the outerwear) were making their way monthly from France to England and on to the colonies by the end of the seventeenth century. By the nineteenth century, fashion news was coming directly to the United States and Canada through ladies' magazines (*Godey's Ladies Book* and *Peterson's* magazine) and the *Sears and Roebuck catalog*.

Later waves of immigrants also came to the United States and Canada wearing whatever they had worn in their country of origin. For example, the Japanese came in kimonos; the Indians, in saris; and the Polish, in kerchiefs. Some of these immigrants quickly adopted the clothing styles of the United States or Canada, while others clung to their traditional dress at least for a

generation or so. Thus, both Canada and the United States have had multiple cultures coexisting throughout their histories, but perhaps more so for Canada.

Historically, the United States has had a culture of assimilation; often referred to as a melting pot, it is a country in which immigrants are quickly absorbed into the dominant culture. This assimilation was assumed to be a one-way process. Thus, Italian immigrants would lose their Italian manners and clothing and become American. Asian Indians would stop wearing saris and put on American clothes. In contrast, Canada has been known for its multiculturalism. In Canada, ethnic groups learn and come to understand the prevailing cultural codes without necessarily relinquishing their own, a process known as *acculturation*. Immigrants are integrated into society legally, economically, and politically but often maintain much more of their ethnocultural distinctiveness than is the case in the United States. This distinction may be better understood in terms of the two countries' histories. The United States was settled primarily by English-speaking people and has retained English as the dominant language. In order for immigrants to become citizens, they must learn English, among other things. So, from the beginning, the United States was set up expecting those who arrived on its shores to adapt. The differences among the colonies that would become the United States, while by no means negligible, were far less profound than the divide between French Quebec and all of the other English-speaking provinces and territories. Thus, there has been less emphasis on adapting to the Canadian way of doing things.

A concept related to acculturation, but slightly different, is *transnationalism*. Silvia Pedraza has described this concept as living in two or more worlds simultaneously. She believes this practice is possible because of the explosion of communication venues. The cost of calling home or even traveling home is no longer exorbitant. The Internet allows families to stay connected practically for free through e-mail, instant messenger service, and photo sharing of pictures and even videos of important events such as weddings, christenings, and graduations. The transnational Indian immigrant lives in the U.S. culture when in the United States and in the Indian culture when in India. Both in the parent and adopted country, designers and boutiques have sprung up to help immigrants seeking to integrate both worlds, and it is only a matter of time before these syncretic designs begin to influence mainstream fashion.

The concept of integration as a different explanation for immigrants fitting into their new country has been explored by Raj Mehta and Russell Belk. Unlike assimilation, which is a one-way concept, integration implies a two-way street. Immigrants who are integrated consider it valuable to both maintain their cultural identity and establish relations with the dominant culture. This model implies that the immigrants influence their new culture as well as the dominant culture influencing them. This is certainly seen in the mixing of cuisines, for example, chow mein, pizza, burritos, and sushi. Similar infusions have enriched popular music. In the realm of fashion and dress this two-way flow has been less profound but is by no means unknown. Today, a good deal of influence on clothing designs comes from the street, and certainly some of the *frisson* of street fashion derives from the intermingling of diverse immigrant styles.

Some groups continue to dress in a distinctive manner in order to maintain their separateness. Hasidic Jews mark their devoutness by the frequency and intensity of their religious observances.

By dressing in a very traditional way, Hasidic boys and men separate themselves from non-Jews and the less devout. By wearing such recognizable clothing, they guard themselves from engaging in sin (e.g., attending a movie theater), because everyone in the Hasidic community would know that they were doing something that was forbidden. They wear dark suits with very long jackets that button right over left. Their dark hats have wide brims. Pants are tucked into socks. White fringes are found at their waists. Adult males do not shave. Some wear their sideburns in a long curl hanging separately from the beard. Hasidic women follow Jewish laws for modesty but otherwise have no distinctive appearance. Like other orthodox Jewish women, they wear long, conservative skirts and sleeves that reach down at least to the elbow. Married women cover their hair, either with a wig or with a head kerchief.

Another group that distinguishes itself through its dress is the Amish, who believe that they should remain separate from the evils of the outside world. Their clothing reflects their beliefs in that it is simple and functional, with an emphasis on humility and a sharp separation from the secular world. Clothes are made at home from fabrics that are often industry leftovers; the basic look remains the same, but the fabrics change. Today's Amish prefer synthetic fibers (such as polyester and nylon) because they hold up better than cotton and require no ironing. Men wear suit coats without collars, lapels, or pockets in dark colors, preferably in true black. Trousers do not have creases or cuffs and are held up by suspenders. A broad-brimmed hat is worn (felt in winter, straw in summer). Unmarried men shave, but married men are required to grow beards but not mustaches. Amish women usually wear solid-colored dresses with full skirts and long sleeves. No jewelry is permitted. Black stockings and shoes are worn. They never cut their hair, which is worn braided or in a bun and tucked into a white cap called a *covering*. The covering is worn under a stiff black bonnet when going to town or to church. In such closed communities tradition is foregrounded, and fashion, if it exists at all, must be quiet and unnoticed.

TRADITION AND POSTMODERNISM

While neither Canada nor the United States have a national costume, both countries have shared a good number of clothing rules or informal traditions. A few of these clothing rules include the following: (1) Design principles should be followed when designing clothes. Proper proportion is achieved by dividing the body into spaces that are uneven and related to the natural anatomy. Balance is judged in terms of bilateral symmetry and also top to bottom (for example, a large hat might make someone look top heavy). One dominant center of interest is sought for good emphasis. A few smaller areas of interest lead the eyes around an outfit, thereby achieving rhythm. (2) Summer clothes are made from cotton, linen, and, beginning in the twentieth century, lightweight manufactured fibers such as rayon. Winter clothes are made from silk and wool and, later, warm manufactured fibers, such as acrylic. (3) One should never wear white before Memorial Day and never after Labor Day. (4) It is not proper to wear red and pink together. (5) Floral patterns should not be mixed with stripes or plaids.

The rules outlined above are just a handful of the unwritten clothing rules that have been challenged by designers in the postmodern era. An article in *W* magazine in July 2007 shows

During World War II, North American women often wore trousers for factory work. Courtesy New York Public Library.

twenty-six creations by John Galliano, a British designer known for his uninhibited avant-garde approach to design. Although his workmanship is impeccable and his fabrics exquisite, many of his designs break one or more design principles. One pink dress has huge feathered sleeves that resemble Clydesdale horses' legs. A brown dress of modest proportions is paired with a hat so gigantic that the observer worries about whether the model's slender neck can support such a huge head covering. One outfit pairs a bright red dress with a hot pink coat.

In the July 2007 issue of *Vogue*, there is a Balenciaga outfit by Nicolas Ghesquière labeled, "So mix-matchy and madcap, it gives us both Left Bank Bohemian and International Intellectual at once." The model is wearing a padded jacket that features orange, with accents of white, black, pink, and purple on the outside, lined with a bright yellow fur that shows at the wrists and as part of a huge upturned collar. The waist is encircled by a wide black leather belt with three buckles. Peeking out from under the jacket is a miniskirt whose predominant colors of purple, pink, black, and white seem quite at odds with the mostly orange jacket.

In the Information Age, clothing has sometimes been used to convey mixed and even contradictory messages. An early-twenty-first-century creation by Antonio Marras is a superb example. The base of the upper garment is a man's wool suit jacket. Inside the hip area, it has been carefully covered with sequins. Ostrich feathers have been sewn along the open front of the jacket. The base of the skirt is made from a painter's drop cloth. On top of that is fine netting. On the netting in the huge train, there are the two patch pockets, which were removed from the jacket front, along with other decorative beading. This whole ensemble is screaming ambiguity. Is it male or female? Is it fancy or practical? Is it for evening or day?

There are other examples of mixed messages. Lydia Klenck of Canada transforms used clothing and scraps of fabric into new designs, which she has described on her Web site as "very much influenced by clothing of bygone eras as well as folk costumes and fairy tales from around the world." One design on her Web site from her Spring 2004 collection has a peasant theme. The bodice of the dress is close fitting, made with light blue sleeves, many colors of scraps making up the collar, and a white lace insert at the neckline. The skirt of the dress has a black base to which multiple scraps of different fabrics have been sewn in a cascade of ruffles encircling the skirt on a diagonal from high on the left side to low on the right side. Note that this practice is done for aesthetic reasons in the postmodern world, whereas it was done out of necessity among the poor throughout much of the history of Canada and the United States. Another company, named Project Alabama, puts elaborate hand beading on used sweatshirt material, thereby creating a garment that cannot be cleaned in any way. Is this high fashion because of the beading, or is it mass fashion because of the used sweatshirt material? In short, postmodernism has evolved a tradition of violating traditions.

FASHION AND ANTIFASHION

Postmodern designers not only break the rules of earlier times; they also mine ethnic and traditional dress for ideas. Fred Davis believes that "since the 1960s designers have ... turned more and more to antifashion for inspiration." By *antifashion* Davis is referring to garb and adornment worn by those outside the mainstream fashion process, those too poor to be engaged, those barred from conventional culture (African Americans, Hispanics, etc.), and those who opted out—groups that see themselves as anti-establishment or counterculture—from Black Panthers to White Survivalists, from hippies to cults awaiting the imminent Second Coming. By definition, the elements of antifashion must be distinguishable from mainstream fashion either by design or by default.

Yves Saint Laurent's 1976 collection inspired by Russian peasant dress is probably the most famous example and was very popular in North America. What would have been made out of an inexpensive cotton fabric instead was made of incredibly rich silk satin. U.S. designer Mary McFadden's signature looks have drawn extensively from exotic textiles found around the world. Far more recently, and less haute couture, has been a fashion predilection for torn or strategically placed artificially worn areas in jeans.

As these examples suggest, antifashion influences range from full-blown themes that inspire a whole collection to selected fabrics, particular features, or even just allusions. In the late 1960s and early 1970s, when dictated fashion failed, designers cast about for ideas from living dress in marginalized populations—groups not caught up in the fashion process. The aim was to infuse the elegance and studied aestheticism of new fashions with a vitality often lacking in authoritative pronouncements from Paris. Just as designers looked to unconventional sources for inspiration to breathe new life into their designs, Stephen di Pietri (curator of the Yves Saint Laurent traveling exhibition) saw the need for clothes to be on the human form to maintain freshness and vitality. He has said:

When clothes have been on display too long the fabrics "die" ... Somehow a dress is "fed" the warmth of the body

A group of Amish children, United States, twentieth century. Their simple, functional clothing reflects their beliefs and emphasizes their separation from contemporary society. Clothes are made at home from fabrics that are often industry leftovers. Courtesy of Phyllis Tortora. Photograph by Vincent R. Tortora.

of the person who is wearing it. But when you have a dress on a cold mannequin, under a light, and with dust falling on it, it loses something. No matter how much you clean it and refresh it, in a funny way it seems to lose its life.

Many antifashion groups are caught up in their own fashion process as members jockey for social leadership. However, antifashion is not institutionalized in the same way as mainstream fashion, being more communal and immediate. For those who actively try to distinguish themselves from the establishment (e.g., the punk look and its descendants), change is necessitated as designers purloin elements of their apparel. Other groups, especially those whom mainstream fashion passes by, are more ruled by tradition, and these, too, are all fodder for fashion.

A key feature of the postmodern world is its discontinuity. Unlike modernism, history is not ignored as inconsequential, but it is brought back piecemeal. Elements are ripped from their context if they have something interesting to say about the here and now, similarly with the borrowing from other peoples and traditions. The result is the mix-and-match ethos so indicative of postmodern fashion.

SUMMARY

The relation between fashion and tradition is not simple; there are at least four possibilities. Fashion and tradition can be seen (1) as opposites; (2) as separate domains of the same continuum marked by different rates of change, expectations of change, and degree of embedding in culture at large; (3) in terms of fashion operating inside traditional constraints, rather like Russian dolls; and (4) more recently, fashion using free-floating traditional elements to breathe life into what might otherwise become an increasingly sterile enterprise. These relationships between tradition and fashion are true today, not just in North America but also across much of the world.

References and Further Reading

Alba, Richard, and Victor Nee. *Remaking the American Mainstream: Assimilation and Contemporary Immigration.* Cambridge, MA: Harvard University Press, 2003.

Bourdieu, Pierre. *Distinction: A Social Critique of the Judgement of Taste.* Cambridge, MA: Harvard University Press, 1984.

Daniels, Roger. *Coming to America: A History of Immigration and Ethnicity in American Life.* Princeton, NJ: Visual Education Corporation, 1990.

Davis, Fred. *Fashion, Culture, and Identity.* Chicago: University of Chicago Press, 1992.

Gailey, Alan. "The Nature of Tradition." *Folklore* 100, no. 2 (1989): 143–161.

Handler, Richard, and Jocelyn Linnekin. "Tradition, Genuine or Spurious." *The Journal of American Folklore* 97, no. 385 (July–September 1984): 273–290.

Kaiser, Susan B. *The Social Psychology of Clothing: Symbolic Appearances in Context.* 2nd ed. New York: Fairchild Publications, 1997.

Kelner, Merrijoy, and Evelyn Kallen. "The Multicultural Policy: Canada's Response to Ethnic Diversity." *Journal of Comparative Sociology* 2 (1974): 21–34.

Mehta, Raj, and Russell W. Belk. "Artifacts, Identity and Transition: Favorite Possessions of Indians and Indian Immigrants to United States." *Journal of Consumer Research* 17, no. 4 (March 1991): 398–411.

Palmer, Alexandra, ed. *Fashion: A Canadian Perspective.* Toronto: University of Toronto Press, 2004.

Pedraza, Silvia. "Assimilation or Transnationalism? Conceptual Models of the Immigrant Experience in America." In *Cultural Psychology of Immigrants,* edited by Ramaswami Mahalingam, 33–54. Mahway, NJ: Lawrence Erlbaum Associates, 2006.

Roach-Higgins, Mary Ellen, Joanne B. Eicher, and Kim K. P. Johnson. *Dress and Identity.* New York: Fairchild Publications, 1995.

Sproles, George B., and Leslie Davis Burns. *Changing Appearances: Understanding Dress in Contemporary Society.* New York: Fairchild Publications, 1994.

Symons, S. "The Great Travelling YSL Roadshow." *Sydney Morning Harold Good Weekend Magazine* (16 May 1987): 16–21.

"Vogue Point of View: Cloud Atlas." *Vogue* (July 2007): 124.

Elizabeth D. Lowe

See also Antifashion; Dress Reform; Dress for Rites of Passage; Masquerade Dress; Immigrants Encounter American Dress; American Immigrants of West European Origin.

Types and Properties of Fashionable Dress

Clothing worn by those who live in the United States and Canada may be classified in a similar way to dress of peoples in any part of the world. Types and elements of dress have been classified by Joanne Eicher and other dress scholars, for example, as body modifications or body supplements, which have such properties as color, volume and proportion, shape and structure, surface design, texture, odors and scents, sound, and taste. Not all of these elements were notable in North American dress. For example, sound is rarely mentioned in regard to mainstream fashion, although in periods before the twentieth century the long, often full and heavy women's skirts, especially when made of silk, made sounds noticeable enough to inspire poets and writers to speak of "the rustle of silk."

How these elements and properties of dress are created and manipulated varies with the culture, the geographic region, and the historic period. In some settings variations are few, and styles in dress may persist for a very long time. Western dress, the dress of people in Western Europe and their descendants who now live in other parts of the world, is much influenced by fashion, which is a social phenomenon that can be defined as a taste shared by many for a relatively short period of time.

Although fashion in Western dress leads to frequent changes in styles, the basic types of Western dress can be seen to exhibit some timeless consistencies. In some parts of the world body enclosures are likely to be made by taking lengths of fabric and wrapping or draping the body. In Western dress, preshaped body enclosures predominate. In making preshaped body enclosures, a seamstress or tailor employs pieces that are cut from cloth or other flexible material and stitched or otherwise fastened together. When joined, these pieces form a shape that encloses some part or all of the body, often following the contours. The contours of preshaped body enclosures contribute significantly to achieving a fashionable silhouette by manipulating volume, proportion, shape, and structure.

Western dress uses both body modifications and body supplements that may be temporary or permanent. Temporary modification of body shape is generally achieved by wearing under- or outergarments that shape the flesh of the wearer by being tight in some areas, looser in others. They may support some parts of the body or garment or can be padded to enlarge areas. If a longer body is desired, footwear or headwear can add height.

Permanent body modification may come through purposeful weight loss or gain that brings individuals closer to the currently fashionable ideal. Cosmetic surgery has been used to modify areas of the body. Permanent ornamentation of the skin is sometimes fashionable.

In each style period preferences for color, surface design, and texture can be identified. In some periods odors and scents, sound, and taste may play a part.

1492 TO 1500

Although individual soldiers, sailors, and explorers came from many different countries, the major sponsors of exploration in the New World were Spain, France, England, Holland, and Portugal. Almost exclusively male, the soldiers, sailors, explorers, and fur traders wore garments that derived from the dress of Europeans of the same period who worked in similar occupations. The most obvious body modifications were of the hair, seen in hairstyles and beards of the fifteenth and sixteenth centuries, and in the shapes imposed on the body by the cut of clothing.

By the end of the fifteenth century, styles were changing regularly, with most fashion cycles lasting about thirty to forty years. For working-class individuals, fashionable garment shapes were modified to make them more functional. Upper-class men wore a garment called *trunk hose* that extended from the waist to the upper thighs and was connected to a stocking-like covering of the leg. Sailors and laborers tended to wear less confining longer or shorter garments cut more like trousers.

Properties of clothing were related to the material from which they were made. Cloth was woven from natural fibers, usually wool or linen. Cotton and silk were luxury fibers, not to be worn for the rigors of navigation, battle, or exploration. Leather was made into body supplements, such as jackets, trousers, shoes or boots, head coverings, gloves, and bags that hung from the shoulder or belt, or were held in the hand. Military men enclosed their heads and bodies in protective metal armor.

Natural dyes provided a wide range of colors for fabrics, but colors often were not very durable, so fibers were also used in their natural colors. Surface design and texture was generally achieved through weaving pattern or texture into cloth or by finishing the fabric. For example, wool was fulled to achieve a dense, heavy fabric. *Fulling* is a process based on the natural tendency of wool fiber to shrink when exposed to heat, moisture, and pressure. Fulling required moistening the fabric with warm water or steam and subjecting it to friction and pressure. The resulting fabric was dense, strong, somewhat moisture resistant, and warm. Fulled wool was a practical choice for those engaged in manual labor.

Body supplements that were accessories to clothing enclosed parts of the body (e.g., gloves, headwear such as hats and helmets, and footwear of leather, usually boots for soldiers or shoes for sailors and laborers). Utility bags served to carry essential supplies.

Explorers and fur traders were the first to adopt useful elements of the dress of indigenous peoples. Moccasins, shirts, and leggings

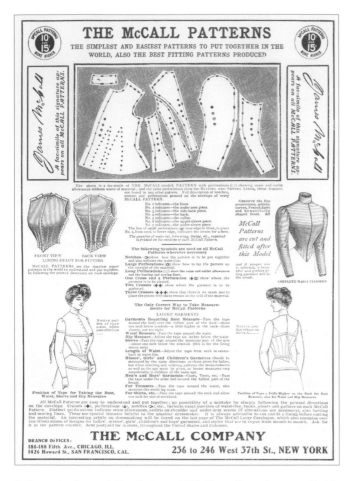

Pattern advertisement, New York, ca. 1900. The pattern pieces provided to seamstresses or consumers by pattern companies such as McCall's will, when sewn together, create the shape of a garment that conforms to the current fashionable silhouette, which is illustrated on the same page. Courtesy of Phyllis Tortora.

of deerskin were practical body enclosures, being more durable than fabrics. Furthermore, the raw material was easily obtained as they moved about the unknown continent. At the same time, some items of North American Indian and First Nations clothing also began to take on some characteristics of European cut.

1500 TO 1800

Once the European powers decided to exploit the resources of the Americas, settlers arrived and the population became more diverse. The first attempts at settlement commenced in the late 1500s. Settlers were male and female, young and older. Individual settlers came from all strata of society and ranged from enslaved people and indentured servants to governors and merchants. Settlements such as the Massachusetts Bay Colony (1620) were founded on religious principles that imposed restrictions on some aspects of dress of sect members. Other religious groups also required adherents to restrict dress styles.

Dress conformed to the basic elements of European styles of the same time period, changing about three times in any one century, although often there was a time lag in getting and adopting fashion information in the Americas. Even Puritans and Quakers wore variations of the customary and fashionable styles of the

1600s. Men wore preshaped garments that consisted of loosely fitted white linen shirts under jacket-like garments. A two-legged linen undergarment known as *drawers* covered the lower part of the body. Over this undergarment men wore a bifurcated garment, either trunkhose or, later, breeches that generally ended at the knee or above.

By the 1700s, upper-class men generally wore breeches that ended at the knee. A vest, called a *waistcoat*, went over a shirt, and outermost was a coat with long sleeves. The skirt of the coat, following fashion, was wider at the beginning of the eighteenth century and narrower by the end.

In addition to accessories noted earlier, which were subject to fashionable variations, body enclosures also had ornamental elements that included jewelry, feathers, ribbons, embroidery, jeweled pins, and lace, which were attached by sewing, pinning, or clipping.

Fashion dictated whether hair was to be worn short or long or whether wigs were preferred to showing one's own hair. Whether the wig should be powdered or natural in color was another fashion decree. Facial hair was in vogue at some times, not at others. British sources speak of cosmetics for men. Americans followed European styles so it is likely that some men may have used cosmetics.

"Fashion dictates" or "fashion decrees"—how and where did these "decrees" originate? By the 1700s, Paris was the major source of new fashion ideas. The French court provided a stage for the display of new fashions, and information about these innovations traveled through printed fashion plates, the first fashion magazines, and the distribution of fashion dolls dressed in miniature versions of the most current styles. Over subsequent centuries, a complex fashion industry developed in the United States and Canada that publicized, manufactured, and distributed new fashions. However, until the second half of the 1900s, most new fashion ideas tended to originate in Paris, which was also the source of most perfumes. For domestically produced scents Americans were more likely to use scented waters and colognes. One popular scent called Florida Water was made of cologne with spices added.

Those women of the seventeenth century who wore body-shaping undergarments placed them over a loosely fitting undergarment called a *chemise*. The extent to which dress served to modify body shape was related to status. To achieve the fashionable body, upper-class women adopted corsets (called *stays* until the early seventeenth century). Essential to providing the correct shape to the stays was a *busk*, a piece of whalebone or wood held in a pocket at the front. The busk provided the desired upright erect posture and flattened the bosom. Fashionable hairstyles for adult women, as for men, included changing the color of hair by powdering.

Until cheaper mass-produced clothing became available in the late nineteenth century, poor men and women and those engaged in manual labor wore more practical clothing made from plainer and cheaper fabrics. Owners provided clothing for the enslaved. Those who worked in their owners' houses were dressed reasonably well, but the few clothing items given to field workers were plain and made from coarse, harsh cloth. A short gown (a loosely fitted overblouse) and a gathered skirt were typical working-class garments of the eighteenth and early nineteenth centuries. Any stays worn by women who had to do physical labor were less confining and more flexible.

The basic pattern of the preshaped body supplements worn by more affluent women was a fitted bodice combined with a

Made from trade materials, this Canadian Blackfoot woman's dress, ca. 1910, shows the influence of both First Nation and Western cultures in one garment. It incorporates Western dress shaping and is ornamented with North American Indian beadwork. Courtesy, National Museum of the American Indian, Smithsonian Institution.

more or less full skirt that, until the twentieth century, usually extended almost to the ground. In the 1700s, women wore a loose linen undergarment, called a *shift* or *chemise*, fitted only at the shoulders. Over this went the stays. A *petticoat*, a full gathered underskirt, was next. In some periods, women wore several layers of petticoats. Petticoats for cold weather were often quilted or made of warm fabric. The outermost layer was a one- or two-piece garment, fitted on the top and with a voluminous skirt at the bottom. Exceptionally full skirts required support by an undergarment into which hoops were sewn. The shape of the hoop varied as the fashionable silhouette was first round, then wider from side to side, and finally fuller at the back.

Accessories worn by women in the colonies included body enclosures such as headwear, gloves, and shoes. Inventories of cargo imported to the colonies indicate a wide variety of items including face masks, jewelry, lace to attach to and decorate sleeves, hand-carried fans, muffs, handkerchiefs, and purses. Aprons—simpler for Puritans and Quakers and more ornate for affluent settlers—tied around the waist.

RELIGIOUS GROUPS AND VARIATIONS OF DRESS

Slight variations from the fashionable norms in the properties of volume and proportion, shape, and structure can be seen in the dress of conservative religious groups such as the Puritans and Quakers. Both were likely to wear a narrower range of colors, most being dark or subdued. Ornamentation was minimal, and undecorated white linen fabrics were used for aprons, collars, and cuffs instead of lace. Headwear shaped like that of fashionable attire lacked the stylish feather and jeweled ornaments. Shoe buckles on plain-colored leather were unadorned. Devout Quaker men did not wear wigs or powder their hair.

Even though preachers from these religiously conservative sects stressed simplicity in dress, contemporary artists depict some Puritans and Quakers in fairly elaborate styles, and the clothes of their more affluent sitters were obviously made of high-quality fabrics. From some of the decorative Quaker garments found in historic costume collections, one must conclude that although church leaders issued strict guidelines about dress, church members followed personal preference and current fashion to a considerable degree.

Some immigrant groups maintained elements of traditional dress from their homelands, especially where communities from one European region were large. Studies of *habitant* dress in French Canada in the 1700s and 1800s have concluded that although it is possible to find examples of ethnically derived clothing in depictions of these early French settlers, the overall styles shown are clearly influenced by current fashion.

THE NINETEENTH CENTURY

A number of the changes in dress in the nineteenth century and on into the twentieth century can be attributed to the Industrial Revolution. Mechanized production of textiles made decorative fabrics less expensive. The synthesis of chemically based dyestuffs in the mid-1800s produced a wider range of durable colors. By the end of the century, the production of clothing was moving from the home to factories. These factories employed women, which, in turn, created a need for more practical clothing. Men's and women's increasing participation in active sports created a market for less confining dress.

One of the enduring changes occurred in men's dress. During the French Revolution men who supported the egalitarian goals of the revolution often wore trousers as a symbol of sympathy with working-class men. Gradually in the early 1800s, after the end of the Revolution, men of all classes in both Europe and America began to wear trousers instead of knee breeches.

MEN'S DRESS, 1800 TO 1900

By the close of the first decade of the nineteenth century, typical garments for men were likely to include undergarments of wool, linen, or cotton. Cotton had become less expensive and more available because it was now being produced in the American South. Over his undergarments a man placed a white linen or cotton shirt and a suit consisting of a waistcoat, a coat, and trousers. This basic pattern continued throughout the century, although there were changes in the form and variety of undergarments and outerwear. For example, by the latter part of the century, men's underwear included one-piece garments called *combination underwear* or *union suits* that united drawers and undershirts. Suit coats might be tail-coats, frock coats, sporty norfolk jackets made with a belt crossing only the jacket back, or, after midcentury, sack jackets that were similar in style to modern-day suit or sports jackets.

One of the properties of men's dress that changed markedly was the color of suits. The colorful upper-class men's suits of the eighteenth century were replaced in the nineteenth century by suits made in dark colors. Except for some fancy waistcoats, men's outer garments for business or social occasions usually lacked ornamentation, surface design, or decorative textures. Dress for recreation allowed more pattern and color. The volume and pro-portion, shape, and structure of these suits changed in relatively subtle ways from decade to decade.

Other than the shapes imposed by the cut of suits, few ex-amples of body modifications are evident except for hairstyles. Hair was shorter or longer, with faces shaven, bearded, or sport-ing mustaches according to the current mode.

Accessories for men consisted of headgear, gloves, shoes, and hand-carried canes. Men were discreet in their choice of jewelry, wearing stickpins, cuff links and shirt studs, rings, and watches.

WOMEN'S DRESS, 1800 TO 1900

The basic elements of women's outer garments continued to be a bodice fitting the upper part of the body and a skirt that, depending on the current fashion, was more or less full. In the nineteenth century, these fashion changes came with increasing rapidity. Styles commonly remained in fashion for about twenty years, with obvious but less dramatic changes throughout the life-time of a fashion trend.

The practice of modifying the shape of the body with a cor-set constructed to suit the volume, proportion, and structure of outer garments continued. For some fashions more than a corset was required to achieve the current look. In the first two decades, many women tied a *bustle* around the waist, a small cushion that was positioned in back and held out the back of the dress.

Dresses worn over these bustles during the Empire period (1800 to 1820) were inspired by the styles of the classical eras in ancient Greece and Rome. The body enclosures of the Greeks and Romans were wrapped and suspended. Empire styles had preshaped bodices that ended just below the bust line and skirts that attached to this elevated waistline. The resulting garments somewhat resembled classical styles. A preference for white linen or cotton fabrics early in the period derived from the mistaken idea that the marble of Greek and Roman statues was unadorned and the classical ideal must have been plain white. Actually, classi-cal statues were painted but had lost their color over time. Gradu-ally, the relatively simple style grew more elaborate, more often made in colors or more ornamental fabric, and had wider ankle-length skirts. By 1820, the elevated waistline had started to move lower, and a changed silhouette emerged.

The outstanding changes in features of women's dress of the late 1820s and most of the 1830s were a waistline at close to the natural anatomical placement; a full skirt that flared out gradu-ally from that waistline and that ended at about the ankle; and extremely wide, full sleeves. Some enormous sleeves required a sleeve pad to hold out the fullness.

Throughout the nineteenth century, women continued to wear a cotton or linen chemise. Although eighteenth-century women had not usually worn drawers (underpants), by mid-nineteenth

Beginning in the nineteenth century and continuing until the latter part of the twentieth century, the colorful, elaborate fabrics that had characterized upper-class men's dress were abandoned and replaced by simple suits and overcoats made in dark and subdued colors. Courtesy of Phyllis Tortora.

century, drawers were almost universally worn. A corset was placed over the chemise. Corsets were stiffened with strips of whalebone until the latter part of the century, when steel was also used. By the third decade of the century, most women wore a corset cover over the corset and also a petticoat cut in much the same shape as the outer skirt. By midcentury and after, some women were wear-ing the garment called a *combination* that was made in one piece and combined the features of drawers and a corset cover.

Around 1837, the skirt dropped to the floor. The wide skirt was gathered to a waist now at about natural anatomical placement.

Starched petticoats supported the skirt. The sleeves decreased in fullness, with any remaining fullness concentrated on the lower part of the arm.

Little change took place during early years of the 1850s, although separate garments for the upper body (bodices) and the lower body (skirts) became more common. After 1857, a structure referred to as either a *cage crinoline* or *hoop*, which was made either of whalebone or steel, supported very wide skirts. The remainder of this period was marked by gradual movement of skirt fullness from a wide circle, to a slightly oval shape, to a concentration of fullness at the back. Along with the back fullness, skirts lost their gathers at the waist, and *gores* (wedge-shaped pieces that are narrow at the top and wide at the bottom) provided a triangularly shaped skirt form.

By 1870, back fullness required a large bustle support to achieve a fashionable silhouette, which was rather like a gradual waterfall of fabric. In the late 1870s, the back fullness diminished; what fullness remained was concentrated low at the back of the skirt, and a wire support at the hem supported fabric concentrated in a train. The upper body was tightly encased in a form-fitting bodice that extended over the hips. In the early 1880s, the bustle returned to popularity, this time with an almost shelf-like rigidity. At the same time, a high-standing collar was a feature of the majority of women's bodices. Throughout this bustle period (1870–1890), the properties of surface design and texture were very important, with much emphasis on elaborately woven and decorated fabrics, plush and velvet textures, and beaded ornamentation.

These properties continued to be important in the period of the 1890s. The bustle was abandoned. Sleeves grew very large and required some padding or stiffening to maintain this shape. Skirts were once again gored, and the overall silhouette has been described as hourglass-shaped.

Fashionable styles could be less than practical for daily use. These garments were also more expensive than many could afford. Consequently, many people continued to wear clothing long after it had gone out of style. The more affluent might pass their outmoded clothing along to poorer employees or relatives. Clothing was often altered to make it conform more closely to the latest styles.

Women's clothing of the 1800s was less practical than men's. Some women's rights advocates saw clothing as a tool to keep women from full participation in society. Rigid corseting was seen as a possible health threat to women. These concerns led some to promote dress reform. Other changes that encouraged the use of more practical clothing were the increased participation of women in sports, their entry into the workforce in larger numbers, and the growing availability of ready-to-wear clothing. The closing decades of the nineteenth century also witnessed the birth of the deodorant. The first deodorant was patented in 1888 and subsequently marketed under the trade name Mum. Prior to this, perfumes and scented powders had served to mask odors.

THE TWENTIETH CENTURY

The foundation of the mass production clothing industry was laid in the nineteenth century. While many women were still making garments for themselves and their daughters in the early 1900s, men's and boys' clothing was more likely to be purchased ready-made. By the close of the twentieth century, the woman who sewed her own clothes was a rarity, and every kind of garment

Women's dresses of the 1920s. In the United States and elsewhere this style was a radical departure from earlier fashions not only because of the short skirts and unfitted lines, but also because the simpler cut of these garments made them easier to fabricate in mass production. Dover Publications, *Authentic French Fashions of the Twenties.*

and accessory was available for purchase. Moreover, practices in the retailing of dress had also undergone many changes.

At the end of the nineteenth century, the fibers from which clothing could be made were still cotton, linen, silk, and wool. The introduction of a wide range of manufactured fibers and the development of techniques for coloring, decorating, and finishing in the twentieth century affected not only price and style but also care and durability. Changes in trade practices toward the end of the century lowered prices while having a negative impact on the domestic manufacturing sector. Although Paris remained a major source of design innovation, designers in the United States and Canada became internationally known as ready-to-wear clothes garnered attention from a fashion press that had formerly reported only on the haute couture.

Fashion changes occurred even more rapidly in the twentieth century, with many fashion periods lasting as little as ten years and sometimes even less. By the late twentieth century, the dominance of one fashionable silhouette had decreased, and women's and some men's fashions tended to be selected according to subcultural affinities.

MEN'S DRESS, 1900 TO 2000

Men's clothing continued to show fewer and less radical changes than women's until late in the century. Fashion change for men was subtle, displaying nuances in cut, fit, preferred fabrics, and details rather than in radical changes of silhouette or components.

By 1900, a pattern of dress for men had been firmly established, and for the rest of the century, both business and formal dress for men in white-collar industries had these components: a suit consisting of a jacket and matching trousers worn with a long-sleeved shirt that buttoned down the front. A necktie was placed at the neck of the shirt, under a collar.

For more than one hundred and fifty years, expectations for how men should dress were firmly established and highly conventional. Then, in the 1960s, dramatic differences in men's styles appeared, and although not all men adopted the newer styles, many did. The fashion press spoke of a "peacock revolution" in menswear. Along with more conservative styles, men found suits made in more decorative fabrics and fitted shapes. Turtleneck knitted shirts replaced the white shirt and tie for some men. Other shirts were made in many colors and vivid printed patterns. Long hair was acceptable. Necklaces and earrings, formerly worn only by women, now appeared on men. Top designers started to create lines of clothes for men.

WOMEN'S DRESS, 1900 TO 2000

The full effect of the social changes of the nineteenth century's last decades was not clearly reflected in women's dress until the 1920s. In the first decade of the twentieth century, women achieved an unnatural shape through steel- or whalebone-reinforced corseting that lifted the breasts, flattened the stomach, and pushed the hips outward at the back. A full bodice front was attained by constructing the front with a wide, full pouch of fabric. Women who were not adequately full-bosomed sewed ruffles on corset covers or padded them. The effect has come to be known as the *monobosom*. Depictions of fashions of this period show skirt lengths ranging from floor length with trains to skirts several inches off the floor. Active women were modifying garments to meet their needs.

The second decade was characterized by rapid changes, brought about largely out of practicality. The monobosom gave way to a revival of Empire styles. Some of the floor-length, straight, and narrow skirts were exceedingly tight at the ankles. This tight *hobble skirt* was replaced by a much shorter and fuller skirt with a slightly elevated but not tightly fitted waistline. This practical style remained throughout World War I (1914–1918) as women often assumed tasks formerly assigned to men. With the end of the war in 1918, styles began changing again.

Women's dress of the 1920s is often seen as incorporating the most radical changes in the history of women's dress in the Western world. Some relate the adoption of these styles to advances in women's rights. By 1920, women in the United States and most provinces of Canada had been granted the vote. Although the adoption of these new styles took place over several years, when the style was fully developed, it had incorporated unprecedented changes.

Skirts were shorter than ever before in the history of Western dress. At their shortest they were as much as eighteen inches (forty-five centimeters) from the ground. Moreover, stockings were flesh colored. Women wore lipstick, rouge, and eye makeup. Prior to this time only disreputable women wore obvious makeup. To achieve the fashionable silhouette, which was flat and boyish, women wore undergarments that flattened the breasts. Most garments either located waistlines or belts at the hip or did away with them. Women cut their hair short. And for the first time women wore trousers, although only for sports or leisure activities.

With the onset of the Depression that marked the 1930s, hemlines dropped, though they gradually moved higher again by the mid-1930s and after. A more womanly figure was preferred, as waistlines returned to the anatomical waist placement. Corsets, now made with new materials that used elastic rather than heavy boning, pushed up the breasts, pulled in the waistline, and confined the hips. By the late 1930s, skirts had risen to a little below the knee and had grown slightly wider; the waist was clearly delineated, bodices outlined the bosom, and shoulders had large pads to make them appear wider. These styles were, in effect, frozen when the United States entered World War II in 1941. Legislation restricted the amount of fabric that could be used in clothing. Shoes were rationed. Many textiles were not available either because, like silk, they came from areas no longer accessible or, like nylon, introduced only shortly before the war, they were utilized by the military. As more women worked in factories, pants were more widely accepted as work and casual dress.

The war ended in 1945. Although U.S. fashion designers had been the focus of fashion magazines during the war, after the war the fashion press once again highlighted Paris as the major source of design ideas. In the spring of 1947, French designer Christian Dior originated the style that would predominate for the next decade. Called "the New Look" by the fashion press, these clothes made a sharp contrast with the wartime styles. Skirts fell to around fourteen inches (thirty-five centimeters) from the floor. Skirts were either extremely wide and made from as much as twenty-five yards of fabric or very narrow, requiring a slit in order that the wearer could take a step. Waistlines were very tight. Undergarments called *merry widows* incorporated nylon featherboning or elastic to create a smooth line though the torso, nipped in the waist, and extended below over a rounded hip. Shoulder pads were rounded and no longer square and exaggerated. This silhouette dominated until the late 1950s.

The styles of the 1960s showed some elements of similarity to the 1920s. Skirts were even shorter than in the 1920s, with miniskirts and micro-minis ending above or at the knee. Dresses were unfitted and given names like the *sack*, the *shift*, the *trapeze*, and the *A-line*. Pantyhose were an essential innovation with such short skirts because stockings held up by garters and garter belts were no longer practical. Until the 1960s, pants and shorts were considered appropriate for sportswear but not for work, school, or more formal occasions. Tailored and dressy pantsuits and hot pants changed that belief. Although men have never adopted skirts, women have since considered pants as appropriate for just about any occasion.

Some fashions of the 1960s and 1970s reflected social turmoil. This tendency could be seen as the civil rights movement in the United States stimulated an interest in African-inspired dress. Some feminists were said to have burned brassieres as a symbol of liberation, leading to an ongoing fashion for the braless look. Anti-establishment groups, such as the hippies, assembled colorful, eclectic elements, including jeans worn as a statement of solidarity with working people. Antiwar activists also chose jeans

In the United States, from the 1960s onward, pantsuits were considered appropriate dress for women at work or at formal occasions. Image Copyright Andresr, 2007. Used under license from Shutterstock.com

as a symbol of protest. These pants, once only for work or sports, became an internationally fashionable garment.

About 1970, the fashion industry in the United States attempted to introduce a new style nicknamed the *midi*. Its midcalf length was a sharp contrast with the fashionable short miniskirt. The attempt to create demand for a sudden radical fashion change failed resoundingly. Gradual fashion change is more common, and by the mid-1970s, women's clothes had become fitted, and their skirts were longer.

Accompanying the recognition of notable U.S. designers in the post–World War II period came the introduction of designer-

named perfumes. Cosmetic companies such as Coty had introduced fragrances around the time of World War I, but the U.S. fragrance industry came of age only in the 1970s.

Until about 1980, it is possible to point to predominant fashion silhouettes and trends that cut across age, economic, and social divisions. But gradually, the notion of a single fashion from which an individual should not deviate has disappeared. Instead, what is considered fashionable is more likely to be determined by the groups to which individuals belong. This is particularly evident among young consumers. Often their dress choices originate within peer groups or relate to singers or music groups they admire. Ted Polhemus has called these subgroups "style tribes."

The concept of style tribes can be extended to all of the population. Choices about dress tend to grow out of formal and informal group affiliations. In U.S. fashionable dress at the end of the twentieth century and the beginning of the twenty-first century, one can identify trends that are widespread but not monolithic. The idea that "fashion dictates" has changed to "my style tribe tells me what fashion is."

References and Further Reading

Baumgarten, Linda. *What Clothes Reveal: The Language of Clothing in Colonial and Federal America*. Williamsburg, VA: The Colonial Williamsburg Foundation, 2002.

Beaudoin-Ross, Jacqueline. "'A la Canadienne' Once More: Some Insights into Quebec Rural Female Dress." *Dress* 7 (1981): 69–81.

Beaudoin-Ross, Jacqueline. *Form and Fashion: 19th Century Montreal Dress*. Toronto: University of Toronto Press, 1992.

DeMarly, Diana. *Dress in North America*. New York: Holmes and Meier, 1990.

Eicher, J. B., and M. E. Roach-Higgins. "Describing Dress: A System of Classifying and Defining." In *Dress and Gender: Making and Meaning in Cultural Context*, edited by R. Barnes and J. B. Eicher, 8–28. Oxford/Washington, DC: Berg Publishers, 1992. (Reprinted in paperback, 1993.)

Hall, Lee. *Common Threads: A Parade of American Clothing*. Boston: Bullfinch Press, 1992.

Milbank, Caroline. *New York Fashion: The Evolution of American Style*. New York: Abrams, 1989.

Palmer, Alexandra, ed. *Fashion: A Canadian Perspective*. Toronto: University of Toronto Press, 2004.

Polhemus, Ted. *Street Style*. New York: Thames & Hudson, 1994.

Routh, C. *In Style: 100 Years of Canadian Fashion*. Toronto: Studdart, 1993.

Severa, Joan. *Dressed for the Photographer: Ordinary Americans and Fashion 1840–1900*. Kent, OH: Kent State University Press, 1995.

Severa, Joan. *My Likeness Taken: Daguerreian Portraits in America*. Kent, OH: Kent State University Press, 2006.

Tortora, Phyllis, and Keith Eubank. *Survey of Historic Costume*. New York: Fairchild Publications, 2005.

Phyllis G. Tortora

See also Evidence about Dress in the United States; Evidence about Dress in Canada; Tradition and Fashion; Snapshot: Jeans; Dress Reform; Children and Adolescents in the United States.

Snapshot: Jeans

The evolution of blue jeans from ordinary working dress into an international fashion classic began in California shortly after the start of the Gold Rush of 1849. Levi Strauss was a Bavarian immigrant seeking to expand the New York–based family-run dry goods business. Strauss arrived in San Francisco in 1853 and established a wholesale fabric supply house. One of his customers was Jacob Davis, a tailor who made blue denim work pants for miners and other laborers. Responding to complaints about pants pockets that kept ripping out, Davis added copper rivets to reinforce the pockets. Demand for these sturdy pants grew, and Davis was unable to fill all the orders. He feared competitors might patent his design, but he was unwilling or unable to pay the US$68 fee to file a patent. Davis was buying his fabric from Strauss. Looking for financial help, he offered Strauss half interest in the product. With this partnership, Levi Strauss entered the retail business in 1873.

These pants were made from a sturdy, twill-weave cotton fabric called *denim*. The word *jean* describes a fabric that is very similar to denim, and the two terms were often used interchangeably. As a result, customers called the pants "jeans." Others called them "Levi's," after the company that made them. From the beginning the color blue was frequently, though not exclusively, associated with this cloth. Indigo, one of the few natural dyes with excellent colorfastness, produced a strong blue color. It was a logical choice for a garment that would be washed often. Blue became the traditional color for these sturdy pants that were first worn by laborers, cowboys, and farmers, and the name "blue jeans" has been applied to these garments ever since.

As customers brought new ideas to the attention of the manufacturer, improvements were made. To the copper rivets that were part of the patented pants in 1873, the company added an orange double arch of stitching as a means of identifying the Levi Strauss product. From 1886 on, a leather patch with a drawing showing two horses trying unsuccessfully to pull the pants apart proclaimed the strength of the pants. Belt loops were added in 1922, and to prevent the rivets from scratching school benches, the back pocket rivets were concealed inside the pockets in 1937. Zippers replaced button fly front closures on some styles in 1954. After 1890, when the patent expired, other manufactures also produced jeans.

Hollywood helped to keep jeans before the public by costuming tough cowboy heroes and villains in blue jeans. *Vogue* magazine featured women in tight-fitting jeans in the 1930s, a style they called "Western chic." Around the same time adolescent girls began to wear jeans as casual sportswear. The Sears Catalog of 1939 advertised blue denim slacks and overalls as "work–play" clothes.

1940s, United States: A diecut advertisement for Lee Riders denim jeans. Jeans were first worn by gold miners, cowboys, farmers, and laborers. Getty Images.

Denim continued to move into the fashion spotlight in the 1940s. Claire McCardell, one of the most innovative U.S. fashion designers of the forties and fifties, used blue denim in a 1943 wraparound dress that she called a *popover*. In one year, more than seventy-five thousand of these house-dresses were sold. She used denim in other casual clothing as well.

Richard Martin and Harold Koda, curators in fashion at the Metropolitan Museum, have singled out the 1955 film *Blue Denim* as an example of the linking of blue jeans with rebellious youth. They have noted that many movies with jean-clad cowboys portrayed them as anti-establishment figures. It is not a great surprise, then, that antiwar protesters adopted blue jeans as a symbol of solidarity with working people and an anti-establishment statement. More surprising was the way that high fashion picked up jeans, and by the 1970s, they were an international style. Americans who wore blue jeans for travel abroad where jeans were not available were besieged by requests to sell them. Famous designers of ready-to-wear each created their own version of blue jeans, put their names on highly visible labels, and sold them for twice the price of an unlabeled pair of jeans. Owning a pair of designer jeans became a status symbol.

At the same time that jeans were becoming fashionable, a trend toward casual dressing for leisure and social activities was accelerating. As a result, men and women considered jeans suitable for all kinds of occasions. Designers began to use blue denim for tailored suits for men, pantsuits for women, skirts, shorts, and evening gowns. The design firm of Versace introduced cologne for men called Blue Jeans.

Blue jeans entered the antiques trade. In April 1995, *Vogue* magazine described a Japanese market for used jeans in which Levi's bearing certain lot numbers with hidden rivets and in good condition commanded prices as high as US$2,000. A front cover of the *New York Times Magazine* on 1 December 2002 featured a photograph of a pair of new jeans on which all of the signs of wear (tears, worn spots, stains, mended areas) had been faithfully reproduced. In the accompanying article the author, Austin Bunn, reported these new jeans sold for US$150 to US$200, then went on to report on two sales of antique jeans for US$25,000. One was a pair of 1880s buckle-back jeans bought in Japan and the other a pair of valuable 1890s Levi's sold in the United States. In his book *Jeans*, James Sullivan has confirmed these astronomical prices, stating that the sales of rare vintage jeans at prominent retailers can bring "tens of thousands of dollars." He continues, "In 2001 the oldest known pair of Levi's in existence, a miner's pair of buckle-back waist overalls from the 1880's, went for US$46,532 on eBay."

It is likely that the closets of many households in the United States and Canada hold at least one pair of jeans. These pants may belong to males or females, children or adults. Depending on when they were made, they might be some color other than blue or some fabric other than denim; the pant legs may end in a straight or bell-bottom cut, or their fit at the waist may be tight or baggy; they may droop at the hip. Each season different design elements may predominate, but it seems reasonable to expect that, like the ubiquitous T-shirts with which they are so often paired, jeans are here to stay as a staple of the international wardrobe.

REFERENCES AND FURTHER READING

Bunn, Austin. "Not Fade Away." *New York Times Magazine* (1 December 2002): 60.

Martin, Richard, and Harold Koda. *Jocks and Nerds*. New York: Rizzoli, 1989.

Ratner, Elaine. "Levi's." *Dress* 1, no. 1 (1975): 1–5.

Sullivan, James. *Jeans: The Cultural History of an American Icon*. New York: Gotham Books, 2006.

Phyllis G. Tortora

Regional Differences in Dress and Fashion

Are there regional differences in dress and fashion trends in the United States and Canada? When queried, fashion professionals say yes. But objective data is hard to find. Scholars have paid little attention to regional differences in fashion in the United States and Canada. National retail firms are likely to evaluate sales in different regions in order to provide a range of stock that will appeal to their customers. Trade publications report the sales volume of items in various regions. Trade associations, such as Cotton Inc., have collected data and from time to time published reports on their findings. Fashion reporters writing for the news media use their observations about regional dress as a basis for feature articles. A few reference works with a regional focus discuss regional fashions. And perceptive well-traveled individuals with a good eye often spot unique aspects of dress in one region as compared with others.

The Web site About.com in the early twenty-first century included a regional fashion forum. Readers could submit their region's style report to the site by completing a short questionnaire that included the following questions: (1) Where do you live? (2) What's everybody wearing? (3) Does your city have a style trademark? (4) What's the biggest misconception people have about your city's style? and (5) What trend doesn't work there and why? The forum included individuals from around the world, providing a capsule view of one person's perception of regional fashion in their locale.

One major conclusion can be drawn from these sources. A few striking differences can be found, but they must be viewed against a background of remarkable countrywide similarity. Residents across the United States and Canada view much of the same media, which provide a primary means of conveying information about fashion. The mobility of both countries' population can also account for similarities. Many families have members living in different regions, and recreational travel takes people from coast to coast and back and forth between Canada and the United States.

The data and conclusions described by the various sources are not always in agreement. This is not surprising, given the complexity of the various regions and the differing reasons and methods used for gathering the information.

REGIONAL DIFFERENCES BASED ON CLIMATE

Almost immediately climate and lifestyle emerge as the primary reasons for the most significant regional differences. Residents of the colder regions in the Northeast, northern Midwest, northern Mountain states, and the Pacific Northwest of the United States and all of Canada have to take into account the climate in their seasonal wear. A high level of interest in outdoor sports in colder seasons is also a factor. Both participants and spectators need to dress appropriately for the outdoor environment.

The Pacific region is often defined as the states of Alaska, Hawai'i, Washington, Oregon, and California. However, within this large regional area, the climate varies greatly. Attire ranges from expedition weight parkas of arctic Alaska to the surf and beach attire of tropical Hawai'i and Southern California, making it necessary to divide this region climatically. A few examples of subregional fashions in the Pacific include the Pendleton plaid jacket (Pendleton Woolen Mills), athletic wear (Nike, Adidas, and Insport), and outdoor apparel (Eddie Bauer, Columbia Sportswear, and REI) of the Pacific Northwest and the surf wear (Volcom, Hurley, and Quiksilver) of Southern California.

Some of the apparel currently favored and worn in this region was developed by apparel companies located in the specific region and based on the regional climate. However, there is crossover: Pacific Northwesterners wear L.L. Bean coats in winter that are produced by a Maine manufacturer, and residents of Maine wear Lands' End coats produced by a Midwestern manufacturer. Residents of these regions are dressed in functional, climate-appropriate apparel very different from what would be worn for winter in the Southwest, Southeast, or Southern California.

Southern California and Hawai'i provide a sharp climatic contrast with the Pacific Northwest. In climate they are closer to the southeastern United States. The climate in all of these areas ranges from moderate to semitropical, and as a result, the climate is a driving force in the apparel that tends to be worn. In the South, merchandisers have reported a preference for light, loose clothing of high-quality cottons and linens. The popularity of more colorful apparel worn in the South is mentioned by several fashion experts. Florida fashion colors and styles are described by some fashion professionals as a separate realm from the rest of the South. Vibrant, tropical colors and tropical prints seem ever-popular in Florida. It also appears that women in the South tend to wear dresses more frequently than in other regions.

REGIONAL DIFFERENCES BASED ON LIFESTYLE

Telephone interviews with a women's wear merchandiser, a women's wear design director, and a menswear design director for apparel companies that sell nationally revealed that they agreed that climate and lifestyle are the two most important factors affecting regional differences.

Pat Fowler, women's wear division manager for Pendleton, a national brand (classically styled apparel for the higher income levels), was interviewed in 2007. Pendleton segmented the country's regional differences into the Southeast, Northeast, Midwest, West, East, and Southwest. In warm climates, such as the Southeast, according to Pendleton, brighter colors are preferred,

The Pendleton plaid women's jacket: A twentieth-century garment from the Pacific Northwest that has become a national brand. Courtesy of Pendleton Woolen Mills.

whereas on the West Coast, earth tones are preferred. For fabric preferences, tailored linen apparel is favored in the South and Southeast, whereas on the West Coast, a more relaxed, deconstructed linen styling is preferred. Fowler commented that the East Coast customers tend to prefer more traditional and preppy styles.

Pendleton divided its target customers into three lifestyle types—one customer type is refined, well-educated, executive; another type is relaxed, dresses down on off time, especially on weekends; and the third type loves the outdoor lifestyle. All of these customer lifestyle types would reside in any of the regions of the United States. Thus, while there are some regional differences in sales, the company does not design their product with those in mind; Pendleton designs for the three lifestyle types they have identified.

David Witkewicz, women's wear design director for Target's store brand apparel, stated in 2007 that Target selected seasonal colors for the company's lines to be consistent throughout the chain. The goal was to deliver a brand message; colors were not segmented regionally. On the other hand, there are regional differences in fabrics, classified into three climate zones: North, South, and Midwest. Heavier-weight fabrics might be selected for winter styles for the Midwest, whereas fabrics with more cotton content might be selected for sale in Southern climates. Sleeve lengths also are adjusted by climate—with longer sleeve lengths for colder regions. For Target, the more fashion-forward styles sold better on the West Coast. Target's store brand apparel was produced for the mass price zone; thus, the need for a huge quantity of products targeted for the masses affects the company's needs to refrain from much regional differentiation.

The menswear design director for Target's store brand apparel, Greg VanBellinger, has stated that climate dictates much of the regional differences. Southern climates allow much more casual apparel. Also, the population's age affects apparel's sales performance. VanBellinger used Sun City, Arizona, and Florida (calling Florida a microcosm of the United States) as examples of style segmentation by age in various regions. Occupational differences were also mentioned: The finance industry in large East Coast urban centers expects more suits and ties to be worn, whereas the more casual industries in California (big computer corporations and the film/TV industries) lean toward more informal attire. Other regional differences are based on the types of outdoor sports popular in specific regions as well as affiliations to local national and university sports teams. VanBellinger mentioned that on the East Coast, sports affiliations are passed down from generation to generation, whereas on the West Coast, fewer residents affiliate with a specific national or university team. He also stated that for many men, clothes do not rank high on their list of importance, and if nobody notices or makes a comment about your clothes, then that is good. Regarding color, Californians might adopt a brighter color earlier than the rest of the country.

In addition to climatic needs influencing the choice of regional fashions, many West Coast residents possess an underlying attitude. It is a spirit of outdoor adventure, living in the "last frontier," and enjoying a more casual lifestyle. To underscore the more casual dress of the Pacific region, the executive vice president of Barney's New York, Michael Celestino, quoted by David Moin in *Women's Wear Daily*, compared merchandise stocked in the new Seattle Barney's store to the Barney's New York store: "Seattle is a casual city … You don't hear me speaking about men's tailored clothing so much. The store is more geared to a sportswear customer, but we do have women's and men's designer [brands]." In fact, the Pacific region seems the most likely region of the United States and Canada to showcase regional differences in fashion.

New England residents tend to view dress in that region as casual. By contrast, the Mid-Atlantic region, with its concentration of large urban centers, is viewed as a source of new fashions and more avant-garde style ideas. Although Midwest urban areas may be a little slower to adopt new styles, they generally move quickly into the fashion mainstream.

Western wear shows up as a factor in the Great Plains, the Mountain States, and the Southwest. The popularity of rodeos and the influences of the rich history of the cowboys have generated an interest in what has been called "cowboy chic." The most popular styles that come out of cowboy dress include cowboy boots, bolo ties worn with sport coats, and jeans worn with cowboy shirts.

In the Southwest, regional styles are influenced not only by the cowboy culture and lifestyle but also by dress that originates with the North American Indian population and with residents of Mexican origin. Influences from Indian groups can be seen in the Indian jewelry and designs that originated with prehistoric Southwest people and adaptations of their daily dress. Mexican styles include felt jackets with embroidered and appliquéd motifs and the Chimayo jackets that are woven locally and use traditional geometric patterns.

Throughout the country a similar style prevails that is related to the American enthusiasm for sports. These are the items of apparel that are used to identify an affiliation with a specific sports team. Sports team apparel and accessories provide definitive regional variations throughout the country, with residents of any given region sporting their favorite "home town" team's logo, whether professional sports teams or university teams.

Climate may have an impact on lifestyle, and as a result, some regional styles can be seen to grow out of both climate and lifestyle. Although the Hawaiian Aloha shirt is seen across the United States, its frequency of wear is probably greatest in Hawai'i. The Aloha shirt is not only a comfortable, practical garment for a tropical climate but also a key factor in representing local or regional identities.

It is evident that while climate is an important explanation for some of the regional differences in dress and fashion, lifestyle is also a very important factor. Lifestyle reflects the attitudes and values of an individual or group. For example, as noted by Sylvia Miller in 2007, "because of climate, people in Florida dress somewhat similarly to people in southern California, but the culture and dress is still quite different." The Southern California culture might include factors such as the focus on the movie industry and its high-glamour, high-glitz lifestyle. On the other hand, many areas of Florida exude a more casual and relaxed feel than even the image of the California lifestyle. Thus, our choice of lifestyle has a strong influence on our fashion decisions.

TEXAS: A DISTINCTIVE AREA

From a fashion perspective, Texas has its own distinctive regional differences separate from other states in the region. Fashion professionals often refer to "Texas style" or "Texas fashion." The television series *Dallas* may have had an additional influence on the segmentation of Texas style as being uniquely different from other states.

Color preferences of Texans are mentioned by several writers: "In a place like Dallas they might wear a traditional suit but it will be bold red. Part of that is due to the climate," observed Jo Cohen, of the COTTONWORKS Fabric Library at Cotton Inc. Monica Kostelnik at Ivy, a division of Kellwood Company, has stated, "The southwest is enamored by hot pink hues mixed with reds—the key is clear color and lots of it." Color is also mentioned by Patricia Marx in "Dressin' Texan" as being uniquely recognizable in Texas: "The Lone Star palette is sparkly sea green, sunshine yellow, lavender flecked with gold, and turquoise—lots and lots of turquoise." Marx provides numerous examples of Texas fashion style, citing a penchant for formal wear, especially glittery and embellished gowns. There are numerous black-tie fundraising events in Houston and Dallas where formal wear is required, and stores in Dallas and Houston merchandise accordingly.

Dressy attire is not just for evening charity events. Texans tend to love to dress up in general. According to Marx, "Dallas/Ft. Worth has more shopping centers per capita than any other city in the country, and … Houston is not far behind." Conversely, the general public outside of Texas may form a stereotypical image of Texas fashion: cowboy boots and hats. A Houston socialite has commented, "I am constantly fighting the Texan stereotype. I've never been to a rodeo, I don't own cowboy boots, and I don't have a ranch."

Twentieth-century cowboy chic in the Southwest, United States: The most popular styles to come out of cowboy dress include cowboy boots, bolo ties worn with sports coats, and jeans worn with cowboy shirts. Copyright Jake Hellbach, 2007. Used under license from Shutterstock.com

COMPARING CANADIAN AND U.S. REGIONS

Climate is clearly a major factor in determining preferred types of dress. The climatic regions of Canada are much less varied than those of the United States, and as a result, Canadian regional dress does not appear to have the kind of marked differences that can be seen in its southern neighbor. New Englanders and residents of the U.S. Northwest would undoubtedly have much in common with Canadians when they dress for winter.

A Web site offering advice to diplomats about how to dress when working in Canada made a number of observations and recommendations. Canadians are described as dressing more conservatively than people in the United States, but they are also told that practices do vary in different regions. Vancouver is said to be more casual. Toronto follows more British styles, and French Canadians dress in more European styles than their fellow Canadians. Men are advised to wear suits and ties for business meetings. Women would be appropriately dressed in conservative suits or dresses.

When asked about regional differences in Canada, Canadians living in the United States will often express the opinion that even though the major business center for the fashion industry is Toronto, residents of Montreal, in the French-speaking (and France-oriented) province of Quebec, are more fashion conscious than other Canadians and closer to Europe in their style. Canadians from western Canada have been described as dressing much like Americans from the Midwest. Most casual observers see very little difference between the dress of Canadians and that of U.S. citizens.

U.S. REGIONAL DIFFERENCES DISCUSSED IN THE MEDIA

Fashion professionals tend to divide the country into these regions: East Coast, West Coast, Midwest, South (or Southeast), and Southwest, with some adding Texas as its own region. For example, an article in *DNR* (a menswear trade publication) reported the top apparel sales purchases for Father's Day (2007) by region: East Coast (sales in New York City were described), Midwest (sales in Chicago), West Coast (Los Angeles sales), Southwest (Dallas sales), and Southeast (sales in Atlanta). Regional differences in fashions purchased are quite evident. For example, cotton plaid shorts were mentioned on the top-sellers list in Atlanta and Dallas, microfiber shorts sold well in Dallas, twill and cargo shirts sold well in Atlanta, cargo shorts sold well on the West Coast, and striped shorts were listed as strong sellers in New York City.

Two companion articles in the *Wall Street Journal* in 2007 focused on fashion differences between the East and West coasts. The first article contains the most succinct and relevant information currently available on this topic. Journalist Christina Brinkley, of the "Style" section of the *Wall Street Journal*, has stated that she always feels underdressed when in New York, with one possible reason being the East Coast tendency to enforce office dress codes. Her discussion focuses on men's regional fashion differences. "Double-breasted suits also carry important messages. A man wearing one in Manhattan looks smart. In the Silicon Valley or Southern California, it will look like he's trying too hard." Brinkley quoted Peter Low, 65, chief executive of Griswold Co., a brokerage firm, about his clothing choices in different cities. In New York, he wears a "daily uniform" of Brooks Brothers suits; in Chicago, he would wear dark slacks and a navy blazer; and in Los Angeles on a recent trip, he wore a casual button-down shirt instead of a spread collar.

Note that the regional differences might be as subtle as the difference between a spread collar and a button-down collar. Or it could be the difference between a woman deciding not to wear hose in Washington, D.C., versus deciding to wear hose in Los Angeles. Brinkley extended her discussion beyond the two coasts, adding these observations: "Residents of the Midwestern United States tend to be more conservative and preppy than either coast—there's a little bit of Washington, D.C., in Chicago

sensibilities. In the South, there's more focus on color for men and women. But the clash between the coasts is particularly strong. People from the West Coast often fail to perceive the importance that Easterners place on dressing up."

In Brinkley's second article, published two weeks later, readers responded to her earlier article by speaking out on their experiences of culture shock between the two coasts. Apparently her original article had struck a chord with many readers, who often felt out of step with the dress codes in their cities because they had moved from somewhere else. One reader listed ten tips "for professional East Coast women who do business on the West Coast and don't want to appear frumpy, stuffy or dowdy." The respondent includes tips such as "don't be afraid to show your ankles—capri pants are just fine" and "dressy, open-toed shoes or sandals are appropriate year round."

In another *Wall Street Journal* article, fashion reporter Teri Agins answered a reader's question about appropriate funeral attire. It appears that there are regional differences in appropriate attire. While black or navy suits and modest dark dresses were said to always be acceptable, "especially when the services take place in houses of worship," for youngsters and residents of the Sunbelt, a spokeswoman for the National Funeral Directors Association has said that "conservative, light color clothing—such as pressed khakis and a white shirt, with or without a tie, are also considered respectful."

Do presidential candidates who traverse the country select their attire to appeal to the region in which they are campaigning? Would a candidate dress more casually when speaking to a local group in the Midwest versus in New York City? In a *New York Times* article, Guy Trebay quoted fashion experts as saying, "Mr. Obama has managed to score hits with wardrobe choices—jackets nonchalantly slung over the shoulder, short sleeves in the heartland, neatly tailored suits on television—that somehow telegraph personal comfort without sacrificing authority." Mr. Obama may have worn short sleeves while campaigning in the heartland to provide a sense of ease with his audience, and his audience with him.

URBAN VERSUS NONURBAN AREAS

Are there noticeable regional differences between fashions worn by urban versus nonurban residents? Several writers commented on such differences. However, fashion choices may be cross-tied to lifestyle as well as vicinity to an urban center. Christopher Dente represents a number of young designers. In research done by Cotton Inc. about regional preferences, he suggested that many of the regional differences are due to differences between an urban and nonurban lifestyle. He has stated, "The definition between work and evening/leisure outfits is very distinct in nonurban areas. In big cities, women need an outfit that will carry them from work to dinner to the theater. Not so in the suburbs. Even outside of New York City, the trends are watered down—women wear different clothes to work than they do to go to a movie or to a restaurant."

An approach to compiling data about regional differences in dress and fashion is to interview people in various regions who are observant about fashion. An e-mail conversation with book editor Sylvia Miller provided some interesting observations. She stated, "New York is a special case. I lived there for 20 years, after living elsewhere, and it was the most distinctive. Everyone wears

The Hawaiian shirt, ca. 2000. A practical, loose-fitting garment for a tropical climate that also has a strong regional identity. Copyright Ocean Image Photography, 2007. Used under license from Shutterstock.com

black, almost all the time. They always wear black shoes. When I arrived from California, it was August and I had white sandals, but I quickly gave them up for black sandals. If they wear colors, the colors are always anchored by a black jacket, black belt, black bag, etc. The bag is very important because it is your car." Miller continued, "There are also clear career differences, for example Wall Street (suit and tie) versus publishing (quite casual, maybe a tweedy jacket) versus advertising (trendy)."

Miller's comment about the popularity of wearing black apparel in New York City is reinforced by other observers. But black apparel is worn frequently in other large urban centers as well. According to the experts interviewed by Cotton Inc., charcoal gray and black prevail in New York, Los Angeles, and San Francisco, while "bright colors pack a punch in the south."

New York City fashion does seem to exude a style that is more fashion-forward than most of the rest of the country. A banner displayed in New York City's SoHo district proclaims New York City the "Fashion Capital of the World." Its residents tend to be more daring or experimental with fashion. While the same garment might be worn by someone in the Midwest, the way a typical New Yorker accessorizes an outfit creates a trendy statement. And, according to Miller, "trends sweep through the streets like so many passing clouds" in New York City.

OTHER FACTORS: ETHNICITY AND AGE

In regions with a large percentage of the population of Hispanic origin, fashions may be quite different from an area of the country with a larger percentage of other ethnic groups. Many regions of the country include neighborhoods with ethnic populations that have their own differences in dress and fashion. A New York resident for twenty years, Sylvia Miller stated, "There are also distinctive ethnic differences in dress in New York City. There is cross-over, but of course kids from Harlem dress differently from kids on the Upper East Side."

For young men's apparel, fashions are very different on the East Coast versus the West Coast. The East Coast young men's fashions are influenced by music and urban culture. FUBU was mentioned as a hot-selling urban streetwear brand name on the East Coast. On the West Coast, the skate and surf industry influences young men's fashions. Favorite brand names include sun and surf favorites Volcom, Quiksilver, Hurley, and Billabong. California young men are especially trend-forward. To those familiar with the styles of apparel produced by these companies, the East Coast versus West Coast differences are very apparent. Additionally, young men are influenced by what their favorite bands in their region are wearing.

The major factors that influence regional differences include climate, lifestyle, occupation, age, urban/nonurban setting, and ethnicity. The interaction of these factors contributes to the rich diversity in dress that is visible in every region of the United States and Canada.

References and Further Readings

Agins, Teri. "Ask Teri" column. *Wall Street Journal*, 7 June 2007, p. D8.

Ballentine, Sandra. "The Luxe Roundup." *New York Times*, 27 August 2006, section 6.

Brinkley, Christina. "Cracking the Dress Code in L.A., New York." *Wall Street Journal*, 14 June 2007, p. D8.

Brinkley, Christina. "Culture Shock, Part II: Readers Speak Out." *Wall Street Journal*, 28 June 2007, p. D8.

Cotton Inc. http://www.cottoninc.com/lsmarticles/?articleID=221 (accessed 13 February 2007).

Fowler, Patricia. Telephone interview conducted 14 June 2007.

Greenwood Encyclopedia of American Regional Cultures. 8 vols. Westport, CT: Greenwood Press, 2004.

Marx, Patricia. "Dressin' Texan." *New Yorker* (19 March 2007): 68–73.

Miller, Sylvia. Electronic communication, 24 June 2007.

Moin, David. "Barneys Goes Bigger in Seattle." *Women's Wear Daily* (5 July 2007): 3.

Montamat, Thibault. "Going for Baroque." *W* (April 2007): 94, 96, 98.

Sander, Libby. "In Land of Khakis, a New Focus on High Style." *New York Times*, 2 July 2007, p. A9.

Trebay, Guy. "Campaign Chic: Not Too Cool, Never Too Hot." *New York Times*, 22 July 2007, section 9, p. 1.

VanBellinger, Greg. Telephone interview conducted 23 July 2007.

Vargo, Julie. "Apparel Performs for Father's Day." *DNR* (25 June 2007): 1, 16, 17, 24.

Witkewicz, David. Telephone interview, 18 July 2007.

Nancy O. Bryant

See also The Geographic and Cultural Region; Western Wear.

The Textile Industry

A ny overview of the textile industry in the United States and Canada will focus primarily on the United States until the latter part of the nineteenth century. So long as Britain maintained its hold on the American colonies, British policy directed commercial activity there. That policy fluctuated, sometimes encouraging local production and sometimes forbidding it. Once the United States gained its independence, it followed its own course in actively developing its textile industry.

Canada, however, remained a British colony until the mid-nineteenth century. During this time period, Britain preferred to supply manufactured goods of all kinds to Canada, while exploiting the raw materials that were found in abundance in the colony. As a result, Canadian industry, including textiles, did not have the opportunity to develop and expand until after the six colonies that made up Canada became a confederation in 1867.

Until 1780, fabrics produced in North America were of locally grown fibers, home-spun and woven, relatively simple in structure and designed to meet specific needs of the home, farm, and settlement. This kind of an essentially home-based industry would have been practiced in all of the British colonies in America. More affluent colonists would have been able to purchase imported goods.

UNITED STATES

As early as the mid-1700s, economic and political pressure in the colonies that would become the United States initiated a movement toward self-sufficiency in several industries, including textiles. Once independent, the need to reshape the United States from an import-dependent to an export-dependent economy encouraged development of a textile industry that was built on technological inventions, entrepreneurial spirit, and, unfortunately, slave labor. Taxes and other restrictions on imported textiles provided protection of the industry from competition of lower-cost imports.

From the earliest settlements textiles played an important part in the life of the colonies. Around 1640, the Massachusetts General Court studied the potential for textile production and identified the number of weavers and spinners as well as the amount of flax and hemp seed. The Connecticut General Court ordered that each family sow flax and hemp and import cotton. In 1645, the Massachusetts General Court encouraged towns to increase sheep flocks through breeding and import and by encouraging people to move to Massachusetts with as many sheep as was convenient. In Beverly, Massachusetts, a completely integrated mill (combining hand-carding, -spinning, and -weaving) was founded by George Cabot in 1787.

Germantown, Pennsylvania, settled in the late seventeenth century by German textile workers, became a center for linen weaving. In the eighteenth century, thousands of displaced British skilled handloom weavers and their families immigrated to Pennsylvania. Textile production concentrated in urban areas where these immigrants settled. Women produced wheel-spun yarns; men wove complex cloth on their own looms using commercially spun or hand-spun yarn or worked the yarn-making machinery called spinning mules in factories. In the 1820s, a switch to factories occurred, but fancy goods, including hand-frame knitting, remained a Philadelphia specialty.

The Society for Establishing Useful Manufactures encouraged development of Paterson, New Jersey, as a textile manufacturing center. That effort collapsed in 1796, ending direct government interest in the location and development of textile mills. From this time, federal support of the textile industry focused on tariffs and protection through granting patents. The 1816 tariff imposed a 25 percent duty on imported cotton and woolen goods and encouraged growth in the domestic textile industry. From 1815 to 1860, cotton production occurred almost entirely on slave plantations in the South, the products of which constituted approximately half of all U.S. exports. In the nineteenth century, the Paterson, New Jersey, venture was revived with factories specializing in weaving, spinning, dyeing, and finishing. In the 1840s, strikes and riots in Philadelphia occurred over disputes between labor, management, and immigrant hiring practices.

By the early eighteenth century, areas north of Maryland focused on commerce while the southern areas focused on agriculture and traded cotton with England. By 1750, South Carolina, Georgia, and North Carolina had a thriving indigo dye trade. Georgia also produced some trade silk. Because of its value, numerous attempts were made to develop a silk industry in North America. In 1833, the Cheney Brothers tried to raise silkworms in Connecticut. Other efforts were made as settlers moved west, but none were successful because of the climate and the labor-intensive nature of silk production.

NEW ENGLAND MANUFACTURING

In New England, large textile factories appeared where there was access to abundant sources of water power and native-born, rural female labor. By the late eighteenth century, New England focused on homespun production, where items were made at home for home use. Textile manufacture was one of the first mechanized industries to incorporate outwork production into its manufacturing procedures. *Outwork*, or commission-based labor, was an important source of income for many rural families in the nineteenth century. Women purchased raw materials or supplies and processed them into finished goods. Outwork industries depended heavily on women's work at home rather than labor from

Wabasso Cotton Mills at Three Rivers, Quebec, ca. 1913. The mule room shown here housed the spinning mules, machinery used to make yarn. McCord Museum VIEW-4981. http://www.mccord-museum.qc.ca/en/

a large number of operatives in factories. Mitten production in Maine allowed women to work at their own pace in exchange for money they could spend in dry goods stores. Handmade lace was outwork in Massachusetts. Prior to the introduction of English lace machines in Ipswich, Massachusetts, in the 1820s, an industry of hand-produced lace (also known as the twist trade) existed. Approximately twelve thousand women hat makers were employed in palm-leaf outwork in 1820 in rural New England. As late as 1850, more Massachusetts women participated in outwork than worked in textile factories.

In 1819, several emigrant English lace workers set up the Boston Lace Company in Watertown, Massachusetts. In 1822, the factory moved to Ipswich. Machines were hand-cranked or treadle-powered modifications of warp knitting and Levers lace-making machines. Ipswich had three factories that produced simple and complex lace. In the 1820s, lace schools in Rhode Island taught young women to embroider machine-made lace.

The U.S. cotton factory system got its start in New England. Samuel Slater had apprenticed in Arkwright's revolutionary water-powered spinning mill in England, during which time he acquired knowledge of textile machinery and principles of factory organization. He moved to North America and gained sponsorship of a Rhode Island merchant. In 1789, he established a cotton spinning mill, based on Arkwright's spinning mill, in Providence, Rhode Island, for Almy & Brown. In 1793, he opened a spinning mill at Pawtucket Falls, Rhode Island, primarily using child labor. In 1798, he founded Samuel Slater & Co. and established mills in Connecticut, Massachusetts, and Rhode Island. Because of the importance of the family in New England, Slater used a partnership or single-ownership model, personal management, small-scale

production, waterpower, and family labor that evolved into a division of labor based on gender and age. Men were supervisors or skilled artisans. Children and adolescents worked in the mill, with their wages going to the head of the household. This model was so frequently followed by manufacturers throughout New England and the Mid-Atlantic states that it became known as the Slater system, the Rhode Island system, or the British system.

In the early nineteenth century, Rhode Island spinning mills needed unskilled labor. Managers convinced families to live in the newly created factory towns of Slatersville and Webster in single-family dwellings with gardens. Children were a tractable workforce; some fathers were mill managers. Married women and widows rarely entered the factories. Many rural women used their looms to weave cloth on commercially spun yarn for a commission (outwork). Often young, single farm women were paid for their work in the mill. This practice eventually evolved into boardinghouse mills to control access to the workforce, to enforce quality standards, and to control mill output.

The Lowell system (developed by Francis Cabot Lowell) was another example of corporate paternalism where company owners provided housing, moral supervision, and entertainment. The Boston Manufacturing Company built a factory in Waltham, Massachusetts, in 1813 that used power looms and combined yarn spinning and weaving in the corporate-owned facility. In the Lowell system, women and girls operated the machinery in large-scale facilities using professional managers. In 1826, Lowell, Massachusetts, was founded by six textile firms. They built boardinghouses for young women employees, mostly from New England farms, who expected to be paid for their labor and treated with respect. With an economic recession starting in 1829 and deepening in the early 1830s to a depression, management tried to cut wages, and the women went out on strike in 1834 and 1836. They formed an early labor organization, the Factory Girls' Association, to maintain wages and limit the working day to a ten-hour day. With a labor glut in the 1840s and reaction to labor movements, management was able to pit one labor group against another and hire Irish and French Canadian immigrants to replace the women workers. In one example, Woonsocket, Rhode Island, recruited its first French Canadian families from Quebec to work in its mills in the 1840s. Eventually, one-third of Quebec's population left Canada for the mill towns of New England. At this time, working days were twelve to fourteen hours long.

Throughout most of the 1800s, textile manufacturing of cotton, woolen, linen, and thread remained in the Northeast of the United States. Access to rivers for water power, shipping (ports, canals, and railroads), and investors from local cities encouraged growth of the New England textile industry. New mills representing both model and substandard facilities were constructed in Connecticut, Massachusetts, New Hampshire, and New York. Woolen mills were established later than cotton mills because of the more complex process requiring more skilled operators. By 1815, however, the wool industry had been established in New England.

By the time of the Civil War, textile manufacturing was concentrated in New England. Both the Lowell and Slater systems employed immigrant and family labor; constructed tenements for workers; exerted some control over the workers' lives and working hours; and had corporate ownership, professional management, and cost accounting. Cotton was produced in the southern states, shipped to New England or England on merchant ships, processed into fabric, and then shipped to retailers, who sold it to individuals who made it into clothes and other textile products for their families or who made clothing for others. Although many New England mills continued into the 1950s, their downfall was imminent. Remnants of New England's textile industry currently exist primarily as museums and interpretive sites.

MANUFACTURING MOVES SOUTH

After the U.S. Civil War, the Reconstruction period began the textile industry's move to the South, particularly to Georgia, North Carolina, South Carolina, and Alabama. This move accelerated during the early 1900s. Reasons for the move included proximity to areas where cotton was produced; abundant streams and rivers for generating water power; lower labor costs; racist, segregationist Jim Crow laws that forced a compliant workforce; readily available capital; tax incentives by local governments; and the success of the International Cotton Exposition held in Atlanta, Georgia, in 1881. It was less expensive to build a new facility with new technology in the South than to remodel obsolete facilities in the North. From 1850 to 1900, the capital of textile mills increased over 200 percent in the southern United States.

Even with tariff adjustments in the 1920s and 1930s, many New England manufacturers shut down or moved to the South. Fashion changes that made rayon and nylon garments popular required expensive new equipment to manufacture these fabrics; new power sources reduced the dependence on waterpower. Other factors influencing the move to the South included the cost of transportation—shipping cotton to New England cost more than processing it closer to where it had been harvested. Southern labor costs and taxes were lower. The South would remain strong in textile production until global considerations moved production offshore.

U.S. technology in knitting advanced through a series of patented inventions, from the Bazier knitter of 1814 and Hibbert's 1849 patent of the latch needle using malleable steel resulting from

A view of Slater Mill from the Congregational Church Tower, Pawtucket, Rhode Island, 1869. Samuel Slater's model for cotton production was so frequently followed it became known as the Slater system. Courtesy of Slater Mill. http://www.slatermill.org

the Bessemer process through Isaac Lamb's V-bed flat knitting machine using latch needles, invented in 1863. The first recorded industrialized knitting mill in the United States was in Pennsylvania in 1825. In 1832, at Cohoes, New York, waterpower was first used to operate knitting machines. In 1880, Kayser developed a warp knitting mill in the United States. The knitting industry grew from 85 establishments in 1850 to 807 establishments in 1890. In the 1920 Census of Manufacturers, hosiery was 43 percent and underwear, 29 percent of all knit goods produced in the United States. In 1940, a U.S. patent was issued for the manufacture of shaped knitted skirts improving drape, fit, and production costs. At various times in U.S. history, hand knitting has been an important social, cultural, and even political pastime.

Changes in the textile industry in the twentieth century included the introduction of new fibers, changes in fashion that required substantially less fabric, the emerging importance of apparel designers, increasing consumer demand for textile goods, and heightened competition from developing countries. By 1921, the small, family-owned textile factories in the South represented the state of the art in spinning and weaving. Textile machinery manufacturers (Saco Lowell and Whitin, Leesona, Draper, and Crompton & Knowles) developed and modified technology to accommodate changes in materials, markets, and labor. Between the 1920s and the 1950s, smaller firms consolidated to increase profits through economies of scale. Following World War II, the textile industry in the United States continually lost business to Asia and Central and South America. By the 1950s, manufacturing productivity had greatly increased as a result of consolidation and technological developments. In the 1960s and 1970s, individual firms and corporations gained control of a significant portion of the market and went on to specialize. Development of highly automated equipment reduced the number of employees needed to operate spinning, weaving, knitting, and finishing facilities. While the number of employees decreased, wages increased because of the need for highly skilled labor.

In the 1930s, machinery converted hand-tufting into a mass production technique. In 1950, the first room-wide (wall-to-wall) carpeting was made. By the mid-1950s, nylon wall-to-wall carpets were readily available and popular in new home construction, as well as remodeling of older homes, and the carpet industry experienced tremendous growth. Early in the 1950s, automated continuous spinning systems were developed for yarn production. In this process, automatic control of each machine and the movement of fibers between machines reduced labor needs.

In the 1970s through the 1980s, increased awareness of environmental hazards due to manufacturing processes associated with the use of textiles resulted in laws and regulations related to air and water quality, disposal of chemicals, and keeping records regarding hazardous chemical use. These regulations and public relations issues forced manufacturers to decrease the use of solvents, organic compounds, and metallic salts in producing and finishing textiles. The discharge of unfixed dyes and particulates into the air and water was reduced.

In the United States, all segments of the textile products industry are responsible for maintaining quality and for complying with legal requirements for labeling. The introduction of new fibers and new processes resulted in truth-in-labeling laws and regulations to protect and inform consumers. Regulations that apply to textile products include the Silk Regulation of 1938, which restricted use of metallic salts on silk to improve their durability;

the Wool Products Labeling Act of 1939, which required fiber content information at point of sale and defined wool, new or virgin wool, and recycled wool; the Fur Products Labeling Act of 1951, which required use of an animal's true English name and country of origin as well as identification of processes designed to improve a fur's appearance; the Flammable Fabrics Act of 1954, amended in 1967, which restricted interstate commerce of highly flammable textile products; the Textile Fiber Products Act of 1960, which identified generic names for fibers and regulated use of trade names in their promotion; and the Permanent Care Labeling Ruling of the Federal Trade Commission of 1972, which required use of standard terms and symbols on care labels.

By the 1980s, mergers, acquisitions, and leveraged buyouts were common. Changes in ownership and corporate structure continued, and by the mid-1980s, competition from the offshore textile industry and movement of manufacturing facilities to developing countries was accelerating. Higher wages for U.S. textile workers made lower labor costs in other parts of the world, and the resulting lower costs of textile goods attractive to many retailers. By the early years of the twenty-first century, free trade agreements, low-cost overseas labor, and gradual phasing out of trade restraints had reduced the U.S. industry to a small portion of its previous strength. The remaining industry is focused in niche markets and areas where trade constraints restrict use of imported textiles.

DYEING AND FINISHING

Copperplate roller techniques appeared in North America in the late eighteenth century. John Hewson, from England, was the first successful textile calico printer in Philadelphia in 1774. In 1823, the Merrimack Manufacturing Company was founded at Lowell, Massachusetts, with roller printing facilities. The forebear of the textile hand screen was patented in 1887 in the United States by Charles Nelson Jones of Michigan. Printing using metal engraved rollers (roller printing) was common until the introduction from Europe of printing using flat screens in the 1930s and roller screen printing in the 1960s.

Finishing is the application of special processes that improve the appearance and serviceability of fabrics. Continuous, open-width finishing of textiles became common practice in the 1930s. In 1937, Campbell and Fennell of the DuPont Company developed a two-stage process for continuous bleaching of cotton with peroxide using a J-shaped storage chamber of stainless steel (the J-box).

Durable water-repellent finishes include reactive pyridinium (introduced in the mid-1930s), silicone (introduced in the early 1950s), and fluorochemicals (introduced in the late 1950s). By the 1990s, fluorochemicals dominated the water-repellent market. Because of the soiling problems associated with the popular durable-press finishes in the mid-1960s, Deering Milliken announced a soil-release finish in 1966 based on polymers incorporating carboxylic acids. In 1967, 3M introduced the fluorochemical finish Dual Action Scotchgard. After 1968, interest in soil-release finishes waned.

DuPont patented DMEU (dimethylolethyleneurea) in 1945 as a possible durable-press agent. Permanent shape was introduced in the United States in 1955 by Korot of California. This innovation received little notice until 1964, when Levi-Strauss introduced "Oven-Baked" pants of 100 percent cotton with the

New fibers such as acetate could be difficult to dye. Disperse dyes were developed in 1922 to improve the dyeability of acetate. Solution dyeing, in which dye was incorporated into the fiber before it was formed, was developed in 1951 to correct problems with fume fading of disperse dyes on acetate. In 1955, an inhibitor was developed that greatly improved protection of disperse dyes from environmental fumes that caused fume fading. Fiber-reactive dyes were developed in 1956 in Europe, but their use quickly spread to North America. The Thermosol process was developed at DuPont in 1947 using disperse dyes and heat. A jet-dyeing machine was developed in 1958–1959 by Burlington Industries and Gaston County that allowed continuous movement of both dye liquor and fabric. After the 1970s, the U.S. dye industry declined in importance because of environmental issues and increased offshore competition.

CANADA

As a late entrant into the textile industry, Canadian practice was influenced by U.S. technology and British tradition. During the last half of the nineteenth century, the factory production of textiles emerged as a significant sector in the Canadian economy partly due to the stimulus of the National Policy of 1878, which introduced higher tariff protection to the textile industry. In 1826, Mahlon Willett had established a woolen mill at l'Acadie in Lower Canada. In 1844, the first limited liability company in Canadian manufacturing established a cotton and knitting mill in Sherbrooke, Quebec, operating until it burned in 1854. A powered knitting mill was built in Ancaster, Ontario, in 1859. Belding Paul & Co. built the first silk mill in Montreal in 1876. Courtaulds (Canada) Ltd. established the first artificial silk (rayon) manufacturing plant in Cornwall, Ontario, in 1925. In 1926, Celanese Canada built a facility to make acetate yarn in Drummondville, Quebec. DuPont established the first nylon production facility in Canada in 1942 during World War II for parachute silk. ICI Ltd. introduced the production of polyester in Canada in the 1950s. During the late nineteenth through mid-twentieth century, the production of cloth in the home either as outwork for the textile industries or craft production remained an important source of income for many families.

Most production facilities were located in eastern Canada—primarily in Quebec and Ontario. These locations were attractive areas for cotton manufacturers because of the provinces' transportation system and natural and human resources. With the North American Free Trade Agreement (NAFTA), plant expansions occurred in the Maritime Provinces and Manitoba. Canada introduced open-end yarn spinning and led in the use of shuttleless weaving machines. Canada leads in production and development of nonwoven fabrics, especially textiles for stabilizing and protecting outdoor areas that are called geotextiles. The United States is an important export market for Canadian textiles and textile products. Canadian textile manufacturing has decreased due to automation, equipment modernization, and technological advances.

Dominion Textile Inc., based in Montreal, was a significant force in the Canadian industry. Begun in 1873 as a cotton mill (spinning, weaving, bleaching, dyeing, and printing), the company merged or consolidated with other companies in the 1880s and 1890s and became Dominion Textile in 1905. Its fiber focus expanded into rayon, flax, and wool in the late 1920s and

---

TIME TABLE OF THE LOWELL MILLS,

Arranged to make the working time throughout the year average 11 hours per day.

TO TAKE EFFECT SEPTEMBER 21st, 1853.

The Standard time being that of the meridian of Lowell, as shown by the Regulator Clock of AMOS SANBORN, Post Office Corner, Central Street.

From March 20th to September 19th, inclusive.

COMMENCE WORK, at 6.30 A. M. LEAVE OFF WORK, at 6.30 P. M., except on Saturday Evenings.
BREAKFAST at 6 A. M. DINNER, at 12 M. Commence Work, after dinner, 12.45 P. M.

From September 20th to March 19th, inclusive.

COMMENCE WORK at 7.00 A. M. LEAVE OFF WORK, at 7.00 P. M., except on Saturday Evenings.
BREAKFAST at 6.30 A. M. DINNER, at 12.30 P.M. Commence Work, after dinner, 1.15 P.M.

BELLS.

From March 20th to September 19th, inclusive.

Morning Bells.	Dinner Bells.	Evening Bells.
First bell,..........4.30 A. M.	Ring out,............12.00 M.	Ring out,...........6.30 P. M.
Second, 5.30 A. M.; Third, 6.20.	Ring in,...........12.35 P.M.	Except on Saturday Evenings.

From September 20th to March 19th, inclusive.

Morning Bells.	Dinner Bells.	Evening Bells.
First bell,..........5.00 A. M.	Ring out,.........12.30 P. M.	Ring out at.........7.00 P. M.
Second, 6.00 A. M.; Third, 6.50.	Ring in,...........1.05 P. M.	Except on Saturday Evenings.

SATURDAY EVENING BELLS.

During APRIL, MAY, JUNE, JULY, and AUGUST, Ring Out, at 6.00 P. M.
The remaining Saturday Evenings in the year, ring out as follows:

SEPTEMBER.	NOVEMBER.	JANUARY.
First Saturday, ring out 6.00 P. M.	Third Saturday ring out 4.00 P. M.	Third Saturday, ring out 4.25 P. M.
Second " 5.45 "	Fourth " 3.55 "	Fourth " 4.35 "
Third " 5.30 "	**DECEMBER.**	**FEBRUARY.**
Fourth " 5.20 "	First Saturday, ring out 3.50 P. M.	First Saturday, ring out 4.45 P. M.
OCTOBER.	Second " 3.55 "	Second " 4.55 "
First Saturday, ring out 5.05 P. M.	Third " 3.55 "	Third " 5.00 "
Second " 4.55 "	Fourth " 4.00 "	Fourth " 5.10 "
Third " 4.45 "	Fifth " 4.00 "	**MARCH.**
Fourth " 4.35 "		First Saturday, ring out 5.25 P. M.
Fifth " 4.25 "	**JANUARY.**	Second " 5.30 "
NOVEMBER.	First Saturday, ring out 4.10 P. M.	Third " 5.35 "
First Saturday, ring out 4.15 P. M.	Second " 4.15 "	Fourth " 5.45 "
Second " 4.05 "		

YARD GATES will be opened at the first stroke of the bells for entering or leaving the Mills.

• SPEED GATES commence hoisting three minutes before commencing work.

Penhallow, Printer, Wyman's Exchange, 28 Merrimack St.

Timetable, regulations, and policies of the Lowell Mills, Massachusetts, for 1853. Courtesy of the American Textile History Museum. http://www.athm.org/

Koratron trade name that were successful in spite of wear problems at creases and cuffs. Men's dress shirts with permanent shaping were the next products to be introduced. In the mid- to late 1960s, cotton/polyester blends helped minimize durability problems from the resin-based finishes. Other chemicals not incorporating formaldehyde have been introduced to reduce environmental problems. In 1972, the Consumer Product Safety Commissions banned the use of TRIS, a flame-retardant compound used on cotton and other fibers.

While most synthetic dyes were developed in Europe, the North American textile industry quickly converted from natural to synthetic dyes. The first production of synthetic dyes in the United States took place in 1864 in New York by Charles and Thomas Holliday. Other early dye companies include the Albany Aniline and Chemical Company, founded in 1868 by A. Bott; the Schoellkopf Aniline and Chemical Company, founded in 1879 in Buffalo, New York; and the Hudson River Aniline Color Works, founded in 1882 in Rensselaer, New York. With the start of World War I and the conversion of most German dye factories to the production of ammunition, North American textile companies needed dyes. Calco Chemical Company was founded in 1915 in New Jersey to manufacture synthetic dyes. Dr. William G. Beckers, with financial support from Eugene Meyer Jr. built the National Aniline and Chemical Company in 1917 in Brooklyn. In the late 1920s and early 1930s, lighter-weight, high strength, and corrosion-resistant dye kettles of stainless steel replaced those of wood, copper, and iron.

1930s and into polyester in the 1980s. Because of the tariff-protected market in Canada, Dominion captured most of the Canadian market with Wabasso bedding, Caldwell towels, and Penman's underwear during the early half of the twentieth century. Production occurred in small towns across Canada but was concentrated in Quebec. In 1948, tariff reductions and competition from the United States and Britain reduced its market share from nearly 100 percent of the Canadian market in 1947 to 47 percent by the late 1950s. In the 1980s, Dominion led the world in denim production until the General Agreement on Tariffs and Trade (GATT) provisions greatly increased competition from countries with low wages and developing economies. In spite of efforts to reduce labor costs, the company collapsed in the 1990s, and the remaining two factories were purchased by a U.S. company.

LABOR UNIONS

Labor organizations in both Canada and the United States date to the early years of the textile industry. Mill workers organized to address wages, working conditions, irregular employment, and working hours. The first organizations were temporary and focused on specific issues. When that issue was settled, they dissolved or became a more general reform or political association.

Two women weavers, United States, ca. 1860. Courtesy of the American Textile History Museum. http://www.athm.org/

The first recorded strike among U.S. mill workers (primarily women at this time) occurred in 1828 in Dover, New Hampshire. Workers protested a wage cut and demanded a ten-hour day. In 1891, the International Union of Textile Workers was formed. By 1900, it was a federation of worker organizations. In 1901, it was formally organized as the United Textile Workers of America (UTWA) and affiliated with the American Federation of Labor. Early in the twentieth century, the UTWA was effective in the North in achieving a shorter workweek and good wages and restricting the time of day that women and children worked. The UTWA was not as effective in the South, with its fewer labor unions, longer workweeks, lower wages, and greater numbers of women and children mill workers. Throughout the twentieth century, union efforts focused on working conditions, wages, shorter workweeks, safe working conditions, health and life insurance, and retirement. Unions in the United States weakened drastically in the 1980s, and by the twenty-first century, most textile work had moved offshore, and textile unions had all but disappeared.

The history of textile labor unions in Canada is similar to that of the United States. The Nine-Hours Movement of 1872, the first significant cross-occupational organization, focused on reducing the working day by several hours. Strikes in the Canadian textile mills occurred in the 1880s. Canadian unions allowed only the most skilled laborers as members, effectively blocking women and children from membership. The short-lived Knights of Labor Movement of the late nineteenth century welcomed all workers. In the first part of the twentieth century, increasing use of machines demanded more skilled labor. By 1950, massive strikes across Canada resulted in the Industrial Relations and Disputes Act, which affected labor relations for decades. Strikes were frequent in the 1960s and 1970s. The need to reduce costs and increase productivity in the 1980s resulted in management demanding a flexible workforce. The possibility of layoffs and downsizing (decreasing the workforce and reorganizing work with the use of technology) resulted in concessions by unions. While unions in the United States were weakening, Canadian unions worked to strengthen their position.

FIBER PRODUCTION

The United States has been a major producer of cotton for more than two hundred years. In 1793, Eli Whitney greatly increased the speed of cotton ginning with development of the sawtooth gin. The hard physical work of growing cotton was forcibly completed by slave labor in the nineteenth century. Slave labor helped keep the production costs of cotton low so that it could be processed into goods available at a range of qualities and costs for low- to high-income people. During the U.S. Civil War, both sides burned cotton fields to prevent their harvest and sale. Sharecropping developed out of the Civil War to allow plantation owners to maintain income from the land, but it was a system that impoverished both black and white farmers, keeping many farm laborers in similar economic, social, and physical circumstances as before the war. Cotton production significantly impacted the development of agricultural chemicals: pesticides for use against boll weevils and other insect pests, chemical fertilizers, and herbicides to control weeds. Selective plant breeding and bioengineering improved the yield and quality of U.S. cotton. Today, much of the U.S. cotton crop is shipped offshore to production facilities in Asia and Europe.

Early settlers produced flax for domestic consumption. However, flax production failed to become a significant part of the textile industry. Today, flax seed is produced for its oil. Wool and the production of sheep had been important from the earliest settlements in the United States and Canada. However, demand for domestic wool has not been high for decades. While wool production continues in both countries, wool is a by-product of the meat industry. Mohair and alpaca are produced at minor levels. In the late twentieth century, interest in organic textiles (organic cotton, color-grown cotton, transition cotton, cruelty-free silk, organic wool) and eco-friendly and biodegradable textiles, including Ingeo®PLA (polylactic acid) from corn, bamboo fiber, Soy Silk, and SilkLatte (from milk), has influenced textile production and consumption.

In 1928, E. I. du Pont and Company hired Dr. W. H. Carothers to head a research program to discover how to form large molecules (polymers). This research led to the development of the synthetic fiber industry. In 1928, manufactured fibers accounted for 5 percent of textile fiber consumption in the United States; today, it is approximately 72 percent. The manufactured and synthetic industry is an important contributor to fashion change. The commercial introduction of rayon in the 1920s, acetate in the 1930s, and nylon in the late 1930s offered an affordable alternative to silk. Lastex, a rubber filament core covered by a natural fiber yarn, changed the silhouette and style for adult undergarments and bathing suits in the 1930s and 1940s. In the 1950s, polyester allowed for wash-and-wear fabrics. Mylar, textured nylon, and spandex allowed for metallic looks and the popularity of pantyhose in the 1960s. Polyester double knits allowed for leisure suits in the 1970s. DuPont's high-performance fibers, such as Cool Max (polyester) and Supplex (nylon), provided comfortable athletic looks in the 1980s. In the 1990s, lyocell, produced under the trade name Tencel, was developed to be a more environmentally safe fiber. "Smart" fibers that incorporated wireless communications or solar power were explored by various research groups in the 1990s and 2000s.

Hemp became a minor crop in Canada in the late 1990s. It is grown under license and is used for textile, paper, concrete, and oilseed products. New applications for hemp fiber and seed include composite building and manufacturing materials, nutritional, cosmetic, and industrial preparations, and biomass applications. Cultivation of hemp in the United States has been restricted because it is in the same botanical family as marijuana. Retailers do, however, sell apparel made from imported hemp, and a number of states have removed barriers to production and research.

Nonwovens are fabrics manufactured from fibers by mechanical, chemical, thermal, solvent, or combination methods. Nonwovens have been used since the 1920s, but they became important during World War II with shortages of high-quality cellulosic fibers. In 1933, C. H. Dexter and Sons began producing wet-laid nonwovens from cellulosic fibers. In 1944, the Minnesota Mining and Manufacturing Company began producing nonwovens for electrical insulation. In 1965, DuPont began producing a spunbonded nonwoven, and they received a patent in 1968 for hydroentangled or spun-lace nonwovens. In the early 1980s, melt-blown nonwovens were introduced to the market. By the mid-1990s, about half of the worldwide nonwoven fabric production capacity was located in North America.

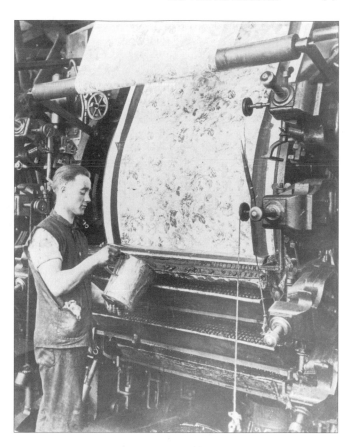

A textile factory worker pours dye into a textile printing machine, North America, ca. 1930. Getty Images.

MARKETING AND TRADE ISSUES

During World War I, lack of availability of British, Swiss, and German dyes forced development of the North American dye industry. The American Association of Textile Chemists and Colorists (AATCC) developed out of a need for standardized testing and consistent dye quality. In 1921, the AATCC was founded by Louis A. Olney and 140 dye and textile representatives. Its purpose was to increase the knowledge of the application of dyes and chemicals, to encourage research on chemical processes and materials, and to promote the exchange of knowledge among members.

The Worth Street Textile Market Rules were codified in 1926. Twelve major textile associations joined together to establish definitions, performance standards, physical testing procedures, and rules of conduct pertaining to the purchase and sale of cotton textiles and related goods. Revised in 1941, 1964, and 1986, they expanded to cover most textile fibers and finished textiles. The rules reflect common and fair business practices. In 1986, the Worth Street Textile Market Rules were approved and endorsed by the American Textile Manufacturers Institute, the Textile Distributors Association, and the Knitted Textile Association. The rules classified fabrics into five groups based on fiber and fabric type.

The American Textile Manufacturers Institute (ATMI) is the trade association for textile material manufacturers. It was established in 1949 with the consolidation of the American Cotton Manufacturers Association and the Cotton Textile Institute.

Other sections of the industry merged in 1958 (National Federation of Textiles, representing the manufactured fiber and silk industries), 1965 (Association of Finishers of Textile Fabrics), 1971 (National Association of Wool Manufacturers), and 1989 (Thread Institute). ATMI focuses on problems and programs from a national, industry-wide perspective.

In the 1950s, the American National Standards Institute published a voluntary set of textile performance standards, the L 22 Performance Specifications for Textile Fabrics, based on fabric end use. They have not been published since 1968. In the 1980s, the American Society for Testing and Materials (ASTM) began updating the L 22 standards to reflect new technology and performance expectations. The first performance specifications from ASTM were published in 1983, and ASTM continues to develop new standards and refine and review documents every five years.

Trade names were important in promoting individual synthetic and manufactured fibers and durable-press and shrinkage-control finishes from the 1950s through the 1970s. Use of trade names decreased drastically in the 1980s. Current use of trade names and trademarks with textile products focuses on specialized products like outerwear and extreme sportswear.

Textile imports from the 1960s through the 1990s were controlled by the Multifiber Arrangement (MFA) of the GATT. The Crafted with Pride advertising program of the 1990s was an industry effort to influence consumers to purchase textile products manufactured in the United States. The quick response system emphasized improvements in manufacturing techniques and reduced the time between new product development and retail stores. Current lead times are in the range of six to nine months for imported fabrics and a few days to three months for domestic fabrics. Social responsibility for textile and other manufacturing companies includes attention to working conditions, environmental impact, and consumer protection.

The overall effect of the 1994 NAFTA on its member countries (Canada, United States, and Mexico) has been to increase both imports and exports of textiles to and from member countries. Even so, globalization has had a negative effect on both Canada and the United States. With the World Trade Organization (WTO) and NAFTA, the North American textile industry has consolidated, innovated, and automated to remain competitive in global markets. The industry has reconfigured itself with a focus on niche markets in the global textile market or on working in areas where barriers to entry exist, such as with automotive textiles.

The industry has steadily become more capital intensive with fewer but more highly skilled workers, more automated equipment, and more vertical integration. Equipment is more sophisticated, more automated, more productive, and more expensive. In the 1980s, capital improvements focused on producing large quantities of moderate-quality fabric at a faster pace and lower prices per yard and requiring larger order minimums. In the 1990s and into the twenty-first century, more flexibility is required to meet consumer needs. In the 1990s, many textile manufacturers established production facilities in Mexico so that textiles would be produced in closer proximity to apparel production. In 2000, the Caribbean Basin Trade Partnership Act (CBTPA) reduced demand for U.S.-made fabrics. Between 1998 and 2002, more than two hundred mills in the U.S. textile industry were closed—more than at any time since the 1930s.

Significant dates in the textile industry in the United States and Canada

1830	John Thorpe devised a ring spinning machine for spinning staple fibers
1910	Rayon first commercially produced in the United States
1924	Acetate first commercially produced in the United States; crimped staple acetate introduced in 1935
1926	Invention of the double godet wheel to increase fiber orientation by stretching filaments
1932	First production of filament tow to be cut into staple
1933–35	First resin finishes applied to rayon and cotton in the United States for permanent shape, shrinkage control, embossed designs, luster, and water repellence
1938	Glass fiber first commercially produced
1939	Invention of the Pacific Converter to change filament tow into staple fiber
1939	Nylon first commercially produced
1940	Process of conjugate spinning developed for rayon
1950	Acrylic first commercially produced
1952	Production of textured filament yarns for stretch hosiery
1953	Polyester first commercially produced in the United States
1954	Triacetate first commercially produced in the United States
1954	Polytetrafluoroethylene fiber first produced
1959	Spandex first commercially produced
1954	Introduction of polyester films for metallic fibers
1957	Introduction of metalizing process to deposit vaporized aluminum on polyester films
1959	Conjugate spinning of bilateral acrylic
1961	Olefin first commercially produced in the United States
1963	Bicomponent self-crimping nylon introduced
1960s	Aramid first commercially produced
1965	Superfine stainless-steel filament (6–12 microns) introduced
1971	Silk-like Qiana nylon introduced
1989	Microfibers first commercially produced in the United States
1993	Lyocell first commercially produced in the United States
2002	Moderate-quality LAPLA first commercially produced

References and Further Reading

Aspland, J. Richard, and Edward A. Vaughn. "75 Years of Change in the American Textile Manufacturing Industry." *Textile Chemist and Colorist* 29, no. 5 (1997): 25–28.

Austin, Barbara, and Henry Mintzberg. "Mirroring Canadian Industrial Policy: Strategy Formation at Dominion Textile from 1873 to 1990." *Canadian Journal of Administrative Sciences* 13, no. 1 (1996): 46–64.

Brandt, Gail C. "Women in the Quebec Cotton Industry, 1890–1950." *Material History Bulletin* 31 (1990): 99–105.

Canadian Museum of Civilization Corporation. http://www.civili zation.ca/hist/labour/labo1e.html (accessed 29 December 2006).

Candee, Richard M. "Lace Schools and Lace Factories: Female Outwork in New England's Machine-Lace Industry, 1818–1838." In *Textiles in Early New England: Design, Production, and Consumption*, edited by Peter Benes and Jane M. Benes. Boston, MA: Boston University Scholarly Publications, 1997.

Glock, Ruth E., and Grace I. Kunz. *Apparel Manufacturing: Sewn Product Analysis.* 4th ed. Upper Saddle River, NJ: Pearson, 2005.

Hartford, William F. *Where Is Our Responsibility: Unions and Economic Change in the New England Textile Industry, 1870–1960.* Amherst: University of Massachusetts Press, 1996.

Kadolph, Sara J. *Textiles.* 10th ed. Upper Saddle River, NJ: Pearson, 2007.

Kowaluk, Russell. *Growth Perseveres in the Canadian Primary Textile Industry.* 1998. http://www.statcan.ca/english/freepub/34-250-XIE/1998/34-250.htm (accessed 15 January 2007).

McMahon, Thomas F. *United Textile Workers of America: Their History and Policies.* New York: The Workers Education Bureau Press, 1926.

Mock, Garn N. "75 Years of Change in Dyeing and Finishing." *Textile Chemist and Colorist* 29, no. 5 (1997): 29–36.

Rivoli, Pietra. *The Travels of a T-Shirt in the Global Economy.* Hoboken, NJ: John Wiley & Sons, 2005.

Sparks, R. P. "The Garment and Clothing Industries, History and Organization." *Manual of the Textile Industry of Canada* (1930): 107–130.

Steed, G.P.F. *An Historical Geography of the Canadian Clothing Industries: 1800–1930s.* Research notes No. 11. Ottawa: Department of Geography and Regional Planning, University of Ottawa, 1976.

Wehrle, Louise. *Fingers of Steel: Technological Innovations in the United States Knitting Industry, 1850–1914.* New York: Garland Publishing, 1995.

Wilson, Kax. *A History of Textiles.* Boulder, CO: Westview Press, 1979.

Sara J. Kadolph and Sara B. Marcketti

See also The Garment Industry and Retailing in the United States; Textile and Apparel Industries at the Turn of the Millenium; The Garment Industry and Retailing in Canada.

The Pattern Industry

The pattern industry in the United States and Canada had as its antecedents a number of earlier attempts to simplify the making of garments. The earliest records of patterns used in clothing construction date from over eight centuries ago. For the majority of people, covering the body was more important than fashion. The first patterns, made by cloistered monks, consisted of only two pieces: a sleeve and a piece from which identical front and back pieces were cut. The resulting garment was tied around the waist. Those twelfth-century patterns were made of slate. One size fit all, or one size fit no one.

In the thirteenth century, French master tailor Charles Daillac began making his patterns out of thin pieces of wood. The tailors' guilds fought the introduction of the thin wood pattern pieces, fearing that general knowledge of trade secrets would lessen the importance of their work. Later in the thirteenth century, Marcel Tassin, tailor to King Jean Le Bon, made his patterns for the king's clothing from cardboard. Eventually, French tailoring guilds accepted this innovation, and by the end of the fourteenth century, dressmakers and tailors had sets of patterns. The use of the cardboard patterns had improved the art of dressmaking and tailoring for tailors and their customers.

In the late fourteenth and early fifteenth centuries, fashion journals began to appear, illustrating and describing the increasingly complex styles of the times. Out of necessity, patterns and designs continued to be refined. Patterns became so important to garment makers that they were referred to in England as "Gods" and were mentioned in wills as a legacy to sons. However, as the number and types of tailors' and dressmakers' pattern shapes increased and became more available than they had been in the past, the importance of garment makers' trade secrets diminished.

As clothing became increasingly complex, so did the garment maker's job. Much skill was needed to form the pieces of a garment and then to join the pieces properly. In the nineteenth century, an increasing number of people, the emerging middle class, wanted the sophisticated clothing worn by the upper classes. Pressure existed to keep prices down so that those in the growing middle-class population in the United States could afford to purchase the newest fashions.

TOOLS AND TECHNIQUES IMPROVE

New tools and techniques were developed to improve garment-making efficiency and to keep costs down. The inch tape measure was developed, and in the early to mid-nineteenth century, the sewing machine was invented.

Various types of systems for *pattern drafting* (making the pieces that were combined to make a garment) were developed also. Proportional drafting systems and direct-measure drafting systems, the former using a special tool to develop measurements and the latter based on direct measurement of the customer, appeared in the early nineteenth century. These were followed by a combination of the two systems that resulted in a complex innovation, the *hybrid drafting system*. The principles upon which the aforementioned drafting systems were based, and the drafting systems themselves, later became the basis for sized and graded patterns. Additionally, new tools were developed that proved useful in the drafting of graded and sized patterns.

Various types of unsized patterns appeared in the nineteenth century. Miniature pattern diagrams appeared in some of the leading fashion magazines, including *Peterson's Magazine* and *Godey's Lady's Book*, in the early part of the century, but these patterns had to be traced, enlarged to scale, and then scaled up or down to fit the user. Additionally, three to four garments were often printed on one page, each defined by a different type of line, from dots, to dashes, to wavy, and to combinations thereof. In the mid-1800s, full-scale patterns appeared, but these, too, had to be traced and fitted to the wearer. Patterns were made in one size only. Full-size or unsized patterns and various drafting systems existed together throughout the early to middle 1800s.

Ellen and William Jennings Demorest were among the business people manufacturing and distributing unsized, full-scale patterns in the mid-nineteenth century. The Demorests may have been the first to introduce them to the United States, and several researchers have alluded to the possibility that the Demorests also developed and introduced graded and sized patterns there. However, no conclusive evidence exists to support this theory.

BUTTERICK AND THE SIZED PAPER PATTERN

Most believe that Ebenezer Butterick invented and introduced graded and sized patterns to the United States. Butterick was a tailor by training and trade and no doubt was familiar with the concept and use of patterns. In 1863, after two unsuccessful attempts to establish tailoring businesses, Butterick, with his wife's help, placed his first graded and sized patterns on the market. The first was for a set of men's shirts and was cut from stiff brown paper. The second was for a Garibaldi suit, a collarless, belted jacket worn with calf-length trousers, for young boys. These first patterns were an immediate success. Patterns were cut and folded by the Butterick family. Soon patterns were cut from tissue, to be easily folded by the producer and then unfolded by the purchaser. Patterns were sold door-to-door and later by the box to retailers.

Ebenezer soon moved his business from the Sterling/Fitchburg, Massachusetts, area to New York City. By 1866, the business was described in *Wilson's Business Directory of New York* as "patterns and fashions for gents', youths' and children's clothing … , 192 B'rdway [sic]."

The Civil War (1861–1865) served as a stimulus to the Buttericks' pattern business because fabrics were scarce and women were looking for inexpensive ways to clothe their families. The

No. 1273.

E. Butterick & Co.'s Pattern

FOR A

BOY'S PANTS.

They are made without Plaits at the Top, and extend half way from the Knee to the Ankle.

1273

This pattern, suitable for cassimere, broadcloth, lady's-cloth, velvet, linen, or any kind of goods used for boys' pants, is in four pieces: Front, Back, Front and Back of Waistband. In cutting goods that has a nap, be careful that it runs toward the bottom of the garment. Place the pockets in between the notches on the outside seam. In sewing on the front waistband (which is the shortest) let the point lap at the seam in front, so that it can be stitched on smoothly across the top of the pants. In sewing on the back waistband, place the centre at the seam in the back, and allow it to extend to the edge of the facing. This facing is cut on the back part at the side seam, and is of sufficient width to allow the front waistband to lap over and button smoothly. Ornament the fronts near the outside seam, and around the bottom, with narrow braid. These pants may be buttoned to a shirt waist, or worn with suspenders.

Usual Age for this size	3	years.
Waist Measure	20	inches.
Length of Leg	8	inches.
Quantity of Material, 27 inches wide	1	yard.
" " Braid for Trimming	10	yards.
Number of Buttons	4	.

PRICE 15 CENTS.

To measure for a pair of pants, ascertain the waist measure by putting the measure around the body, over the pants at the waist, and drawing it closely—*not too tight.* For length of leg, measure from the fork toward the ankle to the point you desire the pants to extend. If this pattern has the waist measure as required, and the leg is longer or shorter than desired, add to or shorten in length as needed.

Allowance for ¼ inch seams is made in the pattern.

Address **E. BUTTERICK & CO., 589 Broadway, N. Y.**

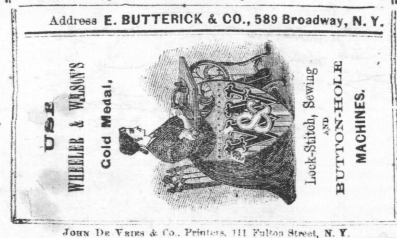

USE WHEELER & WILSON'S Gold Medal.

Lock-Stitch, Sewing AND BUTTON-HOLE MACHINES.

JOHN DE VRIES & Co., Printers, 111 Fulton Street, N. Y.

Butterick pattern, 1869, printed and cut from tissue. Ebenezer Butterick's graded and sized patterns were highly successful in the United States. Many pattern producers also developed working relationships with sewing machine companies, also advertised here. Butterick Pattern #1273. Commercial Pattern Archive (1869.1.URI) Special Collections, University of Rhode Island Library.

war also brought standard sizing for men's uniforms and civilian clothing and, eventually, to women's and children's clothing as well. By the end of 1867, Butterick agents were required to order patterns by number because naming each pattern had become so complex. In 1868, Butterick began publishing the *Metropolitan Monthly* to spread fashion news and increase customer demand.

With fabric and ready-to-wear clothes scarce during the Civil War, Butterick pattern sales rose. In 1867, Ebenezer Butterick and two boyhood friends, Jones W. Wilder and Abner W. Pollard, became partners in E. Butterick and Company. The pattern business grew rapidly, and the Butterick company began printing several publications to advertise its products. Butterick's graded and sized patterns were highly successful. Newspapers such as the *Buffalo Daily Courier* (18 March 1869) even claimed that Butterick patterns were socially redemptive, stating, "Butterick ... solved one of the grave social problems which was tending toward a dissolution of the family ties. The making of their own dresses is an occupation that will prove a blessing to restless women who, in the bans of their idleness have turned after the false gods of suffrage." In 1871, six million patterns were sold by Butterick and Company.

MCCALL'S PAPER PATTERNS

No good and potentially profitable idea goes unnoticed by entrepreneurs, and so it was with thirty-year-old James McCall, a full journeyman tailor who immigrated to the United States in 1857. Mr. McCall gave up the sale of sewing machines in 1873 and invested his money in starting his paper patterns business. He immediately began publishing a tabloid-type magazine titled *The Queen* to promote his patterns, along with a small pattern catalog titled *Catalogue of Bazaar Paper Patterns*. McCall advertised his patterns in *Harper's Bazaar* magazine, undoubtedly taking advantage of the similarity of names. An examination of the early patterns of both Butterick and McCall demonstrates similarity between the two.

In the mid-1870s, Butterick appears to have overexpanded its operations and was having financial difficulties, as were many companies caught in the Panic of 1873. The fact that McCall's was prospering certainly did not help Butterick weather the financial storm. In addition to competition with McCall's, the Domestic Sewing Machine Company (DSMC), well known by many, began making sized garment patterns, calling their pattern business simply Domestic. There is little doubt that the sewing machine operation helped support the pattern business.

By the mid- to late 1800s, several pattern manufacturers or distributors were established. Most flourished only briefly. Women's magazines and family magazines sold patterns by mail order, and pattern companies began to furnish retailers with counter catalogs (called *counterlogs*) for customers to use in the stores. There was no other way for pattern companies to display the full array of their offerings. Advertisements for patterns increased nationwide, many of which were printed by the pattern companies themselves. By the beginning of the twentieth century, pattern companies had also become printing houses.

Early Butterick patterns had no seam allowances, no printing on pattern pieces, not even any perforations to help guide the user. Sometimes there was a small picture of the featured garment attached to the pattern. There were no fabric or yardage recommendations and no directions for assembly of any sort.

There were also no small pattern pieces for facings, pockets, or trimmings.

Competition among existing pattern companies was fierce. In order to distinguish themselves one from the other, the companies developed distinguishing factors such as seam allowances; perforations of different designs; weight and type of tissue paper; and small pattern pieces for facings, trims, and pockets. Very brief instructions began to appear. Home catalogs were published for home use.

The Standard Fashion Company was established in 1887 by Franz Keowing, a former sales manager with Butterick. Standard was successful from the start. Keowing knew that many fabric stores wanted to use patterns to stimulate the sales of fabric and trims. The Standard Fashion company also stated that they sold to only one merchant in an area, bringing exclusivity to their patterns.

Growth was the byword for the late nineteenth century. When James McCall died in 1883, the company was solvent and run by McCall's wife for six years following. In the decade following the death of James McCall, the company changed hands several times.

In 1894, the New Idea Pattern Company was established by Mr. J. W. Pearsall. With very little capital at his disposal, Pearsall purchased patterns from other manufacturers and placed them in envelopes bearing the New Idea Pattern Company name. The ten-cent patterns were sold by mail order through farm journals, newspapers, and a few magazines, with postage-paid delivery. By 1895, New Idea Pattern Company was manufacturing all its own

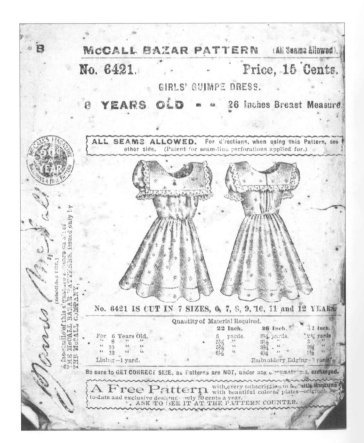

McCall pattern for a girl's guimpe dress, costing fifteen cents. United States, 1900. McCall Pattern #6421. Commercial Pattern Archive (1900.11.URI) Special Collections, University of Rhode Island Library.

patterns, and business was brisk. After all, Butterick, Standard, McCall, and other patterns were selling for as high as thirty cents. New Idea sold merchants on the value of a pattern department as an indirect sales producer. That value persists today.

TWENTIETH-CENTURY DEVELOPMENTS

By the turn of the century, probably a dozen pattern manufacturers existed. Women obviously liked the mass-produced, graded, and sized patterns. Through the use of patterns, fashion could be had by many, and class differences were further broken down. Jeffersonian principles of government, with their hands-off philosophy, helped big business. Volume and revenues in the pattern industry grew steadily.

The sharp economic upturn seen in the early 1900s offered reassurances to business. Mergers and trust formations were common until government regulations, in particular, the Clayton Anti-trust Act of 1914, slowed the activity. Mergers among the pattern companies were not uncommon later in the twentieth century, but the Clayton Act slowed them considerably. The emergence of strong businesses, increased production and new technology, and modes of transportation and communications brought about the existence of a world market in the early 1900s that continued through the century.

Two important pattern interests were formed at the turn of the twentieth century—the Pictorial Review Company in 1899 and the pattern department of *Vogue* magazine in 1905. *Vogue* patterns provided the market with high-fashion pattern styles. Both Pictorial Review and *Vogue* developed publications specifically for the promotion of their pattern products.

Vogue magazine, established in 1894, grew out of a struggling New York weekly society paper. Condé Montrose Nast, son of a prosperous New York family and educated as a lawyer, worked for *Collier's* magazine in the early 1900s. He quit Collier's, established Condé Nast Publications in 1909, and began publishing *Vogue*, which became the premier fashion and high-society magazine of the twentieth century.

Vogue had, in 1905, begun offering patterns to its readers. The patterns, developed by Ms. Rosa Payne and allegedly cut by her on her dining room table, came in just one size, with the only permissible bust measurement of thirty-six inches (ninety centimeters). Customers who did not fit that size could send their measurements to *Vogue* and a custom pattern would be cut—but only in sizes ranging from a 32-inch (80-centimeter) to a 46-inch (115-centimeter) bust. In 1914, Vogue Pattern Company was formed as a subsidiary of *Vogue* magazine.

Butterick purchased the Standard Fashion Company and the New Idea Pattern Company in 1900 and 1902, respectively. For a number of years, the three entities within the Butterick company operated independently except that the expense of securing fashion information was shared and costs were, therefore, reduced. The magazines of the three companies, the *Delineator*, the *Designer*, and the *Woman's Magazine*, became known as "The Butterick Trio." From 1902 until the time this volume was prepared for publication, Butterick has occupied the Butterick Building at 161 Sixth Avenue in New York.

In 1914, with the passage of the Clayton Antitrust Act, the pattern companies were forced to stop making tying contracts with retailers in unfair restraint of trade. Many retailers were able, for the first time, to carry more than one line of patterns in their stock. Competition for customers increased, and many pattern companies did not survive.

Pattern instructions for layout, construction, and finishing of garments improved in the twentieth century. Separate instruction sheets tailored to individual patterns were included in each envelope, though instructions were brief, and there were no layout instructions until the middle of the century. In 1919, the Butterick Company patented its printed instruction sheet, calling it "the Deltor." The term *deltor* is still used in some parts of the United States and Canada to describe the instruction sheet of any pattern company, just as many people use the term *Kleenex* to describe any brand of facial tissue.

In 1919, the McCall Company obtained patents for printing the outlines and construction details of pattern pieces instead of cutting and perforating them. The idea and implementation of

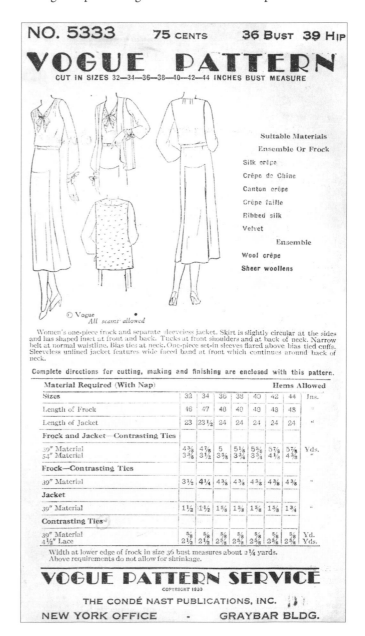

A Vogue pattern for a dress and jacket, United States, 1920. *Vogue* magazine started offering patterns to its readers from 1905 and later formed its own pattern company. Vogue Pattern #5333, 1920. Commercial Pattern Archive (1920.8.JSE) Special Collections, University of Rhode Island Library.

printing patterns revolutionized the pattern industry. When the McCall patents expired in 1938, the method of printing on patterns became public domain. Condé Nast even tried cutting its patterns in three different colors: the lining in brown, the trimming in green, and all other parts in straw-colored tissue.

The biggest challenge for pattern customers was that of selecting the proper size pattern that would result in well-fitting garments. The problem continued in the twentieth century and still goes on, despite the fact that patterns, pattern magazines, counter catalogs, and pattern company publications contain elaborate instructions regarding how to take body measurements in such a way as to ensure the selection of a pattern that fits. Whether or not to allow for seams, and if so, how much, continued to be controversial into the mid-1950s.

World War I had little impact on the pattern industry. However, as is common in wartime, military-influenced fashions became popular, and this was reflected in pattern companies' offerings. Pattern companies also began to introduce small amounts of color, usually light brown or yellow, in counter catalogs. Increasing amounts of information were given in the catalogs, such as fabric suggestions, amounts of trims, and notions needed.

Small pattern companies continued to be formed in the 1920s and 1930s. Technological advances in fabrics and dyes during this time were substantial. Rayon was developed in 1909, and between 1919 and 1920 production increased tenfold. Assisted by hydroelectric power, cotton production increased in the southeastern United States. Fashions changed rapidly as rebellious young women struggled for and found new freedoms. In 1919, women were still wearing ankle-length dresses and confining underpinnings. By 1925, hemlines were scandalously high, stopping just above the knee. The automobile and radio industries grew rapidly. Almost every industry was booming except the pattern industry. Pattern prices were almost as high as the cost of three or four yards of fabric. Increasing numbers of women were working outside the home, ready-made clothing was well made and easily available, and fashion was changing so fast that a home-sewn garment might be out of style before it was completed.

THE SIMPLICITY PATTERN COMPANY

Once again, no good opportunity goes unnoticed by entrepreneurs. Mr. Joseph M. Shapiro, an advertising salesman, saw the imbalance in the cost of patterns (a few pieces of tissue in an envelope) and fabrics. Joseph and his son, James, set about correcting the imbalance and established the Simplicity pattern company.

Simplicity patterns were an immediate success. By the 1970s, retrospective speculation and conventional wisdom in the industry was that Butterick had refused to manufacture a low-priced house brand for the F. W. Woolworth Company in the 1920s (Keane, 1978). It was said that Butterick refused on the basis that it could find itself competing with itself, that manufacturing for a low-priced house would undercut its reputation for creating high-styled fashions, and that the low-priced patterns would not be self-supporting and would cut into profits.

What the Shapiros, including Joseph, James, and home economist Caroline Hutchins Shapiro (wife of James), understood was that patterns had no intrinsic value in and of themselves but that they were the drivers for sales of yard goods, trims, notions, and other sewing supplies. Simplicity immediately enjoyed access to every Woolworth store in the United States. The Woolworth house brand of patterns, manufactured by Simplicity, carried the name DuBarry.

In 1930, just three years after Simplicity was established, James Shapiro founded the company's Canadian and British subsidiaries. Simplicity introduced new marketing techniques and promotions. Other existing pattern companies were forced to become more creative and innovative in their approach to retailers and customers than they had been before. Though other companies had previously founded offices outside the United States, particularly in Canada, none were so successful as Simplicity, which purchased both the Pictorial Review and Excella pattern companies in 1936.

The Great Depression and then World War II actually did more to stabilize the pattern industry than any other event in its history. During the Depression, women sewed to save money. During World War II, ready-to-wear clothing was sometimes scarce and usually expensive, and women sewed to alleviate both problems.

According to U.S. government statistics and research completed under the *National Recovery Act of 1933*, it was found that nine pattern companies existed in 1929. The industry employed over two thousand seven hundred workers, and employment had increased 15.4 percent since 1929. As well, the industry remained labor intensive, with some smaller companies still cutting pattern pieces by hand. All collating, folding, and insertion of pattern and instruction pieces was done by hand; all shelving and picking was also done by hand. By the late 1980s, all of these operations were done by machine and, in some cases, by computer.

Several companies were formed and then vanished in the 1930s, including Hollywood Pattern and the New York Pattern. In 1932, the Advance Pattern Company was established, offering high style at a lower price than Vogue and Butterick. Vogue patterns continued to be successful, and Vogue offices were opened in Canada and England.

Home economist Caroline Hutchins, who had joined Simplicity in 1934 and later married James Shapiro, had been a teacher. She convinced Simplicity owners that if the home sewing market was to be maintained and expanded, it must be done by educating large numbers of young people and others. One of the first magazines targeted for high school youth was *Modern Miss*, first published by Simplicity in the 1930s.

Simplicity's aggressive corporate growth put pressure on the other pattern companies to become increasingly assertive. Nearly all of them instituted educational programs that worked with schools. Most pattern companies sought out and developed working relationships with fabric, sewing machine, notion, and trim companies; department stores; 4-H clubs; and women's clubs, among others.

Simplicity's horizontal and vertical growth was aided by its purchase of the North American Pulp and Paper Corporation, making it the first fully integrated pattern company. The acquisition of the corporation was especially advantageous to Simplicity during World War II, when paper goods for nonmilitary use were in short supply. Not only did the corporation supply Simplicity with all its paper needs for patterns and publishing, but it also also met the needs of other pattern companies and nonrelated industries.

Once again, in the late 1930s and early 1940s, Butterick was trying to rebuild from its most recent financial problems. The company finally began to make money in 1943 and used its earnings to pay off old debts, accumulate capital to move forward, and build its credit. In 1948, a new plant was built in Altoona, Pennsylvania,

Woman sewing in 1943 with a McCall's pattern. The pattern industry followed the ready-to-wear restrictions required by the General Limitation Orders issued by the U.S. War Production Board. The purpose of the restrictions was to conserve fabric. Library of Congress Prints and Photographs, Farm Security Administration, Office of War Information Photograph Collection digital id # fsa 8e00944.

to handle the printing of patterns, pattern envelopes, and bookbinding that had previously been contracted out to other firms.

IMPACT OF WORLD WAR II

When the United States entered into World War II, five companies were selling patterns over the counter: Simplicity, McCall, Advance, Butterick, and Vogue. Sales of patterns skyrocketed as the industry adopted its wartime slogan: "So much for so many for so little." A survey found that in 1940, 6 percent of all women in the United States made at least some of their own clothes or clothes for their families.

The pattern industry followed the ready-to-wear restrictions required by the General Limitation Orders issued by the War Production Board. The restrictions, imposed to conserve fabric, limited the types of facings for garments, the length of skirts, the width of collars and cuffs, and the sweep of skirts. Only bridal gowns, burial gowns, and vestments required by the clergy or judiciary were exempt.

During the war, less paper was used for patterns and instructions, and the quality of the paper used decreased as well. Black-and-white drawings replaced color. All the pattern companies but Vogue produced patterns related to war needs, including some for nurses' and Red Cross workers' uniforms, work clothes, and hospital gowns. Patterns for blouse fronts, dickeys (a small piece to fill in a neckline, made with or without a collar), and collars helped stretch the wardrobe.

The War Production Board was terminated in 1945, and rationing ended, except for sugar and rubber tires. Many women returned to full-time homemaking, and there was an increased interest in sewing. Surveys taken in 1944 showed that 82 percent of all American women sewed at home. Sewing machines were in short supply, and companies featured their repair services and sewing instruction classes instead. By 1945, there were more sewing machines in homes across the country than there were telephones, and sewing machine companies had heavy backlogs of orders. Between 1944 and early 1957, the numbers of girls and women over twelve years of age increased 12 percent, while the increase in home sewers was 52 percent.

Pattern company earnings increased fairly steadily through the 1950s. The Federal Trade Commission (FTC) accused Simplicity of having a monopoly of the pattern business in national chain stores; it filed a complaint against Simplicity in 1954 but dropped it in 1956. All the pattern companies grew in the 1950s, with most establishing offices and distribution in several countries. Though it did not thrive, in 1961 Simplicity was the first U.S. company to introduce patterns sized for the Japanese figure.

Though Vogue contended that its customers were more sophisticated and knowledgeable about sewing than the average home sewer, in 1956, it added an educational department to promote the use of Vogue patterns among young people. However, it continued to sell patterns with only perforations. It was not until 1957 that Vogue distributed patterns that were both perforated and printed. The new patterns were so successful that Vogue modernized further to produce wholly printed patterns.

CHANGING BUSINESS PATTERNS

In 1960, the Butterick Company and Condé Nast Publications entered into a licensing agreement that gave Butterick the right to manufacture and distribute Vogue patterns. Initially, Butterick maintained two separate operations in New York City, with Vogue

This image formed part of a promotion advocating the economical use of patterns and fabric by the U.S. War Production Board, 1943. It shows a simplified waistline and careful placing of the fabric's flower design. Library of Congress Prints and Photographs Division, Library of Congress Prints and Photographs, Office of War Information Photograph Collection, LC-USW33-021693-ZC.

remaining on Lexington Avenue and Butterick designers and other Butterick personnel remaining in the Butterick building. Vogue/ Butterick manufacturing facilities continued in London, Paris, Milan, Toronto, Sydney, Melbourne, Auckland, and Johannesburg.

The general corporate upheaval that followed the pattern industry in the period from the mid-1960s to 2007 seems to have begun in 1968, when Norton Simon was formed as a conglomerate, bringing the McCall Corporation, Canada Dry, and Hunt-Wesson Foods under one conglomerate umbrella. The Vogue/ Butterick Company was purchased by yet another conglomerate, American Can Company, in 1968. The Advance Pattern Company had been purchased by Puritan Fashions and soon disappeared entirely, and then Puritan itself disappeared when Calvin Klein secured a buyout. In 1976, Simplicity had the largest share of the pattern industry market.

In 1984 the stagnated McCall Pattern Company was purchased for US$25 million by Reginald Lewis, an African American former Virginia State football player and a graduate of Harvard Law School. He named his newly formed holding company TLC (The Lewis Company). McCall sales doubled after the purchase, and profits rose to new heights. Three years later, in 1987, TLC sold McCall to the John Crowther Group for US$95 million. In 1990, MP Holdings purchased the McCall Pattern Company, which made home sewing patterns under the brand names of McCall (contemporary), Butterick (classic), and Vogue (couture). MP

Holdings, headquartered in New York, also produced do-it-yourself wall treatments, such as wallpaper borders, cutouts, and murals, under the Wallies brand and published *Butterick Home Catalog* and *Vogue Patterns* magazines.

In 1998, Simplicity Pattern Company became part of the Conso Products Company, which made trims for crafts and home furnishings. Citicorp Venture Capital acquired Conso and took it private, and then Wm. Wright Company acquired Conso in 2006. Simplicity has licensed its name for a variety of products such as sewing machines, dollhouse kits, toy sewing machines, polyester fiberfill, and other sewing and non-sewing-related products.

Small pattern companies in Canada, the United States, and other countries continue to enter the market, some more successfully than others. Many of the small companies are focused on a particular market niche such as historical clothing, Asian clothing, Hawaiian clothing, or clothing of the U.S. Civil War, used by historic reenactors. Favorites among home sewers include Birch Street Clothing and Folkwear, both of which place an emphasis on patterns for ethnic and folk dress.

The men and women who molded the pattern industry believed the production and sale of patterns was an honorable means to a profitable end. Successful pattern makers analyzed the market, considered the needs and desires of potential consumers, and created a way to fulfill those needs and desires. A useful and fashionable product coupled with good marketing techniques, an efficient corporate organization, and good consumer relations created an almost innately successful formula for financial success.

References and Further Reading

Bryk, Nancy Villa. *American Dress Pattern Catalogs, 1873–1909.* New York: Dover Publications, 1988.

Davis-Meyers, Mary L. "The Development of American Menswear Pattern Drafting Technology, 1822 to 1860." *Clothing and Textiles Research Journal* 10, no. 3 (1992): 12–20.

Dickson, Carol Anne. "History of the US Garment Pattern Industry: 1776–1976." Ph.D. dissertation, Ohio State University, 1979.

Gordon, Sarah A. "Boundless Possibilities: Home Sewing and the Meanings of Women's Domestic Work in the United States, 1890–1930." *Journal of Women's History* 16, no. 2 (2004): 68–91.

Kidwell, Claudia B. *Cutting a Fashionable Fit.* Washington, DC: Smithsonian Institution Press, 1979.

LaBat, Karen, Carol Salusso, and Jongeun Rhee. "Home Sewers' Satisfaction with Fit of Apparel Pattern." *Journal of Fashion Marketing and Management* 11, no. 3 (2007): 429–440.

Laboissonniere, Wade. *Blueprints of Fashion: Home Sewing Patterns of the 1940s.* Atglen, PA: Schiffer Publishing, 1997.

Moody's Manual of Investments. New York: Moody's, 1931–1938.

Shapiro, James J. "Patterns of Culture." *Forbes* (1 May 1967): 68.

Waller-Zuckerman, Mary Ellen. "Marketing the Women's Journals, 1873–1900." *Business and Economic History* 18 (1989): 99–108.

Walsh, Margaret. "The Democratization of Fashion: The Emergence of the Women's Dress Pattern Industry." *Journal of American History* 66, no. 2 (September 1979): 299–313.

Wilson's Business Directory of New York. New York: John F. Trow, 1863–1976.

Carol Anne Dickson

See also Writing About Fashions.

The Garment Industry and Retailing in the United States

The U.S. garment industry has followed a distinctive path that at various times has seemed to position it in the vanguard of industrial development and at other times as a stubborn hold-out of archaic production methods. Some characteristics of the industry have remained stable from the start: its dependence on a dense web of subcontractors arrayed in relatively small units of production, its basic workflow organization, its extreme sensitivity to consumer preferences, and its resistance to automation and reliance on a large, fluid labor force that typically includes high percentages of women and immigrants. At the same time, apparel manufacturing has always been noteworthy for its ability to adapt to changing fashions and new economic circumstances. It has continually adjusted in numerous small and large ways, and it has been perpetually on the move, from major northeastern cities, to the rural South and West, to developing countries worldwide. This interplay between its enduring aspects and its ever-changing nature has characterized the industry throughout its history.

DEVELOPMENTS THROUGH THE MID-NINETEENTH CENTURY

In Colonial America, virtually all clothing was custom made, either at home or by professional tailors and seamstresses. Almost the only already-made clothing for sale was secondhand, although the demand in this area was considerable; in fact, the trade in secondhand clothing may well have exceeded that of new ready-made clothing in the United States until the Civil War.

The development of a substantial ready-made garment industry began in the first half of the nineteenth century thanks to entrepreneurial intermediaries who envisioned possibilities for forging a connection between new supplies of cloth, a rapidly increasing reservoir of urban labor, and growing consumer markets that were not linked to traditional channels of supply. By 1850, fully half the U.S. population lived in areas that had not been settled in 1800. The pioneering inhabitants of these regions did not develop the extensive household production that characterized Colonial America, preferring to rely for many goods, including clothing, on an expanding system of market exchange. Widespread commerce in clothing had become possible because advanced production methods in the textile mills of England and the American Northeast began to produce cloth in immense and affordable quantities at about the same time the so-called transportation revolution—brought about by steam-powered riverboats, a canal-building boom, and then railroad construction—made distribution over a broad geographical area feasible. Enterprising businesspeople saw that they could make a profit connecting the two ends of this economic chain with ready-made clothing.

Early clothing entrepreneurs quickly discovered it was most efficient to have skilled tailors cut fabric into component parts and then have less-skilled and lower-paid workers assemble the garments. They also discovered they could reduce overhead costs and minimize financial risks if, rather than hiring workers and gathering them under the same roof, the sewing work was "put out" for workers to do in their homes, at first by rural farm women and then by immigrants who began to collect in U.S. cities. The manufacturer could maintain some control by selection of fabric and supervision of the pattern-making and cutting processes but would not have to bear the costs associated with a large factory or a regular payroll. To be successful in this system, the clothier needed expertise in buying and selling cloth as well as in buying and selling labor; expertise in making clothes was optional, however, because that skill could be purchased. Although some tailors took the initiative to expand into this new arena, at least as often the early clothing manufacturer was a cloth wholesaler, an auctioneer, or simply a merchant in search of a profitable commodity. For example, Henry Sands Brooks bought and sold groceries before deciding to open a clothing store in New York in 1818, thereby launching a business that, by 1855, had been renamed Brooks Brothers and employed as many as fourteen hundred outside workers.

By 1860, clothing was the biggest manufacturing industry in New York City, which was the city with the greatest amount of manufacturing in the United States. A business directory for 1853 indicated the city had eighty-five clothiers specializing in wholesaling and more than four hundred businesses combining wholesale and retail operations. For other industries, high rents, cramped spaces, and lack of access to a good source of water-power made doing business in the heart of the city impractical. In contrast, the clothing maker only needed a loft, some cloth, a cutting table, and a cutter—outside workers would bear the costs of rents, utilities, and whatever technology was required for the actual sewing work. Ready access to raw materials through the city's port facilities and to a densely clustered workforce of immigrant workers made a downtown location ideal.

Three distinct types of clothing manufacturer emerged in the earliest days of the business and remained typical throughout its history. Some operated an *inside shop* where full-time employees worked. In a true inside shop, all aspects of production were completed on the premises of a company-owned factory. In practice, however, some inside shops included only designers, cutters, and inspectors on the regular payroll, with the rest of the work contracted out. More common was the *outside shop* run by a contractor (also called *contract shop*). These firms would fill specific

The sewing room of a shirt factory, Troy, New York, ca. 1907. Library of Congress, Prints and Photographs Division, LC-USZ62-96094.

orders for garments or parts of garments, but they were operated and owned independently of the wholesalers and retailers who merchandized the finished goods. Some outside shops became sizable firms, but the majority of them were small operations existing perpetually on the edge of financial ruin. Finally, there were *jobbers*, who normally did not own either manufacturing or retailing facilities. Almost pure intermediaries, they would accept orders from retailers or wholesalers, then buy cloth, hire a cutter, and turn to the vast network of contractors to create an ad hoc system of suppliers that produced the clothes.

Startup costs in the clothing trade were low, and with each semiannual cycle, clothing concerns sprang up and died off like wildflowers. The proliferation of clothing makers meant contractors competed ferociously. They made their money by underbidding rivals for jobs and then "sweating" out a margin of profit from their workers. Sewing workers were typically paid by *piece rates*—a set amount for each piece of work completed—rather than by the hour or by the week. By continually lowering piece rates, the contractors put unremitting pressure on operators to work longer, faster, and harder. At the other extreme, during the slack season or an economic slowdown, the workers simply received no work or pay. The system greatly benefited manufacturers because it minimized their fixed costs and risks. In addition, the system could quickly adjust products or workforce to meet changing demand, and this flexibility proved perfectly suited—perhaps even necessary—in an industry that was subject to seasonal cycles and constant vagaries of fashion.

The spread of sewing machines beginning in the 1850s may have aided large-scale clothing production, but it did not change its basic organization. Many operations still needed to be completed by hand, and operators still needed to guide fabric through the machine rather than stand back and let it work. This technology also was relatively inexpensive and portable, making continued decentralization possible (and even desirable because the contractor could require workers to assume responsibility for their

own machines). Unlike many industries in the nineteenth century, the garment industry's growth was not fundamentally shaped by technological innovation. On the other hand, the clothing trade was on the leading edge of industrial development when it came to division of labor. Workers who became highly proficient at a single task not only could complete their tasks more quickly but also reduced the need for more skilled (and more highly paid) operators. Already by 1859, an observer in Cincinnati, Ohio, visited a clothing business and reported that it had subdivided the work of making a pair of pants into seventeen different operations that could each be performed by a different person.

From the first, retailers pushed manufacturers to produce within specific parameters. The correspondence of one jobber in the 1830s showed he was continually exasperated by a merchant's demands for special garments and variations, all according to the latest style and delivered within a few weeks. The need for garment makers to be exquisitely attuned to consumer demand reinforced the development of production systems that valued flexibility over economies of scale and, hence, a system of small subcontractors rather than large, self-sufficient producers.

At a remarkably early phase, the garment industry assumed distinctive features that have characterized it ever since. In the twenty-first century, the clothing trade still includes many relatively small production units enmeshed in a web of complex subcontracting relationships and specializations. It remains common for design, pattern making, and cutting to be done at a central location by highly skilled workers but for actual sewing to be done elsewhere by lower-paid workers. The industry has proven remarkably resistant to automation and high-tech production solutions. And, particularly toward the end of the twentieth century, retailers have once again begun to drive production with demands that suppliers meet strict cost, variety, and delivery requirements.

DEVELOPMENTS THROUGH THE EARLY TWENTIETH CENTURY

By the mid-nineteenth century, the clothing trade had undergone impressive growth, but there were two important qualifications to its success. The first was that a large majority of the industry's output was confined to cheaper goods. Broad-based acceptance of ready-made clothing as a respectable middle-class substitute for custom-made goods was still some years off. The second qualification was that most ready-made production involved menswear only. Women's ready-made clothing scarcely existed at midcentury and progressed slowly thereafter, starting with cloaks in the 1860s, tailored suits in the 1880s and 1890s, shirtwaists in the 1890s and 1900s, and finally dresses in the 1910s and 1920s. In contrast, by the 1860s a thriving trade already existed in men's suits, shirts, and overcoats, and by the 1890s the ready-made business had captured the lion's share of the men's market.

All sectors of the clothing industry grew substantially in the late nineteenth and early twentieth centuries, drawing on reserves of economic energy generated by an enormous influx of immigrants into major U.S. cities. This process began early, with the arrival in the 1840s and 1850s of large numbers of Irish and German immigrants fleeing political and economic instability in their homelands. The Irish supplied much hand labor in the industry and for some time often occupied its most skilled positions. Many German immigrants were middle-class Jews with backgrounds as

Sweatshop employees of Mr. Goldstein's Workshop, New York, 1908. Sweatshops were characterized by overcrowding, poor lighting, unsanitary conditions, long hours, and low pay. Library of Congress, Prints & Photographs Division, National Child Labor Committee Collection. Reproduction number LC-DIG-nclc-04455.

merchants or training as business clerks. During the period from 1860 to 1890, they dominated the ownership of clothing firms in most cities with a substantial garment industry.

The last two decades of the nineteenth century and the first decade of the twentieth century saw a surge of immigration that dwarfed any previous arrival of foreigners to the United States. Among them were hundreds of thousands of Russian and Polish Jews who settled in major cities, where they lived and worked in garment districts like New York's Lower East Side. Many came with experience in the needle trades, but others were "greenhorn tailors" who merely found it advantageous to claim such expertise in order to advance in the one economic area that was the purview of their ethnic group. The more enterprising among them became contractors, taking advantage of low entry costs into the clothing business and their ability to tap ethnic networks of potential workers. They started a seemingly endless number of small clothing shops that fueled the industry's explosive growth. At the very end of the century, an enormous wave of Italian immigrants added another important stream of workers into the garment industry. By 1909, it was estimated that workers in the shirtwaist industry were 55 percent Jewish, 35 percent Italian, and 7 percent native born.

The U.S. Census reported that domestic clothing factories manufactured product worth US$489 million in 1909, an increase of almost exactly 1,000 percent since 1849. The majority of this growth—some US$210 million worth of annual sales— had come in the previous ten years. By and large, the industry remained a kaleidoscopic collection of small firms that came and went rapidly, but the rapidly expanding market did create momentum for standardization and efficiency that somewhat favored inside shops, where quality control could be more closely watched. The men's industry began to develop a two-tier system in which a small group of large manufacturers coexisted in a symbiotic if not untroubled relationship with a much larger group of small manufacturers and contract shops. The women's industry

also included both inside and outside shops, but the average size of the manufacturing unit was smaller, probably owing to the need for greater flexibility given the more frequent changes in fashion styles for women.

THE FIRST RETAIL REVOLUTION

Retail outlets for ready-made clothing emerged throughout the country in the nineteenth century. Indeed, a number of the most important manufacturers started in the retail side of the business. Daniel Devlin, for instance, was an Irish immigrant who began manufacturing clothing to supply his own retail store in Louisville, Kentucky. By the 1850s, he occupied a handsome five-story white marble building in New York City, where he sold readymades, maintained a custom clothing department, and employed a crew of cutters whose work kept two thousand outside sewers busy supplying the wholesale market. Top-of-the-line stores like D. Devlin & Co. provided a genteel shopping experience for customers, but more typical establishments were probably like that visited by one journalist in 1848, who described the experience this way: "Stooping, as you enter the low, dark doorway, you find yourself in the midst of a primitive formation of rags, carefully classified into vests, coats, and pantaloons." For many years a men's store might well have a "puller-in" standing in the doorway to drag business in off the street, sometimes literally. Inside the store, little effort was made at display or enticement. Customers encountered the goods heaped on tables and faced high-pressure sales tactics rather than courteous service.

The retail landscape was transformed between 1850 and 1900 by the development of the department store—establishments that offered an immense variety of products accompanied by a one-price policy, access to the store without obligation to buy, and refunds or exchanges for unsatisfactory goods—all merchandising novelties for their day. They sold both men's and women's ready-to-wear clothes and also maintained fitting rooms and alteration services along with custom clothing departments. Some of these merchants, such as Macy's, Wanamaker's, and Marshall Field's, began to manufacture their own clothes, although the intense competitiveness of the industry meant they reaped relatively little cost savings; by 1900, most had abandoned the practice, preferring instead to exercise their considerable influence over the industry by demanding price concessions and other accommodations from their suppliers.

The department store buyers were an elite class among retail employees. Often they were granted considerable autonomy in determining selection, amount, timing, and prices for the inventory in a specific department. The position offered a rare path of upward mobility for working women, who comprised as many as one-third of buyers by 1915. The buyer's ability to predict consumer taste and demand could determine the success of the store, and buyers in the clothing departments of top stores made annual visits to Paris to stay abreast of fashion change. Their network of contacts and personal feel for the market exerted significant influence over the distribution of ready-to-wear clothing in the United States until the 1980s, when new technology and management methods produced new methods of retail management. Around the turn of the century, department stores introduced the Paris-style fashion show to the U.S. mass market. The event quickly assumed familiar form—models on runways, spotlights, musical accompaniment—and by 1915 such shows were held semiannually in every city of any size in the country. They represented the democratization of fashion aspirations in the United States that sparked the spectacular growth of the clothing trade during this time period.

SWEATSHOPS AND UNIONS

In the clothing trade's highly competitive atmosphere, many contractors had little regard for the hours, wages, or working conditions of their workers; as a result, the term *sweatshop* entered the business lexicon toward the end of the nineteenth century. It was an extension of the earlier terms *sweating* and *sweater*, which had been used since at least the middle of the century to describe the determined efforts of contractors to minimize costs and squeeze the last ounce of productivity from workers. In subsequent years, the term *sweatshop* has been used to describe any workplace with long hours or substandard conditions, but in the late nineteenth century, it more specifically referred to an immigrant workroom— usually the shop of a contractor—that was characterized by overcrowding, poor lighting, unsanitary conditions, extremely long hours, and low pay. A New York factory inspector in 1887 claimed that virtually all garment workers in the city's outside shops labored under such conditions.

Some historians have noted how the condemnation of sweatshops by reformers in the late 1800s and early 1900s seemed to incorporate not only concern for the workers but also ethnic prejudice, anti-immigrant bias, and a determination to perpetuate U.S. middle-class standards for the proper role of women, home, and domesticity. There can be no doubt that many workers were exploited, however. Workweeks of eighty hours or more were not unusual, and the contractor had every incentive and inclination to lower piece rates but no incentive at all to spend money on additional space, light, heat, or sanitation.

One consequence of these work conditions was the growth of unions and labor conflict. A government report just after the turn of the century noted, "It is a saying on the East Side that there is always a strike going on somewhere." As with all aspects of the garment trade, the men's and women's sectors developed separately. The major union for the menswear industry was the Amalgamated Clothing Workers of America (ACWA). Formed in 1914, in its early years the union was more than willing to use strikes to pressure manufacturers. The union grew to 170,000 members by 1920, and in the five years between 1919 and 1923, it was involved in an average of about ninety strikes or lockouts each year, many of which won concessions for workers. The key labor organization on the women's side was the International Ladies' Garment Workers' Union (ILGWU), which was formed

Two women tailors on the picket line during the walkout of shirtwaist workers known as the "Uprising of 20,000," New York, 1910. Library of Congress Prints and Photographs Division, George Grantham Bain Collection cph 3a49619.

in 1900. In 1909 and 1910, the ILGWU organized a New York City walkout of shirtwaist workers known as the "Uprising of 20,000." The strikers were only minimally successful, but their efforts paved the way for the "Great Revolt" in the summer of 1910, when up to sixty thousand cloak makers went on strike, eventually negotiating a contract that called for a fifty-hour workweek, an end to homework, and a grievance procedure for worker complaints. This agreement did not survive an economic recession in 1913–1914, when manufacturers used the contracting system to evade its requirements. The ILGWU continued to grow, however, and by 1918 it had 130,000 members.

DEVELOPMENTS THROUGH THE MID-TWENTIETH CENTURY

Overall, the U.S. apparel industry charted a course of growth and prosperity from the mid-1910s through the 1960s, although along the way it was subject to the fluctuations that most U.S. businesses experienced during a period that included the most serious depression in the nation's history sandwiched between two major wars. By the end of this period, both employment and wages in the clothing trade had been rising for years, and apparel manufacture loomed large on the U.S. industrial landscape. In 1960, far more people in the United States were employed making clothing than were making cars, airplanes, steel, furniture, electronics, or just about any other manufactured goods, including textiles. Several significant trends emerged during this time that reflected on long-term prospects for the industry, however.

First, labor unions became a fact of life, at least in those segments of the industry located in its traditional urban centers. Through the 1920s and 1930s, under the skillful and pragmatic leadership of Sidney Hillman, the ACWA continued to grow, becoming a truly national union while forging solid working relationships with major manufacturers. Meanwhile, the ILGWU nearly self-destructed in the 1920s amid bitter infighting provoked by an attempt of Communist members to take over the union. By the time the Communists withdrew, ILGWU membership had fallen from a high of 130,000 to 40,000. Under new leadership in the 1930s, when David Dubinsky became union president, the ILGWU was able to take advantage of the labor-friendly policies of President Franklin Roosevelt's New Deal to restore its influence. In just two years in the early 1930s, ILGWU membership shot up to 200,000, and it remained a force to be reckoned with in ensuing years. In the major urban areas, and particularly

Woman carrying bundle of clothing to be worked on at home, near Astor Place, New York, 1912. Once the allocated task was finished, the bundle would be retied and passed on to the next worker. Library of Congress, Prints & Photographs Division, National Child Labor Committee Collection, LC-USZ62-26831.

in New York—still by far the largest and most important site of clothing production in the country—many manufacturers were willing to accept union shops because they brought some relief from the cutthroat competition and turbulent labor market that had tended to characterize the industry.

In direct reaction to the growth of unions, however, came increasing dispersal of production facilities away from urban centers—and away from union wage scales. As early as 1922, the ILGWU had identified 270 "runaway" shops that had located in rural New York, Connecticut, New Jersey, and Pennsylvania and employed nonunion workers. Though unionization may have prompted this dispersion, the tendency also reflected characteristics the industry had exhibited from its birth, when its dependence on cheap labor, portable technology, and tight profit margins encouraged decentralized production and extreme cost cutting. The attributes that created the fragmented and fluid production environment of urban garment districts also generated momentum for more far-ranging geographical dispersion. From the earliest days, manufacturers often centralized crucial operations, such as design or cutting, while dispersing other, more labor-intensive parts of production; this technique proved adaptable on a larger geographical scale as well. By the 1930s, for example, only cutting operations of major men's shirt manufacturers remained in New York City, while the sewing rooms had all been moved to neighboring states. The search for low-cost labor became a major trend in the industry, beginning with movement out of the urban centers to neighboring states in the 1920s and 1930s, continuing with a shift to southern and western states in the 1950s through the 1970s, and culminating with the globalization of the industry from the 1980s onward.

Southern factories were often located in rural areas and made more standardized apparel lines, such as blue jeans or underwear. These were products where large production facilities and long production runs made sense, and access to highly skilled workers or the latest design information was less important. By the early 1970s, the South had 18 percent of the apparel production facilities and more than 35 percent of apparel workers. The tide had already begun to shift, however, and through that decade an accelerating number of companies began to bypass or leave the South in favor of even less industrialized locations—with accompanying lower wage scales—in the West.

Particularly noteworthy with regard to diffusion of the apparel industry was the rise of Los Angeles as a garment center to rival New York. Los Angeles's assets were in some ways similar to New York's: It was a focal point for dissemination of fashion trends (thanks to its proximity to the entertainment industry), and it experienced a continuing influx of immigrant workers, in this case from Latin America. As Los Angeles's garment industry was gaining momentum, more and more manufacturers were relocating away from New York and its relatively high cost of doing business. By the end of the 1980s, Los Angles had surpassed New York in the size of its apparel workforce.

The basic organization of clothing manufacture remained remarkably stable, although some new wrinkles were tried. Since the beginning of large-scale production, most clothing makers had used the *bundle system*. In this system, cut-up pieces for several garments would be tied up in a bundle and distributed to a worker who performed one key task on its contents—making collars or pockets, for example—then retied the bundle and passed it to the next worker, who performed another task, and so on.

The system allowed for specialization and subdivided work, but considerable production time was lost in handling the bundles. In the early 1930s, an approach called the *straight-line system* was developed. In this system, a factory would be set up like an assembly line, with each garment moving one at a time from worker to worker, each of whom performed his or her specialty operation. This approach reduced handling so that more of the workers' time was spent actually sewing, and it was very efficient when all stations on the line worked smoothly. However, a slowdown or breakdown by one machine or operator could paralyze the whole line, and because of the difficulties in balancing and maintaining workflow along the line, the system was never adopted by a majority of manufacturers. Most shifted to a method known as the *progressive bundle system*, a variation on the traditional bundle system in which work stations on the factory floor were laid out to minimize handling time between operators and individual tasks were subdivided and monitored to the closest possible extent in order to speed production.

LATE TWENTIETH CENTURY RETAIL REVOLUTION

In the mid-1980s, the apparel industry retained many of its historic characteristics. It was still dominated by small firms; in 1986, 58 percent of all apparel manufacturing firms employed fewer than twenty people. Apparel producers were still divided, as they had been a century before, among manufacturers, contractors, and jobbers, and the market remained fiercely competitive. Apparel production occurred in most states, but 60 percent was in either the old-line manufacturing states of New York, Pennsylvania, and New Jersey, or in California. Output continued to grow, and employment stayed strong, with more than one million workers employed in the industry. As late as 1988, department stores were still the largest single category of clothing retailers in the country.

Several trends that would reshape the industry were already becoming apparent, however. The rise and popularity of sportswear for men and women, including the celebrated "jeaning of America" in the 1960s, gave more standardized garments a larger share of the market. The growth of these categories made larger operations and dispersal of production away from fashion centers more feasible. Even larger firms often continued to rely on a dense network of contracting and subcontracting relationships among smaller shops, however. And while the rise of less formal styles sometimes increased standardization, as with jeans, it sometimes multiplied stylistic variation, as with men's dress shirts. In 1962, 72 percent of all men's dress shirts were of the plain white variety; by 1986, that had decreased to 21 percent, to be replaced by a plethora of stripes, patterns, and other colors. In fact, if one considers every size, color, and stylistic variation available in stores, the diversity and number of clothing products exploded in the last quarter of the twentieth century, creating more pressure for short production cycles and rapid adjustments. These tendencies sustained the tough competitive atmosphere and need for flexibility that had always characterized the clothing trade.

Even more pressure was placed upon manufacturers by the consolidation or elimination of many department stores and the rising market domination of mass retailers. From 1988 to 1999, the percentage of apparel sales controlled by department stores shrank from 25.3 to 18.7 percent, while the percentage controlled by discounters rose from 18.7 to 30 percent. The competitive nature of the industry had historically given retailers leverage over manufacturers. The rise of discounters exerted downward pressure on prices that further increased competition, and the immense size of the survivors of this retail shakeout gave them even more power over their suppliers. In 2005, one of the largest clothing manufacturers in the country, V. F. Corp., did about one-sixth of its business with a single customer: Wal-Mart.

Advances in information technology, chiefly bar code scanners and computerized data exchange, further transformed the trade. The day of the semiautonomous retail buyer, who regulated the store's inventory based on his or her feel for the market and judgment of coming fashion trends, was over. Retailers instead collected real-time data on consumer purchases and based buying decisions on that. They adopted just-in-time replenishment standards, cutting their costs for maintaining large inventories and reducing losses from both overstocked or sold-out items. The largest retailers also began to bypass wholesalers and to contract on their own for garments manufactured to their specifications or under their own private labels. In some ways, they were replicating the earliest phases of the industry, when retailers like Daniel Devlin and the Brooks Brothers expanded into manufacturing to supply their own needs.

Retailers began to insist that manufacturers use similar information technology and integrate it with their own systems, as well as adopt uniform standards for sales data, labeling of goods, and methods of material handling. They stepped up the pressure for lower prices and rapid replenishment of stock, often stipulating that goods be delivered already labeled and ready to display. Department stores once placed orders three or four times a year. By the 1990s, large retail chains examined sales data every weekend and placed a new order on Monday, typically requiring that it be filled within a week.

Manufacturers upgraded their technology where they could. They incorporated bar codes and electronic data exchange to schedule and track production. The introduction of automatic cutting machines made it possible to cut increasingly thick layers of fabric accurately. Computer-assisted techniques streamlined the design process and enhanced marker making (the process by which a pattern is laid out on the fabric so it can be cut with the least waste). Virtually all the technological gains were in the pre-assembly phase, however. The limp quality of cloth and the need for regular stylistic changes continued to make sewing operations difficult to automate. By most manufacturing standards, the garment industry remained highly labor intensive.

Clothing makers also experimented with new ways to organize production. In the bundle system, after each operation was completed, bundles were placed in a buffer to await the next step. This approach minimized downtime because operators never had to wait for the next set of work to arrive. It was therefore efficient from the standpoint of overall production, but it lengthened the time for a single item to move from start to finish because a large number of garments were always in pieces on the shop

Garment factory in Zhejiang Province, People's Republic of China. By 2005, China was the largest supplier of imported clothes to the United States. Getty Images.

floor. To offset this, some manufacturers tried a *modular production system*, in which a team of operators was assigned to complete a set of tasks or to produce entire garments. The approach moved individual garments through the production process more quickly. Team members were cross-trained so they could adjust for quicker completion and perhaps avoid the psychological and physical toll that intensely repetitive work produced. On the other hand, worker turnover, absenteeism, or a weak link in the production unit could limit a whole team's output. Other factories used the *unit production system*, a high-tech version of the straight-line approach in which each garment moved down a computer-controlled overhead transport system toward completion. Though computerization made the system more precise, its advantages were still often outweighed by problems balancing work along the line. While some factories had success with these systems and pressures to streamline the production process might prompt further efforts in this area, a 2004 report by the World Trade Organization indicated that the progressive bundle system remained the industry standard.

In another move to protect interests, large manufacturers began to establish multiple brands and target them for different price points, market segments, or types of retailers. For example, although Liz Claiborne's initial success in the 1970s was driven by clothing with the corporate name on the label, by the 2000s the company sold clothing under forty different brand names and expanded its reach by licensing the brands to other companies for products ranging from footwear to wristwatches.

THE GLOBALIZATION OF THE APPAREL INDUSTRY

Without doubt, the most important trend affecting the garment industry in the late twentieth and early twenty-first centuries was globalization. Apparel production within the borders of the United States plummeted, especially after the mid-1990s, while U.S.-owned manufacturers prospered, mostly according to their success in building supplier networks around the world. Manufacturers in the United States had little competition from other countries until the 1950s, when imports of inexpensive cotton blouses from Japan began to raise concerns among domestic producers. Despite attempts at restricting trade from then onward, the value of imported garments in the United States grew from just over US$300 million in 1962 to just over US$80 billion in 2005, by which time more than 90 percent of the garments purchased in the United States were imported.

Concerted attempts to limit apparel imports began in 1957, when the U.S. government pressed Japan to accept voluntary limits on exports. In a pattern to be repeated many times over, attempts to restrict the imports from one country merely spread them to others, in this case to Hong Kong, Taiwan, and South Korea. The Long Term Arrangement of 1962 and its successor, the Multifiber Arrangement (MFA) of 1974, were multinational attempts to address the issue. The MFA created a framework for bilateral agreements among participating countries, but although the United States negotiated import quotas with many countries, they had limited effect. Quotas were not set low enough to prevent increased market penetration by foreign producers, and they were often evaded by slightly modifying garments so they did not fit the agreement's exact specifications or by shifting production to a third country that had more room under the quota system.

In addition, U.S. authorities were unwilling or unable to enforce the quotas consistently. From 1984 to 1988, imports from countries with which the United States had MFA agreements grew by an average of 20 percent a year, even though quotas theoretically restricted them to an annual increase of no more than 6 percent.

By the 1980s, free trade advocates had gained ascendance among U.S. policymakers, and the government began to promote agreements that increased trade rather than restricted it. The *Caribbean Basin Initiative* in 1982 gave special access to countries of that region, and a special exception further loosened rules for Mexico in 1988. The *North American Free Trade Agreement* (NAFTA) of 1994 virtually eliminated trade barriers between the United States, Mexico, and Canada. The next year, negotiations among more than one hundred governments created the World Trade Organization (WTO), an entity designed to promote unrestricted trade and adjudicate trade disputes between countries. The talks that produced the WTO also terminated the MFA in favor of an agreement that called for the elimination of all clothing tariffs and quotas by 2005.

Apparel imports in the United States more than doubled in the years after NAFTA and the WTO, growing from US$36.9 billion in 1994 to US$80.1 billion in 2005. The largest supplier of imported clothes to the United States at the end of this period was the People's Republic of China, which industry officials predicted would ultimately produce 80 percent of the clothing sold in the United States. The next largest suppliers were Mexico, Hong Kong, India, and Indonesia, in that order, but the United States imported at least US$1 billion in apparel from eighteen additional countries (plus the European Union) as well.

The clothing industry was particularly attractive to newly industrializing countries because of the same characteristics that had shaped its development for the previous two centuries: It was labor intensive but did not require an educated or highly skilled workforce, it required little technology and had low startup costs, and its raw materials were readily available. The circumstances that had produced the proliferation of small shops and contracting arrangements in the United States during the waning years of the nineteenth century made the industry a natural starting point for other countries seeking a path to industrialization in the late twentieth century. Domestic producers viewed this as unfair competition because wage levels were far lower in most developing countries, where workplaces were largely unregulated and unions were often unknown. In early debates over trade regulations, U.S. labor organizations and most manufacturers fought to limit imports. Retailers, on the other hand, favored imports because they resulted in lower-cost goods. As retailers gained clout in the industry—along with the willingness and ability to contract directly with foreign suppliers if they wished—and as the creation of NAFTA and the WTO seemed to eliminate any hope of legal protection for domestically produced garments, manufacturers began to support the elimination of quotas and globalize their own production to cut costs.

The result was a new version of the runaway shop—the ultimate extension of the pattern of dispersion the industry had contended with almost since its inception. Using a tried-and-true organizational structure, many companies retained key operations in corporate offices in the United States and used contractors for the rest of work. Liz Claiborne, one of the earliest and most successful upmarket adopters of this strategy, continued planning, designing, and marketing in New York but by the 1990s was producing goods in forty different countries entirely through contractors, spreading the work among more than 250 firms.

Through the end of the twentieth century, the garment industry hung on in major U.S. cities by reinventing itself along familiar historic lines: as a swarm of tiny contract shops with distinctive ethnic character. In both Los Angeles and New York, thousands of workers were employed in shops that perhaps averaged thirty to forty employees each. In both cities, the owners of these firms were most often Asian, typically Korean, and the operators were mostly Hispanic. New York also had a thriving garment district in Chinatown, where native-born and immigrant Chinese Americans served as owners and operators, capitalizing on the ethnic and cultural ties in much the same way the East European Jews had done a century before. For small production runs, perhaps to test a new product or supplement an order for an item that sold unexpectedly well, the planning and time involved in overseas production was not worth the effort to clothing merchandisers, and nearby shops' ability to make changes, produce small batches, and deliver quickly earned them a market niche.

Another vestige of the past that reemerged was the sweatshop. Some researchers questioned whether publicity about this issue exaggerated the extent that sweatshop labor increased in the latter part of the century. Others, however, took the opposite position, claiming that the uproar actually downplayed the persistence of sweatshop labor throughout history. The most widely held view, however, is that by the 1960s, the phenomenon of the sweatshop had been pushed to margins of the industry, only to reemerge with renewed vigor from the 1980s forward. There were numerous well-documented examples that closely fit the definitions that had been in use a century before—immigrant workers in cramped quarters working long hours for low pay in unsanitary, unpleasant conditions. After a couple of particularly dramatic examples made headlines in the 1990s, President Bill Clinton formed a task force that created a code of conduct signed by many leading manufacturers in 1998. Skeptics argued that the code was flawed by its voluntary nature and by an approach that did little to hold manufacturers accountable for the actions of their suppliers, but it showed the depth of public concern that sweatshops once again were creating.

Unions responded in this period with antisweatshop drives that increased attention to the issue, both within and outside the United States. However, their ability directly to affect activity in the workplace was sorely limited by their dwindling numbers and the movement of jobs overseas. In 1995, the successor union of the ACWA merged with the ILGWU to form the Union of Needle-trade Industrial and Textile Employees (UNITE). In 2004, with membership down to 180,000 (about half of what it had been ten years before), UNITE joined with the Hotel Employees and Restaurant Employees International Union to create UNITE HERE, and the new union has continued its agitation against sweatshops while attempting to gain new members from service industries. From the standpoint of employment, the adoption of

Shopping for clothes on the Internet: From the late twentieth century onward, U.S. clothing retailers were generating increasing online sales. Freudenthal Verhagen/Getty.

NAFTA and the WTO in the mid-1990s sent the domestic industry on a downward spiral from which there is little prospect of recovery. By 2005, the U.S. Department of Commerce reported only 260,000 people remained in the trade, a huge drop from its peak of 1.4 million in the early 1970s. Even the immigrant-run contract shops in New York and Los Angeles suffered steep declines as their clients diverted production to other countries.

In terms of clothing consumption, however, the market continued to grow. To meet these demands, U.S. apparel companies faced the continued need to balance their business among multiple worldwide suppliers, multiple brands, and multiple channels of distribution. There was no sign that the historic requirements for flexibility and sensitivity to the marketplace would diminish or that the distribution of work among many subcontractors would fall out of favor. For retailers, one important challenge was the need to integrate Internet shopping into their sales mix. Although some had questioned whether consumers would buy clothing when they could not touch the goods or try them, the convenience and ubiquity of online shopping made it inevitable that clothing sales in this area would grow. By offering generous return policies and attempting to develop online options such as the "virtual dressing room" (in which a customer can view a selected garment as it would appear on a computer image of themselves), clothing retailers generated increasing Internet sales, which were projected to pass US$20 billion in 2007.

Everlasting change has combined with notable continuities to characterize the garment industry in the United States throughout its history; as the clothing trade moves deeper into the twenty-first century, there is no sign that this dynamic will not continue to define the clothing trade of the future.

References and Further Reading

Abernathy, Frederick K., John T. Dunlop, Janice H. Hammond, and David Weil. *A Stitch in Time: Lean Retailing and the Transformation of Manufacturing—Lessons from the Apparel and Textile Industries*. New York: Oxford University Press, 1999.

Bender, Daniel E., and Richard Greenwald, eds. *Sweatshop USA: The American Sweatshop in Historical and Global Perspective*. New York: Routledge, 2003.

Bonacich, Edna, Lucie Cheng, Norma Chinchilla, Nora Hamilton, and Paul Ong. *Global Production: The Apparel Industry in the Pacific Rim*. Philadelphia: Temple University Press, 1994.

Chin, Margaret. *Sewing Women: Immigrants and the New York City Garment Industry*. New York: Columbia University Press, 2002.

Cobrin, Harry A. *The Men's Clothing Industry: Colonial through Modern Times*. New York: Fairchild Publications, 1970.

Dickerson, Kitty G. *Textiles and Apparel in the Global Economy*. 3rd ed. Upper Saddle River, NJ: Prentice-Hall, 1999.

Fraser, Stephen. "Combined and Uneven Development in the Men's Clothing Industry." *Business History Review* 57, no. 4 (Winter, 1983): 522–547.

Gereffi, Gary, David Spencer, and Jennifer Bair. *Free Trade and Uneven Development: The North American Apparel Industry after NAFTA*. Philadelphia: Temple University Press, 2002.

Green, Nancy. *Ready to Wear and Ready to Work: A Century of Industry and Immigrants in Paris and New York*. Durham, NC: Duke University Press, 1997.

Jensen, Joan M., and Sue Davidson, eds. *A Needle, a Bobbin, a Strike: Women Needleworkers in America*. Philadelphia: Temple University Press, 1984.

Kidwell, Claudia B., and Margaret C. Christman. *Suiting Everyone: The Democratization of Clothing in America*. Washington, DC: Smithsonian Institution Press, 1974.

Kunz, Grace I., and Myrna B. Garner. *Going Global: The Textile and Apparel Industry*. New York: Fairchild Publications, 2007.

Levine, Louis [pseud. Louis Lorwin]. *The Women's Garment Workers: A History of the International Ladies' Garment Workers' Union*. New York: Arno Press, 1969. (Originally published 1924.)

Nordås, Hildegunn Kyvik. *The Global Textile and Clothing Industry post the Agreement on Textiles and Clothing*. Geneva: WTO Publications, 2004.

Pope, Jesse Eliphalet. *The Clothing Industry in New York*. Columbia: University of Missouri, 1905.

Rosen, Ellen Israel. *Making Sweatshops: The Globalization of the U.S. Apparel Industry*. Berkeley: University of California Press, 2002.

Schorman, Rob. *Selling Style: Clothing and Social Change at the Turn of the Century*. Philadelphia: University of Pennsylvania Press, 2003.

Zakim, Michael. *Ready-Made Democracy: A History of Man's Dress in the American Republic, 1760–1860*. Chicago: University of Chicago Press, 2003.

Zarantz, Charles Elbert. *The Amalgamated Clothing Workers of America: A Study in Progressive Trades-Unionism*. New York: Ancon Publishing, 1934.

Rob Schorman

See also Textile and Apparel Industries at the Turn of the Millennium.

Fashion Designers, Seamstresses, and Tailors

Throughout the nineteenth century, North American fashion followed the dictates of French design. American dressmakers and tailors looked to Paris for the newest silhouettes and adapted them to the American lifestyle. It was not until the 1930s that independent fashion designers emerged and rejected the idea that all fashion must be inspired by Paris. These early designers created a unique "American look" that was predicated on comfort. This design tended to be more casual, with an air of sophistication and elegance. Moreover, these designers strove to create democratic fashion—good design for the masses at an affordable price. This approach of combining comfort and elegance defined North American fashion design in the twentieth century.

THE NORTH AMERICAN TAILOR

Prior to the Industrial Revolution and the rise of ready-made clothing, both men's and women's garments were custom made. Serving the male community, tailors were skilled artisans. Their talents lay in careful measuring, cutting, and fitting of the fabric perfectly to each individual body. These unique garments were difficult to construct and, therefore, costly.

By the 1830s, however, there was a great demand for fashionable men's clothing that was available to all rather than the wealthy few who could afford the tailor's custom services. Capitalizing on this potential expanding market, tailors began to modify their traditional techniques and create standard measuring methods. These proportionally standardized drafting systems resulted in garments that fit a wider variety of body types. In this manner, nineteenth-century tailors essentially spearheaded the ready-to-wear industry and the democratization of clothing, which would become a dominant theme in North American fashion design.

To increase their economic savings, tailors also began to contract out certain tasks. Every nineteenth-century young girl was taught basic sewing skills, and soon thousands of lower-class women were accepting piecework for pay. Women, the cheapest labor force available, were employed to sew straight seams and attach buttons. Considered unskilled laborers, seamstresses worked at home and were paid pennies for each completed piece.

Once labor- and cost-saving methods were in place for tailored men's clothing, the variety in styles, fabrics, and types of jackets, coats, shirts, and trousers proliferated, albeit within a narrow range. Certainly prior to midcentury, the ubiquitous black suit could be seen on almost every male—a style that essentially would not change until the 1920s. This boon in ready-made clothing for men, however, did not apply to women's garments, which were far more complex and changed form frequently. It was not until the turn of the twentieth century that ready-to-wear garments became commonplace for women. While custom tailors continued to serve upper-class gentlemen who could afford their services, women, regardless of their social standing, were required to patronize dressmakers throughout the nineteenth century for their fashionable wardrobes.

THE NORTH AMERICAN DRESSMAKER

In the early years of the nineteenth century, it was perfectly acceptable for young unmarried women to work and contribute economically to the family household. Once married, however, society demanded that women's concerns involved household management and childcare exclusively. Working outside the home was considered vulgar and undignified. In general, only lower- or middle-class women who had no income or male economic support system found themselves in the unfortunate position of having to earn a living.

Most suitable work for women related to their traditional domestic and caretaking roles. Teaching, nursing, housecleaning, and sewing were among the few appropriate choices. Dressmaking and working as a seamstress figured prominently in these women's lives. In addition to piecework, seamstresses were in constant demand by middle- and upper-class women who continually required the production of household linens, unfitted clothing items, alterations, and repairs on existing garments. These tasks required little design knowledge but much tedious handwork. Seamstresses were often contracted either to perform the work in their own home or to live in the client's household for a number of weeks to complete the required tasks.

While seamstresses were poorly paid, dressmakers were highly regarded. They were often able to advance significantly, both economically and socially. Acquiring their skills through apprenticeships, dressmaking schools, or simple natural ability, dressmakers not only manufactured but also designed clothing. Their highly valued skills included an astute knowledge of fashionable styles, the ability to design flattering garments for clients, and, as women's dress styles became increasingly complex throughout the nineteenth century, providing a perfect custom fit.

Custom dressmaking as a trade provided women with employment that spanned the gap between traditional women's work and the undesirable workplace. Many dressmakers were widows or unmarried women who utilized the only skill they had, sewing. It was not uncommon for dressmakers to work in family groups. Mothers, daughters, sisters, and extended family members often participated in home-based dressmaking businesses. As a group, they enjoyed joint economic success.

Dressmakers who had a superior eye for design and were technical experts in terms of custom fitting were particularly successful. These women were viewed by their clients as artists and generated a local, if not regional, reputation. Some individuals

Dress and slip, 1935, silk, by U.S. designer Elizabeth Hawes. Cincinnati Art Museum, Given in memory of Julius Fleischmann by Dorette Kruse Fleischmann. Accession # 1991.210a, b. http://www.cincinnatiartmuseum.com

were successful enough to employ a workforce of seamstresses who, in time, might establish their own dressmaking businesses. Overall, dressmaking proved to be both a profitable and socially acceptable occupation for women.

THE DEMISE OF THE DRESSMAKER AND THE RISE OF READY-TO-WEAR

The custom dressmaker thrived throughout the nineteenth and early twentieth centuries. Thousands of women across the United States in every city and small town made their living by dressmaking. Maintaining a fashionable wardrobe was highly important to women. Even those who lived outside of major metropolitan areas desired fashionable gowns, and dressmakers profited accordingly. By the third and fourth quarters of the nineteenth century, however, the rise of the department store began to impinge on the success of independent dressmakers. Department store owners recognized the possibilities of developing custom dressmaking salons in their stores. Already providing all the necessary elements for a complete ensemble under one roof—fabric,

trims, undergarments, and accessories—offering dressmaking as a service made these stores even more convenient for the consumer. Dressmakers' clientele began to patronize the highly accessible and less costly custom salons in department stores. Many independent dressmakers and their seamstresses abandoned their own businesses for work in these salons, finding the assurance of a steady wage and better working conditions exceedingly attractive.

In the second decade of the twentieth century, as fashionable styles began to simplify, ready-to-wear clothing for women became more available. Department stores quickly increased their inventory. Small-scale specialty women's clothing shops provided the convenience of ready-to-wear, custom dressmaking, French imported designs, and custom alterations under one roof. By 1920, independent custom dressmaking shops had declined almost to extinction in most urban areas.

THE PIONEERS OF FASHION DESIGN IN THE UNITED STATES

Throughout the nineteenth century, fashionable design in North America was dictated by Parisian couturiers. While upper-class women were able to travel to Paris to be outfitted by the couturier of their choice, most women relied on their local dressmaker to provide them with fashionable clothing. Dressmakers watched carefully for the new silhouettes that emanated from France and were illustrated in women's and fashion magazines. They altered the styling of their offerings, adapting it to local tastes to satisfy both lifestyle and regional differences. Those dressmakers were able to offer the most up-to-date French fashions that were patronized most ardently. By the 1920s, garment manufacturers were creating both licensed and illegal copies of French designs that they produced in the United States at much lower costs in an effort to satisfy North American women's insatiable desire for French design.

It was not until the late 1920s and early 1930s that fashion designers began to emerge in the United States and create styles specifically suited to women without heeding French influence. Many of these early pioneers were women, and they defined what came to be called the American look. From these beginnings, Canadian newspapers and magazines that discussed fashion gave regular coverage to designs shown in New York; as a result, when designers began to be identified by name, they became familiar to Canadians, especially during World War II when there was a hiatus in European imports. By the late 1900s well-known designers based in the United States often were represented in retail outlets in both the United States and Canada.

In 1918, Austrian-born Hattie Carnegie (1889–1956) opened her custom dressmaking salon in New York. While Carnegie is generally considered the first North American designer, she was not an innovator. She imported French models from the major couturiers, including Lanvin, Vionnet, Molyneaux, Chanel, Patou, and Schiaparelli. She offered copies of these imports, and she sold ready-to-wear as well as custom adaptations of French designs. Overall, Carnegie is known for her talent of refining Parisian couture to fit the lifestyle of consumers in the United States.

The first true North American couturier, however, was Elizabeth Hawes (1903–1971), who opened her salon in New York City in 1928. Previously, she had worked in Paris as a copyist, a fashion

Coat and purse, 1966, leather and fur, by U.S. designer Bonnie Cashin. Cincinnati Art Museum, Gift of Stewart Shillito Maxwell Jr. in memory of his mother, Marilyn M. Maxwell. Accession # 2001.169a-b. http://www.cincinnatiartmuseum.com

editor, and for Parisian designer Nicole Groult. Hawes's time in Paris only served to disenchant her with the French fashion industry, and she returned to New York confident that she could create original designs for women in the United States.

Hawes's first collection in 1928 was not the expected shapeless flapper look that was popular in the 1920s. Instead, Hawes created dresses with Empire waists that hugged the body and had flowing skirts to the floor. Weathering even the Great Depression, her salon was successful through the 1930s, and she was patronized by celebrities including Katharine Hepburn, Ingrid Bergman, and Gladys Swarthout. Until she closed her house in 1940, Hawes focused on style rather than fashion. Her classic designs were cut on the bias, fitted to the bust, full over the hips, made to be worn without undergarments, comfortable, and beautiful without overwrought embellishments.

Even while she created couture garments, Hawes was interested in the democracy of clothing and good design for the masses. In the early 1930s, she contracted with several Seventh Avenue manufacturers in an attempt to make affordable but well-designed dresses and accessories. Throughout her career, she envisioned a revolution in clothing design. She advocated trousers for women and skirts for men. She hypothesized that future clothes would be produced chemically in molds and that garments would be cheap and disposable, eliminating the need for doing laundry. Prophetically, she envisioned unisex jumpsuits and clothing that would be designed by artists or the wearers themselves. Many of her ideas were not realized until decades later.

In the 1930s and 1940s, Hollywood also exerted great influence over American fashion. The social and cultural dilemmas of the Great Depression and World War II were managed in part by escaping before the silver screen. Gilbert Adrian (1903–1959), Travis Banton (1894–1958), Irene Lentz Gibbons (1907–1962), Howard Greer (1886–1964), and Edith Head (1907–1981) were the major designers for Hollywood film studios. Women across North America idolized film stars and the clothing they wore. Designing for Hollywood starlets both on and off the screen, these individuals opened their own salons; they were highly successful even though their collections were often dismissed by fashion critics as Hollywood fluff.

ESTABLISHMENT OF THE "AMERICAN LOOK"

Up to this point, North American designers struggled to market their work to a clientele that still idealized French design. This obsession was frustrated during World War II, when North America was cut off from French inspiration. This absence of Parisian influence fostered the growth of purely local design and weaned both designers and consumers from their dependence on Paris.

Women have figured largely in the development of this American look, perhaps because it was they who had been forced to wear clothing that was neither comfortable nor suitable to their lifestyle. Claire McCardell (1905–1958) has been credited with playing a major role in the growth of ready-to-wear in the United States and for helping to define the American look. The philosophy behind her designs was to create garments that were comfortable, practical, and feminine. Utilizing wartime restrictions on fabrics as inspiration, she designed simple inexpensive sportswear and casual ensembles.

Bonnie Cashin (1915–2000) is another early innovative designer and perhaps the most well known. Cashin's beginnings were in theater and dance in the 1930s and 1940s. With this background, it is not surprising that her mature designs were focused on functionality and accommodated the lifestyle of the active woman. Cashin created wardrobes with multiple separates and coordinated accessories. Using the concept of layering, they fit any climate or time of day.

An independent thinker, Cashin rejected the glamour and fitted silhouette popular in the 1950s. She was influenced greatly by her world travels, and many of her designs were based on the simple rectangular and square shapes of ethnic clothing with minimal fit. She pioneered layered dressing and produced garments that were multipurpose and casual yet provided the consumer with a stylish individuality. Coats, ponchos, and capes were paired with jumpsuits, full skirts, and knitted dresses and blouses. These garments were outfitted with roomy pockets that served as substitutes for handbags and funnel-knitted turtlenecks that doubled as hoods. Knits, canvas, tweed wools, and leather were her favorite fabrics. Her signature embellishments were edges bound with leather or suede and metal toggle fasteners instead of zippers or buttons.

THE NEXT GENERATION OF FASHION DESIGNERS IN THE UNITED STATES

It was these early female designers who established and defined the American look. While their innovative designs were primarily based on comfort, ease of movement, and functionality, the next generation of American designers would provide women with elegance and sophistication as well as practicality.

One of the truly outstanding fashion designers of the 1950s was Charles James (1906–1978), who stands alone in terms of style and philosophy. Three of the most accomplished designers of the twentieth century, Paul Poiret, Cristobal Balenciaga, and Christian Dior, collectively acknowledged James as the greatest North American couturier and the individual who raised fashion design from an applied art to a pure art form. Born of Anglo-American parentage, Charles James spent most of his adult life crisscrossing the Atlantic, restlessly studying and designing. In 1939, he settled in New York long enough to establish Charles James, Inc. He continued to operate in both New York and London until his retirement in 1958.

James created garments that were sculptures. He used the female body as an armature on which to build three-dimensional forms. James was not interested in designing collections or multiples. He worked and reworked designs for decades as his concepts evolved.

James was a perfectionist who was obsessed with construction details. When designing a gown, he considered weight distribution, balance, proportion, line, and color. His purest designs were worked solely in black and white. While he did design day wear, he is best known for his sculptural yet elegant evening gowns.

James seems to have been an aberration in North American design in the period. He was a pure artist who produced clothing that conformed to his own ideas. He was more akin to his Parisian counterparts than other designers based in New York. Just as James retired, however, the next generation of designers rejected the extreme structure of James's garments and embraced new materials, new concepts, and the modern lifestyle of the 1960s and 1970s. These individuals included Rudi Gernreich and Norman Norell.

Rudi Gernreich (1922–1985) immigrated to the United States in 1938 from his native Austria and settled in Los Angeles. From 1942 to 1948, he performed with the Lester Horton Dance Company. This experience greatly influenced his clothing designs, which were body conscious and allowed for unimpeded movement. He was destined to become one of the most revolutionary designers of the twentieth century.

Most remembered for his 1964 topless bathing suit, Gernreich was interested in complete functionalism, which translated into clothing that was totally unstructured. His early swimwear designs eliminated the traditional boning that shaped and supported the bust. He designed knitted swimwear that naturally molded to the body and was soon designing dresses in the same manner.

Comfortable, body-hugging knits were Gernreich's fabric of choice. Designing for Harmon Knitwear in the 1960s, he produced collections knitted in geometric patterns and bright colors. He mixed stripes with checks and dots, lime green with orange and hot pink, and he used clear vinyl insets and cutouts to emphasize particular areas of the body. Realizing the earlier ideas of Elizabeth Hawes, Gernreich promoted unisex clothing such

Bulls-eye dress, 1968–1972, wool, by U.S.-based designer Rudi Gernreich. Cincinnati Art Museum, On to the Second Century Endowment. Accession # 1999.58. http://www.cincinnatiartmuseum.com

as floor-length caftans and jumpsuits. He designed the first see-through blouses; the "no-bra" bra, free of padding or structure; and the thong bathing suit.

Gernreich was a phenomenal force in fashion in the 1960s equal to French designers Andre Courrèges and Pierre Cardin. He embraced emerging materials; women's liberation; and the new, free body that defined the period. In doing so, he pushed North American fashion forward.

Existing side by side with the radicalism of Rudi Gernreich was Norman Norell (1900–1972). While Norell was not the revolutionary that Gernreich was, he did espouse some of the same ideas. Having worked for Hattie Carnegie from 1928 to 1940, Norell not only absorbed her sense of style but was also exposed to the finest in French couture.

Norell's hallmark was cleanly proportioned, expertly crafted clothing that was timeless. His contribution was a new elegance that incorporated casual elements. He paired soft sweater tops with full-length evening skirts and introduced fur-lined cloth coats embellished with sequins. He promoted masculine-inspired garments for women such as the jumpsuit and the pantsuit. Norell designed his ready-to-wear day wear in clear, bold colors punctuated with large, contrasting buttons or belts. His graceful "mermaid" evening gowns—form-fitting sheaths covered with glimmering sequins—were elegant yet simple and comfortable.

Norell's primary goal—to simplify dressing for women—was shared by three major American designers who emerged in the 1970s: Geoffrey Beene, Bill Blass, and Roy Frowick Halston. The designs of Norman Norell and Geoffrey Beene (b. 1927) have much in common. Establishing themselves about the same time, Norell in 1960 and Beene in 1962, the latter was always interested in casual chic. Working under the tutelage of Teal Traina, as did Norell, Beene emerged with the idea that women needed easy-to-wear, comfortable clothing with a touch of class. Both Norell and Beene were champions of ready-to-wear clothing.

Like Norell, Beene upset convention by using casual fabrics in his evening wear, and he frequently borrowed elements from menswear. He differed from Norell in his desire to incorporate the unexpected and humorous into his work. One of his most well-known designs is a 1967 sequined evening gown that looks like a numbered football jersey. He constructed bathing suits from sweatshirt fabric, coats from striped blankets, and paired sequined jackets with tweed slacks, all with minimal shaping. Beene is known for combining disparate fabrics and textures into one design. Lace, leather, jersey, and flannel might be mixed or matched in a single gown.

Of the same mind, Bill Blass (1922–2002) used casual fabrics for evening wear, incorporated elements of menswear, and was interested in layering—a concept pioneered by Bonnie Cashin. Blass, however, was dedicated to creating luxurious, high-priced clothing that expertly combined simplicity with glamour.

Perhaps the master of combining these same elements in ready-to-wear was Roy Frowick Halston. Early in his career, Halston (1932–1990) designed millinery for Norman Norell. Establishing Halston International in 1972, he built upon Claire McCardell's American look by reinventing casual sportswear with a touch of sophistication.

Halston was a minimalist who, like Madeleine Vionnet, frequently used the bias. He was a true genius in terms of cut; he could take a piece of fabric and, with minimal cutting and barely a seam, transform a piece of two-dimensional cloth into an exquisite gown. Like Norell, Halston embraced ready-to-wear. He designed shirtwaists in his signature washable ultrasuede that could be worn to suit the individual. The plainness of his garments for women allowed the wearers to participate in the designs by adapting them to their own style.

An overview of North American design would not be complete without mention of Pauline Trigère (1912–2002). Born in France, she arrived in New York in 1937 and established her own house in 1942. Although Trigère was interested in the same simplicity other American designers espoused, she arrived at it by means more akin to those of Balenciaga than Norell or Beene. Like Balenciaga, Trigère used intricate and inventive cut to minimize seaming. She was fond of wool and used it for everything from daytime coats to evening wear. She is noted for her classic, reversible coats and capes that often incorporated an attached scarf. Rarely utilizing elements of menswear, her clothing is unmistakably feminine.

Trigère was interested in creating timeless designs that could be worn for years. Her collections were carefully planned so that clients could mix and match elements from new collections with those from years before. Trigère outlasted most of her peers, continuing to design into her nineties.

While most North American designers were interested in casual sophistication, Canadian-born Arnold Isaacs (b. 1931), known as Scaasi, took a different tack. An apprentice to Charles James in the early 1950s, Scaasi adopted the concept of sculptural dress and, while he has dabbled in ready-to-wear, chooses to focus on couture dressmaking.

Throughout his career, Scaasi has remained dedicated to lavish, structured gowns. His clients include celebrities and stars of film, stage, and politics. Influenced by the 1950s ideal of perfectly accessorized dressing from head to toe, his designs recall a sumptuous elegance of the past. Scaasi fills a void in U.S. design that is primarily focused on the casual.

THE MODERN DESIGNER IN THE UNITED STATES

Two iconic designers of fashions for both men and women are Calvin Klein (b. 1942) and Ralph Lauren (b. 1939). Klein formed Calvin Klein Co. in 1968. A quintessential U.S. designer, Klein is all about minimal construction, comfortable fit, and mass production paired with luxury fabrics.

In 1980, he and fashion photographer Richard Avedon began an aggressive advertising campaign that used overt sexuality as a marketing tool. This was a new concept in fashion advertising and was adopted widely by other designers to sell their products. Klein also generated the branding of a multitude of products beyond his clothing lines, including underwear, fragrances, blue jeans, swimwear, hosiery, eyewear, accessories, and eventually home decor items and cosmetics. While not a new concept to the fashion industry, Klein's product lines were certainly broader than those of any previous designer.

Like Klein, Ralph Lauren has focused on classic, relaxed designs with an elegant touch for both men and women. In 1968, he formed Polo Fashions, producing expensive, classic styles for men. The same expert craftsmanship, fine fabrics, and attention to detail mark his women's collections. He is most noted for his Western wear line developed in 1979. Highly popular, this collection embodied his concepts of a mythic past for the United States that was rugged and athletic with overtones of the romantic. Lauren has also built a massive empire of products that bear his name. He and Klein expanded the idea of fashion designer's using their celebrity to brand a diverse stable of products.

Another designer who has spawned a myriad of divisions within her parent company is Donna Karan (b. 1948). Jeans, menswear, fragrances, luxury nightwear, and accessories are all designed under her Donna Karan, or DKNY, label. When Karan emerged in 1984, she skyrocketed to success by offering modern, integrated wardrobes for women. Based on a basic bodysuit, blouses, skirts, or pants of her design were interchangeable and accessorized with fashionable handbags, belts, and outerwear. It was a dream wardrobe for a busy working mother, young executive, or mature businesswoman.

Isaac Mizrahi (b. 1961) worked for Calvin Klein before forming his own house in 1987 at the age of twenty-six. Taking his cues from Klein and Lauren, Mizrahi's collections fall into the category of luxury sportswear. In 2003, however, he launched a

Dinner dress and belt, 1979, silk and leather, by U.S. designer Roy Frowick Halston. Cincinnati Art Museum, Gift of Joyce Greenberg, Accession # 1987.129a–b. http://www.cincinnatiartmuseum.com

signature line for Target, a discount retail chain. Aimed at women who cannot afford designer clothing, Mizrahi's designs for Target are modestly priced. He has reinvigorated the idea of good design for the masses.

Like their predecessors, this newest generation of U.S. designers—Lauren, Klein, Karan, Mizrahi, and others too numerous to mention—has continued to reinvent the innovations of the originators of the "American look": Elizabeth Hawes, Claire McCardell, and Bonnie Cashin. There is no doubt, in looking at the stars of U.S. fashion, that comfort and sophistication for all has been the goal from the start. There is, and always has been, an inherent democratic essence to design in the United States.

References and Further Reading

Amnéus, Cynthia. *A Separate Sphere: Dressmakers in Cincinnati's Golden Age, 1877–1922.* Lubbock: Texas Tech University Press, 2003.

Daves, Jessica. *Ready-Made Miracle: The American Story of Fashion for the Millions.* New York: G. P. Putnam's Sons, 1967.

Gamber, Wendy. *The Female Economy: The Millinery and Dressmaking Trades, 1860–1930.* Urbana and Chicago: University of Illinois Press, 1997.

Hay, Susan, ed. *From Paris to Providence: Fashion, Art, and the Tirocchi Dressmakers' Shop, 1915–1947.* Providence: Rhode Island School of Design, 2000.

Kidwell, Claudia B., and Margaret C. Christman. *Suiting Everyone: The Democratization of Clothing in America.* Washington, DC: Smithsonian Institution Press, 1974.

Lee, Sarah Tomerlin. *American Fashion: The Life and Times of Adrian, Mainbocher, McCardell, Norell, Trigére.* New York: Fashion Institute of Technology, 1975.

Martin, Richard. *American Ingenuity: Sportswear 1930s–1970s.* New York: The Metropolitan Museum of Art, 1988.

Martin, Richard, ed. *The St. James Fashion Encyclopedia: A Survey of Style from 1945 to the Present.* Detroit, MI: Visible Ink Press, 1997.

McDowell, Colin. *McDowell's Directory of Twentieth Century Fashion.* Englewood Cliffs, NJ: Prentice-Hall, 1985.

Stegemeyer, Anne. *Who's Who in Fashion.* 3rd ed. New York: Fairchild Publications, 1996.

Cynthia Amnéus

See also Evidence about Dress in the United States; Introduction to Fashion; Tradition and Fashion; The Garment Industry and Retailing in the United States.

Textile and Apparel Industries at the Turn of the Millennium

Behind the runway shows and other glitz and glamour of the fashion industry are the textile and apparel firms that churn out the garments and other textile products for U.S. consumers. These are companies that have to deal with serious realities of profit and survival in an intensely competitive environment. Just as fashions are transformed over the years with hemlines that rise and fall and silhouettes that change, the industries and companies that produce the fashions have been completely transformed as well. The turn of the millennium has seen changes in the industries themselves that have been even more dramatic than the changing whims of fashion.

The industry that led the Industrial Revolution in the United States and subsequently transformed the economic and social landscape of the country found itself metamorphosed at the turn of the millennium. Having changed in the eighteenth century how goods were produced, the early textile industry laid the groundwork that other industries followed. By the end of the twentieth century, however, global macroforces had significantly reshaped both the U.S. textile and apparel industries but in vastly different ways for the two sectors. Globalization, with its transforming technologies and communications systems, changed the apparel industry into a highly competitive global sector, but it left the U.S. textile sector in a weakened state.

Therefore, behind the glamour of today's runway are such serious matters as economics; politics and complex trade policies; concerns about profit, loss, and competition; investments in technology; and sophisticated logistics systems that deliver products from remote corners of the world. Despite the sometimes frivolous nature of fashion, these U.S. industries are part of a very large, complex, and very competitive production-distribution sector of world commerce.

For the greater part of the U.S. industry's history, the sector had a large, nearly captive domestic market. Because of the vast size of the U.S. market, the country's textile and apparel manufacturers found ready buyers for the products they made. In the 1950s and 1960s, however, changes began to affect the global environment for the textile and apparel sector. In contrast to earlier years, when a relatively limited number of countries manufactured textile and apparel products for the world markets, several nations, particularly those in East Asia, entered the scene. Many of those countries developed their textile and apparel sectors to become the primary drivers of their respective country's broader development, and U.S. firms began to feel the impact of that competition.

OVERVIEW ON THE TEXTILE AND APPAREL TRADE

As less-developed countries have entered the soft goods industry, at the earliest stages they enter primarily the labor-intensive aspects of the industry—such as assembling garments from imported components. These countries typically do not have the technical skill and capital to produce the higher-value-added fabrics, trims, and other needed components, so they come from elsewhere. At this stage, the industry provides little more than much-needed jobs for the local workforce. However, as a country's clothing industry advances in development, it seeks to provide more of the higher-value-added materials. That is, as these industries become more developed, they start producing their own fabrics and other components. Hence, as this has occurred in country after country, a growing number of proficient textile-producing nations has emerged in the global market.

Although the U.S. textile and apparel industries had experienced growing import penetration for decades, the domestic industry still supplied most of the U.S. market for a very long time. Many foreign textile producers found it difficult to compete with the U.S. industry's efficiency and economies in producing standard fabrics that could be made in large runs. These efficiencies, along with proximity to market and distribution costs, appeared for a time to make U.S. textiles seem viable for many years longer than their apparel counterparts.

During the 1970s, the U.S. textile/apparel industry had taken steps to counter increasing competitiveness in international trade. Adjustments varied, however, in different segments of the industry. Because of the textile industry's technology and capital orientation, modernization and efficiency were more readily achieved by that segment than the labor-intensive and more fragmented apparel industry. Textile producers achieved improved results by investing in new plants and equipment that increased operating efficiency, reduced labor costs, and often boosted quality. Textile industry productivity in the 1970s grew at a much faster rate than the economy as a whole.

As the U.S. population's incomes rose, the apparel industry needed fabrics with more design interest and that were produced in shorter runs to provide an element of exclusivity to both the apparel firms for their lines and the end-use consumer. Consumers with a fashion sense do not want all their garments made from basic commodity fabrics. When approaching the textile

India, ca. 1999. As a country develops, its textile industry is able to produce more of the components needed for apparel production. Published by permission of the International Labour Organization. Photograph by Khemka A.

firms, many apparel producers encountered a "take it or leave it" attitude. Unfortunately, for U.S. textile firms this attitude was in sharp contrast to that of a growing number of firms in other countries, particularly those in East Asia, who were becoming increasingly proficient at production.

As they faced the growing competition, U.S. textile manufacturers realized the importance of becoming more sensitive to the needs of the market and initiated various measures to do so. These included efforts to streamline production, reduce inventory investment, and implement just-in-time (JIT) delivery, quick response, and electronic data interchange (EDI) strategies, processes that permit more rapid manufacture and supply of products without the need to maintain large inventories. Other adjustment strategies included closing or revitalizing outmoded and inefficient plants and investing in the most advanced technology available. However, the fact remained that companies had made huge capital investments in plants and technology designed for large runs of commodity fabrics.

In the 1960s, 1970s, and 1980s, the apparel industry experienced growing levels of competitive pressures from imported clothing. Although several apparel companies had started outsourcing production and U.S. apparel employment had declined gradually (as had textile employment), a large workforce still existed in the United States. As late as 1986, there were still more than one million workers in the U.S. apparel industry.

OTHER WESTERN HEMISPHERE APPAREL PRODUCTION

When U.S. apparel manufacturing began to experience competitive pressure from imports, other low-cost areas of the Western Hemisphere became good production sites for a time. For several decades, a number of special provisions in U.S. trade policies encouraged garment production in the Caribbean, Mexico, and other parts of Latin America. These policies, intended to aid less-developed countries, soon made the apparel industry the leading manufacturing employer in the region. Like most countries in early stages of development, these nations began garment assembly as an important generator of income, employment, and foreign exchange. Having little textile-producing capacity at the time, these countries had to rely on fabrics and other components from elsewhere.

A number of U.S. trade policies for the region gave incentives for the use of U.S. textiles in products that would return to the U.S. market. That is, textile leaders had used their political clout to secure policies designed to create growth markets in the region for U.S. textile firms. These policies required use of U.S. textile components (some specified "yarn forward," which means that products can be made up overseas as long as they use yarn produced in the United States) to qualify for duty-free shipment back to the United States and thus created sales that helped offset the loss from the U.S. textile industry's continually declining domestic market. That is, as the domestic market for U.S. textiles shrank, these preferential U.S. trading policies helped create new markets in Mexico and the Caribbean region. Exporting fabrics to these areas became increasingly important for U.S. textile firms, and over the years it accounted for a significant portion of their total sales.

Despite the preferential trade schemes, other trends in sourcing caused major shifts away from the region. Apparel industry wages in many Asian countries were already much lower than in the Caribbean and Latin America. Further, a significant disadvantage for regional apparel contractors is that they generally were not able to provide full-package programs, in contrast to many Asian contractors. *Full-package production* means that the buyer (whether an apparel company, retailer, or sourcing agent) pays for completed finished garments, rather than contracting for labor only, which was the practice in earlier years.

THE PENDULUM SWINGS BACK TOWARD ASIA

In 1997, the depreciation of the Thai baht, the Korean won, and other currencies led to the subsequent economic crisis that spread to other Asian countries and greatly reduced the costs of doing business with Asian firms. Many of the Asian firms became desperate for work and slashed prices just to be able to keep their factories operating.

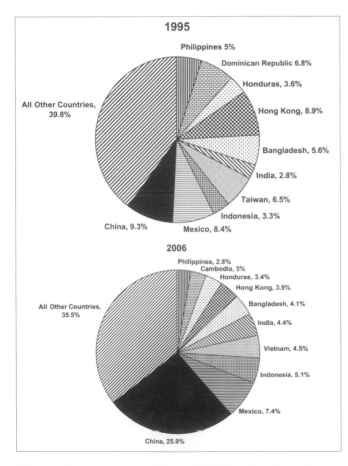

U.S. apparel imports by country, 1995 and 2006. Office of Textiles and Apparel, U.S. Department of Commerce.

Now, rather than handling just the garment assembly, many of the Asian contractors had trained, experienced staff who could handle many aspects of the manufacturing process. Larger ones had their own fabric specialists, who scouted textile markets for fabrics for the client company. At the same time, many Asian textile producers had also become proficient in making very good fabrics, offering excellent selections for the contractors to consider. There was no reason for Asian garment producers to use U.S. fabrics because their own were usually considerably less expensive, and buying from nearby countries saved significant shipping costs.

As Asian contractors grew proficient in providing more and more of the activities involved in the development and production of garments, many of the companies evolved into full-package producers. They took on all the responsibilities of producing a line for a company and delivering finished products to the U.S. apparel firm, many of which had become basically apparel marketing firms by this point. Hence, this evolution in the contracting business has meant that a large portion of the garments produced in Asia use Asian fabrics. This is not to say that Asia has become the only site for production, but it has surely become the dominant one. Trade data tell the story. The sources of U.S. apparel imports changed markedly from 1995 to 2006.

The economic incentives for production in Asia, together with the increased ability there to provide fabrics as well as full-package programs, led to a gradual swing away from production in Western Hemisphere regions. In turn, this led to a shrinking market for U.S. textile firms that had relied on fabric sales to Western Hemisphere markets.

RETAILERS GO DIRECT

The competitive environment for apparel retailers has encouraged similar patterns of production for their private label lines, which account for a growing portion of most retailers' apparel lines. That is, retailers discovered the advantages of going directly to contractors rather than paying to have apparel firms do it for them, thereby cutting out costs paid to U.S. apparel firms. Most major retailers have now assembled large product development teams to handle technical aspects of creating and promoting their own private label lines and to handle overseas sourcing. Similarly, these major retailers have offices throughout their sourcing regions with staff who help to coordinate and monitor production farmed out to contractors. While not the only region for retailers' contracting operations early in the millennium, Asia is by far the dominant one—just as for apparel firms. Retailers use many of the same contractors used by the apparel firms—and use Asian fabrics in the production.

Thus, the sourcing of full-package programs in Asia by both apparel firms and apparel retailers has greatly reduced markets for U.S. fabrics. Not only has diminished apparel production in the United States decimated this market for U.S. fabrics, but also the imported garments coming into the U.S. from full-package suppliers, primarily from Asia, contain little or no U.S. fabric. (Imports from the Western Hemisphere are an exception.)

In summary, the combined advantages of lower costs and full-package production in Asia are too attractive and firmly established with sourcing agents in the U.S. apparel, retail, and importing sectors to expect any reversal of this trend in the near future.

THE ROLE OF POLITICS

The U.S. textile and apparel industry has had a long history of concern over imports and their real or anticipated effect on domestic operations. The U.S. industry was also politically powerful and savvy in getting various forms of government protection from imports. The textile and apparel industries were part of an influential anti-import coalition, well connected to members of Congress and other government officials. Connections in the highest places allowed the industry to have a great influence on trade policy. Even presidents Kennedy and Nixon pressured trading partners to accept restrictive textile trade policies in order to curry the favor (and votes) of the large and powerful textile/apparel coalition.

Exerting their political muscle, U.S. industry leaders successfully influenced the development of a complex quota system under the General Agreement on Tariffs and Trade (GATT), which included a provision called the Multifiber Arrangement (MFA), in 1974. For over thirty years, bilateral agreements under the MFA placed limits on the quantity of textile and apparel products imported into the more-developed countries from less-developed ones. As global competition escalated over the years to the point of having an "overcapacity" of production and products, the quotas helped protect the U.S. industry by shielding the domestic market from the full impact of imports.

The potential tidal wave of imports was slowed by the quota system. However, even when quotas were in place, firms intent on having apparel lines made offshore were able to find ways around them. In many cases, this meant shifting production from quota-controlled countries to those with fewer or no restraints. This strategy often required going to increasingly less-developed and more remote countries, but that did not deter sourcing agents determined to find low-cost production sites. Cambodia, Bangladesh, Sri Lanka, Vietnam, Madagascar, and sub-Saharan Africa are just a few examples.

THE TEXTILE AND APPAREL SECTORS PART WAYS ON TRADE

For decades, U.S. apparel firms found it hard to compete domestically against products made in low-wage countries. Apparel companies gradually shifted from seeing overseas producers as competitors to viewing them as partners. During this time, advancing communication, transportation, and logistics systems were making it easier to conduct international business—that is, to use overseas factories rather than domestic ones.

By the late 1980s, the shifting trade stance of the apparel industry regarding imports became evident. The American Apparel Manufacturers Association (AAMA; now the American Apparel and Footwear Association, or AAFA) announced that it would no longer be a part of the strong anti-import coalition that for years had exerted pressure on policymakers to provide protection for the domestic industry. The reason: Too many of the AAMA members, the apparel manufacturers, were going offshore for production themselves. This was an acknowledgment of how dramatically the apparel industry was changing.

THE POLITICAL ENVIRONMENT CHANGES

Until the mid-1980s, retailers and other importers had little opportunity to have their views represented in textile trade policies. This group had not developed a political base or network to exert influence on policies that greatly restricted their overseas buying potential in the textile/apparel product areas. However, this changed dramatically in the mid-1980s, when retailers and importers began to recognize and activate their enormous political base among the large numbers employed in these sectors across the country. Defeat of a bill detrimental to their business was the first major accomplishment of the new retailer/importer lobby. The Jenkins Bill, nearly passed by Congress, would have put additional restrictions on apparel imports. The defeat was a defining time that reinforced this group's commitment to exert its political power.

Thus, when apparel firms changed their political stance on trade, combined with the political prowess of the retailer/importer groups, this represented a significant counterpressure coalition to provide resistance against the protectionist textile lobby forces. Further, when this situation is considered in light of the declining domestic textile industry's size, it means that the U.S. textile sector was no longer the political powerhouse it once had been. Together, all of these changes meant that the U.S. textile industry was in a weakened position to secure special protection from imports.

Cambodia. In the early stages of a country's development, apparel production is the primary industrial activity. Published by permission of the International Labour Organization. Photograph by Cassidy K.

AN END TO THE IMPORT QUOTA SYSTEM

For many years, the less-developed textile/apparel exporting countries agitated against the quota system. Leaders of these countries felt the quotas stifled one of their major exports. Finally, collective pressure from these nations in the GATT's Uruguay Round negotiations resulted in plans to phase out the quota system over ten years. On 1 January 1995, the GATT became the World Trade Organization (WTO), and the quota phase-out began the first of four stages.

At each stage of the phase-out, the governments of the importing countries identified those product categories that would be integrated into the normal rules of trade for all other sectors under the WTO. U.S. government officials consulted with domestic industry sources in identifying the products to be surrendered (i.e., to be removed from a quota system).

In this process of determining the categories to integrate in each stage, the textile industry engaged in gamesmanship that probably did not serve it well in the long run. That is, textile industry supporters were successful in having nonquota products counted in the categories that were to be surrendered in the first stage. Items were included that had never had quotas, such as umbrellas, parachutes, safety belts, and garments for dolls.

Unfortunately, holding the most sensitive categories until the final phase-out stage simply postponed the day of reckoning for U.S. textile firms. The final stage would have been dramatic anyway, even if implemented as the WTO originally intended. Nearly half (48.65%) of products would have had quotas removed at this last step anyway. However, by first surrendering nonquota items, and second, by keeping quotas on the more sensitive product categories until the end, a tsunami effect at the end of the ten-year phase-out was created. As was expected, when quotas were removed at the final stage, the import surges were dramatic in many of the affected categories.

Additionally, apparel firms and retailers' private label divisions were already proficient at sourcing in Asia. Furthermore, they had shifted increasingly to full-package sourcing, which used mostly Asian fabrics, in plentiful supply by that time. The remaining quotas on the sensitive categories were likely the leading reason they had not already shifted much of this production to Asia. Labor costs in most of Asia were significantly lower than in the Western Hemisphere. However, there were still tariff and shipping cost advantages for Western Hemisphere production. Some production remained in Latin America for retailers' rapid replenishment programs used to replace inventory quickly.

China had become the textile and apparel powerhouse globally. About thirty-five thousand of China's textile and apparel factories were producing for the export market. Even before the end of the quota system in 2005, the U.S. textile sector anticipated this and had begun to pressure for additional safeguard quota protection from the anticipated Chinese import surges. After quotas ended, massive surges did occur in most of the sensitive import categories protected to the end.

Following the surge from China, the U.S. textile industry was successful in securing safeguard quotas on sensitive apparel categories from China during the 2006–2008 period. U.S. companies manufacturing textiles for products in those categories were spared temporarily from some of the surge in completed apparel that would otherwise have come directly from China. By then, however, there was a growing number of proficient producers in other parts of Asia—areas not restrained by safeguard quotas.

IMPACT OF GLOBAL CHANGES ON THE U.S. INDUSTRY

The long-term outlook for the U.S. textile industry has been challenging for many years. Fortunately for the sector, the preferential trade schemes that provided incentives for the use of U.S. textiles in Western Hemisphere production provided a market for the industry, particularly in the 1980s and 1990s. However, that market has been declining as production has shifted to Asia. According

Chinese laborers work at the Youngor Group textile factory in Zhejiang Province, People's Republic of China. A surge of Chinese exports to the United States followed the removal of safeguard quotas in 2005. Getty Images.

to U.S. Department of Commerce data, the textile sector has shown a steady decline in the value of shipments, industrial production, capacity utilization, and employment. Many U.S. textile companies with a proud heritage of contributing significantly to the economy have in recent years declared bankruptcy, some have restructured, and others have shuttered their plants and ended operations completely.

In examining comparable data for the U.S. apparel industry, a significant decline in the value of U.S. shipments, industrial production, capacity utilization, and capital expenditures can also be noted. However, a very different scenario exists here, because we see from apparel retail sales that the market continued to grow significantly. At the same time, the dramatic decline of employment from over 700,000 in 1997 to 238,400 in 2006 shows that the domestic industry was shrinking rapidly.

When these figures are coupled with the growth of apparel imports from over US$47 billion in 1997 to nearly US$72 billion in 2006, one may safely conclude that apparel imports have rapidly displaced U.S. apparel production. In the early part of the twenty-first century, an estimated 90 to 95 percent or more of garments in the U.S. market are produced outside the United States. The percentage of import penetration varies by product category. This represented major market losses for U.S. textile firms that once supplied the fabrics and other components. However, it is primarily U.S. apparel firms and retailers who are importing the garments; thus, these segments remain competitive.

SUMMARY

At the turn of the millennium, both the U.S. textile and apparel sectors have been transformed dramatically by the vastly changing global macroconditions. In the 1980s, it might have appeared that the domestic textile sector would fare better than its apparel counterpart. Textile firms had taken measures to try to remain competitive by making investments in technology, implementing JIT and EDI systems, trying to be more customer-oriented, initiating mergers and divestitures, rationalizing unproductive plants, and even using some foreign-made components themselves. These initiatives simply were not enough to offset the fact that this sector's customers—the apparel producers—went elsewhere to do business.

Sadly, the textile industry, the very one that brought the Industrial Revolution and its accompanying economic and social transformations to the United States in the nation's early years, has fallen victim to a crescendo of vast alterations in the playing field.

Over time, a majority of U.S. apparel firms changed from being apparel manufacturers to apparel marketers, doing business with low-cost overseas producers rather than trying to compete with them. Although the domestic apparel manufacturing industry has been badly hurt, major apparel firms survived by shifting to a variety of offshore production arrangements.

Asian contractors grew in their capabilities to handle full-package sourcing. More and more U.S. apparel firms began to rely on these arrangements, whereby finished products are shipped back from Asia. This shift, made possible by the kaleidoscope of advances in communications, logistics systems, the potential for virtual companies, financial systems that made it less complex to conduct business in different currencies, and the end of most of the quota system, made Asian producers formidable competitors. Moreover, the shift of apparel production from the Caribbean region to Asia added to the escalating evaporation of the former customer base for U.S. textile producers.

Although the apparel industry is already intensely competitive, it has become increasingly complicated by the fact that the industry's own customers—the retailers—are taking on the role of the apparel firm. Just as apparel firms contract for full-package programs, so do the retailers. This becomes an increasing threat to apparel firms as retailers steadily increase the volume of private label lines in their stores, particularly as consumers often consider private label merchandise as nothing special.

The tidal wave of imports into the U.S. market was slowed by the quota system. However, removal of quotas in 2005 opened the import floodgates to the world. Temporary safeguards on products from China provided only that—temporary protection from just one supplier nation. Even if the safeguards on Chinese products had been extended after 2008, doing so would probably have offered meaningless protection to U.S. textile firms. Other prolific Asian countries will quickly fill any slack created by limits on Chinese products. Moreover, importing apparel firms and retailers will now exert their political muscle to stop or reduce further restraints on the products they import.

In summary, behind the glamorous runway fashions is a complex story of global negotiation and cooperation, political tugs of war, sophisticated technological systems, an interconnectedness between business partners who may never meet, and banking systems that facilitate and support these global alliances. Consumers are the beneficiaries of fashion products that truly represent a marvel of this global era.

References and Further Reading

Aggarwal, Vinod K. *Liberal Protectionism: The International Politics of Organized Textile Trade.* Berkeley: University of California Press, 1985.

Barrie, L. *Apparel Sourcing in 2006: What Can Be Learnt from Events in 2005?* Management briefing from online textile information source, Just-style.com. Worcestershire, UK: Aroq Limited, January 2006.

Cline, William R. *The Future of World Trade in Textiles and Apparel.* Washington, DC: Institute for International Economics, 1987.

Destler, I. *American Trade Politics.* 2nd ed. Washington, DC: Institute for International Economics, 1991.

Dickerson, K. "Textile Trade: The GATT Exception." *St. John's Journal of Legal Commentary* 11, no. 2 (Spring, 1996): 393–430.

Dickerson, K. *Textiles and Apparel in the Global Economy.* 3rd ed. Upper Saddle River, NJ: Prentice Hall, 1999.

Keesing, D., and M. Wolf. *Textile Quotas against Developing Countries.* London: Trade Policy Research Center, 1980.

Nordas, Hildegunn Kyvik. *The Global Textile and Clothing Industry Post the Agreement on Textiles and Clothing.* Geneva: World Trade Organization, 2004. http://www.wto.org/english/res_e/booksp_e/discussion_papers5_e.pdf

Rivoli, P. *The Travels of a T-Shirt in the Global Economy.* Hoboken, NJ: John Wiley & Sons, 2005.

Kitty G. Dickerson

See also The Textile Industry; The Garment Industry and Retailing in the United States; The Garment Industry and Retailing in Canada; volume 6, Textile and Garment Manufacture and Retailing in China.

The Garment Industry and Retailing in Canada

The apparel industry is the tenth-largest manufacturing sector in Canada. Apparel is manufactured in all provinces and territories. Quebec accounts for 55 percent of production, while significant concentrations of firms are found in Ontario, Manitoba, and British Columbia. Montreal is the third-largest apparel manufacturing center in North America, after Los Angeles and New York.

Canada's apparel industry produces a wide range of garments for consumer and specialized markets. Major areas of production include men's, women's, and children's fashion clothing, including knitwear, outerwear, denim, pants, shirts, and blouses; intimate apparel and sleepwear; tailored clothing; active sportswear; fur and leather goods; occupational clothing; technical outerwear; hosiery and knitted goods; and other fashion accessories.

While small firms predominate in the industry, Canada also has many large and highly sophisticated manufacturing companies. The majority of these companies are Canadian owned. Only about 2 percent of apparel firms are foreign owned, which are mainly subsidiaries of U.S. multinational corporations. Although computer-assisted technology has made inroads in several stages of apparel production, the apparel-manufacturing industry remains fragmented and labor intensive.

Statistics Canada reports that in 2005, the Canadian apparel industry comprised some 2,150 establishments, employed about seventy thousand workers, and shipped CAN$6 billion of apparel, of which some 40 percent was exported, mainly to the United States. For the same year, the Canadian apparel market was valued at CAN$10.4 billion. In 2007, retail markets are expanding rapidly for plus-size clothing as well as environmentally friendly organic clothing and the tween market for those approximately seven to fourteen years old.

EARLY DEVELOPMENT OF THE GARMENT INDUSTRY IN CANADA

Canada's garment industry developed in the nineteenth century. Company records are sparse or nonexistent, and little other evidence survives to document their activity. Data from Canada's first census, taken in 1871, situate much of the historical work on this important manufacturing sector as of this date, although key industry developments occurred over the previous fifty years.

The industry developed primarily in the cities of Montreal and Toronto and its surrounding areas, including Hamilton, and to a lesser extent in Winnipeg, Edmonton, Vancouver, and Halifax. Montreal and Toronto were suited to become early centers for this industry because of proximity to markets and imported supplies, Montreal particularly because of an abundant rural and immigrant labor supply. In the 1901 census, these two cities together accounted for 55 percent of clothing produced in Canada. By 1928, the provinces of Quebec and Ontario accounted for about 95 percent of the country's garment production. While the industries in the smaller cities cannot compare in the value of their output, apparel manufacturing was still statistically a key sector of employment. For instance, clothing led the way to industrialization in the cities of St. John and in Halifax, where by 1891 the clothing industry was the largest employer. By 1900, the needle trade in Winnipeg, the third-largest garment-producing city in Canada, was a major component of the city's economy.

Garment production did not industrialize with a straightforward transition from home to small shops to larger factories; its trajectory was a very uneven one. For much of its industrial history, apparel manufacturing in Canada was carried out under a wide variety of modes and models. Custom work, homework, and factory work existed simultaneously, and each dominated in various sectors of the trade and at various moments.

The development of the industry in Canada, like elsewhere, is inextricably linked to technology and gender. The numerous Canadian sewing machine manufacturers made technology very accessible to enterprising manufacturers. Women filled the lesser-skilled positions of sewing machine operators, with Canada's industry following gendered patterns of lower wages for women's work. Men almost always held the higher-paying skilled jobs of cutter, presser, and special machine operator. Even through the first half of the twentieth century, men received higher wages than women who performed the same jobs; owners, unions, and society at large agreed this was necessary so that men could support their families.

Immigration and ethnicity also structured and influenced developments in the industry in Montreal and Toronto. Between 1900 and 1920 the Canadian government's open immigration policy drew new labor into these cities. An influx of Jewish immigration gradually shaped not only the clothing workforce in these cities but also its residential communities; in both Montreal and Toronto, the location of the industry developed according to the residential areas of its growing Jewish workforce. The garment industry developed in Old Montreal in the nineteenth century but began to move northward toward Bleury and St. Catherine streets at the end of the century, and then north on St. Lawrence

Boulevard to its current Chabanel Street base in the last three decades of the twentieth century. The Spadina district of Toronto that grew into the garment district in the 1910s was also central to the residential areas of many of the city's Jewish immigrants.

The scant research that examines the development of the industry prior to 1871 focuses primarily on Montreal. In the 1830s, the city's population was expanding rapidly, creating a labor pool, a market, and an exchange economy. The first manifestations of larger-scale clothing production are seen with dry goods establishments, which began to manufacture garments on their premises for sale. An excellent example of this transition from retailer to manufacturer is that of the Moss Brothers, English Jews who arrived in Montreal in the 1830s. Their large establishment sold imported English ready-made clothing. By the 1840s they were manufacturing their own merchandise, using outside contractors. By 1856 they had established a five-story factory, the city's largest plant, employing 800 people. Markets for this early ready-to-wear were essentially rural, as urban dwellers continued to have easy access to custom clothing manufacturers.

Other large establishments followed in the 1860s. A variety of modes of production existed simultaneously. One was the traditional small shop servicing a local market with either custom or ready-made clothing. The majority of these small shops employed fewer than fifteen workers, each with a wide variety of skills. Large in-house shops like John Aitken's shirt factory, employing some three hundred women, had extensive mechanization, a highly developed division of labor, and sophisticated distribution. A third type was exemplified by the large business run by wholesale manufacturer H. Shorey, who employed seventy skilled inside workers who cut and prepared material for making up by many more hundreds of homeworkers.

The protectionist National Policy, adopted in Canada in 1879, increased import tariffs to encourage a strong domestic manufacturing base, and many more businesses developed after it was enacted. Tariffs on imported textiles encouraged manufacturers to support the Canadian textile industry. Canada imposed lower tariffs on imported clothing than the United States did, however, which affected the trade balance. U.S. manufacturers penetrated the entire North American market far more than Canadian manufacturers were able to do. Despite the National Policy's benefits for the industry, imports continued to climb steadily, suggesting that the market was expanding for ready-made clothing of all types, whether domestic or imported.

Menswear was the most developed and specialized sector of the industry throughout the nineteenth century. Shirt-making was one of the first sectors to be organized into industrial large-scale production. By 1905 it was estimated that 80 to 90 percent of Canadian men's clothing was factory made. By 1910 an inspector stated that garments made by tailors offered only the slightest of advantages in quality over ready-made and that ready-made clothing in return offered a cost savings of 30 to 50 percent. From this point onward, Montreal's dominance in menswear production was firmly established.

The industry was slower to take on the manufacture of the full range of women's clothing. Hoop skirts, or crinolines, were being industrially produced in both Montreal and St. John in the 1860s in shops that were simultaneously manufacturers, wholesalers, and retailers. Whitewear (petticoats, corset covers, and drawers) was soon being factory produced. From 1900 to 1905 whitewear production doubled in Canada due to better and faster machinery. The corset industry also began relatively early. Toronto's Crompton Corset Co. was a key Canadian manufacturer;

Garment label from Montreal-based manufacturer-retailer Le Château, showing dealer identification CA number and country of origin, 1980s. ©McCord Museum, Montreal; M2004.79.1. http://www.mccord-museum.qc.ca/en/

Dominion Corset Co., founded in Quebec City in 1886, became a leader throughout North America, Europe, and Australia until it closed in the 1970s.

Around the turn of the century, the range of manufactured garments for women expanded to include shirtwaists (blouses), cloaks, and mantles. Production reached a peak around 1915. In the first decade of the twentieth century a few factories began to manufacture dresses, a sector which only really developed after World War I.

The knitted goods sector included companies like Knit-to-Fit, founded in Montreal in 1902, which remained in business for seventy-five years. Its initial products were one-piece knitted undergarments for both men and women. Stanfield's in Nova Scotia, a company still running in the twenty-first century, began producing knitted undergarments in the 1890s.

Western Canadian companies dominated the workwear sector. The Winnipeg Shirt and Overall Company was founded in 1889. The Great Western Garment Company, whose factory ran in Edmonton from 1911 to 2004, claimed to be the largest garment manufacturer in the British Commonwealth throughout much of its existence. Although some manufacturers identified themselves as producers of boys' wear, much of children's clothing was grouped under the other sectors mentioned previously and has not been accounted for separately.

TWENTIETH-CENTURY DEVELOPMENT OF THE GARMENT INDUSTRY

Until the end of World War I, the demand for factory-made clothing progressed steadily. Many small shops closed, as larger, vertically integrated businesses increased their production and gained a greater market share. Following the war, this trend was somewhat reversed; small entrepreneurs were able to compete successfully with larger factories. Starting a small contract shop did not require a huge outlay for equipment, because technology was not advancing as rapidly as it had in the prewar years, nor did larger shops offer much economy of scale. *Contract shops* could be more flexible in reacting to market shifts, while the larger, more vertically integrated factories had difficulty adapting to the fluctuating fortunes of the interwar years. Small shops often had a symbiotic relationship with the larger factories: They competed with them for the same markets but also subcontracted for them.

The industry progressed through the 1920s with both large factories and contract shops existing side by side. Business failure in the clothing industry was very common. Contract shops often stayed afloat for only a very short period of time. Through the 1920s, an average 12 percent of menswear businesses and 19 percent of women's wear shops closed each year.

Through the first half of the twentieth century, domestic apparel production closely matched domestic demand. Canadian manufacturers remained very concerned about tariffs and protection against imports from low-wage countries, which included Britain. Because the tariff on imported raw materials was the same as that on finished clothing, a great deal of Canadian competitiveness hinged on keeping wages low. In 1928 Canada imported over CAN$10 million of clothing, reporting clothing exports valued at CAN$600,000 to Newfoundland (not yet a Canadian province) and the West Indies. In 1938 manufacturers expressed their hope for a continuing policy of protection in Canada's negotiation of a trade agreement with the United States.

The 1930s brought very difficult economic times with the Great Depression. As markets for clothing were constricted, factories and contract shops alike employed workers for fewer weeks of the year and applied a variety of other cost-cutting measures to wages. Workers fought back by joining unions and striking, making this decade a key period for labor unrest.

When Canada entered the war effort in 1939, the economy was still recovering from the Depression. Work in the needle trades became more lucrative, mainly because of the increased hours of work required for increased production and the introduction of piece rates. A massive demand for work clothing and uniforms sparked a rise in employment in the workwear sector. During the war, labor shortages in the garment industry were also chronic, as workers were required for manufacturing armaments.

The Wartime Prices and Trade Board, set up in 1939, regulated prices, wages, and materials in the industry. It legislated economies and simplifications in garment manufacture to reduce production costs and ensure adequate supply. It also controlled prices in an attempt to stem the inflation that Canadians had experienced in World War I. Wage and price ceilings were gradually eliminated after 1945, until the board was dissolved in 1951.

The postwar economic boom fueled a period of growth, modernization, and increased efficiency in the apparel industry. It marked the beginning of a new era in which some of the traditional craft skills and sweatshops were gradually replaced by assembly lines and larger manufacturing companies. Technical change occurred steadily but more slowly than in other sectors of industry until it began to progress more rapidly in the 1970s. Styling and design became an increasingly significant aspect of the manufacturing process. From 1952 to 1981, rates of profit were seen to increase.

The second half of the twentieth century also marked an increase in government involvement and legislation of the industry, evident in garment labeling. Canada was one of the first countries to legislate the labeling of fiber content in 1956. The Textile Labelling Act of 1971 introduced more stringent fiber-content labeling and stipulated that dealer identity be labeled, recommending the CA number system. Regulations regarding standard sizing were passed in 1962. Care-labeling standards took effect in 1969. In 1974, the Consumer Packaging and Labelling Act marked the beginning of legislated bilingual labeling in garments sold in Canada.

Perhaps the most significant development in the Canadian apparel industry in the second half of the twentieth century is the substantial increase in world trade in apparel, mostly originating from low-wage, developing countries and destined for high-wage, developed countries. By 1948, import protection for the clothing industry became more structured as Canada negotiated with seven countries in the General Agreement on Tariffs and Trade (GATT).

Through the 1950s the industry's concern about imports expanded to include not only those from the United States and Britain but also from Japan and Eastern Europe, followed by Korea, Hong Kong, and Taiwan. Industry representatives increased pressure on the Canadian government to establish import quotas. Negotiations with the Asian nations culminated in quotas known as *voluntary export restraints*. Gradually from the 1950s through the end of the 1960s, Canadian manufacturers found the growth of cheap imports from Asia and the United States was directing them into a higher-style and quality-market niche, for both the large domestic and small export markets.

The factory of the Great Western Garment company in Edmonton, Canada (1911–2004), employed hundreds of sewing machine operators, many of them immigrant women. Courtesy of Provincial Archives of Alberta, Edmonton Journal Fonds, PA.J.181/2.

In the 1960s, in reaction to the import trends, provincial and federal governments multiplied their initiatives to promote Canada's industry and create an export market. In 1968 the federal Department of Industry, Trade, and Commerce sponsored presentations of Canadian fashion in New York, which were very successful in stimulating sales. It led to a federal review of the industry in 1970, following which it established its Fashion Canada agency, giving it a mandate to promote the quality of Canadian apparel both at home and abroad. A year later it established the Textile and Clothing Board as an advisory arm for the industry. In 1971, exports were reported to have more than tripled since 1967. Nonetheless, Canadian manufacturers did not actively seek foreign markets through the 1970s and most of the 1980s. In 1973, exports remained at 2 percent of the industry's total output, and in 1989, at 5 percent.

Attempts to address the imbalances and inequities caused by the growing international trade resulted in two multilateral international agreements. The Multifiber Arrangement (MFA), negotiated within the framework of GATT, lasted from 1974 to 1994. It permitted Canada and other developed countries to impose quotas on imports of apparel and textiles from developing countries. Canada imposed its import quotas in 1976. That year, imports accounted for 45 percent of the market share, decreased to 18 percent by 1981, but were back up to 43 percent in 1985, just before the MFA was revised and extended for the second time.

The import share of the market dropped below 30 percent again in the late 1980s.

The 1980s marked a decade of significant growth for the Canadian apparel industry, interrupted by the Canada–U.S. Free Trade Agreement (FTA), which Canada entered in 1989, and the recession of the early 1990s. The industry underwent significant restructuring. Between 1988 and 1993, some eight hundred Canadian firms closed. Then from 1993 to 1995, shipments and employment increased. So did imports; by 1995, when the Agreement on Textiles and Clothing (ATC) stipulated how MFA quotas were to be gradually phased out over a ten-year period, imports were back above 40 percent of the market share.

The drop in domestic market share from increasing imports, as well as the creation of a single North American marketplace, encouraged many Canadian manufacturers to develop an export orientation. The FTA and the North American Free Trade Agreement (NAFTA), entered in 1994, played a role in shaping a significant export market in the United States for Canada's apparel production. From the enacting of the FTA in 1989 to 1997, exports to the United States had quadrupled. In 2007, exports made up 40 percent of Canadian output. Canadian apparel companies have been adjusting to the new trade environment by shifting and focusing their production on selected North American niche markets, where geographical proximity gives them a competitive advantage.

THE WORKFORCE, WORKING CONDITIONS, AND LABOR ORGANIZATION

Throughout its history, Canada's garment industry has been a highly unstable, competitive, and labor-intensive industry where costs are most easily controlled with low wages. This situation has shaped the nature of the labor pool and the way it has grown.

Through the nineteenth century, Montreal's industry relied heavily on *putting-out*, particularly to rural areas well beyond the city, where women were willing to take on paying work. It has been speculated that homework in Quebec farming communities supported much of Toronto manufacturing as well. By the turn of the century, big clothing manufacturers kept distributing agencies in rural areas to deal out materials and collect the finished product. Advantages of this system to manufacturers included lower wage costs, hiring workers only as seasonally required, and savings on overhead, such as heating, electricity, and machines. This facet of the workforce remains historically invisible. In the 1870s, Montreal manufacturer H. Shorey admitted to being unable to estimate the size of his workforce because of the preponderance of rural families working out of their homes. Homework in the urban milieu also existed, under conditions acknowledged as being little better than in rural areas.

As concerns over labor conditions in industrializing Canada spread, attention turned to both the exploitation of homeworkers and to those in garment industry shops. Ontario passed a Factories Act in 1884 and Quebec, in 1885, legislating minimum worker ages and maximum working hours. Other provinces followed suit in the following decades. The National Council of Women of Canada, founded in 1893, stated as one of its aims the betterment of working conditions of female factory workers. In 1895 the federal government commissioned the *Report on the Sweating System in Canada*, which shed light on the sweatshop practices and difficult homework conditions found in the industry in Toronto.

In the latter decades of the nineteenth century and early decades of the twentieth, Canada received an influx of Jewish immigrants. Many of those arriving in the 1880s through the 1890s had tailoring skills and familiarity with garment manufacture, and they easily found employment in the industry in Montreal and Toronto, where the Jewish community still identifies closely with the trade. One estimate suggested that fifteen thousand Jews, or about half the industry's workforce, were in Montreal's needle trades in 1909. These Jewish garment workers had a significant effect on the way apparel manufacture industrialized. Until World War I, many Jews entered the labor force in the larger factories. By about 1915 many began to start their own small contract shops with a few employees, particularly in Montreal, where the system flourished.

Contract shops were a significant factor in the reduction of homework. Factory operators soon found that contract shops better met their needs. Homework was further reduced with the full employment caused by World War I. Faced with the troubled economic times of the late 1920s and the shrinking markets for goods of the 1930s, manufacturers turned to homework once again in an attempt to find all possible ways to cut production costs. In the 1930s, governments took their first steps toward effective regulation. For example, in Ontario in the late 1930s, homeworkers and employers were required to obtain permits. The full employment occasioned by World War II led to another dip in homework, and the widespread prosperity of the 1950s meant that fewer women

needed to supplement their incomes in this manner. Nonetheless, the industry continued to attract vulnerable people such as immigrants, for whom homework seemed a reasonable option, and thus this practice continued to thrive.

Since World War II, Canada has received an influx of immigrants, many of whom have found employment in the industry. Postwar immigrants who were drawn to the industry were first Italian and then Greek and Portuguese. In 1964, workers of Italian origin were said to make up the majority of the workforce, while Jewish workers had become a minority, holding the most skilled occupations. The labor pool continued to evolve in the following decades with immigrants from low-wage countries in Southeast Asia, the West Indies, and Eastern Europe. In western Canada, the needle trades offered employment opportunities unavailable in other milieux or female professions, particularly to Jewish, Ukrainian, Polish, German, and Russian women. In Manitoba, where labor shortages plagued the industry at several times but perhaps most acutely in 1966, Immigration Canada sponsored the recruitment of overseas workers. The manufacturing facilities that still exist in Canada continue to attract immigrant populations. In the first decade of the twenty-first century, it is estimated that women represent 70 percent of the apparel workforce in Canada and that immigrants supply an estimated 50 percent.

Through the 1980s and even by the late 1990s, concerns were still being raised regarding the conditions of homeworkers in Canada, many of them immigrant women working for subcontractors. Their numbers would appear to be decreasing as the global effects of offshore production have resulted in fewer manufacturing jobs in Canada. Nonetheless, the pressures on manufacturers to keep wages and production costs as low as possible to compete with low-wage countries have never been greater, and concerns over homework and exploitation at home as well as abroad remain a constant theme in the industry's present and future.

Unionization of the garment industry in Canada occurred later and was less spectacular than in the United States. Trade unions have nonetheless played an important role in the economic development of the trade. Unionists joining international organizations saw the industry in a continental context, whereas manufacturers tended to see it only in terms of a domestic market.

In the early decades, the workforce was very difficult to organize. The seasonal nature of factory work meant seasonal fluctuations in union membership. Gender and ethnic divisions did not help labor forge a common sense of purpose. Management resisted unionization with great determination, fully aware that there were always many other unskilled workers to replace factory workers if needed.

In 1910, Montreal garment workers held their first general strike. Again in 1912 and 1913, women strikers protested their everyday working conditions. A 1912 lockout at the Eaton's factory in Toronto had an important impact on future labor movements. The factory managed to continue operating with nonunion labor, but when striking workers returned after a four-month lockout, owners had learned that such protests could not be sustained over the longer term.

The 1930s marked a period of a great many strikes. Some twenty strikes took place between 1930 and 1935 in Winnipeg alone, as young female workers protested lowered wages and increased production demands. In 1937, five thousand women went on strike for three weeks in Quebec and won better working conditions and higher wages. Léa Roback, who helped organize the

Interior of Morgan's Department store, Montreal, ca. 1871. Château Ramezay Museum collection, Montreal.

International Ladies' Garment Workers', Union (ILGWU) for this strike, is recognized as one of the key figures in the history of organized labor in Canada.

While several unions have had a history in Canada, the ILGWU, which Toronto women operators joined in 1907, and Amalgamated Clothing Workers, whose Toronto and Hamilton locals were among the earliest in North America, have had the greatest impact on the industry. During World War II, Canadian unions experienced unparalleled growth. The full employment of that period was one determining factor. Collective bargaining, introduced near the war's end under federal wartime emergency powers, was another.

On the whole, successful mediation and arbitration have characterized labor relations in the industry. In 1995, clothing and textile workers' unions merged to create UNITE (Union of Needletrades, Industrial and Textile Employees), now UNITE-HERE, which in the early twenty-first century represents the majority of Canadian workers in the industry.

The industry has also recognized the benefits of creating a central organization to represent its interests. In 1918, a small group of manufacturers formed the first national organization, the Canadian Association of Garment Manufacturers, which included sectors of shirts, overalls, and work clothing. In 1921, this organization expanded to encompass the entire range of the industry, although by 1930 its members were still only one hundred out of the approximately one thousand garment manufacturers operating in Canada. Postwar, stronger national, regional, and sector-based organizations were created, some to deal with economic problems; others, with a bargaining role with labor; and still others, to provide credit. The Canadian Apparel and Textile Manufacturers Association formed in 1958 and continued until 1966, when a regrouping created the Apparel Manufacturers Council of Canada. This organization received federal government support but lacked the organizational capacity to represent the industry as well as was needed. The Canadian Apparel Manufacturers Institute was founded in 1971 and in 1993, with the support of Industry Canada, was succeeded by the Canadian Apparel Federation, which now acts as the voice of the industry. The Fur Council of Canada represents the fur garment industry.

CANADIAN GARMENT MANUFACTURERS

Menswear has remained the strongest sector in Canadian clothing manufacturing. Peerless Clothing in Montreal is North America's largest maker of men's suits and continues to do a substantial proportion of its manufacturing at its Montreal facility. Montreal-based Ballin, founded in 1946, is considered the leading manufacturer of better men's trousers in North America. Riviera Inc., a well-known high-quality trouser manufacturer, was established in 1917. Jack Victor, a company founded in 1913, has seven hundred employees and exports 70 percent of its production.

In other sectors, Canadian manufacturers with significant longevity and a high national or international profile include the Utex Fashion Group, founded in 1943, a global manufacturer and marketer of men's and women's outerwear and menswear. Nygård International, a Winnipeg manufacturer founded in 1967, has grown to be the largest sportswear manufacturer in Canada and third largest in North America. Joseph Ribkoff International, a manufacturer of women's high-end clothing, celebrated its fiftieth anniversary in 2007. Ribkoff continues to manufacture apparel in Canada and exports extensively.

Gildan, founded in 1946, is a global marketer and manufacturer of knit apparel. Gildan remains Montreal based but in 2007 moved all its manufacturing outside of Canada. McGregor Hosiery was one of the early knit hosiery manufacturers and remains based in Toronto in the early twenty-first century.

Leading names in denim manufacture include Parasuco, a Montreal-based international jeans label originally established in 1975 as Santana. Western Glove Works Ltd. of Winnipeg has been in existence since 1921, selling Silver Jeans throughout North America, Europe, and Asia, as well as manufacturing other high-end private-label brands.

Canada has also had a history of excelling in the lingerie sector. Canadelle, founded in 1939, is a leading manufacturer of WonderBra and Playtex brands. Montreal-based Arianne Lingerie, founded in 1939, is a globally competitive lingerie brand. In swimwear, Christina America is one of North America's largest manufacturers.

Several Canadian garment manufacturers no longer in business have also had a significant presence in the industry in the latter half of the twentieth century in terms of their longevity, success, and renown. Auckie Sanft founded his company in 1935 and remained in business until 1997. Montroy Coat, known for outerwear, was founded in 1928 and closed in 1987. Irving Samuel, founded by Samuel Workman in 1946, ran until 1995. Monarch Wear of Manitoba claimed to have been the national leader of Canadian manufacturing for half a century and in the 1970s was the largest jeans manufacturer in Canada; it closed in 1980. All these companies also collaborated with independent Canadian designers to manufacture their lines in the 1960s and 1970s.

THE T. EATON CO.

The T. Eaton Co. deserves a special mention in a history of Canadian garment manufacturing and retailing. This company was a key player in three different sectors. As a department store, it operated for 130 years, from 1869 to 1999. Eaton's, as the firm was popularly known, became a household name in Canada as a mail order company. As one of the early large manufacturers it led the way in vertical integration.

Eaton's introduced its first mail order catalog in 1884. Timothy Eaton was thus able to offer goods from his Toronto store to rural families throughout western Canada, now more accessible with railroad transportation. While a wide variety of merchandise was sold through the catalog, apparel was the dominant commodity and generated the largest sales volume.

Eaton's had been producing small amounts of clothing for the store in the 1870s, but following the first mail order catalog, it launched into manufacturing shirts, women's undergarments, and boys' clothing. By 1893, Timothy Eaton had established a four-story factory in Toronto for women's coats, capes, and skirts; three years later another factory was built for menswear. By 1904, with its new large factory and specialized machines, it was the leader in Toronto's clothing industry. Becoming the most successful of the emerging vertically integrated garment makers, Eaton's expanded its facilities twice more in that decade, making it the largest single center of garment production in the country at the time. The story of Eaton's manufacturing is also that of the beginnings of labor organization and its difficulties. The previously mentioned strike/lockout of 1912 was one of the most bitter in Toronto's history. Its reported cause was that the factory had become so efficient owing to the introduction of new machinery that the firm was eliminating jobs for workers.

In the 1920s and 1930s, it was estimated that Eaton's had half the market share of all Canadian department stores. Eaton's was at the top in department store sales until 1951, when its competition

This boy's summer outfit was made exclusively for the Montreal department store Henry Morgan and Co. in 1935. © McCord Museum M977.8.1.1-3. http://www.mccord-museum.qc.ca/en/

began to increase. By 1950, with thirty thousand employees, Eaton's was Canada's third-largest employer, after the railways and the federal government. Because of its size and spread across the country, it had an inevitable influence on retail wages in large cities and smaller communities.

By 1958, Eaton's gradually stopped manufacturing its own goods. It ceased its mail order operations in 1976 because of lack of profitability. It continued through these decades as a strong department store, however, and by 1994 the Eaton family still owned ninety stores in nine Canadian provinces but was beginning to experience serious financial and identity difficulties. Although the Eaton's company went out of business in 1999, its name lives on in shopping complexes in Montreal and Toronto, situated where the stores were formerly located.

MAIL ORDER AND GARMENT RETAIL IN CANADA

Mail order catalog sales were a very important means of garment retail in Canada from the end of the nineteenth century onward, particularly from the 1920s to the 1960s. The first Eaton's catalog, published in 1884, was a thirty-two-page booklet listing department store merchandise. In 1903, catalog sales became a separate operation with its own merchandise assortment. By 1905, Eaton's Winnipeg was issuing its own catalog for customers in the Canadian West, where mail order kept customers in remote communities supplied with essentials. Warehouses in Regina and Saskatoon later helped facilitate western shipments.

Mail order retailers adapted their offerings and publications to their markets. Eaton's Winnipeg offered its western customers greater variety in outdoor garments, cold-weather clothing, and workwear for men, than Eaton's Toronto, which targeted a female readership. Its portrayals of women and clothing varied in order to appeal to a vast, heterogeneous clientele in the central and eastern parts of Canada, including both rural and urban dwellers.

While, as previously noted, Eaton's had a significant market share of mail order sales, it also had competition, particularly in the early decades of the twentieth century. In Toronto, Simpson's competed directly with Eaton's as a large mail order company as well as a department store. Simpson's published mail order catalogs regularly after 1894. Many department stores offered localized mail order service in the late nineteenth and early twentieth centuries. The Hudson's Bay Company published a catalog from 1896 to 1913. Woodward's fared well in British Columbia from 1898 to 1953, and Army and Navy offered its discount line via mail order from 1919 to 1986. Montreal's Scroggies and Dupuis Frères also published their own mail order catalogs. Scroggies was offering catalogs in French by 1905, placing it twenty years ahead of its competitors in reaching a French-speaking market. Eaton's launched the French version of its mail order catalog in 1928.

In 1953, Simpson's forged a partnership with the U.S. company Sears and Roebuck, and Simpson's-Sears took over Simpson's mail order operation. Its market share increased dramatically after 1976, when Eaton's discontinued its catalog. Sears Canada took over from Simpson's-Sears in 1978. Sears remains the only major Canadian department store with a national presence that continues to produce a print catalog. It has service centers in Belleville, Ontario, and Regina, Saskatchewan. Sears' mail order operation also offers apparel and other general merchandise at its online store.

DEPARTMENT STORES AND GARMENT RETAIL IN CANADA

Department stores have long played a significant role in the history of garment retailing in Canada. In 1930 they accounted for 42 percent of the market share in women's clothing and 27 percent in menswear. In 1951 the market share of women's apparel had dropped to 33 percent, yet millinery and women's wear industry representatives claimed that the three largest department store groups, Eaton's, Simpson's, and Morgan's, determined seasonally whether or not a manufacturer remained in business. Even by 1977, industry advisors remarked that retail buying power was highly concentrated in department store chains. In the early twenty-first century department stores maintain a strong overall 26 percent of the apparel retail market.

In Canada's major cities, department store buildings were urban landmarks, defining apparel shopping districts. Eaton's Toronto, which opened at the corner of Queen and Yonge in 1883, competed with Simpson's on the opposite street corner as of 1896, creating a retail center for well over a century. Henry Morgan's, founded in 1845, established itself in a prominent new building in Montreal in 1891. When Simpson's opened in Montreal in 1905 in the former Murphy's department store, they both anchored a retail mile on busy St. Catherine Street, known as the city's prime fashion center.

In the 1890s and the first decades of the twentieth century, department stores opened in many Canadian towns and cities. Many of them had strong retail presences in their cities and regions for many decades. Even those that did not branch out of their region were local landmarks. In 1903, Woodward's opened in Vancouver, where until 1993 it was an icon of that city and favorite shopping destination. Montreal's Dupuis Frères department store, with a few branches, was well known from 1868 to its closure in 1978. Ogilvy's, still in business, has served Montrealers since 1866.

The Eaton's company built up to a significant nationwide department store chain. It took hold of the Montreal market in 1925, when it acquired Goodwin's department store. When renovations were complete in 1931, the nine-story building was thought to be the finest in the chain. Eaton's extended its reach in the West in the same decade with stores in Regina in 1926, Saskatoon in 1928, and Calgary and Edmonton in 1929. In 1957, Eaton's in Montreal became the largest department store in Canada. Morgan's remained Montreal based but in the 1950s had branched out in stores throughout the city, as well as in Toronto, Ottawa, and Hamilton.

The Hudson's Bay Company (HBC), Canada's oldest retailer, established in 1670 by royal charter for the fur trade, diversified its activities in 1870 to encompass a network of retail stores. From 1881 to 1892, it opened large stores in Winnipeg, Calgary, Vancouver, and Edmonton, followed by Victoria and Saskatoon in the 1920s. The company reinforced its role in the department store retail arena in 1960, with the purchase of Morgan's stores, and began national expansion as The Bay, although they retained the Morgan's name until 1972.

In 1953, Simpson's continued to operate five existing department stores throughout Canada under that name; over the next few decades it would open many new stores under the name Simpson's-Sears. By 1973, the company began to name new stores Sears to avoid confusion with the distinct operation of the Simpson's company. In 1978, Simpson's stores were bought by HBC, and their names changed to The Bay by the late 1980s. Sears bought out the Eaton's department stores that closed in 1999.

Some Canadian department stores ventured into high-end fashion. In the early decades, department stores incorporated men's tailoring and women's dressmaking departments, adding a custom-order business to the ready-to-wear assortment. In the mid-twentieth century, Eaton's boasted the Ensemble Shop in Toronto and the Salon Français in Montreal, and Simpson's operated the St. Regis Room in Toronto and the Salon Vendôme in Montreal, each of which featured imported international designer fashions.

Holt Renfrew, which began as a furrier in Quebec City and expanded its operations to include department stores in the major cities of Quebec, Ontario, and western Canada, offered superior custom-design services in its Montreal store. In the 1940s, its Salon Marie-Paule featured creations by Montreal designer Marie-Paule Nolin, who managed a couture workroom of some twenty employees in the store. This arrangement with a local designer has no other known parallel in the history of Canadian department stores and fashion design. From 1951 through the 1970s, Canadians could have Dior couture garments made locally, under a licensing agreement with Holt Renfrew. A workroom of fifteen couture seamstresses created these garments in the Montreal store.

Holt Renfrew still operates nine stores in central and western Canada in the early twenty-first century and occupies the niche of high-end fashion department store, grouping several designer boutiques under one roof. HBC operates five hundred stores across Canada under The Bay and Zellers banners, with significant apparel sales. HBC was the fifth-largest Canadian employer in 2003. Sears is Canada's largest and most well-known mass-market department store chain.

BOUTIQUES AND CHAIN STORES IN CANADA

In the 1950s, suburban malls developed rapidly, drawing customers away from downtown cores. Boutiques were on the rise as an alternative to the more traditional department stores and the more expensive specialty shops. Department stores reacted by expanding the number of "boutique" spaces within their walls. Window displays and visual merchandising in clothing stores became much more sophisticated.

Of the 1960s boutiques, outstanding examples were Unicorn and Poupée Rouge in Toronto. In Montreal one incarnation of

the boutique Le Château followed this model, offering fashion-forward youthful styles. Le Château has evolved to become a manufacturer-retailer with a strong market presence in Canada in the early twenty-first century. Numerous Canadian manufacturer-retailers developed through the 1970s, the presence of their boutiques in shopping malls giving them extensive market exposure. By the late 1970s, industry advisors were noting that retailers who were not directly involved in manufacturing were increasingly dictating the design aspect of the manufacturing process because of their market knowledge.

In the 1980s, the market became saturated for Canadian apparel retail. Many of Canada's top fashion retailers expanded into the United States, only to suffer significant losses. The 1980s U.S. expansion of Dylex, the largest clothing manufacturer-retailer in the country and one of its one hundred largest companies, proved disastrous and the company has since folded. Dylex enjoyed two decades of success in Canada and at its apogee owned or had interests in twenty-seven hundred stores.

The apparel market in Canada was particularly hard hit by the 1990–1991 recession. In the 1990s, there was an influx of U.S.

The workroom of Salon Marie-Paule, at Holt Renfrew and Co. department store, Montreal, ca. 1945. The store offered an in-store, custom design service, using the skills of fifteen couture seamstresses. ©McCord Museum, Montreal, Fonds Marie-Paule Nolin. http://www.mccord-museum.qc.ca/en/

retailers into the Canadian market, where they now dominate. A wave of consolidations took place, as newer vendors with discount lines moved in and large department store chains like Eaton's closed their doors.

In 2007 in Canada, apparel specialty chain stores dominated the market, with more than 33 percent of the market share. Many of these chains are in fact manufacturer-retailers.

MANUFACTURER-RETAILERS AND DOMINANT RETAIL CHAINS

Canadian apparel retailing has given rise to several successful chains of manufacturer-retailers. National chains include Reitman's, a family-operated manufacturer-retailer founded in 1926 in Montreal, which has over three hundred forty stores under the flagship banner and more than eight hundred stores in total. In 2002, Reitman's bought out another retailer, the Shirmax Organization, which had been in business since 1957. Le Château, founded in 1959, has found its niche in quick production turnaround time, facilitated by having about 40 percent of its production done in Canada. It continues to operate many Canadian and some U.S. stores.

Boutiques San Francisco, which began in 1978, had as many as 140 stores in Quebec and Ontario in the early 2000s. Jacob and Groupe Dynamite each have a thirty-year history, and each operates some two hundred stores in the United States and Canada. Tristan, with similar longevity, operates some seventy stores in Canada and the United States. Since 1984 Aritzia has promoted a unique boutique concept and has expanded into several locations in the United States as well as across Canada. Other large well-known retail chains include Laura, founded by Laura Wolstein as a single store in Montreal in 1930; its 136 stores across the country sell well-known brands as well as its private-label merchandise. Toronto-based Danier is one of the largest publicly traded specialty apparel leather retailers in the world, with some ninety Canadian stores. Mountain Equipment Coop is the largest retail cooperative in Canada and sells activewear and outdoor gear. Mark's Work Wearhouse, owned by the Canadian Tire Group, sells its private-label apparel in over three hundred locations in Canada.

Some Canadian chains have ventured further afield. Parachute, which began in 1978 and ran until 1993, was the concept of design team Nicola Pelly and Harry Parnass. This manufacturer-retailer expanded into the United States in 1980 and at its height was found in five hundred points of sale around the world, including two hundred in Europe. Roots was established in Toronto in 1973 by Michael Budman and Don Green of the United States and now has more than one hundred and ten stores in Canada and the United States, with thirty Asian locations. Vancouver-based Lululemon Athletica opened its first store in 2000 and has since opened more than fifty locations across Canada, the United States, Australia, and Japan. La Senza, created in 1988 by Lawrence Lewin, operates five hundred stores in thirty countries.

TAILORS, DRESSMAKERS, AND FASHION DESIGNERS

In the late nineteenth and early twentieth centuries, most dressmakers and tailors ran relatively small-scale establishments catering to local markets. Canadian city directories document large numbers of dressmakers and tailors. Outstanding names from this period are those who received patronage from Canada's governor general, whose print advertising included the mention "By Appointment to His Excellency." These included the tailor G.M. Holbrook in Ottawa and dressmakers Stitt and O'Brien in Toronto.

Though names of prominent tailors and dressmakers from the nineteenth and the first half of the twentieth centuries can be documented, their influence almost never extended beyond their hometowns and cities. An exception is the Montreal tailoring firm Gibb and Co., which in the 1850s sent representatives to take orders in such locations as Kingston, Ontario, and Buffalo, New York, and received orders by mail from Boston and Philadelphia. Most small establishments did not enjoy such far-flung reputations, however. In the 1920s and 1930s, Ida Desmarais in Montreal and Martha in Toronto were known locally as producers of high fashion. Similarly, Gaby Bernier catered to the Montreal elite from the 1930s through the 1950s, as did Marie-Paule Nolin, who set up her Montreal couture house in the 1930s and was active until the 1970s.

In the 1950s, however, a concentrated effort took place to establish a Canadian couture industry with a recognizable design identity and media presence. The Association of Canadian Couturiers was founded in Montreal in 1954. Its first president was Raoul-Jean Fouré, a Montreal custom couturier who had established his business in the city in the late 1920s, where bridal couture became his specialty. In the year of its founding, the group produced the first all-Canadian fashion show in New York. Twice a year this group, with the assistance of government and textile manufacturers, presented fashion shows in major Canadian cities. Consolidating publicity and production budgets enabled these individual couture designers to make an impact on a wider market that none of them could have accessed on their own. Among the better-known designers in the association were Montreal's Jacques de Montjoye and Toronto's Federica. In 1968 this group disbanded, but a new generation of talented young designers was already making its mark.

In the 1960s several new Canadian designers managed to reach beyond their local borders with a different strategy. They managed to successfully combine custom business for private clients and team up with established garment manufacturers to produce high-end, ready-to-wear lines under their own name, rather than being employed as anonymous stylists. Two young Montreal designers received national and international attention, in part because of the attention focused on that city in the years surrounding Expo 67. Collections by Michel Robichaud and Marielle Fleury toured Europe as part of a Canadian government initiative to attract attention to Montreal at that time. These collections had strong cultural references; Robichaud showed a coat inspired by a Mountie uniform, and Fleury presented garments of handwoven fabrics by a local weaver.

Robichaud and Fleury, along with a larger group, founded the Fashion Designers Association of Canada in 1974. Also involved were Montrealers Léo Chevalier, whose career spanned from 1966 through the 1980s, and John Warden, who was active in Montreal from 1964 through the 1990s. Toronto designers included Pat McDonagh, who made a splash in the 1960s and continues her active design career some forty years later; Claire Haddad, well known through the 1970s and 1980s, particularly for loungewear; and Marilyn Brooks, whose design career spanned from the 1960s

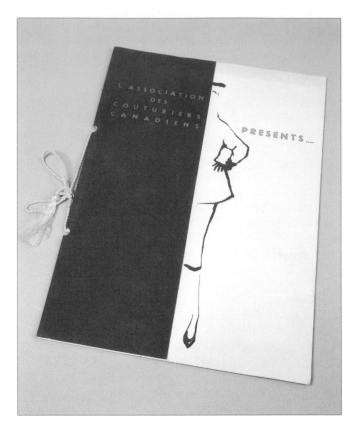

Program from the first fashion show presented by the Association of Canadian Couturiers at the Hotel Pierre in New York, 1954. ©McCord Museum, Montreal; M2007.68.4. http://www.mccord-museum.qc.ca/en/

to 2003. The association, active until 1980, aimed to promote recognition of fashion designers as well as create public awareness of the contribution of fashion design to the Canadian economy and cultural life. Several other designers joined the founding group to present seasonal fashion shows in Montreal and Toronto until it disbanded in 1980. Regional associations continued through the 1980s and 1990s with similar mandates for exposure of independent designers.

Since the 1970s, many Canadian fashion designers have developed significant reputations in Canada and abroad. Alfred Sung is a Toronto designer whose name has appeared on a variety of labels and whose designs were initially featured in Club Monaco, a retail chain which expanded internationally. Montreal's Jean-Claude Poitras has signed a variety of men's and women's lines through the 1980s and 1990s.

Simon Chang, whose design career began in the 1970s, is one of the most commercially successful Canadian fashion designers. Hilary Radley has built a reputation on coat design. Linda Lundstrom is also well known for her Canadian-manufactured winter coats.

Philippe Dubuc has achieved renown since he began his high-end, ready-to-wear men's line in 1993, which expanded to include women's clothing in 2001. Also based in Montreal, Marie Saint-Pierre has enjoyed over twenty years as a high-profile independent designer of women's clothing. Toronto's Lida Baday, active since 1987, is one of the best-known designers in Canada in the early twenty-first century. Vancouver-based Yumi Eto has received international recognition.

In Montreal, Serge et Réal continue a long-standing career in custom couture clothing. In Ottawa, Richard Robinson has also had a significant couture career.

Aside from government initiatives of the past few decades, various other programs have fostered independent designers. The Toronto Fashion Incubator, founded in the 1980s, helps further the careers of designers in that city. Imperial Tobacco established the Matinée Fashion Foundation in 1992 to provide grants and financial support to independent Canadian designers. The program ran until 2003, when it was abolished due to legislation against promotion of tobacco products.

In 2007, the Toronto-based Fashion Design Council of Canada holds L'Oréal Fashion Week in Toronto twice a year. It is billed as the primary vehicle for branding and promoting fashion in Canada and is primarily funded by sponsorship. The Montreal Fashion Network organizes Montreal Fashion Week, also twice a year, which receives private sponsorship as well as public funding. These events show the work of up-and-coming designers and draw media attention to Canadian fashion.

THE CANADIAN APPAREL INDUSTRY IN TRANSITION

In the first decade of the twenty-first century, Canada's apparel industry is definitely in transition, primarily due to the rise in imports following the removal of tariffs and quotas on imported clothing in 2005, in a market where worldwide capacity is twice worldwide demand. Manufacturers continue to lose market share to offshore suppliers. The market share of domestic shipments has declined from 59 percent in 1995 to 33 percent in 2005. The market share of imports, in contrast, has gone up from 41 percent in 1995 to 67 percent in 2005, a 65 percent increase.

Between 1995 and 2005, the total apparel market, driven by rising imports, has risen 18 percent. Total shipments and domestic shipments have followed a pattern of decline since 1995. Statistics Canada records that between 2000 and 2005, Canadian apparel shipments have decreased 24 percent. To offset the continuing decline of the domestic share of total apparel shipments, domestic manufacturers continue to engage in sustained export market expansion. Although there have been slight declines in export volume each year from 2000 to 2005, the export share of total shipments in 2005 showed a 91 percent increase over that of 2000.

Statistics Canada reports that in 2005 the apparel industry allocated some CAN$100.3 million for new machinery, equipment, and buildings. The Canadian apparel industry's investments in machinery, equipment, and upgrading labor skills reflect the industry's drive to sustain its international competitiveness. Currently duty remission programs, managed by the federal Canadian Apparel and Textile Industries Program (CATIP), are designed to help the most vulnerable sectors of the apparel industry adjust to increased competition from low-wage countries and extend to outerwear, shirts, and blouses as well as to fabrics.

References and Further Reading

Baril, Gérald. *Dicomode: Dictionnaire de la mode au Québec de 1900 à nos jours*. Montreal: Fides, 2004.

Gannagé, Charlene. *Double Day, Double Bind: Women Garment Workers*. Toronto: Women's Press, 1986.

Hiebert, Daniel. "Discontinuity and the Emergence of Flexible Production: Garment Production in Toronto, 1901–1931." *Economic Geography* 66, no. 3 (July 1990): 229–253.

Industry Canada, Consumer Products Industries Branch. *Apparel. Part I, Overview and Prospects*. Ottawa: Industry Canada, 1997.

Johnson, Laura C., and Robert E. Johnson. *The Seam Allowance: Industrial Home Sewing in Canada*. Toronto: Women's Educational Press, 1982.

Kinnear, Mary. *First Days, Fighting Days: Women in Manitoba History*. Regina: University of Regina, 1987.

Kuz, Tony J. *Winnipeg 1874–1974: Progress and Prospects*. Winnipeg: Manitoba Department of Industry and Commerce, 1974.

Larocque, Peter J. "'The Work Being Chiefly Performed by Women': Female Workers in the Garment Industry in Saint John, New Brunswick in 1871." In *Fashion: A Canadian Perspective*, edited by Alexandra Palmer, 139–165. Toronto: University of Toronto Press, 2004.

Lewis, Robert. *Manufacturing Montreal: The Making of an Industrial Landscape, 1850 to 1930*. Baltimore: Johns Hopkins University Press, 2000.

MacKay, M. Elaine. "Three Thousand Stitches: The Development of the Clothing Industry in Nineteenth-Century Halifax." In *Fashion: A Canadian Perspective*, edited by Alexandra Palmer, 166–181. Toronto: University of Toronto Press, 2004.

Mahon, Rianne. *The Politics of Industrial Restructuring: Canadian Textiles*. Toronto: University of Toronto Press, 1984.

Palmer, Alexandra. "The Association of Canadian Couturiers." In *Fashion: A Canadian Perspective*, edited by Alexandra Palmer, 90–109. Toronto: University of Toronto Press, 2004.

Reuben, Beth Tzedec, and Helene Dennis Museum. *A Common Thread: A History of Toronto's Garment Industry*. Toronto: Beth Tzedec Reuben and Helene Dennis Museum, 2003.

Routh, Caroline. *In Style: 100 Years of Canadian Women's Fashion*. Toronto: Stoddart, 1993.

Steedman, Mercedes. *Angels of the Workplace: Women and the Construction of Gender Relations in the Canadian Clothing Industry, 1890–1940*. Toronto, New York, and Oxford: Oxford University Press, 1997.

Textile and Clothing Board. *Clothing Inquiry: A Report to the Minister of Industry, Trade, and Commerce*. Ottawa: Textile and Clothing Board, 1977.

Tulchinsky, Gerald. "Hidden among the Smokestacks: Toronto's Clothing Industry, 1871–1901." In *Old Ontario*, edited by David Keane and Colin Read, 257–284. Toronto and Oxford: Dundurn Press, 1990.

Cynthia Cooper

See also The Textile Industry; The Garment Industry and Retailing in the United States; Textile and Apparel Industries at the Turn of the Millennium.

Writing about Fashions

The twentieth century brought many innovations in the fashion world, and those innovations prompted many people to report on new fashions, to analyze them, and even to criticize them. Fashion was, and is, news. Fashion is both an artistic expression and a vital industry that makes significant contributions to a nation's economy. And fashion is a sartorial mirror that reflects a culture's values, beliefs, politics, and technologies. Fashion, then, can also be controversial. With so many facets to its nature, fashion provided an almost endless variety of topics for twentieth-century writers. Some writers loved it and some writers hated it, but fashion was the topic of many written conversations. At the beginning of the century, there were several women's general interest magazines and a few fledgling fashion magazines, but by the end of the century, fashion found its way into a wide array of newspapers, magazines, academic journals, monographs, and history books. Through these media, writers left us a rich legacy of published works about fashion.

FIN DE SIÈCLE

The twentieth century inherited from its predecessor a rapidly evolving world of fashion. Paris dominated the scene, and most consumers viewed that city as the source of all true fashion inspirations. There, couturiers presented their seasonal creations to an elite clientele. Ladies of means traveled to France and spent weeks or even months selecting their wardrobes and enduring numerous fittings. Finally, with their precious cargo carefully packed, they sailed home for another social season. Paris dictated the direction of fashion, but in the United States and Canada, very few women had the financial means to afford Paris couture. Yet at the end of the nineteenth century, many women knew about the latest Paris trends. They owed their fashion education to the diligent reporting of the ladies' fashion magazines, to the fashion editorials in their newspapers, and to the copywriters who wrote for fashion advertisers.

Paris loved all the publicity about its fashions, and it courted the fashion press. The organizing body for the couture industry was the Chambre Syndicale de la Haute Couture Parisienne. This organization coordinated all the Paris couture shows so that retailers, manufacturers, and the press could see all the openings. The Chambre Syndicale also provided press releases about the various couture houses. These press releases afforded the women's magazines, and even some smaller hometown newspapers, official, firsthand reports of the glamorous world of Paris haute couture. Women who could not afford to travel to Paris could still read about the latest fashions and adapt them for their own wardrobes.

During the nineteenth century, many fashion consumers still made their own dresses, or they employed the services of a local dressmaker. There was, however, a new fashion option: *ready-to-wear*, which referred to apparel made to standard sizes by a manufacturer and sold in retail stores or catalogs. This new technology saw its birth in the Civil War when the United States needed to provide uniforms rapidly for the Union army. The manufacturers that developed these technologies during the war continued their efforts afterward by producing ready-to-wear clothing for men. Soon, these manufacturers turned their attentions to the women's market.

DEMOCRATIZATION OF FASHION

The ready-to-wear industry first produced basic, staple items for women rather than more high-fashion garments. They began with simple capes, skirts, and petticoats. With new technologies and an influx of skilled immigrant workers from Europe, the ready-to-wear industry became a growing force in the fashion world by the end of the nineteenth century. This new industry fueled another major change in the fashion world—the democratization of fashion.

Democratization simply meant that at the beginning of the twentieth century, fashion became available to a wider array of consumers. It was no longer just the purview of the wealthy. Manufactured fashions and a cheap source of labor meant that fashion was now affordable to nearly everyone who wanted it. And as women began more and more to work outside of the home, they now had their own incomes to spend on fashion. A new breed of retail emporiums eagerly enticed women with the splendor of their architecture and the promise of a pampered shopping experience, but some entrepreneurs thought that these new consumers needed guidance. As the fashion industry grew, the publishing industry saw new opportunities in the fashion world, and it quickly developed beautifully artistic magazines with the primary goal of reporting on fashion.

FROM WOMEN'S MAGAZINES TO FASHION MAGAZINES

Women's general interest magazines were not new, but they originally offered a variety of topics, not just fashion. By the 1880s, women in both the United States and Canada could choose from a variety of consumer magazines including *Godey's Lady's Book*, *The Cosmopolitan* (later abbreviated to *Cosmopolitan*), *The Queen* (renamed *McCall's Magazine*), *Harper's Bazaar*, *The Ladies' Home Journal*, and *Good Housekeeping*. There was tremendous pressure on the women of the era to create an artistic home in order to guarantee the success of their families, and these general interest magazines guided readers in this cause. The magazines offered some fashion information, but they also provided tips on cooking, gardening, and raising children.

Demorest's Family Magazine, December 1889, p. 124. *Demorest's Magazine* (previously called *Mme. Demorest's Mirror of Fashions*) brought the latest Paris fashion news to U.S. readers. Library of Congress, Prints & Photographs Division, LC-USZ62-115741.

Beyond the practical advice, these publications also provided a literary source. Each month readers could choose from poetry, short stories, and fictional serials, all with a moral undertone that reflected the culture's view of a proper lady. That proper lady, though, was also expected to dress according to the etiquette standards of the time. The correct Victorian lady followed strict guidelines that dictated the proper dress for day, for evening, for calling on friends, and for mourning. With so many rules, combined with the new opportunities in ready-to-wear, the market was ready for a new kind of publication.

In 1892, *Vogue* launched its first edition. *Vogue* targeted both women and men with the latest information on the New York social scene, including news of socialites, theater openings, and book reviews. By 1899, the magazine also offered its readers the opportunity to order paper patterns of the latest fashions. *Vogue* readers could either use the paper patterns to sew their own versions of the newest styles, or they could take the patterns to their favorite dressmaker for her interpretation. However the women used the patterns, this fashion medium allowed its readers to own their own paper copies of the latest fashions. *Vogue* eventually added a sister publication devoted solely to patterns and personal sewing. *Vogue* was initially a weekly publication that used both pictures and prose to guide its readers to the new fashion trends. Fashion was becoming big business. A new, synergistic relationship between fashion and magazine publication was growing as well.

FASHION ADVERTISING

Apparel manufacturers needed a means of marketing their products to the consuming public, and the public was eager for news of the latest trends from Paris. Publishers were delighted to have a new opportunity for readership, but they needed revenue from more than just subscribers. For this reason, a third industry was also growing—fashion advertising. Magazine and newspaper readers culled information from feature stories and editorials, but advertisements offered less objective persuasion as to the correct mode of dress. By definition, an advertisement is funded by an identifiable sponsor. Those sponsors included the manufacturers who produced the fashions and the retailers who carried those fashions in their stores. One might not ordinarily think of advertisements as a source of fashion writing. Fashion ads are often full of beautiful illustrations created by some of the world's top artists, but ads also carry very carefully crafted prose. Skilled advertisers know that the illustrations attract the reader's attention but the words do the persuading. Sometimes those words describe the product, and sometimes the text is aimed at the reader's attitudes, beliefs, and values. The advertising industry grew in size and developed new techniques throughout the twentieth century, and it also came under scrutiny.

In 1892, the *Daily Trade Record* was published for the first time; it was distributed at the Chicago World's Fair (also known as the Columbian Exposition) in 1893. This medium was unique for two reasons. First, it focused on men's fashions, and second, it was a trade publication. A trade publication targets subscribers who work in a particular industry. The *Daily Trade Record* was later renamed the *Daily News Record (DNR)*. *DNR* was originally published daily in a newspaper format, but by the end of the twentieth century, it moved to a glossy paper format with only weekly publications.

DNR's success spawned a sister publication, *Women's Wear Daily (WWD)*, which first appeared in 1910 with a focus on the women's apparel market. It, too, took the form of a daily newspaper with insider information for those working in the trade. *WWD* became known as the bible of the fashion industry and in the early twenty-first century, it is still in print. Each day the paper highlights a different segment of the industry, including subjects such as textiles, cosmetics, sportswear, trade, retailing, employment opportunities, and couture. The paper also covers important issues that impact the fashion industry, including trade regulations, legislation, and business activities. *WWD* is an insider's must-read, but it is seldom available on the newsstand, and subscription rates effectively price the average consumer out of its readership.

At the fin de siècle, or end of the nineteenth century, the fashion world was ready to move into a new era of influence and business. The consuming public was interested in this growing enterprise, and publishers and advertisers were eager to report on every nuance of its activities. From the wonders of Paris haute couture to the ready-to-wear offerings at the local retailer, writers had a rich subject to explore and a reading public hungry for news.

Cover from the U.S.-based *McCall's Magazine*, 1910. Courtesy of Sandra Buckland.

THE FIRST RUMBLINGS OF UNREST

The differences between the two branches of the fashion industry became more pronounced during the twentieth century, and the fashion press grew in both size and influence. As the fashion press expanded its voice, it also flexed its editorial muscles. Editors of major fashion publications, such as *Vogue*, *Harper's Bazaar*, and the *New York Times*, became celebrities and *gatekeepers*, that is, people who edit news of the fashion world for the consuming public. A gatekeeper decides which collections will get the most coverage, which manufacturers or designers will get editorial approval, which designers will be criticized, and which collections will be ignored. Therefore, the fashion press, and particularly the powerful editors, helped to shape the direction of fashion. Consumers viewed the fashion press as an authority on all the nuances of fashionable dress. Initially, twentieth-century consumers followed the directives of the fashion press, but by the end of the century, they had discovered their own power. They became much more discriminating in the advice that they accepted and the advice that they rejected.

The fashion press and the Paris haute couture industry enjoyed a mutual love affair; the press loved Paris couture, and the Chambre Syndicale courted the U.S. press. Until midcentury, Canada lacked its own fashion magazines, so its consumers read U.S. publications or their local newspapers. Paris loved the publicity, but it also carefully controlled the press.

Paris presented its new designs at private shows held in individual couture houses. The designers welcomed stories about their collections, so they provided prewritten press releases. No one, however, was allowed to sketch during a show. U.S. designers Claire McCardell and Elizabeth Hawes began their careers as undercover sketchers. They would attend couture openings and then return to their hotel rooms, quickly sketching everything that they could remember. When the press began using photography, the Chambre Syndicale stipulated that no photographs could be printed for thirty days after an opening. This time lag gave Paris exclusivity before ready-to-wear manufacturers could produce copies called *knockoffs*. A publication that failed to comply with the thirty-day waiting period would be banned from future openings.

Elizabeth Hawes, in her book *Fashion Is Spinach*, later wrote that the news from Paris was so important to the U.S. press that in 1926 there were "over a hundred American fashion reporters in Paris." She continued, saying that there were "many" offices that wrote stories about Paris and sent them home for publication there. In Hawes's opinion, *Vogue* and *Harper's Bazaar* were the largest and were "recognized as the most important publicity agents the French [could] use."

There were two reasons why Paris fashions dominated the U.S. press. The first reason is what Hawes called "the French legend." She wrote, "all really beautiful clothes are designed in the houses of the French couturiers and all women want those clothes." The second reason was owing to the differences between the couture and ready-to-wear industries. The Paris couture industry enjoyed design protection, but U.S. ready-to-wear manufacturers had no such safety net. Therefore, ready-to-wear manufacturers did not hold fashion openings for fear of copying. Retailers held fashion shows after the new designs had been shipped, but these lacked the glamour or the excitement of a Paris opening. Furthermore, many U.S. designs were adaptations of Paris couture designs because many manufacturers believed that U.S. consumers wanted to follow French fashion dictates. Paris fashions were exciting and glamorous, and U.S. newspapers and magazines were delighted to feed the French legend.

U.S. newspapers and magazines like to carry stories about famous people and celebrities, and the public loves to read about them. Readers devour all the intimate details of the lives of the rich and famous, and Paris couturiers were celebrities. Designers from the United States, on the other hand, were seldom, if ever, known to the average consumer. Prior to the 1930s, most garments bore the name of the retailer who sold them. Retailers saw themselves as fashion authorities. They believed that it was much more prestigious for a consumer to wear a garment with a label from Marshall Field's or Sak's Fifth Avenue or Bonwit Teller than to wear one from a manufacturer or from a domestic designer. Therefore, manufacturers struggled for name recognition. If they put their own labels in their garments, the stores simply removed the labels and replaced them with store labels. U.S. designers were even farther behind in name recognition.

The majority of U.S. designers worked anonymously for manufacturers. They were seldom allowed to produce original work; instead, they interpreted the latest Paris fashions for the U.S. and Canadian markets. These talented men and women received no recognition; their names were unknown to the public. They were not celebrities, so they were not newsworthy. Besides, they worked in the ready-to-wear industry. Most readers wore ready-to-wear clothes but dreamed of Paris couture. By the end of the century, however, world events would shift the focus of the media coverage.

WORLD WAR I, THE DEPRESSION, AND WORLD WAR II

World War I brought great hardship to France and, thus, to the Parisian fashion world. The nation suffered from shortages of labor and materials, and their exports to the United States were heavily taxed. North American women were also growing dissatisfied with the ornate nature of couture designs. Instead, even women who could afford couture began patronizing the more Americanized ready-to-wear fashions. *Vogue* continued to report on Paris openings, but fewer buyers attended.

In 1914, *Harper's Bazaar* sponsored a fashion show called "American Clothes for the American Woman." The event was held at the New York Roof Garden on Times Square, and it proved to be a success. In December 1914, *Vogue* reported on a subsequent show of U.S. designs. *Vogue* acknowledged some resemblance to Paris fashions but asked the question, "Is not Paris the master and New York the pupil who, now that the master is otherwise occupied, seeks to prove that by constant study and appreciation it, too, has learned something of the art of making clothes?" The two most influential fashion magazines on the continent were now endorsing U.S. design. They were not just

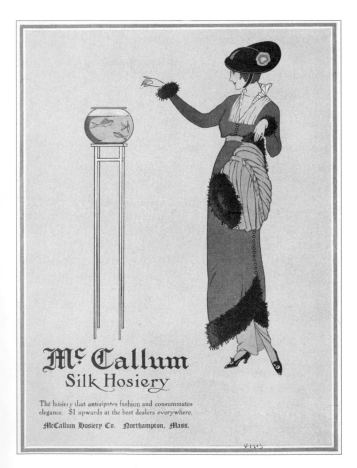

Advertisement for McCallum silk hosiery, 1913. Beautiful illustrations were used in advertisements to attract the reader's attention. Courtesy New York Public Library.

reporting on the events; they were sponsoring and praising them. Their opinions mattered to North American readers, and one can assume that these readers surmised approval for their growing tastes for domestic designs.

The United States was also growing a new source of fashion leadership: the movies. Hollywood fed consumers' need for glamour and celebrities and beautiful garments with larger-than-life productions. U.S. designers such as Gilbert Adrian, Irene, Edith Head, and Howard Greer dressed their stars in all the glamour of a Paris opening. The newspapers and magazines contained stories of all the floodlit openings and celebrity gatherings. The movie studios soon realized that women went to the movies to see the new designs as much as to see the movie itself. The studios capitalized on this phenomenon by releasing ready-to-wear copies of celebrities' wardrobes simultaneously with the release of their movies. Women could wear copies of the same dress designed by Adrian for Joan Crawford. The women knew where to find the dresses because retailers were quick to advertise the garments in the local newspapers, and the women knew the names of the designers. Once again, the media reported the news and influenced, although perhaps inadvertently, the opinions of the consumers.

The 1930s found the world immersed in the Great Depression. Retailers struggled along with consumers, and Paris exports to North America dwindled. Lord & Taylor's vice president at the time, Dorothy Shaver, initiated a new campaign to stimulate lagging sales. She chose a group of designers, including Elizabeth Hawes, and promoted them, by name, with their own labels in the garments. Shaver launched a major advertising campaign in the New York newspapers and magazines, a major and innovative step away from the tradition of promoting French designers. Hawes later wrote that Shaver's move prompted a "flood of articles on American Designers … in newspapers and magazines all over the U.S.A." Shaver acknowledged Paris's leadership, but she also recognized that U.S. designers had something unique to offer to North American consumers. With Shaver's influence as a fashion industry leader and with the authority of major fashion publications, the public moved one step closer to a love affair with domestically designed ready-to-wear.

In the spring of 1940, Paris held its last couture opening until after World War II. Carmel Snow, famous editor of *Harper's Bazaar*, embraced Paris as the heart of all fashion to such a degree that she literally risked her life to attend the shows. She later reported in her magazine that the city showed great courage, and that "Paris was still, and [would] always be, the center of fashion." Snow loved Paris and used her magazine to promote the couture that she adored. But when the Nazis occupied Paris in June 1940, *Harper's Bazaar*, *Vogue*, and every other publication in the free world found themselves without a story line.

The U.S. fashion industry quickly restructured its operations and used the fashion magazines and major newspapers as a means of telling the world that New York was now the fashion capital of the world. For the duration of the war, the United Kingdom, Canada, and South America looked to New York for fashion leadership. The New York industry, however, suffered some growing pains along the way. In 1940, New York's Mayor LaGuardia called a reverse press conference of all the major fashion writers in the city. He wanted to know what was happening in this most important industry. LaGuardia recognized the power of the press to discover, report, and influence its readers.

The fashion magazines and major newspapers were quick to support New York. However, this support required some operational changes. For example, the *New York Times* carried the names of Paris designers in its editorials, but it would not carry the names of domestic designers or retailers. Under the leadership of its famous fashion editor Virginia Pope, the paper quickly changed its editorial policies and soon featured numerous stories about U.S. designers. Throughout the war years, New York, and the nation, worked to turn U.S. designers into celebrities and household names around the world. *Vogue* and *Harper's Bazaar* ran numerous articles about the new American style, but one must also recognize that this coverage was partly out of necessity. After all, there was little news from Paris.

The liberation of France had all the fashion magazines scrambling to be the first to report on Paris couture. Virginia Pope steadfastly reported her allegiance to U.S. design, but other fashion editors were quick to renew their love of Paris. At war's end, the fashion press, the U.S. fashion industry, and the French fashion industry reached an understanding. New York served the ready-to-wear market, and Paris served those few who could afford couture. U.S. designers had gained some recognition, but they were not yet seen as equal with French designers. U.S. designer Bill Blass recalled that upon his discharge from the army after the war, he went to the home of a manufacturer to interview for a design position. He wrote that he did not expect respect for himself, but he thought that at least his army uniform would garner a degree of respect. He was asked to wait in the butler's pantry. Clearly, ready-to-wear designers were not yet celebrities.

READY-TO-WEAR CAPTURES THE SPOTLIGHT

Bill Blass wrote about going to Paris openings in the 1950s and 1960s, when *Vogue's* editor, Diana Vreeland, and *Harper's Bazaar's* Carmel Snow sat down front at the shows in hats and gloves along with the rest of the fashion press. Blass reminisced that it was not until 1968 and Balenciaga's closing that they all realized that they "were witnessing the end of the world." Gradually, over the course of the twentieth century, Paris had been losing its grip on the reins of the fashion world. Paris still offered glamour and luxury, but the culture had changed. Women who could afford couture either did not have the time or lacked the desire to participate in the couture process. In response, Paris made a radical shift and began offering its own ready-to-wear. Middle-class consumers also grew very independent. The youth rebelled against any authority, including fashion. Instead, radical British youth developed their own styles, and North American consumers followed.

Instead of dictating style, Paris reflected the British invasion from Carnaby Street. Street fashion took a leading role through designer Mary Quant's miniskirts and high-fashion model Twiggy's boyish looks. Ready-to-wear dominated fashion, and its designers finally reached celebrity status. Bill Blass called the 1960s "the great American decade," but he did not think this would have happened without the leadership of three people who published fashion news: John Fairchild, editor of *Women's Wear Daily*; Diana Vreeland; and Eugenia Sheppard, writer for the *Herald Tribune*. Fairchild took the ready-to-wear designers from their places of anonymity and instead treated them "like stars." Grace

Vogue magazine editor-in-chief Edna Woolman Chase (center) talking with her editors about the Paris fashion shows, New York, 1937. Time & Life Pictures/Getty Images.

Mirabella, who became *Vogue*'s editor after Vreeland, took a different view of the 1960s and 1970s.

Mirabella watched the designers get rich and too important to talk to fashion editors. From her perspective, the fashion industry became more about gossip and intrigue than good design, and she regretted the lost working relationship between designers and the press. She saw fashion openings as spectacles that forebode the end of true fashion.

The prosperity of the time spread to Canada, which in 1979 published its first fashion magazine, called *Flare*. Canada began to nurture its own fashion designers, such as Alfred Sung, Hilary Radley, and Parachute, and to export their creations to the United States. The glitz of the fashion world also spawned a new venue for writers: fashion television. Fashion had truly come into the venue of the average consumer.

By the end of the twentieth century, *Vogue*, *Harper's Bazaar*, and *WWD* still held leadership positions in fashion publishing. They were joined, though, by a host of newcomers, including *Elle*, *In Style*, *W*, and offspring geared to a specific market, such as *Teen Vogue*. The democratization of fashion was complete. Fashion magazines included photographs of celebrities in combinations of couture, ready-to-wear, and vintage garments, and ready-to-wear designers worked at both the high-fashion and budget levels. The rules of fashion were gone. Some believed that fashion, itself, was gone. Just as it was at the beginning of the century, fashion had its devotees and its critics, but it would always have the fashion press ready to report and influence fashion consumers.

References and Suggested Readings

Blass, Bill. *Bare Blass*. New York: HarperCollins, 2002.

Buckland, Sandra Stansbery. "Promoting American Designers, 1940–44: Building Our Own House." In *Twentieth-Century Fashion*, edited by Linda Welters and Patricia A. Cunningham, 99–121. Oxford: Berg, 2005.

Buckland, S.S., and G.S. O'Neal. "'We Publish Fashions Because They Are News': The New York Times 1940–1945." *Dress* 25 (1998): 33–41.

Hawes, Elizabeth. *Fashion Is Spinach*. New York: Random House, 1938.

Hill, Daniel Delis. *Advertising to the American Woman 1900–1999*. Columbus: Ohio State University Press, 2002.

Hill, Daniel Delis. *As Seen in Vogue*. Lubbock: Texas Tech University Press, 2004.

Levin, Phyllis Lee. *The Wheels of Fashion*. Garden City, NY: Doubleday, 1965.

Mirabella, Grace, with Judith Warner. *In and Out of Vogue*. New York: Doubleday, 1995.

Palmer, Alexandra, ed. *Fashion: A Canadian Perspective*. Toronto: University of Toronto Press, 2004.

Snow, Carmel, with Mary Louise Aswell. *The World of Carmel Snow*. New York: McGraw Hill, 1962.

Sandra Stansbery Buckland

See also volume 8, Fashion Journalism; volume 10, Global Perspectives: Fashion Magazines.

Shoes and Shoemaking

Shoemaking in North America dates back to the establishment of the very first colonies. It was one of the trades that the Virginia Company hoped to establish in Jamestown, and one of the early investors in the Virginia Company was the Worshipful Company of Cordwainers, the shoemakers' guild in London. The first mention of shoemakers, or *cordwainers* as they were known (a term derived from their work with Cordova leather), dates to 1610, when the new governor of Virginia, Lord De La Warr, arrived with shoemakers and leather tanners. Christopher Nelme, who came to Jamestown in 1619, is the first shoemaker known to us by name. Other early shoemakers include Thomas Beard, who was sent on the Mayflower in 1629 to make shoes for the Massachusetts Bay Colony, and Philip Kyrland, who settled in Lynn, Massachusetts, in 1635. By 1648, shoemakers in Boston were well enough established to be granted a charter to form a "company of shoemakers."

EARLY ENGLISH COLONIAL SHOEMAKING

Archaeological evidence from Jamestown suggests that the English had a marked preference for footwear from England, even when it was impractical for colonial use. Jamestown gentlemen, who John Smith wryly commented were in abundance, sported shoes with finely stitched leather uppers and large keyhole latchets secured to the foot with elaborate rosettes or laces. The evidence from Jamestown also suggests that the earliest colonial shoemakers were frequently required to stoop to the level of *cobbler*, a person who repairs rather than makes shoes, due to the lack of supplies. Provisions lists indicate that individuals were also expected to repair their own shoes. A 1618 Virginia Company supply record lists that each man was equipped with three pairs of shoes as well as the materials needed to maintain them.

During Jamestown's "Starving Time" (1609–1610), colonists were in dire need of footwear; many went barefoot or wrapped their hats and even bark around their feet, according to John Smith's handwritten inscription in a copy of his *Generall Historie of Virginia* presented to the Cordwainers' Guild of London. Curiously, wood, a potential shoemaking resource with a long history of use throughout Europe, was rejected by the English. The wearing of moccasins also appears to have been spurned. This stubborn insistence on the familiar footwear of England may have been linked to issues of identity. The psychological comfort provided by familiar signifiers of status and culture seemed to trump practical concerns in the early years of the English colonies.

EARLY FRENCH COLONIAL SHOEMAKING

Shoemaking in New France developed along a slightly different trajectory. As with the English, footwear was an important issue for early French colonists. As early as 1619, French explorer Samuel de Champlain, the founder of Quebec City, recommended that colonial outposts be provisioned with footwear, but the arrival of the first shoemaker cannot be firmly established prior to 1632. In 1634, Jesuit Father Paul LeJeune wrote that tradesmen, including shoemakers, balked at being made to do menial labor such as gathering firewood, complaining that it would make them "forget their trades." French footwear was imported into New France, but unlike in the British colonies, moccasins were also worn. The making and wearing of clogs also distinguished New France from the British colonies. The use of these alternative forms of footwear, coupled with the small colonial market, deterred the early establishment of the colonial shoemaking industry. In addition, there were no tanneries in New France to supply shoemakers until 1648. When tanneries were finally established, they were run as monopolies and employed their own shoemakers, making it difficult for independent shoemakers to obtain leather. In 1663, Louis XIV took control of New France, and the population exploded; by 1666, the first Canadian census listed twenty shoemakers serving a population of 3,215.

HOW COLONIAL SHOES WERE MADE

Despite regional differences, both urban and rural colonial shoemakers made footwear in the same way following established European traditions. Each shoe was handmade using specialized tools. A typical shoemaker's kit included a lap-stone, hammer, stirrup, whet-board, pincers, nippers, shoulder stick, longstick, toe-stick, a variety of knives, an awl, bristles, tacks, wax, a sponge, blackening gum, chalk, rags, grease, channel opener, dogfish skin used as sandpaper, and an apron. The making of a shoe began with a *last*, which is a wooden model of a foot, over which the upper of leather or fabric was stretched, or lasted. Once the upper was lasted, a leather outsole was stitched to the inner *sole*, the inside part of the shoe upon which the sole of the foot rests. The upper would be caught between the inner and outer soles and held in place by the stitching. Experienced shoemakers could make roughly two pairs of shoes or one pair of boots a day.

Durable and inexpensive work shoes called *brogans* were made using heavy cowhide and constituted the majority of shoes made during the colonial era. These hard-wearing shoes were cut with the flesh side facing out and the smooth side worn against the foot so that the shoe did not need to be lined. The rough exterior was

Detail of yellow leather girl's shoes made by Jonas S. Bass, a Boston shoemaker at the end of the eighteenth century. Copyright © 2010 Bata Shoe Museum, Toronto.

blackened with sheep tallow, wax, and lampblack heated together and painted on the upper to make the shoes relatively water resistant. Fine footwear, such as ladies' high-heeled silk shoes and gentlemen's boots, was generally imported.

EIGHTEENTH-CENTURY SHOEMAKING
IN THE ENGLISH COLONIES

By the end of the seventeenth century, shoemaking was firmly established in the English colonies, particularly in and around the urban centers of Philadelphia and Boston. Imported shoes from England remained of importance among the fashionable, but locally made shoes were good enough that last-making and heel-making became viable, independent crafts. Many shoemakers even found it profitable to offer ready-made shoes. Outside the urban centers, itinerant shoemakers met rural footwear needs. In the southern colonies, many plantations had free or indentured shoemakers; some had slaves who specialized in shoemaking.

Throughout the majority of the eighteenth century, most shoemakers worked seasonally, dedicating their time to agriculture during the growing season and making shoes during the colder months. In 1750, however, the arrival of Welshman John Adam Dagyr, "the father of American shoemaking," in Lynn, Massachusetts, ushered in a nascent assembly-line process in which each individual in a workshop specialized in one aspect of shoemaking. Dagyr's influence greatly increased productivity and sowed the seeds for the

industrialization of shoemaking in the next century. The other event that propelled shoemaking forward was the Revolutionary War.

SHOEMAKING IN THE UNITED STATES
AFTER THE REVOLUTIONARY WAR

In the new United States, the needs of the fledgling army, as well as the rejection and scarcity of imports, encouraged greater domestic production. After the war, U.S. shoemakers were also assisted by patriotism, improved transportation, and new tariffs placed on imported shoes. In the Northern states, shoemaker/farmers began to give themselves over to full-time shoemaking as their market expanded in the Southern states as well as the East and West Indies. Increasingly, shoemakers in the North began to employ journeymen and apprentices to meet these demands. In Lynn alone, production increased from 60,000 pairs in 1770 to 175,000 in 1785. By 1788, Lynn was exporting 100,000 pairs of shoes, and by 1795 Lynn had 200 master shoemakers as well as 600 journeymen and apprentices making 300,000 pairs of shoes per year. The shoes being produced in the North were no longer custom made for specific clients or even made on spec for the local market; they were made for intermediary merchants. Merchants became increasingly important at the end of the eighteenth century, often providing the raw materials needed for shoemaking in return for the finished footwear. These "bag bosses" would take one to two dozen pairs of shoes and cart them off to urban

Mid-eighteenth-century yellow brocade shoes, probably made using English Spitalfield silk dressmaking remnants. Copyright © 2010 Bata Shoe Museum, Toronto.

centers for sale. Shoes intended for sale in the South would be put in barrels and shipped to their destinations.

Shoe merchants, however, had no control over the wastage of the material they provided or the quality of the final product. They relied on independent shoemakers, and the increased market had resulted in some shoemakers producing low-quality footwear. This lack of quality control put shoe merchants at a disadvantage and led to the rise of shoe manufacturers, who established central shops from which they could exert increased control. These "shoe bosses" oversaw hide cutting, or *clicking*, to ensure minimal loss. The *binding*, or sewing together of the component parts of an upper, was farmed out to women willing to take piecework. The completed uppers were returned to a central shop for inspection. After inspection, uppers were then redistributed with rough-cut soles to shoemakers who lasted and bottomed them in workshops called *ten footers*. The shoemakers were paid only after the final product was inspected. Shoe manufacturers sold these completed shoes through their own outlets in the South and West and thereby controlled both production and profit. The loss of self-reliance, combined with periodic economic depression, gave rise to shoemaker associations. A case brought by the Federal Society of Journeymen Cordwainers in 1794 in Philadelphia seeking to establish set wages for their work portended the labor issues that would hound shoe manufacturers throughout the nineteenth century.

IMPACT OF MECHANIZATION

Innovation transformed shoe production in the nineteenth century. The first of these new practices was the use of wooden pegs to attach the uppers to the soles of shoes. Although shoe pegging predated the nineteenth century, usually in relation to securing heels or repairing soles, the use of shoe pegs in the construction of new shoes proved revolutionary. Before pegging, soles were laboriously sewn to uppers using heavy thread and a boar-bristle needle. In contrast, nail-shaped wooden pegs could quickly pierce the sole and insole, securing the upper drawn in between the two. Numerous patents were granted relating to this new shoemaking approach. As the century wore on, the momentum toward mechanization steadily increased.

In 1844, the sole cutter was invented by Richard Richards to standardize the size and shapes of soles, followed by the pattern machine of George W. Parrot, which provided the same regularity to uppers. The rolling machine, invented in 1845, was designed to relieve shoemakers of the task of pounding leather by compressing the fibers of sole leather with powerful rollers. The invention of the sewing machine by Elias Howe in 1846, and its adaptation to shoemaking by John Brooks Nichols in 1852, transformed women's participation in the shoe industry by moving them out of the domestic space, where they had done binding by hand, into the central shop. In 1860, frustration over mechanization, wage loss, and the depressed economy reached a boiling point, and Lynn shoemakers called a strike. Soon shoemakers across Massachusetts were striking, and the ranks of the strikers swelled to twenty thousand. It was to be one of the largest strikes in U.S. history.

Despite these labor disruptions, mechanization continued unabated. The next major invention was the McKay sewing machine, which stitched soles to uppers. Introduced in 1862, it became instrumental to the Union during the Civil War, when it was

Bill of sale from 1879 showing the Roos's shoe factory in Galt, Ontario. Copyright © 2010 Bata Shoe Museum, Toronto.

pressed into service by Northern shoe manufacturers to compensate for the reduction in labor due to enlistment. In the South, the Confederacy also needed footwear, but without a large manufacturing base, it remanded most of the Southern shoe manufacturers and put soldiers with shoemaking skills to work in the army camps. Despite these efforts, at the end of the war the South was in need of footwear, and Northern shoe manufacturers responded by canceling the debts of many Southern shoe jobbers and resuming normal trade.

EIGHTEENTH- AND NINETEENTH-CENTURY SHOEMAKING IN CANADA

In Canada, shoemaking developed along similar lines, but its smaller population made the establishment of a thriving shoe trade difficult. When the British took control of Canada in 1763, they counted only 13,000 people living in urban areas and noted the marked difference between the French shoes worn in these centers and the moccasins worn throughout the countryside. With such a limited market and competition from imports and indigenous production, Canadian shoemakers devoted substantial time to agricultural pursuits and made shoes during the colder months in their homes. The British takeover of Canada, however, pushed Canadian shoemaking further as French imports dwindled, leaving the civilian population to fend for itself. This was coupled with the increased number of soldiers also in dire need of footwear, especially with the advent of the Revolutionary War. The ability of Canadian shoemakers to meet these demands was further stretched by the influx of Loyalists, who frequently arrived with nothing more than the clothes on their backs. The first official party of Loyalists, escorted by Captain Michael Grass from New York to Canada, was to be provided 107 pairs of shoes, one pair for each Loyalist, at Sorrel. However, not a single pair of shoes could be found, so shoe soles were given instead. These conditions might have seemed ripe for entrepreneurial shoemakers, but by 1798, only nineteen French and fourteen English shoemakers were working in Quebec City, the administrative capital of Canada. The rest of Canada was no better off for shoemakers. It has been estimated that Upper Canada had only half a dozen by 1800.

French Canadian shoemakers consciously attempted to increase production and increase the size of their shops; in Quebec City, there were thirty-five shoemakers in 1805 and 224 by 1830. By 1829, Canada was even exporting footwear to the West Indies, and in the late 1830s, shoemakers in Belleville, Ontario, organized a public meeting protesting the importation of inexpensive U.S. footwear and advocating that Canadians buy domestic.

It was U.S. shoemakers, however, who brought the first shoemaking machine to Canada and ushered in the industrial age. Champion Brown and William Sullivan Childs imported a rolling machine for use in their shoemaking business in Montreal. Like the shoemakers in the United States, Canadian shoemakers protested the use of machines. The Journey Shoemaker's Society called a protest meeting concerning mechanization and even invited Mr. Brown and Mr. Childs to attend, but when they refused, a strike was called that lasted sixteen weeks. Despite such protests, by 1866, Guillaume Breese of Quebec City had built a factory that was completely mechanized.

INDUSTRIALIZATION IN THE UNITED STATES

In the United States, mechanization continued unabated after the Civil War. The Goodyear welting machine was developed between 1862 and 1875 under the auspices of Charles Goodyear Jr., son of Charles Goodyear, who discovered vulcanized rubber in 1839, thus enabling the development of the sneaker and the rubber boot. Edge-trimming and heel-trimming machines were introduced in the late 1870s and displaced the highly paid whittlers who finished shoes. The lasting machine was invented by Dutch Guianan immigrant Jan Ernst Matzeliger, who arrived in Lynn in 1877. Prior to his invention, it was believed that lasting could not be mechanized, but his tenacity proved them wrong. By 1883, he had received a patent for a machine that allowed operators to last between three hundred to seven hundred pairs of shoes a day, compared with the fifty pairs hand-lasters could make. The hand-lasters soon lamented that Matzeliger's machine taunted them with the song "I've got your job, I've got your job" as it worked. Each of these inventions transformed shoe production and was met by worker dismay.

Pair of wedding boots worn by Margaret Townsend for her wedding to James Plum in New York City on 13 May 1863. Copyright © 2010 Bata Shoe Museum, Toronto.

Pair of early-twentieth-century boy's black leather lace-up boots made in Canada by Sisman Shoe Company. Copyright © 2010 Bata Shoe Museum, Toronto.

By the last quarter of the nineteenth century, the bespoke shoemaker had all but disappeared throughout North America; the wage-earning shoe factory worker had replaced him. Working conditions for many were dismal, with long days and minimal pay. Unions in both the United States and Canada tried to address these issues, and repeated strikes were called to decrease the length of the workday and to limit child labor. Despite these confrontations, the shoe industry continued to grow. However, the reliance on machinery introduced new challenges, such as machine service and maintenance. As early as the introduction of the McKay stitching machine, manufacturers of shoemaking equipment leased rather than sold most of their equipment; receiving a small royalty for each pair of shoes made using their product. The making of shoemaking machinery became a thriving industry in its own right, and in 1899, four of the principal machine manufacturers joined together to form the United Shoe Machinery Company. It became the largest company of its kind and was the target of aggressive antimonopoly interests for much of the twentieth century.

THE SHOE INDUSTRY ENTERS THE TWENTIETH CENTURY

By the turn of the twentieth century, significant shoemaking regions were firmly established. In Canada, shoemaking was a leading industry in Quebec, and Quebec City was the country's main producer. In the United States, Massachusetts led the way with Lynn as the world's leader in women's shoe production; Brockton, for men's shoes; and Haverhill, for slippers. Missouri came next in production, followed by New York, New Hampshire, Ohio, Pennsylvania, and Illinois. Shoe manufacturers were a major employer, and the U.S. shoemaking industry was the largest in the world. Many manufacturers began to manage their own retail stores, and there was a concerted effort at product branding. The famous Buster Brown character of the Brown Shoe Company illustrates this. In 1904, the characters of Buster Brown; his dog, Tige; and his sister, Mary Jane, were purchased from cartoonist Richard F. Outcault to promote Brown's children's shoes. This marketing was extremely successful: The characters became cultural icons, and popular girls' instep-strap shoes began to be known as "Mary Janes," a term still in use in the early twenty-first century.

The outbreak of World War I put an increased demand on U.S. exports to meet the footwear needs of both the European military and its citizenry. By the end of 1915, it was estimated that roughly fifteen million pairs of army shoes had been sent to Europe from U.S. factories. In addition, the U.S. domestic market also experienced an upswing, with female customers in particular demanding a wide variety of fashionable footwear, many with extravagant embellishments such as beading. By 1915, sneakers were being mass produced; both Converse and Keds began to be sold around this time.

When the United States entered the war in 1917, the orders for military footwear grew larger, but leather shortages and limited labor frustrated the industry's efforts. Following the war was a period of unprecedented growth. No longer hidden beneath voluminous skirts, women's shoes emerged as essential fashion accessories, and many high-end shoe retailers began to create sumptuous shoe salons with high turnover throughout the 1920s. The stock market crash of 1929, however, pitched the entire North American economy into a downward spiral. Despite the bleak economic conditions of the Great Depression, by 1937, the four largest shoe companies in the United States—International Shoe Company, Endicott Johnson Corp, Brown Shoe Company, and Florsheim Shoe Company—had combined assets of over US$150 million. The advent of renewed hostilities in Europe also brought the headquarters of one of the largest manufacturers of shoes in the world, the Czech Bata Shoe Company, to North America. Bata's international market presence as well as its manufacturing facilities around the world, including Canada and the United States, made it an early example of the globalization of the North American footwear industry.

The Depression ended with the United States's entry into World War II. As with previous wars, the government placed massive orders for footwear. Efforts were made by the shoe industry to meet the needs of the armed forces; the strength of the U.S. shoe industry was even a point of national pride. Domestic shoe sales were negatively affected by government restrictions. The government's requisition of rubber limited the production of inexpensive footwear, such as sneakers, just as gas rationing created a demand for cheap walking shoes. Shoe rationing, however, was the biggest blow. Ration books containing coupons for shoes were first issued in May 1942. With shoe sales limited by the government, shoemakers began to emphasize the quality of their goods and offer products and advice on prolonging the life of a pair of shoes. Shoe manufacturing also experimented with materials not needed by the war effort.

Once the war was over, shoe production and consumption immediately spiked. Fashion quickly shifted, and the heavier heels of the 1940s gave way to the slender stiletto by the early 1950s. Industrial innovations such as extruded metal and superstrong plastics developed during the war years enabled these slim heels to bear the weight of the wearer. In retail, the youth market emerged as a viable niche market. Increasing numbers of specialized children's shoes began to be offered, from ballet slippers to Girl Scout shoes; the teen fashion market was also targeted. The debut in 1958 of the pigskin suede Hush Puppy, marketed as a distinctively American casual shoe, became a best seller. By 1963, one in ten American adults owned a pair for leisure dress.

Pair of Converse basketball sneakers from the 1940s. From about 1915, sneakers were being mass produced in the United States. Copyright © 2010 Bata Shoe Museum, Toronto.

THE DECLINE OF SHOEMAKING
IN NORTH AMERICA

Although the shoe industry in both Canada and the United States seemed to be thriving in the post–World War II boom, a number of changes signaling its denouement were quietly taking place. In 1958, over twenty-three million pairs of shoes were imported into the United States, twice as many shoes as the year before, and almost half came from Japan. The opening of Pay-Less National in Topeka, Kansas, in 1956 also hinted at shoe-retailing changes. Started by two cousins, Louis and Shaol Pozez, Pay-Less stores were converted supermarkets that promoted a no-frills, self-service shopping experience that translated into low-priced footwear.

In the 1960s, growth in the shoemaking industry began to slow noticeably due to the steady increase of imports. The one bright spot seemed to be the booming (and consuming) youth demographic. The youth market was driven by fashion, but it was also interested in the sneaker, the form of footwear that would come to dominate the market by the end of the century. These young consumers, however, did not show a preference for domestically made shoes: price point, not country of origin, made the sale.

The fitness craze of the 1970s created the next major North American footwear trend and highlighted the growing distance between shoe manufacturers and shoe retailers. As sneakers rose in prominence, many high-end brands became signifiers of privilege whose high-priced innovations promised increased performance. This, combined with the use of celebrity endorsements, made sneakers a fashion essential. As long ago as 1921, Converse had used a sports celebrity to promote its famous Chuck Taylor All-Star basketball shoes, but athlete endorsements were not fully exploited until the last quarter of the twentieth century. The most successful example is Blue Ribbon Sports, which changed its name to Nike in 1978. The company was dedicated to improving running shoes, and celebrated runner Steve Prefontaine's exclusive use of Nike sneakers gave the brand credibility. Its introduction of the waffle trainer in 1974 also confirmed Blue Ribbon/Nike as an industry leader, and it became the best-selling runner in the United States. The combination of innovation and celebrity endorsement became standard in the marketing of athletic footwear into the twenty-first century.

Nike also set the example of having their footwear produced overseas, mainly in Asia, while maintaining company headquarters in the United States. This trend toward Asian manufacture was echoed throughout the footwear industry as the century progressed. For example, U.S. imports of nonrubber footwear increased from 265 million pairs in 1974 to 370 million pairs by 1976. The threat to the domestic shoemaking industry was the focus of many international trade negotiations that sought to reduce imports. However, the tide of imports could not be stemmed. By the mid-1980s, U.S. shoe companies had shifted their focus to brand development, marketing, and sales, leaving offshore suppliers to manufacture the actual footwear. In 2006, the United States imported two billion shoes, 85 percent of which were from China, and shoe imports constituted one of the top five trade imbalances between the two countries. Despite this shift in manufacturing, many U.S. and Canadian shoe companies continue to maintain internationally recognized brands and a dominant global presence.

References and Further Reading

Boot and Shoe Recorder 78, no. 24 through 168, no. 2 (5 March 1921–15 June 1965).

Commons, John R. *Labor and Administrations.* New York: Macmillan, 1913.

Davis, Horace B. *Shoes: The Workers and the Industry.* New York: International Publishers, 1940.

Hazard, Blanche E. *The Organization of the Boot and Shoe Industry in Massachusetts before 1875.* London: Oxford University Press, 1921.

Johnson, David N. *Sketches of Lynn or the Changes of Fifty Years.* Lynn, MA: Thos. P. Nichols, Printer, 1880.

Martin, M. Michel. *Cordonnerie Traditionnelle.* Quebec City: Musée du Quebec, 1977.

McDermott, Charles H. *A History of the Shoe and Leather Industries of the United States.* Boston: John W. Denehy & Company, 1918.

Payne, Fred M. *The Historical Development of Shoemaking in Canada: A Brief Summary of Events and Circumstances Relating to the Birth and Growth of the Industry.* Unpublished paper in the Collection of the Bata Shoe Museum Library, 1985.

Rexford, Nancy E. *Woman's Shoes in America, 1795–1930.* Kent, OH: Kent State University Press, 2000.

Saguto, D.A. "The Wooden Shoe Peg and Pegged Construction in Footwear—Their History and Origins." *The Chronicles of the Early American Industries* 37, no. 1 (1984): 5–10.

Saguto, D.A. "Footprints on the Past: Tracking the First English-American Shoemakers." *Colonial Williamsburg Journal* 22, no. 2 (Summer 2000): 19–26.

Elizabeth Semmelhack

See also volume 8, Footwear.

Snapshot: Hosiery

Before the twentieth century, hosiery (a knitted item of wearing apparel covering the foot and/or leg) had seldom enjoyed the fashion limelight with other accessories of dress because its context had been domestic: the Christmas stocking hung at the fireplace, darning socks as women's work, and the miser's stocking with its hoard of gold hidden away. William Lee, an English clergyman, is credited with having invented the first knitting machine for hosiery in 1589. In 1857, a simple drive mechanism was added so that the machine could be mechanically controlled, allowing for a faster production. These machines made full-fashioned *stockings*, which are stockings that are knitted flat, with the two sides united afterward by a seam up the back.

During the nineteenth century, hosiery was made from cotton, silk, or very fine wool. Those living in the colder climates, such as northern Canada, would have used heavier-weight wool for warmth. Colors for women were dictated by fashion, sometimes matching the dress, petticoat, or shoes. The new synthetic dyes, developed from a coal-tar derivative in 1856, allowed for modern sharp and bright colors. Stripes and embroidered patterns called clocks (small embroidered, woven, or knitted decorations on the back of the heel or side of the stocking) were used. Women wore heavier black stockings with their cycling, bathing (swimming), and other recreational costumes. Children wore hosiery often similar to that of adults. Both sexes wore white calf-height socks before the 1880s. From 1900 to 1914, women's stockings were generally dark- or light-colored cotton lisle (a very fine, smooth, and lustrous yarn) for daytime wear and silk for formal wear.

RAYON

After 1914, rayon stockings were introduced. Also called *artificial silk,* this fiber was manufactured from cellulose. The early rayon was too lustrous, had poor wrinkle recovery, and tended to shrink when washed. Women who wore rayon stockings frequently complained that they became baggy and sagged throughout the day.

As hemlines began to rise in 1924, women focused greater attention on their hosiery, turning it into a fashion item. The new stockings were tan- or flesh-colored, with the more luxurious ones made of silk and the less expensive ones, from rayon. Frederick Allen Lewis, writing of the 1920s in *Only Yesterday,* described young women who rolled their stockings below their knees, revealing shinbones and kneecaps to the "shocked eyes" of the older generation. Garters could be frilly or embroidered, and the popular dances of the time provided onlookers with frequent views. Suspender belts ending in gilt mounts and clips were also used to fasten the short stockings, and these, too, were often visible. By 1928, well-made seamless silk stockings were introduced as a bare-leg look in suntan shades for the hot weather, but sales dropped at the end of the first summer.

On the golf course or in the country, gentlemen were wearing argyle socks with their knickers or plus fours (fuller version of the knickers). Argyle socks, a style that originated in

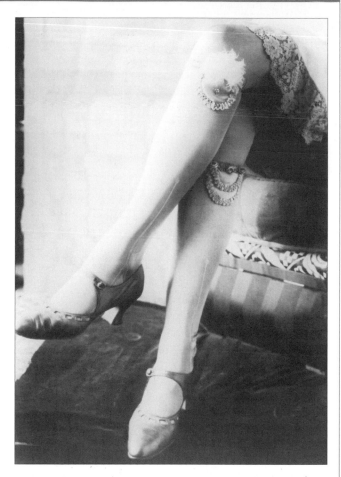

Stockings, 1916. In the United States, as hemlines began to rise, women focused greater attention on their hosiery, turning it into a fashion item. Getty Images.

Scotland, are knitted in a diamond or diagonal plaid pattern using two or more colors. By 1927, men's half-hose (a standard-length stocking that ends halfway between the ankle and the knee) were becoming more available in patterns.

NYLON

Nylon was introduced in 1939 by the DuPont Company. It was the first synthetic fiber (fiber created from chemical components). As a filament, the size of a nylon yarn is measured in denier: the higher the denier number, the thicker the yarn. The term gauge refers to the number of needles per inch on the knitting machine. A higher gauge number means that the stitches are closer together. The denier and gauge together determine the weight or sheerness of hosiery.

DuPont unveiled the fiber at the 1939 World's Fair in New York. The fiber was silky, strong, and wrinkle resistant, and it did not shrink when washed. The term *nylon* entered the U.S. vocabulary as a synonym for stockings; the official launch date of nylons in the United States was 15 May 1940. Over four million pairs of the flesh-toned nylons were sold in the first few hours. At first nylons were only available in the United States and Canada. In 1942, nylon stocking production was halted so that the fiber could be used for military purposes during World War II. Left without their nylons and cut off from silk by the Asian war, some women used leg makeup and drew seams on the back of their legs with eyebrow pencils. Others made do with the sagging rayon stockings. By the end of the war, nylon stocking production was reinstated, and in 1945, the Macy's store in New York City sold their entire stock of 50,000 pairs within six hours.

Ankle socks (a short sock reaching only to the ankle, worn turned down or with an elastic top on the cuff) were used by young girls and women for sports participation. In the 1940s, teenaged girls wore ankle socks so often that teens were nicknamed "bobby-soxers." Men wore more colorful, patterned socks with elastic tops, eliminating the need for garters.

Between 1947 and 1960, women had the choice of seamed nylons (stitched in dark thread with reinforced heels made in dark yarn extending several inches up the back of the ankle) or seamless ones. In the 1950s, through the use of heat-setting treatments or stretch yarns, it was possible to produce a better-fitting seamless stocking, and these started to dominate the market. Antistatic finishes were given to men's socks to prevent them from clinging to the legs of synthetic trousers. In 1954, a standardized method for evaluating the fit of hosiery was realized.

PANTYHOSE

Sheer nylon pantyhose, a garment that is part hosiery and part underpants, were introduced in the early 1960s. They were made very much like the opaque knitted tights worn by dancers that had been sold by the Danskin Company since the early twentieth century. As skirts became shorter, pantyhose became an absolute necessity.

A pattern and color revolution took place in women's, teens', and little girls' hosiery in the mid-1960s. Textured stockings with wild patterns, explosive colors with offbeat combinations, fishnet, and lace patterns were popular. A new over-the-knee sock length appeared for girls. The fashion for clear vinyl footwear in 1966 created the necessity for sandalfoot stockings (stockings with no reinforcement at the toe). Leg warmers, loose footless stockings used by dancers to keep their legs warm, became a fashion item.

To eliminate the gap between sock and leg when a man sat with his legs crossed, a new over-the-calf sock (a sock that extends above the fattest part of the calf) was introduced in 1970. Other sock types available for men in the early 1970s included tube socks (socks without a knit-in heel) and cushion-soled socks (use of a terry pile surface on the inside of the foot portion of the sock to reduce the shock of activities such as running and jumping).

The glaring flaws of pantyhose were poor fit and inconsistent sizes. This problem was solved in 1972, when research results indicated that pantyhose could be fitted properly by knowing a woman's correct height and weight.

In the twenty-first century, new fibers, blends, and finishes are used to bring the consumer the best possible sock or stocking for any activity or foot problem. These include: antimicrobial finishes that do not wash out for the life of the sock and control the growth of odor-causing bacteria; hydrophobic fibers, such as CoolMax and polypropylene, to keep the athlete's foot dry during exercise; Thermax socks, which insulate against heat loss; and support hosiery, which uses spandex, is available to help regulate blood circulation, and provides a range of light to firm support.

Consumers in Canada and the United States have access to the same major hosiery brands, such as Hanes (L'eggs Products), Gold Toe, Burlington, No nonsense, and Hue, through retail stores in both countries. The Gap, Banana Republic, Old Navy, Sears, and Wal-Mart all have stores in both Canada and the United States. Phantom, which produces the Silks brand, is a major Canadian hosiery manufacturer. Consumers worldwide can purchase hosiery through mail order catalogs, such as FootSmart, and a number of online Web sites and hosiery-buying clubs.

REFERENCES AND FURTHER READING

Kay, Sally. *The Hosiery Association Centennial: In Step with the Industry for 100 Years.* Charlotte, NC: National Association of Hosiery Manufacturers, 2005.

Tortora, Phyllis. "Hosiery." In *The Fairchild Encyclopedia of Fashion Accessories,* edited by phyllis Tortora and Bina Abling, New York: Fairchild Publishers, 2003.

Nan H. Mutnick

Accessories of Dress

- Headwear
- Eyewear
- Scarves and Shawls
- Neckties, Handkerchiefs, and Pocket Squares
- Gloves
- Belts
- Handbags
- Small Personal Leather Goods
- Luggage
- Umbrellas
- Fans
- Watches

The accessories industries in Canada and the United States are multibillion dollar industries that include many diverse product categories, from headwear to footwear. Fashion accessories may be defined as fashion items that are carried or worn and that support or accent apparel fashions. They may be mostly functional or strictly for adornment, but in order to be classified as fashion accessories, they should have acceptance by a majority of a given group and should complement popular clothing styles of the time. Common accessories used by consumers in North America include hats and headwear, eyewear, scarves, shawls, neckties, handkerchiefs, pocket squares, gloves, belts, handbags, small personal leather goods, luggage, umbrellas, fans, and watches. Jewelry and footwear are also classified as accessories, but these will be discussed in separate sections. Canada and the United States are primarily consumers rather than manufacturers of fashion accessories. Most fashion accessories are manufactured outside of Canada and the United States because domestic labor costs are much higher in these countries than in developing ones such as China, India, Korea, and Mexico. Because of the large percentage of overseas manufacturing, the importers and wholesalers may become the primary contact for retail store buyers when selecting the merchandise for sale in their store. Retailing of fashion accessories occurs via many different venues, including traditional brick-and-mortar store formats, catalog or Internet retailing, or a combination of these formats. Less common methods of retailing accessories include direct sales, flea markets, and craft fairs. However, these retail outlets are important to local economies.

In a comparison of the numbers of apparel and accessory business establishments in the United States and Canada, there were 12,356 U.S. establishments under SIC Major Group 23 (Manufacturing: Apparel and Other Finished Products Made from Fabric and Similar Materials) and 2,208 such establishments in Canada. Wholesale businesses in the United States numbered 4,242 under SIC Major Group 5137 (Wholesaling: Women's, Children's, and Infants' Clothing and Accessories), and comparable Canadian businesses numbered 339. Comparing the number of apparel and accessory stores in the United States and Canada, there were 185,592 U.S. establishments under SIC Major Group 56 (Retail) and 26,644 such establishments in Canada (*American Business Directory* and the *Canadian Business Directory*).

Trade shows and fashion markets represent opportunities for fashion accessory businesses in nearby geographic regions to come together and conduct business. Generally, exhibitors at trade shows include manufacturers, importers, and wholesalers. Their purpose is to show the upcoming fashion trends to other businesses that might be interested in retailing the merchandise lines in stores. Fashion markets are also scheduled events for manufacturers, importers, and wholesalers to spend time with their retail buyer clients in showrooms looking carefully at lines of accessories. Retail store buyers can place orders on accessories that will be purchased by the store's target customers. In Canada, two of the largest accessory trade activities are located in Toronto, Ontario. One is an annual international trade fair called the Toronto Mode Accessories Show, which features women's hats, scarves, jewelry, hair accessories, sunglasses, belts, handbags, watches, hosiery, umbrellas, and shoes. Toronto is also the location for a regional show called the Luggage, Leathergoods, Handbags and Accessories Show, which is sponsored by the Luggage, Leathergoods, Handbags and Accessories Association of Canada. In the United States, numerous trade shows and market events are held across the country. AccessoriesTheShow is one of the largest trade shows in the United States specifically intended to feature almost all of the accessory categories. Some categories are themselves large enough to have very specific trade shows, such as footwear, leather, fine jewelry, travel goods, and fur (in Canada). Across the United States, market weeks are scheduled in most regions, as often as five times per year. New York, Los Angeles, Las Vegas, Chicago, Atlanta, and Dallas host market weeks throughout the year.

As a general rule, apparel styles influence accessory styles. The popular accessories du jour (of the day) complement or enhance the popular styles of apparel. If the clothing styles do not warrant a particular accessory, then the accessory will not be highly important during that season. For example, an empire waistline on a dress may cause the popularity of belts to wane. A clothing trend toward understated and simple designs will result in the marketing of ornate and larger pieces of accessories and decorative scarves.

Another relationship between apparel and accessories is the use of common art principles and design elements. For example, scale and proportion are balanced between apparel and accessories. Full skirts, flowing clothing, gathering, and other uses of volumes of fabrics result in larger-scaled accessories, like handbags and hats. Popular patterns, prints, and colors are found in both apparel and accessories.

Pervasive fashion trends will also influence accessory fashions. A pervasive trend is a fashion component that can be found across many fashion product categories, including apparel, accessories, and even home fashions. For example, animal print is a pervasive trend: Animal prints are found on handbags, frames for sunglasses, shoe fabrics, skirts, blouses, necklaces, sofa pillows, and bed comforters. The use of fur may also be a pervasive trend at times. It can be found in small and large quantities on apparel, knitted in scarves, and as the fashion fabric of a handbag. The option of real or faux (fake) fur depends on the preferences of the target customer and the intended retail price points.

Profits from the sale of accessories are vital to the success of a fashion business. Salespeople are encouraged to sell accessories to complement apparel when a customer selects an outfit for purchase. Merchandisers know that in order to optimally sell accessories, the items must be placed in high-traffic locations where customers are likely to buy on impulse. For this reason, accessory departments or outposts are most often located near the cash register, along the main aisles, and on the main floor of a store. Even when apparel sales are sluggish, accessory sales tend to create a steady income for businesses. During times of economic hardships, consumers may not be able to afford an entire outfit, but they seem to find enough discretionary income to purchase an accessory or two.

Marketers encourage the concept of accessory wardrobing to further increase sales. *Accessory wardrobing* refers to owning multiple styles of a single accessory so the item will always match the outfit being worn. For example, consumers might own several watches (gold, silver, or leather banded) to coordinate with different outfits in their wardrobe. Sunglasses are also purchased (and sold) in multiples. A customer might buy a brown tortoise frame and a black frame to match different outfits. Even gloves are usually color coordinated with outwear ensembles. The disposable (short-lived) and affordable nature of fashion facilitates the purchase of quantities of the same basic item.

Designer and branded accessories are important status symbols in the fashion industry. The relatively small size of accessories and the proliferation of designers that have entered the accessory business have made status symbols of all types, from shoes to handbags and watches. A consumer may not be able to afford a designer outfit or evening gown, but she can possibly afford a pair of sunglasses, a scarf, or a handbag bearing that same designer's name. Counterfeiting of designer accessories is a huge business in the global economy and of great concern to legitimate businesses. Counterfeit merchandise devalues the brand and affects the company's profits. North American customs officials continually monitor and seize illegal goods, but the proliferation of fakes makes enforcement very difficult. Commonly counterfeited accessory goods include handbags, sunglasses, athletic shoes, and luxury watches. Counterfeiting is not limited to these products and is likely to occur whenever a popular brand or designer name accessory is perceived as a status symbol.

The accessories industry is regulated by numerous laws in the United States under the jurisdiction of the Federal Trade Commission. The Textile Fiber Products Identification Act (a labeling law) covers accessory items such as socks, hosiery, scarves, handkerchiefs, umbrellas, and parasols. These items must be labeled with the fiber content, country of origin, and the manufacturer's identification. All wool accessory items, such as headwear, are covered separately under the Wool Products Labeling Act. The U.S. Federal Trade Commission has set forth voluntary guidelines for luggage, shoes, belts, and handbags. The Guide for Select Leather and Imitation Leather Products covers deceptive marketing and advertising practices, misbranding, special performance finishes (such as waterproofing), and textile content including leather or simulated leather.

The Canadian Competition Bureau is the government agency that imposes regulations on textile products manufactured or

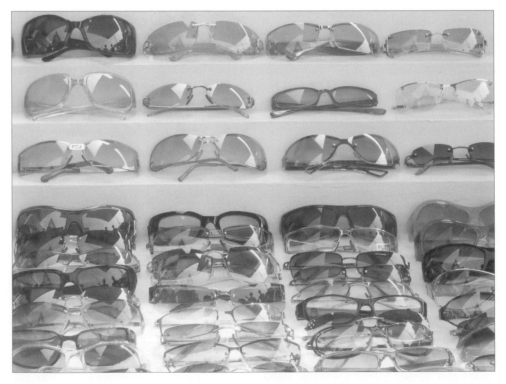

Sunglasses for sale, ca. 2000. Consumers in the United States often buy more than one pair of this popular accessory to match different outfits. Copyright Shi Yali, 2007. Used under license from Shutterstock.com

sold in Canada. The Textile Labelling Act and Advertising Regulations cover almost all accessories made from textile fibers, including hair. False or misleading advertising and marketing are prohibited, percentages of fibers are mandated, and the fiber content is generally required to be bilingual (French and English).

Accessory items that are exempt from the act include shoes, handbags, luggage, carrying cases, parasols, belts, suspenders, and straw or felt headwear. These exempt items (including fur items) are regulated under the federal Canadian Competition Act.

The U.S. leather and fur fashion accessory industries are also regulated by the U.S. Endangered Species Act, which prohibits the sale or possession of products containing fur from any animal on the endangered species list. Both Canada and the United States are among the 173 members of the Convention on International Trade in Endangered Species (CITES), headquartered in Switzerland.

HEADWEAR

The fashion headwear industry produces hats, hair accessories, wigs, and hairpieces. However, hats are the main focus of this section. A common term used to describe hats is millinery. The term is derived from the popularity of women's straw hats from Italy, particularly from the city of Milan, in the sixteenth century.

Hats should always be functional, but in order to be classified as a fashion accessory, they must be fashionable, too. Strictly functional hats lacking fashion appeal will be sold in different departments or retail stores than fashion hats. Over the centuries, hats have evolved in shape and style, from simple linen kerchiefs to high, pointed hennins that look like cones. Cowboy hats are also highly functional, although fashion is somewhat important. The popularity of ball caps has become a noteworthy fashion item for both genders.

Hats are composed of a few basic components, including the crown, brim, headband, and decorative trim. The crown covers the top of the head, while the brim is the horizontal piece that extends from the base of the crown. Some hats have only a brim and no crown, such as a visor. Other hats have only a crown and no brim, such as a knitted winter stocking cap. In the case of the coolie hat, the crown and brim are combined. The headband is the section at the lower portion of the inside of the crown, securing the hat to the forehead. It might be a strip of leather or ribbon. The decorative trim includes ribbons, feathers, artificial flowers, netting, embroidery, grommets, or other ornamentation.

Hats are made of a variety of materials, including suede and leather, fur fibers, woven or knitted fabrics, and straw. Lightweight fabrics, straws, and open weaves are typically fashioned into summer hats, while knits, fur, suede, and leather serve as winter hat materials.

Most inexpensive hats are mass-produced as one-size-fits-all. The sizing occurs when purchasing more expensive hats, like cowboy hats. The hat size is determined by horizontally measuring the circumference of the forehead, just above the eyebrows. An average hat size might be 22–22.5 inches (55–56 centimeters) in circumference. Hats are sized to the nearest one-eighth inch (one-third centimeter).

A certain amount of craftsmanship goes into the manufacture of more expensive hats. This can include hat blocking and steaming to achieve the proper shape and fit, or even handweaving straw to create summer hats. Hat blocks are wooden or metal

forms around which the crown is formed. Women's fashion hats that are handcrafted one-of-a-kind designs are called model millinery.

The market for casual hats has increased dramatically since the mid-1980s. Hat wardrobing is common for both males and females who have numerous hats from which to choose to complete a *total look*. Sales in the more formal hat market remain flat for most customer groups. There are niches of customer groups that are frequent buyers of formal fashion hats, but these groups remain relatively small.

Advanced technology is available for the manufacture of high-performance headwear, such as heat-sensitive models that hold in body heat in cold weather and release it in hot weather and headwear made of ceramic-coated nylon fibers that reflect the sun's harmful rays. However, most headwear is not technologically

A pashmina shawl worn by U.S. musician Ashlee Simpson, 2006. Tom Wargacki/WireImage.

innovative and is sold simply for function and to help the consumer express their individuality.

The hat industry may be classified into three sections: cloth hats and caps (the largest of the sections), hats and hat bodies, and millinery. Most hats are imported from China, Hong Kong, Korea, and Taiwan. Large labor pools and low living wages make offshore production attractive to manufacturers and retailers.

Hats are marketed in several ways. They may be marketed in a special women's hat department called a millinery department, or they may be located alongside other accessories within a larger accessories department. If they are girls' hats, they are probably located in the girls' department. Hats may also be merchandised by lifestyle or end use, such as by placing them in an outerwear section of the store that also features coats, scarves, gloves, and other outdoor use items. Unisex ball caps typically are placed within a boys' or men's department. Catalog and Internet retailing are also popular ways to sell fashion hats.

EYEWEAR

Benjamin Franklin is credited with the invention of bifocals and is frequently depicted wearing eyewear. Sunglasses began to be advertised regularly in the 1930s, and the demand has continued to increase. Sunglass wardrobes are common among young women who are not dependent on the costlier prescription eyeglasses.

Eyewear is influenced by fashion. Whether large, circular lenses or narrow granny glasses, eyewear shapes swing between extremes: very large to very small. It takes several years for this cycle to come full circle, and changes in eyewear fashions may be more gradual than in other, less expensive accessory fashion items. The high investment in prescription frames and lenses tend to retard the fashion life cycle.

Eyewear is composed of two main components: the lens and the frame. The lens ranges from large to small, depending on the fashion. The frame includes the templepiece, earpiece, and bridgepiece and is made of a variety of materials, from plastic to lightweight metals. The templepiece connects the frame to the earpiece, the earpiece fits behind the ears, and the bridgepiece crosses the nose and connects the two lenses.

The part of eyewear most subject to fashion influence is the overall frame: its size, shape, color, and material. From large to small, the size of the frame changes annually. The changes are relatively small and may go unnoticed from one year to the next, but after a few years, older frames begin to look dated and distinctly different. Frame shapes undergo changes in appearance and fashion, too. For example, aviator glasses may be very fashionable but not during a time in which granny glasses are fashionable. Heavy frames eventually give way to minimal frames or rimless eyewear. Fashionable colors and materials may be more a product of the season than of a particular year. Lighter and brighter colors are usually associated with summer, but all colors can be found year-round. Tortoise shell is a perpetually popular color, as are metallic, black, and brown. Plastics are common in lower-priced frames, while titanium is a popular metal for prescription eyewear because of its light weight and high strength.

Italy is the hub of fashion eyewear production. A few large Italian firms create most of the more expensive eyewear on the market today. China and Italy produce the majority of sunglasses.

Fashion eyewear is available through numerous retailing venues. Traditional department stores and specialty stores may have multiple locations on the selling floor to stock and display fashionable sunglasses. Usually, the less expensive sunglasses are positioned near cash registers and in other high-impulse locations. More expensive sunglasses may be located in locked showcases, and a salesperson's assistance may be required to examine a pair. Sunglass specialty stores concerned with inventory *shrinkage*, or theft of merchandise, have made attempts to create both secure and accessible inventories so that customers can easily try on sunglasses without having to wait for assistance from salespeople. The result has been well-lit, accessible displays with retractable wire attachments that secure the sunglasses to the display fixture but allow customers to try on the samples. Early in the summer (which is the peak selling time for sunglasses), discount stores prominently feature sunglass outposts near the front of the store. A discount store may also have smaller displays in various departments throughout the store. For example, the children's department might have an accessory section that includes sunglasses. The health and beauty aids section may feature nonprescription magnified reading glasses on a rotating fixture. The Internet is also a retailing venue for prescription and nonprescription eyewear. Catalog sales of sunglasses are also opportunities for retailers to generate additional profits. Because fit is not a problem, catalog customer returns are reduced.

Stores that stock large quantities of sunglass eyewear usually merchandise the inventory by brand name. This is also true of upper-end stores that carry expensive sunglasses and of eyewear specialty shops that sell frames for prescription glasses. Regardless of the price point for the eyewear, it is common for a manufacturer or eyewear distributor to provide stores with point-of-purchase displays for that company's particular line of products. This both protects the inventory of frames from being poorly merchandised, damaged, or scratched and projects the image of the brand.

SCARVES AND SHAWLS

Scarves are rectangular or square pieces of fabric that have multiple uses. They can be used as functional head coverings; to cover exposed skin, such as shoulders; for added warmth; for decoration; and even to carry personal items. Scarves can be inexpensive, like cotton bandannas used for headwear or neckwear, or hand-painted, designer silk scarves that sell for hundreds of dollars. Winter scarves are usually knitted and part of a set that also includes a knitted cap and gloves or mittens.

Shawls are larger than scarves and cover the shoulders. They are quite often fringed and may be triangular or rectangular in shape. Shawls are generally used for added warmth. A variety of terms may be used to describe unique variations on shawls, including *shrug* or *chubbie*, *wrap*, *stole*, *boa*, *pashmina*, and *capelet*. Each term has a slightly different meaning and denotes various stylings or materials. For example, a *shrug* or *chubbie* is a loose-fitting shawl with armholes, a *wrap* is a fabric rectangle, a *stole* can be a fur piece, a *boa* is long and narrow and often made of feathers, a *pashmina* refers to a scarf or shawl made of very fine wool, and a *capelet* is fitted across the shoulders.

Most scarves are woven fabrics, although the fiber content can be quite varied. Cotton and cotton/polyester blends are common for summer scarves, while acrylic, wool, and silk are frequently used for winter scarves. Because scarves and shawls are worn with apparel, the colors and prints are chosen with this in mind.

Shawls are usually made from fabrics that hold body heat, such as crochets, loose knits, flannels, and woolens. The prestigious pashmina shawls are woven from a special type of wool or a wool/silk blend. The fine wool is obtained from the Capras goat in the Himalaya Mountains. Shawls may also serve to cover a woman's bare shoulders when she wears a strapless evening gown.

The techniques used for merchandising scarves and shawls depend on the selling season, the price point, and manufacturer. During the fourth-quarter holiday season, gift-packaged scarf sets may be brought to the forefront of the accessory department. These are displayed to entice uncertain shoppers to select a present that is already attractively boxed and overcomes fit concerns. During the summer season, chiffon or cotton scarves and bandannas may be hung near the straw hats because it is not uncommon for women to combine the two items. As retail prices increase, there is a greater likelihood that the scarves and shawls will be merchandised by brand or designer name. These are usually folded rather than hung because folded merchandise can be maintained neatly. In addition, folded merchandise is less likely to be snagged by rough hangers or to become shopworn, and flat items can be placed in locked cases to reduce pilferage.

Scarves and shawls are available at all price points and qualities and in most fashion retail businesses. They are sold via many traditional formats, such as department, specialty, discount, and off-price stores, and via nontraditional retailing formats, such as catalogs and the Internet. Because selecting the proper size is not a problem, customers include gift purchasers as well as self-purchasers. Merchandisers understand that a gift shopper may not consider buying a scarf or shawl unless the item is in a highly visible location. By anticipating customers' needs, retailers can strategically improve sales of scarves and shawls.

NECKTIES, HANDKERCHIEFS, AND POCKET SQUARES

For centuries, neckwear has been the ultimate status symbol in men's clothing. Historically, the necktie has been the business power symbol for men. Prior to the modern necktie, the large or small piece of fabric that covered a fashionable man's neck was called a *stock, steinkirk, cravat, ascot,* or *ruff.* These fashions were meticulously folded, pleated, or draped. Neckwear was (and still is) a sign of fashion elegance.

Contemporary modifications of a necktie are the bolo or string tie, the bandanna, and the bow tie. A *pocket square* is an attractively folded square of linen or silk that fits in the breast pocket of a suit jacket. A fashionable and common pocket square is a starched white linen handkerchief. Although manufacturers of neckties make pocket squares of the same fabric, not all men wear both the necktie and pocket square of the same print and fabric.

Neckties are made of a variety of materials, but silk and polyester microfibers are the two most commonly used and provide the characteristic sheen that is desired in neckties. Other fibers include wool, acrylic, and cotton, but these lack the widespread popularity of silk or imitation silk (polyester microfibers). Pure silk ties are the most expensive and have the greatest status of all the fibers. Ties are usually intended to be dry cleaned only. Italy is well known for luxurious silk fabrics and beautiful ties. However, China leads the world in silk fabric and cotton handkerchief production.

Necktie prints or patterns are quite varied and tend to have a cyclical pattern in popularity. This means that a pattern will be quite popular for a few seasons but will eventually wane in popularity. Another pattern will begin to increase in favor, and then it, too, will show a decline. In order to provide consumers with ample choices, several popular prints and colors will be available during a given season. Fashionable colors for men's shirts and suit jackets will also influence tie colors and patterns.

Common necktie prints include rep (repeating stripes), plaid, paisley, foulard (small geometric prints), polka dots or pin dots, club (representing a particular organization, such as a university mascot or logo), abstract, murals (scenes), floral, conversational or novelty (such as cartoon characters or "fun" ties), and solid colors. Some neckties have the design woven into the fabrics, while others are printed designs on the surface of the fabric. Many print and color variations exist, and the merchandise selection must be large enough to satisfy the majority of the customers.

Neckties have four main components: the visible front blade or apron; the under blade or tail; the neck gusset, which connects the front and back blades; and the inner fabrics, consisting of the lining or interlining. The fashion fabric is cut on the *bias,* or diagonal, of the fabric (known as a bias cut). This technique gives the ties greater flexibility and a beautiful drape.

Although most men tend to tie a tie using the same knot variety each time, there are a few alternatives that can be used. The

A diagram illustrating Thomas J. Flagg's patented necktie and watch guard, United States, 1868. M J Rivise Patent Collection/Getty Images.

selection of knot depends on the spread of the collar, the shirt fabric, and the preference of the wearer. The most common is the four-in-hand knot, which is believed to have originated with liveried coachmen needing to secure their tie while handling the reins for a team of horses. Alternative knots are the Windsor and the half-Windsor, favorites of England's King Edward VIII, who later became the Duke of Windsor in 1937. The bow-tie knot is an occasional alternative, but it requires a differently shaped tie. Regardless of how a traditional tie is knotted, the tip of the front blade should hang to the middle of the belt buckle when the knot is tied. The back blade should rest slightly higher than the front blade so that it is not visible during wearing.

Most men who wear ties regularly will have a wardrobe of them in their closet. When buying a suit, merchandisers may encourage a man to purchase a necktie or two, a shirt, and socks to complete the new look. In order to do this, salespersons are trained in coordinating different fabrics of suits and shirts with the unique prints of neckties. In a self-selection department, the neckties should be merchandised close to the dress shirts and suits in order to encourage unplanned purchases. An attractive presentation is important in necktie merchandising, so attempts are made to keep folded (or hung) ties neat and colorized. A designer's collection of neckties will be merchandised separately from the less expensive ties, but the collection will still be colorized.

GLOVES

Although the primary use of gloves is to protect the hands from the elements, gloves also have a long history as a symbolic accessory. To throw down a glove or gauntlet or to slap a person with a glove was the ultimate disrespect and a challenge to a duel. When a woman gave her glove to a knight to wear tied to his arm, it was a symbol of her devotion and a desire for good luck. A person's wealth was judged in part by the number of gloves in his or her wardrobe.

The varied uses of gloves involve work, driving, outdoors or sports activities, and dress occasions. The bulk of fashion gloves are winter gloves, either for driving or protection from the cold. Commonly used cold-weather fashion materials include genuine leather, leather or fur trim, and nylon or acrylic knit. Manufacturers choose supple leathers for gloves, such as calfskin or kidskin. These leathers may lose pliability and become somewhat brittle when wet unless the manufacturer has treated the product with a moisture-resistant finish.

Most gloves consist of fewer than ten components. When nonstretch textiles, such as leather, are used, a closer fit can be achieved by having more pieces. In gloves with multiple pieces, the thumb may be cut in one with the trank, or it may be sewn in separately to give greater movement to the wearer. The *trank* is the rectangle of fabric that is the main piece of the glove and covers the hand. Many inexpensive gloves are knitted entirely as one piece without any seams. The knit construction also creates a close-fitting glove. This knitting technique is known as full-fashioning and is achieved by dropping and adding knit stitches to shape the glove around the fingers and wrist.

Work gloves are purchased with greater frequency than fashion gloves, so manufacturers are adding fashion appeal to traditional work gloves for female consumers. Fashionable prints and colors help increase sales to females, especially for gardening gloves and other types of work gloves.

Athletic or sports gloves, like athletic shoes, are constantly modified to encourage replacement purchases and stimulate artificial obsolescence. This means that replacement purchases are encouraged, not because the old accessory is worn out or unusable but because it is last season's style and thus out of fashion. The most updated athletic glove may feature a slightly newer

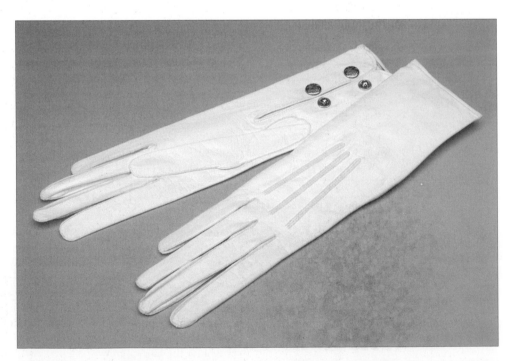

Women's kid gloves manufactured by Émile Bonnet, Montreal, ca. 1900. At this time women were expected to wear gloves whenever they ventured outside the home. © McCord Museum M970.25.26.1-2. http://www.mccord-museum.qc.ca/en/

style, fashion colors, improved (or at least different) fit, and high-performance fabrics and finishes. Teflon coatings or membranes on the nylon or polyester fibers will help repel moisture, wind, and cold. Linings are also important in cold-weather athletic gloves. All these performance characteristics and modifications are designed to increase sales to athletes.

Fashion gloves are varied in style and include driving gloves (often with leather grips), gauntlets with flared cuffs, mittens, shorties or Biarritz gloves, fingerless gloves, lace gloves, and the longer-length glove called a *mousquetaire* (French) or *opera glove* (English). Glove length is measured in buttons, with an eight-button glove reaching to the elbow and a sixteen-button glove reaching nearly to the shoulder.

Most gloves are sold in accessory departments in retail stores. They may be merchandised on hanging racks, displayed on table-tops, or displayed inside cases. Name brand gloves, such as the well-known Isotoners, are often merchandised on a separate fixture from the nonbranded gloves. During gift-giving seasons, gloves may be sold as part of a set with scarves and hats. The easy sizing makes gloves a desirable gift idea. In order to encourage the sale of gloves as gift items, they are prominently displayed near main aisles at prices that encourage impulse buying.

BELTS

Belts are accessories that are dependent on the fashionable styles of apparel. They range in width from skinny belts to wide, corselet-type belts. The placement of the waist on women's apparel will determine which belt styles are mass produced for a season. Waistline placement includes an empire waist, which is just below the bust; a high waist, which is just above the natural waist; a natural waist; a lowered waist, which is slightly below the natural waistline; and hip huggers. If provided, the width of belt loops will necessitate buying a complementary width of belt. Belts in women's wear may be a fashion focal point, or they may serve a more functional purpose. Menswear generally remains stable in belt sales, because the waistline is not relocated each season. An alternative to belts is suspenders or braces. These are intended to be in lieu of a belt and never worn with one. Although acceptable for boy's wear, elastic clip-on suspenders are not considered to be appropriate for men's fashionable apparel. Instead, leather suspenders or braces are worn and are buttoned to the inside of the pant waistband.

Materials for belts include metal, wood, cord, plastic, polyurethane, fabric, leather, and even fur. The materials may be manufactured into chain links, beads, macramé, ribbon, elastic, or self-belts, such as sashes made from the same fashion fabric as the garment. More expensive leather belts may include specialty leathers, such as reptiles and exotics (ostrich, shark, seal, etc.). These tend to be more costly due to the rarity of the hides. Reptiles and exotics are used in higher-priced belts, but the same look can be manufactured at lower price points by using embossed cowhide leather or synthetic leather, such as polyurethane.

Two of the main cost differences in leather belts are the use of genuine or top-grain leather compared to splits of leather and whether the belt is lined with leather or lined with a cardboard backing. *Top-grain leather*, also known as *genuine leather*, is the most durable and comes from the outermost portion of the hide. It contains the natural grain of the hide. The *split leathers* are the less durable layers below the top grain. They may be embossed

to look like top-grain leather, but they lack its sturdiness. The second important difference is the choice of lining or backing material. Less expensive belts, such as those that come with the apparel, are often backed with a low-quality cardboard that tends to crack and break with repeated use. It is recommended that a customer discard the low-quality belt and replace it with a co-ordinating belt that has leather lining or backing. This will last longer and look more professional.

Sizing of belts differs for men and women. Men's belts are sized in 2-inch (5-centimeter) increments, according to standard waist sizes. For example, a single style of a man's belt might be offered in 30 inches (75 centimeters), 32 inches (80 centimeters), 34 inches (85 centimeters), and all the way to 44 inches (110 centimeters). Extra-large sizes may require special orders unless the store caters to that niche market. By contrast, women's belts are usually sized as small, medium, large, and extra-large. If the belt is manufactured as part of an outfit, it will be the same size as the garment.

Belts sold separately as accessories are generally merchandised by color because of the difficulty some customers have distinguishing among darker colors, such as navy, charcoal, dark brown, and black. Within each color category, the available sizes are usually placed in order by size. Retailers may also want to merchandise by brand name, if the brand is well known, and possibly even end use, such as dressy, casual, or Western.

Retailers generally hang belts on special fixtures because this is easiest for customers and department maintenance is relatively simple. Higher-priced belts may be rolled and displayed in showcases, but this style of merchandising requires a salesperson's assistance. Self-selection is the most common retailing format because manufacturers provide the required information either printed on the inside of the belt or as a hangtag.

HANDBAGS

Today's handbags have become an extension of a consumer's personality; their appearance indicates the values of the people carrying them. Handbags should be large enough to accommodate a person's necessary belongings, but it should also be sized in proportion to the wearer's physical size. However, even a petite and small-framed woman needs more than a diminutive-sized bag. Employed women spend more than a third of their day on the go, without ever stopping by home. Their time is spent at work, in transit to and from work, picking up and dropping off children at daycare and school, shopping on lunch hours and after work, running necessary errands, and many other highly mobile activities. These require that she carry a sufficiently large handbag to contain all the items that she will need during the long day. She may even carry two handbags: a large satchel and a smaller purse.

Handbag materials should be durable and attractive. Leather and suede are popular choices, while polyurethane and vinyl simulate the look of leather but are lower priced and can be cleaned with a damp cloth. Nylon microfiber fabric is another popular choice for handbags because it is moisture and dirt resistant. For summer handbags, straws, canvas, denim, lightweight woods, and plastics are common materials.

Handbag designers select colors and prints that complement wearing apparel and are often made from the same popular patterns. For example, if faded denim or French toile print are popular in fashion apparel, they will also be popular for handbags.

Designer handbags are a very important and affordable status symbol for fashion-conscious consumers. From a business perspective, designers have found that a line of related accessories, including handbags, is a lucrative business venture. The number of apparel designers and even retail product developers entering the handbag market is increasing each season.

Because of the status symbol position held by many designer handbags, the problem of fakes is a serious legal and ethical matter. Style piracy is the copying of fabrics, prints, or styles and is usually acceptable in the fashion industry. However, it becomes a legal issue when copyright infringement occurs. The illegal copying of intellectual property rights, trade names, copyrights, and registered trademarks is called *counterfeiting*, and the luxury goods industry, including high-end designer handbags, has been one of the hardest hit. Usually, the counterfeit goods are indistinguishable from or identical to the legitimate product. For example, a Gucci bag that is sold as a counterfeit in the back room of a Manhattan Chinatown vendor may be a line-for-line copy, complete with the interlocking Gs logo in hardware, but it may most likely be made of embossed polyurethane, rather than genuine leather. Counterfeit merchandise is a multibillion dollar global industry and is detrimental to the status and profits of legitimate companies. Customs officials monitor the importing of goods and will seize and destroy shipments of illegal goods, but eliminating the problem is very difficult because only a small percentage of shipments are physically searched.

Handbag construction and components depend on the selected style. The most commonly used parts include the outer covering, made of a fashion material; the *gusset*, which is an inset in the outer covering to allow for expansion; the frame, which gives the bag structure; the *padding*, which covers the frame and softens the appearance; the lining, which covers the frame and padding and prevents seams from showing or small items from becoming lost; the handle; the closure, which might be snaps, zippers, magnets, and so forth; and the trim, which includes functional or decorative piping, appliqué, fancy hardware, and any other surface ornamentation.

Handbags are sold in just about any type of fashion store catering to females because they have a relatively high markup and profit margin. Although many handbags are planned purchases, some are impulse purchases. This refers to customers buying an item in the store without prior planning; they see it and like it, the price is right, and they make the decision to buy. To attract the impulse purchaser, retailers understand the importance of placing handbags in 100 percent traffic areas, which include areas adjacent to escalators, main entrances, and main aisles. In smaller boutiques that offer personalized selling, the handbags are suggested, via interior displays or the salesperson, as a way to complement apparel. This is called "merchandising in the total look." A blouse and slacks, for example, might be presented with jewelry, a pair of shoes, and a coordinating handbag. Most customers appreciate the fashion assistance, and sales usually increase.

Merchandising techniques for handbags include coordination by color and brand. When the handbags are featured at lower price points or the brand name is not important, store merchandisers will usually group purses by color or possibly by material. With higher-priced handbags usually comes name brand recognition, so the collection is shown together for maximum visual impact. Very expensive bags are often placed in locked showcases to deter shoplifting. Locked cases also reduce the incidence of merchandise becoming shopworn; they create an exclusive image for the brand and allow for personalized selling, which also helps to increase sales.

SMALL PERSONAL LEATHER GOODS

Small personal leather goods or flat goods are a category of accessory items that are either carried with or take the place of a handbag. The majority are made of leather, but a few are of other materials, such as nylon or even metals. This accessory category includes wallets, billfolds, key cases, change purses, cell phone cases, eyeglass cases, credit card holders, business card cases, cigarette cases, lipstick cases, planners, and portfolios. The styles change very little from season to season, so the emphasis becomes the materials, decorative design, and embellishments used. Embossed or exotic leathers, fashion colors, designer and brand names, ornamentation, and personalization become chief selling points for small personal leather goods.

Because the sizes of these items are relatively small, the primary factors contributing to the prices are quality or rarity of materials used and brand name.

Many small personal leather goods are for sale in a self-selection area of the department. *Self-selection* means the consumers do not receive salespersons' assistance. Instead, they make the decision to buy based on the information provided by the manufacturer.

The trend toward increased consumption of small personal leather goods has occurred because increasing numbers of

Mock crocodile handbag and purse, United States, ca. 2000. Copyright empipe, 2007. Used under license from Shutterstock.com

white-collar workers desire attractive holders for the items that help them stay organized. Personalized, monogrammed gifts continue to be an important trend in retailing, and small personal leather goods have no fit requirements, so they are often choices for corporate and special occasion gifts.

Both Canada and the United States have trade associations that promote and monitor the leather goods and luggage industries: the Luggage, Leathergoods, Handbags and Accessories Association of Canada and the Luggage and Leather Goods Manufacturers of America.

LUGGAGE

Luggage comes in many textures, colors, materials, and styles, but an observation of any airport will reveal that the most popular luggage is a black, softside nylon, upright suitcase with a retractable handle and wheels. Based on this observation, it can be deduced that durability and function are more important than fashion when it comes to checked baggage. The advantages of this particular version of suitcase are significant. The color black is least likely to show dirt; nylon is extremely durable, scratch resistant, and lightweight; and the retractable handle and wheels allow the traveler to comfortably pull, rather than carry, the luggage through long airport corridors.

Fashion is still a factor in luggage, however. It is especially important in small, carry-on luggage that is selected by the female traveler. To meet this desire for fashion in luggage, manufacturers offer colorful carry-ons in the season's most popular prints.

Luggage materials may be classified as softside, hardside, and molded. *Softside* refers to a pliable textile covering over the exterior of the luggage. The textile may be a heavy-duty woven nylon, tapestry, canvas, or even a leather covering. Softside luggage will collapse to some degree when the suitcase is empty. This type of luggage is less durable than hardside luggage, but most travelers do not object to replacing luggage every few years. *Hardside luggage* would include leather stretched over a boxlike frame or a metal trunk. The frame and outer covering are not collapsible. Molded luggage is an impact-resistant plastic luggage that usually has rounded corners. Generally, molded luggage is a two-piece construction, with each half of the suitcase comprised of a single component with no seams.

The airline industry has very specific standards on the acceptable sizes and weights of filled luggage. Travelers should check with each particular airline before traveling to determine the maximum sizes and weights. Travelers with bags exceeding weight limits may be required to pay additional charges. Manufacturers have complied with airline regulations by creating numerous sizes in each line of luggage. For example, one popular brand offers a line of luggage that includes five sizes of uprights, ranging from twenty-one to twenty-nine inches (fifty-three to seventy-three centimeters) in height. That same line also offers a boarding bag, a carry-on bag, a garment bag, and a computer case. Most consumers prefer compartmentalized luggage no matter what the size, so manufacturers have responded with a variety of interior amenities to help improve the function of the luggage.

In the late-twentieth-century United States, umbrellas became a fashion accessory and are now available in a great variety of styles and colors. Copyright Eric Cote, 2007. Used under license from Shutterstock.com

The purchase of luggage would not be considered an impulse purchase, unless only the smaller carry-on totes are considered. Retailers may choose to locate luggage in lower-traffic areas because consumers typically seek out luggage departments if they are shopping for these items. This allows the main traffic areas within the store to be lined with high-impulse and high-margin merchandise. In airports, expensive and inexpensive luggage may be placed in high-traffic locations near the front of the store because luggage is uppermost in the travelers' minds.

Just as in other accessory categories, the quality of luggage available to consumers will vary, and price points are a good starting indicator of quality. Price alone is not the sole determinant of quality, but it provides the customer with a quality range. Other quality factors include a heavy-duty and stain-resistant covering, such as nylon or a nylon/polyester blend; secure topstitching and bar-tacking at stress points; reinforced lift points; and a retractable handle that can be concealed and protected during baggage handling. If leather is the material of choice, genuine leather or top grain is the most durable; splits may scratch or be torn more easily. As a general rule, consumers should comparative shop both higher-priced and lower-priced luggage before making a selection.

UMBRELLAS

An umbrella is a functional and decorative accessory. The purpose of an umbrella is to keep rain and snow from a person and his or her clothing. If the purpose is to keep the hot sun off the wearer, a parasol or *sunshade* is the appropriate accessory. By comparison, an umbrella should have a water-resistant canopy (usually nylon or plastic) that is sufficiently wide to protect the upper portion of the body during a rainstorm. A parasol may be made of any material that blocks the sun, so straw, bamboo, cotton, silk, and even paper are acceptable materials for a fashionable parasol. Parasols or sunshades generally have a smaller diameter than umbrellas because of their function.

Many styles of umbrellas are available, including compact or collapsible, wind-resistant, bubble, oversized, golf, beach, and many variations and combinations of these styles.

Durability is important to many consumers who are making a planned umbrella purchase. The most important factors to consider are the ability to keep the person dry and withstand wind gusts. A wind-resistant umbrella will be more costly because of the research and engineering that go into its design. Some umbrellas undergo wind-tunnel testing to ensure the strongest resistance to wind shears. Wind resistance applies to the durability of the canopy and the durability of the frame.

Most umbrellas and umbrella components are manufactured in China and other parts of Asia, where labor costs are low due to large pools of workers. In 2002, according to the International Trade Administration, the value of umbrella imports from China was more than US$50 million, and the next closest country was Thailand, with less than US$3 million.

Fashion is important in selling umbrellas to customers in situations other than an emergency rainstorm. On rainy days, a good marketer will bring the umbrella display to the front of the store so that customers can easily make a selection before they leave to go out in the rain again. Having fashionable umbrellas in addition to umbrellas in basic colors will encourage impulse purchases. Umbrella designers will offer canopies in popular prints and colors. Museum gift stores may have printed designs that reflect popular artwork housed in the museum. Designers may offer their own signature, while luxury brands may offer umbrellas with large-scale logos printed on the canopies. Corporate gifts also include a variety of umbrellas, from golf to compacts, with the corporate colors or logo featured in the canopy.

FANS

Fans make up a relatively minor fashion accessory category that derives its greatest popularity from use during special occasions. Bridesmaids and brides are some of the main purchasers of decorative fans. In a wedding, the bride can hold a fan to hide her face from the bridegroom until they are pronounced husband and wife. In this instance, the fan becomes a substitute for a bridal veil. Since the widespread use of air conditioning, the once-functional fan has been relegated to a ceremonial and ornamental accessory in most circumstances. However, in the hot summertime with no air conditioning, a handheld fan circulates air and becomes an important accessory.

In addition to cooling the person, fans convey social meanings. These include love messages, femininity, personal modesty, social status, and appreciation (gift giving). In history, fans communicated love messages between couples. Discreet signals, such as the speed at which the lady fanned herself, coy glances over the fan, resting the fan on her lips, and many other subtle gestures had meanings for the intended receiver. In early America, the beautiful fan motif found its way into quilt patterns. In the Far East, fans are an important part of the tourist trade because they are associated with traditional Asian dress. As a result, North American tourists may purchase these as souvenirs.

Hand fans are comprised of only a few parts: the frame or ribs and handle, which might be separate components or all the same part, and the fan itself, which might be made of parchment paper, feathers, leaves, or fabric. The frame or ribs may be made of bamboo, carved wood or ivory, and molded plastic.

The delicate nature of a fan requires retailers to take special care when merchandising them. It is helpful to have display samples available for customers to handle, but the fans should be kept in plastic sleeves or small boxes to protect them. As with other accessories, fans may be considered impulse purchases unless they are intentionally being chosen for a special occasion, such as a wedding. Retailers should remember that impulse purchases require high visibility and ease of customer access to achieve maximum sales results.

WATCHES

The art and science of keeping time is called horology. A chronograph is a timekeeping device that can be started and stopped (such as a stopwatch). Before the invention of clocks or watches, the sun was the chief timekeeper, and stationary sundials were created to measure time as the earth rotated and the sun appeared to track a path across the sky. In the sixteenth century, German manufacturers produced portable timepieces with rock crystal faces that kept fractions of the hour but not minutes. These were powered by putting tension on a spiral spring that was wound daily. Soon after portable timepieces were invented, they became a fashion item. Portable timepieces adorned chatelaines in the eighteenth century. A chatelaine is a timepiece (or any functional ornament) suspended by a necklace or belt chain. Pocket watches were also popular fashion items from the time they were introduced in the sixteenth century until wristwatches became popular during World War I. As time progressed, the watch movements became more complex. By the early nineteenth century, jeweled watches, with tiny diamonds, rubies, garnets, or sapphires acting as pivotal point bearings, featured precise second hands. It was this special movement that created precision previously unavailable in timepieces. Switzerland became well known for its cottage-industry production of fine watches. In the 1840s, during the Industrial Revolution, watch assemblies became mass produced after the creation of interchangeable watchworks parts.

The most common watches today are analog or digital watches made of electronic components. Analog watches have rotating hands, while digital watches display the precise time in numeric format. Both have a quartz movement that vibrates off the electric current of the battery.

Asia is the hub of inexpensive watch manufacture. Hong Kong, China, South Korea, and Taiwan are important centers of lower and moderately priced electronic watch manufacturing. However, Switzerland is still widely considered a center for fine watchmaking.

Watch designs tend to follow fine jewelry designs. For example, if yellow gold and white gold are frequently mixed in fine jewelry, they will also be mixed in watch designs. Showy fine jewelry translates into highly visible watches, while a minimalist approach to fine jewelry results in the creation of delicate and modest watches. Females aged fifteen to thirty-five are the heaviest purchasers of fashion watches, so manufacturers create designs that will appeal to this target market.

The cost of metals and workmanship affect the price of the watch. Fine watches, like fine jewelry, are made of karat gold or other precious metals and may be encrusted with precious gems. They may costs hundreds or thousands of dollars. Bridge watches, so called because they bridge the price point between fine and fashion watches, may still cost hundreds of dollars. Bridge watches may be made of sterling silver or titanium and semiprecious gems. Fashion watches are the least expensive and are often cost less than twenty U.S. dollars. These may be made of plastic or other inexpensive materials, but their ability to keep time can be as accurate as that of any fine watch.

Licensing agreements between designers and manufacturers abound in most accessory categories, including watches. Designers may license their name to watch manufacturers to create a unique watch line that bears the designer's name and complements the designer's ready-to-wear collection.

Watch manufacturers encourage the concept of watch wardrobing among fashion watch consumers, which means they should own several watches and wear a different watch on any given day to match a particular outfit. Retailers respond to this marketing tactic by carrying fashion watches in a variety of the season's popular colors. These may be featured in displays throughout the store or on mannequins in the windows. Because fashion watches tend to be impulse purchases, they may be located near the cash register or on the main aisles. Salespeople are often trained to suggest fashion jewelry, such as a watch, when a customer is making the decision to buy an ensemble of clothing.

A unique, platinum and diamond-set manual-winding wristwatch made in the United States by watchmaker Franck Muller, ca. 2000. Marwan Naamani/AFP/Getty Images.

References and Further Reading

Accessories Magazine. Norwalk, CT: Business Journals. Published monthly.

American Business Directory. http://library.dialog.com/bluesheets/html/blo531.html (for SIC Major Group 23, Manufacturing Apparel and Other Finished Products; accessed 17 February 2007).

American Business Directory. http://library.dialog.com/bluesheets/html/blo531.html (for SIC Major Group 56, (Retail) Apparel and Accessory Stores, Dialog Database file #533. Accessed 17 February 2007.)

American Business Directory. http://library.dialog.com/bluesheets/html/blo531.html (for SIC Major Group 5137, (Wholesale) Women's, Children's, and Infants' Clothing and Accessories, Dialog Database file #533. Accessed 17 February 2007.)

Bruns, R. "Of Miracles and Molecules: The Story of Nylon." *American History Illustrated* 23, no. 8 (December 1988): 24–29, 48.

Bruton, E. *The History of Clocks and Watches.* New York: Crescent Books, 1982.

Calasibetta, Charlotte, and Phyllis Tortora. *The Fairchild Dictionary of Fashion.* New York: Fairchild, 2003.

Canadian Business Directory. http://library.dialog.com/bluesheets/html/blo533.html (for SIC Major Group 23, Manufacturing Apparel and Other Finished Products; accessed 17 February 2007).

Canadian Business Directory. http://library.dialog.com/bluesheets/html/blo531.html (for SIC Major Group 56, (Retail) Apparel and Accessory Stores, Dialog Database file #533. Accessed 17 February 2007.)

Canadian Business Directory. http://library.dialog.com/bluesheets/html/blo531.html (for SIC Major Group 5137, (Wholesale) Women's,

Children's, and Infants' Clothing and Accessories, Dialog Database file #533. Accessed 17 February 2007.)

Clutton, C., and G. Daniels. *Watches: A Complete History.* Totowa, NY: P. Wilson, 1979.

Collins, C.C. *Love of a Glove.* New York: Fairchild, 1945.

Competition Bureau. "Guide to the Textile Labelling and Advertising Regulations." http://www.competitionbureau.gc.ca (accessed 17 February 2007).

Convention on International Trade in Endangered Species (CITES). *News,* http://www.cites.org/eng/news/party/oman.shtml (accessed 16 April 2008).

"Cross Merchandising: What to Buy, How to Dress." *Women's Wear Daily Advertising Supplement, Accessor-Ease* (24 April 2000): 34.

Cumming, Valerie. *Gloves.* London: B.T. Batsford, 1982.

Federal Trade Commission. *Textile Products Identification Act.* http://www.ftc.gov/os/statutes/textile/textlact.shtm (accessed 16 April 2008).

Federal Trade Commission. *Textile, Wool, Fur, Apparel and Leather Matters.* http://www.ftc.gov/os/statutes/textilejump.shtm (accessed 16 April 2008).

Flusser, Alan. *Style and the Man.* New York: HarperStyle, 1996.

Foster, V. *Bags and Purses.* New York: Drama Books, 1985.

Fur Council of Canada. http://www.furcouncil.com (accessed 16 April 2008).

Kaylin, L. "The Semiotics of the Tie." *Gentleman's Quarterly* 57, no. 7 (July 1987): 112, 115, 117.

National Association of Watch and Clock Collectors. http://www.nawcc.org/Library/library.htm (accessed 16 April 2008).

National Fashion Accessory Association. *FASA Accessory Web.* http://www.accessoryweb.com/main.html (accessed 16 April 2008).

Office of Textiles and Apparel, U.S. Department of Commerce. *Major Shippers Report: Flat Goods, Handbags, Luggage.* http://otexa.ita.doc.gov/msrpoint.htm (accessed 16 April 2008).

Office of Textiles and Apparel, U.S. Department of Commerce. *Major Shippers Report: Silk Neckwear.* http://otexa.ita.doc.gov/msr/cat758.htm (accessed 15 February 2007).

Peltz, Leslie. *Fashion Accessories.* Mission Hills, CA: Glencoe, 1986.

Stall-Meadows, Celia. *Know Your Fashion Accessories.* New York: Fairchild, 2004.

Travel Goods Association. http://www.travel-goods.org (accessed 17 February 2007).

Celia Stall-Meadows

See also The Jewelry Industry.

The Jewelry Industry

From early times, men and women sought to adorn themselves. The making of tools and the creation of items of adornment were skills acquired during approximately the same time period. Both required symbolic and creative thinking and self-awareness. The polished point of an arrowlike projectile arises from a desire for something beautiful rather than a need to create a more effective weapon or hunting tool. The desire to adorn the body answered several needs: communication of identity, including status and kinship, as well as symbols of protection and spiritual beliefs. Jewelry worn purely for ornamentation came later in human history. The desire to express beliefs, status, and affiliations grew as the number of family members grew and the number of families who formed groups expanded. Social complexity and competitiveness gave the use of adornments a fillip. It is certain that jewelry antedates clothing. Whether it was worn for artistic display or utility, we do not know for sure. Most historians and archaeologists believe it was worn for utility and for spiritual protection.

Jewelry has been, and continues to be, made from an almost endless variety of materials including shells, ivory, human and animal hair, feathers, human and animal teeth, bone, and metals. Bronze, silver, gold, platinum, steel, aluminum, and titanium are among the metals that have been used. Glass, precious and semi-precious gems, and stones have been a part of jewelry. All materials used have been further decorated or enhanced by embossing, engraving, and etching. Filigree designs were created with the use of wire or were incised. Melted-glass enamels also played a distinctive role in jewelry.

In Central America, Mayans produced jewelry items made of jade, which they believed had spiritual powers. Items included beads, ear plugs, pectoral pieces, and masks. Interestingly, metals such as gold and silver were not used at all by Mayans until the tenth century C.E. By the ninth century, Mayan culture had fallen into decay, and surviving Mayans began to move north along the Atlantic coast.

NORTH AMERICAN INDIAN JEWELRY

Based on the types of housing built, excavated potsherds, and other items, it appears that perhaps Cherokee Indians of the Northern Hemisphere were descended from the Mayans. Many researchers think that there were many waves of migrants to the Americas, and recent DNA testing by University of Pittsburgh geneticist Andrew Merriwether and others has suggested that evolutionary relationships among North American Indians stretched from northern Canada and Alaska along the Pacific Coast to the southernmost tip of South America and then northward along the Atlantic Coast to the Carolinas and Virginia. Merriwether's findings support the Bering Strait land-bridge theory, which means that in all probability, American Indians, including Mayans, were descended from Asian migrants. If one looks carefully at design motifs in rugs, jewelry, and other designs, it is not difficult to see similarities with design motifs in Asian, particularly Chinese, art.

While many people associate colorful glass beads with North American Indians, they did not have knowledge of glassmaking of any type. Prehistoric native people did use beads made of shells, bone, coral, berries, feathers, hair, pearls, stone, porcupine quills, ivory, and other materials, and they even traded those beads with each other, thus passing along individual skills. Wampum, fashioned from polished shell beads, was especially prized for jewelry and also served as currency for trade. It was not until the mid-1500s that North American Indians frequently began to use glass beads that were traded to them by the Spanish. In the early to mid-1700s, those living in the eastern regions received glass beads in trade with the English, Dutch, and French. Anthropologists and historians can trace the contact of Europeans with North American Indians through the types and colors of beads used by various Indian groups.

Indians, particularly Indian women, preferred the smooth and colorful glass beads over the drab beads they had used in the past. They did not abandon the old-fashioned clay, bone, shell, and quill beads, however, but worked them into new designs with glass beads. Glass beads were easier to manipulate than native-made beads; they were traded in hanks of a certain length and were easier to carry than furs, fabric, or firearms. The most popular glass beads were called pony beads. They acquired that name because the beads were often brought into an area by traders on ponies.

Like other prehistoric people, North American Indians wore pouches around their necks and waists that contained amulets, medicines, or food. In some tribes where the taking of enemy scalps demonstrated skill and bravery, the scalps were hung on a leather thong around the waist as a display of skill and courage in war.

Indians wore feathers to communicate status as well as family and tribal affiliations. The number and types of feathers and how they were worn demonstrated how they were earned: through bravery and valor in war or skill and strategy in hunting. They

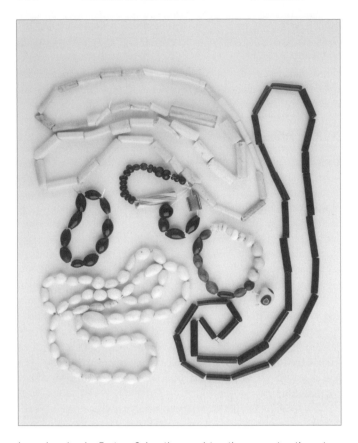

Innu glass beads, Eastern Subarctic, ca. sixteenth or seventeenth century. From the mid-1500s, when the Spanish were the first to trade glass beads to North American Indians, such beads were used to ornament their dress. © McCord Museum M9015A. http://www.mccord-museum.qc.ca/en/

also demonstrated wisdom that benefited the tribe. Feathers were commonly fixed in the hair but were also worn as part of upper-arm bracelets and around the waist fastened to a leather thong. Eagle feathers were most commonly used because they were associated with the spiritual world. North American Indians admired the strength of eagles, their ability to hunt, and the freedom associated with flying.

Again, remembering the Bering Strait land-bridge theory and the attendant DNA evidence cited previously, it is useful to think of the strong trade networks that existed long before Europeans landed in the New World. Asian migrants brought their knowledge of copper and the manipulation of metals with them, as well as their propensity for trade. Approximately 2500 B.C.E., people in the Great Lakes region hammered copper nuggets into sheets and bowl shapes. The flat sheets were fashioned into rolled beads and shaped into bracelets and pendants and other adornments. These items, along with food, animal skins, and household goods, were traded freely among friendly tribes. For unknown reasons, the use and craftsmanship of metalworking declined until the late 1500s and early 1600s, when European immigrants to the Americas gave silver crosses, ornamental collars, and brooches as rewards to Indians.

Silver and copper remained the metals of choice for ornamentation, perhaps because they were less expensive than gold or perhaps simply because of their attractiveness against the brown skin of the wearers. Silver, and eventually gold, were frequently incised and engraved with the symbolic images of individual tribes and

were soon used with jade and jasper and other semiprecious gems found in North America.

INUIT JEWELRY

The environment in which the Inuit people live is far different from that of most North American Indians. Inuit culture grew out of a largely isolated group in Arctic Alaska and northern Canada. Inuit jewelry and carving, like that of the people living on the island of Hawai'i before the arrival of Europeans, carried themes and motifs that demonstrated the jeweler's intimate knowledge of their natural environment and their culture. As in Hawai'i, their access to precious metals and gemstones was limited. Inuit jewelers today use many of the same materials as their ancestors did five thousand years ago.

While many might guess that the Inuit used ivory for carving, they may not know what kind of ivory. Human teeth and animal tusks have the same physical structure and material. The difference is that teeth are inside the mouth and are used for capturing and chewing food, while tusks grow on the outside of the body and are generally used as offensive or defensive weapons. Ivory from the human mouth can be used and carved, but generally humans use ivory from animals, including elephant, mammoth, and warthog tusks and teeth from sperm whales, orcas, hippos, and even bears. The Inuit in particular have used teeth from polar bears and sperm whales, walrus tusks, and the baleen from other whales. The ivory used can be reshaped to the desired form, or it can be scrimshawed, a process of carving or incising designs on its surface. The Inuit also use polar bear claws for jewelry.

EUROPEAN INFLUENCE

An increasing number of Europeans made their way to the Americas, bringing with them their jewelry. Among those who immigrated were skilled metalsmiths. Their skills were put to the practical use of providing necessities, and little jewelry was made in early Colonial America. Pearls, gold, and other materials found in the New World were shipped to Europe in trade for manufactured goods including wine, iron, wood, mercury for refining silver, clothing, textiles for making clothing, farming equipment, and, of course, beads for trade.

Even the wealthiest and most prominent individuals of the Colonial and Revolutionary eras put their disposable resources into more practical items than jewelry. For instance, Martha Washington, wife of the first president of the United States, was considered a very wealthy widow when she married George Washington. However, portraits of Mary Washington and Abigail Adams, wife of the second president, John Adams, show very little jewelry. Some simple adornment of the hair with beads, maybe even pearls, can be seen in portraits. When Thomas Jefferson became the third president of the United States, James Madison became Jefferson's Secretary of State and the Madisons moved to Washington, D.C. Dolley Madison and her husband were socially prominent, and Dolley was often asked to handle the widowed Jefferson's social affairs. When James Madison became the fourth president of the United States, Dolley Madison became known as the most personable and vivacious lady on the Washington, D.C., scene. Yet while Mrs. Madison was famous for the feathered turbans she preferred, we see only a simple strand of beads around her neck in her portraits. America through the eighteenth and nineteenth centuries, known as the Colonial period and the Early Republic by historians, remained conservative in its use of jewelry. The most common jewelry items seen in the Americas were shoe buckles and buttons for both men and women and *chatelaines* (ornamental devices to hold keys and small household tools), simple necklaces, and hair ornaments for women. In such a new republic, ostentatious shows of jewelry would have been considered inappropriate. To be sure, immigrants to America brought their jewelry with them. Those who could afford jewelry generally followed the fashions of Europe with regard to their jewelry as well as their clothing well through the Victorian period.

In any consideration of jewelry in the United States and Canada in the nineteenth and twentieth centuries, the following factors should be kept in mind: (1) With a few notable exceptions, North American jewelers followed European designs and trends. (2) When considering the jewelry produced by U.S. and Canadian jewelers, one should consider the difference between design artistry and craftsmanship in metals, treatment of metals, stones, and other materials and the value of the materials used. (3) One should distinguish between jewelry as an art and a craft and jewelry as a business.

PERIODS IN JEWELRY HISTORY: LATE GEORGIAN AND REGENCY

The period from 1760 to 1837 in England is generally called the Late Georgian and Regency period by historians. While the women and men of the Georgian period were still bound by hoops and shoes with large buckles, respectively, the French Revolution brought simplicity to dress. Those who had fine jewelry made of high-karat gold, high-value gemstones, and other precious materials at the time were likely to have hidden it. Unfortunately, over the decades and centuries since, fine jewelry has often been restyled, reset, and recycled to suit the fashion of the time. For that reason, it is often easier to date jewelry made of nonprecious materials than to date fine jewelry. In the late twentieth century and at the turn of the twenty-first century, jewelry made of nonprecious materials from earlier periods became more valuable for the simple fact that it could be easily dated and was a "sign of the times" antique.

For the most part, most early U.S. jewelers followed the prevalent styles found in Europe in the nineteenth century, almost slavishly. They imported most of their stock from Europe, and most carried a wide variety of items well beyond anything that could be termed jewelry. After all, they made and sold what consumers wanted. There were very few jewelers who demonstrated the creativity that can be found in the mid-to-late 1900s.

Interestingly, the first jewelers to establish businesses in the United States lived in northeastern states, including Rhode Island, Connecticut, and New York. Among the first to set up shop, and to advertise, was Nehemiah Dodge of Providence, Rhode Island. His uncle had been a jeweler, and Nehemiah had learned the trade in Norwich, Connecticut. According to the *Providence Gazette* of 14 November 1794, Mr. Dodge worked in eighteen-karat gold only, making rings, necklaces, and miniature cases. It was later noted that he also found a way to make less expensive jewelry by washing, gilding, or plating gold over a base metal such as copper.

During the War of 1812, the country was flooded with cheap European jewelry, made largely of base metals and glass or faux stones. Some of that jewelry is quite interesting relative to its design and because it was made from base materials. By 1825, in Providence alone, there were over one hundred fifty jewelers or jeweler employees.

VICTORIAN JEWELRY

The year 1837 marks the beginning of what is considered a new era by jewelry historians, the start of the Victorian period (1837–1901) and hence the rise of Victorian jewelry. Notably, 1837 also marks the establishment of what many consider the most famous jewelry establishment in the United States, Tiffany & Co. For jewelry collectors, the period from the 1890s through the mid-1960s marks a period of creativity, richness, diversity, and imagination.

Cartier lace ribbon brooch, ca. 1900. The art nouveau style of Cartier and other designers of this period was particularly popular in the United States. NICOLAS ASFOURI/AFP/Getty Images.

The early Victorian period, also known as the Romantic period, was heavily influenced by Queen Victoria, who ascended to the throne in 1837 and died in 1901. Her choice of jewelry was followed not only by the English court but also by Europeans in general and, thus, by North Americans. Jewels were worn in great abundance, and jewelry that expressed intimate sentiments was especially valued. Naturalism in jewelry design was highly prominent. Brooches of the period displayed flower heads with diamonds mounted as stamens *en tremblant* in the center of the flower. *En tremblant*, literally, "with trembling," was jewelry with a trembling effect when the wearer moved that was produced by elements set upon small springs or stiff wires. Snake motifs were found in rings, bracelets, brooches, cuff links for men, buckles, and other pieces. Coral and cameos were in favor as well. Cameos were worn not only as brooches but also as hair ornaments. Pearls, also, were worn in the hair, around the neck and wrist, and embedded in other materials.

Memorial and mourning jewelry was quite popular, and the design and manufacture of hair jewelry brooches, made from human hair, was as fine as it had ever been or would be. Victorian ladies turned hair-working into a pastime similar to needlework. Full skirts, tight bodices, and low décolletages made the bust the focal point for jewelry. *Parures* (matched sets of jewelry usually consisting of necklace, earrings, a brooch, and one or two bracelets) and *demi-parures* (a less extensive set, such as a necklace, earrings, and pin) were popular and allowed the wearer a justification for wearing several pieces of jewelry at once. Especially sought out were parures and demi-parures that were made of red coral and elaborately handcarved to show the craftsmanship of the artisan.

Married in 1840 to his cousin Victoria, Prince Albert of Bavaria died prematurely in 1861, and the Grand period of Victoria's reign began. Queen Victoria is said to have never fully recovered from Albert's death. She lapsed into a period of mourning for twenty-one years, the same number of years she and her Prince had been married. The Queen's choice of jewelry grew somber, and many in Europe followed her lead, though not for all twenty-one years. There was no longer a place for jewelry that sparkled and was ostentatious in style.

Archaeological discoveries brought to light ancient jewels, which became an inspiration for jewelry designers. Revival styles included Etruscan, Egyptian, Classical, and Renaissance motifs. The use of tortoise shell became popular; soaked in hot liquid and then molded, while still warm, into the desired shape, the shell was then inscribed with a decorative motif of lines and dots and inlaid along the lines and dots with gold or silver. As the shell dried, it shrunk, securing the lines and dots of metal in the surface. This process was called piqué.

By the 1870s, new discoveries of silver, such as occurred at the Comstock mine in Nevada in 1859, had reduced the cost of silver and increased its affordability. Beautifully engraved bangle bracelets and intricately monogrammed rings, brooches, lockets, and other sentimental and whimsical jewelry were created to serve a growing middle market.

The Late Victorian period lasted from the mid-1880s to 1901. Both the queen and her people were ready for change, and the jewelry of the period reflected that. Fun, whimsy, and lightheartedness characterized the spirit of jewelry of the period. With the discovery of diamonds in South Africa in 1867, their use increased substantially. Jewelers adorned their creations with a sparkling

Costume jewelry worn at the 63rd Annual Golden Globe Awards, Beverly Hills, 2006. Kevin Winter/Getty Images.

array of various types of diamonds. Designers and manufacturers created a virtual menagerie of animals, stars, and crescent moons sparkled with diamonds, and flowers were inlaid with diamond dewdrops. Bejeweled insects, griffins, dragons, and beautifully enameled flowers were the rage. Diamond cutters began to experiment with new ways to cut diamonds to satisfy the public's desire for their sparkle. The penchant for novelty and frivolity spread to sporting events and leisure activities, and motifs included golf clubs, fox masks, bridles, stirrups, horseshoes, and saddles—anything to amuse.

ART NOUVEAU AND ART DECO

The time span from 1890 to 1920 is known as the Edwardian period, but it is also identified as the *art nouveau* (new art) period. The Edwardians favored opulence, engraved gift items, and extravagant use of gemstones. Platinum came into use as a lighter-weight alternative to silver. This was the era of such great jewelry designers as Peter Carl Fabergé, René Lalique, and Cartier. The art and jewelry of the art nouveau period was marked by smooth flowing lines and a conscious effort to select materials for their artistic merit and not their intrinsic value. Enamel was widely used, and themes that dominated the period included flowers and flower garlands, bows and ribbons flowing with diamonds, exotic flowers of the East, and smooth, natural female figures. Art nouveau was particularly popular in the United States.

By 1925, hemlines were scandalously high, stopping just above the knee, and dresses featured daringly low backs. The effect was meant to be shocking, and to many it was. During World War I, women had gained new freedoms. After the war many were reluctant to give up those freedoms, which included abbreviated hemlines; short, carefree hairstyles; and an overall androgynous, but sexy, appearance. Art deco jewelry designs grew naturally out of art nouveau—simple but not curving, geometrical, and linear. It was a "break all the rules" period. Necklaces and bracelets, while simple, were copious in their display. Hair ornaments were common but simple. Earrings were long and dangling. Jewelry, in style and materials, was worn to complement and emphasize the dress of the period. Long necklaces, often several, were worn only to highlight the long, slender, boyish look many women sought to achieve, and they were often worn with the greater length of necklace in the back following the low draping back of the dress. The avant-garde borrowed exotic design motifs from Asian, pre-Columbian, and African art.

In the United States, Tiffany & Co. led the way in the art nouveau trend, with Tiffany designer Julia Munson Sherman discovering techniques that became a hallmark for Tiffany's enameled jewelry. Chicago artists and manufacturers, including Clara Welles and William Morris, incorporated into their jewelry artistic representations of American subjects that included American flags, American colonial period design patterns, and American Indian elements. Items were mass produced in silver and jewels that were both artistic and affordable. Aided by the Great Depression, the art nouveau period eventually died—a victim, to some extent, of its own success and overcommercialization.

COSTUME JEWELRY

Costume jewelry, with its roots in the late nineteenth century, was manufactured to give the public an opportunity to own "the look" without having to pay the price for expensive metals and gemstones. Designers and manufacturers of costume jewelry are as familiar as Fabergé and Tiffany, respectively. Chanel, Christian Dior, Anne Klein, and Adele Simpson were among leading designers. Vogue, Napier, Sarah Coventry (which was meant to be sold at home parties), and Trifari dotted the business landscape of designer-manufacturers. The quality of goods varied widely, but all had their market niche and many are considered highly collectible today. One of the most salient reasons for collecting costume jewelry is that because of its relatively low cost, it was less likely to be redesigned than fine jewelry and is therefore more easily dated.

World War II brought an abrupt change to the entire world of jewelry—to designers, to bench jewelers, and to jewelry manufacturers and retailers. (The *bench jeweler* is an artisan jeweler who sits at a workbench and fabricates or constructs jewelry from metals and other materials; *bench* can be used as a verb to describe this process.) Precious metals and gemstones were difficult to obtain. European jewelry businesses were bombed and lost archives and records. Base metal used to make costume jewelry was also used in war materials. Jewelry designers, bench jewelers, and others were drafted into the military. The women who worked in the jewelry industry turned their skills to support the military effort.

Many jewelry businesses in North America turned a portion or all of their capacity to making armaments. The period is notable for its lack of new and creative jewelry design. On the other hand, in unsettling times jewelry is seen as portable wealth.

AFTER WORLD WAR II

Boom times followed the war as the North American and European industries began to rebuild. Feminine dress was in vogue with full skirts, nipped-in waists for bodices and jackets, and heavily embroidered silk satin fabrics for evening. Fur coats and diamonds were de rigueur for the wealthy and those who wished to be counted as such.

Jewelry designs varied widely after the war. Parures and hair ornaments again became popular, and the bib necklace enjoyed a brief period. Tiaras for evening wear were popular through the 1960s. Jewelry was strictly specified for day wear versus evening wear. Women's watches gained new importance, but to wear a watch to an evening affair of any importance was considered a fashion felony. Jeweled watches, though, were popular and featured diamonds and other gemstones. It was only after World

The heiress Evalyn Walsh McLean from Leadville, Colorado, was the last private owner of the forty-five-carat Hope Diamond as well as the ninety-four-carat Star of the East. Photograph taken ca. 1914. Library of Congress, Prints and Photographs Division, LC-USZ62-71454.

War II that the United States was recognized as a world power. Even then, U.S. jewelry design generally followed the trend of Europe.

After President John F. Kennedy's death in 1963, Jacqueline Kennedy continued to influence fashion around the world, from clothing to jewelry. Her taste was judged impeccable. To the casual observer, both her clothing and jewelry appeared to be simple. It was, but it was designed and made by some of the world's top designers. The very simplicity of clothing and jewelry means that any imperfection is obvious.

Jewelry designed and manufactured in India became popular in the late 1960s and 1970s, with combinations of rubies, high-karat yellow gold, and diamonds. While Islamic law indicates that gold is socially taboo for men, Middle Eastern buyers have had a strong impact on the jewelry market from the 1970s to the present. In order to make women's watches acceptable for evening wear, designers in the 1960s began to cover watch faces with hinged or pegged gold or jewelry to give it the look of a bracelet.

The 1980s to the present have been years of prosperity. The late twentieth into the early twenty-first century has already been labeled by some as a period of excess. Tiaras and hair ornaments have been less popular, and small independent jewelers have experimented widely with various metals and other materials. Increased skill and new technology has allowed jewelers to try innovative ways of cutting and carving gemstones, but much of the work, especially handwork, originating in the United States and Canada has been outsourced to foreign countries. Additionally, technological advances, originally developed in San Francisco in the late 1930s and early 1940s, have allowed scientists to produce synthetic, lab-created gemstones, including diamonds, rubies, and sapphires.

A synthetic stone is identical to the natural gemstone it replicates in every way: color, hardness, composition, luster, and looks, except that lab gems have no inclusions or flaws. Emeralds are substantially more difficult to produce in the lab and are therefore more expensive. Gemologists are often challenged to identify a lab-grown diamond. Unfortunately, unscrupulous sellers of gemstones have also found means to disguise flaws in natural stones.

A CLASSIC BUSINESS CASE IN JEWELRY HISTORY: TIFFANY & CO.

In 1837, Charles Lewis Tiffany and childhood friend John B. Young established a business, Tiffany and Young, in lower Manhattan at 259 Broadway, with US$1,000 in startup money from Charles's father. Tiffany was from New England; at the time of the startup, he was twenty-five years old and had previously worked in his father's general store in Connecticut. In 1840, the firm moved to Fifth Avenue in New York, and 727 Fifth Avenue became the company's permanent location. Tiffany and Young was established as a retailer of "fancy goods," including jewelry and silverware, but they also advertised stationery, soap, parasols, jewelry, novelties, and "curiosities of every description." From the beginning, Tiffany advertised and marked prices of all goods as "non-negotiable," which at that time was a revolutionary pricing policy. Tiffany's persistent search for fine and unusual European products fascinated the growing community of wealthy New Yorkers. The firm began to manufacture gold jewelry in 1847, and in 1848, when political unrest in Europe

caused great depreciation in the price of precious stones, Tiffany invested heavily in diamonds, which were sold at a great profit a few years later.

In 1841, Jabez L. Ellis joined the firm, bringing an infusion of new capital. The firm was renamed Tiffany, Young & Ellis. Initially, the imitation jewelry they carried was from France and Germany. By 1844, the firm was purchasing goods from London, Paris, and Rome—the fashion centers of Europe—and some of the jewelry was gold. Advertisements continued to state that the firm sold "curiosities of every description."

By 1845, printing technology allowed for the fairly inexpensive distribution of catalogs, magazines, and black-and-white prints that could be hand colored. In 1845, Tiffany created the Blue Book catalogs that allowed people all over the country to see and order goods from Tiffany. The Blue Books were the first retail catalogs in the United States.

In 1851, Tiffany, Young & Ellis contracted with the operations of silversmith John Chandler Moore. Moore was considered the finest maker of silver hollowware in the United States. Tiffany, Young & Ellis wanted to bring distinction to their silver collections and contracted with Moore to become the exclusive provider of silver products for the Tiffany, Young & Ellis firm. Moore had used the thirteenth-century English standard of .925 for the manufacture of sterling silver. Tiffany & Co. adopted the standard for the manufacture of all its sterling silverware and also for its sterling silver jewelry. Later the standard was adopted as the U.S. standard for silver that was marked sterling silver. John Moore's son, Edward C. Moore, ran the Moore Company after his father retired in 1864.

Charles Lewis Tiffany assumed complete control of the company in 1853 and renamed it Tiffany & Co. (informally known simply as Tiffany's). Tiffany purchased the interests of Young and Ellis when they retired. Within a few decades the firm's emphasis on jewelry was established.

At the beginning of the Civil War, foreseeing that the jewelry business would undoubtedly suffer, Tiffany, ever the quintessential businessman and entrepreneur, turned most of his capital to the manufacture of swords, medals, and similar war material. While other jewelers of the time failed, Tiffany & Co. continued to sell jewelry out the front door and war materials out the back. In 1868, the company was incorporated, and branches were established at London and at Geneva; at that time Tiffany & Co. bought Moore's company, and Edward C. Moore was named a Tiffany director, the chief designer, and the head of the silverware operation.

One of the designs for which Tiffany is best known is the "Tiffany setting," a six-prong diamond solitaire setting that allows a diamond, or any other stone, to receive maximum light and produce maximum brilliance. When the Tiffany setting was introduced in 1886, it became for engagement rings a standard setting that lasted well into the twentieth century.

In 1887, when the store obtained some of the French crown jewels at an auction, Tiffany's fame spread far and wide. The jewels were formerly owned by the Empress Eugenie when she fled Paris in 1870 after Germany defeated France in the Franco-Prussian War. Tiffany bought twenty-four lots for US$480,000 (over US$12 million in 2006).

At the 1900 Paris Exposition Universelle, Tiffany chief designer Paulding Farnham received two gold medals for his designs.

THE JEWELRY INDUSTRY 155

Farnham's designs were more intended as works of art and had become more breathtaking than useful. Farnham had been hired by Tiffany's in 1875 and became its chief designer in the early 1890s. There is no doubt that Farnham was a design genius who has not been well recognized in Tiffany's history; he is called by some "Tiffany's lost designer." In 1907, Charles T. Cook died, and John C. Moore became president. Farnham began to sell his Tiffany stock in 1907 and resigned from the company in 1908. The design impetus is said to have declined substantially after Farnham left the company.

In 1902, Charles Lewis Tiffany died. He was the only Tiffany ever to run the company. Charles T. Cook, vice president of Tiffany & Co., took the reins as president, and Louis Comfort Tiffany became vice president. Cook was the uncle of Paulding Farnham, and Louis Comfort Tiffany was the son of Charles Lewis Tiffany.

Louis Tiffany, born in 1848, was supported by his family and chose a path as an artist rather than going into the family business. He traveled widely across the world and was well known in the 1870s through the 1890s as an artist in interior design and decorative arts. He also designed jewelry, but he is best known for his artistic endeavor in leaded glass.

Necklace by New York jewelry company Tiffany & Co., 2008. Stephen Shugerman/Getty Images.

Even the wealthy cut back on luxury goods after the 1929 stock market crash. During the late 1930s, Tiffany's was losing a million U.S. dollars a year, employees were laid off, and the London store was closed. In 1940, Tiffany was forced to take US$3.6 million from its reserves to stay in business. In 1940, Louis B. Moore followed his father as president of Tiffany's with executive vice president William Tiffany Lusk (great-grandson of Tiffany's founder). Tiffany stock declined to US$5 a share.

When World War II began, Tiffany & Co. shifted a large part of its production in its Newark plant to making precision parts for the military. Wartime production helped Tiffany stay in business, but in 1949, profits were still low, and the company closed the Paris store. Tiffany's 1955 sales were the same as those in 1914.

Harry Maidman, a realtor, became interested in the long-term lease of the land underlying the Tiffany building on Fifth Avenue. Tiffany stock was low, and Maidman quietly purchased about 30 percent of the stock. However, Maidman was unable to secure a seat on Tiffany's board of directors and in 1955 sold his shares to the Bulova Watch Co.

Tiffany and Moore's heirs were shocked at the prospect of hard sell and ringing cash registers (to this day, no cash registers can be heard at Tiffany stores) for inexpensive watches. To prevent Bulova from taking control, the firm and close associates sold 51 percent of their stock for US$3.8 million to the Hoving Corporation, owner of neighboring Bonwit Teller. Walter Hoving took the reins as president of Tiffany & Co. and resolutely maintained its strict standards for quality of goods and service to customers. Walter Hoving inspired renewed energy and creativity at Tiffany's. He gave great freedom to designers, both those who created jewelry, such as Jean Schlumberger, Angela Cummings, Elsa Peretti, and Paloma Picasso, and those such as Gene Moore, who designed Tiffany's astonishingly simple and eye-catching windows. Tiffany's sales grew from US$6 million to US$100 million between 1955 and 1979.

Tiffany & Co. was publicly owned until it was acquired in 1979 by Avon Products. In 1984, Avon Products sold the company to private investors in Bahrain. In 1987, it again became publicly owned. Its stock is listed on the New York Stock Exchange. The firm sells its goods exclusively through nearly one hundred seventy Tiffany & Co. stores and boutiques worldwide, with approximately 85 percent of its sales generated by jewelry.

A BRIEF ANALYSIS OF TIFFANY & CO. AND ITS IMPORTANCE

Tiffany's history is less tumultuous than that of many companies. Tiffany & Co. was founded by an American and is the oldest jewelry business in North America still operating under its original name. In fact, it is among the oldest of all continually operating North American companies of any type. How has it sustained itself or been sustained by others?

The jewelry business is, by its nature, tenuous at best. The business requires artistic and imaginative designers, creative merchandising, and skilled bench jewelers. It is both capital intensive and labor intensive at all junctures.

Using Tiffany as a case in point, one can come to several not-so-obvious conclusions about jewelry and the jewelry industry. Charles Lewis Tiffany was neither a jewelry designer nor jewelry maker. He had no training in either area, nor was he reared in an artistic, jewelry-designing or jewelry-making family or business. His father owned a mill as well as a general store, and Charles worked for him in his younger days. Charles Tiffany grew to be a creative, shrewd, and visionary merchandiser. He and his partners identified their niche of customers, purchased from others what their niche wanted, employed designers, and then hired bench jewelers or artisans to make or manufacture what the company needed.

Neither Louis Comfort Tiffany nor Paulding Farnham were merchandisers. They and others like them were the artists who provided the design ideas, and likely design drawings, to be made by the bench jewelers who worked for Tiffany's and other firms. The designers, the artisan bench jeweler, and other jewelers are rarely if ever named, but without them jewelry companies could not succeed.

One person cannot grow a jewelry business trying to design, bench, and sell jewelry. Jewelers and jewelry businesses require an interdependent complement of qualified experts. One person can play any two of the three roles in a jewelry business but not all three. In distinguishing jewelry as an art form from jewelry as a business, one can see clearly that Tiffany's and other firms like it are businesses supported by gifted artists and artisans.

OTHER NORTH AMERICAN JEWELRY BUSINESSES OF IMPORTANCE

San Francisco in the mid-1800s was home to great wealth and substantial cultural sophistication. Unlike many frontier towns and cities, San Francisco was a law-and-order community with an established and growing infrastructure. It was a port of entry for both supplies and immigrants, and it was an established center for the entire Pacific Coast. Shipping goods from the East was hazardous and time-consuming, and local manufacturing was a necessity. Fortunes were made almost daily, and the wealthy and neowealthy desired and supported trade in luxury goods.

The mid-1800s in Europe, however, were tumultuous. As a result, risk takers who were skilled in a trade, relatively affluent craftsmen, merchants, and capitalists sought their fortunes in California.

In 1852, just four years after the beginning of the California gold rush, half brothers George C. and Samuel Shreve opened the doors of a small jewelry shop, the Shreve Jewelry Store, in San Francisco. The brothers had previously owned a small business in New York. Another brother, Benjamin Shreve, was a partner in a firm known as Shreve, Stanwood & Co. in Boston from 1860 through 1869. Shreve, Stanwood & Co. became the famous Boston jewelry company Shreve, Crump & Low in 1869.

Samuel Shreve died in San Francisco in the late 1850s, and the company was renamed George C. Shreve and Co. The business remained a retail store until 1881, when George Shreve opened a jewelry-making factory. Two years later, he also took up silversmithing. By 1882, George Shreve was advertising that he had a factory with some seventy workers, probably made up of designers and bench jewelers.

After the death of George C. Shreve, the store was incorporated as Shreve & Co. in 1894. George Rodman Shreve, the son of George Shreve, was president. His partner, Albert J. Lewis, was

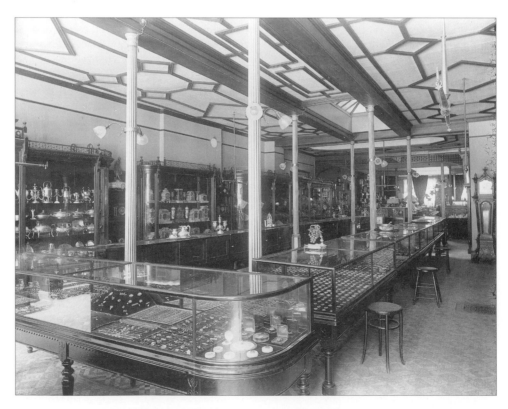

Interior of Henry Birks & Co.'s jewelry store, Montreal, Quebec, about 1890. © McCord Museum VIEW-2518. http://www.mccord-museum.qc.ca/en/

the majority stockholder. Shreve & Co. was located on Market Street in the center of the city.

With money from mines, farming, and the railroads, San Francisco seemed to be virtually afloat in wealth. Men and women wore the latest styles from Europe and the eastern United States, including wide cravats for men that were adorned with diamonds and gold stick pins, gold chains for watches, and rings of every type. Women wore rings, brooches, necklaces, and many jeweled bracelets on each wrist. San Francisco was the Gold Coast of the West.

The great earthquake and fire of 1906 destroyed most of the city, but the Shreve & Co. building withstood the earthquake. While the firm's building and the rest of San Francisco underwent restoration, Shreve & Co. moved temporarily to Oakland for two years. No time was wasted in moving the company forward, and the company published its first illustrated catalogs in 1907 displaying jewelry and novelties, as well as its own silverware designs. A few years later, during World War I, Shreve & Co. shifted to the production of airplane parts for the U.S. government.

George Rodman Shreve sold his stock in Shreve & Co. in 1912 to George Lewis, the son of Albert Lewis. Almost one hundred years after the company was established in San Francisco by Shreve and Lewis, it was sold by Lewis in 1948 to the Hickingbotham family. The business was not to stay in the hands of a San Francisco family. In 1967, ownership of the store went from a noted San Francisco family to Dayton-Hudson Corporation, which also owned the Target Corporation, seller of discount goods. The Shreve & Co. factory was then closed, ending the business run of California's oldest silversmith and the last major regional silversmith in the United States. Shreve & Co. was sold again in 1982 to Henry Birks & Sons Ltd. of Montreal, Canada.

Schiffman Jewelers, established in 1893 in Greensboro, North Carolina, purchased Shreve & Co. from Henry Birks & Sons. Schiffman Jewelers is one of the few jewelry firms in the United States that remains in the hands of the family that established it. The three children of the third generation of the Schiffman family are currently learning the family business and operating several aspects of it.

The oldest continuing jewelry firm in Hawai'i is the Sultan Company. In succession, three generations of Sultans have operated the business since Russian immigrant Edward Sultan established it in 1924, selling jewelry throughout Hawai'i and the Pacific. With a wide range of styles and designs, most of Sultan's jewelry focuses on the mass market, with popular Hawai'i motifs. In 2000, Sultan Company was the eleventh-largest jewelry manufacturing and retailing company in the United States, with retail stores doing business as Hawaiian Island Gems, H. F. Wichman & Co., Jewels of the Sea, Na Hoku, and The Pearl Factory. Sultan Company operates more that sixty retail operations in the United States.

Henry Birks & Sons was a prominent Canadian jeweler selling high-quality merchandise similar in quality to that of Tiffany & Co. Henry Birks & Sons stores catered to a wealthier clientele who could afford their top-of-the-line offerings. They became famous for the Birks "Blue Box" that was quite similar to the renowned Tiffany's Blue Box. Birks has five flagship stores: one each in the cities of Montreal, Toronto, Calgary, Edmonton, and Vancouver.

Henry Birks & Sons, which was founded in 1879, merged with Mayors Jewelers in 2005 to form a new company, Birks & Mayors. Mayors Jewelers was a former partner in the company with Birks, and the majority of its stock was already owned by Birks. The company designed, manufactured, and sold diamond and fine gemstone jewelry, in addition to timepieces and gifts, through approximately seventy stores in Canada and the United States. There are forty stores under the Birks brand in Canada and thirty under the Mayors brand in the southern United States. The company remains in the hands of the family.

Until recently, many museums have not collected much jewelry. The justification has been (1) issues of replication performed by jewelers and (2) the expensive nature of jewelry. Even when outstanding sui generis pieces have been offered for donation, many times museums have taken them only if they could be sold for fund-raising.

The art of jewelry and the business of jewelry are equally important, just as both the art of painters and the business of promoting and selling for painters is important. For jewelers and painters to make a living, they must sell their art. Rarely can an artist make a living on only one-of-a-kind pieces. Jewelry, like other artistic endeavors, is a sign of the times, to be seen as a reflection of a culture, including its love for the land; its ethnic diversity, wealth, and power; its economic and political circumstances; and its social concerns. The challenges faced by jewelry artists are unique and complex. Their art must be expressed in three dimensions. It must be small and convey its message and spirit on a living, moving person.

Snapshot: Hawaiian Jewelry

Island nations and removed cultures, due to the nature of their isolation, developed traditions and art substantially different from those developed by populations living close to each other, trading with each other, and sharing ideas and perspectives on the world as they knew it. Hawai'i, which was until the eighteenth century the most isolated landmass on earth with no metals, no precious gemstones, and, even after European contacts, limited access to the jewelry-making tools that developed in the nineteenth century and after, provides an example of how jewelry evolves in such an environment.

Each wave of Hawai'i's immigrants and visitors, Western and Asian, intertwined its arts with the arts of native Hawaiians and each other. The outcome is jewelry that is artistically and beautifully unique in design and materials. The art and artifice of Hawai'i's twentieth-century jewelers, without realizing it, often combined the simple sophistication of the art nouveau and art deco periods.

The *palaoa*, a fishhook-shaped pendant made by precontact Hawaiians, was worn by Hawaiian *ali'i*, or royalty, to protect against their loss of *mana*, or spiritual power. Whether such adornment is seen as ornamental or reflective of spiritual beliefs or both, its simple, artistic beauty was replicated by Hawaiian jewelers in almost every conceivable material throughout the twentieth century.

Western immigrants in the nineteenth and twentieth centuries brought new jewelry design ideas, but the lack of availability of precious metals and gems induced them to adapt. Once again, Hawai'i's isolation proved helpful. Some Western jewelry was imported, and Hawaiian royalty began to travel occasionally to the United States and Europe. Aided by socially prominent women of Hawai'i, including Queen Lili'uokalani, the engraved and enameled rings and bracelets characteristic of the Victorian period took on distinctively Hawaiian attributes, including the use of Hawaiian motifs and symbols and the use of Hawaiian names. Cultural authentication of the Hawaiian bracelet and ring was complete by the mid-1900s.

While Hawaiians were eager to adopt Western-style jewelry, the reverse was true of Western visitors. The art and artifice of Hawai'i's jewelers gave visitors and *kama'aina* (nonnative Hawaiian residents) alike the opportunity to own wearable art capturing Hawai'i cultural themes.

In 1938, the firm of Ming's was established in Honolulu by Wook Moon and his wife, ShayYung Zen Moon. Moon was one of Hawai'i's own native sons, the first island-born and -reared jeweler of substance to establish such a business in Hawai'i. One of six children, Moon was born to Korean parents who had immigrated to Hawai'i during the early 1900s. At the age of twenty, Moon set sail for the U.S. mainland. He traveled in the United States, Europe, and Asia for several years and returned to his native Hawai'i just prior to World War II.

In the 1940s, increasing numbers of tourists visited the islands looking for jewelry that portrayed the essence of Hawai'i. As the specter of World War II grew into monstrous reality in the early 1940s, sharply rising numbers of military personnel and their families were stationed in Hawai'i, and they, too, sought high-quality, wearable art that reflected the beauty and culture of the islands.

Responding to his own artistic imagination and skill as well as the market, Moon began to design and create jewelry that characterized and captured the magic of Hawai'i. In mid-1943, Ming's advertised, for the first time, its designs of *Hawaiian jewelry*, including an ape-leaf design. A large advertisement in the *Honolulu Advertiser* in 1944 pictured and offered for sale "pin and matching earrings in sterling." The pin and earrings were both priced at US$4.80, a princely sum at a time when wages were often less than US$12 a week.

Advertisements for the first hand-carved ivory pieces designed and created by Moon appeared in the *Honolulu*

Lili'oukalani, Queen of Hawai'i, 1892–1893. As Hawaiian royalty began to travel to the United States they brought Western jewelry back to Hawai'i. Later, the engraved and enameled rings and bracelets characteristic of the Victorian period took on Hawaiian attributes. Courtesy New York Public Library.

Advertiser in 1944. Moon experimented widely and successfully with both painting and dyeing ivory pieces from time to time.

Inspired by the beauty of his homeland, Moon designed and created additional pieces for the Ming's collection continuously until his death in 1989. He used Hawaiian plants and symbols, as well as Chinese motifs, to design jewelry that combined gold and silver with jade, pearls, ivory, and other precious stones. Most of the ivory pieces carry a distinctive signature on the back.

Ever self-effacing, Moon's mind was certainly one of the most fertile, imaginative, and prolific of its time. Simplicity and harmony were the hallmarks of each and every design. While Chinese characters and motifs remained an important factor in his jewelry designs, Moon's interpretations of Hawai'i's flowers, plants, symbols, and artifacts became the standard against which all other Hawaiian jewelry was measured. Moon died in 1983, and in 1999, the Moon family closed the doors of Ming's, refusing to sell the business.

Maui Divers was considered by many to be a young upstart firm, making inexpensive jewelry from black coral found off the shores of Hawai'i. Its young owners, Jack Ackerman and John Stewart, were well known in the islands for their diving ability, performing periodically in Hollywood movies. In a diving expedition off Lahaina, Maui, in the Molokai Channel, they discovered black coral, then pink and gold coral. They harvested the material, experimented with it, and discovered that when polished, it had a luster softer than onyx. In 1958, they established their business, stringing black, pink, and gold coral for necklaces and bracelets. Soon they began carving the coral, and eventually they mounted the coral in gold, combining it with pearls and other gems for sale to the public. Maui Divers still designs and sells Hawaiian jewelry.

CONTEMPORARY HAWAIIAN JEWELERS

Both Merle Boyer and Stanley Shinkawa created in their jewelry imagery that expresses Hawai'i's culture and historical background; it is an artistic delight for its own sake. Boyer came to the islands as an engraver and quickly developed his artistic abilities in jewelry design and manufacturing. Boyer's renditions in gold are both classic and impertinent. The artistic talent and careful craftsmanship of Stanley Shinkawa rivals that of admired 1940s and 1950s jewelry artist and sculptor John Roberts. Shinkawa, a second-generation Japanese American, was educated as a sculptor at the California College of the Arts and has exhibited his jewelry in Hawai'i and on the mainland. Shinkawa carved ivory before its importation was banned. He is, perhaps, the last handcarver of black coral in the United States. His black coral jewelry designs are simple and sophisticated and capture the essence of Hawai'i.

Recognized by the Smithsonian with work in the permanent collection of the Renwick Gallery, Frances Pickens has also been awarded Distinguished Artist status by the Honolulu Academy of Art. Her creation of the pectoral cross worn by Richard S. O. Chang of the Episcopal Church of Hawai'i transcends the boundaries of decorative, spiritual, and Hawaiian themes.

Leland Toy is the tenth of twelve children of immigrant Chinese vegetable farmers. Toy began his artist's career as a sculptor. He obtained his MFA at the Rochester Institute of Technology in Metalsmithing and Jewelry Design. His work has been shown in the "Young Americans" exhibit at the Museum of Contemporary Crafts, New York, and at the American Federation of Arts, New York, among others. Toy owns Leland's, a small jewelry business specializing in custom jewelry design. Toy's jewelry is sculptural in nature.

Perhaps jewelry artist Frances Pickens summed it up best for most Hawai'i jewelry artists: "Themes in my designs often reflect my Hawaiian and Oceanic surroundings. I am committed to the presentation of cultural motifs, especially Hawaiian, transformed and integrated in subtle and sophisticated ways expressed in twentieth-century materials and forms."

REFERENCES AND FURTHER READING

Neich, R., and F. Pereira. *Pacific Jewellery and Adornment*. Auckland, NZ: David Bateman, 2004.

See also Dress in Hawai'i since 1898.

References and Further Reading

Bennett, D., and D. Mascetti. *Understanding Jewelry*. Suffolk, England: Antique Collectors' Club, 2002.

Douglas, F. H. *Plains Beads and Beadwork Designs*. Denver, CO: Denver Art Museum Leaflet, 1936.

Dubin, L. S. *North American Indian Jewelry and Adornment: From Prehistory to the Present*. New York: Abrams, 2003.

Dun & Bradstreet Reports. Short Hills, NJ: D&B, 2007.

Gallagher, F. *Christie's Art Nouveau*. New York: Watson-Guptill, 2000.

Merriwether, D. A., F. Rothhammer, and R. E. Ferrell. "Distribution of the Four Founding Lineage Haplotypes in Native Americans Suggests a Single Wave of Migration for the New World." *American Journal of Physical Anthropology* 98 (1995): 411–430.

Morris, R. L. *The Power of Jewelry*. New York: H. N. Abrams, 2004.

Peacock, J. *20th Century Jewelry: The Complete Sourcebook*. New York: Thames & Hudson, 2002.

Phillips, C. *Jewelry: From Antiquity to the Present*. New York: Thames & Hudson, 1996.

Robb, J. "North American Indian Jewelry and Adornment from Prehistory to the Present." *The Archaeology of Symbols. Annual Review of Anthropology* 27(1998): 329–346.

Romero, C. *Warman's Jewelry*. 3rd ed. Iola, WI: Krause Publications, 2002.

Seton, J. M. *American Indian Arts*. New York: Ronald Press, 1962.

Snowman, A. K., ed. *The Master Jewelers*. New York: Thames & Hudson, 2002.

Thomas, C. *The Cherokees in Pre-Columbian Times*. New York: AMS Press, 1980.

Tortora, P. *The Fairchild Encyclopedia of Accessories*. New York: Fairchild Publications, 2003.

Carol Anne Dickson

See also Evidence about Dress of Indigenous People: Canadian Territory; Influence of the Arts; The Northwest Coast; The Plateau; The Southwest; The Northeast; The Southeast.

Antifashion

The idea of being outside of or above the fashion system has been part of a larger cultural debate for years. Fundamental to this debate are various stigmatized assumptions about fashion itself—that it is frivolous, wasteful, irrational, inauthentic, feminized, or representative of the so-called establishment associated with bourgeois capitalism. Adding confusion, rather than clarity, to the debate are the multifaceted and even contradictory ways in which the term *antifashion* has been used. Antifashion has variously been used to describe everything from countercultural and subcultural styles to traditional or classic forms of dress. Its use has implied an assumption that it is possible to be outside of fashion, with connotations ranging from oppositional tactics to perceived stasis. Complicating matters further is the ambiguity of the prefix *anti-*, which is used to mean everything from opposition to neutralization and protection. *Antiestablishment* evolved as a concept to express sentiments against dominant power and industry. Antibiotics are used to neutralize the damaging effects of microorganisms. Antivirus software protects us from viruses on our computers in today's technologically advanced world.

THE CONCEPT OF ANTIFASHION

In addition to the diverse and overly sweeping uses of the term *antifashion*, there is the problem of the binary opposition it constructs with fashion. That is, fashion and antifashion become mutually exclusive, or "either/or," in character; such binary oppositions lead to oversimplification and mutual exclusivity. The recognition of an *interplay*—rather than merely an opposition—between two categories leads to a more constructive "both/and" (beyond an "either/or") understanding.

The use of *antifashion* typically involves the breakdown of the word into two parts: *anti-* and *fashion*. This approach does not allow *anti-* to modify the meaning of *fashion*. Rather, it refers to being outside of (or beyond) fashion's reach. There is a fundamental flaw in this idea: Remaining outside of fashion actually requires a keen awareness of fashion. How else is one to know that they are wearing antifashion as opposed to fashion?

Allowing *anti-* to work as a modifier, rather than as a separate concept, to *fashion* in *antifashion* leads to a different meaning. The meaning, in this case, would be "fashion used to show difference."

Although offering more flexibility than the previous definition, an inherent ambiguity still remains. What is the fashion used to oppose, and how do we (the viewers) know it is different, especially if the difference is subtle? To understand this, it is necessary to pursue a clearer comprehension of "dressing differently" from mainstream fashion and, beyond that, a plethora of appearances.

Loosely implied in many uses of *antifashion* in contemporary North American societies is the theme of intentionally dressing differently from mainstream fashion in a specific time and space/place. From the zoot suit of the early 1940s to the Beat and biker looks of the 1950s, to hippie and feminist styles of the late 1960s, to the later "subcultural" styles (e. g., punk, goth, emo) of the late twentieth and early twenty-first century, a variety of aesthetic and (at times) political strategies have been pursued to articulate difference from mainstream fashion. What does this actually mean, however? Presumably, the concept of antifashion serves as a kind of thermostat for mainstream fashion itself. If this is so, then by creating an identifiable difference (aesthetically), the wearers of antifashion offer a reference point that helps to define fashion per se.

A review of the fashion scholarship over the last hundred years or more points to another even more fundamental question regarding antifashion: To what is it being contrasted? What *is* fashion? Is it only mainstream, or is fashion a larger process that *incorporates*—even appropriates–opposition to the mainstream?

Fashion itself is loaded with multiple layers of meaning. Over one hundred years ago, the sociologist Georg Simmel described how fashion becomes a complex dialectical process or interplay/dynamic between identification and differentiation, or between conformity and individuality. He was intrigued with fashion's role as a kind of synthesizing process in this interplay—a process that helped to hold a modern society (the "social fabric") together when there were so many differentiating threads within that fabric.

Generally, Simmel pointed to fashion as a social process of construction, enabling individuals and groups to make connections between identity and difference by accepting and rejecting styles. Simmel's conceptualization of fashion has stood the test of time. Research published by Anthony Freitas and his colleagues has demonstrated that it was easier for most of the Californians they interviewed to express in words (e.g., labels) who they *are not* than it is to articulate who they *are* (or *are becoming*). The latter is difficult to articulate verbally, because they include identity-related ambivalences, which can be represented—at least partially—through the nonlinear and visual vehicle of appearance style.

Somewhat similarly, in 1930, J. C. Flügel had developed the idea in his book *The Psychology of Clothes* that multiple fashions may occur within and across social groups. Under Flügel's logic, it is at the point of acceptance by a significant portion of a population that a garment shifts from being simply clothing to becoming fashion. His focus on the processes underlying acceptance (and rejection, by some) casts fashion in a larger role of negotiation, as does Simmel's dialectical process. One could argue that this broader understanding of fashion includes pockets of oppositional dress or even resistance to change. Susan Kaiser, Richard Nagasawa, and Sandra Hutton have described the overall process of negotiation associated with fashion as a collective, ongoing

for anthropological study. Antifashion, in their view, was oppositional to (mainstream) fashion.

OPPOSITIONAL DRESS

In the chapter on antifashion in his book *Fashion, Culture, and Identity*, sociologist Fred Davis has made the case that there should be some differentiation between "antifashion" (oppositional dress) and "nonfashion" (traditional and folk dress that lie outside of the "Western" fashion system). Using *antifashion* to encompass "all of the above," he has suggested, renders an overly broad definition. He has argued that *antifashion* should be restricted definitionally to instances of "dissent, protest, ridicule, and outrage" in opposition to mainstream fashion. He used the term *antifashion* in a manner that is virtually synonymous with sociologist Elizabeth Wilson's use of "oppositional dress" in her book *Adorned in Dreams: Fashion and Modernity*. Wilson described oppositional dress as expressing "the dissent or distinctive ideas of a group, or views hostile to the conformist majority." She illustrated this definition with examples ranging from the male French bohemians of the 1830s (wearing romantic styles), to the American beatniks' use of black (drawing from the existential fashion of postwar Left Bank Paris) in the 1950s, to British youth subcultures (mods, teds) of the 1950s and 1960s, to American hippies of the late 1960s, to punk ("the opposite of mainstream fashion").

The benefits of restricting the concept of antifashion to oppositional dress are twofold. First, such usage avoids confusion; second, it reinforces Simmel's idea of fashion as a dialectical process that subsumes or includes simultaneous and contradictory expressions of conformity or similarity (identification). At the same time, the latter dialectic challenges—even opposes—prevailing norms, as the fashion system absorbs that which is different from the norm.

Key to understanding oppositional dress is an understanding of the zeitgeist (the spirit of the time, at least in dominant culture) in a particular space/place. Oppositional dress need not be organized and worn by a group and may have obvious meanings or very discreet, subtle meanings. Key to oppositional dress, however, is the idea of articulating resistance to dominant culture, including issues of hegemonic masculinity and hegemonic femininity. For example, Van Dyk Lewis has pointed out that the Black Panther style of the late 1960s and early 1970s (black berets, black turtleneck sweaters, black leather jackets, Afro hairstyles) enabled African American men to express their rejection of white bourgeois male culture. The "second wave" feminist movement of the late 1960s and early 1970s expressed stylistic difference from, and hence opposition to, mainstream bourgeois femininity. In the process, there was a rejection of fashion, just as there was in the first wave of feminism in the last half of the nineteenth century. The first wave of feminism had focused on dress reform: freedom from the corset and crinoline, experimentation with bloomers, and a "natural" look. The second wave highlighted freedom from many of the rituals associated with (oppressive) femininity in the twentieth century: makeup, the bra, the girdle, shaving, and high heels. Many of the ideas and symbols of second-wave feminism were appropriated from lesbian culture, which had been strongly influenced by working-class culture.

In some cases, oppositional dress has been even more direct in its response to a given look. For example, in the 1980s, there was a preppy look (very classic, deriving from upper-class

Beatniks outside a coffeehouse in California, 1960. Beatniks adopted styles of dress that symbolized a rebellion against the norms of American society. Time & Life Pictures/Getty Images.

process of imitation, modification, and negation. Analogous to a Wikipedia entry on the Internet, fashion undergoes continual revision as individuals assert their own versions or counterversions to a general theme.

If, in fact, fashion is a process of negotiation and change, then it applies within, as well as across, groups and cultures. However, some of the terminology and frameworks used to characterize diverse forms of dress have oversimplified this process. For example, the development of the fashion/antifashion binary is credited to Flügel's distinction between "fixed" (relatively unchanging) and "modish" (changing) dress. Nearly fifty years later, anthropologists and writers Ted Polhemus and Lynn Procter have modified these terms by equating "fixed" with antifashion and "modish" with fashion, indicating that "the time has come to subdivide the generic subject of adornment into two separate types, fashion and antifashion." Unfortunately, this binary distinction has obfuscated, rather than illuminated, an understanding of fashion as a process of negotiation. Further complicating such an understanding is Polhemus and Procter's use of *antifashion* as inclusive of everything from the dress of traditional cultures and tribes to European and North American "Western" youth subcultures. Fundamental to antifashion's opposition to fashion, in their formula, was the idea that antifashion—traditional folk or tribal dress and "Western" youth subcultural style alike—was fair game

Black Panther demonstration, New York, 1969. Through the Black Panther style of the late 1960s and early 1970s (black berets, black turtleneck sweaters, black leather jackets, Afro hairstyles), African Americans expressed their rejection of white bourgeois male culture. Jack Manning/New York Times Co./Getty Images.

understatements of casualness with branded separates such as polo shirts and khaki pants—ironically derived from the working classes). The branding of polo shirts included little icons such as alligators and polo players on horseback. Expensive designer sunglasses, worn on a protective cord, helped to complete the look. Somewhat predictably, opposition to the preppy concept and to its branded leanings arose: Enter the antipreppy—the individualist who refuses to engage in a status-driven existence. Indeed, he or she goes further and explicitly *mocks* preppy style by cutting off their polo shirts to a ragged midriff length or by collecting little icons that are worn as little badges in another context (for example, an old hooded sweatshirt) or wearing cheap sunglasses on an old rope rather than a cord. The antipreppy look was offensive to preppies; there was little ambiguity in the intended message. Oppositional dress, in this instance, required an obviously strong norm (preppiness) against which to articulate a conflictual, negating message. Probably more typically, the norms of mainstream fashion are not as clear-cut, and hence oppositional dress has multiple meanings—not merely those of conflict or negation.

Culturally and collectively speaking, oppositional dress tends to assume one of at least two major forms: countercultural (*against* dominant culture) or subcultural (resistance *underneath* dominant culture). Generally, the countercultural form tends to involve, at least initially, bourgeois youth striving to challenge the intellectual, political, and aesthetic values of their parents' generation. The subcultural form tends to involve a wider range of youth (especially working-class and minority youth) and to have a less pervasive or less powerful political positioning in relation to the dominant culture. Aesthetically and economically speaking, however, the dominant culture relies upon oppositional dress of all kinds for inspiration and marketing. In both countercultural and subcultural forms, much of the oppositional impetus originates with youth, who, as Fred Davis has noted, are more likely than adults to have the time and inclination to suspend "major institutional commitments" (i.e., career development, family building) for a temporary period. Youth also have the ambivalent "luxury" of rejecting bourgeois culture while also reaping the benefits of it. This was especially true in the last half of the twentieth century, when the marketing category of "teenager" emerged and the huge baby-boom generation (born approximately between 1946 and 1964) exercised a great deal of symbolic energy.

COUNTERCULTURAL STYLE: THE MYTH OF A BOHEMIAN IMAGE

Beginning in the nineteenth century, at least, "romantic" aesthetic experiments have been designed to resist modernity and mainstream fashion, in part by exploring what it means to be natural or authentic. In her book *Bohemians: The Glamorous Outcasts*, Wilson has elaborated on the cultural construction of "Bohemia" as a mythical and contradictory space for ambivalent resistance to mainstream culture. In France, the term *bohemian* had been the term used to describe gypsies, who were mistakenly believed to have come from Bohemia in Central Europe. (Actually, the

Hippies in Los Angeles, 1967. The hippie experimentation with a "natural" look was represented by, among other styles, long hair on males and females alike and blue jeans. Michael Ochs Archives/Getty Images.

language of gypsies—Romany—had been traced to Sanskrit in India, but the term *bohemian* continued to be used to describe people who have a nomadic or alternative lifestyle that is more authentic and day-to-day than the mainstream modern experience.) The nineteenth- and twentieth-century artists, writers, intellectuals, and radicals participating in the bohemian myth (at times involving tangible involvement in an identifiable subculture) exaggerated their individualism and authenticity. Collectively, however, bohemians created a cultural space that highlighted being *against* the dominant culture. According to Wilson, the first bohemians in Paris viewed themselves as "embattled geniuses defending Art against a vulgar bourgeoisie." Few bohemians, actually, had working-class or proletarian backgrounds; Bohemia was basically an oppositional group *within* the bourgeois class. Perhaps this contradiction has contributed to what Wilson has described as "a long-standing, love-hate relationship between Western industrialized society and the culture it has produced"; basic to this ambivalent relationship is the central problem of authenticity. The garments worn were eclectic, accenting a sought-after look of ambivalence about and through material possessions.

Although bohemian culture has essentially been an urban phenomenon, there have been ongoing fantasies about what is authentic, leading to fascination with, and fantasies about, nature. In the latter part of the nineteenth century in California, especially, this form of bohemian culture flourished in San Francisco, as well as in the artist colonies of Carmel and Pasadena. Greenwich Village in New York developed as the most famous of U.S. Bohemias, especially in the 1910s, with its combined culture of grittiness, creativity, and leftist politics.

In the 1950s, bohemian culture flourished but had new labels: existentialist, Beat, and counterculture. Many of the Beat writers and artists in Greenwich Village and the North Beach community in San Francisco were well educated and had bourgeois backgrounds, but antibourgeois sentiments continued; the *real* working class represented a style metaphor for authenticity. Neal Cassady, for example, became an authentic working-class muse for writers and artists. Typical Beat style was meant to be "anti-establishment and anti-grey-flannel-suit," according to Amy de la Haye and Cathie Dingwall in their 1996 book on subcultural style. That is, it was intended as an oppositional, "almost sloppy" affront to mainstream masculinity. More than "studied indifference," Beat style expressed a rejection of bourgeois values and appropriated symbols of working-class style, including khaki pants, white T-shirts, flannel shirts, unpressed corduroy jackets, black leather jackets, heavy workman's shoes, and other separates that defied the business suit concept.

In the hands of the media, the Beat counterculture evolved into the "beatnik," who focused on black—stereotypically, a black turtleneck sweater and a black beret. Part of the bohemian influence of black came from Paris, where those involved in the existential philosophical movement wore black.

Fashion theorists ranging from J. C. Flügel to Fred Davis have noted how people on the political left, between the 1910s and 1960s, had been prone to express some bohemian identification through their dress. Davis indicates that in the 1960s, the oppositional dress of the political left and the cultural (bohemian) left coalesced into "blue jeans mania." The working-class influence prevailed among bourgeois youth (especially college students) in the context of the antiwar movement associated with the late 1960s. The hippies extended bohemian, antibourgeois culture but gave it a more colorful and experimental countercultural turn during the "Summer of Love" in the Haight-Ashbury district of San Francisco in 1967. Part of the experiment involved a return to anything that was perceived as natural, hearkening to the romantic movement of the nineteenth century. The hippie celebration of peace, love, sexuality, and experimentation with natural (often working-class) styles were represented by long hair on males and females alike, blue jeans, blue work shirts, and T-shirts.

The hippie movement expressed ambivalence through the interplay of natural and unnatural experimentation through media ranging from drugs to fashion. Although the hippies of San Francisco had an aesthetic appearance style that was much more colorful than that of the Beats before them, some aspects of the two movements shared the principle of "dropping out" through experimentation with natural (e.g., marijuana) and synthetic (LSD) drugs. T-shirts tie-dyed in psychedelic colors symbolized some of this experimentation, as well as an ethos of do-it-yourself. Attempts to create authenticity through style ranged from tie-dyeing to patchwork, appliqué and embroidery techniques, crocheted halter tops, and home sewing. More basically, the hippie movement can be linked to the nineteenth-century romantic experiment: the desire to construct a bohemian space that was freer, more natural, and more authentic than dominant bourgeois culture.

SUBCULTURAL STYLE

The term *subculture* was coined in the 1940s and has been used as a term to designate social groups who deviate in some way from

Three young men wearing the latest teddy boy fashions, London, 1955. Popperfoto/Getty Images.

mainstream norms. Because cultural values and norms are often based upon the dominant ideals of adult communities, subcultural style has often represented youthful attempts to differentiate itself aesthetically from a parent culture. The youth involved use elements of style from clothing and music alike to express their ambivalent opposition to their parents' values, coupled with resistance to dominant (bourgeois or mainstream) fashion and even to other youth subcultures who resist dominant parental and cultural norms on their own terms. Style becomes a vehicle for aesthetic expression (and "noise") that might not otherwise be possible to articulate culturally or politically. Often, these styles begin with working-class and minority ethnic youth and are later picked up by middle- and upper-class youth.

This description of style fits a variety of North American subcultures: from the zoot suit worn by African American and Latino youth in the early 1940s to contemporary hip-hop. (It is interesting to note how both the zoot suit and contemporary hip-hop style rely upon a looseness of fit on the male body.)

In addition, styles such as the biker style (e.g., jeans, white T-shirt, black leather jacket) of the 1940s and 1950s (as exemplified by Marlon Brando in *The Wild One*) can be traced to working-class youth. However, overall the pattern of subcultures emerging from the working class can be seen most clearly in Britain. From the teddy boys of the 1950s to the mods and skinheads of the 1960s and the punks of the 1970s, British working-class (largely white) subcultures have challenged the hegemony of dominant culture obliquely, through style, according to Dick Hebdige. Through globalization media, movies, and music became devices to deliver fashion to the youth of the world. This phenomenon blurred the lines of where and when the authentic oppositional styles began, creating an opportunity for unique interpretations of similar sentiments.

Many scholars have observed that the identities and appearance of subculturalists are continually in flux, as they experiment with diverse forms of opposition, incorporation, and articulation. This pattern probably fits Simmel's dialectical understanding of fashion as a dynamic force in society.

STUDYING ANTIFASHION IN THE 1990S AND BEYOND

Ironically, while some scholars were attempting to identify, categorize, and fix different forms of dress, poststructuralist and postmodern theories (following feminist theory) were beginning to argue for the unfixing or deconstruction of binary oppositions in favor of fluidity and flexibility. The restructuring of global capitalism in the early 1980s further contributed to a discussion of flexibility and fluid boundaries among categories. Fashion studies scholars, like those in other fields of the humanities and social sciences, began to examine some of the basic assumptions of ongoing changes in appearance styles. In addition to theoretical examining, there were tangible signs of changes in terms of how clothes were being produced, distributed, marketed, and consumed: offshore outsourcing of garment labor, a dramatic increase in new visual media bombarding individuals in everyday life (e.g., music videos and, later, the Internet), the growth of branded merchandise, and a mix-and-match consumer aesthetic (e.g., business casual, separates dressing). If fashion and identity constructions were so fluid and flexible, then how could there be a clear fashion or mainstream target *against* which to resist or rebel? How could any form of dress be fixed?

In an essay on subcultural style in the journal *Fashion Theory* in 1997, fashion historian Caroline Evans critiqued a 1994 exhibition on street style at the Victoria and Albert Museum in London, noting how her students thought the curators had just "gotten wrong" what the students had experienced firsthand. But this was not the primary problem; interviews conducted by Cathy Dingwall for the exhibition indicated that individuals

Skateboarders in New York City, ca. 2000. Photograph by Leland Bobbe/Getty Images.

with ties to subcultures felt "transfixed, immobilized, like a butterfly impaled on a pin in somebody else's butterfly collection." In fact, subcultural identities are probably among the most fluid and mobile of identities, according to Evans; attempts to categorize, label, and analyze them tend to fix or freeze them in time, with little recognition to life changes, space/place, musical or other lifestyle preferences, and other issues associated with identity experimentation.

There is an ongoing dilemma associated with documenting and analyzing subcultural style: Almost at the moment of the verbal labeling of a subculture and a representative visual snapshot of its style, a subculture can become somewhat fixed in the popular imagination. The label becomes associated with a "picture in the head"—the idea of a stereotype, which might carry with it dangerous assumptions. Thus, media and academic interpretations of subcultures cannot help but engage in some of this fixing in order to describe, analyze, theorize, and represent visually. What is the alternative? The curators of the street style exhibit at the Victoria and Albert Museum note in their 1996 book on the exhibit, *Surfers, Soulies, Skinheads, & Skaters*, that the museum has made a commitment to collect "examples of authentic subcultural outfits" along with "examples of high-fashion 'spin-offs.'" Ultimately, everyday style (especially in subcultures) is dynamic and cannot be adequately captured in single "looks," which are frequently appropriated by the fashion industry and which then undergo change so as to maintain some sense of opposition. Yet, it is probably worse *not* to attempt to record, document, and analyze style in everyday life *nor* to acknowledge the importance of subcultures in contemporary culture.

The field of "post-subcultural studies," as expressed in the volume *The Post-Subcultures Reader*, edited by David Muggleton and Rupert Weinzierl, addresses in part the need to move beyond an oversimplified dichotomy between a culturally authentic or heroic view of subcultural style and a view of popular culture (and, indeed, fashion) as a parasite that aims only to coopt, or to capitalize on, subcultural innovations. Furthermore, whether referred to as *oppositional dress*, *subcultural style*, or even *antifashion*, the most ambiguous term, it is evident that the pace of change has accelerated as a function of contemporary capitalism. Processes of oppositional innovation and mainstream absorption and diffusion have become so blurry and complicated as to make the idea of resistance itself a highly challenging feat. If fashion itself is open ended and encompasses multiple options, then it is hard to identify exactly what there is to resist. In Simmel's terms, fashion's dialectic—the continual interplay between identification and differentiation—is simultaneously more individualized, less organized, and more commodified. Yet the dialectic itself continues.

Snapshot: Beats and the Beat Generation

In the late 1940s and into the 1950s, a group of young men began to question the ideals of the so-called American Dream. These were the Beats. This generation of young men rejected many of the basic elements of hegemonic manhood: marriage, economic competitiveness, career aspirations, and the like. According to Gene Feldman and Max Gartenberg, in their book titled *The Beat Generation and Angry Young Men*, the Beat Generation, or Beats, "dig everything" and "implicitly want nothing."

The thrust of the Beat was to reject the norms of the time and rebel against those (the "squares") who mindlessly entered into "the system." Beats were determined to be undetermined, worked hard to not work hard, and focused on the unreal realities of life. Following the existentialist philosophical movement, they believed that life should be more authentic than the façade that is built by living in U.S. culture, asking, "Should we live as slaves to illusions we know to be untrue?"

Although the Beats were in constant search of the truth, they somehow claimed to be apathetic and to accept the uncontrollability of life.

EVOLUTION OF THE BEAT

Different stories circulate regarding the word *Beat*. Steven Watson, an author who has examined the origins of the Beat generation, contends that the word has roots in drug culture and referred to a bad drug deal or being robbed but was appropriated to mean (more generally) living neither with money nor prospects. The term *Beat Generation* is said to have been coined by author Jack Kerouac in his 1950 book titled *The Town and the City*. Through the 1950s, Kerouac and other authors such as Allen Ginsberg, William Burroughs, and Neal Cassady led the charge for a generation who shared their sentiments, referred to as simply *Beats*.

By the late 1950s, the Beats had become a topic for popular media. Articles in popular magazines such as *Esquire* and *Time* were appearing, and a number of books about the Beat Movement were published in the late 1950s. Literature had long been a tool for the expression of Beat ideology, but now, ironically, it was used to parody the movement. The term *beatnik* appeared in a *San Francisco Chronicle* article by Herb Caen, who used it to express similarities to the Beat and the

Russian satellite *Sputnik*. Beats (now called beatniks) were suddenly depicted as marijuana-smoking, coffee-drinking existentialists who wore only black (a black beret and black jeans if male and black tights if female). A Beat man would have a goatee, according to the media depictions.

Although there was no single uniform or look for Beats (the idea was not to care about appearance, which would have been inauthentic), Beat culture did not escape the new, commercialized, and stereotyped beatnik image. Not long after the media depictions of beatniks came out, Hollywood also joined the bandwagon with a 1959 movie titled *The Beat Generation*. It seems the Beat, from that point on, could no longer be authentic—the driving impetus for the movement itself.

Ironically, images of beatniks are now a timeless favorite for commercial use. A Beat (or the now synonymous beatnik) continues to stand for a deep-thinking, coffee-drinking existentialist who has the deepest disgust for the suburbs, consumer capitalism, and the pursuit of the American Dream.

REFERENCES AND FURTHER READING

Feldman, Gene, and Max Gartenberg. *The Beat Generation and Angry Young Men*. New York: The Citadel Press, 1958.

Watson, Steven. *The Birth of the Beat Generation: Visionaries, Rebels, and Hipsters, 1944–1960*. New York: Pantheon Press, 1995.

Snapshot: Lesbian Looks

Inasmuch as the essence of fashion has often been equated with bourgeois (heterosexual) femininity, lesbian looks have often been stereotyped as antifashion. In actuality, the situation is much more complicated, and lesbian style is not outside the realm of fashion. Indeed, lesbian styles have historically influenced the course of fashion change. Fashions ranging from jeans, work shirts, and the "natural" look to black pantsuits or, more generally, to the very idea of women wearing trousers can be attributed to lesbian culture(s). Resistance or opposition to dominant, feminine fashions of the day shaped some of the looks and the ideologies of the first (latter half of the nineteenth century) and second (late 1960s and 1970s) waves of feminism in North America.

Lesbian looks have not only revolved around statements of gender and sexuality; they have also varied within and across time and space in accordance with issues of social class, race, ethnicity, and age/generation. In a compelling personal memoir and critical analysis titled *Butch/Femme: Inside Lesbian Gender*, Sue-Ellen Case has described the concept of "making butch" in the San Francisco lesbian bar culture of the 1970s, extending her previous work highlighting the intersections among class, race, and lesbian identity in the butch/femme

Lesbian activists, United States, 1971. Barbara Gitlings and Kay Tobin Labusen Gay History Papers and Photographs, Manuscripts and Archives Division, The New York Public Library, Astor, Lenox and Tilden Foundation.

aesthetic. Countering the commonplace assumption that lesbian feminism can be characterized unproblematically as anti-fashion, Case has described the hippie butch look arising in the 1970s as stylistically combining elements of the classic butch look with "hippie anti-masculine male fashions" (e.g., 1930s men's clothes and flowing Marlene Dietrich–style pants and silk bow ties). As hippie dykes dedicated themselves to new ways of being and appearing, style became conceptualized as a vehicle for lesbian self-representation. Case has argued that the encounter between classic and hippie butches had more impact on new negotiations of style than the stereotypical image of the overalls-wearing lesbian feminist that dominates characterizations of the 1970s.

At the same time (the 1970s), across the country in Baltimore, Maryland, and in a different context (socialist feminist politics), a recent historical analysis by Laurel Clark has revealed how lesbian and heterosexual feminists alike "dressed down" in order to deemphasize their femininity, to critique consumer capitalism, and to identify with the struggle of the working class. Regardless of sexuality, socialist feminists, who were predominantly white and middle class, dressed androgynously in order to refute both gender and class norms. Clark has argued, along with Sue Ellen Case and other scholars, that middle-class lesbians were less likely to embrace butch/femme roles than their working-class counterparts. Regardless, in the 1970s and 1980s, the fashion and beauty industries appropriated the general oppositional discourse that was created by lesbian culture and second-wave feminism and their intersections. Danae Clark has pointed out that in the 1990s, younger urban lesbians pursued a different discourse—one that exposes the constructed nature of the earlier flannel-and-denim look, for example, and that uses fashion as a site for female resistance and masquerade. Experimentation with style and butch/femme roles resulted in "transgressive self-representations" that were in turn appropriated by capitalism into trendy and chic styles.

These case studies demonstrate how oppositional dress is a multifaceted matter; it does not simply reflect resistance to one thing or idea. The issue of just what was being opposed is context specific and crosscutting within lesbian culture, as a function of factors such as race, class, age/generation, sexual desire, politics, and geographic location.

REFERENCES AND FURTHER READING

Case, Sue-Ellen. "Making Butch: An Historical Memoir of the 1970s." In *Butch/Femme: Inside Lesbian Gender*, edited by Sally R. Munt, 37–45. London and Washington, DC: Cassell, 1998.

Clark, Danae. "Commodity Lesbianism." *Camera Obscura* 25–26 (January/May 1991): 181–201.

Clark, Laurel A. "Beyond the Gay/Straight Split: Socialist Feminists in Baltimore." *NWSA Journal* 19, no. 2 (2007): 1–31.

Hammidi, Tania N., and Susan B. Kaiser. "Doing Beauty: Negotiating Lesbian Looks in Everyday Life." *Journal of Lesbian Studies* 3, no. 4 (1999): 55–63.

Lewis, Reina. "Looking Good: The Lesbian Gaze and Fashion Imagery." *Feminist Review* 55 (1997): 92–109.

Rolley, Katrina. "Love, Desire and the Pursuit of the Whole." In *Chic Thrills: A Fashion Reader*, edited by Juliet Ash and Elizabeth Wilson, 30–39. Berkeley: University of California Press, 1992.

Snapshot: Zoot Suiters

The loose, exaggerated silhouette of the zoot suit distinguished it from other menswear in the late 1930s and early 1940s. Many variations on the origin of the style have been pinpointed, from George Washington to the Duke of Windsor. The more popular theory, reported by Australian historians Shane and Graham White, includes the emulation of Rhett Butler's style in *Gone with the Wind* by a young African American named Clyde Duncan from Gainesville, Georgia. Depending on the theory of who started the style, the date of the style's acceptance also varies. Nonetheless, there is little disagreement that the zoot suit became a popular fashion for many African American jazz musicians and the corresponding dance culture in the late 1930s and into the 1940s. This popularity effectively made the zoot suit a form of subcultural or oppositional dress. By the early 1940s, the *pachucos* (Mexican American youth) were wearing zoot suits on the West Coast. The subcultural dress adopted by the pachucos effectively served to connect Mexican American and African American youth symbolically as oppositional to hegemonic masculinity.

Although the original wearers of the zoot suit may have designed it for purely aesthetic reasons, it eventually symbolized dissent. The specific meaning of the zoot suit depended on who was wearing it and where. In March 1942, only four months after U.S. involvement in World War II officially came to fruition, the War Production Board created a rationing act that affected clothing containing woolen fabric and, therefore, the zoot suit. The act essentially made the production of zoot suits illegal and gave the zoot suit a new spin, making it an "unpatriotic" garment. Technically, it was not illegal to wear a zoot suit, and many African American and Latino young men already owned them. Some perceivers of these young men

U.S. singer, dancer, and actor Sammy Davis Jr. (center) wearing a zoot suit in 1944. American Stock/Getty Images.

in their zoot suits, however, viewed them as unpatriotic and confrontational.

Eventually, the zoot suit became perceived as more than a statement of youth rebellion against U.S. patriotism. Racial implications came into play as some African Americans and Latinos continued to wear zoot suits and as the dominant media stereotyped the young men as hoodlums who disavowed the norms and morals holding the United States together during the war. Zoot suits came to represent excess—excessive material, excessive flamboyance, and excessive leisure. As White and White have pointed out, the latter came from the "dance and music culture that displayed a studied indifference to a work ethic that, for many Americans, seemed even more important as the nation fought for its very survival." Zoot suiters were seen in the dominant popular imagination as blatantly oppositional to this work ethic; the majority of the population was white, but some middle-class African Americans and Latinos adults were also extremely upset with and embarrassed by zoot suiters. While the vast majority of African American and Latino males of draft age did end up in the armed services, there was a significant and obvious minority who did not.

What may well have been an aesthetic, if not an oppositional, choice became a metaphor for social difference, revealing and articulating racial tensions between young white men (especially servicemen) and U.S. men of color dressed in leisure attire. Eventually, tensions rose, as servicemen reacted in what has been dubbed the "Zoot Suit Riots" in the summer of 1943 in the Los Angeles area.

The Zoot Suit Riots resulted in incredible violence, leaving many people injured or killed. The riots did shed light on the reality of the racial tension in the country at the time. Furthermore, the Zoot Suit Riots became the birthplace of two important leaders of future social movements. The Chicano union activist Cesar Chavez (a zoot suiter) first experienced community politics during the Zoot Suit Riots during the summer of 1943. And it was the experiences of "Detroit Red" in similar zoot suit riots in Harlem that inaugurated a political awakening that ultimately led to his emergence as Malcolm X.

Zoot suits eventually became a symbol of resistance to dominant white hegemonic ideals. In a relatively fast evolution from youth expression to musical subcultural dress, to the ultimate banding of the Mexican American and African American subcultures, zoot suits were able to articulate challenges to the norms that subcultural dress had not yet seen. The Zoot Suit Riots have served as an illustration of the potential volatility of subcultural and oppositional dress when deviating from the ideals of the majority.

REFERENCES AND FURTHER READING

Berger, Meyer. "Zoot Suit Originated in Georgia; Bus Boy Order First One in '40." *New York Times*, 11 June 1943, 21.

Cosgrove, Stuart. "The Zoot-Suit and Style Warfare." *History Workshop Journal* 18, no. 1 (1984): 77–91.

White, Shane, and Graham White. *Stylin': African American Expressive Culture from Its Beginnings to the Zoot Suit*. Ithaca, NY: Cornell University Press, 1998.

References and Further Reading

Davis, Fred. *Fashion, Culture, and Identity*. Chicago, IL: University of Chicago Press, 1992.

de la Haye, Amy, and Cathie Dingwall. *Surfers, Soulies, Skinheads & Skaters: Subcultural Style from the Forties to the Nineties*. Woodstock, NY: The Overlook Press, 1996.

Evans, Caroline. "Dreams That Only Money Can Buy ... Or, the Shy Tribe in Flight from Discourse." *Fashion Theory* 1, no. 2 (1997): 169–188.

Flügel, John C. *The Psychology of Clothes*. London: Hogarth Press, 1930.

Freitas, Anthony J., Susan B. Kaiser, Joan Chandler, Carol Hall, Jung-Won Kim, and Tania Hammidi. "Appearance Management as Border Construction: Least Favorite Clothing, Group Distancing, and Identity. Not!" *Sociological Inquiry* 67, no. 3 (1997): 323–335.

Gelder, Ken, and Sarah Thornton, eds. *The Subcultures Reader*. London/New York: Routledge, 1997.

Hebdige, Dick. *Subculture: The Meaning of Style*. London/New York: Methuen, 1979.

Kaiser, Susan B., Richard H. Nagasawa, and Sandra S. Hutton. "Fashion, Postmodernity and Personal Appearance: A Symbolic Interactionist Formulation." *Symbolic Interaction* 14, no. 2 (1991): 165–185.

Lewis, Van Dyk. "Dilemmas in African Diaspora Fashion." *Fashion Theory* 7, no. 2 (2003): 163–190.

Muggleton, David, and Rupert Weinzierl, eds. *The Post-Subcultures Reader*. Oxford/New York: Berg, 2003.

Polhemus, Ted, and Lynn Proctor. *Fashion and Antifashion*. London: Thames & Hudson, 1978.

Simmel, Georg. "Fashion." *International Quarterly* 10, no. 1 (1904): 130–155 (Reprinted in *American Journal of Sociology* 62, no. 6 (May 1957): 541–558.)

Wilson, Elizabeth. *Bohemians: The Glamorous Outcasts*. New Brunswick, NJ: Rutgers University Press, 2000.

Susan B. Kaiser and Ryan Looysen

Body and Dress

All human cultures engage in some form of dress and adornment. From tattoos to tunics, fashion is a means by which bodies become presentable and decent, bringing order to the completely unadorned human form. Although our bodies and the items we put on them might appear to be separate, they, in fact, have a great deal in common and are considerably intertwined. A dressed body represents a complex set of negotiations between an individual, the fashion system, and the social context in which they exist. Fashion reflects the concerns of the group(s) to which a person belongs and also how an individual interprets and expresses these concerns. Codes of dress set parameters but do not entirely determine what clothes or other items individuals might wear. The actions performed may appear routine and mundane, but they reflect a negotiation between individuals and their particular historical context. Thus, fashion is not a simple process of designers making and people wearing. The body and dress are mutually constitutive—dress adds social meaning to the body, and the body gives life to dress.

Bodies and fashionable dress intersect and overlap at a number of places. It is possible to see that unclothed bodies have a fashion. Viewing the dressed body provides evidence of a conversation between bodies and fashion—each influences how the other is understood. It is useful to see this relationship in a model resembling a hair braid—certain fashions emerge and then retreat for a variety of social and cultural reasons, trading off and sharing the podium with other fashionable models. No one model ever completely dominates at any time, so it would be overly simplistic to view fashion as a systematic and homogeneous series of changes. And when a particular fashion goes out of vogue, it does not outright disappear overnight, nor is it prevented from reemerging again twenty or one hundred years later. In fact, what makes fashion particularly democratic is that changes are usually slow and slight, making adjustments from season to season—a process more like tweaking a silhouette than reinventing it altogether.

Singular interpretations of the dressed body are problematic. Instead, a range of frameworks exists for understanding fashion and the body. These begin with debates about how gender is articulated through dress. Historically, fashion has been presumed to be a woman's preoccupation. Evolutions in men's fashion have often been overlooked due to a belief that men's clothing is unchanging or outside of fashion. In addition to gender considerations, an examination of hygiene and modernity, considering how industrialization and advertisements generated new imperatives of bodily health and care, is useful. The section "Natural Bodies and Dress Reform" shows how claims about the nature of bodies have shaped ideas about how to fashionably dress them. "The Beauty Myth" demonstrates how seemingly benign details, such as hair and makeup, help in understanding the social and capitalist framework in which beauty ideals are articulated. "Ideal Bodies and the Contours of Fashion" addresses shape and size and how these ideals have shifted in the nineteenth and twentieth centuries, reflecting broader social complexes.

GENDER AND DRESS

Dress has more than one purpose in Western culture. Its purely functional use is to protect the wearer from the elements and the environment, but it also functions to identify the person in a number of ways. When social scientists began to recognize dress as something more than "frivolous fashion," various viewpoints, which are still debated, emerged. Some theorists argue that Western society is obsessed with gender, and most agree that dress has worked to reinforce ideals of masculinity and femininity. Fashion, therefore, works to reproduce the social order in unassuming ways and helps differentiate the bodies of men and women. Gender differentiation has long preoccupied feminist analyses of fashion. Simone de Beauvoir's path-breaking 1949 text *The Second Sex* unreservedly identified fashion as enslavement. She was critical not only because of the time required to keep up fashion and beauty rituals but also because fashion has limited women's physical movement, preventing them from acting in the world. For de Beauvoir, fashion puts the body on display and traps women in a self-critical cycle of narcissism and voyeurism. In line with de Beauvoir, second-wave feminists have concerned themselves with the danger of fashion culture in its relationship to patriarchy and capitalism. Femininity, in their view, is false consciousness because representations of women do not in fact represent real women at all. In the late twentieth century, feminist essayist Adrienne Rich further argued that women's dress is a form of bondage. For Rich, high heels belong in the same category as purdah, the veil, and foot binding because they are a form of patriarchal control over the female body.

Since the 1990s, feminist theoretical debates have rejected the distinction between biological sex and socially constructed gender roles made by de Beauvoir and Rich. Instead, they argue that sex (the material body) is indistinguishable from gender (the social and historical context) in which bodies exist. Fashion is one mechanism through which the gender of bodies is made culturally visible.

Two young women wearing the latest Paris fashions, ca. 1914. For Simone de Beauvoir, fashion puts the body on display and traps women in a self-critical cycle of narcissism and voyeurism. Library of Congress, Prints and Photographs Division, LC-DIG-ggbain-15048.

Early academic analyses on the subject of gender and clothing suggested that fashion's primary function was to distinguish men from women and attract them to one another. J. C. Flügel's influential *Psychology of Clothes* argued that the fashionable clothing of a given time period emphasized bodily features that were the subject of erotic fascination. James Laver later used the term shifting erogenous zone to describe this phenomenon. For instance, in the depression of the 1930s, families without work made concerted efforts to curb their fertility. Women's fashion trends mirrored this turn by covering the previously bare knees and shoulders; growing out the freedom bob, or short haircut of the 1920s; and marketing corsets that smoothed out the figure, deemphasizing the curves of the reproductive region. Instead, the back was exposed in women's fashions, featuring a safe, or benign, erogenous zone. After World War II, women's fashions and erogenous zones shifted considerably. In conjunction with the post–World War II focus on rebuilding the nation, women's fashions embodied a hyperfeminine ideal, with a return to the cinched waist and buxom

form. Breasts, legs, and fertile hips became the subject of erotic fascination in images of women in this era.

Subsequent analyses of the relationship of fashion and gender have suggested that these theories are too deterministic and that fashion cannot be understood solely as part of the history and evolution of sex roles in the nineteenth and twentieth century. Fred Davis has suggested that instead, fashion operates in terms of a "dialectic of eroticism and modesty" that shifts across time. Clothing is about more than just sex. Shifts in what is concealed or revealed can tell us about the social context in which fashion is created and worn. Self-reflective fashions of the 1980s embodied this concept in a unique way. The look popularized by Madonna's early career—a hypersexual motif that mixed fishnet stockings and evening gloves; the bouffant skirt at mini length; the hourglass shape and the décolletage, pearls, and torn lace—is emblematic of this argument between eroticism and modesty. This motif confused and contradicted traditional erogenous zones and, in some cases, called to the forefront all these zones at the same time. These trends can be firmly planted in the 1980s, a decade of recession and disenchantment, when the desire was to have it all, even if it wasn't functional.

Dress plays a role in delineating masculinity, femininity, and heterosexual relations, but placing fashion in its social context shows that these categories are ultimately unstable and change over time. This fluidity in the gendering of clothing has played itself out numerous times in the last 200 years. The British defeat of France in 1759 in what is now Canada was a turning point in the way fashion was gendered among Montreal elites. Prior to this time, elite fashions were heavily influenced by the vibrant, lavish styles of France. Wigs; tight, colored breeches and stockings; and brightly colored vests were fashionable for both men and women and were not stylistically far apart. While today we might take this as a sign that lines of masculinity and femininity were not as clearly drawn, this was not the case. The elaborately adorned male codpiece was an affirmation that the virility of the male was not subsumed beneath the silk and lace—it was front and center. Not only did these fashion commodities make a statement about what was required of male bodies, they also set leisured men and women apart from the masses. Here, there is evidence of how fashion intersects with broader questions of class and social distinction.

THE BLANKET COAT

The blanket coat provides an example of a garment that played a unique role in the interface between gender and national identity. The years surrounding Canada's 1867 confederation were characterized by a quest for national unity and identity building. The perceived character-building nature of the northern climate made winter sports a popular venue through which to produce moral, hearty British subjects with good, strong bodies. The blanket coat served the Canadian imperial project as a national costume, but it was also emblematic of the masculine rigor that was required to contend with the climate of this northern colony.

Cut and crafted from a blanket and affixed with a hood, the blanket coat was a functional garment for Canada. Most often made of wool, blanket coats were very durable and performed the invaluable task of repelling moisture and retaining heat. The work of historian Eileen Stack has identified the blanket coat as a distinctly Canadian garment and a symbol of a brave and aspiring people.

Thought to be inspired by the blanketing worn by people of the First Nations, hooded coats were popular among French sailors, the military, and settlers. The blanket coat remained popular throughout the eighteenth century among French and English traders and American, German, and British soldiers in Canada, as well as Canadian peasants. The blanket coat continued to prove stylish across class lines when, in the latter half of the nineteenth century, the growing popularity of winter sports called for suitable outdoor dress and the hearty winter coat was adopted by the Montreal Snow Shoe Club, which made the coat widely identifiable and celebrated.

Although it was an emblem of a rough and rugged climate, the blanket coat was worn by men and women alike. Elite women frequently appeared wearing the blanket coat in the popular press and in images produced by the Notman Studio in Montreal. The blanket coat thus became a marker of Canadian identity that superseded gender.

THE MODERN SUIT

In the streets of the 1790s, however, a new style of male attire was making its entrance and gaining popularity. The bright silks, embroideries, and laces of French vogue were being renounced. After the British conquest, many of the Canadian elite fled to France and were replaced in positions of power by nonelite Frenchmen and British officials. With them, ideals of dress and masculinity shifted. London fashions took on greater influence among Montreal's upper-class men, popularizing gray and black wool coats, drainpipe trousers, and natural trimmed hairstyles. Deemed as effeminate thereafter, cumbersome and heavily adorned attire seemed unsuitable for an evolving masculinity focused on efficiency and function. Suits allowed for considerably more movement and were easy to layer on and off to adjust to changing temperatures between home and public spaces. Although the suit has undergone a variety of aesthetic changes, it has remained to this day the standard dress of men seeking professionalism and respectability.

Suits were eventually appropriated by women in the 1940s but with cuts that followed the contour of a woman's curves. Styles were feminized so as to make the female wearer distinguishable from the male. It was thought scandalous in 1930 when Marlene Dietrich wore a men's tuxedo suit in the movie *Morocco* and again in *Blonde Venus* in 1932. Dressed in the tuxedo, Dietrich blurred Hollywood's normally sharp distinction between the sexes. Until the popularity of unisex clothing in the 1960s, gender ambiguity has seldom been well received. Women's clothing took an interesting turn in the 1980s with the "power suit." These office suits for professional women exuded strength and no-nonsense attitude with their padded shoulders and conservative covering of the body. Many of these suits threw erogenous zones out the window altogether, which was precisely the point for women who wanted to be seen as smart and capable professionals and not as objects of the male gaze.

Changing ideals of male dress and the gendering of garments, as with suits that are masculine or feminine, are examples of the contested and often complex relationship between gender, fashion, and embodiment. Sometimes fashion challenges accepted gender roles by making the wearer's sex ambiguous. The emergence of unisex clothing in the 1960s was high in controversy and low in gender distinction, and it did a great deal to blur the

Mr. Murray wearing a blanket coat, Montreal, Quebec, 1861. The coat was worn by both men and women and provided warmth in the cold Northern climate. © McCord Museum I-924.1. http://www.mccord-museum.qc.ca/en/

male-female, masculine-feminine binaries that had dominated dress codes. Rather than seeing dressed bodies as intrinsically masculine or feminine, these examples are a reminder of the changing nature of these categories. Judith Butler's notion of *performativity* offers another interpretive framework for thinking about gender in dress as unstable. Gender norms persist over time because they are performed, or acted out, through daily social rituals. Slacks for women are a good example. Although slacks were not marketed as women's streetwear until the 1930s, working women wore them as early as the 1910s for their functionality. The notion of fashion as performance allows us to see that the gender of dressed bodies is fluid. Styles, along with fabrics, cuts, and colors, are not intrinsically male or female but change over time according to how fashion is lived and practiced.

NATURAL BODIES AND DRESS REFORM

Understandings of what signifies a natural look in fashion have shifted over the course of the nineteenth and twentieth centuries. What is natural is closely aligned with gender norms but also with ideas about ethnicity, class, and nature itself. The natural can also be defined in opposition to what is thought to be artificial, unreal, or unacceptable in a given period. This accounts for shifting discourses around things such as pajamas, corsetry, and underwear that have been thought to be natural and unnatural at different times. The natural body, like the gendered body, is not separate from fashion. What is thought to be natural about the body is more a product of its historical context; it is not a given. The fashion system shapes and is shaped by ideas about the natural body; this relationship is part of an ongoing conversation about what constitutes the fashionable.

Between 1800 and 2000, the regulation of the natural body shifted from the legal arena to public attempts at moral reform and then to private acts of self-governance. Norbert Elias characterizes the development of certain types of clothing, including pajamas and underwear, as indicating that a "shame frontier" surrounding the body developed after 1600. These concerns about modesty offered a way to differentiate bodies in a newly emerging class system. Before 1800, sumptuary laws in the United States mandating plain dress were one way to regulate the fashions of particular social or religious groups. Legal regulation was undermined after 1800 once the laboring classes obtained the financial means to purchase the same consumer goods available to the upper classes. Social standing was no longer self-evident through clothing. Industrialization allowed the masses to share in these goods. New, less opulent goods became markers of distinction and were valued by the wealthy. While formal sanctions were undermined, attempts to regulate dress continued into the twentieth century. Like the legal regulations that came before them, attempts at moral reform were implicitly aimed at preserving a supposedly natural order. Dress reformers often made claims about the nature of bodies in their appeals for public support as part of the broader political agendas of health reform and feminism.

Nineteenth- and early-twentieth-century dress was tight, restrictive, not breathable, and hard to wash. Beginning around 1830, a number of different religious and social communities began to see this confining clothing as a problem. Both male and female members of Robert Owen's Utopian Socialist Community in New Harmony, Indiana, wore loose pantaloons underneath a tunic. Owenites sought less emphasis on sex division and believed clothing should be comfortable rather than frivolous. John Humphrey Noyes, founder of the Oneida religious community, also found women's dress absurd. Oneida women responded by cutting their skirts to just above the knee and using the discarded material to make undertrousers. "Reform Dress" gained wider public attention when it was taken up by proponents of the *water cure*. This movement advocated baths and compresses as a form of preventative medicine. Members of this nineteenth-century movement rejected ideas of female delicacy and insisted that looser-fitting and shorter dress for women would be healthier. Reform-minded groups like these advocated looser clothing for its simplicity, economy, and health benefits, but they were not necessarily supporters of the women's movement. These more marginal groups took up the cause of *dress reform* two decades prior to the most notorious example from this period: *bloomers*.

Bloomers, shortened skirts worn with baggy trousers underneath, were briefly popular in the 1850s. Amelia Bloomer (after whom the garment was named) and Elizabeth Cady Stanton's feminist challenge to restrictive dress gained extensive attention when they adopted bloomers, which were thought to be more practical in daily life. A popular belief among reformers was that

Sheet music cover showing woman wearing a bloomer dress, United States, 1851. Bloomer dresses were advocated by those seeking to reform restrictive female dress of the late nineteenth century. Library of Congress Prints and Photographs Division, cph 3g04586.

the key to liberation was freeing women of oppressive attire. Although bloomers were out by the end of the decade, the movement signaled a desire, perhaps a need, for change, but it may have been too much too soon. Bloomers' failure to become an international sensation may not have been tied to their functionality or ingenuity but rather because they did not gain the support of powerful social and cultural forces. Bloomers were never affiliated with Paris, donned by a famous actress, or advertised in the women's pages of magazines. Instead, they became affiliated with radicalism, religious fanaticism, and the masculinity of the trouser.

Canadian feminists were comparatively silent about the health benefits of plain dress until 1895, when the National Council of Women petitioned the legislature to reduce hours for working-class women. This petition suggested that middle- and upper-class women adopt simpler dress that required less work of seamstresses. Although it did not pass, this act of cross-class solidarity was intended to allow working women more time with their children. Canadian men worked with the Men's Dress Reform Party of England (1929–1940), extolling the virtues of open-necked shirts, looser trousers, and short pants for men

Physicians were the most vocal advocates of plain dress in Canada. Dr. A. Lapthorn Smith instructed Canadian men to admire natural female figures, rather than corseted women, who made sickly (and expensive) wives. By the late nineteenth century, tight lacing was increasingly thought to negatively impact women's reproduction. *Dress and Health*, a book published in the United States and Canada, warned readers that the tight fashions of the middle and upper classes were "slaughtering the innocents," while the "coarse-grained" and loosely attired lower classes were producing healthier babies. Good health was increasingly synonymous with an unmediated and unrestricted natural body.

The eugenic undertones of the dress reform movement underscore an increasingly scientific conception of the nature of bodies in the early twentieth century. While some medical experts continued to promote the belief that physical exertion was damaging to women, new scientific research emerged to suggest that fresh air and exercise were beneficial to women's health. This process was highly contested by critics who were concerned that activities like cycling would endanger women's reproductive abilities and cause them undue sexual excitement. These anxieties about women's bodies played out in the form of concerns over dress. The possibility that underclothes or ankles might be visible while cycling resulted in a variety of bicycle redesigns, including a model whose seat was modified, allowing women to ride side-saddle. By the end of the century, this problem was solved with the introduction of the two-wheeled safety bicycle and the reintroduction of split-legged garments for women. Attempts to regulate women's appearance while playing sports continued as women pushed the boundaries of what was acceptable physical activity. A 1909 textbook on teaching methods for girl's sports explained that basketball required special training to avoid plays that would result in clothing getting caught in midplay and revealing the body in an "unladylike" manner. Often, scientific claims were employed to argue for both sides of the debate over women's physical activity. Where freedom of movement was for some a danger to women, for others it was considered beneficial. Ultimately, the demand for new fabrics and styles won out over moralistic concerns about exposure of the body.

The debate over the nature of bodies shifted again in the 1960s and 1970s, when a new sort of feminist reform dress was popularized. This dress echoed the natural aesthetic of the counterculture of the time: straight hair, invisible makeup, jeans and loose-fitting T-shirts, and tunics. The feminist naturalist aesthetic was not only a symbol of generational tension and change; it was also a critique of the excessive femininity of the 1950s and 1960s. Fashion was seen as a barrier to women's liberation because women were enslaved by the ludicrous accoutrements of the beauty industry. Changes in fashion were seen as rarely useful, serving capitalism instead of need. In turn, some called for women's clothing to be more like men's, focusing on function over form. This was a challenge to the gender order of the post–World War II era and led to accusations of man-hating and lesbianism. It also resulted in a counterclaim that "real women" were those who adopted "feminine" fashions, makeup, and hairstyles. Women who took on public roles risked their reputations and livelihood. One way that this problem was dealt with was to ensure that the femininity of female public figures was never in question. Responding to charges that their golfers were not womanly, in 1968 the Ladies Professional Golf Association (LPGA) began to encourage golfers to glamorize their appearance and later hired a professional image consultant to work with golfers to feminize their look.

Ideas about what is natural have shifted over the course of the nineteenth and twentieth century along with discourses on masculinity and femininity. Claims about nature have never been inherently true or false because their definitions are historically contingent. As with anything else, what is considered natural changes with time. Nature is significant because of its pervasive use in debates about dress and the body. Bodies often appear in these discourses as essentially natural and unchanging. But, as we have tried to demonstrate, the nature of the body and its relationship to fashion cannot be taken for granted.

BIRD HATS

Women were also at the forefront of a lesser-known dress reform movement: the campaign against bird hats. Hats featuring dead birds or their elaborate feathers were at the height of elite women's fashion in the United States at the end of the nineteenth century. Bird hats were part of a vogue in this period for the natural look—signified quite literally through the incorporation of real and artificial flowers, leaves, and small animals into fashions.

Mrs. Augustus Hemenway organized the first boycott against bird hats in Boston in 1896. Hemenway called upon her wealthy female friends to campaign after discovering the "feather-trade" was devastating wild bird populations. Hemenway's group became the first Audubon Society in the United States, and other

A rear tenement room, New York, early 1900s. At this time overcrowding in urban areas was seen as a cause of disease and led to the heavy promotion of hygiene products. Courtesy New York Public Library.

groups formed by upper-class women rapidly emerged in other states. These societies set up libraries on bird protection, organized teas and "home enlightenment" visits, spoke in schools, and created "White Lists" promoting milliners who sold hats without feathers. Men were also active in these societies. They performed audits of bird-nesting groups and negotiated with manufacturers. Audubon Society activism was vital to the eventual passage of the Lacey Act in 1900, which gave the U.S. government the power to regulate and preserve at-risk bird species.

Jennifer Price has argued that beyond conserving birds, Audubon Societies created a public role for women, which confirmed gender norms of this period; "Save the Birds!" called on women, as mothers, to stop the slaughter of innocent animals. Price further noted that Audubon societies called on women as consumers to protect bird species but did not afford the same moral responsibility to (male) hunters and milliners. Audubon societies nonetheless provided women an important venue to voice their concerns about nature conservation. This example also demonstrates one way in which consumers can "talk back" to fashion trends.

HYGIENE AND THE CRISIS OF MODERNITY

The early twentieth century was a particularly pivotal time in the way the natural body was addressed and understood. Although health and hygiene rituals had always existed, new imperatives for cleanliness resulted from industrialization and urbanization. Reformers came to see the natural body as a site for disease

stemming from social ills, such as poverty, prostitution, secularism, and poor health, made highly visible by the urban context. These concerns came out of urbanization and the closeness of human contact in urban spaces. Smells, bad air, dirt, and overcrowding, primarily in the slums inhabited by immigrants and the working poor, were seen as culprits in the spread of disease. By the 1920s, advertisers, along with reformers like the Cleanliness Institute, latched onto this "crisis of modernity." Products became linked to the project of "civilizing the self": loveliness, household cleaning, and bodily hygiene were key to preventing further social decay. This placed responsibility for hygiene squarely on the shoulders of individuals. Ads, in particular, were accused of exploiting these concerns by spinning what used to be considered novelties into necessities.

One example of the promotion of such products can be seen in the introduction in 1890 of the disinfectant cleaner known as Lysol, which became an extremely popular form of feminine hygiene among U.S. and Canadian women. Appearing religiously in magazines in both countries, Lysol advertisements responded to growing concerns about bodily odors. Falling in line with social concerns over halitosis and sweat odor, scare-copy advertisements explicitly warned that vaginal odor threatened to end marriages. However, vaginal odor was not the only problem Lysol promised to resolve. Laws against advertising birth control, before birth control became legal in the 1960s, encouraged advertisers to be tactful in their wording, advising, "The douche should follow married relations as a cleansing and antiseptic agent."

Marlboro billboard with cowboys, Los Angeles, 1997. In advertising, men appear in active poses more commonly than women. Gilles Mingasson/Getty Images.

A 1936 American publication, *Facts and Frauds in Woman's Hygiene*, exposed Lysol as a dangerous feminine hygiene product, warning against its "irritating and toxic action," and illuminated the cautions of the American Medical Association against the use of antiseptics on the genito-urinary tract. Despite attempts to discourage women from using these harmful products to "cure" odors and prevent births, Lysol continued to be used by women into the 1960s.

In advertisements, the crisis of modernity was deemed resolvable through consumption. Mass production created a consumer climate in which these novel products could be bought at much more affordable prices. Health, compromised by industrialism, could be regained through products, such as soap to erase signs of the dirty urban landscape, vitamins to supplement compromised diets, and Ovaltine and cigarettes to calm the nerves of urban life. In short, civilization would become its own redeemer. Roland Marchand has identified a series of what he called "parables" characteristic of advertisements from this period. His "Parable of the First Impression" argues that advertisements presented "tragedy of manners" scenarios where a protagonist's success or failure was determined by their mastery of hygiene practices. In a society where personal interactions had become less frequent and more fleeting, a good first impression was integral to one's success.

Looking healthy also came with the promise of upward mobility—the smallest overlooked aspect of one's hygiene could limit one's progress in the new modern world. "Parables of Affliction" showed what one should aspire to avoid, such as bad breath, yellow teeth, and body odor. In this view, advertisements promised a false equality because products could not eliminate deeper differences of class and ethnicity.

Thus, the consumer curtain opened to reveal an endless parade of products explicitly linked to fashionability and civility. Products that had previously been optional came to be seen as a social necessity. One product was never enough; each was sold as an essential component of a hygiene routine. For instance, tooth brushing was no longer enough to master oral hygiene. The makers of Listerine, an antiseptic that had been used in surgery, dug deep into the medical books in the 1920s to uncover the word *halitosis*. This scientific term for bad breath was used heavily in advertisements to warn consumers of the "social offense" they were liable to commit if they were not using mouthwash.

Alongside mouthwash, underarm deodorants, skin powders, creams and oils, scents, and goods to calm the head and nerves, Canadian and U.S. consumers were offered a complete program for body maintenance.

Some have identified this shift as a turn against the body—a denial of its natural processes and an attempt to control its disruptive potential. One sought to look "smart" in the 1920s, but the list of required products seemed then, much as it does today, endless and necessary.

THE BEAUTY MYTH

Throughout the nineteenth and twentieth centuries, beauty was understood as mainly a female preoccupation. The pursuit of beauty transcended racial and class boundaries. Women of different means and ethnic groups practiced beauty regimes in different ways—from expensive wigs to hot irons and tonics, looking beautiful was related to one's financial means and cultural group. However, nonwhite women's beauty practices have rarely been represented alongside those of white women. A very narrow definition of beauty has prevailed in the more widely disseminated advertisements and images of women. Historically, beauty has been represented as white, feminine, heterosexually appealing, comfortably middle-class, and Christian, but the physical features that constitute the beautiful have changed over time. A few extra pounds here or there, larger eyes, thinner lips—ideals are constantly in flux and cannot be separated from the context or complex of which they are part. Nowhere is this more evident than in the girls and women selected to model fashionable dress.

Fashion modeling developed as a new technique for displaying clothing to consumers in the 1860s. Prior to this time, dolls and fashion plates had been used to disseminate information about new fashions. Mass consumption and the development of shopping as a leisure activity for women were the preconditions that led to the use of live models for regular customers in Parisian department stores. These early fashion models would have been working-class girls.

Modeling became an acceptable career for unmarried middle-class girls in the post–World War II period. Early modeling agencies were training and etiquette schools, many of which were started by women. These schools taught makeup, dress, social graces, shoe selection, and personal hygiene in addition to training potential models to pose for television and print advertisements.

Since the 1960s, some models have become celebrities in their own right, distinctive because they seem to embody a particular look of the time. Twiggy, who personified the wide-eyed and flat-chested ideal of the early 1960s, gave way to a more curvaceous ideal of the 1970s, with women such as Janice Dickenson or Christie Brinkley. The tall, toned, pouty supermodels, such as Naomi Campbell, emerged in the 1990s.

The marketing of fashions through the use of live models, as well as illustrations and later photographs in advertisements, has contributed to the designation of certain physical attributes as ideal and womanly. These ideals have not determined the shape of women's bodies but are part of the broader cultural conversation shaping which kinds of bodies are in fashion.

Idealized images of women led John Berger to argue in the 1970s that in advertising, "men act and women appear." Representations of women emphasize display and passivity and give special emphasis to particular body parts. Men tend to appear in more aggressive and active poses, resulting in a different visual language for men than for women. This trope becomes the basis for the visual language of advertising, reinforcing social relations of power between men and women. The glamorizing of narrow ideals acts as a homogenizing force where a repetitive message confirms certain characteristics as beautiful. Products, and everything that is promised to come along with them, become an end goal—a purchase. The problem, according to Berger, is that advertisements trivialize social relations that are far more complex than they appear.

By contrast, in Naomi Wolf's *The Beauty Myth*, the pursuit of beauty is itself the social issue. She argues that beauty has been used as a "political weapon against women's advancement" and a tool of their social control. The competition built into the beauty myth keeps women divided and powerless. Looking for approval from outside sources leaves women's self-esteem for others to validate, loosening their control of their own bodies and bodily self-perceptions. Wolf's frustration is that, having no other avenue to acquire power, women have been left to rely on their ability to

WARNER BROS. CORALINE CORSETS,
THE LATEST ÆSTHETIC CRAZE.

Advertisement for Coraline Corsets, United States, ca. 1870s. Despite the apparent health risks, corsets were desirable for those who wanted to follow the latest fashions. Library of Congress, Prints and Photographs Division, LC-USZ62-53565.

attract a husband. The Miss America beauty pageant is evidence of beauty as a form of currency. Established in 1921, pageants put every inch of the body under scrutiny. Some have argued that the result of the glorification of self-scrutiny has led to an almost obsessive attention to the details of women's bodies. Wolf accuses the beauty and fashion industries of being complicit in this exploitation of women.

Of course, the beauty myth has had its challengers. Feminists and other nonconformist groups have had a long history of refusing to conform to beauty regimes. However, academic analyses of beauty have also argued that the communication of beauty standards is not one-way. When advertisements are seen as imposing beauty ideals on women, it undermines the power that women themselves have as the receivers and interpreters of ads and makes them victims. Rather than seeing women as passively controlled and lacking agency, it has been suggested that beauty regimes are not oppressive if women want to participate. In fact, some authors argue that women are active contributors in the establishment of beauty standards. Not only do women have choice in the products they purchase, but sometimes the people behind the advertisements and products are women, too. To what degree, then, can advertisements be labeled as products and tools of patriarchal power? This challenges the hard line that beauty regimes are necessarily working against women or are antifeminist.

ETHNICITY AND BEAUTY

Although relations between women and advertising have been widely addressed, debates have often failed to acknowledge the role that ethnicity has played in the construction of beauty norms. Advertisements have worked to solidify whiteness as beautiful. They do this by placing nonwhites in opposition to whites as exemplifying the feared result of not following a particular beauty regime. Scholars have also noted that outside of advertisements produced by and for white readers and consumers, alternative

representations of beauty do exist. Ads produced for Madam C. J. Walker's beauty products did not establish beauty standards with examples of white women's bodies or hair but along lines particular to black women. Madam C. J. Walker's Vegetable Shampoo, Wonderful Hair Grower, and light oil treatment, which pressed the hair with a heated metal comb, proved popular and profitable in the early 1900s. It has been observed that Walker, who was born in 1867 and died in 1919, went against the middle-class belief that women's place was in the home. She encouraged women to earn money and independence by selling her products or by going into business themselves.

Walker's products generated a great deal of controversy over the process of hair straightening that helps make the politics underlying representations of beauty visible. Early-twentieth-century African American intellectuals and leaders were concerned with the practice as a literal and symbolic attempt to be accepted within U.S. society. In tune with this cultural critique, Walker never advertised her products or services as providing hair "straightening." Instead she emphasized the ritual of her beauty system as a path to physical and mental wellness, in step with ideas of racial uplift popular at the time. A model for twentieth-century black women entrepreneurs and a pioneer in the women's beauty industry, Madam C. J. Walker remains one of the most influential individuals in visually representing and constructing identities of African American women at the turn of the century.

In looking at the role ethnicity plays in constructions of beauty, it is also necessary to remember that whiteness is in itself a contested category. Subtle nuances of skin tone were used to make class distinctions between Caucasians. In the early nineteenth century, pale skin was a sign of wealth and the luxury of leisure. Dark skin was presumed to be a signifier of outdoor labor and lower-class status. Thus, anything that kept white women's skin light and even was incorporated into women's beauty rituals. The use of parasols and bonnets (and general avoidance of the sun) were some ways women achieved their goal. Others went to such lengths as drinking vinegar and eating chalk or arsenic, which paled the skin. However, the category of white has proved to be unstable. As industrialization flourished and hard labor moved indoors, a tan became a sign of time for leisure. The raging vogue for tanned skin, beginning in the 1920s, made sun-tanning oils a necessary part of beauty regimes for white women, the consequences of which are coming to light today.

CHANGING FASHIONS IN HAIR

In addition to shifts in hair texture and skin tones, the visibility of flesh and body hair has been an important part of what is considered beautiful. For instance, as hems rose and sleeves became shorter in the twentieth century, hair removal became a part of beauty rituals. Exposed body hair interfered with notions of soft and smooth femininity.

Legs and underarms were swallowed into the realm of cosmetics, and depilatory creams were used to rid women of unsightly hair. In the 1960s, hair removal, as part of women's beauty rituals, underwent scrutiny from some members of the women's liberation movement. For men, only the hair on the face has undergone similar shifts in fashion. In the 1830s and 1840s, the cleanshaven face was an ideal look for men; young rebellious university men grew whiskers in defiance. By the 1850s, the beard had become a sign of virility, power, and wisdom and was adopted widely by professional men but rejected by young fashionable men. The beard became popular again in the 1960s, but it bore completely new meaning through its association with the antiestablishment counterculture.

Hair became a symbol of freedom from beauty norms in the 1960s and 1970s. The 1960s Afro became popular among some radical groups as a symbol of black pride.

The notion of "black is beautiful" eventually became a popular rallying cry and a rejection of white beauty ideals. Similarly, long, straight hair became a symbol of the Red Power movement and was a part of the North American Indian critique of white ideals in the 1960s. The shag hairstyle was adopted by white men as yet another symbol of their rejection of 1950s conservatism. Alternatively ridiculed as dirty hippies, radicals, naturalists, and feminists, these groups were making loud public statements of their rejection of established beauty regimes and their control over the body. Such public rejections of norms demonstrate that beauty ideals are not and never have been universal or monolithic. Politics, ethnicity, class, and gender norms of a given period influence how beauty is expressed and read. Advertisements work to create norms, but the politics and practices underlying and outside of these representations are not as strong and stable as we might think.

IDEAL BODIES AND THE CONTOURS OF FASHION

The shape that bodies take in their clothes and the way that clothes shape bodies has shifted considerably across the nineteenth and twentieth centuries. Body ideals are subject to change.

Body shape is no exception. It has been observed that a frail and almost sickly ideal of womanhood dominated the antebellum United States. Concurrent with reconstruction efforts after the Civil War, a less delicate and plumper ideal of femininity was encouraged. Slenderness came to be seen as a sign of nervous disorder, while a more rounded body was considered healthy. It is unlikely that this new ideal had any physiological impact on men's and women's bodies. Instead, clothing would be padded in order to achieve particular silhouettes. Bustles were an extreme example of this. Fabric was pulled to the back of women's dresses, which exaggerated the size of their bottoms. An examination of the ways that fashion and the body have, literally, intersected will illustrate that fashion not only dresses bodies but also that bodies have a fashion. Fashioned bodies are not arbitrarily shaped by designers or the fashion system; they are part of a broader social complex.

A tight-laced waist was an essential component of early-nineteenth-century women's fashion if one wished to wear dresses as they were intended to be seen. Corsets were necessary to achieve this shape. Usually made of metal or whalebone and lined with cloth, corsets were designed to mold the natural kidney shape of a woman's waist into a round shape. Fitted in early childhood and worn until death, the corset was an intimate piece of many women's daily lives. The preference for an eighteen-inch (forty-five-centimeter) waist was not driven by the corset manufacturers alone. Victorians valued a disciplined mind and

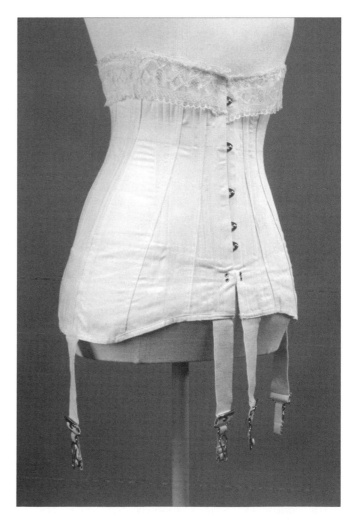

This corset, made in 1915, is lighter than those of the nineteenth century. As women in the United States started to participate in sports such as tennis, there was a need for more comfortable undergarments. © McCord Museum M976.4.5. http://www.mccord-museum.qc.ca/en/

controlled emotions, and the corset can be seen as an extension of this preference for containment. This refined body was also easily distinguished from the unrestrained silhouette of the working class. Corseting was not an uncontested practice. The medical community believed that corsets caused headaches and fainting, as well as numerous unseen internal ailments like spinal disfigurement, uterine problems, and the damage and puncturing of organs by manipulated ribs. Despite the apparent health risks associated with corsets and the labor required to lace them up, corsets were considered to be a necessary garment for fashionable women. Fashionable men of the nineteenth century also wore corsets, but their function was different. Corsetry provided men with a square and robust shape, while they made women appear smaller.

The petite ideal even extended to pregnancy, and women went to great lengths to conceal their swelling bodies. Maternity corsets were designed to reduce the obviousness of the growing torso and make a pregnant woman look as close to the feminine norm as possible. In the absence of maternity clothing, women also altered their dresses by letting out the abdominal area of a dress and taking it back in once they had given birth. Shawls were also a popular means of concealment. Some dress reformers and medical professionals condemned the practice of wearing corsets during pregnancy. They stressed that it had detrimental effects on the development of the fetus. But the distaste with which pregnancy was viewed made public exposure of one's maternal state unfathomable for the fashion conscious. The social and cultural marginality of pregnancy was evident in the invisibility of the female body and maternity clothing in advertisements until the 1910s.

Specialized diets meant to help men and women manage their body shape and size were used as early as the 1800s. The medical community offered its support, arguing that women's delicate digestive systems required that they eat lightly and refrain from meats and starchy foods like potatoes. For a time, eating in public was altogether unfashionable for women. Fads like the *Graham system*, which encouraged a diet "low in pork and ale," or Bantingism, a low-starch diet, were very popular after the 1830s. These diets were initially attached to concerns about digestion, but over the course of the twentieth century, obesity became increasingly problematized. Obesity was perceived as emblematic of moral and personal failure and increasingly seen as unattractive.

Slim bodily standards, however, were not sought by everyone. Among immigrant groups, for whom threats of starvation were persistent, being thin and frail was a sign of failure. Laboring in the fields or in tight quarters made nineteenth-century high fashion unsuitable and ridiculous. Work required development of muscles, freer posture, and more bodily freedom. A full figure was a sign of prosperity. As such, clothing was cut to accommodate movement. Fabrics needed to be sturdier to allow for wear and tear. Practicality won out over detail, and the clothing of working people was less delicate and less ornate than that of the elite.

Another process influencing awareness of body size and shape at the turn of the century was the development of ready-to-wear fashions and, from this, the standardization of clothing sizes. Standardization was not necessarily meant to regulate bodies. What it did do was heighten awareness of body size and shape and draw attention to (seemingly) odd-shaped bodies. The result of standardization was the creation of the category of nonstandard. Oversized clothing for stout men and women was introduced concurrently with industrialization. Hillel Schwartz has argued that large bodies were the wrong scale for contemporary life. New technologies like streetcars and turnstiles did not accommodate heavier people. Insurance companies introduced height and weight tables as obesity began to be seen as an index for mortality. Schwartz believes that by the 1930s, "overweight" was understood less as a variation in body size and more as a deviation from the norm. This was a marked shift from fifty years earlier, when being slim was seen as a sign of poor health. Emerging imperatives on body size and shape were part of a growing cultural consensus between slenderness and health. This idea changed what clothing was made of and what it was supposed to allow the body to do.

PLUS-SIZED FASHIONS

Standardized clothing heightened awareness of body size at a time of increasing cultural condemnation of fat bodies. This fashion for slender bodies in twentieth-century North America did not eliminate the need or desire for stylish clothing for larger people.

Lane Bryant, started in New York by seamstress Lena (Himmelstein) Bryant, began offering clothing for "stout" women by mail order in 1909. Bryant's promise was to give her customers an air of "modish slenderness" regardless of her proportions. Bryant believed the key was to redesign current fashions for larger figures rather than to cut regular sizes bigger. Canada's oldest large-size retailer for women, Pennington's, was developed by William Drevnig and Albert Sherman in 1948 after the men noticed that large women were going around from store to store looking for clothes that would fit them. Like Lane Bryant, Pennington's, "for when a figure needs a friend," staffed its stores with larger women and promised consumers something more fashionable than the matronly large sizes available elsewhere.

When Lane Bryant began, the company's advertisements made discreet references to the availability of clothing for stout figures. Over the last one hundred years this language has shifted, from "oversized" to "plus-sized." Cultural ambivalence about large bodies continues in the twenty-first century, but the market for plus-sized fashion continues to grow.

CHANGING STANDARDS

One of the stories of twentieth-century fashion has been the emergence of sportswear to dress active bodies. New fabrics and fibers were introduced in this period, including nylon, rayon, elastic, Lycra, and spandex, which allowed for softer lines that followed the natural contours of the body. The shape of the physical body in clothes became more visible. Swimsuits offer a particularly revealing example. Men's as well as women's bodies were fully covered while swimming until the 1890s. At this time, it became more acceptable for men to bathe topless, and women were no longer expected to wear a full-length skirt. Women first participated in swimming in the 1912 Olympics, where they wore sleeveless knit costumes that covered their bodies to midthigh. Swimsuits for men and women have become more form fitting over the course of the twentieth century. These changes reflected evolutions in style and function. Not only did lighter (and less) fabric have greater sexual appeal, it helped swimmers to move faster in water.

Family of Polish workers, Baltimore, 1909. Clothes had to be cut to accommodate movement for field laborers. Photograph by Lewis Wickes Hine, Library of Congress, Prints and Photographs Division, LC-DIG-nclc-00009.

Although swimsuits have become progressively smaller, North Americans have been slow to accept nude bathing. Public comfort with the undressed body continues to have its limits.

In the post–World War II era, aerobic exercise and bodybuilding became a way for North Americans to shape their bodies and were emblematic of self-care and self-control. For men, the goal was to build larger muscles and chests, whereas for women, the goal was muscle tone and slimness, not bulk. The feminist response to this change has sometimes been negative. The commercialization of exercise and the discursive links made between slenderness, health, and beauty seem to be another example of patriarchal standards of beauty being imposed on women. Others, including Jane Fonda, believed that "discipline is liberation." Fonda's best-selling workout book proposed that a healthy diet and lots of exercise would enable women to make good life decisions. Whether understood as a question of health or of beauty ideals, the late-twentieth-century imperative to work out represents a major shift in the life style of North Americans. This change has, in turn, influenced fashion. Fitness fashions of the 1980s became

popular streetwear. From tracksuits to yoga pants, fashion trends continue to echo changing North American lifestyles.

In the nineteenth century clothing was used to help shape bodies; by the twenty-first century, the body must be in shape in order to fit into fashions. In this sense, the relationship between fashion and the body has shifted—from the external shaping of the body through clothes, to the internal management of the body for clothes. The irony of this shift is that it is difficult to actually change one's physical shape and size; after all, we do not choose our bodies.

CONCLUSION

Bodies are not simply hangers for clothes. Nor are our bodies before or outside of fashion; they are always mediated by the social context and complex in which they are borne. The body is one category of analysis that leads to a better understanding of fashion. Over the course of the nineteenth and twentieth centuries, ideals in gender, nature, hygiene, beauty, body shape, and size have emerged and retreated. These nonlinear shifts are a product of the dances people do to negotiate personal wants and needs, the fashion system, and their social context. Therefore, fashion is never just fashion; it is an ongoing conversation between bodies and dress.

References and Further Reading

Banner, Lois. *American Beauty*. Chicago: University of Chicago Press, 1983.

Beauvoir, Simone de. *The Second Sex*. New York: Alfred A. Knopf, 1993.

Berger, John. *Ways of Seeing*. London: British Broadcasting Corporation & Penguin, 1972.

Butler, Judith P. *Gender Trouble*. New York: Routledge, 1999.

Canning, Kathleen. *Gender History in Practice: Historical Perspectives on Bodies, Class & Citizenship*. Ithaca, NY: Cornell University Press, 2006.

Craik, Jennifer. *The Face of Fashion: Cultural Studies in Fashion*. New York: Routledge, 1994.

Davis, Fred. *Fashion, Culture and Identity*. Chicago: University of Chicago Press, 1992.

Entwistle, Joanne, and Elizabeth Wilson. *Body Dressing*. New York: Berg, 2001.

Flügel, J.C. *The Psychology of Clothes*. London: Hogarth Press and the Institute of Psycho-analysis, 1950.

Gaines, Jane, and Charlotte Herzog, eds. *Fabrications: Costume and the Female Body*. New York: Routledge, 1990.

Hollows, Joanne. *Feminism, Femininity and Popular Culture*. Manchester, UK: Manchester University Press, 2000.

Kelcey, Barbara E. "Dress Reform in Nineteenth Century Canada." In *Fashion: A Canadian Perspective*, edited by Alexandra Palmer, 229–248. Toronto: University of Toronto Press, 2004.

Laver, James, Amy de la Haye, and Andrew Tucker. *Costume and Fashion: A Concise History*. 4th ed. New York: Thames & Hudson, 2002.

Marchand, Roland. *Advertising the American Dream: Making Way for Modernity, 1920–1940*. Berkeley: University of California Press, 1985.

Palmer, Alexandra, ed. *Fashion: A Canadian Perspective*. Toronto: University of Toronto Press, 2004.

Peiss, Kathy. *Hope in a Jar: The Making of American Beauty Culture*. New York: Metropolitan Books, 1998.

Price, Jennifer. *Flight Maps: Adventures with Nature in North America*. New York: Basic Books, 1999.

Rooks, Noliwe M. *Hair Raising: Beauty, Culture, and African American Women*. New Brunswick, NJ: Rutgers University Press, 1996.

Routh, Caroline. *In Style: 100 Years of Canadian Women's Fashion*. Toronto: Stoddart Publishing, 1993.

Schwartz, Hillel. *Never Satisfied: A Cultural History of Diets, Fantasies and Fat*. New York: Anchor Books, 1986.

Scott, Linda M. *Fresh Lipstick: Redressing Fashion and Feminism*. New York: Palgrave MacMillan, 2005.

Summers, Leigh. *Bound to Please: A History of the Victorian Corset*. New York: Berg, 2001.

Tone, Andrea, ed. *Controlling Reproduction: An American History*. Wilmington, DE: Scholarly Resources, 1997.

Vinikas, Vincent. *Soft Soap, Hard Sell: American Hygiene in an Age of Advertisement*. Ames: Iowa State University Press, 1992.

Wilson, Elizabeth. *Adorned in Dreams: Fashion and Modernity*. New Brunswick, NJ: Rutgers University Press, 2003.

Wolf, Naomi. *The Beauty Myth*. London: Chatto & Windus, 1990.

Woolson, Abba Goold, ed. *Dress and Health: How to Be Strong*. Canadian Institute for Historical Reproduction, CHIM No. 06242. Montreal: J. Dougall, 1876.

Angela Durante and Jenny Ellison

See also Dress Reform; Gender; Dress for Recreational Sports and Professional Sports; Health; African American.

Body Art

- Body Paint
- Dyes and Bleaches
- Tattoos
- Piercing
- Modification of the Skin Surface
- Reshaping

Body art decorates, adorns, emphasizes, and transforms the human body in temporary, semipermanent, and permanent ways with the use of body modifications or supplements. Throughout history, body art has been practiced and displayed not only in the United States and Canada but also by members of all cultures. Body art serves a range of purposes, from indicating social and cultural status to commemorating special occasions and from displaying daily aesthetic adornment to performing theatrical art. Whether temporary adornments (cosmetics or hairstyles), semipermanent adaptations (haircuts or skin dyes), or permanent modifications (tattoos or brands), body art nonverbally communicates information about an individual or group.

Body art functions as a nonverbal or visual language that can communicate status and position, document accomplishments and autobiographies, commemorate loves and losses, and display desires and talismans. In these ways, the human body is a good medium for expressing creativity, innovation, and reinvention, as well as challenging or affirming social and cultural values about aesthetics, appearance, gender, identity, and the body itself. Body art may function as a narrative or simply enhance the appearance of a person.

Body art has been used in preparation for, during, and after social, cultural, and spiritual rituals and ceremonies. Historically, Iroquois League warriors were reported being tattooed with personal animal or spiritual totems as a means of gaining strength and courage. Contemporary rituals also employ body art; however, they are rarely recognized in the same ways as historic rituals. A rite of passage for many U.S. and Canadian teenagers is piercing of the ear(s), nose, lip, or navel.

While body art has been historically associated with ceremonies, rites, aesthetics, identities, or memberships, it also may be a work of art displayed for its own merits. In this way, body art is most commonly associated with performance art, where an artist uses his or her body as a medium and mode for public or private expression. In the 1950s and 1960s, the Happenings movement introduced North Americans to performance art, where the human body was the mode for expression in loosely structured theatrical events. However, individuals had used body art within sideshow performances on carnivals during the nineteenth and twentieth centuries. In the late twentieth century, individual (performance) artists, such as Orlan and Enigma, modified and displayed their bodies in public and private settings.

In North America, body art ranges in type and purpose from face and body paint for Mardi Gras (Fat Tuesday) in New

Dreadlocks are created when hair is allowed to mat, knot, and dread into long, cylindrical, thick locks. Since dreads are most easily achieved with curly or nappy hair, straight hair often requires a "dread perm" and constant care to maintain the dreaded appearance. United States, ca. 2000. Photograph © Therèsa M. Winge.

Orleans, Louisiana, to hook-hanging body modifications for the Sundance ceremony practiced by the Plains Indians. Jewelry, clothing, and body paint are body supplements that temporarily transform a person's body to construct an ephemeral appearance and identity, whereas brands and breast implants are semipermanent and permanent body modifications that can alter a person's body perhaps for their lifetime. Types of body art include, but are not limited to, the following: body paint, dyes, tattoos, piercings, scarification, reshaping, and cosmetic surgery.

BODY PAINT

Body paint is the most temporary of all types of body art because the paint is removable. Body paint is closely associated with works of art. Some designs painted on the body are used to indicate particular events or celebrations, such as rites of passage or street carnivals. Body paint can temporarily transform an individual into a mystical being, a work of art, or even another gender. It can also provide protection, highlight cultural aesthetics, express creativity, or indicate spiritual transformation.

Body paints were historically made from dyes; minerals, such as ochre, chalk, kaolin, iron oxide, and cinnabar; and plants, including charcoal from wood, bloodroot, henna leaves, annatto, and huito. These substances are mixed with oils or fats from plants and animals. In the twentieth century, there were also mass-manufactured body paints in an array of colors and compositions; these are typically used because of their availability, ease of application and removal, and visual appearance.

Cosmetics are types of body paints that are composed of materials, such as creams, paints, polishes, powders, or dyes, that are used to highlight, improve, or transform appearance. The use of cosmetics varies depending on the definitions of beauty within a designated culture. They are also used for medicinal or ritual purposes. Some cosmetics are meant to be seen, while others conceal imperfections in order to create a more desirable appearance. Cosmetics can emphasize gender differences and create illusions of preferred beauty ideals. They can also denote a significant event or rite of passage, such as a prom dance at the end of a school year. Cosmetics allow people to enhance and re-create themselves on a daily basis.

Liquid latex is commercially manufactured fluid rubber. It is painted on the skin and allowed to dry. Layers of liquid latex are used to create close-fitting and body-forming costumes for plays, films, music videos, fetish communities, and dance clubs. Combined with pigments in various colors, it is used in similar fashion to body paint.

Body paint hues may have meanings that are symbolic to specific cultures or events. Red body paint often represented warfare to the North American Indians, who used the sap from the bloodroot plant or red ochre to paint their bodies as part of rituals and ceremonies. Sometimes body paint colors represent affiliation, such as sports fans who paint their faces and bodies with their favorite team's colors. Blackface, a style of body paint once common in vaudeville and minstrel acts, symbolized the transformation of white actors into African American character stereotypes. People paint toenails and fingernails with colored nail polish that reflects their moods or to complement their choice of dress.

Body paints used in connection with rituals and events relating to transitions are often thought to embody protective properties for the wearer. Potawatomi Indians of either gender painted their faces and bodies for protection during ceremonial practices. Drag queens (men who dress as women) use cosmetics and dress in their transition from males to females. Body paint also has practical protective purposes. Baseball and football players wear dark black makeup on the highest parts of their cheeks just under their eyes to reduce glare from the sun when playing, and surfers wear zinc oxide over the nose and cheeks to protect their faces from sunburn. Military personnel also use camouflage paint to protect themselves from enemy detection.

Body paint is often used as a medium for modifying the human within the context of art work, performance art, entertainment, and holidays. Children have their faces painted to resemble animals at street carnivals. Mimes don white face makeup with black accents that represent their transition into a nonspeaking performance art identity. Entertainers, such as the Blue Man Group, professional wrestlers, and the rock band

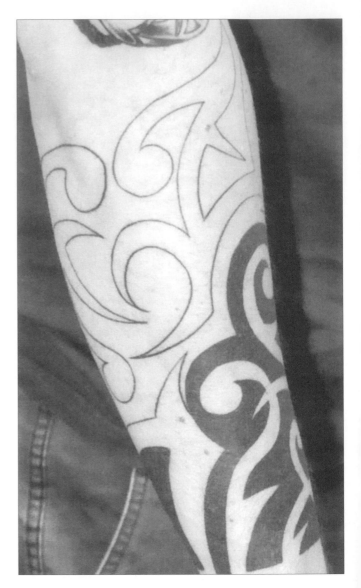

Unfinished tattoo, United States, ca. 2000. Tattoos are typically outlined and then filled with ink, which may require several sittings depending on the size of the tattoo. Photograph © Therèsa M. Winge.

KISS, utilize body paint to alter their appearances in ways that are entertaining to their audiences. Halloween is a holiday in the United States and Canada during which people dress in costumes and body paint to transform themselves into aliens, monsters, or superheroes.

DYES AND BLEACHES

Dyes deposit color and bleaches remove color, but both are used to create body art. Some people dye or tint their skin, hair, fingernails, and toenails, while other people bleach their skin, hair, and teeth. Dyes and bleaches are most often used to achieve cultural ideals of beauty and aesthetics.

Dyes are temporary, semipermanent, or permanent, and colors range from natural hair colors to neon hues. Dye is sometimes only effective when applied to lightened hair. Commercially manufactured red hair dye applied to dark brown hair requires some of the natural hair color to be lifted, and then the dye color is deposited onto the hair. Natural red hair dye, typically made of henna, will tint darker shades of red.

Bleaching or whitening is used to lighten the natural appearance of hair, skin, and teeth. In North America, both genders use bleach to achieve culturally established standards and ideals of beauty. Hair on the head, face, and body is bleached or whitened to a lighter color to minimize its appearance. Skin is bleached or whitened to even out imperfections or achieve a lighter skin shade. Teeth are whitened with commercially manufactured home treatments or by the dentist.

Humans supplement and modify their hair according or contrary to cultural, social, and spiritual ideals and standards. North American Indians often cut their hair to visually express mourning for the passing of a community member or a hardship. Historically, in the dress of females in the United States and Canada, fashion required females to have longer hair than males. Early in the twentieth century, however, females cut their hair as short as males. Currently, hairstyles, cuts, and colors vary greatly; they range from shaved heads to bright pink Mohawks to waist-length dreadlocks.

If a person desires more hair than is naturally growing on their head, they may wear a wig or toupee, weave in hair extensions, or surgically graft hair to the scalp that is made from natural or synthetic hair. Wigs, toupees, and extensions are also used to temporarily modify the length, color, or style by covering a person's natural hair and head.

In North American fashion, the aesthetic ideals for facial and body hair change with time. They modify the growth and appearance of facial hair with bleach, dye, electrolysis, waxing, plucking, laser, depilatories, and shaving.

TATTOOS

The tattoo is a form of body art in which the skin is permanently or semipermanently marked by the injection of pigment, which is deposited in the skin with a sharpened object in designated designs or patterns. Tattoos range from tribal designs to portraits and from dark black to neon colors.

Tattooing is practiced globally. The methods and meanings associated with tattoos vary from culture to culture and person to person. Historically, tattoos were used by North American Indians and First Nations people to indicate identity, membership, power, spiritual totems, medicinal rites, age-grades, and battle victories. In the twenty-first century, tattoos are more often used to communicate an aesthetic or personal statement. In the seventeenth century, Jesuit missionaries reported seeing tattoos on North American Indians. These tattoos communicated social, cultural, and spiritual values and ideals and were often given during or related to a ritual or ceremony. These tattooing methods varied from incisions in the skin covered with dark pigments to marks tapped into the skin with sharpened objects and covered with colored clay.

In the nineteenth century, U.S. naval personnel were among the few non-Indians who had tattoos. Often these decorations related to their travels. During and after both world wars, military personnel could be observed wearing tattoos of U.S. flags, hearts with banners and names of sweethearts, and panthers. These stereotypical symbols were the first stock art on tattoo parlor walls, also known as *flash*. By the late nineteenth century, the trend to display tattoos as body art had spread to other civilian males and females in North America, a change that was facilitated by the patent of the first electric tattooing implement in 1891. Most people concealed these tattoos under clothing. However, some people displayed their tattoos as body art in specific settings, such as sideshows, carnivals, and exhibition settings.

In the twentieth century, tattoos were primarily seen on subcultural groups, such as motorcycle gangs and street gangs, and therefore often associated with males and criminal, deviant, and fringe activities. By the twenty-first century, tattoos had grown in popularity, and some designs and their locus were fashionable. Tattoo designs were incorporated into clothing, and a person could give the illusion of having tattoos by donning an illusion

Body art, such as this Celtic goddess tattoo, may aesthetically adorn the body and represent spiritual significance for the wearer. In the United States, by the twenty-first century, tattoos had grown in popularity. Photograph © Therèsa M. Winge.

knit shirt with tattoo designs printed on the sleeve. Women wear tattoos as aesthetic statements, reclamations, and accomplishments. Breast cancer survivors with mastectomies have reclaimed their bodies and missing breast by tattooing a personal design over the scar. The Dixie Chicks, a country music band, tattoo tiny chicken feet on their feet to acknowledge their major achievements in the music industry.

The widespread popularity of tattoos led tattoo enthusiasts to seek out unique designs, ranging from animal themes to tribal designs. Katzen the Tiger Lady owns a tattoo parlor in Texas, performs musical numbers, and is tattooed all over her body with black tiger stripes. Fakir Musafar owns a body modification studio in California, presents body modification seminars, and sports several tribal blackwork tattoos.

Cosmetic tattoos can mimic eyebrow pencil, eyeliner, lipliner, and lipstick. These tattoos are semipermanent; owing to the use of plant-derived inks and minimal skin penetration, they fade after four or five years. Cosmetic tattoos are applied by tattoo professionals with a tattoo gun or by trained medical professionals through a process called *micropigmentation*.

Temporary tattoos can be inexpensively purchased and come in a variety of designs, typically flash designs. These tattoos simply adhere to the skin and can be applied or removed by the wearer or a person without tattoo training. Henna, or a variant called *mehndi*, is also recognized as a temporary tattoo that stains the skin and eventually wears away as the skin exfoliates.

PIERCING

Piercing is the act of puncturing the skin and underlying tissue to create a hole, as well as the resulting hole. Piercing holes are usually maintained by inserting a body supplement (bone, metal, or jewelry). As with tattoos, ancient mummies found worldwide suggest that piercing has been practiced by people from all cultures.

The Tlingit of southeast Alaska utilized shark's teeth as earrings. Within this culture, ear piercing was directly linked to an individual's rank in society. Only the very wealthy could afford to have their family's ears pierced. The Inuit of Alaska used lip piercing to indicate social status. Both males and females wore body supplements (lip plugs) in their lips, called *labrets*. Young Tlingit girls of Alaska were once pierced before marriage.

In the twentieth and twenty-first centuries, North American mainstream youth pierce their ears, navels, eyebrows, and the sides of their noses according and contrary to social and cultural aesthetic ideals. A piercing is emphasized and maintained by inserting jewelry made from materials ranging from bone to surgical steel, in various designs, into the piercing hole. Some individuals stretch their piercing holes with weights and larger-gauge jewelry.

MODIFICATION OF THE SKIN SURFACE

Scarification permanently modifies the texture and appearance of the skin with scars created in predetermined designs and patterns by using incisions, abrasions, or burns. Healed scars often become raised keloids on the skin's surface due to the migration of collagen during the healing process. Some types of scarification practiced in North America are cutting, skinning, resurfacing, and branding.

Cat tattoo, United States, ca. 2000. The images used for tattoos as body art may represent symbols of good fortune or protection for the wearer. Photograph © Therèsa M. Winge.

During the late twentieth century, many scarification practices were forbidden or outlawed around the world by the local governments. At the same time, North American groups, such as subcultures, body modification enthusiasts, performance artists, and university fraternities and sororities, were practicing scarification. Fraternity alumni Michael Jordan and the Reverend Jesse Jackson have their Greek fraternity letters branded on their bodies, symbolizing the permanency of membership and commitment to their fraternity's ideals and bylaws.

Cutting is a body modification that makes incisions into the surface of the skin with a scarifier, such as a sharpened bone, scalpel, or razor blade. Pronounced scars or cicatrization are produced by placing inert materials, such as clay or ash, into the fresh cuts that heal into keloids. An inking (tattoo) is created by rubbing ink or other pigment materials into the cutting. Inking was historically used by North American Indians to create a type of raised tattoo.

Large areas of scarification are created with *skinning*. A scarifier is used to outline the design. Then the surface of the skin is lifted, cut away, and removed in manageable pieces. Sometimes the skin is lifted and packed with inert materials and allowed to heal. Skinning takes a significant amount of time to heal depending on the amount and locus of the removed skin.

Resurfacing uses friction, lasers, or chemicals to remove the dermis layers of skin. North American subculture members use sandpaper, steel wool, or grinding stones to create visible scars in desired designs and patterns, while members of the mainstream culture use chemicals and lasers to create finer scars, encouraging the migration of collagen to smooth away wrinkles and create a more youthful appearance.

Branding permanently modifies the texture and appearance of the skin by directly applying extreme heat or cold, which destroys layers of skin tissue and encourages a raised scar. Brands as body art range from finely detailed to crude symbol designs. There are basically two types of brands: strike brands and cautery brands.

A common form of branding, *strike branding* employs branding irons made from metals or ceramics, either as complete single units or shaped designs or symbols held by a gripping tool. The strike-branding iron is either heated from an external source or submerged into liquid nitrogen or another cooling chemical solution. Then the branding iron is pressed against the skin to create third-degree burns, which leave permanent scars in the designated design of the brand.

Cautery branding uses electrical devices, such as soldering irons and lasers, to create the desired design or pattern. In the late twentieth century, Steve Haworth, a body modification enthusiast, invented the electrocautery unit, similar to an arc welder, for branding the skin. An electrocautery unit allows the branding artist to have more control over the brand than a strike brand, resulting in more intricate and elaborate designs.

RESHAPING

Reshaping is the practice of modifying the shape of specific body areas in temporary, semitemporary, and permanent ways. Some of the ways by which the body is reshaped in North America are diet and exercise, corsetry, cosmetic surgery, amputation, and splitting.

Diet and exercise are used to reshape the body. While it is typically related to reducing the body's mass, it can also be used to increase mass, as is the case with bodybuilders. North American diet and exercise practices vary according to the desired health and aesthetic outcomes.

Corsets typically constrict and reshape the torso of the human body to a desired silhouette. Both males and females have worn and wear corsets as body-shaping undergarments; however, there is limited information on male corsets in North America. In the early twentieth century, North American women exchanged their corsets for girdles. Corsets would resurface on occasion to

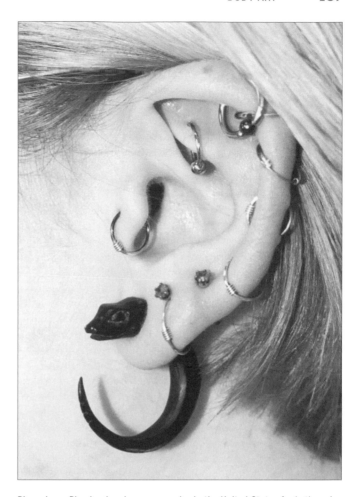

Pierced ear. Piercing has become popular in the United States for both males and females. Individuals often have multiple piercings with various types of jewelry that may adorn and/or stretch the piercing hole to a larger gauge. Photograph © Therèsa M. Winge.

achieve a new fashion. In the late 1930s and again in the 1940s, corsets were responsible for achieving a narrow waist and a more fashionable silhouette. In the late twentieth century, corsets were worn by celebrities such as Madonna on the outside of clothing. By the twenty-first century, corsets were fashionable and available in various colors and designs. Corsets are also used within fetish circles.

Cosmetic surgery can alter nearly any aspect of a person's appearance, not exclusively for health-related issues. Skin, tissue, and fat can be removed or repositioned, and implants can be positioned in order to reconstruct, resurface, or reshape with cosmetic surgery.

Facial augmentation, used for reconstruction and cosmetic purposes, employs a wide array of implant practices. During the late twentieth century, rigid and injection implants were created for facial augmentation. Most facial augmentation in the United States and Canada is done to achieve a youthful appearance; however, some performance artists and body modification enthusiasts augment their faces for cultural or spiritual transformations. The Stalking Catman, from Washington State, has transformed his appearance to that of a cat with facial augmentation, whiskers, tattoos, and green cat's-eye contacts in order to honor his Huron animal totem.

A common temporary facial augmentation is *soft-tissue implant injections*, which eliminate the appearance of lines and wrinkles. Soft-tissue implants include (bovine) collagen, fat grafting, Botox, and Gore-Tex. Collagen implants are usually made from bovine collagen, which is injected into the skin and results in a smoother skin surface. Fat grafting is the removal of fat from an area of the body that is injected into areas to smooth or eliminate wrinkle lines. Botox, a botulinum toxin type A, and Gore-Tex, a porous fluoropolymer membrane, temporarily improve the appearance of facial lines.

Cheek and chin augmentations use soft-tissue and rigid implants to reconstruct and reshape areas of the face and eliminate signs of aging. *Facelifts*, a surgical procedure where loose skin is pulled tight and removed along the hairline and near the ears, are also commonly used to create a more youthful appearance.

Chest augmentations for females are *breast implants*, while males have pectoral implants. Breast implants replace, reshape, or resize the female's breast with round or teardrop-shaped implants. Pectoral implants are flat and circular and placed under the chest muscles, increasing the mass and muscular appearance of the chest. In the early 1960s, plastic surgeons Cronin and Gerow created the gel silicone chest implants, after which they were commercially manufactured by Dow Corning. In 1992, silicone gel implants were banned by the FDA due to health risks, such as arthritis and lupus. In the 1990s, chest implants were changed to saline-filled silicone bags.

Calf augmentation increases the mass and appearance of the calf muscle in the leg with a rigid silicone rubber implant placed under the existing calf muscle. Males and females augment their calves to achieve more aesthetically appealing calves, especially when exercise has not produced the desired results.

Buttock augmentation increases the area and mass of the posterior. This implant is positioned between the gluteal muscles. In North America, buttock augmentations gained popularity in connection to the idealized body of Jennifer Lopez.

The penile implant (prosthetic) or soft-tissue implant, first used in the 1950s, addresses impotence and may increase size. A surgical procedure is used to increase the penis's length, girth, or erection.

Dental implants replace, repair, or improve the appearance or structure of the teeth or the jawbone. In the twentieth and twenty-first centuries, dental implants and related surgical procedures were improved and gained popularity in North America. The appearance of teeth may be improved with the use of veneers, which are thin layers of material attached to and covering individual teeth. Some vampire subculture members either sharpen their incisor teeth or purchase and attach fangs to create the appearance of vampires portrayed in popular culture.

Rhinoplasty is a surgical procedure that alters the nose for reconstructive or cosmetic purposes, also known as a *nose job*. This surgical procedure separates the soft tissues from the underlying structures in the nose in order to reshape the cartilage and bone. Implants are sometimes used to strengthen or change the shape of the nose. In North America, parents sometimes give their daughters or sons a nose job for their sixteenth or eighteenth birthday.

Implants used as body art include, but are not limited to, the following: horns, beads, gauged jewelry, or organic shapes. The modern primitive subculture uses Teflon, surgical steel, bone, or coral implants for subcutaneous body art. Enigma, a body modification enthusiast and performance artist, has two coral

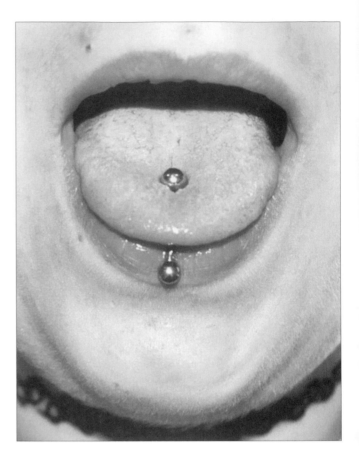

Pierced tongue. Piercing as a body art has become popular in twentieth- and twenty-first-century U.S. culture for both males and females. It is not always visible and has significance to the wearer even if not readily displayed for public view. Photograph © Therèsa M. Winge.

horn-shaped implants on his forehead, along with blue puzzle pieces tattooed all over his body.

Liposuction or *lipoplasty* is a cosmetic surgery that reshapes specific areas of the body by removing excess fat to achieve a personal or cultural ideal. If too much fat is removed from one area, there may be a dimpled or dented appearance.

Laser vision correction or *LASIK* (Laser-Assisted In Situ Keratomileusis) is a body modification procedure that permanently changes the shape of the cornea with a laser. Laser vision correction may eliminate the need for glasses or contact lenses, thereby changing the appearance of the face overall. In North America, performance artists, actors, and the general public also have access to contact lenses that modify the appearance of their eyes, and these lenses vary in type (soft to hard), color (natural colors to neons), and design (normal pupil to cat's eyes).

Amputation is the permanent removal of a body part, such as fingers, toes, leg, penis, or ear. This form of body art is called *amputee art* and is included in body modification festivals, such as the annual ModCon Festival in North America.

Splitting is the permanent separation of a body part, such as a finger, toe, tongue, penis, or ear lobe, for a bifurcated appearance. The Lizardman is a performance artist who has a split or bifurcated tongue, along with tattoos of green scales and a series of Teflon subdermal implants to represent the appearance of a human/lizard hybrid.

References and Further Readings

Beck, Peggy, Nia Francisco, and Anna Lee Walters, eds. *The Sacred: Ways of Knowledge, Sources of Life*. Tsaile, AZ: Navajo Community College Press, 1995.

Camphausen, Rufus C. *Return to the Tribal: A Celebration of Body Adornment*. Rochester, VT: Park Street Press, 1997.

Demello, Margo. *Bodies of Inscription: A Cultural History of the Modern Tattoo Community*. Durham, NC: Duke University Press, 2000.

Engler, Alan. *Body Sculpture: Plastic Surgery for the Body of Men and Women*. 2nd ed. New York: Hudson, 2000.

Gilbert, Steve. *Tattoo History: A Source Book*. New York: Juno Books, 2001.

Haiken, Elizabeth, and Venus Envy. *A History of Cosmetic Surgery*. Baltimore: Johns Hopkins University Press, 1999.

Mercury, Maureen. *Pagan Fleshworks: The Alchemy of Body Modification*. Rochester, VT: Park Street Press, 2000.

Rubin, Arnold, ed. *Marks of Civilization: Artistic Transformation of the Human Body*. Los Angeles, CA: Museum of Cultural History, University of California, 1988.

Winge, T. M. "A Survey of 'Modern Primitive' Body Modification Rituals: Meanings of Pain." In *Meanings of Dress*, edited by Mary Lynn Damhorst, Susan O. Michelman, and Kimberly A. Miller-Spillman, 127–134. 2nd ed. New York: Fairchild Publications, 2004.

Therèsa M. Winge

Dress Reform

Throughout the nineteenth century and in the early decades of the twentieth century, the basic silhouette of women's dress in the United States went through many changes. Many people accepted this ever-changing succession of fashions as a natural phenomenon, an inevitable outward expression of progress; fashion was a sign of modernity. The changing styles of dress and its silhouette were largely dependent on various undergarments—corsets, petticoats, crinolines, bustles, and other supporting devices, rather than the natural body. Consequently, a growing number of individuals began to believe that women's clothing, particularly fashionable dress, was a problem. They argued that the amount of underclothing, the sheer weight of the clothes, and the constriction of the corset were not only harmful to women's health, but because clothing encompassed unnatural forms, they argued that fashionable dress was aesthetically unpleasing as well. For many, fashion was the culprit that destroyed the natural beauty of women's bodies. For others, fashion was a symbol and major cause of women's political and economic oppression. Some considered women to be slaves to fashion. They all desired a change. They had a formidable task: Breaking women's bonds to harmful fashion would not be easy, for fashion was tenacious and remained a central force in the lives and minds of most women.

THE PROBLEM WITH FASHION

Problems with fashion were evident throughout the nineteenth century. An example of a woman getting dressed in the 1880s reveals her troubling situation. First, the process of getting dressed was time-consuming. She might start with stockings, gartered above the knee with elastic bands that could reduce circulation of the legs. A woman then put on drawers, knee-length or longer cotton trousers that buttoned at the waist, and over the drawers she put on either a hip-length knitted vest and a short petticoat or a chemise. The next essential garment was the corset, stiffened with thin strips of whalebone. Over this she put on a corset cover and then a bustle, a contraption made of coils that was tied around the waist and hung in back. Another petticoat was worn over this. Finally, she would put on her gown, which might consist of a boned bodice and stiffened skirt to match. If it were cold, a fashionable woman might wear a jacket decorated with jet beads, which could add as much as ten pounds (4.5 kilograms) to her clothing. In all, her complete outfit could weigh as much as twenty-five pounds (11 kilograms).

Health and beauty were not the only issues regarding women's dress. A number of people linked restrictive clothing to women's

limited roles and what they perceived was their inferior political position in society. Clearly, many women in the nineteenth century could not, or chose not, to focus their lives on being fashionable. As middle-class women became more involved in the public sphere and attended college, they desired to be more active participants in roles outside of the domestic sphere. For these women, being modern meant more than wearing the latest styles in dress. Indeed, in the second half of the nineteenth century, increasing numbers of women were attending college and entering professions and businesses. Women on many fronts sought economic and political power. Reform clearly was not the concern of a single group. Clothing reform was of interest to many organizations and was an international phenomenon, especially from the second half of the nineteenth century through the first decade of the twentieth century. There were many people involved in dress reform, and their persistence over a period of time attests to the continuing problem and interest in creating alternatives to fashionable women's dress. Promoters of women's clothing reform in

The bloomer costume, *Peterson's Magazine*, 1851. As a solution to the problem of restrictive and cumbersome women's dress, the bloomer was championed in the United States during the 1850s for its health benefits and practicality. Courtesy of Patricia Cunningham.

the United States included men and women who were health or hygienic reformers, educators, feminists, physicians, artists, architects, club women, dancers, actresses, opera singers, members of communal and religious groups, and many other educated people. They all sought in some way to alter and improve contemporary styles of women's dress.

In order to make fashion rational, some advocates of fashion reform suggested altering the underpinnings of women's dress—corset, corset cover, petticoats, bustles, pads, and so forth. They wanted to keep the outer dress in compliance with the styles then in fashion, so they devised ways to construct fashionable garments to be less restrictive and cumbersome. Other reformers began to advocate for completely new clothing styles that would not suggest an inferior role and that would allow enough ease in movement for work and active sports. These new styles of clothing went against the norm. As such, they were viewed as less-than-attractive alternatives to fashionable styles of women's dress. These new reform garments took several forms. They included trousers, artistic "aesthetic" gowns, and reform underwear. Together these garments served to make fashion rational. Trousers offered freedom of movement and were modest. The rational underwear systems replaced fashionable, bulky underwear and the tight corset. The new underwear was lighter, less restrictive, and comfortable. Also, it was a less obvious way to reform women's clothing. Artistic dress offered both comfort and beauty.

LADIES IN TROUSERS

One of the first elements of fashionable dress to come under the reformers' fire was the long, full skirt. Long skirts dragged on the ground, sweeping up tiny vermin and debris from the street with the wearer's every step, which was then deposited indoors. Petticoats hung heavily on the waist, cage crinolines could swing out and flip up in the wind, and trains and bustles were heavy and awkwardly balanced. Women's skirts made walking up and down stairs treacherous and running nearly impossible.

The reformers chose a solution that they believed was both practical and modest. They did not elect to reveal women's legs, for that would have been improper, indeed, unthinkable. Rather, they chose to wear a dress made like other fashionable dresses except for its knee-length skirt worn over matching trousers. A similar style was worn by Turkish and Syrian women and had been worn on stage and for masquerade dress. Trousers, called *pantalets*, had also been worn under skirts by women in France in the early 1800s and later became the fashion for young girls. Pantalets were seen on gymnasium outfits as early as 1830. Trousers also were worn by women in sanitariums and in communal societies.

Although fairly restricted in use, trousers caught the attention of a young feminist, Elizabeth Smith Miller. She adopted the costume for her own everyday dress and introduced it to her cousin Elizabeth Cady Stanton and Stanton's friend Amelia Bloomer, editor of *The Lily*, a feminist tract devoted to temperance and women's reform. Amelia Bloomer began wearing the shortened skirt and trousers in 1851, the advantages of which she described in a *Lily* article. The local newspaper in Seneca Falls, New York, *The Courier*, also commented favorably on the style worn by Mrs. Bloomer, and soon newspapers picked up the account and named the style the *bloomer*.

In the 1850s, the bloomer costume gained worldwide acceptance. Supporters in the United States noted the practicality and convenience of the new costume, as well as its health benefits. They saw moral and patriotic qualities in its simplicity. Yet there were many detractors. Some opponents simply believed that it was bad fashion or that it was immoral or unpatriotic because it was based on foreign styles (Middle Eastern). Perhaps the strongest argument used was that the bloomer was incongruous with prevailing ideology regarding women's roles. There was strong antagonism toward women wearing trousers, and those who wore the bloomer in public faced harassment. Numerous cartoons played upon deep-seated fears of people regarding gender and fashion. Eventually, bloomers became associated with the women's rights movement, an effort not wholly embraced by people in the United States. Indeed, feminists did believe that fashionable dress was a symbol of their oppression. They shared Elizabeth Cady Stanton's opinion that women's tight bodices and long, trailing skirts deprived them of all freedom. Yet, notwithstanding the recommendations given in *The Lily* for the bloomer style, many feminists ceased wearing it after a few years because the ridicule became counterproductive to gaining rights for women.

Not all reformers ceased wearing trousers. Indeed, throughout the nineteenth century there were activists for women's rights, temperance, and other causes who continued the effort to reform women's dress by wearing trousers. For example, there were two grassroots efforts toward dress reform that occurred in Ohio during the 1870s. One took place in South Newbury, Ohio, where in September 1870 a group of men and women organized what may have been the first society of its kind in Ohio—the Northern Ohio Health and Dress Reform Association. The organizers announced that its Dress Reform Picnic was for all women having courage to lay aside symbols of their servility and don the "American Costume" of trousers and frock. They celebrated every year by having a Fourth of July picnic where women were expected to wear bloomers. The second such organization in Ohio, the American Free Dress League, held its first meeting in 1874. (*Free* for them meant freedom of the individual to decide on needs and styles of dress, as well as fiscal freedom.) This organization had the support of Mary Tillotson, an ardent reformer. The *Northern Ohio Journal* carried announcements of the meeting and later reported on its activities, including the resolutions offered by Tillotson. They were not favorably inclined toward these more radical conveners and made a point of criticizing Tillotson's clothing, a short dress worn with pantaloons, as "aggressively ugly."

Trousers also continued to be a solution for health reformers who spread their gospel through a number of publications. They could advocate bloomers for health reasons with little public harassment; such reasoning implied that women were inherently weaker than men and thus was less threatening to established ideas about gender roles. Between 1856 and 1864, Lydia Sayer Hasbrouck, an energetic bloomer-wearer and water-cure physician, edited *The Sibyl*, a health publication primarily devoted to improving women's dress. Other health journals, such as the *Water-Cure Journal* (later the *Herald of Health*), similarly promoted sensible dress for women, and its editor, Mary Gove Nichols, also adopted the bloomer style, testifying that it brought her new health and courage. Other water-cure physicians who promoted trousers were Ellen White of the Seventh-Day Adventist Water Cure in Battle Creek, Michigan, and Harriet Austin, who

Elizabeth Cady Stanton wearing a short dress and trousers, a style that was seen as particularly radical at the time. From "The First of the Flappers," *Literary Digest*, 13 May 1922. Courtesy of Patricia Cunningham.

adopted what she called the "American costume" at James Caleb Johnson's Water Cure in Glen Haven, New York, in 1852.

The health aspect of dress reform was also of interest to Canadian women. The dress reform movement in Canada was sparked by a letter written by Clara Graham to the *Public Health Magazine* in 1877. Graham had been greatly influenced by the reform ideas presented by Bostonian Anna Woolson in *Dress and Health* (1874). However, as a whole, Canadian women were far more reticent about dress reform than their counterparts in the United States. Their interest in reform came about much later than the first efforts of U.S. feminists in the mid-nineteenth century.

In the mid-nineteenth century, there was also increasing interest in using exercise as a means to maintain good health. Educators and advocates of physical training believed that an indoor life was physically debilitating to children and women. Indeed, Oberlin and Vassar colleges shared the philosophy of the health reformers and included hygiene, calisthenics, and sports activities in their curricula. At Vassar in 1865, a Venus de Milo cast was even placed in the calisthenics classroom to serve as an ideal standard of natural beauty for the students. Whether at Vassar,

Mt. Holyoke College, or in Dr. Dio Lewis' Academy of Physical Culture in Boston, women wore shortened gowns and loose trousers for calisthenics classes. In 1858, *Godey's* magazine introduced the Metropolitan Gymnastic Costume, which was similar to the bloomer dress. The loose bloomer style of the gymnasium suit became linked more and more with the idea of physical activity for women and thus became acceptable dress for a variety of sports and outdoor activities in the nineteenth and early twentieth centuries. These included mountain climbing, swimming, and bicycling. However, the bloomer style never caught on as a fashionable substitute for everyday dress.

Although many feminists in the 1850s ceased wearing the bloomer, they continued to support the concept of dress reform. In the 1870s, both the National Woman Suffrage Association, headed by Elizabeth Cady Stanton, and the American Woman Suffrage Association, led by Lucy Stone, promoted dress reform in their publications, *The Revolution* and *The Woman's Journal*. Yet it was not until the 1890s that feminists in the National Council of Women established a dress committee to recommend specific styles of reform dress for everyday or public use. Not surprisingly, the styles they chose echoed the earlier bloomer design, now acceptable for women engaged in physical activities. This committee chose three styles, all of which had some type of trouser or leg covering: the Syrian costume, the gymnasium suit, and the American costume. All were recommended by the committee, and speakers on dress reform at the 1983 Columbian Exposition in Chicago wore variations of garments exhibited. Laura Lee, an artist from Boston and one of the speakers, wore several versions of the Syrian costume.

REFORM UNDERWEAR

Many of the objections to fashionable dress were in fact directly related to abuses caused by undergarments. Remember that the fashionable woman of the 1880s wore too much underwear; it restricted her and weighed her down. It could be too hot in the summer and not warm enough in the winter. (Even the cage crinoline that mercifully reduced the number of petticoats allowed air to blow around a woman's legs.) The corset was generally worn too tightly. The many skirt layers created bulk at the waist, and the weight of the clothing was unevenly distributed. If the excess bulk was removed, then a woman would not have to resort to tight-lacing, which, according to many health experts, greatly damaged women's internal organs and caused disease.

One of the first reform undergarments to be promoted in the United States was the "emancipation union under flannel," patented in 1868. This *union suit* combined a knit-flannel waist (shirt) and drawers in one. The "combination," as the union suit was often called, was continuously improved by various knitwear companies and reformers in the United States. Susan Taylor Converse of Woburn, Massachusetts, designed an improved version in 1875 and named it the *Emancipation Suit*. Because the suit was actually a corset and corset cover in one, it reduced the number of undergarments. A gathered section across the bodice freed the breasts from compression, and sets of buttons at the waist and hips helped suspend several layers of skirts. The Emancipation Suit also could have been purchased as two separate parts that buttoned together at the hips.

Several individuals devoted to reform devised whole systems of underclothing that included no corset at all. In the 1890s,

Leglettes and gown forms. Part of the reform underwear system designed by Annie Jenness Miller and presented in *Dress, The Jenness Miller Magazine*, United States, 1894. Courtesy of Patricia Cunningham.

one of the best-known health reformers in the United States, Dr. J. H. Kellogg, developed a dress system at the Battle Creek Sanitarium that was practical, healthful, and artistic. Kellogg believed that a young woman who had not permanently ruined her body by badly constructed apparel could learn to stand like the Venus Genetrix. His dress system attempted to minimize the weight on the hips and shoulders previously emphasized in fashion. Corsets and tight bodices were discarded. The general plan for the system included designs for gowns and undergarments. For the latter, women could choose from the following selections to best suit their needs for warmth and comfort: the union suit, jersey tights (worn over the union suit for extra warmth), a combination suit (instead of chemise and drawers), the Dr. Lindsay divided skirt (knitted for warmth), the "improved" divided skirt (without visible divide), skirt waists (to be sewn or buttoned to skirts), the improved *freedom waist* (with two rows of buttons for attaching the dress skirt and petticoat or drawers), or "umbrella drawers" (a yoked skirt, divided skirt, and ruffled drawers with yoke).

Annie Jenness Miller, a frequent lecturer, author, and publisher on the subject of physical culture and correct dress, also devised a dress system to replace the fashionable chemise and drawers, corset, corset cover, and petticoats. As illustrated and described in her journal, *Dress, the Jenness Miller Magazine*, this system was similar to Kellogg's and included leglettes, chemilettes, and a model bodice. Both systems freed women from wearing heavily boned corsets and sought to distribute the weight of the underclothing and reduce bulk at the waist. The Jenness Miller system also included a bosom support for stout women, a garment similar to a brassiere. Although not necessarily an undergarment, the gown form provided by Kellogg and Jenness Miller was essential as a foundation for the gown; Jenness Miller's form was cut in the princess style and not only replaced the lining of a fashionable skirt but was also arranged so that fabric for a gown could be draped over it, with the weight thus evenly supported by the body. The gown form also eliminated "tie backs" under the skirt and had no band on the waist.

Union suits, knit chemises and drawers, corsets with fewer stays (such as the Flynt and Ferris waists), and the Kellogg and Jenness Miller unboned bodices all eliminated the heavily boned corset as well as reduced excessive bulk and weight. These undergarments could be worn without being readily noticed and were a great improvement over the more fashionable but distorting undergarments.

ARTISTIC DRESS

Many advocates writing of the need for change in women's dress referenced the statue of Venus de Milo as the epitome of natural beauty and contrasted an image of her with one of the distorted body of a corseted woman. They did so to reveal what they believed were the damaging effects of the corset. However, it was the proponents of artistic dress who most heartily adhered to classical ideals of beauty reflected in the Venus statue and who believed in the principles of art upon which these ideals were founded. For them, the artificiality of fashionable dress—the corset, crinoline, bustle, and other disguising elements of fashion—went against nature and thus destroyed the beauty of a woman's natural form.

As with the health reformers, some aesthetic dress reformers saw the need to abandon and reduce the weight of women's clothing, maintaining that without good health, women could not be truly beautiful. Many objected to fashionable dress chiefly on the grounds of taste, rejecting the excessive ornamentation of Victorian design in favor of the principles of simplicity and suitability. Still others decried fashion because it encouraged women to conform to a single style of dress rather than allowing them to choose a style to express their individuality. They believed that women should enhance their individuality through the application of the principles of art to dress.

Artistic (aesthetic) dress in the United States was greatly influenced by the British aesthetic movement. Ideas regarding artistic styles were rapidly dispersed through various print media. Rather than being solely confined to elite circles of artists, artistic dress appeared to have a middle-class following. Indeed, U.S. magazines did not miss the opportunity to report on aesthetic dress. An 1878 issue of the *American Agriculturist* observed that the aim of the "Pre-Raphaelite style" was to "have a thick waist," like the Venus de Medici and Venus de Milo. Furthermore, it reported that artists declared tight waists unartistic and vulgar because the natural beauty of the human figure is lost through the destruction of its healthy proportions.

Annie Jenness Miller, publisher of *Dress, the Jenness Miller Magazine* (1887–1898), continued her efforts toward reform as an outspoken advocate of artistic reform in women's dress. As noted previously, she advocated a system of rational underclothing, but she also stressed the need to adapt artistic principles to life and dress in order to achieve beauty through simplicity, unity, utility, and harmony. The magazine frequently featured examples of artistic dress patterns, which were available for purchase from the Jenness-Miller Publishing Company. An article on artistic clothing that appeared in the magazine noted that the beautiful new gowns presented to the English public by Liberty & Co. of London were created on a purely hygienic plan and were as artistic as they were healthful because they embraced all of the principles of the Jenness Miller system. (In reality the influence was no doubt reversed.) Annie Jenness Miller and her sister lectured extensively throughout the United States. Owing to their efforts, dress clubs began to appear in several cities. One prominent example was the Society for the Promotion of Physical Culture and Correct Dress, an affiliate of the Chicago Women's Club. With a membership of 250 in 1892, the organization condemned the use of the corset and the so-called health waist. Their study committee earnestly recommended that each member supply herself with a photograph of the Venus de Milo and visit the Greek statuary in the galleries of the Art Institute.

The artistic reform styles most acceptable to fashionable American women were *wrappers*, or house gowns, especially the more formal version, the *tea gown*, which first became popular in the 1870s. Taking the lead of the British, Americans designed tea gowns in a vaguely medieval or high-waisted, loose-fitting style known as the *Directoire style*. The gowns were meant to be a type of reform dress. Kate Manvell, a Chicago-based dressmaker, made sure that there would be no doubt. A label in one of her tea gowns identifies her as "Kate Manvell, Dress Reform Artist."

No. 6—JENNESS MILLER JOSEPHINE GOWN.
Price of Pattern, 50 Cents.

A Josephine gown designed by Annie Jenness Miller, one of many tea gowns presented in her publication, *Dress, The Jenness Miller Magazine*, United States, 1894. Courtesy of Patricia Cunningham.

Until the 1890s, etiquette demanded that tea gowns be worn only in the home, where they were appropriate when entertaining close friends. However, *Dress, The Jenness Miller Magazine* observed that women in the 1890s frequently wore tea gowns in public, especially at summer resorts. The designs of a number of Miller's gowns meant to be worn for evening events were, in fact, indistinguishable from her tea gowns.

THE IMPACT OF DRESS REFORM ON FASHION

Clearly, all efforts toward reforming dress had a lasting influence. The loose, Turkish-style trousers that had first inspired sports enthusiasts and then dress reformers metamorphosed as part of the archetypal gymnasium suit worn at colleges and high schools in both Canada and the United States well into the mid-twentieth century. They remained quite acceptable and appropriate for hiking, biking, and many other recreational activities as well. The loose, full trouser style occasionally sees revival as fashion today. Reform underwear—knit union suits, vests, and drawers—continued to be offered by stores and mail order catalogs, largely for warmth. The drop-seat union suit still provides a warm underlayer for skiing and other winter sports.

By 1910, the idea that women could wear loose-fitting, artistically inspired clothing in public was a reality. Indeed, the *Empire style*, a high-waisted silhouette first promoted by the aesthetic dress reformers, was dominant in the United States and Canada between 1910 and 1918. It was seen on day wear as well as evening wear. Designers, dressmakers, and stores selling ready-mades began to offer high-waisted designs, often with layers of soft, drapable fabrics. The new ease seen in women's clothing took off following the earlier success of two of the most celebrated avant-garde designers in the early twentieth century, Paul Poiret and Mariano Fortuny. Fortuny's high-waisted, pleated delphos dresses and Poiret's high-waisted narrow Directoire models offered to the public in 1907 became very popular, especially with the avant-garde. Their styles appear to be direct descendants of the classical Greek-inspired styles of the aesthetic reformers, yet these two men are often credited with freeing women from corsets. It is clear that they were not the innovators. Rather, they were simply nourishing the seed that had been planted by the dress reformers of the nineteenth and early twentieth centuries.

References and Further Reading

Cunningham, Patricia A. *Reforming Women's Fashion, 1850–1920: Politics, Health and Art.* Kent, OH: Kent State University Press, 2003.

Fischer, Gayle V. *Pantaloons and Power, a Nineteenth Century Dress Reform in the United States.* Kent, OH: Kent State University Press, 2001.

Kelcey, Barbara E. "Dress Reform in Canada." In *Fashion, a Canadian Perspective,* edited by Alexandra Palmer, 229–248. Toronto: University of Toronto Press, 2004.

Kellogg, John. *The Influence of Dress on Producing Physical Decadence of Women.* Battle Creek, MI: Modern Medical Pub. Co., 1893.

Miller, Annie Jenness. "Our Own System." *Dress, the Jenness Miller Magazine* 1 (1887): 65–68.

Murray, Anne Wood. "The Bloomer and Exercise Suits." *Waffen und Kostümekunde* 24 (1982): 103–118.

Parker, Francis Stuart. *Dress and How to Improve It.* Chicago: Chicago Legal News, 1897.

Russell, Frances E. "A Brief History of the American Dress Reform Movements of the Past, with Views of Representative Women." *Arena* 6 (1892): 325–339.

Sims, Sally. "The Bicycle, the Bloomer, and Dress Reform in the 1890s." In *Dress in American Culture,* edited by Patricia A. Cunningham and Susan Lab, 125–145. Bowling Green, OH: Popular Press, 1993.

Stearns, Bertha-Monica. "Reform Periodicals and Female Reformers." *American Historical Review* 37 (July 1932): 697–699.

Warner, Deborah Jean. "Fashion, Emancipation, Reform and the Rational Undergarment." *Dress* 4 (1978): 24–29.

Patricia A. Cunningham

See also Antifashion; Functional Dress; Influence of the Arts; Health.

Ecological Issues in Dress

E cological concerns relating to dress arise at various points in the processes used to manufacture textiles and apparel and also as a result of the use of those products. These concerns are similar in both the United States and Canada, and the solutions to these problems are much the same in both countries.

Processing of manufactured fibers, such as viscose rayon, and natural fibers, such as wool, may result in water pollution. Cotton processing produces fine dust particles that can cause lung disease in workers. Chemicals used in dyeing and printing or in special finishing techniques may cause air or water pollution. Environmental regulations in both Canada and the United States have required producers of textile products to develop safe and nonpolluting processes. In some cases, such as the production of cuprammonium rayon and viscose rayon, North American companies have ceased manufacture because of the difficulties of meeting environmental standards. When a textile fabric is ready to be cut and sewn into an item of dress, preconsumer waste is created. Scraps of new fabric are often left after a garment is cut; this material can be recycled.

RECYCLING

Textiles may also serve to minimize disposal of other kinds of waste. Processes have been developed whereby soft-drink bottles, which are made from the same chemical material (polyethylene terephthalate, or PET) as polyester fiber, can be recycled into polyester fibers for use in other products.

In the United States and Canada, consumer lifestyles, in combination with clothing pushed to market by the fashion industry, have resulted in an abundance of used clothing that must be managed through the ecological pipeline. Not only are products consumed at a high level, but consumer goods are also often overpackaged, contributing even more to the waste stream. As concerns for landfill space continue to rise, the costs of dumping will also continue to increase.

Scientists, policymakers, and the general public are becoming increasingly aware of environmental issues as pressures on the earth's resources come to the forefront. When the American Textile Manufacturers Institute (ATMI) initiated the Encouraging

Sorting clothes at Remains, a textile-recycling company in St. Louis, Missouri, ca. 2000. Courtesy of Jana Hawley.

Environmental Excellence (E3) program in 1992, the apparel and textile industry began improving production practices. This ten-point program included the reduction and management of preconsumer manufacturing waste, but, except in the carpet industry, little attention has been given to take-back programs at the postconsumer stage.

Furthermore, municipalities seldom include textiles in their curbside recycling programs. Instead, most postconsumer clothing and textiles enters the waste stream through donations to favorite charities such as Goodwill Industries and the Salvation Army, both present in the United States and Canada. Consumers may not understand that textiles are fully recyclable, so when clothing is worn out, stained, out of fashion, or torn, consumers often put clothing in the trash rather than send it to their favorite charity. Consumers who know that charitable organizations will continue to process clothing through the recycling pipeline when it does not meet the resale needs of the organization are more likely to donate even unusable clothing that can be sold as institutional rags to for-profit used textile dealers that are located throughout the country.

THE TEXTILE-RECYCLING PROCESS

Because textiles are nearly 100 percent recyclable, nothing in the textile waste stream need be discarded. The textile-recycling effort is concerned with recycling and source reduction of both preconsumer waste created during the manufacturing process and postconsumer waste generated after product use. Sources in the recycling industry put the per capita consumption of manufactured cotton, wool, and other fibers at 83.8 pounds (38 kilograms) in 2003. The Council for Textile Recycling reports that on a national level, postconsumer waste in the United States amounts to about 35 pounds (15.8 kilograms) per person, while the textile-recycling industry annually diverts approximately 10 pounds (4.5 kilograms) per capita, or 2.5 billion pounds (1.1 billion kilograms), of postconsumer waste from landfills. Analysis of municipal solid waste indicates that textile waste makes up approximately 4.5 percent of the material in landfills in the United States. This is equal to four million tons of textiles going to the landfills each year.

Many entities participate in the textile-recycling process, including consumers, policymakers, solid-waste managers, not-for-profit agencies, and for-profit retail businesses. *Rag graders*, or rag dealers, are the textile-sorting companies that acquire, sort, process, export, and market pre- and postconsumer textile products for various markets. Most rag-sorting companies are small, family-owned businesses that have been in operation for several generations. However, start-up businesses have started new textile-recycling companies because they perceive it as a low-cost, easily accessible form of entrepreneurship. What many of the start-ups fail to realize, however, is that this business is highly dependent on global contacts that take years of development and fostering in order to have markets to sell their sorted goods.

Depending on the current economic climate (primarily associated with materials availability and the current commodity price for used textiles), for-profit rag-sorting companies realize both success and hardship. Although the primary goal for these small businesses is to earn profits, the business owners also are very committed to environmental philosophies and take pride in their contribution to waste reduction.

These business owners continue to seek, develop, and nurture markets for reclaimed textiles to not only increase their company profits but also continue to increase the amount of pre- and postconsumer textile goods diverted from the landfills.

Many of the textile-recycling companies in the United States are in their third or fourth generation. However, as the competitive nature of the business has increased and profit margins are threatened, the younger generations have opted for careers different from those of their parents. A result has been the closing of several textile-recycling companies in the past decade. A wide variety of markets exist for used textile and apparel. This means that sorting companies have had to evolve with the market and remain sensitive to its requirements, whatever they may be.

THE SORTING PROCESS

Consumers often take apparel that is worn, out of fashion, or no longer their size to charity organizations such as Goodwill or the Salvation Army. Charity agencies then sort the clothes and choose items for the retail store; the leftovers are sold to rag sorters as institutional rags for pennies on the pound. The price per pound of used clothing is dependent on current market value, but it usually ranges from three to six cents (US) per pound. Textile-recycling companies are often located in large metropolitan areas because it is imperative to keep transportation costs to a minimum. It has been found that transportation and sorting costs can be the decisive criteria for profitable business. Used clothing is then taken to the recycling warehouses and emptied onto a sorting deck; then the sorting process begins. Newer employees make the initial crude sorts from the picking belt. Sorted goods in Europe, however, are more carefully scrutinized and packaged.

Crude sorts include the removal of coats and the sorting of trousers, blouses, and dresses. As the process proceeds, the sorts get more and more refined. For example, once all trousers are picked, they are further sorted based on women's or men's, fabric/fiber (e.g., woolens go to cooler climates, while cottons and linens go to hot climates), condition (e.g., tears, missing buttons, and discoloration), and quality. Certain brands and styles (e.g., Levi's, Ralph Lauren, and Harley-Davidson, or Boy Scout uniforms and bowling shirts from the 1950s) are sorted because they are called *diamonds* based on the premium prices they bring in certain markets. Recycling apparel is further compounded today because clothing is often made of a high content of synthetic fiber or blended fibers. This increases the complexity of the issue because (1) synthetic fiber strength makes it more difficult to shred, or "open," fibers, and (2) fiber blends make it more difficult to purify the sorting process.

As the recycled goods are sorted, they are also graded to meet specific markets. It is not uncommon for a fully integrated rag sorter to have over four hundred grades that are being sorted at any given time. The quality of the grading process often distinguishes a competitive advantage of one rag sorter over another. It is not uncommon for the larger textile-recycling companies to sort a semitrailer load of postconsumer clothes per day. This adds up to over ten million pounds (4.5 million kilograms) per year.

Most rag sorters have a division of labor whereby the newest employees are trained to do the crude sorts, that is, sorting into categories such as heavy outerwear and bedding from the rest of the apparel items. As expertise increases, employees are promoted to more complex sorting and fine grading. As workers gain experience, they can eventually tell cashmere from sheep's wool with a quick touch of the hand. Fashion forecasting becomes an important part of the process because vintage trends from used clothing is one of the higher-profit margin areas. Goods that are torn or stained are separated from the wearable goods and used for a wide variety of markets.

While the largest volume of goods (48%) is sorted for secondhand clothing markets, primarily for export markets in developing countries or disaster relief, other sorting categories include sorts that are converted to wiping cloths and new products from *open recycling*, which refers to the process of mechanically or chemically opening the fabric so as to return it to a fibrous form. Mechanically this involves cutting, shredding, carding, and processing the fabric. Chemically it involves enzymatic, thermal, glycolyse, or methanolyse methods. Once the postconsumer textiles are opened, they can be further processed into new products for renewed consumption. Much of the preconsumer recycling that comes in the form of textile scraps, which remain after cutting of garments or other products, is treated in this way. Additional sorts are those sent for landfill dumping or incineration for energy and what is referred to as *diamonds* for the vintage markets. For the most part, volume is inversely proportional to value. For example, the largest volume category (by the pound)

Discarded shoes that have yet to be sorted (United States, ca. 2000). At each stage of the process, sorting becomes more refined and specialized. Courtesy of Jana Hawley.

of used clothing for exports earns a range of fifty to seventy-five cents (US) per pound, whereas the diamonds can bring several thousands of dollars per item, depending on the item's market or collectible value.

In recent years, competition in the rag business has become intense, and rag sorters have realized that in order to stay viable, sort categories must be further refined to meet the demands of unique markets. They also collaborate with textile engineers to design new value-added products from used textiles. Available markets for used apparel flux in the marketplace. For example, the popularity of vintage clothing fluxes depending on whether current looks of the season can be easily interpreted with vintage apparel.

USED CLOTHING MARKETS

Once sorted, the goods are compressed into large bales, wrapped, and warehoused until an order is received for export. Several things are considered when sorting for this category: climate of the market, relationships between the exporters and importers, and trade laws for used apparel.

Used clothing from reclaimed textiles and apparel comprises approximately 48 percent of the total volume of reclaimed goods. The U.S. Department of Commerce estimates that second-hand clothing is the country's eighth-largest export commodity behind automotive parts and wheat. Most of these goods are sorted for export or disaster relief markets. On many street corners throughout the developing world, racks of Western clothing are being sold. The United States exports US$61.7 million in sales to Africa. One of its primary export sites is Uganda, where 95 percent of the population wears secondhand clothing and a Ugandan woman can purchase a designer T-shirt for US$1.20. Clothing from the United States is a highly valued commodity and perhaps serves as the only source of affordable clothing in

many developing countries where levels of income are so low that food and clean water are the primary concerns. Some have argued, however, that the export of clothing to these nations has threatened the traditional dress of many indigenous cultures and, at the same time, may threaten the fledgling textile and apparel industries of those countries. While this is certainly a provocative issue, wearable, climate-appropriate, and affordable clothing is a valuable commodity for most of the population in less privileged areas of the world.

Clothing that has seen the end of its useful life as clothing may be turned into a wiping or polishing cloth for industrial use. T-shirts are a primary source for this category because the cotton fiber makes an absorbent rag and polishing cloth. Bags of rags can be purchased in automotive departments in large retail stores. But in some cases, because of its excellent wicking and *oleophilic*, or oil-loving, properties, some synthetic fiber waste (particularly olefin) is cut into wipers to serve in industries where oily spills need to be cleaned up or wiped. Other variations include wiper rags reclaimed from the sorting process that are sold to a washing machine manufacturer for use-testing of the machines or oleophilic wipers sold to the oil-refining industry. Oil spills are often cleaned up with large "snakes" that are made with a combination of oleophilic and hydrophobic used fibers.

CONVERSION TO NEW PRODUCTS

The material that results from open recycling when it is returned to fibrous form is referred to as *shoddy*, which includes stuffing for mattresses and pet beds, filler stock for automotive components, carpet underlays, building materials such as insulation and roofing felt, furniture upholstery, insulation materials, automobile sound absorption and insulation materials, toy and mattress stuffing, and low-end blankets. The majority of this category is

Chopped shoes for recycling in the United States, ca. 2000. Courtesy of Jana Hawley.

comprised of unusable garments—garments that are stained, torn, or otherwise unusable. But some goods are used for wipers because of their fiber properties (e.g., oleophilic or hydrophilic). The production of shoddy represents an economic and environmental saving of valuable fiber that would otherwise be lost to the landfill. Often this category has a high level of specifications forced upon it by the end-use industries (e.g., building, auto, aeronautics, defense, etc.).

Considerations during the sorting process include color, fiber content, and the removal of *findings*, such as zippers, buttons, and labels. Some virgin fiber (fiber that was never used before) must be added to the recycled fiber; yarns cannot normally be spun using 100 percent recycled fiber because the mechanical processes reduce the original fiber length and therefore the fiber strength. Once the clothing or textile is returned to a fibrous form, several products are made. The following is a brief description of these products.

Wadding and Stuffing. Much of the unwearable (e.g., torn or stained) textile and apparel products are often chopped into small pieces, further pulled apart by carding to return to fibrous form and used for stuffing for mattresses, pet beds, chair pads, toys, and envelope padding. Unwearable used clothing can also be finely chopped, mixed with sand, and used to fill punching bags and other sporting equipment.

Paper. About 36 percent of today's paper contains recycled fibers, including textile fiber. In an effort to enforce Section 6002 of the Resource Conservation and Recovery Act of 1976 and "reduce the municipal solid waste stream," the Environmental Protection Agency now mandates the use of recycled paper when federal funds are used for procurement. This proves to be an increasingly important market for recycled fibers. However, one problem with using postconsumer textiles for paper production lies in the soapy residue that persists from repeated washings of the garment. For example, preconsumer denim is commonly

used in paper making, but when engineers try to use postconsumer denim (old jeans), the suds from soapy residue that has built up on the denim are so profuse that it interferes with the paper-making process. Used fiber is also used in the production of U.S. paper currency.

New Yarn Formation. The process of reducing cuttings or other textile waste materials to fibrous form is known as *opening, picking,* or *garneting.* High-quality used clothing, particularly knits, can be reduced to fibrous form and respun into coarser yarns with industrial spinning methods. Much of this processing occurs in Prato, Italy; Dewsbury, England; and, more recently, in India and the Philippines. In Prato, for example, a used clothing broker locates bales of sweaters from around the world. They are then sorted based on color and fiber content, reduced to fiber, stored until ready for use, spun into yarns, and finally woven into blankets for mass-market consumption. Fiber content varies from acrylic, to wool, to cashmere. IKEA is one company that sources blankets of reclaimed fiber from the Prato, Italy, manufacturer.

LANDFILL AND INCINERATION FOR ENERGY

For some reclaimed fiber, no viable value-added market has been established, so the used goods must be sent to the landfill. Rag sorters work hard to avoid this for both environmental and economic reasons because there is a charge per pound for goods that must be taken to the landfill. In the United States, testing has just begun for the process of incinerating reclaimed fiber for energy production. Although emission tests of incinerated used fibers are above satisfactory, the process of feeding the boiler systems in many North American power plants is not adapted for this procedure. The incineration of used textiles as an alternative fuel source is more commonly done in Europe than in the United States.

DIAMONDS

The diamond category accounts for approximately 1 percent of the total volume of goods that enter the textile-recycling stream, yet this category also accounts for the largest profit center for most textile-recycling companies. These items, once they are cleaned, pressed, and packaged, are valuable in the marketplace either as collectible or trend-right items.

Items that could be classified as diamonds in the United States and Canada include couture clothing and accessories, Americana items such as Harley-Davidson and Levi's, uniforms such as those worn by Boy Scouts, certain branded items, trendy vintage clothes, luxury fibers (e.g., cashmere and camel hair), and antique items. Many of the customers for diamonds are well-known designers, youth trendsetters, or wealthy individuals. Ralph Lauren and Donna Karan both have vintage collections. Other diamond customers include vintage shop owners who sell their diamonds in retail boutiques or on the Internet.

In May 2001, an anonymous seller placed a pair of century-old Levi's on the eBay auction platform. Believed to be the oldest in existence, the jeans (technically denim waist coveralls) were found buried in the mud of a mining town in Nevada. In fair to good condition, the anonymous seller opened the bid on 17 May 2001 for US$25,000. One week later, after a frenetic final few hours of bidding, Levi Strauss & Co. won the bid and paid US$43,532 for the 120-year-old dungarees. This is believed to be the highest price ever paid for denim jeans.

Many diamonds have global markets as evinced by the fact that collectible used clothing and vintage pieces are highly prized in other parts of the world. Japanese collectors continue to be among the highest proportion of buyers of U.S. collectibles and prove to have continued interest in authentic Americana items such as Harley-Davidson or Ralph Lauren Polo clothing or Tommy Hilfiger with the red, white, and blue signature labels. After the 11 September 2001 terrorist tragedy, the secondhand signature red/white/blue Tommy Hilfiger goods realized increased interest in the global market. However, perhaps the one item that has had consistent global interest is Levi's jeans, particularly certain older styles. One rag sorter found a pair of collectible Levi's and sold them on the Paris auction block for US$18,000. Another rag sorter sold a collectible find for US$11,000 to the Levi's corporation. However, it requires a special eye and a sense of trend forecasting to be able to find diamonds in the huge mine of used textiles that rag dealers must sort.

Many owners of vintage shops are members of the National Association of Resale and Thrift Shops (NART). Founded in 1984, this Chicago-based association has over one thousand members; it serves thrift, resale, and consignment shops and promotes public education about the vintage shop industry. Textiles Recycling for Aid and Development (TRAID) is a charity organization that finances itself through the sale of quality secondhand clothing. As evinced here, even though the diamond category consists of only 1 to 2 percent of the volume of reclaimed goods, the profits for these diamonds can make a big difference to the small family-based businesses.

TRADE POLICIES

Policymakers at the local, state, and federal level are involved with setting policy and passing legislation that either supports or inhibits textile recycling. Many trade laws, for example, prohibit trade to certain countries. The Secondary Materials and Recycling Textiles (SMART) organization works with U.S. trade representatives and the Department of Commerce to remove trade barriers so that U.S. used clothing can be exported to developing countries.

As an example, recent negotiations between the U.S. Department of Commerce, the Tanzanian Bureau of Standards, and the U.S. Embassy in Tanzania are concerned with the following:

Japanese buyers selecting vintage collectibles at a U.S. textile-recycling company, ca. 2000. Courtesy of Jana Hawley.

(1) requirement of fumigation certificates; (2) a ban on used undergarments, socks, stockings, and nightwear; (3) a requirement that bales should not exceed 110 pounds (50 kilograms); (4) a requirement for a health certificate to prove the country of origin is free from diseases; (5) certification of used garments; and (6) sampling of consignment. Protectionists cite a list of concerns including infestation of harmful insects, chemicals, and microorganisms. The fact remains, however, that many people in developing nations, even those working in the fledgling textile and apparel industries, cannot afford the clothing that is produced in those factories, particularly clothing that is manufactured with intent for the Western world. Instead, they can buy used clothing imported from developed nations. Even though trade policies prohibit the export and import of certain items, the industry still finds ways to continue trade in the global market while still maintaining trade policies. In an interview one informant revealed to Hawley:

> India has developed a substantial industry of manufacturing wool blankets from used wool clothing. Trade laws between the United States and India do not allow the export of wool clothing from the United States. To meet this market demand, used wool clothing in the United States must be sent through a shredding machine that slashes the garment beyond wearable condition, yet keeping it in one piece so that it can be more easily baled and shipped to India.

Thus, the clothing is no longer clothing, but is, instead, used fiber. Indian manufacturers process the fiber to a more fibrous state, into new yarns, and then into the manufacture of blankets.

FUTURE TRENDS

The ecology of textile recycling is a global consideration with two primary conditions: (1) increased textile waste is being created throughout the world as disposable income continues to rise, and (2) much of the market for used clothing is located in developing nations where annual wages are sometimes less than the cost of one outfit at retail price in the United States. The developing country markets provide a venue where highly industrialized nations can transform their excessive consumption into a useful export. For many of these people, used clothing surplus provides a much-needed service.

As landfill space becomes scarce and costs for disposal continue to increase, so will the ethos for environmentalism. Those in the rag business continue to extend the ecology of used clothing by creating value-added markets. At the same time, consumers must be provided with timely information about these markets and convenient ways to recycle clothing. Finally, policymakers must make it viable for textiles to be recycled, exported, and reprocessed.

References and Further Reading

Berger, Ida E. "The Demographics of Recycling and the Structure of Environmental Behavior." *Environment and Behavior* 29, no. 4 (1997): 515–531.

Gillis, C. "Wringing Out Logistics Costs: In the Used Clothing Industry, Every Penny Counts." *American Shipper* 47, no. 9 (September 2005): 6–10.

Granzeier, Margaret Scully. "The Many Faces of Canadian Environmental Policy: Is Canada Moving toward a Sustainable Society?" *Policy Studies Journal* 28, no. 1 (2000): 155.

Hammer, M. *Home Environment.* Gainesville: University of Florida Press, 1993.

Hanson, J. W. "A Proposed Paradigm for Consumer Product Disposition Processes." *The Journal of Consumer Affairs* 14, no. 1 (1980): 49–67.

Hawley, J. M. "Textile Recycling as a System: A Micro/Macro Analysis." *Journal of Family and Consumer Sciences* 93, no. 5 (2000): 35–40.

Jacoby, J., C. K. Berning, and T. F. Dietvorst. "What about Disposition?" *Journal of Marketing* 41, no. 2 (1977): 22–28.

Nousiainen, P., and P. Talvenmaa-Kuusela. *Solid Textile Waste Recycling.* Paper presented at the Globalization—Technological, Economic, and Environmental Imperatives, 75th World Conference of Textile Institute, Atlanta, Georgia, 27 September 1994.

Packer, G. "How Susie Bayer's T-shirt Ended up on Yusuf Mama's Back." *New York Times*, 31 March 2002, p. 54.

U.S. Census. "US International Trade in Goods and Services." Statistical Abstract, 2005.

Winakor, G. "The Process of Clothing Consumption." *Journal of Home Economics* 61, no. 8 (1969): 629–634.

Jana M. Hawley

See also volume 10, Ethical and Eco-Fashion.

PART 3

Demographic and Social Influences on Dress

Introduction to Demographic and Social Influences

- Age and Gender
- Dress for Work and Play
- Other Aspects of the Culture

Most U.S. and Canadian consumers select dress based at least in part on current fashion trends. Those selections are, however, influenced by the place of the individual in a particular demographic group or social group. The articles in part 3 of this volume examine dress from the vantage point of demographic and social influences. Choices are also influenced by messages about dress carried by films, television, music, sports, work, leisure activities, and religious practice.

AGE AND GENDER

Age often plays a part in choices relating to dress. Choices made by older individuals may be limited by cultural expectations that grow out of ethnic traditions, physical changes that result from aging, or psychological causes. Immigrants may come from cultures that prescribe or limit the kinds of colors or styles thought to be appropriate for older adults. Individuals may continue to wear clothes they preferred at an earlier age—perhaps from a time when they were most satisfied with themselves and their lives—and they may avoid adopting newer styles.

As individuals age, they may find that physical changes can sometimes limit what they wear. Arthritis may inhibit flexibility, making it difficult to pull clothing over the head. Body proportions may change with age, and standard sizes may no longer be suitable. Constance White, who examined shopping trends among older women, has noted, "Clothes that promote sexual attraction and reproduction are, it seems, fundamentally different from those suited to cocooning and reaching maturity in a career or relationship."

Dress at the beginning of the life span is selected by parents and other friends and relatives. The clothing industry even has a name for elaborate dresses for infant and toddler girls. They are known as *grandmother dresses* and are promoted as gifts for newborns. Tradition may affect choices of clothing for infants. For many years the color blue was thought to be appropriate for boys and pink, for girls. Although such traditions have changed, some people still follow this practice. Black was once avoided for young girls, but when it became fashionable for adult women, black was seen in dresses and other clothes for girls. Babies and toddlers were said to look best in pastel colors, but by the late twentieth century, babies as well as older children wore vivid colors.

Gender and age sometimes combine to determine the type of clothing considered suitable for children. The practice of dressing male and female children in skirts until the age of about four or five was carried to North America from Europe and continued until the early part of the twentieth century, when dress for boys gradually switched to rompers or short pants. Some immigrant groups may have strong feelings about appropriate dress based on gender. When school children began wearing jeans to school in the 1970s, some Hispanic parents insisted that their daughters wear skirts. Girls who wanted to conform to practices of their peers often kept jeans in their school lockers and changed into them after they got to school.

As manufactured fibers with special characteristics were synthesized, infants' clothing changed. Stretchable, one-piece, knitted "wash and wear" garments allowed freedom of movement and could, to some extent, accommodate size increases of growing babies. Child psychologists of the 1950s stressed the need for clothing that enabled toddlers to dress themselves in order to allow children to develop a sense of independence.

Psychologists began to study the period of life between childhood and adulthood in the early twentieth century. Childhood had previously been considered to end when individuals began to work, married, and assumed the responsibilities of adult life. For many this happened in the early teens. When the young began to depend on their families for much longer periods of time, however, dependence stretched into the late teens and, for the more

Four- or five-year-old boy dressed in a skirt. In North America, until the early twentieth century, it was common to dress both boys and girls in skirts until they reached about six years of age. Courtesy of Phyllis Tortora.

affluent, to the postcollege years. The teen period, now called *adolescence,* took on a dynamic of its own, with specific fashion and fads unique to that age group. The fashion industry, ever alert to potential new markets, began to target adolescents, who are rather independent in their selection of dress. In the first years of the twenty-first century, retailers found that choices about what styles of dress to wear were being made by even younger girls between the ages of seven and fourteen. They called these customers *tweens* and marketed to them instead of their mothers.

The garment industry promoted fashionable children's clothing at all price levels, with the most expensive and high fashion of these being called *kiddie couture.* Throughout the twentieth century, fashions in adult dress and children's dress exhibited similarities. For example, when women's skirts were short, girls' skirts were short. When men wore more fitted suit jackets, so did boys. When teens wore bell-bottom pants, so did men and women.

The fashion press coined the phrase "youth quake" in the 1960s to describe the dominance of clothing that was especially suitable for the young. From that time on, North American fashions have continued to include a strong focus on what has been called a "cult of youth." Men and women of all ages can be observed wearing clothing that could also be worn by children. Anne Hollander has observed, "A crowd of adults at a museum or park now looks just like a school trip. Everyone is in the same colorful zipper jackets, sweaters, pants and shirts worn by kids." Adolescents can be seen in clothing that in previous periods would have been considered too adult for them. Cosmetic surgery and treatments with Botox gained popularity with older adult women striving to maintain a youthful appearance, a trend that has spread to other developed countries around the world.

Gender-specific clothing exists in most societies, with the assignment of certain types of clothing to men and others to women. Although there are no universal standards, Western dress had, for many centuries, assigned bifurcated clothes (i.e., trousers) to men and skirts to women. With occasional exceptions, this pattern continued until about 1920, when women first began to wear pants in limited and prescribed situations. By the late twentieth century, women could choose to wear pants at almost any time, although some strictures did continue to exist in areas such as attendance at services held by more conservative religions. In the 1960s and 1970s, the fashion press spoke of unisex clothing, and the former identifications of some elements of dress as being masculine and others feminine had largely broken down. For example, men began to wear long hair, necklaces, high heels, and vivid colors. Pantsuits for men and women could be almost identical. Men, however, are still ridiculed if they wear skirts. It is probably no accident that these changes took place at the same time that women were challenging limitations that had long been imposed on their social and economic roles. Even so, men's formal business wear did not change radically. Successful businesswomen were encouraged to wear skirted versions of tailored suits but not with tailored shirts and neckties. Gender distinctions, though much less rigid and possibly more subtle, continue to exist.

DRESS FOR WORK AND PLAY

Dress for the working day may be prescribed, as some occupations require that employees wear uniforms. For many working situations, employees do not wear formal uniforms, but they are expected to wear certain kinds of clothing, something akin to an informal uniform. The specifics depend upon the occupation. Professions such as the law have such well-understood standards for dress that if a recent law school graduate asks for a lawyer's suit at a clothing store that caters to lawyers, the store clerk will know immediately what suits to show. Creative fields such as advertising or commercial art generally have more leeway in dress for the office. In the corporate world, however, the business suit has remained the standard. For their leisure hours, individuals can choose to wear whatever they wish.

The fashion industry in the United States began to differentiate between more formal and less formal clothing in the 1930s. The term *sportswear* was coined to designate clothing for less formal or casual occasions and for leisure time. In the garment industry, this term did not mean clothing for specific sports, such as tennis or baseball. Pants for women, for example, were first acceptable as sportswear. Only in the 1970s did they become acceptable as clothing for the workplace and, even then, only for some occupations. The growth in casual dress can be associated with the growth of suburban areas near cities. Nonworking time in the suburbs called for less confining clothing suitable for time outdoors. In the 1930s and 1940s, housewives wore washable cotton dresses called *housedresses* during the day. By the 1950s, housedresses had been replaced by blouses or knit shirts and shorts, blue jeans, or slacks. Men wore knit shirts with shorts or trousers. Children and adults wore similar clothes for their free time.

Gradually, in subsequent decades, casual dress was accepted for many activities. People adopted casual dress for occasions that

A page from Sears catalog (United States, 1933) which promotes "sportswear"— a category of casual clothing for women that was first called by that name in the 1920s. Dover Publications, *Everyday Fashions in the 1930s.*

previously had required more formal dress such as the theater, parties, and even church attendance. The workplace eventually followed. By the 1990s, some businesses decreed that on Fridays, known as "casual Fridays," employees could wear more informal clothing. The fashion industry promoted some clothing items as appropriate for casual Fridays, especially after employees seemed uncertain about what was acceptable. The men's suit industry experienced a downturn in sales as the trend to casual Fridays and casual dressing in general increased. By the first years after 2000, some businesses began to reverse the casual Friday practice, while others maintained the option. Professionals from minority groups reported that they did not participate in casual Fridays as they felt their hard-won status might be jeopardized.

OTHER ASPECTS OF THE CULTURE

Demographics and membership in particular social groups are related to participation in fashion, but other aspects of the culture also play a role. What individuals see and hear from peers is especially influential for adolescents. And, as noted previously, what the young adopt in fashion often makes its way into adult styles. One of the major sources of fashion information for young people is the music world. Starting as early as the zoot suit worn by African American musicians in the 1940s, fashion designers took note of dress in the music world. With the huge popularity of the Beatles in the 1960s, mod style and longer hair for boys and men soon followed. Adolescents copied the styles of their favorite performers. Hip-hop musicians not only established style trends, but some musicians, such as Sean Combs (trademark Sean John) and Russell Simmons (trademark Phat Farm), also moved into the fashion world as designers.

From its beginnings, cinema has influenced fashions. Notable early examples include the negative impact on men's undershirt sales when Clark Gable took off his shirt and revealed that he was not wearing an undershirt in the film *It Happened One Night*. Joan Crawford's ruffled white evening dress from *Letty Lynton* has been described as "setting off a fashion craze across the United States." A number of other films from more recent decades led to the adoption of fashions inspired by the heroine's way of dressing in *Annie Hall* and twenties fashions of *The Great Gatsby*. The annual Academy Awards presentation serves as a showcase for top fashion designers, who lend dresses to prominent stars in return for the publicity they gain when the event is televised.

Both television and the Internet have had a less obvious function in the genesis of new fashions. They do play a role by providing fashion-conscious consumers with information ranging from what styles are being shown at important fashion shows, advice as to fashion trends to follow, or what is being worn by media stars. They also provide sites for purchase of fashionable goods. As a result, the electronic media play a major part in encouraging consumers to participate in current fashion trends.

Many leisure activities, from participation in active sports to attending sports events, are related in some way to dress. The ubiquitous baseball cap had its origins in spectator sports. Sneakers, now almost universally worn, emerged from professional and amateur athletics. Polo shirts originated as the dress of upper-class polo players. Uniforms worn by Olympic athletes influence the type of clothes worn for swimming, skiing, and snowboarding. Hiking boots moved from practical wear for difficult terrain to fashion for the young. The rise of health clubs, jogging, and other types of exercise led manufacturers to produce comfortable

Several items that were originally part of U.S. sports uniforms, such as the baseball cap, have, in the late twentieth and early twenty-first centuries, come into mainstream dress. Image Copyright Antoine Beyeler, 2007. Used under license from Shutterstock.com.

knit pants and tops suitable for these activities. These styles, easy to wear and simple enough to manufacture in large quantities, rapidly spread throughout the population to become virtual leisure dress for all ages, both genders, and all sizes.

References and Further Reading

Farrell-Beck, Jane, and Jean Parsons. *20th Century Dress in the United States*. New York: Fairchild Publications, 2006.

Hollander, Anne. *Sex and Suits*. New York: Kodansha International, 1994.

Kidwell, Claudia Brush, and Valerie Steele. *Men and Women: Dressing the Part*. Washington, DC: Smithsonian Institution Press, 1989.

Welters, Linda, and Patricia A. Cunningham, eds. *Twentieth-Century American Fashion*. Oxford: Berg, 2005.

White, Constance C. R. "As the Way of All Flesh Goes South." *New York Times*, 6 October 1996.

Phyllis G. Tortora

See also Tradition and Fashion; Regional Differences in Dress and Fashion; Immigrants Encounter American Dress.

Children and Adolescents in the United States

Children's clothing can be especially revealing of a culture's beliefs and values because it is so often used not only to signify the wearer's identity and group association but also to teach cultural patterns to the young. The fashions worn by North American children and youth reveal a history of increasing emphasis on individuality expressed through consumer goods.

BEFORE 1820: COLONIAL NORTH AMERICA

Examples and written records of children's clothing from Colonial North America are rare. Based on limited evidence, it appears that the way in which European settlers clothed their children was determined by three factors: cultural traditions, the availability of imported goods and information, and environmental influences.

The cultural traditions varied among the diverse groups. Calvinist families believed that wealth was a sign of divine favor and dressed accordingly. Quakers adopted the sober garb that would earn them the name "the plain people." Dutch Protestants in New Amsterdam favored dark colors and starched white-linen collars. African slaves brought headwraps and cornrows, even while wearing European clothing. North Americans Indians, influenced by new trade materials, contributed to changes in the colonists' clothing. Fur caps and buckskin trousers, jackets, and moccasins were worn by boys as well as men. One European tradition that traveled to North America was *swaddling*, the practice of wrapping infants in layers of restrictive clothing.

Swaddling survived until the eighteenth century among English-speaking colonists and well into the nineteenth century for settlers from continental Europe. Changing philosophies of child development began to free infants from their swaddling bands in the middle of the eighteenth century.

Fashion in the Colonies. Fashion was followed as avidly by the well-to-do in North America as in Europe. Colonial-era children seen in formal portraits wear styles like those seen in Europe at the same time. In cut and silhouette, fashions in North American cities were only a fraction of a step behind the styles seen in London or Paris. The clothing of Colonial children was also influenced by the demands of an environment that was much different from that of Europe. The harsh winters in the northern colonies made heavier winter clothing and sturdy footwear a necessity. At the other extreme, southern summers demanded lighter clothing, and caps and bonnets were less common.

The end of the eighteenth century brought dramatic changes in many aspects of North American life, including the founding and early formation of a new country and the beginnings of industrialization. The educational philosophies of Locke and Rousseau transformed children's clothing. Child-rearing handbooks and pamphlets appeared in increasing numbers. In general, they agreed on certain principles of dress. First, it should not be too warm. Layers of swaddling and heavy fabrics were condemned as encouraging sickliness and weakness. Caps were to be worn indoors only by infants and in cold weather. Second, both clothing and the body should be kept clean. The hands, feet, and face should be washed daily, and baths, once considered harmful in the wintertime, were encouraged on a regular basis, year-round. Washable fabrics such as linen and cotton were preferred for children's wear. Third, clothing should be simple and unrestrictive. Corseting for little girls drew a great deal of criticism, as did tight infant clothing and swaddling. Simple cotton dresses that hung from the shoulder were popular garments for babies, toddlers, and girls.

The dresses worn by infants and toddlers were remarkable for their scantiness as well as their plainness. Though they were floor length, most had low necklines and short sleeves, exposing more of the body than had previously been acceptable. Many were quite plain, although frocks with embroidery around the hem were not unusual.

White cotton became the standard material for infants' dresses. For centuries, the predominant fiber had been hard-to-dye linen, usually left its natural color or sun-bleached to whiteness. The growth of cotton manufacturing during the Colonial period made cotton more available. Improved dyeing techniques made colorful cotton fabrics possible. Still, for any number of reasons—neoclassical tastes, tradition, or advances in soap-making and bleaching—white remained the color of choice for infants' dresses. Color was added through the use of colored underslips visible through translucent fabrics and through satin sashes in pastel colors.

Similar dresses were adopted for toddlers and older girls. School-age girls wore simple cotton frocks with little or no boning. Some were white, though printed cottons were also popular for everyday wear. The narrower skirts and slightly shorter hems revealed girls' legs, contrary to accepted standards of modesty, leading to the introduction around 1800 of cotton underdrawers, or *pantalettes*. A variant form consisted of tubes of cotton fabric tied around each leg just below the knee.

Little boys wore dresses until they were four or five years old, but they no longer went directly into men's clothing. The *skeleton suit*—a garment comprising long, loose trousers buttoned to a shirt of the same fabric—was introduced in the late 1700s and was worn by boys through the early nineteenth century, establishing boyhood as a stage with its own distinct costume. For older boys, pantaloons and full-length trousers replaced knee breeches beginning in the 1790s.

1820 TO 1890: CHILDREN'S SEPARATE SPHERE

Between 1760 and 1820, children's clothing had gradually moved away from faithful imitation of adult dress. This trend continued through the nineteenth century, with the introduction of distinctive styles for children between infancy and school age and the further subdivision of boyhood into two stages. This reflects a belief in stepwise maturation, with more adult clothing—a child's

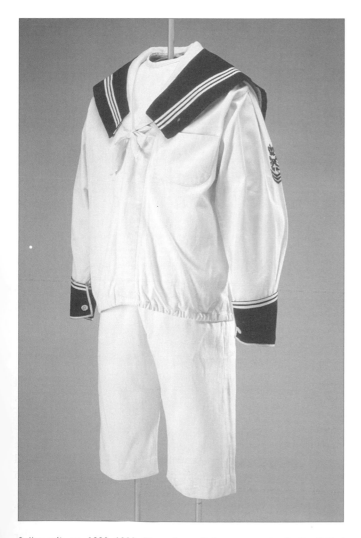

Sailor suit, ca. 1890–1900. The sailor suit became popular in the United States after Queen Victoria of England commissioned a portrait of her son dressed in a child-sized replica of the uniform of the Royal Navy. © McCord Museum M966.159.26.1-6. http://www.mccord-museum.qc.ca/en/

first short dresses, a boy's first kilts or short pants, a girl's first long skirts—being adopted at major milestones. Nineteenth-century parents were concerned that clothing be appropriate to a child's age and not prematurely signify gender.

For most North Americans, childhood in the nineteenth century was brief; young men and women in their teens were assumed to be ready for adult responsibilities. Parallel to the separate sphere for women, the ideal middle-class childhood was a third sphere nestled within the realm of women, at home and at school. Likewise, children's clothing was placed, both in terms of design and production, within the larger universe of women's clothing.

Most of the published advice offered about children's clothing dealt with moral questions, not stylistic ones. Authors were vague about the choices of color, fabric, and design because fashions changed rapidly. Instead, they offered principles to guide mothers in dressing children. Many writers warned that excessive finery encouraged vanity, and they stressed simplicity, even as the plain, easy-fitting styles of the Regency period were going out of style. In reality, simplicity was abandoned as children's clothing followed the increasing elaboration of women's clothing.

When children's clothing finally began to lose its fantastic look in the 1880s, the change was advocated on practical, rather than moral, grounds. Simple, washable clothing was believed to be more hygienic. An emerging conviction that vigorous activity was good for children also did away with clothing styles that were too fragile, restrictive, or hard to clean.

1820 TO 1890: INFANTS' CLOTHING

The styling of infants' clothing changed little throughout the nineteenth century. The traditional pattern of wearing white dresses until the age of one or two persisted. Though no longer swaddled, the well-dressed baby was clothed in layers of garments, including diapers, undershirts, flannel abdominal bands (long strips of woven or knitted fabric wrapped or pinned around an infant's midsection), petticoats, and slips. Finally came the outer dress: long-sleeved, white cotton, often styled with a yoke, and the most elaborate piece of the ensemble.

An infant's first clothes were quite long, to protect the feet and legs from drafts. Women's magazines suggested that baby's dresses be one yard (a little less than one meter) long for daily wear and a yard and a half or two yards long for visiting and christening. If a mother did provide a long, elaborate dress for her child, it was probably worn for several dressy occasions, not just christening.

When the baby was beginning to crawl, his or her skirts, slips, and dresses were shortened to just about floor length. In this way, the newborn's layette could be worn throughout most of the first year. This practice probably limited the extent to which baby clothes could be handed down to younger siblings; short dresses could be reused, but they could not be made long again.

Infants' clothing reflected trends in the styling of women's dresses. In the 1820s, when women's sleeves were short and puffed, baby dresses featured the same style. As women's skirts became fuller in the 1830s, so did baby dresses. The trend toward longer sleeves and higher necklines for more concealing dress was seen in both women's and infants' clothing after 1830. Trim for baby clothes, though lighter and smaller in scale, reflected prevailing tastes in pattern, such as the interest in Greek key borders in the 1860s.

Other trends seen in nineteenth-century baby clothes are uniquely theirs. In the 1850s, small, close-fitting caps fell out of favor and were replaced by larger, face-framing bonnets. A variety of materials were used, depending on the season. Calico, muslin, and straw were popular in the summer or in warm climates, while quilted silk or satin-lined velvet were preferred for winter. The introduction of pastel trimming for baby clothes dates to the 1860s, when pink or blue sashes were added to the traditional white dress. Some German Catholic regions associated blue with the Virgin Mary and girls; some French-speaking areas preferred pink for girls and blue for boys. More often, they were simply "nursery colors," appearing in clothes and furnishings with no gender symbolism.

During this period, babies became more involved in their families' social activities. In the first half of the century, the youngest babies in middle- and upper-class homes rarely left the nursery, and babies under one year rarely left the house. The introduction of the first baby carriage in 1848 eventually made babies' lives more public by making them more portable. Infants' fashions found in magazines from the second half of the century are more elaborate and include many styles for "visiting" or "walking," once occupations of the fashionable lady, which now included her children as well.

1820 TO 1890: CHILDREN
(ONE TO SIX YEARS)

In the eighteenth century, styles distinctly for children had been introduced, separating infancy from adulthood. In the nineteenth century, children's fashions were further subdivided into two groups: styles for school-age children and those for younger children. These new styles appeared gradually over the first half of the century and were commonplace by the 1850s. In the second half of the century, women's magazines featured fashions for children from one to six years much more often than styles for infants or for older children. Fashions for small children, especially boys, combined trends in women's clothing with elements of military or historical men's dress.

Until the very end of the nineteenth century, both boys and girls wore skirts until the age of five or six. The reasons for this range from the practical (ease of dressing and toileting, hand-me-downs) to the influence of larger cultural attitudes toward childhood and gender. Children were not supposed to be aware of sex differences, and distinctive clothing made such differences more apparent. To nineteenth-century parents, a newborn boy was male but not masculine. He would be more masculine at eight and even more so at fourteen. It was considered appropriate to let a child's masculinity or femininity emerge naturally; clothing should reflect those changes, not anticipate them.

From 1820 through the 1840s, fashions for little children were miniature versions of women's clothing, with the main distinctions found in the fit of the bodice, length of the skirt, and choice of fabric. Women's bodices gradually lengthened and became more tapered, extending to a deep V-shape by the late 1840s. The waistline for young children conformed to the natural waistline or fell just slightly above it. Light stays were used for children, but actual corsets were rarely used. In the 1820s, children's dresses became much shorter than women's, usually reaching to a point between the calf and the knee. This revealed the white cotton drawers, or pantalettes, which had been worn by children

since around 1800. Drawers became longer and more elaborate, filling the gap between hem and boot top; some illustrations show their decorative edges extending six to eight inches (fifteen to twenty centimeters) below the skirt.

The fabrics chosen for young children's clothing were somewhat different from those used for older children and women. Many of the prints and patterns popular for women's dresses were too large to be used for children. Instead, small-scale designs such as plaids, checks, and tiny calico prints were often used, in addition to solid-color fabrics. When tiny floral prints went out of style for women in the 1840s, they remained on the market for children's clothing.

It is very hard to distinguish between boys and girls in illustrations dating before 1850. The cut of their clothing was virtually identical. Lace, ribbon, and braided trim were used for both sexes. Sandals were more often worn by girls and boots, by boys. Girls' dresses were made up in floral fabric more often than were boys' styles, and fashion magazines recommended dark neutral colors (brown, black, gray) more often for boys. Girls' hair was sometimes longer, with lovelocks at either side of the face. But most little children in illustrations had chin-length hair very simply parted and combed.

Late in the 1840s, a few styles specifically for boys made their appearance. From the middle of the century to the 1890s, most boys under the age of six wore distinctive skirted styles, unlike girls' fashions. One important influence was Queen Victoria of Britain, who in 1846 commissioned a portrait of the Prince of Wales dressed in a child-sized replica of the uniform of a sailor in the Royal Navy. Engravings of the portrait appeared in women's magazines within months, and the sailor suit became enormously popular. Unlike Prince Edward's suit, which had long trousers, most adaptations for little boys had pleated skirts, mingling traditional boys' costume with naval dress. Similarly, descriptions of the Highland dress worn by the royal family on their visits to Balmoral Castle inspired plaid kilt suits for little boys as well as tartan dresses for both boys and girls.

In the 1840s, dresses gave way slightly in popularity to tunics and coatdresses worn over skirts, particularly for little boys. Other military styles were favored, in addition to sailor suits; the most common was the *Zouave suit*, which featured a short, unfitted, collarless jacket usually trimmed with braid. This same jacket was a vogue for women from the late 1840s through the early 1860s.

The introduction of the sailor suit and Highland costume accompanied a trend that further divided clothing for little boys into styles for toddlers and preschoolers. Boys from one to three years wore dresses and skirts very similar to those worn by girls. From three to about six years they wore kilts or wide, short trousers either gathered at the knee or left ungathered. The ungathered version was referred to as *Garibaldi trousers* and often worn with the *Garibaldi blouse*, with full sleeves and stand-up collar. The gathered style, called *knickerbockers*, first appeared in the 1860s, paired with a variety of jackets and tunics. They resembled Dutchman's breeches, which may have inspired them. As Garibaldis and knickerbockers began to be worn more, pantalettes were left for girls and toddler boys.

While boys were adopting knickerbockers and Garibaldi pants, little girls continued to dress like their mothers. Fashionable dress for women was becoming more complex and elaborate, and styles for girls were no less intricate. Clothing for both girls and boys became more elaborately trimmed between 1840

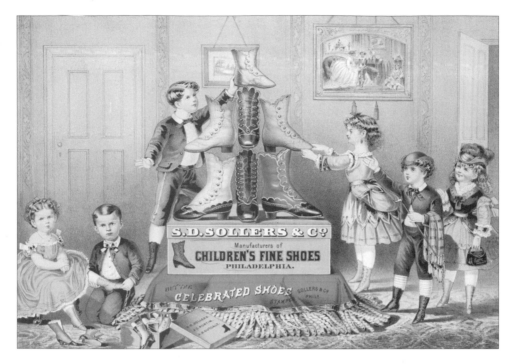

Advertisement for S. D. Sollers & Co., manufacturers of children's fine shoes, Philadelphia, 1874. In North America, the 1870s and 1880s marked the high point of elaborate dress for children. Library of Congress, Prints and Photographs Division, LC-USZC4-2057.

and 1880, primarily due to the availability of inexpensive trimmings and the ease with which it could be applied with the sewing machine. Colors were deep and highly saturated, and heavy, plushy fabrics such as velvet and velveteen were favored for clothing and trimmings. Texture was important, whether in the form of piqué for a simple, washable dress or steel button–studded leather trim on a brown merino dress.

The 1870s and 1880s marked the high point of elaborate dress for children. Closely reflecting trends in women's fashions, a single outfit might be made up in two or three fabrics and feature as many different trims. Every possible historical, literary, and fantastic source was consulted for design inspiration, particularly for little boys, who appeared as sailors, cavaliers, and Highlanders. Gender distinctions became more blurred later on in that period, between a vogue for short *garçon* haircuts for girls and long, curly locks for boys. Multipiece costumes were much more popular than one-piece dresses; most dresses for two- to four-year-olds were designed to look like suits, with bodices, vests, overskirts, and underskirts all sewn into one garment. Waistlines dropped to the hip or lower in the late 1870s, freeing the child's torso but sometimes hobbling the upper legs instead.

The 1880s saw fantastic dress for children reach its height with the Lord Fauntleroy suit craze. This outfit was a boys' dressy suit in the seventeenth-century style that was often made of velvet and worn with a ruffled shirt and wide sash. Frances Hodgson Burnett—the English-born author of both the original 1885 story, *Little Lord Fauntleroy*, and the enormously successful play—did not invent the Fauntleroy style. Illustrator Reginald Burch based little Cedric's suit on a portrait of Burnett's son dressed in a cavalier-inspired velvet suit already in vogue a few years earlier. The popularity of the book and play breathed new life into the style.

Fashions specifically for older girls not quite ready for long skirts began to appear in the women's magazines during the 1860s. For the most part, these featured a *demi-ajuste*, or half-fitted bodice, to accommodate the girl's changing body without drawing attention to it. White and pastel shades were favored for this age group. Fashion periodicals showed young misses' hot-weather dresses in light-colored silk organdy with white muslin mantles, all trimmed with ruffles and lace. The desired effect was feminine and innocent, appropriate for girls who were becoming women but who were not yet part of the adult social world.

1820 TO 1890: OLDER BOYS (SIX TO FOURTEEN YEARS)

Throughout infancy and early childhood, boys and girls led very similar lives in the nineteenth century. By the time they reached the age of five or six, however, their paths were beginning to diverge. Boys were more likely to be educated at school than at home, and they were starting to engage more in masculine activities, whether man's work or boy's play. Accordingly, boys' and girls' clothing styles lost much of their similarity.

A six-year-old boy had already graduated from infants' clothing to short dresses and from dresses to kilts and wide, short trousers. When he reached school age, he was considered old enough to wear styles that were closer adaptations of men's clothing. During the latter half of the century, when long hair for little boys was in vogue, this transition was particularly dramatic because it coincided with a boy's first short haircut.

While magazine descriptions of clothes for girls and little children's clothing typically included expressions of delight and enjoyment of the task of making or selecting their clothes, columns on boy's clothing were less enthusiastic. Once it lost its resemblance to women's clothing in fabric and construction, boys' clothing became more difficult to make at home. Shirts and everyday knickerbockers were still within the skills of the average home seamstress, but suits and coats were often delegated to a tailor. Ready-to-wear clothing was available for this age group earlier than for other children, well before the Civil War.

Older boys' clothing was supposed to be sturdy, practical, and handsome. Sturdiness required heavier fabrics, leaving delicate materials for girls and younger children. A handsome appearance implied dignified good looks, and practicality meant room to move and grow and pockets to stuff with treasures.

Between approximately 1820 and 1870 there were a variety of acceptable styles for older boys, including short Eton-style jackets, flared Zouave jackets (introduced in the 1850s), and even frock coats with flared skirts, just like those worn by grown men. Shirts with flat or slightly raised collars were considered more appropriate for boys than a man's stock and cravat, though some portraits do show boys as young as nine or ten in adult-style neckwear. Long trousers, knickerbockers, and full-cut, knee-length Garibaldis were all worn; by around 1850, however, long trousers were being reserved more and more for boys aged eight and over. Sailor suits, so popular for little boys from the late 1840s on, made little impact on older boys at first. Fashion magazines recommended blouses with sailor collars for boys under eight and regular collars for boys aged eight and up. Similarly, Highland costumes and kilts were shown for boys of six or seven but rarely for older boys.

By 1870, full-length trousers were rarely worn by boys not yet in their teens. The transition from short to long pants was becoming institutionalized as a rite of passage into manhood. Jackets and coats for boys became plainer and more tailored, echoing similar changes in men's clothing. Sailor suits became popular for boys as old as ten or twelve, and other naval-inspired styles made their appearance in the 1870s, such as the reefer jacket and its shorter cousin, the peacoat. Winter sailor outfits were made of dark-colored wool and summer ones, in light wools, linen, or, more rarely, cotton. They were considered too dressy for school, where corduroy or wool knickers were more appropriate, and too playful for church and other more formal occasions, which required a plain serge or worsted knickers suit with a man's tailored jacket. The Fauntleroy style enjoyed some popularity for boys from six to eight years old, but it was never adopted for older boys. By 1890, however, the cavalier style was rejected in favor of the sailor suit, which became much more widely worn by boys of all ages.

1890 TO 1919: THE "MODERN" CHILD

The new century demanded sweeping changes in everyday life. Children's clothing reflected this modern impulse, including the growing emphasis on sports and physical fitness and rejection of picturesque costumes of the 1870s and 1880s. By the 1890s, clothes specifically designed for outdoor play were becoming popular. Denim overalls were worn by both boys and girls as early as 1900. Warm snowsuits permitted children to romp outdoors in the winter as well.

Traditional white dresses for little boys and girls, once chosen because they could be bleached to their original whiteness, were replaced by patterns and colors that showed the dirt less. This reform was part of an effort to rearrange housewives' workloads so that they could spend more time with their children and less

North American children wearing velvet suits inspired by the Little Lord Fauntleroy style, between 1909 and 1932. Library of Congress, Prints and Photographs Division, LC-USZ62-67632.

with their laundry. The modern mother made (or bought) clothing that was easy to maintain, rather than spending hours bleaching and starching white dresses.

Infants' Clothing. Between 1890 and 1919, clothing for infants changed noticeably, influenced by innovations in baby care. Babies were more lightly dressed and were able to move their arms and legs more freely, and their previously all-white wardrobes became more colorful. Some of these changes were prompted by scientific studies. The traditional practice of dressing the baby in many layers of clothing, for instance, was intended to protect the child from "bad air" as well as harmful drafts. Advances in microbiology proved that germs in the air, not the air itself, were the culprits, and doctors were quick to point out that overheated babies were prone to rashes, nausea, and fussiness.

The newest style of dress for babies reduced the number of layers to three garments: a sleeved petticoat, then a sleeveless one, topped with a single cotton long-sleeved dress. If each layer buttoned from neck to hem, the three pieces could be nested into each other and the whole suit put on at once. Concern about ease of dressing was based not only on the time and effort involved but also on the belief that babies could be spoiled by too much handling.

Creeping aprons, or creepers (loose-fitting coveralls), introduced in the 1890s, were originally worn over the baby's dress, not instead of it. By the 1910s, mail order merchants were offering creepers designed to be worn over a child's underwear.

Girls (Two through Fourteen Years) and Little Boys (Two to Four Years). The period from 1890 to 1919 was one of great change for women's fashions. Lightweight, washable dresses and shirtwaists offered comfort in hot weather. Active sports enjoyed growing popularity, as did the clothing associated with them. Hemlines rose to the lower part of the calf during World War I, and women wore lighter underwear and less of it. Likewise, dresses for girls and little boys of the period became simpler and lighter and exposed more of the body. Toddler girls and boys wore dresses that fell in gathers or pleats from shoulder to the hem, often featuring a decorative yoke. Three- or four-year-old children and older girls wore dresses with belts or sashes at about hip level.

For very young children there was little distinction made between boys' and girls' dresses. Pink, blue, gray, and tan were suitable colors for either sex, and boys and girls had similar hairstyles, a simple bob with bangs. Sailor styles were available with pleated skirts for little boys and girls or with shorts or bloomers for slightly older boys. Rompers and overalls were introduced in the 1890s and became overwhelmingly popular for preschoolers' play clothes. *Rompers* were a one-piece garment worn by babies and toddlers, usually featuring a snap or button closure at the crotch for easier diaper changing.

Styles for preteen girls reflected adult trends in colors, trims, and other details, although the silhouettes and length were different. Lowered waistlines were preferred for girls, rather than imitating women's hourglass shapes. Skirts for children under the age of five were usually just above knee length, with short socks leaving an expanse of bare leg. Younger school-age girls wore their skirts at or just below the knee, and girls approaching their teens wore calf-length skirts.

The demands of athletic activities resulted in some additions to girls' wardrobes. Specialized clothing for the gymnasium was adopted, including middy blouses and bloomers, already common in colleges and women's athletic clubs, sized for smaller girls. By the mid-teens, the same styles had been accepted for at-home play clothes.

Boys (Four through Fourteen Years). Creepers and rompers were offering parents an alternative to dresses for very little boys, and boys over the age of three increasingly wore short trousers rather than skirts or kilts. By 1900, suits that combined long tunics with short, full trousers were gaining in popularity for the three- to five-year-old boy. Within the next decade, the tunics and sailor blouses, worn with full knickers, dominated fashion for little boys, and overalls and rompers were worn for play. The costume styles of the 1880s had fallen from favor, although Fauntleroy suits still appeared occasionally in formal portraits.

Clothing for school-age boys included many styles based on men's business dress, in addition to sailor suits and Norfolk jackets. Military influence was strong throughout the period, particularly during World War I. College and professional athletes inspired the adoption of golf- and tennis-style sweaters, baseball caps, and canvas shoes.

1920 TO 1946

Increasingly gender-specific dress for infants and toddlers, the influence of popular entertainers, and the emergence of the teen market characterized the years between the end of World War I and the end of World War II. In the 1930s, economic hardship forced many families to make more garments at home, do more mending and remodeling, or rely on secondhand clothing. Emphasis was placed on styles that could be worn for a variety of occasions or were composed of several interchangeable pieces.

The 1940s brought many changes. As North American industries shifted to wartime production, shortages were felt by consumers. Government regulators could not keep children from outgrowing and wearing out their clothes, though they tried to predict demand based on the population in each age group. Unfortunately, projections of demand were complicated by an unforeseen increase in the birthrate. Births were up 9.9 percent in the United States between 1941 and 1942, precipitating shortages in diapers, rubber sheets, cotton sheets, and wool blankets. Throughout the war, demand for children's clothing continued to far exceed supplies, particularly for items that were quickly worn out or outgrown. Suppliers of babies' and toddlers' shoes reported that barely 20 percent of their orders could be filled.

Clothing styles for children came into their own during this period, as the market became sufficiently well defined to operate separately from women's and men's fashions. Novelty styles, based on children's favorite radio or motion picture heroes, proliferated, even during the Great Depression. Cartoon characters adorned sweatshirts and handkerchiefs; children begged their parents for cowboy suits or aviator's caps.

1920 TO 1946: INFANTS' CLOTHING

Infants' clothing changed dramatically during this period. Dresses became shorter, rompers more popular, and fewer layers were worn. A suggested layette or collection of garments made or purchased for a newborn infant from 1921 included slips (pull-on dresses), night dresses, belly bands, undershirts, *pinning blankets* (an undergarment first worn by infants in the nineteenth century, consisting of a long petticoat of flannel attached to a wide cotton waistband that was closed with a straight pin or ties), underskirts, kimonos, stockings, and booties. By the 1930s, experts recommended that sleeveless undershirts replace the belly band. The shirt and diaper were worn alone in hot weather, and a shirt or dress could be added on cooler days. By the mid-1940s, the layette list included *soaker pants*, knitted woolen underpants worn over a diaper to absorb urine that replaced rubber pants during the war, and a christening gown (by then becoming more traditional).

Once a baby began to crawl, creepers were substituted for the dress. In the summertime, low-cut sunsuits exposed the baby to the sun's rays. Light clothing, already the norm for women's everyday dress, had become the standard for babies as well. Dressing a child in long, heavy layers of flannel and muslin was old-fashioned and unscientific. Baby clothes of this period were increasingly individualized, with the use of colorful fabrics and juvenile motifs, such as nursery-rhyme characters and animals.

Scientific discoveries continued to influence infant care between World Wars I and II. With new information about vitamin D, sunlight was promoted as preventing rickets and curing tuberculosis. Babies were often given sunbaths wearing a sleeveless, low-necked sunsuit, a diaper, or nothing at all.

1920 TO 1946: GIRLS (ONE TO FOURTEEN YEARS)

Like infants, girls of this period enjoyed unstructured lightweight dresses and simple undergarments. Short white anklets replaced long cotton stockings, and sleeveless and short-sleeved dresses gained in popularity over longer sleeves, which looked awkward as the girl outgrew her clothes. Instead, girls wore long-sleeved

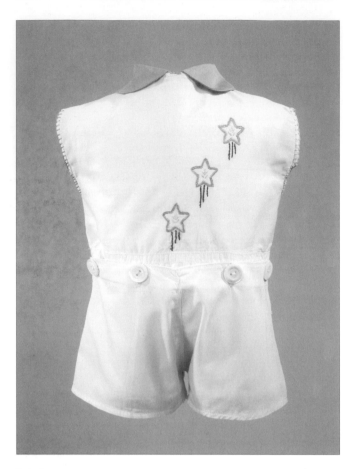

Baby's cotton romper suit with button opening, ca. 1930, North America. Rompers were introduced in the 1890s and became overwhelmingly popular for preschoolers' play clothes. © McCord Museum M965.134.18.1-2. http://www.mccord-museum.qc.ca/en/

1920 TO 1946: BOYS (ONE TO FOURTEEN YEARS)

The trend toward earlier differentiation between boys and girls continued during this period, with new styles for toddler boys. In 1919, a two- or three-year-old boy might have a few dresses in his wardrobe; by the end of World War II, however, only the youngest male infants would wear dresses instead of creepers. Dresses for small boys were no longer a harmless, picturesque tradition but, many experts believed, a threat to the child's self-image that could expose him to ridicule and might undermine his developing masculinity.

Age distinctions in boys' clothing shifted between the 1920s and the early 1940s. Boys born in the 1920s donned knickerbockers around age six and their first real suit with trousers at twelve or thirteen. In many households, the transition to knickers and suit jackets also marked the change from homemade clothing to ready-to-wear for a young boy. The average home seamstress could easily manage to make clothes for boys under the age of six or seven, but tailored suits were beyond her sewing skills.

By the 1930s, there was less distinction between clothing for boys still in infancy and boys nearly ready to start school. Rompers were worn by boys as young as six months and as old as five or six years. Toddlers and schoolboys alike wore knitted shirts, either long- or short-sleeved, over short trousers. Sleeveless full-length bib overalls, with or without a shirt, were extremely common for playwear for boys of all ages, especially in rural areas. Similarly, the differences between boys of six or seven and boys nearly in their teens were less marked, as tailored knickerbockers and short-trouser suits were made available for smaller boys. By 1945, the practice of keeping a boy in short pants or knickers until adolescence disappeared.

Having finally been freed from the influence of women's fashions, boys' clothing from this period drew mainly on three sources: men's clothing, military dress, and sports clothing. The effect of men's fashions was most strongly seen in clothing for older boys, whose dress suits, shirts, and ties became more like those worn by their fathers. Military clothing had long been an important source of inspiration; only the branches of the military changed. Leather jackets and aviator caps replaced naval styles such as sailor hats and peacoats. Sports contributed an enormous range of styles, from argyle golf stockings in the 1920s to ski pants and parkas in the 1930s. Sweatshirts and sneakers, already staples of the U.S. high school boy's wardrobe, became popular for younger boys during this era, as did baseball caps.

1920 TO 1946: TEENAGERS AND THEIR DRESS

The field of adolescent psychology was producing volumes of research on teenagers, much of it quickly translated into popular books and magazines for parents and teachers. Adolescent dress was a persistent theme in these works, as authors noted teenager's interest in their appearance, their intense desire for peer approval, and the conflicts that could be generated by these impulses. Teenagers no longer aspired to look like their elders, and they were equally disinterested in being dressed like children. They asserted their identification with their peers by adopting styles that were either local in origin or that were based on those worn by popular entertainers.

sweaters, with easily rolled cuffs, over short-sleeved dresses. Waistlines returned to women's fashions in the 1930s, but little girls' styles continued to fall loosely from the shoulders.

While girls wore dresses most of the time, all kinds of alternatives were available for play clothes. From dresses with matching panties to denim overalls and dungarees to pajamas, girls were wearing pants in many forms. In the 1940s, playsuits consisting of a one-piece romper with a separate skirt were worn by school-age girls.

The red-and-white polka-dot dress Shirley Temple wore in *Stand Up and Sing* (1934) sold millions of copies on both sides of the Atlantic, and her curls inspired popular hairstyles. Princesses Elizabeth and Margaret Rose of Britain were also influential, with their simply tailored, classic styles. The war in Europe influenced girls' fashion in the late 1930s. Dirndl skirts, inspired by the folk costumes of occupied countries, were immensely popular, and tulips and "Dutch girl" caps honored the well-publicized resistance fighters in the Netherlands.

The emergence of a strong teenage market during the war years provided an important new source of fashion influence for younger girls. Where once little girls had dressed like their mothers, more and more of the trends for grade-school girls were set by high school and college students. This was especially true of girls in the preteen age group, who were anxious to distance themselves from their younger sisters.

Although teenage boys could dress like men, most adults frowned on permitting adolescent girls to dress like women. The timing of a girl's first brassiere, stockings, and makeup became an increasing source of conflict in many households. Typically, daughters began to lobby for less childish clothing and more adult styles at age twelve or thirteen, while parents wanted to postpone their acquisition of women's clothing and grooming until around sixteen years. In practice, most girls began shaving their legs, wearing stockings, and using makeup when they entered high school, at fourteen or fifteen. More clothing designed for teenage girls appeared in stores, often in separate "junior" departments. These first teen styles were in many ways a compromise between girls' demands for more sophisticated styling and their parents' desire to dress them in clothes that were feminine but not too mature. So, while teen styles mirrored adult trends in basic silhouette, hem length, and other details, they also featured elements that had come to connote youthfulness—puffed sleeves, long-torso bodices, fuller skirts, and fanciful trims.

Inspiration for high school fashions came from a variety of sources. Movies were important, of course, as they were for North Americans of nearly every age. The long white gown with ruffled short sleeves worn by Joan Crawford in *Letty Lynton* (1934) unleashed a flood of imitations for high school and college proms. Western films inspired many styles in the 1930s and 1940s, including blue jeans and "Apache" skirts (twisted into irregular pleats on a broomstick while still wet). College students were popular role models. The "babushka" style of large, printed head scarves was first worn by college coeds, as were three-quarter-length hooded "stadium coats" and twin sweater sets. The "Sloppy Joe" style of the 1940s, consisting of an oversized man's shirt and rolled-up dungarees, originated on campuses before becoming the teenage girls' afterschool uniform. Teenage boys, looking to collegiate athletes and BMOCs (big men on campus) for fashion leadership, adopted college-style letter sweaters and crew cuts. Military styles also proliferated during the war for teenage boys and girls alike, particularly in the form of coats and jackets.

CHILDREN'S CLOTHING SINCE 1946: THE BABY BOOMERS AND THEIR CHILDREN

The importance of the nuclear family, a trend toward fewer children, and the growth of an affluent middle class since World War II have resulted in a child-focused consumer culture. In addition, there has been a tendency to condense and accelerate childhood and prolong adolescence. Formal education begins earlier and lasts longer, well into young adulthood. This acceleration has carried over into children's social lives and sexual development, particularly for girls. Adolescent styles (and more recently, children's clothing) has reflected this sexualization. Cosmetics for teenagers are no longer controversial, and makeup is marketed to preteens as well. Finally, the children's fashion industry has expanded dramatically since the 1950s, due initially to the post–World War II baby boom but continuing to grow even when the birthrate leveled off in the 1960s. Larger disposable income controlled by children and youth, coupled with the success of advertising directly to children, has resulted in several generations of child consumers with a taste for fashion change and self-expression.

In general, children's fashions since World War II can be characterized as appealing to children's sense of fun and self-expression and adults' desire for status and vicarious nostalgia. They have also been designed for rapid obsolescence, in the manner of most post–World War II consumer goods. Dramatic seasonal fashion change in children's wear meant more garments sold because hand-me-downs carry the double stigma of being both used and out of style. More highly gendered clothing for boys and girls has also translated into increased sales at a time when smaller families were threatening to lower the demand for children's clothing.

Beyond these general characteristics, there are differences in the dress of the three generations of children born since 1946. Some of these differences are reflections of adult fashion trends, while others are the result of shifts in parental attitudes toward child rearing and the influence of popular youth culture.

BABY BOOM FASHIONS, 1946 TO 1963

From a mother's point of view, perhaps the biggest change in children's clothing after the end of the war was the introduction of fibers, fabrics, and finishes that reduced the amount of ironing she had to do. Polyester–cotton blends for shirts and school dresses, dressy no-iron nylon frocks, and knitted T-shirts and polo shirts

A young boy wearing a cowboy suit, United States, ca. 1940. American Stock/ Getty Images.

were popular innovations. Babies, too, wore more and more knits, which were not only easier to care for but also less trouble to put on and take off. The one-piece knitted stretch suit, worn day and night, was introduced in the late 1950s and soon dominated the infants' wear market.

Self-help clothing for toddlers and preschoolers, featuring elasticized pull-on pants, large buttons, and easy-to-use zippers, was popular for its confidence-building qualities. Besides encouraging independence, clothing was invested with even greater psychological importance by post–World War II experts. "Good" clothing gave children a sense of security and encouraged creativity. "Bad" clothing sowed the seeds of irresponsibility and feelings of inferiority. Conformity was encouraged; children wanted to belong. Odd or unfashionable clothing would make them feel left out and possibly antisocial, the experts believed.

School-age children's clothing of this period had changed little in some respects since the late 1930s. Plaid full-skirted dresses with white collars and cuffs were the staples of a typical schoolgirl's wardrobe. Jumpers were a popular alternative, especially around 1950, in the nostalgic form of pinafores. Corduroy was a frequent choice for girls and boys alike; the boy's school "uniform" was a pair of corduroy pants and a striped knit shirt. Military styling continued long past V-J day; Eisenhower jackets and Coast Guard slickers were among the favorites.

There was a sense of fun and frivolity in many children's styles as well, a kind of everyday costume party. Western styling was a very strong influence, with cowboy shirts and Indian-style dresses. Special dresses inspired by *Alice in Wonderland* or *Heidi* appeared in girls' departments; Walt Disney characters adorned slippers, pajamas, T-shirts, and many other garments; and Davy Crockett coonskin caps were enormously popular. Girls could enjoy being "sisters" to dress-alike dolls, some of them life size. The ultimate dress-up was mother–daughter dressing.

Teenage clothing diverged more sharply from children's wear and from adult fashions. Girls rejected frilly or too-detailed school dresses in favor of separates, usually a tailored blouse or sweater and a full skirt. Boys adopted chinos—satin-weave cotton trousers—sports shirts for school, and blue jeans for casual wear. Slacks, pedal-pushers, and shorts were also popular for afterschool and weekend wear for girls.

THE QUESTIONING YEARS, 1964 TO 1978

After the conformity of the post–World War II years, the early 1960s gave way to a period of experimentation and innovation in fashions for all age groups. Inspiration came from every conceivable direction in time and space. Nostalgic granny dresses in soft calico prints coexisted with mod minis from London's Carnaby Street. Southern California surfing styles alternated with exotic looks from India and Africa. For parents of small children, selecting clothing was considerably less complicated than governing the appearance of teenagers. A child of six or seven would still wear the clothes favored by their parents. For this age group, nostalgic fashions won out; Sears's Winnie-the-Pooh line, introduced in 1965, mingled an old-fashioned look with modern easy care and durability. The classic styles favored by the Kennedy mothers also won widespread acceptance. The short skirts of the mini era were translated very successfully into clothing for toddlers and small girls, even while they were controversial choices for teenagers and adults.

Clothing for older children, especially teenagers, became increasingly troublesome for parents, manufacturers, and retailers. For many parents, the confusing smorgasbord of youth fashion offered few acceptable choices. Mod styles; surfing styles; and the exotic, hippie-style looks of the late 1960s, with their countercultural association with sex, drugs, political protest, and rock 'n' roll, made many parents and teachers highly uncomfortable.

The front line of defense against outrageous teenage dress was the school dress code. Schools added forbidden items to the dress code constantly, it seemed, and shifting standards made enforcement difficult. Boys' hairstyles that seemed long in 1966 were laughably short by 1970, when even some male principals had long hair and sideburns. In 1966, many schools dictated that hemlines could be no shorter than one inch (two and a half centimeters) above the knee and forbade girls to wear trousers; by 1969, skirts were so short that pants were a relief. By the early 1970s, dress codes had largely been abandoned as antiquated and unenforceable.

The other major issue in children's clothing was that of gender stereotyping. The women's liberation movement and the arguments over pants for women and long hair for men had heightened people's awareness of how dress expresses and influences gender roles. In the early 1970s, the idea of nonsexist, or unisex, child rearing encouraged many parents to dress their children more androgynously. Boys wore brightly colored, patterned clothing and often had long hair, for the first time since Lord Fauntleroy. Girls wore overalls and striped, knitted T-shirts once favored by boys. Blue jeans were ubiquitous for all ages, even adults.

By the mid-1970s, however, children's fashions were less experimental. Dresses reappeared in girls' wardrobes, as soft knitted styles replaced the stiff, more restrictive styles of the 1950s and 1960s. Boys and men were returning to traditional norms of masculine appearance, with shorter hair and less experimentation with color and design. Styles inspired by athletes found new favor among boys and girls, from football jerseys to Dorothy Hamill haircuts.

One of the interesting features of children's fashions in the 1970s was an emphasis on safety. The Flammable Fabrics Act of 1972 required flame-retardant fabrics for children's sleepwear. No-skid socks were introduced for beginning walkers, and protective bicycle helmets were advocated for babies and older children alike. Children were protected from more physical dangers than their parents were as children, the result of innovations in technology coupled with parental concern.

CHILDREN'S FASHIONS SINCE 1978

Three main trends mark the last quarter of the twentieth century: increasingly gender-specific clothing for infants and young children, popular culture influences from the entertainment industry reaching younger consumers, and the reemergence of dress codes and school uniforms.

From the early 1970s to the mid-1980s, feminist child-rearing philosophies had resulted in a brief reversal of the gradual trend toward more gender-specific clothing begun a century earlier. But between 1982 and 1986, several innovations signaled the end of unisex infants' clothing: a sharp increase in the practice of ear piercing for baby girls, a vogue for feminine decorative headbands (especially popular for baby girls with no hair), and the introduction of pink and blue disposable diapers. At the same time, infants' clothing departments offered more gender-specific styles and fewer neutral options, particularly in the United States.

U.S. teenagers, ca. 1950. Teenage girls at this time favored separates and boys adopted chinos.
George Marks/Retrofile/Getty Images.

While popular media had been an important influence on teenagers' clothing for decades, its impact on young children had been mitigated by their parents' tastes and preferences. The last quarter of the twentieth century witnessed not only proliferation of media (most significantly, music videos, cable television, and the Internet) but also an increase in the amount of advertising directed at children. Clothing trends inspired by Madonna, Michael Jackson, Kurt Cobain, Marilyn Manson, and dozens of other artists were adopted not only by teenage fans but by children as young as elementary school. Specialty stores for children proliferated, from adult spin-offs such as the Gap to Club Libby Lu, a chain of stores featuring makeup and clothing for preteen girls. Cultural critics blamed heightened gender distinctions and popular media culture for the premature sexualization of children and eating disorders; others decried the overemphasis on materialism that resulted in children being targeted for violent attacks because they were wearing expensive jackets or spending hundreds of dollars on designer jeans and sneakers. The institutional response to this pop culture–driven consumerism has been a return to school dress codes, even to

the extent of requiring uniforms in some school systems. Uniforms had long been associated with private schools, but in the 1990s, an increasing number of public schools in the United States adopted them, beginning with elementary schools and eventually spreading to high schools. The reasons usually given were to create a safer environment (citing violence over expensive clothing and the use of clothing to signal gang membership) and to refocus students' attention on learning, rather than on socializing.

Children's clothing in the United States has been completely transformed since its colonial beginnings. Where children were once either genderless infants or miniature adults (and in both cases reflected mainly their parents' tastes), today's children and youth are highly gendered, individually expressive juvenile consumers. In some ways, this reflects trends in adult clothing—mass consumption and planned obsolescence are part of the grown-up world as well—and in some ways children's clothing is different. Adult women and men have many more choices in dressing themselves than their children, whose wardrobe options are more gendered than any time in modern history.

Snapshot: The "Fauntleroy Plague"

The last two decades of the nineteenth century were years of tremendous change in U.S. men's and boys' fashions. While these changes were related, they neither appeared at the same time nor proceeded at the same rate. Men's clothing had been undergoing an evolution from colorful, individualistic, and expressive to drab and conformist. In the 1880s, when the business suit was gaining wide acceptance for men, the convention of elaborate, picturesque dress for boys was at its apogee, with a widespread vogue for velvet suits associated with the fictional character Cedric Errol, also known as "Little Lord Fauntleroy."

Little Lord Fauntleroy, written by English-born Frances Hodgson Burnett, was published as a serial in the children's magazine *St. Nicholas* in 1886; a book version appeared the same year. In it, Cedric and his widowed mother are summoned from the United States to England so that Cedric may meet his paternal grandfather, an earl, and take his rightful place as Lord Fauntleroy, heir to his grandfather's estate. The grandfather dislikes people from the United States and refuses to meet his daughter-in-law, insisting that the boy live with him, apart from his beloved mother. Gradually, the earl discovers that Cedric is a courageous, chivalrous boy with a strong sense of right and duty—due mainly to the influence of his U.S. mother, who is allowed to rejoin Cedric and enjoy the respect of her father-in-law. Cedric's appearance is important to the story because it is a sign of his own natural nobility and his mother's efforts to raise him as a gentleman, despite her straitened circumstances. We first meet seven-year-old Cedric running down the New York streets, in the words of a devoted servant: "An' ivvery man, woman and child lookin' afther him in his bit of black velvet skirt made out of the misthress's ould gound." Later, Cedric wins a footrace wearing a suit of cream-colored flannel, his long golden locks streaming behind him. In this way, Burnett introduces Cedric as princely yet every inch an active, energetic U.S. boy.

Velvet suits and picturesque dress had been acceptable fashion for middle-class boys for some time, and boys in the United States had already been dressing like Little Lord Fauntleroy for several years. *Peterson's* magazine described a "boy's knickerbocker suit of black velvet … trimmed with fur" in 1865. During the 1880s, cavalier suits (seventeenth-century-style suits in black velvet) were among the most popular styles for boys from the ages of four to eight. An 1885 photograph of Burnett's son Vivian in a cavalier suit was sent to illustrator Reginald Birch as a model for Cedric Errol.

The book was eventually translated into twelve languages and sold over one million copies in English. An important factor in its popularity was the 1888 stage adaptation. A New York reviewer called it "an ideal picture of childlife," and another remarked on actress Elsie Leslie, the first of many women and girls to portray Cedric: "She is a lovely figure in Cedric's dainty costumes and her photograph … will be in the shop windows before too long." By the spring of 1889, the Fauntleroy mania

Theater poster, ca. 1888. The popularity of the Fauntleroy suit in the United States was in part due to the stage adaptation of Frances Hodgson Burnett's book, *Little Lord Fauntleroy*. Library of Congress Prints and Photographs Division, Theatrical Poster Collection, var 0599.

had spread throughout the country, with two New York productions, five companies in other cities, and over a dozen touring companies.

The Fauntleroy suit enjoyed its greatest popularity in the fall and winter of 1889–1890. *Godey's Lady's Book* provided a description of the style: "For small boys nothing has met with such universal favor as the Fauntleroy suit … It is usually made of black velvet or velveteen, with a broad collar and cuffs of Irish point lace, with a sash of silk passed broadly around the waist and knotted on one side." Eventually, the Fauntleroy craze subsided, and boys' fashions began to rapidly echo the conservative trend that had already gradually occurred in men's dress. Did the 1886–1890 Fauntleroy craze postpone this revolution by a few years, or accelerate it?

Consider that acceptance of the Fauntleroy suit was not entirely universal. The boys and fathers of the United States had not been polled. Newspapers carried rumors of boys deliberately ruining their velvet finery. There is even one story of an eight-year-old in Iowa who burned down the family barn to protest his mother buying him a Little Lord Fauntleroy suit. When the *New York Times* polled four hundred boys in 1895 about the best books for children, the list included *Ivanhoe*, *The Three Musketeers*, and several works by Dickens—but no Frances Hodgson Burnett. Perhaps even more telling is the fate of Little Lord Fauntleroy when the boys of 1888 reached manhood. By the 1920s, "Little Lord Fauntleroy" had become a synonym for a pretty, effeminate mama's boy. The Fauntleroy suit also underwent a change in definition. In 1889, the name denoted a very specific style, made of velvet and featuring a lace collar and a broad sash. By 1910, the term was used to describe velvet suits in general; eventually, it became a generic label for dressy suits with fancy collars. Apparently, the Burnett character and the clothes he inspired provided a focal point for rejecting picturesque clothing for boys. Ironically, Burnett—and many of her readers—saw Cedric as an ideal: a mother's perfect son. *Little Lord Fauntleroy* is the story of the power of a mother's influence on her child. It was mothers who brought their children to see the play and mothers who created or bought velvet suits for their sons.

The 1880s witnessed the return of fathers to the nursery. After two generations of women's domination of the home, the opinions and influence of the father grew in importance, especially concerning the raising of boys. Articles on boys' fashions began to take fathers' preferences into account. An 1887 article in *Godey's* advocated sailor suits for preschool boys instead of kilt suits, which "father and boy dislike." With their own sartorial questions settled with the acceptance of the business suit, fathers may have seen cavalier suits in a different light than mothers. The Fauntleroy craze, which at an earlier time would have been just one more brief fashion, was instead the last straw. Unknowingly, Frances Hodgson Burnett may have provided the catalyst that translated the new image of the U.S. man into the new, more masculine image of the U.S. boy.

REFERENCES AND FURTHER READING

Burnett, Frances Hodgson. *Little Lord Fauntleroy*. New York: E. P. Dutton, 1962.

Burnett, Vivian. *The Romantick Lady*. New York: Charles Scribner's Sons, 1927.

Paoletti, Jo B. "Clothes Make the Boy: 1880–1910." *Dress* 9 (1983): 16–20.

Thwaite, Ann. *Waiting for the Party*. New York: Charles Scribner's Sons, 1974.

A Version of this article appeared as Paoletti, Jo B. "The Fauntleroy Plague" in *Historic Fashions of Women and Children*, http://www.sallyqueenassociates.com/fauntleroy.htm, 9 October 2002. By kind permission of Sally Queen Associates.

References and Further Reading

Cable, Mary. *The Little Darlings: A History of Child Rearing in America*. New York: Scribner, 1975.

Caller, Alma A. *Our Baby: How to Dress and Feed It*. Boston: Charles A. Marsh, 1886.

Calvert, Karin Lee Fishbeck. *Children in the House: The Material Culture of Early Childhood, 1600–1900*. Boston: Northeastern University Press, 1992.

Chudacoff, Howard P. *Children at Play: An American History*. New York: New York University Press, 2007.

Cross, Gary S. *The Cute and the Cool: Wondrous Innocence and Modern American Children's Culture*. Oxford: Oxford University Press, 2004.

Earle, Alice Morse. *Child Life in Colonial Days*. Bowie, MD: Heritage Classic, 1997.

Ewing, Elizabeth. *History of Children's Costume*. New York: Scribner, 1977.

Fass, Paula S., and Mary Ann Mason. *Childhood in America*. New York: New York University Press, 2000.

Griffith, John Price. *The Care of the Baby*. Philadelphia: W. B. Saunders, 1895.

Griffith, Nancy. *Wee Warriors and Playtime Patriots: Children's Military Regalia, Civil War through the Vietnam Era*. Atglen, PA: Schiffer, 2001.

Hardy, Kay. *Sewing for the Baby*. New York: M. Barrows and Company, 1944.

Hiner, N. Ray, and Joseph M. Hawes. *Growing Up in America: Children in Historical Perspective*. Urbana: University of Illinois Press, 1985.

Illick, Joseph E. *American Childhoods*. Philadelphia: University of Pennsylvania Press, 2002.

Macleod, David I. *The Age of the Child: Children in America, 1890–1920*. New York: Twayne, 1998.

Picken, Mary Brooks. *Maternity and Infants' Garments*. Scranton, PA: Women's Institute of Domestic Arts and Sciences, 1921.

Reinier, Jacqueline S. *From Virtue to Character: American Childhood, 1775–1850*. New York: Twayne, 1996.

Rose, Clare. *Children's Clothes since 1750*. New York: Drama Book Publishers, 1989.

Warwick, Edward. *Early North American Dress*. New York: Benjamin Blom, 1965.

West, Elliott, and Paula Petrik. *Small Worlds: Children & Adolescents in America, 1850–1950*. Lawrence: University Press of Kansas, 1992.

Worrell, Estelle Ansley. *Children's Costume in America, 1607–1910*. New York: Scribner, 1980.

Jo Barraclough Paoletti

Aging

C lothing serves as a source of ego support, self-image enhancement, social acceptability, and personality expression throughout a person's life. Problems occur, however, when appropriate clothing is not available or marketed to certain segments of the population, particularly older persons and those with a disability. Design problems may relate to the fit, cut, function, and appropriateness of the item(s), while marketing problems may relate to communicating the product(s) to the consumer. Fashion reflects the zeitgeist (spirit of the times), including the social, economic, political, technological, and artistic expressions of an era: It reflects a society's prevalent expression of its culture through such diverse consumer products as clothing, cars, and electronics. In postindustrial society, fashion helps process a barrage of information about consumer products, including beauty, clothing, and accessories. In the latter half of the twentieth century, fashion houses and retailers focused on youth. At the same time, people lived longer and maintained a more active lifestyle. In the early twenty-first century, the changing clothing needs of older persons began to be realized by clothing designers and retailers. They began to consider these consumers' lifestyle and changing physical needs as they selected fabric and designed, labeled, marketed, and sold their products.

DEMOGRAPHIC AND PSYCHOGRAPHIC TRENDS

Market researchers use demographic and psychographic studies to classify groups within a population into market segments to understand consumer needs and desires. They use statistical studies of a population relative to its size, density, distribution, vital statistics, and lifestyle indicators to segment groups within the population. An aging population is changing demographics in the twenty-first century because of increased life expectancy and slowing growth rates. The U.S. population was about one hundred fifty million in 1950, had reached almost three hundred

million by 2005, and is projected to be over three hundred sixty million by 2030. A growth rate of 1.7 percent for 1950 to 1960 was recorded for the United States; the growth rate is projected to be 0.9 percent for 2000 to 2010 and 0.8 percent for 2020 to 2030. The population of Canada was about fourteen million in 1950, close to thirty-three million in 2005, and is projected to be over thirty-nine million by 2030. A growth rate of 2.7 percent for 1950 to 1960 was recorded for Canada; the growth rate is projected to be 0.9 percent for 2000 to 2010 and 0.6 percent for 2020 to 2030. In 2007, the United States was the third most populous country, behind China and India, whereas Canada ranked thirty-sixth.

Following World War II, a dramatic increase in population between 1946 and 1964 created a *population cohort*, or group of people who experienced similar events within a time period, known as the *baby boomers*. They were followed by the *baby bust* cohort, the smaller number of people born between 1965 and 1976, and *baby boom echo*, baby boomer children born between 1976 and 2000. Since the rise of baby boomers, many sociocultural changes have occurred: More women are working outside the home, postponing childbearing, and having fewer children. The participation of women in the workforce expanded greatly in the 1970s and 1980s and has continued to increase, although more gradually.

Data from the U.S. Census Bureau graphically illustrate the 2005 population pyramids and 2025 projected pyramids for the United States and Canada. For the United States, the 2005 midyear population of people fifty-five years and older was sixty-seven million; the projected population for 2025 is more than one hundred four million. For Canada, the 2005 midyear population of people fifty-five years and older was close to eight million; the projected population for 2025 is over thirteen million. By 2014, minorities will constitute more of the U.S. labor force: Hispanics, almost 16 percent; Asians, 2.8 percent; and African Americans, 1.6 percent.

Baby boomers have been and continue to be a major cohort that has shaped both U.S. and Canadian cultures in many ways, including fashion and dress. An aging population and an increase in eating out have led to increased body girth; concurrently, there is a greater interest in low-fat food and fitness activities. Consumer lifestyle trends place a value on time, including personal and family time; comfort, including more casual business attire; home, including cocooning, entertaining, and working at home; and technology, including e-commerce. Fashion houses and retailers must consider lifestyle factors as they design, develop, and market their fashion products.

BODY CHANGES AND PHYSICAL LIMITATIONS

Age-related anatomical, physiological, and pathological changes occur as a person ages, leading to dissatisfaction in the design and fit of clothing. Major body changes include a reduction in height, spinal curvature, and forward rounding of the shoulders, creating a less erect posture. This causes a shortened front length and longer back length as the back becomes rounder and is accompanied by the neck angling forward, an increase in waist girth, and abdominal protrusion. Other changes include a flatter derrière, flabby upper arms, sagging breasts, dry skin, facial wrinkles,

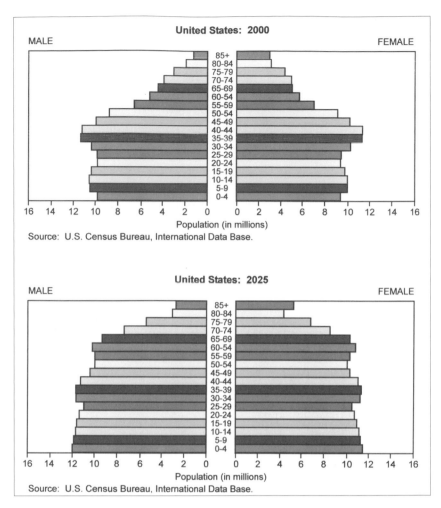

The U.S. population was about one hundred fifty million in 1950, almost three hundred million by 2005, and is projected to be over three hundred sixty million by 2030. Courtesy of U.S. Census Bureau.

droopy eyelids, double chin, and crepey neck. These changes are caused by shrinkage of the vertebral column, loss of muscle tone, shifts in fat distribution, loss of skin elasticity, and less production of oil. In addition, the hair thins and changes color, age spots increase, and dilated blood vessels become more noticeable. Body changes occur gradually and affect people individually to broaden market segmentation in the apparel industry.

Problems in donning and doffing, or putting on and taking off, clothing may be caused by physical disabilities that occur as a person ages, leading to limited range of motion, poor coordination, muscular weakness, and the use of assistive devices such as wheelchairs, walkers, scooters, canes, or braces. Missing body parts, loss of vision, and incontinence, or the lack of control of the bowel or bladder, also affect clothing design.

MEETING CLOTHING NEEDS OF OLDER PERSONS: BACKGROUND

In the mid-twentieth century, occupational and physical therapists, clothing designers, and home economists applied their knowledge of body mechanics, functional limitations, clothing design and construction, and social psychology of dress to developing clothing solutions for older persons and those with a disability. *Disability* is a physical impairment that results in a handicap or decreases a person's ability to function at the highest level. *Handicap* is a broad term referring to physical, social, cultural, emotional, mental, financial, or educational constraints that limit a person's functional level. Many people have socially acceptable, correctable physical handicaps, including vision problems requiring glasses, hearing losses requiring hearing aid(s), or dental problems requiring tooth replacement. Functional and fashionable clothing is necessitated when a person's activities of daily living (ADL), such as donning and doffing clothing, are limited by medical or age-related conditions.

In 1982, the United Nations adopted the International Plan of Action on Aging in an effort to assist governments and civil society to deal effectively with aging citizens. This was followed in 1991 by adoption of the U.N. Principles for Older Persons, including independence, participation, care, self-fulfillment, and dignity to enhance the quality of life in the years added to life. The United Nations designated 1999 the International Year of Older Persons (IYOP). In 1997, the U.N. IYOP Clothing Initiatives Committee was formed with representatives from the United Nations, the International Textile and Apparel Association (ITAA), the

Sporting Goods Manufacturers Association (SGMA), and the American Association of Family and Consumer Sciences.

The U.N. IYOP Clothing Initiatives Committee actively worked to communicate the clothing needs of older persons to key fashion industries and the public. Design criteria were developed for the Active & Ageless consumer that related to body changes, including fit, design, fabrications, labeling, and care. *Active & Ageless*, trademarked by SGMA, was developed to promote active aging and describe consumers based on lifestyle rather than age. The SGMA Sports Apparel Products Council adopted the design criteria in recognition of older consumers' changing needs and the desire to build inclusive brands. In 1998 and 1999, the ITAA Design Exhibitions included a plus-fifty-five design category. A 1999 symposium and fashion show in New York City targeted baby boomers: Symposium speakers were from the United Nations, the fashion press and industry, academia, e-commerce, government agencies, marketing and senior organizations, and also featured older athletes and models. Designs from the 1998 and 1999 ITAA Design Exhibitions were featured in a Boston Museum of Science exhibit on aging that opened in April 2000 and traveled to six cities over four years. In 2000, the committee participated in a clothing workshop and fashion show during an international rural aging conference in West Virginia that represented forty nations on six continents.

MERCHANDISING CLOTHING TO OLDER CONSUMERS

The baby boomer cohort was youth obsessed as they aged; therefore, as boomers tried to maintain their youth, many firms skewed their businesses to youth. As baby boomers reached age sixty, this practice turned away key customers. They wanted to look fashionable but were unable to find age-appropriate clothing. Design houses and retailers responded to the loss of this customer base by opening retail concepts for mature customers with classic fashions or reinstating previous merchandising formulas. Designs for older consumers should focus on lifestyle rather than age and look good on a mature body. The challenge is to design fashionable clothing that is not geared to the young adult market. As the population advances in age, design features that accommodate functional limitations will need to be incorporated, possibly through *universal design*, that is, functional, fashionable designs that work for a wide range of people.

CONSUMER-CENTRIC DESIGN MODELS

Design houses and retailers can employ a consumer-centric design model to create and market clothing for older consumers. The Functional, Expressive, and Aesthetic (FEA) consumer needs model aids in the development of clothing design criteria and does not distinguish between functional or fashion design. The Clothing Purchase Decision (CPD) model includes price, appearance, and care. Appearance factors are related to dress and the body and include the functional, aesthetic, and symbolic values of dress and the Forms, Expression, and Motions (FEM) of the body.

The Apparel Product Appearance Factors (APAF) model was created by merging the FEA and CPD models. The consumer is at the model's core in the context of clothing and culture in relation to dress and the body. The FEA and CPD factors were combined, resulting in the following FEA/FEM factors: Functional, including comfort, protection, mobility, fit, and independence; Expressive, including fashion, group affiliation, beliefs, values, roles, status, and self-esteem; Aesthetic, including fit, quality, design, body/garment relation, color, style, and fabric; Forms, including body size and shape, posture, and variations from the norm; Expressions, including skin and hair color, eye color and shape, and hair texture; and Motions, including a person's gait, range of motion, and use of limbs and assistive devices.

FIT AND SIZING ISSUES

U.S. apparel sizing was developed to produce and market apparel for a mass market. Body dimensions are used to denote size proportions for menswear; women's size codes do not. The first U.S. sizing system developed for women was based on 1940 data of primarily young, single, white women, underrepresenting those over fifty-five. A second sizing standard, PS 42-70, used the same database, simplifying size categories to reduce height variation. Age differences were implied by size categories: Juniors', young fashion figures; Misses', average adults; and Women's, mature figures. Juniors' and Women's sizes lead to problems for petite older women and younger women with a mature figure. Complications also arise because manufacturers generate their own sizing specifications to differentiate their brand or use *vanity sizing*, smaller size designations for higher-priced garments.

Sizing for older women began to be considered by the apparel industry only in the 1990s. The Civilian American and European Surface Anthropometry Resource (CAESAR) project features collaboration between the automotive, aerospace, furniture, and apparel industries to develop a body measurement database for designed products. Between 1997 and 2002, three-dimensional body scans and forty body measurements were taken on approximately twenty-five hundred U.S. and Canadian men and women and two thousand European men and women, eighteen to sixty-five years old. In 2002, SizeUSA was initiated with a goal of collecting 10,000 body measurements of representative adults using body scanning. A *body scanner* uses cameras with white light or lasers in a 360-degree view to record a cloud of body measurement data points; linear measurements can be extracted and the rotated body shape observed on a computer screen.

In 1990, the American Society for Testing and Materials (ASTM) surveyed 6,657 women age fifty-five and older, collecting 57 measurements, resulting in the 1994 ASTM national body measurement database. A range of consumers could be accommodated by segmenting the market with body-type sizing, using the ASTM database and developing a sizing system with fewer sizes than the current sizing system, and employing custom fit. To reduce frustration with the present chaotic sizing system, the International Standards Organization proposes using a body pictogram, or line drawing, and specific body measurements to eliminate individual size codes in different countries.

DESIGN AND STYLING

A viewer's perception of another person's body is affected by the clothing worn. Clothing can be used to create illusions that enhance the body, bringing it closer to the cultural ideal of beauty. Apparel designers can design clothing to make the body appear larger, smaller, taller, or shorter; conceal or reveal the body; and allow or impede movement. This can be done by manipulating

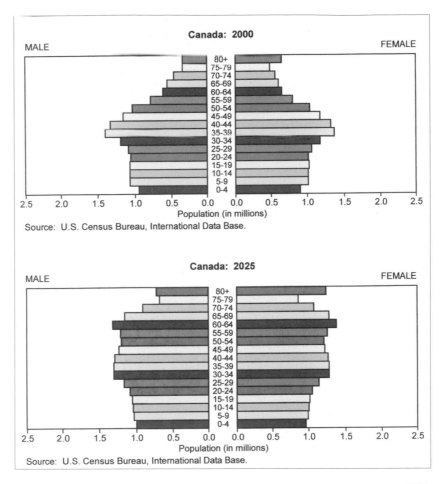

Canada: 2000

MALE   FEMALE

80+
75-79
70-74
65-69
60-64
55-59
50-54
45-49
40-44
35-39
30-34
25-29
20-24
15-19
10-14
5-9
0-4

2.5   2.0   1.5   1.0   0.5   0.0   0.0   0.5   1.0   1.5   2.0   2.5
                Population (in millions)
Source: U.S. Census Bureau, International Data Base.

Canada: 2025

MALE   FEMALE

80+
75-79
70-74
65-69
60-64
55-59
50-54
45-49
40-44
35-39
30-34
25-29
20-24
15-19
10-14
5-9
0-4

2.5   2.0   1.5   1.0   0.5   0.0   0.0   0.5   1.0   1.5   2.0   2.5
                Population (in millions)
Source: U.S. Census Bureau, International Data Base.

The population of Canada was about fourteen million in 1950, close to thirty-three million in 2005, and is projected to be over thirty-nine million by 2030. Courtesy of U.S. Census Bureau.

design elements such as the silhouette; structural and style lines of the garment; and fabric/trim color, texture, and print. A systems analysis approach is helpful in developing industry product design specifications by analyzing the proposed use of the product(s), identifying the requirements of all design components, producing a design, and incorporating feedback into the design process.

Garment styling occurs when a design team puts together a seasonal clothing line. Decisions need to be made, including those regarding fabric and trim in relation to personal coloring, seasonal colors and weights, care, and end use; garment openings and closures relative to donning and doffing; structural and design style lines; and garment fit in relation to body contour, ease allowances, and body movement. Safety issues and use of assistive devices also should be considered for this market segment.

Ease, the difference between the body and garment measurements, allows for body movement and design effect: *Basic ease* is the difference between the body and pattern that accommodates body movement, while *design ease* is extra allowance that creates a specific design. Ease allowances range from tight to basic, relaxed, or generous depending on the backgrounds of the target consumers, or intended users, because people from different racial and ethnic backgrounds have different preferences for the garment/body relationship in regard to fit. This becomes more important as demographics change.

Older people desire to be independent in dressing; as people age, their range of motion may be more limited. Designers should consider garment openings and closures to accommodate this need. Back openings may be difficult for women who have limited range of motion. Pull-on and pullover styles, front openings, and side openings are easier to don and doff for both sexes. Garment fasteners should be selected wisely because small fasteners are difficult for people with hand limitations. Possible choices include larger buttons, shank buttons, easy-to-use buttonholes, zippers with large zipper pulls, wrap-style dresses, pretied neck ties or bows with hook-and-loop closures, prebuttoned cuffs using elastic thread, and hook-and-loop shoe closures.

Body contours, such as size, shape, proportion, and posture, affect clothing design for men and women. Because the waistline becomes more prominent, garments that are looser at the waist are more comfortable and flattering. A protruding tummy can be camouflaged with no-waistline-seam dresses and pants or skirts with trouser tucks or pleats. Pants can be designed with a full elastic waistline, a front band with back elastic that is visible or hidden in a band, or side button tabs to adjust the waistband. As people age, the derrière becomes flatter and should be considered in pant development. To accommodate a dropped bustline, dresses and tops can be designed with bodice gathers, dart tucks, dart pleats, or released darts. Postural changes can be camouflaged by designing tops with longer back length and upper-back yokes.

Sleeve designs may allow for unimpeded range of motion by using kimono sleeves, dropped armholes, raglan sleeves, action pleats, and gussets. Changes in the upper arms can be covered by using elbow-length or longer sleeves. Temperature management can be achieved with appropriate fabric selection and layering short-sleeve or sleeveless shells with short- or long-sleeve tops.

Safety should be considered in the design of clothing for this market segment. Pant legs that are moderate in width and length help to prevent falls. Fitted long sleeves or those with controlled fullness will decrease sleeve flammability and are less likely to cause a fall. Long tie belts or neck scarves should be avoided. Pockets can be included in many garment categories as aids for persons with limited mobility and should be positioned and designed to avoid the possibility of getting caught and causing a fall.

Wheelchair users need pants to be adapted for a seated figure, including long back and short front crotch length. Easy-to-reach pockets can be included on the front or pant leg. For people with incontinence, pants with a full waistband and a drop seat facilitate toileting.

FABRICATION

Fabrication involves all components and processes required to assemble a garment. Clothing systems should be designed for maximum comfort, including the fabric and garment design. The outer fashion fabric is the most visible element and should be selected because of its color, texture, weight, and hand in relation to the target consumer and end use. *Fabric hand* is the tactile quality, including the feel, softness or firmness, thermal character, and drapeability, of a fabric. Other components, such as lining or trim, should be selected because they coordinate with the care requirements, fashion fabric, companion pieces, or because they reflect the zeitgeist. Warmth and moisture management are important considerations for older consumers.

Color is the first thing consumers see when they shop for clothing. It is an important aspect of a garment, as it should enhance the person's coloring. As coloring changes over time, a person may need to change the color palette worn previously. Softer colors, such as pastels, work well for many people. The following colors can be problematic: brown, if it calls attention to brown spots; reddish-blue and purple, if dilated blood vessels show through thin skin; orange near the face, if eyelids have reddened; beige and some grays, if they are too close to the person's coloring. Bright colors may be more flattering as accents because a person's coloring changes to a softer palette as they age. For this reason, makeup that once was suitable may no longer be flattering. Color has great implications for the apparel and beauty industries for both sexes.

Texture, weight, and hand are important textile qualities because these can be used to enhance a person visually and make him or her more comfortable physically. Shiny fabrics should be avoided near the face because they may reflect the light and call attention to wrinkles. As people age, they may be more comfortable with lighter-weight but warmer fabrics. Fabrics with smooth textures will be more comfortable for people whose skin is dry and easily irritated.

LABELING

Labels are any printed elements that are sewn into, printed on, or hanging from a garment; used in a store; or used for garment care.

Because of age-related eye changes, older persons prefer easy-to-read labels. High contrast between the font and background and a large, easy-to-read font facilitate reading garment labels and hang tags. Garments should be labeled clearly with all necessary information about garment size, fiber content, care, and special styling details. It is better if permanent garment labels are smooth and nonirritating. Care labels should be easy to locate within the garment.

When good lighting is used on retail sales floors and in dressing rooms, older consumers can locate pertinent information easily. In addition, older persons can determine garment care instructions and read directions related to laundry products, at-home dry-cleaning products, and laundry equipment when home and commercial laundry areas are well lit. Garment care-related product package designers should accommodate this growing market segment.

CARE

Care factors that need to be considered by designers, manufacturers, and retailers who are targeting older consumers include performance and ease of care, which relates to the cost and amount of time and effort required for garment upkeep. In making this assessment, garment fiber content and recommended care need to be assessed. Easy-care garments and those that require little or no ironing are preferred by many consumers.

Performance relates to how well the garment will perform over its life. Consumers may be willing to spend more or less on a garment in anticipation of the cost-benefit ratio, including the cost of care in relation to where and how often the garment will be worn. A person may be willing to spend more for a shirt or blouse that has a no-iron finish because the garment will be a staple wardrobe item and will require less time to care for it. Garment care design considerations include using fasteners, trims, underlinings, linings, and interfacings that are compatible with the fashion fabric so that the most desirable method of care can be recommended. Soil-repellent finishes may be desirable on clothing items such as shirts, ties, and pants for persons with a disability who have difficulty holding eating utensils steadily and may spill food. For those with incontinence, it is desirable to use fabrics that can be laundered in hot water. People with limited vision may need assistance with clothing care, including the use of marking systems for clothing items, laundry aids such as sock fasteners, and a computer-based storage and retrieval system to assist in wardrobe coordination. Garment care product designers should consider the color of laundry detergent in relation to the color of the pour cap for low-vision older consumers.

COMMUNICATING FASHION TO OLDER CONSUMERS

Into the early twenty-first century, very few design houses and retailers were willing to use older models to show customers aging. That trend gradually changed as leading-edge baby boomers reached their sixties. The tide has shifted from a youth obsession to a more inclusive focus where fashion is presented as a state of mind and lifestyle. Fashion and lifestyle magazines have offered fashion advice since their inception. *Harper's Bazaar* publishes monthly age-appropriate fashions for women from twenty to

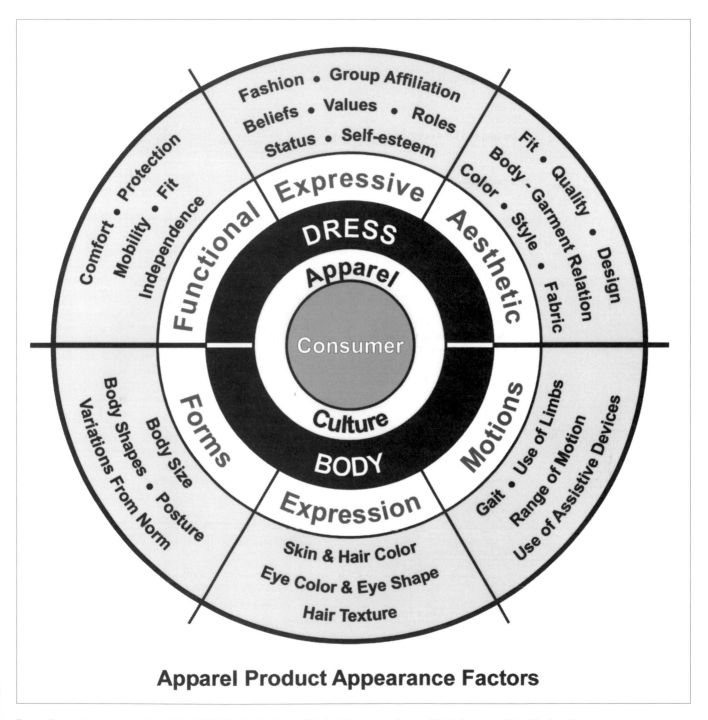

Apparel Product Appearance Factors

Twenty-first-century merchandising in the United States: the Apparel Product Appearance Factors Model. Courtesy of Nora MacDonald.

seventy-plus. *Vogue* extended the range of its annual age fashion feature in 2006 to encompass women from age twenty through ninety-plus. *More*, a lifestyle publication, features a real-people model search for women over forty.

Many retailers follow a multichannel marketing approach by offering goods, services, and support to consumers using two or more distribution channels, such as stores, catalogs, online shopping, kiosks, and trunk shows, to facilitate shopping by older consumers. This consumer can be accommodated by having senior discount days, holding fit seminars, arranging for alterations, and offering styling services. Retailers can enhance their physical accommodations by having seating, well-lit dressing and checkout areas, and installing well-placed, full-length mirrors. Training sessions for employees can cover appropriate communication with consumers of all ages and abilities as well as design features for people who use a wheelchair or have gross- and fine-motor impairments or visual limitations.

FUTURE DIRECTIONS

As the population ages, the challenge is to seek readily available clothing that is both fashionable and functional for people of all ages and abilities in a socially responsible and sustainable environment. Manufacturers need to adopt an international sizing system that more accurately reflects the population and to develop clothing with universal design features. Active sportswear and textiles that have been developed for technical applications increasingly will influence the design of ready-to-wear clothing. Smart textiles will incorporate nanotechnology to color textiles; weave fiber-optic cables or electric wires into fabric to connect personal electronics or monitor vital signs; improve stretch, colorfastness, breathability, and antibacterial qualities; impregnate vitamins into yarns; and more. Technology will become more commonplace in clothing design for people of all ages, including virtual body-scanning technology and motion studies to refine fit and function; Global Positioning Systems (GPS) incorporated into accessories for tracking people; inflatable air channels for temperature maintenance; handheld reading devices that convert text to speech and tactile images incorporated into computers for people who are blind; and more.

References and Further Reading

Bye, Elizabeth, Karen L. LaBat, and Marilyn DeLong. "Analysis of Body Measurement Systems for Apparel." *Clothing and Textiles Research Journal* 24, no. 2 (2006): 66–79.

Fiore, Ann Marie, and Patricia Anne Kimle. *Understanding Aesthetics: For the Merchandising and Design Professional*. New York: Fairchild, 1997.

Flügel, J.C. *The Psychology of Clothes*. New York: International Universities Press, 1930.

Frings, Gini Stephens. *Fashion: From Concept to Consumer*. 8th ed. Upper Saddle River, NJ: Prentice Hall, 2005.

Goldsberry, Ellen, Soyeon Shim, and Naomi Reich. "Women 55 Years and Older: Part I. Current Body Measurements as Contrasted to the PS 42-70 Data." *Clothing and Textiles Research Journal* 14, no. 2 (1996): 108–120.

Goldsberry, Ellen, Soyeon Shim, and Naomi Reich. "Women 55 Years and Older: Part II. Overall Satisfaction and Dissatisfaction with the Fit of Ready-to-Wear." *Clothing and Textiles Research Journal* 14, no. 2 (1996): 121–132.

Hoffman, Adeline M. "Clothing." In *The Daily Needs and Interests of Older People*, edited by Adeline M. Hoffman, 286–299. Springfield, IL: Charles C. Thomas, 1970.

Hoffman, Adeline M. *Clothing for the Handicapped, the Aged, and Other People with Special Needs*. Springfield, IL: Charles C. Thomas, 1979.

Kaiser, Susan B. *The Social Psychology of Clothing: Symbolic Appearances in Context*. 2nd ed. New York: Fairchild, 1997.

Kallal, M. Jo, Sandra Keiser, Nora MacDonald, and Maria Stefan. "The Potential for Emerging Technologies to Positively Impact the Apparel Needs of the Plus-55 Consumer." In *Proceedings EASYtex 2002: 1st International Conference on Clothing and Textiles for Disabled and Elderly People*, edited by H. Meinander. Tampere, Finland: VTT, 2002.

Karimzadeh, Marc. "Youth Isn't Everything: Brands Chase Boomers with the Power to Spend." *Women's Wear Daily* 192, no. 54 (12 September 2006): 1, 30.

Lamb, Jane M., and M. Jo Kallal. "A Conceptual Framework for Apparel Design." *Clothing and Textiles Research Journal* 10, no. 2 (1992): 42–47.

Langner, Lawrence. *The Importance of Wearing Clothes*. New York: Hastings House, 1959.

MacDonald, Nora M., Pisnu Bua-Iam, and Ranjit K Majumder. "Clothing Purchase Decisions and Social Participation: An Empirical Investigation of U. S. and U. K. Rehabilitation Clients." *Journal of Rehabilitation* 60, no. 3 (1994): 44–50.

MacDonald, Nora M., Maria D. Stefan, M. Jo Kallal, and Sandra Keiser. "Bridging the Divide: Diverse Entities Work to Meet the Apparel Needs of Older Consumers." In *Proceedings EASYtex 2002: 1st International Conference on Clothing and Textiles for Disabled and Elderly People*, edited by H. Meinander. Tampere, Finland: VTT, 2002.

Newman, Cathy. "Dreamweavers." *National Geographic* 203, no. 1 (2003): 50–73.

Salusso, Carol J., John J. Borkowski, Naomi Reich, and Ellen Goldsberry. "An Alternative Approach to Sizing Apparel for Women 55 and Older." *Clothing and Textiles Research Journal* 24, no. 2 (2006): 96–111.

Schofield, Nancy A., Susan P. Ashdown, Janet Hethorn, Karen LaBat, and Carol J. Salusso. "Improving Pant Fit for Women 55 and Older through an Exploration of Two Pant Shapes." *Clothing and Textiles Research Journal* 24, no. 2 (2006): 147–160.

Toossi, Mitra. "Labor Force Projections to 2014: Retiring Boomers." *Monthly Labor Review* (2005): 25–44.

United Nations. "International Year of Older Persons." http:/www.un.org/esa/socdev/iyop (accessed 31 May 2000).

U.S. Census Bureau. "IDB Summary Demographic Data for Canada." http://www.census.gov/cgi-bin/ipc/idbsum.pl?cty=CA (accessed June 2007).

U.S. Census Bureau. "IDB Summary Demographic Data for United States." http://www.census.gov/cgi-bin/ipc/idbsum.pl?cty=US (accessed June 2007).

Watkins, Susan M. *Clothing: The Portable Environment*. 2nd ed. Ames: Iowa State University Press, 1995.

Nora M. MacDonald

See also Introduction to Demographic and Social Influences; Care of Dress.

Gender

Gender remains the basic distinction in dress, currently and historically, in U.S. and Canadian society as well as others. Masculinity or femininity is reflected in the presentation of dress by the individual and is categorically interpreted by others according to societal norms. Although many people use the terms interchangeably, *sex* and *gender* do not have the same meaning. *Gender* is determined psychologically, socially, and culturally and refers to acceptable behavior and dress for males and females. Appropriate male and female behavior varies according to time and place. *Sex* refers to the biological aspects of maleness and femaleness. Primary sex characteristics are the anatomical traits essential to reproduction. This would seem to be a clear-cut means of identifying the sex of an individual; however, some babies are born *intersexed*, a broad medical term used to classify people with some mixture of male and female biological characteristics. Parents would work in consultation with a physician to assign the child as female or male. Clothing would be a secondary way of reinforcing this identity. Secondary sex characteristics distinguish one sex from another. These are physical traits such as breast development, quality of the voice, distribution of facial and body hair, and skeletal form. These secondary sex characteristics can, along with dress, be used to identify gender.

A body ideal consists of a size, age, and a combination of physical attributes that society deems to be the most desirable for each gender. The current body ideal for women in the United States and Canada is very different from what it was in the early twentieth century. The ideal for early-twenty-first-century women is a slim, youthful, athletic, and well-toned physique. Unfortunately, the possibility of taking this conformity too far by some young women can be witnessed in the rise of disordered eating and exercising, including *anorexia nervosa* and *bulimia*, eating disorders characterized by an unrealistic fear of weight gain. At the beginning of the twentieth century, fashion dictated a well-corseted but nonetheless rounded physique. Changes in body ideals are an essential part of fashion change for both men and women. Men of the early 2000s also aspire to the ideal of being tall, youthful, attractive, muscular, and well toned.

CRITICAL ANALYSIS OF THE BODY AND DRESS

In North American culture, a slim waist for women and men is emphasized along with large breasts and hips for women and broad shoulders and slender hips for men. These ideals of beauty are similar to ancient Greek body ideals of perfect proportions. Minoan artifacts, which date from 2900 to 1150 B.C.E., depict men and women with extremely small waists. Some scholars speculate that this could have been the result of artistic convention, while other authorities suggest that young boys around the age of twelve or fourteen wore belts that constricted the waist. These constrictions of the waist may have begun with men and boys and were adapted by women during later Minoan periods. There have been other periods in history when men adopted the corset to achieve the fashionable silhouette of the time. Manipulation of the body to achieve a fashionable silhouette is not unique to either gender.

Given the persistence in Western culture of an ideal of perfect body proportions, U.S. obsession with the body comes as no surprise. Common phrases regarding the body include "one can never be too rich or too thin"; "no pain, no gain"; "thin-buttoned"; and "tall, dark, and handsome." Photographs of bodies depicted in magazines are often modified by using computers or airbrushing, allowing models to appear unrealistically beautiful,

A suit from the Jean-Louis Scherrer Spring/Summer collection, United States, 1983. In the 1980s the style of professional women's dress in the U.S. corporate world copied the masculine shape, which symbolized the idea of having an equal status with men. Hulton Archive/Getty Images.

thin, and blemish and wrinkle free. Body doubles in popular movies mean that the viewer assumes they are seeing one person when in reality they are seeing two or more. The models themselves cannot attain this ideal. Few people can. Some models have recently admitted to resorting to near-starvation or binge-and-purge eating to lose weight. This is largely because clothing, in order to sell, must have "hanger appeal" and fashion models have become walking hangers. Many individuals try to approximate ideals through diet, exercise, and sometimes plastic surgery. Although these ideals are prevalent in North American culture, the research of nutritionist Sheila Parker and others has indicated that white and African American adolescent girls do not have the same response to these social pressures. African American girls receive positive feedback from their community when they develop a style of their own, while the white group gets support for their success in copying the difficult-to-reach ideal.

GENDER AS A SOCIAL CONSTRUCTION

Gender, and by extension dress, is a cultural and social construction. Viewing gender as a fluid concept allows scholars studying clothing and appearance to understand gender relations as more than men and women "dressing their parts." Gendered dressing is more than complementary role-playing; power relations are inextricably involved. Jo Paoletti and Carrol Kregloh have argued that women's adoption of pants in the twentieth century, therefore, represents a redefinition of femininity but not necessarily an adjustment in power.

That is why an examination of global cultures, current and historical, reveals wide variations in how gender is expressed through appearance. For example, there can be seeming similarity in the dress of both men and women. Subtle differences, such as head covering or shoes, along with secondary sex characteristics make a relatively subtle distinction in the dress presentation between the genders. In contrast, current veiling practices of women in some countries where Islam prevails create a sharp and defined difference between how men and women appear in their dress. In the broad Western culture as seen in the United States and Canada, fashion change has been an area where political, economic, and religious issues, as well as social roles of men and women, are reflected in gendered presentations.

Fundamental to any examination of dress is the symbolic separation of men and women through dress. The forms of gendered dress have changed over time (fabric, silhouette of clothing, colors), but the idea of gender difference has endured. Humans are socialized into appearance and dress that is either masculine or feminine, which varies historically and culturally. Gendered fashions often become examples of how tensions between genders are visibly displayed. For example, female college students in the United States were not allowed to wear pants on campus until the late 1950s to early 1960s, a change that may have been a result of the women's movement of the 1960s. Still later in the 1980s, U.S. women's dress-for-success was a symbolic and visible assertion of their ascension in the ranks of corporate America, which had always been traditionally male. John Molloy's best-selling book *Dress for Success* prescribed women's professional dress that moved away from traditional feminine symbols and more closely emulated men's business attire.

The sociologist Gregory Stone, in his classic article "Appearance and the Self," emphasizes the importance of identification of gender in order to select the appropriate language for discourse. He notes that we need not inquire to establish the other's gender, because to do so would "impugn the very gender that must be established. The knowing of the other's gender is known silently, established by appearances."

What is noticed when individuals encounter one another? Skin color, age, body language, appearance (particularly if it is perceived as different or deviating from the norm), and most critically, what is perceived as the person's sex. At least we think that we see whether an individual is male or female. In truth, what is seen is an individual's gendered appearance, which may be identified correctly or incorrectly as a sign of the sex. People fit what they experience into what they believe to be gender norms for dress. Clothing itself does not have inherent meaning; rather, it is defined both socially and culturally. For example, the Scottish kilt, traditionally worn by Scottish men, closely resembles what is called a skirt in American society. Few U.S. or Canadian men would wear a skirt or even a kilt unless they were of Scottish ethnic origin. A *skirt* is defined as a nonbifurcated garment, or one that is not divided below the waist. Members of the presidential guards in Athens, Greece, wear what look like skirts (actually a modification of the ancient toga with a belt); they are far from feminine in appearance. This uniform is a socially and culturally accepted presentation of masculinity in the Greek profession of presidential guards.

DRESS, GENDER, AND SOCIALIZATION

The response of others to gender-specific colors of attire encourages what is socially designated as gender-appropriate behavior toward that child. Stone has observed that dressing a newborn in either blue or pink in the United States begins a series of interactions. Norms governing gender-appropriate attire are powerful. Gender-specific attire enhances the internalization of expectations for gender-specific behavior. Through the subtle and frequently nonverbal interactions with children regarding both their appearance and behavior, parents either encourage or discourage certain behaviors often related to dress, which leads to a child's development of his or her gender identity. When a boy decides he wants to play dress-up in skirts or makeup or a daughter chooses to play aggressive sports only with the boys, parents may redirect the child's behavior into a more socially acceptable and gender-specific activity. Even the most liberal and open-minded parent can be threatened if a child does not conform to appropriate gender behaviors. Research has shown that children as young as two years of age classify people into gender categories based on their appearance.

Dress and gender, from a historical viewpoint, stimulate awareness of the shifts that have occurred regarding appropriate dress for boys and girls. For example, the expectation that blue is for boy babies and pink is for girl babies has not always been the case. Jo Paoletti and Carrol Kregloh have observed that, in 1918, contrary to later practice, the color rule was pink for the boy and blue for the girl. Pink was interpreted then as a stronger and more assertive color, and blue, more dainty and delicate.

As late as the 1950s, boy babies still wore white dresses despite some popularity of rompers, overalls, and footed sleepers. During the twentieth century, many more changes have been made to boys' clothing than girls'. After World War II, the color preferences for boys and girls reversed. When a girl baby is lacking hair,

and women's dress continued to follow an elaborate set of rules or expectations. As a result, men assumed a highly restricted dress code with the decline of the European aristocracy and the advent of industrial capitalism. Thus, distinctions between men's and women's dress increased in the nineteenth century, a situation that continued into the twentieth century.

During the early twentieth century through the 1950s, men generally wore clothing limited to angular design lines, neutral and subdued color palettes, bifurcated garments (i.e., pants) for the lower body, natural but not tight silhouettes, sturdy fabrics and shoes, and simple hair and face grooming. This uncomplicated and more restricted appearance allowed them to focus on work and accomplishments rather than on how they looked. Their attire (except for perhaps a tie) did not impede physical activity. The negative impact of men's uniformity and conformity in dress is that men may dress to conceal aspects of their identity. Fear of social ridicule drives men to assert an image of masculinity, which leads to the all-purpose business suit that could be worn for both formal and office wear. Stone's research has suggested that men are motivated to avoid wearing clothing styles that may be viewed as feminine for fear of ridicule.

In contrast, women had an elaborate code for appearance through the 1950s. Their unlimited options for fabrics, colors, design, lines, and silhouettes gave them a useful bag of tricks for attending to their *hedonic role*, emphasizing the pursuit of beauty and physical being. Women were encouraged to spend considerable time on clothes, hair, weight control, and makeup to render themselves beautiful for men (who were expected to marry and support women to have children). Women's involvement in appearance, along with attending to men and children, could easily distract them from pursuing a full-time career. Recent studies indicate that men are catching up with women in their overall concern with their appearance.

Beginning in the 1960s, androgyny in gendered appearances became widespread. *Androgyny* is a mixture of masculine and feminine styles in one person's appearance. The term *androgyny* is derived from the Greek words *andro* (male) and *gyn* (female). The term defines a condition in which the characteristics of the sexes and human impulses expressed by men and women are not rigidly assigned. Therefore, the term refers to perceptions of identity as well as characteristics of physical appearance.

One arena where androgyny is particularly exaggerated is the music industry. Many popular culture music stars (e.g., David Bowie and Annie Lennox) have effectively used androgynous appearances to distinguish themselves from other artists. A 2007 exhibit at the Louvre's Musée de la Mode et du Textile featured the collaborative work of fashion designer Jean-Paul Gaultier and ballet choreographer Régine Chopinot from the 1980s. Not only were the fashion show format and the ballet mixed, but clothing was a mixture of masculine and feminine characteristics.

Throughout the history of Western dress, women have borrowed elements of men's dress. Frequently, this has been related to women's participation in activities such as riding, outdoor exercise, or hunting. For example, in the late sixteenth century, women commonly adopted men's hats and doublets. In the late seventeenth and early eighteenth centuries, women appropriated men's formal jackets. In the 1850s, derogatory cartoons of women were published that included them in bars, smoking cigars and wearing pants; these were fueled by men's fear that if women

The ceremonial changing of the guard at the parliament building in Athens, Greece, 2007. The "skirts" worn by the guards (tsiolias) are not considered feminine in appearance and are a culturally accepted presentation of masculinity. Copyright Cristina Ciochina, 2007. Used under license from Shutterstock.com

parents often adorn her with elastic, pink-satin headbands so that no one is confused about her gender. Babies are also often color coded prior to their arrival. Often, nursery rooms are painted in blue colors for boys and pink for girls. If wallpaper is selected, the themes are often coded by gender, for instance, frog, snake, and turtle designs for boys and flower, unicorn, and fairy princess designs for girls. Parents describe their newborns in terms of gender. In a study of girl and boy babies of the same weight and length, twenty-four hours after birth, Jeffery Z. Rubin and colleagues asked parents to describe the newest addition to their family. Boys were described as strong, having large hands or feet, and demanding. Girl babies were described as sweet, cuddly, and cute.

DRESS AND GENDER: A HISTORICAL LOOK

Dress of the European aristocracy changed in the 1800s, when men's dress became a means of communicating economic success

began to wear pants and achieved the right to vote, they might turn into men. In the twentieth century, women began adopting men's trousers, an idea that had been promoted by Amelia Bloomer as early as the 1850s. At the beginning of the twenty-first century in the United States and Canada, women enjoy many freedoms regarding wearing men's dress. Indeed, the once forbidden pants have become a common wardrobe staple.

In contrast, men, despite the counterculture approach to appearance and increase in informality initiated in the 1960s, are still very unlikely to wear women's attire, particularly skirts. Braveheart: Men in Skirts, a 2003 exhibit at the Victoria and Albert Museum in London, explored masculine identities related to the wearing of skirts in Western society. Andrew Bolton has described the wearing of skirts by men "as a utopian ideal and contemporary lifestyle decision."

In the United States and Canada, how does the society arrive at these proscriptions related to dress? Social gender conformity is a central factor, but one deeper meaning of this dress behavior relates to *object relations theory*, which posits that external objects (such as dress) play a crucial role in the psychological development of an individual. In this view, males are seen as being more fragile in their presentation of gender. They need to be seen as not female, whereas girls, being female, have a connectedness and positive identification with the mother and, as a result, have more freedom in gender presentation. The result, according to this theory, is that in contemporary Western societies, most girls can wear either pants or skirts, while boys wear only pants.

Jean-Paul Gaultier designed skirts for men in the 1980s, although this was never established as a major fashion trend. He has challenged traditional conceptions of Western dress for men, suggesting that there is no clothing that is intrinsically male or female with the exception of the brassiere. By creating skirts for men, he is making the sartorial point that gender inequality exists between the sexes, with the overwhelming majority of historical changes occurring from men's to women's dress. The most recent has happened in the twentieth century, with women adopting men's pants, now a fashion staple for them. Gaultier, as a contemporary designer, points out that women can now wear pants comfortably for most social occasions while a skirt for a man raises questions about his masculinity. Gaultier's designs symbolically challenge symbolic male roles in contemporary Western society.

In 2005, the term *metrosexuals* was widely used to describe a market niche of heterosexual, urban males who adopted dress behaviors indicating a comfort level with feminine expression. Metrosexuals used perfume and cosmetics and wore jewelry and tight, low-slung blue jeans. For instance, David Beckham, an English soccer player, essentially followed pro basketball player Dennis Rodman's previous example by mixing feminine dress with a masculine career. Neither Beckham nor Rodman successfully changed the traditional dress for men.

Men's business attire has been linked to a display of power facilitated by the uniform nature of dress. In examining differences in the ways that uniforms can facilitate communication, Nathan Joseph has pointed out that uniforms exert a degree of control over those who must carry out an organization's tasks, encouraging members to express the ideas and interests of the group rather than their own, thus promoting the group's ability to perform its tasks. The opportunity for men to relax at work on casual Fridays has not released them from burdens of conformity, because they

The baby boy in front is dressed in blue while the two baby girls behind are in pink, showing that gender distinctions in dress are made from an early age. Interestingly, in 1918, contrary to later practice, the color rule was pink for the boy and blue for the girl. Copyright digital skillset, 2007. Used under license from Shutterstock.com

frequently adopt a uniform of trademarked polo shirts and khaki pants. This symbolic allegiance to work and career also signals a privileged access to economic and political power in postindustrial society, namely, occupational success. Women's conservative dress-for-success appearance of the 1980s can be analyzed as an appearance cue that announced women's intention to ascend the corporate ladder.

As early as the turn of the twentieth century, both Georg Simmel and Thorstein Veblen had noted that with the rise of the urban bourgeois, women who were without title or other claims to social status were denied access to business, politics, and government. They demonstrated their rising status through clothing, interior decorating, and other consumer activities.

Today in U.S. culture, adolescents are often allowed leeway in experimentation with gender and dress. Some adolescent girls may shave their heads, and some adolescent boys may have shoulder-length or longer hair. Adults, however, are generally expected to adhere to their societies' rules regarding appropriate gender dress.

GENDER, DRESS, AND THE PUBLIC, PRIVATE, AND SECRET SELF

Study of the self and dress has led to some insights into the differences in the way women and men view and use some aspects of dress. Joanne Eicher has proposed this model for viewing dress and three different aspects of the self: The public self is the part of the self the individual allows everyone to see, the private self is the part of the self that only family and friends see, and the secret self is seen by no one or only close intimates. From this analysis several questions arose. Is dress for the secret self (what Eicher calls *fantasy dress*) more restricted for men than women? Do U.S. women feel more freedom to dress out fantasies than men? In other words, are women allowed to purchase fantasy dress for the secret self more so than men?

In searching for an activity in which fantasy dress is worn so that these ideas could be examined, Kimberly Miller has focused on historic reenactment, asking historic reenactors about their use of costume during living history events. What she found was that the women reenactors she surveyed have more sexual fantasies about dress than men. Female reenactors also reported more childhood memories about dress than men, indicating that boys and girls are socialized differently about dress.

She also reported that among costumed reenactors, females dressed in costume primarily to assume another persona, whereas males dressed in costume primarily because of their love of history. Male reenactors distanced themselves from descriptions of their hobby as fantasy, costume, and dress-up. Women, on the other hand, embraced these terms and indicated that people do not dress in costume only on the weekends (for reenactments) but for every day. Additional research across cultural groups is needed for a more complete understanding of gender differences in expressing aspects of the self through dress.

GENDER MARKERS

Some dress items mark the gender of an individual more than others. Examples include a corset, an interest in fashion, a codpiece, and maternity apparel. Corsets have been associated with female morality, that is, the tight-laced woman is moral while the unlaced woman is "loose" and immoral. In addition, corsets have been blamed for displacement of internal organs and disfigurement of the female body during the 1800s; however, these accounts are generally considered few in occurrence and possibly overstated. Many writers have commented on the erotic appeal of corsets, and Valerie Steele has used representations of the corset

David Bowie, ca. 1970. Androgynous looks have been adopted by many U.S. and U.K. music performers. Michael Ochs Archives/Getty Images.

in art, illustrations, and advertising to show that the corset shares a close association with female erotic beauty.

Corsets have also been worn by men, although less frequently than by women. Fashion plates from some periods during the nineteenth century depict men's waists that are unnaturally small. Cartoons showing men in the process of dressing emphasize the areas of the body that were to be rounded by padding (shoulder, chest, hip, and calf). Tight corseting created a small waist, and it emphasized the padded areas of the body by contrast.

Women are often accused of being excessively interested in fashion. But throughout history, one can find examples of men who also took a strong interest in fashion, such as the very fashionable King Louis XVI of France (ca. 1700), or the British dandy Beau Brummel (1778–1840), whose name has become synonymous with style leadership. It is more difficult to identify male fashion leaders of more recent times from the United States or Canada. Their interest is demonstrated more indirectly by their willingness to follow the fashions set by international figures. In the 1930s, the Prince of Wales (later King Edward VIII) visited the United States, and his example inspired fashion trends such as full pants called *plus fours*, argyle socks, Windsor neckties, and polo coats. More recent celebrities such as the Beatles, television and film personalities, and musicians have also served as role models, demonstrating that many U.S. and Canadian men are consistently interested in appearing to keep up with fashion.

Some items of dress are gender markers for one or the other sex. The codpiece is an example of a relatively early gender marker exclusively for men. In the sixteenth century, this pouch of fabric joined the separate legs of hose, providing space to accommodate the male genitalia. From 1500 to 1560, the codpiece increased in size and was padded, slashed, decorated, and prominent.

Maternity apparel, like the codpiece, is gender specific. Examination of illustrations of pregnant women over time indicates that the public perception of pregnancy has greatly influenced the style of maternity apparel available. Maternity career apparel became available during the last half of the twentieth century largely because popular opinion held it acceptable for women to work while pregnant. This approach is in contrast to the Victorian era, when pregnant women were said to be "in a family way" and were expected to remain at home and out of public view. Juxtapose the Victorian image of a pregnant woman with a more recent image of Demi Moore, nude and pregnant, on the cover of *Vanity Fair* in the early 1990s, and it is obvious that the societal perception of pregnancy has changed over time.

Gender as a social and cultural construction needs—indeed, demands—the appropriate props to successfully convince the audience that an individual's gender presentation is authentic. Dress is layered with many meanings, such as culturally appropriate gender behavior, gender socialization via dress, codes of dress and gender, historical perspectives of dress and gender, dressing parts of the self, social resistance, and gender markers.

References and Further Reading

Bolton, Andrew. *Bravehearts: Men in Skirts*. London: V&A Publications, 2003.

Damhorst, Mary Lynn, Kimberly Miller, and Susan Michelman. *Meanings of Dress*. New York: Fairchild, 2005.

Eicher, Joanne B., Sandra Evenson, and Hazel Lutz. *The Visible Self: Global Perspectives on Dress, Culture, and Society*. 2nd ed. New York: Fairchild, 2000.

Joseph, Nathan. *Uniforms and Nonuniforms: Communicating through Clothing*. New York: Greenwood Press, 1986.

Kidwell, Claudia, and Valerie Steele. *Men and Women: Dressing the Part*. Washington, DC: Smithsonian Institution Press, 1989.

Michelman, Susan O. "Appearance for Gender and Sexuality." In *Meanings of Dress*, edited by M.L. Damhorst, K.A. Miller, and S.O. Michelman, 153–159. New York: Fairchild, 2005.

Miller, Kimberly. "Gender Comparisons within Reenactment Costume: Theoretical Interpretations." *Family and Consumer Sciences Research Journal* 27, no. 1 (1998): 35–61.

Molloy, John T. *Dress for Success*. New York: P.H. Wyden, 1975.

Newman, David M. *Sociology: Exploring the Architecture of Everyday Life*. Thousand Oaks, CA: Pine Forge Press, 1995.

Paoletti, Jo, and Carol L. Kregloh. "The Children's Department." In *Men and Women: Dressing the Part*, edited by C. Kidwell and V. Steele. Washington, DC: Smithsonian Institution Press, 1989.

Parker, S., M. Nichter, N. Vuckovic, C. Sims, and C. Ritenbaugh. "Body Image and Weight Concerns among African American and White Adolescent Females: Differences That Make a Difference." *Human Organization* 54, no. 2 (1995): 103–114.

Rubin, J.Z., F.J. Provenzano, and Z. Luria. "The Eye of the Beholder: Parents' Views on Sex of Newborns." *American Journal of Orthopsychiatry* 44 (1974): 512–519.

Simmel, Georg. "Fashion." *American Journal of Sociology* 62 (1957): 541–558.

Steele, Valerie. "The Corset: Fashion and Eroticism." *Fashion Theory* 3, no. 4 (1999): 449–474.

Stone, Gregory. "Appearance and the Self." In *Human Behavior and Social Processes: An Interactionist Approach*, edited by A. Rose. New York: Houghton Mifflin, 1962.

Veblen, Thorstein. *The Theory of the Leisure Class*. New York: Mentor Books, 1953.

Susan O. Michelman and Kimberly Miller-Spillman

Class

To understand the current relationships between class and dress in the United States and Canada, it is necessary to review the most important theories that have been put forth about class and dress in Western Europe. There are nearly as many opinions about the nature of class as there are people. These opinions vary widely, ranging from, "class explains everything" to "it no longer exists." To many, social class has become just a metaphor for varied access to resources, a way to describe the uneven distribution of wealth. Even with dramatically increasing disparity in wealth in recent years, class structure has not crystallized; instead, there has been a shift from a collection of fairly stable classes in the early days of U.S. colonization to a blurred class structure in the postindustrial, postmodern world of the early twenty-first century.

Writing in the mid-nineteenth century, the philosophers and authors of the *Communist Manifesto*, Karl Marx and Friedrich Engels, put the idea of class in the forefront of social consciousness. They set forth ideas of social class as a manifestation of who possessed power in the workplace. The bourgeois captains of industry were the owners of the means of production, with power over everyone who worked for them. The *proletariat*, or working class, consisted of those who sold their labor and had no power over anyone else. Thrown in as a sort of in-between class were the *petite bourgeoisie*, merchants who bought and resold goods. Marx predicted that the bourgeoisie would amass more and more of society's wealth over time to the point that the upper class would own everything. At that point, the proletariat would rise up and overthrow the bourgeoisie, thereby ending capitalism and ushering in a golden age characterized by the ethos "from each according to his means, to each according to his needs." What emerged instead was a triumph of the middle class.

At the end of the nineteenth century, economist Thorstein Veblen expressed his ideas about social class and dress in his book *The Theory of the Leisure Class*. He described the leisure class as dressing to show that they did not have to engage in productive labor. He coined the term *conspicuous consumption* to indicate that the leisure class could flaunt their wealth through extravagance. In as much as other classes might wish to emulate the leisure class, Veblen's work pointed the way to sociologist Georg Simmel's 1904 trickle-down theory of fashion change. Simmel's main idea was that fashion is driven by the human needs of imitation and differentiation, and this is played out along class lines. As soon as the middle class began to wear clothing similar to the upper class (imitation), the upper class had to adopt new styles to maintain distinction (differentiation). Here power and differentiation were maintained by the upper class based on leisure, rather than work, as was the case with Marx's theory. This picture has to some extent been turned on its head today, where members of the upper echelon take pride in competing with one another over how hard they work.

Many twentieth-century sociologists thought three classes were not enough, and typically an upper-middle class and lower-middle class were introduced as intermediate categories. Class membership was seen as an amalgam of income, education, and occupational prestige. Unfortunately, while these three scales correlate with one another (e.g., education tends to go up with income), those class boundaries become somewhat arbitrary. Another term, *status*, has emerged that does not try to group members of a population into vertically stratified subpopulations; instead, income, education, and occupational prestige are used to project members upon some vertical continuum. There is little disagreement that people arrange themselves and others along some sort of scale; how they do this, or how they should do this, remains far more controversial.

Writing a century after Marx, French sociologist Pierre Bourdieu has proposed that social class is composed of three kinds of capital: *social capital*, derived from one's network of acquaintances, or who one knows; *cultural capital*, what one knows; and *economic capital*, the financial resources at one's disposal. The classes sort out by how much of each type of capital they possess. While this system allows for a more realistic depiction of inequality and how it is maintained through time, it does not create distinct, homogeneous groupings. Social capital may be high if someone plays golf with the chief executive officer of a corporation. Cultural capital may increase with the number of academic degrees possessed. And economic capital goes up with increased salary or winning the lottery. Into which classes would this system put the following individuals, all of whom have an income of US$50,000 per year: a college professor, an owner of a small grocery store, and a bus driver? Marx would put the storeowner above the college professor and bus driver. Veblen and Simmel would not put any in the upper class. To Bourdieu, the professor would probably outrank the other two.

What seems to have emerged in the late twentieth century is what fashion scholar Diane Crane has described as *hypersegmentation*. Social classes, she maintains, have been broken into finer and finer categories to the point that they are meaningless. Instead, she (and most marketers trying to sell to consumers) views the social structure as "continually evolving lifestyles based on leisure activities, including consumption." In this view consumer fashion has replaced class fashion. *Class fashion* was a top-down approach. A few designers came up with remarkably similar designs and presented them mostly to the elite. With *consumer fashion*, there is much more stylistic diversity. She argues that the haute couture associated with class fashion has been replaced by luxury designer fashion, industrial fashion, and street fashion.

Luxury designer fashion is created by designers and sold with their names on the label; Ralph Lauren, Geoffrey Beene, Yves Saint Laurent, Oscar de la Renta, Giorgio Armani, Karl Lagerfeld, and Valentino are just a few of the best-known brands that are

Upper-class women in New York City, ca. 1910. Affluent women wear clothing made from decorated, fine fabrics.
Library of Congress Prints and Photographs Division, George Grantham Bain Collection, LC-USZ62-77905.

available in the United States and Canada. More and more, these luxury brands carry visible labels because consumers want others to know this is a Coach bag, for example, and not to have to guess from the stylishness and quality of the leather. Recently, there has been a consolidation of disparate luxury brands into a few international powerhouses (Louis Vuitton, Gucci, etc.) peddling everything from fine brandy to expensive purses and jewelry.

Industrial fashion is produced by manufacturers who advertise heavily. Often, it is selling an attitude or lifestyle more than clothing styles. In most Guess advertisements, for example, the sensual look on the model's face and her often provocative posture are what sell the clothes, which often cannot even be seen clearly. These brands are used to define personal identity (at least identity for the moment), a state of mind, rather than just a look.

Street styles derive from urban subcultures. Punks of the 1970s and 1980s seemed wild at first, with their strangely colored hair and use of safety pins for earrings. But over a remarkably short period of time, these styles were adapted by designers and marketed as mainstream styles. Over the ensuing decades the number of subcultures has proliferated as have their influence. Crane's analysis of the postmodern world seems to capture the multifocal reality of fashion and the social order of the early twenty-first century better than the earlier writers Marx, Veblen, Simmel, or Bourdieu.

DRESS AND FASHION

Before looking at the relationship between class and what people wear, it is useful to differentiate between the terms *dress* and *fashion*. Dress involves everything that is used to cover or decorate the body, including clothes, accessories, cosmetics (e.g., makeup, perfume, lotion), and body modifications (e.g., hairstyles, tattoos,

scarification, piercings). By this definition, humans have been dressing for a very long time indeed. David Reed and his colleagues have found evidence of body lice from 540,000 years ago. They suggest that this may indicate that clothing went back that far because lice need either a very hairy animal or clothing in which to develop. What people wear makes a host of statements about identity—about who they are—and, historically, dress has been a primary indicator of class and status. *Fashion* or the *fashion process* refers to the rapid and incessant changes in clothing styles that have occurred since the early Renaissance. In this process, one style replaces another not because of any inherently superior qualities but because people value the new.

To understand the interplay of fashion and class, two features of fashion (affluence and competition) must be addressed. A necessary condition for fashion is affluence. After all, for fashion to exist, things must be discarded before they are worn out. Fashion is not a hallmark of subsistence economies. To a first approximation, the more affluence in a society, the more fashions it is likely to have. In the twenty-first century, fashion pervades much more than clothing styles. It is seen in kitchen design, cell phones, laptops, food, child-rearing practices, and fashionable places to vacation. By definition, there is more affluence at the top of the economic order, so this is where fashion should have its primary arena.

Like capitalism, fashion is fundamentally about competition, in this case social competition. Fashion helps sort the social leaders from the followers. At the heart of class, regardless of how it is envisioned, is a focus on economic winners and losers. And insofar as winners in one arena are winners in the other, fashion leaders would be expected to be near the top of the economic order. Certainly most would agree that individuals near the top of the economic hierarchy are far more competitive than those near the bottom.

Throughout much of history, class and dress have been intimately connected. In some eras, class distinctions seemed quite obvious. The peasants knew their place in relation to the aristocracy, and this was reflected in their dress. No one mistook a member of the nobility for a peasant or vice versa. Later, with the rise of a middle class in the late medieval Europe, sumptuary laws were enacted, regulating who could wear what. One had to do with how long the pointed toe could be on men's shoes in the fifteenth century. The higher men ranked in society, the longer their pointed toes could be. Likewise, the greater a lady's status, the higher her hat and the longer the train of her dress could be. The American colonies included sumptuary laws in their legislation.

In the West, clothing is generally cut and sewn as opposed to being draped like the Roman toga or the Indian sari. In a deep sense this probably reflects a greater emphasis on the individual in the West as opposed to the community/group in many other societies. As a result, better-fitting garments tended to distinguish the upper class from peasants. The upper class also used finer fabrics in more vivid colors. They decorated their clothes and wore jewelry.

To understand class and its impact on dress and fashion in Canada and the United States, it is necessary to understand the way the economies have changed. Here, this change is sketched by dividing U.S. and Canadian dress history into four periods. This is a variation on the conventional periodization, which is most commonly divided into preindustrial, industrial, and postindustrial eras (the latter sometimes referred to as "late industrial" to lend a subtone of contemporary decay

and dissolution). It seems useful to distinguish nineteenth- and twentieth-century industrialization—what are called here early and late industrial economies—rather than pretend the same relationship held between class and dress and fashion in the 1950s as in the 1850s. Perhaps not coincidently, this arrangement more nearly mirrors major periods in art and architecture.

AGRARIAN ECONOMY

Up until the Industrial Revolution, despite a quickening in technology and a burgeoning trade, most people in the British colonies and later, the United States, made their livings off the land, farming and trapping. For Canadians this agrarian economy persisted until the early twentieth century. Class structure was well defined and fairly stable. The upper class (often consisting of large landowners) imported custom-made garments from Europe. The middle class was made up of professionals, craftsmen, and the clergy. Their clothing tended to be made by local dressmakers and tailors. The working class included farmers, laborers, servants, and slaves. By and large they wore styles similar to those of the upper classes, but less fabric was used. Clothes did not fit as well and were often made of yarn spun by the housewife and woven into cloth at home. The resulting fabric was coarser and less colorful than that enjoyed by the upper classes. Because cloth was so precious to this group, they often used partially worn-out or cast-off clothes to underline newer skirts or to be refashioned into more updated looks for themselves or clothes for children.

In North America, extremes of wealth were lacking compared to Europe. All money tended to be "new money." Class was neither as extreme nor as entrenched as in the Old World. New opportunities for wealth creation were constantly opening up, bringing a constant stream of nouveau riche into the well-to-do.

EARLY INDUSTRIAL ECONOMY

From the Age of Machines (the Industrial Revolution) up until roughly World War I, economic emphasis was on production. Steel was manufactured and used to build railroads, locomotives, and ships. The Industrial Revolution did much to make clothing more affordable to the masses. Invention of the cotton gin and steam-powered loom lowered the cost of fabric without sacrificing quality. What had been a huge responsibility for the housewife in earlier times was lifted. Now she could afford to buy ready-made fabric. While Canada lagged a few decades behind the United States in industrialization, its inhabitants benefited from Britain's early industrialization. Even more than the United States, Canada looked to Britain and Europe for inspiration and traded raw materials (e.g., fur pelts, coal, lumber) for fashions and fabrics.

The invention of the sewing machine made it possible to construct garments more quickly and efficiently, leading eventually to factory production beginning in the nineteenth century (for example, men's uniforms in the U.S. Civil War) and intensifying in the twentieth century. This invention and others brought with them accompanying lower prices. Dressing well was no longer a purview of the rich. More and more people were drawn into the fashion process.

Industrialization not only made clothes cheaper but also made nearly everyone richer. Industrialization blossomed just as the United States was running out of land. Near the end of

A typical group of mill boys in South Carolina, 1912. Class distinctions in dress were obvious at this time since the poorer classes could afford only a few items of clothing. Library of Congress, Prints & Photographs Division, National Child Labor Committee Collection LC-DIG-nclc-02532.

the nineteenth century, as free land became scarce in the United States, there was an accelerated migration to Canada, which still had plenty of open spaces. This flow of people into Canada expanded its labor pool, thereby contributing to its ability to industrialize.

Two offshoots of the Industrial Revolution, seen quite clearly in the nineteenth century, were that as men went to work in factories, they fairly abruptly changed their clothing to a more sober, even drab appearance compared to their forefathers. No longer did upper- and middle-class men display their wealth in their own clothes. Instead, their women wore elaborate gowns to show off the family wealth, demonstrating what Thorstein Veblen had dubbed conspicuous consumption. However, almost as soon as Veblen identified the concept of conspicuous consumption in 1899, it began to disappear.

LATE INDUSTRIAL ECONOMY

After World War I up through the 1960s, emphasis in the economy shifted from production to consumption. In the early twentieth century, Henry Ford introduced the concept of mass production for making cars more cheaply. Much of the prosperity of the 1920s was the result of using mass production to create affordable transportation; household appliances, such as refrigerators, toasters, and radios; as well as clothing for men and women. Mass-produced items cost less and thus brought consumer goods, including ready-to-wear clothing, within the range of most consumers.

Class distinctions could still be discerned in what people wore. The upper class wore silk, fine wool, and better-woven cotton, and they sometimes traveled to European couture fashion shows to return with Parisian creations. The middle class bought mass-produced copies of the couture items. And the working class bought cheaper, mass-produced ready-to-wear. With the dawn of modernism in the twentieth century, complexity gave way to simplicity and functionality, and clothes, even for the wealthy, became less fancy and more practical for women as they had for men in the previous century. Three major events helped level the playing field between men and women. First, women got the right to vote, beginning in 1918 in Canada and in 1920 nationwide in the United States. Second, the next huge advance was the introduction of the birth control pill in 1960. In 1968, a popular writer (a woman!) ranked the importance of "The Pill" with the discovery of fire and the development of toolmaking. For the first time in history, women had a very reliable means for timing and limiting their pregnancies. The third notable advance in the women's movement occurred in the postindustrial economy.

Just as Veblen had summarized the early industrial social order as it was coming to a close, sociologist Herbert Blumer explained the late industrial age as it was ending. He saw that Veblen's notion of class differentiation and emulation did not work in the latter half of the twentieth century. Rather, he believed that fashion proceeded as a series of choices made by designers, manufacturers, retail buyers, and consumers. According to him, fashion is a form of collective behavior that is influenced by elite choice but not driven by it.

Consumption had become king by the 1960s, composing over two-thirds of the U.S. gross domestic product, and mass production and economies of scale ensured that consumption remained top-down. Producers made what they thought consumers

Model on the runway at the Project Alabama 2006 Spring show, Olympus Fashion week, New York City. The designs of Project Alabama use recycled fabrics in combination with the couture techniques of hand-beading and hand embroidery. Class tension has given way to another kind of tension, where one part of a garment or outfit contradicts, rather than complements, another part. Fernanda Calfat/Getty Images.

should want and then marketed their products. For the most part, consumers dutifully accepted what was presented to them. That changed in the 1970s.

POSTINDUSTRIAL ECONOMY

The third notable advance in the women's movement occurred in 1971, when over 50 percent of women were in the workforce for the first time in history. In the twenty-first century, well over 50 percent of women work, including those with young children. It is no longer the exception but the expectation that women will work outside of the home. As women took on more responsibility outside of the home, female clothing became more action oriented, and there was a blurring of gender boundaries. Women adopted the man's trousers and suits to wear to work.

The postindustrial economy is truly driven by demand. The Information Age affords a host of new technologies for tracking consumer attitudes and preferences. Sales are tracked daily. Many surveys and focus groups do research on what consumers want so that producers can make it for them. Mass production is giving way to mass customization and global sourcing.

There is no doubt that globalization has made the world more complicated. Paris, once the center of fashion, has become just one of a number of centers. Today, clothing is designed and manufactured all over the world. A quick inventory of most closets in Canada or the United States would find clothing made in such places as Taiwan, Israel, Sri Lanka, Honduras, Macau, Thailand, Jordan, Mexico, China, Brazil, and Guatemala.

The plethora of choices has led to fragmentation. The old rules of social order and even fashion adoption do not work anymore. The trickle-down of fashions from the upper class to lower classes has been replaced by street culture as one of the main engines of fashion. In fact, fashion in the postmodern world often takes its cue from marginalized groups of people, such as young African American men in prison giving rise to the hip-hop style of baggy pants worn with the crotch close to the knees and boxer shorts showing at the waist above them. This transgressive look was later picked up by designers, who put it in stores at prices most of the originators of the style could not afford, and it was adopted by white adolescents living in the suburbs. Elegant styles, such as a classy Coco Chanel lace gown, have given way to edgy styles, illustrated by an Antonio Marras creation that combines parts of a man's wool suit with lace, sequins, feathers, and other feminine features. Another postmodern fashion concept that mixes up the rules combines meticulous beading on preworn sweatshirt material from Project Alabama. The recycled fabric looks worn out but is combined with the couture technique of hand-beading. Class tension has given way to another kind of tension, where one part of a garment or outfit contradicts, rather than complements, another part. As society has become more casual and less formal, the rich of the twenty-first century are less likely to flaunt their wealth through fashion than was the case in Veblen's day. They may think nothing of pairing a US$10 shirt from Target with a US$4,000 Armani suit from Saks Fifth Avenue.

The modern media has transformed how fashion is communicated and who the fashion leaders are. Celebrities in the twenty-first century have much more influence than their moderate wealth would indicate. Madonna, Brad Pitt, Britney Spears, and their handlers exert enormous sway over fashion. Information no longer flows through well-established channels. Waiting for the latest issue of *Vogue* to arrive has lost ground to where to buy a publication like *Lucky*; home-shopping channels on TV; or going online to see fashion shows, browse catalogs, and find out what the beautiful people are wearing to the Oscars, all with the click of a mouse. Fashion information is available around the clock.

Postmodernism has brought with it discontinuity, diversity, and decentralization. Up until the late 1960s, there was an identifiable look for clothing of each decade of the twentieth century (e.g., tailored, knee-length suits worn with white gloves and hats for the 1940s). Perhaps in response to the outright rejection of the midi-length skirt by miniskirt-wearing women in 1971, designers no longer could present a unified look and find acceptance. Instead designers took a kind of buckshot approach, sometimes showing mini-, midi-, and maxiskirts along with pants in the same season. There was little continuity between designers or even within one designer from year to year.

Diversity was evident as consumers had plenty of choices. This diversity is amply illustrated by a sampling of some of the looks presented in the March 2007 issue of *Vogue*, published in the United States but showing fashions that originated around the world, a reflection of the international nature of the marketplace. Featured in this issue were sculpted leather dresses that exaggerated the size of the hips (Dolce & Gabbana); a classic halter top and fitted slacks (Anne Klein); a hot pink minidress with a low neckline (Versace); a floral-print dress with the hem a few inches above the ankle (Ellen Tracy); a black-and-white, pin-striped, tailored pantsuit (Jones New York); a bright red, skirted suit with ruffles along a neckline opening all the way to the waist (Escada); a strapless dress, tight at the bust and ballooned out at the hem above the knee (Oscar de la Renta); an ill-fitting camisole worn with wrinkled pants that bunch up at the ankle and a scarf that reaches to the knees (Gap); and a floor-length, shirtwaist dress with a slit open to the upper thigh (Carolina Herrera).

Along with postmodernism came decentralization. Gone were the days of a small group of designers dictating the look of the season. Gone also was the rather comforting knowledge that one could be fashionable by pursuing the look presented in *Vogue* magazine and then purchasing items at a respectable store like Saks Fifth Avenue. Today, as Crane has put it, fashion is "presented as a choice rather than a mandate." Consumers are free to choose whatever look they think expresses who they are at a particular time in their lives or in a specific situation.

Most likely, it is not a coincidence that a huge interest in brands developed in the 1970s and 1980s. Brand names were built with meticulous determination. With a traditional social class system and fashion order no longer relevant, consumers found comfort in the security of buying name brands and designer goods. Labels migrated from inside the garment to the outside so that the whole world could appreciate that the savvy consumer was wearing Calvin Klein jeans or carrying a Gucci handbag. Brands have displaced class as a primary mechanism for fashion diffusion. This is a far more democratic approach, because in a competitive marketplace brands rise or fall based on the way people vote with their wallets.

Both Crane and Joseph Turow have argued that class in the postmodern world has fragmented into lifestyles, which resemble "image tribes." Each tribe is contextual—a single individual is allied with different sets of other individuals in various contexts. More and more individuals, especially in the more affluent and metropolitan sectors of the population, can no longer be sorted into nonoverlapping segments, whether they are called "lifestyles" or "classes."

By the early twenty-first century, class has become context specific. Possibly related to a decline in a sense of community, people interact with different sets of individuals in different contexts (e.g., work, church or synagogue, garden club, son's Little League games, volunteer work, college alumni functions, hiking group, etc.). The result has been a movement from coherent self-identity to an expanded identity in which it is possible to be more upper class in some contexts and more lower class in others and to dress accordingly. What has evolved is a more active consumer, one who is constantly making choices about "what identity to wear" and is not simply consigned by birth and upbringing to a particular group.

TWENTY-FIRST-CENTURY SOCIAL CLASS STEREOTYPES VERSUS REALITY

Class in the twenty-first century is enveloped in some fascinating contradictions. As the disparity in wealth has increased and the struggle to get ahead has become progressively more intensified,

A woman modeling a tailored Simon Massey suit, 1947, in typical style of the 1940s. In North America, there was an identifiable look for clothing of each decade of the twentieth century until the 1960s. Chaloner Woods/Getty Images.

where are class boundaries today? The ability to place a random individual in his or her proper class has evaporated. That said, it is noteworthy that there still is a good deal of collective agreement about the stereotypes of social classes. Upper-class people live in big houses, drive luxury cars, take exotic vacations, and wear designer clothing and accessories. Lower-class people rent, take mass transportation, do not take vacations, and wear clothing from thrift shops. Middle-class people own modest houses, drive nonluxury cars, take simple vacations, and wear ready-to-wear clothing.

Another example of social organization may clarify this seeming paradox between people's definite idea of social class and reality. The same paradox exists in people's notions of the ideal family. The overwhelming majority of people will describe the nuclear family as the ideal with mom, dad, and the kids all living under one roof. The interesting fact is that less than 20 percent of families fits this pattern. Like social class, the concept of the family is perfectly clear. The reality, however, has changed considerably in the postmodern era. And like the hypersegmentation of class that Crane has discussed, families are seen in a growing array of forms: single-parent, blended families, same-sex partners raising children, empty nesters, and so forth. In fact, there has been a blurring of boundaries for gender, social class, childhood, family composition, and a host of other social arrangements in the postmodern era.

With the blurring of social class, there has not been an accompanying demise of status. In fact, studies show that there is a widening gap between rich and poor in the United States and around the world for that matter. Everyone is on a status elevator. Consumers might be moving up or going down, but there are no clear floors to exit onto and find a class full of like-minded individuals. Retailers know this and so no longer market to classes. Rather, they market to lifestyles, to the idea of class, to a society obsessed with getting ahead, thereby reinforcing existing stereotypes of class.

Further, retailers realize that consumers lead serial lives. A waitress in a uniform by day can become a glamour queen at night, dressed in designer clothes. Status symbols are no longer out of reach of all but the wealthy. Luxury brands often come out with a somewhat cheaper version aimed to hook a younger generation. BMW and Mercedes already have autos for US$30,000, with plans to introduce some versions for US$25,000. Some save for years to be able to buy a Rolex watch, while others simply go into debt to buy a status symbol, thereby indulging in the ever more prevalent practice of status compensation.

In summary, class as a metaphor for inequality can never be severed from the fashion process, which is inherently about social competition. Dress and fashion have become aspirational; they are not only about who one is but also who one might be. Therefore, class stereotypes often permeate and infuse fashion communications, which in turn perpetuate those stereotypes.

Both dress and the fashion process reproduce and reinforce the social structure of society. The social class system of the agrarian and industrial ages was far more structured than it has become in the postindustrial era. As this social structure has fractured, classes have fragmented and fashion has become multifocal. It no longer proceeds from an apex down the social pyramid or outward from a single center to the rest of the world. Today, nearly everyone participates in the fashion process, regardless of socioeconomic standing. Multiple dress codes coexist. Fashion has moved from a predictable, top-down process to a scrambled, often bottoms-up approach. Paralleling that "anything goes" approach to fashion has been a blurring of clothing clues to definitively indicate a person's social class.

References and Further Reading

Barnard, Malcolm. *Fashion as Communication.* 2nd ed. London and New York: Routledge, 2002.

Blumer, Herbert. "Fashion." In *International Encyclopedia of the Social Sciences*, edited by D. L. Sills, 341–345. New York: The Free Press, 1968.

Bourdieu, Pierre. *Distinction: A Social Critique of the Judgement of Taste.* Translated by Richard Nice. Cambridge, MA: Harvard University Press, 1984.

Crane, Diane. *Fashion and Its Social Agendas: Class, Gender, and Identity in Clothing.* Chicago: University of Chicago Press, 2000.

Fussell, P. *Class: A Guide through the American Status System.* New York: Summit Books, 1983.

Giuntini, Parme, and Kathryn Hagen. *Garb: A Fashion and Culture Reader.* Upper Saddle River, NJ: Pearson/Prentice Hall, 2008.

Keller, Bill. *Class Matters.* New York: Henry Holt and Company, 2005.

Lowe, Elizabeth D., and John W. G. Lowe. "Quantitative Analysis of Women's Dress." In *The Psychology of Fashion*, edited by Michael R. Solomon, 193–208. Lexington, MA: D.C. Heath and Company, 1985.

Marx, Karl, and Friedrich Engels. *The Communist Manifesto.* Introduction by Martin Malia. New York: Penguin, 1998.

Morgado, Marcia A. "Coming to Terms with Postmodern: Theories and Concepts of Contemporary Culture and Their Implications for Apparel Scholars." *Clothing and Textiles Research Journal* 14, no. 1 (1996): 41–53.

Palmer, Alexandra, ed. *Fashion: A Canadian Perspective.* Toronto: University of Toronto Press, 2004.

Reed, David L., Vincent S. Smith, Shaless L. Hammond, Alan R. Rogers, and Dale H. Clayton. "Genetic Analysis of Lice Supports Direct Contact between Modern and Archaic Humans." *PLOSBiology* 2, no. 11 (2004): 1972–1983.

Sapir, Edward. "Fashion." *Encyclopedia of the Social Sciences* 6 (1937): 139–144.

Simmel, Georg. "Fashion." *International Quarterly* 10 (1904): 130–135.

Turow, Joseph. *Breaking Up America: Advertisers and the New Media World.* Chicago: University of Chicago Press, 1997.

Veblen, Thorstein. *The Theory of the Leisure Class: An Economic Study in the Evolution of Institutions.* New York: Macmillan, 1899.

Zweig, Michael. *The Working Class Majority: America's Best Kept Secret.* Ithaca, NY: Cornell University Press, 2000.

Elizabeth D. Lowe

See also Uniforms as Work Dress for Civilians and Military; Conventional Work Dress and Casual Work Dress.

Functional Dress

Functional dress may either serve as a protective barrier between some hazard and its wearer or as an enhancement, adding capabilities to the body. The word *dress* generally connotes items made of flexible textile materials, but functional dress may incorporate major areas of hard goods or be made entirely of rigid materials. A functional garment, whether it is flexible or rigid, can be conceptually differentiated from other products or environmental structures, such as vehicles or buildings, by two criteria: it is attached to or supported by the body, and it is portable. Some of these *portable environments* may be fully encapsulating and life supporting.

Among the items of functional dress that serve as protective barriers are space suits, deep-sea diving gear, clothing for the military, extreme cold weather ensembles, protective sports equipment, chemical/biological (C/B) and hazardous material (HAZMAT) suits, body armor, firefighting gear, and surgical and other medically related clothing such as X-ray-shielding aprons.

Functional dress that enhances body function includes garments that increase a wearer's visibility; flotation devices for water safety; braces, orthotics, and other devices for individuals with injured or paralyzed body parts; clothing that has been modified for easier use by an individual with handicaps; exoskeletons that give the body superhuman strength; and a wide range of computer wearables that adapt to changes in the environment or the individual.

Unless individuals are under the most severe, life-threatening conditions, functional dress is generally not entirely devoid of fashion or, at the very least, some consideration for aesthetics and body image. While the design of both protective and function-enhancing apparel focuses on the more physical aspects of the body, for many users of functional dress, the image they project while wearing it influences their decision whether or not to wear it.

Functional dress is both influenced by fashion and, in turn, influences fashion. One only has to look at the "moon boots" of the 1970s to see how passions concerning the astronauts' first walk on the moon combined with the more down-to-earth construction of a ski boot to produce a fashion hit. In addition to influencing the visual aspects of fashion, many technical advances in protective clothing items eventually evolve into innovations in everyday clothing.

Five types of functional dress will be explored here as illustrations of the complexities of protective barriers: extravehicular activity (EVA) suits for outer space, firefighting clothing, chemical/biological protective gear, protective sports equipment, and clothing for the military. Three types of clothing will serve as examples of how functional dress enhances body function: flotation devices, high- and low-visibility clothing, and clothing for people with disabilities.

EVA SPACE SUITS

Perhaps the most well-known item of functional dress is the EVA suit for outer space. Outer space is a frontier that involves many hazards that are not faced on Earth, among them (1) extreme temperatures, (2) lack of the atmospheric pressure that keeps tissues of the body from flying apart on Earth, and (3) micrometeoroids, which are tiny, sandlike particles of rock that travel at extremely high velocities. The totally enclosed system needed to protect astronauts from these and other conditions in outer space creates additional problems, such as how to allow for freedom of movement and ease of communication.

Whether in space or on Earth, the basics of protection from heat and cold boil down to one simple principle: A balance needs to be struck between the heat an individual produces and loses and the heat and cold provided by the environment so that the body remains within a survivable temperature range. Clothing may provide a barrier so that heat cannot escape from the body, or it may work to remove excess body heat.

Most clothing systems for preserving body heat use air as the primary insulator. Still air is the poorest conductor of heat. Clothing materials such as fleece and down incorporate a lot of still air that can provide resistance to body heat as it tries to pass through them into the environment. Aluminized fabrics and films may also be used to radiate body heat back toward the body or to insulate against environmental heat. Because metals are highly conductive, when aluminized materials are used within a garment, they are most effective if they're used with a spacer, that is, a low-density material filled with air that creates a space between layers. Spacers are placed between an aluminized layer and the skin surface and between each of a series of aluminized layers so that heat is not simply conducted from one layer to the next.

The suit used by the Apollo astronauts in their first mission to land on the moon was comprised of several separate garments layered over one another. The outermost garment incorporated both still air and aluminized fabrics. It was a fourteen-layer suit that provided a barrier to both the extreme temperatures and micrometeoroids. Among the materials in this suit were five layers of aluminized Mylar, each separated by a thin, nonconductive spacer layer of nonwoven Dacron. The outermost layers of the suit were made of a nonflammable material that remained flexible in temperature extremes. Under this many-layered thermal protection, the Apollo astronauts wore pressure suits that were inflated to mimic the pressure of the earth's atmosphere on the body.

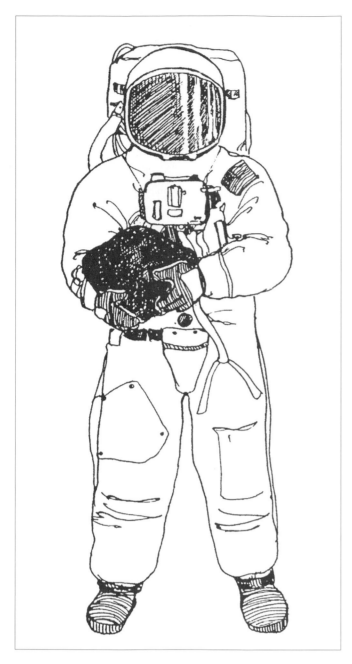

The EVA suit worn by Apollo astronauts, United States, ca. 1960. Courtesy of Susan Watkins.

The extremes of thermal protection presented a problem for space suit designers that is often faced in everyday clothing: It is possible to insulate the body so well that it can overheat, causing sweating, which wets insulation and destroys its crucial air spaces. The totally enclosed and protected astronaut needed some method for heat to be dissipated before too much built up inside the suit. This was provided by a stretch-mesh bodysuit laced with tubing that circulated cool water. Suits based on this concept have also been developed for use by workers in close proximity to high-intensity fires in industry.

As the space program evolved, rigid materials replaced increasing portions of the flexible fabric suits. The manner in which both inflated fabric and rigid suits provide for freedom of movement is a testament to design ingenuity.

CLOTHING FOR FIREFIGHTING

Firefighting clothing provides a good illustration of the way in which advances in functional dress can alter the activities of people wearing it. Early firefighters wore their everyday clothing and stood at a distance from burning structures. When firefighting jackets made of rubber or a finished-cotton duck cloth began to be used, they provided no significant protection from flame. They simply kept firefighters dry and protected from the spray of the hoses as they remained at a safe distance from the fire.

Turnout gear (the coat, pants, and boots worn by a typical firefighter to most fires), made a major advance in protection when flame- and high-heat-resistant fibers such as Nomex *aramid* were developed in the 1960s. Garments made of aramid fabrics allowed firefighters to move closer to the fire. While they could not actually walk into the flames, the heat and flame resistance of the materials meant that they could enter buildings that were on fire. Being in close proximity to both water and extreme heat, however, created the danger of steam burns, and this posed a conflict for designers. A firefighting garment needed to be waterproofed to prevent water from destroying insulation and to keep steam from penetrating the clothing, but waterproofing also would prevent the ventilation of any built-up body heat and moisture within the system.

One solution to this problem came about in the 1970s with the development of Gore-Tex, a microporous film that could be laminated to water-resistant fabrics. The result was a waterproof but breathable material; it ventilated to remove moist vapor from the skin surface while keeping rain and other liquids in the environment out of insulation. Other microporous coatings and nonporous laminations have since been developed and applied to firefighting gear and many consumer items, such as breathable rainwear.

With the advent of microporous materials, water and steam protection began to be laminated directly onto the underside of the outer shell of firefighting gear rather than existing as a separate liner. Although micropores allowed steam to penetrate the clothing system, they did so at such a gradual rate that the skin was not burned.

High heat and water are only some of the hazards present when firefighters move closer to a fire. Masks and self-contained breathing systems have been added to firefighting ensembles because there is little or no oxygen in a fire environment. The smoke-filled areas inside a building make visibility even more difficult. High-visibility tapes on clothing and equipment are thus very important for locating injured firefighters, and any high-visibility materials must be heat resistant and easy to clean. Early leather helmets provided only a minimal shield against heat and water. Once firefighters move into a building, helmets also need to provide protection from the impact of falling portions of the burning structure.

Fasteners also merit special attention because metal closures can heat up and cause a burn, and many plastics will melt in high temperatures. Therefore, high-temperature-resistant solid plastics or hook-and-loop fasteners are used, and many of those must be covered by a flap of aramid or the more recently developed outer-coat fabric polybenzinidazole (PBI) to keep them from being degraded by heat or frozen together by the spray from the hoses in winter weather.

As firefighters move closer to the fire, interfaces between the various components of the ensemble (i.e., the coat, pants, gloves,

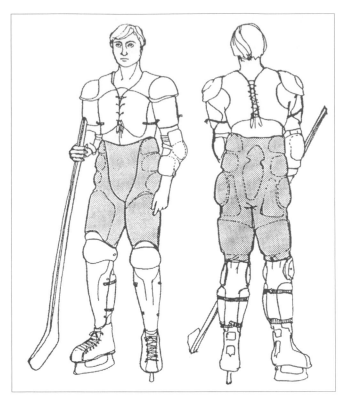

The Cooperall, a stretch pant that houses lower-body protective pads for ice hockey (Canada, ca. 2000). Courtesy of Susan Watkins.

boots, mask, and helmet) become an increasing concern. Different companies generally produce these components, and gaps in protection occur if they do not fit together properly. Most firefighters now wear a heat-resistant hood that bridges the gaps between the helmet, mask, and coat to prevent burns from occurring between those items. Some garments incorporate inner and outer extensions that form complete seals between the pants and boots and the glove and coat sleeve.

Entry suits, in which firefighters can actually walk through flames, have been created by aluminizing the outer surface of heat-resistant fabrics and forming fully enclosed ensembles that incorporate a self-contained breathing apparatus (SCBA).

Terrorist threats in the early twenty-first century added the potential for chemical and biological hazards to be in the environment of the average firefighter. Thus, basic firefighting gear has begun to incorporate features that could modify the ensemble to be more completely enclosed and life supporting.

CLOTHING FOR CHEMICAL/ BIOLOGICAL PROTECTION

Clothing for C/B hazards ranges from the apron and gloves worn by a farmer mixing chemicals for pesticides to the full HAZMAT suits worn for cleaning up chemical spills. Many of the principles used to develop these garments are also used for items such as surgical gowns that protect an environment from being contaminated by people.

C/B hazards may be in the form of solids, powders, liquids, gases, and aerosols (fine liquid sprays). In an operating room or clean room (a facility in which sterile supplies, precision instru-

ments, microchips, and the like are produced) the form of the threat is often known, and the conditions of the environment can generally be controlled. When pesticides are being prepared and sprayed, the level of danger to workers is generally known but may change with each job, and different ensembles are prescribed accordingly. However, in situations such as chemical warfare or a mysterious outbreak of disease, the specific threat may be undetermined, and even known threats can be altered by environmental conditions such as wind or rain. In those situations, the safest garment is a C/B suit, which is fully enclosed with a self-contained breathing system.

The materials for C/B protection may be either impermeable, permeable, or what is called *permselective*, that is, permeable to some substances but impermeable to others. Impermeable materials have no pores through which gases can pass; to be effective in C/B clothing, they also must not react chemically to a hazardous substance. Many impermeable materials used in C/B clothing are continuous films of substances such as polyvinyl chloride (PVC). Others are woven materials that have been coated to make them impermeable, for example, nylon coated with butyl rubber. Because both the fabric and the garment constructed from it must be impermeable, materials for C/B protection should also be easy to join by a method that makes seams impermeable as well. Seams are generally fused rather than stitched, using some form of heat sealing (heating materials and pressing them together until they merge).

Some garments include a combination of materials. Surgical gowns, which could be too hot if made entirely of impermeable materials, often use tightly woven but permeable materials for the main portion of the garment with sections of waterproof or water-resistant protection from midchest to knees in front and in the lower arm of the sleeve, the areas closest to the operating table where the surgeon could be in contact with blood and other fluids.

Permselective materials incorporate a substance that traps or neutralizes toxins. Many military ensembles for chemical warfare are impregnated with charcoal that has active sites that attract molecules of chemical agents, while allowing other molecules in the air to pass through. Toward the end of the twentieth century, various types of permselective materials began to appear in hospital garments and consumer goods in the form of antimicrobial and antiflu garments.

The design of a clean-room garment provides a good example of how the interaction of workers, the hazards, and the environment affects garment design. Clean rooms limit the number and size of contaminants, such as dust, hair, skin cells, and bacteria, in the work area. Therefore, the fabrics used to keep workers from contaminating products must serve as filters, and garments must be free of lint, static, and design details in which particles could lodge.

Thermoplastic filaments of polyester and nylon are the most lint-free fibers suitable for clean rooms, but they both tend to build up a static charge. This attracts dust that can be shaken off onto a work surface. Therefore, many materials used for clean-room clothing contain electrically conducting (static-dissipating) metallic fibers woven in at intervals. Fabrics are woven rather than knitted because tight weaves of filament fibers serve as filters. Seams must either be heat sealed or stitched so that there are no exposed raw edges. Designs have no outer pockets, no gathers or pleats, and as few seams as possible.

Worker protection from toxic chemicals is the subject of much litigation. The U.S. Occupational Safety and Health Administration (OSHA) and Canada's Center for Occupational Health and Safety (CCOHS) have both published guidelines for selecting protective clothing for chemical protection, but they have stopped short of mandating their use. The need for protective clothing in many fields often sets up a legal and political battleground. Some workers may refuse to wear it if they feel it affects their efficiency, while others demand it from an employer who may find it too expensive to provide.

PROTECTIVE SPORTS EQUIPMENT

The primary purpose of most protective sports equipment is (1) to keep objects from breaking through the skin surface and entering the body and (2) to cushion the effects of an impact on the skin surface so that the skin and the body tissues beneath it are not injured.

Protective equipment for sports generally consists of (1) a combination pad, a rigid plastic plate shaped to conform to the surface of a body part; and (2) an energy-absorbing material, generally a closed-cell foam, that is, a foam in which each bubble of gas is completely surrounded by the rubber or Neoprene material that forms the foam. The air in closed-cell foam cannot be squeezed

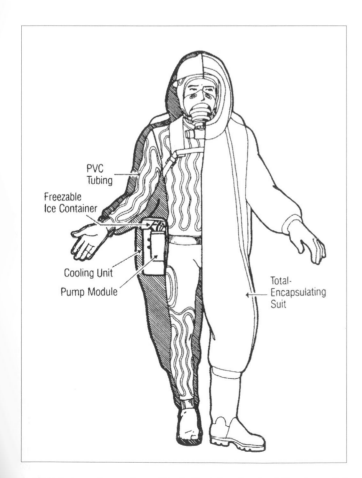

A whole-body cooling system with plastic tubes for circulating ice-cooled water. In the late twentieth century, designers in the United States tried this system both for space suits and for people working in close proximity to high-intensity fires in industry. Courtesy of Min Safety Appliances Company.

out as it can in open-cell foam, such as a kitchen sponge. In some protectors, rigid plates or foam padding may be used alone; in others, rigid plates may be backed with a special type of open-cell foam.

One purpose of a rigid protector is to spread out the force of an impact over a wider body area, decreasing its effect on any one area. Another may be to bridge over a sensitive area, keeping any impact at all from reaching that part of the body surface. The foam further dissipates the energy of the blow and cushions the skin. Because closed-cell foam is compressed, no air escapes, and thus it cannot bottom out and leave an athlete unprotected. Instead, upon impact a person will sink slowly into the material as the bubbles of gas compress.

Protective equipment for football illustrates one use of these materials. This equipment consists of shoulder pads and a helmet, both with a rigid outer layer lined with foam; a semirigid, segmented rib pad; and stretch pants with combination rigid/foam pads in pockets over the vulnerable body areas. Housing separate padding in a stretch garment is an approach used for many sports. It ensures that protection will stay located over the most vulnerable body areas while allowing the wearer maximum mobility.

Because movement is so critical to an athlete's performance, sports equipment is often formed in a working position, that is, the position in which a wearer will be most of the time, or pads are hinged or segmented so that it is easy to move into the working position. Hockey elbow protectors are shaped with the elbow bent, because that is a player's most typical position. A football quarterback's shoulder pads are hinged so that the arm can be raised easily when throwing.

Consideration must also be made for providing thermal protection and ventilation in sports equipment. In some sports equipment, spacers are used to allow ventilation near the skin surface. They form a type of sling that holds impermeable pads away from the skin surface so that air can flow over the skin. Phase-change chemicals are also being applied to clothing for active sports. When chemicals change phase (from solid to liquid, for example), they emit or absorb heat. Fabrics treated with phase-change chemicals can absorb body heat when a wearer's skin becomes too warm and add heat when the skin surface begins to cool.

Whether impact protection is being planned for athletes, construction workers, or soldiers, protection is planned according to (1) the potential for serious injury or death, (2) the areas of the body most likely to be impacted, and (3) how critical movement is in the areas needing protection. Athletes may prefer to play without equipment that they believe hampers their abilities. Therefore, many sports governance groups mandate that specific equipment be worn for officially sanctioned events, and in some cases, they require equipment to meet specific standards. Because head injury is a serious threat to life, helmets are worn for many sports and a number of occupations and are subject to both mandatory and voluntary standards in the United States and Canada.

CLOTHING FOR THE MILITARY

The environment of a ground soldier contains perhaps the most complex threat combination of any occupation. Among the many hazards with which a soldier is confronted are extreme weather conditions, bullets and fragments from explosions, chemical and biological agents, nuclear and radiation hazards, directed energy weapons and flame, detection by the enemy, disease, puncture and impact from falls and collisions, and biting animals. Soldiers need to carry weapons and ammunition, and many carry communication equipment and detection devices.

Designing military clothing involves many trade-offs. Designers face the challenge of how to provide enough protection without bulk and weight that would compromise soldiers' ability to move quickly enough to perform their missions. Even well-designed body armor interferes with heat loss needed in arid climates. Adding an air-cooled system to desert gear may create a heat signature that is visible to an enemy holding an infrared detection device. Modern military gear provides an excellent example of how designers can minimize or even eliminate some of these trade-offs by using multifunction materials and components.

A major step toward integration of functions was the Soldier Integrated Protective Ensemble (SIPE) program of the late 1980s and early 1990s. The SIPE program looked at the soldier as a system and attempted to create an ensemble in which each item supported the function of every other item. In the proposed SIPE ensemble, headgear provided basic ballistics and impact protection, but it also added respiratory support, hearing protection, laser eye protection, communications, high-visibility detection

An entry suit for firefighting, United States, ca. 2000. Courtesy of Susan Watkins.

devices (i.e., infrared sighting), a weapons interface that allowed a soldier to aim a weapon visually rather than by hand, and a computerized display system that provided information such as the location of the enemy, the status of other troop members, vehicle repair instructions, and so forth. Body armor and supply belts were combined into one unit, with vests fitted with features that could carry ammunition and other supplies. Multifunction materials served an integrative function as well. The aramid fiber Kevlar was used to provide not only ballistics protection but also protection from flame, heat transfer, and cuts.

Subsequent design research by the military resulted in air- and water-cooled systems for hotter climates. One program added an ergonomic backpack frame that increased the mobility of the system. Technological developments in detection systems forced changes in camouflage techniques.

Major advances have also been made in protection from bullets and fragments from explosives, which pose some of the most critical threats to the life of a ground soldier. Although the impacts involve tremendously magnified forces, the principles used for protecting from bullets are the same as those for other impacts.

Thick, heavy, rigid ceramics and metal plates were used in early body armor for seated individuals such as helicopter pilots or tank crew, but they were too heavy for ground troops. As lighter metals such as titanium were added to vests, metal armor became more appropriate for a foot soldier. Lightweight ceramics such as boron carbide are used in standard-issue body armor today.

During the Korean War, flexible nylon ballistics vests began to be used for the foot soldier. The most significant change in body armor, however, came about with the development of the aramid fiber Kevlar and later, the high-strength extended polyethylene fiber Spectra. These lighter, more flexible fabrics made possible soft body armor for soldiers and police and were thin enough for undercover agents.

Spider silk has been explored as a ballistics material, and nanotechnology offers the potential for tiny particles to be incorporated into flexible fabrics that will become rigid the instant they are struck by a significant impact. These new materials also hold promise for ensembles for bomb squads and those who work in ordnance disposal in the military.

FLOTATION DEVICES

Clothing items are used to achieve buoyancy for survival in military and civilian air and water travel, for safety in boating and watersports, and in helping divers descend and ascend in the water. Flotation devices change the buoyancy of a body by adding significantly more surface area than they do weight. A life vest, for example, adds bulk to the body, but because it is filled with air, it adds very little weight. A body with a vest on, then, becomes less dense than the water surrounding it. In some cases, inflation is used to achieve this. In others, the body is surrounded by closed-cell foam.

Most life vests are made of closed-cell foam because they will continue to function even if they are punctured. If a piece of closed-cell foam is cut, only the air in the cells where the cut occurs will be lost, whereas a puncture of an inflated vest would allow all of its air to be released. In addition, the many pockets of still air in closed-cell foam provide insulation that is much to the advantage of someone who is in the water following an accident.

Inflation, on the other hand, is space saving. It has the advantage of allowing a clothing item to be collapsible until it is needed, so it is often selected for use for individuals such as navy pilots, who must wear survival equipment at all times when they are flying, or backpackers and others who have limited storage space.

While some survival vests can be inflated by mouth, most are generally inflated by pulling on a cord that punctures a small container of compressed carbon dioxide. The released gas then flows into the vest, filling it until it conforms closely to the body of the wearer. Some life vests inflate when they are submerged in water rather than counting on wearers, who might be incapacitated or confused, to pull a cord and start inflation.

Wet suits for scuba diving are also made of closed-cell foam. Fully suited divers are so buoyant that they have difficulty sinking below the surface of the water. To descend, they put on weight belts that will sink them to the lowest level they want to explore. As they descend, the air in the cells of the wet suit compress, and the buoyancy of the suit itself decreases. In order to ascend or remain at a specific depth, divers wear an item similar to a life vest called a buoyancy compensator. As air is fed into the compensator from the diver's tank, the diver becomes more buoyant.

Dry suits, which completely exclude water, were initially made of a thin, flat sheet of rubber or Neoprene and worn over insulating underwear. In the late 1960s, a dry suit was developed using a foam laminated to a four-way stretch nylon and an air- and watertight zipper developed for the U.S. space program. The suit was warmer than previous dry suits and strong enough to be inflated so that it could serve as its own buoyancy compensator. Air fed into the suit also affected thermal insulation.

For extreme deep-sea diving, rigid suits are needed to keep the extremes of pressure from crushing a diver and to avoid the need for decompression when returning to the surface. Variations of these atmospheric diving suits (ADS) have existed since the nineteenth century. They are basically diving bells shaped in the form of the human body and articulated. The manner in which articulation is provided is similar to that of a rigid space suit.

HIGH- AND LOW-VISIBILITY CLOTHING

Most high-visibility clothing works because it reflects a light source. Modern high-visibility clothing uses what is called retroreflection. When a headlight, for example, strikes a reflective stripe on a jogger's clothing, the ray of light is retroreflected, that is, bent and then reflected, so that the light bounces back into the eyes of the motorist rather than being bounced off to the side of the road or scattered.

Rigid retroreflectors began being used on highways as early as the 1920s, but it was not until the 1950s that 3M developed Scotchlite flexible tapes with retroreflective glass beads adhered to them. These were developed for use on shoes and children's clothing but eventually found important uses on uniforms for firefighters and traffic police. As technology advanced to allow the production of more stable retroreflective materials, including those that could be laundered, they became prevalent in many items of activewear for cycling, jogging, or walking along roadways.

In the late twentieth century, light-emitting features began to be used in clothing and footwear. Motion-activated lights in the heels of children's sneakers became commonplace, and light-emitting diode (LED) garments that display text messages were developed for a variety of end uses.

Camouflage clothing provides an interesting example of how changes in technology force a constantly evolving relationship between user needs and protective clothing. Woodland, desert, arctic, and urban visual camouflage patterns were developed by the U.S. Army to match the types of light and shade that could be seen by the naked eye in those environments. When infrared detection devices were developed, soldiers in camouflage garments could be seen through a detection device by opposing forces because of the heat their bodies generated. Because specific dyes reflect infrared rays differently, camouflage materials were then developed with dye patterns that reflected heat in a similar manner to each terrain. As each new detection device is developed, technology of the times provides a way to block its use for detection.

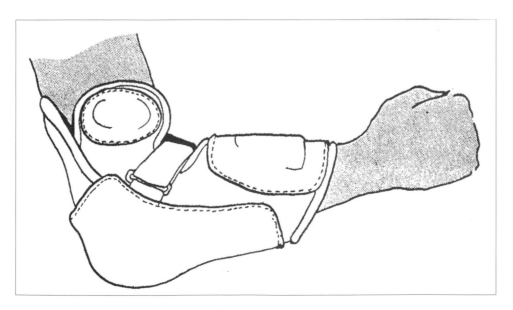

Elbow protector, ca. 2000. Hockey players in the United States use elbow protectors that are shaped with the elbow bent, because that is a player's most typical position. Courtesy of Susan Watkins.

CLOTHING FOR PEOPLE WITH DISABILITIES

A wide array of clothing has been developed for individuals who have temporary or permanent disabilities. In addition to clothing that has been modified to meet the needs of people with handicaps, a number of medical devices have been made portable and inserted in clothing so that patients no longer need to be tied to hospital beds. Personal status monitoring has been incorporated in many of these medical items as well as in clothing for sports, the military, outer space, and firefighting.

The key to many items of clothing for people with disabilities lies in two factors important to all functional dress: (1) fasteners and (2) suspension systems, that is, the way clothing is attached to the body. Hook-and-loop fasteners such as Velcro placed in easy-to-reach openings or a wraparound design have made dressing much easier for those with functional limitations and allow precise fitting of orthotics and splints. Garments with adjustment features and pockets allow portable medical devices to become almost part of the body. One vest monitors a patient's heart and delivers a shock treatment if the heart goes into a life-threatening condition. Others hold nutrition that is fed directly into the bloodstream or provide for the elimination of waste.

Inflation allows flexible fabrics to become rigid and fit closely to the body so that they can provide support. It also allows garments to be worn flat and then expand to provide impact protection when it is needed. An inflatable collar, triggered by a seizure, has been developed to protect the heads of people with epilepsy. Proposals have been made for similar inflated hip protectors for the elderly. Inflatable garments can also provide pressure on the skin of burn victims, serving as an alternative to stretch burn covers.

Innovative methods of suspension have been developed because an anchor point on the body is either missing, not in a typical position, or not able to tolerate the pressure of garment suspension. For example, a lower-arm immobilizer attached to a waist belt was developed as an alternative to a sling that would otherwise hang over an injured or sensitive shoulder.

THE FUTURE

Many items of functional dress owe their existence to technological developments in non-clothing-related fields. Others come about because a designer takes several technologies—even those already developed and on the market—and combines them in nontraditional ways to create a unique design. It is anticipated that future protective dress will no longer just be passive applications of technology but will increasingly link protection and enhancement, responding to changes in the body and changes in the environment with active, dynamic garments.

Snapshot: Mobility in Pressurized Garments

Preserving survivable pressure is a critical function of many items of functional dress. Space suits are pressurized to preserve at least part of the pressure of the earth's atmosphere on the body; rigid diving suits maintain a constant pressure on divers' bodies to keep them from experiencing the bends and other conditions that occur with pressure change. A slight inflation is also used in many HAZMAT suits so that if they are accidentally punctured, air flows out, pushing toxins away rather than letting them flow into the suit.

It can be difficult to move in air-filled garments. The materials used to make them are generally stiffer than most clothing fabrics, and even if the materials are flexible, it is difficult to bend when what is essentially an inflated balloon surrounds each body segment. Inflated sleeves, for example, tend to balloon outward into rounded shapes, so they often contain circumferential restraints to hold the sleeve closer to the arm.

One solution that was used in early space suits was to place rigid rings circumferentially in flexible fabrics only in the area surrounding each body joint and to restrain the rings to a constant length along the axis of motion of that joint. A pressurized leg covering that contained circumferential rings at the knee could expand in length over the front of the knee and contract at the back as the leg bent, but a restraint along the joint's axis kept the leg covering from expanding in length there.

In the space suits developed during the 1960s and 1970s for the Apollo and space shuttle programs, a separate restraint layer covered the bladder, the pressurized portion of the suit, to keep it from rounding out and overinflating. Each garment segment was composed of many shaped fabric sections that allowed increased length over the back of a hinge joint, such as the elbow, when it was extended and folded into pleats when the joint was contracted. A nonstretch material was firmly stitched down along the axis of motion of the joint.

For joints such as the shoulder, where a more complex range of motion was possible, or the wrist, where the rotation of the hand was needed for its full use, metal rings were often used to join garment sections. Wrist rings on sleeves joined to rings on gloves with a ball-bearing rotating joint. This allowed the gloved hand to turn freely as the two rings slid around within one another.

Rigid suits also use ball-bearing joints, but these joints link cylinders that have angled edges. The segments then come together at an angle and form what is called a *stovepipe joint*. When an elbow is bent in this joint, for example, the wider portion of the segment slides around to the point of the elbow, and the narrower portion rotates toward its crook. Rigid joints may be powered in a fashion similar to that of a self-propelled

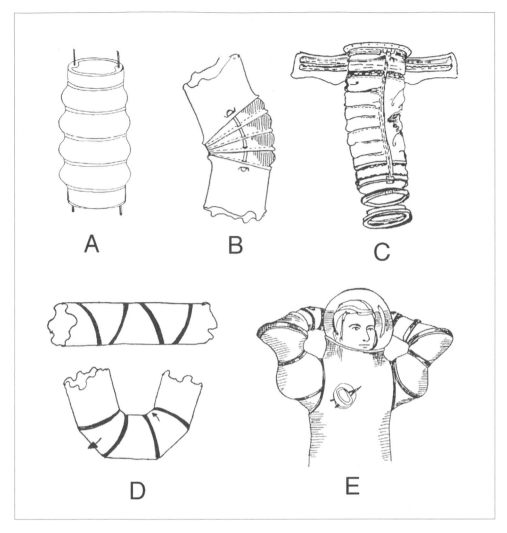

In pressurized garments developed in the United States, movement is made possible using a number of different structures. A. Circumferential restraints on a sleeve segment. B. A knee joint with rigid hoops restrained along the axis of motion, like those used in early space suits. C. The restraint layer in a Shuttle space suit, with rigid wrist rings. D. A stove-pipe joint extended and bent. E. A stove-pipe joint on a rigid space suit. Courtesy of Susan Watkins.

lawn mower so that movement requires very little effort on the part of the wearer. Increasingly, proposed designs link computerized programs to rigid suits so that they will follow the design movement patterns of specific users or even move independently. Thus, a rigid suit of the future would require no effort to lift its sleeve or move a leg within it, and in cases where the wearer was injured, it could be "thought" into walking a nonmoving wearer out of harm's way.

Snapshot: Textile Design and Functional Dress

New materials may be developed in response to specific needs, but often, by making modifications in some aspect of the original material—its fiber, yarn structure, fabric construction, or fabric finish—a designer can create innovative end uses for materials that are quite different from the original purpose for which they were designed.

One example of this can be found in the logging industry, where there have been a variety of approaches to keeping loggers from being cut by chain saws. Early protection involved the use of cut-resistant leather chaps just over the upper legs, where the saw was most likely to fall if knocked from the hands. When aramid fibers were developed, several layers of woven

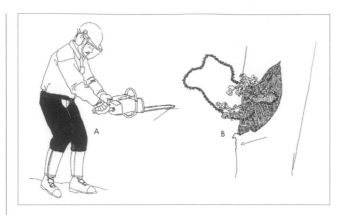

Protective material for loggers in North America, ca. 2000. When a chain saw comes into contact with a knit of strong fibers, the fibers pull out of the material and tangle in the saw, shutting it off. Courtesy of Susan Watkins.

Kevlar were used in chaps or added to pant linings in the thigh area. Aramids were lighter and more flexible and provided more time for lumberjacks to take evasive action, although the last layer of aramid could still be penetrated and considerable damage done to the body before the saw fully stopped.

An innovative solution came about when a designer noted an interesting aspect of the behavior of Kevlar in a knit structure. In a weave, the material simply provided cut resistance, but in a complex knitted structure, the first response of the yarns was to pull out of the structure. When touched by the chain saw, they caught in it and wrapped around it, tangling the chain and quickly jamming it long before the saw could penetrate the whole knit structure. Thus, the saw was deactivated even if a logger still had a thumb on the switch. Placing knitted Kevlar in pants and chaps produced lighter, more flexible, and more protective garments.

References and Further Reading

Braddock, Sarah E., and Marie O'Mahoney. *Techno Textiles: Revolutionary Fabrics for Fashion and Design.* New York: Thames & Hudson, 1998.

Federal Emergency Management Agency and U.S. Department of the Army. "Personal Protective Equipment Study Guide: Second Edition." http://www.emc.ornl.gov/EMCWeb/EMC/CSEPP_Slides/PPE_2002_Student_Guide.pdf (accessed February 2007).

Gupta, Sanjay. "Design Innovation and New Technologies." http://www.techexchange.com/thelibrary/designinnov.html (accessed February 2007).

Harris, Tom. "How Body Armor Works." http://science.howstuffworks.com/body-armor1.htm (accessed February 2007).

Hatch, Kathryn L. *Textile Science.* Minneapolis: West, 1993.

National Aeronautics and Space Administration (NASA). "Apollo Operations Handbook Extravehicular Mobility Unit, Volume I." http://www.hq.nasa.gov/alsj/alsj-EMU1.pdf (accessed February 2007).

National Aeronautics and Space Administration (NASA). "Future Space Suits." http://quest.nasa.gov/space/teachers/suited/8future.html (accessed February 2007).

Ornhagen, Hans. "Thermal Problems in Diving." http://www.ornhagen.se/Thermal%20problems%20in%20diving%2020050106%20Hemsida.pdf (accessed February 2007).

Renbourn, E. T., E. T. Rees, and W. H. Rees. *Materials and Clothing in Health and Disease.* London: H. K. Lewis & Company, 1972.

Santa Clara County Fire Department. "Protective Clothing: Hazmat Gear." http://www.sccfd.org/clothing_hazmat.html (accessed 4 June 2008).

Watkins, Susan M. *Clothing: The Portable Environment.* 2nd ed. Ames: Iowa State University Press, 1995.

Susan M. Watkins

Dress for Rites of Passage

- Birth
- Coming of Age
- Marriage
- Young Adulthood
- Aging and Retirement
- Death
- Postmodern Subcultural Identities

A *rite of passage* is a series of ritualized acts moving an individual from one stage of life to another, a formal and public marking of changing status and position within society. *Rituals* are repeated patterned actions that serve to reinforce and publicly announce beliefs and values to both the participating initiate and a culturally aware audience. Dress as a visible sign of social position is very often used within rites of passage as a public symbol of changing identity and a means of expressing and reinforcing shared values and beliefs.

Traditional rites of passage commonly include three stages, each marked by some form of a public ritual. *Separation*, the first stage of the social process, formally severs the ties between the initiate and his or her current social identity. This stage can be marked by the removal of dress related to their current social status or, in some cases, body modifications or changes. The intermediate stage, *liminality*, is a developmental stage. The initiate is literally between two social identities, preparing to assume the new role and also furthering distancing him- or herself from the former position. This stage is characterized by dress that places the initiate outside of formal social positions, symbolically marking the lack of a defined social role at this stage of the rite of passage.

The third stage, *aggregation*, is typically the most elaborate and publicly celebrated. This final culminating ritual moves the initiate into their new status and role within society. Dress is commonly used in this stage to mark the new identity and to express the values and responsibilities that come along with the newly earned position.

In the postmodern era, social identities have become negotiable and elective, with individuals choosing to either participate or not participate in traditional coming-of-age rituals and, at times, electing to join subcultural groups through a formal or semiformal rite-of-passage ritual. Rites of passage might be divided into traditional rites of passage linked to the life cycle and rites of passage in postmodern society in the marking of subcultural or subversive identity.

BIRTH

The first rite of passage in the human development cycle is experienced by the expectant mother as she separates from her former social identity: moving from an individual status to that of a woman carrying a baby, into the liminal pregnancy stage, and finally the aggregation stage marking the entrance into the world of a new mother, father, and child. In the United States and Canada, the formal confirmation of pregnancy marking separation of the woman from her earlier status role is commonly experienced in a medical environment, often preceded by a home-administered pregnancy test. The increasing use of medical interventions, such as *amniocentesis* (a test of amniotic fluid for evidence of genetic birth defects in the fourth month of pregnancy), has affected the duration of the separation stage for many modern mothers, with some not fully separating themselves from their former role until after the test results are known.

While the separation stage may not be formally marked by dress, the liminal stage, lasting from the point that a woman accepts her pregnancy until the weeks directly following her child's birth, has a history of being significantly marked by dress in U.S. and Canadian society. Liminality is often a stage of rites of passage where individuals are physically moved away from the center of social interaction and then dressed to symbolically express their invisible social status. In the pre–World War II era, married women were not physically removed from society, but in terms of visibility, they were often shielded from public attention and kept away from events that would expose their physical condition. Phrases such as "in the family way" and "with child" masked the link between sexuality and pregnancy.

Dress as a visible symbol formally marked the invisibility of pregnancy during this era because there was a noticeable lack of clothes distinctly designed for pregnant women to wear in the public sphere. It was assumed that women would stay at home and remain unobserved as their bodies changed and developed; therefore, public dress styles accommodating the developing pregnant body were not designed and marketed. In the last four decades, the liminal stage of pregnancy has become publicly observed, with pregnant women moving freely outside of their homes and into the work and public sphere more generally. Moving from the 1970s T-shirts with large arrows on the front advertising the physical location of the baby on the woman's body, dress styles in the early twenty-first century are now slick and trendy and show the distinct shape of the female belly as it grows and expands.

The aggregation stage of pregnancy results in the emergence of three new identities: a mother, a father, and a new child. Each of these three identities is marked by dress, appearance, and behavioral changes. Some of these rituals and dress changes happen directly after birth. For example, a new father smokes a cigar as a symbol of his passage into fatherhood, male maturity, and assumption of adult responsibilities. Some rituals, such as the baby shower, happen in advance of the actual birth, preparing the young mother and baby for their new roles and identities with a series of gifts. For the new mother, moving out of maternity dress and into normal clothing marks the end of the liminal stage and the beginning of a new identity. Attention is often paid to the outfit a new mother wears home from the hospital, with pictures taken to mark the event. For a young father, the carrying of the diaper bag for the first time or the first purchase of a T-shirt supporting his child's nursery school may be emblems of his new identity.

A young woman wears a traditional Hmong outfit at the Hmong New Year Celebration, Wisconsin, 2004. For the Hmong Americans this time of year has become a significant public display of emerging adulthood. Darren Hauck/Getty Images.

For the infant, first identity is experienced as an act of investiture bestowed on the new child by his or her parents, family, and hospital caregivers. The planting of a blue stocking cap on a newly born male baby by the hospital staff immediately marks the entrance of the child into the gendered U.S. world as a "normal" male baby. In a more extreme and dramatic sense, the surgical changing of a sexually ambiguous infant into a well-defined male or female, a common solution for infants born with both male and female genitalia, is a physical marking of entrance into a society built on a conceptual foundation of distinct male-female sexual difference. Other identities of the child are marked as well. In the Christian tradition, baptism is often marked by a handmade or specially purchased dress marking the occasion of being accepted as a member of God's larger family. In the Jewish religion, the *bris milah ceremony*, in which a male baby is circumcised in a ritual attended by family and friends, similarly marks the new baby as a member of God's chosen. Popular culture values are bestowed as well, as the logos of college or national sports teams find their way onto baby T-shirts, baby bibs, and the little boy's first ball cap.

COMING OF AGE

Adolescent rites of passage to adulthood are some of the most elaborately marked because they signal the transition from sole reliance upon family and parents to the beginning stages of adult responsibility and autonomy. Within traditional and more closed and homogeneous societies, the aggregation stage of adolescent rites of passage often features dress styles that symbolize the ties of the newly emerging adult to the past and to long-standing values and traditions. In multicultural modern societies, emerging adults often use their heritage as a means of interpreting or responding to current realities. Multiple identities that may be in conflict within a young person at this stage of development are often expressed and negotiated on the visible body at this public stage of emerging adulthood.

The United States, as a relatively young country composed of immigrants and refugees, has a long history of teenage rites of passage being used as a means of exploring a newly emergent U.S. identity. U.S. ethnic groups who commonly have abandoned traditional dress for everyday use often return to those traditions as they mark young people's entrance into adulthood. For example, among Hmong Americans, the New Year celebration, with the playing of the traditional courtship ritual ball-toss game between male and female adolescents, has become a visible and significant public display of emerging adulthood in communities throughout the United States and, to a more limited extent, Canada. While young women still wear styles linked to traditional dress of the past, they have enlivened the ensembles with modern North American decorative elements and an emphasis on fashion change. By wearing the newest version of traditional styles, they simultaneously mark both their commitment to their Hmong heritage and express a modern Western sensibility that is open to change and eager to express a new look. Young Hmong men, much more heavily charged with paving a practical road into the pragmatic world of business and commerce, wear more Western-inspired suit styles to the New Year, symbolizing their emergence into responsible adult roles of financial support for the immediate and extended family. With growing assimilation the Hmong traditional coming-of-age New Year celebration in St. Paul, Minnesota, expanded in 2007 to include a New Year for the Hmong GLBT (gay/lesbian/bisexual/transgender) community, including a ball-toss ritual and beauty contest featuring male-to-female cross-dressed contestants wearing versions of traditional dress styles.

Coming-of-age rituals in modern societies are also utilized by young people and their communities to redefine or reconstruct male and female gender roles to keep current with changing realities and to attempt to revise racist or sexist stereotypes. African American debutante balls emerged in the post-Emancipation period as a public display of the value, social class, and propriety of young women within urban black communities. As a part of the wider uplift movement, the balls emerged as a public display staged by the black urban elite showcasing the wealth and the accomplishments of educated African Americans. The young women from prominent families presented at the early balls thus served as symbolic emblems of the value and accomplishments of their sponsoring families.

Contemporary African American debutante balls in the rural Midwest have moved in the direction of stressing the academic accomplishments and community service records of the participants, rather than their social standing. To minimize the impact of socioeconomic background on the event, many sponsoring organizations provide scholarships or economic assistance for needy young women so that they are able to participate. African American debutantes wear white wedding-gown styles and are presented by their fathers or other older male relatives. The presentation is accompanied by commentary that speaks to the young woman's character, intelligence, and value to the community. The sponsoring female organizers of the event stress that the ball is an opportunity for a positive portrayal of young black women, pointing out that both historically and in the current media, black women are not always depicted as exemplars of value and character.

Thus, historical and contemporary stereotypes depicting black women as promiscuous or lacking in intelligence and grace are confronted within this ritual by a public presentation of young women of scholastic merit wearing quintessential symbols of purity: formal, white wedding-style dresses. This concept of reconstruction is a primary theme underlying African American culture and community. Noted African American scholar Henry Louis Gates used the term when he observed that U.S. "blacks seem to have felt the need to 'reconstruct' their image to white probably since the dreadful day in 1619 when the first boatload of us disembarked in Virginia." In this case, the coming-of-age aggregation stage becomes a point of reconstruction not only for the young woman but also for the community at large.

MARRIAGE

Weddings are one of the most celebrated and public rites of passage. While a coming-of-age ritual marks a young woman or man

as eligible for courtship and dating, a marriage moves the participants into responsible roles within the family and the community. With weddings accounting for as much as one out of every eight retail dollars spent in the North American market, this rite of passage is the most heavily promoted in the United States and Canada. Young women grow up with fantasies of their wedding day, and dress is central to the vision they conjure in their imagination.

While certainly a wedding between a man and a woman is a formal rite of passage for both participants, the symbolism of transition is more clearly defined for the bride. Despite four decades of gender renegotiation, the traditional wedding in which the bride is "given away" by her father to her new husband still is a central feature of many contemporary ceremonies. In this case, the white dress symbolizes her prebridal innocence, the departure of her father after walking her down the aisle marks the separation stage, and lifting the veil for the first kiss and the triumphant walk back down the aisle with her new husband marks the aggregation stage.

While this traditional ceremony is culturally constructed as timeless, a tradition that has always been there, in fact it became

A bride wearing a white wedding dress. In the United States, the convention of the single-use white fantasy wedding dress established itself from the 1950s onward. Copyright Francois Etienne du Plessis, 2007. Used under license from Shutterstock.com

the norm relatively recently, beginning in North America in the early twentieth century. The tradition of wearing a white wedding dress purchased exclusively for this one special day is rooted in British upper-class society, dating back first to the royal family of Queen Victoria. Most British brides wore more practical multiuse dresses from the Renaissance period to the turn of the nineteenth century. White dresses gained momentum in Britain throughout the nineteenth century, climaxing in the Victorian period with the emergence of the white wedding dress as symbolic of innocence and virginity. By the 1880s, the single-use white wedding dress was the norm among most societal groups in Britain.

The tradition of the white wedding dress was picked up more slowly in the United States. Early colonists and later immigrants had limited means and access to high fashion and often wore colored gowns that were worn for other dressy occasions. By 1850, the upper classes favored the single-use white wedding dress, but it was not until the 1890s that the white wedding dress tradition began to affect the larger population, and even in this instance, the dresses followed contemporary fashion trends in terms of styling and length. The crystallizing of the single-use white fantasy wedding dress emerged most clearly in the 1950s. With the return of soldiers from World War II and the return of women to the domestic sphere, the fantasy wedding gown symbolized a return to more clearly marked gender differences and roles. Throughout the later part of the twentieth century, the experimentation with female gender was expressed in female wedding apparel. However, overall, the fantasy constructed in the 1950s, then echoed with highly publicized weddings such as that of Prince Charles and Princess Diana, embedded the single-use wedding gown in the imagination of young women as the ultimate symbol of this highly public rite of passage.

YOUNG ADULTHOOD

Rites of passage also occur within the adult world of work. In many cases these rites of passage are private, for example, the buying of a briefcase for a young, just-out-of-college professional. In other cases, the rite is public and includes more of the three formal stages of separation, liminality, and aggregation. For those entering into the military, formal rites of passage are often very significant, performed by groups who begin the process together and aggregate in their new role together at the end. Marine paratroopers go through a separation stage together when they first enlist. Their civilian dress is removed, their hair is cut uniformly short, and they physically move into training facilities away from their communities and families. The liminality stage is the training stage, which for paratroopers culminates in a required ten training jumps.

As is typical of rites of passage, the aggregation stage is the most vividly marked by dress and appearance. In this case, newly trained U.S. Marine paratroopers receive their *golden wings*, pins with two half-inch (1.25 centimeter) protruding points on the back, which are worn on the front chest of their uniform to mark their new rank. The symbolic meaning of "becoming a Marine" is also often a part of this aggregation ceremony. With the U.S. Marines known as the toughest group among the armed forces, the final rite of passage often involves not simply pinning the wings on the chest but proudly thumping the prongs of the pin into the chest of the new male initiates to symbolize their new, tough military identity. While in most cases this gesture draws a small

amount of blood, in some reported cases this ritual has resulted in repeated pounding of the pins into the chests of the young men by their older peers—with some labeling the practice as barbaric. This association of aggregation rites with hazing most commonly occurs within groups of young men who use this final stage of rites of passage to test the virility or strength of the new initiate. Similar problems have emerged in fraternity initiations, leading to regulation of these ceremonies on many college campuses.

AGING AND RETIREMENT

Rites of passage also mark retirement and the entrance into middle or older age groups. Leaving of a long-term position through retirement often includes a gift of a wearable symbol of loyalty and contribution to the work organization, such as a watch. For women, the recent emergence of Red Hat Society organizations provides a rite of passage for women moving from roles of caregiving into a period of their life where they are free to focus on themselves. Sometimes, as is the case with Red Hat Societies, a privately experienced rite of passage becomes a group rite of passage.

Red Hat Societies began in 1997, when founder Sue Ellen Cooper bought a red hat while she was on vacation and discovered that by wearing it she felt younger, more carefree, and more positive about herself as an older woman. Cooper enjoyed this feeling so much that she wanted to share it with other women. As a result, she began buying red hats for her female friends who were reluctantly celebrating fifty-plus birthdays. In doing this for her friends, Cooper also gave her friends a copy of the poem "Warning" by Jenny Joseph, which relates the wearing of outrageous red hats and purple apparel to aging with spirit and spit. In Jenny Joseph's words: "When I am an old woman I shall wear purple, and a red hat which doesn't go and doesn't suit me."

Just for fun, Cooper and her friends created the first Red Hat Society and began to wear their regalia in public; they quickly gained public recognition and positive attention from the mass media. Older women throughout the United States and Canada began to take notice of Cooper's group, leading to the development of a Web site and extensive e-mail networking among those interested in starting their own chapters of the organization. Red Hat Society membership has grown to include chapters officially registered on Cooper's Red Hat Society Web site (41,000 as of this writing) and regionally based unofficial chapters, with a total official membership numbering over one million and spanning over thirty countries. Once women from across the country began e-mailing Cooper, she decided to begin the official "disorganization" of the Red Hat Society as the official queen mother.

The three formal stages of rites of passage exist within the standardized Red Hat Society guidelines developed by Cooper. Red hats are exclusively reserved for women who are fifty years of age or older. Those younger than fifty interested in participating in a Red Hat Society chapter are encouraged to wear pink and lavender hats, thus marking their liminal status. At the age of fifty, Red Hat members go through what the queen mother refers to as a "red-uation" in which women formally become proper Red Hat Society members. Red-uation ceremonies captured on public Web sites typically feature a formal ceremonial presentation of the red hat, a story-telling session by friends of the new initiate, an exchanging of symbolic gifts, and a public and visible party for the new member. Red-uation includes both the separation stage

Members of the Red Hat Society (founded in the United States in 1997), which provides a rite of passage for women who are fifty years of age or older. Copyright Lise Powell, 2007. Used under license from Shutterstock.com

and the aggregation stage: Initiates arrive at the ceremony wearing a pink hat, which is removed at the stage of aggregation and replaced by a red hat. The public display of youthful, fun behavior characterizing the red-uation ceremony is central to the mission of the Red Hat Societies. By acting young together and wearing very visible and attention-getting apparel, these societies have actively worked to deconstruct negative impressions of female aging prevalent in modern youth-oriented culture.

DEATH

The rites of passage surrounding death are most visibly expressed by those losing a loved one. The wearing of mourning dress by those attending a funeral marks the sorrow of the separation stage. The wearing of mourning apparel over a long period of time following a death, or more simply an item of dress that reminds you of the loved one, marks the liminal stage—the stage of attempting to accept the death. The moving back into normal dress styles, or the final removal of the wedding band by a widow, marks the aggregation stage, the moving back into normal life after loss. The modern tendency to avoid confronting death has led to less visible displays of mourning, with the liminal stage often privately experienced but not publicly displayed.

POSTMODERN SUBCULTURAL IDENTITIES

The ability to continually renegotiate identity in the postmodern era opens up the possibility for rites of passage marking entrance into a range of new identities throughout the life cycle. Often in these less formal rites of passage, the stages of separation and liminality are not vividly marked by dress and appearance; however, the aggregation stage often includes the donning of a newly appropriate look symbolizing entrance into the adopted subculture.

For example, when author and punk researcher Lauraine Leblanc formally entered into the subcultural world of punk, she cut her hair in the characteristic Mohawk style with the help of her new group members.

The adopting of dress and appearance styles from outside one's own tradition and past is typical in this type of subcultural initiation. The adoption of other forms of North American Indian dress and appearance were used in the late 1960s and 1970s among countercultural groups living communally in small Indian-style villages. Living in Plains Indian tepees in the Pacific Northwest, young, white, suburban adults dressed in moccasins, headbands, and fringed leather, using dress to visibly announce their chosen new identity posed in rebellion against the suburban affluence and uniformity of the 1950s and early 1960s.

North American rites of passage, like those throughout the rest of the world, often focus on marking different stages of the life cycle. As individuals move from birth, to adolescence, to young adulthood, to first job, to marriage, to middle age, to retirement, and finally death, dress and appearance are used to mark the transitions for the initiate and for the surrounding audience. In addition, in the postmodern era, dress and appearance are also used to mark entrance into electively selected subcultural worlds within which individual members sometimes stay all their lives but that they often visit only briefly before moving on to another identity. The entrance into a new subcultural identity is often marked by appearance changes, either in a formal public or a private sense.

References and Further Reading

Cunnington, Phillis, and Catherine Lucas. *Costumes for Births, Marriages, and Deaths*. London: A. and C. Black, 1972.
Davis-Floyd, Robbie. *Birth as an American Rite of Passage*. Berkeley: University of California Press, 2003.

Deloria, Philip J. *Playing Indian*. New Haven and London: Yale University Press, 1998.

Gates, Henry Louis. "The Trope of a New Negro and the Reconstruction of the Image of the Black." *Representations* 24 (1988): 129–155.

Geffen, Rela M., ed. *Celebration and Renewal: Rites of Passage in Judaism*. Philadelphia: The Jewish Publication Society, 1993.

Leblanc, Lauraine. *Pretty in Punk: Girls' Gender Resistance in a Boy's Subculture*. New Brunswick, NJ, and London: Rutgers University Press, 2002.

Lynch, Annette. *Dress, Gender and Cultural Change: Asian American and African American Rites of Passage*. Oxford: Berg, 1999.

Lynch, Annette, Marybeth Stalp, and M. Elise Radina. "Growing Old and Dressing Dis-Gracefully." In *Dress Sense*, edited by Donald Clay Johnson and Helen Foster. Oxford: Berg, 2007.

Monsarrat, Ann. *And the Bride Wore: The Story of the White Wedding*. London: Dodd, Mead, 1973.

van Gennep, Arnold. *The Rites of Passage*. Chicago: University of Chicago Press, 1960.

Vida, Vendela. *Girls on the Verge: Debutante Dips, Drive-Bys, and Other Initiations*. New York: St. Martin's Griffin, 1999.

Annette Lynch

Influence of the Arts

The relationship of art to dress in any part of the world and at any time is complex, as is the case in the United States and Canada. Both art and dress reflect and share not only aesthetic elements but also parallel cultural, social, philosophical, geographical, technological, political, gender, and religious influences of any particular era. This confluence, or zeitgeist, characterizes the spirit of the times and defines the prevailing style. Yet even while sharing the formal visual elements of shape, color, texture, and line, art and dress differ in terms of purpose. Theorists and historians have debated about the hierarchical classification of art and dress within the continuum of visual expression, attempting to place dress within the fine arts or decorative arts.

In addressing the definition and purpose of art, the scholarly and curatorial community now define pure, inspired, original self-expression as *art*, relegating functional pieces—such as *dress*—to *decorative art* or *applied art* categories. Thus, painting, sculpture, and printmaking (termed *major* or *fine arts*) were separated from the *applied arts* (also known as *minor* or *decorative arts*). During the nineteenth century, the Industrial Revolution further separated the maker from the conceptual development, or the idea behind the work. As fashion became more industrialized and mass produced, dress and fashion were pushed further away from the core definition of art, which focused on self-expression and allowed for spontaneous leaps of the imagination during the creative process. However, during the past fifty years there has been a conscious blurring of these classifications and an overt attempt by artists to transcend previous categorization. Crafts have become more individually artistic; photography and film have become accepted as art; and some dress is now considered wearable art.

Despite these divisions, there is remarkable unity among visual expressions in any one period or culture. Shapes, forms, colors, proportions, and other visual characteristics are usually consistent if the artistic expression, or *style*, is truly embedded in the fundamental culture. North American fashion and dress developed from a Eurocentric foundation built upon centuries of stylistic evolution, which continue to be revived and to inspire fashion designers while also developing a recognizable American aesthetic.

PRIMARY SOURCES FROM EARLY CULTURES

Parallel phenomenon in art and dress can be seen in the earliest civilizations. Influences from these early forms of dress are the archetypal foundation for all Western dress and fashion, and they link to a continuous living tradition. A few examples from the period before Europeans settled in the Western Hemisphere illustrate this point. The 1920s and 1930s art deco style incorporated ancient Egyptian images, icons, and symbols. Minoan art from the island of Crete included distinctive "Mother Goddess" figures with tightly cinched waistlines; exposed breasts; and full, bell-shaped skirts. This hourglass figure dominated Western dress for four hundred years, from the sixteenth to mid-twentieth centuries. A further revival can be seen in the mid-twentieth century of small, corseted waistlines and deep, décolleté necklines contrasted with full, crinoline-supported skirts in the post–World War II New Look of 1947. It completely changed fashion at that time and prevailed throughout the 1950s.

Another example of enduring aesthetic influences is represented by the proportions and draped garments of the classical Mediterranean civilizations of Greece (500–323 B.C.E.) and later, Rome. The Hellenic raised-waistline style belted under the breasts has been consistently reinterpreted in Western fashion, during the Renaissance, the neoclassical Empire period in France, the aesthetic movement of the late nineteenth century, and periodically throughout the twentieth century, such as when Mariano Fortuny (1871–1949) working in Venice, Italy, took his vision of Greek Delphos dresses into production, creating graceful, pleated silk gowns. These sensuous dresses became signatures of many artistic North American women of the cultural and social elite. In the 1930s, U.S. designer Gilbert Adrian (1903–1959) glamorized classicism in many of his designs for Hollywood film goddesses, including Marlene Dietrich, Greta Garbo, and Jean Harlow, in both Metro-Goldwyn-Mayer films and in real life through his own couture fashion atelier in Beverly Hills, California. Other twentieth-century U.S. fashion designers also embraced this look.

U.S. actress Joan Crawford in the film *Letty Lynton*, 1932. U.S. designer Gilbert Adrian, who was influenced by classical styles, designed the dress. George Hurrell/John Kobal Foundation/Getty Images.

The legacy of the Byzantine period (ca. 330–1453 C.E.) has continued to inspire textile and fashion designers periodically. Notable are Italian Gianni Versace's (1946–1997) collection of 1991 and those of U.S. designers Oscar de la Renta (1932–) and Mary McFadden (1938–), making the heavily embellished references immediately recognizable in its many reiterations. Medieval tunic-style garments and cloaks served to inspire similar proportions and bold, graphic qualities in women's wear during the 1960s, when minidresses were embellished with bold graphic designs by French couturier André Courrèges (1923–), English designer Mary Quant (1934–), and U.S. designer Rudi Gernreich (1922–1985), who specialized in knitwear. Full-length, stretch-leg tights enabled the proportions and visual effect of his designs to be identical to the parti-colored men's costumes of the fourteenth and fifteenth centuries.

THE ITALIAN RENAISSANCE, BAROQUE, AND ROCOCO (FIFTEENTH TO EIGHTEENTH CENTURIES)

The interdependent synergy in art and dress is seen most vividly during the Renaissance, when the glorification of the individual included rich, elaborate dress. During the nineteenth century, *renaissance*, the French word for "rebirth," became the accepted term for this era. The legacy of the Renaissance is seen most clearly in the work of the aforementioned Mariano Fortuny, who invented many unique techniques to reinterpret Renaissance

textiles, primarily his luminous printed velvets designed for high-fashion robes, coats, and jackets worn over his pleated Delphos dresses. His work has subsequently inspired U.S. couturiers Mary McFadden and Marian Clayden of California. Their interpretations of dyed, printed, and voided velvets take the luxurious, sensuous textiles of Renaissance dress into the twenty-first century. They have, in turn, inspired many other U.S. "wearable artists" who have pursued the art of dyeing cloth for their artisanal clothing, which has become a version of U.S. couture.

While Italian Renaissance dress reveled in sensuous opulence, the northern countries adapted a more controlled approach based on Spanish aesthetics. Shared stylistic characteristics of symmetrical balance, stiff deportment, broad proportions, and conventionalized embellishment typify the dress of the sixteenth century. An extraordinary copperplate engraving by Simon van de Passe (1616) portrays North American Indian Pocahontas (ca. 1596–1617) dressed in full English formal fashion befitting an urban, middle-class Englishwoman documenting her visit to London with her American husband, John Rolfe. This rare early image records the first official marriage between a North American Indian woman, daughter of an Algonquian chief, and an Englishman. Subsequent images and reworkings of Pocahontas's story presented her as an emblem of the potential for North American Indians to be assimilated into Euro-American society.

The baroque period that followed abandoned the geometric emphasis in favor of robustly curvilinear shapes, rounded forms, and asymmetrical treatments of drapery and accessories. The toned-down version of this style came to early America as Puritan dress—dark, plain, simplified baroque fashion. The basic silhouette and design lines were shared; the fabrics, trims, and detailing, however, were in direct contrast to one another.

The historicism of the nineteenth century often revived selected baroque features in quantities of bulky trimmings, bouffant sleeves, and swags of drapery. A later example was Charles James's richly sculptural gowns (active ca. 1930–1950s).

In reaction to the elaborate pomp characteristic of baroque art, the form changed, moving toward lighter, smaller, more tightly curved decorative patterns. *Chinoiserie*, or Chinese-inspired design elements, added exoticism to rococo arts, especially textile and furniture design. This style had little to do with the realities of North American life during the eighteenth century. Playing against the lively French rococo aesthetic was the Dutch and English Puritan Protestant ethic of sobriety, restraint, practicality, and austerity. These were the roots planted in the New World that laid the groundwork for the development of the North American aesthetic.

NORTH AMERICA (SIXTEENTH TO EIGHTEENTH CENTURIES)

During the sixteenth through the eighteenth centuries, as North American colonies were being established in the New World, localized styles reflected basic English, French, Spanish, Dutch, German, Scottish, and Swedish influences imported by the new arrivals. Little original cultural innovation could be expected while the Europeans established their regional dominance and patterned life after their homelands, but there were local variations.

The dress and decorative embellishments that mixed European cuts and styles with indigenous materials and surface designs ultimately created a uniquely North American synthesis.

Examples include Western European styling and shaping of frock coats in the painted caribou hide coats worn by both non-natives and natives in Canada (from 1700 to 1930). The Europeanized cut is thought to have been influenced by the European cloth *presentation coats* given by the French as a token gift for diplomatic and public relations purposes. Similarly, nineteenth-century frontier explorers and settlers adapted the native fringe trim designed to conduct moisture from the surface of leather garments. This combination of frontier practicality and simplicity punctuated by North American Indian aesthetics is the essence of Americana perpetuated through the fashion designs by Ralph Lauren (1939–), purveyor of "iconic American looks," and the Sundance company of Colorado owned by actor Robert Redford. European glass trade beads reinterpreted indigenous quill-work embellishment on dress by the Plains Indians tribes and French-influenced floral beadwork by the Northeast/Woodland tribes from the nineteenth century on. The Northwest Coast tribes received Hudson Bay blankets from whalers, which were adopted for ceremonial regalia and embellished with abalone shell—later replaced by European buttons. Today, Northwest Coast native artist Dorothy Grant creates appliquéd versions of Northwest Coast totemic icons in contemporary cashmere garments.

Initially, these hybrid styles were exceptions to the garments worn by early immigrant townspeople, who generally followed European styles or directly imported clothing from England and France. With time, however, a decidedly North American style began to emerge. Despite the differences in materials, early North American art, architecture, and dress shared these common stylistic characteristics, which have continued to define the continent's design aesthetics: simplicity, austerity, and functionality. These aesthetic roots prevailed until emerging wealth and cosmopolitanism developed into colonial prosperity by the mid-eighteenth century, creating the desire and means to emulate European neoclassical aesthetics.

NEOCLASSICISM AND LATER NINETEENTH-CENTURY ART MOVEMENTS

The refreshing simplicity of neoclassicism was totally embraced by the founding fathers of the United States as symbolic of the democratic republic. The influence of neoclassicism was evident in early U.S. dress because it incorporated the typical columnar silhouette and raised waistline highlighted by elegant symmetry and orderly simplicity in fabric, trim, and accessories. The rapid spread of this style was also a major step in the democratization of fashion because more people could participate with the relative simplicity of cut and fabric. The high-waisted silhouette and innocence of the neoclassical style returned once again around 1910. U.S. ready-to-wear designer Claire McCardell updated the essence of neoclassicism in her 1946 "baby doll" look, which included a high-waisted cocktail dress with small puffed sleeves and drawstring neckline rendered in black wool jersey, and later in evening dresses draped from nylon tricot (ca. 1950). Similarly, California designer Jessica McClintock reintroduced the appeal of neoclassical, Victorian, and prairie styles during the 1970s through the 1990s.

During most of the nineteenth century, as industrial and technological advancements began to radically change daily life, European and North American artists utilized different stylistic

"Gibson Girl," by Charles Dana Gibson, ca. 1900. The U.S. version of art nouveau was epitomized by Gibson's illustrations, which captured the young, active "new woman" ideal of the twentieth century. Courtesy New York Public Library.

approaches now identified as neoclassicism, romanticism, realism or naturalism, and ultimately, impressionism. This time of revival styles in architecture and eclectic syntheses ultimately led to original developments, such as the arts and crafts movement's shingle style in North America. Dress and fashion paralleled some aspects of these movements, but rather than moving toward modernism, high fashion turned back to revivals of familiar past styles and reinterpretations of designs from the court costumes of the seventeenth and eighteenth centuries. The House of Worth, the first haute couture house in Paris, founded in 1858, took an authoritative lead in these nostalgic fashion revivals, and North Americans followed. For the remainder of the nineteenth century, it was the hallmark of class distinction and elitism among North American high society to be dressed by Worth and other French couturiers—the very opposite of egalitarian democracy.

Fashion and art were inextricably linked throughout the nineteenth century. In mid-nineteenth-century Victorian England, a group of reform painters adopted the cryptic label of "Pre-Raphaelites" to signify their belief that art history had taken the wrong direction during the Renaissance. In producing their emotionally charged but painstakingly rendered paintings of beautiful models dressed in medieval and Renaissance dress, they required historically accurate props and costumes based on fifteenth- and sixteenth-century dress that were already a reinterpretation of classical Greek and Roman styles. This art movement was the origin of *aesthetic dress*, as the models adopted the styles for themselves and inspired many followers who rejected cumbersome bustle fashions. Thus, the Pre-Raphaelites awakened admiration for a more graceful, fluid silhouette in fashion, which, although considered controversial at the time, gave new impetus and opened up the possibilities for change and reform in mainstream fashion.

Aestheticism spread from its origins in English literature to the fine and applied arts, elevating applied arts to a level in which dress design became recognized as an area of legitimate concern for the artist. English art critic John Ruskin advocated the rejection of crass materialism and the distinction between the so-called major and minor arts. Interior decoration, as well as dress design, which had formerly been entirely in the hands of artisans, now took on dimensions of a major social and artistic mission to be accomplished. Ultimately, this struggle to resolve the dichotomy between art and industry that had proliferated the rampant revivalism and reproduction of historic styles during the nineteenth century, evolved into the arts and crafts movement, which greatly affected North American design. Fundamental to this movement is the notion that all visual expressions in daily life should be in artistic harmony, a concept derived from Japanese aesthetic philosophy.

What Americans did help initiate was the incorporation and acceptance of Japanese influences into Western European art traditions. Artists collected porcelain, fans, textiles, and kimonos and incorporated them in their artworks. These new works also featured asymmetrical compositions, a major characteristic of Japanese art found in the woodcut prints. Such works showed Asian art as worthy of the admiration by the fashionable classes and helped to spread its popularity. Japanese fabrics and kimonos became widely popular from the 1860s onward.

The design-conscious aesthetic movement, with its cult of beauty and focus on the harmonious relationship of furniture, decorative objects, and even clothing with the décor of a room, together with the Japanese aesthetic, served as the seed of the American Arts and Crafts movement at the turn of the twentieth century. It is also the core of the late-twentieth-century North American wearable art movement.

THE UNITED STATES IN THE NINETEENTH CENTURY

Although the United States had been politically independent since 1776, the country continued to maintain its European cultural heritage. However, by the nineteenth century, a sense of U.S. nationalism was being expressed in romantic landscape paintings as well by the Hudson River school group (early-nineteenth-century native U.S. landscape and genre painters, many of whom lived in the vicinity of the Hudson River and the Catskill Mountains). This influence on dress may be less direct, but it helped to reinforce the sense of place that the new frontier held.

Another artist of the early nineteenth century, John James Audubon (1785–1851), became intent on painting pictures of all

Model wearing a costume designed by Erté. Erté (1892–1990) designed for Hollywood films, as well as opera and ballet productions. His highly theatrical style influenced U.S. fashion in the first half of the twentieth century. Evening Standard/Getty Images.

the birds of North America in their natural habitats. In addition to being valuable documentation of the birds, these images were also elegant works of art. They became a valuable tool later in the fight to protect birds from extinction at the hands of plume hunters seeking to meet the demand for feathers to trim the huge hats that were at the height of fashion at the turn of the twentieth century. One result was the establishment of the National Audubon Society (1905), which not only successfully thwarted this ecological disaster but also serves as a model for the ongoing efforts to restrain fashion's use of endangered species for garments.

For the most part, however, U.S. patrons still preferred European artists. And so, too, the patrons of high fashion continued to flock to European couturiers for their wardrobes. U.S. dressmakers copied the European styles, undermining any serious support for the development of original domestic high fashion in the early twentieth century.

U.S. reliance on French fashion leadership began to change during the 1890s as the arts and crafts movement that had originated in England took root in U.S. design. The goal of this movement's leaders was to have consumers surround themselves with good design produced by handmade processes, including hand-loomed and hand-printed fabrics and garments, and to influence the improvement of industrial design in this way. The Philadelphia Centennial Exposition of 1876 displayed handicraft, antique furniture, needlework art from Europe, and a number of reform garments, including a woman's "emancipation suit," which combined a chemise, drawers, corset, and corset cover. Also exhibited were Japanese textiles and ceramics that inspired the craze for *Japonisme* that swept the United States afterward. This Centennial Exposition provided the key link between the British aesthetic movement and the evolution of the arts and crafts style in the United States.

Japanese theories of design and lifestyle were also being integrated into the U.S. aesthetic through the works of many influential designers and architects who adopted the "total design" concept and were involved with clothing. Frank Lloyd Wright designed textiles for his architectural commissions and garments for his wife that were executed by a seamstress. Gustav Stickley began publication of *The Craftsman* in 1901, advocating that U.S. women free themselves from the "treadmill of fashion … because dress as an expression of character, as related to daily living, as part of personality like one's home and friends, is very closely and inevitably woven in the woof of life." Stickley's Craftsman Workshops, in fact, followed the core arts and crafts principles by creating textiles that utilized linen and flax, the simple bast fibers of early cultures; muted, natural colors of tan, ecru, brown, or green rather than harsh tones from aniline dyes; and hand-block-printed patterns and handwoven textures. Some would consider any textile of flat, abstracted, stylized pattern with bold outlines, created through appliqué or embroidery, to be in the arts and crafts style.

The basic tenets of the arts and crafts movement affected fashion by advocating simplicity, honesty, health, and individuality. Form follows function. An emphasis on health combined with natural beauty led to reform of the fashionable silhouette that complemented, rather than contorted, the human form and was in harmony with the proportions of the body. A preference for natural fibers, cotton, silk, and linen garments modestly embellished with embroidery was the hallmark of the North American arts and crafts style.

ART NOUVEAU: THE BIRTH OF MODERNISM (1890 TO 1910)

The style in the decorative arts that eventually came to be known as art nouveau originally emerged from nineteenth-century ideas expressed in writings on aesthetics. The term *art nouveau* was defined as art that refused to accept the prevailing cult of the past. The return to observation and imitation of nature translated into an emphasis on curves, floral motifs, abandonment of the straight line, and a vogue for Gothic and Japanese forms.

In this spirit, fashion adopted the straight-front corset, which created an elongated torso and thrust out the hips in art nouveau's characteristic whiplash curve. The figure was further heightened by enormous hats and narrowed skirts. Sinuous S-curves defined the silhouette as well as embellishments and trims that followed seaming and construction lines to create graceful, fluid fashions that typified the Edwardian era in England and *La Belle Epoque* in France.

The U.S. version of art nouveau was epitomized by "The Gibson Girl," named after illustrator Charles Dana Gibson, whose drawings captured the young, active "new woman" ideal of the twentieth century. Newfound freedom resulting from the long campaign for dress reform gave Gibson girl fashions a lighter, looser look, although the monobosom and small waist were still securely corseted, and collars were still high and stiffened with boning. Between 1890 and 1900, as more women joined the workforce outside the home, "separates" consisting of a skirt smoothly fitted over the hips worn with a blouse with leg-o-mutton sleeves (or "shirtwaist" blouse) gained popularity. This more practical, tailored apparel became a national uniform combining simplicity, utility, and practicality. In addition, increased physical activities and sports began to play a significant role in women's lives requiring lighter, more sensibly designed garments.

As early as 1907, the voluptuous, S-shaped female figure began to be replaced by a slender, willowy figure that would evolve into the abstracted, androgynous body type reflecting the geometric, cubistic art of the 1920s.

POSTIMPRESSIONISM/EXPRESSIONISM/ FAUVISM (1900 TO THE 1920s)

The vibrant European postimpressionist paintings of Vincent Van Gogh, Paul Gauguin, and Paul Cezanne released a joy through vivid color, bold brushwork, and sensual pleasure in nature. That legacy was passed to *Les Fauves*, or "The Wild Beasts," as they were initially called in their first Paris public showing in 1905. There was no common stated manifesto for the Fauves, but rather an intuitive reaction against the morbid styles of the 1890s. They freed color from its traditional role as the description of the local tone of an object and helped prepare both artists and public for the use of color as an expressive end in itself. Moving away from narrative and story-telling traditions in pictorial art, the formal visual components became the subjects of these paintings.

The leading practitioner was Frenchman Henri Matisse (1869–1954) whose art is founded upon his instinctive love of nature, of color and pattern, and of joyous subjects but with very special and very French qualities, expressed as "simplicity, serenity, and clarity." In addition to a lifetime devoted to painting, he also designed costumes for theater productions. Many of his paintings include patternings and textures based on his collection of world textiles and costumes. According to the book *Matisse, His Art and His Textiles: The Fabric of Dreams*, "textiles were the key to Matisse's visual imagination," and examples from Africa and the Middle East, as well as Europe, surrounded him in his studio. Matisse's love of color and simplified pattern influenced the overall future direction in textile designs created for daytime fashion and resortwear, especially.

CULTURAL EXOTICISM IN THE 1910s

The second decade of the twentieth century witnessed the cultural explosion inspired by the 1909 Paris performances by the Ballets Russe and French couturier Paul Poiret (1880–1944). "Oriental" influences from the Middle East, China, Japan, and Russia were combined to produce a colorful renaissance of peasant styles and non-Western aesthetics. Poiret commissioned artists to illustrate these new fashions for his own books *Le Robes de Paul Poiret* (1908) and *Gazette du Bon Ton* with bold, graphic *pochoir* prints that completely revolutionized fashion illustration,

Art deco evening dress, 1925. Art deco characteristics popular in North American fashion at this time included a flat, rectangular silhouette and beads, rhinestones, and sequins placed to catch the light while dancing. © McCord Museum M985.1.2. http://www.mccord-museum.qc.ca/en/

paving the way for art deco's new aesthetic. (*Pochoir* is the French term for an art technique whereby color is applied by hand to a print using a stencil. It is not silk-screening but creates a similar flat tone of color in selected areas of a printed outline image.)

Romain de Tirtoff, known as Erté (1892–1990), emigrated to Paris in 1912 and worked briefly with Paul Poiret before branching out on his own. His flamboyant, yet meticulous, fashion illustrations strongly influenced North American fashion from 1915 to 1936, during which time he designed 240 covers for the U.S. fashion magazine *Harper's Bazaar*. Highly theatrical and imaginative, his unique style also led him to design costumes for the Folies Bergère and briefly for Hollywood films, as well as for opera and ballet productions. The direct influence of his work has continued in show costumes worn in Las Vegas revues and in the work of U.S. designer Bob Mackie, who did much work for Cher during the last quarter of the twentieth century.

Many North American clients of French couture embraced this change toward escapist, fantasy styles—heavily influenced by exotic Middle Eastern and Asian aesthetics—which was in direct contrast to the simplification and controlled austerity seen in the abstract paintings of Georgia O'Keeffe and Charles Demuth in their steady march toward modernism.

Moreover, the exotic aesthetic legacies of both Paul Poiret and Erté inspired an entire generation of North American artists and designers of the late twentieth century to create the wearable art movement that began in the 1960s. Their wit, panache, and aesthetic daring spurred the generation to rebel against the mass-produced, conformist clothing of the 1950s.

THE TWENTIETH CENTURY: FASHION, ART, AND TECHNOLOGY

Advancing technologies stimulated changes in both art and fashion in the late nineteenth and early twentieth centuries. As painting began to compete with the new realism of the camera, more experimental approaches were called for. The impact of photographic realism pushed artists to seek new directions for their art that can be summarized as a series of "isms." *Constructivism* and *cubism* looked at structure, movement, and the fragmentation of form and reflected the enormous impact of the new phenomenon of moving pictures on the static art of painting. *Impressionism* and *fauvism* experimented with light and color. *Modernism* embraced machines' movement and speed. *Surrealism* questioned inner perceptions and what the mind sees. All of these movements had an influence on fashion and other decorative arts—both directly and indirectly. The legendary Armory Show held in New York in 1913 crystallized the debate that had persisted in U.S. cultural life since the mid-eighteenth century: Should U.S. art be rooted in the U.S. environment and subject matter? Or should the U.S. artist take a more global point of view and look to Europe for inspiration? Fashion was at the same crossroads.

As handmade production was replaced with industrial mass production, there was a natural trend toward simplification and standardization imposed on style in order to speed output and maximize profit. When the sewing machine was first introduced in the 1840s, the tendency was to proliferate trims and embellishments, resulting in the overloaded ornamentation characteristic of the Victorian period. However, as factories were established during the 1890s to produce shirtwaist blouses, among other clothing items, designs became relatively more simplified.

In the arts of painting, sculpture, and architecture, as well, ultimately the image of the machine and symbols of speed were portrayed through the use of metallic surfaces and simplified, curved forms. A fascination with this progress fueled art deco and streamline moderne styles, as well as surrealism in the 1930s, which carried through to all aspects of the decorative arts. Art deco was the second all-inclusive aesthetic, after art nouveau, to sweep across all forms of visual expression.

One pioneering U.S. artist whose abstract paintings evolved from her own authentic vision of modernity was Georgia O'Keeffe (1887–1986). The simplicity of her enlarged close-up images of flowers, the spare austerity of her Southwestern landscapes, and the precise geometry of her urban cityscapes all demonstrate her innate understanding of modern abstraction. This pursuit of the essence of form is the same direction that clothing was taking throughout the twentieth century.

1920s CUBISM, MODERNISM, AND THE INTERNATIONAL STYLE

The 1902 Turin (Italy) Exhibition was dedicated to modern decorative arts, with its main purpose to consolidate and encourage the spread of an international style. The international style advocated utter simplicity and elimination of ornamentation—"form follows function." In its quest for universal geometric purity, it also played cubistic solids against voids, giving each equivalency. This reductionist philosophy stripped away nonessentials and provided cold, clean abstract shapes and uncluttered surfaces that eventually led to minimalism.

The culmination of this trend in the pictorial arts is the iconic, geometric, totally nonobjective painting titled *Composition with Red, Blue, and Yellow* (1930) by Dutchman Piet Mondrian (1872–1944), which was quite literally translated into a dress by French couturier Yves Saint-Laurent in 1965. The color blocks contained in black-outlined rectangular shapes allude to the steel frameworks of skyscrapers and perfectly echo the rectangular silhouette of the dress, a revival of the 1920s chemise. This led to countless knockoffs by North American fashion, especially for sportswear and activewear, where bold color blocking became synonymous with team logos and branding.

Following the international style direction in the 1910s, French couturiere Gabrielle "Coco" Chanel (1883–1971) popularized the aesthetic of freedom, comfort, and simplicity, which became the modern ideal, merging this with the classical French values of elegance and restraint. She also introduced *jersey*—knitwear fabric that had been used for fishermen's sweaters and underwear—as outerwear, and her "sportswear" became streetwear. It was her belief that the streets would be the true source for new modes of expression.

Chanel also understood the massive changes provoked by World War I. She proposed that clothing should be uniform rather than idiosyncratically unique—an idea that was the antithesis of haute couture's one-of-a-kind custom dressmaking. Standardization and repetition of clothing, just like the assembly-line, industrially produced Model T Fords and ready-to-wear clothing, promoted simplicity and architectural structure. Chanel was also predisposed to wearing her boyfriend's clothing for its practical comfort and rebellious symbolism, resulting in abstracted and flattened curves of the female figure echoing the geometry of cubism. This tailored silhouette became the most enduring fashion for women's wear throughout the twentieth century.

ART DECO (1920s AND 1930s)—AND AMERICAN SWIMWEAR

Replacing the naturalistic curving forms of art nouveau, art deco adopted geometric abstraction and nonrepresentational approaches to imagery and patterning. This aesthetic reinforced fashion's flat, rectangular silhouette and the geometric surface patterns that enlivened it. *Streamline moderne*, a variation of art deco, was forward looking, capitalizing on machine-age aerodynamic styling designed for speed and use of metallics and shiny, reflective, machined surfaces. Movement was a key dynamic in this new aesthetic. Short flapper dresses covered with beads, sequins, and rhinestones—all designed to catch the light while dancing—were a ubiquitous embodiment of North American ease, youth, and movement.

Quick to incorporate art deco and cubist-inspired style elements into modern sport and swimwear, French designer Jean Patou and textile artist Sonia Delaunay both produced revolutionary, bold graphic patterns for resort fashions. U.S. knitting mills in Portland and California seized upon this idea—a perfect application of the naturally geometric motives produced by knitting technology—and transformed Paris haute couture inspiration into knitted, tubular, one-piece swimwear for the masses.

In 1921, the Portland Knitting Company of Portland, Oregon, perfected the "elastic" or "rib" stitch, which offered twice the elasticity of plain jersey and clung to the body like a second skin. This brilliant U.S. technology eliminated excess bulk and weight from bathing suits. In 1917, the company sold about six hundred bathing suits. By 1930, having changed its name to Jantzen Mills after founder Carl Jantzen, it was the world's leading manufacturer of swimming suits, selling over 1.5 million units. They also pioneered the branding of Jantzen as "The National Swimming Suit" through the use of the "Red Jantzen Diving Girl" logo that was sewn to the outside of each suit from 1920 on. This brilliant marketing image was reproduced in the form of a variety of trinkets and gadgets and even made into windshield decals and a hood ornament for Model T Fords. This perfect combination of U.S. technical ingenuity and promotional marketing, which capitalized on the Western climate and outdoor, sporting lifestyle, laid the foundation for the West Coast fashion industry that was built on sportswear.

Two knitting mills based in Los Angeles, similarly specializing in mass-produced underwear and sweaters, also went into the swimsuit business in the 1920s, changing their names to Catalina and Cole of California. Fred Cole, located next to Hollywood and the burgeoning film industry, incorporated glamour into swimwear and continued to experiment with fabrications and styling expressive of this look. Combined with film studio public relations and media hype, these looks began to revolutionize bathing suit design internationally by the 1930s. A new "California beauty" with long, tan legs and sporty outdoor freshness redefined the fashion ideal representing U.S. freedom.

Ultimately, it was U.S. knitwear designer Rudi Gernreich who revolutionized swimwear with his "Topless Suit." Evolving from a series of cutout suits that he presented over the span of several years, he finally produced the suit that bared the breasts in 1964—after making a prediction that "bosoms will be uncovered within five years" in 1962. This was followed by the revolution in undergarments starring the "No-Bra bra" and then bralessness. The fact that these fashion developments coincided with the era

U.S. music-hall and jazz artist Josephine Baker, ca. 1926. She helped popularize *l'art negre* in the 1920s. Gaston Paris/Roger Viollet/Getty Images.

of availability of birth control pills, the height of the feminist movement, and legislated equal opportunities for women only added to its cachet as a trend-setting symbol of women's emancipation.

OTHER INFLUENCES: PICASSO AND AFRICAN ART

In the United States, art deco and the subsequent art moderne style were embraced by architects, artists, and fashion designers alike. The signature tubular silhouette of fashion during the 1920s incorporated similar motifs through beading, embroidery, and surface patterning. The continuing U.S. search for a native

vernacular appropriate to modern decoration turned to films and photography. The silver screen provided the perfect format to present sleek gowns made of light-reflective silk satin and crepe de chine or beaded and covered with paillettes to highlight movement in dance and performance.

Sources for art deco style include a mixture of exotic and historic aesthetics and can be seen as being rooted in the displays of colonial artifacts at international expositions as well as post–World War I waves of nationalism. The exotic was a vital component of modernity. Rarely used as a derogatory term, *exotic* suggested an exciting, sensual, and decorative vision that carried the dynamics of nineteenth-century colonialism into a global future. Perhaps the richest field for the study of the taste for the exotic is the vogue for *l'art negre*, a phenomenon largely of the 1920s. It came to signify modernity in fashionable Parisian interiors, in the frenetic world of the cabaret, in the monumental projects of colonial enterprise, and in the search for an African American identity.

Jazz music, in both Europe and North America, was an integral component of the vogue for l'art negre. Born of the fusion of European musical forms, complex West African rhythms and syncopations, and American blues and ragtime, jazz came to simultaneously symbolize the exotic and modern urban living. The parallels between the complex patterns of jazz and the energetic geometric forms of art deco were clear, and as a result, the style was often known as *jazz moderne*. As a later musicologist wrote, it seems that the striking qualities of jazz are found again in the ornamental arts, in the fine arts, as well as in the arts that one terms *applied*—the same sense of symmetries, oppositions, repetitions, and accidents of rhythm and counterpoint. By the early 1930s, the vogue for l'art negre was beginning to

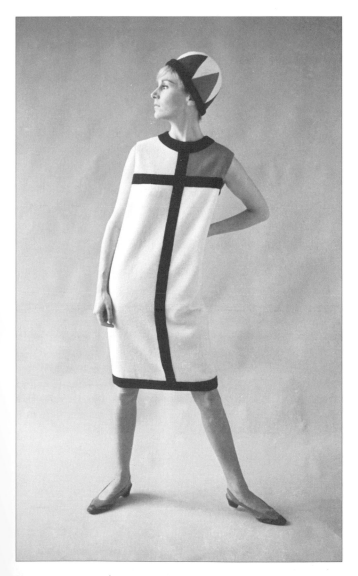

Mondrian-influenced sleeveless dress by Yves Saint-Laurent, 1965. Mondrian's art also influenced U.S. fashion designers of the 1960s. Terry Fincher/Getty Images.

wane. However, the draw of the fantasy exotic was no less powerful during the 1930s, though the passion for things African was replaced by a growing fascination with North American Indian and pre-Columbian art. Ultimately, for the mainstream culture that art deco represented, the appeal of the exotic would diminish in the later 1930s as Nazi cultural politics created a fatal association between the primitive or the exotic and the hedonistic degenerate.

FANTASY: DADAISM AND SURREALISM (1920s TO THE 1940s)

As a result of World War I, European intellectuals and artists began to question the premises on which their entire culture had been based. This is reflected in art movements such as *Dadaism* (1916–1922), in which nonsense, anti-art, and calculated irrationality were primary ideas. The only law respected by the Dadaists was that of chance and the only reality, that of their own imaginations. *Surrealism* (1924–1940s) was the successor to Dadaism. Both of these movements had a greater impact on European art than North American. Surrealist theory is heavily laden with concepts borrowed from psychoanalysis and was linked to fashion by its preoccupation with the female body, the world of real objects, and the life of objects in the mind—as interpreted, as modified, as in dreams. Its goal was to make the familiar strange. Generating surprising juxtapositions of imagery and objects, surrealist artists such as Salvador Dalí and Jean Cocteau collaborated closely with French haute couture designer Elsa Schiaparelli (1890–1973) to create some of fashion's most memorable expressions of the twentieth century.

Surrealism did not become acclimated in the United States until several of its European leaders emigrated in the late 1930s and early 1940s. Enigmatic photographs by Horst P. Horst, Cecil Beaton, and Man Ray (1890–1976) were published in U.S. fashion magazines and popularized some of these fashion ideas that continue to fascinate designers. Surrealism juxtaposed ordinary, everyday objects in extraordinary settings—creating the unreal through association.

Dadaism and surrealism reflected the confusion and disillusionment of the interwar years experienced primarily within the European community. One spectacular dress by California designer Gilbert Adrian from 1945 captures the post–World War II U.S. surrealist era. A rather modest black rayon crepe afternoon dress with a gathered skirt incorporates a black-and-white photographic image of a pitcher of milk printed on the bodice and a sliced loaf of bread on the skirt, symbols of the nurturing role of women. It represents life and hope.

NONOBJECTIVE ART (1945 TO THE 1960s)

The legacy of surrealist artists, many of whom came to the United States to escape European persecution during World War II, strongly influenced the nonobjective artists that began the abstract expressionist movement. This style was about the act of painting and the anxiety faced in real life; it emphasized liberation and creative freedom. The subject was paint and how it reacted on the canvas. This so-called action painting combined chance effects, a frenzy of psychophysical action, and captured the "furious energy of the process of painting, the sense of risk, of a challenge successfully—but barely—met" (Jansen 1971, 365).

Action painting marked the international coming of age for U.S. art. Its link to fashion was visually through the textile designs that it inspired. But the release of creative freedom set the stage for the creative revolution of the 1960s.

Evolving from this was the much quieter color-field painting (mid-1950s–1960s), which reduced imagery to simple abstracted rectangles of richly blurred, brushed-on color. Related to the classic color theory experiments of Joseph Albers, these artists isolated the essence of painting on canvas cloth and enlarged the scale (7 1/2 feet, or 2.3 meters, tall) for dramatic backdrops for modern architecture and interior design. The result created the purest subdued, contemplative stillness with an impressionistic softness, in direct opposition to the aggressiveness of action painting. In a similar vein, Helen Frankenthaler and others pioneered these ideas in the 1960s through their "stain paintings," in which thin, translucent color washes of acrylic paints were left to drift over the canvas surface, their patterns left to chance. A technique reminiscent of Rorshach inkblots, the random patterns used in psychological tests, these works suggested amorphous images and impressions beyond the control of the artist open to the viewer's interpretation, which were also seen in the tie-dyed clothes of young hippies.

All of these trends had more impact on contemporary textile designs than on the form or silhouette of fashion. With the increasingly simplified rectangular shapes of garments predominating during the 1960s that served as virtual canvases, the body became a moving art form. This led directly to North American wearable art, especially as hand-dyed, handwoven, and hand-knitted textiles generated unique one-of-a-kind textiles for the geometric clothing forms based on the kimono.

In opposition to these chance effects, many artists turned away from action painting in favor of the hard-edge style, with flat areas of color carefully delineated and controlled. American Frank Stella, inspired by Mondrian, evolved a nonfigurative, self-contained style based on shaped canvases, eschewing the rectangular and emphasizing impersonal precision and an object more than a picture. Also spawned by Mondrian, *op art* was concerned with optics, the physical and psychological process of vision. Devoid of emotional appeal and more related to science and technology, it extended optical illusion to nonrepresentational art. These stylistic developments created the era of super graphics and bold, simple, colorful designs for clothing.

POP ART (1960 TO THE 1970s)

Fashion lies at the nexus of commerce and art. *Pop art* pushed the art world into that raw, lowbrow world of commerce and popular culture that thrives on advertising, magazine illustrations, comic strips, and celebrity. Unlike Dada, pop art was not motivated by despair or disgust with present-day civilization; it viewed commercial culture as raw material to be celebrated. Playing on the principles of repetition and enlarged scale, common subjects such as soup cans, silk-screened images of celebrities, U.S. flags, and comic strips were shown on the walls of leading museums. Fashion similarly developed its love of incorporating company logos into clothing designs that became walking advertisements, removing all subtle references and any doubt as to whose label was being worn. Signature logos are now standard elements in fashion clothing and accessories even for the highest couture designer lines: the final triumph of commerce over art.

Dior-inspired floral-print dresses by Claire McCardell, modeled at Bloomingdale's, United States, 1956. McCardell played a major role in developing U.S. ready-to-wear designs, creating clothes that were comfortable, practical, elegant, and affordable. Paul Schutzer/Time Life Pictures/Getty Images.

THE U.S. AESTHETIC

These qualities—simplicity, functionalism, and practicality—define the U.S. aesthetic that can be traced through nineteenth- and twentieth-century fashion. This lineage connects rural and frontier clothing with U.S. sportswear and ready-to-wear. It also reflects the eclectic patchwork of ideas that fashion has borrowed from its many source cultures, both native and nonnative—truly a melting pot that combines and synthesizes selected bits into something uniquely American.

Whereas nineteenth-century British designer William Morris returned to medieval Europe for inspiration, U.S. artists and artisans returned to their own regional heritage. Interest in regional heritage crafts, rag rugs, lacemaking, and embroidery all underwent revivals during the 1890s as women's groups sought to preserve and expand upon their own historical arts, as well as generate income for themselves. There was developing interest in the indigenous arts of the Southwest such as North American Indian textiles, which were collected by crafts enthusiasts, as well as handweaving from the southern highlands of Kentucky and Tennessee and North Carolina's Appalachian area. Chicago, on the other hand, was profoundly influential as the midwestern frontier and pioneered with skyscrapers and modern machines, no longer reliant on imitating East Coast and European prototypes. And in California and the Far West, the Spanish-Mexican culture, along with the *mission style*, was incorporated into frontier concepts of truly continent-wide proportions. Architecture was integrated with the landscape through horizontal design lines and native materials. Clothing reflected a functionalism derived from pioneer homesteaders, Hispanic gauchos and cowboys, and the rural work ethic.

The Navajo of the Southwest were also affected by contact with nineteenth-century white settlers and they adopted the European long "broomstick-pleated" skirts and velvet blouses as their everyday dress. Examples also exist of embellished U.S. Army officer's coats worn as "wedding coats" by North American Indian brides during the nineteenth century. These reciprocal influences are later evident in the fashion styles worn by Millicent Rogers, a New York socialite and tastemaker who adopted this Southwestern style of dress when she moved to New Mexico in 1949 and which she subsequently introduced into the pages of *Vogue* magazine, also popularizing Navajo silver jewelry as a fashion item. This look is one of the perennial favorites in the collections of Ralph Lauren since 1985.

Similarly in Florida, the now famous Seminole patchwork clothing was a direct result of contact with nineteenth-century Europeans, inspired by the settlers' patchwork quilts and then developed further as sewing machines became available to the natives, who produced their own distinctive diagonal-strip constructions. This technique was later adopted by U.S. quilters and fashion designers who have perpetuated it in late-twentieth-century wearable art.

Overall, arts and crafts reformers were concerned with the improvement of public aesthetic taste: the incorporation of art into daily life for all classes of people—part of the social liberalism that characterized the age of suffragettes and labor reform—and the development of a simple, natural, and functional aesthetic. North America had finally discovered its sources for an authentic, democratic aesthetic expression.

The most authentic, democratic North American fashion that emerges from these early aesthetic and philosophical ideals are *jeans*, denim work pants that were originally created for the gold miners in California in the 1870s. The pants and the Levi's brand have endured and dominated the international fashion scene throughout the twentieth century. Fancy Western wear was also pioneered in California by a transplanted New Yorker named Nudie Cohn, the original "rhinestone cowboy." His mixture of Western styling with the Hispanic love of color, glitz, and spangles created the unique show costumes worn by "singing cowboys" such as Roy Rogers and Gene Autry. These perpetuate and build on the early design innovations seen in the Wild West shows of William "Buffalo Bill" Cody, who modified North American Indian costumes for his show business purposes.

Corporate CEO Ralph Lauren, probably the most representative of U.S. designers, has successfully implemented his regional vision in the fashion business. Identifying several key North American themes, Lauren interpreted classic looks for his fashion and interior design collections as if designing for Broadway stage or Hollywood film productions, role-playing in fantasy environments and clothes to evoke distinctly American regional aesthetics. He creates highly desirable "sets and costumes" for the U.S. consumer that are also wildly popular overseas.

"MESSENGER OF AMERICAN MODERNITY" (THE 1940s AND 1950s)

When World War II broke out and many French couturiers closed their doors and went into exile, an opportunity was presented to U.S. designers to step out of the European fashion shadow. Through the efforts of Dorothy Shaver, president of Lord & Taylor, and Eleanor Lambert, U.S. designers became recognized names.

Claire McCardell (1905–1958) has been hailed as the most important U.S. ready-to-wear designer of the twentieth century—and can be considered the ultimate expression of the democratic ideal. She is credited with creating the U.S. style of progressive, casual dress in the twentieth century that was without precedent: comfortable, practical, elegant, and affordable. There were other North American designers at this time, but McCardell was a pioneer (in the 1940s–1950s), refusing to visit the Paris collections or to be influenced by the current New Look European fashions. She resisted the trend for Eurocentric taste—yet was, herself, heavily influenced by the use of bias-cut designs of French couturier Madeleine Vionnet of the 1920s and 1930s and Chanel's use of jersey knits and pragmatic design elements based on menswear.

Butterfly evening dress by Elsa Schiaparelli, 1937. Schiaparelli was influenced by surrealist artists such as Salvador Dalí, and her collections were widely publicized in the United States. Lipnitzki/Roger Viollet/Getty Images.

The concept of fashion as art had not been fully developed since the widely publicized Schiaparelli collections of the 1930s, which incorporated the work of surrealist artists including Salvador Dalí. What inspired California art gallery owner Frank Perls to hold a twenty-year retrospective of McCardell's work in 1953, and what the United States had long recognized, was the pure design genius inherent in McCardell's entirely undecorated visions of women's clothing—the design of the garment itself, its cut, its functionality—its "McCardellism." Believing only in that which withstood constant erasure, Claire McCardell had mastered the art of design.

WEARABLE ART: ARTIFACTS FOR THE WALL OR THE WEARER

The American wearable art movement evolved from the abstract expressionist era, when figurative art had been abandoned. It put the figure back into art and introduced movement in combination with textile paintings. Largely inspired by Japanese kimonos, which are often displayed on the wall, the simple, geometric pieces of cloth that make up of most of these garments create the perfect canvas for the textile artist. Most artists are not interested in the structure or design of the garment, which merely became the vehicle for virtuoso textile designs, whether handwoven, crocheted, knitted, printed, or dyed. The tie-dyed and hand-embellished jeans of the 1960s hippies slowly evolved into sophisticated, handmade, one-of-a-kind clothing and accent garments concurrent with a renaissance of textile arts inspired by global aesthetics and traditions.

The impulse to create wearables also grew from a rejection of standardization and mass-produced clothing and a nostalgia for artisan handcrafts that were being lost to industrial processes. Clumsy, awkward, and often humorous in the beginning, wearable art has evolved into highly sophisticated North American artisan couture. The garment format provided a means for artists to enliven their textiles through fashion shows, photographic images, and performances. Be they narrative, abstract, highly personal, or based in tradition, the images, colors, and patterns explore every subject, feeling, emotion, and theme that art addresses. The fact that more women are practicing artists and that museums and galleries have accepted this blurred category provides even greater impetus to this genre.

Installations of nonwearable art based on clothing forms have also become more prevalent for many of these same reasons. Creative explorations of objects of dress, including corsets, bustles, high-heeled shoes, wedding dresses, and other powerful female signifiers, are popular artifacts for exhibitions such as The Empty Dress: Clothing as Surrogate in Recent Art (1993–1995) and Discursive Dress (1993), which raise questions about the social and cultural meaning of fashion as art, as sculpture, as surrealist dream, as historical reality, as metaphor, and as subject. These explorations of the role of clothing in cultural self-definition have

also stimulated a new body of writing, publishing, and scholarly inquiry. The early twenty-first century appears to have closed the gap between art and fashion—for the moment.

References and Further Reading

Ayers, Dianne, Timothy Hansen, Beth Ann McPherson, and Tommy Arthur McPherson II. *American Arts and Crafts Textiles*. New York: Harry N. Abrams, 2002.

Benton, Charlotte, Tim Benton, and Ghislaine Wood, eds. *Art Deco 1910–1939*. London: V&A Publications, 2003.

Blum, Stella. "Introduction." In *Designs by Erte: Fashion Drawings and Illustrations from Harper's Bazaar*, by Erté. New York: Dover Publications, 1976.

Brunner, Kathleen, Ann Dumas, Jack Flam, Remi Labrusse, Hilary Spurling, and Dominique Szymusiak. *Matisse, His Art and His Textiles: The Fabric of Dreams*. London: Royal Academy of Arts, Thames & Hudson, 2004.

Bullis, Douglas. *California Fashion Designers*. Layton, UT: Peregrine Smith Books, 1987.

Dale, Julie Schafler. *Art to Wear*. New York: Abbeville Press, 1986.

Felshin, Nina. *Empty Dress: Clothing as Surrogate in Recent Art*. New York: Independent Curators, 1993.

Galassi, Susan Grace, Margaret F. MacDonald, and Aileen Riberiro, with Patricia de Montfort. *Whistler, Women, & Fashion*. New Haven, CT: The Frick Collection, New York, and Yale University Press, 2003.

Garner, Philippe, ed. *The Encyclopedia of Decorative Arts 1890–1940*. London: Quarto Publishing, 1978.

Hall, Marian, with Marjorie Carne and Sylvia Sheppard. *California Fashion: From the Old West to New Hollywood*. New York: Harry N. Abrams, 2002.

Jansen, H.W. *The History of Art for Young People*. 2nd ed. New York: Harry N. Abrams, 1971.

Koda, Harold. *Goddess: The Classical Mode*. New Haven, CT: Yale University Press and the Metropolitan Museum of Art, 2003.

Lencek, Lena, and Gideon Bosker. *Making Waves: Swimsuits and the Undressing of America*. San Francisco: Chronicle Books, 1989.

Leventon, Melissa. *Artwear: Fashion and Anti-Fashion*. London: Thames & Hudson and Fine Arts Museums of San Francisco, 2005.

Martin, Richard. *Fashion and Surrealism*. New York: Rizzoli and the Fashion Institute of Technology, 1987.

Martin, Richard. *Cubism and Fashion*. New York: The Metropolitan Museum of Art, 1999.

Steele, Valerie. *Women of Fashion: Twentieth-Century Designers*. New York: Rizzoli, 1991.

Wollen, Peter, with Fiona Bradley. *Addressing the Century: 100 Years of Art & Fashion*. London: Hayward Gallery Publishing, 1998.

Yohannan, Kohle, and Nancy Nolf. *Claire McCardell: Redefining Modernism*. New York: Harry N. Abrams, 1998.

Jo Ann C. Stabb

Film

Perhaps nothing in the twentieth century has influenced North American clothing more than film or, to use the more prosaic term, the movies. Many authors have written about the role of the designer throughout the past hundred years, claiming that the fashionable style and look comes essentially from that rarified source, but a close look at the history of the movies and their pervasive role in modern society suggests otherwise. From their beginning in the 1890s, films have fascinated, captivated, and subtly, even if perhaps unwittingly, acted as tastemaker, trend recorder, and guide. Today, it is hard to define specifically the role of movies in influencing clothing; the question, of course, remains: Who copies what? Do the movies, which reflect contemporary life, simply copy what is out there, or do they capture the essence of the times, reinterpret it to tell their stories, and in the process, in that indefinable mix of storytelling, art, technology, and sensitivity to the times, provide the models needed to enable individuals to express their current lives? The answer is cloudy at best, but there can be no doubt that the movies have influenced dress.

EARLY YEARS

Even during the first years of moviemaking's emergence in the United States, patterns of interaction were clearly being established: The magnetic attraction between filmmakers and audiences was evident from the beginning. Even before filmmaking left New York and New Jersey around 1910 for the constant sunshine of California, where outdoor filming could go on all year round, enamored young moviegoers began demanding to know the names of their favorite actors, who had, before then, gone unrecognized. Once actors' names appeared on U.S. screens, fans wanted to know more about them. And once they demanded to know, various venues of information sprang up to answer their call.

Prime among these were the movie or fan magazines. In a happy coincidence—or perhaps not a coincidence at all—photography had matured hand in hand with the rise of cheaper magazine publication, offering pictures, immediate and captivating, of the new stars. The publishers quickly responded by writing articles on the beautiful young people who gravitated to California and the movies, telling avid readers about their lifestyles, making up glamorous, upper-class lives for these rare people, most of whom had emerged from gray, working-class existences. In creating the legends, details of all sorts, true and false, appeared in the fan magazines. They even wrote about the clothes the actors wore,

selling ideas and even the garments themselves as they went. Article after article discussed in fervid language, calculated to tempt, the choices (or those made for them) that the actors preferred, where they wore these beautiful clothes, how they looked in them (back and front), and what movie in the near future would feature, if not these exact garments, then ones similar or even more beautiful. The magazines were read by hundreds of thousands each month.

The movies themselves introduced new style and new ideas to a wide audience, even as early as the 1910s. Mae Marsh, for example, in 1912 agreed to bare her legs (risking scandal in the doing) in a caveman scene for director D. W. Griffith after other actresses had demurely refused. At about the same time, Mack Sennett's Bathing Beauties picked up on this daring to give up the sedately covering swim dresses, with long black stockings and suitably baggy bloomers that had been the only acceptable fashion for half a century, in favor of a newer, lighter, barer bathing suit worn without stockings. Thus, even before World War I, the seeds of modernity in swim clothing had been sown and, most important, had been broadcast around the world.

So pervasive were the movies and their influence that during this same period, German and English manufacturers became aware of a notable rise in demand for things American—not just clothing, but other goods as well—as their fellow citizens saw them in movies. As a result, to the distress of European businessmen, U.S. imports rose sharply. This situation continued throughout the entire Golden Age of the movies. The irony of this was that the circumstances of these goods—what they stood for in U.S. life—never really existed for the average person in the United States. The things the audiences saw—the beautiful houses with vast rooms, high ceilings, and gracious stairways; the racy motor cars; the elegantly dressed men and women; the dazzling jewelry; the luxurious hotels, spas, resorts, and clubs that spoke "American" to the audiences who wanted them all as a result—were in fact the products of the moviemakers' imaginations. They were the creations of immigrant moguls who themselves wanted, like Jay Gatsby in F. Scott Fitzgerald's novel *The Great Gatsby*, to fit in. The life they presented in the movies, especially the opulent, leisured, and moneyed life, was their dream, their vision of America, and almost never reality. But so successful were they in creating this extraordinary movie world that audiences everywhere unquestioningly accepted the images presented and were prompted in turn to demand the goods they saw on the screen. As for clothing, by the 1920s, the movie star costumes that photographed well fell into the same categories as all the rest of the consumer goods portrayed on screen. People saw them; people wanted them.

It is difficult to discuss the relationship between dress and the movies without taking into consideration the bodies that wore the clothing. Between the beginnings of the movies and the 1920s, actors realized that the camera tended to make them seem heavier than they actually were. Tiny sixteen-year-old Mary Pickford, on coming from the stage to the Biograph Company in 1909, was aghast at her on-screen image. Much later she declared, "I had no idea I was so stocky." She was five feet and one inch (about 1.5 meters) tall and weighed 115 pounds (about 52 kilos). From then on, during her film career, she kept her weight at 95 pounds

The swim dresses of Mack Sennett's Bathing Beauties represented a revolution in swimwear that did away with long black stockings and baggy bloomers. Washington, D.C., 1919. Library of Congress Prints and Photographs Division LC-USZ62-99823.

(43 kilos). She was perhaps the first to realize how the camera lens changed her image but certainly not the last. A leaner, sleeker body that looks as if it were the product of diet and exercise has stayed as an ideal for good or evil ever since. It is a body that both enhances and is enhanced by beautiful clothing. Movie stars work hard to keep that ideal body, one that wears clothes well.

FROM SILENCE TO SOUND

The movies of the 1920s, silent still, followed the pattern established earlier, drawing audiences all over the world to the look of the United States, which had taken on a golden aura—it had won the Great War. The movies capitalized on that ideal, presenting for the most part a world of brilliant comedies, beautiful youth, idyllic lives, and happy endings amid elegant surroundings. In them, the world saw a new and youthful fashion look emerging in the United States based on clothing for sport.

As the new technology of sound was just on the horizon, other new ideas in clothing were appearing as well. The lower-calf-length waistless dresses that gathered low on the hip and were the rage in the early years of the decade, failed to show off the lean, sleek bodies of the young actresses who came to epitomize the Flapper Age of the waning years of the 1920s. By 1927 and 1928, a startling change in young women's movie costumes was seen: They began to fit the body, showing flat bellies; slim hips; narrow waists; and long, shapely legs to their best advantages. Clara Bow, in *It* (1927) and Joan Crawford, in her first major starring role in *Our Dancing Daughters* (1928), wore tight, waist-revealing short dresses; trim, pleated skirts and fitted sweaters; and menswear shirts and jodhpurs, while most of the other women wore the more conventional low-waist, loose styles. Paris at that time still showed straight-waist dresses. It seems clear that the young stars pushed a new look forward to display their slim figures.

After talkies arrived and movie musicals invaded the scene, the dance clothes, both practice and show, also introduced a new world of acceptability. All those practice sessions in all those movie musicals showing all those legs in all those shorts, tiny pleated skirts, and sporty tops finally broke the barriers of clothing propriety. Clearly, the movies introduced new ways of wearing clothes.

By the 1930s, commerce found a way to profit from the overwhelming demands of the fans. In a new interaction between the studios, the manufacturers, and the retailers, the clothing audiences saw on screen became available to them almost instantaneously in select stores. Perhaps the most famous of all these, mentioned in almost every book on movie costumes, was the white, sheer, two-piece Adrian-designed dress with enormous ruffled sleeves that Joan Crawford wore in *Letty Lynton* (1932). That year, Macy's claimed to sell fifty thousand inexpensive copies of it, and three years later, Paris still showed dresses with those amazing sleeves in shop windows—proof that by that time, the movies influenced not only the clothing of the audiences but also the designers as well. The boundaries between fashion leadership and the movies had blurred.

THE DESIGNERS

Hollywood had brought famous designers to work on costumes as early as the 1910s; Chanel came in the 1920s to dress Gloria Swanson, but Swanson hated the dark, spare, clean, unadorned lines that photographed poorly and failed to enhance her. A new breed of designers appeared, though, one that understood the relationship between star, film, and fashion. Perhaps Adrian was the most successful of them all. Out of this stable of famous costumers came Edith Head, who learned her craft on the job assisting Travis Banton, another well-known designer of the 1930s who was best known for dressing Marlene Dietrich.

Edith Head's success lay in her ability to please her stars, to dress them in contemporary American style, and to design

U.S. actor Mary Pickford in 1918. During her film career, she kept her weight at ninety-five pounds (forty-three kilos), conscious of how the camera lens changed her image. Library of Congress Prints and Photographs Division LC-DIG-ppmsca-18840.

wearable clothing that would let the actress shine rather than the dress. Her clothes always expressed the essence of the time. For example, in 1947, when Dior introduced the New Look with its much longer skirts, Head refused to "pick a length" in her movies until the furor of major change had finally settled. Only at the very end of the 1940s do we see Head designing the new, longer skirts; only then are they photographed to be seen. From 1947 until that time, her characters were never shown in long shots that showed the actresses' skirt lengths. Her definitive New Look statement came with 1950's *All about Eve*, where Bette Davis's full-skirted, bare-shouldered, cocktail party dress became iconic. Edith Head continued her career into the 1980s. For her efforts, she won eight Academy Awards (she was nominated for over forty), still the most ever won in Hollywood by a single individual.

In the 1950s, the role of the designer took a radical change away from the Hollywood system when the young Audrey Hepburn asked the Parisian couturier Hubert de Givenchy to design the clothes for her new movie *Sabrina* (1955). Edith Head did the studio work on the costumes, but it was the magical chemistry between Hepburn and Givenchy that created the Hepburn Look that influenced the next decade, including its most famous devotee, Jacqueline Kennedy. Ironically, of all six nominations for Academy Awards from that production, only one won—Edith Head, who claimed to but did not design the dazzling Sabrina dress so much copied thereafter. From that time on, fashion

designers worked on films. Givenchy, in a string of Hepburn movies, led the way. Famously, another designer appeared in 1980. *American Gigolo* featured newcomer Richard Gere wearing another newcomer's, Giorgio Armani, gorgeous clothes in an edgy turnaround that ignored women's clothing to highlight men's. The "dressing scene" made history on screen, giving permission to men to enjoy the combinations of color, texture, line, drape, and beauty every bit as much as women did.

FILMS GIVE BIRTH TO FADS AND FASHIONS

Sometimes the clothing in the movies almost accidentally set off instantaneous fads, as in the torn-neck sweatshirt and dancers' leg warmers featured in *Flashdance* (1983). Young women all over North America appeared overnight garbed in this combo, which turned out to be the most memorable feature of that movie. As the latter years of the twentieth century drew in, then, costuming was often as much a matter of shopping for as it was of designing for. This is certainly true of both film and television costuming, where entire seasons depended on dressing the actors in clothing shopped for by the designer. Patricia Fields, designer for *Sex and the City*, was famous for this approach, earning two Emmy nominations for her "trend-setting" looks.

Looks of stars still mattered, but the way of handling glamour was now different. One constant remained: Many movies of the last decades of the twentieth century still showed audiences how to wear their clothes. Some even turned into fashion shows from beginning to end, following a decades-long tradition. *Pretty Woman* (1990), which made a superstar of Julia Roberts, is an example. Audiences loved the Cinderella story that had the heroine shopping and changing clothes at every turn. Ironically, though, perhaps the most enduring influence from that movie was from Roberts's prostitute's outfit of tall, tight, high-heeled boots; midriff-baring top; and short, short mini skirt. Of all the costumes in that movie, this was the one that became the look of the young in the 1990s, a sort of street-walker look that prevailed for years.

Contemporary Seventh Avenue designers have often costumed movies, but never has their own style taken over that of the character. The costumes remain handsome and unobtrusive. Calvin Klein, Donna Karan, and Ralph Lauren, to name three, have all worked with Hollywood productions, the latter most famously with Diane Keaton in *Annie Hall* (1977). Keaton wore her own clothes in her own style, but they were Ralph Lauren clothes and influenced years of women's wearing men's clothing in a free, casual, Annie Hall way. It is one of the few examples where an actor's personal style actually influenced the look of the movie and, as a result, the look of the times.

THE FASHION SHOW

The connection between the fashion show and the movies goes back to the early years when Lucile, Lady Duff Gordon, designed for Lillian Gish, Mary Pickford, and Billie Burke on screen. Lucile promoted her work through newsreels as well, even prior to 1920. From then on, the notion of the fashion show within a film has been a staple of moviemaking. Some, as with *Pretty Woman*, were subtly woven into the story line, but others were blatant appeals to women and their devotion to fashion. Probably the most famous of these is *The Women* (1939), which stops the action of

Audrey Hepburn on the set of the film *Sabrina* (United States, 1955) wearing a Hubert de Givenchy–designed suit. Her look and his designs influenced the styles of the following decade. Hulton Archive/Getty Images.

the movie for a good twenty minutes to have the main characters and, thereby, the audience, too, sit in the luxury of a Technicolor world inserted into the midst of a black-and-white potboiler. Other movies prior to that made no attempt to cover up the purpose: *Vogues of 1938* (1937) was one (a less successful *Vogues of 1937* had preceded it), blatantly broadcasting the message even in its title. Set in a fashion house in New York, the entire movie was a display of beautiful clothing, calculated to enchant the typical moviegoing audience, which consisted of nineteen-year-old girls and their families and friends. The credits, which run for several minutes, list many of the leading designers of the times, including Irene, Omar Kiam, and Sally Victor as designers of the costumes. To top off the importance of fashion in film, the entire movie was filmed in the new process Technicolor, a full two years before Dorothy found herself in Oz. Made as the Depression still held sway, these movies took audiences out of the doldrums, giving them fashion inspiration and ideas and delighting them in the presentation.

The 1940s and 1950s certainly continued to give audiences much fashion to look at—*Funny Face* (1957), designed again by Givenchy and Edith Head, was another movie centered on the fashion industry and without doubt was the best of them all. But although Audrey Hepburn appeared in the next decade in great clothes, the movie that retains best the fashion-show-within-the-movie cliché was *That Touch of Mink* (1962), which featured first

a fashion show of Norman Norell clothes, then the star, Doris Day, wearing them for the rest of the movie so the audience can see how they look on a "real" person. From then on, as it had done previously as well, the look of current styles became an integral part of the movies themselves, until, as noted previously, *American Gigolo* appeared in 1980, turning the traditional pattern of showing clothes for women on its ear. The idea of the fashion show has been so lasting throughout the past century that its worth to moviemakers and fashion purveyors alike has been proven over and over.

TEENAGERS

Another major category that relates to the movies is that of the *teenager*. As late as the 1930s, that awkward period between childhood and adulthood still had no name. The Depression played a role in identifying a new and separate segment of society, one that had remained relatively invisible before. Up through the 1920s, young people left school early to get jobs to help the family finances. With the disappearance of work during the Depression, however, those same young people stayed in school longer, and by the end of the 1930s they more often than not finished high school. Thus, throughout North America, more young people were educated than ever before. It was not until 1941, though, that the term *teenager* was coined, and from the beginning, it was tied to the market value this segment of the population represented. The movies were with them every step of the way. Indeed, the movies had helped build awareness as the youth of the day grew into their new role in society: The *Andy Hardy* series lasted throughout the 1930s, and Judy Garland and Deanna Durbin were among the highest-paid stars in Hollywood at the time. The notion of "If we had a barn, we could put on a show!" became a standard of American get-up-and-go. And it was firmly rooted in the high school age group.

By the 1940s, those same young people were going to war or to work in the munitions factories and elsewhere. And they had money to spend. The new field of market research realized the potential spending power of those earners and encouraged retailers, magazine publishers, and moviemakers to cater to them, coining the term that has identified them ever since in the process. Thus, long before the appearance on the scene of James Dean and Marlon Brando, the stage had been set to tempt teenagers. World War II interrupted the progress, but the market had been established, and the buyers were waiting. Movies helped. After the war, movies directly appealing to teens appeared: Shirley Temple, grown now over the war years from a mop-headed child into a teenager, starred in a 1947 hit *The Bachelor and the Bobby Soxer*, set, among other places, in a high school. Fashions of teenaged girls—bobby socks, saddle shoes, pleated skirts, and pullover sweaters—filled the screen, once again showing audiences how to put it all together, or, by this time, reinforcing the style already popular in North America.

Biker look: U.S. actor Marlon Brando as he appeared in the film *The Wild One*, 1953. Popperfoto/Getty Images.

Thus, by the time the edgier, seamier movies of the early 1950s came along, the path had been set. Marlon Brando and his biker look in *The Wild One* (1953), perhaps the ultimate juvenile delinquent movie of the 1950s, was hailed as a new kind of antihero, and a sexy one, too, in his jeans, jacket, T-shirt, and boots. The other exemplar, of course, was James Dean in *Rebel Without a Cause* (1955), who wore his jeans, T-shirt, and red windbreaker into a lasting place in U.S. culture. The fashion world had shifted.

The movies showed what to wear as a teen, whether girl or boy. Natalie Wood's costumes in *Rebel*, more conservative than the jeans the "fast" boys wore routinely or the "nice" boys changed into after school, were the uniforms of teenaged girls everywhere in the 1950s. But the boys in that movie showed what was possible. The T-shirts they wore had been underwear until the outer shirts came off to stay, creating a new kind of casual, practical clothing. It took some years for jeans and tees to be acceptable everywhere, but the first volleys had been sounded, and the teenaged world was alert to new ideas to express themselves through their clothing.

PERIOD COSTUMES

A word should be said about period films and their role in influencing contemporary clothing. One might even claim just the opposite: Contemporary dress influences the looks of the movies being made if they are historically set. As a rule, U.S. moviemakers have been reluctant to accurately costume historically set films, preferring rather to let their stars shine in looks that modified historic dress to appeal to the fans who pay to see the movie. Almost invariably, the stars keep their own look. Vivian Leigh as Scarlett O'Hara comes to mind, wearing costumes that reflected the 1860s but keeping her 1939 hairstyle and makeup intact. The further viewers are removed from when the movies were made, the more keenly aware they are of the influence of the decade when the movie was made. Some, however, have inspired new looks in the fashion world, a memorable case in point being *Dangerous Liaisons* (1988). The V-shaped stays that characterized the eighteenth century, to name one example, appeared almost instantaneously in fashion magazines for evening wear, ushering in a short period of reminiscence for a style some two hundred years in the past.

U.S. movies, then, have influenced dress from the very beginning of their existence. Designers have come and gone throughout the same history, but few have left their mark on the movies overall. What has remained is that fascination of sitting inside a dark hall, surrounded by strangers, watching, noting, and ultimately trying to copy later, however unaware the viewer may be of doing this. The movies have been an irresistible juggernaut of twentieth-century ideas, molding, pushing, and forming opinions and desires as they entertain. They have shown viewers who they are. The movies have helped North American viewers to become American, and throughout their history, they have taught moviegoers how to dress.

References and Further Reading

Balio, Tino. *Grand Design: Hollywood as a Modern Business Enterprise 1930–1939*. Edited by Charles Harpole. Vol. 5, *History of the American Cinema*. New York: Charles Scribner's Sons, 1993.

Basinger, Jeanine. *A Woman's View How Hollywood Spoke to Women, 1930–1960*. Hanover, NH: Wesleyan University Press, 1993.

Bruzzi, Stella. *Undressing Cinema: Clothing and Identity in the Movies*. London and New York: Routledge, 1997.

Eckert, Charles. "The Carole Lombard in Macy's Window." *Quarterly Review of Film Studies* 3, no. 1 (Winter 1978): 1–21.

Eyman, Scott. *Mary Pickford, America's Sweetheart*. New York: Donald I. Fine, 1990.

Fuller, Kathryn H. *At the Picture Show*. Washington, DC: Smithsonian Institution Press, 1996.

Gaines, Jane, and Charlotte Herzog, eds. *Fabrications Costume and the Female Body*. New York and London: Routledge, 1990.

Palladino, Grace. *Teenagers: An American History*. New York: Basic Books, 1996.

Seeling, Charlotte. *Fashion: The Century of the Designer, 1900–1999*. Cologne: Könemann Verlagsgesellschaft mbH, 2000.

Thorpe, Margaret Farrand. *America at the Movies*. New Haven, CT: Yale University Press, 1939.

Warner, Patricia Campbell. "The Americanization of Fashion: Sportswear, the Movies and the 1930s." In *Twentieth-Century American Fashion*, edited by Linda Welters and Patricia A. Cunningham, 79–98. New York: Berg, 2005.

Patricia Campbell Warner

Masquerade Dress

Masquerade rituals and entertainments popular in North America were initially derived from European tradition and fashionable practices. Mummering and Mardi Gras, both forms of masked celebration that had roots in the Middle Ages in Europe, took on their own unique character in the specific regions of Canada and the United States where they persisted. When the European vogue for public masquerade declined at the beginning of the nineteenth century in favor of private, fancy dress balls and parties without masks, North American preferences followed suit. Fancy dress parties and balls were similar in many ways to those held in England and France that inspired them, but they were underpinned by preoccupations, such as national identity and issues of social class, that were unique to the United States and Canada. These forms of masquerade were closely tied to popular nineteenth-century constructs of public performance and spectacle. In the twentieth century, as structured fancy dress entertainments went into rapid decline, North Americans gradually channeled their propensity for playful dressing up into Halloween, a uniquely North American custom. Much activity that involves disguise and masking is informal in nature, and as a result, it is typically not well documented historically. The more structured and ritualized masquerade activities of the past two centuries are thus those that are the best understood and most well known.

The ludic, or playful, function of costumed performance has been recognized as a constant in many cultures across time. Disguise or dress-up provides imaginative freedom, allowing a participant to embody qualities of an imaginary persona. Wearing a costume can provide an extraordinary and exciting tactile and visual experience. The nature of social interaction changes radically in a masquerade context. Individuals are cast in new roles of either performers or audience, or they participate simultaneously as both. Because activities that involve masking, disguise, or fancy dress without masks give license for departure from social norms of behavior, and perhaps role inversion and reversal, they are almost always contested terrain. Tension and controversy rarely center on matters of dress itself but rather on aspects of the behavior and social pressures that ensue.

EUROPEAN ROOTS

In Europe, Carnival masking has ancient and complex roots. *Carnival* was (and is) the period of festivities extending from Twelfth Night to the beginning of Lent, during which a temporary reprieve from the normal social order was condoned. Amusements during this period typically involved disguise that promoted reversal of gender and class; men dressed as women, and people made fun of their social superiors. Animal heads were also worn as masks. Masked or disguised entertainments were particularly characteristic of the last six days prior to Ash Wednesday, ending on *Mardi Gras*, or Fat Tuesday.

Eventually Protestant countries abolished Carnival, focusing their winter celebrations around Christmas but retaining some of the masking traditions associated with Carnival festivities. *Mummering*, or visiting houses in disguise to perform a play or generally display disorderly behavior, followed by a request for payment to leave, persisted at Christmas time in England and Ireland and was transported to Newfoundland. Catholic countries retained Carnival, which grew to its most elaborate in Italy, particularly in Venice in the eighteenth century; the custom of celebrating Mardi Gras with masked revelry was brought with the French to Louisiana.

MARDI GRAS

Carnival was not only a familiar custom to those who brought it to Louisiana, but it also served as a means of asserting French national identity in a continent dominated by Anglo-American influence. Mardi Gras, the final day of European Carnival, has come to denote several days of festivities in the Gulf Coast area of the United States. In New Orleans, Mardi Gras has grown to become an important tourist and commercial event, one that defines the city and sets it apart from the rest of the United States. Mobile, Alabama, is also renowned for Mardi Gras festivities; in rural Louisiana, masked activities mark the holiday as well.

Mardi Gras in New Orleans has long been a multicultural festival, reflecting Louisiana's French and American backgrounds and African and Caribbean connections, and it has been shaped and continually redefined by various conflicts over inclusion, exclusion, and assertion. Since the late twentieth century, the celebrations have been touted as a symbol of the city's racial, ethnic, and class harmony, although a historical perspective reveals an event in which rituals have underscored race and class tensions.

Masked balls were long typical of the Carnival period; an early one is documented in 1828 along with an advertisement for a costumer who dressed ballgoers. At balls, company was mixed, although at the first Mardi Gras costumed parades in New Orleans in the 1830s, Anglo-Americans were typically spectators. These early parades were thought to be informal and impromptu processions of young Creole (Louisiana-born and French-speaking) men. The black population of the city also took part in processions at this time in a temporary subversion of the city's racial order.

Composite photograph of a fancy dress skating carnival at the Victoria Rink, Montreal, 1870. Notman Photographic Archives, © McCord Museum, Montreal. http://www.mccord-museum.qc.ca/en/

The year 1857 marks a major transformation of the way Mardi Gras was celebrated in New Orleans. The Mistick Krewe of Comus was formed by a group of Anglo-American men who presented both a themed nighttime procession for public viewing and a private ball. Character representations for Comus's first parade were primarily devils, inspired from The Demon Actors in John Milton's *Paradise Lost*. In its next year, it took inspiration from Greek gods and goddesses. Within the next fifteen years, other *krewes*, or groups of paraders, formed, the most well known of which is Rex, the self-appointed king of the festivities. The krewe of Rex established a daytime parade, presenting tableaux on decorated floats. As additional krewes shaped the festivities of parades, tableaux, and balls, the resulting separation between maskers and audience added structure, which helped to control the threat of disorderly behavior and made the festivities more respectable. The krewe structure also established Mardi Gras as a U.S. festival, albeit one based on Creole tradition. As further krewes emerged, many mocked what had come to be viewed as traditional Mardi Gras at the same time as they appropriated it.

Mardi Gras Indians began a black masking tradition sometime in the second half of the century and paraded through black neighborhoods of New Orleans. The krewe of Zulu, whose black members parodied African stereotypes, was formed in the early twentieth century from a more loosely organized group, but by the 1980s, it had integrated white paraders.

Women in male attire, often presumed to be prostitutes, were always on the fringes of the more structured festivities in the nineteenth century. By the 1920s, the participation of female maskers was being advertised as an element of the appeal of Mardi Gras. Men are also documented as dressing as women, frequently in provocative and immodest dress. Cross-dressing eventually became an important component of gay Mardi Gras celebrations, which became widely known only in the 1970s in spite of having existed for much longer. Gay balls are very much part of the contemporary celebration.

By the turn of the twentieth century, Mardi Gras and, specifically, the Rex parade had been recognized as a lucrative commercial opportunity for the city, and krewes developed the parades and events with a heightened consciousness of tourism. Festivities were suspended at the time of World War I and resumed in the 1920s. New krewes have been formed as recently as in the 1990s. Renowned for its traditions of public costumed parades and parties, which serve to transform the city into a public setting for festive and unrestrained behavior, Mardi Gras in New Orleans continues to be an important commercial and tourism event for the city.

MUMMERING IN NEWFOUNDLAND AND PHILADELPHIA

Mummering (also known as *mumming*) refers to costumed parading or house visits and is known to have been practiced in Newfoundland since the beginning of the nineteenth century. At that time, it appeared to arrive with recent immigrants, but it was not generally endorsed by the inhabitants already established there. By 1861, public mummering or dressing up had been banned in Newfoundland because of the offensive behaviors to which it gave rise, including drunkenness and rioting. Mummering that involved visits to people's homes persisted in spite of this law until the mid-twentieth century and has enjoyed a revival in recent decades.

Two varieties of Newfoundland mummering have been distinguished: urban and outport, or village mummering. *Urban mummering* in St. Johns and some other large towns took the form of both parades and private performances. Parade costume was based on role reversal of both gender and class: men dressing as women or as upper-class ladies. Costumed performances were put on in the houses of the upper class by working-class mummers, who were given money to leave. The play performed by Newfoundland mummers followed a plot typical of those found throughout England, Wales, and Scotland, probably from the fifteenth century onward. Characters usually included a hero such as St. George, an antagonist who challenged him to a battle in which one of the two was killed, a doctor who revived the victim, and a man dressed as a woman whose role varied. This form of mummering disappeared when outlawed.

Outport mummering took place in the small Newfoundland coastal fishing villages, a tradition that dated back to the early 1800s in some areas and was present in all communities by the early twentieth century. Outport mummering was more egalitarian in nature because it was practiced among social equals and did not involve the class reversals found in the urban tradition. It began on Christmas Eve and continued every evening for the twelve days of Christmas. Women were costumed participants, unlike in the city where mummering was a solely male activity. Costumes worn by outport mummers masked their faces and concealed their hands to disguise their identity entirely, and it was often based on a gender-role reversal or grotesque assemblage to alter body size, posture, and gait, rather than an attempt to create a particular character. Mummers demanded entry to a house in a disguised speech generally described as ingressive, caused apprehension to its residents with boisterous behavior, but then unmasked themselves, altering to their regular selves before they left, usually after being offered a drink or money. This sort of mummering declined rapidly in the 1960s and 1970s as the family-based labor structure was replaced with wage labor and industrialization penetrated to these areas.

An annual 1 January parade in Philadelphia is also known as a mummers' parade. A form of New Year's Day parade had existed through the nineteenth century, but was not known to involve masquerading of any sort. An act outlawing public masquerade was repealed by 1859, reflecting a change in public opinion. By this time, a mummers' club known as the Chain Gang was known to exist and to parade on either New Year's Day or Mardi Gras. Following the Civil War, the New Year's parade became one where fancy dress figured prominently, as did loud noisemaking. By the early 1880s, but probably not before, these costumed paraders had come to be known as mummers. A city-sponsored mummers' parade began in 1901.

Various mummers' clubs were formed through the late nineteenth and twentieth centuries. Each participates with costumed paraders and floats on various themes. Costumes are frequently spectacular and occupy a great deal of physical space beyond the wearer's body. Comic Clubs, each with many brigades, start off the parade with comic floats and individuals dressed as clowns who strut with parasols. Fancy clubs provide further scope for fantastical costume themes. The String Band division presents large groups of musicians, all costumed according to a theme. Fancy brigades with elaborately dressed captains perform indoors.

FANCY DRESS PRACTICES IN THE NINETEENTH AND EARLY TWENTIETH CENTURIES

In the very early nineteenth century, British and North American society found the licentiousness of masquerade and masked entertainments to be anathema to its values. Masquerade was even being outlawed in various locations. Masquerade dress came to be generally supplanted by *fancy dress*, or dress-up costume that does not obscure one's identity or constitute a disguise. Fancy dress entertainments began to grow substantially in popularity in North America as well as in Europe. From the 1850s onward, opportunities for fancy dress multiplied and included parlor theatricals, such as tableaux vivants (living pictures); skating carnivals; private and public balls; public parades; and historical pageants. A large amount of print and iconographic evidence exists to document fancy dress practices in the nineteenth and very early twentieth century. Unlike earlier and later costumed activities, many of these events were highly structured and commemorated.

The North American predilection for fancy dress has been viewed as underpinned by the theatricality of the social conduct of middle-class society. North American social life of this period has been equated with a performance of gentility. Dressing up offered a socially acceptable outlet for escapist fantasy, as an embodied participation in an activity predicated on fantasy, albeit one circumscribed by its own set of conventions and tacit rules of social behavior that still fit within the larger framework of Victorian social preoccupations. The sort of heightened and emotional aesthetic involvement in such activities has been described as "saturated."

Tableaux vivants were at the height of their popularity in the 1850s and 1860s. While they were typically a domestic amusement having pride of place in the repertoire of parlor theatricals so popular at this time, they could also be performed publicly. Tableaux consisted of the representation of a work of art or scene, typically a climactic moment of literary, dramatic, or historical inspiration, where participants dressed as the figures and held the pose for the audience to guess at, often behind a gauze drapery. Typical subjects were paintings and sculptures, historical events, and scenes and events taken from poetry and literature. Allegorical scenes were also very popular. Regardless of the setting, tableaux had to be designed and rehearsed, and choosing appropriate costume for the participants was an important aspect of the activity. Frequently tableaux were gendered with primarily female performers and male spectators. Public tableaux and drills

Costumed attendants at a fund-raising fair, Montreal, 1887. Notman Photographic Archives, © McCord Museum, Montreal. http://www.mccord-museum.qc.ca/en/

continued to be popular forms of entertainment, and ideas for themes were provided in books, newspapers, and magazines. A broom drill was inspired by a military parade, with female marchers carrying brooms and mops.

By the 1860s, fancy dress was an important component of fund-raising events staged by women in the United States, particularly those to support the Sanitary Commission. A group of women wore fancy dress on a similar theme, and later in the century, thematic representations expanded to comprise a decorated booth. As international exhibitions grew in number at the end of the nineteenth century, these also shaped fancy dress preferences in more modest fund-raising exhibitions and events such as bazaars, where international themes became fashionable.

Skating carnivals were a favorite Canadian entertainment. Newspapers indicate that most Canadian towns and cities held one large fancy dress carnival a month in the 1860s through the 1880s, but by the 1890s in Montreal alone there were two a week. The effect of large numbers of skaters in costume created a shared feeling of otherworldliness. Carnivals in Montreal, Ottawa, and other Canadian cities were occasionally documented in large composite photographs, copies of which were then sold to participants. The most well known of these images was William Notman's "Skating Carnival at the Victoria Rink of 1870."

Fancy dress balls ranged from small to very large affairs. Some private parties still allowed some form of masking. Large balls often had one or more themes and might include a series of *quadrilles*, or theme-based dances, on which all members of a set based their costumes. The fancy dress events that received the most media attention in the late nineteenth and early twentieth centuries were the large balls held by the most socially prominent individuals in the United States and Canada. These balls were widely reported on with extensive and detailed descriptions of costumes, decorations, security, music, and dancing. Illustrations, both engravings and photographs, and even commemorative souvenir albums were frequently published.

By the first decade of the twentieth century, community pageants featuring hundreds or even thousands of costumed participants had supplanted other forms as the most popular and elaborate fancy dress activity. These events used the appeal of fancy dress to provide a memorable experience to both performers and audience, who enacted a carefully defined version of their community's past and often presented a progressive vision of its future.

Beyond the individual and social concerns, the attribution of altruistic purposes to fancy dress events added legitimacy to the individual pleasures of choosing and acquiring a costume and assuming a fantasy character. Fund-raising was one such purpose; educational goals lay behind historically themed balls, and a desire for collective betterment drove participation in costumed community pageants. Likewise, the wearing of costume could also be employed to make otherwise serious events seem playful and amusing.

FANCY DRESS COSTUME

In North America, a variety of publications offered advice on fancy dress costume. *Godey's Lady's Book* and other North American magazines sometimes featured fashion plates illustrating fancy dress costumes with their descriptions. Frequently variations on these suggested costumes were adapted and published in other magazines. The *Canadian Illustrated News* from 1869 to 1883 did likewise. Widely available in the United States and Canada were two British books by Ardern Holt, *Fancy Dresses Described, or What to Wear at Fancy Balls* (published in six editions between 1879) and *Gentlemen's Fancy Dress: How to Choose It* (also in six editions from 1882 to 1905). In the United States, Butterick published its own guide to fancy dress, *Masquerade and Carnival: Their Customs and Costumes*, in 1892. Weldon's, an English company, sold costumes and paper patterns through catalogs distributed in North America well into the 1920s and 1930s.

The Dennison Crepe Paper Company of Framingham, Massachusetts, sold publications describing how to make paper fancy dress and Halloween costumes in the early twentieth century.

Fancy dress costumes were acquired in a variety of ways. Costumes for domestic amusements were usually made at home, in contrast to those worn to fancy dress balls. For a ball, women might adapt a regular evening dress for fancy dress wear or combine elements of several different cast-off garments. Rental was a popular option, and New York costume rental firms Lanouette and Koehler were known to rent garments not only in that city but also much further afield, including in Canadian cities. London's Nathan and Company is also known to have supplied costumes to North Americans. Major department stores often advertised that they would make fancy dress. Extant garments worn in North America bear labels of tailors and dressmakers, including that of Worth, a prominent Parisian couturier.

By allowing its wearers to step away from the constraints of fashionable dress and to draw on a much wider range of potential styles, a costumed performative identity was felt to offer possibilities that were more reflective of an individual's true self if one knew how to choose properly. The ideal choice was based on knowledge of both personality and self on the one hand and body type and flattering clothing styles on the other. It was recognized that the choice of an appropriate character and costume was a minefield where temptation might lead one to portray oneself as one wished rather than in accordance with one's socially constructed self. The dilemmas surrounding the choice of fancy dress amplified the discourse of middle-class fashion and consumption, which required simultaneously that one look one's very best and appropriate or slightly superior to one's station in life while avoiding excessive preoccupation and expense.

The nature of the appeal of fancy dress was highly gendered. Women could expect to enhance their sexual attractiveness by displaying good physical features more prominently and appropriating the mystique of a fantasy persona. For men, the experience of wearing a costume was far more divergent from regular dress than it was for women. Choosing and wearing a fancy dress was tantamount to a male foray into the feminine sphere, which led to a spectrum of reactions from exceptional pleasure to utter revulsion. Evidence shows some men being more or less coerced into wearing costumes with minimal effort, placing themselves on the margins by wearing regular evening dress to a fancy ball, or simply avoiding an event altogether.

A strong moral code pervaded fancy dress entertainments held prior to World War I. Fancy dress could transform the self but only in accordance with accepted moral principles of modesty in dress. While fancy dress allowed wearers to flout some of the conventions of dress, many others could still not be transgressed. Men might reveal their legs in short breeches and tights; never would they display arms above the elbow or bare chests, however. Women might reveal ankles and calves and wear their hair long and loose, but beyond the legs they would almost never reveal more of their bodies than they would in regular evening dress. Nonetheless, a heightened sense of sexual excitement is almost always discernible in reports of fancy dress balls and costumed activities. In New York in 1840 at a ball at the home of Henry Brevoort, two young people eloped and found a preacher at 4:00 A.M. while they were still in costume. This reported occurrence encapsulated the fear and distrust of disguise that existed widely in the nineteenth century and helped to shape the moral conventions of fancy dress activities. Minus the moral baggage of the previous century, in the late 1910s throughout the 1920s and 1930s, fancy dress events were still popular, but they were understood to be much more lighthearted forms of entertainment.

FANCY DRESS CHARACTERS

The characters chosen for fancy dress balls prior to World War I fall into categories that reflect various facets of nineteenth-century life and experience. Historical impersonations enjoyed the widest popularity. Such costumes usually tended to resemble fashions of the period in which they were created more than those of the period they were trying to emulate. Ardern Holt, author of *Fancy Dresses Described and Gentlemen's Fancy Dress*, stated that her period's devotion to matters of taste and culture required that educated people research their costumes. Nonetheless, authenticity in historical dress was a construct conflated with beauty far more than with accuracy and fidelity to the past. The compliment "historically correct," seen frequently in press descriptions, implied that the wearer was simultaneously cultured, tasteful, and attractive. In the United States, historical impersonations were in great majority inspired by the colonial past.

The wearing of elements of extant historical costume for fancy dress enjoyed popularity where it was available. The flurry of centennial and colonial revival fancy dress activities in the United States often involved elements of ancestral garb. In Canada, ancestral costume was not as widely worn, probably because it was owned by fewer people, but it was almost always used to draw attention to an illustrious ancestor or to a family's longevity in the country. Such elements were often transformed; many eighteenth-century women's garments have bodices altered to fit a nineteenth-century corseted torso. Incongruous elements of costume were often juxtaposed; in an 1898 fancy dress portrayal of a heroic military ancestor, a headdress from 1759 was worn with military accessories from the war of 1812 and a reproduction military coat created for the event.

A *poudré* (powdered) costume implied one worn with hair done in imitation of eighteenth-century hairstyles and powdered white; while a wig might suffice, advice manuals strongly recommended doing one's own hair. Poudré was worn with both eighteenth-century-style historical fancy dress, or for a poudré ball, it could imply powdered hair with regular evening dress.

Literature was another common source of fancy dress inspiration, and many of the characters it yielded also wore historical costume, though usually as described by the novelist or as portrayed by a stage actor. Sir Walter Scott's characters Rowena; Ivanhoe; and Mary, Queen of Scots, were seen at many fancy dress events. Shakespearian characters such as Romeo, Hamlet, and Portia were also frequently represented. Mythology-inspired portrayals such as Diana the Huntress were also popular; Mary Mary Quite Contrary was a common nursery-rhyme-inspired costume.

Exotic characters drew on stereotypes of those seen as "other" because of ethnocultural or geographical origin. It was widely recognized at the time that such portrayals were grounded in fantasy. They often comprised elements of non-Western dress or other exotic elements combined incongruously. An Ottawa man attired as a Chinese Mandarin in 1876 wore a woman's Cantonese theater costume. A man attired in aboriginal costume in 1896

Miss Stevenson as "Photography," Montreal, Quebec, 1865. At this time, "photography" was commonly depicted in a short dress trimmed with photographs, wearing a camera on her head. Notman Photographic Archives, © McCord Museum, Montreal. http://www.mccord-museum.qc.ca/en/

entertainments, such as plantation or minstrel parties, advocated the wearing of blackface.

Pastoral or peasant dress was favored very much by women only, often colored by historical, literary, or exotic inspiration. Such representations were highly romanticized interpretations of imagery such as the Dresden china shepherdess, Italian peasant girl, or Longfellow's Acadian peasant heroine Evangeline.

Emblematic costumes were inspired by an object or concept, such as "Rose Trellis," "The Press," "Night," or "Chess." In contrast to the historical characters, these provided far more scope for creativity. They also allowed as little or as great a departure from standards of fashion as the wearer wished. They usually comprised a dress trimmed with odd objects and images to render the concept. In the 1860s, "Photography" was usually depicted in a fashionable but short dress trimmed with photographs and wearing a camera on her head. She wore bracelets on her wrists and ankles and carried a fan trimmed with photographs.

Costumes that highlighted new technology also fell into this genre. Although few and far between, they remained vivid in the public imagination for long afterward. At the New York ball Fanny Ronalds hosted at her home in 1864, she appeared dressed as the Spirit of Music. On her head she wore a miniature harp surrounded by musical notes illuminated with gas jets (fed by a small tube running through her hair). Her Parisian dress of heavy white silk was embroidered with bars from Verdi's *Un Ballo in Maschera*, and her bright red boots were adorned with tiny tinkling bells. Later at the Vanderbilt ball in 1883, Mrs. Cornelius Vanderbilt came as "The Electric Light," with tiny lightbulbs in her hair powered by batteries and a white satin gown trimmed with diamonds. Although unusual for men to adopt such a category of dress, in Toronto in 1897 a group of men dressed as telephones, wearing the devices on their chests.

At most large events, invitations indicated that certain categories of fancy dress were banned. These included costume of religious orders, as well as men impersonating women. While women were not warned against impersonating men, there is no photographic evidence of a women appearing in visible trousers for any fancy dress ball held in the nineteenth century in Canada. There is occasional evidence of men dressing as women, though usually these costumes were intended to provoke laughter and poke fun at a particular stereotype, either a bashful young girl, a buxom matron, or an emancipated woman. Women also portrayed and parodied such stereotypes of female emancipation.

Calico balls encouraged guests to make costumes out of printed cottons and other lower-cost fabrics. *Domino balls* required the hooded cape that had become the trademark of the Venetian carnival in the eighteenth century. Children also enjoyed fancy dress activities, and their costumes were based on similar sources of inspiration, as illustrated by fashion plates, advice literature, and extant photographs.

HIGH-PROFILE FANCY DRESS BALLS

While many fancy dress activities were held within parlors or small town halls, large fancy dress balls, both public and private, were widely reported on in the press. In the first half of the nineteenth century, newspapers reported only briefly, but as the century progressed, more and more papers devoted ever more columns of type to chronicling preparations and listing guests, their costumes, and the evening's proceedings. With their widespread

is seen wearing the extant shirt backward in his portrait photograph. Skin was occasionally darkened in such guise, usually by men more than by women. Frequently such characters performed stereotypical behavior at the ball or party. It has been argued that exotic dress in the United States was viewed as feminine, and, by implication, neither aggressive nor exploitive; nonetheless, at the most prominent Canadian and British balls there are many documented examples of men undertaking such portrayals. While it has also been argued that an element behind the appeal of exotic dress was embodying the other entering into a community rather than expressing aggression or a power relationship, it is undeniable that such representations played into ethnocentric stereotypes of those perceived as others. In many cases, blackface fancy dress was considered in poorer taste than other sorts of exotic portrayals. Some such characters appeared at Canadian skating carnivals but were almost never photographed or illustrated in images for public consumption. Sometimes specific

publicity, these high-profile events became benchmarks for lavish entertainment. Many guests commemorated their participation in portrait photographs.

By the late 1820s, fancy dress balls and their preparations were being announced in the newspapers of Boston, New York, and Philadelphia. A ball held by Mrs. Charles Brugiere in 1829 is remembered as the earliest large fancy dress ball held in that city. A ball reported on in Toronto in 1838 is thought to be the earliest-known Canadian recorded event.

Queen Victoria's three major fancy dress balls, in 1842, 1845, and 1851, doubtless had an influence on the genre in North America because they lent it the legitimacy of aristocratic approval. Each of these balls had a historical theme, also setting the tone for the preference for historical fancy dress throughout the rest of the century. Historical accuracy was encouraged, and historian J. R. Planché was brought in to suggest designs for costumes. Organized quadrilles on historical themes, each composed of a different group of guests, also set a precedent for the way large aristocratic fancy dress balls were structured.

In the case of Queen Victoria's balls, controversy around the economic impact of these events was hotly debated in the press, a tradition that was to continue for the major North American fancy dress balls. Queen Victoria positioned her first ball as a means of providing opportunities for tradespeople in a time of economic difficulty. The need for large numbers of supposedly authentic costumes justified the weaving of special fabrics and the design and manufacture of accessories and jewelry, all of which was an impetus to trade. In Britain such intentions went largely unquestioned, however, controversy in the press became

an expectation on the other side of the Atlantic, and the large and costly events held by aristocrats on North American soil were hotly debated. The criticisms usually had to do with an elite host imposing the need to spend on large numbers of guests for their own glorification. The hosts almost always offset the criticism by invoking the financial benefits to their city's economy because of the impetus to spend.

By the 1890s, almost every noteworthy hostess invoked her social responsibility by touting a higher educational and moral purpose to her fancy dress ball. In Canada, this uplifting purpose materialized in the creation of public historical imagery, foreshadowing that which would be put forth in pageants in the following decade.

In North America, a ball held in 1864 stood out as a benchmark for a decade. Fanny Ronalds (Mrs. Pierre Lorillard Ronalds) sent invitations out to her 300 guests three months ahead of time to allow them to have costumes made, which may even have included ordering them from Paris. Nonetheless, stories of the Ronalds ball were not published or circulated in the press, so it does not really foreshadow the status-enhancing events held by Mrs. W. K. Vanderbilt and Mrs. Bradley-Martin.

In 1876 in Ottawa, Canada's governor general, the Earl of Dufferin, held a ball for eight hundred guests. The viceregal retinue wore costume of the period of James V of Scotland. Guests were given complete freedom of costume choice, and several ballgoers came in costume inspired by Canadian experience, including an allegory of The Dominion of Canada accompanied by a personification of Jacques Cartier. As it was the U.S. centennial year, many guests with U.S. ties also came dressed in patriotic fancy

Fancy dress ball for Anna Cowans' coming out, Mount Royal Hotel, Montreal, 1924. Notman Photographic Archives, © McCord Museum, Montreal. http://www.mccord-museum.qc.ca/en/

dress, including George and Martha Washington costumes and a portrayal of The Stars and Stripes. Controversy surrounded the political choice made by the British aristocrat to import this lavish form of entertainment into a colonial setting that could ill afford to adopt British class attitudes and the obligation to spend on entertainment. Some of the contradictions were encapsulated in the reporting on Dufferin's own costume. He was praised for setting an example with the simplicity of his dress, despite knowledge that he had purchased and rejected two other garments from London and New York prior to settling on an Ottawa tailor to provide him a costume with forty-eight hours notice.

Alva Vanderbilt's housewarming ball of 1883 had an estimated cost of US$250,000 and was held as an attempt to bring her parvenu family into New York society. Alva herself dressed as a Venetian princess in a costume taken from a painting by Cabanel, while her husband, Willie K. Vanderbilt, dressed in yellow with a black cape, a copy of a portrait of the Duc de Guise that hung in his own collection. Twelve hundred guests were invited, including society doyenne Mrs. Astor, whose acceptance was the key to the success of this ball. The most salient feature of the evening was the Hobby Horse Quadrille, where costumes were constructed to make it appear that guests in riding habits were sitting on hobby horses. It was followed by a Mother Goose Quadrille, a Dresden China Quadrille, and a Star Quadrille, each with guests dressed according to the theme. Dancing lasted until 6:00 A.M.

In 1897, Mrs. Bradley-Martin set out to unseat the Vanderbilt ball as the benchmark and host the fancy dress ball that would become the new standard of magnificence in New York. The Bradley-Martins had come into their money some fifteen years earlier on the death of her father, also making them new wealth. The hostess's arrangements were estimated at US$370,000, a figure that was decried in newspapers across the country as a lead news item. Various editors argued over whether the expenditure should not be made at all at a time of economic difficulty in many U.S. cities, or whether the effect of the amount being put into circulation among laborers in the city would be beneficial. The Bradley-Martins attempted to save the reputation of the event by suggesting it was spreading upper-class wealth to various categories of tradespeople, but many guests backed out because of the controversy. Although twelve to eighteen hundred guests had been invited, only about half attended, and many made a point of leaving after the first half-hour of dancing. The hostess's theme was historical costume of the sixteenth through the nineteenth centuries. She herself chose the character of Mary, Queen of Scots. Mr. O.H.P. Belmont appeared in a suit of solid-steel armor said to have cost US$8,000, with a Henry VIII costume beneath it.

Again in New York in 1905, James Hazen Hyde held a fancy dress ball on the Louis XV theme; while the outlay was nowhere near that of the Bradley-Martins's ball, this event had the distinction of being extensively photographed on site. The rumored extravagance of the event was later fatal to Hyde's career as chairman of an insurance company.

FANCY DRESS AND NATIONAL AND COMMUNITY IDENTITY

People in the United States dressed in costumes inspired by their colonial past for a variety of activities, which allowed them to embody symbols of U.S. identity and simultaneously contrast the ancestral past with the modern present, evincing a strong sense of progress. At Sanitary Fairs, it was the early American farmhouse and kitchen that inspired fancy dress. Women's colonial costume typically portrayed the domestic past, while men's, less popular, took inspiration from military heroes. A dual function of patriotic veneration combined with amusement was characteristic of almost all colonial costumed representations.

Centennial tea parties and Martha Washington teas and receptions were very popular in the mid-1870s, as were more high-profile centennial balls. Extant historic garments were often incorporated in the fancy dress costume worn to such events and highlighted a family's pedigree and long presence in the United States. The Colonial Dames and the Daughters of the American Revolution (DAR) in the United States were sponsors of many Americanizing activities using historical guise, again in a very gendered context.

Toward the end of the nineteenth century, the use of fancy dress balls to foster national identity became very prominent in Canada. In 1896, the Countess of Aberdeen, wife of the governor general, held the Historical Fancy Dress Ball in Ottawa. Guests were marshaled into nine organized sets, each of which represented a period in Canadian history. A Viking set led off the proceedings and was followed by a Jacques Cartier set, an Acadian set, and a United Empire Loyalist set. Guests were expected to research their historical characters and costumes, extensive descriptions of which were published in all the newspapers.

In 1897, Lady Aberdeen organized a ball in Toronto to celebrate the Diamond Jubilee. This event comprised twenty-four organized sets; individuals in each set dressed and performed dances on themes related to the benefits of the British Empire to Canada. A North American set featured women dressed as allegories of natural resources and men, as their controllers, for instance, "Forests of Canada" was accompanied by "A Lumberjack." British literature and sports provided themes for two other sets, and science and inventions for still others.

In 1898, Lady Aberdeen was guest of honor at the widely publicized Historical Fancy Dress Ball organized by the Ladies Antiquarian and Numismatic Society in Montreal, which was structured similarly to her Ottawa event. Guests dressed in seventeenth-, eighteenth-, and some early-nineteenth-century-style costumes to impersonate French viceroys and explorers and British governors of early Canada.

Because of their structure and intent, these three Canadian events share aspects of historical pageantry, which was also becoming very prominent around this time. Fancy dress representations of history were gradually being assimilated into a larger body of public historical imagery.

By the early twentieth century, thousands of North Americans were acting out dramatic episodes from the history of their area. Historical pageantry, in which fancy dress played a significant role, had become a central part of civic celebrations. Pageants offered officials a means of boosting civic pride; performers, a form of costumed recreation; and audiences, a spectacle and educational entertainment. Such pageantry was based on an assumption that history could be made into a dramatic public ritual through which the residents of a community, by acting out the right version of their past, could bring about some kind of future social and political transformation. Performers might number in hundreds or thousands. The American Pageant Association was founded in 1913, a reflection of the strong pageant fervor existing by that time and that persisted through the 1920s.

While civic pageants were initially best suited to the organizational capacities of small North American towns, large urban pageants had appeared by the end of the first decade of the twentieth century. In Quebec City in 1908, a tercentenary pageant celebrated the founding of that city. The ten-day event involved 4,500 costumed participants who reenacted a different period of the French regime each day on the Plains of Abraham. The Pageant and Masque of Saint-Louis in 1914 was the ultimate expression of the pageant medium in the United States with a cast of 7,000. It surveyed three centuries of local development, from aboriginal dwellers through French and Spanish explorers and settlers, to the nineteenth-century American city.

CHANGES IN TWENTIETH-CENTURY PRACTICES

Costume balls continued to be popular in the 1920s and 1930s, with many of the same types of impersonations that had been popular in the nineteenth century. While the number of historical representations declined somewhat, poudré remained popular, and clowns and pierrot costumes for both men and women added to the repertoire. Products and their advertisements also provided a new source of inspiration. (These had occasionally been seen in the 1860s but only worn by men.) Life Savers candy and brands of toothpaste were portrayed in costume. While costly ensembles were still occasionally turned out by costumers and couturiers, the trend was turning toward more amateur and ephemeral fancy dress garments and accessories. Instruction books for making paper costumes were widely available. Women revealed more of their bodies in fancy dress in the 1920s and 1930s, just as they did in mainstream fashion. In monied circles in the 1920s, fancy dress balls marked the coming out of socially prominent debutantes.

Fancy dress pageantry persisted as well but as more of a feminine pastime. Fiesta San Antonio began as a series of annual public parades and historical pageants in the early twentieth century and evolved into an ongoing event featuring pageants of young women dressed in allegorical costume. In spite of the decline of the pageantry movement in the 1940s, this particular event has flourished, and young women continue to make their debut in its elaborate pageants today.

Occasionally the masked ball genre has been revived, and the most highly publicized example was the Black and White Ball held by Truman Capote at the Plaza Hotel on 28 November 1966. The elite guests wore black or white evening dress with a mask.

DRESSING UP ON HALLOWEEN

The most popular contemporary venue for costuming and disguise in the masquerade and fancy dress traditions is Halloween. This ritual but informal festival has become a representation of North Americanness, both for new immigrants and in places where North American culture is transplanted and marketed. Halloween has transcended its ethnic roots, appropriating and transforming some of its aspects but reinventing and creating new referents for a great many others. While the date of 31 October is a fixture in the calendar, the way in which Halloween has been marked has had a very fluid nature without official origin or sanction, though by the twenty-first century, it has definitely been appropriated by commercial interests.

In mid-nineteenth-century North America, the observation of Halloween was thought to be the prerogative of first-generation Irish or Scottish immigrants. Middle-class families may have practiced contemporary versions of ancient divinatory rituals at home in their parlors, but for lower-class men, the event was marked by pranks outside the home and in the streets. Some form of disguise, perhaps as simple as smearing soot or burnt cork on the face, may have been part of the ritual as it had been with entertainments such as Mardi Gras, but it did not bear similarities to the fancy dress vogue that coexisted alongside it. In the late nineteenth and early twentieth centuries, college and university students used the evening for pranks, which had some impact in adding the holiday to the North American cultural calendar as well as its associations with youthful exuberance and rowdiness. By the turn of the century, most places in North America had rid themselves of festivals that inspired raucous behavior by outlawing them, institutionalizing them with parades, or domesticating them entirely. It followed that Halloween, as a final holdout of transgression on the margins of mainstream commemorative practices, would invigorate older traditions of masking as they became more circumscribed elsewhere.

Through the very early twentieth century and by the 1920s, at the height of the civic pageantry craze, fancy dress parties or more structured street parades had become an optional way for both children and adults to mark the evening of 31 October. The icons of bats, black cats, witches, and goblins, as well as the traditional colors of orange and black, were well in place and commercialized by this time, and they were featured in the Dennison Crepe Paper Company's *Bogie Book*, first published in 1909. The commercial importance of Halloween thus became established. Through the interwar years, while civic organizations were behind an increasing number of structured Halloween celebrations, which often included fancy dress competitions, these did not serve to eliminate or reduce the pranks and public mischief as was hoped. The tension between the fancy dress carnivals being promoted as family entertainment and the anarchic aspect of the entertainment appropriated by adolescents led to a popular misconception that a children's holiday was being overtaken by adults and adolescents.

The children's trick-or-treating ritual as it is known today was introduced in the late 1930s, but it really did not gain momentum and wide acceptance until the 1950s, transforming Halloween into a rite of consumption and giving it strong retail potential. Children's Halloween costumes were produced in increasing number and variety by manufacturers over the course of the century. As the entertainment industry grew, characters inspired by television, movies, and particularly the frightening Halloween Hollywood movie genre became part of the repertoire.

By the 1970s, Halloween as a children's celebration, characterized by costumed trick-or-treating, had become entrenched in North American mass culture. Simultaneously, Halloween has gradually been appropriated by adults, whose participation is driven by retail and leisure industries. Halloween dressing up by adults is usually used as an unstructured means of parody. Because of the outlet for transgression Halloween provides, in many urban areas, gay cultures have used Halloween costumed parades and parties as reaffirmation. Halloween at the end of the millennium has become an event for adults, with an estimated 65 percent of North American adults participating beyond just giving out candy to children.

A reenactment of Henri IV and Queen Marie de Médicis leaving the throne in 1608, presented at the 2nd Pageant, Quebec Tercentenary, Quebec City, Quebec, 1908. Notman Photographic Archives, © McCord Museum, Montreal. http://www.mccord-museum.qc.ca/en/

NEW DIRECTIONS IN MASQUERADE

In the twenty-first century, the ludic function of dressing up has been recognized as an important facet of children's play. No longer do children have to improvise costumes for play; toy stores and departments carry a range of dress-up clothing. Adult dressing up is focused primarily around Halloween. Recent attention to the mummering traditions in Newfoundland ensures that this tradition will continue, as does the tourism impact of the Philadelphia Mummers' Parade and New Orleans Mardi Gras. For adults, beyond Halloween, outlets for dressing up in the masquerade tradition for themed social events are perhaps most frequently found in science fiction group events, as well as historical reenactments.

References and Further Reading

Cooper, Cynthia. *Magnificent Entertainments: Fancy Dress Balls of Canada's Governors General, 1876–1898.* Fredericton and Hull: Goose Lane Editions and Canadian Museum of Civilization, 1997.

Cooper, Cynthia. "Dressing Up: A Consuming Passion." In *Fashion: A Canadian Perspective,* edited by Alexandra Palmer, 41–67. Toronto: University of Toronto Press, 2004.

Cooper, Cynthia, and Linda Welters. "Brilliant and Instructive Spectacles: Canada's Fancy Dress Balls, 1876–1898." *Dress* 22 (1995): 3–21.

Galembo, Phyllis. *Dressed for Thrills: One Hundred Years of Halloween Costume and Masquerade.* New York: Harry N. Abrams, 2002.

Glassberg, David. *American Historical Pageantry: The Uses of Tradition in the Early Twentieth Century.* Chapel Hill and London: University of North Carolina Press, 1990.

Gordon, Beverly. "Dressing the Colonial Past: Nineteenth Century New Englanders Look Back." In *Dress in American Culture,* edited by Patricia Cunningham and Susan Voso Lab, 109–139. Bowling Green, OH: Bowling Green Popular Press, 1993.

Gordon, Beverly. *Bazaars and Fair Ladies: The History of the American Fundraising Fair.* Knoxville: University of Tennessee Press, 1998.

Gordon, Beverly. *The Saturated World: Aesthetic Meaning, Intimate Objects, Women's Lives, 1890–1940.* Knoxville: University of Tennessee Press, 2006.

Halpert, Herbert, and G. M. Story, eds. *Christmas Mumming in Newfoundland: Essays in Anthropology, Folklore, and History.* Toronto: University of Toronto Press, 1969.

Halttunen, Karen. *Confidence Men and Painted Women: A Study of Middle-class Culture in America, 1830–1870.* New Haven, CT, and London: Yale University Press, 1982.

Haynes, Michaele Thurgood. *Dressing Up Debutantes: Pageantry and Glitz in Texas.* Oxford: Berg, 1998.

Huber, Leonard V. *Mardi Gras: A Pictorial History of Carnival in New Orleans.* Gretna, LA: Pelican Publishing, 1989.

Louisiana State Museum. "Mardi Gras: It's Carnival Time in Louisiana." http://lsm.crt.state.la.us/mgras/mardigras.htm (accessed May 2007).

Mitchell, Reid. *All on a Mardi Gras Day: Episodes in the History of New Orleans Carnival.* Cambridge, MA, and London: Harvard University Press, 1995.

Nelles, H. V. *The Art of Nation-Building: Pageantry and Spectacle at Quebec's Tercentenary.* Toronto: University of Toronto Press, 1999.

Ribeiro, Aileen. "The Old and New Worlds of Mardi Gras." *History Today* 36 (February 1986): 30–35.

Rogers, Nicholas. *Halloween: From Pagan Ritual to Party Night.* Oxford: Oxford University Press, 2002.

Sider, Gerald M. "Mumming in Outport Newfoundland." *Past and Present: A Journal of Historical Studies* 71 (May 1976): 5–31.

Skal, David J. *Death Makes a Holiday: A Cultural History of Halloween.* New York: Bloomsbury, 2002.

Welch, Charles E., Jr. "'Oh, Dem Golden Slippers': The Philadelphia Mummers Parade." *The Journal of American Folklore* 79, no. 314 (October–December 1966): 523–536.

Cynthia Cooper

See also Dress for Avocational and Historic-Site Reenacting.

Television

- The First Era of Television: The Golden Years
- The Rise of Fashion Television
- The Golden Age of Fashion Television
- Reality Television: Pushing Fashion Television to New Heights

In 1948, when Wayne Cox of the Federal Communications Commission (FCC) pronounced that television is here to stay, he could not have predicted the real impact this new force unleashed. Writing in 1964, Marshall McLuhan had a better grasp of the situation, claiming that television had potential to transform the world into a "global village." Television is a powerful tool that gains its power through its ability to express ideas through sight and sound. Fashion and television began a symbiotic relationship as early as 1956. Julia Meade, a writer for the *Los Angeles Times*, observed in April of that year that television had done more than anything yet conceived to make women clothes conscious.

Television is a mechanism for persuasion. Advertisers, who support programs, are hoping that U.S. and Canadian consumers will purchase their products. Although any visual image has the potential to be persuasive, when coupled with a person that a viewer admires, the viewer is likely to want to look or dress like that person. Hairstyles, clothing, and jewelry worn by television personalities are frequently copied. The expansion of cable television with the MTV network extended the influence of music on fashion starting in the early 1980s. Satellite accessibility expanded program offerings. Television became a venue for shopping, and in most recent years, fashion has become a dominant feature of many reality shows. Canadians have access to many U.S. programs, but they also have developed their own fashion programs. While there has been considerable interest in fashion television, the costumer designers and stylists who dress the shows have received little recognition until recent years.

THE FIRST ERA OF TELEVISION: THE GOLDEN YEARS

A man by the name of Philo Farnsworth succeeded in developing the first television broadcast on 7 September 1927, but only in 1944 did the Image Orthicon tube provide the technology that allowed television to take off. When the programming improved, television gained viewer support. This came in 1948 with Milton Berle and his success with *The Texaco Star Theater*. Other new shows included the family-friendly *Kukla, Fran and Ollie* and the *Dave Garraway Show*. In the early 1950s, television moved into what has come to be known as the Golden Age of Television. It also saw the expansion of cable access in both Canada and the United States. The early 1950s brought situation comedies—*I Love Lucy*, *The George Burns and Gracie Allen Show*, and *The Jack Benny Show*. *The Ed Sullivan Show* combined culture, comedy, and current hot performers such as Elvis (1950s) and the Beatles (1960s).

Jackie Gleason offered the humorous *Honeymooners*, a situation comedy. *Your Show of Shows*, with Sid Caesar and Imogene Coca, provided ninety minutes of comedy skits, songs, and dances. Family-based situation comedies included *The Adventures of Ozzie and Harriet*, *Father Knows Best*, and *Leave It to Beaver*. The kids' show *Davy Crockett*, which moved on to become a film, was replaced by the adult Western: *Gunsmoke*, *Cheyenne*, *Wyatt Earp*, and *Maverick* (a Western mocking the Western). *Hawaiian Eye*, *The Untouchables*, and *Sunset Strip* provided an emerging genre: the action/adventure/detective series fraught with violence. *The Twilight Zone* was an alternative, offering science fiction.

The clothing worn by women on television had great potential to be copied. Arlene Francis, a permanent member of the show *What's My Line*, wore a heart-shaped diamond necklace that was copied and worn by many women. The necklace had been a gift from her husband; it was not a television prop serving as a promotional tie-in. The ball gowns that Loretta Young wore to introduce her weekly series were a favorite of women viewers and helped set the style for evening gown fashions in the 1950s. The *I Love Lucy* series featured the comedian Lucille Ball, who became

American actors Don Johnson as Crockett and Philip Michael Thomas as Tubbs in the TV detective series *Miami Vice*, ca. 1988 (United States). Men's fashion was strongly influenced by the two leads in *Miami Vice*. Crockett always dressed in casual trousers and T-shirts in pastel shades of turquoise, pink, or lavender while Tubbs dressed in more traditional dark suits and neckties. Getty Images.

pregnant during the run of the show. Rather than hide her pregnancy, the decision was made to incorporate the pregnancy into the story line. The two-piece styles that she wore on the set were an instant success with the public. Many boys in the mid-1950s who watched Disney's *Davy Crockett* series were sure to purchase a coonskin cap or perhaps even a fringed suede jacket.

Many feminist scholars have noted the sanitized, middle-class version of family life depicted on such shows as *Father Knows Best* and *Leave It to Beaver*. The effect was to solidify a woman's role as a glorified homemaker; however, no real homemaker's daytime dress looked like what was seen on the set: high heels, hose, and a tight-fitting, full-skirted shirtwaist dress.

Music and fashion came together when Elvis's slick, combed-back hairstyle, as seen on television, began to be copied by high school students. Youth, like the character Kookie on *77 Sunset Strip*, were seen constantly combing their hair. Pat Boone's white bucks were another television fashion influence. *American Bandstand* was one of the first music venues on television. Largely a pop music show that managed to keep up with new music styles, it was dealt a deathblow with the rise of MTV.

The golden era ended in the early 1960s, when new programming became full of gimmicky sitcoms and stereotypes. Even the successful *Dick Van Dyke Show* mocked television. Spy detective series became popular, inspired by the James Bond movies, no doubt. These included *The Wild, Wild West*; *Secret Agent*; *The Man from U.N.C.L.E.*; *I Spy*; and *Mission: Impossible*. Medical dramas also became popular—for instance *Dr. Kildare*, *Ben Casey*, and *Perry Mason*. *Star Trek* aired from 1966 to 1969 and had a passionate following that merged into a worldwide popular culture phenomenon. *Peyton Place*, based on the novel, captured the attention of many viewers as an evening soap opera series.

Much of fashion in the early 1960s was influenced by Jacqueline Kennedy and styles worn in the late 1950s. By mid-decade, mod influences were coming from England, including simple shift dresses that became shorter and shorter. The events surrounding San Francisco's Haight-Ashbury neighborhood, especially during the "Summer of Love," and the creation of a hippie way of dressing became news. Television news and talk shows that reported on these events served as a medium of communication about the new hippie subculture. The Beatles and other musical groups appeared on television, furthering their sartorial influence.

The decade was one of a growing youth culture that desired a look of its own. The Beatles early on adopted suits, but they quickly shifted to mod styles. Motown music productions in Detroit had great success with groups such as the Supremes, whose carefully chosen appearance, especially their hairstyles and dress, also was copied by their youthful admirers. Television in the 1960s, then, provided viewers with images of fashion: the earlier more conservative, high-fashion style of the Kennedys, as well as the new look of youth—the mods; the hippies; and the folk, rock, and pop music performers. *American Bandstand* (which aired until 1989) featured musical artists popular with the disco set. Chubby Checker made the twist, a dance, popular during the mid-1960s. The Beach Boys solidified a focus on youth, beach attire, and dance music. Their appearance made plaid Pendleton shirts and tennis shoes hot items for teens, who were tuned in to the music and surfing craze.

It was during the 1970s that most people in the United States and Canada began to have access to color TV. Popular shows were *Maude*, *All in the Family*, and *M*A*S*H*, as well as the live skit comedy *Saturday Night Live*, a production that gave Johnny Carson's *The Tonight Show* keen competition. Nostalgia for the 1950s was apparent in the teenage comedy *Happy Days*, based on the film *American Graffiti*, which centered on teenagers of the 1950s. *The Carol Burnett Show* had continued success. PBS expanded its success of *Sesame Street* (1969–) to Jim Henson's *Muppet Show* (1976–1981). *The Mary Tyler Moore Show* (1970–1977) provided a model for single women looking for success in a career. Diversity came to the fore with *Julia* and *Barney Miller*, both depicting diverse characters on the screen. The police stories *Columbo* and *Police Story* satisfied viewers as well. Most people watched the Watergate hearings for the unfolding story of scandal within the U.S. presidency. News became central, with the news magazine *60 Minutes* becoming the most-watched series.

Charlie's Angels was thought by some to be "jiggle" television, yet others saw the Angels as strong women in traditionally male roles. Fashion influence became apparent when women began copying the appearance of Charlie's Angels, such as Farrah Fawcett's hairstyle and the pantsuits worn by the stars of the series. The most outrageous fashions on television were designed by Bob Mackie for Cher of the *Sonny and Cher Variety Show*, which first appeared on television in the early 1970s. Mackie became known for glitzy Hollywood fashions and as the designer for *The Carol Burnett Show*. He won seven Emmy Awards for his television designs and was nominated for an Academy Award for film design three times.

THE RISE OF FASHION TELEVISION

The 1980s saw many changes in television. The Fox network came into the picture, as well as additional cable stations such as ESPN, providing sports; the Weather Channel; and CNN, Ted Turner's twenty-four-hour cable news network. In addition, MTV was significant in providing a new outlet for music. Popular television programs included serious drama, such as *LA Law*, *Cagney and Lacey*, *St. Elsewhere*, and *Hill Street Blues*. *Star Trek: The Next Generation* provided an examination of time-displaced social problems. Comedies of note were *Cheers* and *The Bill Cosby Show*. Romantic comedy favorites were *Remington Steele* and *Moonlighting* (a spoof of detective shows).

The 1980s were important for fashion television. While television programs often portray individual characters with style, it was not until the 1980s that flamboyant current fashion appeared on television. Hence, it can be argued that television moved from costuming characters to fashioning contemporary style. The evening soaps, especially *Dynasty* and the detective series *Miami Vice*, along with the new cable networks CNN and MTV, became a powerful source of fashion news and influence in the 1980s and beyond.

Miami Vice was one of the groundbreaking police programs of the 1980s, along with *Hill Street Blues* and *Cagney and Lacey*. *Miami Vice* aired from September 1984 until July 1989. The two leads, Crockett and Tubbs, were cast as opposites. Tubbs was a street-smart cop from New York, and Crockett was a tough guy from the South. Men's fashion was strongly influenced by the two leads in *Miami Vice*. Crockett always dressed in casual trousers and T-shirts in pastel shades of turquoise, pink, or lavender, while Tubbs dressed in the more traditional dark suits and neckties. Crockett's penchant for wearing no socks with his loafers

into one more facet of consumer culture. By 1985, rock and roll had become mass culture, and MTV was an ongoing, almost subliminal fashion show. Mick Rock, a video photographer who worked in the medium in the 1970s, noted that the video would be nowhere without fashion.

Rock fashion became big business in the 1980s. Young girls desired to dress like Madonna and Cyndi Lauper, two of the early female musicians on MTV with "girl" appeal. It did not take manufacturers and retailers long to discover that the carefully cultivated images of rock stars created consumer desire. The shopping mall and department store were sites for female leisure culture. The look of Madonna was everywhere. One mall was called "Madonna Mall" because so many girls who shopped there tried to look like her. Cyndi Lauper's style also proved to be an inspiration for ready-to-wear manufacturers and retailers. Yet it was Madonna whose persona and look inspired the greatest fandom.

The Associated Department Stores recommended that its member stores open FTV (fashion television) departments. With rock videos blaring, Macy's opened in-store boutiques called "Madonnaland" and "Girls Just Want to Have Fun" where they sold "cropped sweaters ($30) and cropped pants ($21)."

While MTV was appealing to adolescents, *Dynasty* captured the attention of their parents, especially their mothers. ABC came up with *Dynasty* in 1981 in response to the success of *Dallas* on CBS. The show followed the life of the wealthy oil magnate Blake Carrington, played by John Forsythe; his new bride, Krystle, played by Linda Evans; and his family, acquaintances, and business associates. The producers soon added Joan Collins as the beautiful, sexy, powerful tycoon Alexis Morell Carrington Colby Dexter Rowan, who was Blake Carrington's ex-wife and mother of his children. Alexis hated Krystle and continually schemed to break up her marriage to Blake. Krystle and Alexis represented a dichotomy of good and evil.

One of the most significant aspects of both characters was that they personified beauty beyond youth, a relatively new idea to North Americans. One of the central characteristics of the show, of course, was its look. The look of *Dynasty* was based on fashions created by Nolan Miller, who had his big break with this show. Miller had designed costumes for previous shows, including *Charlie's Angels, Matt Houston, Hotel,* and *The Love Boat.* The producers wanted the characters' clothing to fit an idealized picture of the rich and famous. Miller not only decided what the characters would wear, but he also designed much of the clothing himself.

The clothing can best be characterized in a single word: glamorous. *Dynasty* has been described as an hour-long commercial for clothes. It emphasized a kind of out-of-date glamour with ornate clothing in bold colors and glitter. Miller's clothes for Alexis made the statement that she was rich and ruthless. Miller designed Krystle's clothes to reflect her character. He tried to keep the clothes soft in order to show her kindness and understanding. Often she was adorned in white to signify her purity. Her day wear had uncharacteristically large shoulder pads, which gave Evans a pleasing triangular silhouette. *Dynasty* reflected the fashion of the 1980s but also introduced and popularized others. It made white popular and also popularized shoulder pads, columnar evening gowns, and tailored suits. After *Dynasty,* however, women's wear took on a more feminine look, with hats, gloves, jewels, large ruffled sleeves, soft and sensuous fabrics, and expansive décolletage.

Madonna's look was widely copied in the 1980s. U.S. department store Macy's met the demand for rock fashion by providing in-store "Madonnaland" boutiques. Courtesy of the University of Texas Irwin Center, Austin, TX.

became a fashion statement. And his preference for casual clothes and soft colors soon caught on with men's fashion, especially the Versace invention of wearing jacket with a T-shirt instead of with a collared dress shirt and tie. A new masculine type seemed to be in the making with this series. Neither Crockett nor Tubbs fit the stereotype of the ideal male for the era, yet they both had sex appeal, and it is clear that sex was an element of desire in *Miami Vice.* Don Johnson was dubbed "the sexiest man on television" during the run of the show. The show's costume designers, Milena Canonero and Richard Shissler, provided a new and enduring casual look for men. *Miami Vice* also was a milestone in that it confirmed for the networks the potential of fashion and music in appealing to an audience. The truth of this lies in the history of television since the 1980s.

By the time *Miami Vice* took off, MTV had become the emblematic innovation of the decade. MTV began on 1 August 1981 as a twenty-four-hour cable channel with no programs, just rock-and-roll music geared toward viewers between the ages of twelve and thirty-four. In essence, it was a new way to reach the teenage market. MTV immediately captured the attention of the young baby boom generation, perhaps the richest consumer group in the history of the world. By marrying rock and roll to the pervasive power of television, MTV transformed the music

Indeed, the effect of *Dynasty* on fashion was astounding. It did not take long for Twentieth Century Fox to try to cash in on the popularity and license merchandise inspired by *Dynasty*. Nolan Miller at one time had his name on eight different product lines. December 1983 brought the Carrington's Christmas clothing line to Marshall Field's. The fashions displayed on mannequins were made to look like *Dynasty* characters.

It was during the late 1980s that shows devoted to current fashion began to appear. Producers at MTV clearly saw the links between MTV and fashion. They created a series of half-hour segments called *House of Style*, hosted by fashion model Cindy Crawford. *House of Style* drew on a fast-paced format of singers, music, and rap to show fashions meant to appeal to teenagers and young adults. They featured designs by Betsey Johnson and Katherine Hammett, a British designer.

MTV was not the first network to see the benefits of a program on fashion. The ground was broken when *Style with Elsa Klensch* first appeared on CNN in 1980. It was the first original, regularly scheduled, exclusively fashion and design program in the United States. Klensch's subjects ranged from the sportswear of Tommy Hilfiger and the classic fashions of Ralph Lauren to the avant-garde designs of Jean-Paul Gaultier and the trend-setting styles of Japanese designers such as Yohji Yamamoto.

During the 1980s, shopping channels also appeared on television to offer viewers opportunities to shop from home. The initials

McCall's pattern, 1984. Nolan Miller's designs for the U.S. TV series *Dynasty* set trends in the 1980s, popularizing shoulder pads and tailored suits. Courtesy of University of Rhode Island Library, Commercial Pattern Archive (1984.19. URI) Special Collections.

of QVC, the shopping network founded by Joseph Segel, stand for Quality, Value, and Convenience. The show has been on television since its first appearance in 1986. It has become a multinational corporation with presence on the Internet since 1999. It broadcasts in four major countries to 141 million consumers.

During the 1990s, there was further expansion of both cable and satellite television. *Dallas* and *Dynasty* spawned more youth-oriented shows: *Beverly Hills 90210* and *Melrose Place*. Heavily watched comedy included *Seinfeld, Friends, Roseanne,* and *Mad about You*. Dramas took center stage, such as the popular *NYPD Blue, ER, Chicago Hope, Law & Order,* and *The Sopranos,* all of which were grittier than earlier shows in the genre. The examination of social issues was apparent in *Picket Fences* and the high school dramas *My So-Called Life* and *Buffy, the Vampire Slayer,* which also offered paranormal content. Dramas with some paranormal aspects included *Northern Exposure, Twin Peaks, The X-Files,* and *Star Trek: The Next Generation*. One of the most popular shows was the series comedy *Friends,* which continued until 2004. One of its stars, Jennifer Aniston, became a fashion role model when many young women began to copy her hairstyle. This show and others like it (e.g., *Beverly Hills 90210*) were youth oriented and had potential to influence clothing choices.

THE GOLDEN AGE OF FASHION TELEVISION

Television in the 1980s and early 1990s had a significant impact on fashion, especially the evening soaps, music videos on MTV, fashion advice programs, and new shopping channels. Between the late 1990s and 2007, successful programs included the comedy series *30 Rock, Two and a Half Men, Sex and the City,* and *Desperate Housewives*. Well-liked dramas during the period included *Alias* and *Lost*. Popular shows in the twenty-first century tended to be serialized stories—soaps, comedies, or thrillers: *24, Lost, Desperate Housewives, The Office,* and *Scrubs*.

The symbiotic relationship between fashion and television really took off with the comedy series *Sex and the City* on HBO. The multiple-award-winning show was introduced in 1998 and ran until 2004. It continued in subsequent years with reruns on a regular basis. The show was enormously influential: There had been no previous show with such fashion impact or such press devoted to the fashions it featured. The clothes were important to the show in making it seem real; they were almost like another character. Costume designer Patricia Field's deft styling turned the characters of *Sex and the City* into small-screen fashion icons. Their clothes sparked trends including stilettos, high-end handbags, fabric flowers, bobbed hair, greatcoats, and designer weddings. The characters' favorite designer labels were Manolo Blahnik, Richard Tyler, Jimmy Choo, Dolce & Gabbana, Fendi, Dior, Blumarine, Chanel, Chloe, Prada, and Roberto Cavalli.

Each of the characters had a distinct style carefully developed for her: The style of Carrie (Sarah Jessica Parker) ranged from uptown chic, to whimsy, to sexy, with stilettos a staple and a frequent mix of designer clothes with flea market finds. Samantha (Kim Cattrall) wore sexy styles that exuded confidence loud and clear through strong styles and bold colors. Charlotte (Kristin Davis) had a sweet, preppy style that was always accompanied by the proper bag and shoes. Miranda (Cynthia Nixon) looked like a very well-dressed career woman, with stylish corporate suits.

As soon as *Sex and the City* ended, new shows began to fill the gap. The primetime series *Desperate Housewives* soon began to fulfill the viewers' desire for fashion ideas. Teri Hatcher, Susan in the show, became the spokesperson for the U.S. fashion label Badgley Mischka in 2007. Part of the popularity of the show was that its fashion offered viewers a relief from the police uniforms, hospital garb, and grubby *Survivor* gear that ruled the small screen. With between five and twelve changes per episode, there was plenty to scrutinize.

The key players are Susan Mayer (Teri Hatcher), a divorced single mother who illustrates children's books; Bree Van De Kamp (Marcia Cross), an icy perfectionist whose children refer to her as "the mayor of Stepford"; sizzling Gabrielle Solis (Eva Longoria), an ex-model who is looking for love in all the wrong places; Edie Britt (Nicollette Sheridan), the neighborhood's serial divorcée and unabashed sex machine; and Lynette Scavo (Felicity Huffman), who traded the executive suite for four children under age six and a husband who is never home. The costume designer, Catherine Adair, used dress to express the personality of each character. Susan wears designer jeans and T-shirts; Bree is the show's reigning domestic diva, clad in prim suits, pastel twin sets, and an ever-present string of pearls. Gabrielle also has a decidedly unsuburban way of dressing, with a preference for plunging necklines, short skirts, and megawatt jewelry. With her cleavage-baring bustiers and low-slung satin Gucci jeans, Edie is a vixen. Adair dresses Edie in everything from Dolce & Gabbana outfits to sweats from American Eagle Outfitters. Lynette often appears disheveled in jeans and a shirt.

Kristin Davis, Sarah Jessica Parker, Cynthia Nixon, and Kim Cattrall on location for *Sex and the City: The Movie*, 21 September 2007. The show had an enormous influence on fashion, and each of the characters had a distinct style specially created for her. Wirelmage.

REALITY TELEVISION: PUSHING FASHION TELEVISION TO NEW HEIGHTS

Back Channel Media listed 166 fashion genre programs on television for the week of 27 August 2007. That number did not include worldwide broadcasts, and it did not include programs (comedy, soap, or drama) with a fashion interest, such as *Desperate Housewives*, *Sex and the City* (now in reruns), *Ugly Betty*, and *Fashion Hoax*, nor did it include the new Tim Gunn's *Guide to Style*.

The most popular fashion genre shows also have Web sites to provide their viewers access to more information about their favorite shows. Many of these shows are reality shows. Some of the reality shows for 2007 included *What Not to Wear*, *Project Runway*, *America's Next Top Model*, *Queer Eye for the Straight Guy*, *Sports Illustrated Swimsuit Model Search*, *Fashion*, *Victoria's Secret Fashion Show*, *Queer Eye for the Straight Girl*, *Trinny and Susannah Undress*, *Project Jay*, and *Fashion Police*. Web sites such as Fashion Television and Full Frontal Fashion keep viewers updated on the latest fashion television programs. The popularity of shows such as *Project Runway* owes to their ability to demystify fashion and bring it to the masses. Viewers feel as if they are part of the fashion game, and they get fashion news without actually looking for it; it is just there on the small screen. In demystifying fashion, viewers also come to realize that fashion is art, it is creative, and it is hard work and not fluff.

Canadians have access to many U.S.-produced shows, but they also have developed their own networks, such as FT-Fashion Television, which has been around for twenty years. *Raw* is new in the lineup, but other shows are *Larger than Life*; *In Fashion*; *Naked in the House*, and *The Art of the Photograph*. Canada also has its own version of *Project Runway*, produced by Insight Production Co., Ltd. The model Iman is host for the show.

Fashion Rocks is the name of a Condé Nast magazine and a special television show. The show is presented by the publisher every September. Together these continue the association of television with music and fashion as they were first presented by MTV in 1981. MTV promoted itself using its own clothing line beginning in 1989. As popular music moved from rap to grunge and hip-hop, the clothing worn by musicians has continued to be copied by fans. Music stars have gone beyond the success of earlier groups like the Rolling Stones, who in 1989 produced their own line of clothes—leather motorcycle jackets with studded epaulets and bandannas. In the twenty-first century, the trend has taken off; superstar musicians have made clothing big business by moving to mainstream mass fashion. Gwen Stefani has an apparel line L.A.M.B.; Sean "Puffy" Combs has found success with his Sean John label. Their lines have moved beyond the concert venue and are found in many large department stores. The musician/designer has become commonplace and clearly visible as a personality; they are celebrities in their own right, an element that aids sales. As this trend continued in 2007, MTV altered its programming to include soaps, such as *Laguna Beach: The Real Orange County* and *The Hills*, that influenced the desire of teens for upscale luxury items. Another twist on the fashion-music connection is the decision of the Italian fashion brand Diesel to launch its own music label.

There have been Academy of Television Arts and Sciences Emmys awarded for excellence in costume design since the 1970s. The first winner was Bob Mackie, who styled Diana Ross, the Supremes, and the Temptations, as well as Cher and the costumes for *The Carol Burnett Show*. Yet many television costume designers remain unknown. With recent television shows having such an impact on fashion, some of the designers, such as Patricia Field for *Sex and the City*, have gained recognition. In the past few years, the FIDM Museum in Los Angeles has had a special exhibition of TV costumes that earned their designers Emmy nominations. Nominated costume designers for the 2007 Emmy Awards included Eduardo Castro, for his work on *Ugly Betty*, a fashion-focused program (eleven nominations); Andrea Galer's costumes for *Jane Eyre* (nine nominations); April Ferry, with the show *Rome* (seven nominations); Catherine Adair's styles from *Desperate Housewives* (six nominations); and Joan Bergin, with the show *The Tudors* (four nominations).

References and Further Reading

Akass, Kim, and Janet McCabe. *Sex and the City*. London and New York: I. B. Tauris, 2004.

Benedik, E. "Inside Miami Vice, Sex and Drugs and Rock & Roll Ambush Prime-Time TV." *Rolling Stone* (28 March 1985): 56–62, 125.

Blackwell, R., and T. Stephan. *Brands That Rock: What Business Leaders Can Learn from the World of Rock and Roll*. Hoboken, NJ: John Wiley & Sons, 2004.

Buxton, D. *From The Avengers to Miami Vice: Form and Ideology in Television Series*. Manchester, UK: Manchester University Press, 1990.

Champlin, S. "Nolan Miller Woos and Wins Dynasty's Women with His Razzle-Dazzle Fashions Every Week." *People Weekly* (19 December 1983): 66–68.

Clerk, C. *Madonnastyle*. London: Omnibus, 2002.

Conrad, P. *Television: The Medium and Its Manners*. Boston: Routledge, 1982.

Coulson, Clare. "How to Carrie It Off." *Daily Telegraph* (14 July 2003).

Cunningham, Patricia A., Heather Mangine, and Andrew Riley. "Television and Fashion in the 1980s." In *Twentieth-Century American Fashion*, edited by Linda Welters and Patricia A. Cunningham. Oxford and New York: Berg, 2005.

Gripsrud, J. *The Dynasty Years: Hollywood Television and Critical Media Studies*. London: Routledge, 1995.

Lewis, L.A. "Consumer Girl Culture: How Music Video Appeals to Girls." In *Television and Women's Culture: The Politics of the Popular*, edited by M.E. Brown. London: Sage Publications, 1990.

Nonkin, L. "Prime Time Style." *Vogue* (May 1984): 280.

Oldenberg, Ann. "TV Brings High Fashion Down to the Everyday." *USA Today* (12 July 2006).

Pollen, M. "The Vice Look." *Channels* (July/August 1964): 24–28.

Ross, A. "Miami Vice: Selling In." *Communication* 9 (1987): 305–334.

Schwichtenberg, C. "Sensual Surfaces and Stylistic Excess: The Pleasure and Politics of Miami Vice." *Journal of Communication Inquiry* 10, no. 3 (1986): 45–65.

Patricia A. Cunningham

See also Music and Dress in the United States; Music and Dress in Canada.

Music and Dress in the United States

- Songs and Music Videos That Focus on Dress
- Fashion Designers, Merchandising Fashion, and Dress
- Performances That Combine Music and Dress
- Music Genres and Dress: Folk Music
- North American Indian Music and Dress
- African American Music Traditions
- The Impact of Jazz
- Musical Theater and Dress
- Swing Sentiment and Patriotism
- Country Music
- Early Rock and Roll
- The British Invasion
- Further Evolution of Rock Music
- Electronic Media, Music, and Fashion
- Rap and Hip-Hop
- Grunge, Goth, and Rave
- Music Festivals
- Venues for Fashion Display
- Print Media and Film

The music and dress of the United States reflects its diverse and multicultural population made up of indigenous and immigrant groups, from North American Indians to Irish immigrants. The United States has a wide variety of music styles, from folk music to hip-hop, and related dress trends, from broomstick skirts to hubcap medallion necklaces.

The United States of America has a rich history of interplay between music and dress, and this reciprocal relationship is evident in all forms of popular media, from films to magazines. The movie *Zoolander* (2001) features two male runway models, as well as runway music and fashions. *MF Magazine: Music + Fashion* is a periodical dedicated to the intersections of independent music and fashion. The movie (and later Broadway play) *Hairspray* (1988), by John Waters, features a young woman who struggles to find her place as a plus-size fashionable teen, while embracing music that crosses racial boundaries. The musical *Hair* (1967) discussed issues of dress in the 1960s from nudity to long hair within narrative songs. The song "Fashion" (1980), by David Bowie, satirically positions fashion against the backdrop of dance (runway) music.

SONGS AND MUSIC VIDEOS THAT FOCUS ON DRESS

Dress is often the focus of songs. Consider these examples, the titles of which highlight items of dress: "Blue Suede Shoes" (1955),

by Carl Perkins; "Itsy Bitsy Teenie Weenie Yellow Polka Dot Bikini" (1960), by Brian Hyland; "Devil with the Blue Dress On" (1964), by Fredrick "Shorty" Long; "These Boots Are Made For Walkin'" (1966), by Nancy Sinatra; and "Forever in Blue Jeans" (1979), by Neil Diamond. Still others are "Tiny Dancer" (1971), by Elton John; "Pretty in Pink" (1981), by the Psychedelic Furs; "I'm Too Sexy" (1991), by Right Said Fred; "Chain Hang Low" (2006), by Jibbs; and "Fashion Zombies" (2006), by the Aquabats.

There are also songs written about holiday dress: "Easter Parade" (1948), by Irving Berlin; "Yankee Doodle Dandy" (1942), by George M. Cohan; "Dead Man's Party" (1985), by Oingo Boingo; and "Santa Baby" (1953), by Eartha Kitt. The Metropolitan Museum has put together a collection of songs about dress titled *The Songs of Fashion*, featuring "Diamonds Are a Girl's Best Friend" (1953), by Marilyn Monroe, and "Puttin' on the Ritz" (1930), by Harry Richman.

Music videos may be the most significant and tangible connection between music and dress. It is with the popularity and availability of music videos on the major music channels—MTV, VH1, and BET—that fashion icons and trends are born, spread, and established within the mainstream culture.

U.S. musician Jennifer Lopez with models wearing garments from her Sweetface fashion brand at Olympus Fashion Week, New York, 2006. Louis Dollagaray/WireImage.

The music videos range from discussing fashionable accessories in "Raspberry Beret" (1985), by Prince and The Revolution, and "Sunglasses at Night" (1984), by Corey Hart, to commenting on fashionable erogenous zones in "Physical" (1981), by Olivia Newton-John, and "Legs" (1984), by ZZ Top. In "Vogue" (1990), by Madonna, the artist encourages posing with fashionable style on the dance floor. "Barbie Girl" (1997), by Aqua, brings to life a U.S. fashion icon—the Barbie doll. India.Arie's music videos "Video" (2001) and "I Am Not My Hair" (2006) both discuss the artist's personal and casual style and dress. In "The Real Slim Shady" (2000), Eminem features numerous Slim Shady clones, indicating the rap artist's impact on music and fashion trends.

FASHION DESIGNERS, MERCHANDISING FASHION, AND DRESS

Fashion designers dress musicians for music videos, award shows, television appearances, and everyday life. In 1992, Snoop Doggy Dogg was dressed in hip-hop fashions by Tommy Hilfiger for his *Saturday Night Live* television appearance. In 2000, Jennifer Lopez was dressed for the *Grammy Music Awards Show* in an extremely deep-cut and scandalous Versace gown. Musicians also recognize the importance of their dress when on stage and often rely on designers to create a desired stage image. In 1990, Jean-Paul Gaultier dressed Madonna in attention-grabbing fashions for her Blond Ambition tour.

Music industry executives have recognized the possibility for profit from a combination of music and dress. The most notable examples are the fashion brands Phat Farm and Baby Phat. In 1992, the cofounder of Def Jam Records, Russell Simmons, launched Phat Farm, a clothing company that merged urban culture, fashion, and music. Simmons and his wife, Kimora Lee Simmons, also created Baby Phat, the female version of Phat Farm.

Musicians are branching out into fashion design and using their celebrity status to promote their fashion brands. In 2001, Jennifer Lopez joined with Andy Hilfiger to create Sweetface Fashion, which has control over the JLo fashion brand. In 2004, numerous musicians, such as Paula Abdul, Boy George, Hilary Duff, Reba McEntire, Mandy Moore, Lil' Romeo, LL Cool J, and Queen Latifah launched fashion brands. Some of the most successful musicians who have founded fashion brands are Gwen Stefani and her brand L.A.M.B., which stands for Love Angel Music Baby, and P. Diddy and his Sean John collection. Other music celebrity clothing brands include Vokal and Apple Bottoms, by Nelly; Shady, by Eminem; Fetish, by Eve; Shago, by Bow Wow; Boomer 129, by DMX; Rock Star Baby, by Tico Torres from Bon Jovi; Bushi, by Busta Rhymes; Wu Wear, by Wu-Tang Clan; I Am, by Will.I.Am from The Black Eyed Peas; and Dragonfly, by Nikki Sixx from Mötley Crüe. These musicians often promote their fashion brands by wearing their clothing and accessories in music videos, at awards ceremonies, and at media events.

PERFORMANCES THAT COMBINE MUSIC AND DRESS

Musicians are also experimenting with dress that makes music. Jon Fishman, from the prog-rock band Phish, had a tunic-style dress made from woven audiotapes, which was playable by gloves containing audiotape heads. Fishman composed a song about the dress's debut using the gloves and audiotape fabric of the dress. Audio Gruppe creates "sonic costumes" and "audio uniforms" for its performers to make sound and music within their performances. This performance dress uses light sensors to electronically transfer body movements into sound and music.

Other areas of the performance arts utilize dress to emphasize or complement the musical component of the presentation. In opera, ballet, modern dance, and musical theater, costumes are created to help communicate the specific storyline. At festivals such as Renaissance Faires, performers dress, act, and play music that help evoke and create an atmosphere conducive to the festival theme.

Retail stores utilize music and feature musicians within the store for a more integrated experience between music and fashion. DJs spin records at clothing stores, such as Diesel in New York City and For Breakers Only in Hollywood, to create a dance club atmosphere. Specialty stores, such as Crash Bang Boom in Philadelphia, Pennsylvania, cater to musicians' fashion needs and feature live music. Hard Rock Cafés around the United States display fashions worn by musical legends and sell music-inspired fashions, while featuring related music and musicians.

Dress also can be designed to accommodate emerging music technologies. The fanny pack was a popular accessory to transport and listen to the Walkman (a brand and now also a generic term for portable cassette players and radios with small, corded headphones). MP3 players and iPods allow for the downloading of songs as electronic data from the Internet for personal listening. These players are designed small to allow for easy transportation in a pocket or purse. Clothing companies have also designed garments, ranging from outerwear to sportswear, with MP3 pockets and holes for headphone cords to pass through. Headphones are designed to be accessories in fashionable colors for fashion-conscious music listeners.

Fashion shows naturally bring together music and dress in a variety of ways. Olympus Fashion Week, in New York City at Bryant Park, draws music celebrities as high-profile attendees for many of the urban fashion designers. Glam Live Rock Fashion Shows held in major cities around the United States and Voltage Amplified in Minneapolis, Minnesota, feature musical performers, attempting to blur the boundaries of music and fashion. Funkshion: Fashion Week Miami is held in Miami, Florida, and attempts to celebrate and merge music and fashion. JLo, Heatherette, and Alexander Crocker have had runway shows during Funkshion. The VH1/Vogue Fashion Awards show recognizes the connections between musicians and fashion.

MUSIC GENRES AND DRESS: FOLK MUSIC

Genres of music in the United States are complex and intricate because the inspirations for styles of music come from diverse areas and established styles evolve into new ones. The chronology of music is also complicated because some genres continue from inception, some fade away and later have resurgence, and others completely disappear. Consequently, dress associated with genres of music has an equally serpentine existence.

Folk music has narrative lyrics that reflect U.S. culture or a group's ethnic and cultural origins, such as the Aanishanabe culture of the Ojibwa Indians or Irish culture. The exact origins and beginnings of U.S. folk music are difficult to identify; however, it was most notable in the 1800s. Stephen Foster is considered the "father of folk music"; he wrote: "Oh! Susanna" (1848), "Camptown Races" (1850),

The Great Omaha powwow dance of the Cheyennes in Montana, ca. 1891. Participants wear colorful dress with abundant eagle feathers and fringe to represent grass. Library of Congress, Prints and Photographs Division, LC-USZ62-101168.

and "My Old Kentucky Home" (1853). Other folk songs from the period include "Turkey in the Straw" (ca. 1820s), "Yellow Rose of Texas" (1858), and "Oh My Darling, Clementine" (1884).

Folk music experienced a resurgence in the 1950s and 1960s with the music of Bob Dylan, Woody Guthrie, and Joan Baez. This folk music was closely associated with the hippie counterculture and political movement. Hippie dress included long hairstyles, decorated jeans, ethnic shirts, and hemp sandals. In the late twentieth century, culture-specific folk music was performed by bands such as The Pogues and The Knitters. This later generation of folk music performers often donned folk costumes that represented the cultural origins of their music.

NORTH AMERICAN INDIAN MUSIC AND DRESS

The North American Indians were the first inhabitants of what is now the United States. They had and still have a wide array of music and related dress, primarily displayed during rituals or ceremonies for spiritual and cultural rites and prayers, as well as cultural celebrations. Each group had a culturally specific type of folk music, often spiritual in nature. Vocals were important components of ancient North American Indian music, ranging from solo and group to call-and-response songs. Drums and rattles were commonly used to keep the beat for the singers and dancers, but music varied with vocal accents and shouts, along with drums that gained speed and intensity.

Singers and dancers dress according to gender, song, culture, and dance related to the specific ritual or ceremony. Throughout the history of the North American Indian groups there have been handmade garments for rituals and ceremonies, which included music that varied from group to group. The North American Indians crafted their garments from various materials, such as cloth, leather, or fur, depending on available resources and climate. The garments made for cultural and spiritual rituals or ceremonies were often adorned with embroidery or beadwork, and some included headwear.

Men's dance dress varies depending on the specific dance and ritual or ceremony, often requiring the dancers to secure eagle feathers, sinew, and specific animal skins. In the 1890s, the Ghost Dance circulated throughout the various Great Basin Indian groups. Young men wore "ghost shirts" decorated with mystic imagery believed to protect the wearer. The Straight Dance is a formal dance style that has origins in the war dance. The dancer wears a roach headdress with one eagle feather, leggings, and an otter skin down his back. The Fancy Dance was created on reservations to attract visitors. Men dance in broad movements and colorful dress, specifically a two-piece bustle made from dyed turkey feathers. The Sun Dance and Grass Dance are the foundations of the pantribal powwows. The Grass Dance originated from the Omaha Grass Dance and also utilizes broad movements and colorful dress with abundant eagle feathers and fringe to represent grass. The Traditional Dance is commonly seen at powwows and is considered the warrior's dance because it demonstrates through dance one's martial accomplishments. The Gourd Dance is not a powwow dance but instead is used for the Grand Entry into the powwow.

Women's dance dress also varies depending on the dance and occasion, usually requiring intricate designs made from embroidery, ribbonwork, or beadwork. The Jingle Dance has its origins in a vision and is quite popular at powwows. This dance has small movements, but the jingles of the rolled metal or shells on the dress emphasize the dancer's movements with sound and reflective light. The Fancy Shawl Dance has broad and intricate movements and most notably uses a shawl to accentuate the movements of the female dancer. The Traditional Buckskin Dance is an elegant dance and utilizes beadwork on the garments. The Southern Cloth Dance is similar to the Buckskin Dance, but the women wear garments made from fine cloth and ribbonwork.

In the twenty-first century, North American Indians are often grouped together under the umbrella of pantribalism, which impacts the music and dress for rituals and ceremonies. Still, there are distinct differences from one ritual or ceremony to another. Contemporary North American Indian music draws from traditional and pantribal music as well as soul, funk, jazz, and rock music. Performers' dress ranges from pantribal garments to contemporary fashions and a mixture of both styles.

AFRICAN AMERICAN MUSIC TRADITIONS

The *spiritual* is a music genre in North America that has been around in North America since before the 1800s. These songs were originally sung by enslaved African Americans as expressions of sociocultural struggles and spiritual faith. Songs included "Swing Low, Sweet Chariot" and "Deep Down in My Heart." In time, the spiritual was associated with religious services (not necessarily within a church) and African Americans dressed in their "Sunday best," choir robes, or finest garments reserved for church services. However, spirituals were also sung in the fields and were not necessarily associated with a specific type of dress.

The *minstrelsy*, or *minstrel show*, was prevalent in the United States from 1820 to 1900 and included music, comedy, acting, and dancing. These shows spread African American music and dress around the United States, and eventually became popular within mainstream culture. Minstrelsy included influential narrative songs about African American nostalgia and history set to syncopated dance beats, such as music by Stephen Foster, America's first popular songwriter. Originally, the dress associated with the minstrelsy included blackface and stereotypical slave styles. As racial tensions increased in the United States, blackface was eliminated, and dress styles became elaborate and lavish.

Work songs are rhythmic, a cappella songs that repeat phrases and sometimes include call-and-response lyrics. Work songs were usually sung by people doing physical labor to coordinate repetitive movements. In the United States, work songs were commonly sung among sailors, military personnel, and enslaved African Americans. Songs such as "She'll Be Coming Round the Mountain" and "Casey Jones" might have been sung while picking cotton, weaving a textile, or stitching a quilt. Due to the purpose of work songs, the songs were often associated with dress that was practical, distressed, and used for physical labor.

Blues originated in the African American communities in the area of the Mississippi Delta in the late 1800s. Blues music

U.S. blues performer Howlin Wolf in 1950. Many blues performers dressed in suits or elegant gowns; this may have been a way of illustrating how far they had come from slave and laborer roots. Michael Ochs Archives/Getty Images.

began as unaccompanied narrative or call-and-response songs by African American laborers, with regional variations and distinctions throughout the United States. Eventually, the guitar became the primary blues instrument. The blues were the foundation for much of modern U.S. popular music, such as country, jazz, and rap. Many blues performers dressed in suits or elegant gowns, possibly to differentiate themselves from their slave and laborer roots. *The Blues Brothers* (1980) movie prominently featured twentieth-century blues music and fashion, such as dark sunglasses, thin ties, and dark suits with a white shirt.

Ragtime is a form of dance music that originated in African American communities and peaked in popularity from 1896 to 1918. The "Big Three" fathers of ragtime were Scott Joplin, James Scott, and Joseph Lamb. This genre of music featured piano with melodic accents that occur between metered beats, which encouraged the listener to move and dance along with the beat. Popular ragtime dances were the Two-Step, Slow Drag, Classic Rag, and Folk Rag. Ragtime fashions usually included garments that allowed for ease of dancing, such as loose pants or dresses with knee-length full skirts.

Tin Pan Alley was music resulting from the sheet music and songs sold by the New York City music publishers and songwriters during the late nineteenth and early twentieth centuries. Music publishers in Chicago, Philadelphia, New Orleans, Detroit, St. Louis, and Boston sold regional hits to New York publishers, and the songs were then made available for listening and purchase around the United States. The North American music industry has its origin with Tin Pan Alley. Fashions associated with Tin Pan Alley were primarily transmitted to the mainstream culture by the images on the front cover of sheet music; however, some fashions were communicated through the lyrics of the songs.

THE IMPACT OF JAZZ

Jazz music originated in Louisiana at the beginning of the twentieth century, and it soon spread to Charleston, North Carolina; Chicago, Illinois; and St. Louis, Missouri. Jazz music began in African American communities, which drew inspirations from ragtime and military marching band music, with regional variations. Jazz was a form of dance music. The 1920s in the United States became known as the Jazz Age, and radio stations helped establish jazz as a sophisticated and "cool" genre of music. Over the decades, jazz continues to be a significant genre of U.S. music and has branched out to subgenres, such as Latin jazz, smooth jazz, acid jazz, and jazz fusion.

Stylish and avant-garde dress has often been associated with jazz music, both for performers and listeners. In the 1920s, jazz music was associated with the speakeasy and the flapper style, that is, short hair, boxy silhouette, knee-length dress, and a long necklace. In the 1940s, zoot suiters were associated with jazz music. The zoot suit was worn by Chicano and African American males; it was a long suit coat with wide shoulders and lapels and high-waisted, pleated pants tapered to narrow pegs at the ankle. The zoot suit was completed with a wide-brimmed hat and a watch on a chain that hung down from the suit coat. In the 1950s, jazz musicians, such as Thelonious Monk, Miles Davis, and Dizzy Gillespie, played bebop jazz and were known as hipsters. At this time, jazz music was closely associated with the beatnik movement and Beat writers, such as Jack Kerouac and Allen Ginsberg. The jazz style of dress included black berets, goatees, scarves, and sunglasses, and these fashions are still seen in jazz fashions. In the 1960s and 1970s, jazz performers integrated African dress with fashion-forward styles.

MUSICAL THEATER AND DRESS

Vaudeville shows were popular in the United States during the nineteenth and early twentieth centuries. Shows included comedy, songs, acting, and dance that drew from U.S. popular culture. Vaudevillian performers included Jack Benny, Judy Garland, the Three Stooges, Kate Smith, Buster Keaton, and the Marx Brothers, most of whom went on to have careers in Hollywood. Vaudevillian dress encompassed various costumes for stage.

Burlesque emerged from minstrelsy and vaudeville in the mid-nineteenth and early twentieth centuries. Burlesque shows often had highly ornate scenery, theatrical lighting, ambient music, and variety acts, such as puppets, opera, satire, comedy, dancers, and striptease. Most burlesque performers were females, and their costumes were lavish and colorful but usually minimal in fabric and coverage. In the late twentieth and early twenty-first centuries, burlesque had a revival as *neoburlesque*. Burlesque-inspired fashions were shown on runways by fashion designers, such as Betsey Johnson and Heatherette, and worn by performers, such as the Pussycat Dolls and Chris Owens.

The *Ziegfeld Follies* were elaborate theatrical revues on Broadway in New York City from 1907 to 1931. These shows were inspired by the Folies Bergère from Paris, France, and resembled a high-scale version of vaudeville shows, including various musical performances. Follies performers wore elaborate costumes that were often heavy and cumbersome, making it difficult for performers to sing, dance, or even move. Las Vegas performances featuring showgirls are compared to the Follies.

SWING SENTIMENT AND PATRIOTISM

Swing dance music was popular during from the 1920s through the 1940s and is still heard in dance halls around the United States. Big bands, such as those led by Benny Goodman and Glenn Miller, popularized swing dance music among young North Americans. Swing fashions focused on dress that emphasized dance moves and has not changed much in its overall appearance since its inception. Female swing fashion often included a dress or blouse and skirt, comfortable dance shoes, and underwear that may be seen during spins or throws. Male swing fashion usually included a suit or pants and a shirt, comfortable dance shoes, and a hat.

Music during World War II played an important role as it related to in the sociopolitical fabric of the United States, especially the troops. U.S. troops listened to the Armed Forces Radio, except when in heavy combat. U.S. wartime music was often sentimental (e.g., "Sentimental Journey," 1945, Les Brown), nostalgic ("White Christmas," 1942, Irving Berlin), confident ("Praise the Lord and Pass the Ammunition," 1942, Kay Kyser), and patriotic ("Boogie Woogie Bugle Boy," 1941, Andrews Sisters). Performers' dress often resembled military uniforms from the time period. This broad-shouldered silhouette was also seen in the everyday fashions of the U.S. audiences.

COUNTRY MUSIC

Country music, also known as *hillbilly* or *country and western* music, originated in the Appalachian Mountains and was influenced by U.S. folk, Celtic, blues, and gospel music genres. Country music also borrowed instruments, such as the Irish fiddle, German dulcimer, African banjo, and Spanish guitar, and related musical styles from the "melting pot" of U.S. cultures. Country music is often associated with the southern United States, but it is performed and listened to across the United States (and the globe). Themes of country music range from love and loss to everyday American life. Jimmie Rodgers and the Carter Family are thought to be the originators of country music. Many genres of music have been influenced by country music: bluegrass, zydeco, honky-tonk, and rockabilly.

Country music performer dress is often associated with "average American" or blue-collar dress. Country music fans felt validated in their chosen dress when they saw their favorite performer wearing jeans and a plaid shirt on the Grand Ole Opry. A notable exception is the use of the *Nudie suit*, which was created by Ukrainian American tailor and designer Nudie Cohn. Nudie established a business of designing country music dress by dressing Porter Wagner in a peach-colored suit covered with embroidery and rhinestones in the shape of wagon wheels, with a covered wagon on the back of the jacket. Later Nudie suits often featured European folk floral designs and symbols specific to certain performers. By the 1970s, the Nudie suit and similar styles were no longer the country music image. However, by the late twenty-first century, Marty Stuart began wearing Nudie suits again in homage to past country music icons. In the twenty-first

Jazz style: Duke Ellington (at the piano) and Dizzy Gillespie (second from left at the front) during a jam session (United States, 1942). Gjon Mili / Time Life Pictures/ Getty Images.

century, with few exceptions, it is often difficult to distinguish country music performers due to their dress.

Country music continues to have a unique relationship with dress. Shania Twain caused commotion among U.S. country music fans when she wore tops that exposed her midriff. In 1999, Twain allowed Revlon to use her song "Man! I Feel Like a Woman!" for an advertisement campaign. Billy Ray Cyrus donned a lengthy mullet hairstyle (short in front and sides but long in back) in his music video for "Achy Breaky Heart" (1992). The Dixie Chicks have chicken feet tattooed on them; each tattoo represents one of their musical accomplishments, such as their Grammy awards.

Zydeco is a form of North American folk music that originated among the Francophone Creole people in Louisiana during the early twentieth century and continues into the twenty-first century. Zydeco is dance music that integrates sounds, beats, and styles from blues, bluegrass, reggae, rock and roll, and hip-hop. The dress associated with zydeco music reveals its rural Louisiana origins, and performers' dress is not usually distinctive from fans' dress.

EARLY ROCK AND ROLL

Rock and roll was a genre of U.S. music that began in the 1940s and became popular in the 1950s when it was associated with youth. By the twentieth century, this genre was better known as *pop(ular) music* and had given birth to numerous subgenres, such as rockabilly, surf, disco, new wave, glam rock, heavy metal, grunge, and techno. Elvis Presley was one of the first rock and roll performers to impact fashion in a major way. From his pompadour hairstyle to his custom-dyed boots, North American youth copied his style and dress. This established the pattern for rock and roll audiences to mimic their favorite performer's dress.

Surf music was a subgenre of rock and roll in the 1950s and was associated with the surf culture. It had upbeat lyrics about surfing and a medium to fast tempo. The most notable surf band was the Beach Boys. The original fashions of surf performers were similar to those of their surfer fans: Hawaiian print shirts, baggy shorts, and deck shoes.

In 1959, Motown Records was founded by Barry Gordy in Detroit, Michigan. The Motown record label brought African

American music to a broad audience, primarily offering soul, blues, rhythm and blues, and funk music. Since the 1960s, Motown performers have included Smokey Robinson, the Temptations, Marvin Gaye, Diana Ross, Teena Marie, Debarge, Queen Latifah, Erykah Badu, Boyz II Men, and India.Arie.

Motown performers were always dressed in the latest fashions. In the early 1960s, men and women wore fashionable suits and gowns, and groups dressed similarly to one another, which established a standard for African American youth to dress with a flair for style. By the late 1960s, performers had a more relaxed appearance and sometimes wore clothing that had African origins, which was reflected in the African dress worn by many American youth regardless of race. In the 1970s, U.S. youth were dressing similarly to the band Jackson 5: Afro hairstyles, fringe vests over broad-collared shirts, and bell-bottom jeans. Motown performers continued to set and follow the latest fashion styles into the twenty-first century.

Psychedelic music in the 1960s had a rock and roll tempo with surreal effects and lyrics. Bands such as Strawberry Alarm Clock and Iron Butterfly made psychedelic music popular among the hallucinogenic drug countercultures. Related fashions followed current silhouettes with colorful fabrics inspired by hallucinations, or "trips," and surreal accessories. Rowan and Martin's *Laugh-In*, a 1960s comedy television show, further popularized psychedelic music and dress.

THE BRITISH INVASION

The British Invasion was an influx of British bands (such as the Beatles, the Rolling Stones, and the Who) and their music into North America during the mid-1960s. The British musicians were influenced by North American rock and roll but had modified the sound to be distinctly British. During the early part of the British Invasion, the Beatles introduced the *mop-top* hairstyle to North American youth, along with the Edwardian collarless suit. Later, during the psychedelic era in the late 1960s, the Beatles introduced brightly colored paisley shirts and floral-patterned pants.

In the late 1960s, the Beatles traveled to India for spiritual enlightenment and returned with Indian-inspired music and fashions, such as tunics, sandals, and beads. The Rolling Stones traveled to North Africa for inspiration and returned with Moroccan-inspired fashions, such as beaded and embellished tunics and embroidered bell-bottom jeans. These fashions were the inspiration for the 1960s bohemian style.

FURTHER EVOLUTION OF ROCK MUSIC

In the 1970s, people were listening and dancing to *disco* music at clubs such as Studio 54 in New York City and dressing like John Travolta's character from the movie *Saturday Night Fever* (1977) or Farrah Fawcett from the television series *Charlie's Angels*. Disco performers who influenced fashion included Rick James, Donna Summer, and the Bee Gees. Disco music and clubs attracted models, fashion designers, and celebrities who were interested in the latest disco-inspired fashions. The glitz and glam of disco fashions included for women, lamé dresses or satin jumpsuits with feathered hair and platform shoes, and for men, unbuttoned shirts with skintight, wide-legged pants and multiple gold necklaces.

A poster for The Famous Rentz Santley Novelty and Burlesque Co., ca. 1900. Most burlesque performers were female and wore highly decorative and colorful costumes with minimal fabric and coverage. Library of Congress Prints and Photographs Division, Theatrical Poster Collection, LC-USZC2-1394.

Glam rock of the 1970s was closely associated with disco music, but it had more of a rock and roll edge. Fashions associated with glam rock were often associated with "gender-bending" or androgyny. Glam rock performers who influenced fashion were David Bowie, KISS, Alice Cooper, and the New York Dolls. Each of these performers experimented with dramatic makeup and elaborate costumes.

Funk was a genre of African American dance music in the 1970s. Funk performers who influenced fashion included Sly and the Family Stone, the Commodores, and George Clinton. Funk fashions were similar to disco: dramatic makeup, lamé jumpsuits, sequin dresses, platform shoes, and large gold jewelry. Rick James is featured on the front of his funk retrospective album, *Rick James Anthology* (1979/1980), wearing a white cowboy hat and long hair, with a white leather ensemble that is embellished with red and blue stars and lightning bolts, and white thigh-high boots with heels.

In the late 1970s, *punk* music was imported from Great Britain into the United States with the Sex Pistols. U.S. punk musicians included Patti Smith, the Ramones, and the Dead Kennedys. Punk music was cacophonous, confrontational, and rebellious. Punk bands wore ripped T-shirts, distressed jeans, spiked dog collars, and Dr. ("Doc") Marten boots, with spiky hair. Punks also had body modifications, such as facial piercings and tattoos of punk symbols. Many of these fashions were conceived and designed by Malcolm McLaren and Vivienne Westwood. In the late 1990s, punk music resurfaced with bands such as Green Day and Rancid, and punk fashions emerged as highly stylized and commercial versions of the original punk dress.

Beginning in the late 1970s, North American youth were introduced to *reggae* or *rasta* (Rastafarian) music. Reggae songs were primarily commentaries about social issues in Jamaica, as well as love, spirituality, women, and drugs. Reggae musicians who influenced fashion were Bob Marley and the Wailers, Steel Pulse, Peter Tosh, Mighty Diamonds, and Black Uhuru. The reggae style included clothing with the same colors as the Ethiopian flag (red, gold, and green) and dreadlocks, as well as the marijuana-leaf motif, which symbolized the desire for the decriminalization of marijuana. Reggae music and style still has a presence in the United States among small counterculture groups.

ELECTRONIC MEDIA, MUSIC, AND FASHION

The 1980s brought opulence, superficiality, and excess, which was evident in the abundance of music and fashion styles. Prior to the 1980s, music was disseminated through sheet music, radio, and on media such as vinyl records, eight-track tapes, and cassette tapes. In the 1980s, compact discs (CDs) were readily available for North American consumption, which stimulated the synergy between music and technology. In 1981, MTV (Music Television), a cable station, broadcast the first music video, introducing the U.S. public to visually portrayed music. Unlike radio stations, MTV did not limit the music videos that it broadcast to a certain style or genre. This open-programming format exposed a vast audience to a broad range of musical styles, and in this manner, music influenced dress in ways it had not been able to in the past.

MTV not only played music videos but also explored other ways of knowing music and musicians, for example, with interviews, parties, music news, award shows, and game shows. MTV capitalized on music and musicians; however, musicians also

gained from this new musical medium. The music video and MTV catapulted pop musicians into new arenas and provided them with a platform from which to be heard. Some performers used the MTV platform to launch their music careers, while others addressed world issues (hunger, natural disasters, and AIDS) and still others simply enjoyed the spotlight. Regardless the reason for being on MTV, the audience was watching and mimicking their favorite musicians, particularly their dress. Even MTV video jockeys (VJs) had an impact on their audiences' dress; J. J. Jackson, for example, wore a red leather jacket similar to Michael Jackson's in the video "Beat It" (1983), and Nina Blackwood wore the latest rock and roll hairstyles.

Madonna became a fashion icon for women by introducing several successful styles through her music videos (and concert performances). She introduced corsets and other lingerie as outer garments, or at least visible through clothing; leggings under skirts with high-heeled shoes; and crucifixes and rosaries as jewelry. Other female musicians who introduced new fashions through their music videos included Cyndi Lauper, who presented a layered look both in dress and jewelry, along with brightly colored, asymmetrical haircuts in the video "Girls Just Want to Have Fun" (1983); Terri Nunn, from the band Berlin, who had blond hair with black tips and sophisticated 1940s-inspired clothes in the music video "Take My Breath Away" (1986); Annie Lennox, from the band the Eurythmics, who introduced masculine dress for women with her tailored men's suits fitted to her slim physique in the video "Sweet Dreams" (1983); and Pat Benatar, who introduced the gauze dress with handkerchief hemline in her video "Love Is a Battlefield" (1983).

Male musicians also introduced new fashions through their music videos. Boy George and Culture Club presented dramatic makeup and body-disguising clothing to create an androgynous image in his music video "Do You Really Want to Hurt Me?" (1982). A Flock of Seagulls popularized asymmetrical haircuts with their video "I Ran (So Far Away)" (1982). Bon Jovi presented the fringe leather jacket in their music video "Livin' on a Prayer" (1987). Duran Duran made fashionable the tailored suits, skinny ties, and eyeliner from their music video "Rio" (1982).

MTV also opened the door for the second British Invasion with synthpop, new wave, and new romantic music videos. The second British Invasion included bands such as The Clash, ABC, Human League, Madness, Adam and the Ants, Wham!, and Soft Cell. These bands' music videos introduced U.S. audiences to preppy dress, androgyny, and exaggerated silhouettes.

MTV featured weekly shows that introduced lesser-known music styles. *Headbangers Ball* was one such show that premiered in 1987; it featured interviews with and music videos of *heavy metal* performers, ranging from Mötley Crüe to Motörhead. *Headbangers Ball*, named for the rhythmic head-thrashing that the heavy metal performers and fans did to the beat of the music, reintroduced the United States to long hair for men (often teased and heavily hairsprayed); leather pants and jackets; denim jackets covered with heavy metal band patches; animal-print Lycra pants; bandannas tied around the head, wrists, and pant legs; band tour T-shirts; and metal-inspired tattoos.

Heavy metal music videos were also played on MTV during regular rotation. Many of these bands were referred to as *glam metal* or *hair metal* for their use of makeup and overly teased hairstyles. Music videos by Mötley Crüe, Ratt, Def Leppard, and Whitesnake, for example, popularized many heavy metal fashions

U.S. singer and musician Elvis Presley performs with his band on *The Ed Sullivan Show*, New York City, 28 October 1956. Elvis was one of the first rock and roll performers to impact fashion in a major way. This established the pattern of rock and roll audiences mimicking their favorite performer's dress. CBS Photo Archive/Getty Images.

among metal fans, as well as fans from other music genres. Heavy metal bands completed their bridge to fashion when fashion models were included in their videos. Whitesnake used fashion model Tawny Kitaen in their music video "Here I Go Again" (1987).

Other music genres also included fashion models in their music videos. George Michael featured models Naomi Campbell, Linda Evangelista, Christy Turlington, Cindy Crawford, and Tatjana Patitz in his music video "Freedom 90" (1990); and Beverly Peele, Linda Evangelista, Emma Sjoberg, Estelle Hallyday, and Nadja Auermann in his music video "Too Funky" (1992). Duran Duran featured fashion models in a number of their videos, including "A View to a Kill" (1985), "Notorious" (1986), "Skin Trade" (1987), "Femme Fatale" (1993), and "Electric Barbarella" (1997). Further establishing the connection between the music video and fashion, MTV introduced *House of Style* in 1989, hosted by Cindy Crawford, which featured the latest fashions and rock star styles.

RAP AND HIP-HOP

Music videos ensured that rap and hip-hop music not only reached a diverse audience but also popularized the associated urban African American style of these music genres. In the 1980s, rap and hip-hop artists, such as Run DMC and Grandmaster Flash, wore brand-name, oversized clothing; tennis shoes; and baseball caps, along with large, heavy gold jewelry. Will Smith and Kid 'n Play introduced the hi-top fade hairstyle; Salt-N-Pepa wore oversized "door knocker" earrings; and LL Cool J popularized the name-brand tracksuit and tennis shoes.

In the 1990s, musicians such as Queen Latifah and Public Enemy expanded the rap and hip-hop fashions to include traditional African styles. These fashions included kente cloth garments, kufis, headwraps, and dreadlocks. Sportswear, such as Raiders starter jackets and Chuck Taylor tennis shoes, was also made fashionable by rap and hip-hop musicians. During the mid-1990s, the *gangsta* style was made popular by Ice-T, N.W.A. (Niggaz with Attitude), and Tupac Shakur. Gangsta style was influenced by gang members and prison inmates. In time, brand names such as ECKO Unlimited and Lugz fostered relationships with rap and hip-hop musicians. And name brands, such as FUBU, Phat Farm, and Baby Phat, were created within the African American community to respond to the styles desired by the rap and hip-hop community.

In 1999, B.G., or Baby Gangsta, made the song "Bling-Bling," which referenced the elaborate and ostentatious jewelry, fashion, and lifestyle of the rap and hip-hop artists. Rap and hip-hop musicians popularized *bling-bling* fashions, such as grills (jewel-encrusted metal teeth coverings), large jeweled earrings and rings, and fashions with visible brand names. Fashion designers began incorporating faux and real jewels into their garments, as well as prominently featuring brand names on garments and accessories.

GRUNGE, GOTH, AND RAVE

In direct contrast to the opulence of the rap and hip-hop music scene, in the late 1980s *grunge* music emerged in Seattle, Washington, from bands such as Soundgarden, Pearl Jam, and Nirvana. Grunge was deemed an *alternative* music genre for the disillusioned youth of Generation X. Grunge music was loud and raw, with guitar-oriented music and disenchanted lyrics. Kurt Cobain, from Nirvana, and Courtney Love, from the band Hole, were considered the royalty of grunge. Cobain established the fashion of thrift store cast-offs: worn jeans, distressed plaid shirts, out-of-date cardigans, and uncombed hair. Love wore baby-doll dresses, Mary Jane shoes, disheveled makeup, and unkempt hairstyles. In the mid-1990s, Marc Jacobs designed a fashion collection that reflected the grunge style.

U.S. rap artists Run DMC, 1970s. Along with other hip-hop and rap artists, their look included large, heavy gold jewelry. Michael Ochs Archives/Getty Images.

Earlier in the 1980s, the *goth* or *gothic* subculture emerged, inspired by bands such as Souxsie and the Banshees, Bauhaus, and the Cure. The music dealt with dark literary themes: star-crossed love scenarios, philosophical quandaries, and apocalyptic predictions set to dark and heavy dance music. Goth musicians and fans dressed in primarily black clothing, had extremely pale complexions highlighted with heavy black and red makeup, wore silver jewelry of religious symbols, and had black hair that fell dramatically over the face. In the 1990s, Marilyn Manson popularized goth music for mainstream audiences; he also introduced an updated gothic style of dark and dramatic makeup, black hair, and fetish garments.

In the late 1980s, the *rave* subculture emerged as a dance culture whose members were often associated with the drug ecstasy (MDMA), techno and acid house music, and brightly colored clothing. Raves are all-night dance parties in warehouses or large campsites where DJs mix house music with dance beats and bass lines. DJs, sound system groups, and ravers travel around the globe to participate in rave parties. Ravers dress in layered clothing; glow-in-the-dark and candy accessories, such as pacifiers and glow ropes; and platform shoes, along with the yellow smiley-face buttons that symbolize the acid house music scene. Ravers rhythmically swing their glow-in-the-dark accessories as they dance to create trippy light shows. The rave scene continues into the twenty-first century.

MUSIC FESTIVALS

Music festivals play a significant role in disseminating music genres and associated styles. The Woodstock Music and Art Festival took place on a farm in Bethel, New York, in 1969. Five hundred thousand people attended the free event to celebrate peace, love, and music. *Woodstock* (1970), the documentary film by Michael Wadleigh and Martin Scorsese, won an Academy Award and confirmed stereotypes about this time period and its youth—the 1960s were about the hippie generation: young Americans who protested the Vietnam War; listened to Jimi Hendrix, Crosby, Stills, Nash, and Young, Joe Cocker, and Jefferson Airplane; and dressed in the bohemian style. The Woodstock Music and Art Festival was held again in 1979, 1989, and 1999, but the impact of original music festival was never duplicated.

In 1971, the Seattle Arts Festival hosted an international music festival in Seattle, Washington, which was renamed Bumbershoot: Seattle's Music and Arts Festival in 1973. This music festival attracts international performers and audiences, as well as a global array of dress. The Bumbershoot music festival continues to take place into the early twenty first century. Similar to many music festivals, Bumbershoot sells a large number of promotional and commemorative T-shirts with various festival-related graphics.

In 1976, the National Old Time Country and Bluegrass Festival was established as an annual U.S. music event. Musical styles at the festival include traditional country, bluegrass, ragtime, zydeco, western, hillbilly, and folk. Performers and fans dress in similar fashions, such as a Western shirt, jeans, and cowboy boots or a music festival T-shirt with jeans and a cowboy hat.

Lollapalooza, which started in 1991, is a North American music tour and festival organized by Perry Farrell, former leader of the band Jane's Addiction. Lollapalooza features bands ranging from Nine Inch Nails to Ice-T and Body Count and attracts a diverse audience and dress. At this annual music festival, numerous vendors sell not only Lollapalooza and band T-shirts but also specialty garments, such as tie-dyed clothing, Grateful Dead T-shirts, and hemp jackets.

In 1996, Sharon and Jack Osbourne, the wife and son of Ozzy Osbourne, created Ozzfest as an annual touring music festival. Ozzfest features heavier rock bands, such as Korn, Danzig, Fear Factory, Ozzy Osbourne, and Slayer. Performers and fans tend to dress in primarily black, typically in their favorite band tour T-shirts, black jeans, and black tennis shoes.

Into the late 1990s, some version of the Grateful Dead toured, primarily in the United States. Grateful Dead concerts resemble music festivals because of their large fan base, called *Deadheads*, and the number of vendors that attend their shows. Deadheads were dedicated to following the band from one concert location to the next. A large number of fans and vendors sold Dead paraphernalia, such as pipes, cassette tapes and CDs, and clothing. Grateful Dead clothing typically had a tie-dye base, with graphics of skulls or dancing teddy bears.

Kurt Cobain, lead singer for the U.S. band Nirvana, ca. 1990. Cobain established the grunge look of worn jeans, out-of-date cardigans, and uncombed hair. Kevin Mazur Archive 1/WireImage.

VENUES FOR FASHION DISPLAY

In the mid-1980s, the red carpet became a significant venue for musicians to display their fashion style. When musicians attended award shows or charity events, they were photographed on the red carpet entering the event and thus were visually connected to their choice in fashions. So-called fashion police were then allowed to review these visuals on television and critique each musician's style or lack thereof. This resulted in musicians hiring stylists and fostering relationships with fashion designers to ensure that their red-carpet moments were fashion perfect. Beyoncé is known as a trendsetter, not only because of her style in her music videos but also because of her continuously successful red-carpet appearances. Gwen Stefani is another musician who has had successful appearances on the red carpet, with her music-inspired fashions, platinum blond hair, and striking red lipstick.

Music awards ceremonies are opportunities for musicians to demonstrate their style of dress. Some U.S. music awards shows include the Grammys, the American Music Awards, the Billboard Music Awards, the Native American Music Awards, the Country Music Awards, the MTV Video Music Awards, and the Rock and Roll Hall of Fame Induction. The most notable music awards show that gives musicians a chance to make a fashion statement is the MTV VMA (Video Music Awards).

Beginning in 1984, MTV introduced the VMA show, which allowed musicians to walk the red carpet, many for the first time. At the 1984 VMAs, Madonna performed "Like a Virgin" in a corset-style short wedding dress with her Boy Toy belt. In 1990, she wore an extremely revealing Marie Antoinette–inspired costume to perform "Vogue." At the 1992 VMAs, the Red Hot Chili Peppers performed "Give It Away," and Anthony Kiedis, the band's lead singer, wore a checkered suit. At the 1993 VMAs, RuPaul, dressed in drag, had a verbal exchange with Milton Berle about how Berle had once worn dresses, too, but now he wore diapers. In 1998, Rose McGowan wore a see-through dress to the VMAs. In 1999, Lil' Kim wore a purple ensemble that completely exposed one of her breasts except for a sequin circle that covered the nipple. In 2001, Macy Gray wrote on her gown the release date for her new album for all to read when she walked the VMA red carpet. In 2002, Christina Aguilera put her teenybopper image aside when she wore a revealing ensemble. In 2003, Madonna dressed as a groom to perform "Like a Virgin" with Britney Spears and Christina Aguilera, who were dressed as brides on stage, and Madonna kissed both Spears and Aguilera during the performance. In 2005, MC Hammer performed "U Can't Touch This" from 1989, wearing the peg-legged, long-crotch, parachute pants seen in his music video for the same song.

Some musical performers combine dramatic music, scenery, lights, and dress or costume in their live performances to create a theatrical experience. Meat Loaf wore an unbuttoned tux shirt, dress pants, suspenders, and a red handkerchief to perform operatic rock and roll. Elton John wore outrageous costumes, including an Amadeus Mozart costume with an oversized white wig, a duck costume with oversized glasses and feathered bustle attached to a flamboyant jumpsuit, in live performances, and he became closely associated with round eyeglasses and bowler-style hats. Liberace performed in suits encrusted with jewels, large rings, and a pompadour hairstyle. James Brown was known for having his assistant drape a cape over his back when he was done performing, which was usually thrown off in a dramatic gesture to indicate that he had no desire to stop performing. Cher wore Bob Mackie body-revealing fashion designs for live performances, award shows, and her variety show with Sonny Bono.

Music and dress are featured and promoted in media, such as television, magazines, books, and movies. *The Ed Sullivan Show*, a variety television show, gave American viewers their first opportunity to see musical acts, such as the Beatles and Elvis Presley, and their fashions. *Saturday Night Live* and *Late Night with David Letterman* introduced audiences to new musical groups and their alternative fashions. *Star Search* and *American Idol* presented potential musical artists, who dress in styles that are relevant to their individual musical styles, to the U.S. television audience for critique and entertainment. *American Bandstand* and *Soul Train* featured fashionable youth dancing to popular music or performers.

PRINT MEDIA AND FILM

In 1993, Quincy Jones founded *Vibe* magazine, which focuses on urban culture, including lifestyle, fashion, and music. *Rolling*

Stone magazine primarily focuses on music-related articles and often includes articles about musicians and their chosen fashions. Teen magazines, such as *Teen Beat*, *Tiger Beat*, and *BOP*, present U.S. teenagers with pop rock artists and their fashions.

There are many books written about specific performers and their fashions, such as *Elvis Fashion: From Memphis to Vegas* (Julie Mundy, 2004); *The Story of Gwen Stefani* (Amy Blankstein, 2006); *Destiny's Style: Bootylicious Fashion, Beauty, and Lifestyle Secrets from Destiny's Child* (Tina Knowles and Zoe Alexander, 2002); and *Madonna in Art* (Mem Mehmet, 2004). *Rock Style* (2000), by Tommy Hilfiger, is a book about the fashions worn by the icons of rock and roll music. *Rock Fashion* (2002), by Joshua Sims, features fashions and styles associated with rock and roll music. *Fever: How Rock 'n' Roll Transformed Gender in America* (2005), by Tim Riley, examines the construction of gender through the fashions and styles of rock and roll music and performers.

Musical movies present audiences with fashion through period costumes, current fashions, and fantasy projects. The movies *Grease* (1978), *Dirty Dancing* (1987), *The Wedding Singer* (1998), *Chicago* (2002), and *Dreamgirls* (2006) introduced audiences to music and fashions from another time in U.S. history. *Victor/Victoria* (1982) introduced audiences to cross-dressing and androgyny through music. *Purple Rain* (1984) fictionally chronicled the rise to fame of the musical performer Prince and his unique, often purple fashions. The cult classic *Rocky Horror Picture Show* (1975) featured Meat Loaf and Tim Curry as singing and dancing aliens from the planet Transsexual, with unique styles of dress, often fetishistic in origin.

References and Further Readings

Blush, Steven. *American Hair Metal*. Los Angeles, CA: Feral House, 2006.

Crawford, Richard. *An Introduction to America's Music*. New York: W. W. Norton, 2001.

Davis, Mary. *Classic Chic: Music, Fashion, and Modernism*. Berkeley: University of California Press, 2006.

Easely, Erica. *Rock Tease: The Golden Years of Rock T-Shirts*. New York: HNA Books, 2006.

George, Nelson. *Hip Hop America*. New York: Penguin Books, 1998.

Grossberger, Lewis. *Turn That Down!: A Hysterical History of Rock, Roll, Pop, Soul, Punk, Funk, Rap, Grunge, Motown, Metal, Disco, Techno and Other Forms of Musical Aggression over the Ages*. Cincinnati, OH: Emmis Books, 2005.

Heth, Charlotte, ed. *Native American Dance: Ceremonies & Social Traditions*. Golden, CO: Fulcrum Publishing, 1993.

Hilfiger, Tommy. *Rock Style: A Book of Rock, Hip-Hop, Pop, R&B, Punk, Funk and the Fashions That Give Looks to Those Sounds*. New York: Universe Publishing, 2000.

Hodkinson, Paul. *Goth: Identity, Style and Subculture*. Oxford: Berg, 2002.

Jasen, David. *Tin Pan Alley: The Composers, the Songs, the Performers and Their Times*. London: Omnibus Press, 1990.

Mcrobbie, Angela. *In the Culture Society: Art, Fashion and Popular Music*. London: Routledge, 1999.

Mundy, Julie. *Elvis Fashion: From Memphis to Vegas*. New York: Universe Publishing, 2004.

Perkins Gilman, Charlotte. *Music Reference Collection, #193: The Dress of Women: A Critical Introduction to the Symbolism and Sociology of Clothing*. Westport, CT: Greenwood Press, 2001.

Polhemus, Ted. *Style Surfing: What to Wear in the 3rd Millennium*. London: Thames & Hudson, 1996.

Riley, Tim. *Fever: How Rock 'n' Roll Transformed Gender in America*. New York: St. Martin's Press, 2005.

Sims, Joshua. *Rock Fashion*. New York: Omnibus Press, 2002.

Southern, Eileen. *The Music of Black Americans: A History*. 2nd ed. New York: W. W. Norton, 1983.

Starr, Larry, and Christopher Waterman. *American Popular Music*. New York: Oxford University Press, 2003.

White, Shane, and Graham White. *Stylin': African American Expressive Culture from Its Beginnings to the Zoot Suit*. Ithaca and London: Cornell University Press, 1998.

Therèsa M. Winge

Music and Dress in Canada

C anadian musicians have struggled with many of the same issues that challenge Canadian artists of all persuasions: primary among them, the proximity and overwhelming influence of U.S. culture. The Canadian journalist Robert Fulford described Canadians as living a "two-tiered life" in that they absorb the culture, politics, and social issues of both the United States and Canada.

This problem of the two-tiered life applies to all aspects of Canadian culture, and Canada's music and dress is no exception. The Canadian Radio-Television and Telecommunications Commission introduced a quota system for Canadian broadcast content in the 1970s that remains in place today. This system has achieved great success in both creating audiences for Canadian music in Canada and the United States and in giving Canadians an opportunity to develop as artists in their own country. This undoubtedly supported the homegrown market for Canadian music, which otherwise would have been largely obliterated by the power of much larger audiences for U.S. and also British music in Canada. To the credit of the Canadian music industry, the country has had a disproportionate number of musical successes relative to its small population (thirty-three million in 2007). At just over one-tenth the size of the population of the United States, many of Canada's most important artists have left the country to go south of the border to achieve levels of success that are unobtainable for them in their home country. Some of these artists proudly retain their ties to Canada and their allegiance to all things Canadian. Nevertheless, to distinguish Canadian musical artists from their U.S. counterparts and to present Canadian musical influences within dress in ways that are culturally differentiated from similar U.S. influences proves a difficult task. The Canadian musicians featured in this article, while not an exhaustive list, have all made a significant and unique contribution to Canadian popular music since the 1960s, and through their work, they have influenced dress in Canada and, in some cases, dress throughout North America and other parts of the Westernized world.

BUFFY SAINTE-MARIE: A CANADIAN ABORIGINAL ACTIVIST

Buffy Sainte-Marie (1941–) is a Canadian Cree First Nations musician, singer, and songwriter. She is also an artist, educator, and social activist. She developed her own distinctive musical and visual folk style, and along with fellow Canadian musicians Joni Mitchell, Neil Young, and Leonard Cohen, she apprenticed herself by playing in the coffeehouses in Toronto's Yorkville district in the early 1960s. Her protest song "Universal Soldier," from her first album *It's My Way* (1964), became an emblematic peace anthem of the Vietnam War period. Between 1976 and 1981, Buffy regularly appeared on the children's TV show *Sesame Street* with her son Dakota Starblanket Wolfchild, teaching kids about aboriginal life and culture. She received an Academy Award for Best Song in 1982 for the cowritten "Up Where We Belong" from the film *An Officer and a Gentleman*. Buffy is a striking aboriginal woman, and in her early career she made her native American style of dress an important part of her musical presentation. While in her early performances she mainly wore jeans and short skirts with a Western hat, in the 1970s, her increasing identification with aboriginal culture in her music and politics was reflected in her dress. For publicity photos and performances she adopted full Cree regalia, including feathered and beaded headdresses; bead, bone, shell, and feather necklaces, earrings, and adornments; long, fringed, First Nations blankets and woven wool dresses; and Western hybrids of First Nations dress, such as jeans with tooled leather belts, jackets with leather fringes and shells, Western hats, and moccasins. Although it would be difficult to prove that the popularity of North American Indian influences in the dress of young men and women of the 1960s and 1970s counterculture is directly attributable to her mode of dressing, it may well have been one of the factors in the popularity of such styles. Her dress was at the same time theatrical and culturally emblematic, and it made a significant statement about her personification as an aboriginal spokeswoman and role model. Buffy Sainte-Marie is a highly successful representative of First Nations music, and she has been recognized for her achievements and contributions to North American and Canadian culture with many awards and honors. She is an officer of the Order of Canada.

JONI MITCHELL: FREE-SPIRITED SELF-PORTRAIT

Joni Mitchell (1943–) is one of Canada's most well-loved singer-songwriters. An exceptionally versatile musician, Joni has performed equally successfully in folk, rock, and jazz styles as a musician, singer, and songwriter. An accomplished painter and photographer, she has illustrated most of her album covers with her paintings and self-portraits and describes herself as "a painter derailed by circumstance." Joni Mitchell left her native Alberta and began her career as a folksinger in the coffeehouses of Toronto in the 1960s. Greater opportunities called south of the border, and she left Canada for California, where she became a leading light in the folk-rock scene of the early 1970s and had major hit songs from her second album *Clouds* (1969) with "Both Sides Now" and "Chelsea Morning." *The Ladies of the Canyon* album (1970) established her fame as a singer-songwriter with the hit singles "Big Yellow Taxi," which was covered by Bob Dylan, and "Woodstock," famously covered by Crosby, Stills, Nash, and Young. She followed this success with a change of musical direction and the starkly revealing musical self-portrait *Blue* (1971), which featured the evergreen songs of Canadian longing, "River," in which Joni invokes her wish at Christmas for winter snow and "a river I could skate away on," and "A Case of You," in which she reprises the Canadian national anthem, singing "In the blue TV screen light, I drew a map of Canada, Oh Canada, with your face sketched on it twice." Both songs have also been widely covered by international artists such as Prince and Tori Amos and Canadian artists such as k. d. lang, Sarah McLachlan, Diana Krall, and Madeleine Peyroux.

As the young of North America who were known as flower children or hippies rejected the established culture and focused on peace, love, and idealistic values, Joni Mitchell created her flower child persona with her 1970s albums and performances. Her music, her art, her pacifist political leanings, and her dress were all part of a strong sense of self-awareness, image, and ambition. Joni's long, straight blond hair has been a consistent feature of her look over the years, but she evolved her dress throughout her career to include variations on the hippie flower child as she matured. Velvet knickerbockers and knee-high, flat leather boots were featured in the photographic cover of *For the Roses* (1972). When she donned an artist's black felt beret for *Hejira* (1976), photographed by Norman Seef, she heralded her ongoing romance with hats. Headdresses of all sorts have featured in Joni's dress; floral garlands; big, floppy brimmed hippie hats; felt berets; knitted cloches, fedoras, and trilbys; and straw hats of all varieties. Another photo session with Seef, for *Don Juan's Reckless Daughter* (1977), shows her wearing a black top hat and flowing black pantsuit. Seef captured the sophisticated side of Joni Mitchell in numerous photo sessions over the years, portraying her as a cool, artistic, cigarette-smoking chanteuse. Joni's stage dress throughout the 1970s and 1980s continued to combine hippie styles and ethnic influences with long dresses and skirts, caftans, peasant blouses, and her love of First Nations silver jewelry. In 1988, Joni

Canadian singer-songwriter Joni Mitchell, during a shoot for *Vogue* magazine, 1968. Mitchell's long straight blond hair has been a consistent feature of her look over the years, but she evolved her dress over her career, to include variations on the hippie flower child, as she matured. Jack Robinson/Hulton Archive/Getty Images.

appeared on the cover of the album *Chalk Mark in a Rain Storm* and in the video of her song "In My Secret Place," with British artist Peter Gabriel, both clad in Navaho blankets and fedora hats. On her *Turbulent Indigo* album (1994) she portrayed herself as a troubled Van Gogh look-alike, emulating his characteristic swirling brushstrokes to paint her self-portrait, wearing a heavy winter coat and classic Canadian fur-lined hat with ear flaps. The cover of *Taming the Tiger* (1998) shows another self-portrait of Joni in a shawl and wide-brimmed straw hat, cradling her cat in her garden, while in *The Beginning of Survival* (1994) she paints herself crouching on the earth, in workingman style, wearing jeans, a denim jacket, and a porkpie hat. On the compilation *Dreamland* (2004), she portrays herself as a blue-coated Joan of Arc figure, wearing a white dress and holding orange day lilies in front of a fiery background. Joni Mitchell is an individual and a consummate artist who maintains as much control of her image and dress as she does of her musical and artistic life.

Joni Mitchell's musical and stylistic path has been multifaceted, unpredictable, and difficult to pin down. In her own words, she acknowledges that her musical style has been described as folk/rock/country/jazz/classical, even though she never cared much for any of these labels. She has delighted in using her dress style to reflect her musical directions and to express her changes of musical mood. Joni's fans have sometimes struggled to keep up with her highly idiosyncratic musical and stylistic stances, but this has not been her concern. She forges ahead in whatever direction appeals to her current interests and her enquiring musical and poetic talent.

CANADIAN ROCK AND ROLLER: NEIL YOUNG

Neil Young (1945–) is a Canadian singer-songwriter and musician who was born in Toronto and grew up in Winnipeg, Manitoba. His deeply personal, outspoken lyrics; his distinctive high voice; and his individual (Gibson Les Paul) guitar style are all his hallmarks. Young had remarkable success in the late 1960s with the band Crosby, Stills, Nash, and Young. The band performed at Woodstock and covered Joni Mitchell's song on the album *Déjà Vu* (1970). Young's song "Helpless" from that album has become a signature Canadian anthem, with its opening line, "There is a town in north Ontario …" The same year, the band had an important hit with their song "Ohio" (1970), which was written after the Kent State massacre of 4 May 1970. Neil Young's solo albums *After the Gold Rush* (1970) and *Harvest* (1972) became important rites of passage music for many Canadian teenagers. Neil Young dressed as the personification of the working man. His long, straggly hair looked as if it rarely saw a comb, and he always dressed in jeans, work boots, and corduroy or checked flannel shirts. Young also wore battered cowboy hats and boots and truck driver's caps. Neil Young's dress displayed the antithesis of concern about image and made a powerful symbolic statement about nonconformity and rejection of wealth. His look was highly imitated and became a staple for Canadian high school kids in the 1970s and onward. The Canadian comedian Mike Myers based the distinctive parody of Canadian dress, look, and mannerisms for some characters in the *Saturday Night Live* series and the spin-off film *Wayne's World* (1992) on a version of this dress that was widely adopted by Canadian teenage boys. The dress commonly worn by grunge bands in the 1980s and 1990s, such as Nirvana and Pearl Jam, consisted of thrift store items, outdoor clothing, and flannel

Canadian singer-songwriter Neil Young in concert, 1970. His long hair looked as if it rarely saw a comb, and he always dressed in jeans, work boots, and corduroy shirts or checked flannel shirts. Young's dress showed the antithesis of concern about image and made a powerful symbolic statement about nonconformity and rejection of wealth. Al Pereira/Michael Ochs Archives/Getty Images.

shirts, as well as a general unkempt appearance that can trace its original influences back to Neil Young.

K.D. LANG: CROSS-DRESSING SINGER AND LESBIAN ADVOCATE

k.d. lang (1961–) was born in Edmonton, Alberta, and grew up on the Canadian prairies. She has built a career on her powerful showboating voice and her playfulness and bravery with her image and dress. A celebrated musical artist who came out as a lesbian in 1992, she managed to offend her fellow Albertans less with her sexuality than her refusal to eat beef. She first came to public attention when she recorded a stunning duet version of "Crying" with Roy Orbison in 1987. They appeared together on *The Tonight Show*, with k.d. dressed in a silver jacket, black shirt, black jeans and boots, and her short, dark hair slicked back in an androgynous incarnation of a young Elvis. In 1989, k.d. lang won the Grammy Award for best female country vocal with her album *Absolute Torch and Twang*. On the cover of the album and in the video for "Trail of Broken Hearts," she portrays herself not as a cowgirl but as a cowboy, clean faced and wearing a ten-gallon hat, denim worker's coveralls, and a leather rancher's coat, standing tall in a wheat field against a big blue sky. On *Ingénue* (1992), k.d. lang left her country influences behind and had her first big hits on an album of contemporary pop songs, with the singles "Constant Craving" and the tongue-in-cheek "Miss Chatelaine," named after a popular mainstream Canadian teenage girls' magazine. In the video for "Constant Craving," she played on her sexually ambivalent looks, appearing again as a pretty-boy Elvis look-alike with a distinctive "young rebel" tapered pompadour haircut, a man's high-collared and long-cuffed white shirt, and a black suit jacket. In the video for the song "Sexuality," from *All You Can Eat* (1995), she is provocative in a black trench coat and leather trousers with Dr. ("Doc") Marten boots, a style adopted by the young around this time; in another scene, she wears a Scottish kilt worn in a mannish style with an old, woolen cable-knit sweater, heavy socks, and hiking boots. On her 1997 album *Drag*, a play on words using the reference to cross-dressing to describe what is in actuality a collection of songs based on cigarette addiction, k.d. performed "The Air That I Breathe" wearing a man's black, pinstriped jacket and waistcoat with her signature high-collared white shirt and a red cravat.

k.d. lang cemented her reputation as the premier female interpreter of Canada's balladic anthems on her 2005 outing *Hymns of the 49th Parallel*, a best-selling album of covers of songs by Canadian singers such as Leonard Cohen, Neil Young, Bruce Cockburn, Ron Sexsmith, Joni Mitchell, and Jane Siberry. k.d. lang revisited her Western theme both musically and visually with *Reintarnation* (2006). A photo shoot for the album shows her sitting on a stockyard fence wearing full Western regalia: a heavily embroidered green cowboy hat; fringed shirt; neckerchief; white-fringed, green-leather chaps over jeans; matching gloves; and cowboy boots. And k.d. is not just dressing up; she can ride, too, and she is shown in her Western gear mounted on the back of a bucking bronco. Using her mainstream musical popularity, k.d. lang has championed gay rights and broken down the barriers of female representation in pop music in North America and throughout the world. She pioneered boyish lesbian themes and dress in her music, and as a consequence, she has influenced a whole generation of young lesbian women, particularly in North America, liberating them to celebrate their sexuality with boyish hairstyles, grooming, and dress.

SHANIA TWAIN: ADVOCATE OF INDEPENDENCE IN DRESS

Shania Twain (1965–) is a Canadian country/pop music, multi-Grammy-Award-winning singer-songwriter who has enjoyed phenomenal success. Her third album, *Come On Over* (1997), is listed as one of the best-selling albums in the history of country music. Shania grew up in Timmins, Ontario, with her mother and four siblings, as the adopted daughter of an Ojibwa First Nations father. Life was hard, and Shania helped to support her family from an early age by singing in local clubs and bars. Success brought clothes, and Shania is a woman who clearly enjoys dressing up. She even has her own fragrance, Shania, promoting her "beauty, spirit, and independence." In the video for "That Don't Impress Me Much" (1997), she is shown hitchhiking on a highway in an oilfield, wearing leopard spots from head to toe: a full-length, hooded, flowing coat over a leopard-spotted bra and flared pants, with long gloves and high-heeled boots, carrying an oversized leopard-spotted hat box and turning away the many male offers she receives. The lyrics of her song "Man! I Feel Like A Woman!" (1997) praise female independence in dress and behavior.

In the video for "Man! I Feel Like A Woman!," she parodies the Robert Palmer "Addicted to Love" (1985) video, and she performs backed by four male models, all of whom clearly have less idea of how to play their instruments than how they should wet their lips and sway their hips. Shania fronts the band, dressed in a top hat with a fishnet-lace veil covering her eyes and a floor-length black dress coat, which she later drops to reveal a short black bustier dress with thigh-high black boots and three-quarter-length black gloves. In her song "Shoes" (2005), Shania sings an ode to the numerous pairs and sorts of shoes a girl needs, in which she plays on an extended metaphor comparing different types of shoes to different types of men: "A girl can never have too many of 'em … men are like shoes."

CELINE DION: GLAMOUR AND FEMININITY

Celine Dion (1968–) is a French Canadian pop singer renowned for her technical skills as a vocalist, with sweeping, classically influenced ballads that show off her powerful vocal abilities. She grew up in a large family in Charlemagne, Quebec, and became a young star in francophone Canada. It wasn't until the 1990s, with the release of a series of anglophone albums, that she became a successful singing star. Her song "My Heart Will Go On," from the album *Let's Talk about Love* (1997), was written by James Horner as the love theme for the Academy Award–winning blockbuster film *Titanic*. The song went on to become an enormous hit and has been adopted by Celine as her theme song. Celine competes with Shania Twain for the title of one of the world's best-selling female pop artists, with her record company announcing that she has sold over two hundred million albums worldwide. But in the fragrance category she wins hands down, with her own complete line of women's and men's fragrances. Celine's dress is ultra-feminine, conservative, with a hint of old-school show business and glamour. She rarely performs or does a photo, video, or commercial shoot wearing anything less than a full-length, full-blown gown. In 2003, Celine moved to Las Vegas to perform full time in her own show *A New Day…*, a long-running extravaganza staged at Caesars Palace.

Both Celine Dion and Shania Twain can legitimately be seen as Canadian pop music divas, and they both know how to dress for the job. Both stars share a real-life story of humble beginnings that, through raw talent, dedication, grinding hard work, and some great breaks, has led them to dizzying heights of stardom and fame.

Celine's "grown-up woman" style is highly influenced by grand dame film actresses such as Barbara Stanwyck and Bette Davis. She follows in the footsteps of artist Barbra Streisand, in the grand tradition of high-end entertainers. Wearing a glamorous Caroline Herrera gown at the 1999 Grammy Awards, she carried off two awards, including record of the year for "My Heart Will Go On" from the film *Titanic*, and she was voted the best-dressed star on the red carpet. Celine makes it her business to show off her success, wealth, and style to her public by getting dressed up. She is a feminine icon with her divine designer gowns, over-the-top (real, not fake) diamonds and jewelry, and perfect hair and makeup. Celine Dion's dedicated fans are mainly female, and they have responded to her Caesars Palace Las Vegas shows by making them special events—an occasion to get dressed up and go out on the town with their favorite artist.

Shania Twain's music is considered to be a country/pop crossover, and her dress style vacillates between these two influences. It is fair to say she mainly wore jeans until she teamed up with her husband/producer Robert "Mutt" Lange in 1995 to write and record her album *The Woman in Me*. They formed a highly successful musical partnership, and her music and image crossed over from country to pop with their second collaboration, *Come on Over*, in 1997. She grew up stylistically with these albums, taking influences from other top artists in her dress. Her appearance in the video for "Man! I Feel Like A Woman" is clearly an homage to Madonna's "Erotic" (1992) look, which was in turn paying homage to Liza Minelli's portrayal of the erotic dancer Sally Bowles in the film *Cabaret* (1972).

SK8ER GIRL

Avril Lavigne (1984–) is a Canadian pop musician who came from humble beginnings, growing up in the small rural Ontario town of Belleville and later moving to the smaller nearby town of Napanee, where she was raised in a devout Christian household. She had enormous success with her debut album *Let's Go* in 2002, which went multiplatinum with sales of over eighteen million copies worldwide. Her hit songs "Sk8er Boi" and "Complicated" (2002) tell tales of turbulent confrontations between skater kids, like her, and preppy kids, whom she portrays as uniformly stuck up, dumb, and fake. Avril adopted an outsider style of dress, and she wears a combination of punk and skater gear, mixing black jeans, T-shirts, and Converse Hi-Top sneakers with motorcycle boots or Doc Martens, studded black-leather wristbands, striped socks, and skinny men's neckties. Avril denies that either her music or her look is punk, maintaining that she acts and dresses as herself, but her look is punk rock influenced. Avril sets off her pale skin and long, straight blond hair with heavy black eye makeup and bare lips. Invariably the preppy girls on the sidelines of her early videos are wearing plaid, pleated skirts and Fair Isle sweaters and looking miserable, as if they either loathe her, feel threatened by her, or secretly wish they could be more like her. Avril has championed "girl power" with her dress and reveled in very bad girl behavior in her videos, including swarming malls with other skaters, smashing guitars, jumping on the roofs of cars, and giving the camera the finger, showing off her black nail polish. In 2007, with her album *The Best Damned Thing* and with the influence of her Hollywood career, Avril Lavigne's dress has become more mainstream. The addition of short skirts and pretty dresses, fishnet stockings, and high heels to her repertoire has caused some of her fans to complain that she has sold out to the style-conscious, preppy crowd that she originally ridiculed.

IDIOSYNCRASY: INDEPENDENT, CONTEMPORARY CANADIAN ARTISTS

Melissa auf der Maur (1972–), former bassist with Hole and Smashing Pumpkins, is a Canadian musician and songwriter based in Montreal who has been working as a solo artist since 2004. That year, she released her eponymous debut album and appeared on the CBC national TV show *The Greatest Canadian* as social activist David Suzuki's celebrity mentor, raising both awareness of her music and her ecological consciousness. Her second release, titled *Out of Our Minds*, is part of a multidisciplinary Viking-themed project that includes a short film and a comic book. The project draws on the theme of blood and the heart to draw together three narratives and time periods within

Canadian musician Melissa auf der Maur at the New Musical Express (NME) awards, 2004. Jo Hale/Getty Images.

a short movie and a hand-drawn conceptual fantasy world. "Vikings are a symbol of a male archetype I channel into the making of rock music … These male forces help balance the woman in me," she has explained. Drawing on her education as a photography major specializing in self-portraiture at Montreal's Concordia University, Melissa has developed an individualistic, artistic, sexy, look—part waif and part gothic witch. Her early incarnation mirrored fellow Hole artist Courtney Love's rock-and-roll tramp persona with torn stockings, secondhand clothes, and ultrashort skirts revealing lots of pale skin, set off by her long, unruly red hair and darkly made-up eyes. Her look has become more sophisticated as her music has matured, and while stopping short of making her dress into a fashion statement, she clearly enjoys dressing up. Melissa portrays herself as a woman who is confident and revels in her idiosyncratic "art-rock chick" image.

One of the most popular Canadian independent bands of the new millennium is a group out of Montreal called Arcade Fire. Their first album *Funeral*, released in 2004, became album of the year for music magazines in Canada, the United States, and the United Kingdom. The band was featured on the cover of the Canadian edition of *Time* magazine in April 2005, dressed in black suits with pale shirts and ties and with the two women members wearing elegant, long black gowns. The reference is apt—husband and wife founding members Régine Chassagne and Win Butler, along with the rest of the band and collaborators, use their considerable musical talents within an instrumental section of piano, violin, mandolin, accordion, drums, guitar, and flute to layer their highly orchestrated music. In support of their sound, the group dress for performances and videos like a classical music sextet, with a formality that echoes their music and a style that some of their fans emulate at concerts.

Indie/folk/rock artist Leslie Feist (1976–), daughter of Toronto-based artist Harold Feist, is a singer-songwriter who enjoyed a phenomenal rise to fame with her second solo album *Let It Die*, recorded in Paris and released in 2004, and her Canadian Juno Award–winning performances with Toronto indie rock band Broken Social Scene. Her stage act, which includes sock-puppet sequences, synchronized dance routines, and miming, and her music and dress style can best be described as sweet. Feist usually appears wearing little or no discernible facial makeup with a fresh, direct "take me as I come" look. Sweetly girlish, with a seductive mix of shyness and self-confidence, Feist takes a personal approach to her image that is as indefinable and individualistic as her music. She lists the Kinks, Etta James, and Marvin Gaye as musical influences on her MySpace page, and this eclectic circle of stylish artists has also influenced her stage dress. She still manages to look like the little girl who is getting dressed up for her high school play. Her performance in the video for "My Moon Man" (2007) shows her posing, dancing, and flipping out on an airport moving walkway dressed as a stylish but slightly prim and reserved airline traveler. Her hair is tied into a neat side bun, and she is wearing a smart, belted 1960s-style trench coat over a prim and pretty, waisted cotton dress with matching pale tights and heels and carrying a white valise. In her publicity photos, Feist wears a heavy, knitted-wool, shawl-necked sweater and a fur hat to complete her "I'm ready for a Canadian winter" look. But it was her outfit in a music video for her song "1234," from her album *The Reminder* (2007), that gave away her penchant for Motown glitter. Feist throws herself about and is carried around by her dance crew, who are wearing colorful boiler suits (overalls or coveralls).

Canadian singer-songwriter Leslie Feist, ca. 2000. Feist lists the Kinks, Etta James, and Marvin Gaye as musical influences, and this eclectic circle of stylish artists has also influenced her stage dress. Courtesy of Stephen McGrath.

She is wearing an all-in-one, royal blue, sequined, strapless jumpsuit with pale high heels. She ends up looking slightly out of place, as if she found herself accidentally all dressed up, and she is enjoying every minute of it. Feist's style is idiosyncratic, with some retro influences, but updated to suit her individual style; still, she has something of the "little girl all dressed up" quality of an Audrey Hepburn about her.

Another Broken Social Scene graduate and former Concordia University student is the singer Emily Haines from the band Metric. Her pale blond looks and relaxed, unisex dress style of jeans, *hoodies* (hooded sweatshirts), and T-shirts takes a back seat to her voice and dreamlike musical performances. Sometimes she performs blindfolded and insists she never knows what will happen next when she is on stage. Emily is not interested in influencing young women with her dress, which is really a sort of antistyle: "I try not to focus on gender," she has said, "but everybody needs people to inspire them. The most valuable make you want to be more yourself, not more like them."

Haines's casual style of dress is an antifashion statement and a reflection of the sort of dress that her university audience would probably wear to a Broken Social Scene concert. It says that she is one of them, that this is where she comes from, almost "I'm like you; you could be me."

The style statements of Melissa auf der Maur, Emily Haines, Leslie Feist, and Avril Lavigne are distinctive, but they share a slight form of exaggeration. This exaggeration may be an effort by these artists to distinguish themselves as Canadians and to differentiate themselves from their U.S. pop counterparts. They have shown Canadian women of the new millennium that they can dress comfortably and with style, that it is cool to mine their "Canuck" roots, and that they can pick and choose from different periods and different looks—from retro, to punk, to country to the relaxed classics—and combine contemporary fashion with thrift shop treasures to create their own eclectic, and distinctly Canadian, style of dress.

Canadians feel more closely connected to Europe than they do to the United States, and they express their difference from U.S. culture through their music and dress. The influence of Europe gives Canadians a conduit to a more sophisticated, self-aware, and nuanced style. The single most distinctive Canadian influence on dress is still the ability to and love of dressing up for harsh winters. No pop music artist can call themselves Canadian if they have not been photographed in a big coat, hat, boots, and, in Joni Mitchell's case, skates, on some frozen pond in the middle of a Canadian winter.

Canadian fans have the same interest in distinguishing themselves from their U.S. counterparts as the artists do. And like all fandom, not just in Canada and the United States but worldwide, some hardcore fans emulate their idols, while most enjoy the images and videos as entertainment, fantasy, and escape.

References and Further Reading

Bufwak, Mary A., and Robert K. Oermann. *Finding Her Voice: Women in Country Music, 1800–2000.* Nashville, TN: Vanderbilt University Press, 2003.

The Canadian Encyclopedia. http://www.thecanadianencyclopedia.com/ (accessed August 2008).

Canadian Radio-television and Telecommunications Commission. http://www.crtc.gc.ca/eng/welcome.htm (accessed August 2008).

Gale Reference Team. "The Gospel According to Arcade Fire." *Winnipeg Free Press,* 5 March 2007, d3.

Lull, James. *Popular Music and Communication.* Newbury Park, CA: Sage Publications, 1991.

O'Brien, Karen. *Joni Mitchell: Shadows and Light.* London: Virgin Books, 2002.

Pareles, John, Holly George-Warren, and Patricia Romanowski Bashe, eds. *The Rolling Stone Encyclopedia of Rock and Roll.* New York: Fireside Original/Simon and Schuster, 2001.

McQuaig, Martin, ed. *Music Directory Canada.* 8th ed. St. Catharines, ON: Norris Whitney Communications, 2001.

Shuler, Roy. *Understanding Popular Music.* 2nd ed. Oxford: Taylor and Francis, 2007.

Smith, L.D. *Elvis Costello, Joni Mitchell, and the Torch Song Tradition.* Westport, CT: Praeger Publishers, 2004.

Starr, Victoria. *k.d. lang: All You Get Is Me.* New York: St. Martin's Press, 1995.

Strudwick, Leslie, and Krista McKlusky. *Great Canadians: Singers.* Calgary: Weigl Educational Publishing, 2000.

Thornley, Joe. *Avril Lavigne.* London: Virgin Books, 2003.

Tracey, Liz, and Sydney Pokorny. *So You Want to Be a Lesbian?* New York: St. Martin's Press, 1996.

Young, Neil, and James McDonough. *Shakey: Neil Young's Biography.* New York: Random House, 2002.

Martha Ladly

See also Music and Dress in the United States.

Uniforms as Work Dress for Civilians and Military

The fringed hunting shirt that was widely used by U.S. soldiers in the Revolutionary War is shown in this German print of 1771. The hunting shirt was basically a smock made of either white leather or white linen, ornamented with fringes (including one or more fringed capes). Anne S. K. Brown Military Collection, Brown University Library.

Uniforms are distinctive but standard forms of dress associated with particular occupations or social institutions and either supplied or regulated by the associated institution. In donning a uniform, one assumes a social role. Because uniforms are often worn by persons in intensely hierarchal institutions, relatively minor distinctions that indicate status within the hierarchy are important. Anyone wearing the same uniform can be expected to perform in a similar fashion in a given situation.

A group of teens voluntarily affecting the same style of dress are not in uniform, while a similar group attending a private school with dictated dress regulations are considered to be wearing uniforms. There are, of course, cases not as clear cut; a biker gang wearing patches or colors according to the rules of the club might be considered, despite the individuality of dress, to be wearing uniforms. Corporations might have strict dress codes for executives, to present another example, but because the dress is not distinctive or tied to the occupation and corporation, these probably should not be considered uniforms.

While identification is often the most important reason for wearing a uniform, uniforms are useful in other ways. Some uniforms have been characterized as "functionally mandatory." That is, one must dress in special gear in order to safely and effectively perform one's assigned task. Many aspects of combat uniforms and the dress of firefighters (when fighting fires) exemplify this principle. Other uniforms, such as those of cooks, mechanics, and nurses, may be utilitarian. Wear and tear on ordinary clothes is avoided by wearing the uniform while working.

MILITARY UNIFORMS IN COLONIAL NORTH AMERICA

From 1689 until units of the regular French army were sent to Canada in 1755, colonial troops, the Compagnies Franches de la

Marine, were the major defense of New France. Their dress uniform followed the style of the French regulars, but when on duty in the interior, the coat was dispensed with in warm weather, and gaiters and shoes were replaced by Indian leggings (which, like gaiters, reached to midthigh but lacked the twenty-five or so troublesome buttons) and Indian moccasins.

On occasion the British also adapted their uniforms to the frontier conditions in North America. In the expedition against Ticonderoga in 1758, Lord Howe had his troops cut down both the brims of their tricorne hats and the tails of their coats. All lace was removed from their uniforms. As part of this same expedition, the "80th Foot" had been formed and designated as light infantry and clothed in brown rather than red.

THE CONTINENTAL ARMY

With the outbreak of the American Revolution, the Continental Congress faced a chaotic situation in matters of dress. States raised and clothed their own regiments. To the diversity of authorized uniforms were added problems of supply, leading Continental troops to dress in anything available, including captured British uniforms.

Problems in uniform procurement led to the adoption of a purely U.S. style on the battlefield. The *hunting shirt*, of leather or linen, developed on the North American frontier and was basically a smock ornamented with fringes (including one or more fringed capes). Initially, in the American Revolution it served as the dress of regiments such as Morgan's Virginia Riflemen, raised on the frontier and armed with the Pennsylvania rifle. Many conventional units adopted the hunting shirt as their working dress. Regimental or unit distinction was provided by dyeing all the hunting shirts the same color, such as the garish purple (with red capes and cuffs) of the Fourth Independent Company of Maryland worn at the battle of Long Island in 1776.

THE WAR OF 1812

When Britain and the United States clashed in the War of 1812, the U.S. infantry was initially clad in dark blue coatees with red collars and cuffs. White lace adorned the collar, cuffs, and button holes. The black cylindrical *shako* bore a white plume rising above the white-metal shako plate. In all, the silhouette of the U.S. infantryman was remarkably like that of his British foe. Strangely, both sides authorized similar changes in shako form in 1813, each adopting a shako with a high false front. Thus, the U.S. leather shako resembled the "Belgic" or "Waterloo" shako, which was authorized for the British army. That same year, the regulation uniform of the U.S. infantry was simplified, with the collar and cuffs becoming the color of the coatee and most of the lace being removed.

It became impossible to supply even this simplified uniform, however. This led to an incident that had a great impact on the uniform in the United States. Early in the war, the color gray had been associated with uniforms worn by the U.S. militia, troops easily swept aside by disciplined British infantry. Supply problems caused the well-trained line infantry regiments under the command of Winfield Scott on the Niagara Peninsula to be dressed in gray uniforms. At the battle of Chippawa (5 July 1814), the British saw the gray-clad troops before them and expected an easy victory. The steadiness of Scott's men led the surprised British commander to shout out, "Those are regulars, by God!" Tradition attributes the adoption of gray uniforms for the cadets of the U.S. Military Academy (West Point) to the performance under fire of Scott's men.

THE CIVIL WAR

Amateur soldiers drilled and marched throughout the United States during the nineteenth century, forming into volunteer units under state jurisdiction. When conflict broke out between the Union and the Confederacy in 1861, these amateur soldiers marched to their respective flags in a great variety of uniforms. Gray became the official color of the uniforms of the Confederacy, but the 7th New York marched to the Union cause in gray uniforms. Initially, blue uniforms were not uncommon for troops fighting for the Southern states. All this led to tragic battlefield errors in the first major battle of the war, Bull Run.

Mention must be made of the popularity of *Zouave* uniforms. The French conquest of North Africa had led to the recruitment of local troops wearing a fez, white turban, baggy red trousers, and short jackets. These troops fought in the Crimea against the Russians and received a great deal of coverage in the world's emerging illustrated press. Added to this publicity was that generated by an 1860 tour of the eastern United States by the U.S. Zouave Cadets, a drill team raised in Chicago by Elmer Ellsworth. It challenged local volunteer units to drill competitions and spread the reputation of the Zouave uniform and drill. As a result, when war broke out, a large number of Zouave units were raised to fight for each side. Ellsworth himself raised the 11th New York Volunteer Infantry (the New York Fire Zouaves) recruited from New York City firefighters.

The problems faced by the Union in supplying its vast armies during the Civil War led to an addition to the English vocabulary. *Shoddy* had long existed as a noun meaning recycled wool fibers gathered from the factory floor and reused in the milling process. The poor quality of uniforms supplied by many contractors led to the word's usage as an adjective, both to describe the "shoddy" uniforms and the "shoddy" contractors who profited from the sale of such substandard uniforms to the army.

The problems faced by the federal government in supplying the Union Army were dwarfed by those faced by the Confederacy. Officially, Confederate soldiers should have worn gray coats with light blue trousers and gray kepis, but in reality, most wore whatever they could acquire, often homespun dyed a uniform butternut or drab and a slouch hat. The necessities to keep the Confederate soldier as comfortable as possible in the field were folded in a blanket roll worn over the left shoulder.

For most of the nineteenth century, the U.S. military, like the rest of the world, patterned its uniforms, particularly its dress uniforms, on those of France. A shock came in 1870–1871 with the defeat of France by Prussia. The cavalry and other mounted troops immediately adopted the spiked helmet of Prussia, and the infantry followed suit in 1881. This was for full dress and was worn on parades in garrison; while on campaign, however, troops enjoyed considerable latitude, often wearing more comfortable items of civilian dress purchased privately rather than the issued campaign uniforms.

THE WORLD WARS AND AFTER

From the time of the Indian Mutiny, khaki had been worn by the British army in India. In 1885, it was made official for wear in India, and in 1896, it was approved for use in all foreign stations. In 1902, it became the service dress for the entire army. Other armies adopted khaki, with those of the United States, Japan, and Imperial Russia being the first three to dress in uniforms of that color. While the United States had officially adopted khaki prior to the Spanish-American War of 1898, it fought that war in Cuba in the old army blue. Subsequent campaigns in the Philippines against insurgents and in China against the Boxer Rebellion were waged by troops clothed in khaki. The official title of the U.S. uniform color became "olive drab" in 1902, although it remained within the range of hues that have been designated khaki.

When the U.S. army sailed "over there" to join in the Great War, soldiers replaced their campaign hats with British-style steel helmets, donned British gas masks, and wrapped their calves and ankles with puttees. Exceptional in appearance on the Western front, however, was the 369th Infantry. This was a black National Guard regiment from New York City. The French were more willing to serve alongside these men from Harlem than were their fellow Americans, so they were employed in a French division. For logistic reasons, they were equipped with French arms.

Cadets of the U.S. Military Academy (West Point), ca. 1900. The gray uniform is said to commemorate the dress of the American regular infantry, clad in provisional gray uniforms at the Battle of Chippawa in the War of 1812. Anne S. K. Brown Military Collection, Brown University Library.

U.S. Zouave cadets, 1860. U.S. Zouave soldiers dressed in a uniform derived from that of the French Zouaves. They wore baggy red trousers, a red sash, and a light blue shirt with a dark blue short Zouave jacket. As headgear they wore a red kepi with a dark blue band rather than the red fez worn by the French Zouaves. Courtesy Dora Hood Rare Book Room, Dana Porter Library, University of Waterloo, Waterloo, Ontario, Canada.

Over their drab U.S. Army uniforms they wore French leather equipment, and on their heads they wore the horizon blue French Adrian steel helmet. This regiment spent more days at the front in the trenches than any other U.S. unit.

In the initial battles of World War II, the soldiers and sailors of the United States still wore the British-style steel helmet, but soon the new distinctively U.S. style was in universal use. Indeed, each of the major powers in this war had a distinctive form of protective headgear. While the adoption of khaki and olive drab were designed to reduce the visibility of troops, further attempts to mask the presence of troops even more through camouflage patterns were experimented with by both sides. Winter conflict led to the utilization of white overalls to blend with the snow.

The Korean War was largely, for the U.S. armed forces, fought in World War II uniforms. The marines who stormed Inchon Harbor wore the same uniforms their uncles and cousins had worn when storming Tarawa or Iwo Jima. Late in the conflict, however, relatively lightweight body armor was introduced, and this would continue as a vital aspect of dress in later conflicts.

Other than reinforce the importance of both camouflage and body armor, the quagmire of Vietnam did not have a heavy impact on U.S. combat uniforms, but it was a time for the institution of both the green service dress uniform and the recognition of the beret as the headgear of the soldier. The early involvement of the United States in the conflict focused on extensive use of the U.S.

Army's Special Forces. Like other elite units (the British Royal Marine Commandos and the French Foreign Legion), the Special Forces wore a green beret and indeed came to be known as the *Green Berets.*

The role of women in the army (as well as in the other services) has changed through time. During World War II, a feminized version of service dress, with a skirt rather than trousers, was adequate given their duties as clerks, drivers, and so forth. Later, as their duties have carried them close to and into the combat zone, they have been issued normal combat dress.

UNIFORMS OF THE U.S. NAVY, MARINES, AND AIR FORCE

Naval uniforms developed later than army uniforms, and the naval uniforms of the world exhibit a great similarity. Both of these facts derive from the fact that in naval combat, it is the ship that must be identified, not the personnel who man her. Working dress aboard ship varies with the task, but the ordinary seaman in the U.S. Navy has expressed a fondness for the bell-bottom trousers and the blouse with scarf and sailor collar that have long marked the identity of a seaman. In 1973, this uniform was replaced under the direction of Admiral Elmo Zumwalt; the unhappiness of the sailors over this move led to the reintroduction of the old uniform within five years.

A unique feature of dress in the U.S. Navy is the sailor's cap, which differs in form from that worn by the remainder of the world's navies. It may well be that the association of the latter style with Donald Duck led to its unpopularity among U.S. sailors.

The nickname of the U.S. Marines, "Leathernecks," derives from the custom of wearing leather stocks in the early nineteenth century, a practice that distinguished them from sailors of the ships on which they both served. In basic form, the evolution of their dress paralleled that of the army described previously. However, unlike the U.S. Army, the U.S. Marines have exploited the publicity value of units appearing on parade in full dress.

As part of the U.S. Army through World War II, the U.S. Air Force wore army uniforms with special badges. When it became a separate service after the war, for dress uniforms and service dress it adopted the light blue of the Royal Air Force and the Luft-waffe. From the first, the necessity of pilots and other air crew to adapt to the physical conditions of the altitude and speed of their flight has meant that they must wear clothing that is functionally mandatory, allowing them to survive and perform their duties.

CANADA'S MILITARY

As part of the British Empire, Canada dressed its troops in a fashion almost identical to that of Britain. Indeed, some units in the Canadian Army wore uniforms identical to regiments in the British Army and could be distinguished only by their buttons. There were some distinctions. The *Wolseley helmet* was widely worn in Canadian full dress after 1912. (It was also part of the full dress of the British Royal Marines and was in wide use among cavalry regiments in the Imperial Indian Army.) Both world wars were fought by Canadians in the dress of the British "Tommy," but with distinctive patches marking Canadian units. The Canadian version of the British battledress jacket was of such superior quality that it was widely sought after by British troops during World War II.

In 1968, Canada merged the Canadian Army, the Royal Canadian Navy, and the Royal Canadian Air Force into the Canadian Forces and provided a single rank structure and a single uniform. It was 1971 before all personnel had received the new dark green dress. By 1985, general unhappiness led to the authorization again of three different uniforms for the Canadian Army, Navy, and Air Force.

POLICE UNIFORMS

Following European examples, U.S. cities began to dress their police forces in uniforms in the 1840s. At first the police themselves resisted this, equating uniforms with servants. Soon, however, the police uniform became equated with authority, and resistance ceased. For the most part, municipal police in North America wear navy blue or black uniforms with the forage cap. Sheriffs' departments and state police often wear khaki or gray. Headgear may be the forage cap, a *Stetson*, or a cowboy hat. Police utilizing motorcycles of necessity use helmets and protective clothing suitable to their transport.

Female police officers have increased in number through time, and their uniforms have changed from a militarized feminine uniform to one no different from that of their male colleagues. This has paralleled a change in their roles, which have broadened to include the same sort of assignments as pursued by men in the force.

At the start of the Civil War Elmer Ellsworth recruited personnel from New York City firefighters to form the 11th New York Volunteer Infantry. They dressed in a modified Zouave uniform, continuing to wear the red shirts of their firefighter uniforms. National Archives photo no. 111-B-6343.

As police forces have had to deal with hostage takers and terrorists, special squads (SWAT teams) have been formed that are heavily armed, wear body armor, and very much resemble in dress the combat infantry.

Municipal police in Canada dress in a fashion nearly identical to their U.S. counterparts. The provincial police of both Ontario and Quebec wear dark blue uniforms, while the remainder of the provinces at the provincial level are policed by the Royal Canadian Mounted Police. For normal duties they wear a brown tunic. The RCMP also are present at Canadian airports, but they probably go unrecognized by the average tourist who fails to note the distinctive dark blue trousers with their yellow stripe and their dark blue forage cap with its yellow band.

In an effort to assert authority, private security companies often clothe their employees in uniforms much like those of the police.

AIRLINES AND THE HOSPITALITY INDUSTRY

Naval styles have had a strong impact on the dress of air crews. This is partially from the early relationship of the navy to "air ships"—the pilot of the airplane is "the captain," and rank among air crews on commercial airlines is, as is the case with officers in the navy, marked by gold braid on the cuffs of the sleeve. This rank structure and uniform probably serves to instill passenger confidence in the skills of the crew. For the flight attendants in the cabin, the military style of their dress serves two functions. It establishes for both the passengers and themselves that they are not simply waiters and waitresses, despite the fact that much of their time on normal flights is spent dispensing drinks and food. It also gives them an aura of authority, allowing them to deal effectively with nervous or unruly passengers.

Staff of hotels, restaurants, and cocktail lounges usually are in uniform. This serves to identify such staff to the clientele of the establishment. These uniforms also serve as a rough guide to the price range of the establishment. A waitress in a "greasy spoon" is clad in a different sort of uniform from that worn by a server in a posh and expensive restaurant. Uniforms of staff in chain establishments are stamped from a nationwide mold, similar to the food that they serve.

THE MEDICAL PROFESSION

Some have likened the wearing of a white lab coat by doctors in certain settings to a uniform, but because this is not enforced by any authority, it is different from other cases of uniform discussed here. The scrubs worn in the operating theater are closer to what most would consider a uniform.

For nurses, throughout much of the twentieth century, a white uniform with a cap that indicated the place at which she trained (male nurses did not wear a cap) was prescribed dress. A revolt in the 1970s led to the dispensing of the cap and a shift to colored uniforms, usually pastel, and often a trouser suit of material resistant to stains.

CLERICAL DRESS

Uniform dress among clerics, with distinctive dress for various religious orders, actually predates the adoption of military uniforms (the Salvation Army is an exception, patterning its dress consciously on that of the military), but clerical dress has had little impact outside the church except for providing the pattern for academic robes. Also, the uniform dress of many monastic orders is seldom or never seen outside the monastery. Rules for uniform dress in the Roman Catholic Church relaxed considerably in the second half of the twentieth century. For the most part, nuns in North America ceased to wear the habit but instead wore the conservative dress of other devout Catholics. Still, the dress of the Roman Catholic priesthood, like other uniforms in hierarchal institutions, provides clear distinctions that allow those who are knowledgeable to see where the wearer stands in the church hierarchy.

SPORTS UNIFORMS

In team sports, the wearing of distinctive clothing by each team certainly facilitates both offensive and defensive play by allowing quick recognition of who is on which team. George Catlin illustrated Choctaw lacrosse players, in what was probably a practice dating back to an era before European contact, dressed and painted like fellow members of the same team and differently from their opponents.

U.S. Army Officer in khaki uniform, ca. 1905. This officer is dressed entirely in khaki a decade prior to the outbreak of World War I. On the battlefields of Europe, the slouch hat with its gold cords and the sword would be replaced by a steel helmet and firearm. This small card, which is perforated so the figure pops out and stands as a paper soldier, was issued by Recruit Little Cigars. Courtesy of Thomas S. Abler.

The modern baseball uniform had its origins in 1867, when the Cincinnati Red Stockings opted to wear knickers to show off their red socks. Previously, baseball players had worn ordinary trousers. The utility of playing in the baggy pants led to their widespread use.

The evolution of sports uniforms has been influenced by technical developments in plastics and synthetic fibers. In football, plastic helmets and shoulder pads replaced earlier versions made of leather, and jerseys of synthetic fibers replaced those made of wool. Several writers have commented on how the football uniform has evolved through time to present what is almost a caricature of hypermasculine form.

The marketing of sports, either at the professional or the amateur level, has been a prime mover in the evolution of sports uniforms. Originally the uniforms only displayed numbers, forcing those attending the game to buy programs to identify the players. When attracting viewers to telecasts of games became more important than attracting them to the arena or stadium, players' names came to be displayed upon the uniforms. With the growing market in sports memorabilia and souvenirs, it became important that teams have distinctive and attractive logos. For the most part, National Football League teams wore helmets of a single color until the marketing potential of selling souvenirs replicating the helmet, with a distinctive logo identifying the team,

was realized. This practice has spread from professional to collegiate football in the United States.

Uniforms among workers and the military in North America copied or paralleled developments in Europe, with Britain, France, and Germany all being influential on North American practices. While utility is clearly a factor in the wearing of uniforms, in both the military and in the commercial world, the fact that a uniform leads to the recognition of the social role expected of the individual wearing it is perhaps the paramount reason that it is worn.

Snapshot: Canada's North West Mounted Police in London, 1897

Canada joined the rest of the empire in celebrating Queen Victoria's Diamond Jubilee in London in 1897. The celebrations provided a glamorous array of uniforms worn by the empire's military around the globe. Along with representatives of its small army and militia, Canada sent a contingent of the North West Mounted Police (NWMP), the unit ancestral to the current Royal Canadian Mounted Police (RCMP), the famous Canadian "Mounties."

The NWMP was formed in 1873. Initial uniforms for the rank-and-file were a scarlet Norfolk jacket, a pillbox cap worn

tipped to the right side of the head, and breeches of various colors. New uniforms were authorized in 1876. Breeches were dark blue with yellow stripes (gold for officers). The tunics remained scarlet, and those of the officers in full dress exhibited elaborate gold braid. Both officers and men wore white helmets in full dress. The pillbox cap was retained for undress.

The detachment that went to London for the jubilee, however, did not wear the full dress with its gold braid and white helmets. Instead, it wore the plain scarlet serge undress tunic

The contingent of Canada's North West Mounted Police in London for Queen Victoria's Diamond Jubilee (1897) wore an undress uniform. This included blue trousers with yellow stripes, a red serge undress tunic, and a brown Stetson. This dress very much resembles the current full dress of the famous Canadian "Mountie." Library and Archives Canada/PA-202921.

and the Stetson. The crown of the Stetson was indented, forming what would later be termed in the U.S. Army a "Montana peak." The Stetson was not yet official, having been adopted as practical working headgear when patrolling on the prairies of western Canada. Perhaps because of the contrast with the glitter of other imperial contingents, the NWMP made a fine impression indeed.

The uniform worn in London very much resembled what is now the full dress of the RCMP. The Stetson officially replaced the helmet as full-dress headgear in 1904. There have been other, relatively minor, changes; this red-coated icon that is so widely associated with Canada firmly established itself in the world's consciousness in that parade in London to mark the Diamond Jubilee of Queen Victoria in 1897.

References and Further Reading

Chartrand, René, and Serge Bernier. *Canadian Military Heritage.* 3 vols. Montreal: Art Global, 1993–2000.

Craik, Jennifer. *Uniforms Exposed: From Conformity to Transgression.* Oxford: Berg, 2005.

Fussell, Paul. *Uniforms: Why We Are What We Wear.* Boston: Houghton Mifflin, 2002.

Noonan, James Charles. *The Church Visible: The Ceremonial Life and Protocol of the Roman Catholic Church.* New York: Viking, 1996.

Roach, Mary Ellen, and Joanne B. Eicher. *The Visible Self: Perspectives on Dress.* Englewood Cliffs, NJ: Prentice Hall, 1973.

Ross, David, and Robin May. *The Royal Canadian Mounted Police 1873–1987.* London: Osprey, 1988.

Schreier, Barbara A. "Sporting Wear." In *Men and Women: Dressing the Part,* edited by Claudia Brush Kidwell and Valerie Steele, 92–123. Washington, DC: Smithsonian Institution Press, 1989.

Steele, Valerie. "Dressing for Work." In *Men and Women: Dressing the Part,* edited by Claudia Brush Kidwell and Valerie Steele, 64–91. Washington, DC: Smithsonian Institution Press, 1989.

Todd, Frederick P., and Fritz Kredel. *Soldiers of the American Army 1775–1954.* Chicago: Henry Regnery, 1954.

Windrow, Martin, and Gerry Embleton. *Military Dress of North America: 1665–1970.* London: Ian Allan, 1973.

Thomas S. Abler

See also Dress for Rites of Passage; Conventional Work Dress and Casual Work Dress; Dress for Recreational Sports and Professional Sports; Dress for Avocational and Historic-Site Reenacting.

Conventional Work Dress and Casual Work Dress

Clothing of men and women who lived and worked in the United States and Canada since the beginning of the nineteenth century through the start of the twenty-first century has presented a microcosm of societies' changes. Agriculture was the primary means of livelihood at the outset and continues to play a role for a small portion of the population. Rag pickers, rug weavers, and quilters wore and reused fabrics; therefore, not many examples of work dress have survived. Early sewing machines of Germany, Austria, and France spurred U.S. inventors Walter Hunt, Elias Howe, and Isaac Singer to struggle with patenting, production, and marketing of reliable machines by 1840. Patented inventions reflected design and tailoring advances in mechanization and factory production. Prior to those innovations, clothing worn by workers at virtually every occupation was hand-stitched and often handed from one stratum of society to another. With only natural fibers and dyestuffs available, laborers of all strata were clothed in the common denominators of utilitarian fabrics and drab colors. The servant dressed in livery (an often colorful uniform), so ubiquitous in Europe, was seldom found in America and then often clothed in plain garb. Before the late eighteenth century there were three primary categories for workers: professional, managerial, and laborers. The first comprised solely males in medical, teaching, legal, and clerical occupations, who wore either academic robes or somber suits of woolen cloth with plain linen or cotton shirts and a silk necktie. The businessmen and farm managers, including engineers and mechanical workers, wore trousers with jackets or suits, perhaps of a slightly inferior grade and tailoring detail but always with shirts and ties. Laborers purchased used garments of no particular fit or fabric to do the manual jobs associated with farming, mining, and semiskilled work of all types; ties were superfluous for most.

DRESS OF UNSKILLED LABORERS

Appropriateness for the occupational needs of the wearer was less considered than necessity of coverage. No reliable records of problems or accidents were kept to compare to today's safety evaluations. Under the doctrine of Manifest Destiny, the United States appropriated land and encouraged movement westward. During the decades of high immigration from 1840 to 1920, both Canada and the United States gave jobs to hundreds of thousands of unskilled workers who wore clothing of ethnic European styles. Railroads were built, towns established, and farms homesteaded. Historic photographs depict men digging trenches wearing felt hats, ankle boots, and two- and three-piece woolen suits, sometimes with ties at their necks! There are images of Southern tenant farmers and slaves who wore little more than a wide straw hat with cotton pants and shirt. Footwear was not made with left and right differences, nor was safety a consideration. Through the nineteenth century, bare feet in summer was the order of the day for some adults and many children in both factory and farm work.

A breakthrough came in the 1850s in the Californian gold fields when the Levi Strauss company began selling strong work pants from brown canvas that was originally imported to make tents. Strauss soon switched to blue denim (*serge de Nimes*, twill from Nimes, France); his example was followed by several manufacturers in the East who catered to the railroad and mining company stores. By 1870, twill weaves and indigo-dyed jeans became ubiquitous for workers across the continent. Jeans were made by nationally recognized companies such as Carhartt, in Kentucky; Lee, of Kansas; Oshkosh B'Gosh, from Wisconsin; Dickies, in Texas; Red Kap, in Tennessee; and in 1936, Great Western Garment, in Alberta, among many others. Farmers, miners, oilmen, herders, and cowboys have worn jeans for over a century for practicality, ease of maintenance, and low cost. Bib overalls and coveralls (boiler suits) have been women's choice since Rosie the Riveter and her compatriots entered the workforce. Studies have shown jeans to remain useful with regular wear for longer than a year, thus providing economical cover.

DRESS TO MEET SPECIAL NEEDS IN THE WORKPLACE

In the nineteenth century, thermal protection, essential for many outdoor workers in the cold winters of North America, was provided primarily by layering of woolen items (often felted from frequent washings), sometimes in conjunction with hide or fur coats. French Canadian coureurs de bois (traders) took clues from North American Indian populations and insulated their boots with moss linings, stuffed grass between sweater layers, and bordered coat bottoms and sleeves with fringe to channel moisture away. Lewis and Clark were outfitted in similar leather garments as they trekked across North America in 1804 to the Pacific coast. Coats made of buffalo hide as well as coyote, wolf, and beaver pelts for the Northwest Mounted Police of Canada (later renamed the Royal Canadian Mounted Police), established in 1874, were adopted by herders and hunters of the plains north and south of the forty-ninth parallel. When polar expeditions were mounted and Arctic oil drilling commenced by U.S. and Canadian groups, they initially looked to the Inuit for clothing clues. The challenges of frostbite protection are critical in such extreme conditions. Enormous strides have been made in development of clothes for cold weather, and much of the research has been done by military-sponsored research. As synthetic fibers were introduced in the mid-twentieth century, their uses have increased exponentially. Fabrics were developed to wick moisture;

to create barriers against heat, light, and fluids; to promote or reduce airflow; and to maintain special environments within garments. The space program was instrumental in making textiles available such as Gore-Tex, Kevlar, and Tyvek, which have revolutionized garments for police and rescue personnel in addition to those for astronauts. Lightweight synthetic fiberfill replaced heavy layers of wool and knitted textiles for polar and winter wear. Late-twentieth-century clothing designs by the Canadian firm ROOTS were made using microfibers and worn by Olympic athletes of both the United States and Canada. Their designs have been copied worldwide.

PROTECTIVE GEAR FOR WORKERS

Unionized workers began to demand specialized clothing and protective gear for their members about 1860, initially without success. When miners asked for protective headgear and steam engineers demanded gloves, boots, and waterproof coats, suppliers in Boston, Montreal, and Philadelphia met their challenges. Bowler hats had been adapted for use in mines by the addition of a candle or gas lamp at the rigid front brim; this was further improved by Thomas Edison in the early twentieth century with an electric cap lamp. Centuries at sea brought clothing adaptations to answer needs of sailors and fishermen: whale-oiled canvas

coats, for example. Some fishermen's gear with waterproof features was adapted for firemen, but rubber replaced whale oil for waterproofing after Goodyear patented his invention in 1844. In 1820, volunteer fire brigades in Boston wore "lobster-tail" hats to prevent water flowing down their necks, patterned after the "souwesters" worn at sea; fire companies everywhere followed that lead, and helmet design changed very little over two centuries. Patents from 1870 were issued for firemen's coats and pants (turnouts); supply companies, such as Globe of Lynn, Massachusetts, have remained in business since that time. Twenty-first-century firemen have added specialized hazardous material cleanup to their responsibilities, which requires extremely specialized protective gear. Their firehouse clothing is generally a soft-collared shirt with belted trousers, with athletic shoes that can be kicked off to place feet into their turnouts.

Hardened hats were not produced until 1915, when Bullards of San Francisco produced a helmet, similar to one worn by doughboys in World War I, to protect workers on the Golden Gate Bridge project from falling rivets. The black-lacquered, steamed-canvas headgear was quickly adopted by miners and construction workers nationwide. The steel-and-rigid-plastic hard hats worn in construction today are direct descendants of those designs. Federal and state regulations for wearing of protective headgear apply to workers in all states, provinces, and territories,

Miners in Red Star, West Virginia, 1908. In the mid-nineteenth century workers began to demand protective clothing, such as the headgear shown here. Library of Congress Prints and Photographs Division LC-DIG-nclc-01078.

and accident statistics show a reduced rate of injury over the past fifty years. Respirators and safe-breathing masks were gradually improved following the experiences of soldiers with poison gas in World War I for use in mines and the burgeoning chemical industries. Underground mining has increased the use of equipment worn for safety: hats, boots, breathing apparatus, eyewear, protective jackets, and the like. The Mines Safety Appliance Company in Pennsylvania, established in 1914 and expanded to Canada by 1934, is typical of suppliers to gas and oil development, mining, construction, firefighting, HAZMAT, police, general industry, and the military. They produce safety equipment from head to toe—from simple eye protection to sophisticated HAZMAT suits.

UNIFORMS FOR WORKERS

Influences of the Industrial Revolution upon clothing were not limited to factory floors. The increasing wealth of the middle class was demonstrated in their clothing, not only in a conspicuous manner, as described by Thorstein Veblen, but also in uniforms worn by retail clerks, bank tellers, Pullman porters, waitstaff, service personnel, ushers, and hundreds of others who served them. The person wearing the insignia and colors of a company uniform was seen as an ambassador to the public and recognized as capable in their role. Uniforms were to be worn during work hours and not to be seen when the employee was off duty. Laundry, dry cleaning, and other upkeep of uniforms was often, but not exclusively, the responsibility of the establishment, while employees paid for and maintained their personal undergarments and shoes. Some businesses required employees to pay for their uniforms, taking a portion from the salary each week, including companies such as the Canadian National and Pacific Railways, John Deere dealers, and retailers such as Woolworth's. As unionization took hold in the 1930s, some employers deferred costs by requiring workers to wear their own clothing. In today's complicated society, people look for recognizable signs to reassure them of security in their surroundings. The postal worker, the United Postal Service deliveryperson, and the General Motors service mechanic are dressed in uniforms for just that reason.

FOOTWEAR FOR WORKERS

A category of workwear that was mainly purchased by the individual was footwear. No records have been found regarding the cost for footwear required by any particular company's policies, except to find reference to items in dress codes, which do exist, such as "plain black oxfords must be worn," or "no open-toes shoes will be allowed." Use of high-gloss patent leather, developed in 1818, was discouraged except for a few occupations such as dancers and stage actors. Sturdy oxfords and rubber-soled shoes have been the primary shoes in dozens of occupations that require workers to be on their feet during service. Fashion styles such as high heels, pointed toes, and platform soles known to cause foot and back problems continue to be worn because working females insist on following styles. Since a New York subway strike during the 1980s, some working women began to wear athletic shoes to walk to work and to change into dress shoes on the job. How widespread this trend became is not certain, but women dressed for the office except for the sneakers they are wearing can still be observed carrying shoe bags in midtown Manhattan.

Laced boots that protected the ankle and lower leg were worn by miners and construction laborers throughout the nineteenth and early twentieth centuries and often featured a double-leather toe cap. Steel-toed workboots were readily accepted for their safety features after World War I, when returning soldiers recognized their usefulness in heavy industry, farming, and construction. In the past fifty years, several regulatory statutes specific to workboots have been passed by the Occupational Safety and Health Administration (OSHA) in the United States and by Canada's Standard Association, with certificates to be displayed for the buyer. On Canadian hang-tags, a green triangle indicates a heavy-steel toe cap and puncture-resistant sole, a yellow triangle indicates a basic steel toe cap and puncture-resistant sole, and no triangle means no toe cap. A white square indicates electrical protection, a yellow square indicates antistatic protection, a red square shows electrical conductivity, and a fir tree indicates protection against chain saw injury. Similar categories exist in the United States. However, any regulations are only as good as the buyer insists upon, and policing is negligible except where regulated by union contracts.

Specialized footwear has been worn in commercial and restaurant kitchens and hospitals. Cooks have eschewed leather shoes in the kitchen because of their tendency to slip on greasy or wet surfaces, and clogs with either rubber or nonskid soles are their primary choice. Surgeons, who until the advent of sterile technique around 1900 wore their suits and shoes while operating, began to change into rubber boots and later into clogs similar to a chef's by the 1920s. Nurses across the United States and Canada were shod in black or white oxfords with low or Cuban heels for over a century until the 2002 invention of the "Croc," a plastic slip-on clog with nonskid tread, originally designed for boaters. The Crocs brand became an overnight sensation and was endorsed by several nursing associations, which severely reduced demand for oxford styles. Not only did the clog make sense from a comfort level, but it was also easy to clean and did not require white shoe polish. Recent studies are showing increased incidents of blood and infectious punctures through the decorative holes in addition to accidental falls of personnel wearing the popular footwear. Hospitals in Sweden have banned clogs for hospital and clinic duty since 2006, and hospitals in Manitoba and Pennsylvania have followed suit.

One group who generally do not bother with polishing their boots are cowboys; their triangular-toed boots with high, angled heels contribute to their ease of slipping forward into the stirrups and anchoring the foot when the wearer requires bracing for tasks. The calf-high leather protects the lower legs from chafing against the mount and rough brush in the environment. These utilitarian boots worn in casual and work situations have remained almost unchanged since the Spanish invasion of North America.

As motor vehicles changed transportation, a plethora of uniformed personnel sprang to the fore: mechanics and auto-body workers in one-piece overalls; salesmen in a shirt, tie, and jacket; and petrol (gasoline) pump attendants, with their jaunty caps and crisply creased shirts and pants. Although the workers on Henry Ford's first assembly lines in 1914 wore their own clothes, including aprons and hats, a one-piece coverall was substituted by the early 1930s that protected the workers' clothing, added company identity to all workers, and prevented some accidents caused by clothing being caught in machines.

WHITE COLLARS AND BLUE COLLARS

The nineteenth-century upper-class men's shirts were exclusively white and with long sleeves. Collar styles changed as the white cravat gave way to the simpler knotted silk tie, but the front-button placket and cotton fabric remained almost constant in the offices of the nation. Bleaching, starching, and ironing were all necessary for shirt maintenance, and legend has it that a housewife in Troy, New York, in the 1820s invented removable collars when faced with the task of daily shirt maintenance for her blacksmith husband. He demanded a clean white shirt each evening, so his wife cut off his collars, bound the edges, and washed the collars to save work. It is said that the idea was soon copied by other housewives. This story may be apocryphal, but what is known is that collars began to be manufactured in Troy, New York, which is known as "the collar city."

The detachable collar allowed for some relief to the laundress, and when celluloid appeared in the 1870s, it enjoyed a brief flirtation with men's fashions as material for collars. Paper collars were cheaper for the occasional wearer to add formality to his appearance. Clerical or roman collars had always been detachable and worn with a "dickie-front" over a banded, collared shirt. Often the simple banded shirt would be worn as casual dress and could be quickly converted as necessity demanded. The Hathaway Shirt company started in 1837 and built a strong business in the eastern states with very limited advertising. In 1951, they launched their first national campaign, featuring a man in a Hathaway shirt wearing an eye patch; the image instantly became synonymous with their brand. Since 1851, The Arrow Shirt Company has made men's shirts, and in 1905, they launched the very successful advertising campaign featuring the handsome Arrow Collar Man. The company is still in business in the United States and Canada.

White-collar and blue-collar differentiation has denoted status within segments of the economy since the early nineteenth century. *White-collar* workers usually wore a tie and jacket with their shirts. The *blue-collar* worker's covering garment, however, was almost universally an apron. From the leather-fronted blacksmith to the Harvey girl in her white apron or the carpenter's nail pouch, the apron has been the longest-used protective device in humanity's closet. Social class, education, and opportunity played roles in choosing a clerkship over a laborer's job; society dictated rules (written and unwritten) for dressing appropriately.

DRESS CODES

Dress codes have been an elusive topic for several reasons. They are not often published for public perusal; they tend to change frequently; and they are often initialized in response to customer complaints, hierarchical tastes, societal mores, and other elusive factors. The computer company IBM has had a reputation for its dress code; however, company archives do not support the claim. Although the sales and office staff of IBM were often referred to as the "wing-tipped warriors," no evidence has ever been shown of a written policy for workers. Interviews with former IBM employees confirm that during the presidency of Thomas Watson all were aware of the unwritten rules, which included wearing a shirt and tie with jackets, polished shoes, and tidy hair. Craft or assembly workers are exempt from any clothing constraints, while the software and sales staff at U.S. IBM sites are conservative and still compliant with Watson's preferences. Young executive candidates at 3M and Cargill are introduced to tailors as part of their induction into company procedures, along with golf lessons. A retired executive from AT&T recounted that no written policy existed but that peer pressure "to conform to the conservative image" was always present.

Off-the-record personal interviews with staff of the Mayo Clinic have revealed that policies were in effect to promote that staff be "neatly groomed," but few specifics were learned: no leather or fur clothing was allowed, cultural accessories such as turbans may be worn, but no jeans or sandals may be worn in the clinic or hospitals, except where clogs are part of the uniform. Doctors have followed the lead of the 1892 founders, William and Charles Mayo, who wore three-piece suits to the office. Other notable medical facilities, such as Johns Hopkins, Cleveland Clinic, UCLA, Mount Sinai in New York, and others, require their medical staff to wear white coats over their personal clothing. This may have been a response to early research into infection control, which promoted separation of institutional and private clothing; more recent studies have failed to produce the same statistical evidence. Companies as diverse as Home Depot and Best Buy require their employees to wear signature-colored aprons or shirts,

Uniformed bellboys at the Hotel Martin, Utica, New York, 1910. Library of Congress Prints and Photographs Division LC-DIG-nclc-03432.

which allow customers to identify them. During the late 1950s, attempts were made to relax the strictures of business wear by allowing "dress-down" or "casual" work clothes on Fridays. Soft-collared shirts and casual pants, even jeans, were encouraged for all levels of workers in many companies. Since about 1990, this practice was gradually reduced in acceptance by customers according to anecdotal reports; bank personnel in jeans do not evoke a professionalism expected by their clientele. Statistical evidence is difficult to gather on such arrangements, but a few companies have asked their employees to substitute khakis for jeans on casual Fridays.

The white lab coat worn by medical doctors has been a universally accepted identifier of professional men and women in a variety of occupations, including dentists, veterinarians, researchers, scientists, and even cosmetologists who want to have the cachet of scientific trust. Whereas doctors had the option of lab coats over their suits, nurses and other medical professionals have universally been required to wear uniforms. From their inception as members of a profession by Florence Nightingale, nurses wore starched aprons, collars, and cuffs over their floor-length, long-sleeved dresses. Starched veils or caps to conceal or bind their hair were de rigueur. Nurses' uniforms followed the mainstream fashion in silhouette and skirt length through the twentieth century until the pantsuit was adopted in the 1960s, which revolutionized their workwear. Not only were the pantsuits more practical than the fashionable miniskirts when caring for patients, but they also allowed the freedom from wearing pantyhose, slips, and foundation garments of the time. Over the following three decades, white uniforms were replaced by colors, initially to make nurses look friendlier to pediatric patients and later to allow for recognition of departmental specialties, such as emergency room, obstetrics, surgery, and so forth, for attending staff and patients alike. The acceptance of scrubs for every level of personnel has created homogeneity at the same time, making for some confusion of roles.

BUSINESS SUITS

The business suit as it is now known was first produced in the United States following the lead of British tailors who were influenced by fashions for men, such as George (Beau) Brummell, a friend of the English regent of the early nineteenth century. By 1818, Henry Brooks and his brothers had established their New York tailor shop, and by 1850, they were nationally recognized for their quality menswear. Samuel Lord and G. W. Taylor in 1826, also in New York; Harry and Max Hart, who started in Chicago in 1872 to answer clothing needs following the Great Fire; and John Wanamaker in Philadelphia, in time for the Centennial Exhibition of 1876, were early contributors to U.S. men's sartorial splendor. The 1830s frock coat with stirrup trousers had given way to the more practical sack coat with hemmed trousers. Only the wealthiest customers could afford the bespoke suit (individually made to measure from cloth saved for just one customer), but as pattern systems, standardized sizing, and simpler construction methods evolved, suits were purchased ready-made. The surge in production that gave workers choices happened after 1850 and was spurred by demands of the Civil War in the United States and the increased immigration to both Canada and the United States. Manufacture started with men's suits and overcoats and later cloaks and skirts for women entering the

workforce in droves. Although names of early tailors in Canada were not nationally known, following World War I, many Italian tailors immigrated to supply the demand for quality menswear. Ready-to-wear retailers with mail order catalogs, such as those of Sears Roebuck and Montgomery Ward of Chicago and Hudson's Bay Company and T. Eaton's of Canada, offered economical choices. The number of buttons on the jacket was determined by modifications in fashion, as were lapel shapes and width, pocket placements, vent choices, and cuff or no cuff on trouser legs. A matching vest was routinely included as part of the businessman's suit, which sold with two pairs of trousers until World War II, when fabric was rationed. Somber colors with faint chalk stripes as an occasional choice were worn by all. Tweeds were worn only for sporting or leisure until 1945, when returning GIs headed for colleges and later to white-collar jobs nationwide. The *sport coat*, with contrasting trousers, was accepted in some business circles, particularly those who desired to present a friendly and welcoming atmosphere, such as car and real estate salesmen. The 1955 book *The Man in the Grey Flannel Suit*, by Sloan Wilson (and subsequent movie with Gregory Peck in 1956), depicted the fashion demanded in post–World War II U.S. business. The suit was somber gray worsted wool without a vest worn with a white shirt and plain tie. It became the prototype for businessmen everywhere. Some men's suit fashions have failed to gain such long-lasting acceptance, such as the Nehru jacket with its banded collar, the completely collarless style worn by the Beatles on their foray into North America in the mid-1960s, or the white linen suit sported by such figures as Colonel Harlan Saunders and the writer Tom Wolfe. They remained almost caricatures in their category.

Women in business have been restricted by more than their clothing choices. With the gradual acceptance of women in the roles of typist, telephone operator, and retail clerk, the dark-colored skirt with a simple white blouse served almost as a universal uniform for female workers. Conflicts that sent men to war opened doors in business for females who readily undertook the tasks. Fashions at the time demanded skirts; jackets were added to complete an executive image, and thus the *dress suit* emerged for women. Immediately following 1945, many women returned to their domestic duties, and their business suits hung unused. It took until the late 1960s for trousers to be acceptable for women in the executive business setting; cut in men's suiting fabrics, pantsuits became wardrobe regulars. Blouses were almost universally worn beneath the jackets, with accessories such as soft bowties and plain jewelry of gold or silver. Women who wanted to attain ranks above the "glass ceiling" were discouraged from wearing bright colors or alluding to their sexuality with clothing; prim was proper in the office. An occasional female executive, such as Katherine Graham of the *Washington Post*, could wear dresses or bright colors without censure, but most women adhered to somber tones.

Guidebooks were published for businessmen, such as *Dress for Success*, by John T. Molloy, in 1975. In 1987 *Color Me Beautiful*, by Carole Jackson, featured grooming and fashion hints for women in business. These were closely followed by individual counseling and home party demonstrators who taught techniques and sold products to willing customers with a desire to improve their image. Dozens of titles were published over the decades on similar themes, some of which have become reliable references in law schools and business colleges for up-and-coming entrepreneurs.

Descriptions of "power ties" and advice on choosing name brands, such as Brooks Brothers, Ralph Lauren, Donna Karan, Gucci, Rolex, and others, are offered by authors with little else than popular culture to back their claims. Like so much in the clothing field, research has failed to gather more than sketchy retail data.

By the early twenty-first century, clothes worn for work depended on the occupation; the environment or conditions in the workplace; regulations specific to the job; identification associated with tradition, status, hierarchy, or company policies; and in some instances, gender distinctions. As of late 2007, the Department of Labor in the U.S. Commerce Department lists 821 detailed occupations grouped into 449 broad categories, with 23 major and 96 minor divisions. Many of those have special clothing requirements in the form of OSHA-specified regulations. Fashion always plays a role in dressing for work, perhaps less in some occupations than others.

References and Further Reading

Copeland, P. F. *Working Dress in Colonial and Revolutionary America.* Westport, CT: Greenwood Press, 1977.

Corbin, H. A. *The Men's Clothing Industry: Colonial through Modern Times.* New York: Fairchild, 1970.

Fire and Emergency Manufacturers and Services Association, Inc. *FEMSA Official User Information Guide* 22. Lynnfield, MA: Author, 1996.

Kidwell, C. B. *Suiting Everyone: The Democratization of Clothing in America.* Washington, DC: Smithsonian Institution Press, 1974.

Kidwell, C. B., and V. Steele. *Men and Women: Dressing the Part.* Washington, DC: Smithsonian Institution Press, 1989.

Molloy, J. T. *Dress for Success.* New York: Warner, 1975.

Molloy, J. T. *New Women's Dress for Success.* New York: Warner, 1996.

Rubenstein, R. P. *Dress Codes: Meanings and Messages in American Culture.* Boulder, CO: Westview Press, 1996.

Stavros, A. G., and S. G. Pore. *The Globe Odyssey: The Story of an American Enterprise.* Concord, NH: Globe Manufacturing Company, 1996.

Veblen, Thorstein. *The Theory of the Leisure Class; an Economic Study in the Evolution of Institutions.* New York and London: Macmillan, 1899.

Waugh, N. *The Cut of Men's Clothes 1600–1900.* London, Boston: Faber and Faber, 1964.

Wilcox, R. T. *The Mode in Footwear: From Antiquity to Present Day.* New York: Charles Scribner's Sons, 1948.

Colleen Gau

Dress for Recreational Sports and Professional Sports

Sport is any athletic activity that requires physical skill, rules, or customs and specific dress and environment in order to participate. *Recreational sport* is any athletic activity that a person may participate in to occupy one's spare time enjoyably, as a diversion from work or school. Some people participate in recreational sports to help manage a healthy lifestyle and improve their physique. There are a multitude of sports in which North Americans participate. Special types of dress that facilitate participation in the activity are often associated with recreational sports. By contrast, a *professional sport* is any athletic activity that a spectator may view to admire the participating athletes' physical skills. Uniforms or other types of dress that contribute to the ease of performing the skills needed for the sport are usually worn. North Americans watch a multitude of professional sports. In order to provide an in-depth look at dress worn for both types of sport, two examples, the most popular of those recreational sports and professional sports in the United States and Canada, are examined in depth.

Football, ice hockey, baseball, basketball, tennis, skiing, walking and running, swimming, and golf are but a few of the very popular sports in the United States and Canada. Each has its own type of dress. Influences from the professional practice of sports frequently transfer quickly to the kinds of clothing and accessories sold to recreational practitioners of the sport or to the general public. Notable examples include the baseball caps that have become ubiquitous in the North American wardrobe, sneakers for basketball and other sports that are manufactured in all colors and styles and sometimes serve as inspiration for fashionable high-heeled shoes, and knit golf shirts that are longer in the back so they do not pull out of the pants during a swing of the golf club. Special dress for sports such as tennis evolved from mandatory, conservative white outfits to fashionable colors, with the breaking of that color barrier meriting national headlines in sports publications. High-tech, form-fitting skiing outfits for Olympic games and international ski tournaments quickly moved into retail ski stores. Most children own a cap, a sweatshirt, or a T-shirt that proclaims their loyalty to a local or national sports team.

EXERCISE WALKING

The two most popular recreational sports for adults in Canada and the United States are exercise walking and swimming. *Exercise walking* is the number-one recreational sport for adults in Canada and the United States because it is a gentle, low-impact activity with numerous health benefits. It is accessible to people of most income levels and is relatively safe. Exercise walking also does not require learning a new set of skills or rules, and it can be performed in a variety of cardiovascular intensities on almost any surface and climate, with the appropriate dress.

Ever since humans became bipedal, walking has been a very efficient means of gathering food, moving from place to place, herding animals, fighting battles, surveying land, and even racing between villages. The concept of exercise walking is rather new, with the first club chartered in 1864 in Germany; it was called the Black Forest *Wanderverein* (hiking club). Photographs from the late 1800s show men and women dressed in knickers and sturdy walking shoes and carrying walking staffs.

Exercise-walking programs typically begin with the individual walking for small periods of time, usually for ten minutes around his or her neighborhood. Then, as the individual builds endurance, the program generally increases by five-minute increments until the individual is content with their set program.

A policeman measures the distance between the knee and the bathing suit in Washington, D.C., 1922, following an order that suits must not be over six inches above the knee. Library of Congress, Prints & Photographs Division, LC-USZ62-99824.

Some walkers choose to walk indoors, using a treadmill or indoor track, especially in geographical zones that are too cold or when the weather is inclement. Exercise walkers are recommended to watch their posture, to stretch before and after exercise to prevent injury, and to drink plenty of water to avoid dehydration. The dress chosen depends on the setting for the exercise.

Each weekend in Canada and the United States, cities host a variety of exercise-walking events, from ones for novices that cover short distances such as 5 kilometers (3.1 miles), to ones that are very competitive and cover long distances, such as the marathon, at 42.2 kilometers (26.2 miles). Many of these events are cause-related, such as the March of Dimes Walk-A-Thon, which promotes infant health research, and the Susan G. Komen Race for the Cure, which promotes breast cancer awareness and research. No matter the level of intensity, distance, or cause, similar philosophies of dress exist between exercise walkers.

EXERCISE-WALKING DRESS

The activity of walking itself influenced the creation of footwear so that individuals could be protected from rough terrain while conducting everyday activities such as hunting and gathering. The first items of footwear, dating from around 1600 to 1200 B.C.E., were sandals discovered in the Mesopotamia region by archaeologists. When it comes to the recreational sport of exercise walking, footwear is also used for protection, specifically from impact, unstable surfaces, and environmental conditions.

Exercise-walking footwear has evolved substantially over the last century. When the sport established itself in the 1860s, walkers typically wore their everyday stitched-leather footwear, which was relatively unstructured. In areas of the world where *plimsolls*,

more commonly called *sneakers*, were available, they were very desirable because they had vulcanized rubber outsoles that kept the foot more protected from water and provided traction and some cushioning, owing to the springy nature of rubber. The vulcanization process also created a more stable platform so that the walker would less likely overpronate on uneven surfaces. These shoes usually had an upper composed of canvas, which also made the footwear more compliant and breathable than leather.

Since the late 1800s, exercise-walking footwear has become very specialized and diverse, depending on the terrain type, climate, and skill level. Today, there is walking footwear designed for cold, snow, and water and ones designed for light weight, heat management, and breathability. Upper materials used are also diverse, ranging from Gore-Tex performance leathers to thin, breathable sandwich meshes made out of synthetic yarns. Outsole and midsole materials have evolved as well and include injected foams and high-density rubbers that improve cushioning and durability.

Much like footwear, exercise walkers originally wore their everyday apparel for walking. Wool and cotton woven materials in form-fitting silhouettes, such as tailored jackets, shirts, trousers, and long skirts, have now evolved into easy-to-care-for synthetic, knitted, or stretch-woven tops and bottoms that help wick sweat to aid in its evaporation, have night visibility, and can even protect the skin from ultraviolet rays. Two styles are typically seen with modern-day exercise-walking dress. One style that is more athletic and technical looking in nature is typically worn by younger participants because the silhouettes are more body conscious, dynamically colored, and blocked with stripes and geometrics. This style was also influenced by the jogging craze of the 1970s, when tracksuits became a staple necessity for participants. Today, this

North American ice hockey team, ca. 1910. Leather shin guards were modified for better protection by stuffing them with newspapers and magazines. Goalkeepers adopted shin- and kneepads from the sport of cricket to protect them from the high-speed puck. Library of Congress, Prints and Photographs Division, LC-DIG-ggbain-11853.

style has also been adopted into many high-end fashion collections. It is very common to see renditions of exercise-walking (also known as *active sportswear*) dress from upscale fashion design firms such as Prada, Hugo Boss, and Donna Karan each season. Even major athletic companies such as Nike and Adidas produce high-end options for the consumer who is looking for something special and different from what is available at mass retailers.

The second style seen in exercise walking is more traditional and conservative. The silhouettes are loose, monochromatic, and made of materials in a similar hand and appearance to the participant's everyday dress. Walking apparel products come in a variety of silhouettes, which can accommodate bodies of all ages, shapes, and sizes, especially in countries such as Canada and the United States, where multiple ethnicities and body shapes exist.

In addition to the footwear and apparel worn for exercise walking, there are many accessories that people use or carry along to facilitate the activity. Some of these include walking canes, to add balance and help leverage the body over hills and poorly maintained trails; hats of many shapes, which help maintain body heat or block the sun from radiating onto the face and neck, along with sunscreens and lip balm; pedometers, heart-rate monitors, and sport watches to measure mileage, steps, and time; bottled water, performance drinks, and gels, to keep the exercise walker hydrated and his or her electrolyte balances intact, especially in extreme heat and over long distances; and socks and gloves, to protect extremities. Customized walking accessories, such as orthotics and heel lifts, help support the arch and reduce pain from *plantar fasciitis*, a stress injury to the bottom of the foot. Fanny packs and backpacks allow for longer walks and the ability to carry additional footwear, apparel, and provisions for climate and environmental changes. Portable music is also a popular accessory and over the last fifty years has seen the most evolution and innovation in the marketplace. Portable, hand-held radios and boom boxes have developed into Walkmans (1970s) and Discmans (1980s). Most recently portable music has evolved into MP3 players and multifunctioning devices, such as the Apple iPhone (2007), with which one can listen to music, feel safe by having a portable telephone, and even watch workout movie clips all with one device.

Because modern exercise-walking dress is very practical and comfortable, many social groups have adopted it into their everyday wardrobe. It is very common to see parents attending their children's extracurricular activities and doing the weekend gardening in walking dress. Many tourists and retirees have also adopted walking dress because it is comfortable to wear on long-haul flights and sightseeing and does not need special care or dry cleaning.

RECREATIONAL SWIMMING DRESS

Recreational swimming is the second most popular sport for Canadian and U.S. adults. Many consider it a great way to relax and destress while enjoying a healthy workout. Like exercise walking, recreational swimming is accessible by many social classes, but it does require a little skill to keep afloat.

Although recreational swimming is a very old sport, depicted by the Egyptians and practiced by the Romans, it was not until the seventeenth century that it became popular and encouraged by government officials for its health and medicinal benefits in Europe and Japan. Throughout the years before, swimming was often banned because of public health and safety issues, such as the plague, and the basic fact that many people did not know how to swim. Swimming was most often done nude in classic antiquity. In cases where swimming dress was worn, it consisted of a two-piece outfit that covered the breasts and genitals and that resembled the bikini of the mid-1940s. Documentation from 350 B.C.E. also showed people wearing togas while swimming. Given that recreational swimming was abandoned for centuries for health and safety reasons, the need for swimming-specific dress was not really critical until the eighteenth century.

During the eighteenth century, therapeutic spas where men and women engaged in public bathing began appearing in France and England and then migrated over to North America. By the early 1800s, a trend began when people flocked to the beach for seaside recreation such as swimming, surfing, and diving. Technological innovations such as the railroad made public beaches even more accessible. Swimming pools started to become popular, and after the modern Olympic games in 1896, the popularity of swimming grew even more.

Most recreational swimmers swim with their head out of the water and keep afloat with an underwater arm recovery technique such as the breaststroke, sidestroke, or doggy paddle. Most participants today swim in public pools, where the water is calm and clean. However, beaches, lakes, swimming holes, creeks, rivers, and canals are also popular locations for recreational swimmers.

The earliest form of modern-day swimming dress for women was a smock called a *bathing gown*. This type of swimming dress was far from ergonomic or comfortable; women often attached lead weights to the hems of their gowns to prevent them from floating up and exposing their legs. The bathing gown evolved into bloomers and stockings around 1855, to prevent exposure, and by the 1880s, the *princess cut* was introduced, consisting of an all-in-one blouse and trouser. Some women also wore a separate skirt that fell below the knee and buttoned at the waist to conceal the midriff. By the end of the nineteenth century, recreational swimming had become a form of entertainment as well as an intercollegiate and Olympic sport.

One of the most famous female swimming entertainers was Annette Kellerman. She was an Australian synchronized swimmer who revolutionized the swimsuit aesthetic by wearing a provocative swimsuit in 1907 that exposed her arms, legs, and neck. Although she was arrested when visiting the United States for her "indecent" exposure, her swimsuit dress aesthetic was highly influential to the appearance of the modern-day swimsuit. Conservative swimsuits that fully covered the body evolved to ones that uncovered the arms and legs up to midthigh. Formal collar lines receded from around the neck down to the top of the breast. By 1910, the one-piece tank became the accepted silhouette for women.

The development of new fabrics with synthetic and elastic fibers allowed for comfort and practicality. The first *bikinis* were introduced after World War II in the late 1940s. They were named after Bikini Atoll, the site of a nuclear weapons testing area, for their "explosive" effect on the viewer. Up until the 1960s, the lower part of the bikini always covered up to the navel. From the 1960s onward, the bikini shrank in all directions until it sometimes just covered the nipples and genitals. Today there are many varieties of women's swimsuits deriving from the tank and bikini. Some of them include the topless *monokini* (designed by Rudi Gernreich), the *thong*, suits with different ways of suspending parts of the garment known variously as *slingshot* or *suspender* (having a Y-shape), and the *pretzel*, which twists around the body.

Men's recreational swimsuits are a little less complex and tend to be known as *surf* or *board shorts*, *cut-off shorts*, *shorts*, *trunks*, and *jammers*; occasionally men may wear thongs, g-strings, and bikinis. The male upper body is almost always left uncovered. However, in the early part of the twentieth century, it was illegal for men to be topless in the United States.

There are many accessories worn for recreational swimming. In the late 1800s, ruffled caps and straw hats were almost always worn by women as part of the outfit; today, headwear such as rubber bathing caps are worn to keep the hair from getting wet or from clogging up filters in public pools. For recreational swimmers who are more athletic and sporty, there are rubber fins, snorkels, and goggles, which allow one to maneuver more efficiently through the water and see more clearly. Nose and ear plugs are also used to help prevent water from entering the ears and nose. In the outdoors, recreational swimmers will also don bronzer or sunscreen to enhance their suntan and prevent sunburn.

RECREATIONAL SWIMMING DRESS IN MAINSTREAM FASHION

Recreational swimwear has influenced many other forms of dress. Gym, dance, and running apparel, along with body, scuba, and speed-skating suits, are all types of dress that have taken inspiration from swimwear through its materials, body-conscious fit, and aerodynamic functionality. It has also been adopted as a device to display the "perfect" female body. This idea first started with glamour photography of the 1940s and 1950s and then moved into beauty pageants, where today much public debate continues about how it objectifies the female gender. Magazines such as *Sports Illustrated* still use the swimsuit as a mechanism to portray what the perfect body looks like and to attract a large male readership with its annual swimsuit issue.

PROFESSIONAL SPORT: ICE HOCKEY

A wide range of professional sports is played in Canada; however, ice hockey is the most popular. The object of ice hockey is to get the puck into the opposing team's net, which is defended by a goalie, by maneuvering the puck with a stick while on ice skates. The term *hockey* comes from the French word *hoquet* (shepherd's stick) and was originally played in the early 1800s in Nova Scotia by the Micmac tribe of First Nations people. The sport was influenced by field hockey and the Irish game of hurling, and it was spread throughout Canada by immigrants from Scotland and Ireland as well as by the British army. Montreal students from McGill University (1879) created the rules still followed today, and by the late 1880s, several clubs and professional leagues were established in Canada, including the National Hockey League (NHL). The NHL is the most popular ice hockey league in the world and consists of players from the United States and

An American football player in 1916. Players wore soft, pliable leather "head helmets" with nose guards. Pants were made of brown cotton canvas. Courtesy New York Public Library.

Canada, but for many years almost all players were Canadian. The winning team of the annual NHL playoffs is awarded the Stanley Cup. Ice hockey was added to the Winter Olympics in 1920, where it is one of the most popular events.

ICE HOCKEY DRESS

The first ice hockey players wore very little protective and specialized equipment compared with what is presently worn. Skates, sticks, and pucks have always been compulsory. In the beginning, skates were merely metal blades rudimentarily attached to shoes, and sticks were made from tree branches. James Whelpley, of New Brunswick, created the first ice hockey skate in 1857. His invention, called the *long reach skate*, consisted of a blade that had to be fastened to the skater's boot with leather straps and buckles. In 1863, Forbes and Thomas Bateman, from the Starr Manufacturing Company in Nova Scotia, invented the modern-day hockey skate that revolutionized the sport with blades that were attached to the bottom of the boot with nails. The first hockey sticks were carved by hand and used a strong wood called hornbeam. They looked more like the sticks used for field hockey because the blade curved up, and they were short and heavy. As hockey grew in popularity, mass production became more favorable, and the Starr Manufacturing Company also began manufacturing hockey sticks. They called their sticks *Mic-Macs*, after the name of the original First Nations players. For many years, the blades on sticks were completely straight, but in the 1950s experimentation with the curve began, and this shape is still used today. Folklore tells that the original ice hockey pucks were balls, stones, lumps of coal, frozen animal dung, or even potatoes. Wooden pucks were also used for many years. Today's ice hockey puck is made from vulcanized rubber and molded into a disk.

As for protective equipment, players began wearing padded gloves in 1917. Leather shin guards were also worn and modified for better protection by stuffing them with newspapers and magazines. The goalkeepers also adopted their own protection—shin- and kneepads from the sport of cricket to help them protect themselves while in the goal and facing high-speed pucks. The first mask worn for ice hockey was also borrowed from another sport, fencing, in 1927. Clint Benedict, a goalie, designed the first official hockey mask, but the popularity of wearing masks among players was meager. Most players wore masks only when recovering from major injuries, such as broken skulls and jaws, and lacerations. It was not until the NHL passed a mandatory helmet rule at the start of the 1979–1980 season that newly signed players were officially required to wear head protection.

Along with all of the specialized and protective equipment worn for ice hockey, there are also uniforms. The first home and away uniforms were used in 1910 and consisted of a black-with-white-trim uniform for home games and white-with-black-trim uniforms when playing away. Like most other team sport uniforms, the invention of synthetic fibers and sophisticated material constructions greatly influenced the aesthetic of the modern-day ice hockey uniform. Original uniforms consisted of everyday dress (trousers, shirt, and sweater) and were made of natural fibers such as wool and cotton; today, uniforms (jersey, pants, and socks) are made from polyester and nylon. Like many other team sports, jerseys contain the name and number of the player and team logo for on-ice identification. The first time numbers were used in the NHL was in 1979, when player Wayne Gretzky

used 99. In the 1970s, there was also an attempt to streamline the very bulky and aerodynamically slow ensemble, with an all-in-one, body-conscious concept called the *Cooperall*, but players rejected it because it was too feminine. However, most recently, at the 2006 Winter Olympics, Nike outfitted many teams in new ergonomic, streamlined uniforms that were lighter, cooler, and more mobile in attempt to address the bulkiness of the entire ensemble worn by ice hockey players.

PROFESSIONAL ICE HOCKEY DRESS IN MAINSTREAM FASHION

Given the variety of specialized and protective equipment worn for ice hockey, the shift of the exact ensemble into mainstream fashion is not as straightforward as in other sports. The most common items that have been adopted into mainstream fashion include the skates and uniform jersey. Ice hockey skates are seen on many recreational skaters as an alternative to the figure skate, in order to achieve a more masculine and sporty look on the foot. Fans of ice hockey will also don their favorite team's jersey with their everyday dress as a statement to others of their interest in ice hockey and what team they support. Dedicated fans will own jerseys in home and away colors, with names of their favorite players, and will collect them each season to remember all of the year's highlights.

AMERICAN FOOTBALL

The sport of American football derived from rugby. Soccer (known outside of North America as *football*) has also been noted as a relative to American football. The sport came to the United States in the mid-1800s and was played by many northeastern colleges; in 1876, Harvard and Yale universities met together in Massachusetts to formalize the rules of American football. The game is played between two teams, each with eleven players. The players can be substituted in and out of the game in between plays, which is different than in soccer and rugby, where players can be substituted only during breaks. The object of the game is to move the egg-shaped ball across the goal line by kicking, throwing, or running with it. The team that acquires the most points in four quarters wins. The National Football League (NFL) is the most popular and only major professional league in the United States. The NFL consists of thirty-three professional teams located in major cities across the United States. Each team plays sixteen games between early September and the end of December. The annual championship game, called the Super Bowl, is watched by 50 percent of all U.S. television households. Millions of U.S. sports fans also watch college football throughout the autumn, and some communities, particularly in rural areas, place great emphasis on their local high school football team.

AMERICAN FOOTBALL DRESS

When the Professional Football League (now the NFL) began in the 1920s, there were no rules regarding the equipment players wore. Teams only provided players with long-sleeve, knitted-wool jerseys and socks in team colors and logos. Many players used the equipment that they acquired at college, if they attended. To protect the head from contact, players wore soft, pliable leather

American football players in 2007. Throughout the twentieth century, elaborate equipment was developed for the players, including pads made with high-density plastics and foams for the neck, thighs, hips, groin, ribs, knees, shoulders, and sometimes the forearms. Copyright Laurin Rinder, 2007. Used under license from Shutterstock.com

head helmets with nose guards, though some players felt that long hair was good enough. Pants were knicker length and made of brown cotton canvas (reminiscent of the original Levi's). Players also wore cleats to enhance traction when running, especially in the mud. Throughout the 1900s, elaborate equipment was developed for the player, including pads made with high-density plastics and foams for the neck, thighs, hips, groin, ribs, knees, shoulders, and sometimes the forearms. Many of the equipment developments during the last century were created by players themselves or by equipment managers. Over the pads, the players usually wear a knitted cut-and-sewn jersey, knee-length pants, and socks, all in team colors and made of synthetic fibers that provide durability and thermal comfort. Like many other sports, jerseys contain the name and number of the player and team logo for on-field identification. Today, players also wear proper, durable helmets with face and mouth guards. Light-weight cleats are worn for different field environments such as grass or synthetic turf. Gloves are sometimes worn for warmth and to provide a better grip on the ball. Even the ball has gone through a series of changes, making it more durable, aerodynamic, and easier to handle.

PROFESSIONAL AMERICAN FOOTBALL DRESS IN MAINSTREAM FASHION

Like ice hockey, fans wear their favorite team's jersey with their everyday dress as a statement to others of their interest and what team they support. Dedicated fans also will own jerseys in home and away colors, with names of their favorite players, and will collect them each season to remember all of the year's highlights. Unlike ice hockey, the American football jersey has also been adopted by the hip-hop culture along with the basketball jersey. Even high-end designers such as Geoffery Beene adapted the American football jersey graphic in 1968 into an evening wear line, all in sequins.

References and Further Reading

Bensimon, Kelly Killoren. *American Style.* New York: Assouline Publishing, 2004.

Buxbaum, Gerda, ed. *Icons of Fashion: The 20th Century.* New York: Prestel, 1999.

Costantino, Maria. *Fashions of a Decade: The 1930s.* New York: Facts on File, 1992.

Feldman, Elaine. *Fashions of a Decade: The 1990s*. New York: Facts on File, 1992.

Herald, Jacqueline. *Fashions of a Decade: The 1920s*. New York: Facts on File, 1991.

Lee-Potter, Charlie. *Sportswear in Vogue since 1910*. New York: Abbeville Press, 1984.

McDonough, Will, Paul Zimmerman, and Peter King, eds. *75 Seasons: The Complete Story of the National Football League 1920–1995*. Atlanta: Turner Publishing, 1994.

O'Mahony, Marie. *Sportstech: Revolutionary Fabrics, Fashion and Design*. New York: Thames & Hudson, 2002.

The Culture Statistics Program, Culture, Tourism and Centre for Education Statistics, Statistics Canada. *Sport Canada: Sport Participation in Canada: 1998 Report*. Gatineau, QC: Minister of Public Works and Government Services Canada, 2000.

U.S. Bureau of the Census. *No. 412, Selected Spectator Sports: 1985 to 1994*. Washington DC: U.S. Census Bureau. http://www.census.gov/prod/2/gen/96statab/parks.pdf (accessed 23 March 2009).

Susan L. Sokolowski

See also Functional Dress.

Dress for Avocational and Historic-Site Reenacting

- What Are Reenacting and Historical Interpretation?
- Dress as a Key Ingredient in Reenacting
- Why Reenact History?
- A Case in Point: Confederate Civil War Reenacting
- Dress Authenticity as a Measure of Confederate Reenactor Competence
- Dress Authenticity as a Measure of Meaning

In both Canada and the United States, human history is of interest and fascination to many people, and for some, inhabiting a historical period by virtual time travel to the past is a form of entertainment, hobby, or in some cases, when employed by a museum, a vocation. Those individuals who re-create a historical event or period as a hobby are referred to as *reenactors*, while those who are financially remunerated are commonly referred to as *historical interpreters* (similar to a reenactor, but they perform under the auspices of a museum). In all cases, these individuals create a virtual past by establishing a historical persona or *impression*, by donning historical apparel, and by mastering the use of other artifacts and tools from their selected time period. Serving as a historical interpreter at a museum site can bring history alive to the attending public. On the other hand, reenacting the past as a hobby can offer participants an opportunity to seek meaning in their contemporary lives.

WHAT ARE REENACTING AND HISTORICAL INTERPRETATION?

Reenacting the past can take on multiple forms, and the form taken may dictate how the activity is referred to or defined. For example, historic sites such as Colonial Williamsburg in Virginia fill their locale with as much accurate historic artifice as possible, including individuals who dress and act the part of the original inhabitants, which adds flavor and depth to the public's experience. Individuals creating historical impressions at a museum or historic sites are often, but not always, financially remunerated and prefer to be referred to as interpreters. Museum-site historical interpretation is typically done under the supervision of a site director or curator, and the more fastidious historic sites will require that their interpreters be well informed about the time period and location being represented. Furthermore, historic interpreters are required to look the part of the historical inhabitants. Under the guidance of the site director, effort is applied to create reproduction garments and associated material culture that accurately represents the time frame of the historic site. Original artifacts would rarely, if ever, be used by interpreters because of potential for damage. Research sources for reproduction garments include actual historic artifacts held by museums, such as period photographs and artwork, as well as historic patterns of period garments, if available. To the extent possible, reproduction garments are produced with fabrics, dyes, and buttons

that are historically accurate. For practical purposes, compromises are sometimes made in areas that would not ordinarily raise public notice or concern, such as substituting machine sewing for hand sewing during garment construction. In sum, a professional site director will ensure that interpreters create an accurate representation of historical events and time periods. Achieving historical accuracy may or may not be the case for hobby reenactors, discussed later.

Representing a very different form of reenacting was Thor Heyerdahl's 1947 voyage on the ship *Kon-Tiki*, which he designed and modeled after primitive sailing vessels, to demonstrate the possibility that the ancient inhabitants of pre-Columbian South America were capable of navigating the Pacific Ocean to eventually inhabit the islands of Polynesia. In a similar vein, but more recently, the British Broadcasting Corporation and History Channel funded a 2001 reenactment of one of Captain James Cook's Pacific voyages to gain insight into the physical and emotional challenges that those voyages entailed. Though the participants in the Cook reenactment did not dress the part of the original seafarers, they sailed on a replica of Cook's ship, *The Endeavor*, and ate historically accurate foods. They also performed the ship's operations in a manner akin to Cook's sailors on the original voyage. The purpose of this event, as with the preponderance of other reenactments, was to entertain and inform the public.

The most common form of reenacting is considered more of a hobby and is popular in both Canada and the United States. The sheer number of hobby reenactors in North America dwarfs in size that of historical interpreters working at museum sites or those participating in reenacted research explorations, such as the *Kon-Tiki* voyage. The hobby typically focuses on commemorating and celebrating past events that simultaneously reside in the popular consciousness and are considered to be of historical importance. For the most part, it is Canadian and U.S. history that is reenacted; however, other seminal eras predating the existence of the two countries, such as medieval Europe, are also popular.

Hobby reenactors should be distinguished from amateur historical scholars who, as avocational historians, study and master a time period in detail but from an armchair's distance. The primary feature that distinguishes reenactors from amateur scholars is that reenactors choose, in a manner of speaking, to travel backward in time to a period or event of their historical interest through a form of physical and perhaps psychological immersion. In essence, reenactors inhabit a historical period by donning the dress, mastering the associated material culture of the time, and mimicking, as much as possible, the habits and behaviors of the time they wish to explore and emulate. The ultimate accomplishment in this form of reenactment is the magic moment when reenactors personally feel as though they have been literally propelled backward in time. Some reenactors refer to this hobby and this behavior as *living history* (another term for reenacting or historical interpreting). Though there are physical, intellectual, and psychological limits to how accurately an impression of the past can be reconstructed, reenactors remain undeterred in their zealousness to reach historical perfection. An accomplished reenactor will invest energy into studying the history of the chosen time period; however, beyond analysis of the broad sweep of historical

A pair of Confederate cavalry soldier reenactors photographed at the battle of Chickamauga national reenactment in Tennessee, ca. 2000. Military accoutrements complete the overall historical impression, such as a musket with bayonet and a set of traps, otherwise referred to as *leathers*. Dress authenticity is the metric upon which the reenactors sort each other by competence. Courtesy of Mitchell Strauss.

events, the reenactor will often focus intensely on the personal life experiences of people from the past, as well as the dress and related material culture of that time.

Typically, reenactments are publicly staged events designed to create a relatively large-scale emulation of a historical time period. The size of a reenactment varies depending upon whether they are local or national in ambition, ranging from several hundred to thousands of participants. As stated earlier, dress and other material culture artifacts are central elements to reenactments. They serve as elemental stage props to create the atmosphere of the time period being reenacted. For example, avid buckskinner reenactors, who emulate the Rocky Mountain fur-trading rendezvous period of the early mid-1800s, invest heavily in historically accurate fringed-leather outfits and replica North American Indian tepees; they may also practice so as to master rendezvous competitions, such as hatchet throwing.

DRESS AS A KEY INGREDIENT IN REENACTING

Of all the reenactor's props, dress is arguably the most important. Reenacting is all about constructing a past identity, often referred to as an impression, and the reenactor's costume allows the individual to drape history upon his or her shoulders. Dress is the key foundational ingredient in the equation for adopting a valid historical impression. Without historical dress, the reenactor cannot create the necessary temporal distance from extant quotidian life. In essence, dress creates the initial recognition or signal that the hobbyist is entering into another time realm. In fact, individuals will initially judge each other in terms of reenactor efficacy almost entirely on dress appearance. Of course, developing a reputable and efficacious historical impression requires that the reenactor go beyond simply dressing the part. For example, mannerisms of the original historical inhabitants must be studied and emulated as well.

Large-scale cottage industries have developed to support and profit from reenacting hobbies, and their focus is largely on dressing the reenactors. From these enterprises, the more serious reenactors may spend thousands of dollars on their kits. Suppliers, frequently referred to as *suttlers*, will develop and sell a broad array of period products for reenactors to purchase. Suttlers attend reenactments and set up on-site shops, while the more sophisticated enterprises offer catalogs via mail and Internet services. Suttlers vary in the quality of reproduction items they offer for sale, leaving the burden upon the reenactor to sort out the accurate from the not-so. To aid reenactors, there are periodical journals available to help them recognize accurate or authentic products. For example, in Civil War reenacting, the monthly *Watch Dog* or the *Camp Chase Gazette* serve as consumer digests.

The history that hobbyists choose to reenact is wide and varied, though most periods reenacted are, by popular consensus, important and well-known historical times. Some of the more popular reenactments in the United States include

- Medieval periods
- French and Indian War
- American Revolutionary War
- Buckskinner/Rocky Mountain culture of the 1825-to-1849 period
- U.S. Civil War
- World War II

Common Canadian reenactments include

- Medieval periods
- War of 1812
- The North West Riel Rebellion of the late 1800s
- U.S. Civil War (50,000 Canadians fought in that war)
- World Wars I and II

A pair of Confederate reenactors photographed at the battle of Chickamauga national reenactment in Tennessee, ca. 2000. These men are reenacting infantry soldiers. Their dress would be considered reasonably authentic from a historical standpoint. Courtesy of Mitchell Strauss.

While some reenactments occur close to or at the original sites, such as the Gettysburg Civil War gatherings, it is not a necessary ingredient for the hobby to be enacted. Original historical sites are most often preserved and precluded from reenactments and thus protected from damage. For example, a reenactment of the pivotal Civil War battle of Pea Ridge annually takes place at a public park in Keokuk, Iowa, whereas the original battle took place miles away in the Ozark region of Arkansas. In other instances, the original sites might be a continent away, thus economically infeasible to enact authentically from a geographic standpoint. Consider medieval reenacting, European in origin, but still very popular in the United States and Canada because of the romance of the period as well as strong European roots existing among much of the population. Despite the cognitive dissonance created by reenacting events that originally occurred across the Atlantic Ocean, the activity occurs merrily across North America. On the other hand, Europeans have been known to enjoy reenacting the U.S. Civil War, with reenactments occurring in locations such as Belgium and Germany. In sum, fealty to the original location of the historical event is not a necessary requirement for reenactors to happily engage in their hobby.

While there are numerous historical eras to reenact as a hobby, the interests are not evenly spread, with some time periods being more popular than others. For example, those who reenact World War II–era Russian soldiers are relatively rare in the United States. On the other hand, medieval reenactors are quite popular throughout North America. The largest group of reenactors, by far, in the United States is involved with the Civil War period. Because Canadians also participate in Civil War reenacting, most subsequent examples discussed will be drawn from that particular era. Nevertheless, concepts and behaviors discussed about Civil War reenacting will often be exhibited in other forms.

WHY REENACT HISTORY?

Different points of view have been taken to account for the popularity of reenacting. From a leisure and social standpoint, reenacting is an opportunity to pretend, dress up, play, and escape from the humdrum of quotidian life, entering into an imaginary environment with others of like mind. From the perspective of gender analysis, there is a strong element of masculinity construction exhibited during reenacting. For example, it is the rule rather than the exception to find in the various genres of reenacting manifest opportunities to gallantly brandish, in raucous faux battles, all manner of military hardware, including daggers, swords, pikes, pistols, muskets, and even artillery. When men feel emasculated by disruptions in the economy, feminism, and political correctness, reenacting affords an opportunity to recapture, whether appropriate or not, archetypal, heroic representations of masculinity. For example, in the United States, use of weapons and reenactment of violence reach back to the core elements of the U.S. national character, which is grounded in frontier mythology, a concept deeply ingrained within male self-perceptions of virility and masculinity.

This is a time when many closely held existentialist notions are under constant reconsideration and deconstruction. Identities are fluidly shifting, swirling, and reconstituting in new forms, and individuals' perceptions of themselves as individuals and parts of a greater whole are no longer grounded in bedrock but instead on shifting sands. In recompense, reenacting can be an attractive defense to postmodernism because of the innate sense that the past offers less ambiguity and complexity than does the present. To that end, the creation of a reenactor's historical impression gives the individual a concrete existence. Taken another way, reenacting gives the participant a feeling of well-being, grounded in the rejection of an uncertain present, to be replaced instead with the nostalgic and mythical sense of a more predictable past. Furthermore, there is satisfaction to be derived from developing a deep sense of knowledge about a clearly delineated historical time frame, as well as mastery of the material artifacts that physically represent, symbolize, and define that past. In sum, a comforting stability of self can be found in the re-creation of what is perceived, by reenactors, to be an authentic re-created past. In fact, achieving the perception of authenticity is the ultimate measurement of reenactor competence.

Considered in the political context, reenacting can be viewed as quite subversive. Despite claims among participants, sometimes patina thin, that reenacting creates an isomorphic simulacrum of the past; the historical representations are, in reality, somewhat more elastic. Bending to the will of the reenactor, the past, as presented, can be more invented than authentic, and invented past can be used as a tool to manipulate perceptions in the present. For example, though historical evidence suggests otherwise, buckskinners incorporate inauthentic, hippie-like aspects to their impressions, which suggests a countercultural motivation to their reenacting activity.

A CASE IN POINT: CONFEDERATE
CIVIL WAR REENACTING

While the focus of the remainder of this discussion will be on Confederate reenacting, the concept of reenactor authenticity is fairly universal across all reenacting genres and can thus be generalized to a great extent from what follows. To place the extent of this activity within proper perspective, it is the predominant form of historical reenacting in North America. Civil War reenactments occur at two basic levels, regional and national, with participants ranging from hundreds to thousands in number. There is a routine, perhaps ritual, nature to the events that lend commonality to most Civil War reenactments. In brief, reenactments typically occur on weekends, with the participants arriving early evening on Friday. The locations for regional events are usually public parks, and the reenactors stake out the property with separate areas for Confederate and Union troops. Neat rows of canvas tents, cook fires, stacked weapons, and battle flags characterize the living arrangements. The more serious reenactors might eschew tents and sleep out in the open, as would actual campaigning soldiers. Separating the two armies is usually an area for civilian reenactors and suttlers, who supply material needs for hobbyists. Lending a carnival atmosphere to the regional events are food vendors that may or may not be serving period-related fare.

Saturdays and Sundays consist of marching drills and staged battles enacted before a public gallery. The battles themselves are highly ritualized and bear little resemblance to actual Civil War encounters. They begin with a cacophonous exchange of period cannon fire, followed by a balletic display of cavalry combat, with horsemen from opposing armies crossing sabers gingerly to ensure horse and human safety. Afterward, the infantry face each other across the field of battle in orderly lines and rake each other with musket fire, loaded with blanks, of course. Attempting to create a semblance of reality in the proceedings requires that some reenactors fall in the throes of simulated death, with the occasional more accomplished reenactor emulating the "battlefield

bloat" of the dead, made famous by Matthew Brady's Civil War photographs. In sum, reenacted Civil War battles are scripted beforehand, orderly, civilized, and with an eye on safety. For the sake of fairness, the Confederacy prevails in battle one day and the Union, the next.

DRESS AUTHENTICITY AS A MEASURE
OF CONFEDERATE REENACTOR COMPETENCE

As with most human enterprises, social forces come into play, and status hierarchies are created. In Civil War reenacting, participants gauge and stratify each other based on internal hobby-driven status markers. Obviously, the possession of historical knowledge about the war is quite important to earn peer standing, but the core measure for status stratification in Civil War reenacting is authenticity of an individual's historical impression, with the most immediate and visible marker being dress. Authenticity as a status marker is true for most other forms of reenacting as well. In other words, if it were possible to completely and exactly copy an actual Confederate Civil War participant of the past, then the most serious reenactors would attempt to do so. For example, purist Confederate reenactors will ensure that all their garments are hand sewn, based upon the prevailing belief that Confederate soldiers did not own machine-produced uniforms. Achieving authenticity can become quite expensive. Typically, the more authentic the item, the more expensive it will be.

For the Confederate reenactor, dress includes a complex collection of apparel items and military accoutrements. The dress kit includes a basic military uniform consisting of trousers and a jacket. Other apparel items, civilian in origin, typically include a shirt and vest, long underwear, and socks. There are also several basic apparel accessories, including brogans, a hat, and braces to hold up the uniform trousers. The elements of dress that complete the overall historical impression are military accoutrements, which include a musket with bayonet and a set of traps, otherwise referred to as *leathers*, which include a shoulder-strap-suspended cartridge pouch and a separate waistbelt upon which is hung a smaller cap pouch and bayonet scabbard. In addition, for the campaigning reenactor, a blanket, tarp, and haversack for rations are included to complete the kit. Finally, it should not go unmentioned that a host of smaller material culture elements can add depth (and expense) to an impression, such as period eyeglasses or the perfect eating utensils as well as tallow soap and sugar in the form of a hardened brown cone. Reenactors are always on the lookout for a new addition to add interest to their historical impressions.

Based upon a scaled measure of authenticity, reenactors visually assess and make inferences about each other's seriousness and accomplishment. This behavior of ranking each other by status is one of the leading causes of friction among hobbyists. The authenticity of a reenactor is inversely proportional to the number of flaws found in the reenactor's dress-based impression. For example, the most authentic reenactors are referred to in the hobby as the "hard core," and they present to the viewer a virtually flawless impression. The most accomplished reenactor appears to have walked out of an original Civil War photograph. Their reproduction uniforms and accoutrements will be made to the exacting dimension of museum specimens. To that end, some hard-core reenactors are referred to as "stitch counters" because of

This man is a Confederate reenactor at the battle of Vicksburg national reenactment in Mississippi, ca. 2000. Typical among some reenactors is his inauthentic apparel, including nonperiod glasses and boots. His excessive armament, including two pistols and a leg knife is also not characteristic of an actual Confederate infantryman. Courtesy of Mitchell Strauss.

the insistence that their uniform's seams contain the historically appropriate number of stitches per inch. Being hard core is more than wearing a perfect uniform; it must be worn appropriately, too. It cannot be too new or too clean. In fact, many of the most serious reenactors adopt a ragged, somewhat haggard look, emulating a soldier long in the field.

The slightly less authentic reenactors are actually very good; however, they may suffer from minor flaws, such as the uniform being too neat or orderly. Compared to the entire population of hobbyists, the top-tier, highly authentic reenactors are actually a minority in the hobby population. The more mainstream reenactors, which make up the largest portion of the population,

typically wear generic uniforms, failing to identify themselves with a specific time period or geographical region of the war, as the more authentic reenactors do. Their appearance is also usually marred by visual flaws in their period material items: uniforms made of inauthentic materials, such as manufactured fibers; inappropriate footwear; or the careless wearing of accoutrements, such as a cap pouch on the wrong side of the body.

The least authentic reenactors are referred to as the "farbs." The etymology for the word *farb* is debated, but the meaning is clear. Farbs are considered offensively inauthentic and a bane upon the hobby by more accomplished reenactors. Farb impressions are characterized by egregious flaws, which might include nonperiod apparel, such as cowboy boots; hats reflecting other time periods, such as a Vietnam War–era bush hat; or the wearing of modern-day sunglasses. The flaws exhibited by farbs are considered by other reenactors to destroy all sense of historical credibility. As a group, farbs are reviled and even ostracized by other participants. In sum, dress plays a major role in how Civil War reenactors assess and relate to each other. Dress authenticity, which is based upon exacting fealty to the past, is the metric upon which the reenactors sort each other by competence.

The dictates of dress authenticity might require reenactors to wear and use actual historic artifacts; however, such artifacts are rare and easily damaged. In fact, reenactors would frown upon the use and potential injury of actual artifacts. Using reproduction dress items and accoutrements are the expected means of achieving an impression. To that end, serious reenactors spend a great deal of time and effort researching their dress impressions. There are publications such as the *Time-Life: Echoes of Glory* series that document, with museum-quality imagery, historical artifacts that the reenactors use to design or purchase their reproduction items. It is also not unusual for reenactors to visit museums to view actual artifacts as a means of researching their impressions.

DRESS AUTHENTICITY AS A MEASURE OF MEANING

Some enter Civil War reenacting to seek their own personal meaning by identifying with the conflict in some way, shape, or form. Identifying with the varying aspects of the war permits the reenactors to express themselves in a public manner. For example, for some Confederate reenactors there is the romance of the underdog Southern forces gamely holding their own against the more numerous and better-equipped Northern army. It is distinctly American to identify with the beleaguered fighter against overwhelming odds, as the outsized reputations of Custer's Last Stand and the Alamo testify. On a different plane of expression, there is a strong element of gender construction underpinning the motivations of Southern reenactors, with masculinity enhancements created by excessive displays of weaponry. With the common but inappropriate perception of flexibility in Confederate dress impression, many reenactors absorb into their impressions more knives, daggers, derringers, and pistols than historical analysis could justify.

The self-expressions among Confederate Civil War reenactors can take on subtle political undertones as well. A reenactor's appearance, the setting that the reenactor places himself within, and the verbal articulations of the reenactor can be examined to interpret meaning from the activity of reenacting. For example, reenactors see themselves as serving an important role of interpreting history for the public. But how that history is presented to the public can be influenced by a reenactor's own personal predilections. For example, some Confederate reenactors present a biased form of Civil War history to the public, inappropriately downplaying slavery as a cause of the war, instead speaking to the gallantry of Confederates protecting their homeland from unwelcome invaders and specifically citing the violation of state's rights as the primary circumstance underpinning the conflict. This "Lost Cause" interpretation of the war was actually developed during the post–Civil War period to undermine Reconstruction efforts and preserve white hegemony in the South.

Photograph of the author in Confederate attire, ca. 2000. Dr. Mitchell Strauss spent three years in the field with U.S. Confederate reenactors, studying the meaning of their activity with a focus on dress authenticity. Courtesy of Mitchell Strauss.

Thus, one interpretation of contemporary Confederate Civil War reenactors purveying Lost Cause history to the public suggests that preservation of white hegemony in the United States is still a relevant political expression that is encoded within their historical impressions. Preservation of white hegemony is a subtle, symbolic form of racism and, in today's political climate, considered a stigmatic behavior. Nevertheless, by donning a Confederate uniform and reenacting their own chosen form of Civil War history, reenactors can express their disdain for erosion of white hegemony in a publicly palatable manner.

References and Further Reading

Agnew, V. "Introduction: What Is Reenactment." *Criticism* 46, no. 3 (2004): 327–339.

Allred, R. "Catharsis, Revision, and Re-Enactment: Negotiating the Meaning of the American Civil War." *Journal of American Culture* 19, no. 4 (1996): 1–13.

Belk, R., and J. Costa. "The Mountain Man Myth: A Contemporary Consuming Fantasy." *Journal of Consumer Research* 25, no. 3 (1998): 218.

Hall, D. "Civil War Reenactors and the Postmodern Sense of History." *Journal of American Culture* 17, no. 4 (1994): 7–11.

Handler, R., and W. Saxton. "Dyssimulation: Reflexivity, Narrative, and the Quest for Authenticity in 'Living History.'" *Cultural Anthropology* 3 (1988): 242–260.

Horwitz, T. *Confederates in the Attic: Dispatches from the Unfinished Civil War.* New York: Pantheon Books, 1998.

McCalman, I. "The Little Ship of Horrors: Reenacting Extreme History." *Criticism* 46, no. 3 (2004): 477–486.

Strauss, M. "A Framework for Assessing Military Dress Authenticity in Civil War Reenacting." *Clothing and Textiles Research Journal* 19, no. 4 (2001): 145–157.

Strauss, M. "Pattern Categorization of Male Civil War Reenactor Images." *Clothing and Textiles Research Journal* 20, no. 2 (2002): 99–109.

Strauss, M. "Identity Construction among Confederate Civil War Reenactors: A Study of Dress, Stage Props, and Discourse." *Clothing and Textiles Research Journal* 21, no. 4 (2003): 149–161.

Thompson, J. *War Games: Inside the World of Twentieth-Century War Reenactors.* Washington, DC: Smithsonian Books, 2004.

Turner, R. "Bloodless Battles: The Civil War Reenacted." *The Drama Review* 34, no. 4 (1990): 123–126.

Mitchell D. Strauss

Leisure

*S*portswear, *casual wear*, *business casual*, and *casual Friday* all suggest variations on leisure dress intended for a relaxed or less formal approach to dressing. The concept of dressing for leisure that emerged at the end of the nineteenth century and continued throughout the twentieth was different from that of earlier periods. Leisure dressing occurred across gender and class lines and involved a steady erosion of occasion-specific dressing. Women borrowed traditionally male attire for sport and leisure, and both men and women appropriated casual attire for all but the most formal occasions. Although the seemingly unstoppable transition to a casually attired lifestyle occurred in other areas of the world, it had its roots in both lifestyle and geographic transformations in the United States and Canada. Also fundamental was the ability of the ready-to-wear industry in the United States, founded to a large extent on production of sportswear separates, to supply both quantity and quality clothing to the masses. And while fashion may sustain seemingly infinite variations in a multitude of levels of formality, the overall trend in the last century has been toward casual dress.

To discuss this century-long progression requires beginning with the premise that leisure time became available to more than just the upper classes. Without some measure of free time and the opportunities for dress adaptations this afforded, a more casual style could not have evolved. It is therefore natural that the beginnings of sport and casual dress appeared concurrently with changes in lifestyle and work patterns. This occurred with increased speed between 1890 and 1910 as more women entered the workplace and as college attendance for both men and women expanded. Although the forty-hour workweek did not become the norm until mid-twentieth century, the length of the average workweek began to decrease in the first decades of the century. Increases in the number of men and women who worked as clerks, typists, and salespeople in offices and stores (white-collar positions rather than manual labor, or blue-collar, jobs) more clearly differentiated work clothing from leisure clothing. Clothing worn for manual labor, then and now, fell into the category of casual wear.

Change in dress did not occur in a continuous and uninterrupted evolution, nor did it occur exactly the same for men and women. However, a few generalizations can be made. In many instances, what created the perception of leisure was not the clothing worn but rather what was *not* worn. Although clothing does not need to be revealing to be considered casual, transitions to a more relaxed style are interrelated to changing attitudes about modesty. For women, this meant the gradual forgoing of corsets and other support garments and, indeed, the eventual transition of unseen undergarments to acceptable visible attire. Initially, it also meant more leg exposure. For men, the identifying garments of formal or business attire were, and continue to be, the suit and tie. For over a century, to remove either signified a relaxation of prevailing dress codes. While women have always had a more varied dress code, the adoption of pants in various styles indicated more casual appearance than did a skirt. Change for either men or women did not come without controversy. In examining over a century of transformations, it is important to place style modifications into the context of each period and to understand that what may appear formal to the contemporary eye, could, in an earlier time, have represented a significant leap toward informality.

THE BEGINNINGS OF LEISURE STYLE

The last decade of the nineteenth century set the stage for an evolution to leisure attire that continued unabated through to the early twenty-first century and was shaped by a multitude of often interrelated influences. In addition to identifying specific styles, it is essential to examine critical lifestyle changes that influenced dress transformations. Early transitions to casual dress depended on increased leisure time and occurred simultaneously with both the rising popularity of sport activities and the increased freedom that new modes of transportation afforded. Evidence of the latter is apparent in the last decades of the nineteenth century with the bicycle, arguably an invention that revolutionized society and dress. Cycling provided freedom and, for women, the opportunity to travel independently. The amazing popularity of the bicycle led women in particular to seek more practical attire. While some sports, particularly horseback riding, required a rigidly defined set of clothing, the bicycle, as a new invention, did not have established dress standards. The woman cyclist retained considerable freedom and flexibility in adopting new sporting attire. This provided an initial challenge to the long-standing taboo against women wearing bifurcated garments. While those who adopted trousers were often criticized, and even occasionally arrested, it opened the door to acceptance of less restrictive apparel.

The development of the ready-to-wear industry provided another striking opportunity for changes in dress that set the tone for more casual style. Both men and women could avail themselves of ready-to-wear in most categories of apparel by the early 1900s, but especially notable for women was the rise of the ready-to-wear shirtwaist and skirt. The Gibson Girl, a powerful fashion and lifestyle symbol at the turn of the century, created a visual link between leisure style and the shirtwaist. Created by illustrator Charles Dana Gibson, she was the personification of a sporty and athletic young woman. The Arrow Collar Man functioned as the masculine counterpart to the Gibson girl. Illustrated by J. C. Leyendecker, he was depicted as a healthy and athletic male shown not only without either formal suit or coat but often with his sleeves rolled up as well, the picture of casual relaxation.

SPORTS AND LEISURE DRESS

By 1900, the middle class played croquet, tennis, and golf; swam; did calisthenics; and engaged in team sports. Country clubs began to be established, some of the earliest as golf clubs in Canada. These sports required some type of specialized equipment and attire that eventually developed into separate apparel categories and exerted an influence on everyday streetwear. Leisure items of the late nineteenth and early twentieth centuries that became part of an informal wardrobe included knit sweaters, less constructed jackets, and canvas shoes. Athletes also became role models, both for apparel styles and for breaking ground on what was considered acceptable dress. Indeed, the first athletic product endorsement occurred in 1923, when the Converse Company added basketball star Chuck Taylor's name to the logo of its All Star athletic shoe, naming it the *Chuck Taylor All Star*. This canvas shoe with white-rubber toe and sole soon became a fashion classic.

While not everyone participated in sports, watching sports became a leisure-time activity. For this, a new style of casual clothing appeared called *spectator sportswear*. Usually a modification of daytime dress, it included more comfortable elements common to sport clothing and yet remained apart from the function-oriented apparel of the playing field or swimming pool. In addition, apparel companies such as Spaulding, Jantzen, and Munsingwear began to mass-produce sport clothing and gear in the first decades of the twentieth century. Retailers stocked and advertised it, bringing these styles to a wider audience.

Increases in the number of men and women who attended college contributed to a desire for casual dress, and indeed, college students set casual dressing trends throughout the twentieth century. As costume historian Patricia Campbell Warner has pointed out in *When the Girls Came Out to Play*, as colleges introduced women to physical education and sports, they had nothing functional to wear for these strenuous activities. This gave rise to the gym suit and to the adoption of bloomers, initially worn only with other women. Eventually, some of this comfortable clothing began to sneak out of the gymnasium and onto the street. It was not until the 1930s, however, that sportswear became firmly established for occasions other than sport participation or for watching sports activities.

One leisure activity that created a market for casual attire was tourism, and as the automobile became more affordable, people traveled for recreation. Many more gained easier access to the beach or other resorts with the introduction of Henry Ford's affordable Model T in 1908. As resort areas grew in popularity, new casual clothing styles appeared, including bathing suits with increasingly more body exposure. The attraction of automobiles and the freedom they allowed continued unabated throughout the twentieth century. By 1940, the number of cars registered in the United States alone reached thirty-two million. Traveling for recreation exploded in the 1950s, as larger baby boom families took to the road, wearing casual and comfortable clothing.

In the 1940s and 1950s, as the population moved out of the cities and into the suburbs, casual dressing truly came into its own, with backyard patios and informal neighborhood get-togethers. Popular sports for the suburbs included not only bowling and other already common pastimes such as golf and tennis, but also do-it-yourself projects for the home. The popularity of separates permeated both men's and women's fashions. The U.S. ready-to-wear industry produced all manner of casual pants, skirts, and sport shirts for relaxed suburban dressing for leisure and for sports. And yet, these casual styles still did not make the transition to work attire for men or women until much later.

It was in the 1970s that a craze for running and jogging created demand for a range of jogging-related apparel—styles that

A walker in typical hiking gear, 2007. The influence of sports was crucial to the acceptance of leisurewear in twentieth-century North America. Copyright Val Thoermer, 2007. Used under license from Shutterstock.com.

quickly became casual streetwear and not just for exercise. In addition to jogging clothing, sales of running shoes rose dramatically. The Nike Company, founded in 1972, became a major source of athletic shoes and apparel and from the start sought athletes' endorsement. These aided in making athletic footwear the shoe of choice for all activities. Indeed, many younger boys and girls soon owned only athletic footwear.

In the 1980s, women created a demand for spandex exercise clothing that also came out of the exercise studio onto the street. This included bright-colored tights, leotards, wrap skirts, and leg warmers, often worn in a multitude of layers and combinations. Shoe manufacturers again recognized the marketing potential and produced shoes designed specifically for aerobic exercise. These also became popular for everyday wear. By the 1990s, Generations X and Y popularized extreme sports (sports done to enhance a sense of excitement or challenge). Both skateboarding and snowboarding grew in popularity, and a subculture of fashion style arose associated with these sports, frequently involving baggy or oversized clothing.

The influences of sports and transportation were critical to the acceptance of leisure dress. While initially only for leisure activities, casual dress began to suffuse into all parts of daily life, from the workplace to traditionally formal occasions, including religious and ceremonial events.

However, it took the better part of the twentieth century for clothing associated with leisure activities to make the transition to even occasionally acceptable attire for the office.

SPORTSWEAR AND THE READY-TO-WEAR INDUSTRY

There exist endless variations on attire for sport activities, from equestrian dress to swimwear. It was, however, the transformation of the elements of athletic sport dress to acceptable streetwear, office wear, and even sometimes formal dress that marks the unique twentieth-century progress to an almost all-inclusive casual approach to clothing. Sportswear as a clothing category retained at least some of the comfort of athletic sports clothing and became widely available through the marketing of mass-produced, off-the-rack apparel. While today it seems to know no limits, the rise of the ready-to-wear industry and the availability of clothing for the masses allowed a casual dress code to begin to supplant the influence of high fashion focused on couture and custom clothing.

Ready-to-wear apparel for men appeared in substantial quantity after the U.S. Civil War and can perhaps be linked to a less structured suit shape. The U.S. women's apparel industry began its rapid rise with the more casual look of the shirtwaist and skirt. Although the industry also, of course, produced dresses, it was in the realm of casual sportswear that it excelled. U.S. manufacturers quickly developed the ability to produce affordable and well-made clothing, and ready-to-wear designers recognized and responded to the shift to a more casual lifestyle. Indeed, it was, to a great extent, ready-to-wear designers who formulated the image that has become the casual dress uniform: one of comfort, of mix-and-match pieces, and of layering those pieces for function and for style. Although some early introductions of casual- or sport-inspired design came from couture designers, including Chanel's jersey knits and menswear inspirations and Jean Patou's high-end spectator sportswear, these remained rooted in the couture tradition. Mass-produced sportswear became the standard dress of all classes, and sportswear became the bread and butter of the ready-to-wear industry. Numerous businesses and designers achieved success creating separates for customers around the world, not just in the United States and Canada. Ready-to-wear designers also expertly interpreted athletic sport styles into clothing for all times of the day or evening.

CASUAL DRESS AND YOUTH

Innovative fashion often arises from youth culture, and this, in turn, is often in rebellion against the perceived staidness of adult dress. The concept of youth style as separate from that of adults, although not defined as the *teen* market until the 1930s, began to appear early in the twentieth century. While what constituted style rebellion varied both geographically and over the course of the century, it almost always entailed a more casual expression of dress. Some youth fashions arose through creative variations in how off-the-rack clothing was worn, while other styles were appropriated from working-class dress.

The beginnings of separate teen fashion occurred at a time in the 1910s and 1920s when adolescents stayed in school longer. This provided an opportunity to interact with peers, to develop a sense of separateness, and, as a result, to adopt behavior in opposition to parental standards. In the 1910s, the *flapper* appeared, a young adolescent girl whose dress, although similar in form to that of adults, was looser and had fewer decorative details. By the 1920s, the term also applied to older teens and to unmarried women in their early twenties. Flappers wore knee-length skirts, a first for women, and rolled their stockings down in an ultimate expression of casual and relaxed style. Some also sported "flapping" unbuckled rain galoshes. These new modes of dressing, along with innovative bathing suit styles, pushed the limits of acceptable body exposure. Young men also adopted casual styles, including full-legged trousers called *Oxford bags*. The youth styles of the 1920s were spurred by introduction of new forms of popular music and dance, including fast and sexy dances such as the Charleston and the tango. This connection between youth, music, and fashion represented the beginning of a trend that has continued into the twenty-first century.

Within the fashion industry, teen and youth culture were increasingly recognized as a separate market by the Depression years of the 1930s, but, as always, teens combined individual pieces of clothing into their own unique style. The casual look that began in the Great Depression and continued through the 1940s went hand-in-hand with swing music and dances like the Lindy and the Jitterbug. Portions of the look derived from Hollywood, particularly the popular press images of actors and actresses portrayed in their everyday life. This more casual West Coast style tended to be more youthful and less constricting than urban East Coast fashion, with looser sport shirts for men and trousers for women. Other casual youth styles of the 1940s included dungarees or jeans for both girls and boys and thick bobby socks and loose, oversized shirts or sweaters for girls.

One of the most iconic examples of casual attire grew out of teen culture: blue jeans and a T-shirt. Initially working attire, it was adopted by teens and college students but had little appeal otherwise. However, by the last quarter of the twentieth century, it became a standard across almost all markets, supported by the aging baby boom generation who continued to wear jeans, albeit in a fit and style that was often different than the style worn by the new, younger generation.

By the 1960s, surfer style, another California creation, entered the casual dress lexicon with proponents who sported longer, bleached hair and a continual tan. Part of the look included *baggies* (long swim trunks) or, for streetwear, *chinos* (also known as *khakis*) and windbreakers. Popular footwear included flip-flops and huarache sandals. Hippie styles of the late 1960s came from a variety of influences and included both jeans and a fad for second-hand clothing that would mark youth and casual wear trends later in the century.

Hip-hop began in the 1970s in the South Bronx with a cross-cultural blending of Jamaican and black styles of music, but it soon become one of the most influential cultural movements of the last quarter of the twentieth century. For break-dancers, hip-hop artists, and, into the 1980s, rap artists, fashion was an essential component of their identity. Many wore expensive athletic shoes and oversized jogging attire, an appropriation of athletic dress to subcultural youth fashion. Variations of these styles continued into the twenty-first century. For boys in their teens and early twenties, the clothing was extremely oversized with loose jeans, usually bagged at the ankle, and oversized shirts and hooded sweatshirts worn with either heavy boots or athletic shoes. For adolescent girls, fashion included hip-hop looks but more often a combination of styles from the 1960s and inspirations from female rock performers. Grunge, an alternative youth music and fashion style of the 1990s, borrowed the casual look of work dress along with a revived trend for secondhand clothing.

TECHNOLOGY AND COMFORT

Technological advances in textiles did not necessarily create a demand for casual clothing, but fiber and fabric advances certainly affected style and comfort and added to an overall sense of relaxation and even perhaps to more relaxed posture. Clothing deemed casual in the earliest decades of the twentieth century would seem confining to a contemporary body accustomed to spandex and other high-performance fabrics. At the beginning of the twentieth century, flexible knitted textiles provided comfort and a more casual appearance. But advances in synthetic fiber technologies not only imparted comfort, flexibility, and easy care; they allowed for more body-conscious clothing as well.

The wonder fiber of the 1930s that changed style and silhouette for both men's and women's undergarments and bathing suits

U.S. actor Lex Barker in a Lacoste shirt, 1960. The polo-style shirt with collar can be credited to tennis player René Lacoste, who developed and marketed the original in the 1930s. RDA/Getty Images.

was *lastex*, with a core filament of extruded latex (a synthetic rubber) covered by layers of cotton, rayon, or silk yarns. Lastex was lightweight and washable and created fit and control without sagging and without structured boning in women's garments. The stretch allowed designers to create swimsuits with a sleeker and closer-to-the-body silhouette.

Spandex, introduced by E. I. du Pont de Nemours & Company in 1959, replaced lastex and provided more stretch and comfort and easier care. Spandex became integrated into mainstream fashion by the late 1970s as part of the jogging and fitness craze. By the 1980s, women created a demand for bright-colored spandex exercise clothing, including leotards, tights, and leg warmers worn in a variety of layers. Tracksuits and other active sport clothing cut from stretch fabrics influenced both day and casual evening wear for men and women.

Technology influenced casual dress in an indirect way in the late 1980s and throughout the 1990s. The rise of a computer culture, with mostly young, male "techies," created a revolution in office dress because they preferred casual dressing (jeans, chinos, and T-shirts) over the traditional suit and tie. Beginning with high-tech firms in Silicon Valley, companies around the country offered dress-down Fridays as a perquisite for employees. The casual dress code soon expanded to other days and then was succeeded by everyday business or corporate casual attire. This arrangement of apparel separates has no precise definition, but it is a middle ground between traditional office attire of a suit for women or suit and tie for men and streetwear. As on most occasions, women retained more leeway than men. In 1998, 60 percent of U.S. companies allowed some degree of casual dress.

ICONS OF LEISURE DRESS

Casual dress is not only about a particular style but also about how it is worn, whether with a rolled-up sleeve, untucked shirt, or loafers worn without socks. Casual dress in the early twenty-first century encompasses a wide range of styles and frequently is an outlet for personal expression. Certain garments, however, evolved to be considered classics of leisure-time attire despite periodic variations in silhouette, fabrics, and cut. Despite its name, however, the *leisure suit* cannot be considered a classic of casual dressing. A relatively short-lived fashion for men in the 1970s and more akin to the Western jacket in style, it was designed as a more casual alternative to the traditional two- or three-button suit.

The gradual acceptance of slacks is perhaps the most significant style change for women over the course of the century, and pants of all types are now classic casual attire. Adoption occurred gradually, and until the 1920s, the cut of casual clothing tended to more or less follow the cut of more formal attire, although there were exceptions. By the late 1920s, a relaxed pajama style with full legs became popular for casual and at-home wear. In the 1930s, the more avant-garde Hollywood actresses inspired some gradual acceptance of women in trousers for activities other than active sport. But it was the rapid entry of women into the workplace in the 1970s that brought the question of trouser wearing for professionals to the forefront. That it continued to be debated is a telling sign of the controversy of this casual attire for women. While trousers, shorts, and other bifurcated garments can now be worn for anything from casual to semicasual to formal occasions, pants are still frequently viewed as more casual than skirts.

Jeans and a T-shirt are to contemporary leisure style what the shirtwaist was for women in the early 1900s—almost a uniform of dress despite infinite silhouette and detail variations. Both have undergone dramatic transformations from working-class apparel to acceptable dress for almost all occasions. The jeans and T-shirt combination came into its own in the 1960s with the baby boom generation, although it was still not acceptable for work or other professional circumstances. By the late 1970s, however, various young ready-to-wear designers appropriated jeans style, and the transition to acceptable fashion garment for all but the most formal occasion began. Soon, jeans were worn with blazers to transform them into acceptable work attire. In what has been described as a postmodern approach to fashion, the intermixing of individual pieces can transform casual clothing into acceptable attire for anywhere. Designers even borrowed the basic T-shirt and morphed it into countless variations, including long and sequined versions for evening wear.

Chinos or khakis, casual pants made of cotton or cotton-blend twill, began to cross over from a military staple into civilian wardrobes in the 1950s. By the 1990s they were, with jeans, a casual dressing staple for both men and women. Described by one apparel producer as the perfect bridge between casual weekend and business wear, they became the pants of choice, over jeans, for many middle-aged men and women. Even the New York Stock Exchange declared a casual dress day in 1997, with thirty-five hundred traders in khaki pants. *Cargo pants*, baggier than regular khakis, were originally designed for outdoor activities, with large, sometimes pleated pockets, belt loops, and heavy-duty top-stitching. Youth and teens initially adopted cargos almost as a uniform in the 1990s and into the twenty-first century. Some even had zippers around the leg that allowed a transformation from long pants to shorts.

One of the most ubiquitous casual shirt styles, the *polo shirt* with collar, can be credited to tennis player René Lacoste in the 1930s, who developed and marketed the original, with the alligator logo. Paired with any of the casual pants styles for men or women, it has become a preferred shirt for casual business attire.

References and Further Reading

Grossbard, Judy, and Robert S. Merkel. " 'Modern' Wheels Liberated 'The Ladies' 100 Years Ago." *Dress* 16 (1990): 70–80.

Lee-Potter, Charlie. *Sportswear in Vogue since 1910.* New York: Abbeville Press, 1984.

Martin, Richard. *All-American: A Sportswear Tradition.* New York: Fashion Institute of Technology, 1985.

Martin, Richard. *American Ingenuity: Sportswear 1930s–1970s.* New York: The Metropolitan Museum of Art, 1998.

Routh, Carol. *In Style: 100 Years of Canadian Women's Fashion.* Toronto: Stoddart Publishing, 1993.

Warner, Patricia Campbell. *When the Girls Came Out to Play.* Amherst and Boston: University of Massachusetts Press, 2006.

Wass, Ann Buermann, and Clarita Anderson. "What Did Women Wear to Run." *Dress* 17 (1990): 169–184.

Jean L. Parsons

See also Conventional Work Dress and Casual Work Dress; Dress for Recreational Sports and Professional Sports.

In most environments on Earth, clothing provides needed protection from the elements and from other hazards, both inanimate and animate. Yet, over the past two centuries, dress has been vilified as a source of disease and death or lauded as a device for improving health and physical vigor. Writers have often directed their prescriptions and proscriptions toward women's dress, but they also critiqued men's and children's apparel. This article deals first with problems and solutions connected to microbes and dermatological hazards, followed by consideration of mechanical risks and remedies, especially those related to the confinement of the body by undergarments and footwear.

MICROBES

Enlightened physicians of the late 1870s and early 1880s embraced the *germ theory*—the idea that minute organisms caused diseases—and rejected the so-called *zymotic theory*, which suggested that diseases such as typhoid, diphtheria, and malaria arose from foul-smelling air and general filth. Gradual acceptance of germ theory influenced many patterns of living, including dress. Skirts that trailed along the dirty streets stood condemned for bringing dangerous germs into the household. To remedy this, some daytime skirts of the 1890s shortened just enough to clear the pavement. Through the 1900s and 1910s, skirts inched upward and became narrower, culminating in the knee-level skirts of the mid-1920s.

Men did not escape hygienic censure, either. Physicians commonly wore street clothing to perform surgery and went from patient to patient without washing their hands. Beards marked the mature professional or businessman. As the acceptance of germ theory widened, white (and later green) surgical gowns and beard bags came into use. By the early twentieth century, the "unhygienic" beards themselves disappeared, first among physicians and anti-tuberculosis crusaders and then among educated young men in general. Assiduous hand-washing reduced the spread of germs between patients. Within the broader population, disposable tissues eliminated the germ-bearing potential of cloth handkerchiefs.

WOMEN'S SANITARY PRODUCTS

One special case of hygienic reform involved the development and marketing of women's sanitary products, both as components to

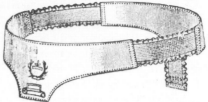

Early advertisement for commercial sanitary pad (towel) and supporting belt, from *Peter Van Schaack & Sons Annual Price Current*, 1889. Courtesy of Dr Jane Farrell Beck.

assemble at home and as fully manufactured disposable pads and later, tampons. Until the late 1880s, women routinely wore woven-cloth diapers or crocheted or knitted pads to catch menstrual fluid; these were washed and reused, creating a disagreeable laundry task and potential source of infection. Tampons were known but only for internal application of medicines by a physician.

U.S. patenting of menstrual hygiene devices began with the 1854 suspensory belt of Alfred A. Starr, followed over the ensuing century by various patented suspenders and belts. Hiram Farr invented a pad-and-belt combination in 1884, but a more practical breakthrough came with Horn & Company's 1887 marketing of disposable "antiseptic and absorbent pads," carried primarily by drugstores. Lady agents sold various brands of pads and belts door-to-door, and very timid or embarrassed customers could order from Montgomery Ward's catalog by the mid-1890s. By 1917, three years before hugely successful Kotex pads went on the market, both sanitary napkins and the cotton batting and cheese-cloth to make napkins had become staple commercial articles in department stores.

U.S. women gradually accepted disposable products, encouraged, perhaps, by improved knowledge among physicians and nurses about antiseptic management of childbirth and postnatal care. These reforms helped reduce the alarming levels of maternal deaths from sepsis in the United States. Disposable pads that nurses used to absorb *lochia* (postpartum discharge) may well have introduced many women to the convenience and hygienic advantages of pads that could be discarded, usually by burning. Popular home health manuals also preached the virtues of disposables for maintaining perineal cleanliness.

The design of sanitary pads and supporters showed marked influence from apparel styles, including both underwear and outerwear. Bulky pads and supporters easily hid beneath the full skirts of the 1850s and 1860s and the protuberant bustles generally in fashion from 1870 to the late 1880s. Slimmer styles of skirts with smooth backs appeared first in 1889 and continued into the early 1900s; these modes pushed pad and belt makers

to devise more compact products. Also influential was the emergence in the 1890s of closed-crotch drawers, which gained wider acceptance in the early 1900s. When drawers consisted of separate legs sewn to a waistband, bulky pads were relatively easy to change, but closed drawers called for trim pads and belts. Slimmer dresses, many in light colors, stimulated the production and marketing of moisture-resistant undergarments, including pants for holding a pad and various types of washable, rubberized back aprons to prevent leakage onto the outer garments.

In addition to their discreet name and clever advertising, Kotex pads featured a relatively trim shape, which was necessary for use with sheer 1920s dresses. More pronounced clinginess took hold in fashion, beginning with 1929's hip-hugging styles and continuing throughout the 1930s. Even tapered pads could not hide under these dresses, prompting the patenting and sale of menstrual tampons in 1935 by Wix, followed in 1936 by Tampax.

DERMATOLOGICAL PROBLEMS

Allergens (substances that induce an allergic reaction) and *pathogens* (disease-causing microorganisms) can cause skin problems. General acceptance of what historian Nancy Tomes has called "The Gospel of Germs" failed to convince most of the U.S. population that dangerous illnesses did not arise from the chilling of the body. Indeed, the idea of "catching a cold" persists in the twenty-first century. Warmth in clothing so dominated nineteenth- and early-twentieth-century ideas of hygiene that multiple layers of apparel and woolen underwear were considered de rigueur, even in mild weather. Lacking scientific weather forecasting or a radio or television broadcasting the day's weather, many North Americans chose to dress for a drop in temperatures, however unlikely. Wool in both under- and outerwear supposedly maintained the body's temperature and drew noxious discharges away from the skin. Wool could absorb water or perspiration without feeling clammy, another assumed advantage to justify swimsuits being made of woven or knitted wool well into the twentieth century. Advocates of cotton in underclothing, emphasizing its superior washability compared to wool, waged an uphill struggle and only began to succeed in the early 1900s, when a general lightening up of dress gained acceptance.

One argument on the side of cotton advocates was that rashes from scratchy wool afflicted babies and some adults and was only partially remedied by *plating* (spinning the wool with a silk outer layer), a process that made the fortune of Minneapolis underwear manufacturer George Munsing. Dermatologists, whose specialty was just beginning to organize in the late 1800s, described a range of skin eruptions provoked by wearing wool. Flannel underwear, chest protectors, and stockings were blamed for inflammations such as eczema (surface dermatitis), *dermatitis* (inflammation of the skin), or *tinea versicolor* (a fungal skin infection causing discolored patches) and a maddening itch called *pruritus* (intense itchiness caused by allergy, infection, or other diseases). Physicians prescribed more frequent laundering of underwear or the substitution of linen or other undyed undergarments to remove the possibility of a reaction to dyestuff.

Aniline- or arsenic-based dyestuffs appeared often as the culprits in dermatology textbooks and articles. Red, magenta, and black had especially bad reputations. Further experimentation convinced a few dermatologists that arsenical *mordants* (dye fixatives) were the true causes of skin rashes. However, the most

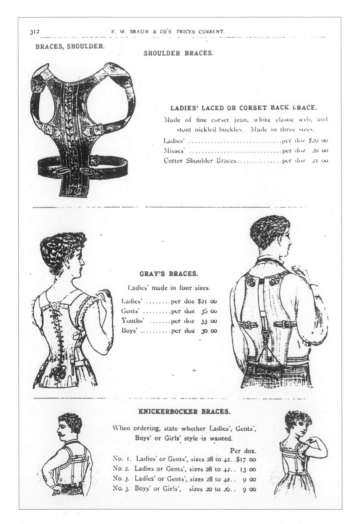

Commercial, over-the-counter back or shoulder braces. *F. W. Brown & Co. General Prices Current*, 1903. Courtesy of Dr Jane Farrell Beck.

prominent controversy of the late nineteenth and early twentieth centuries centered on a natural black dye, logwood, mordanted with metallic salts in the production of *crape* (stiff, crinkled black silk worn during deep mourning).

Doctors regularly denounced this stiff, crimped fabric that convention prescribed for widows into the early 1900s. Anyone of respectable social standing had to adopt English crape, famously made by Courtaulds, for a period of months or years after the death of a family member. Medical critics charged crape with causing skin rashes, nasal allergies, and damage to the eyes. Social reformers railed against the emotional damage of wearing crape. Beginning in the 1890s, opinion slowly evolved away from prolonged public expression of grief to a more private way of honoring the dead. With this, the depth and length of mourning diminished, and crape was replaced with sheer black veils and dresses, put aside much more quickly than in the nineteenth-century heyday of mourning rituals.

Other canons of gentility and modesty also became more flexible during the transition from the late 1800s to the early 1900s, prompting a reduction in the bulk and weight of clothing for women, men, and children. Adults' dresses or suits narrowed and shortened; even men's trousers skimmed the ankles. Stiff shirt collars yielded to soft ones; stiff corsets, to elastic styles. The latter trend benefited from the effort to conserve metal for armaments during World War I. Supposedly 8,000 U.S. tons (7,257.5 metric tons) of steel were saved annually by curbing the use of metal boning. Babies continued to be swathed in long dresses and petticoats, flannel belly bands, and blankets, only gaining relief when they began to toddle. In fact, preschool and school-aged children wore less burdensome clothes than either infants or adults.

CORSETS

Corseting loomed as a major bugbear of many physicians, health reformers, and women's rights advocates. In fact, just as the fires of social reform began to ignite in the United States in the 1830s, corseting evolved to a form designed to provoke censure. After rising and relatively loose waistlines from the 1790s to the 1820s, waistlines descended and narrowed. This silhouette could be achieved only by confining the torso in an hourglass corset. For fifty years, until about 1880, the style of corset changed very little. From then until about 1910, the corset gradually lengthened, became even tighter and, starting in the late 1890s, assumed a straight front that distorted posture.

Not only adult women but also adolescent girls and even children wore some form of stay or corset in order to mold the torso into a narrow waistline with full breast and hips. In the 1800s, soldiers employed corsets under tight dress uniforms. Fashion exerted its pressure on women and girls, physically and psychologically, but so did social expectations for reserved demeanor and the avoidance of physical or moral "looseness." The aesthetic opinions of many North Americans favored (and still favor) a trim waistline. Even the so-called health corsets designed and promoted by doctors and other reformers forced a front-tilting posture that produced an array of physical symptoms. Recent scholars have questioned the prevalence of tight lacing, but even if these were laced loosely with a gap in the back, corsets produced negative effects. Physicians decried the prevalence of digestive disorders such as *dyspepsia* (indigestion or impaired digestion) and *chlorosis* (an iron deficiency in young women often associated

Young woman in mourning attire, including crape, Astoria, Oregon, mid-1880s. The material used (crape) was denounced by the medical profession for causing a number of maladies. Courtesy of Elizabeth Callan-Noble.

with insufficient food, and a forerunner of anorexia nervosa); reproductive ailments such as falling (*prolapse*) of the uterus, which slipped out of the body cavity in the worst cases; spinal curvature and loss of muscle tone; and lung impairment. Colleen Gau's experiments in the late 1990s confirmed a decrease in lung capacity of corset-wearing living-history reenactors. These volunteers also experienced diminished appetite, muscle tone, and ease of movement.

Physicians of the late 1800s and early 1900s rarely censured corsets per se, because these were so much a part of the style and mores of the era. Also, most doctors had less social prominence or professional authority in that era than they have today, and they rarely communicated with the general public, so their criticisms did not have widespread impact.

Some of the orthopedists who dealt with scoliosis, or lateral curvature of the spine, actually used corsets of their own design to improve their patients' posture. Physicians who attributed scoliosis to weakness of the bones favored corsets, while their colleagues who believed muscular weakness was the culprit pre-scribed exercise as the primary therapy. Scoliosis corsets varied from heavy, abrasive plaster-of-Paris instruments of torture to reinforced-cloth styles that could harmonize with wearing fashionable clothing. Other types of supporters resembled a leg brace more than a corset. Some corsets were used postoperatively. Drugstores sold nonprescription braces over the counter into the mid-1910s, but after that period, sturdy styles of brassieres supplanted the braces, with claims to support the back more comfortably and fashionably. Looser styles of clothing popular in the 1920s helped to mask mild cases of scoliosis, decreasing the urge to use heroic correctives.

Ultimately, it was not dress reform or health reform that shifted women away from corset wearing but changing activities—athletic, educational, occupational, and recreational—that prompted changes in external fashions and made the corset less necessary. Small-waisted silhouettes yielded gradually, between 1908 and the 1920s, to a loosened waistline, which was initially placed above the anatomical waist, lowering in the 1920s to hip level. The slim-hipped style prevailed between the late 1910s and the 1930s, with a gradual return of the waist definition after 1930. Overall slenderness was prized, to be achieved by diet and exercise or more dubious methods based on massage or sweating. Women's clothing hung from the shoulders in a manner long advocated by dress reformers. New shape-making undergarments arose from these fashion changes and from technological advances, notably brassieres and flexible girdles.

BRASSIERES AND GIRDLES

When Luman L. Chapman, a Camden, New Jersey, corset maker, patented a breast supporter in 1863, he intended it to provide shoulder bracing and to relieve friction on the breasts. To this end he used "breast puffs," a rudimentary form of cups. In 1870s Boston, a center of dress reform, modiste Olivia Flynt designed and produced hygienic underwear, including "bust supporters," for mail order sale. The goal of the inventors was to support the breasts, the hosiery, and other undergarments without compressing the waist. By the 1890s, a variety of mail order companies were producing "short stays" or "bust girdles" to harmonize with the raised waistlines of empire dresses. These dress styles offered an alternative to the usual hourglass shape, appealing to pregnant women and apparel aesthetes.

None of the early breast supporters enjoyed the popularity of the "brassiere," as the garment was christened in 1904. Several companies mass-produced brassieres in standard sizes for sale in department stores and specialty shops. Early brassieres began as slightly reinforced *corset covers* (a thin undergarment like a camisole, worn over the corset) to wear with a short hip confiner, harmonizing with the fashionable dress silhouette. In 1906, the smooth-lined princess silhouette replaced blousy styles of dress, increasing the demand for the brassiere because it smoothed the roll of flesh that ordinarily swelled over the top of a corset.

Gradually, brassieres shortened and evolved from covered shoulders to narrow straps, a style called the *bandeau* (narrow brassiere with narrow straps), similar to present-day bras. Contouring was minimal, particularly between the late 1910s and early 1924. Women ready for a more curvaceous dress style, and perhaps dismayed by the breakdown of breast tissue from binding brassieres, expressed interest in a true uplift garment. Beginning

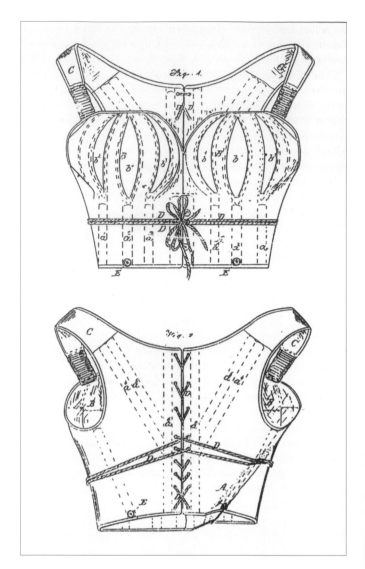

Patent illustration of the first U.S. breast supporter, designed by Luman L. Chapman, 15 December 1863. Courtesy of Dr Jane Farrell Beck.

in 1923, several patentees devised curvy designs, subsequently manufactured by Maiden Form (sic), Model, G. M. Poix, and other companies. Gabrielle Poix's front-fastening brassiere drew an enthusiastic response from nurses for its accommodation of nursing mothers.

Nurses' involvement in the problems of breast care increased with more accurate understanding of breast structure and function, plus improved nursing education fostered by Canadian and U.S. nurse leaders. Aseptic care of the lactating breasts called for elaborate washing and lubrication. The mother's comfort and health required breast support in the form of contoured binders and brassieres. Because a bandage-like binder required assistance to put on, supportive brassieres became a practical option when a new mother went home with her flannelly bundle of joy.

Other health-related brassieres were the postsurgical and therapeutic styles produced by S. H. Camp & Company and Leading Lady. In 1922, Canadian nurse Laura E. Mailleue won the first U.S. patent for *mastectomy* (surgical removal of all or part of a breast) pads. Breast surgery had been known even before the twentieth century, but it became more common in the 1920s.

Brassiere departments participated in educating women about breast self-examination starting about 1952, in an effort to catch cancer while it was treatable.

The outbreak of World War II brought thousands of women into armaments plants, where bras were employed for health and safety. (*Bra* became the usual name about 1934.) No-nonsense cotton bras and reinforced girdles did duty in postural support. Situations calling for more serious protection of the breasts required plastic or molded-fiber, vulcanized breast protectors, which were shaped like and worn over the regular bra.

Athletic bras debuted in 1904, when Laura Lyon patented a cloth style that had similar dimensions to a present-day sports bra but lacked the high technology of support. Improvements followed sporadically in the 1920s through 1940s, but more serious efforts came to fruition in the 1950s, with hookless pullover bras. Improved synthetic elastics, including lastex (1931) and spandex (1959), made it easier to fashion bras that "gave" with the movements of the wearer, including the popular Sarong bras by Canadian Corset Company. However, a fully fledged jogger's bra did not become available until 1979. Many efforts have been made over the ensuing decades to reduce painful, harmful "bounce" while facilitating competitive sports and fitness routines.

Experimentation with rubber and its substitutes contributed to other changes in women's *foundation garments* (corset, girdle, or corselet, the latter with an integral bra). During the mid-1910s, para rubber replaced unyielding cloth in fashioning the girdle, a welcome substitute for the corset. Fewer bones or laces and more elasticity made girdles popular with young and relatively slim women and also pleased the anticorset campaigners. However, for the less-than-slim, rubber "reducing" girdles were sold from the early 1900s to about 1930. Loose styles of dress gave many women the impetus to abandon corsets and girdles between about 1919 and 1924. When brassieres gained contour in late 1924, increasingly shapely dresses also revived the popularity of garter belts and light girdles. Two-way stretch girdles of the new lastex fiber saved many manufacturers and retailers from disaster during the 1930s Depression. A scissors-shaped silhouette for women, with full breast and narrow hips and thighs, made girdles ever more popular in the late 1930s. Women who wore slacks usually felt a need for a panty girdle, which was first manufactured about 1934 and gained popularity through the 1940s and 1950s. Nylon (1940–1942; after 1945) and spandex (in the late 1950s) made girdles lightweight. Even in the supposedly ungirdled 1960s, various styles of high-waist, short-hipped girdles and panty girdles offered smooth lines under fitted styles of dresses and pants.

Although girdles generally exerted less harmful pressure than corsets, physicians and health advocates warned about wearing sizes that were too small or so tight in the legs that they restricted circulation. Corselets, all-in-one bra-and-girdle combinations, sold from the 1920s through the 1950s posed special hazards to the breasts by pulling them down. This problem, decried by doctors, diminished when the bra top of the corselet became more of an uplift during the 1930s.

MATERNITY CLOTHES

Pregnancy made the healthful use of foundation garments even more difficult. During the late 1700s and early 1800s, high-waisted dress styles had provided a comfortable space for the expanding uterus. The problem arose when dress waistlines descended and became snug in the 1830s. Alternative garments, such as loose wrappers, short *matinees* (a woman's short smock of thin material, intended for indoor use), and *tea gowns* (long gowns, often of fragile material, for wear at home), served some women well, but these styles were unacceptable in public. Surviving dresses from the mid-1800s reveal remodeling to permit advancing pregnancy. Some had the front waistline released from tight gathers or pleats and run onto a drawstring, for letting out as needed through the months of gestation. In the 1820s through 1850s, practitioners of the alternative "water cure" medical movement instructed pregnant women to wear an uncorseted ensemble of trousers plus a short, loose-fitting overgarment. In addition to making the woman more comfortable, the outfit would mask her condition, although it would not shield the wearer from ridicule of her nontraditional garb.

In the late 1800s, the utility day gown called a *Mother Hubbard* accommodated pregnancy. Loose jackets over conventional-looking skirts helped to conceal a woman's swelling abdomen when she went out in public. Women's periodicals published patterns for maternity dresses and wraps, at first euphemistically labeling gravidity a "delicate condition" but by the later 1890s openly declaring maternity wear. The early 1900s brought the first factory-made maternity garments, such as the Fine-Form Maternity Skirt (1908) and Lane Bryant's negligees and dresses for childbearing women (starting in 1911). Easy-fitting styles of the later 1910s and 1920s proved kind to the pregnant figure. By 1930, a prominent nurse educator recommended clothes that would allow a mother-in-waiting to enjoy sports and a normal social life, for both mental and physical health.

Of much greater concern than maternity outerwear was corseting, because cramping the uterus was believed to produce deformities and even to precipitate miscarriage. Inventors responded to the problem with a variety of styles of maternity "bandages," supporters, or *trusses* (a belt, sometimes with a pad, for support in cases of rupture or hernia) patented between the early 1860s and the early 1900s. A few provided a slinglike support to the abdomen and were marketed for corpulence as well as pregnancy.

FOOTWEAR

Jeremiads about corsets and girdles abounded in the professional and popular literature of the 1800s through mid-1900s. Curiously, another serious problem of confinement drew only sparse comment: ill-fitting and physically hampering shoes. These afflicted women through much of the nineteenth century and, with short respites, most of the twentieth. Between 1900 and about 1920, men wore sharp-toed shoes that pushed the bones of their feet out of alignment and raised corns and calluses. Even some military sketches delineated boots with pointed toes.

At the heart of the problem lay a collective blindness to the real proportion of the foot to the rest of the body. As Vickie Lynn Dirksen has observed, there was not much difference in the depiction of a North American woman's foot versus that of a Han Chinese woman with bound feet. The shape and proportions were disturbingly similar. Human faces, hands, and feet are comparable in dimensions, but feet and hands were routinely shown half that of normal size in fashion illustrations from the early 1800s through the 1930s. As photography supplanted sketching as the main vehicle for reporting fashion, the scope for distortion decreased and sketches became slightly more realistic.

U.S. fashion illustration showing abnormally small feet. May Manton, "Practical New Patterns," *The Ladies World*, April 1916. Reproduced with permission of the University Archives, Iowa State University, Ames, Iowa.

Physicians gave relatively little attention to women's feet, partly from an exaggerated idea of modesty about feminine limbs. However, beginning about 1870, medical articles began to reveal foot problems, such as corns, calluses, and exacerbated *bunions* (abnormal enlargement of the joint at the base of the large toe). Poor fit and design of shoes impeded walking and discouraged exercise, resulting in harm to the whole body. Blood circulation slowed, and swelling of the feet and legs ensued. High heels threw the body out of alignment and precipitated back problems.

Medical specializations of the late 1800s included *chiropody*, the forerunner of podiatry, whose practitioners took a new interest in the health of the feet. There was much for chiropodists to lament. Heels had been almost flat on women's shoes from the 1800s through the 1850s, and low heels typified 1860s footwear. During the 1870s, heels rose and have never flattened since. In addition to high heels, pointed toes and overly small sizes put stress on the feet. The nineteenth-century practice of making shoes internally symmetrical for wear on either foot spelled discomfort and ignored the inherent asymmetry of a normal foot. In vain doctors explained that a pretty shoe would generally create an ugly foot. Feet were usually covered, at least by hosiery, even at the beach. Finally, the acceptance of bare-legged swimming and sunbathing in the 1920s revealed damaged feet.

Yet practical footwear sold to few patrons, except for the athletic shoes that were beginning to be promoted at the start of the twentieth century. Men's foot problems became a public issue in the mid-1910s, with the recruitment of soldiers for service in World War I. By the 1920s, men's shoes generally exhibited wider toes and realistic proportions, except for some formal styles. Men, women, and children got an alarming (and dangerous) view of the bones of their feet with the X-ray machines commonly used in shoe stores during the 1920s. Doctors were also more attentive to examination of the feet and did not hesitate to prescribe corrective appliances, sometimes to their own financial benefit.

Unlike the corset and tight girdle, which have faded from fashion, damaging styles of shoes are still much in evidence. True, many people in the United States and Canada spend their youth and adult leisure hours in athletic shoes, and low heels are available.

However, dressy occasions and some business settings still encourage women to wear high, narrow heels and pointy toes. Heels make the foot look shorter and the woman taller, so their appeal persists. The war between fashion and physical health rages on.

References and Further Reading

Dirksen, Vickie Lynn. "Health Problems Associated with Women's Fashionable Shoes, 1870–1930." Master's thesis, Iowa State University, 1998.

Donegan, Jane B. *"Hydropathic Highway to Health": Women and Water-Cure in Antebellum America.* Westport, CT: Greenwood Press, 1986.

Farrell-Beck, Jane. "Medical and Commercial Supports for Scoliotic Patients, 1819–1935." *Caduceus* 9 (Winter 1995): 142–163.

Farrell-Beck, Jane, and Elizabeth Callan Noble. "Textiles and Apparel in the Etiology of Skin Diseases, 1870–1914." *International Journal of Dermatology* 37 (1998): 309–314.

Farrell-Beck, Jane, and Colleen Gau. *Uplift: The Bra in America.* Philadelphia: University of Pennsylvania Press, 2002.

Farrell-Beck, Jane, and Laura Klosterman Kidd. "The Role of Health Professionals in the Development and Dissemination of Women's Sanitary Products, 1880–1940." *Journal of the History of Medicine and Allied Sciences* 51, no. 3 (July 1996): 325–352.

Gau, Colleen R. "Historic Medical Perspectives of Corseting and Two Physiologic Studies with Reenactors." Ph.D. dissertation, Iowa State University, 1998.

Kidd, Laura K., and Jane Farrell-Beck. "Menstrual Products Patented in the United States, 1854–1921." *Dress* 24 (1997): 27–42.

Moon, Cassandra Curry. "Selecting and Adapting Clothing for Pregnancy in the Nineteenth Century." Master's thesis, Iowa State University, 1995.

Tomes, Nancy. *The Gospel of Germs: Men, Women and the Microbe in American Life.* Cambridge, MA: Harvard University Press, 1998.

Jane Farrell-Beck

See also Dress Reform.

Care of Dress

Until the twentieth century, the care of clothing generally meant unrelieved drudgery—arduous, backbreaking, and undertaken by females. Traditionally, outer clothing was protected from the body, even as the body was protected from the outer clothing, by linen shifts, shirts, petticoats, and sometimes drawers. For most people, these items were washed only when absolutely necessary, perhaps once every three or four months, by using the age-old ritual of soaking the items, often in a nearby stream or pond; scrubbing; beating; wringing; and finally draping them on grass to dry in the sun. As for the rest of the clothes, until the age of cotton, which began in the late eighteenth century, most simply were never washed at all. Eventually, as the population moved into urban centers, heated water replaced the once nearby streams for soaking. Wash day then took on a different, albeit equally arduous, ritual—one of toting water, filling tubs, scrubbing clothes, changing water, wringing garments, and hanging them out to dry. Soap was a luxury, expensive and rare—indeed, in England it carried a luxury tax until the mid-nineteenth century—so many housewives had recipes, often based on the traditional lye, for making their own well into the late nineteenth century.

Cleanliness had become a mark of status by the eighteenth century. Laundry, then, became more and more important, if still avoided as much as possible. The Industrial Revolution, begun at the end of the eighteenth century, inaugurated the age of cotton and ensured both its wide production and its desirability. One advantage of the popular, newly available fabric was its ease of laundering. Even so, as late as the first decades of the nineteenth century, only the very rich had enough clothing and household linens to put off doing the wash for more than a single week. For all others, the laundry became a weekly chore. It was regarded as the worst burden of women's lives, variously described as "the Herculean task which women all dread" or "the weekly affliction." In this period, when the relatively new custom of a weekly wash had become a necessary part of keeping house, its backbreaking steps were both inevitable and carefully outlined by household advice authorities. Its methods changed little throughout the entire century, even with the introduction of scrubbing boards and dollies, available as early as the late eighteenth century, and primitive washing machines by the 1850s. In the end, even with the tools dedicated to the task, doing the family wash depended more on brawn than orderly household management. Indeed, not until the 1910s, with the introduction of soap products and new electrified laundry machines, was there much relief.

The eighteenth century had seen the introduction of handheld tools to work the heavy wash load. The dolly was one: a simple wooden contraption that looked very much like a four-legged milkmaid's stool with a wooden extension rising up from one of the legs, cross-barred to make a handle to raise and lower the entire thing into and out of the soapy water to agitate the clothes. It was, at best, heavy. Another was a primitive washboard, first made entirely out of wood, but later, in the nineteenth century, improved with a galvanized-metal corrugated scrubbing surface and finally with a textured glass surface embedded in the wood frame. These last two are still available in the twenty-first century. An early washing machine, patented in 1837, consisted of a set of rollers in a tub that were hand turned by an attached handle in order to squeeze the water out of the wet clothes. It becomes immediately evident that all of these, though invented to aid the laundry process, required strength, muscle, and determination to achieve the desired results. In North America, women hired immigrant workers, often the Irish who were desperate for work, to help with the wash, hence the stereotype of the brawny, crude Irish washerwoman. However untutored she may have been, she was a necessity. Later, another stereotype, the Chinese laundry, became a fixture in many cities across North America. This, too, was grounded in reality—the Chinese established themselves and their good laundries to do the work the resident populations refused to do themselves.

THE PROCESS OF THE WEEKLY WASH IN THE NINETEENTH CENTURY

It is very difficult to find specific information on laundering prior to the nineteenth century, but undoubtedly the best source for understanding what doing the weekly wash actually looked like during the nineteenth century is Catharine Beecher's *Treatise on Domestic Economy*, published in 1841. Beecher was the ultimate authority on domesticity of her time. So valuable was this book, which outlined every imaginable household task that young women needed to master to become capable housewives, that it remained a best seller throughout the rest of the nineteenth century. In it, she devoted three chapters to doing the laundry. Only with her meticulous guideline are we able to see what the chore entailed and why it was so hated.

To summarize, Beecher stipulated Monday as wash day and Tuesday for ironing. This ritual was probably time honored, but it continued throughout much of the twentieth century, until women entered the workplace in large numbers after the 1970s, happily depending on their automatic washing machines, dryers, and detergents not only to do their work for them but also to do it at the time the owner chose. Beecher tells us that in her day, "it is a common complaint in all parts of the Country that good washers are very rare"—referring, of course, to the people who did the washing, rather than to the machines. She expressed her dismay that "nice articles" were put into the wash, only to have them "returned yellow, streaked and spotted." To solve these problems, she set out to teach the housewife to maintain an eagle eye and a tight control over the work of her washerwoman.

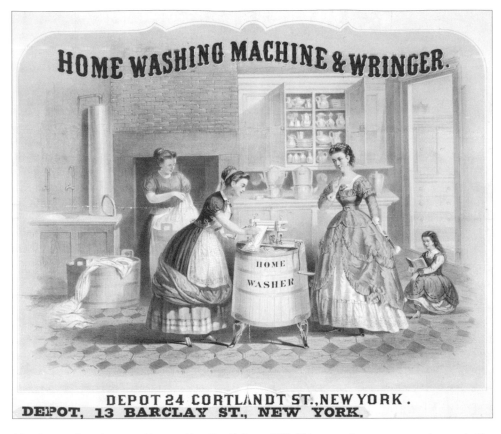

Advertisement for a home washing machine, New York, ca. 1869. This scene shows a woman using a primitive washing machine as her employer looks on. Library of Congress Prints and Photographs Division, LC-USZC4-4590.

Any good housewife needed, first of all, a good water supply, preferably soft water, to fill the wash tubs. The water, of course, some fifty gallons (189 liters), or four hundred pounds (181 kilograms), per wash, would have to be toted by hand from the source. Then she needed four tubs, two for suds and the other two for bluing water and for starch. They were all large and heavy, each weighing some forty to fifty pounds (18 to 22 kilograms) dry, and all needed to be moved into place. Beecher then mandated several pails for soaking and for moving water, a large wooden dipper, a grooved washboard, a clothesline, a wash stick and a wooden fork (or perhaps a dolly) to stir the clothes, bags to hold the sorted clothes when they are being washed, a brass or copper kettle for boiling clothes, and various cleansing agents. Six to eight dozen clothes pegs or clothes pins—a relatively new invention in the 1840s, because Beecher describes what they are to her reader—would be needed to hang the clothes to dry.

After the preparation of the equipment, the process of washing begins. Beecher lists the steps: Sort the items by color and coarseness of fabric and soak them overnight in tubs of warm water to "release the grime." Then, in a series of washings the next day, wash the finest first, going through all the steps of soaping, rinsing with water, and then rinsing with other agents to freshen the colors and fabrics; work through, one after another, to the heaviest and dirtiest items, until all the clothes had been washed. Every transference demanded wringing, "hard the last time." The articles that needed stiffening then went into the starch tub. As for the final step, hanging the clean clothes out to dry, Beecher was well aware of the problems of color fading in the days before aniline dyes, and she cautioned her readers to hang the white clothes in the sunshine but to make sure that the dark or colored clothes were in the shade.

Once dry, the clothes were ironed, using flatirons to smooth the cloth. These were heated on the stove and had detachable handles to make rotation of the hot irons easy and enabling the ironer to have a hot iron constantly available. A household would usually have two or three irons heating or in use at the same time in order to speed the chore. The irons, like the wash itself, were heavy.

The principle of heating flat metal in order to smooth cloth goes back to the Chinese in the first century B.C.E., and various adaptations of it have been in use ever since. Several sources of fuel to heat the irons were attempted, but many became fire hazards and were abandoned. A first electric iron was patented in the United States in 1882, and the first iron with a thermostat was patented in 1922. The ironing board was another invention of the mid-nineteenth century, but many women continued to use their kitchen tables, protected by layers of cloth, for the purpose.

COMMERCIAL LAUNDRIES

By later in the nineteenth century, domestic gurus were beginning to lament having to do the laundry at home, individually, suggesting that central town laundries run by professionals made much better sense. Harriet Beecher Stowe, sister of Catharine Beecher (and author of *Uncle Tom's Cabin*), was one of these: in 1868, she wrote that her ideal village would be organized with this concept at its core. "Whoever sets neighborhood laundries on foot will

Wash day in the tenements of New York City, ca. 1905. Library of Congress, Prints & Photographs Division, Detroit Publishing Company Collection, LC-DIG-det-4a18586.

do much to solve the American housekeeper's hardest problem," she wrote. Interestingly, such group laundries had already been established, notably by the Chinese after their mid-century immigration and settling into U.S. life, and even earlier at some of the women's colleges being established. In those cases, students did the work in teams. The idea of a central town laundry finally became a reality by the end of the century when commercial laundries had become fixtures in urban centers.

THE ARROW COLLAR

The problems of doing the laundry even brought about change in the way men dressed in the nineteenth century. The need to keep a crisp, pristine shirt front exacerbated the laundry chore because laundering men's shirts took up a considerable portion of the family wash and, therefore, much time and energy. Around 1820, in answer to this constant headache, a woman in Troy, New York, made a shirt for her husband with a removable collar and shirt front, enabling her to launder each small piece separately without the additional task of washing the entire shirt. A collection of seven separate collars allowed a clean appearance each day of the week. Her creativity sparked an industry that lasted for a century and earned Troy the label "Collar City." Cluett Peabody became the company famous for manufacturing these prestiffened, button-on collars, offering hundreds of different styles to wear with a standard shirt body. When, around 1905, Cluett Peabody began an ad campaign

using the image of an almost impossibly handsome young man to sell these stiff, highly starched collars, by now appearing under their company name, Arrow, the Arrow Collar Man was born. Arrow shirts are still a staple of menswear in the twenty-first century. During World War I, wartime expediency demanded a simpler and cheaper production method for making the shirts of the U.S. Army uniforms. Attaching collars to the body of the shirts solved this problem and, in the process, gave their youthful wearers a taste of comfort they had not known in the past. Not coincidentally, electric washing machines came into wider use after the war. By 1920, doing the laundry had become easier.

THE ELECTRIC WASHING MACHINE

The first electric washing machine was introduced sometime during the first decade of the twentieth century. Although it was a leap forward, taking much of the backbreaking work off the housewife's hands, it presented problems of its own. The electric motor rotated the tub, but water tended to drip onto the motor below, causing shorts and shocks to the user. By the 1920s, with the improvements made on the machines, more and more urban people served by electricity used the new devices. As for people outside the cities, before 1936 and the Rural Electrification Act, only some 10 percent of rural U.S. households had access to electric power. Even so, by 1940, 60 percent of the twenty-five million wired homes in the United States had an electric washing machine, many of which featured a power wringer. These machines, though much better than their predecessors, still required many steps to do the job. As with today's chore, sorting still had to be done prior to the task itself. The machine was placed adjacent to permanent laundry tubs built into the wall of the house, one empty to accept the used water from the machine, the other filled with clear water for rinsing. After the wash cycle was done, the operator of the machine (by this time, the housewife herself—the Irish washerwoman was a thing long past) had to pluck the items from the tub of the washer and feed them into the wringer to fall into the clear rinsewater tub. Once rinsed, the procedure of wringing was reversed before the entire wash could be hung on the line to dry. Clotheslines sometimes were in the backyards of houses, but they were also a fixture of basements everywhere. For those who could not afford the new washing machines, laundromats (self-service laundries) made their first appearance in 1934.

By 1937, the Bendix Corporation had invented the front-load automatic machine, but its production was stalled by World War II. When it finally was presented to the public in 1947, it was marketed to the select few, costing the modern-day equivalent of US$2,500. That same year, General Electric introduced a top-loading machine that, with little modification and technological updates, remains the standard automatic machine in North America today. By the 1950s, in spite of the high costs, manufacturers had a hard time keeping up with the demands for automatic machines, and the wringer washers, though still made, fell more and more into disuse.

Until the 1930s, women had used various soap products but found that soap tended to dim the colors and surfaces of the fabrics being washed and left a residue on their new machines that was difficult to remove. The soap industry, notably Procter & Gamble in the United States, responded by creating synthetic laundry detergents. The first marketed in the United States was Dreft, introduced in the late 1930s. Although it solved some of the problems, it was too gentle for the new machines. In 1943, a newer, tougher detergent that Procter & Gamble called Tide was formulated. Not until after World War II, in 1946, was it offered to the public; it became an instant success. The synthetic detergents washed clothes more thoroughly and prepared the way for the introduction of easy-care clothing that used textiles made of manufactured fibers.

The automatic clothes dryer's lifetime parallels that of the electric washing machine. A rudimentary version appeared in the 1900s and slowly improved over the course of the next fifty years. The dryer as it is known today appeared more or less in tandem with the automatic washing machine, and it has been marketed as part of the laundry pair ever since.

Dry cleaning, so called because it did not require a total wet wash as laundering did and used chemical solvents instead, was discovered in the mid-nineteenth century by a Frenchman who noticed that kerosene removed spots on fabric. It was a valuable tool for cleaning fabrics that could not take soap-and-water cleaning. Various improvements in solvents aided the process, and it remains a staple of today's cleaning methods.

Women at work in a U.S. laundry, ca. 1905. Library of Congress Prints and Photographs Division, LC-DIG-ppmsca-05917.

Electric washing machine, ca. 1950. The electric washing machine was to revolutionize housework, greatly reducing the time and effort needed to wash clothes. Library of Congress Prints and Photographs Division, Office of War Information Photograph Collection, LC-USW4-019833.

MANUFACTURED FIBERS

The last invention to be considered in the care of clothing is manufactured fibers. The earliest successful one, an attempt to imitate silk, was rayon, first called *viscose rayon* when it appeared in 1894. Its commercial manufacture began around 1910. Rayon is a regenerated fiber made from cellulose materials. Nylon was the first successful manufactured synthetic fiber, created from chemicals in 1938 by DuPont and first displayed to the world at the New York World's Fair in 1939. After World War II, other textile products using synthetic polymer bases came on the market. By the 1960s, polyester became the fiber of choice. With its introduction, care of clothes changed radically. Polyester was inexpensive and virtually indestructible, unless it melted from contact with

excessively high temperatures. Because of polyester, clothing then entered the easy-care, throwaway era. Mass production and cheap clothing made from inexpensive cloth changed the patterns of consumerism. Laundry of these new products, with the new machines, became a simple matter of turning on the washer, turning on the dryer, smoothing the garments, and putting them on.

CHANGES IN ATTITUDES TOWARD CLOTHING MAINTENANCE AND CARE

For all of history, before the introduction of manufactured fibers, clothing had been much more expensive and much less plentiful. Its major cost lay in the fabrics that the clothes were made from. As a result, people cherished their clothes, making and remaking them, bringing them up-to-date in style or cutting them down for smaller members of the family. Indeed, few extant dresses from the eighteenth century are in their original condition, having been tweaked, redraped, and recut as the century wore on. Some were saved and turned into nineteenth-century fashions. Nineteenth-century gowns today bear evidence of warm bodies, of middle-aged spread, with let-out seams and waistbands. Good-quality silks and wools, even cottons, were mended as a matter of course, to be worn again and again through the years, even with discrete patches here and there. Alteration and mending were a part of clothing care into the 1960s.

With the twentieth century and its mass manufacturing, these careful, thrifty reuses and recyclings began to fall away, vanishing almost entirely after the advent of polyester and its cousins at the end of the century. Today, it is more likely that a ripped or stained garment, one that no longer fits correctly, or one of which the owner is simply tired, will be thrown away or recycled. Even clothing that has been washed too many times is rejected. So the care of clothing by the twenty-first century has become easy. It is second nature to wear clean clothes, a luxury previous generations could ill afford. But easy care today has taken its toll in the appreciation and value of clothing at the beginning of the twenty-first century.

Snapshot: Wash Day at Mount Holyoke Seminary

Mount Holyoke Seminary (later Mount Holyoke College, founded in 1837) devised a creative system of student-run domestic labor, one that guaranteed the smooth running of the school as cheaply as possible. Mount Holyoke's meticulous organization to solve the problem of the entire school's laundry, for both students and teachers, predated Harriet Beecher Stowe's ideal community-based laundry by more than a generation.

Lucy Goodale, who came to the seminary a year after it opened, tells of the process in letters home to her parents. She gives us a very early and vivid glimpse into the task a number of years before Catharine Beecher's more general and prescriptive commands in the ensuing decade.

The entire school was divided up into groups that Lucy called "Circles." They had a variety of tasks for "extra work," such as

pie baking, table setting, sweeping, dusting, and cleaning, and each group (four in all and representing perhaps half the entire student body) was responsible for the general laundry, including the sheets, towels, and tablecloths. The remaining half of the circles had other domestic chores around the school.

The laundry routine for the seminary wash was as follows: Their leader, usually an experienced student, got her circle up at half past three in the morning, an hour later than the designated girl whose task it was to light the fires under the boilers to heat the water. This first team washed until the rising bell woke the rest of the students, at five o'clock, after which the other three circles each took turns until the entire wash was completed, sometime around eight o'clock. The task of ironing, an hour at a time, was also broken down into the circles and came a few days later.

Mount Holyoke Seminary students, Massachusetts, 1871. A group of students wearing the clothing they had to contend with when they did the laundry for the entire college. Courtesy Mount Holyoke College Archives and Special Collections, South Hadley, Mass.

Lucy mentions that a "washing machine" was available only on Thursdays, but because the rollers that helped to squeeze out extra rinsewater did not appear until the 1850s, perhaps some contraption like W. Hovey's Washing Machine, patented in 1837, helped them out. As for doing their own clothes, another carefully plotted timetable had to be followed, this one beginning at four in the morning. The circles were divided into two groups, and there were two rooms, each with a tub. Each girl had her own pail and could suds her things in that (using soda, Lucy tells us, rather than either expensive soap or harsh lye) before switching to the tubs for the heavier things. Girls would trade off pails for tubs. An alarm rang at five o'clock, warning that they had five minutes to finish up before the next group came in.

As part of their "extra work," some students were assigned to tend to the boilers, to get them refilled and heated for the next group coming in after them; others were to rinse, hang out, bring in, or sort. "Of course," Lucy tells us, some of these tasks "were larger than others"—only two girls were needed to "bring in," while eight or nine were needed for rinsing.

Preparations for the wash required extra planning, extra muscle, and extra time but could buy off the task of actually doing the laundry. Again, Lucy explains in a letter to her parents, datelined "Wed. eve. 9 o'clock": "I have not sat down since five o'clock except at supper. After supper ... I filled three boilers, brought in the wood and tubs, which occupied me an hour and therefore I shall not wash tomorrow morn." Finally, in a later letter, she reveals what the task takes out of her: "This is washing day ... and I have just completed my part of the ... division.... I feel much the same as after washing at home, not much in the mood for accomplishing anything."

This procedure was carried on for decades at the school. Insights and updates as the years go by are gained from other students writing to their families. New girl Melissa Usher wrote in 1852: "We have to furnish basket and pins, soap and bluing. I am not going to practice boiling my clothes, for the old pupils say they look worse than before washing. So many being boiled together and so long." Her reluctance to boil was an issue much debated for the next half century. Many manuals instructed readers to boil their clothes, but Catharine Beecher warned against it, and the students seemed to have learned from experience that it did not help. Another student the next year, in 1853, confessed in her diary, "Today is a day to be remembered in the catalogue of my trials. It was my first washing day. I blistered my fingers, and was so tired that I felt more like going to bed than anything else." Although exhausted, she still had energy enough to editorialize: "I did not boil my clothes, for they say it makes them look very yellow and I am sure mine look bad enough without my help."

Students complained throughout the rest of the century; some even devised tradeoffs to get out of doing the laundry. Eventually, the central laundries of Harriet Beecher Stowe's dreams took over the task.

References and Further Reading

Cowan, Ruth Schwartz. *More Work for Mother*. New York: Basic Books, 1983.

Matthews, Glenna. *Just a Housewife*. Oxford: Oxford University Press, 1987.

The Soap and Detergent Association. *Soaps and Detergents*. 2nd ed. New York: Author, 1994.

Strasser, Susan. *Never Done, a History of American Housework*. New York: Pantheon Books, 1982.

Walkey, Christina, and Vanda Foster. *Crinolines and Crimping Irons: Victorian Clothes. How They Were Cleaned and Cared For*. London: P. Owen, 1978.

Warner, Patricia Campbell. "'Washed Again Today, the Skin Was Gone from My Hands': Early Women's Colleges and the Laundry, 1840–1890." *Dress* 30 (2003): 38–47.

Patricia Campbell Warner

PART 4

North American Indian/ First Nation Peoples

Introduction to the North American Indian and First Nation Peoples

The North American Indians and First Nations people are descended from those living in North America at the time that Europeans began to explore, trade, and establish settlements. The societies established by natives of North America were different not only from those of Western Europe but also from one region of this continent to another. The interaction of the native people and the Europeans had profound effects on many aspects of the lives of both groups, including their dress.

Regrettably, there is no written history of North America before the fifteenth century. What is known about the dress of North American Indians and First Nations people is what has been written and drawn or painted by Europeans or learned from elements of the material culture that have been saved by native people or found by archaeologists and anthropologists. Some North American Indian and First Nations peoples have oral traditions that can amplify what is known about the past, but these have not always been believed and valued by non-Indian people, nor are they always accompanied by a cultural context adequate for complete understanding.

Areas of the current United States and Canada were inhabited by different Indian nations. The encroachment of settlements on the territories of native people often resulted in their mandatory or voluntary removal from the regions they had occupied previously. Sometimes these movements displaced other Indian nations or tribes. How then can a comprehensive picture be provided of the dress of native people?

CULTURE AREAS

While it would be possible to include the dress traditions of North American Indians and First Nations people in a discussion of fashionable dress or as just another among several ethnic groups in the United States and Canada, it is also possible to address them by region. The Smithsonian *Handbook of North American Indians* identifies ten such regions, calling them *culture areas*. These are regions in which tribal groups or nations live in contiguous areas and/or have similar cultures and history. To quote volume 4 of the *Handbook*, this division does "not imply that there are only a few distinct ways of life in the continent. … all neighboring peoples are similar in some ways and dissimilar in others. The lines separating the culture areas represent a compromise among many factors and sometimes reflect arbitrary decisions."

Carl Waldman, archivist and author of books about North American Indians, using a similar organizational plan in the *Atlas of the North American Indian* has noted that the divisions are a convenience. He goes on to remind the reader that the environment of any area has an impact on the way that inhabitants live,

including the development of their dress, and as a result, those who inhabit a particular geographic region are likely to share some cultural traits. Anthropologist June Helm, too, has observed the impact of geography. She writes, "Physiography and resources are paramount in determining the direction and course of intercultural contacts," and she notes that this is the reason the cultural areas identified correspond to major physiographic zones. She also acknowledges that the boundaries set for regions may be disputed, especially where more than one tribe may lay claim to the same area.

Within each region live many different tribal or national groups. For some, relatively little information is available; for others, more research and better records exist. Gathering information about dress is particularly difficult. The materials from which items of dress are made are often perishable and do not survive. Documentation of how and why changes in styles occurred may not exist. For these reasons, the information provided may vary widely from group to group and region to region.

The Smithsonian Institution has chosen to use the following ten regional divisions: the Arctic, the Subarctic, the Northwest Coast, California, the Plateau, the Great Basin, the Southwest, the Plains, the Northeast, and the Southeast.

The northernmost region is the Arctic. This region stretches across the top of the North American continent from Labrador on the east to beyond Cook Inlet on the west. The native people who live in this area are thought to have arrived in North America relatively late, perhaps about 2500 to 1000 B.C.E. The people prefer to be called by the name *Inuit*, because *Eskimo*, the name formerly used, is not an Inuit word and is considered pejorative as it means "raw meat eaters." The people who live in the Aleutian Islands are sometimes known as *Aleuts*.

South of the Arctic region is the Subarctic region. Like the Arctic region, it stretches across North America from the Atlantic to the Pacific, ending in the east at Newfoundland and the Gulf of Saint Lawrence and on the west at Cook Inlet. Its northern limit is bounded by Hudson Bay, and the southern border skirts the northern shore of Lake Superior. With long, harsh winters, most of the native people living in the area were migratory. Linguistic study of the population classifies the languages spoken by most tribes as belonging to one of two broad language groups.

The Northwest culture area is located along the shores of the northern Pacific Ocean and stretches from the Oregon-California border on the south to the Copper River Delta on the Gulf of Alaska, while extending inland to mountain ranges in Alaska (the Chugach and Saint Elias), British Columbia, and the Cascades in the Pacific Northwest of the United States. Fortunate in having plentiful food supplies and a mild climate, the Indians of the Northwest Coast lived in established communities with complex cultures. Many readers will be familiar with the art produced in this region.

The California culture region is situated approximately, though not exactly, in the same position as the state of California. Although it does extend south along the Baja Peninsula into Mexico, the Mexican area is not included in the discussion in this

North American Indian children in cadet uniforms, Carlisle Indian School, Pennsylvania, 1880. Getty Images.

volume. Blessed with a diverse and copious natural food supply, the population was relatively dense, and many different small groups, sometimes called *tribelets*, have been identified.

A small portion of northern California, eastern Washington, northeast and central Oregon, northern Idaho, western Montana, and an area extending into British Columbia are the areas identified as part of the Plateau culture region. An abundance of rivers but a limited supply of undergrowth in dense forests meant the people here had a good supply of fish but few large mammals, because these animals required more vegetation as a food source. As a result, human populations were not so dense as in the Northwest culture region; tribes tended to be nomadic in warm weather and settled into villages during the colder months.

The Great Basin culture region is described as occupying about four hundred thousand square miles (1,036,000 square kilometers) of the area between the Sierra Nevada Mountains on the west and the Rocky Mountains on the east. This includes the states of Nevada and Utah; a large part of Colorado; areas of southeastern Washington, southern Oregon, Idaho, and Montana; and small parts of northern Arizona and New Mexico.

Surrounded by higher-elevation lands, the region is arid and has few large mammals; life was probably difficult for the small bands of hunters that made up the population.

The Southwest region is identified as touching on Utah, Colorado, Arizona, New Mexico, Texas, California, and Oklahoma and extending into Mexico. This volume excludes the Mexican part of the region. But given the proximity to Mesoamerica, many connections can be identified. The dry climate makes it possible for archaeologists to identify many prehistoric cultural traditions. Agricultural traditions in settled communities with complex architecture seem to have existed along with nomadic traditions in response to a very arid climate. Crafts among tribes such as the Hopi and the Navajo are widely known.

The Plains culture region extends as far north as Manitoba, Saskatchewan, and Alberta and as far south as Texas. Roughly analogous to what modern North Americans call the Great Plains, this region was not forested but consisted largely of open, grassy flatlands. What is known of culture of the region dates largely from the Indians' acquisition of horses after their contact with the Europeans. Ideally suited to covering large distances, the horse caused changes in patterns of settlement and modes of food acquisition as well as significant migration of native peoples into different areas. Most of the stereotypes usually associated with North American Indian dress originated in the Plains area.

Starting at the Atlantic coast, the Northeast culture region extended west to the Mississippi Valley. On the north were the Great Lakes, and the region extended east to the coastal area of Virginia, south into North Carolina then, skirting the Appalachian mountains, southwest to Tennessee. Woodland areas predominated, even in more mountainous areas. Although some food was obtained by hunting and gathering, Northeast region peoples also engaged in agriculture and, especially in coastal and streamside areas, fishing.

The Southeast culture area was bounded on the south by the Gulf of Mexico and the east by the Atlantic Ocean as far north as mid–North Carolina. It extended west as far as Texas, touched on Oklahoma, and stretched gradually northeast ending in Maryland. Like the Northeast region, it was heavily wooded. The geography of the region was varied, with extensive coastal areas, riverside floodplains, plateaus, and mountains. The climate was moderate, and agricultural skills were well developed, although hunting and gathering were apparently also used to expand the food supply.

LIMITATIONS OF INFORMATION ABOUT DRESS

The picture that will be provided of the dress of the native people now residing in each of these culture regions is limited. Not only is the historical record sparse, but what exists is often tainted. As Bruce Trigger, anthropologist and archaeologist, has stated, "It now seems unlikely that the earliest European accounts of any ethnic group in the Northeast describe a way of life that is totally uninfluenced by European contact."

A few generalizations can be made about dress of the North American Indian and First Nations peoples. Choices about dress were shaped by climate and available raw materials. In many areas, furs, skins, hides, and other animal materials, such as bone, were most available. In regions where populations lived in settled communities, construction of dress from plant materials was more likely. Decoration of the body was common. Methods included painting, tattooing, and cutting of hair into various patterns or insertion of ornaments into the skin.

Although North American Indian and First Nations groups consider themselves separate nations, they also reside within and participate as citizens in the United States and Canada. They are, therefore, subject to influences from the larger cultures of these two countries. Throughout the period from first contact with Europeans until the present, their dress has preserved some aspects of traditional styles and also incorporated new materials and construction techniques and contemporary fashions. Among the earliest examples of the adoption of material gained in trade was the acquisition of glass beads, which became an important part of the ornamentation of tribal dress soon after the arrival of the first explorers. As early as 1501, Indians in the area now occupied by the state of Maine possessed Venetian glass beads. Fabrics were another prized trade item that was incorporated into dress. At the same time, Europeans found Indian moccasins superior in comfort to the hard leather of their boots and began to wear them instead. Explorers in Arctic regions spoke admiringly about the completely waterproof garments natives made from sea-mammal gut. Some of these garments can be found in museums around the world, testimony to the willingness of explorers to trade for these garments.

With the arrival of the first European settlers came opportunities to expand the repertory of materials for dress. In some periods, native people were coerced into wearing Western dress; at other times they chose such garments. Fashion was not absent from these choices. And sometimes the choice was a mixture of traditional and fashionable dress. In the essays that follow, readers will find descriptions of the enormous variety of choices made by indigenous people and their descendants.

References and Further Reading

Helm, June, ed. "Introduction." In *Handbook of North American Indians. Vol. 6: The Subarctic.* Washington, DC: Smithsonian Institution, 1981.

King, J.C.H. *First Peoples, First Contacts.* Cambridge, MA: Harvard University Press, 1999.

Mann, Charles C. *1491 New Revelations of the Americas before Columbus.* New York: Vintage, 2006.

Meltzer, David J. *Search for the First Americans.* Montreal: St. Remy Press, 1993.

Trigger, Bruce G., ed. "Introduction." In *Handbook of North American Indians. Vol. 15: The Northeast.* Washington, DC: Smithsonian Institution, 1978.

Waldman, Carl. *Atlas of the North American Indian.* New York: Facts on File, 2000.

Phyllis G. Tortora

See also Evidence about Dress of Indigenous People: United States Territory; Evidence about Dress of Indigenous People: Canadian Territory.

Shared and Unique Traditions and Practices

- Influences of Environment
- Historic Changes in Cultural Patterns
- Clothing for Specific Purposes
- Symbolic Associations
- Reflections of Status and Social Position
- Clothing as Statements of Cultural Identity

Whether for everyday wear or special occasions, clothing throughout native North America reflects many important aspects of the lives of the people who made and wore these garments and body adornments in the past. Contemporary clothing incorporates the same styles found throughout North America and the Westernized world in general, but ceremonial attire still differs markedly. Clothing sends clear messages about those people who wear it; contemporary clothing styles attest to the survival of native people, and the garments they don for weddings, or coming-of-age rituals, for example, testify to a continuation of world views that could not be eliminated, no matter how hard European newcomers tried. The past coexists with the present for people of native North America in ways that are stronger than they are for many other people. Clothing and body adornment are clear reflections of this.

The vast geography of native North America, ranging from the Atlantic Ocean to the Pacific and from the Arctic to northern Mexico, demands a great range of creative methods of fashioning clothing to deal with the environment on a basic level as well as to reflect worldviews in more complex ways. Clothing styles have changed markedly since the time of European contact as new materials became available, and native people incorporated those materials they wanted into their clothing and body adornment. Materials were, however, traded from great distance even before European contact: grizzly bear teeth, for example, came from the Rocky Mountains to the Great Lakes region and the Southeast during the archaeological era. Rare materials such as these appear to have been controlled by leaders and, based on later comparisons, were probably signs of social position. So, too, as Europeans brought glass beads, wool yarns, cloth, and ribbon into North America, these became important signifiers of status. Not everything that Europeans offered, however, was readily accepted. For the people of the far Northeast, specifically the Micmac (Mik'maq), as well as for some people of the Southeast, such as the Creek, red and white are colors with strong associations that made them the favorite color choices in glass trade beads. White is associated with peace and well-being, and red, with both life for many people as well as with war for others; in either case, it is the visual connection to blood that is suggested by red beads. Delicate, lacy embroidery patterns in white against dark trade cloth, sometimes edged in red, were common in parts of both the Southeast and the Northeast, and they appeared on many types of garments ranging from tailored European-style coats to shoulder bags based on the design of European shot pouches.

INFLUENCES OF ENVIRONMENT

However, materials indigenous to one's home territory provided the major basis for the manufacture of clothing in the past. Fur and hide from whatever animals filled a specific area, naturally occurring fibers as well as cultivated cotton, and hard materials that could be sculpted, such as wood, shell, and stone, are but a few of the materials employed in diverse ways. Carefully manufactured clothing designed to best protect its wearers from the specific environmental conditions in which people live is a practical and realistic aspect of native North American cultures. Whether that clothing is fur lined for winter wear in the Arctic or hide that is heavily fringed to help deflect insects, such as biting flies in the Subarctic region of Canada, clothing is functional. In warm parts of the continent, such as California or the Southwest, the body did not need to be covered as thoroughly. Clothing was augmented by body paint and tattoos as well as other kinds of ornaments in these areas and others throughout North America, particularly for special occasions, to mark life transitions such as a young girl's coming of age, or to indicate achievements. As Europeans entered these regions, they imposed their ideas of appropriate behavior and dress upon native people, resulting in dramatic changes.

Breechcloth, Eastern Woodlands, North America, ca. 1900. The red wool cloth is elaborately sewn with multicolored glass beads. The wool and glass beads brought by Europeans were used in clothing to symbolize status. © McCord Museum M1551. http://www.mccord-museum.qc.ca/en/

Items of clothing that were found throughout much of the continent during the eighteenth, nineteenth, and early twentieth centuries include soft-sided hide shoes or moccasins fashioned differently dependent upon the culture. Some moccasins have cuffs and are seamed up the front, while others have a separate inset vamp. Each type might be ornamented in various ways with bird or porcupine quillwork, again varying by area; as glass trade beads became readily available, these increased the vocabulary of decoration. Many artists explored a wide array of floral, geometric, or abstract floral patterns on the vamps and sometimes on the cuffs of the moccasins as well. For some cultures in the Southeast and Great Lakes and adjacent Prairie regions, the cuffs of moccasins provided an opportunity for the exploration of asymmetrical design with one cuff per moccasin bearing one pattern and the second cuff another; generally the two inside cuffs had matching designs and the two exterior ones had another. Many cultures, including those of the Plains and parts of the Great Lakes and Northeast, either did not use cuffs or, when they did, the designs were symmetrical.

In the more northern regions of the Arctic and Subarctic, footwear providing heavier insulation was vital. *Mukluks*, or fur-lined boots, are well known from the Arctic and provide their wearers with the necessary protection against the harsh cold. These were generally not embellished with such materials as beads when created for everyday wear, although the use of different furs on both mukluks and heavy *parkas* provides intriguing patterns, with lighter furs alternating with darker ones. Women's special-occasion mukluks, however, might be embroidered with silk thread in elaborate floral patterns.

HISTORIC CHANGES IN CULTURAL PATTERNS

With the change to a cash economy in the twentieth century and the necessity for many native people to work in cities, additional changes in clothing occurred. While in most cases contemporary clothing might be all but indistinguishable from that worn by nonnative people, in some cases specific clothing styles remain closely associated with native people. In the past, many men in the more moderate climates wore loincloths, leather leggings, and leather shirts when necessary. As cotton trade cloth became available, men in the Southeast, for example, began to wear long cotton shirts. Among the Seminole of present-day Florida, patterned cottons or calicos were the most highly desired. Seminole women in the Everglades of Florida began to experiment, sewing strips of plain cotton together to form banded patterns. When the supply of calico was cut off during World War I and hand-operated sewing machines became available, women introduced what is known as Seminole patchwork as they cut and folded designs from one color of fabric and sewed these onto another fabric; these complex bands of patchwork are then sewn together to create garments that have become clear signs of Seminole cultural identity. Clothing styles also changed among the Seminole when men began to work outside their own communities. The old-style men's long shirt, worn without trousers, was replaced for most with a shorter-style shirt and Westernized slacks. Women's garments changed as well, with longer capes replacing shorter midriff-bearing tops found offensive by nonnative people, especially missionaries, in the region.

While influences from European-style garments on those of native people are perhaps better known, the reverse also happened

with some frequency. Fur parkas of the Arctic are but one example. Arctic hunters developed a specialized, unique garment that became highly sought after by Russian whalers when they entered the region in the eighteenth century. These lightweight parkas are fashioned from animal intestine, generally walrus, that has been cleaned, dried, split, and carefully sewn together with sinew. The parkas are not only light but also waterproof; the sinew expands when the garment gets wet, providing extra protection to prevent water from seeping between the seams. Weighing far less than the heavy gear the Russian and subsequent North American hunters brought into the region, gut-skin parkas remain prized and very practical items of apparel.

CLOTHING FOR SPECIFIC PURPOSES

Some items of apparel are practical because they assist the wearer by making a task easier. Hunters among the Aleutian Islands of the Arctic coast are known for specific hats or visors associated with whaling. Fashioned from steamed and bent wood, these hunting visors protect the wearer from the sun's glare on the water, but their decoration of painted bands of various colors of spiraling patterns placed at specific locations—sea lion whiskers attached to the top of the visor, large-scale trade beads, and small-scale ivory carvings of sea mammals attached to the open crown—visually unite the hunter with the animal being hunted while simultaneously honoring those very animals who provide continuing life to the Aleuts.

While many people could make various items of apparel, in some cases the creation of specific garments was limited. In the nineteenth century, some Plains cultures had beadworking or quillworking societies for women to work together. The Northern Arapaho Seven Old Women, who each owned one of the seven existing sacred quillworking bags, is perhaps the best known of these; members of this society were women of virtue who had achieved, partially through their age, great knowledge of the Northern Arapaho worldview. Only they could take on the responsibility of quilling specific kinds of work. Quilled robes were one of those creations limited to these respected women who sometimes took on the task as part of a vow to ensure that a son or other relative would return safely from war or, after the establishment of off-reservation boarding schools and the subsequent ravages of disease at those institutions, that a child might safely return from a distant school. In other cultures, such as the Hopi of the Southwest, only men initiated into the ceremonial societies of the culture could create specific ritual paraphernalia, including headdresses or masks. Among various native people of central and northern California, the great skill involved in creating ceremonial headdresses, bustles, and other dance regalia is widely recognized, and those who excel in these arts are held in high regard.

With great frequency, ritual specialists were responsible for the creation of some items of apparel or for dance regalia. Among the most diversified masks and headdresses in native North America are those created by the Yupiit people of Alaska. Here, many masks and headdresses are used by shamans to recount their travels through time and space. The materials employed vary, but wood with sea lion whiskers, topped by feather tufts that move on the springy whiskers as the dancer moves, take a great variety of forms, ranging from highly abstract to far more realistic carvings of game animals. Dance mittens fashioned from

R. J. Kidston, Royal Canadian Mounted Police, wearing a fur parka, Pond Inlet post, Nunavut, 1928. Fur parkas were adopted by Europeans as they were lighter, warmer, and more practical than Western winter clothes. © McCord Museum MP-1986.71.207. http://www.mccord-museum.qc.ca/en/

hide to which puffin beaks have been attached provide percussion to accompany the drummers and dancers.

In the far Northeast, fitted hide coats with inset gussets (diamond-shaped pieces that allow easy movement) and often collars, while based on European style, were made wholly native with painted imagery applied to them. Innu hunters of the Quebec-Labrador peninsula who dreamed powerful images would then have them painted on their coats, generally by the man's wife. While most of these paintings are abstract rather than representational, with straight lines, curving circular and spiraling forms, and geometric shapes rendered most frequently in red, blue, or black and yellow natural pigments against the light hide of a caribou skin, occasionally a figurative form appears. Such coats were considered powerful and brought success in caribou hunts, but the coats were good for only one year. After that, a new coat had to be made in response to another dream or vision that would again bring power to the hunter. On the Plains, visions were suggested but not fully represented by paintings on shields that, by the nineteenth century, when guns were readily available, had become much smaller and less effective in offering physical protection than earlier, larger shields had been. These smaller shields with vision designs placed on them offered spiritual protection, however, and also told the enemy that the shield's owner was fighting with supernatural power.

SYMBOLIC ASSOCIATIONS

Some naturally occurring materials were selected for their symbolic value as well as their availability. Specific animals that are strong fighters for their size, such as weasels or ermine, are admired not only for their fur but also for their tenacity. Ermine pelts were particularly prominent on chiefs' headdresses along the Northwest Coast, and they had a strong presence in the Subarctic and Arctic areas where these white relatives of the weasel live and blend in well with snow, which covers the ground for a significant portion of the year. In other parts of native North America, otters carried similar associations, and their hides covered turbans, arm and leg bands, and quivers, among other items of clothing.

Selection of particular stones and shells for adornment also frequently follows a set symbolic system. Many people of native North America have color symbolism associated with the directions, often four for the cardinal or semicardinal directions, sometimes six, adding an Up and Down to the initial four. The Dené, or Navajo, of the southwestern United States connect directions to specific stones and shells that occur in a variety of colors. White is the color of the east and the rising sun; white shell carries these associations. Blue is the color of the south, and turquoise is the stone connected to that direction. Obsidian reflects the darkness of the north, and abalone reflects the yellow of the west in twilight. Jewelry fashioned from these materials continues these associations.

Dress is symbolic in other ways, both in style and in the materials used in its creation. On one level, clothing carries messages of gender. Men and women dress differently, even in cultures that require heavy outer garments for frigid temperatures. These differences may appear subtle to those unaccustomed to noticing them. A man's parka, for example, might have long, white pointed inserts at the chest linking him, visually, to the tusks of the walrus that he hunts. A woman's parka might have a much wider hood, offering room for a child to ride behind her or next to her body sharing in her warmth, or it may also allow her to move the child to the front of the her body to nurse without exposing the child to frigid weather.

Some beadworkers incorporate specific images such as U.S. or Canadian flags, eagles, and other animals into their work. These are readily recognizable in work from the Plains, Plateau, and Great Basin, in particular; many flags are also found in beaded work from the Great Lakes region. Other types of embellishment on clothing are more subtly symbolic. In the dry region of the Southwestern United States, where Pueblo people are often farmers dependent upon extremely limited rain during the growing season, much of ceremonial life revolves around supplications for moisture. Clothing worn during dances reflects abstracted representations of mountains with rain clouds rendered as dark stacked triangles embroidered on white woven cloth for men's kilts and sometimes on women's mantas or shawls. Within the dark borders of these garments, the embroiderer allows narrow white zigzag lines to show through from the white cloth underneath to suggest lightning against the dark sky. Other parts of the clothing for dances for Pueblo men and women vary but often include evergreen branches and stepped wooden headdresses or tablita for women, each also referencing clouds, rain, and the green growth of a successful season.

REFLECTIONS OF STATUS AND SOCIAL POSITION

Clothing also makes statements concerning status and social position. For native men in the heaviest fur-trapping regions of the Subarctic and the Great Lakes, clothing became elaborately embellished with glass trade beads after contact with Europeans. Fur companies such as Hudson's Bay stocked large numbers of glass beads at their trading posts because native men would not bring furs to them unless the Europeans had sufficient amounts of high-quality beads to give them as payment. The beads, in turn, were taken to the hunters' families, and beadworkers fashioned lavishly beaded clothing that spoke simultaneously of the hunter's status in being able to hunt successfully and trade for large numbers of beads as well as the artist's creativity and skill at sewing and embroidery.

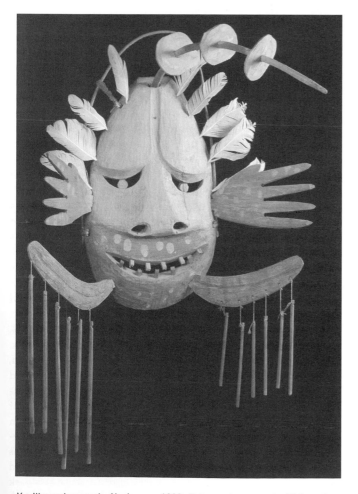

Yup'ik wooden mask, Alaska, ca. 1900. This mask represents *Walaunuk*, or bubbles, as they rise through the water. Courtesy of the National Museum of the American Indian, Smithsonian Institution.

Clothing also speaks of the accomplishments of its wearers in other, more dramatic ways. Nineteenth-century men from the Prairie regions of native North America and on the Plains placed a high value on bear claws. The bear was a powerful animal, both physically and spiritually, and a man who wore a necklace of bear claws was an established leader and a recognized brave man. So, too, some Plains warriors who had achieved significant success in battle during the nineteenth century wore shirts or robes painted with cryptic representations of those battle encounters. Body paint as well might indicate successes in battle, with abstract representations of pipes standing for war parties led and black stripes suggesting enemies killed. Such garments and paint, again, announced to all the bravery of the man who wore them. No one dared lie about such achievements, as the artist George Catlin noted when he traveled amid the Upper Missouri River people in the 1830s, for it would not be safe to do so when everyone in the village would have recognized the falsehood for what it was.

Richly embellished clothing is a part of the culture of native North America. The creativity of the artists who embroidered their clothing and that of their families with stone and shell beads, animal teeth, and porcupine quills, and later, when they became available, with metallic objects, silk thread, and glass trade beads, is evinced throughout native North American cultures. In some cases, patterns used in beaded embroidery, for example, were considered the property of specific artists, and they might be handed down from mothers to daughters. People in small, closely connected communities recognize the work of individual artists even after much time has passed.

For major, life-altering events such as a young girl's coming of age, special clothing might be made to be worn as an indication of her new role as a woman capable of motherhood as well as the additional responsibilities she now has in life. Among the Tanaina of the Canadian Subarctic, every month during her menses, a young woman wore a beautifully embellished, long, beaded head covering with a veil-like side and back that effectively hid her eyes from men, who were not to look at her, nor she at them, during this time of great power. Another time of change for some native people came when someone died. Close family members would then wear only coarsely woven fiber clothing as a sign of their mourning and their new status. Marriages were, in the past, very formal alliances among families along the Columbia River Plateau region in Idaho and adjacent areas. As signs of these new unions, great quantities of gifts were exchanged between the two families. Among those gifts were items of clothing and the raw materials necessary to manufacture those items of apparel. Finished clothing, as well as food, were gifts from the woman's family, while the man's relatives supplied meat and hides.

CLOTHING AS STATEMENTS OF CULTURAL IDENTITY

Clothing and its embellishment are strong reflections of cultural identity. The style of bead or quillwork as well as the cut of a garment could mark its wearer as a member of a specific Plains group, for example. Northern, Central, and Southern Plains tribal styles varied from each other both in the number of animal skins that might be used for a woman's dress and in the manner of ornamenting it. Southern Plains and Great Basin hide clothing more frequently included large, solidly painted areas than did clothing from other parts of the Plains. Such differences become even more visually striking in the areas where one region or style area came into close and frequent contact with its neighbors; clothing plays an even greater role as cultural identifier in many such locations.

Intermarriage and trade, as well as simple visual contact, were among the forces that encouraged clothing styles to change over time; they remain active forces today. Large-scale powwows, where many people from different native nations gather to dance and visit, bring vibrant and creative artists together. In dances, clothing that appears to relay the body in motion in a more effective manner, with specific placement of feathers, fringe, or metal cones to add to the motion of the dance, might well be emulated, at least in part, by others as they make new clothing. Contemporary native clothing retains its connections to the past, but, like the clothing of the ancestors, it, too, changes to reflect new materials, styles, and experimentation.

Creating beautifully embellished garments for children is also seen throughout native North America but perhaps most dramatically during the early reservation era on the Plains. Many Lakota women, for example, created fully beaded dresses for their young daughters and completely covered small vests and trouser leggings for little boys with beadwork, despite the fact that these children would soon outgrow these garments. In such a time of intense trauma, when traditional life was being replaced by a stagnant reservation existence and the federal government was trying so desperately to assimilate native people, Lakota women dressed their families in strong outward signs of their culture as a way of instilling in them their Lakota identity and as a way of fighting against the forces of assimilation. When young Plains children went away to off-reservation boarding schools, often hundreds of miles away, mothers frequently dressed them in these fine clothes as a continuing sign of their culture.

Clothing also reflected changes in lifestyles adopted by native people. Especially prominent in the early twentieth century are garments associated with both Wild West shows and rodeos. Elaborately embellished chaps, vests, and gauntlets or gloves with large cuffs were adopted by native men even though such garments were of nonnative origin. They quickly became cultural signifiers, however, as successful rodeo contestants posed for many photographs wearing such decorated clothing that spoke of their new position. Women who made such garments would also be recognized as the industrious, creative artists that they were. Beadworkers remain highly regarded today, and some of these types of clothing continue to be made. They are augmented by more contemporary items, such as beaded tennis shoes, but the spirit of beauty and expression of identity remain the same.

In other parts of native North America, clothing unmistakably relays information concerning the wearer's family heritage or clan. This is most obvious among the people of the Northwest Coast on Vancouver Island, British Columbia, and Alaska. Here, images of animals and humans, or crests, are associated with families, and one inherits the right to certain crests. The well-known crest poles, often called *totem poles*, of the region are visual statements of crests; the same can be said about clothing. When a Tlingit man from Alaska wears a wooden crest hat carved with an image of a killer whale, with the animal's head appearing directly above the man's face and the mammal's large dorsal fin projecting above, there is no doubt that he owns the right to the killer whale crest; the two are visually united. Other Northwest Coast cultures create crest or clan hats in different media; the Haida of

Headdress with feathers and ermine fur, Northern Plains, ca. 1875–1925. The ermine was seen as a strong fighter, and its fur was used on headdresses and other items of clothing as a symbol of this strength. © McCord Museum M5347. http://www.mccord-museum.qc.ca/en/

the Queen Charlotte Islands are well known for woven basketry hats on which crest figures are painted. Other garments also reflect crests. Tunics can be woven in extremely abstracted patterns, but these, too, center the face of the crest in the chest or midbody area. Known as *Chilkat* tunics and blankets, these textiles woven from mountain goat wool are among the finest in native North America and are named for the Chilkat Tlingit, who specialized in making them; they were, however, widely traded and remain prized possessions. Crest images might also be apparent on trade cloth blankets, generally termed *button blankets*, as the crest is represented by sewn buttons placed on the back of the blanket. Early forms of button blankets used shell instead of buttons as embellishment, but, as mother-of-pearl buttons became available, they became the standard objects to be appliquéd to what are generally dark wool trade cloth blankets that have upper and lower borders of red wool. Such blankets are worn on many occasions, including dances; when the dancers turn their backs toward the audience and open the blankets outward, the full crest is visible.

The more than five hundred native nations of North America have long, diversified histories of creating clothing and body adornment that can only be suggested here. Clothing is a reflection of identity, social position, heritage, and achievement, as well as personal taste. Creative outpouring and practical considerations coexist today, just as they have in the past and will undoubtedly continue in the future in ways that both connect native people to their histories and suggest their firm resolve to survive.

References and Further Reading

Burnham, Dorothy K. *To Please the Caribou: Painted Caribou-Skin Coats Worn by the Naskapi, Montagnais, and Cree Hunters of the Quebec-Labrador Peninsula.* Seattle: University of Washington Press, 1992.

Catlin, George. *Letters and Notes on the Manners, Customs, and Conditions of North American Indians.* New York: Dover, 1973. (Originally published in London, 1844.)

Dubin, Lois Sherr. *North American Indian Jewelry and Adornment from Prehistory to the Present.* New York: Harry N. Abrams, 1999.

Duncan, Kate C. *Northern Athapaskan Art, A Beadwork Tradition.* Seattle: University of Washington, 1989.

Glenbow-Alberta Institute. *The Spirit Sings, Artistic Traditions of Canada's First Peoples.* Toronto: McClelland and Stewart, 1987.

Her Many Horses, Emil, ed. *Identity by Design: Tradition, Changes and Celebration in Native Women's Dresses.* Washington, DC: Harper Collins and National Museum of the American Indian, Smithsonian Institution, 2007.

Heth, Charlotte, ed. *Native American Dance: Ceremonies and Social Traditions.* Washington, DC: National Museum of the American Indian, Smithsonian Institution, 1992.

Hudson, Charles. *The Southeastern Indians.* Knoxville: University of Tennessee, 1976.

Oakes, Jill, and Rick Riewe. *Our Boots, An Inuit Women's Art.* London: Thames & Hudson, 1995.

Roediger, Virginia More. *Ceremonial Costumes of the Pueblo Indians, Their Evolution, Fabrication, and Significance in the Prayer Drama.* Los Angeles: University of California Press, 1991. (Originally published 1941.)

Wroth, William, ed. *Ute Indian Arts & Culture from Prehistory to the New Millennium.* Colorado Springs: Taylor Museum of the Colorado Springs Fine Arts Center, 2000.

Joyce M. Szabo

The Arctic

In an environment where temperatures are below freezing for much of the year, appropriate clothing is vital. For the native peoples of Arctic North America, until about the mid-twentieth century, survival largely depended on women's skills to create clothing that provides insulation against the cold and protection from snow, ice, and water. At the same time, the garments are lightweight and durable, and their designs provide the freedom of movement required for carrying out everyday activities.

However, as in other parts of the world, not only the functional aspects of clothing are important. Clothing also reflects connections with the social and natural environment. In this way, it illustrates both the differences and the commonalities between native peoples from across Arctic North America and provides a window on past and present life in the Arctic.

THE IMPORTANCE OF CLOTHING

The North American Arctic is the area on the shores of the North American continent around and to the north of the Arctic Circle. Today, there are about one hundred forty thousand native people living here: the Aleut, Alutiit, Yupiit, and Iñupiat in Alaska; the Siberian Yuit in Alaska and Siberia; the Canadian Inuit; and the Greenlanders. Historically, these peoples (except the Aleut) were collectively known as *Eskimos*. In the late twentieth century, especially in Canada, this word has been replaced by the term *Inuit*.

The cultures of these peoples are based on the hunting of sea mammals and caribou. This subsistence pattern goes back some four thousand years in the Bering Strait region and spread eastward in two major waves from around 2000 B.C.E. and 1000 C.E. In many parts of the Arctic, hunting and fishing, supplemented by some collecting of plants and berries, provided the basis for subsistence until about the mid-twentieth century. The seasonal round of activities varied regionally, depending on the availability of specific resources in the area. Animals were not only important sources of food; their skins, sinews, and bones, as well as walrus tusks, caribou antlers, and whale baleen, were used for making a variety of tools and in the construction of houses and tents, dog

sleds, and so forth. Skins, sinews, and sometimes intestines provided materials for clothing. Survival, therefore, depended on the ability of hunters to provide food and important raw materials by hunting and fishing. To a large extent, the comfort, efficiency, and success of the hunters was dependent on appropriate clothing for use in the Arctic environment.

Traditional clothing was highly effective in fulfilling two basic requirements posed by environmental conditions. First, it kept the wearer warm in a cold environment. Due to its northern location, in many parts of the Arctic, temperatures are below freezing for much of the year. Thus, warm clothing is essential, especially for hunters who spend much time outside. Second, in the Arctic, wet garments freeze quickly, especially in winter, which may lead to hypothermia and eventually freezing to death. Therefore, it is vital to keep dry at all times. Garments were made to protect both from

Inuit woman, Arctic Bay, Nunavut, 1926. Her parka has a slit on either side to allow freedom of movement, with front and back flaps for extra warmth. © McCord Museum MP-1984.127.33. http://www.mccord-museum.qc.ca/en/

moisture from the outside, such as snow or rain, and to prevent perspiration and accumulation of moisture inside the garment. At the same time, clothing was designed to allow the freedom of movement necessary for carrying out daily activities. Durability was another important concern because damaged clothing may be life threatening in an Arctic environment. Because of these characteristics, traditional clothing of skin or intestines often proved superior to European clothing, and it was held in high esteem by those European, U.S., and Canadian explorers and traders who chose to adopt it. Skin clothing also contributed significantly to the success of expeditions in the Arctic and Antarctic, such as the voyage of Roald Amundsen (1872–1928) to the South Pole in 1911.

Protection from cold and humidity, ease of movement, and durability were achieved through the cut of the garments, the materials used, skin preparation, and sewing techniques, as well as knowledge about the use and maintenance of the clothing. The following sections give an overview of the main features of traditional Arctic clothing as it was used until about the mid-twentieth century.

TYPES OF CLOTHING AND CLOTHING DESIGN

Insulation from the cold and protection from moisture was in part achieved through clothing design. A traditional outfit includes four basic types of garments: a jacket or parka, trousers, boots, and mittens. In its basic form, the *parka* consists of a front and a back part, sewn together at the shoulder and at the sides. The sleeves, made from separate pieces of skin, are attached at the shoulder. The parkas of the Aleut and Alutiit of southern Alaska reach down to the feet and are cut wide to allow freedom of movement. Their fur and bird-skin parkas are hoodless, with a high collar, although at sea or in cold or rainy weather, they might use hooded gut-skin parkas or separate hats or caps. Further to the north in Alaska, Canada, and Greenland, parkas are usually hooded and may reach down to the middle of the thighs. To allow freedom of movement, they are often slit on the side, and the bottom ends in two flaps. The length and shape of the flaps varies regionally, reflecting the gender and sometimes the age and marital status of the wearer. The back flap is generally somewhat longer than the front flap. In this way, it protects against draft and may be used to sit on.

In the past, the parka had no pockets. Small items were carried in a bag around the neck or over the shoulder. In some parts of the Central and Eastern Arctic, women wore boots or leggings with extensions forming pouches, which they used to store their knife, sewing kit, or material for diapers.

With the exception of the Aleut and Alutiit of southern Alaska, trousers were used across the Arctic, with designs varying regionally. For instance, in the Canadian Arctic, trousers were cut straight or flaring, usually reaching to the knee or slightly below, and held up with a drawstring or belt. In eastern Greenland, both knee- and ankle-length outer trousers were known for men, while women's trousers reached to midthigh. Indoors, eastern Greenlandic men and women wore very short, tight-fitting pants (*naatsiit*).

Except for the Aleut and Alutiit, who reportedly did not or only rarely used footwear, Arctic people had a variety of different types of footwear for different purposes in different seasons. For instance, in the Canadian Arctic, hunters might wear a pair of inner boots or stockings, a pair of outer boots, and, when needed,

additional socks and stockings and a pair of external thermal slippers. Soft, pleated soles are characteristic of boots (*kamik*) from the Central and Eastern Arctic, while hard, pleated soles and ankle straps are typical for boots or mukluks from the western Canadian Arctic and Alaska. The length of the leg section varied regionally and depending on the type of the boot. Men's boots often were about knee high, while women's boots in some areas were longer, reaching up to midthigh. The vamp and leg section might be elaborately decorated with inlays, appliqué, trimming, or beadwork, reflecting local and regional styles and often also the gender of the wearer.

Mittens commonly were made with one thumb. However, in Greenland, hunters used a special type of mitten with two thumbs, one on each side, when kayaking. In this way, the mitt could be turned around when one side had become too slippery from ice.

Traditional clothing is designed to keep the wearer warm by using air as a thermal insulator. This is achieved by wearing two, sometimes more, layers of clothing, the inner layer with the fur turned inward toward the body and the outer layer with the fur turned outward. In this way, the warm air trapped between the multiple layers of clothing, and the body serves as insulator. Additional insulation may be provided by dried grass that was put in boots or mittens. In summer, when it is warmer, garments often consisted of only one layer of clothing or were made of less warm materials.

To reduce drafts and prevent warm air from escaping, upper garments have no side and front openings, and the edges of adjacent garments overlap. Wide shoulders and armholes allow the withdrawal of the arms from the sleeves and allow them to be wrapped around the body for warmth, while providing the freedom of movement necessary for hunting, fishing, and other activities. At the same time, the loose fit of the garments permits air circulation and ventilation. Throwing back the hood or taking off the mittens further helps to regulate heat by allowing humid air and heat to escape, preventing the accumulation of sweat inside the garment.

To prevent garments from becoming wet, snow and ice had to be removed regularly. Fur, and particularly furs with uneven hair length that were used for ruffs around the hood, for instance, allowed snow and ice crystals to be brushed off easily. A particularly elaborate type of ruff, characteristic of Alaskan parkas, is the so-called sunshine ruff or sunburst ruff (called *isigvik* in Iñupiaq), which is made of several layers of long wolf and wolverine hair or dog hair. Ruffs and trims had the additional advantage of strengthening the edges of the skin, preventing tears and coiling up.

In rainy weather or when fishing or hunting at rivers or at sea, raincoats of gut skin were put on over skin clothing. Bird-skin garments, with the feathers to the outside, served the same purpose. In Greenland, hunters wore waterproof clothing of seal skin over their clothes when kayaking and whaling suits of waterproof seal skin are known from western Greenland, Labrador, and northern Alaska, where they were put on during whale hunting and *flensing* (cutting of whale blubber). These whaling suits were hooded, all-in-one suits that only left the face uncovered and were entered through an opening on the front, which was then closed with drawstrings. They could be inflated to protect whale hunters from drowning in case of an accident. In addition, they allowed the wearer to do part of the flensing under water so that the whale did not need to be pulled ashore entirely.

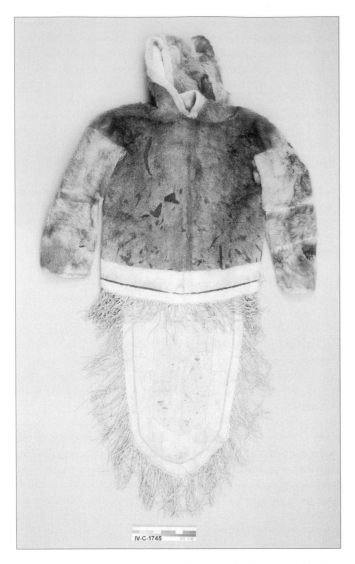

Netsilingmiut parka, Nunavut province, Northwest Territories, roughly nineteenth or twentieth century. This fur parka has a white trim, and the back flap could be used for sitting on. © Canadian Museum of Civilization, artifact IV-C-1745, image D2002-009508. http://www.civilization.ca/

Men's and women's clothing was similar in many ways. However, in Canada and Greenland, women used a special type of parka when carrying a baby or a young child. The back of this parka is especially wide, forming a pouch in which the child could be kept warm and comfortable on its mother's back, close to her naked body. In Inuktitut, the language spoken by the Inuit in the Canadian Arctic, this parka is called *amauti* or *amautik*, after the characteristic pouch at its back. The hood of this parka is very large—roomy enough to protect both mother and child. The parka also has broad shoulders, which allow the mother to bring her baby from the pouch at the back of the amauti to her breast for nursing without exposing it to the cold. In Alaska and the Mackenzie Delta, women's parkas were pouchless, but they were cut wider at the back to make room for the child. To prevent the baby from slipping down, women used a belt around the outside of the parka.

There is little information on children's clothing before the early twentieth century. It seems that children's clothes generally resembled the clothes of adults, although they were usually made of the soft skin of young animals. Where a baby spent the first years of its life in its mother's amauti, its first set of clothes might consist of a parka and small boots. In the Canadian Arctic, children would wear a combination suit (*atajuq*) when they started to walk around. As children grew older, their clothing increasingly resembled that of adults.

Comparing clothing from different parts of the North American Arctic shows that although environmental conditions influence the clothing in important ways, culture and history play an important role in shaping the clothing as well. This is particularly evident in variations in clothing designs, such as the form and the length of the front and back flaps in men's and women's parkas, and in decoration. Occasionally, it seems as if fashion and aesthetic considerations may have been more important than practical considerations, especially in women's clothing. For instance, among the Siberian Yuit, the women's *khonba*, a combination of trousers and parka, had a large neck opening that left neck and shoulders exposed to the cold, while the long sleeves often interfered with work. In eastern Greenland, women's trousers did not reach down to their boots, leaving parts of their thighs uncovered, often resulting in frostbite.

MATERIALS

In the past, native people of the North American Arctic made clothing using skins from a wide range of animals, including caribou, ringed seal, bearded seal, polar bear, Arctic fox, hare, dog, and wolverine, among others, as well as from birds and fish. The decorative and functional qualities of the skins depend on the age and gender of the animals and on the season in which the animals were taken. Skins were carefully selected, taking into account their warmth, water-repellent qualities, lightness, durability, and the firmness with which the hair was attached to the skin. Aesthetic considerations, such as the color of the skin, played a role as well. To a large extent, the choice of materials has reflected the local availability of game animals, although materials were sometimes obtained through trade with neighboring peoples.

In most parts of the Arctic, caribou skin and the skin of various seal species are the main materials for making clothing. Caribou skin is the preferred material for winter clothing because it is particularly warm. The hair growth is twice as dense as on seal skin, and air is trapped inside the hollow guard hairs, providing additional insulation. Caribou leg skins, which shed hair less easily, are used for mittens and boot uppers, where the toughness of the material is especially important.

Although seal skin is less warm than caribou skin, it has the advantage of not shedding hair as easily, and it is less heavy than caribou skin. Seal skin also contains natural oils that make it water resistant. These characteristics make it ideal for garments worn in the wetter seasons (i.e., spring, summer, and fall) or for clothing made for kayaking. Being particularly tough and thick, bearded seal skin was the preferred material for boot soles across the Arctic.

In contrast to their neighbors in northern Alaska and the eastern Arctic, caribou and seal skin are less central in the clothing made by the Yupiit of southwestern Alaska. Instead, they could take advantage of the wide range of fur-bearing animals found in Alaska, which provided a variety of materials for their parkas and other articles of clothing.

Bird skin and intestines were important materials for making clothing as well. Bird-skin clothing is known from across the North American Arctic. Worn with the feathers to the inside, bird-skin clothing is very warm and provides lightweight winter clothing, especially in areas where there are no caribou. In the rainy coastal areas of southern and southwestern Alaska, bird-skin parkas also served as a raincoat when worn with the feathers to the outside or in combination with a gut-skin parka.

Gut-skin parkas were made of the intestines of bear or sea mammals, an extremely light and flexible, waterproof material. They were made of strips of intestine sewn together horizontally or vertically using a special waterproof stitch and threads of grass or sinew, which expanded when soaked to make the seams waterproof. Everyday garments were sparsely decorated and usually could be fastened with drawstrings around the hood and at the cuffs. They were worn over skin parkas when it was raining or when at sea. In eastern Greenland, parkas of white, frost-bleached gut skin (*ikkiaq*) provided camouflage when stalking seals. For festive and ceremonial occasions, the Aleut also made hoodless gut parkas (*kamleika*), preferably of bear intestines and often elaborately decorated with bands of colored skin at the collar, cuffs, and hem.

SKIN PREPARATION AND SEWING TECHNIQUES

In the past, women's skills as seamstresses, acquired by watching and helping their mothers and other women, were as important for survival as men's hunting abilities. Skin preparation and sewing was women's work, although men might help with skin preparation and do repairs when necessary. Making skin clothing is arduous and time-consuming, and even experienced seamstresses might work for several weeks to make winter clothing for their families.

Before sewing can begin, skins have to be properly prepared to make them soft and pliable as well as long-lasting. Skin can be prepared in many different ways. The exact methods used depend on the type of skin, the desired qualities (e.g., warmth, water resistance, decorative qualities), and local traditions. Important steps include removing blood and fat. If this is not done, or not done well, the skin will turn yellow and decay more quickly. The fatty tissue on the inside of the skin is removed with an *ulu*, a semicircular woman's knife. The hair side of the skin is cleaned by rubbing with sand and gravel; washing in salt water, urine, and (more recently) soapy water; or by rinsing the skin in cold water or snow to harden the oil and then scraping or beating it off. Other important steps are stretching out the skin to dry on a wooden frame or on the ground and softening the skin. The latter is achieved by a variety of techniques, including rubbing, twisting, rolling the skin into a ball and stomping on it, scraping with a dull scraper, and chewing.

The hair may be left on if warmer skins are desired, or it may be removed to make the skin more water resistant or to produce a decorative whitish color. To enhance the water resistance, the hair may be shaved or plucked off, leaving the epidermis, the outer layer of the skin, intact. Seal skin treated in this way could be used for waterproof boots and for clothing worn while kayaking. Another method, aging, involves removing the hair together with the epidermis and yields a less water-resistant skin. To this end, the skin is soaked in blubber or in hot water, or rolled up and

Red trimmed boots, Sachs Harbour, Northwest Territories, Canada, roughly nineteenth or twentieth century. The patterns on boots reflect regional styles and the gender of the wearer. © Canadian Museum of Civilization, artifact VI-D-2205a-b, photo M. Toole, 1992, image S93-728. http://www.civilization.ca/

left in a warm place until the hair and epidermis loosen and can be removed with a dull scraper. If the skin is dried in freezing temperatures afterward, the result is a bleached skin of a whitish color. No longer water resistant, bleached skin was used for festive clothing and decorations, such as fringes and appliqué. To obtain different colors, bleached skin could be dyed, smoked, alder barked, or (more recently) painted.

Clothing, like other equipment and tools made by Arctic peoples, is made to fit the wearer. Seamstresses used hand, string, and eye measurement, and old garments might serve as a model. Patterns are symmetrical, using the skin's longitudinal center line along the spine as axis. Often parts of the skin are used for corresponding parts of the garment. For instance, the rump skin of caribou may be used for the seat of trousers, the head skin for the parka hood, and the leg skins for making boots or mittens. The fur flow on the body of a garment usually goes from top to bottom; however, practical consideration and local traditions play a role as well. For instance, on edgings, the fur flow is usually horizontal to prevent tears and curling.

Seams are often placed in areas that are less subject to stress so as to prevent the tearing of seams. For instance, on parkas, the shoulder seams are often placed at the back of the garment, while the sleeves are attached at the middle of the upper arm. Commonly used stitches include the overcast stitch, the running stitch, the tucked overcast or running stitch (where one of the skins is gathered), and several kinds of waterproof stitch. The latter are common on clothing intended for use in wet conditions, such as waterproof seal-skin boots, clothing used when kayaking, and gut-skin parkas.

To prevent decay and shedding of hair and to keep the garments soft and pliable, proper maintenance is essential. Before entering a house, snow and ice are beaten off the clothes to prevent the clothing from becoming wet from the melted water. Outer garments are taken off inside the house to dry. When they have dried, the garments are stiff and need to be softened again before the next use by scraping or chewing.

MEDIATING THE RELATIONSHIP WITH ANIMALS AND SUPERNATURAL BEINGS

In the past, to be a good hunter was not only a matter of having adequate equipment and clothing and mastering certain technical skills; the success of a hunter also was believed to depend on the respectful treatment of the animals hunted, both by the hunter and his family. Further, it was important to follow certain rules, such as norms for sharing meat and skins or norms relating to the division of land and sea animals. This was thought to make the hunter attractive to the animals so they would come to him. Clothing played an important role in this, and many norms related to the preparation and wearing of clothing. For instance, in many parts of the Arctic, the preparation of caribou-skin clothing had to be finished before the start of the seal-hunting season in order not to offend the animals. Hunters used beautiful tools and, in some areas, dressed in beautiful garments to please the animals. Such norms had to be followed in order not to offend the animals and supernatural beings, although some may have had practical aspects as well. For instance, garments that were considered beautiful were, above all, well made, sewn with small and regular stitches, and either new or in an excellent state of repair.

Clothing and the amulets attached to it also protected the wearer from supernatural threats (e.g., preventing illness or hunting accidents) and transferred to him or her the characteristics of the animal or the previous owner, such as speed, strength, fertility, or luck. Amulets were worn by men, women, and children. Often the mother wore amulets attached to her clothing on behalf of her children while she carried them in her parka. When the child started to walk and got his or her own clothing, the amulets were attached to the child's clothes.

Amulets often consisted of animal parts, such as claws, beaks, or teeth, but parts of tools or clothing, especially of clothes that a person had used as a child, were used as well. Some of the qualities of the animals or previous owners were preserved in the objects, and it was thought that their spirits would come to the support of the wearer when needed.

In Greenland, an only child whose older brothers and sisters had died was often dressed in uncommon clothing to protect it from evil spirits. For instance, a girl might be dressed in boy's clothing and vice versa, or the child might wear nonmatching boots (e.g., one boot of haired seal skin and one of waterproof seal skin), buttons, or a loose cap. Dressed in this way, it was believed that evil spirits would become confused and not recognize the child.

Before the arrival of Christianity, the shaman was considered to have special powers that allowed him or her to communicate with spirits and animals. In this way, shamans could determine, for instance, the reasons for an illness or for the scarcity of animals and suggest remedies. In the North American Arctic, shamans wore everyday clothing but sometimes with distinctive accessories, such as headdresses or belts. In Canada and Greenland, their upper body was often naked during seances, while Alaskan and Siberian Yuit shamans wore gut-skin *kamleikas*. However, among the Siberian Yuit, shamans used special white clothing during the whale ceremony, and Qingailisaq, a nineteenth-century shaman from the Canadian Arctic, reportedly had a special caribou-skin coat, hat, and mittens made for himself after an encounter with *ijiqqat* (supernatural beings).

TRADE: IMPORTED MATERIALS

There is relatively little information on clothing used by indigenous peoples in the Arctic before the twentieth century. Clues to changes in clothing over time are provided by some archaeological finds of figurines and clothing, most famously perhaps at Qilakitsoq in western Greenland and Utqiagvik in northern Alaska, dated to the fifteenth century and about 1500–1826 C.E., respectively. From the sixteenth century onward, accounts of European explorers, traders, and missionaries, as well as sixteenth-century depictions of Inuit captured in Canada and Greenland, are available. Clothing in museum collections dates back to the late eighteenth century, but most are from the late nineteenth and twentieth century.

Contact with Europeans, Canadians, and Americans had a profound impact on the clothing of indigenous Arctic peoples. In the eastern Arctic, European trade goods were available from whalers and fishermen who visited the Davis Strait from the early sixteenth century. Trade relations became more regular from the eighteenth century after the establishment of small trading posts in western Greenland and eastern Canada. On the other side of the continent, Russian fur hunters first reached the Bering Strait in 1648. In 1784, the Russian American Company established a trading post on Kodiak Island, followed by several posts in the Yukon-Kuskokwim area in the 1820s. In northern Alaska and in the western and central Canadian Arctic, trade increased from the mid-nineteenth century with the arrival of whaling ships and later the establishment of trading posts. However, before then, Western goods were available indirectly through trade with Siberian Yuit and Chukchi and with Algonquian peoples, respectively.

Trade goods included, among other things, metal tools, such as needles or knives; materials used for trim and decorations, such as beads, colored ribbons, decorative braid, rickrack, and bias tape; fabric for making garments and lining; and commercially made articles of clothing, such as shirts, underwear, trousers, or caps and hats. Over time, the range of goods offered became more diverse.

Manufactured goods were quickly adopted. Initially, they were incorporated as decoration into traditional skin clothing without significantly altering basic clothing design. For instance, Iñupiaq women used small pieces of red yarn in the trim of parkas, boots, gloves, and caps. From the 1890s, a geometric trim, known as *qupak* or Delta trim, became popular. It consisted of small pieces

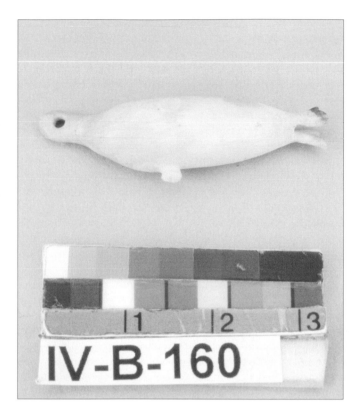

Amulet, Newfoundland and Labrador, roughly nineteenth or twentieth century. This amulet was probably worn to bring luck on a seal hunt as it was believed that the characteristics of the animal were preserved in the object and could be transferred to the wearer. © Canadian Museum of Civilization, artifact IV-B-160, image S2001-2537. http://www.civilization.ca/

of light and dark caribou skin sewn together to create geometrically patterned strips that were used as decoration on the hem of the garments or along major seams.

Coins, buttons, brass bells, pewter jingles (made by recasting pewter spoons), and other things were used as pendants attached to the hem of the parka or to the ends of beaded strings, jingling at festivities and dances. Beads, in particular, were popular. At first, they were used singly or in small strings, replacing earlier, locally made beads of animal teeth, bones, and other materials. With the intensification of trade relations, beads became increasingly plentiful, and the European traders soon adapted to local preferences for particular colors and shapes. In the Canadian Arctic, women's (and in some areas, men's) parkas were lavishly decorated with beads. In Nunavik and Baffinland, the chest of women's parkas was decorated with strings of beads, each with the same number and color of beads, creating the impression of alternating dark and light horizontal bands. In the central and western parts of Arctic Canada, beads were sewn to panels of dehaired skin or fabric and attached to the chest and the back of the parka.

Information on the meaning of colors and designs is often lacking. In many cases, it seems that colors and designs were selected according to the preferences of the seamstress, taking into consideration the materials available. Local and regional styles developed as seamstresses were inspired by the work of others and by reusing beadwork from worn-out garments. However, among the Yupiit of southwest Alaska, the meaning of many designs is recognized, and many are associated with stories and myths. For instance, the linear trim on the hem of the garment, called *qamuuraq*, is said to symbolize sled tracks in the snow. Bands of white skin and arrow tassels recall the escape of an ancestor, Apaanugpak, from an enemy attack. Certain motifs, or the use of particular pieces of fur in parts of the garments, are associated with particular villages or families.

While imported materials initially were used only for decorating skin clothing, giving rise to increasingly elaborate and diverse decorations, starting in the mid-nineteenth century garments and linings were increasingly made of fabric. However, traditional designs were often retained. Elements of Western dress were incorporated into traditional skin clothing. For instance, in western Greenland from the mid-eighteenth century, men's trousers were commonly made with pockets to hold handkerchief and snuffbox. In the twentieth century, in many parts of the Arctic, skin parkas were often made with zippers and a textile lining.

Before trade, whaling, and the church offered employment opportunities, occupational differentiation was lacking in the Arctic, and there was little status differentiation except among the Aleut and Alutiit. Differences in men's hunting success, however, as well as in women's sewing skills, were often reflected in clothing through the use of skins that were rare or difficult to obtain, such as polar bear or wolverine skin; the use of trimmings and decorations; and the quality of the needlework. Later, the use of imported goods not only reflected differences in skills but, increasingly, differences in occupation and wealth as well. People employed at trading posts, missions, or on whaling ships often had better access to trade goods and frequently were the forerunners in adopting items of Western clothing, such as caps, shirts, trousers, or underwear.

Becoming involved in the fur trade often led to a shift in subsistence strategies as hunters concentrated their efforts on animals whose skin would achieve the highest prices. Such skins were traded rather than used by the hunters and their families, contributing to the shift in materials used for clothing. For instance, in the eighteenth century, bird skin increasingly replaced sea-otter and fur-seal skin as material for Aleut women's garments because the furs were bought up by the Russian American Company; from the mid-nineteenth century, skin clothing was largely replaced by Russian-style dress. Over time, this resulted in an increasing dependence on trade goods also for necessary food, clothing, and equipment.

MISSIONARIES: CHRISTIAN NORMS AND BELIEFS

While traders, fur hunters, and whalers brought Western goods, missionaries introduced—and often imposed—beliefs and practices associated with Christianity and Western civilization more generally. They arrived in western Greenland and southern Alaska in the eighteenth century and expanded their activities to northern Alaska, the Canadian Arctic, and northern and eastern Greenland in the nineteenth and early twentieth century. As part of their efforts to convert and civilize the native population, missionaries discouraged or suppressed the pagan and "savage" practices that they deemed incompatible with a Christian, "civilized" life. Objects associated with such practices, including clothing, provided a tangible focus for their efforts. Drums, masks, and other dance paraphernalia, as well as amulets, were particularly suspicious and often confiscated and burned, because the missionaries often associated them—rightly or wrongly—with shamanic rituals and "heathen superstitions."

While simple masks of seal skin or wood were known in most parts of the Arctic and used to amuse or frighten children, or in connection with festivities or ceremonies, masks were particularly elaborate among the Yupiit of southwest Alaska. Different types of masks were made for different purposes. Carved of wood, painted, and with feathers or carved appendages attached to the mask itself or the concentric bentwood hoops surrounding it, masks were used during ceremonies, for dances at festive intra- and intercommunity gatherings, and by shamans during seances. Powerful masks reflected the visions of the shaman, representing animal spirits or the shaman's spirit helpers and human-animal transformations. Through the influence of Catholic and Moravian missionaries, traditional ceremonies and dances had virtually disappeared around 1900, along with the objects associated with them. However, in the 1960s a revival of dancing, including masked dances, was encouraged by Father René Astruc. Intracommunity dances evolved into large regional festivals in the 1980s and 1990s.

As part of their civilizing efforts, missionaries also fought against clothing that offended their sense of decency, such as the short trousers of eastern Greenlandic women that exposed parts of their thighs or the widespread practice of undressing almost completely when indoors. Similarly, tattoos disappeared after contact, perhaps due to changing religious beliefs and changing standards of beauty. Before contact, facial tattoos for women, most common in the form of vertical lines marking the chin and diagonal or horizontal lines on the cheeks, had been common across the North American Arctic. Tattoos were most varied in Alaska and Siberia, where both men and women were tattooed. They often seem to have had magical aspects, such as ensuring hunting success or fertility; women's tattoos often were linked to puberty or marriage.

By the late nineteenth century, hooded cloth covers (called *atikłuk* in Iñupiaq and *qaspeq* in Yup'ik) had become common for men and women in Alaska. By the 1920s, they had spread to the western Canadian Arctic, where Kenmek and Etna Klengenberg, wife and daughter of the local trader, had introduced them to the Copper Inuit. Worn over the skin clothing, they were advantageous in keeping the fur garments dry and clean. Women's cloth covers, also known as "Mother Hubbards," reaching down

below the knee and with ruffles at the bottom, resembled Western dresses. Worn without the skin lining, they could be used as indoor dress as well.

FESTIVE AND ETHNIC DRESS

Festive clothing, for use in church on Sundays as well as on Christian holidays and for celebrations such as christenings, weddings, Easter, or Christmas, developed in the wake of Christianization. Before contact, there had been no specific festive clothing, but people had used their best clothing or newly made garments.

In contrast to everyday clothing, and especially clothing used for hunting or traveling in winter, where traditional skin clothing proved superior to Western clothing in its functionality, imported materials and Western design elements were most prominent in festive clothing. Homemade or store-bought European garments, such as shirts, trousers, caps, and dresses, were popular as well. Festive dress often was European dress, especially for men, while women might wear either Western dresses or clothing in traditional designs, if not materials. The cloth covers mentioned previously or, in Canada, the cloth amauti, made of white cloth following traditional amauti designs, are examples.

Similarly, in western Greenland, festive clothing combines both traditional and Western designs and materials. In the late twentieth century, men's festive clothing consists of hooded, hip-length parkas (*annoraaq*) of white cotton, with black trousers and black seal-skin boots. Women's festive clothing (*kalaallisuut*) includes a red or blue silk blouse (annoraaq); a multicolored, almost waist-length bead collar (*nuilarmiut*); short trousers of haired seal skin (*seeqqernit* or *takisut*); long white or red outer boots of seal skin; and a long inner seal-skin boot with the hair turned inward, with edgings of black, haired seal skin. Women's trousers, and men's and women's outer boots, are decorated with *avittat*, or bands of geometric appliqué of bleached and painted seal skin. Avittat are also known as "skin embroidery" because the mosaiclike patterns of tiny pieces of seal skin have been compared to the petit-point stitch. While this western Greenlandic festive clothing is worn in all parts of Greenland, women in northern and eastern Greenland may choose to wear distinct regional festive clothing. In northern Greenland, this is characterized by long white boots of bleached seal skin, with an inner boot of caribou skin and an edging of polar bear skin, while eastern Greenlandic women started using white cotton amauti (amaat in Greenlandic) for festive occasions in the 1980s.

Since the 1970s, in the wake of land claims movements in Canada and Alaska and the creation of the Homerule Government in Greenland in 1979, traditional-style garments have become powerful symbols of ethnic identity. This reflects the increasing

Avittat sampler, Eastern Arctic, early twentieth century. Made by the Kalaallit from seal or walrus skin, the sampler has a cotton-fiber backing sewn with black. Young girls sewed the difficult and complicated skin mosaic to record and store the art of the Kalaallit. © McCord Museum ME933.3. http://www.mccord-museum.qc.ca/en/

pride in ethnic identity among indigenous Arctic people as well as their increasing political power through native corporations in Alaska and some degree of self-government in Canada and Greenland. Increasing participation in international contexts, where ethnic and national differences are salient, plays a role as well. Political leaders often wear traditional clothing to make a statement about ethnic identity and indigenous rights.

CLOTHING IN THE TWENTY-FIRST CENTURY

Today, people wear a mixture of traditional and Western clothing, depending on personal preferences as well as on the occasion. Manufactured clothing, such as jeans, T-shirts, and sweatshirts, are widely worn indoors, within the community, and during the summer. Traditional clothing is used in winter, especially when hunting or traveling, and usually in combination with manufactured clothing. In most parts of the Arctic, it is also worn on festive or ceremonial occasions, especially by women.

Traditional clothing, and the knowledge and skills associated with it, plays an important role in the cultural revitalization that started in the 1970s. Numerous projects across the Arctic seek to document the knowledge of elders and pass it on to younger people in school, in evening school courses, or in culture camps. In Greenland, skin-sewing workshops, supported by the municipalities, offer employment opportunities to local women while keeping traditional knowledge and skills alive. They make festive costumes, or parts thereof, on commission for locals but also smaller, less expensive items that are popular with tourists, such as mittens or slippers.

Since the 1990s, there is increasing concern about protecting traditional designs to prevent their alienation and appropriation by outsiders. Given the collective nature of the ownership of the designs, this is difficult within the current legal framework. Pauktuutit, the Inuit Women's Association of Canada, has been particularly active in seeking protection for the amauti, an important cultural symbol for Canadian Inuit.

In the late twentieth century, an increased mixing of local and regional styles can be observed. To a large extent, this is due to increased contact and exchange between communities, as well as between people of Greenland, Canada, Alaska, and Siberia. While seamstresses in the past learned mostly from their mothers and other women in their community, today they may get inspiration from published sources as well as from personal observation and discussion with seamstresses from other areas. This may be in connection with international events, such as the Inuit Circumpolar Conference or the Arctic Winter Games, or national meetings, such as those of Pauktuutit.

Individual seamstresses and designers, as well as larger companies, create clothing in modern designs using a variety of materials, including commercially tanned skins and fabric. For instance, two Greenlandic companies, Great Greenland and Eskimo Pels, have been successful in making fashionable garments of commercially tanned seal skin for customers in Greenland and Denmark. Popular articles include jackets, waistcoats, and bags.

Thus, in spite of the increasing use of manufactured garments, traditional clothing remains important. For certain purposes, some types of traditional-style clothing are still preferred over manufactured garments. In addition, the making and use of such clothing also helps to keep traditional knowledge and values alive and provides a striking symbol of cultural identity for native peoples of the North American Arctic.

Snapshot: Snow Goggles

Snow goggles were used by peoples across the North American Arctic, from southwestern Alaska to Greenland, to protect the wearer from direct sunlight and sharp reflections from snow and ice.

Snow goggles known from southwestern and northern Alaska, Canada, and Greenland from the nineteenth and early twentieth century were usually carved of wood but were occasionally made of seal skin, caribou antler, or musk ox horn or bone and fastened with a string of sinew or leather. They were made to fit the nose and completely covered the eyes, with a horizontal slit or a round opening over the eye. Depending on the size and shape of the eye opening, they were found to reduce harmful ultraviolet light to between 2 and 8 percent of what it would be otherwise. Sometimes they were blackened on the inside with soot, a practice that further increased the protection from ultraviolet light.

An unavoidable side effect of the small eye openings is the restriction of the visual field upward and downward, a disadvantage especially when traveling on uneven ground. On the other hand, due to their optical qualities, snow goggles could correct minor myopia, and they also improved visual acuity in people with normal vision. Furthermore, snow goggles protected the eye from cold and draft. In contrast to Western glasses, they had the additional advantage of not misting over or getting coated with ice, and they remained comfortable to wear even in cold weather, when the metal frame of Western glasses might cause frostbite.

Snow goggles were used in the Arctic long before optical glasses were invented in Italy in the late thirteenth century, as is evident from a pair of ivory snow goggles from the Ipiutak culture (about 0–900 c.e.) that was excavated at a village site near Point Hope in northern Alaska. The advantages of snow goggles were recognized by early European explorers such as W. E. Parry (1790–1855), who employed Inuit people to make snow goggles for his crew on his 1821–1823 voyage in search of the Northwest Passage.

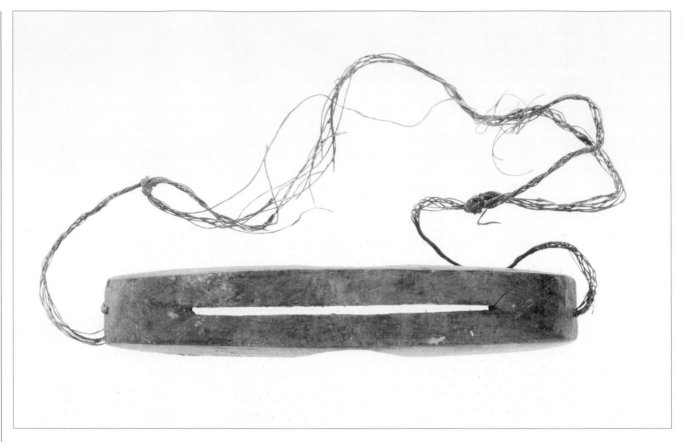

Wooden snow goggles, Arctic, nineteenth century. Worn to completely cover the eyes except for a tiny slit, snow goggles are designed to reduce the amount of ultraviolet light entering the eye. © McCord Museum ME982X.86.2. http://www.mccord-museum.qc.ca/en/

In southern Alaska, Aleut and Alutiit hunters did not use snow goggles but wore bentwood visors over their gut-skin parkas when at sea. These were usually elaborately decorated with polychrome paintings, ivory carvings, sea lion whiskers, feathers, and glass beads. They not only protected the wearer from sun and glare but also expressed prestige. Beautiful garments were also thought to attract sea mammals, especially sea otters, and were thus believed to be necessary for a successful hunt. Wooden eye shades, often elaborately decorated, were also used by hunters in Greenland and southwestern Alaska when at sea.

In the late twentieth century, traditional snow goggles and eye shades have been replaced by mass-produced Polaroid sunglasses in modern designs developed for outdoor use. Some people, and not only hunters, use sunglasses almost daily, while others normally do not use them.

REFERENCES AND FURTHER READING

Black, Lydia T. *Glory Remembered: Wooden Headgear of Alaska Sea Hunters*. Juneau: Alaska State Museums, 1991.

Norn, Mogens. "Eskimo Snow Goggles in Danish and Greenlandic Museums, Their Protective and Optical Properties." *Meddelelser om Grønland, Man & Society* 20 (1996): 1–25.

References and Further Reading

British Museum. "Annuraaq—Clothing in the Arctic." http://www.thebritishmuseum.ac.uk/explore/online_tours/americas/clothing_in_the_arctic/annuraaq_clothing_in_the_arct.aspx (February 2001) (accessed 1 July 2008).

Buijs, Cunera. *Furs and Fabrics: Transformations, Clothing and Identity in East Greenland*. Mededelingen van het Rijksmuseum voor Volkenkunde, no. 32. Leiden, The Netherlands: CNWS Publications, 2004.

Buijs, Cunera, and Jarich Oosten, eds. *Braving the Cold: Continuity and Change in Arctic Clothing*. CNWS Publications, vol. 49. Leiden, The Netherlands: Research School CNWS, School of Asian, African and Amerindian Studies, 1997.

Damas, David, ed. "Arctic." *Handbook of North American Indians*. Vol. 5. Washington, DC: Smithsonian Institution, 1984.

Driscoll, Bernadette. *The Inuit Amautik: I Like My Hood to Be Full*. Winnipeg: The Winnipeg Art Gallery, 1980.

Fienup-Riordan, Ann. *The Living Tradition of Yup'ik Masks: Agayuliyararput—Our Way of Making Prayer*. Seattle: University of Washington Press, 1996.

Fitzhugh, William, and Aron Crowell, eds. *Crossroads of Continents: Cultures of Siberia and Alaska*. Washington, DC: Smithsonian Institution Press, 1988.

Hall, Judy, Jill Oakes, and Sally Qimmiu'naaq Webster. *Sanatujut: Pride in Women's Work*. Hull, QC: Canadian Museum of Civilization, 1994.

Hansen, Jens Peder Hart, Jørgen Meldgaard, and Jørgen Nordkvist, eds. *The Greenland Mummies*. Washington, DC: Smithsonian Institution Press, 1991.

Hatt, Gudmund. "Arctic Skin Clothing in Eurasia and America: An Ethnographic Study." English translation by Kirsten Taylor. *Arctic Anthropology* 5, no. 2 (1969): 3–132.

Hickman, Pat. *Innerskins/Outerskins: Gut and Fishskin*. San Francisco: San Francisco Craft and Folk Art Museum, 1987.

Issenman, Betty Kobayashi. *Sinews of Survival: the Living Legacy of Inuit Clothing*. Vancouver, BC: UBC Press, 1997.

King, J.C.H., Birgit Pauksztat, and Robert Storrie, eds. *Arctic Clothing of North America: Alaska, Canada, Greenland*. London: British Museum Press, 2005.

Oakes, Jill E. "Copper and Caribou Inuit Skin Clothing Production." *Canadian Ethnology Service Mercury Series Paper*, vol. 118. Hull, QC: Canadian Museum of Civilization, 1991.

Oakes, Jill E., and Rick R. Riewe. *Our Boots: An Inuit Women's Art*. Vancouver, BC: Douglas & McIntyre, 1995.

Varjola, Pirjo. *The Etholén Collection: The Ethnographic Alaskan Collection of Adolf Etholén and His Contemporaries in the National Museum of Finland*. Helsinki: National Board of Antiquities, 1990.

Birgit Pauksztat

The Subarctic

Clothing was a fundamental and striking feature of the cultures of the Algonquian and Athapaskan peoples of the Subarctic region of North America when Europeans first encountered them in the sixteenth, seventeenth, and eighteenth centuries. Garments made from tanned animal hides afforded protection against a harsh northern environment; beautifully decorated with porcupine quillwork, fringes, and earth pigments, they also provided an important outlet for artistic expression, signified ethnic identity, and conveyed information about individual physical, social, and spiritual well-being.

The arrival of Europeans on the northeast coast of the continent in the sixteenth century initiated a period of rapid cultural change for the indigenous peoples of the Subarctic. In clothing and adornment, three major trends characterized the Post-Contact period: the long-term retention of some traditional forms of hide clothing, particularly in remote regions and for winter wear; the emergence of a variety of new, distinctive, aboriginal fashions in which indigenous and imported clothing materials and fashion ideas combined; and the ever-increasing popularity of clothing made from imported textiles styled after current European or Euro–North American models. The latter trend ultimately prevailed: By the late twentieth century, most Subarctic indigenous peoples dressed in factory-made clothing similar to that worn in other rural communities in Canada and Alaska. Nevertheless, into the twenty-first century, in communities across the Subarctic but particularly in Canada's Northwest Territories, hide-tanning and sewing abilities and skills in working with porcupine quills and beads remain respected activities, and a few women carry on these cultural traditions, making native-style clothing for family and friends and to sell.

THE LAND AND ITS PEOPLE

The North American Subarctic spans the width of the continent, extending from the Cook Inlet region on the Pacific Ocean to the coast of Labrador on the Atlantic Ocean. In ethnographic studies, this vast region often is divided into western and eastern components on the basis of the languages spoken by its indigenous peoples. West of Hudson Bay, people speak languages of the Northern Athapaskan family; to the south and east, Algonquian languages are spoken. These linguistic differences notwithstanding, Subarctic peoples across the region share many cultural attributes and a similar history, including aspects of dress practices.

The Subarctic landscape is dominated by northern coniferous forests, which extend in a broad belt across the region, interrupted by numerous lakes, streams, and areas of muskeg; by high mountain ranges in the west; and by arctic tundra in the central area. Woodland and (in winter) barren-lands caribou, moose, and black bear, and smaller mammals such as muskrat, marten, fox, lynx, wolf, beaver, porcupine, and snowshoe hare, are found in forests and river valleys across the region. The many waterways provide habitats for a variety of waterfowl and fish. Dall sheep, mountain goats, woodland caribou, grizzly bears, and ground squirrels live on the rocky slopes, alpine pastures, and foothills of the mountainous regions and wood buffalo in the grasslands south of Great Slave Lake. The tundra is home to ground squirrels, Arctic foxes, wolves, grizzly bears, and in summer, herds of caribou numbering in the thousands. These natural resources provide inhabitants with furs and leather to provide the warmth necessary to dress for survival in a harsh climate.

The climate is similar from east to west across the continent. Winters are long and very cold, with daily temperatures averaging from −20 to −40 degrees Celsius (−4 to −40 degrees Fahrenheit) from November to March. During this time, the sun appears only briefly above the horizon; rivers and lakes are deeply frozen; and fine, powdery snow covers the land. Temperatures moderate in March and the days lengthen. Snow and ice begin to melt quickly and migratory waterfowl return to the waterways. As spring turns to summer, there is a dramatic efflorescence of plant life, and "the bugs"—clouds of blackflies, mosquitoes, and other biting, stinging insects—reappear with a vengeance. Daytime temperatures may rise as high as the mid-30s Celsius (mid-90s Fahrenheit) during the brief weeks of summer. These seasonal factors are obviously related to the choices made about items of dress.

Over the millennia, the indigenous peoples of the Subarctic developed ways of life uniquely adapted to the climate, terrain, and resources of this northern land. They lived by hunting and trapping large and small land mammals (moose and caribou were of primary importance), fishing, and gathering roots and berries. For most of the year, people lived in small, highly mobile family groups, moving camp frequently in response to seasonal changes and the behavior of animals. They traveled long distances in all seasons and all kinds of weather, on foot and in birch-bark canoes in summer and on snowshoes in winter. They carried young children, camp equipment, and personal belongings on their backs or, in winter, dragged them behind on toboggans.

These aforementioned material goods were few and mainly limited to items that were easily portable and of a utilitarian nature. Warm, well-fitting clothing was a necessity, protecting against snow and intense cold in winter and against insects and rough terrain in summer. But, the practical concerns satisfied, clothing served Subarctic peoples in other important ways as well. For both makers and wearers, clothing provided outlets for artistic creativity and aesthetic expression. It functioned, as well, as a form of nonverbal communication, proclaiming ethnic identity and informing others of a man's ability to provide well for himself and his family and of a woman's expertise in highly esteemed skills such as tanning, sewing, and decorative work. In both general and specific ways, it also served in communications with the spirit world: Through handling clothing materials with respect and skill and in making and wearing fine clothing, people honored the spirits of the animals who sustained life; decorative motifs executed in porcupine quills or earth pigments could represent a more direct appeal for assistance from the spirit world.

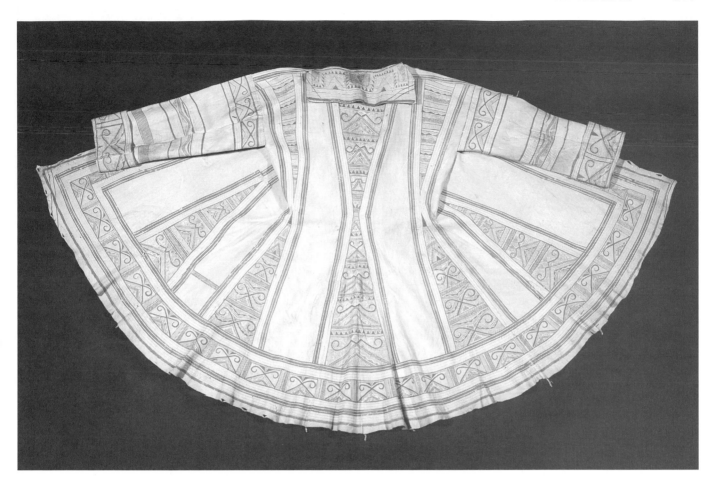

Innu man's painted caribou hide coat, early eighteenth century, Subarctic. The style is distinctive in that the cut echoed a European man's cloth frock coat, which had flaring skirts, a front opening, and a collar. © Canadian Museum of Civilization III-B-590, image E598-14.1.001. http://www.civilization.ca/

The act of getting dressed, particularly for important social or ceremonial occasions, did not stop with the donning of clothes but included as well attention to self-adornment. People painted and tattooed their faces; applied grease, ochre, beads, and feathers to their hair; and wore earrings, bracelets, and necklaces made from beads, bones, and shells. They carried a variety of small decorated bags and containers—knife sheaths, personal charms, and containers for face paints and fire-making equipment—on their persons, looped under belts, and suspended from the neck.

INDIGENOUS CLOTHING: MATERIALS AND STYLES

In earlier times, Subarctic peoples obtained virtually all clothing materials from the land. Caribou and moose were of paramount importance, for they provided not only large hides of excellent quality but also a range of other products useful to clothing production, such as bones for scrapers, brains and spinal fluid used in tanning, sinew for sewing, and hair for decorative work.

Dehaired, tanned caribou or moose hide is soft and pliable yet strong, lightweight, and porous. It was used extensively for summer clothing. Winter clothing commonly was made from furred caribou hide, which has a remarkably high insulating capacity relative to its weight. Whether for winter or summer wear, garments generally were designed to fit and cover most of the body yet enable the wearer to move easily and quietly—important considerations for hunting peoples who were often on the move. Footwear was soft soled, practical for use with snowshoes in winter or for travel in birch-bark canoes in summer. In very cold weather, people wore two layers of clothing: The inner garment had the fur to the inside for warmth and comfort, and the outer had the fur to the outside, where it would shed snow and moisture. Hide robes, furred or dehaired according to the season, often were worn over fitted garments.

The furred hides of smaller mammals—including beaver, muskrat, marten, lynx, and (regionally) mountain goat and sheep—also were used for clothing. Garments made from the soft, fluffy pelts of snowshoe hares were particularly common, worn by adults and children alike. Snowshoe hare pelts are relatively fragile and easily torn, and they required special treatment if intended for clothing. First, the skin was peeled off the carcass in its entirety, then cut spirally to form a continuous strip about two and a half centimeters (one inch) wide. This strip was washed, dried, twisted, and joined to others to form a long, furry cord, then worked (using a looped netting technique) into winter robes, parkas, trousers, and hoods.

Seamstresses used animal hair, earth pigments, bird feathers, and porcupine quills in diverse and ingenious ways to add color and beauty to the garments they sewed. Porcupine quillwork was a particularly important form of clothing decoration. Quills were cleaned, sorted by size, and dyed with plant and berry

Gwich'in Hunters. Colored lithograph based on a sketch by fur trader Alexander Hunter Murray, at Fort Yukon (Alaska) in 1847–1848. Gwich'in men would commonly add life to old clothes by adding woven yarn sashes, long knives in beautifully quill- or bead-decorated cases, small beaded cloth tobacco bags, pillbox hats of velvet and beads, and moccasins made from smoked hide decorated with silk embroidery. Courtesy of Judy Thompson.

juices. They were applied to garments using a number of different techniques, the most common of which were weaving, folding and sewing, and wrapping. Designs executed in porcupine quills were geometric, usually combinations of rectangles, triangles, and diamond shapes. Paint also was applied to clothing, particularly in the eastern Subarctic, where garments often were elaborately decorated with curving, linear motifs in red and brown earth pigments and in yellow derived from fish roe. In the western Subarctic, painting on clothing was far less extensive and complex. Typically, lines were drawn in red ochre (a substance believed to confer spiritual protection) around necks, wrists, and hemlines and over seams.

Almost all work associated with the making of clothing was performed by women. Girls began learning hide-tanning and sewing skills at a young age by watching and helping their mothers and grandmothers. Their training intensified as they reached puberty, during which time a girl lived apart from her family and community for several weeks or even months, restricted her activities, observed numerous taboos, and wore special garments and accessories. Athapaskan girls, for example, wore large, hooded robes of caribou hide that hid their faces and obstructed their vision; special hair ornaments; and necklaces from which hung drinking tubes and head scratchers. Older women instructed pubescent girls in proper social and ritual behavior and in practical skills required for adult life. Girls spent much of their time learning and perfecting sewing and decorative art skills, such as porcupine quillwork, while they were secluded.

The process of making clothing began with the tanning of hides, a time-consuming activity requiring practice and skill as well as physical strength. Procedures for preparing caribou and moose hides for use as clothing were similar throughout the Subarctic. Briefly, raw hides were cleaned by washing and scraping; they were soaked and worked in solutions of caribou or moose brain; and they were stretched, dried, and softened by further scraping. A light smoking of the hide, which colored it golden brown on one side, was a final, optional stage.

Large numbers of tanned hides were required to clothe a family. For example, just to provide warm winter outfits for her husband, herself, and two children, a woman would have required more than twenty furred hides, each tanned on the flesh side. For summer clothing, the same number again would be needed, and these hides would have to be dehaired and tanned.

Some clothing styles—for example, parkas, trousers, and hoods made from netted hare skins and robes of furred or dehaired caribou or moose hide—were worn across the region. In general, however, Algonquian and Athapaskan clothing styles differed. Algonquian clothing typically was of smoked moose or caribou hide. Men wore shirts, closely fitted leggings that reached to the thigh, breechcloths, mittens, and a robe. Women wore sleeveless pullover dresses supported with straps over the shoulders and drawn in at the waist by a belt; separate sleeves secured with ties across the upper chest and back; and leggings tied below the knees with garters. The upper portion of the dress bodice folded over to the outside of the garment, forming a bib that was elaborately decorated with quillwork and fringes; the skirt was decorated with painted designs and fringed along the bottom edge. Both men and women wore soft-soled moccasins.

A typical Athapaskan clothing outfit comprised two garments made from white (unsmoked) caribou hide: a sleeved tunic and a one-piece lower garment in which trouser and soft-soled

Woman's clothing from the Great Slave Lake Region, Subarctic, mid-nineteenth century. The smoked moose hide dress is of a traditional style modified by European styling details: a collar, bead-edged stroud cuffs and epaulettes. The short leggings were made from smoked hide or stroud, and long, rectangular hoods were made from red, black, or navy blue stroud decorated with cloth appliqués. Also typical was a moccasin with seamed, tapered toe. © Canadian Museum of Civilization, image S95-24009. http://www.civilization.ca/

moccasin were combined. (Some eastern Athapaskan peoples, for example, Chipewyan, Slavey, and Dogrib, appear to have worn a variation of the *moccasin-trouser*, a moccasin-legging held up by ties and a belt, which also supported a breechcloth.) An Athapaskan man's tunic hung to about knee level and was cut to a deep point at center front and back. Sleeves were wide at the armhole and set deeply into the lower sides of the garment, enabling easy movement of the arms, particularly in a forward motion. Mittens joined by a braided cord (which ensured they would not easily be lost) and a detached hood often completed an outfit. Women's clothing outfits were very similar to men's. Their dresses differed from men's tunics mainly in being straight cut across the front and longer and slightly dipping in the back. Once able to walk, children wore miniature versions of adult garments.

Athapaskan summer tunics and dresses were decorated with fringed bands of quillwork that curved across upper fronts and backs. On moccasin-trousers, a band of quillwork was worked down the center leg and around the ankle, and a quill-worked garter was attached around the leg, below the knee. Summer hoods and mittens were similarly decorated with porcupine quills and fringes.

THE EARLY POST-CONTACT PERIOD

The first contacts in historic times between the indigenous peoples of the Subarctic and Europeans probably began about 1500 C.E. on the East Coast, with encounters between Innu (formerly known as Naskapi-Montagnais peoples) and fishermen from Brittany, France. Jacques Cartier's voyage up the St. Lawrence River in 1535 and the subsequent formation of French settlements in the St. Lawrence River valley led to more, and sustained, contacts. By the late sixteenth century, increasing numbers of Algonquian peoples (especially Cree and Northern Ojibwa) were trapping furs, particularly beaver, for trade with the newcomers. After 1670, posts on Hudson Bay attracted Algonquian and Athapaskan (primarily Chipewyan) bands to trade.

On the western shores of the continent, contacts between Europeans and Athapaskans began in the mid-eighteenth century with the arrival on the North Pacific Coast of European vessels intent on exploration and trade in furs, particularly sea otter. Dena'ina of the Cook Inlet region of Alaska, the only Athapaskans to inhabit a seacoast, probably were the first to experience direct contact, around the third quarter of the eighteenth century. For most Athapaskans, the first face-to-face meetings with white people came as European explorer-traders extended their quest for furs into the remote interior of the continent. Alexander Mackenzie's two expeditions from Fort Chipewyan on Lake Athabasca, in 1789 and 1793, were key events in this regard. His first voyage, north along the river that was later to bear his name, brought him into contact with Slavey, Dogrib, and Gwich'in; during his second expedition, he traveled westward across what is now northern British Columbia, encountering other Athapaskan peoples: the Beaver, Sekani, and Carrier.

Word of white-skinned strangers and some examples of their marvelous technology usually preceded direct encounters. The indigenous peoples were eager to acquire European goods and well accustomed to trade. With respect to clothing, ready-made garments and imported textiles (particularly wool blankets, wool cloth in fine [*stroud*] and coarse [*duffle*] weaves, and printed cotton cloth) were highly sought after, appreciated for their practical and aesthetic qualities and for the prestige they conferred on their owners. Other new materials—braids and ribbons, silk embroidery thread, and glass beads—also were in great demand as new media for the decoration of clothing.

Contact with foreigners and access to trade goods ultimately had a profound effect on Algonquian and Athapaskan clothing and adornment styles. Change did not happen overnight, however, nor was it uniform across the Subarctic. Face painting, tattooing, and elaborate hair dress gradually were relinquished, perceived as outmoded by aboriginal people modeling

Athapaskan man's jacket, with fringes, fur trim, and decorative panels. Subarctic, early twentieth century. © Canadian Museum of Civilization VI-S-4, (NegativeS95-24052). http://www.civilization.ca/

themselves after the newcomers. Distinctive regional clothing fashions emerged as traditional and new materials and styles were combined in creative ways. One such new-style garment worn by men in the central Subarctic (Algonquian-speaking Cree and Ojibwa, and *Métis*, the term used in Canada to refer to people of mixed blood, usually First Nations and either French Canadian or British Canadian) in the late eighteenth century was a striking, elaborately decorated coat made from moose hide. The coat was long (ankle length), sleeved, and open down the front. It was decorated with bands of woven porcupine quillwork and quill-wrapped fringes on the shoulders and with painted designs in red, green, yellow, and brown down the center back and bordering front and bottom edges. The materials used in such coats and the techniques and motifs employed in their decoration conformed with aboriginal traditions, but their ample length and front opening suggest European fashion influence. The prototype for this moose-hide coat design may have been similarly styled garments worn by French and English traders at posts on Hudson Bay. Similarly, in the eastern Subarctic around the same time, the Innu began making a distinctive style of hunting coat, the cut of which echoed a European man's cloth "frock" coat in that it had flaring skirts, a front opening, and a collar. The Innu garment, however, was made from caribou hide, their local sewing material, and it was decorated with painted motifs reflective of Innu cosmology and spiritual beliefs. Worn by a hunter to propitiate and please the spirit of the caribou and ensure a successful hunt, the painted caribou-hide coat functioned within Innu society as a powerfully spiritual, intrinsically aboriginal garment. With minor modifications to cut and decoration, hunting coats of this style continued in use in Innu communities until the early twentieth century.

These two examples refer to instances where aboriginal seamstresses used traditional, indigenous clothing materials in the making of garments styled after European prototypes. It also happened that clothing of traditional aboriginal design was made from imported materials. For example, around 1800, perhaps earlier, Cree women were using stroud instead of tanned caribou or moose hide to make men's breechcloths, hoods, and thigh-high leggings and women's robes, strap dresses, detachable sleeves, leggings, and long, rectangular hoods. Other imported materials—especially silk ribbon and glass beads—were used to decorate these cloth garments.

In the western Subarctic, Athapaskan peoples, too, responded in diverse ways to the influx of new clothing materials and fashion ideas. As was the case elsewhere, changes to aboriginal modes of dress and adornment were more pronounced, and happened more quickly, among groups living in close proximity to trading posts, whose members had frequent contact with fur-trade personnel and greater access to trade goods. Younger people often were the leaders in fashion change. For example, at mid-nineteenth century, at the heart of the Northern fur trade in the Great Slave Lake region, fashionable clothing for young native men included several garments of smoked moose or caribou hide, more or less modified by trade goods and European fashion. These included a pullover shirt decorated with European military-style cloth (red and black stroud) epaulets; front-placket, long fringed leggings; and mittens and moccasins trimmed with trade cloth. A long sash of bright-red yarn (a popular trade item, often called an *Assomption sash* because of its manufacture in the Quebec village of that name) wrapped around the waist and a powder horn and shot pouch attached to bead-edged cloth bands were common accessories. Comparable clothing for young women consisted of smoked moose-hide dresses of a traditional style modified by European styling details—a collar, bead-edged stroud cuffs, and epaulets—and by a variety of trade materials (glass beads, red and blue wool cloth, and pieces cut from tin containers used to carry tea, tobacco, and foods into the North) incorporated into the garment's decoration. With such dresses, women wore short leggings made from smoked hide or stroud and long, rectangular hoods made from red, black, or navy blue stroud decorated with cloth appliqués (a style of headgear probably influenced by more elaborately decorated Cree women's hoods).

The common footwear, worn by adults and children alike in the Great Slave Lake region at mid-nineteenth century, was a moccasin with a seamed, tapered toe; a small, U-shaped upper; and a wraparound ankle cuff. This was a very different garment from the combination moccasin-legging or moccasin-trouser observed by the first European visitors to the region in the previous century. The origin of this pointed-toe moccasin style is unknown; most likely it originated with Algonquian peoples to the east, possibly with the Cree. Its diffusion into Athapaskan territories may have begun in pre-Contact times, and the movement, via the fur trade in the nineteenth century, of eastern Subarctic peoples and fashions into the far Northwest would have accelerated this process. During the course of the nineteenth century, the pointed-toe moccasin superseded earlier footwear styles throughout much of Athapaskan territory.

Late-nineteenth-century moccasins often were decorated with floral motifs worked in silk embroidery threads or glass beads on

Tsekwitsele, an Athapaskan girl, Fort Norman, Northwest Territories, September 1921. Photograph by P. R. Lang, O.M.I. © Archives Deschâtelets, Ottawa.

the upper. This form of decoration represented a dramatic break with earlier artistic traditions involving mainly linear or geometric patterns executed in porcupine quills or in paint. Silk threads and beads, and the steel needles and scissors used to work them, were of European origin, brought into the Subarctic by fur traders. Floral designs and embroidery techniques also were European, introduced and popularized in the Subarctic mainly through two agencies: Christian mission schools and the Métis.

Catholic missions were established by Jesuit priests in the eastern Subarctic in the seventeenth century. An Anglican clergyman, Reverend John West, set up a mission school on the Red River in the Canadian Plains (Manitoba) in 1820, and later in the century, Anglican missions were established farther west and north. The Roman Catholic Order of the Grey Nuns founded a mission school in Red River in 1844 and, in subsequent years, established a number of other schools along the fur-trade route to the Great Slave Lake region. As a result of missionaries' activities, by the late nineteenth century, most Subarctic peoples were at least nominally Christian, although traditional spiritual beliefs often coexisted and remained strong.

In mission schools, Algonquian, Athapaskan, and Métis girls were taught European domestic skills, including embroidery techniques and motifs that the nuns themselves had learned when young. Native girls returning to home communities further disseminated these skills. Métis of the Red River area (who were mainly of French Canadian and Algonquian heritage) were particularly influential in this regard. Early on, they espoused and perfected floral art, becoming known as "flower beadwork people." Key participants in the fur trade, Red River Métis traveled throughout much of the Subarctic, often settling and intermarrying with local Athapaskans and Algonquians and influencing local fashions of dress and adornment.

FUR-TRADE PERIOD FASHIONS

By the end of the nineteenth century, Subarctic peoples had adapted to a new way of life, one that was to continue until several decades into the twentieth century. Traditional knowledge and customs remained important, but the economy now centered on individual trapping of furs and annual or semiannual visits to the trading post to exchange these furs for products of European material culture. With respect to clothing, the influences of imported goods and technologies, fur-trade lifestyle and society, mission-school training, and styles introduced by the Red River Métis (and peoples of other cultures) combined in a colorful Northern clothing fashion worn particularly by men. Characteristic of this style were jackets of a European cut (short in length, straight cut across the lower edge, and open down the front) made from moose or caribou hide smoked to a deep amber color and decorated with fur trim, fringes, and porcupine quill- and beadwork (on shoulders, across the upper back, on either side of the front opening, and on cuffs). Other items of men's wear in this style included mittens of smoked hide with floral work in beads or silk embroidery thread, thigh-high leggings (usually worn over cloth trousers) made from stroud and decorated with floral-beaded side panels, silk ribbon rosettes, and beaded or quill-worked garters tied below the knee. Accessories included belts of woven porcupine quillwork, braided yarn sashes, and tobacco pouches and cartridge bags made of dark velvet densely worked with floral beadwork or embroidery.

During the same period, Euro–North American styles of dress were increasingly popular and accessible to most; by the early twentieth century, the contents of a trader's store included a variety of clothing and sewing materials and accessories. Native people bought some items ready made, such as shawls, scarves, men's three-piece wool cloth suits and broad-brimmed black-felt hats, and braided yarn sashes. Dry goods, such as stroud, velvet and plaid tartan cloth, also were purchased, from which women made clothing closely patterned after current Euro–North American styles. For the aboriginal owner, such clothing was prestigious, a mark of modernity, and a symbol of skills in hunting, trapping, and trading.

These trends notwithstanding, some traditionally styled garments continued in use, worn especially by people who lived in remote areas or by those who could not afford to buy from the trader's store. In particular, the practicality of old-style winter

Innu woman: Moisie, Québec, 1912. Labrador Innu women wore ankle-length, full-waisted skirts of wool or cotton cloth, smoked hide moccasins, and imported shawls: clothing similar to that worn by many Subarctic women of the time. © Canadian Museum of Civilization, Photograph by Frank Speck, image 20361. http://www.civilization.ca/

clothing ensured its survival long after summer equivalents were abandoned. Thus, until several decades into the twentieth century, Gwich'in women and children wore dresses and moccasin-trousers of furred caribou hide when traveling in winter, and children in isolated communities across the Subarctic wore parkas, pants, mittens, and hoods made of netted hare skins. Moccasins of tanned caribou or moose hide, cut large to allow for the addition of liners, continued in use as the optimal winter footwear for all ages: They were warm and perfectly suited to walking on snowshoes.

Pan-Subarctic trends, such as the adoption of Euro–North American styles of dress and the popularity of indigenous fur-trade fashions involving floral-decorated, smoked-hide garments, inevitably led to a greater uniformity of clothing styles across the region than had been the case in earlier times. Nevertheless, regionally or culturally distinct modes of dress and adornment still were in evidence. For example, at the turn of the twentieth century, Innu women in Labrador wore ankle-length, full-waisted skirts of wool or cotton cloth; smoked-hide moccasins; and imported shawls—clothing outfits similar to those worn by many Subarctic women of the time. The Innu women's hairstyles and hats were, however, unique to their culture. On each side of the head, over the ears, Innu women wrapped their hair around small rectangular pieces of wood, which were then bound with cloth or beads. A conical hat made from six sections of alternated red and black (or dark blue) stroud, with the upper portion folded over to the front, rested above the hair wraps. Similarly, the generic appearance of the two- or three-piece suits of dark wool cloth owned by many Subarctic men at this time often was modified by the addition of accessories, made by wives and mothers, that reflected local tastes and fashions. For example, around 1900, Gwich'in men dressing for a visit to a trading post gave old, worn-out cloth jackets and trousers style and color by adding to the ensemble woven yarn sashes, long knives in beautifully quill- or bead-decorated cases, small beaded-cloth tobacco bags, pillbox hats of velvet and beads, and moccasins made from smoked hide decorated with silk embroidery.

As the twentieth century progressed, Euro–North American style clothing made from imported materials largely replaced indigenous equivalents in the native wardrobe. However, for reasons of economy, practicality, and aesthetics, native-style garments made at home using products from the land did not entirely disappear. Until at least the 1950s in small, remote communities, some children were dressed for winter in parkas and pants of netted hare skins or, in the far Northwest, in combination moccasin-trousers of furred caribou skin. Women continued to make jackets similar to those popular in the early twentieth century, of smoked hide decorated with embroidery as well as bead- and quillwork for summer wear or of furred hides with attached hoods for winter. They also made winter mittens of smoked hide with duffle (a heavy woolen fabric) liners and hats of beaver and other furs. Moccasins still were a popular form of footwear, although their cut had undergone further modification. The new style, which became popular in the 1930s, had a round toe and a large upper (usually decorated with floral beadwork), around which the hide forming the bottom unit was gathered. Another new style of footwear introduced around the same time was a boot made from smoked hide and fabric, usually called a *mukluk*, after an Inuit prototype.

In the early twenty-first century, most Subarctic indigenous peoples live in permanent communities that have houses, schools, nursing stations, police detachments, and stores with imported food, clothing, and other supplies. Hunting, fishing, and trapping are still important, for both economic and cultural reasons, but people rely as well on wage labor and government subsidies in order to make a living. Most communities are small and distant from large urban centers, but they are linked to the outside world by radio, television, computer, telephone, and airplane. Through local stores, mail order catalogs, online shopping, and travel to larger centers, people have access to a wide variety of manufactured goods.

Most people, on most occasions, dress in factory-made clothing similar to that worn by nonnative people in rural communities across Canada and Alaska. Nevertheless, a few women carry on cultural traditions of tanning and sewing caribou and moose hide and working with porcupine quills and beads. Although they often incorporate a variety of modern sewing materials (wool and cotton textiles, zippers, glass beads, wool yarn) into their work, the clothing they make retains a distinctly native character.

Native-style clothing has both practical and symbolic functions in modern Subarctic communities. Parkas, jackets, mittens, and footwear may be worn for everyday or, more commonly,

Athapaskan wedding outfits, made in 1986 by Therese Pierrot, Fort Good Hope, Northwest Territories, Canada. © Canadian Museum of Civilization, image T2007-00001. http://www.civilization.ca/

reserved for special occasions, such as religious ceremonies, school concerts, and holiday visiting. In Yukon and Alaska, such clothing often features in the gift-giving that is part of the ritual of the potlatch. At both the community level and in the broader society, the wearing of native-style clothing proclaims pride in aboriginal ancestry.

A few Algonquian or Athapaskan individuals or organizations have entered the mainstream of contemporary fashion design. For example, D'Arcy Moses, of Slavey ancestry, became one of Canada's most recognized native fashion designers in the late 1990s, known particularly for his fur creations. Moses went on to spearhead the development of *Nats'enelu*, a Northern fashion house situated in Slavey country in Fort Simpson, Northwest Territories. Another Northern enterprise, named Dene Fur Clouds, produces an internationally marketed line of knitted fashion accessories (scarves, hats, vests, leg warmers) made from locally trapped furs such as snowshoe hare and beaver.

In the late twentieth and early twenty-first centuries, faced with the loss in some communities, and the rapid decline in others, of knowledge related to traditional clothing manufacture, some Subarctic aboriginal groups and individuals initiated projects aimed at recovering or reviving this aspect of their heritage. Particularly in the Northwest Territories, hide tanning, porcupine quillwork, and traditional clothing design have been the subject of community workshops. A large project, aimed at repatriating knowledge and skills related to the making of traditional caribou-hide clothing and involving several years' work on the part of over forty seamstresses, was undertaken by the Gwich'in Social and Cultural Institute in the late 1990s. The Gwich'in Traditional Caribou Hide Clothing Project reached a successful conclusion in early 2003, with the completion of five multipiece summer outfits, one for each Northwest Territories' Gwich'in community.

References and Further Reading

Brasser, Ted J. *Bo'jou, Neejee: Profiles of Canadian Indian Art*. Ottawa: National Museum of Man, 1976.

Burnham, Dorothy K. *To Please the Caribou: Painted Caribou-Skin Coats Worn by the Naskapi, Montagnais and Cree Hunters of the Quebec-Labrador Peninsula*. Toronto: Royal Ontario Museum, 1992.

Hail, Barbara A., and Kate C. Duncan. *Out of the North: The Subarctic Collection of the Haffenreffer Museum of Anthropology, Brown University*. Bristol, RI: Brown University, The Haffenreffer Museum of Anthropology, 1989.

Oberholtzer, Cath. "All Dolled Up: The Encapsulated Past of Cree Dolls." In *Papers of the Thirtieth Algonquian Conference*, edited by David H. Pentland, 224–242. Winnipeg: University of Manitoba, 1999.

Oberholtzer, Cath. "Material Culture of the Mistassini Cree: Local Expression or Regional Style?" In *Papers of the Thirty-Sixth Algonquian Conference*, edited by H.C. Wolfart, 287–321. Winnipeg: University of Manitoba, 2003.

Phillips, Ruth B. "Like a Star I Shine: Northern Woodlands Artistic Traditions." In *The Spirit Sings: Artistic Traditions of Canada's First Peoples*, 51–92. Calgary: Glenbow-Alberta Institute, 1987.

Richardson, Sir John. *Arctic Searching Expedition: A Journal of a Boat-Voyage through Rupert's Land and the Arctic Sea, in Search of the Discovery Ships under Command of Sir John Franklin*. London: Longman, Brown, Green, and Longmans, 1851.

Thompson, Judy. *From the Land: Two Hundred Years of Dene Clothing*. Hull, QC: Canadian Museum of Civilization, 1994.

Thompson, Judy, and Ingrid Kritsch. *Long Ago Sewing We Will Remember: The Story of the Gwich'in Traditional Caribou Skin Clothing Project*. Gatineau: Canadian Museum of Civilization Corporation, 2005.

Turner, Lucien. *Ethnology of the Ungava District, Hudson Bay Territory*. Quebec City: Presses Coméditex.

Judy Thompson

The Northwest Coast

The Pacific Northwest Coast has long been known for its elaborate and distinctive art styles. This attention to form and expression is no less true for clothing, especially ceremonial clothing, than for totem poles and masks. On the Northwest Coast clothing conveys identity, status, and wealth among its indigenous people, wrapping wearers in their clan and familial identities. Today, this is most clearly seen in ceremonial regalia worn on important public occasions; but dress has always provided more than protection from the elements. Many communities along the Northwest Coast featured a ranked hierarchy of individuals and families whose social status was denoted by items of dress reflective of the prerogatives and rights owned by the person or clan. This expression of social position could also reflect a link between the human and supernatural realms, again confirming the powerful position of high-ranking individuals. Conversely, the lack of these visual markers of status would convey the social ranking of someone further down in the community hierarchy.

CLIMATE AND GEOGRAPHY

Typically defined as stretching from Yakutat Bay to the Columbia River, the Northwest Coast covers a wide range of climates and geographical environments. In each area, the mountain ranges define the interior boundaries. In Alaska, these mountains come almost straight down to the shoreline, leaving only small areas of habitable coastline along the bays and waterways. In British Columbia, an archipelago of islands, including the Queen Charlotte Islands and the larger Vancouver Island, provides sheltered coves and inlets, while river valleys penetrate deeply into the interior ranges. In Washington State, some groups inhabited the interior fjords of Puget Sound while others faced the Pacific Ocean.

The marine environment of the Northwest Coast is moderated by the Pacific Ocean, which cools the air in summer and warms it in winter, leading to relatively cool summers and mild winters. The north-south mountain chains influence precipitation patterns, leading to heavy rains on the western, windward slopes and drier rain shadows on their leeward sides. Heavy snowfalls accumulate at higher elevations in the coastal ranges, feeding the rivers that flow seaward. Nations living in or near these coastal ranges developed clothing to cope with these conditions, including fur robes, moccasins, and snowshoes. However, with few exceptions, bare feet were the norm.

In all places, the most frequent means of travel was by water; the oceans, rivers, shorelines, and lakes provided transportation as well as sustenance. The seas were the highway on the Northwest Coast, as travel over water was much easier than slogging through the dense old-growth forests and mountainous inlands. Villages were arranged in the littoral zone between forest and sea; houses faced the water so their inhabitants could welcome home family, greet guests, and keep a lookout for enemies. Everyday dress on the Northwest Coast had to accommodate the needs of wet weather, maritime travel, and resource gathering.

CLOTHING BEFORE EUROPEAN CONTACT

In good weather, little clothing was needed. Men frequently went without clothing, and women might wear a simple skirt made of cedar during warmer months. Clothing for the ubiquitous wet and cold seasons was made from a variety of materials along the Northwest Coast. The most utilitarian piece of clothing was the woven cedar-bark blanket, which could be wrapped around the body in numerous ways: draped over the shoulders, tied or pinned over one shoulder and secured by a cord around the waist, or doubled over and worn around the waist only.

CEDAR

The most important resource for Northwest Coast people was the cedar tree. The yellow cedar (*Chamaecyparis nootkatensis*) was more common in Alaska but can be found in the subalpine regions of British Columbia. The western red cedar (*Thuja plicata*) is common from southeastern Alaska down to Puget Sound. Indeed, the red cedar was ubiquitous along most of the coast, accounting for as much as 50 percent of the area's vegetation at one time. It was used to build houses, canoes, and totem poles as well as to make clothing. Men worked with the wood of the cedar tree; women fashioned many items of clothing out of cedar bark.

The best single resource for uses of the cedar tree is Hilary Stewart's 1984 volume titled *Cedar: Tree of Life to the Northwest Coast Indians*. The outer bark of the western red cedar provided a key material for clothing. Both red and yellow cedar bark was used for clothing items, including skirts, capes, dresses, and hats.

Cedar bark is collected in the spring and early summer months when the sap in the tree is running, allowing the bark to be more easily removed. Harvesting is a precise activity; only a certain

Conical hat, British Columbia, Canada. These hats were made from finely twined spruce root and cedar bark. They were worn by great chiefs and whalers in the region. One of the first hat forms reported by explorers was worn by the chiefs on the west coast of Vancouver Island. © Canadian Museum of Civilization, artifact VII-F926, image S97-14907. http://www.civilization.ca/

amount is taken from each tree, after which it is left to heal over time and continue to grow. The process of harvesting includes an understanding of the proper protocol to address and thank the spirit of the tree for its gifts. This respect ensures the continued health of the trees and future supplies of bark. Once harvested, the inner bark is separated from the coarser outer bark, and the long strips of the soft inner bark of both red and yellow cedar trees are dried and stored for later processing. When the time comes to work the dried strips of the inner bark, they are placed over the edge of a board and beaten until the fibers are shredded to create a soft and pliable material. Yellow cedar bark needs soaking, to aid in the shredding process, and a different type of tool—a flat pounder with grooves—is used in the processing of the bark. Alternately, the inner bark can be separated into layers and then split into long, thin strands for use in the creation of mats, baskets, hats, and other woven items.

In the Puget Sound area, women often fastened a belt around long dresses of cedar bark. Cedar-bark robes were worn in a number of ways, often either over both shoulders or under one arm and pinned on the other shoulder. All along the coast, both sexes used cedar-bark capes and hats to protect from the rain. The rain capes were woven from strips of cedar bark or tule grass in the southern regions. Cedar-bark capes were waist length and often finished with a fringe at the bottom edge; they were occasionally lined at the neck with strips of fur. Cedar-bark robes woven from the softer

shredded and beaten bark were elaborated with decorative designs and worn on ceremonial occasions. In wet weather, clothing made from shredded and oiled cedar bark provided both protection from the rain and ocean spray and insulation against the cold.

Cedar-bark skirts were often constructed in two layers: a fine inner layer next to the skin and a coarser outer layer on top. Skirts were woven on a tripod loom that allowed for continuous weaving. Capes and blankets were woven on a two-bar loom. Examples of looms found in archaeological sites measured five feet (1.5 meters) in height and six feet (1.8 meters) in width. The top and bottom bar were affixed to two uprights dug into the ground. The lower bar could be moved to change the tension. With this arrangement the weaving could be rolled around the frame so that the weaver could continually weave as she moved the material along. On the northern coast, some cedar-bark capes were decorated with painted designs on the exterior to display the status and *crest* (a human, animal, or supernatural creature that is the hereditary privilege of a particular family or clan, often depicted in painting, weaving, or sculpture) of the wearer to others; in more southern areas, designs adorned the interior of the cape, more privately bringing the protection and guidance of spirit helpers to the individual wearing the cape.

Other styles of skirts were made either of free-hanging cords of cedar bark secured to bark braid around the waist or shredded cedar bark hanging from a twined waistband. Cedar-bark capes

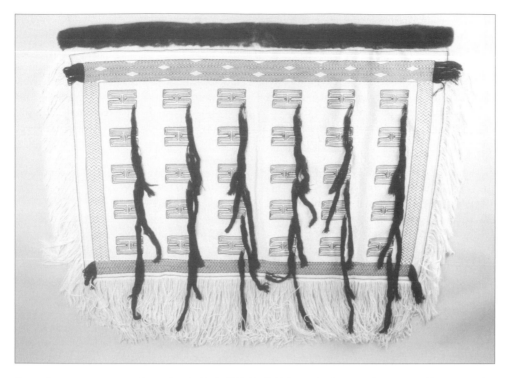

Twenty-first-century ravenstail weaving by Marie Oldfield (Haida), made of wool and trimmed with sea otter fur. The ravenstail style is typical of the Pacific Northwest Coast. Courtesy of the Burke Museum of Natural History and Culture, Catalog Number 2004-2/417.

were made of a continuous length of woven cedar bark, with a hole in the center to pull over the head. It was fitted at the shoulders and expanded over the upper body to allow for freedom of movement.

In addition to cedar bark, many other plant- and animal-based materials were incorporated into weaving and sewing, including nettle fiber, cattail leaves, spruce root, kelp, human hair, fireweed cotton, mountain goat and dog wool, animal intestines, and sinew. In the Puget Sound and Columbia River areas, bird down or down-covered strips of twisted bird skin were incorporated into cedar-bark blankets to add warmth, softness, and insulation. Occasionally, a bark blanket was lined at the neck with fur trim.

A key item in any wardrobe was a cedar-bark or spruce-root hat. A good hat kept the rain off and cut the glare off the water. Some hats were double walled or incorporated a hat band that kept the hat from resting directly on the head, increasing its ability to shed water. There were many different cedar-bark and spruce-root hat styles along the coast. While most everyone would own a plain cedar-bark work hat, a high-ranking person might have spruce-root hats with painted crest designs, ermine-tail tassels, or a particular woven shape to show his or her status. Some hats included designs woven into the outer surface. One of the first hat forms reported by explorers was worn by the chiefs on the west coast of Vancouver Island. A conical hat with a dome at the top, it was woven of finely twined spruce root and cedar bark and was the marker of the great chiefs and whalers of that region.

FUR AND HIDE

In the Puget Sound region, blankets were constructed of wool from a species of dog kept specifically for their fur. These wool dogs were noted by the early explorers to the region, but the decline in indigenous textile weaving in the Puget Sound area led to the extinction of this breed. An 1847 painting by Paul Kane shows the interior of a Puget Sound Salish house, with a small white dog sitting next to a woman weaving a blanket. Kane noted that the dogs were kept isolated on small islands to keep the breed pure, and they were combed for their hair. This was then cleaned, dyed, and spun for use in the weaving of blankets and capes. Dog wool was often combined with mountain goat wool for blanket weaving.

Kane depicted a loom of the two-bar type, where a continuous warp is wrapped around the top and bottom bars of the frame. Women who were accomplished blanket weavers were specialists in their trade. However, Salish weaving practices diminished when commercially made woolen blankets became readily available, although indigenously produced blankets were kept for ceremonial occasions. The practice was resurrected in the late twentieth century, and there are now a number of weaving masters teaching a new generation of students.

Further north on the coast, animal hide and fur were often combined with clothing made from plant materials. Daily dress was not extravagant and included breechcloths and blankets made of hide. Haida women wore a simple tunic of tanned hide. Most men went naked in warm weather and wore a hide or cedar blanket across the shoulders in inclement weather. Cedar-bark robes might be edged with fur, or the shredded and spun cedar bark itself might also be twined with mountain goat wool for weaving into prestige robes known as *chilkat weaving* to Europeans, because of their persistence in that Tlingit area; the robes are known as *naaxein* by the Tlingit and Haida and *gwish-halait* by the Tsimshian. These five-sided robes are the only known example of weaving that includes truly round design forms made possible by the combination of twining and braiding used by the weaver. They were first produced near the beginning of the nineteenth century. Because they could display detailed crest images in the characteristic style of Northwest Coast art, they grew rapidly in popularity and soon replaced the earlier style of robe—the *ravenstail* style—which featured geometric patterns similar to those found on basketry. Both of these types of blankets were made of mountain goat wool collected during the spring shed, when the animals left clumps of their discarded winter coats on trees and bushes. Fur was also processed from animals brought in by hunters throughout the year. Women spun the wool on a wooden spindle into a single-ply twine and then thigh-spun it into a two-ply twine for weaving. This multi-ply yarn could be composed purely of mountain goat wool if used for the more ancient weaving of the ravenstail type or combined with yellow cedar bark for use in the naaxein-type weaving warps. These robes were woven on a frame—rather than a true loom—with free-hanging warps attached to a single bar at the top of the frame. While a very few women continued the practice of naaxein weaving through the twentieth century, ravenstail techniques were lost soon after the turn of the nineteenth century. In more recent years, both ravenstail and naaxein weaving have experienced a renaissance, with weavers producing new garments each year.

One of the most luxurious and precious items of clothing on the coast was a cloak made from pelts of sea otter (*Enhydra lutris*). These were restricted to those of the highest rank. To make a full-length cloak, cedar-bark twine was used to sew together multiple furs. Paintings made by English artist Sigismund Bacstrom in 1793 provide a keen glimpse into the type of clothing used by high-ranking individuals of Haida Gwaii (the Queen Charlotte Islands). They wear a variety of apparel, including sea otter cloaks, cedar-bark blankets, and European clothing received in trade. The women are adorned with labrets in their lower lips and facial paint on the lower portion of the face. Farther south on the coast, the attire of chief Maquinna of Nootka Sound was described by John Rodgers Jewitt, a blacksmith and sailor who spent two years as Maquinna's captive after an attack on his ship, *The Boston*, in 1803. Jewitt wrote that the chief wore a sea otter–skin cloak that hung to his knees and was fastened by a painted or woven belt, clearly expressing Maquinna's power and status.

The trade in sea otter pelts was so intensive that the species was driven to extinction in the region by the early nineteenth century, turning the fur trade to land-based animals. Other animal-fur sources included bear, antelope, deer, elk, mountain goat, and seals. Smaller animals such as beaver, squirrel, rabbits, marten, and marmot provided skins that would either be sewn into larger units or cut into strips and twisted into spiral cord for weaving.

ARMOR

There were a number of different types of armor and warrior's gear along the coast. Among the Tlingit in Alaska, rod-and-slat armor or heavy garments of thick hide served to protect the warrior. Hide armor was often made of elk hide and occasionally walrus hide. Rod-and-slat armor, when worn over a hide tunic, could stop arrows or even musket shot. Some pieces of armor were reinforced with rows of Chinese coins from the fur trade. Tlingit and Haida warriors wore heavy wooden helmets as well. In the central coast, Kwakwaka'wakw warriors used thick ropes sewn into a protective vest to guard against enemy daggers. Along the Columbia River, elk-hide armor was prevalent and was produced for local use as well as traded to more northern groups.

Interestingly, as the use of armor diminished throughout the nineteenth century, the forms of protective gear were retained in the ceremonial clothing of some groups. The Tlingit, for example, developed beaded collars that mimicked the shape of hide bibs worn by earlier warriors. The hide bibs were painted with crest designs just as the later collars depicted beaded crest designs. Daggers, too, remained a part of ceremonial ensembles in many parts of the coast.

BODY MODIFICATION

Body modification was an important status marker on the Northwest Coast. It included piercing of the nose and ears by both sexes, piercing of the lower lip by women, and tattooing by both sexes, as well as head-shaping for girls in the central and southern parts of the coast.

Head-shaping is an ancient practice apparently done as early as first millennium B.C.E., as evinced by archaeological explorations at the mouth of the Fraser River in lower British Columbia. This practice seems to have been most common among the bilateral descent groups of the central coast area, but it was practiced in the most southern regions as well. There were several methods of head-shaping in practice in the eighteenth and early nineteenth century, resulting in various degrees of high, flat foreheads or a flat elongation of the back of the skull. In all cases, the malleable skulls of infants were shaped through pressure applied while in the cradle, using materials such as cedar bark, wooden pads, or kelp. The resulting shape of a high forehead and flattened back of the skull was a sign of beauty as well as prestige and was restricted to those of high rank.

Other practices of body adornment, like head-shaping, transformed the natural skin of the body into a canvas for social markings. Piercings, tattooing, and body painting were ways of visibly asserting one's rank or status. These types of changes were regulated by class; slaves, for instance, were not allowed to change their appearance. Most of these additions focused on the head and face, but tattoos were applied to other parts of the body as well. Hands—like the head—generally remained uncovered and thus were an important area for marking through tattooing. Like other status-changing events, receiving a tattoo required a *potlatch* (a ceremonial feast at which family privileges are displayed or transferred and witnesses are paid with gifts for their acknowledgment of what transpired) and was only available to high-ranking individuals. Tattoos featured crest designs owned by individual clans and families. Some tattoos featured geometric motifs similar to those seen on basketry or other weavings.

Each culture had criteria for which parts of the body were appropriate for tattoos. The Haida covered most parts of the body, including the chest; the full length of the arms and legs, including the back of the hands and the top of the feet; and, on occasion, even the cheeks and back were decorated. Potlatches celebrating marriages, the building of a new house, or the giving of names were occasions in the nineteenth century for ritual tattooing. The marking of high-ranking children was conducted at a potlatch during which children were given proprietary names, had their ears pierced, and were tattooed. The details and ceremonial protocol for this occasion differed from region to region on the coast,

Tlingit "chilkat" or *naaxein* blanket, made of yellow cedar bark and mountain goat wool, typical of the Pacific Northwest Coast (nineteenth century). Courtesy of the Burke Museum of Natural History and Culture, Catalog number 1-1587.

but at each, the goal was the same: to raise the status of both children and parents, transferring a visual mark of wealth and rank onto the younger generation. Among the Tsimshian, these alterations to the skin through tattooing and piercings signified the connections that high-ranking individuals had to the super-natural—those of high rank were considered immortal spirits in human covering. Among the Haida, it was not until a full comple-ment of tattoos around the body was completed, perhaps being applied over a number of years, that a person was considered suit-ably ornamented as would befit a noble elder.

Tattoos inspired by or copied from published images of Northwest Coast art have grown popular in the nonnative pop-ulation of North America, especially in the Pacific Northwest. This practice has distressed members of the indigenous nations who see the practice as infringing on cultural intellectual prop-erty rights and an appropriation of family- and clan-owned crest designs by those who lack the appropriate inherited privileges.

PIERCINGS

Both men and women had their ears and sometimes their noses pierced. Ears often had multiple perforations adorned with string, feathers, abalone, or, in post-Contact times, silver and gold ear-rings. Both sexes had their noses pierced as infants. Unlike ear-rings, which might be worn daily, nose rings were only worn on ceremonial occasions and were often made from whalebone, aba-lone, copper, or silver. Only women on the northern Northwest Coast had their lips pierced. Like head-shaping, the use of labrets is an ancient practice with evidence dating back to 1000 B.C.E.

The recorded practice of lip-piercing documents that the custom was initiated when a girl reached marriageable age, at which time her lower lip would be pierced with a small pin. The opening would be expanded over time, with labrets of ever-increasing size inserted at status-changing moments in a woman's life. Each ex-pansion was marked with a public ceremony and payment of the witnesses. While the custom of large labrets ceased in the early nineteenth century, many young women still wore a small silver pin in their lower lip at the end of that century. The practice vir-tually ceased in the twentieth century, with a small resurgence among today's young people as a result of both renewed cultural practices and the current interest in body piercing throughout North American popular society.

All of these piercings were restricted to men and women of the upper classes. They were considered requisite marks denoting that a family had properly and publicly presented their children at a potlatch with the appropriate protocols and payment of wit-nesses. Reverend W. H. Collison, who worked among the Haida from 1876 to 1883, noted that it was not uncommon for a man of rank, if insulted by an inferior, to point to his own ear and remind his insulter that he had never had his ear pierced, which was the equivalent of saying, "You are a person of very little consequence." George Emmons, a U.S. naval officer, recorded a similar practice among the Tlingit, whose women could use the presence and size of their labret to silently express the hierarchy of rank.

Some scholars have focused on the capacity of some types of adornment to provide internal protection. Anthropologist Martine Reid contends that the original function—dating back thousands of years—of personal adornments hung from the ears,

Necklaces from many parts of the Pacific Northwest Coast show a great range of materials, including animal teeth, shells, and bone. It has been argued that their original purpose was to prevent seepage of the soul through joints. In 1864, a Haida woman reported that her halibut tattoo with the face of her chief on its tail would protect her and her kin from drowning in the sea. © Canadian Museum of Civilization, artifact VII-C-7682, image S97-16442. http://www.civilization.ca/

nose, and lips was to protect these orifices from a departure of the soul. Arm and neck bands, finger rings, and necklaces could prevent seepage of the soul from the joints. Tattoos on the joints of the hands may have served a similar shielding function. Some Haida believed that their tattoos provided amuletic powers. In 1864, a Haida woman reported that her halibut tattoo, with the face of her chief on its tail, would protect her and her kin from drowning in the sea.

PERSONAL ADORNMENT

The popularity of copper, brass, and iron ornaments was noted by the English blacksmith John Rodgers Jewitt during his time at Nootka Sound. He wrote that women's ornaments included earrings, necklaces, bracelets, rings, and anklets, all of which were most often made of copper or brass, and small nose ornaments made from a shell or bead suspended from a thread. He also noted that commoners wore skin or cedar-bark bracelets and anklets while those of higher status valued long strings of dentalium shells as necklaces. Necklaces from many parts of the coast show a great range of materials including animal teeth, shells, bone,

and indigenous copper. Post-Contact, large, blue-glass beads manufactured in Europe were highly prized trade items and were most often incorporated into necklaces. The Tlingit were the only Northwest Coast nation to adopt beadwork, using smaller seed beads to decorate ceremonial gear.

Dentalium shells were used as both personal adornment and currency on the coast in pre-Contact and early Contact times. The *hiqua* is a long, tubular mollusk whose white cylindrical shell is approximately three inches (seven and a half centimeters) long. The shells were sewn onto garments and hats as decoration and were strung into long strands and worn to denote the wealth of a family. They were harvested off the coast of Vancouver Island and were traded as far as California, Alaska, and even into the Northern Plains region.

Abalone was also a valuable trade item used to decorate many items of ceremonial regalia. Although abalone is native to the Northwest Coast, the indigenous people preferred the blue-green shells traded up from California. These large shells were cut into pieces to use as earrings and nose rings. They were sewn onto *button blankets* (blankets decorated with buttons and appliquéd material displaying the crest of the wearer), hats, and headdresses or inlaid into masks. The shimmering quality of the iridescent shell caught the sunlight or the firelight, bringing a radiant quality to whatever it decorated. Among the Kwakwaka'wakw, wearing abalone earrings and a painted spruce-root hat was reserved for women of the highest status, specifically those whose marriage debt had been repaid four times over.

FACE PAINTING

Face painting was common on the Northwest Coast both for ceremonial adornment and everyday utility. Wearing an application of minerals mixed with oil provided the skin a layer of protection from the sun, wind, and insects, especially when traveling long distances. Women painted their faces during mourning. A variety of materials were combined for this purpose, including ochre, trade vermillion, tree fungus, charcoal, tallow, and tree pitch. Paint was applied freehand with fingers or brushes or stamped using wooden stamps incised with heraldic designs.

In the central and southern coast area, early explorers noted the use of a black glittering powder mixed in with face paint. The inclusion of mica dust in red ochre or other minerals mixed with oil made faces shine and shimmer.

In the northern reaches of the coast, face painting was also common. The penchant for increasing the sheen of the face was occasionally accomplished by the application of pieces of abalone adhered directly to the skin. Among the Haida, this use of abalone symbolized the sun.

HAIR ORNAMENTS AND JEWELRY

Women's hair was often long and plaited with ornaments attached at the nape of the neck. These were made with a variety of materials, including deerskin decorated with dentalia and, later, beadwork. Often a half-moon or V-shaped ornament of copper, iron, or silver was attached at the top of the braid.

Northwest Coast jewelry dates back thousands of years. Some of the oldest artifacts include canine tooth pendants and labrets from 1500 B.C.E. Bracelets and rings made of indigenous copper date back twenty-five hundred years on the coast. Bone bracelets

Kwakwaka'wakw huxwhukw mask, used for ceremonial dancing (Port Hardy, 1963). Photograph by Bill Holm.

with engraved geometric designs first appeared around I C.E. The importance of items of personal adornment is evinced by the inclusion of copper bracelets and amber beads in the graves of warrior-chiefs from archaeological sites.

At the time of European contact, indigenous jewelry included copper and iron bracelets and anklets, as was noted by explorers at harbors from Nootka Sound to Alaska. In the southern part of the coast, mountain goat–horn bracelets with engraved Salish designs were a valued marker of status. Further north, Sigismund Bacstrom's paintings of the Haida show a chief's daughter as she appeared in 1793, wearing a skirt, possibly made of cedar bark, adorned with blue buttons, a hide shirt, and a trade cloth robe. Additionally, she has a large labret and wears copper bracelets and anklets as well as a European silver fork as a pendant on a long necklace of blue and white trade beads.

The history of silver and gold bracelets on the Northwest Coast follows much the same pattern as that of other post-Contact art forms, such as button blankets. Native artists took introduced materials or designs that sparked their interest and molded them according to their own aesthetic. Unlike copper and iron, which were used on the coast before Contact, silver was first brought to the coast by Europeans and Americans in the late eighteenth and early nineteenth centuries. Silver spoons and forks were made into pendants, and whole coins were used as nose rings and sewn onto clothing for ornamentation; later, silver and gold coins were

pounded down to make engraved bracelets, earrings, pins, and other jewelry. These precious metal bracelets became signifiers of wealth and status, were important potlatch payments, and were sold commercially to earn an income for native artists, as they still are. Bracelets were decorated with traditional crest designs as well as a variety of motifs introduced by the Euro–North American presence along the coast. Jewelry remains one of the most popular Northwest Coast art forms, among both indigenous and nonindigenous patrons.

CEREMONIAL REGALIA

Ceremonial regalia was treated with high regard and decorated in ways meant to enhance the visual and aural presence of the wearer. Many items were painted or appliquéd with the unique style of flat design particular to the area. On the northern Northwest Coast, that meant the use of *formline design*, which was characterized by the use of red, black, and blue-green elements (plus yellow in weaving) particular to this design system. The eye forms, called *ovoids*, and other graphic elements, such as the U-form and other formline shapes, were combined in standardized ways to portray creatures, both natural and supernatural, which symbolized the crests, prerogatives, or histories of individuals and clans.

This art style was shared widely among the Northern cultures, and certain aspects were incorporated into the less codified aesthetics of the central coast region. In both areas, however, the purpose of decorated ceremonial regalia was to identify an individual's social standing and his kinship connections.

Among the Tlingit and Haida, basketry hats were an important element of ceremonial dress. Woven of spruce root, the most prized of hats were topped with a set of potlatch rings (*sgil* in Haida) signifying the high status of an individual who had hosted numerous potlatches. The surface of these hats was often painted with crest designs. Among the Tlingit, and occasionally the Haida, wooden crest hats were carved in the form of an animal associated with an individual's clan associations.

Headdresses with wooden carved frontlets were a key piece of regalia from the northern through the central coast areas. The carved wooden frontlet represents a family crest and sits atop a headdress. Carved and painted, the frontlet is often surrounded by inlaid pieces of abalone or copper and, on the northern coast, topped with a line of flicker feathers. This hardwood carving is attached to a frame, which itself is covered in cloth, and the sides and back of the frame are ornamented with fur or swan skin thick with down; an ermine-skin trailer depends from the rear of the frame, covering the back of the dancer with numerous white pelts that sway with their movements. The headdress is crested with sea lion whiskers, holding a loose stuffing of eagle down. The "chief's headdress," as it was commonly known, was often worn during a welcome dance that greeted visitors to the village, although they were worn at other times during ceremonial occasions as well. In addition to the headdress, the speaker or dancer would often wear a woven robe or tunic of the naaxein style, although button blankets were used as well, especially in the central coast region. A truly rich ensemble would include a beaded or painted apron and leggings. Among the Tlingit alone, beaded collars and eight-tabbed, beaded octopus bags were added to ceremonial regalia. The ensemble worn by chiefs and other high-ranking individuals at times of ceremony represented all the wealth and family connections available to them.

In the central coast area, many ceremonial masks and regalia included a shredded cedar-bark costume covering parts or most of the dancer's body. In the *Tseyka*, one of the most well known dance cycles of the Kwakwaka'wakw, the *hamsemala*, or bird dancers who are associated with the cannibal spirit *Baxwbak-walanuxwsiwe'*, appear during the taming dances for the *hamat'sa* initiate, who is motivated by the cannibal spirit. The *hamsemala* have large wooden masks whose beaks clap open and shut. The dancers' bodies are covered in a garment of shredded cedar bark that sways with the syncopated rhythm of the dancers' high-stepped movements. The hamat'sa initiate himself would appear in a variety of costumes, beginning with a skirt, head-ring, and wrist ornaments of hemlock boughs. Throughout his taming, his costume would reflect the state of his wildness, from unprocessed hemlock to shredded cedar bark, ending with a robe of tanned hide or fur decorated with symbols of his supernatural experiences. Indeed, all along the coast, cedar bark was made into ceremonial headgear to mark dancers with spirit powers.

Ceremonial clothing functioned at more than just the visual level. Many blankets, tunics, and aprons were adorned with items that would amplify the aural presence of the wearer. Sewn-on deer hooves and puffin beaks would rattle as the dancer or speaker moved. With the introduction of trade metals, thimbles, snuff-lid tin tinklers, or locally made miniature "coppers" (a shield-shaped plate of sheet copper that symbolized wealth and status on the Northwest Coast and was often engraved with heraldic imagery) were added.

In addition to the static display of visual wealth on potlatch participants, the kinetic qualities of ceremonial regalia enhanced the effect of the spectacle. Bird down floating down around a dancer would create a flurry of white, drifting in the firelit darkness of a bighouse. The jingling sound of miniature coppers or tin tinklers on a dancer's apron accentuated movement through sound. The swaying of cedar-bark regalia or the fringe of a naaxein blanket blurred the edges of the dancer's profile and emphasized the particular motions of ritualistic choreography.

MASKS

Ceremonials masks were used in many parts of the coast. Among the Tlingit, masks were generally reserved for shamanic use, while headdresses and crest hats were worn by dancers on other ceremonial occasions. Among the Tsimshian and Haida, masks appeared during secret society dances. They could embody animal, human, or supernatural creatures, some with a high degree of realism, others of fantastical variation. In the central coast area, the Kwakwaka'wakw mastered the art of theatrical drama with an endless variety of masks, both static and transformative. The supernatural bird masks that accompanied the hamat'sa dancer would snap their beaks to evoke the skull-crushing abilities of the man-eating hamsemala. Whale masks could move their fins, and sea monsters could blow water from their spouts.

The most famous masks of the Nuu-chah-nulth and Makah are the wolf masks of the *Tlookwana* or *Tlookwalli*, the winter ceremonies of these groups. While the wolf masks have come to symbolize these ceremonies, there were many other masks that might appear during the winter dances. Age-grade clubs would dance the *o'ocinuk*, or "imitating dances." Club members would all dress as a certain animal and imitate its movement. Often the animals would refer to the property rights of the dance host. These dances were described by anthropologist Philip Drucker in 1951, who listed masks that represented codfish, squirrels, cormorants, deer, devilfish, woodpeckers, and sea cucumbers, among others. Dancers might appear with painted faces or masks representing their creature. These dances account for the multitude of Nuu-chah-nulth animal masks that, while related to the Tlookwana, depict creatures other than wolves.

Among the Coast Salish, the secret societies' dances are closed to everyone but previously initiated members. The spirit dancer's relationship with his or her guardian spirit is a personal and private one. A person's guardian spirit is a closely kept secret, and though the winter dance song or costume might provide a hint at the source of the power, the identity of the spirit is known only to the individual. Even in present times, it is the source of his or her skill, and in past times, it was the basis for that person's profession. Unlike other areas of the Northwest Coast, Coast Salish ceremonial clothing provided only the most general clues to the source of spirit power, in contrast to the public displays of hereditary privilege seen further north. The song that a Salish initiate receives determines whether he or she will be a red-face (*sqaíp*) or black-face (*tubcádad*) dancer, whose painted face will reveal this association. The new initiates, or "babies," wear one of two types of headgear: a collection of loose wool strands depending from a raised crown that covers the head and upper body, or a similar arrangement made from cedar bark and raffia. Often

From the first contacts with European explorers and traders in the late eighteenth century, not only blankets but also items of European clothing were highly valuable trade items. Long-standing indigenous trade networks meant that the native people were well prepared to evaluate and incorporate new materials from this unexpected source. Almost immediately, European goods were transformed into new items to meet indigenous needs: Heavy woolen cloth and Chinese coins were incorporated into Tlingit armor, bolts of fabric were transformed into new clothing styles, and buttons were appliquéd onto woolen blankets, creating the previously mentioned button blanket that quickly surpassed in popularity the more labor-intensive, woven ceremonial robes. By the second half of the nineteenth century, cedar-bark clothing disappeared almost entirely, replaced by store-bought clothing or clothing made from imported cotton and woolen fabrics. Imported clothing was often covered by a woolen blanket. Men wore hats in the European fashion, and women most often covered their heads with colorful handkerchiefs or shawls. Men also adopted European clothing styles. Military regalia was especially valued for the connotations of power that adhered to military uniforms.

Many travel writers of the late nineteenth century commented on the indigenous preference for colorful outfits, often considered gaudy by uninformed observers. In actuality, the uses of numerous different pieces of cloth had social status connotations not known to those outside of the native communities. Among the Tlingit, ownership of certain strips of calico or blankets demonstrated the owner's attendance at the potlatch where these items were paid to the guests. These strips were often combined into items of clothing without regard to a European aesthetic that would require similar or complementary colors of fabric be used. Wearing a suit made of a patchwork of fabrics received at several different potlatches signified an individual's participation in the most important occasions of social validation.

Sheep were introduced to Vancouver Island in the mid-nineteenth century by the Hudson's Bay Company. Native women in the Cowichan valley quickly took to using sheep wool in their industries and learned to knit from European settler women. When prepared by hand, the natural lanolins in the sheep's wool made clothing both warm and water resistant. The wools were used in their natural colors—brown, black, white, and gray—and sweaters, vests, hats, mittens, and other items were knitted in a Fair Isle stitch, with native designs passed down through the generations of women knitters. Their products provided both clothing and much-needed income for families, especially during the first half of the twentieth century. The sweaters, known as *Cowichan sweaters*, gained national renown and have spawned many nonnative copies over the years.

CLOTHING AND THE EXPRESSION OF IDENTITY

One's dress articulated a particular social position; adornment was an additional layer indicating social status or class. In addition, regalia could express a connection between the human and supernatural worlds, presenting spiritual experiences in a concrete form. According to poet and historian Robert Bringhurst, there are "tales of Haida princes arriving at feasts wearing necklaces of live frogs, and their wives with live rufous hummingbirds tied to their hair." These experiences are re-created in the crest objects worn on ceremonial occasions—a hummingbird button blanket or a gold necklace of interlaced frogs.

Tlingit artist Nathan Jackson in his ceremonial regalia including headdress frontlet, beaded collar, leather tunic, woven apron, and naaxein blanket, 2002. Headdress by the artist and chilkat robe by Dorica Jackson. Photograph by Kathryn Bunn-Marcuse.

the head coverings have feathered tops. Tunics might be knit or embroidered, sometimes featuring small wooden paddles. Leggings may be adorned with sewn-on deer-hoof rattles. Each initiate carries a fir-sapling spirit dance staff decorated with wool and feathers and with a pointed end. Many of the special attributes of the costumes are brought out and validated during the work (or potlatch) section of the evening.

POST-CONTACT CLOTHING

With the arrival of European traders on the coast, woolen blankets became a highly sought after item. Blankets became a base unit of trade all along the coast; the cost of many items of trade was figured in numbers of blankets for both trade between Euro-Americans and the indigenous populations and for trade between indigenous nations. Most blankets were supplied by the Hudson's Bay Company and were black or navy blue stroud cloth. By the second half of the eighteenth century, button blankets were a frequent item of ceremonial attire all along the coast.

Hummingbird copper dress, 1989, designed by Dorothy Grant. The four detachable panels each contain identical hummingbird designs. Grant uses a Western cut adorned with Northwest Coast imagery, a style that has inspired many other designers in the region. © Canadian Museum of Civilization, artifact VII-B-1846 a-c, photo M. Toole, 1990, image S91-791. http://www.civilization.ca/

As already discussed, clothing indicated rank; additionally, hierarchies of rank could be expressed through items of ceremonial regalia. For instance, among the Tlingit, as lower-ranking members of the community moved into positions of rank left empty due to population decline caused by disease at the beginning of the twentieth century, they wore beaded tunics, collars, and caps, as well as button blankets. They did not have the status or inherited claim to higher-prestige items, such as naaxein blankets and the conical hats adorned with potlatch rings (sgil). However, the repeated appearance of these lower-ranked articles of regalia at Tlingit potlatches and the payments to witnesses made at the time served to increase the prestige of the lesser clothing through long-standing protocols of social validation.

TWENTY-FIRST CENTURY DRESS AND DESIGN

Contemporary clothing for Northwest Coast indigenous people can be as varied and personal as that for the nonnative population as a whole. U.S. and Canadian fashion has been the norm for everyday wear for well over one hundred and fifty years. Ceremonial regalia, however, has retained a strong link to the standards of dress used on social occasions in the late nineteenth century,

with button blankets, woven robes, hide tunics and aprons, headdress frontlets, and spruce-root hats serving as the main articles.

The most famous contemporary designer on the coast is Kaigani Haida artist Dorothy Grant, whose line of haute couture garments began in the 1980s as a collaborative effort between Grant and Haida artist Robert Davidson, who provided some of the original designs appliquéd to dresses, capes, and suits. Grant now creates all her own designs, and her line of Feastwear clothing has inspired many other contemporary artists to design both casual and formal attire in a Western cut adorned with Northwest Coast imagery. Everyday clothing, such as raincoats, T-shirts, baseball caps, and jewelry, adorned with Northwest Coast designs can now be seen on members of all generations at any given time. Ceremonial wear now includes regalia inspired by nineteenth-century practices as well as vests, suits, shawls, and dresses of a Western cut appliquéd or printed with indigenous designs. Contemporary clothing, both ceremonial and quotidian, continues to be an expression of individual and clan identity and experience, as well as a marker of indigenous status and pride.

Decoration and ornamentation were everywhere on the Northwest Coast. It is only natural that people adorned themselves as lavishly as they did their houses, canoes, and poles.

Clothing and body modification convey information about gender, rank, and status in both ceremonial and nonceremonial contexts. Additionally, personal adornment can be a marker of social and individual connections; items of regalia handed down through the family might display one's crest and be a personal link to a grandparent or other clan relative, doubling its significance as a symbol of both familial associations and clan heritage. Certain items of adornment can signify specific privileges owned by the wearer; alternately, some ceremonial clothing is intentionally vague about the wearer's spiritual connections. The ability of clothing to communicate expressions of identity is as honored and understood today as it was in the past.

References and Further Reading

Amoss, Pamela. "Ceremonies of the Indian Way." In *Coast Salish Spirit Dancing*, 87–120. Seattle: University of Washington Press, 1978.

Bringhurst, Robert, and Ulli Steltzer. *The Black Canoe: Bill Reid and the Spirit of Haida Gwaii*. Seattle and Vancouver: University of Washington Press and Douglas & McIntyre, 1991.

Bunn-Marcuse, Kathryn. *Precious Metals: Silver and Gold Bracelets from the Northwest Coast*. Seattle: University of Washington Press, 2007.

Castille, George Pierre, ed. *The Indians of Puget Sound: The Notebooks of Myron Eells*. Seattle: University of Washington Press, 1985.

Chalker, Kari, Lois S. Dubin, and Peter M. Whiteley. *Totems to Turquoise: Native North American Jewelry Arts of the Northwest and Southwest*. New York: Harry N. Abrams, in association with the American Museum of Natural History, 2004.

Chittenden, Newton H. *Exploration of the Queen Charlotte Islands / Newton H. Chittenden*. Vancouver, BC: G. Soules, 1984.

Collison, W. H. *In the Wake of the War Canoe: A Stirring Record of Forty Years' Successful Labour, Peril & Adventure amongst the Savage Indian Tribes of the Pacific Coast, and the Piratical Head-Hunting Haidas of the Queen Charlotte Islands. B.C.* London: Seeley Service, 1915.

Drucker, Philip. *The Northern and Central Nootkan Tribes*. Vol. 144, Bulletin. Washington, DC: Smithsonian Institution, Bureau of American Ethnology, 1951.

Drucker, Philip. *Indians of the Northwest Coast*. Special members' ed. Garden City, NY: Published for the American Museum of Natural History [by] the Natural History Press, 1963.

Dubin, Lois Sherr. *North American Indian Jewelry and Adornment: From Prehistory to the Present*. New York: Harry N. Abrams, 1999.

Emmons, George. *The Tlingit Indians*, edited by Fredrica de Laguna. Seattle: University of Washington Press, 1991.

Fitzhugh, William, and Aron Crowell. *Crossroads of Continents: Cultures of Siberia and Alaska*. Washington, DC: Smithsonian Institution Press, 1988.

Glinsmann, Dawn. "Northern Northwest Coast Spruce Root Hats." Ph.D. dissertation, University of Washington, 2006.

Gustafson, Paula. *Salish Weaving*. Seattle and Vancouver: University of Washington Press and Douglas & McIntyre, 1980.

Holm, Bill. *Northwest Coast Indian Art; An Analysis of Form*. Seattle: University of Washington Press, 1965.

Jewitt, John Rodgers. *The Adventures of John Jewitt, Only Survivor of the Crew of the Ship, Boston, During a Captivity of Nearly Three Years among the Indians of Nootka Sound, in Vancouver Island, Edited with an Introduction and Notes by Robert Brown, with Thirteen Illustrations*. London: C. Wilson, 1896.

Jonaitis, Aldona, ed. *A Wealth of Thought: Franz Boas on Native American Art*. Seattle: University of Washington Press, 1995.

Kan, Sergei. *Symbolic Immortality: The Tlingit Potlatch of the Nineteenth Century*. Washington, DC: Smithsonian Institution Press, 1989.

Kew, Michael. "Central and Southern Coast Salish Ceremonies since 1900." In *Handbook of North American Indians*, edited by Wayne Suttles, 476–480. Washington, DC: Smithsonian Institution Press, 1990.

Liscomb, Robie. "The Story of the Coast Salish Knitters." *UVic Knowlege* 1, no. 7 (2000): 1.

Miller, Jay. *Tsimshian Culture: A Light through the Ages*. Lincoln: University of Nebraska Press, 1997.

Niblack, Albert P. *The Coast Indians of Southern Alaska and Northern British Columbia*. Washington, DC: U.S. National Museum, 1888.

Paterek, Josephine. *Encyclopedia of American Indian Costume*. Santa Barbara: ABC-CLIO, 1994.

Reid, Martine J. "The Body Transformed: Body Art and Adornment among Prehistoric and Historic Northwest Coast People." In *Totems Toturquoise: Native North American Jewelry Arts of the Northwest and Southwest*, edited by Kari Chalker, Lois S. Dubin, and Peter M. Whiteley, 54–64. New York: Harry N. Abrams, in association with the American Museum of Natural History, 2004.

Samuel, Cheryl. *The Chilkat Dancing Blanket*. Seattle: Pacific Search Press, 1982.

Samuel, Cheryl. *The Raven's Tail*. Vancouver: University of British Columbia Press, 1987.

Smetzer, Megan. "The 1904 Potlatch." In "Assimilation or Resistance? The Production and Consumption of Tlingit Beadwork." Ph.D. dissertation, University of British Columbia, 2007.

Stewart, Hilary. *Cedar: Tree of Life to the Northwest Coast Indians*. Vancouver: Douglas & McIntyre, 1984.

Suttles, Wayne. "Productivity and Its Constraints." In *Indian Art Traditions of the Northwest Coast*, edited by Roy L. Carlson, 67–87. Burnaby, BC: Archaeology Press, Simon Fraser University, 1983.

Suttles, Wayne. "Spirit Dancing and the Persistence of Native Culture among the Coast Salish." In *Coast Salish Essays*, edited by Wayne Suttles, 199–208. Seattle: University of Washington Press, 1987.

Suttles, Wayne, ed. *Handbook of the North American Indians: Northwest Coast*. Vol. 7 of *Handbook of North American Indians*, edited by William C. Sturtevant. Washington, DC: Smithsonian Institution Press, 1990.

Vaughn, Thomas, and Bill Holm. *Soft Gold: The Fur Trade & Cultural Exchange on the Northwest Coast of America*. Portland: Oregon Historical Press, 1990.

Wright, Robin K. *A Time of Gathering: Native Heritage in Washington State*. Seattle: Burke Museum, University of Washington Press, 1991.

Kathryn B. Bunn-Marcuse

See also Snapshot: History of the Graduation Button Blanket.

Snapshot: History of the Graduation Button Blanket

Each spring, when the First Nations Haida secondary school graduates receive their button blankets, they are part of a centuries-old tradition of learning their identity and also a new tradition that celebrates their academic achievements.

Button blankets are a relatively recent art form of the Haida, who live on the forested archipelago of Haida Gwaii (also called the Queen Charlotte Islands) off the west coast of British Columbia. For centuries, they have carved, painted, and otherwise displayed their clan crests on totem poles, jewelry, house fronts, storage chests, and in tattoos. When the first European and Euro-American traders arrived on the islands in the late 1700s, the Haida readily exchanged sea otter pelts for Hudson's Bay Company blankets (usually made of white wool with broad stripes of color), bolts of wool fabric, and Chinese mother-of-pearl buttons. They used these materials to fashion a new ceremonial crest garment: the button blanket.

The first button blankets were usually dark blue or black, with a red border and an appliquéd crest. Hundreds of buttons outlined the crest and blanket border. By the mid-1800s, these garments were common among the Haida and other First Nations of the Northwest Coast.

Between 1876 and 1951, however, few button blankets were made or worn. These were the silent years of the Canadian government's suppression of First Nations language, gatherings, and ceremonies. Cultural expression has slowly returned to Haida Gwaii, each decade marking rediscovered old arts and reconfigured new ones.

Today's button blankets are made of contemporary fabrics and embellishments. Different weights of wool have replaced blankets, and polyester is often chosen for children because it is light for dancing and easy to wash. Mother-of-pearl, abalone, and mussel-shell buttons are frequently used, but more often plastic ones are chosen for lower cost and lighter weight. This is a consideration when a single blanket might have five thousand buttons! As in the past, both men and women wear button blankets for celebrations, Haida dancing, and feasts.

Since 1980, a special button blanket—the *graduation blanket*—has been made for each Haida finishing secondary school. The communities wanted to encourage students to complete their schooling and to proclaim their Haida heritage.

The village councils of Old Massett and Skidegate give fabric and buttons to each graduate: black wool for background, red wool for crest and border, and hundreds of different-sized plastic buttons for embellishment. Each blanket is measured across the length of the wearer's outstretched arms, fingertip to fingertip.

Blanket-making falls to the family, who must first select the crest. Often an eagle or raven is chosen, as every Haida belongs to one or the other clan, following his or her mother. Some choose a special crest belonging to the mother's family, perhaps killer whale, hummingbird, bear, or shark. A carver in the family, one who creates totem poles, boxes, or gold jewelry, is usually asked to draw the design. This ensures that the crest has the precise designs essential to Haida art.

Raven graduation button blanket. Button-embellished red and black ceremonial crest garment of a Haida Raven clan member, British Columbia, ca. 2000. Photograph © Sandra Price.

The maker is most often the graduate's mother or a maternal aunt. She will sometimes use fabric other than the wool provided by the village. *Ultrasuede* (a synthetic, suedelike fabric) is prized because it is easy to cut and does not fray. Different colors might be chosen: a red background instead of black or a white or royal blue crest. Choices are inspired by graduation blankets from previous years.

Most makers use the buttons provided, but all add special features to the crest—perhaps a large abalone eye for an eagle or a spray of beads above the blowhole of a killer whale. Occasionally, buttons cut off a very old and tattered button blanket are used. Families may collect embellishments for years just for this blanket.

Some sew on buttons only around the border. Others use a range of button sizes around different parts of the crest, including tiny Barbie-doll buttons for minute detail. Sometimes family members help sew on buttons. The graduate, however, rarely sees the blanket in the making.

The entire village is invited to the ceremony in each community hall when the graduation blankets are presented. Each graduate's family sets a table with their best linens, candles, and tableware. They prepare a special meal—usually turkey, ham, or fish with salads, fresh-baked buns, fruit, and an assortment of desserts.

After the meal, the graduates come up on stage, one at a time. The maker carries the folded button blanket, and several family members accompany her. The graduation blanket is opened and held up for those in the hall (except the graduate) to see. Cheers, applause, and the flash of cameras greet each presentation. The maker puts the blanket around the shoulders of the graduate and adjusts its chest-high tab. Sometimes the maternal grandmother then gives the graduate a Haida name, one that had belonged to a deceased relative or one especially suited to the graduate. Those in the hall bear witness to the name-giving by following the age-old oral tradition of saying the name aloud three times in Haida.

Speeches follow. Clan chiefs and village officials stress the importance of the event. Speakers praise the graduates' accomplishment in completing this part of their schooling and recognize that many will go off-island, some for further education and some for work, while others will remain on Haida Gwaii. No matter where they are, the graduates are told, each time they wear their button blanket and when they hang it on their wall, it will remind them of who they are: Haida. They know their clan, their family, and their Haida name.

The dancing of the blankets completes the program. First, the young women place their hands at their waist and circle the stage, turning to right and to left in a stately three-step pattern. Then the young men take over. Crouching low with their arms straight and firmly grasping the edges of their blankets, they dance energetically to a strong drumbeat. Thousands of buttons reflect the lights and bring the crests to life. The graduates' pride in their new blankets permeates the hall.

The ceremony ends. The first thing every graduate does, without exception, is take off their graduation button blanket to see it finished for the first time.

REFERENCES AND FURTHER READING

Blackman, Margaret B. *During My Time: Florence Edenshaw Davidson, A Haida Woman*. Seattle and London: University of Washington Press; and Vancouver/Toronto: Douglas & McIntyre, 1982.

Jensen, Doreen, and Polly Sargent. *Robes of Power: Totem Poles on Cloth*. Vancouver: University of British Columbia Press and UBC Museum of Anthropology, 1986.

Sandra Price

California

In spite of the fact that California once supported a native population of more than three hundred thousand individuals who spoke as many as eighty mutually unintelligible languages, the clothing worn by the native peoples was remarkably similar from one tribe, and even one region, to another. When Spanish colonists first arrived in 1769, a priest described two of the natives they met. "The man went entirely naked, as all the rest of them [i.e., men] do; the girl was covered decently with bunched threads in front and deer hides hanging from the waist behind." That could have been a description of the dress worn almost anywhere in California at the time of this first contact.

The terminology used here will follow the forty-eight tribal territories and names set out for California in volume 8 of the Smithsonian Institution's *Handbook of North American Indians*. For simplicity, the regional divisions are slightly modified from four of the six laid out by anthropologists Robert F. Heizer and Albert B. Elsasser in *The Natural World of the California Indians*. The fifth region (the Great Basin) and the sixth (Colorado River) are covered by other articles in this volume. Northwest California is marked by steep, forested mountains and deep river valleys, and many areas experience up to one hundred inches (250 centimeters) of rain a year. Most settlements were riverine or coastal, so the easiest form of travel was by dugout canoe. The tribes here (Yurok, Karok, and Hupa) were culturally similar to those of the Northwest Coast. There were no chiefs. Rather, influence was based on the private ownership of resources. Northeast California, home to the Achomawi and Atsugewi, is less rugged and forested than the Northwest and less rich in resources. Though salmon streams and acorn-bearing oaks are found in the western portion, further east the people depended more on gathering roots and grass seeds and hunting deer, antelope, rabbits, and waterfowl. Their cultural influences came from the Columbia Plateau to the north.

Central California is a very large region including a wide variety of environments: ocean shorelines, forested mountains, wide interior valleys of grass and marshland, and chaparral-covered foothills. Throughout this region, oaks were widely abundant, so tribes from the Miwok of Yosemite Valley to the Costanoans around San Francisco Bay relied on acorns, grass seeds, hunting, and fishing for most of their food. The heaviest area of settlement in the Southern California area was along the coastline, including the offshore islands. From there it shaded off into the drier, less populated interior to the east. Along the coast, people took not only fish but sea otters, seals, and shellfish. The Chumash of the Santa Barbara region traveled and traded widely. Many of the southern tribes achieved a high level of artistry and craftsmanship. The coastal Salinan, Chumash, Gabrielino, Luiseño, Ipai, and Tipai (formerly called Diegueño) were the first to be colonized by the Spanish.

California's geographic location and its history has both helped and hindered knowledge of native dress. European explorers visited the coast as early as 1542, and some early explorers left brief descriptions of the natives they encountered on their infrequent visits to California during the next two and a quarter centuries. The Spanish came to stay in 1769, and they, as well as English, French, and Russian visitors, described and sometimes drew the natives they saw. Most of the rest of the natives of California remained almost completely unknown until the time of the U.S. conquest (1846–1847) and the subsequent gold rush and statehood. With every new wave of foreign settlement into previously isolated parts of California, native societies were altered or destroyed at almost the same time they were discovered. One new tool, photography, was introduced to the state during the gold rush and was used from that time on as an indispensable way of recording the appearances of native peoples. Though there were earlier attempts to preserve evidence of what was, in fact, a rapidly vanishing people, it was the ethnographic accounts and artifacts collected by pioneer anthropologists such as Alfred L. Kroeber and his colleagues in the late nineteenth and early twentieth centuries to which we owe our most detailed knowledge of the native Californians, including their ways of dress. Tragically, between the arrival of the Spanish in the last half of the eighteenth century and the end of the nineteenth, the native peoples of California suffered a decline in population of approximately 90 percent. Tribes were scattered and dispossessed of their land, and murder, disease, and starvation left comparatively few survivors. Many of those who lived to give testimony were unborn or small children when their people last wore indigenous dress.

DAILY DRESS

Unconsciously echoing the description of the first California Indians encountered by the Spanish, anthropologist Alfred Kroeber summed up the subject of native dress in 1929 when he wrote that "the standard clothing of California, irrespective of cultural provinces, was a short skirt or petticoat for women, and either nothing at all for men or a skin folded about the hips." Throughout California, nudity for men seems to have been the norm before conquest and colonization. Often, a sarong-like hip wrap of deerskin made from dehaired buckskin was used by men in warm weather and in cold from deer hide with the hair turned inward. Also well documented are belts of cord, buckskin, or human hair wrapped several times around otherwise naked men's waists and short kilts of hide or buckskin that appear in descriptions and drawings from the Northwest.

Despite Kroeber's certainty about universal male nudity in pre-Contact California, it is hard to know what to make of the descriptions of additional garments by later informants. Many claimed that their people wore breechcloths of either shredded

Karok hat, California, ca. 1875–1915. Basketry techniques were used to make hats, which were usually ornamented with geometric or stylized designs. © McCord Museum ME928.51.6. http://www.mccord-museum.qc.ca/en/

fiber or cordage, or else of buckskin or furs. In many cases these may have been a fairly late introduction, traceable to increased contacts with tribes from outside California or to European influences. For example, the Sierra Miwok living in and around today's Yosemite National Park called the breechcloth a *taplawū*, which is probably derived from the Spanish term for a breechcloth, *taparabo*. It is possible that in this case the garment was introduced by North American Indians from the Spanish missions who escaped into the interior. The Spanish introduced the taparabo to the formerly nude native men of the Central and Southern regions.

Shirts are reported in ethnographic accounts for men and women in the Northwest and Northeast regions, as well as in the Sierra Nevada Mountains of Central California. The Shasta were said to have made knee-length shirts from two deer hides sewn up the sides and across the shoulders. The seams were often painted and fringed. In winter, a similar shirt was made from several raccoon or fox skins pieced together and worn with the fur facing inward. For additional warmth, two fox skins were worn; one over the chest and the other the back. They joined over the wearer's left shoulder and tied under each arm.

Shirts are also said to have been used elsewhere in California, usually where the people were more subject to cold. The Tolowa and Yurok in the Northwest and the Foothill Yokuts, Miwok, and

Monache of the Sierra all are said to have worn shirts at times. Tubatulabal men, women, and children living in the southern foothills of the Sierra Nevada were said to wear sleeveless coats and vests of buckskin in cold weather. But it must have been purely for status that Chumash men of the Santa Barbara Channel wore fur vests that fitted closely to the body. These were sleeveless and reached only to the waist, leaving them naked from there downward. The fur side of the hides faced outward. Raccoon and fox skin were used. Only captains or boat owners could wear vests made from bearskin.

Californian women usually wore separate front and rear aprons. The front apron was narrower, while the rear piece was wider and usually wrapped forward to cover the sides of the legs. Aprons usually ended somewhere just above the knees to midshin and were made from either plant fibers, animal skins, or combinations of the two. Plant fibers included grasses, reeds, and softened strips of the inner bark of trees. These were woven onto fiber or buckskin cords and tied about the waist.

Other skirts were more spectacular. Northwestern tribes, such as the Hupa and Yurok, wore a buckskin back apron and a front apron of buckskin or braided grass decorated with paint and rows of shells. Edges were cut into long fringes that were strung with berry, nut, or seed beads and abalone or obsidian tinklers that rattled and rang as they moved. The Chumash in the Southern region also used paint, abalone, and other shells to decorate their buckskin skirts, while wealthy women pieced together one or more luxurious sea otter skins for their back aprons.

Throughout California, there are reports of unexpected garments such as one-piece skirts worn by both men and women among such tribes as the Yurok in the Northwest. There are accounts of clothing that covered the upper bodies of women, not just the shirts already described but also buckskin camisoles or even full buckskin dresses. It is difficult to know whether these reports might not have come from descendants remembering the coverings added in the nineteenth century under the force of Victorian notions of modesty. Or perhaps these were well-intentioned efforts to hide their ancestors' nakedness. Yet early accounts from the Channel Islands seem to confirm some use of garments by women that covered their torsos. On Santa Catalina Island, women were said to wear a covering of seal skins reaching from their breasts downward, while the "Lone Woman" of San Nicholas Island, discovered living with no companions in 1852, was said by eyewitnesses to be wearing "a kind of gown, leaving her neck and shoulders bare, and long enough when she stood up to reach her ankles." This gown was skillfully made of seabird skins, cut in squares and sewn together with the feathers pointing downward. In most places, prepubescent boys and girls and elderly men and women went naked.

Capes or cloaks provided protection against the elements. These were worn in various ways: over the shoulders; wrapped around the body; or over one shoulder, under the opposite arm, and fastening in front. Both capes and the longer cloaks were often made of deer, coyote, bear, bobcat, fox, and raccoon hides. Coastal tribes enjoyed sea otter- and seal-skin coverings. In marshy areas of Central California, rain capes were made of shredded tule reeds or the inner bark of trees. Often garments were worn with the hair turned inward for warmth or outward to shed rain. Bird skins sewn together were used by some groups for capes. Tribes from many regions used blankets made from strips of fur or feathers twisted into cords and woven together. These served as both bedding and clothing.

The use of muffs made of fur or bird skins and worn singly or on each arm seemed confined to colder regions.

Throughout California, the native peoples almost always went barefoot except in cold weather or for long journeys. As a general rule, moccasins were found in Northwestern, Northeastern, and Central California, while sandals were used in the South. Moccasins were usually made from a single piece of buckskin, with one seam up the front and another up the heel. Separate soles could be added, though some believe that this was a nineteenth-century development. The buckskin formed a cuff around the ankle that was worn up or down; sometimes reaching as high as the calf. In cold weather, moccasins were insulated with grass stuffing.

Sandals were made of rawhide or wrapped yucca fiber. Not all authorities believe that they were prehistoric.

Leggings were rare, though they were used sometimes for work or for long journeys, especially through snow. Usually, these were of buckskin, often with the hair turned inward. Some Northern tribes, including the Shasta, were said to wear fringed leggings reaching from ankle to hip. The Eastern Pomo sometimes used leggings and moccasins made of woven tule reeds.

Most native Californians, especially men, went bareheaded, the exceptions being caps of buckskin or fur that were worn as

A Hupa mother (Northwestern California, 1923) wears a necklace of many strands of dentalium shells. Her hair is braided, and she wears a basketry hat with geometric designs. Her child is covered by a cloth wrap and bound into a carrying basket. Library of Congress, Prints & Photographs Division, Edward S. Curtis Collection, reproduction number LC-USZ62-110505.

far north as the Shasta on the Oregon border and as far south as the Yokuts of the Sierra Nevada foothills. Throughout California, hairnets made of native fibers were often used as ceremonial dress, but they were also used daily in some tribes. These nets were often decorated with small beads and might have had feathers, pendants, and hairpins inserted into them.

Basket caps belonged primarily to women. Dome shaped or flat topped, they were woven just like baskets—and California Indians are among the world's finest basket makers. Originally, caps may have been created to protect the forehead from the tumpline used to carry burdens. Among many tribes, a basket cap was only worn when carrying. But in the Northeast and Northwest, caps were an important part of women's daily dress. Men would only wear these caps for work, such as the fishermen of Northern California who supported their great dip nets with their heads.

Hair was worn to at least shoulder length by both men and women. If trimming of bangs was needed, hair was singed with a live coal or cut with an obsidian knife. Men and women tied their hair back into loose ponytails or braided queues. People of the Northwest parted their hair in the middle and formed braids or clubs on either side of the head or doubled into a club down the back. Braids or clubs were often wrapped with ribbons of buckskin or fur, much like the Plains and Plateau Indians. Tolowa, Karok, Yurok, and Hupa women wore ribbons of otter, mink, or fisher fur with pendants of feathers, seeds, and shells hanging from the ends. Many men wore their hair gathered into a knot on top of the head or at the back of the neck. Knots might be held in place by a string or bone or by wooden hairpins that were often ornamented with feathers, shell pendants, and other decorations. In many areas, the hair was cut or singed off close to the head as a sign of mourning.

Men sometimes grew mustaches or even beards. Otherwise, unwanted hair anywhere on the body was removed either by singeing, plucking, or tweezing.

BODY MODIFICATIONS

In addition to the use of paints to decorate themselves, especially on festive or ceremonial occasions, *body modification*, such as tattooing, was practiced by most of the tribes. Women applied tattoos most often on the face and sometimes on the neck, arms, and body. A Hupa man might have marks for measuring his shell money tattooed on his forearm.

Endless kinds of body supplements were inserted into pierced ears and nasal septums. Ear sticks of wood or bone were often decorated with feathers, incising, and pendants. Among the Chumash, rodlike wooden containers of powdered tobacco were carried in the ears. Ear pendants of shell, bone, stone, and seed beads, singly or in strings, were common throughout California, while feathers, bones, sticks, or even shells were worn in the septum.

Necklaces and bracelets of almost every combination of shells, stones, bones, wood, and seeds were used. Iridescent abalone was found along California's coast, and slender, curved dentalium shells arrived over trade routes extending as far north as Vancouver Island.

Cranial modification was common among the Achomawi and Atsugewi of the Northeast and the Shasta of the Northwest. This was done in infancy by compressing the child's forehead with a flat board or tight binding.

SPECIALIZED DRESS

When hunting, sometimes an entire deer- or antelope skin was thrown over the hunter's shoulders and back, or the antlers were tied onto his head and the skin draped over his body. Bent over and wearing this disguise, the hunter was able to move close enough to hit his target.

In much of California, men dressing for war did little more than paint themselves and take up their weapons. However, the Yana of the Central region wore a larger-than-normal hairnet for war that was so filled with white eagle down that the netting could not be seen. In the Northwest and Northeast and as far south as the Pomo living above San Francisco Bay, warriors could adopt armor that was similar to that of native peoples of the Northwest Coast. Corselets made of wooden rods twined together with fiber or buckskin cords made a stout defense against arrows. An elk-skin collar could give the neck added protection. Others used tunics of elk or bear hide, sometimes with a coating of fine gravel glued to it. These tunics were usually worn alone, but some were used beneath the rod armor for the greatest protection. Northwestern tribes used helmets made of rawhide. The Yurok hung a thick hide curtain from their helmets. Such costly panoplies were impressive, but rare.

Hupa female shaman from northwestern California, wearing headbands made of several types of shells, dentalium shell necklaces, and holding up two baskets, ca. 1923. Library of Congress, Prints & Photographs Division, Edward S. Curtis Collection, reproduction number LC-USZ62-101261.

Transvestites were accepted members of society in some California tribes, at times even serving as shamans. The Spanish colonists and missionaries found transvestites well established among the tribes of the central and southern coast. Not only did they dress as women and do women's work, but they were often married to nontransvestite men. The adoption of the woman's role and dress could also include the facial tattoos reserved for women. Reports of female transvestites are rarer. Among the Wiyot in Northern California, some women were said to dress like men and to hunt.

Girls' puberty rites required many rituals and prohibitions, some of which involved clothing. In Northeastern California, girls wore only old clothes during their initiation, as well as a headband, wristbands, anklets, and a belt of braided fiber or buckskin. In the Northwest, there were special ways of braiding the hair and painting the face during female initiations. The belief that the gaze of a girl during her first menses had destructive power was common, so whenever she went outside, the girl would cover her head with a robe or blanket, a basket, or a specially made visor.

CEREMONIAL CLOTHING

Ceremonial clothing and regalia of California was distinct from much of the rest of North America and was characterized by a brilliant use of natural materials, especially feathers. Celebrations surrounding the concept of "world renewal" were typical of Northwestern California. Male priests held annual rites to ensure the tribe's health, productivity, and the availability of resources. One of the most spectacular rites is the White Deerskin Dance, which is still performed every year among the Hupa. The regalia consist of civet cat or deerskin aprons, numerous dentalium necklaces, and headbands of wolf skin shading the eyes. Plumes rising from the center of the headdress combine several black and white eagle or condor feathers to look like one giant feather whose quill is decorated with the scarlet scalps of woodpeckers. Each dancer in the line holds a long pole that supports the skin of a white, black, gray, or mottled deer, decorated with more woodpecker scalps. Other participants wear netted headdresses with a diamond pattern that fall back from the forehead and end below the shoulders in a fringe of even more woodpecker scalps. Two men bearing huge obsidian blades wear netted headdresses as well as headbands with the large hooklike canine teeth of sea lions projecting outward like a crown.

The term *Kuksu cult* is used to describe a religion practiced mostly in Central California. It was known for its secret societies of men, and sometimes women, who practiced elaborate rituals and rites of passage in order to gain wisdom and status. Elaborately dressed participants might represent gods or spirits, and the typical regalia included long bands composed of the pinkish-orange and black quills of the red-shafted flicker. These bands were most often worn across the forehead and fastened to either temple so that the trailing ends moved freely. Pins inserted into a mass of hair confined in a hairnet held the headdress in place.

Frequently, the hairnets were also filled with white down that floated off the wearer as he moved. Capes of feathers from hawks, crows, eagles, or other birds were formed over netted foundations. Those who represented gods might wear a long, feathered cape that completely covered the body and head.

Other types of ceremonial regalia common to Central California were worn by societies that initiated boys, called *Hesi*. These groups had one dramatic headdress composed of 50 to 150 wooden wands, about two to three feet (two-thirds to one meter) long and colored red. The wands radiated out from the wearer's head and were tipped with white feathers.

Among the Pomo, Coast Miwok, and Patwin, some men ritually impersonated bears by wearing entire bear skins.

Rituals involving the hallucinogenic datura plant (also known as *toloache* or jimsonweed) were believed to give visions and powers to its users. These rites were most widespread among the tribes of the South but also performed in the coastal areas of Central California. Very typical of ceremonial costume in the South were skirts made of strings with white down twisted into them and ending in feathers. Also, feathered topknot headdresses were used. This was a central cluster of long, upright feathers attached to a central foundation and surrounded by a radiating ring of shorter feathers. A Chumash shaman was photographed wearing both a feathered skirt and a feathered topknot headdress in 1878.

THE MISSION ERA AND THE RUSSIANS

A vital component of the Spanish plan to settle California was the chain of missions that they began to establish as soon as they arrived in 1769. The missions had the goal of incorporating the native peoples into Spanish society.

One of the inducements offered to California Indians to enter into life at the missions, and to stay there, was clothing. The Franciscan missionaries sought to cover the naked bodies of the natives who joined their settlements. Though many of the converts remained "much addicted to nudity," as one missionary wrote, Indians saw clothing as valuable and thus a mark of status. However, it was not Spanish-style clothing that was given to the majority of converts. For reasons of cost, supply, and a system for rewarding accomplishment, the majority of the Indians at the missions received something much simpler.

The popular image of Indian men dressed in white pajama-like clothing and women modestly clad in ruffled chemises and bright petticoats is simply not true. This image can probably be traced to historians. Fr. Zephyrin Englehardt, O.F.M. (1851–1934), wrote of the mission experience in a rather idealized way, and illustrations that he commissioned for his books portray stereotypical dress. He described the dress of the converts as "a linen shirt and pantaloons … also a woolen blanket" for the men and "a chemise, gown, and blanket or shawl" for the women. In fact, documents in which the missionary fathers themselves described what they provided tell us that the men and boys wore the *cotón*, "a woolen shirt with sleeves which reaches to about the waist," and the taparabo, a breechcloth "of cotton or wool about a yard and a half long and over a half yard wide" (smaller for the boys). Women and girls also wore the *cotón* and a woolen skirt.

Pictorial evidence, especially the watercolors and lithographs made by Russian artist Ludwig Choris based on his visit to California in 1816, give a good impression of the appearance of California Indians throughout the mission system. The men wear taparabos and blankets of striped cloth, no doubt locally woven wool. Some wear the cotón. No skirts can be seen on the women in these pictures, who wrap the striped blankets around their waists and do not wear shirts. Continued use of traditional hairstyles, tattooing, personal ornaments, ceremonial dress, and persistent seminudity gives a richer, more accurate image than that of white pajamas. A painting of Mission San Gabriel (near Los Angeles) dating from around 1833 by German traveler Ferdinand Deppe does include young women dressed in the petticoats and chemises that Englehardt described, but a man standing by them wears just the breechcloth.

Certain converts were rewarded with the privilege of wearing Spanish-style clothing, part of the plan to mold the California Indians into useful citizens of the Spanish colony. As one padre wrote, "To those who show more effort in some labor or service, we give clothes such as the *gente de razón* [i.e., whites] use." A Spanish woman who issued clothing to the converts at one of the missions wrote that unskilled *vaqueros* (cowboys) did not receive anything except their cotón, blanket, and taparabo. But those who had gained the skills of a vaquero were dressed like Spaniards in a shirt, vest, jacket, breeches, hat, leather leggings, shoes, and spurs. In addition, they received a large silk or cotton kerchief and a sash of Chinese silk. There is no clear evidence that women were ever rewarded with Spanish-style clothing for skill and service in the same way as men.

Russian settlements were established in the Pomo and Coast Miwok regions north of San Francisco Bay starting in 1812. The Russians, trying to grow food to supply their fur-trade establishments in Alaska, also used clothing as payment to the local peoples for work such as harvesting. Here, however, the effect on native dress was almost minimal. Near the end of their twenty-nine-year

Illustration by G. H. von Langsdorff, ca. 1812, entitled "The Dance of the Indians at the Mission of San José in New California." The bodies of the dancers, who are clad in loincloths, are painted in elaborate designs. Their head-dresses are ornamented with feathers. Library of Congress Rare Books and Special Collections, LC-USZ62-8107.

experiment in colonizing California, a French visitor was dismayed to find that the Pomo living near the Russian settlement either continued to wear their own clothing or used various combinations of men's and women's garments regardless of the sex of the wearer. He describes the chief and his principal warriors as presenting themselves in the center of the settlement for an official visit, naked but for their weapons, paint, and ornaments.

THE MEXICAN ERA AND THE U.S. CONQUEST

Mexico's independence from Spain in 1821 began the movement toward dismantling the missions that was finally completed in 1836. The native peoples of the southern and central coasts were cast adrift by this secularization of the missions. Impoverished, their clothing no longer supplied by the missions, they often returned to a state of near-nudity or else sought cast-off clothing. At about this same time, foreign settlers began arriving in California, exposing new populations to Western influences, including dress.

One of these foreigners, John Sutter, a Swiss adventurer, received from the Mexicans in 1839 a huge grant of land belonging to the Nisenan and Miwok tribes of the Great Central Valley. Building his fort and settlement, he, too, paid his native workers with food and clothing. He also formed a small guard of young native men that he armed, drilled, and dressed in uniforms ordered from Russian tailors in Alaska. One visitor in 1846 described his unskilled seasonal laborers as "clothed in shirts and blankets, but a large portion are entirely naked. They are paid so

much per day for their labor, in such articles of merchandise as they may select from the store. Cotton cloth and handkerchiefs are what they most freely purchase."

California was conquered by the United States in 1846, during the Mexican War. It was at Sutter's sawmill in 1848 that gold was first discovered in California, setting off a rush of immigration that transformed the state. The effect on the native peoples of California was predictable. Once again, North American Indians became foreigners on their own land. Hunted, massacred, and exploited by the newcomers, their ancient ways of life, including their ways of dress, were overthrown.

By the 1870s, when pioneer ethnographer Stephen Powers wrote about the tribes of California, tribal dress was retained only by the elderly or for ceremonies. Writing of the Karok in the Northwest, Powers noted: "The young people of both sexes dress in the American fashion, and I have seen plenty of them appareled in quite correct elegance—the young men in passable broadcloth, spotless shirt-fronts, and neat black cravats; the girls in chaste, pretty, small figured stuffs, with sacques, collars, ribboned hats, etc." In photographs from the second half of the nineteenth century, one sees the widespread use of printed dresses, ready-made trousers, shirts, coats, and shoes that are only occasionally mixed with traditional items.

THE NEW RELIGIONS

In 1870, the first Ghost Dance arrived in California. A messianic belief in the destruction of their foreign oppressors and the

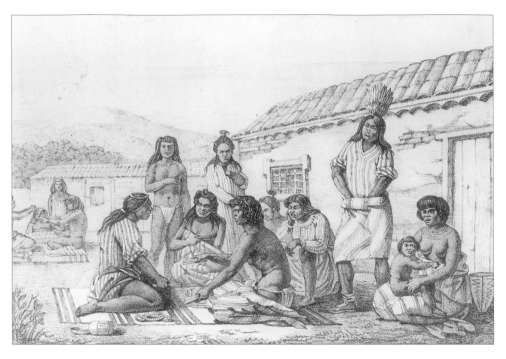

Lithograph after a drawing by Louis Ludwig Andrevich Choris, ca. 1822. North American Indians at a mission near San Francisco wear a variety of garments including loincloths and European-influenced styles of shirts, dresses, skirts, and wraps made in striped cloth. Library of Congress, Rare Book and Special Collections Division, LC-DIG-ppmsca-02900.

revival of native peoples, the Ghost Dance movement arose first among the Nevada Paiute and spread to many parts of the West. In California, it took hold especially in the Central region. Ironically, Ghost Dance clothing was largely composed of cloth created by the very people the rituals were intended to eliminate.

Almost immediately upon its arrival in California, the Ghost Dance was taken and modified into several cults, the most important of which was called the *Bole-Maru*. Combining the revival of native peoples taken from the Ghost Dance with shamanistic healing practices and rituals and morality drawn from both the Kuksu cult and Christianity, the Bole-Maru followers likewise used cloth as the basis of their regalia. Hand-colored photographs of Bole-Maru "Big Head" ceremony from around 1920 show a male dancer wearing the headdress of long rods described previously but tipped with crepe paper instead of feathers. He wears a white-cloth short-sleeved shirt and ankle-length skirt appliquéd with rows of symbols in black fabric. Other dancers retain some elements of more traditional Central California regalia, including flicker headbands, but they are worn with long underwear and cloth petticoats.

DECLINE AND REVIVAL

The last two decades of the nineteenth century saw the native population of California dip to its lowest point—less than twenty thousand. This was due, in part, to many native peoples submerging themselves in the general culture through intermarriage and movement out of tribal areas into more urban settings. By the beginning of the twentieth century, even ceremonial dress was increasingly transformed. At the same time that native Californians were losing access to traditional clothing materials, they were gaining access to new ones: cloth, coins, glass beads, crepe paper, and commercially tanned leather. In many cases, tribes lost their knowledge of how to make things, especially ceremonial regalia, as the old people died off. Increasingly, new influences on ceremonial clothing intruded, especially clothing from the Plains region. Beaded vests and moccasins, cuffs, and other garments appear with increasing frequency in twentieth-century photos of California Indian dance clothing.

In the twenty-first century, this trend continues. In California, as in many parts of the United States, to dress as an Indian means dressing like a Plains Indian. Plains Indian dances and music, too, are becoming universal. There are some notable exceptions, such as the White Deerskin Dance of the Hupa in the Northwest. Others, too, are making the effort to revive and continue native Californian dress. This is seen especially in the creation of feather work for ceremonial regalia. It might be difficult to completely revive native Californian clothing traditions, given that true authenticity would involve some degree of nudity. But North American Indian dress and arts have always been subject to fashion and innovation. There may yet be a way of changing to meet new challenges while still remaining truly Californian.

References and Further Reading

Aginsky, B. W. "Culture Element Distributions: XXIV. Central Sierra." *Anthropological Records, University of California* 8, no. 4 (1943): 393–468.

Barrett, S.A., and E.W. Gifford. "Miwok Material Culture." *Bulletin of the Milwaukee Public Museum* 2, no. 4 (1933): 117–277.

Bates, Craig D. "The California Collection of I.G. Voznesenki." *American Indian Art Magazine* 8, no. 3 (1983): 36–41.

Bates, Craig D., and Brian Bibby. "Flicker Quill Bands of the Maidu; Ceremonial Art of Central California." *American Indian Art Magazine* 5, no. 4 (1980): 62–67.

Bates, Craig D., and Brian Bibby. "Collecting among the Chico Maidu; The Stewart Culin Collection at the Brooklyn Museum." *American Indian Art Magazine* 8, no. 4 (1983): 46–53.

Blackburn, Thomas C., and D. Travis Hudson. *Time's Flotsam: Overseas Collections of California Indian Material Culture.* Menlo Park, CA: Ballena Press, 1990.

Driver, Harold E. "Culture Element Distributions: X. Northwest California." *Anthropological Records* 1, no. 6 (1939): 297–433.

Drucker, Philip. "Culture Element Distributions: V. Southern California." *Anthropological Records* 1, no. 1 (1937): 1–52.

Englehardt, Zephyrin. *The Missions and Missionaries of California.* 4 vols. Santa Barbara: Mission Santa Barbara, 1932.

Essene, Frank. "Culture Element Distributions: XXI. Round Valley." *Anthropological Records* 8, no. 1 (1942): 1–97.

Geiger, Maynard, and Clement W. Meighan. *As the Padres Saw Them. California Indian Life and Customs as Reported by the Franciscan Missionaries, 1813–1815.* Santa Barbara: Santa Barbara Mission Archive Library, 1976.

Harrington, John P. "Culture Element Distributions: XIX. Central California Coast." *Anthropological Records* 7, no. 1 (1942): 1–46.

Heizer, Robert F. *Handbook of North American Indians: California.* Vol. 8. Washington, DC: Smithsonian Institution, 1978.

Heizer, Robert F., and Albert B. Elsasser. *The Natural World of the California Indians.* Berkeley: University of California Press, 1980.

Holt, Catharine. "Culture Element Distributions: XXIV. Central Sierra." *Anthropological Records* 8, no. 4 (1943): 393–468.

Holt, Catharine. "Shasta Ethnography." *Anthropological Records* 3, no. 4 (1946): 299–349.

Hudson, Travis, and Thomas C. Blackburn. *The Material Culture of the Chumash Interaction Sphere, Volume III: Clothing, Ornamentation, and Grooming.* Santa Barbara: Santa Barbara Museum of Natural History, 1985.

Hurtado, Albert L. *Intimate Frontiers; Sex, Gender, and Culture in Old California.* Albuquerque: University of New Mexico Press, 1999.

Kroeber, Alfred L. *Handbook of the Indians of California.* New York: Dover Publications, 1976.

Kroeber, Theodora, Albert B. Elsasser, and Robert F. Heizer. *Drawn from Life; California Indians in Pen and Brush. Socorro.* Menlo Park, CA: Ballena Press, 1977.

Malinwoski, Sharon, and Anna Sheets, eds. *The Gale Encyclopedia of Native American Tribes.* Vol. 4. New York: Gale, 1998.

Paterek, Josephine. *Encyclopedia of American Indian Costume.* Santa Barbara: ABC-CLIO, 1994.

Perez, Eulalia. "An Old Woman and Her Recollections." In *Three Memoirs of Mexican California,* edited by Thomas Savage. Berkeley, CA: The Friends of the Bancroft Library, 1988.

Powers, Stephen. *Tribes of California.* Edited by Robert F. Heizer. Berkeley: University of California Press, 1976.

Vane, Sylvia Brakke. *California Indians: Primary Resources: A Guide to Manuscripts, Artifacts, Documents, Serials, Music and Illustrations.* Menlo Park, CA: Ballena Press, 1990.

Vogelin, Ermine W. "Tubutulabal Ethnography." *Anthropological Records* 2, no. 1 (1938): 1–90.

Vogelin, Ermine W. "Culture Element Distributions: XX. Northeast California." *Anthropological Records* 7, no. 2 (1942): 47–251.

Webb, Edith Buckland. *Indian Life in the Old Missions.* Lincoln: University of Nebraska Press, 1982.

David W. Rickman

The Plateau

The traditional dress of Columbia River plateau natives reflected the abundance of their regional landscape and their access to far-reaching trade systems. Prior to contact with outsiders, Plateau attire was crafted from animal hides and adorned with various organic materials. During the nineteenth century, their attire shared many common traits with contemporaneous Plains Indian clothing. As new trade goods appeared, aboriginal clothing styles were modified, and new styles developed. Increasing trade with Euro–North Americans prompted the widespread adoption of cotton and wool clothing. At the beginning of the twenty-first century, commercially produced clothing is worn as everyday wear, while traditional-style garments are reserved for special occasions.

PLATEAU LANDSCAPE AND ECONOMY

The Columbia River plateau lies in the interior of western North America. It is bounded on the west and east by the Cascade and Rocky Mountain ranges, on the north by the upper Fraser River drainage, and on the south by the Great Basin. In political terms, it covers portions of southeastern British Columbia, eastern Washington and Oregon, northern Idaho, and western Montana.

The plateau is a generally temperate and arid expanse containing diverse landscapes and ecosystems. The Snake-Columbia river system, the Fraser River, and numerous tributaries bisect the area. Riverside villages and fishing industries figured prominently in its transportation and settlement patterns and trade systems. Speakers of two main language groups—Interior Salish and Sahaptian—and of several smaller linguistic isolates populate the area. Despite language differences, centuries of alliances formed through intertribal marriages and shared economies and political concerns produced a commonality of regional cultural traits.

The average elevation of the plateau is about five thousand feet (fifteen hundred meters) above sea level. Some river gorges

extend down almost to sea level; the highest peaks are nearly ten thousand feet (three thousand meters) high. In the northwestern periphery, mixed coniferous forests and grasslands predominate. The north and north-central plateau is forested but broken by grasslands and river valleys. The southern plateau is a sagebrush and bunchgrass steppe that is wooded along its eastern and western high-elevation borders.

Rivers, streams, and the variations in elevation provided the residents of the plateau with diverse and abundant food resources. These included fish species, deer, elk, and other mammals as well as numerous roots, berries, and plant foods. Some communities spent much of the year living near fisheries, while others maintained a seasonal round, moving from location to location as food resources became available.

The Plateau economy also extended onto the Great Plains. Several present-day Plateau groups once lived along the eastern flank of the Rockies. Although the Blackfoot drove them west into the plateau, they continued hunting Plains buffalo. Before

Two Yakama girls, late nineteenth century, Yakama Indian Reservation, U.S. Columbia River Plateau. These young women appear in classic late-nineteenth-century Yakama attire. They are wearing tail dresses, panel belts, twined basketry hats, and shell jewelry. Their braids are wrapped in fur, and they carry woven handbags. Courtesy Lee and Lois Miner, Yakima, Washington.

the arrival of horses, the Nez Percé also hunted buffalo on the Plains, sometimes staying for six months or more.

Southern Plateau peoples acquired horses during the early eighteenth century and quickly developed equestrian-based societies. Local rangeland provided an excellent environment for the expansion of their herds. By 1800, the southern plateau was home to the largest horse population in native North America. With equestrian technology, Plateau peoples hunted on the Plains in increased numbers. Protracted hunting expeditions frequently allied diverse groups to provide mutual protection from Plains enemies.

A defining feature of the aboriginal Columbia River plateau was its regional trade system. The Dalles of the Columbia was the focus of this far-flung network. A great North American trade market was located there, about two hundred miles (three hundred twenty kilometers) above the mouth of the Columbia. During the summer months, peoples from throughout the Pacific Northwest congregated to trade at the Dalles. In addition to the idea exchange that occurred there, different groups brought regional specialties to exchange for goods that were made or harvested elsewhere. Plateau traders were also active farther east, and the presence of Plateau people is noted throughout the Rocky Mountain fur-trade accounts.

After 1810, the fur trade developed in the plateau along a network that appropriated existing indigenous systems. The Pacific Company, the North West Company, and the Hudson's Bay Company (HBC) established their major regional depots on the lower Columbia River. The river remained the artery by which goods were transported.

The Oregon Trail provided further cross-cultural trading opportunities. The Wallowa Band Nez Percé and Cayuse greeted emigrant trains coming through Oregon's Grand Ronde Valley with fresh stock, fresh vegetables, roots, and fish. Emigrant diaries report that weary travelers traded old clothing, tired cattle, ammunition, rifles, knives, cloth, and other items for foodstuffs and horses.

Early written records most often describe the Plateau peoples living adjacent to the Snake and Columbia rivers or along the Oregon Trail route. These texts generally reference the residents of the plateau living south of the U.S.-Canadian border. Plateau dress as described here focuses on these peoples and not the Plateau-based First Nations people living in the wooded areas of interior British Columbia.

WOMEN'S DRESSES

When first encountered by outsiders, Plateau residents were almost universally attired in animal-skin clothing. Oral traditions recall, however, that regional people once wore garments woven from vegetal fibers and that they had once been more lightly dressed.

Throughout the protohistoric and historic periods, Plateau peoples tanned hides for clothing using the brain-tanning technology common throughout native North America. Winter-weather garments and accessories were often made from the hides of fur-bearing animals, but skins taken from mammals of the *Ovis* genus (mountain sheep) and Cervidae family (deer and elk) were most commonly used. Early observers note that individuals owned two or three sets of clothing. Everyday attire was generally unadorned, while decorated clothing was reserved for special occasions.

Women generally wore loose-fitting, fringed leather dresses. These were made from two tanned animal skins. They were sewn so that the animals' tails had a place of prominence in the front and back center of the garments. The forelegs of the animal skin formed a partial sleeve that extended about to the elbow.

Women in equestrian groups living along the western flank of the Rockies, from northern New Mexico to the plateau and then eastward into the northern Plains, shared this tail-dress style. The full cut of the dresses allowed a woman to ride astride a horse.

The decorative elements applied to the yokes of these dresses followed the contours of the skins in a generally horizontal and often highly contrasting pattern. The decoration also emphasized the presence of the animal tails. Early observers noted that the garments were highly ornamented with dentalium (shells shaped like a pointed tooth) or other shells; glass beads; pieces of bone, brass, or copper; elk teeth; or porcupine quills. Hawk bells (small bells like those used in hunting with hawks), thimbles, and glass beads were added after the advent of the fur trade.

At the beginning of the twenty-first century, tail dresses remain in popular use. Animal tails are no longer always kept intact on the front and back of the garments, but beaded areas representative of the tails are generally visible. The beaded yoke decoration is still applied in a horizontal format.

When they became available, commercially produced textiles were highly desired. Woolen, flannel, corduroy, and other garments were brightly colored, lightweight, and more easily handled than animal hides. Plateau women fashioned these textiles into what is known as a wing dress. The pattern for these was inspired by earlier aboriginal designs.

Throughout the region, long-sleeved cotton dresses are worn beneath wing dresses. Many wing dresses were often not overly decorated, although some were adorned with elk teeth, dentalium, cowries, and other shells. The ornamental treatment generally mirrored that appearing on hide dresses.

WOMEN'S ACCESSORIES

Women's dresses were often secured at the waist with a belt. In about 1870, the U.S. government began issuing harness leather to the native population. Plateau women used this base material to produce finely beaded belts of various widths. Geometric designs were standard on these. This *panel belt* tradition was shared with many Plains groups.

A variety of tools were attached to women's belts. Among these were a knife and sheath and an awl and awl case. Special belt bags containing sewing materials, ration cards, and other personal items also appeared on belts, as did rectangular woven wallets.

Plateau women's leggings generally came up only to the knee. With the arrival of commercial textiles, leggings were usually made from pieces of *trade cloth* or blankets and trimmed with ribbon. By the turn of the twentieth century, southern Plateau women preferred to wear leggings adorned with beaded floral designs. These were matched with undecorated leather moccasins.

Moccasins were most commonly created using a side-sewn design. During the nineteenth century, the flaps around the ankles were usually four to six inches (ten to fifteen centimeters) high. This height increased during the twentieth century until some flaps extended up above midcalf.

Two Yakama women, ca. 1910. These women are wearing blankets over wing dresses, typical of the U.S. Columbia River Plateau, with long-sleeved underdresses. The hairstyles, jewelry, and pictorial beaded bags are characteristic of the early twentieth century. Courtesy Lee and Lois Miner, Yakima, Washington.

WOMEN'S HEADGEAR

Fez-shaped basketry hats are signature accessories for Plateau women. They were originally woven from *Indian hemp* (*Apocynum cannabinum*), *beargrass* (*Xerophyllum tenax*), and other plant fibers.

The hats average six or seven inches (fifteen to eighteen centimeters) in height and are of a similar diameter. Many have *buckskin* thongs attached to their crowns. Feathers, beads, bells, dentalium shells, and other items adorn the end of these thongs. On the Warm Springs Reservation, one attached feather identifies a single woman, while two feathers appear on the hats of married women.

Head scarves have replaced twined hats as everyday women's wear. The hats are most often seen at ceremonies and on formal dress occasions. Each year, Plateau people hold seasonal feasts to thank the Creator for the return of sacred foods. The women responsible for gathering, preparing, and serving these honored foods will wear basket hats if they have them. During the twentieth century, bead artists adopted and modified the traditional twined-hat shape, and many hats now carry allover beaded designs with bright geometric or pictorial motifs.

Prior to contact, headbands were worn throughout the plateau. Two-inch- (five-centimeter-) wide leather headbands with beaded decorations have been popular since about 1920. Young women serving as powwow and rodeo royalty commonly wear these. In many cases, a single upright eagle feather at the back of the head completes their look. Since the middle of the twentieth century, these same women have also routinely worn beaded crowns adorned with geometric, floral, or pictorial imagery.

BEADED FLAT BAGS

During the last third of the nineteenth century, flat handbags appeared as popular feminine accessories. Most of these are about twelve inches tall by ten inches wide (thirty centimeters by twenty-five centimeters). The bag form evolved from large aboriginal woven-root storage bags. After the 1855 advent of the reservation system, white settlement limited access to traditional root foods and the plant fibers necessary for weaving. The size of woven bags then diminished, and twined and beaded handbags began to be produced and popularly used.

With a few exceptions, woven handbags are decorated with geometric motifs. Some beaded flat bags are also adorned with geometric designs, but since the 1880s, most beaded flat bags have displayed pictorial images.

MEN'S SHIRTS

When first observed by outsiders, Plateau men were wearing fringed buckskin shirts, skin robes, leggings, and painted moccasins. Their shirts were styled much like women's tail dresses, only cut shorter. They also had wide shoulder bands that were individually decorated with porcupine quills or beads.

In 1828, Samuel Black, chief trader at Fort Nez Perces, the HBC post at the confluence of the Walla Walla and Columbia rivers, wrote an important period description of regional native peoples. He reported that local North American Indian men routinely wore shirts and leggings garnished with porcupine quills and other ornaments, scalps, human hair, horse hair, fringe, and the occasional scarlet cloth.

Men's two-skin shirts were usually assembled from four pieces: front, back, and two arms. Apart from some shaping at the neck opening, the fronts and backs were identical. Northern Plateau shirts were often cut with a straight bottom edge. Elsewhere, the shirts retained the outline of the animal skins, and the leg extensions were considered ornamental.

The front and back neck flaps on Plateau shirts were often triangular, but some were also rectangular. While Plateau skin shirts shared many traits with contemporaneous Plains examples, the Plateau garments were usually a little shorter, often extending to or slightly below the waist.

During the first half of the nineteenth century, the embroidery decoration on men's shirts was generally idiosyncratic. This changed after about 1860 with the introduction of glass seed beads. Tribal and regional beadwork styles then appeared throughout North America. Southern Plateau peoples and the Plains-dwelling Crow together developed a unique geometric style that utilized more colors than were used by other Plains groups.

This shared beadwork style has been associated with the Crow because anthropologists and collectors first associated it

accounts, but they disappear from the historical record by the mid-nineteenth century. Perforated shirts are thought to have been inspired by individual dreams. Many of them were observed during the post-Contact period. In about 1821, fur trader Alexander Ross described the basic attire of Nez Percé, Walla Walla, and Cayuse war chiefs. In addition to headdresses and other accessories, these men wore "a shirt or garment of thin draped leather, cut and chequered into small holes." Shortly thereafter, Samuel Black noted men trading at Fort Nez Perces who had the bodies of their shirts cut with a network of small round or square holes.

Men's perforated shirts are further mentioned in writings and shown in paintings from the 1840s. They also appear in turn-of-the-twentieth-century photographs. Like transmontane beadwork, the perforated-shirt tradition is shared with Plains peoples. On the plateau, they appear within a broad region bounded by the Warm Springs, Yakama, Nez Percé, Spokane, and Flathead peoples. On the Plains they are well documented among the Blackfoot, Gros Ventres, and Assiniboines. They are, however, unknown among the Crows.

Speaking of Nez Percé men, explorer Meriwether Lewis noted that the article of dress upon which the "most pains and ornaments" were bestowed was a collar made from a strip of otter skin about six inches (fifteen centimeters) wide. This was dressed with the hair on; a hole was cut lengthwise in it near the head of the animal to allow for the passage of a human head. When worn, the tippet hung in front of the body and sometimes reached below the knees. Pieces of shell, beads, pieces of cloth, and other ornaments were applied to its front. Lewis's companion, William Clark, noted that one Nez Percé tippet he observed was formed of human scalps and ornamented with the thumbs and fingers of men whom the wearer had slain in battle.

MEN'S ACCESSORIES

Plateau men's leggings were usually quite long, extending from the ankles upward to the waist. They were formed from a single deer, antelope, or mountain sheep hide with appendages (legs and head) attached. The side of the leggings were generally fringed. During the 1830s, eastern Plateau men routinely wore leggings ornamented with colored scalp locks, porcupine quills, and small blue and white beads. They were also ornamented with fur, paint, or pendants of bone, stone, or other items.

Cloth leggings appeared after about 1830, and they were generally made of woolen felt or blanket material. Many styles of cloth leggings were popular, as were diverse methods of applying fringe. Panels beaded with geometric designs were often applied to the lower registers of cloth leggings.

Early breechcloths were made of fringed hides. An 1850s account also describes Yakama men wearing breechcloths made from woven cedar bark. By the late nineteenth century, breechcloths were commonly made of cloth and were ankle length. Early-twentieth-century photos reveal that long, woolen, plaid breechcloths were then popular among southern Plateau men.

Men's belts supported their breechcloths and leggings. As with women, belts of commercial leather were adopted after harness leather became available during the 1870s. Masculine belt attachments included a knife and sheath and a medicine bag or belt pouch.

Nineteenth-century men's moccasins were decorated with quills or paint. They were also decorated with seed beads after

Marilyn Miller, Margaret Jim, and Anita Puyette, Yakama tribe, U.S. Columbia River Plateau. Their outfits are excellent examples of mid-twentieth-century feminine attire. Courtesy Lee and Lois Miner, Yakima, Washington.

with them. Although the "Crow" designation is still sometimes used, the beadwork is more correctly called *transmontane*, which means "across the mountains." This refers to the fact that the style appeared among the Crows, who live east of the Rocky Mountains, and among Plateau peoples, Utes, and others living west of the Rockies.

By the 1870s, the shoulder strips on Plateau and Crow men's shirts were beaded using transmontane motifs. Other items that both groups commonly decorated in the style included men's and women's leggings, men's mirror bags, and horse gear. Transmontane beadwork on otter-skin quivers, bandoliers, blanket strips, gun cases, and laced cradles was generally of Plateau origin. Conversely, only Crow artists made lance cases and six-tab cradles and decorated them with transmontane designs.

In addition to producing similar beadwork, Plateau and Crow artists shared a quill-wrapped horsehair tradition. This decorative technique wraps flattened quills around slender strands of horsehair to produce ornamental panels and rosettes. Plateau quill-wrapped horsehair most commonly appears on men's shirts. The earliest known examples are rosettes on triangular neck flaps. By the 1870s, a few shirt shoulder strips were constructed using this technique.

Two masculine clothing items—perforated shirts and otter-skin tippets—appear as standard Plateau attire in early written

about 1860. Throughout the southern plateau, men's moccasins were usually more highly decorated than those of women.

Men's vests are a post-Contact phenomenon and were not worn aboriginally, except perhaps among the Wishxam. Heavily beaded vests appeared throughout the plateau during the reservation period, and their production peaked about 1910. Many of them were worked with ornate floral designs on white or light blue. Pictorial imagery was also common on twentieth-century vests. They are popularly worn for social events and dancing.

Fringed *gauntlet*-style gloves appeared during the late nineteenth century. Like vests, they were adorned with floral and pictorial imagery. Gauntlets are, however, more associated with cowboys and competitive equestrian events. They were especially worn to dress up men at rodeos. During the first few decades of the twentieth century, beaded gauntlets were popular among both North American Indian and non-Indian rodeo aficionados. At that time, many pairs were made for sale to non-Indians.

ROBES AND BLANKETS

During aboriginal times, tanned buffalo robes and elk skins were common outerwear for both men and women. Some of these were painted; others were embroidered with quills or beads and fringed with various materials. When small beads became prevalent, wide blanket strips with multiple rosettes covered the seams of large tanned robes. These strips were initially embroidered with blue and white beads. As more colors and seed beads appeared, blanket strips were made using transmontane beadwork designs. A few blanket strips were also made wholly or partially of quill-wrapped horsehair.

When Lewis and Clark crossed the plateau in 1805–1806, red and blue wool blankets had already appeared there. Navajo and Spanish blankets became fairly common after Plateau people made peace with the Shoshone during the 1820s. Southwestern textiles were then procured through a trade network that extended along the west flank of the Rocky Mountains and employed Navajos, Pueblo people, Utes, and Shoshones. As was common with buffalo robes, beaded blanket strips were sometimes attached to wool trade blankets and to a variety of Navajo Chief blankets.

Pendleton Woolen Mills, the famous manufacturer of Indian trade blankets, was founded in 1893. Its plant is still located near the Umatilla Indian Reservation in Pendleton, Oregon. For several decades following the 1890s, five major manufacturers produced colorful geometric-design blankets for the Indian trade. These were very popular and soon became a ubiquitous part of plateau attire.

Coats were unknown until after the advent of the fur-trade era. Capote-style blanket coats (similar in style to the coats worn by white men) were then popular until the early twentieth century. They were so common at the middle of the nineteenth century that the publication describing the 1841 visit of the U.S. Exploring Expedition to the interior Pacific Northwest portrayed blanket coats as representative of contemporary male dress.

HEADDRESSES, HATS, AND CAPS

Historically, Plateau headgear was too diverse and idiosyncratic to describe in general terms. Horned feathered bonnets were worn aboriginally. So were "Blackfeet-style" stand-up eagle-feather headdresses. Plains-style eagle-feather headdresses were a late addition to the masculine wardrobe, arriving after the introduction of the horse and even as late as the reservation period.

Fur hats and caps were common throughout the region and were worn by both sexes. Men wore fur hats year round; women generally wore them only during the winter months. Close, form-fitting fur caps were made from a variety of animal furs; feathers were often attached to their crowns. Other caps were fashioned from the heads of wolves, deer, buffalo, or other animals. Some of these were designed specifically for hunting.

Hats made from birds were also common throughout the plateau, and they were sometimes worn for purely fashionable reasons. A few bird-skin hats, particularly those incorporating much of the body of the bird, were worn for spiritual and religious reasons and for specific events. In general, Plateau women did not wear caps made from bird skins.

Sam Morris (left) and Jim Morris (right), ca. 1910–1920, Nez Percé tribe, U.S. Columbia River Plateau United States. Sam Morris here wears a hide shirt decorated with transmontane-style beaded strips, cloth leggings with beaded panels, a cloth breechcloth with attached ribbon and sequins, and beaded moccasins. His braids are wrapped with fur strips. Jim Morris is wearing a cloth shirt and pants with a beaded vest and moccasins. Both are adorned with an abundance of shell jewelry. Unknown photographer. Photographic print RC2006.012.16 Photographic Study Collection, National Cowboy and Western Heritage Museum Oklahoma City, OK.

Women sometimes wore folded pieces of hide on their heads as sunshades. Their male counterparts, both those who hunted buffalo on the Plains and those further west, wore a style of rawhide sunshade more commonly associated with central Plains peoples. This was constructed from a decorated rawhide rectangle with a circle at one end. The interior of the circle was cut to allow passage of the crown of the head; the remaining portion of the rectangle formed a visor.

During the 1840s and 1850s, *peaked Scotch bonnets* were very popular with Plateau men. The caps were a longtime HBC trade item, and the 1853 Pacific Railroad Survey also carried them for trading purposes. Tacks were sometimes added to their leather visors (peaks), and otter or other fur trim often surrounded the bodies of the hats.

A few top hats were worn regionally. These usually belonged to chiefs who had received them as gifts from outsiders. Ostrich and other feathers were often attached to them. Between about 1870 and 1920, several styles of broad-rimmed hats were more widely worn. These were decorated with feathers, plumes, and other attachments.

HAIRSTYLES, FACIAL PAINTING, BODY PIERCING, AND JEWELRY

Hair was historically combed and oiled, often with bear, deer, elk, or even fish oil. It was usually worn long, although in many areas, people cut it above the shoulders when in mourning. Men often spent more time arranging their hair than did women. Both sexes commonly braided their hair into two plaits, while the hair of children remained loose. Braids were frequently wrapped with strips of otter, mink, or other fur.

Bangs were seldom worn, although many Eastern Plateau men had their hair cut short in the front but combed backward or upward to form a pompadour. Some Nez Percé men also wore side braids and let their hair hang loose in the back. Across the plateau, eyebrow hairs were often plucked. Beard hairs were also plucked with fingers or tweezers.

Hair ornamentation was both prevalent and idiosyncratic. Lewis and Clark found the Nez Percé decorating their hair with mother-of-pearl, dentalium, and feathers. In 1829, Samuel Black reported that hair ornaments included beads, quillwork, bits of tin, brass, small buttons, and "anything polished Sparkling or Shining they can pick up." He also observed one man wearing the socket of a brass candlestick in his hair. Some years earlier, the North West Company's David Thompson had encountered a man whose head was adorned with the handle of a teakettle.

Facial painting was common throughout the plateau. In many instances, its specifics were linked to a man's or woman's guardian spirit. Black noted regionally available pigments of white, red, green, blue, yellow, and other colors, and that these were used to "paint their faces in the most strange fantastical manner possible." Charcoal and lamp or kettle black supplemented the naturally occurring colors. He noted that faces painted with a red ground to which spots and lines of black and white had been added were often seen. He also reported that black lines passing across the eyelashes and lines running across the temple from eye to ear were "a favorite mark of beauty" for men.

During the 1830s, pioneer Protestant missionary Samuel Parker stated his belief that Plateau men painted themselves less than their Plains contemporaries. He noted that vermilion mixed with red clay was a common facial and hair covering. A Catholic missionary reported this same convention a decade later.

Throughout the plateau, the wearing of jewelry and the decoration of hair and body reflects individual status and preference. Historically, both sexes pierced their ears. The ears of children were usually pierced at a young age. Ear bobs and pendants were fashioned from diverse species of shell; strings of beads were also hung from the ear. Some shell ear pendants were incised or carved. Others had brass tacks attached to them.

Northern Plateau and some Lower and Middle Columbia River people routinely pierced the nasal septum. Single dentalium shells were often placed through septum holes. Lewis and Clark observed some Nez Percé doing this, but the practice ended shortly after their visit. The *Nimiipuu* ("The People") came to be called *Nez Percé* during the nineteenth century. This French fur trade–era term leads outsiders to believe that pierced noses were common among this people group. In fact, it was not. Some Nez Percé believe their current tribal name comes from a past misunderstanding of Indian sign language. A pinky finger moving across and down the nose does not refer to the piercing of a nose but rather to people coming down from the mountains to hunt on the Plains.

Before the arrival of glass beads and other trade goods, jewelry was made from handmade stone, bone, or shell beads or from elk and other teeth. These were frequently combined with fur or feathers to produce showy ornaments. Diverse materials were also strung together to produce necklaces and bracelets. With the arrival of glass and porcelain beads and metal items, this decorative vocabulary greatly expanded.

Lewis and Clark noted bead bracelets, beaded sashes worn on opposite shoulders and crossing at the chest, and bear-claw necklaces and collars being worn by men. David Thompson, writing in 1811, found prodigious use of dentalium among people living along the Columbia River between the Okanogan and Snake rivers. He noted several villages where the women were wearing dentalium *fillets* (headbands), dentalium bracelets, and dentalium armbands. Many women along this same stretch of river also wore the shells in their noses. Several years later, Alexander Ross found Okanogan women securing their dresses with dentalium belts.

Half a century later, many North American Indian men at Fort Colvile wore necklaces made from grizzly bear claws, while women wore "armlets and rings, and strings of hawk bells, large beads, or thick rolls of small beads, round the neck."

THE ADOPTION OF CITIZEN'S DRESS

Coastal traders began plying the waters off the Pacific Northwest Coast during the 1780s. Shortly thereafter, European and North American clothing found its way into the hands and wardrobes of Plateau peoples.

As fur trappers and other visitors began traversing the plateau, they soon recognized the value of cloth garments given in trade or as gifts. One 1814 fur-trade journal lists the type of gifts given to Columbia River chiefs. These included gingham shirts, cloth jackets and trousers, and soldier's coats. During the following decade, Samuel Black reported that the Nez Percé, Cayuse, and the wealthy among the other tribes had European clothing, "of course," and that they wore these as "a change and badge of riches." Their poor neighbors were still clothed in leather garments.

During the 1830s, striped cotton and calico shirts were the universal attire of the Euro–North American men working in

William Lemon, Nez Percé tribe, ca. 1910–1920, United States: Columbia River Plateau. William Lemon poses in a cloth shirt and beaded vest worked in floral designs. He is wearing beaded moccasins, and his cloth leggings and breechcloth have beaded decoration. He also wears a beaded belt pouch, cuffs, and arm garters. His hair is combed into a front pompadour, and his braids are wrapped with fur. Unknown photographer. Photographic print RC2006.012.22 Photographic Study Collection, National Cowboy and Western Heritage Museum Oklahoma City, OK.

the southern plateau. The HBC's annual Snake Country Expeditions carried a stock of the garments as trade items as early as the 1820s. After 1836, the Protestant missionaries noted their popularity, and one requested and received quantities of "coarse common shirts rather long, calico or domestic" from his eastern supporters because he found them to be useful trade items. He paid his Indian laborers with them at a rate of a single shirt for four to five days' work.

Published Nez Percé accounts record that the missionaries held native dress to be inherently evil and tools of the devil. During the early 1840s, one missionary woman at the Waiilatpu Mission (west of present-day Walla Walla, Washington) taught European sewing techniques and pattern usage to local Indian women. Her diary specifically mentions assisting with dress and bonnet construction.

At the Clearwater Mission, near present-day Lewiston, Idaho, missionary Eliza Spalding taught young women to card, spin, weave, and knit. Her husband made numerous handlooms to assist the enterprise, and these were used for the production of both cloth and wool blankets.

North American Indian demand for European clothing far outstripped the reserves held by the fur companies and the missionaries. Ever-increasing numbers of Oregon Trail emigrants helped supply quantities of the desired items. Arriving in Oregon's Grande Ronde and Umatilla River valleys in the fall of each year after 1841, the settlers met and traded with local native people. One overland traveler reported that Cayuse men were generally "dressed as the white man" and that the women wore calico dresses. Another noted the Cayuse "fondness for our dress" and that they "uniformly charge a shirt for every service they perform." This trade phenomenon also continued downstream along the Columbia River to the Dalles, especially at locations where native guides helped ferry emigrant wagons across rivers.

EARLY TWENTY-FIRST CENTURY DRESS

At the beginning of the twenty-first century, the everyday wear of Plateau peoples is much like that of their nonnative neighbors. However, many tribal people regularly wear small items referencing their ethnic identity. The standard attire for religious or cultural events is markedly different. At these events, women normally wear wing or beaded hide dresses, often with moccasins, leggings, and beaded hair ties and other accessories. Some wear twined hats and others wear head scarves. Ribbon shirts are popular with many men. If they have them, men may wear beaded hide shirts. These are frequently worn with moccasins, breechcloths, leggings, and accessories.

Attire at powwows and some social events can be dramatically different. While regional clothing styles may appear for traditional dance events, Plateau powwow clothing is generally similar to the powwow attire worn elsewhere in North America.

References and Further Reading

Ackerman, Lillian A., ed. *A Song to the Creator: Traditional Arts of Native American Women of the Plateau.* Norman: University of Oklahoma Press, 1996.

Baird, Dennis W., ed. *"Faithful to Their Tribe and Friends": Samuel Black's 1829 Fort Nez Perces Report.* Moscow: University of Idaho, 2000.

Grafe, Steven L. *Beaded Brilliance: Wearable Art from the Columbia River Plateau.* Oklahoma City: National Cowboy & Western Heritage Museum, 2006.

Harless, Susan E., ed. *Native Arts of the Columbia River Plateau: The Doris Swayze Bounds Collection.* Seattle: University of Washington Press, 1998.

Heard Museum. *Glass Tapestry: Plateau Beaded Bags from the Elaine Horwitch Collection.* Phoenix, AZ: The Heard Museum, 1993.

Holm, Bill. "Quill-Wrapped Horsehair: Two Rare Quilling Techniques." In *Studies in American Indian Art: A Memorial Tribute to Norman Feder*, edited by Christina F. Feest, 53–68. Altenstadt, Germany: European Review of Native American Studies, 2001.

Horse Capture, George P., and Richard A. Pohrt. *Salish Indian Art from the J.R. Simplot Collection.* Cody, WY: Buffalo Bill Historical Center, 1996.

Lewis, Meriwether, and William Clark. *July 28–November 1, 1805.* Vol. 5 of *The Journals of the Lewis and Clark Expedition*, edited by Gary E. Moulton. Lincoln: University of Nebraska Press, 1988.

Lewis, Meriwether, and William Clark. *March 23–June 9, 1806.* Vol. 7 of *The Journals of the Lewis and Clark Expedition*, edited by Gary E. Moulton. Lincoln: University of Nebraska Press, 1991.

Loeb, Barbara. "Classic Transmontane Beadwork: Art of the Crow and Plateau Tribes." Ph.D. dissertation, University of Washington, 1983.

Schlick, Mary Dodds. *Columbia River Basketry: Gift of the Ancestors, Gift of the Earth.* Seattle: University of Washington Press, 1994.

Shawley, Stephen Douglas. "Nez Perce Dress: A Study in Culture Change." Master's thesis, University of Idaho, 1974.

Walker, Deward E., Jr., ed. *Plateau.* Vol. 12 of *Handbook of North American Indians*, edited by William C. Sturtevant. Washington, DC: Smithsonian Institution, 1998.

Steven L. Grafe

The Great Basin

The *Great Basin* is a large, semiarid region of western North America that was host to several indigenous tribes and groups prior to the coming of Europeans to the New World. Most were culturally as well as linguistically related. They included groups speaking Uto-Aztecan languages of the Numic branch: Northern Paiute, Bannock, Owens Valley Paiute; Panamint, Western, Northern, and Eastern Shoshone; and Southern Paiute, Chemehuevi, and Western, Northern, and Southern Ute. The Washoe, also traditionally included, spoke a language affiliated with the

Wuzzie George, Stillwater, Nevada, Northern Paiute tribe, ca. 1956. She wears a twined sagebrush bark dress made by her to illustrate the old style. Note also her sagebrush bark shoes, bulrush stem hat, shell bead necklace, and white face paint. Courtesy of Special Collections, University of Nevada-Reno Library.

Hokan stock of languages centered in California. In early times, the cultural similarities of all these groups included their manner of dress and personal adornment and the methods and materials that they used in manufacturing them. However, after Euro–North American contact, as in many other parts of the New World, many of the groups underwent different changes as they adapted to the new looks of the local newcomers and assimilated the new material goods that they introduced. Their clothing and accessories became distinctive by subregion and then continued to change and diverge as yet more ideas and materials became part of their lives. Today, indigenous Great Basin people maintain some of that regional and subregional distinctiveness in dress for important social and ceremonial occasions, but for everyday life, they keep pace with U.S. regional and global cultures and their influences.

CLOTHING IN DEEP TIME

Interior western North America, including the Great Basin and the Southwest, are unique in that they are very dry areas, and this dryness is conducive to excellent preservation of textiles, especially in protected caves and rock shelters. Among the earliest textiles from the region, found in Oregon and Nevada, are twined sandals of several styles made of the shredded bark of sagebrush (*Artemisia tridentata*) and juniper (*Juniperus* spp.) as well as tule (*Scirpus* spp.) fibers, some dating back more than twelve thousand years. Nevada was the location of finds of other remains from this early time. There are blankets made of twisted strips of rabbit skin twined together with plant fiber and dating at least to 9400 B.C.E. People also made skin moccasins at this time and what are likely skin aprons or breechcloths. Additional garments of skins and fibers were likely worn, although the direct evidence is not as strong. There are also technically sophisticated mats of plant materials, specifically split-tule warps (lengthwise yarns) with dogbane or Indian hemp (*Appocynum cannabinum*) cordage wefts (crosswise yarns) that could have been used for body wrapping.

Although there are not comparable items from all areas within the region for this early period, what is available indicates that people in different subregions in Oregon, Nevada, and Utah preferred at a minimum different styles in footwear. In later years (5000–2000 B.C.E.), in western Nevada, front aprons made of twisted cordage suspended from belts further held together with a few rows of horizontal twining are present. These are sometimes beautifully decorated with rows of olivella shells (shells of a marine snail, *Olivella biplicata*, also called "purple olive") and bird down and at other times are plain. Archaeological sites such as Lovelock Cave in Nevada contain as well hundreds of shell disk beads and whole olivella shells carefully strung into necklaces and armbands. Buckskin moccasins and presumably other garments are also decorated with shell beads, most of which came from the Pacific Coast through trade. Capes of twisted and twined bird-skin strands and rabbit-skin strips occur as well, as do yet additional sandals with different types of weaves. There are sizes (and perhaps styles) of sandals and moccasins for men, women, and children, although it is not clear whether there were such differences for other garments.

Man draped in a rabbit-skin robe with rabbit-skin or bobcat-skin boots. Robes often doubled as sleeping blankets. Stillwater, Nevada, ca. 1890. Courtesy of Special Collections, University of Nevada-Reno Library.

NORTHERN AND CENTRAL GREAT BASIN (1700s TO THE 1880s)

By the time early explorers began to document the Great Basin's indigenous peoples, the clothing they described varied by subregion and season of the year. In the northern and central part of the region (Great Basin Desert), which is marked by temperatures that can range from −10 degrees Fahrenheit (−23 degrees Celsius) in the winter to 100+ degrees Fahrenheit (37+ degrees Celsius) in summer and vary as much as 50 degrees Fahrenheit (25 degrees Celsius) from day to night, people were flexible in clothing themselves. Washoe, Owens Valley and Northern Paiute, Western Shoshone, Southern Paiute, and Western Ute men in some areas often went without clothes in the summer or wore only a belt with a skin or plant-fiber breechcloth with flaps front and back. Women wore a small front apron and a larger back apron of shredded bark or of small skins (duck, rabbit, marmot, etc.) sewn together and suspended from a belt. In colder weather men added a poncholike shirt made of one whole tanned deerskin or a two-skin shirt of tanned mountain sheep or pronghorn sewn loosely at the sides and with shoulder flaps or short sleeves. In winter, women wore a two-skin dress of tanned whole deer or mountain sheep hides that reached below the knees. The uncut skins were joined at the shoulders, leaving a neck hole and a folded flap of skin that had been the animal's neck front and back. They also were stitched up the sides to form shoulder flaps or short sleeves of the animal's front quarters. Skins were in short supply in some areas, so winter garments, especially for women, were often made from plant fibers, including shredded sagebrush bark, cliff rose (*Cowainia neomexicana*) bark, and occasionally tules twined together with cordage. Men added skin leggings that reached from ankle to calf or thigh or twined-bark leggings that

Western Shoshone Bill Kawich and wife, ca. 1900, south-central Nevada. Kawich wears the feathered outfit for the South Dance, with twisted eagle-down skirt and collar, each tipped with magpie feathers, and a magpie feather headdress. His shirt appears to be painted. His wife's net-beaded collar is also part of dance dress for women seen among Southern Paiute and Owens Valley Paiute people and also the Mohave of the Southwest in the early 1900s, and farther north among the Northern Paiute and Washoe by the 1920s. Nevada Historical Society.

were tied in place around each leg to cover the thighs and sometimes the calves. Rabbit-skin capes and robes gave added warmth. Capes required roughly fifty rabbit skins; robes required as many as one hundred, and they often doubled as sleeping blankets.

Twined basket caps were common for women in the central region (except Washoe), especially in summer and in fall for piñon nut collection. They protected those gathering the nuts from the sticky pitch secreted by the trees. Most caps were small, reaching to the ears, except in Owens Valley, where they often came down over the ears and were large enough that women could twist their hair underneath. Most tribes made slightly different shapes and had their own designs for decoration. Men occasionally wore either a headband of skin or a small skullcap of hide, sometimes decorated with a feather or two from birds such as eagles, hawks, or owls. They plucked their beards except in central Utah, where facial hair was prevalent among the Pahvant Ute. Both sexes wore face paint (usually of red ochre) in summer to protect from sunburn, although for healing, white paint was applied, as were other mineral colors (blue and yellow). Charcoal was used for certain ceremonies. Designs included dots and lines, with patterns largely controlled by individual preferences. Shell bead, animal- and bird-claw, deer dewclaw, duck, and other bird-bone necklaces were worn by both sexes, and in the north and west among the Northern Paiute, men sometimes pierced the nasal septum and inserted a bone tube. Earrings of a single bone or shell suspended by cordage were reported for both sexes.

Footwear in summer varied with activities. Both men and women often went barefoot in camp, but when on the trail, sandals or moccasins were preferred. Again, as in the deep past, patterns for sandals varied by subregion, with twined and plaited styles made by different groups out of local fibers including yucca (*Yucca* spp.) in the south and east and tules and sagebrush in the west. Deer- and mountain sheep–hide moccasins were often stuffed with plant fibers for added warmth in winter, or boots of tanned rabbit or badger skins covered the feet. Children's clothing generally mimicked that of adults, especially after roughly age twelve. Young children rarely wore much clothing of any kind before this age, although in winter they were often wrapped in small rabbit-skin robes or other garments to keep them warm.

SOUTHERN GREAT BASIN (1700s TO THE 1800s)

In the southern Great Basin (Mojave Desert), summer temperatures can reach 120+ degrees Fahrenheit (48+ degrees Celsius); winters are usually milder (40–60 degrees Fahrenheit daytime; 4–15 degrees Celsius), but nights are chilly (20–40 degrees Fahrenheit; –6 to 4 degrees Celsius). Panamint Shoshone, Chemehuevi, and some Southern Paiute groups wore few clothes in summer or in winter, the major garment being a breechcloth and belt for men and a short front and longer back apron for women, the latter commonly of shredded bark. A poncho-type skin or bark shirt might be added in winter, as was a twined skirt of bark for older men and women and ankle-to-thigh leggings for men and occasionally women, also of bark. Shredded-bark sleeveless dresses were also reported for some groups. Very few skin clothes were made or worn by either sex in warmer climates, but all used the rabbit-skin robe or capes of tanned skins with the fur remaining for winter warmth. People went barefoot in camp, and sandals of different styles, mostly made of yucca or rawhide, were preferred.

Pah-Ri-Ats, Northern Ute tribe, in winter dress. He wears an older-style buckskin shirt, slim leggings, cotton (or perhaps Navajo textile) breechcloth, and plain moccasins. Note the side fringes on his leggings and shirt sleeves and the flap (likely painted) at the front of his shirt. He has a beaded bag suspended from his plain belt. Uintah Valley, Utah, ca. 1874, stereo card. Library of Congress Prints and Photographs Division, LC-DIG-stereo-1s00862.

A liner of the inner bark of the Joshua tree (*Yucca brevifolia*) was often added for winter.

Men in southern areas often wore caps made from the head hide of young mountain sheep with the horns attached, or they made larger buckskin caps with two short peaks drawn up to simulate horns. An alternative for good hunters, especially among the Chemehuevi, was a skin cap decorated with quail topknots and red woodpecker feathers. Women wore twined basket caps of different styles in most areas, although the Panamint Shoshone and Moapa Southern Paiute also made their caps by coiling. Both sexes wore their hair loose and generally parted in the middle. Earrings of shell or bone and bone and juniper berry necklaces are reported for both sexes. Children wore little clothing except on cold days; their clothing mimicked that of adults once they reached adolescence.

NORTHERN AND EASTERN GREAT BASIN (1700s TO THE 1800s)

Clothing in the northern and eastern parts of the Great Basin for Southern and Northern Ute and Eastern and Northern Shoshone, Bannock, and Oregon Northern Paiute people may have started out in the 1700s as similar in style to that described earlier for the northern and central Great Basin region—basically alternating between plain skin garments and those made of plant fibers. Their clothing may always have been more commonly of skin, however, given that they were in better large game–hunting territories in and around the Rocky Mountains. But certainly by the time they were observed and described by outsiders in the late 1700s and early 1800s, many people were already dressing more like some of their neighbors to the south and east who had also acquired horses than their western Great Basin cousins. The Southern Ute and Eastern Shoshone may have been some of the first peoples to adopt the horse after its introduction by the Spanish and, thus, to begin the trend toward Plains-style dress. This trend would continue well into the reservation period, especially for those who had earlier chosen to take up the lifestyle of hunting bison with horses. For those who remained more localized and followed a mixed hunting-gathering lifestyle, changes were less dramatic, and older styles persisted longer.

Northern and Southern Ute and at least Eastern Shoshone men by the early and mid-1800s wore several styles of shirts, some subregionally popular. One was made of a single deer or mountain sheep skin with separate sleeves from a second hide sewn in—a more tailored approach than that farther west. After the introduction of glass beads in the early 1800s, these hide shirts often had lazy-stitch or appliqué beadwork on vertical shoulder strips and sometimes horizontal sleeve strips similar to central and southern Plains styles. They also included fringes on shoulder seams and down the midline or back of sleeves. Some had small triangular bibs in front and back and occasionally painted motifs, bells, and fur trimming. Southern Ute shirts of this type were most like those worn by the Jicarilla Apache and Taos Pueblo men of the Southwest.

A second shirt style, popular especially among the Northern and Southern Ute by the 1860s, had hide sleeves with fringe and a cloth body (cotton), sometimes plain and sometimes painted. Variations included shirts made with cloth bodies and sleeves but with beaded strips on shoulders, sleeves and buckskin fringes at the arm seams and down the back of sleeves, and also shirts that combined a cloth-and-hide body with hide sleeves. By the 1890s, Ute shirt shoulder strips in beadwork were narrower than their Plains counterparts, but some men wore human-hair locks attached as in central Plains designs of the Arapaho, Cheyenne, and Sioux.

Men in the eastern and northern Great Basin also wore tanned skin breechcloths with front and back flaps suspended from a belt. By the 1860s, many were made of wool and were either plain with white (nondyed) edges or had the long edges bound with ribbon, woven tape, or cloth of contrasting color. After 1890, they were decorated with beadwork (geometric and floral patterns among the Eastern and Northern Shoshone; geometric for the Ute), brass tacks or metallic sequins, ribbons, or commercial braid.

Men also wore leggings that covered ankle to hip and were attached to a belt. These were often of skin and tight fitting, with long fringed tabs at the ankles. Some had either a single- or double-wide flap at the sides that might be decorated with a two-inch- (five-centimeter-) wide beadwork strip at the outside edge. Ute leggings were sometimes painted with vertical lines or lines and dots, or solidly stained yellow. They might also be decorated with beadwork at the ankle and on the outside of the wide flaps. Other groups fringed the narrow leggings along the sides and used tribal beadwork designs to decorate those with wide side flaps. By the 1860s, some leggings, especially those with wide side flaps, were being made in a coarse wool fabric called *stroud* that were either blue or red but were similarly decorated.

Men wore hide moccasins, often plain for everyday wear (some with rawhide soles) and heavily beaded for more formal occasions, such as dances. Patterns and colors of beadwork varied by tribe, with each developing to some degree its own designs based on regional models. Southern and Northern Ute beadwork patterns show more central Plains affiliations with those of the Cheyenne and Sioux, which had basically a white field and geometric patterns consisting of large and small squares and triangles in red, blue, and green. They occasionally traded for and likely made some items in *transmontane style* (basically Crow patterns and colors), such as shoulder bags called *bandolier bags*. Eastern and Northern Shoshone beadwork affiliates more with the transmontane style, with some additions of floral patterns likely introduced into the region in the 1890s with the spread of the Grass Dance. Trade relations and influences during this period were particularly complex and led to several exchanges in styles, including in basic clothing as well as decoration.

Northern Shoshone and Bannock men seem to have preferred large hoop earrings with a perforated single-shell disk, metal-studded wide belts, hairpipe breastplates, or multistrand looped beaded necklaces and multistrand hairpipe chokers. Hairpipes were originally long, narrow pieces of bone, shell, copper, or stone, but after European traders realized the importance of these ornaments, they also provided trade beads of this shape and

Chief Ouray and Chipita, Northern Ute tribe, ca. 1870–1880. Ouray wears a fringed hide shirt decorated with a beaded flap and ermine tails, as well as wool cloth leggings with white borders and a wool breechcloth. His hair is side-parted and he has long, thin braids. Chipita wears a classic Ute dress of two mountain sheep hides. Note the extra beaded hide down the sleeves and the red wool cloth appliquéd pieces and lane beadwork at the bottom of her dress. She wears a wide hide belt ornamented with brass tacks and lane beadwork, and possibly beaded leggings with plain moccasins. Her hair is parted in the middle and hangs loose. Library of Congress, Prints and Photographs Division, LC-DIG-cwpbh-04477.

size. They sometimes wore an otter-fur tippet across one shoulder. They wore their hair parted on the side and in two braids (sometimes thin ones on each side, with the remainder of the hair left loose), which were wrapped with otter fur for important occasions. They had bangs pulled to the side, or sometimes standing up, and a single eagle feather at the back of the head. They plucked their beards and sometimes their eyebrows. Northern and Southern Ute men preferred to part their hair in the middle and wear two braids, either plain or wrapped. They sometimes added silver Navajo *concho belts* (made of oval silver pieces) over their shirts. They also wore silver bracelets from the Southwest and occasionally metal cuffs. Feathered bonnets, largely of Plains style but with fewer feathers, were worn by important men from all groups on important occasions. Hair *roaches* (crests of their own or added animal hair) likely came into these areas around 1890 and were worn for dances and other occasions largely by young men, as were streamers of brass or German silver hair

Northern Paiute cowboys in Stillwater, Nevada, dressed in working ranch clothes, including denim pants, jackets, vests, broad-brimmed hats, and neck scarves. This style of dress came into the region with the European settlers, and men began wearing it in the 1870s. Courtesy of Special Collections, University of Nevada-Reno Library.

plates. Armbands of beadwork were also part of dance regalia, but many men wore them as part of regular dress as well.

Women's dress in the northern and eastern Great Basin was also closely patterned after Plains styles, at least by the mid-1800s. Women tended to wear *tail dresses* made of two hides, with the tails turned to the outside at the neck. These were like dresses in the Columbia River plateau but also central and northern Plains styles from roughly 1820 onward. By the 1870s, they were also making dresses with separate yokes and sleeves from a third hide joined to a two-skin lower dress or with detachable yokes that could be worn over a plain skin or cloth underdress. The yokes were often heavily decorated with multiple undulating rows of beadwork or elk teeth, and the dresses were often fringed on the bottom border and at the sides. Those made by Ute women were similar in layout to Jicarilla Apache dresses; those farther north more closely patterned Blackfoot, Nez Percé, and Sioux designs, depending on the time period. Southern Ute women often wore Pueblo woven sash belts with Navajo concho belts or wide beaded belts over them, and they carried tail bags and trinket bags.

Women in northern areas wore brass-studded belts from which a knife, an awl case, and a trinket bag were suspended. They carried square beaded bags or sometimes Nez Percé twined-fiber bags, at least for special occasions. Northern and Eastern Shoshone women wore breechcloths under their dresses. They tended to wear their hair parted in the middle and hanging loose or, occasionally, in two braids. Ute women had similar hairstyles and occasionally wore hairpipe chokers and sometimes loop earrings.

For footwear, both men and women wore soft-soled or hard-soled skin moccasins, either plain or heavily beaded depending on the occasion. Beaded ankle cuffs were added for men, whereas women wore either tall beaded moccasins or shorter moccasins with leggings to midcalf. Their leggings were beaded with a wide row at the base and a vertical row up the sides and might also have German silver or brass conchos.

Clothing for children in the northern and eastern areas tended to mimic that of adults, but they appear to have worn these styles at an earlier age than farther west. Many children had complete buckskin or cloth outfits like those of their parents from the time

Ute bridegroom, United States, 1906. He wears a mixture of clothing styles typical of the period from the 1870s to the 1920s, including a vest with beadwork, silk neck scarf, and armbands over his collarless shirt as well as red wool leggings with beaded side panels and beaded moccasins. Library of Congress Prints and Photographs Division, LC-USZ62-112569.

they were three or four years of age, at least on dress occasions. Many early photographs show children basically as miniaturized adults, complete with fully beaded outfits and accessories.

By the 1870s in all areas of the Great Basin, traditional clothing of the types just described was seen less often except on important occasions or perhaps for dances and ceremonies. People throughout the Great Basin had quite thoroughly adapted their everyday clothing to that of their nonnative neighbors who were ranchers, farmers, and town dwellers. Even earlier, many young people had been making these transitions, while older adults retained at least some aspects of traditional dress. At first some of the clothing was likely worn-out clothing from local non-Indians. But as native women became more adept at needlework, they began to buy or trade for local cloth in the form of sacking or bolts in stores. Cotton and wool were especially popular, and women very carefully stitched garments for their families that in many ways resembled the clothing of their Euro–North American frontier neighbors, but they were not strict copies. Women made and wore mostly full-length, two-piece calico dresses with flared skirts, and men wore calico shirts and serge or broadcloth pants. Older women and most children preferred moccasins for footwear, while working men replaced moccasins with boots or shoes. Little girls wore loose-fitting sack-type dresses, and little boys wore a loose-fitting shirt that came to the knees. Women, especially in the central and western Great Basin, added silk head scarves, and men wore mostly flat-brimmed, high-crowned unblocked hats. Many groups and individuals added innovative touches that still allowed them to distinguish themselves, such as beadwork armbands, hatbands, and plain or beaded vests for men and beadwork belts or necklaces for women.

THE 1890s TO THE 1930s

Trends begun in the Great Basin with nonnative settlement continued to develop in the different subregions through the latter part of the 1800s and into the early decades of the 1900s. While older adults remained somewhat conservative in dress, younger people innovated as they began to attend boarding schools or reservation schools, and they abruptly made the transition to Euro–North American dress. Descriptions and photographs throughout this period show children, young people, and adults in various types of handmade and store-purchased clothing, sometimes with added distinctive accessories. Older styles of clothing, especially plant-fiber clothing and the simpler skin garments, largely disappeared during this period in favor of introduced cloth styles, especially in the western, central and southern Great Basin. However, the fringed and beaded clothing of the eastern and northern Great Basin was retained in those areas, especially for important occasions. It also filtered into areas to the west and south, so that these styles came to be associated with "traditional" clothing for much of the region somewhat independently of what had gone before. A few groups, such as the Washoe of western Nevada and the Panamint, Western Shoshone, Chemehuevi, and Southern Paiute groups in the Mojave Desert areas, did not adopt much in the way of this type of dress, even for important occasions. A few individuals may have favored it, but most preferred lighter cotton garments accessorized with beadwork.

In the central and western Great Basin, as well as to some degree in the north and east, men's clothing generally moved to cotton shirts, sometimes worn with an additional cotton undershirt, and work pants, such as denim or Levi's. Most shirts had long and rather full sleeves and band collars. Most men wore either buckskin or cloth vests, with various types of decoration on them, especially in the north and east. Decoration included loom-beaded strips or appliquéd beadwork, metallic fringe, brass studs or tacks, ribbonwork, and so forth. Vests in the western and central area were usually plain and store-purchased rather than handmade. Men in this subregion normally wore them buttoned, whereas in the east and north, they were often left open. Men in the north and east more typically wore either garters or beaded armbands around their forearms and either beaded, metal, or rawhide stamped cuffs. Many men, especially in the west, also wore denim or other work jackets or, sometimes, suit coats over their shirts. Men in most subregions wore bright silk bandannas knotted loosely at the throat or with the knot to one side, like local cowboys or buckaroos. Felt hats (Stetson type) of several varieties, most with broad brims but some narrower, high-crowned and lower or flat, unblocked and blocked to various shapes, distinguished individuals, especially in the west and central areas. Men in the northern and eastern areas (Northern and Eastern Shoshone, Bannock, and Ute) seem to have favored wide-brimmed, high, unblocked crowned hats or occasionally small sombreros (Southern Ute). Women made plain buckskin

Chemehuevi mother and child, 1907, typical of the Mojave Desert area. She wears a handmade one-piece dress, with a scarf and blanket shawl. Library of Congress, Prints & Photographs Division, Edward S. Curtis Collection, LC-USZ62-112235.

gloves for working ranch hands in all areas, and many men had heavily beaded gauntlet gloves for important occasions.

Men accessorized their outfits for special occasions with beadwork: beaded ties that were either long and narrow or larger and diamond shaped (Western Shoshone, Northern Paiute), attached to a beaded choker, or they wore long loom-beaded bands that went behind the neck and came down on either side in front, reaching to the waist (Washoe, Northern Paiute, Western Shoshone). Older or high-status men wore wool blankets wrapped around the waist and over one shoulder. Southern Ute men sometimes substituted Navajo wearing blankets for these.

In the western and central areas, most women, but especially older women, made and wore long, two-piece dresses with long sleeves and various bodice shapes. The skirts were full, gathered at the waist, and either had a second tier below the knee or a bottom ruffle about six inches (fifteen centimeters) deep. Fabrics included prints of various kinds, usually matching but sometimes not. A long white or light-colored cotton apron was worn over the front of the skirt. Twined basket caps continued, but most women wore brightly colored head scarves, with some differences as to how these were tied about the head and face. Washoe women tended to tie the scarves under the chin in such a way that the scarf partly shaded the face, whereas Northern Paiute women tended to tie them behind the neck and tighter to the head. Scarves, when not on the head, were worn tied loosely around the neck. Most women, especially in cooler weather, also wore a wool plaid fringed blanket as part of regular attire. Little girls wore the same styles, including head scarves, but the latter seem almost mandatory by adolescence. Older women preferred ankle-high moccasins; younger women and girls occasionally wore moccasins but mostly shoes.

This type of dress was accessorized with beaded bands, including a beaded belt and long beaded bands worn around the neck and reaching to the waist or knees, and occasionally a beaded choker and beaded wristbands. The Southern Paiute, Owens Valley Paiute, Western Shoshone, and Northern Paiute also began to wear large, lacework-beaded collars around 1900. These are similar to those of southern California and lower Colorado River tribes (e.g., Mohave) but with local differences. Most of the beadwork accessories were worn at dance time or when people wanted to dress up.

Women's cotton dresses in the eastern and northern Great Basin tended to be of slightly different styles, most emulating the previous skin dresses in that they either had a separate yoke and elbow-length sleeves or they were single-piece dresses with elbow-length sleeves worn with a belt. They tended to be one color rather than print, although there is some variation. Accessories included wide beaded belts, and most older women continued to wear moccasins and short leggings. Sometimes they wore a second underdress, especially in cold weather. Older women occasionally wore scarves, but most women in the north and east preferred to go without head covering. Plaid fringed blankets were occasionally worn, as were Navajo wearing blankets and Pendleton blankets.

THE 1930s TO THE EARLY
TWENTY-FIRST CENTURY

With more and more experience outside regional areas, in schools and in the military during the war and afterward, clothing in the Great Basin changed to that of mainstream U.S. society. In rural

Ute women, ca. 1899, United States. Five Ute women in handmade cloth dresses in the style of the turn of the twentieth-century, showing a variety of decorations in beadwork, cloth and buckskin fringe, some with underdresses. They wear traditional hairstyles and large hoop or shell earrings along with bead chokers (one with neck scarf) and various bead/shell long necklaces. Library of Congress, Prints and Photographs Division, LC-USZ62-111566.

areas, men still dress like local cowboys and buckaroos, with big hats, bright bandannas, and armbands. Otherwise, men and women show the usual variation in style of dress by occupation and age. Several native communities as well as surrounding non-native communities, have developed special occasions where more traditional clothing is seen. These include pageants, powwows, parades, rodeos, and similar events. Some communities have ceremonial occasions, such as the Ute and Shoshone Sun Dances, the Ute Bear Dance, western and central Great Basin Round Dances, or harvest festivals (pine-nut dance, girl's puberty dance, etc.), where traditional clothing is still appropriate, but today they may be mixed with various features of modern dress. A number of women throughout the region still make fine beadwork accessories for clothing as well as skin and cloth dresses decorated with beadwork. Some still make much older plant-fiber clothes, which are often worn over cotton garments for parades and other special occasions. Powwow clothing, in particular, has taken on a new look with multiple layers of detailed cloth appliqué work on dresses, leggings, men's vests, and shawls, along with the addition of ribbonwork, silk and rayon fringe, sequins, and many other materials. Dance outfits for Fancy Shawl Dances, Jingle Dances, Grass Dances, Women's Traditional Dances, War Dances, and others continue to show the creativity and ingenuity of many Great Basin women and men as a continuation of a long and changing legacy of dress.

References and Further Reading

Bates, Craig D. "An Artistic Style Uniquely Their Own: Basketry, Parfleches and Beaded Clothing of the Ute People." In *Ute Indian Arts and Culture*, edited by William Wroth, 143–187. Colorado Springs: Taylor Museum of the Colorado Springs Find Art Center, 2000.

d'Azevedo, Warren L., ed. *Great Basin*. Vol. 11 of *Handbook of North American Indians*, edited by William C. Sturtevant. Washington, DC: Smithsonian Institution, 1986.

Fowler, Catherine S. *In the Shadow of Fox Peak: An Ethnography of the Cattail-Eater Northern Paiute People of Stillwater Marsh*. Cultural Resources Series #5. Portland, OR: U.S. Fish and Wildlife Service, 1992.

Scherer, Joanna C. *A Danish Photographer of Idaho Indians: Benedicte Wrensted*. Norman: University of Oklahoma Press, 2006.

Steward, Julian H. "Culture Element Distributions, XIII: Nevada Shoshone." *University of California Anthropological Records* 4, no. 2 (1941): 209–360.

Steward, Julian H. "Culture Element Distributions, XXIII: Northern and Gosiute Shoshone." *University of California Anthropological Records* 8, no. 3 (1943): 263–392.

Stewart, Omer C. "Culture Element Distributions, XVIII: Ute-Southern Paiute." *University of California Anthropological Records* 6, no. 4 (1942): 251–356.

Catherine S. Fowler

The Southwest

North American Indian dancers at a powwow in Arizona, 2007. The metal cones on the dancers' skirts jingle when the dancer moves, giving rise to the term *jingle dress*. Image Copyright Jim Parkin, 2007. Used under license from Shutterstock.com.

The U.S. Southwest and northwestern Mexico compose a culture area that is called the Greater Southwest. This designation reflects two geographical orientations: one extending north from Mexico and the other from the eastern United States. The area encompasses the states of Arizona and New Mexico; small parts of Colorado, Texas, Nevada, California, and Utah; and the Mexican states of Sonora, Chihuahua, and Sinaloa. (Sometimes geographical areas and societies farther south into Mexico are also included.) The area is bordered by the Plains, Great Basin, and California culture areas.

One of the Southwest's most important characteristics is that it is home to strong enclaved societies with integrated, functioning cultures of great historic depth and unbroken continuity to the present. This is reflected in phenomenal archaeological remains, historic accounts, and oral traditions as well as in attire. Although the Southwest's native peoples have been engulfed by colonizing Spanish, Mexican, and Euro-American nations and have been greatly affected by foreign governmental policies since the sixteenth century, they have retained their traditional worldviews and philosophies as well as portions of their original homelands. All groups have a profound connection to their lands that is supernaturally sanctioned and expressed symbolically in all their arts, including dress. The clothing styles worn thousands of years ago are still seen in the ceremonial attire of many groups.

Another defining feature is an arid environment with subregional and local ecological diversity due to altitude, longitude, riverine, and mountainous terrains. Because of the environmental and social landscapes, the Southwest has always been multicultural. Although the Puebloan peoples are often considered the region's most advanced culture, that is, the culture climax or most "typical" culture, this is a misperception and essentialization based on the fact that the Puebloans lived in settled, permanent villages of stone houses and practiced irrigation agriculture, which Europeans admired. But many other people lived in less permanent settlements because their homelands could not support villages or their economic systems required seasonal, annual, or periodic movement to effectively utilize scarce resources. Individualized and constant adaptation to local resources is thus another regional hallmark of the culture area, as is the fact that

in 1848, the region was bisected by two nation-states with different governmental policies and clothing styles and fashion trends. Indigenous dress styles through time have been affected by the introduction of mass-produced attire and the subsequent reduction in handmade, culturally specific dress, except as special-occasion wear.

REGIONAL INFLUENCES, TRADITION, AND INNOVATION

In 2010, the Southwest's indigenous cultures are component members of the United States and Mexico but are treated differently because of distinctive government policies concerning native peoples. They are also affected by the sartorial norms of each country and by regional styles as well as by globalization, tourism, and fashion fads and styles in the twenty-first century. This is clearly seen in the dress of young people that, except during extraordinary events when portraying unique cultural identities and honoring heritage is expected or required, is normally indistinguishable from general urban or rural attire. In the United States, 60 percent of North American Indians live in urban areas and not on their home reservations for extended periods of time, working in the same types of occupations, with the same dress expectations, as members of the general society. Blue jeans and T-shirts for students, ranchers, farmers, and construction workers rule the day. Professional men and women and elected officials wear business suits, dresses, short-sleeved cotton shirts, and khaki pants, as well as the latest fashions, obtained from upscale department stores or native, New York, and Parisian haute couture, as long as they are suitable for the hot summers. (Fur coats or parkas, for example, are rarely seen.) Those working in professions requiring uniforms wear attire that is no different from their nonnative colleagues; Opata miners in Mexico wear hard hats, Navajo ranchers wear cowboy hats and boots, and O'odham or Maricopa tribal police are easily recognized by their blue uniforms, as are the Western Apache's famous firefighting contingent, who wear protective clothing when battling wildfires in the western United States. Elders living on reservations, particularly in isolated or remote regions, or in border towns tend to wear older styles of attire or housedresses, skirts, and blouses, holding onto workable but outmoded or classic clothing traditions in the same manner as rural Euro-North Americans or Mexican families living among or near indigenous groups. Some of the most traditional Tarahumara or Navajos, who still do not have access to electricity, will wear their traditional attire when herding sheep. The poor, of whom a disproportionate number are North American Indians in both Mexico and the United States due to the lack of employment opportunities in isolated areas, wear secondhand clothing from thrift shops or obtained from charities. This can be seen especially among those living in Mexico, along the international border, or in border towns, as well as among those who work off reservations as seasonal or migrant laborers.

Despite the twenty-first-century range of styles that reminds us that North American Indians are members of U.S. and Mexican societies; have different educational, wealth, and class distinctions; and are affected by their common sartorial cultures, it is not unusual for native individuals to wear adornment symbols. These might be silver and turquoise jewelry or classic hairstyles (long and straight for both men and women or tied with head scarves, beaded barrettes, or woven hair ties) to establish and emphasize their native identity through easily recognizable visual cues that make them distinct from the general population. For example, Navajo politicians often wear turquoise jewelry, which has symbolic importance to their people. Leaders among the Central and Eastern Pueblos carry silver-headed canes given to them by the Spaniards and, later, President Abraham Lincoln as signs of their sovereignty. These canes are handed down to each succeeding leader and visibly symbolize his responsibility to his community. Traditional wear, the beautiful and colorful attire that is seen in tourist brochures, books about specific cultures, or on television specials, tends to now be reserved for a wide variety of special occasions. These include when people are being honored or participating in a ceremony requiring symbolic designs. Other situations include when people are participants in weddings and life-cycle events (such as puberty ceremonies or ceremonial or ritual events), selling art to peoples from other cultures who like to see costumed artists as part of their buying experience, giving entertainment or dance performances, or participating in beauty

Chiricahua Apache in Arizona, 1898. The man wears a European-style suit, the seated woman a European-style blouse, and the young girl a traditional hide garment. Both the woman and the girl wear shell necklaces. National Anthropological Archives, Smithsonian Institution NAA INV 06411300.

pageants, rodeos, and powwows. Time-honored attire that has been appropriately adapted to the modern world serves as valued and beautiful markers of who people are and distinguishes them from other social and cultural groups. Such attire is worn with pride and is felt to be a right reserved for members of each society rather than a privilege that anyone with enough money to purchase reproductions can wear. It is this traditional attire that will be the main topic of the rest of this article, which will concentrate on how culturally specific clothing and traditional apparel has changed through time.

What is considered tradition and traditional is an evolving, adaptive concept in any society. Some cultures change faster than others; some cultures like change, while others distrust it. A core of bedrock tradition is always present, but so is innovation, experimentation, diffusion or borrowing, modification, and ultimately rejection or acceptance based on the needs and philosophies of the community over time. Tradition is adaptable and has been so since the beginning of each culture's creation. Even before the arrival of the first Spanish explorers in 1540, the Southwest has been a meeting ground of peoples, with a constant infusion of new ideas and materials. However, the Southwest does not exist in a vacuum and never has. There is great evidence of trade and intermarriage with neighboring peoples in the archaeological and protohistoric record and also recounted in indigenous oral histories, which include the importation of raw materials for clothing and adornment (buffalo robes, shells, and feathers) and ideas on how to cut tanned deerskin and leather for dress and shirt styles. In turn, clothing from the Southwest was traded to peoples living on the area's borders; the most famous examples are handwoven textiles made by the Hopi, Zuni, and Navajo, which became items reflecting great social status on the North American Plains. This is where the designation for the Navajo "chief blanket" came from: Only chiefs could afford them.

Trade with different peoples, language differentiation, historic origins and paths, as well as where each group lived and the resources they could exploit, produced cultural and subregional specificity in sartorial styles. These styles had, and still have, the stamp of tradition—that is, what were gifts of the Creator, Holy People, or ancestors and have proven to work well over time. Dress (especially as a holistic ensemble) has always been and remains a multivocal art form with condensing symbolic qualities used as cultural identity markers and indicators of political status, age, gender, marital status, accomplishment, alliances, values, and social status, as well as indicators of spirituality and respect. These sartorial cues are easily read and can be seen from a distance. O'odham women could immediately recognize Chiricahua Apache apparel from a great distance during the raiding periods of the eighteenth and nineteenth centuries and would quickly hide. Pueblo women's marital status was seen in their hairstyle. The young know that their attire is the gift of their relatives and makes them part of their communities. Clothing also instills pride. Navajo Tamara S. Nez has said, "I feel very special [when I wear my traditional dress]. I am very proud of the clothes that I'm wearing. It makes me proud and strong, and I am glad to be a Navajo." Dress also makes people who they are. Navajo historian Ruth Roessel has said, "We are strong by the way we dress. We identify ourselves as Navajo women, from our ancestors—who were called Asdzání—that means 'one sits down and has her skirt laid out beautifully.'"

This cultural pride and people's sense of themselves, as well as the region's frontier nature as part of the American West and as a Mexican hinterland and remote trading area, has meant that external influences have affected each culture's attire. But enforced colonial change in Mexico was different from that in the United States, and here the native cultures were not affected to the same extent as those in the eastern United States. Since 1848, the dimension of the international border, with its unique blended culture, has also affected clothing, what materials are available to make clothing, what people ought to wear, and the occasions on which types of attire can be worn. This can be seen in U.S. policies about attire over time: the types of cloth given to people in return for relinquishing their lands as defined by treaties, the requirement to wear uniforms in government boarding schools, the inability of people who had lost part of their land base to find enough of traditional materials (especially animal skins) to produce time-honored clothing, and Christian missionaries' ideas of modesty and proper appearance as they strove to civilize "primitive" peoples. As a result, traditional standards of proper attire have changed; no women go topless, and no men wear loincloths. Instead, blouses are added to traditional styles, skirts are now made in manufactured cloth, and loincloth aprons are worn over pants. Adaptation can also be seen in the desires of indigenous

peoples for new materials for jewelry (brass, silver, and gold), soft cotton cloth that was more comfortable than twined yucca fiber, and manufactured apparel, which traders readily brought to them in the nineteenth and twentieth centuries. Forced changes and new sartorial and adornment desires affected all groups over the last two hundred years, but the ways in which this has occurred makes a discussion of Southwest Indian clothing a discussion of groups of cultures, of simultaneous change and retention of tradition through constant adaptation to materials, styles, silhouettes, and moral and cultural values.

THE SOUTHWEST'S CULTURES

The Greater Southwest is composed of a large number of cultures, many of whose ancestors have lived in the area for tens of thousands of years. Others have migrated from central Mexico, the Great Plains, or California during the pre-Contact past, while still others have moved in historic eras and recent times. These peoples can be divided into four basic groups that existed at the time of European contact and most of whom still exist today. In most cases, people retain portions of their homelands. These four groups are the Pueblo Villagers, Apachean Bands, Rancheria groups, and groups that, until the late nineteenth century, subsisted primarily on hunting and gathering.

Pueblo Villagers are people who live in autonomous villages composed of multifamily and multistoried stone houses in Arizona and New Mexico. These groups have many commonalities but vary based on language group and interactions with neighbors and trading partners. They are divided into Eastern Pueblos, who live along the Rio Grande River and its tributaries and include the Tanoans, which are further subdivided into Taos, Picuris, San Juan, Pojoaque, San Ildefonso, Nambe, Tesuque, Santa Clara, Isleta, Sandia, Puaray; the Piro, who moved out of their homelands along the southern Rio Grande in the eighteenth century and became the Tegua near El Paso; and Keresans, who can be further divided into the Cochiti, Jemez (with Pecos population), San Felipe, Santo Domingo, Santa Ana, and Zia. The Central Pueblos include the Keresan Acoma and the Laguna and the Western Pueblos who practice dry farming and have important rituals designed to supernaturally affect climate. This group includes the Zuni; the Hopi, with their ten villages on three mesas; and the Hopi-Tewa, Tanoans from the Galisteo Basin area in New Mexico who moved to First Mesa after the Spanish returned following the Pueblo Revolt of 1680.

Apachean Bands are Athapaskan language speakers; they have a hereditary relationship and similar worldviews, social structures, and ceremonial organizations, but they express cultural variation as a result of differing social contacts and microenvironmental adaptation. This has resulted in Eastern Apacheans resembling Plains Indian groups and Western groups adopting some Puebloan cultural features. Due to a war-raiding complex, Apacheans historically acquired reputations as raiders who made forays from mountain strongholds and attacked sedentary groups such as O'odham and Pueblos. Eastern Apache societies live in New Mexico and are called Northern Chihuahua, and those who live in western Texas are the Lipan, Jicarilla, and Mescalero. (The Kiowa Apache are more prevalent in the Plains region.) Western Apache societies residing in Arizona and western New Mexico are the Arivaipa, Apache Peaks, Cibecue, San Carlos, Carrizo, Fort Apache, Pinal, Mazatzal, Southern Tonto and Northern

A woman of the Isleta Pueblo, United States, ca. 1910. She wears a cotton blouse beneath a traditional garment called a *manta* that fastens on the right shoulder. Over the *manta* she has placed a printed skirt. Her footwear consists of ankle-high boots that are covered from the ankle with wrapped whitened strips of hide or cotton cloth that extend to the knee, a style known as *puttees*. Library of Congress, Prints and Photographs Division, LC-DIG-ppmsca-09507.

Yuman rear skirt made of strips of inner willow bark, Arizona, ca. 1900. Cocopa women wore twined fore-and-aft aprons of shredded willow bark. Courtesy, National Museum of the American Indian, Smithsonian Institution.

Tonto, White Mountain, and Payson Apache bands, which are identified by the area in which they lived. Other groups are the Chiricahua (including the Gila or Mimbreños) Apaches and the Navajo (Diné).

Rancheria groups are the largest group of peoples in the Southwest. They are irrigation and rainfall run-off farmers and formerly lived in the south in autonomous communities spread along a river. They were greatly influenced by Spanish clothing styles until the twentieth century. They include a subdivision called River or Lowland Yumans (also called Colorado River Tribes), who farmed along the Colorado River. Others in this grouping were the Cocopa, Maricopa, Kaveltcadhom, Yuma (Quechan), Mojave (Mohave), Kamia, Halchidhoma, Kohuana, Halyikwamai, and Kamii. The O'odham are Uto-Aztecan speakers who occupied the southern half of Arizona and northern Sonora following a mixed strategy of irrigation and dry farming. Included in this group are the Pima (Akimel O'odham), Tohono O'odham (Papago), Pima Bajo (Lower Pima), and Cahitans (Yaqui or Yoeme and Mayo). The Chihuahuan groups include Concho, Huichol, Opata, Tepahuan, Cora, Tepecano, Warihio, and Tarahumara (Ramamuri). (Most Mexican groups will be discussed in other volumes.)

Groups that until the late nineteenth century subsisted primarily on hunting and gathering foods, along with minimal agriculture in marginal and extremely mountainous areas, include the Plateau or Upland Yumans (Yavapai or Apache-Mohave: Tolkepaya, Eastern Yavapai, Keweyipaya, Northwestern Yavapai), Walapai (Hualapai), and Havasupai. The Seri of the coastal areas of Sonora lived by fishing, and the Paiutes lived in the northwestern part of Arizona and southern Nevada and Utah.

BASIC CLOTHING STYLES OF THE SOUTHWEST

Clothing as protection from the elements is influenced by climate, available technology, and raw materials. From the beginnings of human occupation in the Southwest, people wore clothing of tanned animal skins (deerskin and buffalo hide or rabbit-skin

robes) and gathered plant materials that they twined or coiled into a number of useful items, such as sandals, shirts, hats, and belts. From the earliest times (time immemorial according to indigenous groups or the initial settling of the area in the Paleo-Indian period according to archaeologists: 12,000 to 20,000 B.C.E.) men wore only loincloths (often referred to as *breechcloths, breechclouts, flaps,* or *clouts*). A *loincloth* is a long rectangular piece of cloth, twined fiber, or soft, tanned animal skin worn between the legs and tucked over a belt so that the flaps fall over the groin and buttocks. In the earliest periods, emergence and then the great migrations (referred to as the Archaic period by archaeologists), tanned animal skins and woven or twined fibers were used for all apparel. (Children generally went naked until age six or seven.) While few examples of these perishable items remain, several styles have remained basically unchanged until the early twentieth century. Tarahumara runners don cloth fitted loincloths, along with shirts and sandals, for their marathon races through the Sierra Madre Mountains.

For thousands of years women wore fiber aprons of twined strips of yucca or other plant and animal fibers (Indian hemp, fur, feathers, mountain sheep wool, and human hair). These were twisted into cords or woven into rectangles that were sometimes sewn together or worn one in the front and one in the back of the body and tied with thongs to cover the groin and buttock area. This style has been termed a *fore-and-aft apron*. These aprons were often fringed and decorated with the same paints used to decorate the body and hair; they still form the basic silhouette of much of the region's feminine attire. Like men, women wore animal skin or woven-fiber ponchos in inclement weather; people in the west wore rabbit-fur blankets made of pelt strips woven on yucca cords in a simple pattern. Peoples in Mexico and the O'odham made blankets of domesticated turkey feathers woven in the same manner.

While people generally went barefoot, when necessary both sexes wore woven yucca sandals, with either square or round toes, tied to the feet with a thong. The latter style was often decorated with colored strands in geometric patterns. Buckskin moccasins were only worn by tribes living adjacent to the Great Plains. In

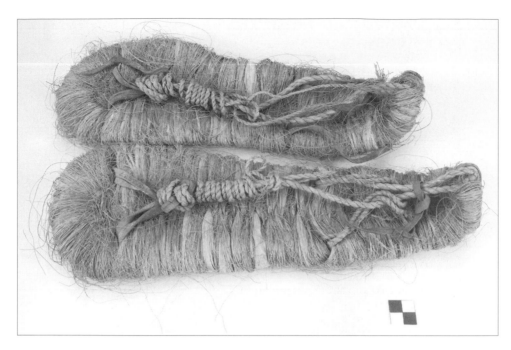

Twisted cord and fiber sandals worn by Yavapai or Apache Moha Plateau Yumans, Arizona, ca. early twentieth century. Courtesy, National Museum of the American Indian, Smithsonian Institution.

addition, unfitted, tanned deerskin ponchos were used by both men and women in the north, and leggings of deerskin or woven plant fibers, such as yucca or hair (including human hair), protected both men and women from abundant cacti thorns and prickly plants. Leggings were long tubes, one for each leg, that were tied at the back to the loincloth or apron belt. Leggings of animal skin were often made from the legs of a deer and were lightly decorated with tribal symbols.

Hair adornment included basketry caps, especially in the north and west, and headbands with macaw and turkey feathers in the south. Twined bags, belts, and *tumplines* (a strap running from the top of the head to the bottom of a pack) were painted with mineral pigments or decorated with shell beads. Abalone-shell and turquoise jewelry was worn by both men and women. These were great trade items, as was catlinite (pipestone) from as far away as Minnesota and coral from the Gulf of Mexico. Beads and pendants were made of these materials and worn as earrings, necklaces, and sometimes earplugs.

With the development of agriculture and the introduction of cotton around 1000 C.E., loincloths began to vary. The ancestors of the Pueblos, O'odham, and groups in parts of northern Mexico began to wear loincloths of woven cotton rather than tanned deerskin loincloths, as did those who retained hunting lifestyles. In addition, clothing styles began to differentiate: Some groups developed an apron style. They tucked the loincloths through a twisted fiber or a woven belt, which kept it in place over the crotch for a more fitted look. Other loincloths were worn loose; some had panels of the same lengths, while others had fronts shorter than rear cloths, over which a decorated apron was worn. Ancestral Puebloans developed woven *kilts* (rectangular pieces of woven and often embroidered cloth wrapped around the waist, extending to the knee, and held in place with a woven sash) that are still used today in ceremonials. Accessorizing these woven kilts and aprons were braided or twined sashes with a long fringe

made by finger-weaving. These are still worn today by all the Pueblo groups. Woven cotton shirts (rectangular woven cloth with a hole cut in the center to insert the head, side ties, and attached square-cut sleeves) replaced tanned deerskin ponchos. For rituals, the men are bare breasted but covered in symbolic body paint. In a few groups, women wore fitted breechcloths, always covered by fore-and-aft aprons.

From pre-European Contact times, clothing in the Southwest has been geographically differentiated and culturally specific. Each culture had styles that marked an individual as a member of a group, distinctive from all others. Similarly, each society had elaborate attire for special occasions and rituals. The next section describes the historic traditional attire of several main groups at the time of European contact, including major changes stemming from European contact, such as the introduction of sheep, which influenced the attire of the Puebloans and the Navajo. One group in each section is highlighted as emblematic of essential styles due to space limitations.

GROUPS OF NORTHERN MEXICO

Little has been recorded about the clothing worn by most of the groups of Chihuahua and Sonora and how their clothing has changed through time. Many groups were amalgamated into the general Mexican population during the long Spanish occupation and the Mexican period and adopted what quickly became basic regional and, later, national attire—loose white-cotton pants and overshirt for men; and a floor- to knee-length, gathered full skirt; apron; flounced, short-sleeved blouse or rebozo; and head shawl for the women. People used fiber sandals and later added shoes and straw hats for the men. Most of these items are no longer handmade but purchased in local markets; in the early twenty-first century, young people wear shorts and pants. Identity markers tend to be robes and adornment.

Jicarilla Apache brave in typical costume, northern New Mexico, 1874. stereo card. Library of Congress, Prints and Photographs Division, LC-DIG-stereo-1s00414.

Peoples inhabiting the most remote regions or those who were able to keep the Spanish at bay, like the Yoeme (Yaqui), retained their traditional attire longer than groups whose homelands were quickly overrun because of their good farmland or mining opportunities. Today this dress, which includes cotton and woolen textiles, is used in a rich ceremonial life. The Seri, who inhabited the hottest desert areas, wore minimal desert-style clothing that consisted of wraparound kilts for men, fox-skin loincloths, deerskin skirts, woven-fiber aprons, pelican robes, and twined and coiled basketry hats, belts, armbands, and sandals until the early twentieth century. The main form of body decoration was body painting and tattooing, in a wide variety of patterns, supplemented by multiple shell bead necklaces and nose plugs. Since the mid-twentieth century, men have worn the typical Mexican rural attire with minor stylistic variations over time, while women's attire has been more distinctive. Women produce handmade loosely fitted, long-sleeved, brightly colored shirts tucked into the waists of ankle-length, unembellished full shirts or fitted jackets. Sometimes contrasting colored piping is added. Their long hair is parted in the middle, worn loose or in braids, and covered with a cotton shawl. More recent items include straw cowboy hats and sunglasses and, for those men who still wear their long hair tied in a braid at the back, a bright cloth front apron over trousers, a substitute for their older pelican-skin loincloths and a sign of ethnic identity. Face painting had disappeared by 1950 except in religious ceremonies.

The Tarahumara who live in the rugged mountains of Chihuahua have worn leather sandals, deerskin clothing, rabbit-fur robes, and agave-fiber aprons and robes since pre-Contact times. In warm weather, males wore loincloths, sandals, a headband,

and a finely woven warp-faced belt. Later, shirts or short ponchos were added for those living in isolated areas, while Tarahumara living near mestizo communities adopted Mexican attire: cotton trousers and shirts. Women historically wore very wide skirts, a light blouse, and a headband. Women traditionally have gone barefoot; in cold weather they wear extra shirts and skirts. Jewelry consists of decorated belts. The Tepehuan, Concho, and Mayo have since Contact worn typical rural Mexican attire: jeans, ready-made cotton shirts, and woolen or cotton sashes for men and a cotton blouse, short skirt, seed and shell necklaces, and head bandanna for women, except in the most remote areas where old styles prevail. Women weave cotton or wool striped blankets for cold weather.

YUMANS OF THE LOWER COLORADO RIVER REGION

The Yuman-speaking cultures who lived along the Colorado River wore clothing that in many ways resembled the traditional attire of the groups in California as well as the dress of the other groups in the Southwest. All groups wore minimal clothing because of the intense summer heat on the lower Colorado and Gila rivers. Men and children generally went naked during the hottest times of the year; at other times they wore narrow loincloths of woven willow-bark strips held up with a thong belt, without leggings. With increases in trade, men wore large kerchiefs over their loincloths. Men used no head coverings and let their hair grow to waist length, which was often rolled into twenty or thirty braided strands. Sometimes the braids were pulled back with a thong tie or wound on top of the head and painted with white clay. For ritual occasions or warfare, one or two feathers were fastened to the hair. Men also wore shell pendants in the nasal septum when young. After Spanish Contact and until the coming of the railroad, men wore small, more fitted loincloths held in place by a cloth girdle around the hips. They traded for cotton bandannas, which were worn as neckerchiefs. Men also began to wear cotton loincloths. Each group was distinguished by a different style of hair wrapping and hairstyle.

Mohave, Cocopa, Quechan, and Maricopa women were bare breasted until the turn of the twentieth century, but they never went naked. They always wore one or two twined fore-and-aft aprons of shredded willow bark over a short underapron made like a loincloth of finer bark. The back of the top apron was sometimes twined to stand out like a bustle. In inclement or cold weather, women donned rabbit-skin robes of their own manufacture or acquired blankets from the Southern Paiutes or Walapai or Hopi. Men and women in the northern groups later traded for Navajo-made ponchos, which symbolized that the wearer had wealth. Women wore their hair long or shoulder length, with bangs in styles that indicated their cultural affiliation. Like men, most women went barefoot and used fiber sandals of untwisted bundles of mescal woven over a looped cord, which formed a sole, mainly when traveling. The Cocopa also made rabbit-hide sandals. When trade cloth became available in the 1800s, women began unraveling it into long red or blue strands and intertwined it into their front aprons.

Yuman-speakers did not have special ceremonial attire, but adornment was quite extensive. From pre-Contact times to the present, both men and women wore strings of clamshell disk beads obtained from the West Coast; turquoise obtained from the O'odham or Hopi; bead and shell necklaces, earrings, and bracelets; and feathered articles. Sometimes these were woven into one long strand, which was wrapped around the neck as a choker, with long strands hanging down the chest. Women and men had facial tattoos and used extensive face and body paint made from plant and mineral pigments in culturally specific designs and colors; children obtained their tattoos in a ceremony at puberty. Quechan men had wavy lines over their bodies, while Mohaves used straight lines. Men used black pigments to signal their readiness to go to war. Women in all groups had straight vertical lines on their chins and often painted white highlights in their hair. People who were not tattooed were thought to be unable to go to the afterworld. Some groups, such as the Cocopa living in Mexico, continued tattooing until the late twentieth century.

Women who had status and wealth wore highly regarded neckwear that often covered the breast. These came to be called *Mojave collars*. They were originally made of twined fibers that were woven into diamond, fret, triangular, and hexagonal patterns in a netted openwork weave. Attached to these were rare or valuable items as pendants; the most well known were made of blue and white seed beads, which were first obtained in trade from the tribes of Southern California. In the nineteenth century, these collars were made by both men and women. Both men and women also wore braided or finger-woven belts and carried bags of fiber and, later, commercial yarn.

For all these groups, clothing began to change due to missionaries and government agents who considered bare breasts immodest. People also began to wear rawhide sandals and, later, shoes bought in stores. With the coming of the railroad and through the efforts of U.S. Indian Service agents, educators, and missionaries, men began donning different clothing: white pants and shirts for groups in Mexico and, in the United States, white cotton shirts followed by trousers in the 1890s. During the twentieth century, men gradually adopted Western wear: blue jeans, boots, neckerchief, belts, and Stetson hats. Women began wearing plaid fringed shawls in cold weather, a cotton shawl fastened in front, or cotton blouses, which were more comfortable than fiber and lasted longer. By the early twentieth century, women wore cotton-print full skirts with wide ruffles at the bottom and a cotton sash.

UPLAND YUMAN ATTIRE

Nonagricultural groups living in upland and mountainous regions, such as the Walapai and Havasupai, wore buckskin attire. Havasupai men wore sleeveless shirts, short loincloths, leggings, a headband, and moccasins. The Walapai also wore shredded and twined juniper bark and a short-sleeved hide shirt and coiled yucca-fiber sandals. Textiles were obtained from trading with the Hopi and Navajo and were highly prized. Ornamentation for both sexes was not elaborate and consisted of highly prized shell necklaces and chokers with pendants and earrings, which also served as amulets against disease; these were obtained in trade from the Mohaves and Quechans. Both Walapai and Havasupai made temporary face painting of red hematite, and some women tattooed the lines on their chin with ground charcoal. Hair was worn long or shoulder length for both sexes and held back with hair ties or headbands by men; women wore bangs and let the rest of their hair hang long without headwear. After the 1860s, these materials were slowly replaced with the type of mixed attire described for the Western Apaches as well as manufactured woolen and cotton work shirts, blue jeans, workboots, and large straw hats. Loincloths, manufactured shorts, and wraparound cloths are used in modern sweat lodges, and Hopi and Navajo blankets are still used as well as commercial blankets and shawls.

Traditional Walapai women's clothing consisted of a double fore-and-aft apron belted at the waist and buckskin leggings to protect the legs while traveling. Havasupai women's dress consisted of a two-piece length of buckskin, reaching from neck to ankles, worn over a short underapron and held in place with a leather belt or a Hopi sash. The Havasupai's front dress was looped over the neck and tied at the waist with a breast flap that was usually plain or minimally decorated with loops, hem, and side fringe. A similar dress, dyed red, was worn at the girl's puberty ceremony, even after cloth replaced leather attire. Dress styles followed the Anglo norms of the day and had fitted long sleeves, high necklines, and long, full skirts in the early nineteenth century and, after World War II, standard U.S. rural attire. Moccasins were commonly worn, and, in inclement weather, rabbit-skin blankets were used, which were later replaced by Navajo-made blankets.

The earliest traditional attire of the three Yavapai groups was similar to their Walapai neighbors, although they also used willow-bark blankets and hide ponchos in cold weather, especially in the mountains. There was some regional variation in styles around the time of early Euro–North American contact; some groups living nearest the Western Apaches sewed their hide dresses at the sides or wore a top, Apache-style dress, and Apache-style boots when traveling. Only the poor wore fiber

Navajo girl, Granado, Arizona, 1926. She wears a belt decorated with silver conchos and a silver squash blossom necklace on top of a shell necklace. Courtesy New York Public Library.

clothing. Both men and women wore their hair loose, with bangs cut at the eyebrows; women cut theirs at the shoulders and wore it loose, while men's hair was longer and tied in the back. Red clay was used by both sexes on their bodies as sunscreen. After the period of military encounters with the Euro–North Americans, Yavapai, especially those who were incarcerated with the Western and Chiricahua Apaches, adopted their clothing and adornment styles; those incarcerated with the River Yumans accepted their styles of attire and manufactured apparel and cloth obtained through government rations and trade.

O'ODHAM ATTIRE

Like the River Yuman groups, O'odham peoples wore basically identical clothing, which changed through time in the same way and at approximately the same time. The main lifestyle differences among the groups were first whether they lived on major rivers and could practice irrigation agriculture or lived in harsher areas of the desert, which required them to have seasonal residences. When they came under the influence of Mexicans and later Euro–North Americans, O'odham men wore the standard desert-style loincloth of cotton with little or no flaps, and to protect them during travel, they wrapped undecorated pieces of deerskin around the leg and fiber sandals. Rarely were poncho-style shirts worn because of the intense heat. Later, men adopted the Mexican-style white-cotton pants and shirt. Men always wore sandals and never adopted moccasins.

Similarly, women wore basic desert-style clothing of a wrap-around skirt and a fiber fore-and-aft apron of cottonwood or willow bark. Later, after Christian missionaries insisted, women wore a sarong dress of commercial cotton fabric that extended from the shoulder to the ankles and covered the breasts. Hopi robes, Mexican sarapes, and commercial blankets were also worn by the O'odham, over the shoulders for women and around the waist for men. Later, O'odham women adopted the Apache-style camp dress, but they added a bottom ruffle to the skirt and used inset, full-length sleeves to distinguish them from other groups. The blouse hung over the shirt and is seen today on many occasions.

Both men and women wore their hair long and loose, with bangs as protection from the sun. Like the River Yumans, men braided their hair and wore it turban fashion, sometimes adding horse hair to increase its thickness. In the nineteenth century, some O'odham men added long, woven, fringed sashes, twisted in changing fashionable styles in their hair. A deerskin hood with eagle feathers was worn by warriors to signify their bravery. While headbands were worn, the O'odham did not use hats until the late nineteenth century. Accessories and jewelry for both men and women was always minimal, except for shell bead necklaces

Zuni moccasin, United States, ca. 1880–1930. The colors are produced by painting the leather. © McCord Museum ME937.17.1-3. http://www.mccord-museum.qc.ca/en/

and earrings; garment decoration was typically simple bands. Face and body painting was saved for special occasions and is rarely seen today except in special ceremonies among the Tohono O'odham and Pima Bajo.

APACHE ATTIRE

Hunters and later ranchers, such as the Apacheans who inhabited areas of canyon, high grasslands, and mountains, at first wore clothing made of fringed and painted tanned deer and buffalo hide, which were stylistically influenced by the Plains groups to the north and east: ponchos and leggings for men; two-piece dresses for women. These were decorated with beaded strips on the shoulders and the arms and fringing. For groups such as the Mescalero, Lipan, and Chiricahua, they stained the deerskin yellow as was done by Plains groups in Texas. In summer, men wore only breechcloths, and women wore a short skirt. The knee-length attached leggings and moccasins were decorated with culturally specific designs. Hair was held in place by a buckskin or cloth band. Men occasionally wore brightly painted buckskin caps.

About the time that game used for clothing began to become scarce, commercial cloth became available. This turned out to be an advantage because, due to their subsistence lifeways, Apaches often had to move quickly and often had no time to tan or weave. This increasingly became the case when the Mexican government armed Plains tribes, such as the Comanches, to stop Apachean raids on Puebloan, O'odham, and northern Chihuahuan communities. Apacheans acquired the clothing of the communities they raided and then made it their own. Men in the east and south began in the early nineteenth century to wear standard Mexican attire: large, white-cotton, knee-length breechcloths, loose white-cotton pants, and cotton shirts with fitted sleeves that hung over the pants and breechcloth. Mexican sarapes and shawls were extremely popular. Footwear also changed from a two-piece, Plains-style moccasin with a front seam and attached leggings to a knee-high boot with upturned toes, rawhide soles, and buckskin uppers, decorated with short fringe and metal conchos. The tops of the boots could be folded to make carrying pouches.

The famous photographs of Chiricahua Apache warrior Geronimo and his relatives resisting the attempts of the U.S. military to confine them to reservations depict the clothing that popular culture considers appropriate for Apache warriors of the nineteenth century. Men wore white loincloths with or without boots; handmade white shirts in the Mexican style; leather belts and loaded cartridge belts; Euro–North American vests, jackets, and kerchiefs; colorful cloth headbands; high leather boots; protective jewelry; fringed, U-shaped carrying pouches; and the accoutrements of war. Following the Apaches' confinement to reservations and the forced removal of some Mescalero, Lipan, and Chiricahua to reservations in Indian Territory (Oklahoma), Apaches began to adopt Euro–North American attire acquired through Indian Service and military rations. Now poor with no way to acquire clothing in their time-honored ways, men's clothing became a mixture of Mexican-style trousers and blue jeans, dark vests, colored-print shirts, and suit coats. From these colored shirts, the groups in Oklahoma developed the ribbon shirts that are seen at rodeos, powwows, and special events throughout the Southwest and, indeed, at all North American pan-Indian gatherings.

Apache women wore wraparound hide skirts and went bare breasted in warm weather or donned sleeveless ponchos of tanned deerskin for cold nights before adapting the Plains-style, T-shaped deerskin dress. This widespread style consisted of three tanned animal hides, two for the torso and skirt sewn at the sides and a third folded over to form a yoke attached to the basic dress. These were decorated with long fringes on the sleeves and hems and painted a solid color, often a rich yellow or tan. Women also wore wide leather belts decorated with brass tacks or metal conchas and beaded headbands. This style of dress has great symbolic importance and can be seen in the late twentieth and early twenty-first centuries as the Jicarilla and Mescalero girls' puberty dresses. The puberty ceremony is a multiday ritual in which an adolescent girl becomes a woman and learns important values, knowledge, and behavioral practices that prepare her to be a valued member of the community and a future mother. At this time, all unmarried women wear their long hair pulled back and tied to the base of the neck with a *nah-leen*, a dumbbell-shaped ornament covered with red cloth and brass buttons.

After the U.S. government confined Apaches to reservations, women began to develop a new dress style that has become traditional wear for Western Apaches, Upland and River Yumans, and O'odham. This is the camp dress. A *camp dress* is a modification of a Victorian style called the *Mother Hubbard dress* and consists of a full, floor-length cotton skirt composed of two to four gathered bands and a matching, loose, hip-length overblouse with flounced, short or elbow-length sleeves and a round-necked, square-cut yoke. These nineteenth-century dresses were made of plain or patterned calico obtained through rations or trade, or purchased from stores. They were decorated with rickrack, bias tape, braid, lace, and ribbon in contrasting colors. Today, these dresses are used for all special occasions, including parades such as the celebration for the opening of the National Museum of the American Indian in 2005, annual rodeos, building dedications, marriages, and community ceremonies. The camp dress is also used for the girl's puberty ceremony by all Western Apache bands; it is made especially for the young woman by her female relatives in either cotton or satin.

Jewelry was predominantly beads, showing heavy Plains and Pueblo influence and utilizing geometric styles, some of which carried symbolic meaning. In the Western Apache groups, a special choker called a *big bertha collar* was made of open network and seed beads, similar to the Mohave and Quechan necklaces. Face painting and body painting was generally reserved for ritual occasions and warfare; these later were individual and culture-specific designs.

Navajo clothing has changed considerably through time and in different directions than other Apachean bands. Following contact with Pueblo groups, the typical Apachean tanned-skin clothing with high boots and turquoise jewelry was augmented by cotton and then wool garments. Women became renowned weavers and developed unique styles of robes, blankets, and dress. Women wore a two-piece, fore-and-aft dress of black wool pinned at both shoulders, with top and bottom end panels that depicted symbolic designs of the Navajo homeland, also seen in ceremonial baskets. This dress was cinched at the waist with a woven cotton belt and, later, a silver concho belt and worn with Puebloan puttee-style leggings and boots. Men wore Mexican-style white muslin trousers split to the knee and fastened with silver buttons, a woven sash, decorated leather pouches, and a V-necked cotton shirt by the 1840s; they had special attire and headwear for warfare. Both sexes wore extensive turquoise and bead jewelry.

Hopi girl, United States, ca. 1921. Unmarried Hopi girls wore their hair in two whorls, while married women arranged their hair in braids. Library of Congress, Prints and Photographs Division, Edward S. Curtis Collection, LC-USZC4-8858.

In the late nineteenth century, following the return of the Navajo from captivity at Bosque Redondo, clothing styles began to change radically to new traditional styles. Solid-colored velveteen or colored V-necked calico shirts with inset sleeves and tucks were worn by both sexes. These shirts were decorated with silver fluted buttons as the Navajo became renowned silversmiths. Stetson hats and blue jeans became common for men, and full, long cotton skirts for women became standard and highly distinctive apparel. Ankle-high moccasins, fastened across the instep by a silver button, were worn by both men and women. Hair was long and usually tied in an hourglass bun worn low on the neck. Long, narrow, handwoven belts, garters, and hair ties were characteristic as decoration, combined with large quantities of silver, shell, and turquoise jewelry. Manufactured Pendleton blankets and coats replaced the Navajo blanket, which was itself superseded by rugs made for external markets.

PUEBLOAN ATTIRE

The agricultural Pueblo relied on woven cloth for their clothing. Up until the beginning of the nineteenth century, Pueblo men wore only fitted-cotton loincloths or kilts, decorated along the lower edge. Those made for ritual use were decorated with culturally and ritually specific embroidered or painted symbols. On ritual occasions, male performers decorated their torsos and faces with body paint in appropriate symbols. The Pueblos did little body or face painting on a daily basis. In cool weather, a plain or embroidered poncho-style shirt (with or without square-cut sleeves) or woven robes of rabbit skin, cotton, or wool were added. At Acoma, Hopi, Zuni, and Laguna, the men wove, and the women embroidered. Around 1800, men at Acoma, Laguna, and the Rio Grande Pueblos adopted the Mexican-style loose white-cotton pants and shirts; western pueblos followed some years later. These, in turn, were replaced by blue jeans and Western-style shirts in the twentieth century.

Footless, knitted, white calf-length stockings of open-knit weave, looped twinning, and later crocheting, held in place by an instep strap, were worn with colored hide and beaded moccasins until they were replaced by machine-woven socks and shoes bought in stores. These stockings are still used for ceremonial attire; however, only a few are still produced by Zuni and Hopi men. At Rio Grande, Pueblo men also wore calf-high boots of buckskin with painted rawhide soles, first acquired from Apacheans and then decorated to reflect each Pueblo's design elements and patterns.

In the eighteenth and nineteenth centuries, Eastern and Central Pueblo men wore robes composed of painted deerskin or buffalo hide. Rabbit-skin robes slowly went out of style as commercial cloth and jackets became available in the mid-1800s. Textile robes were especially conspicuous at Taos Pueblo, where they marked social relationships: one *moiety* (an extended social clan) wore white; the other, red. By the turn of the twentieth century, most photographs and paintings of Taos men show them depicted with a robe worn over the head. Other groups are depicted with robes worn over the shoulders and without hats, except for kerchief bandannas serving as headbands.

Since the 1850s, most Pueblo men and women let their hair grow long unless they were in Indian Service boarding school or the military. This pattern continues today, as does the twentieth-century trend of cutting the hair to the shoulders or jawline and using a cloth headband. Occasionally men at Acoma would wrap a piece of calico cloth like a turban, but this was a short-lived style. Earlier, men had bangs and knotted their long hair in back, secured with a strip of cloth. Both men and women also wore a special Southwestern style called the *chongo* (in which the hair is coiled at the nape of the neck in a figure eight and bound at the crossing with beaded or woven hair ties), which is still seen today worn with traditional dress. Female hairstyles also signified age and social status. Hopi unmarried girls wore their hair in two whorls, while married women sported braids.

Pueblo women wore handwoven, one-piece *mantas*, elongations of the basic fore-and-aft apron covering the breasts, which went under the left arm and fastened above the right shoulder. A long, narrow, finger-woven belt cinched the dress's waist. Each Pueblo used different colors. At Acoma, sashes were of red or red and green wool. Some Pueblos also embroidered bands; at Acoma these were red, blue, yellow, and green. For ceremonial occasions, Pueblo men add woven garters and armbands to which religious paraphernalia is attached. All Pueblo women wore ankle-high boots with this dress. The boots usually had undecorated tops and painted rawhide soles. Pueblo women also wrapped their legs with clay-whitened leather strips, which were later replaced in the

Western Pueblos by strips of heavy, handmade cotton. This was called the *puttee* style and is a marker of Puebloan fashion.

By the 1890s, Eastern and Central Pueblo women began to wear a cotton, calico-sleeved blouse or underdress beneath the manta dress. Within twenty years, lace edging and ribbons were added to the underdress. Since World War II, the underdress has become a flowered blouse or housedress, and the manta is constructed of commercial black wool. The fancy aprons were added for special occasions around 1920, while large shawls were draped over the head at all pueblos. Especially valued after World War II at Hopi and Zuni were elegant, tightly woven, soft wool shawls from Czechoslovakia, Romania, and Hungary.

Jewelry for both sexes included silver, abalone, and olivella-shell and turquoise necklaces, belts, earrings, rings, bracelets, and buttons in styles that changed over time. At the time of Spanish Contact, the Acoma wore turquoise nose pendants and earrings. Then Spanish-imported Italian coral became popular, as did necklaces of silver crosses interspersed with silver beads, which the Eastern Pueblos traded from the Spanish, Mexicans, and later Navajo and Zuni. Men generally made and wore more jewelry than women until the mid-twentieth century. Also ubiquitous was dyed cotton or wool sashes, worn by both men and women. At Acoma, which was known for its extraordinary embroidery until the early 1900s, these were decorated in red, black, or green and had tassels rather than fringe.

References and Further Reading

Adair, John. *Navajo and Pueblo Silversmiths*. Norman: University of Oklahoma Press, 1989.

Basso, Keith, and Morris E. Opler, eds. *Apachean Culture, History and Ethnology*. Anthropology Papers No. 21. Tucson: University of Arizona, 1971.

Bennett, Wendell C., and Robert Zingg. *The Tarahumara, an Indian Tribe of Northern Mexico*. Chicago: University of Chicago Press, 1935.

Cordell, Linda S. *Prehistory of the Southwest*. 2nd ed. San Diego: Academic Press, 1997.

Douglas, Frederic H. "Basic Types of Indian Women's Costumes." *Denver Art Museum Leaflet Series* 108 (1950).

Driver, Harold. *Indians of North America*. Chicago: University of Chicago Press, 1961.

Griffin-Pierce, Trudy. *Native Peoples of the Southwest*. Albuquerque: University of New Mexico Press, 2000.

Kent, Kate Peck. *Pueblo Indian Textiles: A Living Tradition*. Santa Fe, NM: School of American Research Press, 1983.

Kluckhohn, Clyde, W. W. Hill, and Lucy Kluckhohn. *Navaho Material Culture*. Cambridge, MA: Belknap Press, 1971.

Kroeber, Alfred. *The Seri*. Southwest Museum Papers, No. 6. Los Angeles: Southwest Museum, 1931.

Kroeber, Alfred, ed. *Walapai Ethnography*. Memoirs of the American Anthropological Association, No. 42. Menasha, WI: American Anthropological Association, 1935.

Ortiz, Alfonso, ed. *Southwest*. Vol. 9 of *Handbook of North American Indians*, edited by William Sturtevant. Washington, DC: Smithsonian Institution Press, 1979.

Parezo, Nancy J. "The Indian Fashion Show: Manipulating Representations of Native Attire in Museums Exhibits to Sight Stereotypes in 1942 and 1998." In *The Representation of American Indian Culture as Artifact or Artwork*, theme issue of *American Indian Culture and Research Journal* 31, no. 3 (2007): 5–48.

Parezo, Nancy J., and Richard V. N. Ahlstrom, eds. "Dress and Adornment of the Pueblo Indians by Matilda Coxe Stevenson." *The Kiva* 52, no. 4 (1987): 275–312.

Paterek, Josephine. *Encyclopedia of American Indian Costume*. New York: W. W. Norton, 1994.

Roediger, Virginia M. *Ceremonial Costumes of the Pueblo Indians*. Berkeley: University of California Press, 1991. (Originally published 1941.)

Roessel, Ruth. *Women in Navajo Society*. Tsaile, AZ: Navajo Community College, 1981.

Sheridan, Thomas, and Nancy J. Parezo, eds. *Paths of Life: American Indians of the Southwest and Northern Mexico*. Tucson: University of Arizona Press, 1996.

Smithson, Carma Lee. *The Havasupai Women*. Anthropological Papers 38. Salt Lake City: University of Utah, Department of Anthropology, 1995.

Spicer, Edward. *Cycles of Conquest; the Impact of Spain, Mexico, and the United States on the Indians of the Southwest, 1533–1960*. Tucson: University of Arizona, 1962.

Spier, Leslie. *Yuman Tribes of the Gila River*. New York: Dover, 1978. (Originally published 1933.)

Wood, Margaret. *Native American Fashion: Modern Adaptations of Traditional Design*. 2nd ed. Phoenix, AZ: Native American Fashions, 1997.

Nancy J. Parezo

See also volume 2, Latin America and the Caribbean: Overview of Mexico.

The Plains

The Plains is a vast region comprising the central portion of the entire North American continent, extending from the Mississippi River west to the Rocky Mountains and from Alberta and Saskatchewan down to Texas. The native landscape is dominated by short-grass prairies and tall-grass high plains. Very little is known about the dress of the prehistoric inhabitants of the Plains, although there is evidence of Paleo-Indian human occupation dating back at least 13,000 years. These early inhabitants originally hunted mammoths and, later, pursued the buffalo herds that roamed the great expanses of grassland, as well as elk, deer, antelope, and mountain sheep. A few ornaments, primarily bone, stone, shell, and copper beads and pendants, and hideworking tools such as bone scrapers and awls have been recovered from the archaeological record. Dry conditions on the southern Plains have preserved some woven items, including yucca-leaf sandals. There is evidence that marine shells were traded to the region from the Gulf of Mexico and Pacific Coast and that copper was imported from the Great Lakes.

Plains Indian culture as a recognizable and shared regional identity emerged more recently. The archaeological record shows that by 900 C.E., horticultural tribes had established themselves along the Missouri River, where they cultivated corn, beans, squash, and sunflowers and hunted seasonally. These tribes are ancestral to the Mandan, Hidatsa, and Arikara that were encountered in the early 1800s. More ephemeral are other populations that relied more heavily on hunting buffalo, practicing a seminomadic hunting-and-gathering lifestyle. While there is evidence of a long regional history of intertribal trade and exchange, contact and trade with Europeans dramatically affected the configuration of native occupation in the region. Both intertribal contacts and contacts with Europeans brought residents of the Plains a variety of new ideas about dress. By 1730, Spanish horses imported from the Southwest to the southern Plains had become an integral part of life across the region, transforming the modalities of travel, hunting, and warfare and defining the Plains cultural pattern as equestrian. The reliance on horses required adaptations to dress. The resulting mobility meant that items of dress had to be readily portable, as groups moved from place to place. At the same time, a series of devastating epidemics caused by European diseases (smallpox, measles) decimated the indigenous populations. Of at least forty villages before the 1781 epidemic, fewer than a dozen remained along the upper Missouri by the time of the Lewis and Clark expedition of 1804–1806. The few survivors after a second outbreak in 1837 merged together to form a single village at Like-a-Fishhook in North Dakota.

The eighteenth and early nineteenth centuries saw substantial movement of tribes. As a result, communication among tribes led to exchanges of information and skills, and thus, individual elements of dress cannot always be attributed to individual tribes. For instance, various Siouan groups were pushed out of the western Great Lakes onto the central Plains because of conflict with the Ojibwa, who had been armed with guns by the French. By 1750, they had reorganized and settled in an area that spanned from the Black Hills to the Mississippi River. The northern Plains (including Canada) were occupied by the Sarcee, Plains Cree, Plains Ojibwa, Blackfoot, Stoney, Assiniboine, Gros Ventre, Crow, Mandan, Hidatsa, Arikara, and Plains Métis (people of mixed First Nations and Euro-Canadian descent). Besides the various divisions of the Sioux—Teton (Lakota) to the west, the Yankton and Yanktonai (Nakota) in the middle, and Santee (Dakota) to the east—the central Plains were home to the Northern Cheyenne, Arapaho, and Pawnee. The Osage, Kansa, Ponca, Quapaw, Omaha, and Otoe-Missouria were occupying the lower Missouri region; these related tribes had migrated from the prairies onto the eastern Plains in the seventeenth century. The Southern Cheyenne, Kiowa, Kiowa-Apache, Comanche, Tonkawa, Wichita, and Lipan Apache were on the southern Plains below the Arkansas River.

AESTHETIC TRADITIONS

Both the wearing and the making of dress were and continue to be core elements of social, cultural, and religious expression across native North America. Dress offers a structure to recognize individual and community accomplishments, rights, and responsibilities. Women not only provided for their families but honored them by making beautiful clothing. Women outfitted the new brides of their sons and brothers to demonstrate generosity to their new kin. Male regalia were distinctive displays of rank and valor.

Often, both men and women shared in the production of a single piece of clothing. Its decoration would depend on its function. For the most part, men painted clothing with images and symbols relating to warfare, hunting, religion, and personal and tribal histories. Men often made their own ceremonial regalia and decorated it with images they obtained through prayer and fasting, and recognized artists or spiritual men were sometimes commissioned to create specific items. Military and dream societies (membership in the latter was based on having had a dream or vision of the animals or supernatural beings who were patrons of a given society) provided the context for the communal expression of a man's position and achievements. Women crafted and embellished objects using abstract and geometric designs in a variety of methods, most notably embroidery with porcupine quills, beadwork, and painting.

Man's hide shirt, ca. 1835, Mandan. An upper-Missouri-style shirt with quilled shoulder strips and painted war honors. Founders Society Purchase with funds from Richard A. Manoogian. Photograph © 1987 The Detroit Institute of Arts.

Porcupine-quill embroidery is arguably one of the most ancient of women's techniques for clothing decoration, and a great deal of formal ritual became attached to its traditions. The most accomplished Cheyenne, Arapaho, and Lakota quill workers belonged to quilling societies whose members possessed exclusive knowledge about symbolic designs and colors used for ceremonial quillwork for the tribe. Designs often came in dreams and with ritual instruction. Membership in the society was an indication of social status and a statement of great artistry. One of the greatest accomplishments was to have quilled thirty buffalo robes, and women who had done so gave testimony about these achievements in the same way that men recounted their war deeds. Quills were stained by boiling them with various pigments from bark, roots, black walnuts, and powdered minerals but also with scraps of red and blue trade wool; bright aniline dyes became commercially available at the end of the nineteenth century. Quilling was done by wrapping, plaiting, weaving, or sewing.

1800 TO 1850

Plains material culture was influenced by encounters between the different peoples meeting in the region, and an examination of dress cannot ignore the impact of materials acquired in trade, both prior to the arrival of Europeans and especially after. The incorporation of foreign items into an indigenous framework reflects the dynamic nature of economic forces and shows how they affect people in their everyday lives. After some time of use, many foreign items become culturally authenticated, that is, they acquire the significance of native objects. European glass beads are a prime example of this process because they greatly affected Plains dress by supplementing (and almost displacing) native materials such as porcupine quills. Bead embroidery was much easier and faster than quillwork and also permitted a wider range of designs and patterns. Blue and white *pony beads* (their name refers to how traders transported them) were used since the first half of the nineteenth century and were most often sewn in rows, just as quillwork was executed. By the 1840s, the smaller *seed beads* became readily available in larger quantities and in a greater variety of colors; steel needles made it easier to sew them onto buckskin.

Between the eighteenth and nineteenth centuries, the impact of Spanish, French, British, and later, U.S. trade goods, including items of manufactured European dress, greatly affected the dress of Plains tribes. Ledger book entries for garments included coats, tall hats, blankets, cloth and silk handkerchiefs, shirts, and items such as flags and feathers worn as status symbols by chiefs, as well as rings, bracelets, beads, paint, and combs. The *capote*, a hooded coat made from Hudson's Bay blankets, was elaborated strictly for this market and widely worn by northern tribes.

MEN'S GARMENTS

What we know of dress in the early nineteenth century is primarily based on the few garments in collections and accounts from explorers and traders. As they traveled the length of the Missouri on the first official U.S. diplomatic mission to the region (1804–1806), Lewis and Clark encountered many different Plains tribes—Otoe, Omaha, Yankton Sioux, Lakota, Blackfoot, Mandan, Hidatsa, and Arikara—and exchanged objects with them. Several painters have contributed to the record, including Peter

Tanininyan Wakuwapi (Reuben Chase-in-sight) wears an eagle-feather headdress with a fully beaded vest, armbands, and cuffs (United States, 1913). National Anthropological Archives, Smithsonian Institution BAE GN 3670.

Rindisbacher, living on the northern Plains in Canada in the early 1820s; Jean Louis Berlandier and his protégé Lino Sánchez y Tapia, in Texas about 1830; George Catlin and Karl Bodmer, both traveling in the Missouri River region in the 1830s (Bodmer as the artist for the famed expedition of Prince Maximilian zu Wied); and Paul Kane, Rudolf F. Kurtz, and Seth Eastman, on the north-central Plains during the following decade.

Beyond distinctions between northern, central, and southern Plains, prior to the 1840s it is hard to discern tribal distinctions in dress beyond very broad regional styles. Items of dress were often traded and thus might be collected from people other than their makers. For instance, the Crow sold finished garments and sought Lakota painted robes, while the Métis in Manitoba traded their own delicately embroidered items all across the northern Plains. Sometimes there were varying preferences about specific trade items. A record from 1794 shows requests for blue cloth by the Omaha and Ponca, while scarlet cloth was very popular among the Lakota in the 1830s. Lewis and Clark brought with them glass beads in several colors to give as gifts but found that blue was the most sought-after color, followed by white. The basic male outfit was composed of moccasins, leggings, and breechcloth. Women wore a long dress, leggings, and moccasins, and both men and women used buffalo robes for warmth. Bodmer's portraits of 1833–1834 in particular convey the richness and elegance of outfits and the dignity of the men and women wearing them.

Moccasins were soft soled and made from a single piece cut and folded so as to have a side seam along the outer edge of the sole. A more eastern variation of this style had the seam running down the center of the moccasin top and with ankle flaps that could be folded over. In the early nineteenth century, rawhide was added to the bottom to make a hard sole, and eventually women started making a two-piece moccasin with separate tops and hard bottoms; the tongue and cuffs might also be added as separate pieces. Winter moccasins were stuffed with buffalo wool or made from scraps of old buffalo robes with the fur on the inside. Everyday moccasins were not decorated, but quillwork and beadwork were applied on the upper vamp of moccasins worn on special occasions. Moccasins on the southern Plains have very little beadwork but a fringe along one side of the upper and on the heel, often tipped with small metal cones and dragging on the ground.

Men's leggings were originally made of tanned antelope, big-horn, deer, or elk hide and were secured to the breechcloth belt with thongs. Early shapes were tubular, sometimes with long tabs at the bottom or a triangular flap extending off the sides; many were painted with personal power symbols or a tally of deeds. The most ubiquitous decoration was a fringe along the seam down the length of the leg, and the amount and style of quillwork or beadwork varied. Common on the northern and central Plains were vertical strips two or three inches (5 to 8 centimeters) wide, quilled or beaded separately and attached along the outer edge, sometimes in combination with painted designs. Crow leggings often have a broad horizontal panel along the bottom portion. By the 1820s, wool trade cloth was used frequently to make leggings.

Men's shirts and headdresses were specialty regalia that indicated social status. Generally, upper Plains men's shirts were made from two hides of medium-sized mammals (deer, mountain sheep, elk, antelope), retaining their natural shape and sewn like a poncho across the top so that the forelegs formed the sleeves (open or partially sewn under the forearm) and the hind legs hung front and back far below the wearer's torso. The part of the hide that had been the animal's head was retained and formalized into a decorated triangular neck flap. Long fringes made of locks of human or horse hair and buckskin were attached to the arms, shoulders, and sides. Strips decorated with elaborate quillwork and beadwork were attached across the shoulders and along the length of the arms. The Blackfoot, Assiniboine, and others in the north favored drops made from ermine furs, large rectangular neck panels, and large quilled rosettes placed on the front and back. The southern style was more fitted to the body, with long and narrow sleeves, sewn sides with a slit at the bottom, and a longer triangular neck flap. They were usually painted (especially in yellow and green), with very little beadwork edging and long, twisted fringe attached to shoulders, neck flaps, sleeves, and elbows.

The most distinctive feature of several early shirts collected along the upper Missouri are the paintings that depict the shirt owner's military exploits and serve as a tally of his war honors. Plains shirts have been, unfortunately, referred to by white observers as *scalp shirts* or *war shirts* because of the belief that the hair locks were scalps taken from enemies. Rather, these ceremonial or *honor shirts* were regalia of political and military office and important symbols of rank and prestige. The human-hair locks attached to these ceremonial shirts were given as an act of allegiance to a recognized political leader, while horse hair indicated horses stolen in raids and other war honors. Men who

had undertaken leadership roles had the right to wear them, as did older men belonging to one of the headmen's associations. Among the Lakota, four appointed *shirt-wearers* oversaw the welfare of the group, with responsibilities such as choosing the best camping and hunting sites. Their shirts were made in pairs, one of which was painted blue on the upper portion and yellow on the bottom while the other was red and yellow, signifying earth and sky and other connotations of power.

Much of the regalia worn by men represented their position within military and religious societies and included sashes, pipe bags, otter-skin capes, bear-claw necklaces, and lances. The most famous headdress is the *eagle-feather bonnet*, with sweeping feathers and one or two long trailers. Only honored warriors would have the right to wear such a headdress, as eagles are considered sacred messengers of the Thunderbird, the winged being that generates thunderstorms by flapping its wings and flashing lightning from its eyes. The Lakota, Cheyenne, Mandan, Hidatsa, and Crow in particular are associated with this style. The Blackfoot wore a version without trailer and with the feathers standing upright, decorated with ermine-skin drops. Headdresses with split antelope or bison horns and with elaborate trailers appropriated the powers of those animals and were worn for the hunt. Many Pawnee, Omaha, Osage, Ponca, Otoe, and Missouria men on the eastern Plains wore a *roach* (a section of hair made to stand erect) made of porcupine and deer hair dyed red and attached to the *scalplock*. This item was associated with a warrior society called the *Iruska*, whose other significant regalia was a crow-skin bustle.

WOMEN'S GARMENTS

An early style of woman's dress on the northern Plains was made from two large rectangular pieces of hide (elk, deer, or antelope) sewn along the sides, with the top folded down and suspended with two wide hide shoulder straps; separate sleeves could be added on. Related to this style is the *side-fold dress* of the upper Missouri area, fashioned with a single hide folded over and sewn along the side, held with one shoulder strap. These dresses were out of fashion by the 1830s, and fewer than a dozen exist today. They are extremely elegant, with decoration elaborated horizontally to encircle the body. A couple of these dresses are painted, but most of them combine thin parallel rows of quillwork with beaded rows across the shoulders, chest, and bottom. A fringe and rows of tin cones embellish several of these dresses.

By the first quarter of the nineteenth century, two-hide dresses, made from two large skins, were common. To make one of these dresses, the rump portion of the animal was folded over, forming a cape or yoke, and then sewn, leaving a neck opening and the two tails hanging on the chest and back. The hind legs formed open sleeves, and the forelegs hung from the sides at the bottom. Hide dresses were variously decorated, more elaborately for wear on special occasions, with thick bands of blue and white pony beads across the shoulders and thinner bands across the chest area and along the bottom contour of the hide. Pieces of red trade cloth framed with beadwork created elegant accents of color and texture, and a fringe several inches long usually decorated the sleeve extremities, the bottom edge, and at various points across the body. One of the richest decorations among the Crow, Cheyenne, Lakota, and Kiowa were rows of elk teeth fastened to the yoke and sometimes to the entire dress. Because the canine teeth of the elk were extremely valued, a dress so decorated indicated a

Kiowa woman wearing an elk-tooth dress, United States, 1892. Elk teeth were a status symbol because only the two eyeteeth of each elk were used, thereby demonstrating the prowess of the hunter in taking many elk. National Anthropological Archives, Smithsonian Institution NAA INV 626 8200.

following a narrative sequence and executed in the conventional schematic form of representational painting done by men. Regalia, hairstyles, weapons, and historical events are accurately represented. A different style of robe also worn by men is painted with a large feathered circle, possibly representing a feather bonnet. Many of the robes from this time period, be they painted or not, also have a beautiful strip of quillwork or beadwork attached along the length of the hide, two or three inches (5 to 8 centimeters) wide and interspersed with four rosettes. This appliqué was intended to be displayed horizontally across the body when the robe was worn and sometimes covered a seam (the easiest manner of skinning a buffalo was to cut along the back and sew the hide back together once it was processed). Women's fancy robes were decorated in two styles. One had a painted red-and-black geometric design articulating along the perimeter with solid elements in the center, descriptively referred to as a *border-and-box pattern* or, for the southern version, a *border-and-hourglass pattern*. The other had narrow, parallel rows of quillwork extending across the wearer's back, said to represent the paths one takes in life. Among the Lakota, both these designs are reported to be associated with a girl's ritual adoption and puberty ceremonies.

BODY ORNAMENT

Ceremonial face and body painting were commonly employed by men to indicate deeds and accomplishments. The custom of painting one's face black when returning from a successful war party expedition was common, and white signified having lost members of one's war party. Red was the color most widely used, but red, green, yellow, and black designs on the face and torso were applied prior to departure for war, for ceremonies, for dances, and for formal treaty signing.

Tattooing was not uncommon although more extensive on the southern Plains. Among the Assiniboine, Mandan, Hidatsa, Crow, Osage, and Kansa, men were tattooed on the chest, arms, or shoulders to signify war and other honors. Wichita men marked the eyelids and made short lines near the eyes and down the sides of the mouth, and references to a boy's first bird-hunting accomplishment and to a man's war honors were also created on the hands, chest, and arms. Assiniboine girls might be tattooed at puberty, with a round spot on the forehead and lines extending from both ends and the middle of the mouth down the chin, transverse lines on cheeks, and rings around wrists and upper arms. Among the Osage and Ponca, daughters of chiefs and wealthy men were tattooed extensively on most of their bodies. Further south, Tonkawa and Wichita women tattooed black stripes and triangles on their chins and cheeks, back, and abdomen, as well as concentric circles around their breasts.

Until they were about ten years old, Osage children had clan haircuts, with some areas shaved but leaving tufts, ridges, or circles with varied significance. Osage, Omaha, Kansa, and Pawnee men shaved the head, leaving only the roach (a narrow strip of hair extending along the top from about the middle to the back, cropped, and greased to stand straight) and two braided strands grown from the center of the scalp (*scalplocks*). Most other tribes let their hair grow but arranged it variously. Using a heated stick, Crow men coiffed their hair with a distinctive pompadour that rose high above the forehead. Among northern groups, certain men of rank wore a topknot coiled and bound to stand high above the forehead. Very fashionable in the 1830s were squared-off side

woman's wealth and status. On the southern Plains, the Kiowa and Comanche employed a whole third skin for the yoke, but the Lipan Apache made the skirt and cape as separate pieces. Beadwork decoration was applied conservatively along borders, but many dresses were stained with yellow, red, blue, and green pigment and featured long, abundant fringe (often twisted and tipped with small metal cones).

Women's leggings covered the bottom of the leg, reaching just under the knee, and were considered part of the footwear. Decoration was applied on the lower portion visible under the dress. Kiowa and Comanche women wore a moccasin boot rather than two separate pieces, with the top portion folded over at the knee and either fringe or a decorative side flap hanging down along the side and minimal decoration (one or two beaded rosettes and a thin border on the foot and thin, vertical beaded strips along the length of the leg with a parallel line of round metal studs).

Both men and women wore buffalo robes (the entire animal's hide, with or without the fur, tanned, and rendered supple) around the shoulders and held overlapping in front. Among the most spectacular robes predating 1850 are several belonging to high-ranking individuals. These are painted with their owner's military exploits,

bangs, sometimes with a short lock over the bridge of the nose. Hair arrangements also reflected society and war honors. Among the Lakota and Cheyenne, there were specific meanings associated with braiding the hair on one or both sides and with the kind of wrapping used (otter fur or red or black wool cloth).

Most Plains women wore their hair parted in the middle and with two braids, although Comanche women cut it. Their hair part was painted red with vermillion to symbolize the path of the sun. Sometimes married and unmarried women wore their hair differently from each other, as among the Osage and Quapaw, where girls rolled their braids and their mothers tied a single braid. Mourning rituals often included the cutting of one's hair and generally not taking care of dress or appearance for one year.

Almost universally, men plucked facial hair, and all adults wore ornaments of shell, bone, and metal dangling from pierced ears. Drops, feathers, pieces of cloth and fur, carved wooden pins, necklaces (the Crow made a loop, one with many rows of strung beads), hairpipe bone breastplates, and chokers and ear drops made with strung rows of dentalium shells were worn as hair and body ornaments. The Crow wore long hair attachments made of human, buffalo, or horse hair decorated with rows of

dots of white clay. Particularly fashionable in the 1830s among young men up north were small rawhide bows tied to the hair above the temples. Further south, native metalworkers cut and stamped German silver into various pectoral ornaments, bracelets, brooches, rings, and *hair-plates* (a leather drop secured to the hair and with a series of large metal disks or *conchos* mounted in graduated size and reaching to the ground).

1850 TO 1900

Plains tribes were engaged in resistance to and negotiation with the incursion of white settlers on their lands for two decades after 1850. The California gold rush of 1849 attracted a steady stream of emigrants across the territory of the Sioux, Cheyenne, Arapaho, Crow, Assiniboine, Mandan, Hidatsa, and Arikara, prompting the Treaty of Fort Laramie in 1851 between the U.S. government and the tribes to negotiate access. Erosion of those boundaries came soon, especially after gold was found in the Black Hills and George A. Custer was gloriously defeated at the Little Bighorn in 1876, and the tribes were confined to small reservations. Tribes further south faced similar encroachment and aggression. The Treaty of Medicine Lodge (1867) forced the Comanche, Kiowa, Southern Cheyenne, Arapaho, and Plains Apache to move to reservations in Oklahoma, where they joined eastern tribes that had been sent there after the Indian Removal Act (1830). Osage, Otoe, Ponca, and other prairie tribes also relocated to Oklahoma as a result of several treaties.

The reservation system placed the tribes under the direct control of the U.S. government and under the management of Indian agents. Native customs, dress, language, and religions were banned, and a policy intent on "civilizing" the North American Indians was carried out through government and Christian boarding schools. From the agents' point of view, the early reservation period was a time of transition, waiting for the old ways to disappear and for a new generation to grow up assimilated. One measure of "progress" was how many natives adopted white modes of dress. Before-and-after photographs of children sent to boarding schools were taken upon their arrival in their native outfits (which were promptly removed and the boys' hair cut short) and again some time later in their school uniforms. Many young men donned their native garb as soon as they came home, in an act of defiance. As women's cloth dresses were deemed acceptable, the agents were more focused on transforming male attire, and resistance to abandon traditional dress was viewed as subversive (the unfortunate expression "going back to the blanket" referred to the perceived regression of Indians from assimilation efforts).

Strictly speaking, this *citizen's dress* consisted of commercially manufactured clothing (or homemade but adhering to the same patterns; women made simple, everyday wool and cotton dresses sewn in a T-shape) worn in a manner consistent with Euro–North American styles. Such clothing was, for instance, required by the authorities for school or administrative employment (teachers, agency and school staff, and students). Even when they wore citizen's dress, however, North American Indians continued to maintain an overall native ensemble by wearing moccasins and wrapping a blanket around their shoulders. Many men worked as cowboys and dressed accordingly, but on special parade occasions they sported buckskin coats, trousers, and vests decorated with floral quillwork or beadwork.

With an increasing distinction between citizen's dress and *fancy dress*, the latter became closely tied to events of cultural

Rosa White Thunder wearing a trade cloth and elk-tooth dress with long dentalium earrings (United States, twentieth century). National Anthropological Archives, Smithsonian Institution BAE GN SI 8384.

celebration when performances of traditional dances and rituals could take place. Ironically, the best opportunity on the reservations to dress in fancy outfits was Fourth of July celebrations organized by reservation officials as demonstrations of patriotic progress. In addition, many Plains Indians also participated in Wild West shows and formed exhibition troupes at World's Fairs, where they would set up a replica of a village and perform dance demonstrations.

Understanding of Plains dress since the mid-1800s has benefited from the advent of photography. Another and more nuanced source of information are drawings made by Kiowa, Arapaho, Cheyenne, and Lakota artists during the early reservation period. They recorded personal and tribal histories as well as social and religious customs, often on the pages of ledger books. Their depictions of how people dressed are exquisite, accurate, and provide a representation of tribal fashions from the native perspective, depicting outfits that were meaningful and the context in which they were worn. For instance, there are many portrayals of courting in the customary manner: A young man would wrap himself and his sweetheart in his wool trade-cloth blanket (red or blue, with a strip of beaded rosettes) so as to have a private conversation with her. Actual garments collected from this time period complement this visual record and help to assess both continuity and innovation in dress fashions.

An increasing emphasis on distinctive tribal styles of dress, and particularly its beadwork decoration, can be discerned. This was in part stimulated by the introduction of steel needles and seed beads and the formalization of preferred techniques and modes of design for their application to clothing within local communities. Floral quillwork done by Métis who had settled in South Dakota influenced Lakota and Dakota artists. The Cheyenne and Lakota employed the *lazy stitch*, consisting of short parallel rows of beads with a slightly loose effect over large areas and with a preference for white or blue background and geometric units within. The Blackfoot used a tighter *spot stitch* that kept the beads flat on the surface, while the Crow composed large geometric forms in blue, pink, red, and yellow and outlined them in white. Rosettes and a netted stitch distinguished the restrained southern look, although the Kiowa also innovated with large, abstract floral elements derived from Prairie tribes that were resettled in Oklahoma.

The early reservation period saw an efflorescence of craft, and beadwork became more intricate, with a tendency to cover clothing and accessories completely. Vests, neckties, glove gauntlets, baby bonnets, sets of shirts and trousers for boys, dresses, moccasins, pipe bags, as well as saddle blankets, horse masks and gear, carrying bags, and baby carriers, were fully beaded, a trend extended to objects of commercial manufacture such as purses, shoes, travel bags, violin cases, and watch fobs. Lakota artists innovated with figurative designs of mounted warriors, sacred beings, animals (elk, deer, eagles), U.S. flags, and scenes of courting and camp life, while the Crow adopted floral designs.

FANCY CLOTHING STYLES OF THE RESERVATIONS

The strong influence of trade goods was primarily in terms of materials rather than in the structure of the ensemble. The most significant changes were the use of trade-cloth blankets (especially

A woman's trade-cloth dress decorated with dentalium shells, Sioux tribe, nineteenth/twentieth century. Founders Society Purchase, Clarence E. Wilcox Fund. Photograph © 1996 The Detroit Institute of Arts.

Hudson's Bay blankets) replacing buffalo robes; the increased use of red and blue trade broadcloth for dresses, leggings, and breechcloths (always with the undyed selvage as a decorative border element); and the men's adoption of cotton shirts (solid colors, calico, striped). The removed tribes from the east, with their long traditions of clothing made from trade materials, proved very influential over clothing styles in later nineteenth-century Oklahoma. Overwhelmingly, the male attire most represented in drawings is an ensemble comprised of a cotton shirt, decorated leggings (most commonly of wool), a long woolen breechcloth, moccasins, and a vest. Vests were part of citizen's dress of the time but were also obtained by cutting off the sleeves of a jacket. They became extremely popular in the period from 1880 to 1910 and were decorated with elk teeth, quillwork, ribbon trim, or beadwork. The Lakota in particular beaded them in their entirety, front and back.

Men's hide shirts continued to be associated with social status and with a position of respect. Those made later in the century tend to have the bottom and sleeves cut with a straighter edge, resulting in a more tailored look. A thick buckskin fringe often replaced the hairlock tassels, while the beaded bands applied along the arms and across the shoulders became wider. Distinguished leaders who traveled to Washington, D.C., to meet with the president dressed in their full chiefly regalia.

One particular male dance outfit style originated from the Pawnee Iruska society, with its distinctive regalia of a porcupine-head roach with two eagle feathers inserted in a spreader and a crow-skin bustle. A *roach spreader* was a device, often of bone, with a hole through which the scalplock could be pulled to form a base for attaching an artificial roach. Within a few years, the rights to the regalia and the associated dance had been transferred among most tribes across the Plains. The Lakota purchased the Omaha's version (*Hethuska*) around 1860 and called it the "Omaha Dance." It became the "Grass Dance" further north, while variations on the original name persisted on the southern Plains (Osage *I'Lonska*; Kiowa *O-ho-mah*).

The Omaha/Grass Dance complex became mostly associated with social dancing and replaced many functions of the now-irrelevant military societies. The outfit retained the core elements of roach and bustle, but the latter became more elaborate, taking the shape of a circle of fluttering feathers with a long trailer decorated with eagle feathers. A short woolen breechcloth, a string of bells along the length of each leg and around the knees, a belt, skunk-fur anklets, moccasins, sometimes a cotton shirt (but no leggings), an otter-skin cape decorated with small round mirrors and ribbons, metal or quilled armbands, hairpipe or quilled breastplates, long necklaces, feather fans, and a variety of other ornaments completed the outfit. After 1900, long underwear was added to the ensemble. On the southern Plains, the crow belt was eliminated altogether. The resulting Straight Dance had a breechcloth with a long trail and a short apron in front, worn with a long cloth shirt, wool leggings, garters, knee bells, moccasins, the roach, a yarn sash with long fringe drop, a silk neckerchief, and an *otter-tail dragger* consisting of a long strip of otter fur trimmed with ribbons and beaded rosettes.

On the north-central Plains, women's hide dresses became more elaborate, with a third hide added to make a larger yoke, which was now completely beaded (a finished dress might weigh upward of 40 pounds, or 18 kilograms). On the southern Plains, women maintained an understated beauty with a preference for white tanned buckskin and contained, yet elegant, trimwork accented by rosettes and thin borderwork with long fringe. Crow, Cheyenne, and Kiowa used three or four hundred elk teeth (real and bone imitations), which were now supplied by traders.

Wool trade-cloth dresses were made from a single length of cloth in the basic T-shape, with the sleeves unsewn and the cloth's woven selvage edge at the bottom of the dress and at the edge of the sleeves, and two side gussets inserted at the bottom. The two principal types of decoration of cloth dresses consisted of elk teeth and dentalium shells. The latter was a particularly popular style among the Lakota between 1890 and 1900. The shells were sewn in concentric parallel rows (about ten) circling out from the neck and completely covering the upper portion of the dress, to a stunning effect. The bottom portion of the dress was trimmed with colored ribbons, sequins, and more shells. Around 1910, though, the elk-tooth dress made a comeback, even mirroring the dentalium pattern in the arrangement of the bone pieces. Sometimes cowrie shells or coins were applied instead of elk teeth. Some very special dresses were painted with the war records of a woman's husband or close male relative and were worn to honor them at public events.

After the 1860s, women adopted the men's graduated concho hair plates to wear as belts, with the long drop hanging down one side. Other belts were beaded, or the leather was studded with brass tacks. Lakota, Cheyenne, and Kiowa increasingly formalized the belt into a specialty set representing the female tool kit: a small bag or pouch, an awl case, and a knife sheath, all decorated in matching beadwork. A long necklace made with vertically strung bone hairpipes was also very popular. The blanket remained an integral part of a woman's outfit. Navajo *chief blankets* were worn well into the 1890s, although most women wore a commercial wool blanket lighter than the trade broadcloth type

and most commonly with a plaid pattern. When they danced, they wrapped the blanket around the waist but left the concho side drop visible.

The fancy clothing styles of the Osage, Kansa, and Ponca looked to the traditions of the prairies as expressed among those tribes, now neighbors that had been removed to Oklahoma, Kansas, and Nebraska. *Ribbonwork appliqué* (consisting of bands of colored silk ribbon folded or cut with curvilinear designs and sewn to form patterns in contrasting colors) and elaborate *abstract floral* or *prairie beadwork* were the most distinctive decorative elements applied to women's wraparound skirts and blankets and men's leggings, aprons, and shirts. These were all made of wool cloth and worn with cotton shirts, with a preference for bright patterns and calicos. Women's cotton blouses often had ruffles and were decorated with rows of silver brooches pinned across the chest, a style that originated in the Ohio valley during the late eighteenth century. In a tradition unique to the Osage and stemming from an episode of tribal history, Osage brides wore a special military-style, three-quarter-length jacket said to derive from gifts given to Osage delegations in Washington. These blue-and-red-wool *wedding coats* were decorated with silk-ribbon appliqué, brass buttons, silver brooches, and braid trim and were worn with a finger-woven sash over the traditional blouse and skirt and with a hat decorated with a silver band and tall, colorful plumes.

DRESS OF REVITALIZATION MOVEMENTS

Special garments are associated with *revitalization movements* that emerged in the 1890s in reaction to the poverty and cultural anguish engendered by federal North American Indian policies and the disenfranchisement of reservation life. Several charismatic individuals experienced visions where they were given instructions to prepare their people for a better life in the future. The best known is the *Ghost Dance*, based on the prophet Wovoka's belief that a cataclysmic event would cleanse the earth of white people, the buffalo would become abundant again, and North American Indians would be reunited with their dead relatives and return to their own ways of life. The Ghost Dance spread among many tribes and took the form of large open-air dances, where participants exerted themselves until they fell in a trance and had their own visions. The Ghost Dance is now indelibly associated with the tragic massacre of Big Foot's unarmed band at Wounded Knee on the Pine Ridge reservation in South Dakota, which effectively put an end to Lakota participation in this religious movement.

Lakota Ghost Dance shirts and dresses were made of muslin, sometimes flower sacks, and cut in a simple T-shape, while Cheyenne, Arapaho, and Kiowa made theirs from hide following traditional cuts. What distinguishes Ghost Dance garments are the designs painted on them, which refer to cosmological symbols that were both protective and symbolized renewal: crows, magpies, and eagles with outstretched wings; crescents, moons, stars, crosses, rainbows, and lightning bolts; dragonflies, turtles, and buffalo tracks. The Lakota, who faced a hostile military occupation, developed a belief that these garments would protect them from bullets and sometimes included the representation of a hail of gunfire. The Arapaho painted the background in blue, green, red, or yellow and placed rows of large five-pointed stars across the entire surface of the garment.

At about the same time, William Faw Faw, an Otoe-Missouria from the Red Rock Agency in Oklahoma, also experienced a

Faw Faw Coat, Otoe tribe, ca. 1890. Coats of this type had a European cut and were decorated with religious symbols related to a version of William Faw Faw who was inspired to create a ceremony and distinctive garments. Museum purchase, Flint Ink Foundation and Edgar A.V. Jacobsen Acquisition Fund. Photograph © 2006 The Detroit Institute of Arts.

vision that called for the refutation of the corrupting ills brought by white society (such as drinking) and instructed him to create a ceremony and distinctive garments. The most striking are men's coats, made in European cut and decorated with religious symbols relating to Faw Faw's vision. Executed in the Otoe style of beadwork, these include human figures with horses, cedar trees, bison skulls, and a striped ladder motif on the back.

POWWOW DANCE REGALIA

The most visible displays of Plains regalia in the twentieth century have been in the context of large intertribal social dance celebrations called *powwows*. Women and men of all ages compete in dancing and outfit style categories. Powwows grew out of the Fourth of July celebrations, fairs, and homecomings honoring veterans returning from the world wars of the twentieth century. These gatherings demonstrate the vitality and creativity of contemporary native cultures. Great amounts of time, resources, and skill are employed to make beautiful regalia, and it continues to be a point of honor and pride to outfit one's family members.

There are six styles of powwow dress, three for each gender, and each is associated with particular footwork and dance moves. The outfits are conceived as an ensemble, so the various components have matching beadwork and colors. The women's *Traditional* (northern) and *Cloth Dress and Buckskin Dress* (southern) categories consist of the dresses examined so far but with a more standardized set of accessories: a long-fringed shawl folded over the left arm, a feather fan, a belt with complete women's tool kit, and a long hairpipe necklace. For the *Fancy Shawl Dance outfit*—representing a butterfly with outstretched wings—the women wear a shawl over their shoulders and dance with high jumps, holding it by the front corners. A solidly beaded or sequined cape with a long fringe is worn over a satin dress with matching belt, leggings, and moccasins. The *jingle dress* is characterized by parallel rows of tin-cone jingles attached across the entire satin dress, worn with a neckerchief, a belt, leggings, and moccasins. Most women wear a plume in their braided hair, barrettes, and jewelry and carry a variety of other accessories.

Men's powwow regalia reflect the history of exchange between the tribes and contemporary connections across the Plains. All contemporary styles derive from the Omaha/Grass Dance complex, defined by the head roach (with two eagle feathers) and the feather bustle with a trailer. The *Northern Traditional* is essentially a more elaborate version of that silhouette, with a large, U-shaped eagle-feather bustle, worn with a cotton shirt, a vest or an otter cape, an apron (over shorts), a beaded belt with long side tabs matched to cuffs and armbands, knee and ankle bells, fringed garters, fur anklets, moccasins, a hairpipe breastplate, and bandolier necklaces. Dancers use face paint and carry feather fans, shields, clubs, staffs, and hoops. Its counterpart on the southern Plains is the Straight Dance already described. The *Fancy Dance outfit* emerged in the 1920s on the southern Plains, when men added a second feather bustle to the upper back and feather rosettes on the shoulders and forehead, and it is associated with a dancing style characterized by extremely athletic footwork. In the early twenty-first century, the two back bustles have reached enormous proportions, with ribbons and plumes in bright colors streaming from the feather tips. The *Northern Grass Dance style* has eliminated the bustle altogether, and now the defining element is a thick and colorful yarn fringe attached to cape, apron, and pants. The fringe is a dynamic element that moves and sways in unison with the dancer, to great effect.

Contemporary artists are energized by the opportunities presented by new materials and balance elegantly between tradition and innovation. In recent times, new dress and dance styles have been created, and native communities are becoming increasingly empowered. Undoubtedly, the twenty-first century will continue to see such growth and the passing on of traditional values. Just as her female ancestors celebrated warriors returning from battle by performing victory dances wearing their husbands' regalia, today Vanessa Jennings honors all veterans when she wears her *battle dress*—a traditional wool-cloth elk-tooth dress that incorporates her own husband's military patches from the Vietnam War. As has always been the case with the artists who created the traditions of Plains Indian clothing, Jennings draws upon the many generations that preceded her to create clothing with meaning and significance for her community in the twenty-first century.

References and Further Reading

Bailey, Garrick, and Daniel C. Swan. *Art of the Osage*. Seattle: University of Washington Press, 2004.

Berlandier, Jean Louis. *The Indians of Texas in 1830*. Edited and with an introduction by John C. Ewers. Washington, DC: Smithsonian Institution Press, 1969.

Berlo, Janet C., ed. *Plains Indian Drawings, 1865–1935*. New York: Harry N. Abrams, 1996.

Berlo, Janet C. "Creativity and Cosmopolitanism: Women's Enduring Traditions." In *Identity by Design: Tradition, Change, and Celebration in Native Women's Dresses*, edited by Emil Her Many Horses, 97–147. New York: Harper Collins Publishers, 2007.

DeMallie, Raymond J., ed. *Plains*. Vol. 13 of *Handbook of North American Indians*, edited by William C. Sturtevant. Washington, DC: Smithsonian Institution, 2001.

Ellis, Clyde. *A Dancing People: Powwow Culture on the Southern Plains*. Lawrence: University Press of Kansas, 2003.

Erekosima, Tonye V., and Joanne B. Eicher. "Kalabari Cut-Thread and Pulled-Thread Cloth." *African Arts XIV* 2 (1981): 48–51.

Greci Green, Adriana. *Performances and Celebrations: Displaying Lakota Identity, 1880–1915*. Ann Arbor, MI: University Microfilm, 2001.

Hail, Barbara A. *Hau, Kóla! The Plains Indian Collection of the Haffenreffer Museum of Anthropology*. Bristol, RI: Brown University, 1980.

Hansen, Emma I. *Memory and Vision: Arts, Cultures, and Lives of Plains Indian People*. Seattle: University of Washington Press, 2007.

Horse Capture, George, Anne Vitart, Michael Waldberg, and W. Richard West. *Robes of Splendor. Native North American Painted Buffalo Hides*. New York: The New Press, 1993.

McLaughlin, Castle. *Arts of Diplomacy. Lewis and Clark's Indian Collection*. Seattle: University of Washington Press, 2003.

Nasatir, A. P. *Before Lewis and Clark: Documents Illustrating the History of the Missouri, 1785–1804*. 2 vols. Lincoln: University of Nebraska Press, 1990. (Originally published: St. Louis: St. Louis Historical Documents Foundation, 1952.)

Newcomb, W. W., Jr. *The Indians of Texas*. Austin: University of Texas Press, 1961.

Penney, David W. *Art of the American Indian Frontier: The Chandler Pohrt Collection*. Seattle: University of Washington Press, 1992.

Taylor, Colin F. *Buckskin and Buffalo. The Artistry of the Plains Indians*. London: Salamander Books, 1998.

Thomas, Davis, and Karin Ronnefeldt. *People of the First Man. Life among the Plains Indians in Their Final Days of Glory. The Firsthand Account of Prince Maximilian's Expedition up the Missouri River, 1833–34*. New York: Promontory Press, 1982.

Adriana Greci Green

The Northeast

Three broad regions based on geographical and cultural boundaries make up the Northeast: Coastal, Saint Lawrence Lowlands, and Great Lakes–Riverine. The Northeast covers a large area, resulting in many regional differences. During prehistoric times, tribes adapted to climatic changes and cultural innovations introduced by other native groups. New technologies and practices generally occurred first in the southern regions and then spread north along waterways and trade routes. At the time of contact with Europeans, North American Indians and First Nations people were organized into small autonomous bands that sometimes formed alliances or confederacies with other groups. Europeans called these confederacies *tribes*, and through their written descriptions, they facilitated the development of tribal identity. The names by which North American Indians and First Nations of the Northeast are recognized in the early twenty-first century came from these early written sources.

The Coastal region stretches from the Atlantic provinces of Canada, including Newfoundland, along the coast of New England and the mid-Atlantic as far south as North Carolina. It is bounded by the Appalachian Mountains to the west. Coastal tribes spoke variations of the Eastern Algonquian language, allowing communication among trading partners. The Coastal region was home to the tribes known as the Beothuk, Micmac, Maliseet-Passamaquoddy, Abenaki, Nipmuc, Pennacook, Wappinger, Massachuset, Wampanoag, Narragansett, Pequot, Mahican, Mohegan, Montauk, Delaware, Virginia Algonquians, North Carolina Algonquians, Nanticoke, Powhaten, Secotan, Susquehannock (Iroquoian speakers), and Tuscarora (Iroquoian speakers).

The Saint Lawrence Lowlands includes southern Ontario, upstate New York, and the valleys surrounding the Saint Lawrence and Susquehanna rivers. The language spoken was Iroquois. In the Saint Lawrence Lowlands region were the Cayuga (Iroquois), Mohawk (Iroquois), Oneida (Iroquois), Onondaga (Iroquois), Seneca (Iroquois), Erie, Huron, Susquehannock, Petun, Wyandot, Neutral, and Wenro.

The Great Lakes–Riverine region includes Ottawa and the territory below the Great Lakes. Michigan, Illinois, Indiana, the Ohio Valley, western Pennsylvania, and the eastern parts of Wisconsin belong to this region. The tribes spoke Central Algonquian and Siouan languages. The Great Lakes–Riverine region was home to the Algonquin, Menominee, Ottawa, Potawatomi, Ojibwa, Chippewa, Winnebago, Fox, Illinois, Kickapoo, Mascouten, Miami, Sauk, Shawnee, and Nipissing.

An Algonquian woman and child of the Pomeiooc tribe of North Carolina. Watercolor by John White, 1585. Getty Images.

PREHISTORY

The thousands of years before Europeans began exploring the New World is termed *prehistory* because North American Indians and First Nations did not have a system of writing to record events and circumstances. Only when explorers came to the Northeast in the sixteenth century and wrote about what they saw does the historical record begin. Thus, scholars seek evidence for the cultural traits of North American Indians and First Nations in the archaeological record. This evidence comes primarily from burial grounds but also from material objects left at dwelling sites, such as spear points, fishhooks, tools, ceramics, and so on. These objects have been found by chance when someone or something disturbed the soil where they were intentionally or accidentally placed. Almost all of these objects are made from materials such as stone or metal. Organic materials that decompose quickly in the wet, acidic soil of the Northeast, such as animal skins and plant materials, are called *perishables* by archaeologists. They are very rare. Occasionally perishables are preserved when in direct contact with metal objects. Copper was mined near the shores of Lake Superior and traded throughout the region; thus, it is not uncommon in burials, where its presence preserved textiles.

Evidence indicates that humans first came to the Northeast at the end of the last Ice Age, around 10,500 B.C.E. These people hunted deer, bear, elk, caribou, beaver, raccoon, fox, squirrels, and other animals; they fished, captured birds, and gathered nuts, grains, and plant materials. How these proto-Americans dressed is not known because hardly any clues survive.

Many millennia later, during the period 3000–300 B.C.E., hunter-gatherers left enough evidence to provide a rough idea of dress and appearance. A variety of objects from sites across the Northeast suggest production of perishable materials, including sewn clothing and footwear. Scrapers were used to process skins and hides for body coverings, pouches, and bags. Needles, pins, and copper awls indicate sewing. Heavy bone needles have been found in the Great Lakes area that are similar to needles used in recent centuries to make snowshoes. Weaving tools also survive, which would have been used for the production of twined objects. *Twining* is analogous to weaving, but instead of interlacing horizontal elements (*wefts*) through stationary vertical elements (*warps*), flexible elements are twisted together in between rigid elements.

The Boucher site in northwest Vermont, dated at approximately 1000–100 B.C.E., preserved many more perishable objects that might have been clothing than other sites in the Northeast. Finely twined textiles for use as upper-body garments and carrying bags survived. Fibers included animal hair and fibrous materials from wild plants such as Indian hemp or milkweed. Sometimes strands of animal gut formed the rigid elements in twined structures. Some of the bags may have been ritual pouches, also known as *medicine bags*, because they contained animal bones.

Items for personal adornment appear in burials, more so as time went on. Strands of copper, shell, and stone beads in the form of necklaces and bracelets have been found on bodies. Stone pendants, stone or shell gorgets, and animal teeth were some of the other objects that inhabitants of the Northeast hung around their necks. A *gorget* is an object perforated with holes and hung on a string at the throat. In many burial sites, red ochre is found. Occasionally yellow ochre is present. North American Indians and First Nations people may have rubbed this ground pigment on their skin as body paint in prehistory; most certainly they covered their burials with red ochre because large amounts have been excavated.

During the period from 300 B.C.E. to 1000 C.E., the peoples in the Northeast began to practice agriculture as a result of favorable climate change. The Hopewell culture, about which much is known, appeared from western New York to the area around Kansas City. People of this culture buried their dead in mounds with numerous grave goods. Large amounts of similar ceramics, beads, and shells survive across the various sites, suggesting widespread exchange. Some of the ceramics are impressed with textile cordage, which provides evidence for the transmission of spinning and twining technology among tribes. Twined fabrics adhering to copper breastplates may have been garments or shrouds. Other

Woman wearing traditional handmade Seneca clothing. Photograph copy of a lost hand-tinted daguerreotype with the image laterally reversed, ca. 1850, United States. Braun Research Library, Autry National Center of the American West, Los Angeles; CT.673.

items such as copper ear spools, feathers, pearl beads, and an antler headdress reveal the variety of objects with which people of the Hopewell culture ornamented themselves.

Omission of certain types of artifacts can be telling, too. In other parts of North America, native people made sandals out of plant materials. Substantial numbers of these have survived in caves in the Southwest. Indians of the Northeast did not make this type of footwear, as far as we know, with a few exceptions. The Iroquois twined cornhusk slippers for summer wear, while the Delaware used them for temporary footwear.

On the eve of first contact with Europeans, the archaeological evidence indicates that the people of the Northeast had a similar broad development but that regional differences existed. Agriculture was more prevalent in the south and hunting and fishing, in the north. Natives lived in dispersed villages consisting of no more than ten to twelve houses. While agricultural groups settled near valleys, those that fished and hunted tended to be seminomadic, moving seasonally between territories. The people wore garments and footwear made from skins and furs of the animals that they hunted. They also twined plant materials into fabrics for garments and carrying bags. They decorated themselves with pendants, gorgets, and strands of beads made from copper, shell, and stone. However, to gain a more precise description of their appearance, it is necessary to consult the accounts written by the early explorers.

CONTACT PERIOD

After Christopher Columbus reached America in 1492, explorers and fishermen began making regular voyages to the New World. The tribes along the coast and the St. Lawrence River had more interaction with Europeans than those in the interior. Sailors on fishing expeditions made the first contacts, but soon traders dominated communication between Europeans and the indigenous population. Contact during the sixteenth century was only occasional, and as a result, native lifeways remained more or less undisturbed.

The first European to write extensively about North American Indians and First Nations people was Giovanni da Verrazano, a Florentine explorer under the command of Francis I. He voyaged from the Carolinas to Newfoundland in 1524, commenting on the natives he met along the way. He found the Indians encountered along Narragansett Bay in Rhode Island to be "the most beautiful" and "most civil" of all. He described the men as tall, bronze colored, and "naked," wearing only deerskin "worked like damask with various embroideries." This may have been porcupine quillwork or shell beadwork. The men had wide chains of different-colored stones around their necks, and their long black hair was carefully arranged. Women also were described as "nude" except for deerskins covering their lower torsos; some wore furs over their shoulders. The women and girls braided their hair in different styles, which varied according to marital status. They decorated their hair with ornaments and hung trinkets from their ears. Verrazano's crew learned that coastal tribes admired bells, beads, and trinkets, but they were indifferent to silk and gold.

By the late 1500s, the French, British, Dutch, and Spanish had begun efforts to colonize the New World. At Roanoke Island in North Carolina, Sir Walter Raleigh attempted to establish a British colony in 1585. John White, a member of the party, made a series of detailed watercolors that provide the first credible visual images of the dress and appearance of North American Indians in the Northeast. He depicted men, women, and children in indigenous dress.

Although the Roanoke colony failed, the cultural exchange between Europeans and natives continued because of the fur trade. Europeans desired beaver pelts to be manufactured into the luxurious hats that had come into fashion in Europe. Numerous seventeenth-century accounts provide good explanations of the dress and appearance of the native people living along the coast. While the details vary, the writers describe similar dress and appearance.

Europeans often commented favorably on the skin color and stature of the natives. They appeared "tawny" to a number of observers. Traveler John Josselyn, who explored the coast of New England, described their bodies as "soft and smooth as mole-skin." He found them to be tall and handsome, with good complexions and white teeth. He described the young women as "very comely" with plump, round faces and bodies.

Throughout the Northeast, natives wore garments made of animal skins. The hides of white-tailed deer, plentiful in this part of North America, were common to all tribes. They were scraped to remove the flesh, then tanned and oiled to achieve a pliable, water-resistant material. The skins could be painted, fringed, or decorated with beads, copper rings, or quillwork. Men wore breechcloths of a single deerskin; the skin was passed between the legs and secured to a belt, with a panel hanging over the front and back. Women wore a parallel garment, often described as an apron of two hides secured by a belt. It was typically longer than the man's garment. Both men and women donned robes or mantles of animal skins, sometimes with the fur removed and other times with the fur left on. These were usually worn over the left shoulder, leaving the right arm free. During the summer, the mantles were of lightweight skins, such as deerskin. During the colder months, mantles of beaver, otter, fox, bear, or other fur-bearing animals covered their shoulders, with the hairy side worn toward the body for warmth. Babies were swaddled in skins and strapped to cradleboards until the age of three. Young children often went naked, although they wore jewelry.

Samuel de Champlain, writing at the start of the seventeenth century, described robes of grasses and hemp that reached to the thighs. These may have been especially for the summer months because he observed this attire on Cape Cod in July. John White illustrated a mantle of "silk grass" worn in North Carolina, indicating that use of body coverings of twined plant fibers may have been widespread.

Many sources mention capes made with turkey feathers, although none have survived. They are described as curious, prettily worked, and as precious to their wearers as velvet was to a European. Made by securing the base of the feather into a yarn of vegetable fiber, only the iridescent feathers showed when made into a garment of capelike proportions to cover the shoulders. Older men and women reportedly made them for children, although adults wore them, too.

The *moccasin*, from the Algonquian word *mocússinass*, was the main form of footwear. Moccasins were often made from deerskin, but moose hide was preferred where available because it was thicker and more durable. The style and pattern of moccasins changed from area to area. Some were cut and sewn from a single skin, while others were pieced. The Iroquois and Huron favored black-dyed skins for their moccasins. In the northern areas, moccasins were often cuffed. They were decorated in various ways, often with shell beads or quillwork. In winter, moccasins could be combined with deerskin leggings that tied to a belt that held the breechcloth in place. Together, these functioned as trousers. Indians had not figured out how to join tube-shaped pieces at the crotch to create bifurcated garments (e.g., pants or trousers), but the combination of moccasin, legging, and breechcloth covered almost all of the lower half of the body. The same principle applied to sleeves, which were separate and attached by ties or laces at the armholes.

In cold areas, natives devised snowshoes that they strapped to their feet to move easily across the winter snow. Josselyn has described these as large rackets like those that Europeans used to play tennis. These were made from bent ash wood strung with rawhide strips. The Micmac, the Iroquois, and the Huron are known to have made snowshoes. The Micmac made two different types: one for light, fluffy snow and the other for snow with a frozen crust. The Huron of Lorette sold snowshoes at the Quebec market along with other native-made products.

North American Indians and First Nations people regularly carried bags and pouches to store personal items. When traveling, they packed food into these bags. While some were made of leather, such as those for tobacco, others were twined. By

This portrait of Sa Ga Yeath Qua Pieth Tow, Mohawk by Jan Verelst, North America, 1710, shows him wearing a scarlet mantle, moccasins decorated with porcupine quills and red ribbons, a native-made belt, and feathers. Library and Archives Canada, Acc. No. 1977-35-2.

interchanging threads of different colors, it was possible to create complex designs by twining that impressed Europeans because it reminded them of their own needlework.

The hairstyles of North American Indians and First Nations people received much comment from the early ethnographers. Observers have noted that they took great pains to dress their hair, oiling and dyeing it to improve its appearance. Styles ranged greatly within and among tribes, denoting age, occupation, and marital status among the community.

Men's hair showed great variation. It could be worn long and loose or tied up "like a horse tail" or cut so that one side was long while the other was "short like a screw." Sometimes the hair was bound with headbands or coronets decorated with feathers, especially for the *sachems*, or chiefs. Young men, who were the hunters, shaved one side of their heads so that their hair did not interfere with the bowstrings. Men did not like hair on their faces, however, and pulled out any whiskers by tweezing them with a pair of clamshells or other tool. One hairstyle that was worn by males across the Northeast was the *roach*. This can be described as a crest of hair from the forehead to the nape of the neck. Roaches could also be hair accessories made of deer bristles fastened to a hemp base.

Women wore their hair long and loose, gathered at the nape of the neck, or braided. Among some tribes, the bangs were fringed. Headbands and thongs tied around the head served as supports for beads and feathers. Age and marital status was signified by hair and hair ornaments. For example, in early-seventeenth-century New England, young women who were seeking a mate wore a red leather cap for a period of twelve months, according to Thomas Morton, a British colonist in North America.

Throughout the Northeast, North American Indians and First Nations people painted their bodies in a variety of colors. They painted the exposed skin with red or yellow ochre, white pigment, and ground-up charcoal. In some regions, observers noted that the skin had been colored completely red. The Beothuk of Newfoundland, for example, mixed red ochre with oil or grease and spread it over their bodies, hair, and caribou-skin garments. Native people also greased their bodies with animal fat to discourage mosquitoes in summer and to retain body heat in winter. They tattooed their arms, legs, and face with representational images as well as geometric designs. First, a sharp instrument raised the skin; then the area was rubbed with charcoal or another coloring agent. The tattoos of the Iroquois were particularly impressive, ranging from simple geometric designs to clan crests.

The Iroquois crafted masks to wear during rituals for secret societies. The masks, carved out of wood or made from cornhusks, carried special powers and had to be specially treated. Those in museum collections date from the nineteenth and twentieth centuries.

A universal observation by Europeans was that the natives loved jewelry. Both sexes and all ages adorned themselves with necklaces, bracelets, earrings, and pendants of shell beads, bone, stones, and copper. The types of jewelry crafted in the prehistoric period continued in the Contact period. Sometimes the ears were pierced and distorted to receive metal ornaments. Occasionally bone combs were placed in the hair.

One of the most highly prized types of ornamentation was wampum. *Wampum* is an Algonquian word for small shell beads. These were made on the coast of southern New England and Long Island from whelk, which yielded white beads, and quahogs,

Denny Sockabasin, daughter of Francis Joseph Neptune, Passamaquoddy chief, North America, 1817. She wears the peaked wool cap characteristic of Abenaki and Micmac women with a wool dress and leggings. A doll swaddled to a cradleboard can be seen resting on the table leg. National Anthropological Archives, Smithsonian Institution OPPS NEG 748342.

which produced purple beads. The latter were more valuable. The beads were strung together on two-ply strands of Indian hemp for necklaces or bracelets. The beads could also be woven into bands suitable for use as belts, bandoliers, or headbands. By mixing purple beads with white beads, imagery such as birds, animals, and geometric motifs could be created. Sometimes the shell beads were intermixed with copper beads, which preserved them in burials. The making of wampum was the work of women. Although collected and manufactured only on the coast, wampum was traded far inland. During the Contact period, wampum became a form of currency for trade with other tribes and with Europeans. Depictions of North American Indians and First Nations peoples from this period also show liberal use of wampum. Among the Iroquois, it remained important long after it ceased being used as currency.

European influence on sartorial choices was felt even before permanent British colonies had been established at Jamestown in 1607 and Plymouth in 1620. Early accounts tell of North American Indians along the coast wearing European-style clothes. Bartholomew Gosnold, in the earliest English description of New England, described an encounter with eight Indians who came out to his ship in 1602. One of the visitors wore a waistcoat, cloth breeches like those of British sailors, hose, and shoes. Obviously,

Gosnold and his crew were not the first Europeans encountered by this tribe. Later accounts describe tailored clothes of wool, silk, linen, or cotton given to natives during the 1620s and 1630s. Several writers say the recipients did not wear them for long, finding them too confining. Among the Nanticoke in the Chesapeake, however, those with high status wore English clothes exclusively by the 1640s.

These exchanges also resulted in widespread epidemics that decimated the native population. In some coastal areas, tribal numbers were reduced over 70 percent after exposure to smallpox, measles, influenza, and other European diseases for which native people had no resistance. The English interpreted the epidemics as divine intervention for their plans to take over tribal lands and colonize the New World.

COLONIAL PERIOD

Nearly all tribes in the Northeast had encountered Europeans by the latter part of the seventeenth century. This was due to the fur trade, which began along the Atlantic Coast and inland waterways and was especially intense in the northern areas where furs were thicker and more desirable. As the animal population dwindled, fur traders ventured further inland, reaching the upper Midwest via the Great Lakes and establishing trading posts by the last quarter of the seventeenth century.

The French, British, and Dutch dominated the fur trade: the French in Canada and along what is now the northern border of the United States, the British along the Atlantic coast, and the Dutch in the Hudson River valley. Traders proffered cloth, beads, trinkets, guns, and various tools in exchange for furs of all types, especially beaver.

Traders sold many varieties of cloth but mostly coarse thick woolens of similar weight and flexibility to deerskin. Called *duffels*, *trucking cloth*, or *trade cloth*, it substituted for skin garments and accessories. In some regions, it came to be known as *stroud* cloth. Sold in lengths of approximately one and a half to two yards (about one and a half to two meters), North American Indians and First Nations people used woolen fabric "as is" for mantles. These mantles were sometimes described as blankets. Trade cloth also found its way into breechcloths, skirts, headgear, and bags. Merchants noted color preferences for blue, red, green, purple, and sometimes white, which they transmitted to their factors in Europe, who bought and sold goods on commission. The natives acquired linen and cotton goods, sometimes already made up into shirts or stockings. Ready-made coats and suits of clothes were traded, too. Metallic trimmings have been found in Contact-period burials; some of these were rolled up, indicating that natives did not use them as decorative edgings for garments as Europeans would have done. For example, the captivity account of Mary Rowlandson described how a tribal leader attached lace trimming to his linen shirt like a tail.

North American Indians and First Nations people sought glass beads and metal ornaments such as bells and rings with which to ornament their clothing and accessories. They incorporated glass beads quickly, sewing them onto leather and cloth in decorative patterns. These were widely used, especially on moccasins and bags. Ribbons also found acceptance as trim.

Increased disputes over land rights resulted in the Pequot Massacre in 1637, King Philip's War in 1675, and Bacon's Rebellion in 1675–1676. Conflicts continued into the eighteenth century along

Full-blood Chippewa Indian, ca. 1918. Typical garments included feather headdresses and moccasins. Library of Congress, Prints and Photographs Division Washington, LC-USZ62-118480.

the frontier and in the borderlands between French and British territories. Tales of whites taken into captivity reveal how native people had adapted European goods into their lives. Captives were requested to sew shirts and knit stockings because natives did not generally know such skills.

After the skirmishes diminished, a transitional period ensued. Descriptions of North American Indians in written accounts lessened. The images that survive, along with sparse documentary sources, show the varied response to living among whites. Many were removed to reservations, where they continued some aspects of traditional life. Some lived in British-style frame houses and worked as indentured servants. Along the coast, many natives mixed European-style clothing with their own.

Still others settled in "praying towns." The colonists tried to "civilize" them by making them Christians. Missionary efforts included getting them out of the clothing of "savages" and into European-style clothing. A 1766 portrait of Samson Occum, the famous Mohegan preacher who led the Brothertown movement (e.g., removal of North American Indians from southern New England to Brothertown, New York, and later to Brothertown, Wisconsin), depicts him in coat, waistcoat, cleric's collar, breeches, stockings, and shoes. He is indistinguishable from any other preacher of the era.

Portraits of four Iroquois sachems who traveled to London in 1710 show how they blended European and native attire while being feted around town. Three wore linen shirts and crimson-wool mantles with native-made belts and moccasins; tattoos appeared on their faces and arms. The fourth sachem wore British dress and held a large wampum belt. Such intermixing of European and native styles characterized the Colonial period.

In the interior, where natives interacted with whites primarily at trading posts, native forms of dress were retained through the Colonial period and into the nineteenth century, sometimes even into the twentieth century. However, garments formerly made of skin were gradually replaced with wool. In northern New England, Canada, and the Upper Great Lakes area, women wore skirts or tubular dresses of wool with jackets, cloth leggings, blanket-like mantles, and moccasins. Men wore cloth breechcloths and leggings, sometimes with European-style shirts or coats. Special goods were developed for the North American Indian trade. The Hudson's Bay Company sold blankets with size and thickness denoted by small stripes, or "points"; these became known as *point blankets* and were sold throughout Canada and the United States. North American Indians and First Nations people wore them as blanket wraps.

Some interesting regional forms evolved despite the sameness of the goods traded. Abenaki and Micmac women, for example, developed a pointed cap of dark blue wool, which was beaded, embroidered, and trimmed with ribbons. Given to a girl at puberty by an older female adult relative, it was worn for the rest of her life. These caps first appeared in the eighteenth century, yet photographic evidence reveals that they were still worn in the early twentieth century.

THE NEW REPUBLIC THROUGH THE VICTORIAN ERA

As the young United States began to expand westward into lands inhabited by North American Indians, rapid settlement of territory east of the Mississippi River created tension between settlers who intended to farm the land and North American Indians who wanted to fish and hunt just as their ancestors had done. The U.S. government intervened through the Indian Removal Acts of 1830, which were intended to relocate the North American Indians to unsettled lands west of the Mississippi. Some bands from Ohio, Michigan, and Wisconsin left for Kansas and then to Oklahoma, where they now reside on reservations. Others remained on reservations in the East.

Paintings by George Catlin and others document what tribes in the Upper Great Lakes area were wearing in the 1820s and 1830s. Their attire can best be described as transitional, combining European materials in aboriginal forms. The Chippewa, for example, wore woolen leggings, blankets, and tubular dresses with moccasins and feather headdresses. Other tribes wore shawls as turbans and wove belts of green and red yarn.

This portrait of a chief at Oka shows him wearing wampum belts over a shirt, waistcoat, and trousers (Montreal, 1870). © Copyright symbol McCord Museum I-48873. http://www.mccord-museum.qc.ca/en/

Over the course of the nineteenth century, however, native garb faded from view along with the old lifeways. Little by little the traditional wigwams and teepees were replaced by frame houses. Indians were taught to read, write, spin, weave, and sew in missionary schools. The aboriginal languages began to die out. By 1900, only a few native speakers of some languages remained when ethnographers sought them out to gather linguistic information. During the second half of the nineteenth century, clothing had shifted to Westernized Anglo-American styles. Victorian-era photographs depict men in trouser suits and hats. The women wore modified Victorian dresses or skirts and blouses in cotton calico or wool trade cloth. Often these dresses were embellished with bells, beads, and ribbonwork that identified them as native. Hairstyles also retained features such as braids for women or longer hair for men, which signaled ethnicity. Footwear was another clothing item that North American Indians and First Nations retained. Whites liked native footwear, too, and for some tribes living on reservations, the manufacture of moccasins for sale to outsiders brought needed cash.

A factor that diluted native culture was intermarriage with non-Indians. From the earliest years of European settlement, when the Powhatan girl Pocahontas married Englishman John Rolfe in Virginia in 1614, interracial marriages occurred. Prior to the Civil War, some free blacks and escaped slaves sought refuge on reservations, resulting in offspring of mixed heritage. Farther north, the French had long been open to taking native women as brides. Their children became known as *Métis*. Such families tended to conform to the dominant culture's standards, dress included.

THE TWENTIETH CENTURY AND BEYOND

At the beginning of the twentieth century, knowledge of the old ways of dress had disappeared along with the languages. North American Indians and First Nations, especially in the coastal areas, had experienced a loss of identity. This was partially due to the U.S. ideal of the melting pot, a response to the large influx of immigrants that entered the country in the late nineteenth and early twentieth centuries. The culture encouraged all newcomers to "become American." This conformity extended to looking American as well as being American, an ideal that spread to native communities, too.

Then a cultural revival known as the *pan-Indian movement* began. Intertribal celebrations, called *powwows*, began to flourish. The Indian Reorganization Act of 1934 renewed interest in tribal incorporation, and intertribal organizations developed. University-trained ethnographers who had visited reservations in the Northeast published studies on tribal culture based on oral histories and extant material culture. All of this encouraged the creation of a North American Indian dress.

Dress was an important component of the powwows. Lacking their own ceremonial attire, tribes in the Northeast concocted a pan-Indian costume based on Plains Indian dress. This was due to the Wild West shows that featured North American Indians dressed in Plains Indians attire. Buffalo Bill Cody had started his

shows in 1883, when the material culture of the Plains Indians was still abundant. He performed throughout the country, and his show was well known. In 1907, he made a spectacular visit to the Connecticut grave of Uncas, the famous sachem of the Mohegan tribe, dressed in full regalia accompanied by Plains Indians on horseback. Other costume ideas were borrowed from the Brothertown, Wisconsin, and Saint Regis Mohawk Indians communities. This pan-Indian ceremonial costume consisted of a buckskin shirt and trousers, moccasins, and long, braided hair for men. An important component was a feathered headdress. Most impressive was the chief's war bonnet. This type of headdress was not indigenous to the Indians of the Northeast, who had worn a circlet with upright feathers instead. Women wore a long dress based on skin prototypes, with a feather in their braided hair.

During the social upheaval of the 1960s, North American Indians organized and formed the American Indian Movement in Minneapolis, Minnesota. The racism experienced by North American Indians found a sympathetic response from the counterculture, who expressed solidarity with the movement by wearing beaded headbands and fringed shirts. Borrowing style details from the North American Indian and First Nations repertoire eventually became a fashion trend. By the late 1970s, the celebration of cultural difference was encouraged among all ethnicities, not just Indians.

When the 1980s arrived, North American Indians and First Nations in the Northeast enjoyed celebrating their cultural heritage through dress and appearance. They wore their hair in Indian-inspired styles and donned native-made jewelry. A general association with the tribes in the North American West, where the Indian presence is much stronger than in the Northeast,

Pan-Indian dress is on display at this annual tribal powwow of Narragansett Indians at an old Indian Meeting House, United States, 1925. Courtesy of The Rhode Island Historical Society, RHi X3 7083B.

spurred the wearing of blue jeans, cowboy boots, ten-gallon hats, and bollo ties. The making of native crafts was revived, and creative tribal members made leather goods, jewelry, beaded or twined handbags, and wood-splint baskets. Guides to making North American Indian and First Nations crafts were published. For example, Margaret Wood developed fashionable styles based on historical prototypes, including skirts and shirts with traditional Iroquois embroideries and ribbon shirts based on Great Lakes styles.

The Indian Gaming Regulatory Act of 1988 allowed the operation of gaming establishments such as casinos and bingo halls on North American Indian land. In 2008, the largest-grossing Indian gaming operation is Foxwoods Casino and Resort on the Mashantucket-Pequot Reservation near Ledyard, Connecticut.

The tribe owns and operates a museum and research center near the casino where visitors may see a replica of a pre-Contact Pequot village and dressed figures from post-Contact Pequot history.

Powwows and other festivals are the only places where full Indian attire, or regalia, is worn. Some outfits are still based on the old pan-Indian styles popular at the beginning of the last century. However, some tribal members create garments that are more faithful to the attire of their ancestors through careful research in documentary and visual sources. Many tribes have their own powwows. The Mashantucket-Pequots, with their successful casino Foxwoods, sponsor an annual intertribal festival called Schemitzun, the Feast of Green Corn and Dance, every August. In addition to competitive rodeo and dance events, visitors can see how North American Indians dressed.

Snapshot: Twined Bags

A number of twined bags made by North American Indians of the Northeast survive from the seventeenth and eighteenth centuries. These bags, which were used to carry personal items, display themes of continuity and change endemic to all material culture of this region.

Twining can be defined as twisting two or three flexible elements around rigid elements to create a fabric. Archaeological finds from prehistoric sites indicate that twining of indigenous plant materials, such as Indian hemp, milkweed, nettle, and the inner bark of the basswood tree, was well developed prior to contact with Europeans. While few actual prehistoric textiles have survived the acidic soil conditions of the Northeast, impressions of twined textiles on pottery shards are frequent and attest to the widespread practice of twining.

Seventeenth-century accounts mention bags, commenting favorably on the clever designs and beautiful workmanship. Daniel Gookin, superintendent of the Indians of the Massachusetts Bay Colony from 1656 to 1687, wrote that many bags were "neat ... with the portraitures of birds, beasts, fishes, and flowers, upon them in colours." Sometimes these bags were gifted to colonists, which is how they arrived in museum collections.

One of the earliest extant bags is credited to the Narragansett Indians. It was donated to the Rhode Island Historical Society in 1842 with the story that it had been given to Dinah Fenner by a native woman in gratitude for providing some milk during King Philip's War of 1675–1676. The warp is basswood, while the wefts are cornhusk and deteriorated red-wool yarns. Wool was not used in bags prior to the availability of European cloth in the Northeast. The maker of this basket-like bag probably unraveled fibers from trade cloth and reworked them to add color to the bag. Ironically, the red

wool has nearly disappeared, while the basswood and cornhusk remain.

Another late-seventeenth-century bag was reputedly given to Susannah (Eastman) Wood Swan while in captivity in northern New England during the French-Indian wars. According to family tradition, an old North American Indian woman packed it with food and a blanket and gave it to Susannah upon her release with directions to a nearby white settlement. It has remained in the family since Susannah's death in 1772. Made of reddish-brown basswood and pale straw-colored wefts (possibly rush grass) on a basswood warp, the bag displays fine geometric designs. It was converted for use as a sewing bag in the early nineteenth century and is now bound at the top edge with a printed cotton chintz fabric. The family called it a "wampum bag."

A third bag is actually a pocketbook. It was made by Molly Ockett (1740–1816), a Pigwacket Indian, and gifted to Eli Twitchell of Bethel, Maine, sometime around 1785. The warp is Indian hemp, and the weft is moose hair in different colors. While the materials and techniques of the outer fabric are pure North American Indian in origin, the pocketbook form is European. It is a trifold design typical of men's billfolds in the eighteenth century, lined with green flannel and closed with a silver clasp dated 1778. Molly created the fabric; however, it is unlikely that she made the pocketbook itself.

Molly Ockett successfully negotiated two worlds, that of her local band of Abenaki Indians and that of Colonial New England. The pocketbook is evidence of the conjoining of these two worlds. She lived in wigwams, traveled by canoe on area rivers, and knew native herbal remedies for physical ailments. She had spent time with a white family in her youth, knew how to communicate in English, and was a devout Christian. She was a skillful negotiator when it came to financial dealings, evidence of which lived on after her death in rumors of a coin-filled teapot buried in the woods. Every year, her memory is honored at Molly Ockett Day, a summer celebration in Bethel, Maine.

REFERENCES AND FURTHER READING

Bethel Historical Society. "*Molly Ockett and Her World.*" http://www.bethelhistorical.org.//molly_ockett_and_Her_World.html (accessed 4 August 2007).

Drooker, P. B. and G. R. Hamell. "Susannah Swan's 'Wampum Bag.' " In *Perishable Material Culture in the Northeast*, edited by P. B. Drooker, 197–215. Albany: New York State Museum, 2004.

Gookin, D. "Historical Collections of the Indians in New England." Massachusetts Historical Society Collections, Part 1, 1. Boston: Apollo Press, 1792.

Ulrich, L. T. *The Age of Homespun: Objects and Stories in the Creation of an American Myth.* New York: Alfred A. Knopf, 2001.

References and Further Reading

Becker, M. J. "Matchcoats: Cultural Conservatism and Change in One Aspect of Native American Clothing." *Ethnohistory* 52, no. 4 (2005): 727–787.

Champlain, S. *Voyages of Samuel de Champlain 1604–1618.* Edited by W. L. Grant. New York: Charles Scribner's Sons, 1907.

Drooker, P. B., ed. *Perishable Material Culture in the Northeast.* Albany: New York State Museum, 2004.

Lindholdt, P. J., ed. *John Josselyn, Colonial Traveler.* Hanover, NH: University Press of New England, 1988.

Petersen, J. B., ed. *A Most Indispensable Art: Native Fiber Industries from Eastern North America.* Knoxville: University of Tennessee Press, 1996.

Trigger, B. G., ed. *Northeast.* Vol. 15 of *Handbook of North American Indians*, edited by William C. Sturtevant. Washington, DC: Smithsonian Institution, 1978.

Welters, L. "From Moccasins to Frock Coats and Back Again." In *Dress in American Culture*, edited by P. A. Cunningham and S. V. Lab, 6–41.

Bowling Green, OH: Bowling Green State University Popular Press, 1993.

Willmott, C. "From Stroud to Strouds: The Hidden History of a British Fur Trade Textile." *Textile History* 36, no. 2 (2005): 196–234.

Willoughby, C. C. "Textile Fabrics of the New England Indians." *American Anthropology* 7 (1905): 85–93.

Wood, M. *Native American Fashion: Modern Adaptations of Traditional Designs.* New York: Van Nostrand Reinhold, 1981.

Wroth, L. C. *The Voyages of Gianni da Verrazzano, 1524–1528.* New Haven, CT: Yale University Press, 1970.

Linda Welters

See also The Geographic and Cultural Region Evidence about Dress of Indigenous People: Canadian Territory; Immigrants Encounter American Dress.

The Southeast

THE SOUTHEAST

The North American Indians of what is today the Southern or Southeastern United States possess a rich system of dress that can be traced from the late pre-Colonial period through the Colonial era to the present. As this is done, patterns of continuity and change over time can be seen as can the ways that native and nonnative materials, forms, and practices were creatively blended by native peoples to formulate regionally and locally distinctive modes of dress. In pre-Colonial times, the peoples of Southeastern North America developed a highly ornate and extremely distinctive mode of dress and decoration, one that reflected the socially stratified, ritually elaborated, artistically fertile civilization that is known to archaeologists as *Mississippian*. Southeastern native dress and adornment after contact with Europeans both maintained older distinctive characteristics and developed new ones while incorporating European materials obtained in trade as well as European techniques. Since the late nineteenth century, Southeastern Indian peoples have preserved and refined the clothing styles established and formulated in the late Colonial and early U.S. periods in a new context. These modes of dress and adornment have transitioned from daily use and become forms of national dress emblematic of community identities. The term *national dress* is used in this contemporary context to refer to locally marked styles of dress that, while sharing regional characteristics, are understood to index membership in a particular native nation or tribal group. Such national dress is worn today in a variety of special-event contexts, both religious and secular. While national dress preserves common features found in the clothing of the Colonial frontier, including elements shared by most native groups as well as many held in common with peoples of European and African ancestry, national dress of the modern period has evolved in ways that emphasize distinctive, community-specific features and that reflect local cultural history.

THE SOUTHEASTERN CULTURE AREA AND THE STUDY OF DRESS

Understanding the dress practices of the Southeastern peoples requires knowledge of the relations between these three regions: the Southeast, the Northeast, and the Plains. The boundary between the Northeast and the Southeast as cultural areas is perhaps the weakest, most arbitrary one in North America. No sharp environmental dividing line exists between them. There has always been much cultural exchange and human movement between the two regions. Cultural and social movement intensified further when many were forced by the U.S. government onto lands west of the Mississippi River. As a result, scholars regularly speak of the Northeast and Southeast as subregions of a larger whole known as the Eastern Woodlands; therefore, the term *Woodlands* will be used when the wider region embracing the Northeast and Southeast is intended. The dress practices of the Northeast and the Southeast share many characteristics through time.

In contrast, the Plains area is separated from the Southeast by a relatively dramatic environmental change and marked cultural differences. It is only with the contemporary eastward spread of the *powwow*—a set of social dance institutions and practices based on older traditions of the Plains peoples—that Plains ways of crafting clothing and dressing and adorning the body have had a significant influence on the peoples of the Southeast. Historically, the two regions possessed distinctive art, craft, and adornment traditions. The sedentary farming peoples, residing historically in the Missouri River drainage, developed a way of life that expressed a synthesis of the distinctive lifeways found to their east in the Woodlands and to the west on the Plains. Their dress styles integrated such Woodland features as floral appliqué beadwork, center-seam leggings, and finger-woven textile belts with Plains elements, such as feather-bonnet headdresses and dance bustles.

Scholarly work aimed at differentiating subregions within the Southeast has often relied on close study of material culture. Studying the beadwork styles found on items of men's dress such as *bandolier* (shoulder) bags and baldrics, researchers have described western and eastern subregions within the Southeast. In these genres, peoples of the western Southeast, including the Choctaw, Alabama, and Koasati, have a markedly different beadwork style than was characteristic of more easterly groups such as the Muscogee, Seminole, and Cherokee.

DRESS IN THE PRE-CONTACT SOUTHEAST

Study of indigenous dress for the Southeastern region before the era of European contact relies on the database provided by prehistoric archaeology, which spans the period of the region's initial settlement by hunting and gathering peoples through the development of settled societies increasingly dependent on horticulture through the emergence, and partial decline, of hierarchical chiefdoms that sometimes integrated peoples of differing linguistic and geographical backgrounds into larger, multiethnic polities. The Mississippian period covers, approximately, the span from 1000 B.C.E. to the time of contact with Spanish Europeans somewhere around 1521 C.E.

Archaeological materials from the Spiro Mounds site in Le Flore County, Oklahoma, reveal some general patterns in Mississippian body art. Mississippian societies were characterized by political and religious elites who presided over relatively stratified societies. These characteristics generated a complex artistic

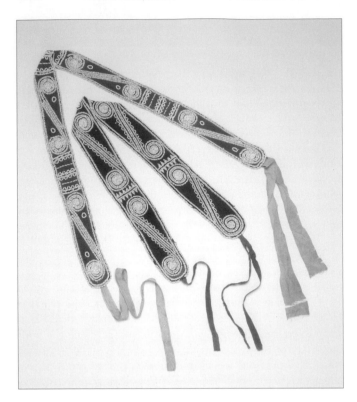

Two Choctaw shoulder sashes, made of wool stroud cloth and glass beads from Mandeville, Louisiana, ca. 1870. Penn Museum objects 38472, 38473, image #151917.

tradition, known especially from those genres of art and craft executed in durable materials. Throughout the Mississippian world, worked marine shell was widely traded and was highly valued, especially when elaborately engraved. Shell was used to produce pendants and beads that were incorporated into dress practices. Engraved shells also offer glimpses of humans and humanlike beings wearing clothing and body decoration. While these images may reveal style of dress associated closely with mythology and belief rather than everyday practice, they do seem to offer clues into actual dress practices. When these engraved shell objects feature abstract designs, they provide clues into the general artistic systems characterizing Southeastern societies. In both abstract imagery and the realistic evocation of certain patterns of dress and decoration, there are remarkable continuities linking pre-Contact practices and more recent, even contemporary usages.

Humans and humanlike beings in the shell-image corpus show figures wearing little clothing but significantly and distinctively adorned with body decorations. These include bead necklaces, large *gorgets* (neck coverings) of shell or copper, arm- and wristbands, knee and ankle bands, and decorated textile waist sashes, typically with side tassels hanging decoratively at the wearer's side. Decorative textile sashes are a reoccurring item of Southeastern dress from Mississippian times to the present day.

In addition to such elaborate but everyday forms of body decoration, the engraved shell images, as well as elaborate images worked in copper *repoussé* (hammered relief designs), picture what seems to be dancers and other ritual participants wearing ceremonial clothing, including masks, elaborate headdresses, and other accessories intended to represent, or to transform the wearer into, birdlike beings. While separated by considerable

time from later practices and beliefs documented ethnographically, these images can be understood in light of the ceremonial dances, mythology, and artistry of southeastern Indian peoples of contemporary times.

Pottery effigy vessels from the region often feature full human figures, typically seated. These figures suggest the commonality of tattooing of the face and chest, as well as the piercing of earlobes and the use of distinctive but varied hairstyles.

In addition to the images preserved in shell, pottery, and copper, there are surviving artifacts that themselves likely constituted key forms of body decoration during this period: large, finely crafted ear spools of copper and pearl beads that were almost certainly worn as necklaces and in other jewelry forms. Later and indirect evidence indicates the key importance of hide clothing and of woven-fiber textiles (of both plant fibers and animal wool), but such materials themselves are not generally preserved in pre-Contact sites. Based on records of the earliest Contact period, it appears that during the long warm season of the region, people—men, women, and children—wore minimal clothing, particularly in everyday contexts. For special occasions they would have adopted elaborate forms of dress that would have included distinctive hair treatments, body and hair painting, bead jewelry, and, for elites, such things as copper and engraved shell adornments. Tattooing was clearly practiced throughout the region before Contact, but it would have marked special social statuses, probably of a religious nature as well as keyed to gender and the life course. In a pattern characteristic of much of native North America over time, children would have been decorated in small, symbolic ways indicative of both the child's gender and his or her fully human status, but these forms of decoration would probably be tokens not necessarily of a materially elaborated sort. As the individual matured, it is likely that dress would have grown more complex as an indication of both progressive acquisition of knowledge and experience and, for some, of social prominence and community leadership.

Knowledge of pre-Contact patterns is enhanced by historical sources, including illustrative material, from the early Contact and Colonial periods. In the wake of Contact, massive population declines flattened the social hierarchies of the region's peoples. Because these shifts generally happened outside the direct observation of European peoples, they do not appear in written sources. When the documentation becomes richer in the early Colonial period, social transformations had ended the production of many emblematic genres of Mississippian art, but everyday dress in the region seems little changed in the gap between the Mississippian and the early Colonial period.

DRESS IN THE COLONIAL PERIOD

The Colonial period in the Southeast spans the vast period from first contacts in the region to the emergence of an independent United States (ca. 1783), a time when the colonials sought to incorporate the region's native peoples into the Atlantic world. Seen from a native perspective, this period was one in which peoples of European and African ancestries were progressively and actively woven into a native world that continues to thrive and expand.

At the beginning of the Colonial period, Southeastern Indian dress was like that described for the pre-Contact period. The ways that European materials, techniques, and styles were selectively, actively, and creatively incorporated into native dress repetoires dominate the story of the region's dress after Contact. This process began first on the coastlines, where Contact happened earliest, but it soon ran ahead of actual European exploration of the interior, as knowledge of Europeans travels inland and as native groups begin to trade European goods among themselves. Such trade items as glass beads, small metal bells, and tin cones were among the first items of European manufacture to become incorporated in this way into native systems of dress. Thus, in the early stages, European goods enhanced indigenous modes of dress just as exotic indigenous trade goods, such as engraved marine shell, long had. Like these pre-Contact analogs, European manufactured goods were scarce, and their acquisition and use was a hallmark of high social status and cosmopolitan social ties.

Used with caution, and in combination with textual sources and comparative evidence, the pictorial evidence left behind by early European observers of native life in the Southeast can be a means of understanding dress during the early Colonial period. Determining the reliability of visual documents left by historical observers requires careful study. One of the most closely considered artists is John White, an English artist living in the middle to late sixteenth century who pictured life in the British colonies located on the coast of what is today North Carolina during 1585.

CAROLINA ALGONQUIANS, 1585

The White drawings, supplemented with textual observations, make it possible to characterize native dress in the early Colonial period, at least for one corner of the Southeast. In this time, place, and cultural setting, both men and women practiced extensive and exuberant body modification and body decoration while wearing relatively simple clothing forms. Adult bodies were often, but not uniformly, painted or tattooed. Designs were in a dark pigment and were typically geometric in design. Women's tattoo designs encircling the upper arm and the neck—upper chest region reappear in the images. Great care was taken in working the hair into an array of different cuts and styles that seem to suggest not only personal preference but also age, gender, and social status distinctions. Ears were pierced and decorated with several kinds of treatments, including single feathers and what seem to be short fur strips passed through the earlobe. Men are shown wearing one or more individual feathers protruding from their hair. Unlike the better-known feather headdresses from native North America in later periods, these feathers seem to be used simply, in unmodified form.

White pictured the Coastal Algonquian peoples that he encountered wearing a variety of necklaces. The evidence suggests that native beads were made from a variety of materials including seeds and shell. Necklaces were probably strung on string twisted from plant fibers, although animal sinews may also have been used. The basic garment for men and women was a fringed, front-and-back apron of what was almost certainly animal hide. Some individuals are pictured without clothing, while some elite men are shown wearing knee-length, togalike garments suspended from one shoulder. The leading men wear a variety of sleeveless upper-body coverings, including one example that appears to be a woven-textile, rather than hide, garment. Other evidence indicates that, in this region and time, cloaks or mantles were woven of bird feathers.

Children in the White drawings are shown comparatively undressed and undecorated, reflecting patterns throughout native

A North American Indian wearing a tasseled sash, ca. 1590, from a painting by John White. Getty Images.

North America in which dress becomes more elaborate with adult status and maturation across the life course. White pictures one prepubescent girl wearing a simple necklace; a loose, fringed hairstyle; and pubic covering held in place with a vertical string that is tied to a second horizontal string encircling her midsection.

White's drawings of peoples on the Atlantic seaboard focus on societies that were beyond direct involvement in the Mississippian cultural sphere that was centered in the interior of the Southeast, but what is generally true of the Coastal Algonquian around 1585 was probably also true for other regions of the Southeast during this time period. For men and women, body adornment and body modification were highly elaborated, while everyday clothing was simple and utilitarian, although not devoid of decorative elements. Personal identity, social status, and individual expression were not signaled first and foremost through garments, although these were surely significant. The body's communicative work was carried on through temporary decorations and permanent modifications that drew upon local codes and customs about which we know little by way of detail, except through analogy to better-known peoples of later periods.

REGIONAL DRESS IN THE EARLY EIGHTEENTH CENTURY

Another glimpse of Southeastern dress can be gained in the notes and color images made about 1736 by the eighteenth-century German adventurer and bureaucrat Philip von Reck during his travels on the frontiers of the British colony of Georgia not long after its founding. The native peoples pictured in von Reck's images are of two groups—the Muscogee (Creek) and the Yuchi (Euchee). Both peoples live today as neighbors in eastern Oklahoma, to which the U.S. government forced them in the 1830s. The Muscogee were, and are, the demographically larger people. Muscogee society, while changing over time, represents a confederation of autonomous towns and differing ethnolinguistic groups, many of whom spoke Muskogean languages, including Koasati, Alabama, Hitchiti, and Muscogee proper. The Yuchi have a different Colonial-era history and continue, into the twenty-first century, to speak their own unique language—a language isolated and unrelated to other known tongues. During the period documented by von Reck, as in the late twentieth to early twenty-first century, the Yuchi people held themselves to be a separate people from the Muscogee, despite periods of historical cooperation, and since the period of removal, their political encompassment within the government of the Muscogee (Creek) Nation. Despite the distinctions characterizing the two peoples, they shared, and today share, some cultural practices, including dress.

Von Reck's portraits of Muscogee and Yuchi individuals in 1736 show the increased prevalence of European manufactured goods in the everyday and ceremonial dress of native peoples. In contrast to the Coastal Algonquians pictured by White a century and a half earlier, the native peoples neighboring the Georgia colony in the 1730s made extensive use of wool trade cloth. The "Uchi King" Senkaitschi was pictured wearing close-fitting leggings of blue wool (covering the legs from ankle to midthigh), a red-wool breechcloth, and a rectangular mantle or match coat of tanned buffalo hide on which the fur had been retained. He wears moccasins of tanned hide sewn of a single piece, with a vertical seam at the ankle and a single center seam running along the top of the foot. This simple, often undecorated, soft-sole moccasin type is the common type throughout the Woodlands. Senkaitschi is shown with extensive tattoos in geometric patterns on his chest, and he wears his hair short atop his head and shoulder length in back. A second Yuchi man, Kipahalgwa, identified as the "supreme commander of the Yuchi Indian Nation" (suggesting he held the status of war chief), was pictured wearing red-wool leggings of a similar type with a long white shirt of probable European manufacture. In his portrait, Kipahalgwa, unlike Senkaitschi, wears extensive face paint, an elaborate topknotted hairstyle, and complicated ear decorations composed of what look to be downy, white bird feathers. He shares with his contemporary elaborate chest tattoos in geometric patterns and soft sole moccasins of the regional type.

The von Reck images are less useful as documents of the dress of Yuchi women and of Creek people in general. Senkaitschi's wife, the "Queen of the Uchi," is pictured facing away from the viewer. Her feet are uncovered, and she wears a knee-length dress or skirt, with a light-colored wool blanket wrapped around her upper body and partially covering her skirt or the skirt of her dress. Her hair is shoulder length, and no other adornment or jewelry is visible in her portrait. An uncolored sketch of a different Indian woman, unidentified as either Creek or Yuchi, pictures her seated and at work weaving a cane basket or mat. She may be uncovered above the waist (the image is unclear), but she clearly possesses tattoos (or perhaps painted designs) running the length of her right arm, from wrist to shoulder. The design is comprised mainly of a line of small arrow shapes pointing upward in succession toward the shoulder. A pair of geometric designs graces her wrist. Only one of von Reck's subjects is presented with enough evidence to identify him reasonably certainly as Muscogee as opposed to Yuchi. This portrait pictures a seated man wearing a dark blanket. His hair is worn short, but the other characteristics of his dress are obscure, except in the form of absences—no moccasins, no face or body paint, no elaborate tattoos, and no wool or hide leggings.

A group of three men, unidentified as Muscogee or Yuchi, are pictured by von Reck in hunting attire. One wears an elaborately decorated hide blanket in geometric designs similar to those better documented for the Quapaw, a people whose homeland was on the western frontiers of the Southeastern region. Another of these men wears a light-colored wool trade blanket, while a third wears a shirt that falls to just below the waist. All three of these men wear the common type of soft-sole moccasins, and two wear leggings of trade wool. One of the three hunters wears a hide shoulder pouch suspended to the side at waist height. This object prefigures the elaborately beaded wool bandoliers made by Southeastern Indian women and worn by Southeastern Indian men in the early to mid-nineteenth century. The two other hunters each carry bundles of equipment and provisions on their backs. These bundles are carried with a single shoulder strap that passes horizontally around each shoulder. This same carrying technique was used in the Southeast when carrying large pack baskets woven of river cane. Straps could be of hide or of native woven textiles.

In his writings and images, von Reck documented some other items of Creek and Yuchi dress. In an annotated colored image, he pictured and described a belt of otter hide decorated with tube beads of deer bone and to which deer hooves were attached. In native North America, clusters of deer hooves (dew claws) are attached in bunches to clothing in this way to produce a gentle rattling sound. Such ornaments are often worn with dance clothing.

Other images in the von Reck corpus show the use, by men and women, of trade-cloth blankets as upper-body coverings. In several images, including one made of a summertime War Dance ceremonial, men are pictured wearing only a simple breechcloth, but in each case, this is made of trade wool (called *strouding* or *stroud cloth*) in the two main colors then available—red and blue. The most common and basic haircut for Yuchi men at this time appears to be a topknot in which the hair, relatively short, was tied up at the top of the head, resulting in a single, relatively short protrusion of hair standing straight up from the scalp.

Regrettably, no children, Muscogee or Yuchi, appear in the von Reck images. We do learn more about the native dress in the artist's writings. Speaking in general of the North American Indians, he reported on the use of face paint, where the preference seemed to be for black "shaded with red." Faces were painted in multicolors for war to create effects intended to be as frightening

Ester Littlebear leads the women of the Duck Creek community in a performance of the Yuchi Ribbon Dance during the town's Green Corn Ceremony, 2005. The women wear full cotton skirts or dresses. They bind rattles to their legs and attach ribbons to combs in their hair. Around their waists they wear yarn belts with long tassels. Photograph by Jason Baird Jackson.

as possible. Both men and women were described as having stripes on faces, necks, and bodies.

Heads were uncovered. Hair was short and black and tied up on the crown. Each nation had a distinctive haircut. Short hair was tied with a red band. Men were beardless and were said to "tear out what little bit [of hair] does grow." Body coverings included a short "blanket" (i.e., breechcloth), and sometimes a wrapping of deer- or sheepskin. Other items described included "white woolen leggings" that covered from foot to thigh and were worn for hunting and as protection against rattlesnakes, which were said to be unable to bite through the material. Shoes were of deerskin and laced to close.

Concluding his description of North American Indian dress, von Reck notes that women were fully clothed, describing them as "almost like the peasant women in Germany." Even those with no clothes covered themselves with wool cloth and "thereby show more modesty than the English ladies." He reports that women braided their hair, except for widows, who let it hang around their faces.

This account, quoted by Danish parliamentary librarian Kristian Hvidt, is among the most comprehensive European descriptions of native dress available for the Colonial-era Southeast.

To the extent that the forms of Yuchi and Muscogee dress pictured by von Reck can be taken as a token of Southeastern trends in this period, continuities and emergent patterns can both be isolated. Add to this archaeology and historical documentation, and these conclusions are possible. For this period, painting, tattooing, and hairstyle remain key indicators of social status, although the details behind these practices are mostly unknown, except by analogy to practices among more westerly peoples

documented later in time. Beads remain present but are not used in vast amounts. Archaeological and historical evidence clearly documents the increasing use of European glass beads during this period. This trend is reflected in the declining use of beads of native manufacture. Wool is the most widely used trade cloth and completed garments, particularly men's shirts, are being traded to native people in finished form. Although we lack pre-Contact examples or documentation, continuity in time is almost certainly observable in the use of the basic regional moccasin type. This widespread type of footwear is fundamentally unchanged from the oldest-known evidence to the present, and its distribution is synonymous with the Eastern Woodlands. Face and body paint, including the occasional painting of the hair, is characteristic of this period.

REGIONAL DRESS IN THE EARLY NINETEENTH CENTURY

A richer set of documents picturing Southeastern Indian dress is available for the early eighteenth century, representing practices characteristic of the time just before and just after the forced removals by which the U.S. government pressured many of the region's native peoples to cede their homelands and relocate to areas west of the Mississippi River. Among the artists picturing Southeastern Indian peoples during this period were the U.S. painters John Turnbull (1756–1843), George Catlin (1796–1872), and Charles Bird King (1785–1862). In the work of these artists, one can glimpse the antecedent clothing forms that came to characterize the national dress of the twentieth century. The sample of reliable images for the early nineteenth century represent a wider array of subjects, with Creek, Cherokee, Choctaw, and Seminole individuals being pictured most frequently. While subregional, tribal, local, and individual differences in dress surely existed during this period, there is a strong regional commonality characteristic of men's and women's dress not only across the Southeast but in the Woodlands as a broader whole. A key variable in the study of native dress for this period is the existence, in public and private collections, of surviving examples of early-nineteenth-century dress.

During this period, blankets continued to be used as warm outer garments by both men and women, but they recede in importance, replaced by more tailored clothing. For men, the upper body was clothed in knee-length cloth shirts over which were frequently worn knee-length hunting (frock) coats of wool or homespun. For women, more tailored shawls could be added atop a cloth blouse. Men's shirts were obtained as finished trade goods, but during this period, more and more trade-cloth clothing was being made by native seamstresses. Shirts featured formal features found in nonnative dress on the frontier, including ruffle shirt collars and front plackets and gusseted sleeves. Both men's and women's dress from this and later periods shows patterning in which women tore rather than cut seams; thus, patterns are based on the use of rectangular and square elements.

Some hide dresses are pictured in the images of this period, but the common style of women's dress is a cloth blouse, often with a round, full-body cape (related in form to a *bertha collar*), worn with a long cloth skirt. The capes characteristic of women's

blouses were often (as among some groups today) decorated with silver (later, nickel-silver) brooches.

When covering their feet, women and men both wore the same simple single-piece, soft-sole Woodland moccasins that were common in earlier periods. For this period, there are surviving Southeastern moccasins embellished with an attachment of wool on which appliqué beadwork with glass seed beads in curvilinear technique has been executed. The beadwork found on such moccasins matches, in technique and visual style, other genres of beaded clothing documented for this period. While moccasins were worn by both men and women, there are two items of beaded dress characteristic of men in this period—bandolier (shoulder) bags and rectangular belts or shoulder sashes. In all these forms of dress, appliqué beadwork was stitched onto blue or red wool using a two-thread technique. Many observers would recognize, as native people clearly did, these beaded items, which are found in local variation across the Woodlands, as among the most elaborate and beautiful of post-Contact native arts in eastern North America.

In addition to shirts and frock coats, men's dress included simple cloth breechcloths, which were generally not visible underneath knee-length shirts, and cloth or hide leggings. While we know that hide leggings continued to be worn by men, they do not generally appear in the portraits made of native leaders in the early nineteenth century. Shown instead are wool leggings of native manufacture that are continuous in basic form with those of the early eighteenth century. Common throughout the Woodlands at this time are relatively tight-fitting leggings with a seam running

Yuchi Chief Simon Harry leads the people of the Duck Creek community, Eastern Oklahoma, in a performance of the Old Folks Dance during the town's annual Green Corn Ceremony, 2002. The women wear full cotton skirts or dresses similar in style to those worn during the nineteenth century. The men wear Yuchi jackets, based on hunters' frock coats, which feature a ruffle trim, a large cape collar, and a vertical front opening that can be closed with a yarn sash, but that lacks buttons or other means of closure. They are made from solid colored cotton or cotton blend fabrics. Photograph by Jason Baird Jackson.

vertically up the front of the leg. This seam was often decorated with silk ribbon and, sometimes, shoe buttons. This legging type seems to usually have been held in place at the bottom by a stirrup that passed under the foot and by a tie that ran up the front of the leg, positioning the top of the legging at midthigh.

Finger-woven textiles were worn in a couple of ways. When wearing cloth leggings, men wore garters just below their knees. These garters were rectangular in form, with yarn fringe at each end. They were tied closed by knotting the fringe at the front of the leg. Based on later garment styles, women probably sometimes wore knee-high leggings secured in place with cloth or finger-woven garters, but such garments are undocumented in the images for this period. The largest, most elaborate, finger-woven textiles were large men's waist sashes, items that were sometimes also worn across the upper body as a baldric. These sashes were comprised of a large rectangular panel of fingerweaving, finished on each end with a large number of long, heddle-woven tassels ending in a pom-pom or tassel of yarn. When worn as a belt, such a sash could close a coat and would be tied in an elaborate bow at one side of the waist. When worn as a baldric or bandolier, the sash would similarly be tied at the side at waist height. Appliqué beaded sashes of wool, mentioned previously, would also have heddle-woven yarn tassels, like those characteristic of finger-woven sashes, attached at each end and would be worn similarly. In the case of both finger-woven garters and sashes, white seed or pony beads were worked into designs, being strung onto the yarns out of which the textile was woven.

The emblematic item of men's clothing during this period was an elaborate cloth turban. These were comprised of a shawl or other piece of commercial cloth wrapped around the head and usually held in place with a silver turban band. Feathers, including large exotic species obtained in trade, were worn tucked into, or attached to, such turbans.

During this period, silver jewelry obtained in trade and, increasingly, made by native silversmiths was prominently worn by both men and women. In addition to turban bands, men wore large crescent-shaped gorgets, upper-arm bands, and earrings. Women wore rings, earrings, brooches, and other smaller items. Although revived as a general North American practice in the twentieth century, tattooing using indigenous techniques and styles seems to have ceased during the early to middle nineteenth century, but face and hair painting, for both men and women, continued to be practiced during this period.

Focused on portraits of native leaders, the available images do not address the clothing and decoration of native children in this period. As in earlier and later periods, children's dress was probably simple and comfortable.

In this period, some affluent native leaders chose to wear Euro–North American dress in nonnative fashion, but the main pattern is one in which native garments came to be modeled upon, but then differentiated from, European antecedents. Men's coats, for instance, were clearly patterned on European prototypes but quickly came to express a distinctly native style. Similarly, women's clothes were adapted from European frontier types, but these increasingly incorporated native aesthetic principles in such areas as color choice, combination of different elements, and embellishment, with cloth appliqué decoration, for instance. Native dress practices also persisted, such as the use of leggings rather than pants, the use of red-earth paints, and, for some groups such as the Shawnee, the use of nose rings and the decorative cutting of

outer earlobes. The region-wide dress characteristics of this period provide the foundation for understanding twentieth- and early-twenty-first-century dress.

REGIONAL DRESS IN THE TWENTIETH CENTURY

The key twentieth-century transformation in Southeastern Indian dress is the adoption of Euro–North American styles for everyday dress and the concurrent emergence, in many but not all native communities, of native styles as a form of national dress worn on special occasions of cultural significance, especially community-wide ceremonial or social gatherings. As native dress became national dress, it localized in community-specific ways while retaining features of the widespread regional tradition formulated in the early nineteenth century. The discussion that follows focuses on contemporary native dress as found among Woodland, especially Southeastern, peoples in Oklahoma. Similar national dress traditions can be found among other Southeastern peoples outside Oklahoma, among, for example, the Choctaw in Mississippi, the Cherokee in North Carolina, and the Seminole in Florida. Among the latter three groups, the processes of differentiation in national dress were accelerated when these peoples became, after the removal era, isolated for a time from other native communities.

The Yuchi people wear distinctive clothing when they gather today for rituals and dances at one of three town ceremonial grounds associated with one of their three townships. The most important of these town ritual events is the annual Green Corn Ceremony, held each summer in connection with the ripening of the corn crop. One component of the Green Corn Ceremony is collective dances in which all the town's people, along with guests from other Yuchi towns and from other native communities, participate. For these dances, women wear cotton skirts or dresses similar in style to those worn during the nineteenth century. A very loose cotton skirt, often in a calico or other print fabric, can be combined with a matching blouse, either one with a matching bertha collar or in some other historic or contemporary cut. Alternatively, a woman might wear a one-piece dress with either a round bertha collar or a tab collar, both drawn from nineteenth-century frontier styles. Whether a skirt or dress, the garment is cut very full and loose to accommodate the large leg rattles that are worn tied around the lower legs. These rattles, comprised of many tortoise shells or, representing a twentieth-century innovation, tin cans strung together, are used by women and girls to provide the rhythmic accompaniment to singing, which is done by male participants.

With their Indian-style dress or skirt, women will wear a yarn waistbelt with long side tassels. These belts are derived from the finger-woven belts worn by Southeastern Indian men during the nineteenth century. While they may be finger woven today, they are more likely to be woven on a box loom or with a heddle—less time-consuming techniques. These same multicolored yarn belts are also worn by men. In addition to such Southeastern yarn belts, a woman might choose instead to wear a silver *concho belt* derived from (if not obtained from) the native people of the Southwestern United States.

Women wear their newest and best native clothes for the annual Ribbon Dance, a part of the Green Corn Ceremony in which only women participate as dancers. The hallmark of this performance is the wearing of long ribbons in many colors attached to the hair. While they can be attached to modern hairclips or barrettes, the use of nickel-silver hair combs of nineteenth-century style is common. Such combs are worn as a part of women's traditional dress among other Woodland peoples, but today only Yuchi women use them to suspend their dance ribbons. While Muscogee (Creek) people also have their own version of the Ribbon Dance in which women wear colored ribbons, Creek dancers wear them pinned to their clothes rather than attached to their hair. Such patterns of minor, but very self-conscious, differentiation characterize modern national dress.

Into the twentieth century, Yuchi women wore cloth leggings and soft-sole moccasins, but these garments are now moribund. In the early twenty-first century, Yuchi women wear street shoes of various types with their Indian clothes. Given the strenuousness of Yuchi dance and the rustic, outdoor setting in which ceremonials are held, athletic shoes were most common in the late twentieth to early twenty-first century. During ceremonies, when participants are not dancing, as during the preparation and consumption or meals, during ceremonial games, and during informal socializing, women wear everyday clothes. Given the centrality of large-scale, outdoor cooking to women's ceremonial activities, kitchen aprons have become an elaborate item of handmade clothing.

When dressed for ceremonial dances, women wear a wide variety of both nonnative jewelry and items of native-style jewelry made both by local and distant native artists. Native jewelry includes silver and nickel-silver jewelry in Woodland, Plains and Southwestern styles as well as pan-Indian style beadwork jewelry, including beaded necklaces, hair decorations, and other items. In continuity with all earlier styles of native dress, strands of bead necklaces remain an iconic part of women's dress.

Face paint, for both men and women, continues to be a part of native dress practices among Woodland peoples. For the modern Yuchi, in partial contrast with their ancestors, paint is today worn only during two important ritual events. It is worn by men and women during the Green Corn Ceremony, and it is worn by the deceased during his or her funeral ceremonies. This reflects the contemporary Yuchi view that Indian paint (but not modern cosmetics) is a special kind of signal to the Creator and to Yuchi ancestors, a token not only of tribal membership but also of the proper fulfillment of enduring collective and personal ceremonial obligations. When worn thus, the modern Yuchi use a consistent set of designs. For men, this entails the use of two or three horizontal bars placed beneath each eye. The number used signifies membership in one half of the dual division in which Yuchi men are divided—the chiefs' or the warriors' societies. Some Yuchi women wear similar designs, but others disagree with this, holding that these designs are emblematic of men and that the proper woman's design is a circle placed on each cheek. This latter design is widespread among Woodland women today.

For ceremonial and celebratory occasions, Yuchi men wear loose *ribbon shirts*, which are modern versions of nineteenth-century frontier shirts. These sometimes feature modern collars and sometimes have an older style of tab collar. Like older shirts, they can include an elaborately constructed front placket. Ribbon shirts today are made from solid or print fabric, with calico being seen as old-fashioned. They take their name from ribbon trim and ribbon dangles that can decorate the front and back. Traditionally long-sleeved garments, they are also made in short-sleeve forms today.

The most emblematic item of men's dress among the Yuchi is a local form of the nineteenth-century hunter's frock coat known as a *Yuchi jacket* or as a *Green Corn jacket*. Once an item of everyday clothing, in the early twenty-first century this jacket is worn only as part of national dress. It is most often worn during the most visually elaborated phases of the Green Corn Ceremony. This jacket, today made from solid-colored cotton or cotton-blend fabrics (sometimes also from shiny, satinlike fabrics), is patterned on the older coats common to the region. In the present-day Yuchi form, it has been shortened somewhat to hip length, but the garment retains its distinctive features—ruffle trim, a large cape collar, and a vertical front opening that can be closed with a yarn sash but that lacks buttons or other means of closure. Like its antecedents, the Green Corn jacket is worn above a shirt, either a modern store-bought garment or a ribbon shirt.

Yuchi men stopped wearing breechcloths with wool leggings and garters in the earliest years of the twentieth century. Since then they have worn European-style pants and commercial overalls. At contemporary ceremonies, slacks, blue jeans (most common), and denim overalls can all be seen worn as part of national dress. Yuchis wore moccasins of Woodland style into the twentieth century, but they were preserved mainly for wear around the house. Sturdier shoes became standard in most contexts, and today, if Yuchi people generally have and wear moccasins, they will be obtained from another tribe. As with women, any kind of shoe can be worn with Yuchi traditional clothes, but whereas athletic shoes are most common for women, girls, and boys, Western cowboy boots are most common for adult men.

In addition to Western boots and belts, a final item of North American Western wear is central to modern Yuchi national dress and to that of most Woodland peoples in contemporary eastern Oklahoma. This is the Western hat thought of by many North Americans as the "cowboy hat." Like the men's turban of the nineteenth century, the Western hat is the emblematic item of men's dress among Woodland peoples of eastern Oklahoma. Its status as native headgear is signaled by how it is accessorized. For both everyday and ceremonial occasions, it will be augmented with a native-style hatband, often beaded. For ceremonial occasions such as a dance, it will have a feather tied or attached to it. The prominence of the so-called cowboy hat as an emblem of native dress is expressive of two wider post-Contact processes revealed in Southeastern Indian dress. One is the manner in which European and Euro–North American materials, clothing styles, and consumer goods have consistently been incorporated and then modified within the clothing systems of the region's native peoples. The other is the way that this general process has led, in a context of both cultural conservatism and cultural differentiation, to the greater relative retention of certain European clothing traits among native peoples than among North American peoples of European ancestry. The fact is that many young Yuchi women regularly wear clothes quite comparable to those worn not only by their own great-great-grandmothers but also by the great-great-grandmothers of their classmates of African and European heritage. At the same time that patterns of cross-cultural similarity and differentiation can be observed, so can patterns of innovation and cultural continuity.

A final pattern can be observed in the dress practices of Southeastern native peoples at the turn of the twenty-first century. Beginning in the 1980s and accelerating in the 1990s, more and more Southeastern Indian peoples took up an interest not only in contemporary forms of "traditional" dress but also in researching, and reviving, its historical antecedents. This intensification of the national dress pattern, with its focus on revitalizing and enriching

An original painting by Charles Bird King depicts Chief Tuko-See-Mathla, also known as John Hicks, of the Seminole North American Indians, 1826. Getty Images.

local heritage culture, has led to extensive formal research by native clothing enthusiasts and to the creation of new events and circumstances in which such antique clothing is being worn. The target for these efforts are the elegant prototypes of national dress documented by the European painters of the early nineteenth century. In the early twenty-first century, one can see such clothing worn by native politicians in their inauguration ceremonies and by native (and nonnative) participants in historic reenactments of nineteenth-century battles between native and U.S. soldiers. Among the Florida Seminole, these trends have progressed a further step, with clothing artists and enthusiasts creating retro dress in styles found at every point along a historical continuum from the early nineteenth century to the present. Such clothing is worn extensively in a host of social and ceremonial gatherings.

At the same time that such historical impulses shape national dress in the present, there are also innovations. One simple example on which to end this discussion is the technique of ribbon appliqué adapted by seamstress and craftswoman Julia Winningham to the decoration of Yuchi ribbon shirts and vests—vests themselves representing a slightly earlier addition to the men's dance clothes repertoire. This technique, which involves the complex folding and sewing down of multicolored ribbons, produces a rainbow effect. This evokes the image of the women's Ribbon Dance described previously, and in both instances, the image is an icon of the rainbow, which figures prominently in Yuchi sacred narrative. The Yuchi word for *rainbow* is also the word for the ceremonial ground at which dances and rituals take place. Literally translating as "big house," the rainbow is the heavenly manifestation of the earthly ceremonial ground. In Mrs. Winningham's vest, we catch a glimpse of the ways that techniques and materials from outside the Yuchi tradition can be turned toward the most deeply significant Yuchi ends.

References and Further Reading

Bailey, Garrick. "Osage." In *Plains*, edited by Raymond J. DeMallie, 476–496. Vol. 13 of *Handbook of North American Indians*, edited by William C. Sturtevant. Washington, DC: Smithsonian Institution, 2001.

Bailey, Garrick, and Daniel C. Swan. *Art of the Osage*. Seattle: University of Washington Press, 2004.

Braund, Kathryn E. Holland. *Deerskins and Duffels: Creek Indian Trade with Anglo-America, 1685–1815*. Lincoln: University of Nebraska Press, 1993.

Brown, James A. *The Spiro Ceremonial Center: The Archaeology of Arkansas Valley Caddoan Culture in Eastern Oklahoma*. Memoirs of the Museum of Anthropology 29. 2 vols. Ann Arbor: Museum of Anthropology, University of Michigan, 1996.

DeMallie, Raymond J., ed. *Plains*. Vol. 13 of *Handbook of North American Indians*, edited by William C. Sturtevant. Washington, DC: Smithsonian Institution, 2001.

Ellis, Clyde, Luke Eric Lassiter, and Gary H. Dunham, eds. *Powwow*. Lincoln: University of Nebraska Press, 2005.

Feest, Christian. "North Carolina Algonquians." In *Northeast*, edited by Bruce Trigger, 271–281. Vol. 15 of *Handbook of North American Indians*, edited by William C. Sturtevant. Washington, DC: Smithsonian Institution, 1978.

Feest, Christian. "John White's New World." In *A New World: England's First View of America*, edited by Kim Sloan, 65–77. Chapel Hill: University of North Carolina Press, 2007.

Fogelson, Raymond D., ed. *Southeast*. Vol. 14 of *Handbook of North American Indians*, edited by William C. Sturtevant. Washington, DC: Smithsonian Institution, 2004.

Fundaburk, Emma Lila. *Southeastern Indians Life Portraits: A Catalogue of Pictures, 1564–1860*. Reprinted. Tuscaloosa: University of Alabama Press, 2000.

Gallay, Alan. *The Indian Slave Trade: The Rise of the English Empire in the American South, 1670–1717*. New Haven, CT: Yale University Press, 2002.

Galloway, Patricia, ed. *The Southeastern Ceremonial Complex: Artifacts and Analysis*. Lincoln: University of Nebraska Press, 1989.

Goggin, John M. *Indian and Spanish: Selected Writings*. Coral Gables, FL: University of Miami Press, 1964.

Hatt, Gudmund. "Moccasins and Their Relation to Arctic Footwear." *Memoirs of the American Anthropological Association* 3 (1916): 147–250.

Hudson, Charles, and Carmen Chaves Tesser, eds. *The Forgotten Centuries: Indians and Europeans in the American South, 1521–1704*. Athens: University of Georgia Press, 1994.

Hvidt, Kristian, ed. *Von Reck's Voyage: Drawings and Journal of Philip Georg Friedrich von Reck*. Savannah, GA: Beehive Press, 1990.

Jackson, Jason Baird. "Dressing for the Dance: Yuchi Ceremonial Clothing." *American Indian Art Magazine* 23, no. 3 (1998): 32–41.

Jackson, Jason Baird. "A Yuchi War Dance in 1736." *European Review of Native American Studies* 16, no. 1 (2002): 27–32.

Jackson, Jason Baird. "Yuchi." In *Southeast*, edited by Raymond D. Fogelson, 415–428. Vol. 14 of *Handbook of North American Indians*, edited by William C. Sturtevant. Washington, DC: Smithsonian Institution, 2004.

Jackson, Jason Baird, and Raymond D. Fogelson. "Introduction." In *Southeast*, edited by Raymond D. Fogelson, 1–13. Vol. 14 of *Handbook of North American Indians*, edited by William C. Sturtevant. Washington, DC: Smithsonian Institution, 2004.

Sloan, Kim, ed. *A New World: England's First View of America*. Chapel Hill: University of North Carolina Press, 2007.

Smith, Marvin T. *Archaeology of Aboriginal Culture Change in the Interior Southeast: Depopulation during the Early Historic Period*. Gainesville: University Press of Florida, 1987.

Sturtevant, William C. "John White's Contribution to Ethnology: 1. The Carolina Algonkians." In *The American Drawings of John White, 1577–1590*, edited by Paul Hulton and David Beers Quinn, with contributions by W.C. Sturtevant, C.E. Raven, R.A. Skelton, and Louis B. Wright, 37–43. Chapel Hill: University of North Carolina Press, 1964.

Sturtevant, William C. "Seminole Men's Clothing." In *Essays on the Verbal and Visual Arts: Proceedings of the 1966 Annual Spring Meeting of the American Ethnological Society*, edited by June Helm, 160–174. Seattle: University of Washington Press, 1967.

Viola, Herman J., and Carolyn Margolis, eds. *Seeds of Change: A Quincentennial Commemoration*. Washington, DC: Smithsonian Institution Press, 1991.

Walker, Willard. "Creek Confederacy before Removal." In *Southeast*, edited by Raymond D. Fogelson, 373–392. Vol. 14 of *Handbook of North American Indians*, edited by William C. Sturtevant. Washington, DC: Smithsonian Institution, 2004.

Young, Gloria, and Michael P. Hoffman. "Quapaw." In *Plains*, edited by Raymond J. DeMallie, 497–514. Vol. 13 of *Handbook of North American Indians*, edited by William C. Sturtevant. Washington, DC: Smithsonian Institution, 2001.

Jason Baird Jackson

Influence of North American Indian and First Nations Dress on Mainstream Fashion

- Borrowing Indian Designs and Ideas for Fashionable Dress
- Jewelry-Making and Design
- Fashionable Garments and Accessories Designs
- Objectives of the Designers
- Sources of Inspiration and Use of Local Materials
- Snapshot: One First Nations Fashion Designer's Journey

Fashion designers of First Nations and North American Indian ancestry began to feel confident about being referred to as fashion designers only by the early 1970s. Fashion has not always been important to indigenous people, but telling a story has. Through their work these designers believe they are telling the story of their people; they are passionate about their work and especially passionate about how it supports their communities. The difference between North American aboriginal design and mainstream design within the fashion industry is that these designers intend to reflect their own culture, identity, and individual rights to use traditional art. Many Indian designers are knowledgeable about the meanings behind clan and tribal designs that relate to their rights and their ancestry. For example, First Nations designers from Canada speak of strong ties with their ancestors, especially their grandparents, and they say that they see it as their duty to find ways to instill pride in the younger generations by reviving the culture and traditions of their people.

Some designers describe much of their work as "wearable art." The designs that they create for customers reflect aboriginal art. It has been estimated that 90 percent of these designers create custom orders and have little or no focus on mass production. When commissioned to design a piece for a customer, these artists are not just taking directions from the customer; they are also including a touch of their culture in the piece. Sometimes they may be commissioned to replicate a fabulous traditional piece.

Designers do not ignore mainstream Western fashion and European design, because the overall trends for what is new for the next season tend to originate there. Designers do the research necessary to keep current the fashions that incorporate their art. As relative newcomers to producing fashionable items, many North American Indian and First Nations designers are only just learning to work as entrepreneurs; the Canadian and U.S. ways of doing business are new to them. Access to education was limited for most of the parents and grandparents of the present designers. The previous generations of First Nations people in Canada were allowed to go to school only until the eighth grade and could not go on to higher education. In the United States, educational policies were directed toward trying to use schools to turn Indian children into "Americans" and toward erasing their language and culture.

BORROWING INDIAN DESIGNS AND IDEAS FOR FASHIONABLE DRESS

The earliest contacts between North American Indians and Europeans led Europeans to adopt some elements of the dress they saw in native communities. The materials from which Indian dress was made or with which it was decorated were especially interesting to them. Europeans prized fur from beaver for use in making felt for hats, and in the Pacific Northwest, the Russians harvested otter skins for the China trade, nearly wiping out the otters in the process. Deerskin garments were a practical alternative for explorers, and eventually fringed deerskin or leather became a hallmark of the stereotypical cowboy dress. European shoemakers quickly added moccasins, a style new to them, to the types of shoes they produced. These have continued to be a fashionable foot covering ever since. To this day, *blanket coats*, originally made from blankets obtained in trade by native people in the early days of European settlement, can be bought in both the United States and Canada.

Indian design motifs from both North and South America have become part of the repertory of decoration in some art movements. The *art deco style* of the 1920s and 1930s is particularly notable in this regard. Decorative elements in some art deco architecture (especially in cities in the southwestern United States), interior design, and textiles include motifs that derive from North American Indian and First Nations ornament. In the early twentieth century, U.S. fashion designers were seeking to establish something that could be seen as a truly "American" fashion, in contrast with the European and Parisian focus that predominated. Art historian Mary Donahue, in an article published on the Internet, has described how designers and museums collaborated because the museums allowed the designers access to their collections of artifacts and artworks in their North American Indian collections. She reports that in displays of dress in an exhibit at the American Museum of Natural History in 1919 called Exhibition of Industrial Art in Textiles and Costumes, designers were identified as basing designs on ornament and style from "Plains Indians," "patterns and styles associated with the Northwest Coast and Plains Indians shirts," and items described as "Pueblan." A bead company identified Woodlands traditions in displaying "Modern Uses of Beads in Dress Accessories." Donahue also notes that it is possible to find "blouses reminiscent of Plains Indians shirts and bathrobes inspired by Pueblan textiles" from 1918 to the 1920s in the Sears mail order catalog.

Sometimes an individual has been responsible for stimulating interest in North American Indian styles. Millicent Rogers, heiress to the Standard Oil fortune, spent much of her life in New Mexico. She was one of the fashion icons of the 1930s and 1940s and an individual with a highly original fashion sense. Her adoption of elements of Navajo art and dress focused attention on the styles she preferred. Her interest in Navajo garments and jewelry has continued to inspire twenty-first-century designers. Designers Jeff Mahshie and Julie Chaiken cited Rogers and the styles she wore as the "starting point" for their codesigned collection of February 2007.

Hand-sewn quillwork jacket, ca. 1860–1870, Canada. The embroidery, typical of that produced by the Huron First Nation people of Quebec, is thought to have been sewn by a Huron woman at L'Ancienne-Lorette. This example of Huron floral embroidery on fashionable feminine clothing at this time appears to be unique. © McCord Museum M7417. http://www.mccord-museum.qc.ca/en/

Fashion designers from New York to Paris have incorporated aspects of Indian design in their couture and ready-to-wear lines. Rifat Ozbek's 1989 collection used North American Indian feathers and beads on black-velvet sheath dresses. The fashion press reported that Anna Sui showed fringed suede in 2005, as well as North American Indian embroidery and Navajo jewelry. Issac Mizrahi, in 1991, designed what he called a "totem pole dress." North American Indian designers have noted that designer Ralph Lauren's use of materials and themes related to the art of the Southwest Indian tribes has served to educate the general public about the beauty of these materials.

North American Indian–inspired elements also appeared as one of the many eclectic elements in the dress of those who were part of the hippie movement of the 1960s. Perhaps the hippies identified with another countercultural group that was struggling for its rights, or they may have been attracted to Indian spiritual connections to nature and the earth that seemed to be different from mainstream Judeo-Christian beliefs. Headbands, fringed leather garments and purses, beaded decoration, and silver jewelry were some of the many items that showed up in hippie dress. Some North American Indians became participants in the hippie movement.

JEWELRY-MAKING AND DESIGN

Archaeological excavations show that the earliest people to arrive in North America used both local materials and those that traveled over continent-wide trade routes to create jewelry. After they began to trade with Europeans and Asians, new materials, such as glass beads and silver brooches, were added. Although some limited production of jewelry for trade or sale existed earlier, it was not until the 1930s that more widespread commercial production of jewelry for sale to those outside the community began in the Southwest. Indeed, it was only in the mid-nineteenth century that Navajos began making the silver jewelry that has become so popular. Turquoise was incorporated only in the latter part of that century, and concho belts made from silver shell-shaped disks began to be made about the same time.

By the end of the twentieth century, jewelry designed by talented North American Indian and First Nation designers and inexpensive copies of the traditional designs were available from coast to coast in both the United States and Canada. Among the more popular traditional motifs in earrings are feathers, which are a metaphor for birds and for the powers of the sky, and *dream catchers*, a netted hoop design intended to catch bad dreams. *Squash-blossom necklaces* of silver or silver and turquoise are widely sold. Missionaries discouraged the use of traditional beadwork design motifs, so designers incorporated them into the ornamental jewelry. In areas such as Alaska, local designers utilize bone and fossil ivory in necklaces, bracelets, and earrings that are bought as souvenirs by tourists. Some top designers not only create traditionally based designs but also have become known nationally for their original creations.

FASHIONABLE GARMENTS AND ACCESSORIES DESIGNS

At first designing was a hobby for most of these designers; they were trying to find a way to incorporate traditional designs in a contemporary way. When they found they were passionate about their chosen field, they struggled to do what they loved in a way that would earn them a living and reach a wider audience. Some designers began by applying art to clothing they already had, and they continued their work when they realized people were interested in their designs. Some chose to go back to school to better their skills.

In the more than forty years since the first designers began to gain recognition, the number of fine artisans from Canada, the Northwest Territories, and regions of the United States has grown and continues to grow. Some Canadians, such as Pam Baker and her T.O.C. Legends project, have become fairly well known. Tammy Beauvais is a Mohawk designer with her own fashion design company that opened in 1999. Her creations are sold in more than forty boutiques in Canada and the United States. She is especially well known for cashmere shawls she created for the wives of thirty-four heads of state when they attended a Summit of the Americas in Quebec. D'Arcy Moses is a member of the South Slave Dene nation and lives in the Northwest Territories of Canada. He gained a strong reputation for work in fur. The hallmark of the work of Dorothy Grant is designs she creates that incorporate Haida art. Sold in stores in both Canada and the United States, she includes men's and women's coats, handbags, briefcases, and wallets in her collections. Angela DeMontigny lives and works in Ontario and uses elements from Chippewa, Cree, and Métis art in hand-painted and beaded work. Her creations are sold not only in the United States and Canada but also in Europe. Ronald Green, who distributes work under the trade name Ronald Everett, is from the Tsimshian community of Lax KwaLaams in northern British Columbia, and his inspiration is drawn from his heritage. He develops ideas that he says grow out of stories, masks, powwows, and potlatches. Dene Fur Clouds, a design firm based in the Northwest Territories of Canada, has

This 1920s bathrobe (center) is printed with geometric designs similar to those used by North American Indians of the Southwest region. Dover Publications, *Everyday Fashions of the Twenties.*

developed a line that specializes in fur. Products include fur knits made into sweaters, vests, and a wide range of accessory items.

In October 2006, the Indian Craft Shop and the Interior Museum of the U.S. Department of the Interior joined together to present a fashion show called "The American Indian Influence in Fashion." Among the North American Indian designers whose work was featured were Virginia Yazzie-Ballenger (Navajo) and Kathy "Elk Woman" Whitman (Mandan, Hidatsa, Artikaras). Virginia Yazzie-Ballenger has been the designer for a firm called Navajo Spirit Southwestern Wear since its founding in 1984. The firm makes both contemporary Western wear and traditional Navajo garments. Kathy Whitman is a sculptor and is also known for her jewelry. Hand-painted shawls made by Red Nations Art were also shown.

Patricia Michaels lives and works in New Mexico. Her work is known for use of unusual textures, and she stresses that it is important to her to blend tradition and contemporary style. Margaret Wood, a Navajo, creates wearable art and quilts. After working for more than twenty years, she is known for her modern adaptations of traditional garments, and she presents some of these ideas in her book *Native American Tradition.*

OBJECTIVES OF THE DESIGNERS

A similar theme runs through the statements made by and about these designers. Their objective, no matter where they are located or what their native heritage, is to express their tradition through the medium of dress. Those traditions may relate to the materials used for their creations, the vocabulary of ornament that they incorporate, or the style of dress that is intrinsic to the items produced.

Only toward the end of the twentieth century have First Nations designers begun expressing themselves through the medium of dress. When asked why she chose fashion design as their medium of expression, designer Pam Baker explains:

> Dress equals identity. These designers have come a long way from the way the Residential School era had crushed our pride. Now we are working towards gaining and instilling pride back into the communities, especially our youth. We are selling our stories, and educating about where we have come from. We love the art, then we experiment with fine fabrics, traditional fabrics. On the West Coast many of the Northern tribes, upon trading in the 1800s, became familiar with wool, and utilized this fabric for traditional regalia; for button blankets with their crests appliquéd. The button blanket of my relations inspired me, the beauty, and the strength of the family crests, clan design. Many of our designers use the fabrics and designs that they view at potlatches and pow-wows.

The aforementioned designers usually utilize their tribal designs in their work or incorporate art that reflects their heritage or creates contemporary versions of these traditional ideas. The customers for their work vary. Some customers are First Nations and North American Indian people. Most items designed are for women, although native men sometimes order replicas of the traditional dress of their fathers or grandfathers or ask to have a wedding garment designed. Some buyers are collectors of wearable art. These may include celebrities and art enthusiasts. Museums take great interest in the work. On occasion non-natives want the opportunity to enjoy the beauty of these cultures through dress.

Many designers do only custom orders, and people say that they enjoy going through the design process and fittings and having an opportunity to provide input. Designers also work on special orders and traditional wear. When designers have the opportunity to replicate something that had been worn by their ancestors, they speak of the joy of seeing a piece that may have been checked out of a museum that allows them to view and look closely at the work of their people.

Many of these designers receive a lot of attention from the media. Sometimes several designers will join to showcase their work together. Involvement in the fashion industry is difficult, often due to lack of resources. Funding is hard to obtain, and designers speak of how more training in the field of business would assist more potential designers to be financially successful. At the same time, attitudes in the mainstream fashion industry show a lack of understanding of some of the goals of native designers. One designer reported that when she met with industry representatives, she was told, "I can sell your product all day long, without the artwork." This is not the message First Nations designers want to bring to their customers. Instead, they see their objective as educating the public about who they are. They want people to know that there are First Nations people working on being self-sufficient, moving away from dependency. They believe that the next generation will have the foresight and tools to succeed more quickly, yet retain their unique identity.

North American Indian and First Nations designers are not immune to the globalization that the fashion industries have undergone. With many artists now moving toward entrepreneurship, they want to move into new products, such as accessories and footwear. They have taken advantage of the lower production costs available in China and arrange for manufacture there or elsewhere in Asia. They expect that keeping costs lower will make their products and designs more accessible.

SOURCES OF INSPIRATION AND USE OF LOCAL MATERIALS

North American Indian and First Nations designers utilize design motifs and materials that they know from having been raised in their own particular culture. In the Northwest region, elements of clan designs play an important role. But a designer will use

Chilkat cape, ca. 2000. The design is inspired by the chilkat blanket, traditionally made by the Tlingit people of the Pacific Northwest Coast. Courtesy of Pam Baker.

only designs appropriate to his or her clan and then only limited elements of the designs. Button blankets made of wool with mother-of-pearl buttons and chilkat blankets made of goat wool are another source of inspiration that might be tied into contemporary design. The ornamentation on a button blanket represents a particular clan, and the designs on them represent the thunderbird, killer whale, and the like. Chilkat blankets showcase hierarchy, chieftainship, or royalty. But care is taken not to offend members of the community by making exact reproductions.

In the Southwest, some of the designs produced have had an interesting historical journey. Both the Navajo and Apache women adapted the Victorian dress that they saw Anglo women wearing in the mid- to late nineteenth century. The Navajo style that developed had a velvet or velveteen blouse worn with a long, full-tiered cotton skirt. Present-day Navajo designers, in turn, have produced items of dress that derive from these garments. This is one of the styles associated with the aforementioned Millicent Rogers, who adopted it and helped to make it popular. During the Victorian period, Apache women wore full gathered skirts and loosely fitted overblouses. This *camp dress*, as it was called, has also served as a basis for designs by North American Indian designers.

The culture and history of the region from which the designer comes may be related to the kinds of materials that a designer favors. Several designers and design firms from Canada place special emphasis on using fur in their designs, whereas Navajo designers from the Southwest may choose velvet or velveteen and cotton. White pearl buttons on dark backgrounds appear in some of the designs from the Northwest. Patchwork designs, associated with the Seminoles of the Southeast, have been reproduced. Fringing in leather or fabric is often associated with Plains Indians and is incorporated into some designs.

However, designers do not feel themselves limited to the materials associated with North American Indians and First Nations people. Pam Baker speaks of progressing from early designs where she worked with the wool fabrics associated with her tradition to manipulating more upscale fabrics; taking velvet, for example, throwing it in the washer, applying a devore printing process, which burns out some of the fibers in a design, and then dyeing it.

The success of some designers and the notice that has come to their work will probably stimulate other designers to enter this field. But not all native people appreciate what the designers are doing; some people object to the use of cultural material in their work. The designers respond that many nonnative companies are promoting their versions of aboriginal art and making a profit. They believe it is better for them to create these styles than to have it be done by those who do not know and respect the culture. Native designers, they say, are very aware of what lines that they cannot cross.

Snapshot: One First Nations Fashion Designer's Journey

Pam Baker, whose ancestral name is Hi-mi-ka-las, is a fashion designer of First Nations heritage who lives and works in North Vancouver, British Columbia, Canada. This snapshot provides a glimpse into the path that she followed in seeking to incorporate unique aspects of native traditions into her designs of items of dress. While the route she followed will not be exactly the same as that taken by other designers of native heritage, the role of heritage in inspiring the designer is echoed in statements made by almost all First Nations and North American Indian designers.

As a child growing up on the Capilano Indian Reservation in the Squamish Nation traditional territory and attending public school, this future designer did not take much interest in her father's Coast Salish traditions and culture. But she did become strongly connected to the traditions and art of her Kwakiutl mother. Here, she found artists reviving both traditional and contemporary arts. She found role models, respected the elders, and loved the traditional dance, the language, and the art. Her family participated in the spiritual event called the potlatch.

Her first connection with fashion came when she was seventeen and enrolled in a fashion-merchandising program in order to get some job training. Unexpectedly, she enjoyed the classes and realized that she could apply an interest in art to her work with clothing. As a young adult, she left the Northwest and after a few years took a job in retailing, followed by a job with an American Indian Employment and Training Program. Here, a more serious interest in fashion began, as she began assisting in coordinating fashion shows. From this experience she felt that the fashion show would be the kind of experience that would help young girls in the reservation community to develop self-esteem.

Acting on this idea, Pam started designing in 1988 when she established workshops that she called "Touch of Culture." She has said of her entry into the fashion field, "I personally fell into it, by loving clothes and the art of my people." Her objective with Touch of Culture was to provide creative First Nations people a stage on which they could showcase their culture. Most of the participants were aboriginal women and teens. The fashion shows they presented provided opportunities to display the talents of First Nations models, designers, and artists.

After two years leading Touch of Culture, she realized that additional training was necessary if she wanted to move the project ahead. She entered Capilano College in North Vancouver and majored in textile arts. Pam has said about her decision to go back to school, "I felt that I was not smart enough as a young girl to go to college, until a role model entered my life." That role model, the owner of the Blanche McDonald Modeling School in Vancouver, was a First Nations woman. Eventually Pam was hired to teach and design a program to teach self-esteem to young First Nations individuals.

After earning a diploma at Capilano, she saw the need for additional technical expertise in fashion design. She moved with her two children to Los Angeles, where she entered Otis College of Art and Fashion Design, earning a B.F.A. degree in 1997. The designer credits Otis College with providing her with the necessary understanding of the fashion industry in North America, business acumen, and the essential technical skills that have enabled her to accomplish her goals. She returned to Canada determined to share her experiences and education with her people. Her objective was to develop a viable long-term business that would employ First Nations people. Beginning by creating wearable art that incorporated her unique First Nations designs, she moved on to this new undertaking.

In 1998, T.O.C. (Touch of Culture) Legends opened its doors. Located on the Capilano Reserve in North Vancouver, Canada, the venture incorporates an accredited/designated school of design, a production facility, and an office where Pam can design. The underlying purpose of the enterprise is to provide First Nations people with the opportunity to explore how modern technology and style can be blended with traditional values and symbols.

Pam Baker's description of her own design inspirations illustrates how First Nations and North American Indian designers utilize their heritage in design. She says,

> I design with my Kwakiutl and Coast Salish background. I am of Squamish/Kwakiutl/Tlingit/Haida ancestry; my father was Squamish from Coast Salish Territory, Southern B.C., and my mother is Kwakiutl of Kingcome Inlet/Fort Rupert, Northern Vancouver Island. Kwakiutl art is renowned with art collectors, including totem poles and masks. The Coast Salish art has been a little slower in reviving the art of the past; recently, there has been more research by our people.

She credits close relatives who were instrumental in reviving tribal art forms. They included Mungo Martin, who was active as an artist, made replicas of artifacts from the Kwakiutl culture, and was a skilled restorer of totem poles. Henry Hunt, an artist and principal carver at the British Columbia Provincial Museum, was her uncle. His son, Tony Hunt, was an influ- ence, not only for his art but also in his efforts to establish apprenticeships for First Nations artists so they could preserve Northwest Coast carving traditions. From her research, the designer, who had been focusing on her Kwakiutl background, also began incorporating Salish styles in order to represent both of her parents' tribes.

These experiences have contributed to the structure of the training that students undertake at T.O.C. Legends. The students begin designing pieces that reflect their culture and nation. Through research they find their own identity and become aware of what symbols and designs they can (and have the right to) use. They learn the answers to questions such as: What clan do I come from? What was the clothing worn by my ancestors? How can I make this contemporary? Part of the focus of their course of study is on recognizing the contributions of others. Students in the school are assigned research on renowned twentieth- and twenty-first-century First Nations (Canadian) artists such as George Little Child and Norval Morreseau and Canadian Emily Carr, a renowned artist from the Northwest region.

Each year the Touch of Culture Native Training Institute holds an annual fashion show that raises funds for First Nations youth. It is attended and supported by the community and individuals who are interested in the art. The students' pieces are showcased at this gala event, which also provides the students with opportunities to work with and coordinate fashion shows on their own and with their classmates and alumni.

How this designer became part of the fashion world is, in some ways, not unlike the route that any designer might take. Her interest in design developed, she saw the need to get the necessary skills and tools through training, and she got that training. Mentors were important influences. Her work gradually came to the attention of the fashion world and was recognized. But what her work, and the work of other First Nations and North American Indian designers, has that is different from the mainstream fashion business is that it is inspired by unique traditions that they can interpret not only to their customers but also to their communities.

References and Further Reading

Berlo, Janet C., and Ruth B. Phillips. *Native North American Art*. New York: Oxford University Press, 1998.

Conn, Richard. *Robes of White Shell and Sunrise. Personal Decorative Arts of the Native American*. Denver, CO: Denver Art Museum, 1974.

Donahue, Mary. "Modern American Fashion Design American Indian Style." In *PART*, online journal of the City University of New York's Ph.D. program in art history. http://dsc.gc.cuny.edu/part/part9/identities/articles/donah.html.

Her Many Horses, Emil. *Identity by Design*. New York: Harper Collins; and Washington, DC: Smithsonian Institution, 2007.

Native American Expressive Culture. Washington, DC: Smithsonian Institution, AKWE:KON Press, and the National Museum of the American Indian, 1994.

Wood, Margaret. *Native American Fashion: Modern Adaptations of Traditional Designs*. Phoenix, AZ: Native American Fashions, 1997.

Pamela C. Baker and Phyllis G. Tortora

See also Western Wear.

PART 5

Cultural Groups in the United States and Canada

Introduction to Cultural Groups

- Dress as Communication
- Dress and Cultural Groups
- Movement of Culturally Based Styles into Mainstream Fashion

Dress is a part of the material culture of the society in which it is worn. *Material culture* consists of the artifacts created or utilized in a society or community. Through the material culture of a society, it is possible to explore the nonmaterial culture: the values, ideas, attitudes, and assumptions present in that society. Elements of the material culture, such as dress, are often related to the nonmaterial culture of a society in complex ways.

DRESS AS COMMUNICATION

Some scholars who study dress consider it to be a nonverbal means of communication. Visual clues can be provided through various elements of dress. If the observer understands the "language of dress" of a particular culture, in some situations words may not be needed. For example, in North America, uniforms can suggest occupation. A soldier, sailor, or marine in uniform is readily identifiable as a member of the military forces, and even beyond that, many people in the United States would be able to tell whether they were looking at a soldier, sailor, or marine. The Royal Canadian Mounted Police have a distinctive uniform with a unique hat style. An item worn on a chain around the neck, such as a cross or a star-of-David, or a head scarf can convey religious affiliation. A tuxedo can announce participation in some kind of formal event. Dress does not replace the spoken language but augments it.

In turn, the spoken language may reflect messages from dress. For example, "war paint," specific ways of painting the body and the face in various North American Indian and First Nations tribes, was used to signal hostile intentions. In twentieth-century North American slang, the term *war paint* referred to elaborate makeup worn by women who were out to conquer the figurative "war between the sexes." The phrases *blue-collar workers* and *white-collar workers* immediately identify people as laborers or office workers.

Within a larger culture, smaller groups of people who voluntarily affiliate are known as *subcultures*. Members of subcultures often announce their membership by adopting dress that is unique to that subculture. Sometimes the messages sent are obvious, but often they are so subtle that nonmembers do not notice them. Lesbian, gay, bisexual, or transgendered (LGBT) communities have developed some symbols that other members understand. The use of the astrological sign for the planet Mercury signifies that a person is transgendered. The masculine is represented by the crescent moon at the top and the feminine, by the cross at the bottom. The ring stands for the individual, and the female and male are balanced at either side. The Greek letter

The spoken language may reflect messages from dress. *War paint* is a U.S. expression that refers to the face paint North American Indians applied when they were about to engage in warfare. In the twenty-first century, some use it to refer to the makeup applied by women when preparing to go out and enter a different kind of warfare between the sexes. Image Copyright Adam Borkowski, 2007. Used under license from Shutterstock.com

lambda (λ) was used to symbolize the gay liberation movement in New York in 1970 and in 1974 by the International Gay Rights Congress, after which it became popular internationally.

Clothing can serve as a public signal of group affiliation. Probably the most obvious example is the T-shirt. T-shirts are produced with a wide variety of printed slogans, graphics, and logos. The text can proclaim membership in groups ranging from fans of a particular musician or music group to male and female members of motorcycle-riding groups. A T-shirt may make it evident that the wearer is a privileged member of a group that visited a famous place or participated in an important event. Baseball caps may signal support for a particular sports team, possibly in the hope of meeting others who share their passion. Other items of dress, such as class and school rings or tattoos for members of street gangs, proclaim "I am a member of this exclusive group."

DRESS AND CULTURAL GROUPS

Entering a new environment can lead to changes in cultural practices in relation to dress. Immigrants to a new land may combine elements of dress from several cultures. A number of scholars who study dress have looked at how people make these adaptations. Mary Ellen Roach and Kathleen Musa have called such styles "mixtures." Tonya Erekosima and Joanne Eicher have called the process through which these mixtures are formed *cultural authentication*, and they note that styles are rarely adopted without some changes. Explorers and settlers in North America after 1492 tended to come from Western Europe. These settlers transplanted their own culture and forms of dress. What they brought with them and, later, the supplies they had shipped to North America came from their home or other European countries. Some groups, such as the earliest French settlers in Quebec, Canada, the *habitants*, preserved some aspects of local peasant dress in their clothing, but Canadian dress historian Jacqueline Beaudoin-Ross has reported that "on the whole, much of what the Quebec rural women wore throughout the centuries seems to be similar to that worn by many in America."

Information about current fashion was sought from European sources. Explorers started to wear mixtures of dress more quickly because they began wearing North American Indian and First Nations items, such as moccasins and deerskin leggings and shirts. These garments were far more practical for the rugged environments that they encountered in their travels than stiff, heavy boots and woven fabrics. In part 4 of this volume, articles describe some of the adoptions and adaptations of European dress made by native people, but overall, settlers remained firmly Eurocentric and adopted rather limited mixtures of dress.

Eurocentric or Western fashionable dress predominated in the United States and Canada from the arrival of the first European settlers until the twenty-first century. Later immigrants, however, came not only from Europe but from all parts of the globe. Often their dress was markedly different from that of the Western dress of the North Americans who had arrived in earlier decades and centuries. The results of their encounters with new forms of dress varied widely. Enslaved people had virtually no control over the dress they were required to wear. Their clothing was given to them by their owners. The first generation of African Americans might carry permanent body modifications made in their native lands, but not only were opportunities to practice rites related to dress gone, but subsequent generations were also likely to be separated from others who shared their places of origin. As a result, valued traditions could not be preserved. Only a few examples of contemporary dress, such as the bandanna head scarf, can be ascribed to their African origins.

Some groups immigrated as intentional communities. An *intentional community* is a small community that purposely joins together because of certain attitudes and values that unite them. The intentional community may have a basis in a particular religion or may be organized around certain secular attitudes and values. Examples of religious intentional communities include the Amish, the Hutterites, the Old Believers, and the Shakers. Secular intentional communities are often utopian groups such as the Oneida Society or the Amana Colony.

Those intentional communities that are religiously based often establish specific dress practices that exemplify tenets of their faith. To this day, the Amish display their antimilitaristic values

by eliminating any display of buttons from their clothing. This is said to grow out of the persecutions they suffered at the hands of soldiers wearing uniforms with prominent brass buttons.

The dress of a number of religious communities is based on passages from the books on which their faith is based. Old Believers and Amish people believe that the Bible requires men to refrain from cutting their hair or shaving off their beards. Orthodox Jews avoid wearing any fabric made from a mixture of linen and wool, forbidden by the Torah because it was sacred to the ancient Egyptians. Some groups from the Judeo-Christian tradition base the requirement for women to wear a head covering of some type on Biblical exhortations telling women to cover their heads when praying.

Secular intentional communities also based their dress on their beliefs. The Transcendentalists of Brook Farm in Massachusetts refused to wear cotton because slave labor was used in its harvesting or to wear wool because it was taken from sheep without their consent. Equality of the sexes was stressed in the Oneida Community, and women wore shorter skirts over long bloomers, a style that allowed them greater mobility than the mainstream fashions of the mid-1800s.

Members of many religious groups may not choose to live apart from the society of which they are a part, but they do wish to conform to the dress requirements of their faith. Examples

Second-generation Greek American woman and third-generation Greek American child dressed in Greek ethnic styles in order to perform in a dance at a Greek Festival in Honolulu, Hawai'i, ca. 2000. Courtesy of Victoria Shiroma and Nicholas Tortora.

include the wearing of a head scarf by Muslim women, special hairstyles for men of some Hasidic sects of Orthodox Judaism, or turbans worn by followers of the Sikh religion. Schools may sometimes attempt to restrict the wearing of religious symbols, and court actions may follow. In one incident in 1994, a Quebec school in Canada forbade a young Islamic woman to wear the *hijab*, a head scarf worn by devout Muslim women. Her family brought the case to the Quebec Human Rights Commission, which ruled that "Quebec schools did not have the right to prohibit any student from wearing religious attire (be it a Sikh turban, a Jewish yarmulke, a Christian cross, or Islamic hijab)." The commission, in another case, ruled against a Muslim school in Quebec that required non-Muslim teachers to wear the hijab while teaching.

As immigrants arrived in greater and greater numbers, they had to make various adaptations to living in new countries. The United States and Canada took somewhat different approaches to their immigrants. In the melting-pot approach of the United States, immigrants were expected to become Americans, and while they might call themselves "African Americans" or "Italian Americans" and preserve elements of their heritage, they were expected to blend into the larger community. The Canadian pattern has been called a "mosaic," an approach enshrined in the Canadian Multicultural Act of 1988.

Some immigrants do not want to stand out as different and try to conform to local standards of dress as quickly as possible. During the huge waves of immigration to the United States around the turn of the twentieth century, immigrants spoke of not wanting to appear to be greenhorns or new arrivals. In the museum at Ellis Island, the point of arrival for immigrants in the nineteenth and early twentieth centuries, visitors can read about settlement houses in New York City in the 1920s where donated American hats and dresses were provided for kerchief-wearing immigrant women who arrived before their husbands. When the spouses arrived later, they would be greeted by "modern-looking" women who were on their way to becoming "real" Americans.

In Canada, the choice to wear ethnic clothing in the workplace is protected by law unless there is an occupational requirement to wear a particular type of dress or if wearing an ethnic garment would present a safety hazard. In 1990, a Sikh officer in the Royal Canadian Mounted Police objected to being required to wear the traditional Mounties' felt hat, and he eventually won the right to wear his turban as part of his uniform.

But although the law is on the side of Canadians who prefer to wear traditional dress to work, they may experience prejudice from their fellow workers. One worker reported that a colleague had commented that her dress was inappropriate because it was ethnic.

Sometimes ethnic groups may develop their own styles in dress. Until the 1960s and 1970s, African Americans tried to conform to mainstream fashion. With the advent of the civil rights movement, the slogan "black is beautiful" came into being, and styles inspired by African textile arts and dress styles were adopted by many African Americans. Popular elements of dress included African fabrics, such as the colorful, traditional *kente cloth* from Ghana; the *dashiki*, a colorful, collarless man's shirt; and hairstyles such as the *Afro* and *cornrow braids*. Religious motivations may underlie some forms of ethnic dress, as in the aforementioned Muslim head scarves or the Russian peasant–inspired shirts and dresses of Old Believers.

Other groups use ethnic dress for special occasions. Greek Americans often wear traditional Greek dress at festivals where dances of their country of origin are performed. The Hmong people who immigrated to the United States after the Vietnam War are especially known for their use of colorful traditional dress and emphasis on wearing these garments and accessories for holidays and celebrations. Use of traditional dress as costume for dancing groups is common when the dancers come from a culture with known dress traditions. One of the best known of the styles associated with North American Indian and First Nations people is the *jingle dress*, made to wear while dancing. The metal jingles add sound to the beauty of the dance.

MOVEMENT OF CULTURALLY BASED STYLES INTO MAINSTREAM FASHION

The use of traditional dress as an inspiration for mainstream fashion is not new. Examples of ethnically inspired fashions can be found in the work of fashion designers in Paris and in other fashion centers. In the years after 1907, women's styles showed strong influences from traditional Chinese and Japanese dress. In many fashion publications of that period, one can find examples of garments in which the cut and shape is clearly based on that of the kimono. Asian design motifs were evident in surface patterns. Hats based on the so-called coolie hats of China were worn.

Some ethnically derived styles have become staples that reappear when the current fashion line is congenial. Wide, gathered *dirndl skirts*, based on those from Germanic folk dress; fabric frog closures that are part of traditional Chinese dress; and fringed leather items based on North American Indian styles are but a few examples.

Fashions resulting from the constant search by designers and merchandisers for new styles are sometimes hard to distinguish from spontaneous adoptions by young people of ethnic styles that carry a symbolic statement. The popularity of the distinctive black-and-white Palestinian head scarf, the *kaffiyeh*, worn

Hip-hop clothes. This style emerged in the 1970s in South Bronx, New York City. Mainstream elements of hip-hop fashion include baseball caps worn backward, baggy pants worn without a belt, and sneakers worn with untied shoelaces. Image Copyright Tatiana Sayig, 2007. Used under license from Shutterstock.com

by some young Americans in the late 1980s, was most likely a political statement of support for the Palestinian people. But by 2007, the *New York Times* was reporting that the head scarf was being wrapped around the neck. When asked, those wearing the scarf said that they were not Palestinian sympathizers but were simply trying to appear fashionable. The woven patterns of the traditional kente cloth fabrics of Africa moved from being an authentic part of the "black is beautiful" symbolism of the 1960s to mainstream fashion when these designs appeared in printed products ranging from neckties to umbrellas.

It is not always easy to assign style origins to a particular ethnic group. Hoop earrings have long been associated with gypsies and are frequently a basic element of a child's Halloween gypsy costume. But hoop earrings are part of the traditional dress of many cultures. Archaeologists find them dating back as far as 3000 B.C.E. The specific styles of hoop earrings can range from small, discreet hoops encircling the earlobe to hoops so large they almost brush the shoulder. This latter style gained great popularity in the years shortly after 2000. One of the media stars who was associated with them is Jennifer Lopez, a Hispanic singer, so some fashion writers saw them as having origins in Hispanic dress. Others may disagree, seeing their origins in the dress of some African regions and connecting them to hip-hop styles.

The fashion industry in North America and in other parts of the world is constantly trying to find new fashion ideas. When something new appears, fashion designers use it as a basis for their designs. Hip-hop, a *street style* that first appeared in the late 1970s in the South Bronx in New York City where young African Americans lived, illustrates the process particularly well. Hip-hop beginnings are associated with the appearance of a new kind of music called *rap music* and a style of street dancing to accompany it called *break dancing*. Gradually a new and distinctive dress style was embraced by the mostly African American musicians and dancers. As the popularity of rap music spread beyond the inner city so did these fashions. Fans were the first to copy the clothes. Soon, many elements of hip-hop fashion spread into mainstream fashion, especially among the young. Baseball caps worn backward, baggy pants worn without a belt, and sneakers worn with untied shoelaces were among the first items to be copied. Certain fashion designers became status symbols in the hip-hop world and benefited from the attention. Some of

these designers, such as Sean Combs, moved from the performing world into the fashion world. Subsequently. Sean Combs won a number of fashion awards. Unlike many fashions that have a short life span, hip-hop has not faded away and has remained a factor for several decades.

References and Further Reading

Alvi, Sajida, Homa Hoodfar, and Sheila McDonough, eds. *The Muslim Veil in North America: Issues and Debates.* Toronto: Women's Press, 2003.

Beaudoin-Ross, Jacqueline. "'A la Canadienne' Once More: Some Insights into Quebec Rural Female Dress." *Dress* 7 (1981): 69–81.

Bhandari, Aparita. "Workers Bring Culture to Their Cubicle." *Globe and Mail*, Toronto, Canada, 28 September 2005.

Erekosima, Tonya V., and Joanne B. Eicher. "Kalabari 'Cut Thread' and 'Pulled Thread' Clothing: An Example of Cultural Authentication." *African Arts* 14, no. 2 (1981): 48.

Kaiser, Susan. *The Social Psychology of Clothing: Symbolic Appearances in Context.* 2nd ed. New York: Fairchild, 1997.

Khan, Sheema. "Banning Hijab in Canada: It Can Happen Anywhere." http://www.soundvision.com/Info/news/hijab/hjb.canada.asp (accessed 29 March 2007).

Kim, Kibum. "Where Some See Fashion, Others See Politics." *New York Times*, 11 February 2007.

McCracken, Grant. "Clothing as Language." In *Culture and Consumption: New Approaches to the Symbolic Character of Consumer Goods and Activities*, 57–70. Bloomington: Indiana University Press, 1991.

Roach, Mary Ellen, and Kathleen Musa. *New Perspectives on the History of Western Dress.* New York: Nutriguides, 1980.

Yu, Haekyung L., Chanju Kim, Juhyeon Lee, and Nayoung Hong. "An Analysis of Modern Fashion Designs as Influenced by Asian Ethnic Dress." *Journal of Consumer Studies and Home Economics* 25, no. 4 (2001): 309–321.

Phyllis G. Tortora

See also Antifashion; Music and Dress in the United States; Music and Dress in Canada; Influence of North American Indian and First Nations Dress on Mainstream Fashion.

Western Wear

North American Western style is known by some familiar materials and details, including embossed or fringed leather, silver conchos used to prevent leather ties from pulling through leather garments, and patterns woven in bright earth tones or primary colors. These materials and patterns did not rise spontaneously but developed over a five hundred–year period. The history of Western style began in Salamanca, Spain; picked up influences from non-Western frontiersmen such as Davy Crockett and Daniel Boone; and added elements of Mexican vaquero (cattle herder) and cowboy dress, as well as motifs from North American Indians. The elements of Western style developed from patterns that seemed appropriate in particular times or in response to environmental conditions and to changes in technology and culture. Six main influences shaped what is now defined as Western style: Spanish dress, frontier dress, North American Indian design, cowboy dress, rodeo clothing, and movie costume. Two of these influences—Spanish dress and North American Indian designs—came in and out of favor because of larger political events. Technology has also had a profound effect on the ways that North American Western style has been interpreted over time.

SPANISH DRESS

Most historians acknowledge Spain as the origin of the New World cattle culture, which included the dress of Spanish landholders who wore low-crowned hats, bolero jackets, sashes, tight-fitting trousers, and spurred boots. The dress of the *charro*, the gentleman rancher of Mexico, began to influence ideas of Western style by the 1830s. These included the use of embroidery and braid; silver embellishments, including conchos and buttons; and tooled leathers that are still defined as Western. Overt Spanish influence remained strong in popular images and the gear of cowboys until the Spanish-American War of 1898. Interestingly, when Owen Wister's *The Virginian*, a book about Wyoming cowboys, was portrayed on stage in 1904, Trampas, the villain, was dressed in Spanish-style clothing. It was not until the 1910s, when rodeo cowgirls began wearing sashes and boleros with their leather, divided skirts, or jodhpurs, that Spanish influences reappeared in Western style. By the end of the 1920s, rodeo cowgirls dressed in flamboyantly Spanish-styled bell-bottomed trousers trimmed

Cowgirl and cowboy on horseback, Newton, Kansas, 1908. Library of Congress Prints and Photographs Division LC-DIG-ggbain-02211.

with braid and brightly colored embroidery along with fringed sashes and boleros that matched their trousers.

FRONTIER DRESS

Stereotypical frontier dress consisting of fringed leather is also an important part of Western design. The fringes that edged leather garments were practical as well as decorative. Rain would run along the fringes and then get flipped away instead of puddling along seams and hems. Images of frontiersmen Davy Crockett and Daniel Boone usually show them wearing fringed leather coats and trousers. Fur traders and mountain men found that leather withstood the rigors of frontier life far better than cloth clothing; furthermore, leather pants and shirts could be made on the frontier when manufactured fabrics were not available. Buffalo Bill, the originator of Buffalo Bill's Wild West Show, and his cronies wore fringed and fur-trimmed leather as well as broad-brimmed hats when they performed on stage in dramas depicting cowboys, gun sharps, and buffalo hunters. Buffalo Bill's leather coat was even imitated by General George Armstrong Custer, who is famous for losing the Battle of the Little Big Horn. Annie Oakley and other women who performed in Wild West shows included fringe as part of their costumes when they appeared in front of adoring audiences. Theodore Roosevelt affiliated himself with the West during his 1904 presidential campaign by being pictured in a fringed leather shirt along with a wide-brimmed Stetson hat.

Wealthy Easterners such as Roosevelt and Owen Wister made the West a popular vacation spot, especially as railroad travel became easier by the late nineteenth and early twentieth centuries. It was not long before ranchers began to accept paying guests who were known as *dudes*, and the ranches became known as dude ranches. Western dude ranches catered to the Eastern upper class with a taste for adventure and created yet another venue for the development of fringed Western style. Larry Larom, owner of Valley Ranch dude ranch in Wyoming, was often pictured in his fringed leather shirt as part of the advertising campaign to lure Eastern dudes to the not-so-wild West of the 1930s. Fringed leather skirts and jackets were almost required for the dude-ranch wives who were expected to be gracious hostesses as well as behind-the-scenes managers. Fringed garments, even in the twenty-first century, are instantly recognized as Western style worldwide.

NORTH AMERICAN INDIAN DRESS

North American Indian designs that are the most integral part of Western style include not only fringe but beadwork—long beads, known as *hairpipes*, that are made from wing bones—as well as silverwork inlaid with turquoise, silver belts, velvet blouses, and concho buttons. North American Indian style was not in favor during much of the nineteenth century because of conflicts caused as Euro–North Americans encroached on territory originally occupied by native tribes, which were often portrayed as brutal savages by artists. By the 1890s, most nomadic Great Plains tribes were confined to reservations, and artists tended to picture a romantic "noble savage," doomed to extinction. This created a desire to learn more about these people and their arts. Among the first to take advantage of this curiosity was Buffalo Bill, who included Chief Red Cloud of the Lakota Sioux Nation and other Plains tribes as part of his Wild West show, thus exposing people to North American Indian designs.

Among the most popular North American Indian designs was the swastika, popular in cowboy gear from the late nineteenth century until the 1930s. When Hitler chose it to represent Nazi Germany, the symbol became unacceptable to Europeans and North Americans. Zigzag and diamond patterns, influenced by motifs used in beadwork, often appeared in hard goods such as spurs or decorated revolvers and in spur leathers and chaps (leather leg coverings). North American Indians often decorated their rifle butts with nail heads, and these patterns reappeared in spots (domed metal brads) that decorated all kinds of cowboy leather goods, including hatbands, wrist cuffs, chaps, and spur leathers.

In addition, Navaho woven blankets and those woven by the Pendleton Woolen Mills for the Indian trade also became part of Western style. Blankets were used as cold-weather and ceremonial wraps by North American Indians and also were made into simply constructed coats similar to capotes (blanket coats) that were made from Hudson's Bay blankets. Most Western-wear catalogs still sell colorful blankets, and some sell outerwear for women and men made from the blankets.

Dude ranchers were also responsible for the popularity of North American Indian design because ranch stores in the northern Rocky Mountains offered Plains Indian beadwork and leather goods while those in Arizona and New Mexico offered Southwestern woven goods and silver. During the golden years of dude ranching in the 1920s and 1930s, wealthy dude-ranch visitors often spent summer months on ranches in Wyoming or Montana and, during the winter, vacationed at Arizona or New Mexico dude ranches. This helped to create a Western style that blended both northern and southern North American Indian designs and materials. Images of dudes show that they bought gloves with beaded gauntlets and beaded vests as well as silver squash-blossom necklaces and concho belts. A photograph of three dudines (female dudes) and the dude-ranch wife at Valley Ranch in Wyoming shows them wearing a blend of Western styles. One woman is wearing a squash-blossom necklace, velvet blouse, jodphurs (riding pants that are loose at the outer thigh but narrow at the knee), and knee-high boots, and she is holding a high-crowned hat. The second woman is wearing a broad-brimmed hat, a white shirt with rolled sleeves under a fringed vest, and denim overalls (a common term for denim trousers during the early twentieth century) with rolled hems to expose decorated cowboy boots. The third woman, the dude-ranch wife, is wearing a high-crowned, broad-brimmed hat with a satin shirt, fringed leather skirt, and cowboy boots decorated with reverse appliqué. The fourth woman is dressed Eastern style in a white shirt, woolen riding jacket, jodphurs, and knee-high boots.

COWBOY DRESS

The most important influence on Western style, however, is the cowboy. Studio portraits of cowboys wearing large hats, silk bandannas, fringed leather chaps, and high-heeled boots were sent by thousands of still adolescent boys to their families back East to prove that they had risen to the high rank of cowboy. In 1878, Teddy Blue Abbot described clothing that he bought in North Platte, Nebraska, after being paid for a cattle drive from Texas, as the kind of clothing that top hands (very skilled cowboys) wore. His new clothing, consisting of a Stetson hat (US$10), pants (US$12), and a laced-front shirt, made him feel as though he was perfectly dressed as a cowboy, which was worth so much more than the month's pay he spent to buy them. Most cowboys' clothing was functional, but even functional dress had some cowboy flair. The most symbolic of cowboy gear were chaps, which often had tooled leather belts and were decorated with fringe and metal or leather conchos that prevented leather lacing from tearing the somewhat brittle oak-tanned leather. Wooly chaps, most often made of Angora goat hide, originated among California vaqueros but were readily adopted by cowboys riding the range on the cold, windy northern plains.

Stetson hats were familiar all over North America, but those worn by cowboys were often distinctive because of the way they shaped the crowns and brims. John Rollinson, a Wyoming cowboy, wrote that in the 1890s most cowboys wore expensive, good-quality, high-crowned Stetson hats showing the results of hard wear. Much cheaper hats were used until cowboys could afford better ones. In his memoirs of working on the DHS ranch in Montana, John Barrows wrote of the brim of his cheap hat blowing down into his face. Frederick Remington's illustrations showed many cowboys wearing floppy brimmed hats that were likely made of cheap felt that would not hold shape, especially after suffering the abuse of wind, rain, and snow.

Cowboys wore a variety of types of pants; the most common on the northern Plains were woolen trousers that were intended for dress. They were more comfortable to wear than Levi's, which were made of stiff denim, but they were much more expensive. An example at the National Cowboy Museum in Oklahoma City is a pair of woolen trousers that has a square-cut top rather than the familiar slant-opening pocket; the square-cut top is still recognized as a feature of Western-cut trousers. Even though woolen trousers were preferred, many cowboys wore cheaper denim trousers. An advertisement for Levi Strauss in the *Yellowstone Journal* of Miles City, Montana, a ranching community, shows that Levi's overalls were marketed in the area. Major William Shepherd, an Englishman who traveled through Montana and Wyoming in 1884, wrote about seeing cowboys wearing new blue trousers with the paper label exhibiting the trademark and size still sewn to the waistband, indicating that denim overalls were also commonly worn.

Several of the reminiscences of cowboys say that they wore work shirts made of "hickory," which is described in an 1894 dry goods dictionary as a type of coarse shirting fabric that had hickory-like wearing quality. A shirt at the Cowboy and Western Heritage Museum is a type of hickory shirt that has an attached collar and placket front characteristic of work shirts. Images of cowboys show that they occasionally wore dress shirts without the starched removable collars normally attached to collar bands. Another favorite style worn by cowboys included shirts described in the Sears and Roebuck Catalog as laced-front "bicycle shirts."

Bandannas, an important wardrobe item, originated in India. The word *bandanna* comes from the East Indian word *bandhana*, which means tie-dyed in intricate patterns in two or three colors. These silken imports were eventually replaced by less expensive printed-cotton bandannas still familiar in the early twenty-first century.

High-heeled cowboy boots, said to have been developed in Coffeyville, Kansas, were another distinctive article of dress that marked cowboys in how they looked and also how they walked. John Rollinson remembered his first pair of real cowboy boots as nearly knee high with pull-on straps at the sides and having a five-inch star sewn in red and white thread at the front of each

one. His feet hurt because he bought the boots a size too small, the practice of most cowboys, until an older man showed him how to stretch the boots by filling them with oats that swelled when he poured water into them. When the boots had stretched enough to fit, he wore them until they dried.

Horses were goaded into action by spurs made in a wide variety of styles of plain steel or steel with silver inlay. A 1905 Western supply catalog listed the plainest styles for only US$5.00, while the most expensive, silver-inlaid spurs cost US$24.00. Spurs fastened to the boots with leathers that were usually decorated in floral or even North American Indian designs. The *rowels* (small wheels with radiating points) that fastened to the end of the spurs jingled with movement, but some spurs had additional jingles hanging near the rowels to provide additional sound.

Although firearms are not technically dress, no cowboy considered his outfit complete without one. Cold-weather gear rarely included expensive fur and fur-lined coats, but most cowboys could afford canvas coats with quilted or flannel linings that are now known as *chore coats*. The coats usually have a corduroy collar, which is more comfortable around the neck, and large patch pockets handy for gloves or tools. More expensive shearling coats made of sheep skin that appeared in the mid-twentieth century have become associated with Western style even though they were too costly for most ranchers.

RANCH WOMEN

Ranch women, who did outdoor jobs, generally wore clothing unsuited to their work but acceptable to society at large. An 1890s photograph of three Colorado girls branding cattle shows that they made few concessions to their work: They wore dresses with long skirts over tight-corseted waistlines, wide-brimmed hats, sturdy shoes, and leather gloves. Photographs taken of the Buckley sisters of Jordan, Montana, in about 1912 show them wearing mannish coats and boots with spurs but more acceptable skirts as they did their work. Even in rural ranch country there was pressure for women to conform to generally accepted standards of female dress. For example, in 1895, Evelyn Cameron, an English immigrant to Montana, wrote about her divided skirt with a modesty panel that buttoned over the front to disguise the fact it was bifurcated: "Although my costume was so full as to look like an ordinary walking dress when the wearer was on foot, it created a small sensation. So great at first was the prejudice against any divided garment in Montana that a warning was given me to abstain from riding on the streets of Miles City lest I might be arrested!" Many women rode sidesaddle rather than buck generally accepted opinion about appropriate female riding dress. Even modified riding habits could be dangerous. Kathleen Lindsay, of Montana, hung upside-down when she was bucked from her horse, and her skirt caught on the pommel of her sidesaddle. A friend, wrote, hearing the news, "I was so extremely sorry to hear of your accident on Dynamite, what a very narrow escape you had. What must your feelings have been when hanging onto the pommel by that fraud of a SAFETY skirt!!" By the 1890s, conventional sidesaddles were still most common, but riding-astride saddles, or *cross-saddles*, made specifically for women were more readily available, indicating that there was a corresponding change in attitude about women wearing dress appropriate for riding astride.

Three dudines (female dudes) and the dude-ranch wife at Valley Ranch in Wyoming wearing a blend of Western styles. One woman wears squash-blossom necklace, velvet blouse, jodhpurs, knee-high boots and holds a high-crowned hat. The second woman wears a broad-brimmed hat, a white shirt with rolled sleeves under a fringed vest, and denim overalls (a common term for denim trousers during the early twentieth century) with rolled hems to expose cowboy boots. The third woman, the dude-ranch wife, wears a high-crowned, broad-brimmed hat with a satin shirt, fringed leather skirt, and cowboy boots decorated with reverse appliqué. The fourth woman is dressed Eastern style in a white shirt, woolen riding jacket, jodhpurs, and knee-high boots. Buffalo Bill Historical Center, Cody, Wyoming; Gift of I.H. "Larry" Larom; P.14.69.1.

RODEO COWBOYS

Rodeos began during the open-range period of ranching history, which ended in the early twentieth century. They were contests between the cowboys of various ranches during the annual spring and fall roundups. Later, rodeos switched to cowboy-like activities (bulldogging, calf roping, saddle bronc, bareback bronc, and bull riding) performed in front of an audience and judges. The clothing they wore for these contests spanned from sports dress to more formal dress. Because most cowboys considered rodeo another form of athletic performance, some cowboys wore tight-fitting sweaters that were part of athletic dress in the early twentieth century. Other cowboys wore dress shirts and neckties along with their chaps and boots. Some rodeo companies regulated the types of clothing allowable, especially those that hired cowboys and cowgirls for exhibition rodeos that toured from Madison Square Garden in New York City to the Pendleton Roundup in Oregon. The dress for these rodeos included high-crowned hats and woolly chaps as well as large bandannas with long tails that bounced along with the Angora goat hair on the chaps. Batwing chaps, which were introduced to the cowboy trade during the 1890s, were chosen by rodeo cowboys because the flaps at the outer edge would flap wildly when the cowboys were riding bucking animals. Spots added to the edges caught the light, providing flash in addition to motion, especially when cowboys did not buckle the bottom snaps that held the chaps against their legs. Twenty-first-century rodeo cowboys wear chaps that are designed specifically for rodeo performances. These chaps, often embellished with Mylar overlays, buckle only to the knee, and the outer edges are trimmed with one-foot (one-third-meter) fringes that provide even more flash than woollies or the spot-trimmed batwings. In addition, some rodeo cowboys wear padded vests to protect them from slashing hooves of broncs and bulls. Helmets with face guards are new elements of rodeo dress that a few safety-minded cowboys are wearing. Most still wear the wide-brimmed hats that are such an important part of cowboy tradition.

No description of rodeo cowboy dress would be complete without discussing the *trophy plate* (a flat buckle that attaches to a belt), which cowboys receive as evidence of their skills. Trophy plates once included devices that resembled military metals hanging from ribbons and miniature spurs that were inscribed to illustrate where and when the prize was won. An early trophy plate bearing the legend "Worlds Champion Best All Round Cowboy Glendive Roundup 1919 Won by Geo. F. Gardner" was riveted to a wide bucking belt like those worn by some cowboys to protect their backs. By the end of the 1910s, plate buckles were wearable trophies awarded to champion cowboys along with saddles as prizes for their rodeo skills. The plates came in a variety of sizes, from wearable ones measuring one and one-half inches by two and one-half inches (about four centimeters by six centimeters), most common from the 1910s through the 1940s, to late-twentieth-century examples that measure seven inches by nine inches (about eighteen centimeters by twenty-three centimeters) and are too large to wear comfortably. The motifs on the earliest plates usually consisted of a written legend that showed where and when it was awarded and sometimes included the event, the location of the rodeo, and the name of the person who received it. By the 1920s, it was common to include the date, rodeo location, and image of the event edged with twisted-rope motifs to frame the plates. During the 1940s, red stones, probably garnets but called

"rubies," commonly embellished flowers that were placed in the corners of the fanciest trophy plates. These trophy-style plates are very common in the early twenty-first century.

There are many silversmiths that supply local and national rodeos with embellished gold and silver trophy buckles. Even Westerners who are not rodeo performers consider their wardrobes incomplete without a fancy plate buckle embellished with Western themes, and visitors purchase fancy cowboy buckles and stamped or carved belts as trophies of their visits.

RODEO COWGIRLS

Cowgirls were active participants in the rodeo by the late nineteenth century when they performed in many of the same events as their male counterparts. Women who participated in the rodeo generally began as children doing ranch chores, as did Lucille Mulhall, who became an excellent roper and rider on her family ranch near Guthrie, Oklahoma. She began performing in Wild West shows in 1897 and then went on to enter rodeo contests in riding and roping. Fanny Sperry Steele worked alongside her father and brothers as they broke horses on their Montana ranch and then began as a relay racer in the rodeo arena in 1904. She earned the title of Lady Bucking Horse Champion of the World at the Calgary Stampede in 1912 by sticking to Red Wing, a bucking horse that had killed a cowboy just the day before. For her ranching chores and bronc riding in the rodeo, Sperry Steele chose to wear divided skirts, but she and her team wore racing silk jackets and jodphurs for the relays. It seems odd that this form of dress would be acceptable for racing but not for bronc riding, especially because bronc riding was so much more dangerous and made even more so by cumbersome clothing. Prairie Rose Henderson, another ranch daughter, began bronc riding in the Cheyenne, Wyoming, Frontier Days in 1910, when she made her appearances in costumes she stitched herself. She was known for her colorful silk vests trimmed with ostrich feathers. It is possible that her flamboyance helped to raise her score for riding events. Tillie Baldwin had an unlikely background for a rodeo star; she was born and raised in Norway, where she was involved in skiing, skating, and canoeing before she immigrated to Canada. She wore lightweight blouses and bloomers that enabled her to perform riding tricks that would have been impossible in the most preferred form of dress for rodeo women during the 1910s: divided skirts made of leather.

Photographs show that rodeo cowgirls adopted more practical dress in the early 1920s. Most women wore jodphurs and cotton blouses with loosely tied bandannas; Western, high-heeled boots; and wide-brimmed, high-crowned hats. Even though most women were selecting more comfortable clothing, some clung to divided leather skirts. Vera McGinnis is said to have been the first woman to wear trousers in the arena. She chose to do so in England, where she did not expose herself to public condemnation as she would have at home. By 1927, nearly all rodeo cowgirls had abandoned divided skirts in favor of trousers.

In 1955, cowgirls were no longer permitted to participate in bronc riding or other activities considered too dangerous for women. Instead, barrel racing, performed by riding a horse around three barrels in a cloverleaf pattern as fast as possible, replaced the events in which women had competed since the late nineteenth century. The clothing worn by barrel racers did not vary too much from that worn by their bronc-riding predecessors

Fancy roping at a cowboys' camp, ca. 1905. An Oklahoma cowboy twirls a rope, as six others watch. This cowboy is wearing woolly chaps/trousers. Library of Congress Prints and Photographs Division, LC-USZ62-56646.

in form, but the styles changed to follow changes in mass fashion. Barrel racers wore trim trousers, Western-cut blouses influenced by film cowgirls, pastel hats, and decorative boots. During the 1960s and 1970s, wrinkle-resistant polyester made its way into rodeo cowgirls' wardrobes. In the twenty-first century, rodeo cowgirls are wearing clothing that includes Lycra for comfort and function because Lycra shirts stay tucked and pants with stretch are comfortable for activity. The shirts often include colorful patterns and applied fringes that illustrate Western style.

PERFORMING COWBOYS AND COWGIRLS

The first U.S. feature film was *The Great Train Robbery of 1903*, a Western starring Bronco Billy Anderson, who was dressed like a Wild West Show cowboy in brass-studded wrist guards, fringed gauntlets, and a huge bandanna worn loosely, point down in the front. Most movie cowboys of the 1910s, 1920s, and 1930s were dressed in variations of this costume, which sometimes included *ten-gallon hats* (very large cowboy hats), very woolly woollies, silver-embellished leather vests, and Western-cut trousers tucked into highly decorated boots. During the 1930s, singing cowboys brought even more decorative details to Western style. Rodeo Ben and Nudka "Nudie" Cohen were the most well-known tailors who created elaborately embroidered and appliquéd shirts, pants, and jackets for stars such as Tom Mix, Gene Autry, Hopalong Cassidy, Roy Rogers, and Dale Evans. The many shirts made by Rodeo Ben and Nudie Cohen included shaped yokes now recognized as distinctly Western style, *smile pockets* (curved vent style) trimmed with points at each end, gauntlet-shaped cuffs with ornate plackets, V-shaped shirt yokes as well as more elaborate yoke shapes, and contrasting piping along seams and collar edges. It

was Rodeo Ben who put the first snaps on Western shirts in 1933. Pants included embellishments similar to those used on the shirts. Jackets for singing cowboys during the 1930s and 1940s were often shorter than regular men's suit jackets, perhaps a reference to the Spanish bolero jackets that inspired cowboy dress.

The *dust coat* or *duster* is another garment that was influenced by movies filmed during the 1990s. Although it was never part of a real cowboy's wardrobe, it was quickly adopted as a part of Western style, and nearly every Western supply catalog includes dusters as part of its offerings. The real cowboy garment that most closely resembled the duster was the *slicker*, usually called a "Fish" after the Fish brand slickers most cowboys preferred to use.

While some country-and-western music stars have continued the tradition of flamboyantly decorative Western dress, others, such as Garth Brooks, have adopted the style of Western dress worn by working men. Brooks's CD covers show him wearing wide-brimmed cowboy hats, colorful shirts, tooled leather belts with fancy Western-style buckles, and *stacked jeans* (pant legs that wrinkle over the boots) over workboots. On some covers he also wears denim jackets, another stereotypical characteristic of the working cowboy.

THE FUTURE OF WESTERN STYLE

Western style has waxed and waned as part of mainstream fashion, except in the West, where it is considered a classic style, so new elements of design that have come to represent Western style are added every now and then. One of these is the *broomstick skirts* (characterized by crinkled fabric) that were likely influenced by the velvet skirts worn by Navaho women. There are a large number of companies that have built their business on Western style; there is even the Western English Sales Association, which promotes the West to potential clients at enormous trade shows in Denver, Colorado, and Dallas, Texas, each year. Western style interpreted by designers such as Ralph Lauren builds on a nostalgic view of the West as a place where men were fiercely independent, with beautiful women at their sides. Western style is a uniquely U.S. style that is a combination of elements rising from functional clothing worn by cowboys but adding color and pattern from Spanish America, North American Indians, and costumers who clothed movie and singing stars. Western style is now part of U.S. folk dress and unlikely to disappear any time soon.

References and Further Reading

Abbott, E.C. *We Pointed Them North: Recollections of a Cowpuncher.* Norman: University of Oklahoma Press, 1989. (Originally published 1939.)

Barrows, John R. *U-Bet: A Greenhorn in Montana.* Lincoln: University of Nebraska Press, 1990. (Originally published 1934.)

Beard, Tyler. *100 Years of Western Wear.* Salt Lake City, UT: Gibbs-Smith Publisher, 1993.

Bishko, C.J. "The Peninsular Background of Latin American Cattle Ranching." *The Hispanic American Historical Review* 32, no. 4 (November 1952): 491–515.

Buffalo Bill and Larom Collections. Buffalo Bill Historical Center, Cody, WY.

Cary, Dianna Serra. *The Hollywood Posse.* Boston: Houghton Mifflin, 1975.

Chap Collection. Range Rider Museum, Miles City, MT.

Cisneros, José. *Riders across the Centuries.* El Paso: Texas Western Press, 1984.

Cole, George S. *Dictionary of Dry Goods.* Chicago, IL: J. B. Herring Publishing, 1894.

Dary, David. *Cowboy Culture.* Lawrence: University Press of Kansas, 1981.

Doubleday Photograph, Grandee Garment, and Trophy Plate Collections. National Cowboy and Western Heritage Museum, Oklahoma City, OK.

Evelyn J. Cameron and Ewen S. Cameron papers, 1893–1929. Montana Historical Society, Helena, MT.

Friedman, Barry. *Chasing Rainbows: Collecting North American Indian Trade and Camp Blankets.* New York: Bulfinch Press, 2002.

Larson, Jack Lenior. *The Dyer's Art Ikat, Batik, Plangi.* New York: Van Nostrand Reinhold, 1976.

LeCompte, Mary Lou. *Cowgirls of the Rodeo.* Urbana: University of Illinois Press, 1993.

Old West Trading Company. *R. T. Frazier Saddlery Catalog.* Colorado Springs, CO: Old West Trading Company, 1995. (Originally published 1914.)

Photographic Archives. Montana Historical Society, Helena, MT.

Pitman's Treasures & Co. *Main-Winchester-Stone Co. Catalog.* San Gabriel, CA: Pitman's Treasures & Co., 1989. (Originally published 1903.)

Rickey, Don. *$10 Horse, $40 Saddle: Cowboy Clothing, Arms, Tools and Horse Gear of the 1880s.* Ft. Collins, CO: Old Army Press, 1976.

Rollinson, John K. *Pony Trails in Wyoming.* Lincoln: University of Nebraska Press, 1988. (Originally published 1941.)

Shepherd, Major William. *Prairie Experiences in Handling Cattle and Sheep.* New York: O. Judd, 1885.

Taylor, Lonn, and Ingrid Marr. *The American Cowboy.* Washington, DC: Library of Congress, 1984.

Westermeier, Clifford P. *Man, Beast, Dust: The Story of Rodeo.* Denver, CO: World Press, 1947.

Wilson, Laurel E. "'I Was a Pretty Proud Kid': An Interpretation of Differences in Posed and Unposed Photographs of Montana Cowboys." *Clothing and Textiles Research Journal* 9, no. 3 (1991): 49–58.

Wister Collection. American Heritage Center, Laramie, WY.

Laurel Wilson

Religion and Dress

- Uses of Dress in Religion
- Religion in North American History
- Catholic Dress Practices
- Customary Dress Practices
- Christian Groups Prescribing Dress
- Jewish Immigrants and Dress
- Dress as a Symbol of Religious Affiliation

Organized religion, defined as an institutionalized set of beliefs about supernatural power or powers, has generally seen dress as a topic of concern. The degree to which dress is an essential element of worship and/or religious practice varies widely. Within a worldwide religion such as Catholicism or Islam, dress practices may be global or instead confined to a particular locality. In countries such as the United States and Canada, with populations that include immigrants from all over the world, there can be much variation in practices not only from religion to religion but also within the same religion.

USES OF DRESS IN RELIGION

Many religions specify how individuals with a particular status, such as minister, priest, monk, or nun, should dress. These requirements are usually established by religious ruling bodies. Religions that have an established hierarchy may use dress to denote the place of an individual within the hierarchy. The Roman Catholic Church and some Orthodox Christian churches are good examples of this practice. Most Canadian and U.S. practitioners of these religions would immediately recognize where a member of the clergy fits into the governing structure of their religion.

The dress of the lay members of a religion may also be prescribed to a greater or lesser degree. Failure to conform to the prescribed dress may, in some religions, be severely sanctioned, even to the extent of expulsion from the religious community. In other religions, certain forms of dress may be customary, with members of these groups tending to follow particular practices but having the freedom to make independent choices without penalty.

Both prescribed and customary dress of lay persons or those with unique status in a religion may change over time or in different places. For example, Quakers in North America in the eighteenth century were expected to dress in subdued colors. Women were to wear a type of bonnet with a wide brim that fitted closely around the face and came to be known as a *Quaker bonnet*, and men wore a wide-brimmed peaked hat. In the twenty-first century, members of Quaker congregations dress no differently than their neighbors. The Doukhobors ("Spirit Wrestlers"), a radical Christian sect that emigrated from Russia to Canada about 1898 to escape persecution for their belief in pacifism and communal lifestyle, initially wore Russian peasant dress. By 2007, their dress is described as being like that of any of their Canadian neighbors.

Unique dress practices will be especially visible when ceremonies are performed. In Christian churches in the United States and Canada, prescribed or customary dress may be seen when a child is baptized, experiences communion for the first time, and is confirmed as a member of a church, or when an individual is married or attends a funeral. Specific requirements for dress are very often based on what is written in the holy books of a particular religion. Old Order Amish (an Anabaptist Christian group that practiced adult baptism) and Old Believers (a group separated from the Russian Orthodox Church) both require adult males of their congregations to have beards because of biblical exhortations to refrain from cutting facial hair.

RELIGION IN NORTH AMERICAN HISTORY

Religion and dress in the United States and Canada cannot be separated from the history of the settlers and immigrants who came to North America after 1492. Although the first to arrive were explorers, traders who were interested in profits, or military men who intended to add territory to that already claimed by their home country, some were accompanied by Roman Catholic missionaries who sought to convert the native population to Christianity. The Protestant Reformation in Europe during the sixteenth century led to the formation of a host of Protestant churches, which were often intolerant of dissent in their communities. As a result, many of those who came as settlers to North America made the journey because they were looking for a place where they could practice their religion freely. From the Massachusetts Bay Colony (1620) with its roots in Puritan England, to the Maryland settlements (1632) where British Catholics sought refuge, to the Swiss-German Anabaptists of southeastern Pennsylvania (1683), such groups formed communities based on religious affiliation.

The thirteen British colonies that became the United States avoided establishing a national religion and enshrined that principle in the U.S. Constitution. Settlers in Canada during the time that France was the colonial power were largely Roman Catholic. When the British assumed control in 1763, the Protestant Church of England became the dominant religious authority, although the population in Quebec remained, and remains until this day, predominantly Catholic. Scholars differ as to whether the Church of England was at any time a legally established state religion in Canada, as it is in Britain, but the rights of varying faiths are acknowledged in the Canadian Charter of Rights and Freedoms (1982), which guarantees "freedom of conscience and religion."

Immigrants of differing religious persuasions arrived in North America knowing that they could freely follow their consciences. North Americans also felt free to take some small subgroup of the "mother" church in a different direction, knowing that conformity would not be enforced by state or local governments. Totally new religions were established, such as the Church of Jesus Christ of Latter-Day Saints (often called *LDS* or *Mormons*). Most members of religious groups saw themselves as part of mainstream society and could not be distinguished on the basis of dress from their neighbors as belonging to one or another church. However, some groups viewed themselves as a people apart, adopting dress that was different from that of their fashion-following neighbors. In these faiths, dress was prescribed at least to the extent that individuals could be identified as members of a particular sect and often to the point of being an absolute requirement.

The majority of immigrants to the United States and Canada in the seventeenth to the nineteenth centuries were European and Christian. Jewish populations were small. The enslaved Africans brought by force to North America were unable to continue practicing the religions of their homelands and were converted to Christianity. Missionaries also worked hard at converting North American Indians and First Nations people to Christianity, although some elements of their spiritual practices remained. As part of these conversions, native people were often required to give up native dress. In the twentieth century, larger populations from Eastern Europe, Asia, and the Middle East began to arrive, and the variety of religious faiths increased. The Canadian census, unlike that of the United States, includes data on religious affiliation. The 2001 Canadian census indicated the percentages of Canadians in the following religions: 43.6 percent Roman Catholic, 29.2 percent Protestant, 1.6 percent Christian Orthodox, 2.0 percent Muslim, 1.1 percent Jewish, 1.0 percent Buddhist, 1.0 percent Hindu, and 0.9 percent Sikh. Individuals with no religious affiliation made up 16.2 percent of the population.

First communion dress, ca. 1940. White dress and veil worn by Roman Catholic girls for their first communion ceremony. In the twenty-first century, the communion dress style includes the same components. Courtesy of Janice Ruotolo.

In the United States, providing this information is voluntary. Self-identification of religious affiliation shows that in the year 2000, Christians, including Catholics and Protestants, were reported to be 76.5 percent of other U.S. population. Nonreligious citizens accounted for 13.2 percent; practitioners of Judaism, 1.3 percent; Islam and Buddhism, each at 0.5 percent; and Hinduism, 0.4 percent. Other much smaller groups included Wiccans, Pagans, or Druids; native American religions; Baha'i; Sikhism; Scientology; and Taoism. Muslims, Buddhists, Hindus, and native American religionists all grew by more than 100 percent between 1990 and 2000.

CATHOLIC DRESS PRACTICES

The Christian group claiming the largest single membership in both the United States and Canada is Roman Catholicism. Dress plays an important part in the Catholic Church as a means of distinguishing the clergy from the laity and, within the clergy, of establishing the hierarchical ranking of prelates. Elements of dress are also determined by the liturgy and the church calendar, with special colors, garments, and accessories assigned, each of which carries symbolic meanings. In a church with such a strong emphasis on ceremony, dress has and continues to play a major role.

Prior to the Second Vatican Council (1962–1965), specific dress was assigned to religious orders (groups of men and women who were usually not ordained as priests but dedicated their lives to working for their church). For nuns and monks, these traditional garments were known as *habits*. However, after Vatican II recommended modifying habits that inhibited the activities of religious orders, many U.S. and Canadian orders of nuns ceased wearing habits and instead donned simple clothing, perhaps a modest blouse and skirt or other secular attire, and a distinctive cross or pin of their specific order or congregation. Some orders or individual nuns continued to wear short veils and knee-length, simplified habits; others preferred to maintain their traditional dress. Men who belong to religious orders will sometimes wear prescribed traditional dress and sometimes dress in the same way as the population that they serve.

The dress practices of the lay membership of the Catholic Church in the United States and Canada were, until the second part of the twentieth century, a combination of customary dress and prescribed dress. Women were expected to cover their heads with a veil, scarf, hat, or other head covering when inside a church. Dress that was too revealing was not considered appropriate. Pants were never worn to church. After Vatican II, many women ceased to cover their heads, although some older women or those from more conservative ethnic backgrounds may continue the practice. Complaints about lack of modesty in dress can be heard among the laity and sometimes from the pulpit. There are also former Roman Catholics who rejected the changes brought about by the Second Vatican Council. These congregations insist on pre–Vatican II requirements stated as "no dresses cut deeper than two fingers breadth under the pit of the throat," sleeves that cover the arms to the elbow, and skirts that are longer than just below the knee.

CUSTOMARY DRESS PRACTICES

Among the many Christian religious groups represented in the United States, dress practices tend to be based on custom, rather than prescription. Ceremonial occasions are marked by customary types of dress. At one time, in churches that practice infant baptism, both male and female infants were dressed in a long, elaborate white gown. By the latter part of the twentieth century, it was more likely that male babies would wear white one-piece outfits with short pants. Greek Orthodox infants are dressed in white, but it is required that their clothing must be entirely new and cannot have been worn, or even tried on, before the ceremony of baptism.

In the Catholic Church, special dress is worn for the ceremony at about age seven or eight when children participate in the rite of receiving communion for the first time. U.S. and Canadian merchandisers sell the appropriate clothing, which for girls consists of a rather elaborate white dress worn with a white headdress and a veil. For boys, there is greater choice. Suits shown on the Internet by merchandisers range from white to black, gray, or beige and include white jackets worn with dark pants.

Many Christian churches hold confirmation ceremonies that publicly proclaim the individual's willingness to be a practicing member of the church after the candidate has completed a course of study of the tenets of the religion. One Catholic church posting advice on its Web site as to how to dress for this ceremony advises the boys and their sponsors to wear a suit or sport jacket and dress pants, a dress shirt and tie, dress socks, and shoes (but not sneakers). The wearing of jeans is forbidden. Girls and their women sponsors are given a choice between dresses, dressy skirts and blouses, pantsuits, or dressy pants and blouses, worn with dress shoes. Skirts must be knee length or longer and the chest, back, and shoulders must be covered. The request is made for participants to use modesty in choosing their outfits. In other congregations, children wear loose choir robes for this ceremony.

Weddings can be occasions in which very elaborate garments are worn by the bride and her attendants. The mother of the bride and the groom also choose their dresses carefully. Formal clothing is worn by the groom and his attendants as well as by the fathers of the couple. Fashion plays a very large role in the selection of the women's clothing, and fashion trends in wedding clothing can be traced over time, with white continuing since the mid-1800s to be the preferred color for the bride. By the 1920s, fashionable weddings had attendants dressed in identically styled dresses, usually in matching colors. By the twenty-first century, preferred styles were changing so rapidly that it became necessary for brides having large, formal weddings to consult bridal magazines to determine the latest fashions in colors and styles. During the last decades of the twentieth century, wedding gowns became sleeveless and more revealing but remained traditionally white or ivory.

Black has long been associated with mourning. Dark, somber colors are preferred for most Christian funeral services, although in the Greek Orthodox Church the color white is traditionally worn by mourners.

What individuals wear to attend church services has varied greatly from one Christian denomination to another. Ethnicity may play a part. African American churches have long been renowned for the handsome dresses and suits and elaborate hats worn by female congregants. But the informality of contemporary U.S. fashion has penetrated even to these churches. In her study of African American dress, Gwendolyn O'Neal described what is found in many churches today as a little bit of everything, from the "overdressed, sequined, beaded shoes, gold, silver, all the way to a very, casual look—jeans and baggy pants for men, to low-rise pants with the midriff showing for young women." Her summary: "You see the complete gamut in the church." Women in Greek Orthodox churches prefer that churchgoing women dress in attractive clothing, preferably dresses; however, now that pants have been accepted so completely as part of women's wardrobes, suitably dressy pants are acceptable.

CHRISTIAN GROUPS PRESCRIBING DRESS

Some Christian denominations combine the wearing of clothing that conforms to contemporary fashion in the United States and Canada with dress that is mandated as a part of religious practice. The Church of Jesus Christ of the Latter-Day Saints (LDS or Mormons) is one such church. Within the LDS temple, which only members of the church can enter, only white clothing is worn. (The color white symbolizes purity.) Men wear all-white suits, and women wear floor-length white dresses and a veil that is worn off the face except during prayer, when it covers the face. Under the exterior clothing, both men and women wear special white undergarments that are given to them after they meet the requirements that enable adults to worship in the temple. The garment is described as being made from any of a variety of lightweight fabrics. The length and cut is meant to ensure modesty, and the garment "bears several simple marks related to gospel principles of obedience, truth, and discipleship in Christ." Once church members receive the garment, they are expected to wear it at all times except for activities during which that would not be possible, such as swimming.

Latter-Day Saints families are expected to teach their adolescent children to dress modestly and avoid the fashionable extremes that lead to immodesty. Excluded from their wardrobes are short shorts or short skirts, tight clothing, bare midriffs, revealing attire, and clothing cut low in the front or the back. All Latter-Day Saints are expected to undertake a missionary period (two years for men; eighteen months for women) during which they travel and proselytize. Retired couples may also become missionaries. Their church provides them with a very detailed list of clothing they are expected to take with them. The prescribed clothing is conservative in styling and cut, and women are advised to take "outfits of modest design" with skirts that are midcalf length. Pants are not included on the women's list.

A number of Christian groups have viewed themselves as a "people apart" and choose to live in communities separate from others whom they view as too modern or too secular. Some of these groups, such as the Ephrata community in Pennsylvania, founded in the eighteenth century, have not survived; others, such as the Quakers, have ceased to dress differently from their neighbors. Anabaptist groups of Amish, Mennonites, and Hutterites or the Russian Old Believers continue to live apart and dress in distinctive, prescribed clothing that is based in their unique histories.

JEWISH IMMIGRANTS AND DRESS

Although there were Jewish residents of both the United States and Canada from the earliest days of immigration, their numbers were few. By the latter part of the nineteenth century, numbers of Jewish immigrants increased until, by the beginning of the twenty-first century, they made up over 1 percent of the population of

Members of the Hare Krishna sect wearing traditional saffron robes, United States, 1967. Time & Life Pictures/Getty Images.

each country. Large numbers of Jewish immigrants arrived when the garment industry was in its infancy. Many found work in the clothing industry in the metropolitan areas where this industry thrived. They became, and remain, key players in the growth and development of this industry as skilled workers, managers, owners, and designers.

Within the Jewish communities of the United States and Canada in the twenty-first century, religious practice ranged from strict observation to minimal acknowledgment of religious rules. Reformed or Liberal Jews considered themselves Jewish by birth and culture, but they did not accept many of the teachings of their more conservative coreligionists. They dress no differently than their gentile neighbors. By their own description, Conservative Jews wish to conserve the traditional elements of Judaism while also allowing for reasonable modernization. No absolute rules are given about dress, although it is appropriate for men to cover their heads when praying, usually with a *yarmulke* (a skullcap) or a hat. For women, modest dress is recommended. Within one of the books holy to Jews, the Torah, it is written: "A man's item shall not be upon a woman, and a man shall not wear a woman's garment." Some rabbis (a *rabbi* is defined as one who is trained to interpret Jewish law) have interpreted this as meaning women should wear only skirts and not pants. Other rabbis say

that within contemporary Western culture, pants are no longer solely men's garments; they can also be worn by women even for religious observances.

Orthodox Jews live very strictly by the rules of their religion. Dressing modestly is stressed. Head coverings are required for men and married women. Men wear a hat, which may be a yarmulke, a black hat, or a fur-trimmed hat called a *streimel*. Depending on the branch of Orthodoxy, the hat styles worn will vary. Married women are required to cover their hair with a scarf, a wig, or a hat, to cover the upper arms to below the elbow, and to avoid low necklines. Within Hasidism, a particular branch of Orthodoxy, both the head coverings and the clothing worn are used to establish religious status.

In addition to weddings and funerals, the rituals of circumcision (the *bris*) and the bar or bat mitzvah are important in Jewish practice. Perhaps as a result of the influence of the suits customarily used at baptism, merchants now offer special bris garments, which are white suit tops with a skirtlike lower half instead of pants so that the operation of the circumcision can be easily performed. When they reach the age of thirteen, Jewish boys and girls are considered to be mature enough to participate actively in religious life, which is marked by the *bar* or *bat mitzvah* for boys and girls, respectively. Originally a ceremony for boys, in the twentieth century it became the practice for girls as well. Only some of the more Orthodox congregations reject celebrating this event for girls. No prescribed clothing is worn, but lavish parties are given to celebrate the event, and fashionable clothing is worn by the young participants, their families, and their friends.

DRESS AS A SYMBOL OF RELIGIOUS AFFILIATION

Ever since the attack on the World Trade Center on 11 September 2001 by men who were members of a violent, fundamentalist Islamist group, those members of the Islamic faith within the United States and Canada have been singled out for special attention if they wear outward symbols of their religion. They may be subject to greater scrutiny in security checks while traveling or may be discriminated against in school or at work.

As with other religions, the requirements related to dress differ in various versions of Islam. Some Muslims do not believe that they are subject to any dress requirements. Others believe that to fully participate in their religion, there are dress codes that must be followed. Because Islam is an important religion in so many different parts of the world, a wide variety of local practices have developed. Islamic immigrants in the United States and Canada and their offspring, as a result, have usually followed the practices of their country of origin.

Within the United States, the number of adherents of the Muslim faith is growing. African American Muslims first came to the attention of the general public through the group called the Nation of Islam, which was seen as racially divisive. A more moderate group broke away to form the Muslim Society of America, which embraces a more orthodox Islam. By 2007, the membership of the Nation of Islam had fallen to about twenty thousand. According to a survey commissioned in 2006 by the American Muslim Council, African Americans make up about 24 percent of the Muslim population of the United States. Little information is available about the dress practices of the more orthodox African American Muslims, but they have not adopted the long white dresses and veils that cover the hair and are worn by women of the Nation of Islam.

One aspect of Islamic dress that is very obvious and therefore receives particular attention is the veil or head scarf. Relatively few women in North America wear veils that cover the entire body, as is done in a number of Muslim countries with very conservative branches of Islam. But many Muslim women choose to wear the *hijab*, a head scarf, as a symbol of their religious belief. Debate about whether Muslim religious practice requires a head covering rages within the Muslim community in Canada and the United States. In Canada, attempts by civil authorities or business or industry to restrict the wearing of veils has led to the filing of a number of lawsuits. The courts have generally rejected attempts to coerce individuals to either remove religiously symbolic dress or to wear such dress within a nonreligious environment. However, in Quebec, an electoral officer did not permit fully veiled Muslim women to vote because they could not be adequately identified. The Justice Department of the United States has generally defended Muslim women's rights to wear head scarves. Court cases in many states have ruled affirmatively on the right of Muslim women to wear head scarves in their photographs for drivers' licenses.

Some Muslim women who dress in Western fashions make choices and modifications to maintain the modesty they believe is required by their religion and appropriate within their community. For example, they might wear form-fitting pants and tops but choose a long top that covers the midriff and arms.

A relatively small proportion of the population of the United States and Canada follow the Sikh religion, a monotheistic religion founded about five hundred years ago in what was then northern India. Sikhs are very visible because their religion requires that certain items of dress be worn. Both men and women must never cut their hair. They must have a steel bracelet (*kara*), a small sword (*kirpan*), a wooden comb (*kangha*), and long underpants (*kach*). Men wrap a long, thin strip of material around their heads to form a turban, replacing the formal turban worn in public with a smaller one (*keski*) at home. Women cover their head and shoulders either with a long scarf (*chuni*) or a turban. Courts in both Canada and the United States have upheld the right of Sikhs to wear these items, including the kirpan, in all circumstances. One particularly remarkable instance was when a Sikh member of the Canadian Royal Mounted Police was granted the right to wear his turban when in uniform.

Many in North America have taken an interest in the philosophical teachings of Buddhism. They may or may not affiliate with a Buddhist temple or congregation. Others are immigrants from Asian countries in which their families have been Buddhists for centuries. For the most part North American Buddhists are indistinguishable from their non-Buddhist neighbors unless they become one of the small number of Buddhist monks, who wear a traditional multilayered robe of saffron or ochre (a red-orange color). Visitors to Buddhist ceremonies are reminded that they should not point their feet toward the altar or the teacher, as this is considered disrespectful.

Hare Krishna adherents, believers in a faith coming out of Hinduism that was founded in the United States, were particularly active in the 1960s and 1970s. They dressed in saffron-colored robes and saris and danced and chanted and sold their teacher's books on the streets and at the airports of major U.S. cities.

Some beliefs and practices of North American Indian and First Nations spirituality have survived in spite of attempts by nonnative settlers and immigrants to extinguish them. As the issues of care for the environment and dealing with global warming have come to prominence, interest in these practices and beliefs that stress the need to respect nature has grown. As a result, some North Americans have added items to their dress that are symbols from native cosmology. Examples include jewelry with motifs such as eagle or other feathers, the figure of Kokopelli (the flute player), and the circle of life. T-shirts have become a particularly popular place to display North American Indian motifs. Members of religious groups may also wear religious symbols as jewelry. The most commonly seen examples are crosses worn by Christians and Stars of David worn by Jews. Specialized Web sites sell a wide variety of jewelry with symbols unique to the Latter-Day Saints. Islamic teaching instructs men not to show off their wealth by wearing gold jewelry. As a result, jewelers who cater to an Islamic clientele do not offer gold-colored jewelry for men.

References and Further Reading

Arthur, Linda B., ed. *Religion, Dress and the Body*. Oxford, UK: Berg, 1999.

Freedman, Samuel G. "Of Disparate Faiths, but of Like Mind on Dress Code." *New York Times*, 14 July 2007.

John–Hall, Annette. "Millinery Maneuvers." *Philadelphia Inquirer*, 24 June 2004, D01.

Kaiser, Susan. *The Social Psychology of Clothing*. New York: Fairchild Publishers, 1996.

Klassen, Pamela. "The Robes of Womanhood: Dress and Authenticity among African American Methodist Women in the Nineteenth Century." *Religion and American Culture* 14, no. 1 (2004): 39–82.

La Ferla, Ruth. "We, Myself and I." *New York Times*, 5 April 2007.

Miller, Kimberly A., and Susan O. Michelman. "Dress and World Religions." In *The Meaning of Dress*, edited by Mary Lynn Damhorst, Kimberly A. Miller, and Susan Michelman, 455–461. New York: Fairchild Publications, 2000.

O'Neal, Gwendolyn S. "Casual Sundays: 'Sunday Best' No Longer in Vogue for Church Services, According to K-State Apparel Professor." 20 May 2005. http://www.k-state.edu/media/WEB/News/NewsReleases/casualsundays52005.html.

Poll, Solomon. "The Hasidic Community." In *Dress Adornment and the Social Order*, edited by Mary Ellen Roach and Joanne Bubolz Eicher, 142–157. New York: John Wiley & Sons, 1965.

Wallace, W. S. "Religious History." In *The Encyclopedia of Canada*, vol. 3, edited by W. Stewart Wallace, 186–191. Toronto: University Associates of Canada, 1948.

Phyllis G. Tortora

See also California; Snapshot: Identity and Gender in Traditional Jewish Dress; Snapshot: Amish, Mennonites Hutterites, and Brettu; Snapshot: Quakers and Shakers; Snapshot: Old Believers; Middle Eastern; volume 10, Global Perspective Dress and Religious Practices.

Snapshot: Identity and Gender in Traditional Jewish Dress

Over the past few decades, North American Jews have increasingly contested and reshaped norms of Jewish gender and identity through ritual and everyday dress. Novel patterns on prayer shawls allow Jewish women to challenge long-standing male privilege during prayer and in the synagogue while nonetheless asserting a commitment to religious tradition and continuity. Skullcap or *yarmulke* designs increasingly draw on U.S. pop culture to uneasily balance Jewish religious particularity with cultural assimilation. Last, many young Jewish adults today announce on caps, shirts, and even undergarments their desire to transform Jewishness from a religious and historical heritage into an ethnic identity that is hip, sexy, and cheeky.

MATRIARCHS IN PASTEL: WOMEN'S PRAYER SHAWLS

The Hebrew Bible (Torah), in Numbers 15:37–41 and Deuteronomy 22:12, specifies the affixing of "fringes" or "tassels" (*tsitsit*), along with a blue thread (*tekhelet*), to the corners, hem, or scallops of Israelite garments. These ornaments visually reminded the Israelites to "recall all the commandments of the Lord and observe them, so that you do not follow your heart and eyes and go whoring."

Fringes, tassels, cords, and ornamented hems in the ancient Mediterranean world served as official insignia of rank, power, and authority. Clay imprints of fine hems functioned as legal seals. Overall, sartorial ornaments denoted nobility. In the biblical context, however, fringes had a slightly different meaning: they represented all Israelites, and no other nation, as God's elite.

The blue thread supports this interpretation. The ancients extracted blue dye from a still unidentified marine animal (likely the hypobranchial gland of the murex snail). The dyeing process was labor intensive, restricted to coastal Phoenicia, and extraordinarily expensive. Blue normally colored the garments only of the wealthy. But if all Israelites were so adorned, then the entire community, yet again, would appear regal. The message was not one of democracy. Rather, the fringes and blue thread symbolized the divine election of Israel above all other peoples.

In the postbiblical era, the command to wear fringes evolved into two mandatory items of masculine Jewish attire: an everyday undergarment (*tallit-katan*) and a ritual prayer shawl (*tallit*). Both garments display fringes at the four corners, tied into a series of windings and knots that communicate mystical meanings. The classic rabbis interpreted these fringed garments as enveloping men in holiness; they represent divine protection. Indeed, a famous rabbinic tale tells of a pious Jew who would have succumbed to illicit lust had it not been for his fringes, which slapped him across the face.

By the eighth century, the source of the blue dye had faded from collective memory. The fringes were, and largely remain today, white. Recently, though, a group of devout Jews living in Israel claims to have rediscovered the source of the blue dye. They now sell blue fringes, largely on the Internet, so that Jews can once again fulfill the original commandment. But there is considerable debate on this matter in Orthodox circles.

In the early twenty-first century, only Orthodox men wear the fringed undergarment, starting at age three. They also, along with men from the less traditional Conservative movement of Judaism, require the use of prayer shawls by all men over the age of thirteen (or only married men) during morning devotions and certain other ritual occasions. Reform Judaism formally abandoned this practice as mandatory in the late nineteenth century. Prayer shawls are commonly presented to Conservative boys at the time of their bar mitzvah; they are a popular souvenir from quasi-religious pilgrimages to Israel.

Orthodox consensus generally holds that the prayer shawl is an obligatory entitlement of men and not women. This ruling of Jewish law (*halacha*) arises from complex linguistic analysis of the original Hebrew. Yet several Orthodox rabbis demurred and permitted women also to wear the garment. In the main, though, the prayer shawl, like the yarmulke and phylacteries (*tefillin*), has symbolized masculine privilege.

But no longer. Since the 1970s, many daughters of Israel, especially among Conservative Jews, have asserted their legitimate right also to wear fringed prayer shawls in the synagogue. They seek to reshape traditional Judaism into an egalitarian religion that no longer excludes women from its ritual prerogatives. The shawl communicates a desire not so much to modernize Judaism as to right a historical injustice that blocked women from a divine commandment intended for all Jews, not just men.

Orthodox denominations reject this reshaping of tradition as a violation of immutable divine law. Jews who abide by orthodox sensibilities yet also reject traditional gender roles, and so permit or encourage women to wear prayer shawls, must form their own independent congregations. Reform Judaism sees this and all ritual accoutrements as a matter of personal choice, regardless of gender. When a Reform synagogue recommends the use of prayer shawls by policy or convention, though, it must do so for men and women equally because the movement formally embraces egalitarianism. Consequently, the adoption of the prayer shawl by women as part of a broader effort at transforming how traditional Judaism approaches and literally enwraps itself in the sacred pertains mainly to Conservative Jewry or small congregations of progressive yet Orthodox Jews. So attired, a Jewish woman announces her commitment to traditional worship as well as modern feminism—to continuity through change.

Contemporary prayer shawls display a wide variety of styles. What was once the generic, unmarked, or unnamed norm in shape and decoration, worn by men, is now dubbed "traditional." This tallit is white, typically woven from wool, striped with black or perhaps blue, and possesses an ornamental collar.

A member of the feminist movement "Women of the Wall," wearing a yarmulke (skullcap) and tallit (prayer shawl) during morning prayer (Jerusalem, 2004). In Orthodox Judaism, women are generally not permitted to wear the prayer shawl. GALI TIBBON/AFP/Getty Images.

Novel styles of prayer shawls today aim specifically to appeal to women. These garments incorporate stereotypically feminine artistic characteristics and names. They are often made from silk, hand painted with pastel colors, and usually depict delicate, curved images of flowers, Jerusalem, and especially dancing matriarchs. Myriad online Judaica shops offer prayer shawl styles called Miriam's Tambourine, Queen Bathsheva, Galilee Silk Pink Flowers, Four Mothers, Dancing Girls, Doves over Jerusalem, Cream Pink Poppies, Lilies of the Valley, and so forth. Because many women who decide to wear a prayer shawl find the act deeply personal and meaningful, women tend, far more than men, to create their own prayer shawls—from a wedding dress, say, or a deceased father's neckties or with a group of friends. This feminine aesthetic not only personalizes the sacred for women, but it also allows devout women to avoid violating a traditional Jewish edict, anchored to Deuteronomy 22:5, against cross-dressing. Women can thus join men without appearing to emulate them. Ironically, though, this sartorial shift toward egalitarianism sometimes also sustains gender differences by enwrapping women in garments that specifically appeal to traditional, if not stereotypical, feminine aesthetic sensibilities.

In Israel, where the avowedly Orthodox chief rabbinate oversees all Jewish religious sites, women are legally forbidden to pray aloud, chant from the Torah scroll, and wear prayer shawls at the Western Wall. Since 1988, a group called Women of the Wall (WOW) has actively campaigned to reform this law. During their devotions at the Wall, WOW members were cursed, called Nazis, spat upon, and dragged away by state security guards. Ultra-Orthodox men hurled chairs. The chief rabbinate vilified WOW as an affront to God. To raise awareness and funds, WOW sold on the Internet special prayer shawls featuring flowers and the names of the biblical matriarchs, as well as the fringed undergarment. They also set up a "tallit table" in Zion Square, Jerusalem, inviting women who had never done so to try on a prayer shawl and chant the appropriate blessing. An Ultra-Orthodox man smashed the table. For WOW, the prayer shawl became a focal symbol for the group's egalitarian efforts.

TRADITIONAL YARMULKES

The history of the Jewish skullcap or yarmulke (*kippah* in Hebrew; while the word *yarmulke* is popularly thought to be Yiddish, scholars have debated its etymology) remains unclear. The Hebrew Bible nowhere prescribes headgear as an everyday obligation. Canonical compilations of rabbinical texts between the second and twelfth centuries also fail with any uniform voice to require male caps. (Vestimentary regulations assigned European Jews distinctive and often demeaning garb, including headgear, from the eleventh through eighteenth centuries.) Historical reconstructions and evidence from illuminated Hebrew manuscripts suggest that various types of headgear, but rarely yarmulkes, emerged as the ritual norm for European (Ashkenazic) male Jews sometime between the fifteenth and the eighteenth centuries.

The yarmulke itself seems not to have emerged as the most distinctive form of public Jewish dress until the early decades of the twentieth century, largely for two reasons. First, in the late nineteenth century, ritual garb shifted to the forefront of debates about Jewish identity when the Reform movement shed headgear so that modern Jews, even when praying, resembled everybody else. In consequence, the wearing of headgear by Jewish men as part of everyday attire emerged as a key sign of one's commitment to traditional Judaism. Modern Jews doffed their caps. Traditional Jews retained them. The presence or absence of a hat now became a self-conscious sign of a Jew's relationship to Judaism.

Second, head coverings gained uniquely Jewish associations in contrast to the rest of society, when secular male attire in North America and Europe regularly excluded hats from formal and everyday occasions in the early decades of the twentieth century. As bareheadedness became the societal norm, Jews increasingly appeared distinct because of their caps. Hasidic and Ultra-Orthodox (*haredi*) men retained their hats (beneath which they also wear yarmulkes). Other Jews, such as Modern Orthodox, who assimilate in dress, found the yarmulke an acceptable compromise that enabled the retention of tradition while acceding to non-Jewish aesthetic norms. The yarmulke marked Jewish masculinity in a relatively unobtrusive manner. In fact, the yarmulke shrank in size during the twentieth century.

In contrast to the Hasidic, Ultra-Orthodox, and Modern Orthodox movements, Conservative Judaism requires men to don yarmulkes only during ritual and in holy spaces such as the synagogue sanctuary. Reform Jews see yarmulkes as a wholly optional, although increasingly recommended, ritual accessory. The degree to which the yarmulke is a special garment or an integral part of everyday attire indexes a male Jew's commitment to religious Judaism.

SKULLCAPS AND SPONGEBOB SQUAREPANTS: CONTEMPORARY YARMULKE DESIGNS

Several variants of yarmulkes emerged during the twentieth century, each more or less representing a distinct denomination or religious affiliation. In the 1950s, a small, typically multicolored, crocheted or knitted yarmulke called a *kippah serugah* gained popularity in Israel among a Zionist youth movement. This yarmulke, typically made by female kin, friends, and romantic interests, came to represent religious Zionism and the settler movement. To secular Jews, the kippah serugah denotes religious fanaticism; to traditional Jews, it signals religious frivolity.

Modern Orthodox Jews tend to favor smallish knitted, somewhat colorful, or suede yarmulkes. Often, these yarmulkes are fastened with a bobby pin—or, more recently, the "kippah clip."

Traditional Orthodox and Hasidic Jews, including many students at *yeshivas* (religious day schools), see the smaller, colorful yarmulkes of Modern Orthodoxy as an unacceptable endorsement of liberalism and modernity. Instead, they typically wear large black velvet and satin yarmulkes that cover upwards of three-quarters of the head. To enhance the public display of piety, moreover, these Jews, as noted previously, may also wear black hats. (They are often called "black hat Jews.") The placement of the yarmulke also conveys meaning: Traditional sentiments push it toward the front of the head; liberalism, toward the back. Similarly, the presence of a crease reveals that the wearer stores his yarmulke, folded and forgotten, in a pocket or drawer.

The yarmulkes of Conservative Jews are especially interesting. They tend to wear lined satin, velvet, moiré, or suede yarmulkes, often with a thin silver or gold ornamental border, acquired as a souvenir on the occasion of a major ritual occasion such as a wedding or bar/bat mitzvah. On the lining is a ceremonial autograph: the honoree's name as well as the date and type of ceremony. Yarmulke embossing began in the late 1950s, gained in popularity during the next decade, and by the mid-1970s was almost de rigueur for large, lavish ritual celebrations among North American Conservative Jews. Synagogue bins brim with these yarmulkes—as do the closets of many Jewish families. This uniquely North American fashion weds consumer capitalism, conspicuous consumption, the personalization of ritual, and Jewish identity.

Recently, a vast repertoire of icons, insignia, and slogans from North American pop culture have appeared on yarmulkes. The major yarmulke manufacturers in the United States, largely based in Brooklyn, New York, still dominate the market, but a sizable number of competitors have appeared on the Internet, thus fueling innovation. Where once the options were mainly Brucha Yarmulkes, A1 Skullcap, Weinfeld Skull Cap, and Mazel Skull Cap, today there are Ego-Kippot, Kippah King, KoolKipah, and Lids for Yids as well as online Judaica shops. Yarmulkes now display professional and college sports logos, cartoon characters such as SpongeBob SquarePants and Bob the Builder, and superheroes such as Superman

Two boys wearing yarmulkes (skull caps). In the twenty-first century, caps are available in a wide range of designs; these particular caps feature symbolic support for the 2004 U.S. presidential candidates. GALI TIBBON/AFP/Getty Images.

and Spiderman. Yarmulke designs show Thomas the Tank Engine, poker hands, the Lacoste alligator, yin-yang patterns, James Bond's 007, Pikachu and other Pokemon creatures, the Simpsons, Blues Clues, Scooby-Doo, characters from *Toy Story*, the Nike Swoosh, a Hershey's Kiss, hearts, U.S. flags, Yoda from *Star Wars*, and so forth. You can announce your musical preference for the Grateful Dead or cast a symbolic vote for the next U.S. president. In 2002, the Gore-Lieberman campaign issued yarmulkes in Hebrew and English. During the 2008 political season, Jewish supporters of Senator Barack Obama could proudly wear the "Obama-kah." Also available for purchase is the "kosher kippot," certified by the Progressive Jewish Alliance to be "sweatshop-free."

Many yarmulke designs are clearly intended for children, such as Hello Kitty, Ariel from *The Little Mermaid*, and *Beauty and the Beast*. Disney is a big hit with this crowd. Some yarmulkes comment wonderfully on the prominence of ethnic fluidity and multiculturalism, such as a pink yarmulke with a painted image of Dora the Explorer, the animated Latina girl from the widely popular television series shown by the Nickelodeon cable network.

Many of these yarmulkes appeal to youth and, indeed, some traditionalist Jewish day schools have banned them. But other yarmulke slogans and motifs cater to the sentiments and humor of adults. In all cases, recent yarmulke designs continue to wed Jewish ethnicity with consumer capitalism. They also communicate a contrary sense of identity. The yarmulke evolved into the quintessential sign of Jewish identity—a sign that, outside of Orthodox traditions, no longer pertains solely to men. But yarmulke designs today also display two quintessential signs of North American identity: individualism and pop culture. They allow Jews to both accept and resist assimilation.

REBELLION THROUGH DRESS

Shortly after the turn of the millennium, several distinct groups of young North American Jews—decidedly urban, progressive, intellectual, and rebellious—established several Webzines, blogs, and organizations devoted to reinventing Jewish identity. These communities, real and virtual, are centered on the Internet, although what many consider to be the flagship institution of this movement, *Heeb Magazine*, also publishes in print. Other influential venues are jewcy.com, jewschool.com, and rebooters.net.

These "hipster Jews," as they are often called, or *Generation-J*, wish to redefine Jewishness in ways that challenge the hegemonic discourses, ideologies, and institutions of North American and mainstream Jewry. They are progressive, heterodox, politically active, and postdenominational. They see established modes of Jewish identity as anachronistic and alienating, inert and dull, rooted in stale theology, and linked to historical events such as the Holocaust that offer limited resonance and relevance to twenty-something Jews. The "New Jews" want to lend youthful Jewish voices to wider debates over multiculturalism and the politics of identity and to push Jewishness, as they did, to the forefront of cutting-edge contemporary culture. They want, in short, to make Jewishness cool.

The "New Jew Cool," as the online magazine *Reform Judaism* called this movement, expresses Jewish identity through tones that are irreverent, sardonic, playfully aggressive, and scandalously erotic. Jewishness became fashionable. Not surprisingly, Jewish slogans and images appeared on all manner of fashion: caps, T-shirts, tank tops, men's boxer shorts, women's thongs, and so on. Youthful Jewish identity is now expressed as "Jewlicious" and "Jewtastic." It is a shirt with the figure of a Hasid clutching a rifle saying, in homage to Clint Eastwood's cinematic persona Dirty Harry, "Go Ahead, Make My Shabbos." Another shirt announces "Jews Kick Ass" and displays portraits of North American Jews who diverge greatly from the stereotypical image of Jewish masculinity, including Bob Dylan, Sammy Davis Jr., William Shatner of *Star Trek* fame, and Henry Winkler, who played the role of "The Fonz," the leather-jacketed Italian American auto mechanic in the popular sitcom *Happy Days*. Other shirts say "Moses is my homeboy," "Jesus was a kike," "Shalom Motherfucker," "Jew. Lo" (a parody of J.Lo, or Jennifer Lopez), and "W.W.B.D.?" ("What Would Barbra [Streisand] Do?)." One can even purchase women's underwear printed with slogans such as "A Great Miracle Happened Here" and "Chanukah Bush," as well as the "yarmulkebra" fashioned from two actual yarmulkes.

Both the form of these garments and the literary and pictorial expressions intentionally call into question the established conventions of upper-middle-class Jewish American taste and identity. A company called YidGear boasts "the shirts your rabbi warned you about." One of their items proclaims "Eat Me, I'm Kosher," accompanied by the logo of the Orthodox Union, one of several rabbinic organizations that certify kosher food. YidGear withdrew the shirt after the organization complained. JewSchool sells skimpy women's panties that say "Really not tznius," a mockery of the rabbinic concept of modesty (*tznius* in Hebrew), mainly incumbent on women. Indeed, young Jews use dress to express their distaste for the traditional forms and decorum of Jewish masculinity and femininity, especially the muting of overt aggression and sexuality.

All these garments, too, express Jewish identity as an ethnicity, not a religion, and so firmly situate Jewishness in the wider trend of contemporary U.S. culture that attaches cachet to proclamations of ethnic particularity. The more youthful Jews use dress to announce the validity and relevance of Jewishness as a unique identity, the more they do so in ways and voices, and from motivations, that seem thoroughly assimilated.

To critics, these exclamations of Jewishness lack substance. They are as flimsy as the cloth on which they are printed. But that, indeed, is the very message young Jews wish to communicate: the fluidity and mutability of Jewishness. Jewish identity today is unstable, multiple, and shifting—slipped on yet discarded like a fashion accessory, just another commodity, for better or worse, in the marketplace of self-invention.

REFERENCES AND FURTHER READING

Baizerman, Suzanne. "The Jewish Kippa Sruga and the Social Construction of Gender in Israel." In *Dress and Gender: Making and Meaning in Cultural Contexts*, edited by

Ruth Barnes and Joanne B. Eicher, 93–105. Oxford, UK: Berg, 1992.

Emmett, Ayala. "A Ritual Garment, The Synagogue, and Gender Questions." *Material Religion* 3, no. 1 (2007): 76–87.

Herz, Rebecca Shulman. "The Transformation of Tallitot: How Jewish Prayer Shawls Have Changed since Women Began Wearing Them." *Women in Judaism* 3, no. 3 (2003) http://www.utoronto.ca/wjudaism/contemporary/articles/Tallitot/a_shulman_herz_1.html (accessed 25 July 2008).

Krauss, Samuel. "The Jewish Rite of Covering the Head." In *Beauty and Holiness: Studies in Jewish Customs and Ceremonial Art*, edited by Joseph Gutmann, 420–467. New York: Ktav, 1970. (Reprinted from *Hebrew Union College Annual* 19 (1945–1946): 121–168.)

Metzger, Thérèse, and Mendel Metzger. *Jewish Life in the Middle Ages: Illuminated Hebrew Manuscripts of the Thirteenth to the Sixteenth Centuries.* New York: Alpine Fine Arts, 1982.

Milgrom, Jacob. "Of Hems and Tassels." *Biblical Archaeology Review* 9, no. 3 (1983): 61–65.

Ochs, Vanessa L. "Women and Ritual Artifacts." In *Women of the Wall: Claiming Sacred Ground at Judaism's Holy Site*, edited by Phyllis Chesler and Rivka Haut, 310–334. Woodstock, VT: Jewish Lights, 2002.

Schnur, Rabbi Susan, and Anna Schnur-Fishman. "How Do Women Define the Sacred?" *Lilith* 31, no. 3 (2006): 20–27.

Zimmer, Eric. "Men's Headcovering: The Metamorphosis of This Practice." In *Reverence, Righteousness, and Rahamanut: Essays in Memory of Rabbi Dr. Leo Jung*, edited by Jacob J. Schacter, 325–352. Northvale: Jason Aronson, 1992.

Eric K. Silverman

Snapshot: Amish, Mennonites, Hutterites, and Brethren

Anabaptists derive their name from the fact that the early practitioners of this branch of Protestantism sought to be rebaptized as adults, although they had been baptized as children. There are four major Anabaptist groups—Hutterites, Mennonites, Brethren, and Amish—with subgroups within each category. Dress is an important means used by many Anabaptist groups to define their affiliation with a particular church, indicate their humility and willingness to submit to church discipline, and demonstrate their separateness from mainstream culture. Anabaptists may seek to differentiate themselves by avoiding changing fashions and adhering to strict rules of dress determined by each Anabaptist community. In the early twenty-first century, this separateness is most visible when adherents practice what is known as "plain" dressing. *Plain* implies a lack of ornament, modest silhouettes, garments that do not conform to changing mainstream fashions but instead to church discipline, and some type of head covering. For men, it may mean wearing a beard. Each group uses distinctive dress as a means of group identity.

The Anabaptists first appeared in Zurich, Switzerland, as dissidents who objected to political compromises made by the Protestant reform minister Ulrich Zwingli and the Zurich City Council. The dissenters believed that only adults could promise to adhere to Christian teaching and thus must be rebaptized to confirm their commitment. They advocated the absolute authority of the Bible to determine religious practice and the conduct of daily life, including modes of dress, thus superseding the authority of the religious establishment and the government of Zurich. This had wide ramifications because infant baptism not only bound the person to the established church but also conferred citizenship, with its obligation to pay taxes and defend the state. The state also promulgated *sumptuary laws* regulating dress. Neither the civic nor the religious leadership could tolerate the flouting of authority and civil law. The first Swiss Anabaptist martyr was killed as a seditionist in the spring of 1525. Thus began more than two hundred years of persecution of Anabaptists. These are recorded in *The Bloody Theatre or Martyrs Mirror*, a compendium of the tortures, harassments, and deaths of thousands of Anabaptists at the hands of Roman Catholic, Protestant, and civil authorities.

In the 1527 *Schleitheim Articles*, the Swiss Anabaptists, known as the Swiss Brethren, stated seven aspects of their beliefs: adult baptism, the ban of errant members from communion, communion only for baptized members, separation from the world, leaders from upstanding members within the community of baptized members, the rejection of violence, and the refusal to swear oaths. Anabaptism spread rapidly as those fleeing persecution zealously spread their religious ideas, and adherents were found over time in Switzerland, Austria, Moravia, Alsace, Germany, the Netherlands, Poland, the Ukraine, and North America. However, Anabaptists are not

Mennonite women of rural Pennsylvania (ca. 1970) wear lightweight, printed summer dresses of a conservative cut. On their heads are small, white, net prayer coverings that are prescribed by their local congregation. Not all Mennonites wear these caps. Photograph by Vincent R. Tortora.

all of the same persuasion, and the movement developed into groups with differing religious convictions within an Anabaptist heritage.

In 1525, Johannes Kessler wrote that the first Swiss Anabaptists "shun costly clothing ... expensive food and drink, clothe themselves with coarse cloth, [and] cover their heads with broad felt hats." In 1568, the Strasbourg conference of Anabaptists decreed that "tailors and seamstresses shall hold to the plain and simple style and shall make nothing at all for pride's sake ... brethren and sisters shall stay by the present form of our regulation concerning apparel." As persecution decimated the ranks of urban Anabaptists, a majority of members came from the peasantry. The dress of sixteenth-century Anabaptist peasants working in the fields was probably similar to that of other field hands, which consisted of coifs, broad-brimmed hats, shirts, simple dresses for women, simple jackets and hose for men, and the shoes of laborers. Anabaptist clothing did change over the centuries but slowly and only after careful deliberation within each group regarding what change might mean to the community's sense of identity.

HUTTERITES

The Hutterites began as a faction of the Moravian Anabaptists in the late 1520s, taking their name from Jakob Hutter, an Anabaptist preacher. Hutterites live communally with common ownership of property and thereby differ from other Anabaptist groups. Their early history was fraught with divisive internal leadership quarrels, persecution, plague, and relocation until by 1819 they had ceased communal living. However, from 1859 through the 1870s, three different groups of Hutterites reestablished communal colonies. In the late twentieth century, there were some four hundred thirty Hutterite colonies, each with about one hundred people, in the United States and Canada. Colony life separates Hutterites from the general population physically, and contact with life outside the colony is strictly controlled, as is access to modern media. Hutterites use modern equipment for farming as well as for the home, but they reject what they see as mainstream social values. All real property is owned by the colony, and except for certain designated items, individuals have no personal possessions. Clothing is acquired communally and is given out to each person by the colony manager about once a year. The men wear beards and, depending on the group, a mustache. Clothing is practical for farm work, and in some groups men wear collarless coats, while others have turned-down collars. Women wear garments made for ease of movement, usually sleeveless printed dresses with modest, longer skirts; blouses; head scarves; and sometimes aprons. Some groups specify that women should tie the apron in front, some tie it in back, and other groups do not wear aprons. One group of Hutterite women in Saskatchewan, Canada, wears polka-dot head scarves as a distinguishing characteristic. As with other Anabaptists, different Hutterite colonies have different standards of dress. An individual choosing to leave a colony may take only the few things considered personal and the clothes he is wearing.

MENNONITES

An early Anabaptist leader in the Netherlands, Menno Simons, had been ordained as a Roman Catholic priest but left the church in 1536. His influence was so pervasive that many Anabaptists were subsequently called *Mennonites*. Menno Simons advocated a strict simplicity in dress, as did others of the early leadership. However, in the more tolerant Dutch society of the seventeenth century, many urban Mennonites became prosperous. Wealthy Dutch Mennonites practiced great sobriety of dress but did not spare the luxuries of fine linen, fur, or high-quality silks, as can be seen in a number of Rembrandt portraits of Mennonites. In 1683, Mennonites began arriving in North America and settled in Pennsylvania. In 2008, Mennonites are the largest and most diverse group of Anabaptists. Their clothing choices reflect the degree of conservatism adopted by each congregation and cover a wide spectrum. Many Mennonites are fully assimilated into mainstream Western culture with no real differences in dress. Others seek separation through abjuring all traces of modernity, as do Old Order Mennonites who use *plain dress* and the horse and buggy for transportation. The more conservative the group, the more likely it will be to prescribe plain dress for members. Mennonites traditionally include printed textiles in their garments, as do the Hutterites.

Amish women from Lancaster, Pennsylvania, ca. 1965. They wear typical black bonnets and black dresses over blouses of various colors. Photograph by Vincent R. Tortora.

BRETHREN

The seven Brethren groups are now considered part of the Anabaptist tradition that originated in 1708 in Germany when a group of German Pietists merged their beliefs with those of the Anabaptists. Pietists sought to make the spirit of Christian living more important than doctrine. There is a wide divergence of practice, with a small number of adherents rejecting modernity and retaining not only plain dress but the horse and buggy, while others are fully assimilated into modern life. Settlements of Brethren are often close to those of Mennonites and Amish, and the degree of conservatism is reflected in attitudes toward dress. The Brethren have suffered schisms, as have the other Anabaptist groups over attitudes toward dress.

AMISH

Another sect of Anabaptists formed in 1693 when Jacob Ammann, leader of a group of Swiss Brethren in Alsace, called for religious practices that were rejected by other Swiss Brethren. Ammann, from whom the Amish take their name, taught against trimming beards and fashionable dress. He prohibited buttons, and Amish men became known as *Häftlers*, or "hook and eyers," and Mennonites as *Knöpflers*, or "button people." Amish women were restricted both then and now to pinning their garments with straight pins. As a result of schisms, the Amish are made up of four major subgroups. Although they may live and work with non-Amish, they do not assimilate into modern life and have devised means of remaining separate, largely through regulating dress, the use of the German language, modes of transportation, and use of electricity.

"Bonnets, beards, and buggies" is a common saying that identifies major aspects of Amish life. In 2008, the largest settlement of Amish is in Ohio, with the second largest in Pennsylvania.

In 1837, one hundred years after the first Amish arrived in Philadelphia, the Amish ministers' conference noted that Amish prosperity had brought about "awful pride in clothing, namely with respect to silken neck-cloths on their children." Tailors were forbidden "to make new or worldly styles of clothing for members of the church" but were "to follow the old style and such as is indicated by the ministers and older people of the church." Attempts at reconciliation in the matter of dress failed to convince the conservatives, and by 1865, the resulting division yielded the Old Order Amish. As was the case with the first Anabaptists, the dress of the Amish in the eighteenth and nineteenth centuries was not as dramatically different from the rest of agrarian society as in the twentieth century, when increasing affluence and rapid communication of changing fashions affected agrarian and urban populations alike. Much dissension in Amish society centers on dress, which is considered a critical outward sign of the submission of individual will. Adherence to rules of dress indicates the commitment of the individual to the unwritten rules for the way things are done in the specific community, so the slightest variation of these defining garments becomes cause for concern within the group. Dissension often cannot be contained, and church groups may split over issues of dress or the interpretation of other aspects of the unwritten rules that govern daily life. As a result, congregations have slightly different rules of dress that are especially obvious in women's dress but also affect men. For example, the width of the hat brim, the hatband, and the height of the crown of the Amish man's hat, the one item of apparel that has changed the least in four hundred years, vary from group to group. The style of sleeve on a woman's dress, the way the skirt is pleated into the waistband, the fabrics and color choices permitted, the style of bonnet—all of these are aspects that differentiate one group of Amish from another within the same geographic area. The Amish color palette has many hues and values of purple, blue, green, wine, brown, gray, and in the early twenty-first century, pastel shades such as pink and yellow for children. Black is reserved for mourning and communion services and white for death. Wedding apparel is not distinguished in line or color from other garments. Rules of dress do change to accommodate perceived needs within the congregation. For example, in the nineteenth century, black was considered worldly, and gray and brown were commonly used for Amish men's suits. However, as the twentieth century progressed and fashionable apparel for men became more colorful, black came to be considered more appropriate. As natural fibers became more expensive and less available, all but the most conservative Amish congregations have allowed synthetic fabrics. This has considerably diminished the need for ironing, a particular advantage to the Amish wife who is, on average, the mother of seven children and has little if any access to electricity. For the Amish, plain dress means no printed textiles, ornaments, or jewelry of any kind, including wedding rings. In the early twenty-first century, buttons are allowed on men's work coats and children's clothes by some groups but not on the suits that men wear to church.

CONCLUSION

Anabaptists of all persuasions have flourished in the United States and Canada since the first immigrant adherents arrived. The importance of dress as a defining aspect of religious commitment is underlined by the attention paid by each community to what each member wears.

REFERENCES AND FURTHER READING

Braght, Thieleman J. van. *The Bloody Theater or Martyrs Mirror of the Defenseless Christians, Who Baptized Only upon Confession of Faith, and Who Suffered and Died for the Testimony of Jesus, Their Savior, from the Time of Christ to the Year A.D. 1660*. 15th ed. Translated by Joseph F. Sohm. Scottdale, PA, and Kitchener, ON: Herald Press, 1987.

Hostetler, John A. *Amish Society*. 4th ed. Baltimore and London: The Johns Hopkins University Press, 1993.

Kraybill, Donald B. *The Riddle of Amish Culture*. Baltimore and London: The Johns Hopkins University Press, 1989.

Kraybill, Donald B., and C. Nelson Hostetter. *Anabaptist World USA*. Scottdale, PA, and Waterloo, ON: Herald Press, 2001.

Scott, Stephen. *Why Do They Dress That Way?* Intercourse, PA: Good Books, 1986.

van der Zijpp, Nanne, and Dirk Kossen. "Art." *Global Anabaptist Mennonite Encyclopedia Online*. 1955. http://www.gameo.org/encyclopedia/contents/A78ME.html (accessed 8 March 2008).

Yoder, Paton, and Steven R. Estes. *Proceedings of the Amish Ministers' Meetings, 1862–1878 (Die Verhandlungen der Diener Versammlungen 1862–1878)*. Goshen: Mennonite Historical Society, 1999.

Jean L. Druesedow

See also Religion and Dress.

Snapshot: Quakers and Shakers

While the names are similar and the groups are often confused in the popular imagination, Quakers and Shakers have distinctly different histories and precepts. Both sects originated in England—the Quakers about 1650, under the leadership of George Fox, and the Shakers in 1774, under the leadership of Ann Lee. Quakers (also known as *Friends* due to their official name, the Religious Society of Friends) believe that all individuals carry an "Inward Light," a direct, inner contact with Christ's energy. Quaker doctrine includes the principles of equality, community, harmony, and simplicity. Friends were expected to use restraint in their dress because excessive attention to fashion would lead them away from the inner world. (As stated in *The Quaker Message*, "Where the adornment of the spirit was so important and so varied a task, and so absorbing, why piffle with jewellery [sic] and furbelows, powder and paint?") Shakers (officially, the United Society of Believers in Christ's Second Appearing) believed that "Mother Ann" embodied the Christ energy in a female form and her followers were daily manifesting God's kingdom on earth. Their principles included celibacy, equality of the sexes, and separation from the world. As they lived in communal "families" under a hierarchical social structure, their clothing was produced in central workshops. It, too, was generally restrained, but the emphasis was on relative uniformity and practicality.

Specific restrictions about dress were not inherent to either religion. Seventeenth-century Friends wore simplified versions of everyday English dress, but they did not consistently interpret that concept. Some Quaker men wore wigs, for example (William Penn had several styles), while others considered them too fancy. The earliest Shakers, similarly, wore whatever they had before they joined the church; it was only after those garments wore out and the community began to centrally provide clothing for its members that there was more conformity in appearance. Eventually, as the styles of the outside world continued to evolve and the adherents of both sects clung to what they had worn before (i.e., individual dress elements became "fossilized"), they increasingly stood out as different. North American Quaker men wore broadbrimmed hats and collarless cuffed coats (with some even retaining wigs), for example, well into the mid-nineteenth century when such garments were exceedingly dated. They remained clean shaven when non-Quaker men usually sported facial hair.

Old-fashioned-looking dress set members of these groups apart from the world at large, underlining the separatist nature of the sects and their inward-looking values and serving as a shield against worldliness. North American Friends established formal dress guidelines in 1800, when Quakerism was well established. Discipline of this sort was seen as a way to encourage group cohesion, which was important when Quakers were no longer subject to external persecution. Individuals spoke of consciously choosing to "go plain" or "put on" these clothes as a way of showing their dedication to inner truth. North Americans were stricter than their English counterparts at this time.

Notably, when there was more overall uniformity, small dress details became highly communicative. Regional differences in elements such as the shape of the Quaker hat or bonnet, for example, were easily recognizable within the Friends community.

Drawings of various items of Quaker dress, ca. 1800 to 1860. Reproduced from Elizabeth McClellen's *Historic Dress in America*, published 1904–1910. Courtesy of Phyllis Tortora.

Head coverings also held symbolic, often metonymic, meaning. To insiders, the man's beaver hat (a fossilized version of the Cavalier-era style, without the extravagant plume that was made from felt containing beaver fur) was associated with Quaker solidarity and pursuit of religious freedom. In the early years of persecution in England, Quaker men had worn their hats at all times, even indoors and in front of judges and other authorities, as a sign of equality; they owed subservience to no one. To outsiders, the hat became an emblem of Quaker conservatism and, by the late nineteenth century, of wholesomeness. (The iconic figure on Quaker brand products still embodies this in 2008.) Women's hat styles changed repeatedly over the course of Quaker history, but it was the *pokebonnet*, worn from about 1820 to 1885 and made with an exceptionally broad brim that obscured the face, that captured the public imagination. It became a shorthand symbol of the Quaker woman, generally evoking a kind of romanticized goodness. Paradoxically, however, it also came to be seen by some outsiders as "bewitching" and carried somewhat erotic overtones.

Shaker leaders also codified dress codes to promote group unity about 1800. Their dated and plain styles were also

Shaker sisters from the late nineteenth century (United States) wear one-piece dresses consisting of fitted bodices and gathered skirts and over each dress either a wide collar called a bertha that was made of matching material or a scarf of another, contrasting fabric. Over time Shaker dress styles varied slightly, but changes were slow and styles always lagged behind contemporary fashions. A white cap was worn by adult women, similar to caps worn indoors by many women in the United States until about the middle of the nineteenth century. Such caps are still worn by Amish and some conservative Mennonite women in the twenty-first century. Unknown photographer.

fascinating to worldly people, although the erotic edge was absent in outsiders' comments about celibate Shaker women.

Stereotypes aside, it is important to clarify that clothing styles were never really static in either group. While the rate of change was slow and clothing was out of date, modifications were influenced by worldly fashion and materials. Shaker men, like Quakers, originally wore knee breeches and *cravats*, broad, soft neckcloths that tied in the front. But like outsiders, they replaced these with trousers and premade, stiffened *stock collars* by 1810. Shaker sisters wore a one-piece dress in most eras. In the early nineteenth century it was relatively narrow, in keeping with Empire fashion; by midcentury it had a much fuller skirt. They wore triangular fichu-like bodice scarves or neckerchiefs in the first part of the century, but they modified this by the 1870s to a separate shoulder cape (a *bertha*) that was more in keeping with Victorian styles. In the twentieth century, it was further simplified to a vestigial cape of the same fabric as the dress. Significantly, Shaker clothing was always of high quality and comfortable. Shaker women did not wear restrictive undergarments or excess fabric that impeded movement. They also never eschewed tasteful decorative details. Sabbath bodice scarves were made from beautiful silk fabrics—some were even tie-dyed—and berthas sported braided trim. Rich colors were typical, reflecting the essential joyfulness of the religion. Shakers also had a relatively large number of clothes, and in Isaac Young's words, spent "a great part of [their] attention, time and earnings" on their wardrobes.

Shaker men abandoned distinctive dress by the last quarter of the nineteenth century. Women still made their own dresses throughout the twentieth century, although there was much individual variation and the adoption of some purchased garments. (There were four remaining Shakers in 2007.) Quakerism thrives today, but Friends gave up their distinctive dress by about 1900.

REFERENCES AND FURTHER READING

Connerley, Jennifer L. "Quaker Bonnets and the Erotic Feminine in American Popular Culture." *Material Religion* 2, no. 2 (2006): 174–203.

Gordon, Beverly. *Shaker Textile Arts*. Hanover, NH: University Press of New England, 1980.

Gordon, Beverly. "Fossilized Fashion: 'Old Fashioned' Dress as a Symbol of a Separate Work-Oriented Identity." *Dress* 13 (1987): 49–60.

Groves, Nancy Alice. "A Study of Quaker Costume." Master's thesis, University of Wisconsin, 1951.

Gummere, Amelia Mott. *The Quaker: A Study in Costume*. New York and London: Benjamin Blom, 1968. (Originally published 1901.)

Lucas, Sidney. *The Quaker Message*. Walingford, PA: Pendle Hill, 1948.

Whitman, Leanna Lee. "Silks and Simplicity: A Study of Quaker Dress as Depicted in Portraits, 1718–1855." Ph.D. dissertation, University of Pennsylvania, 1987.

Young, Elder Isaac N. *A Concise View of the Church of God and of Christ on Earth Having Its Formation in the Faith of Christ's First and Second Appearing*. New Lebanon, NY: n.p., 1856.

Beverly Gordon

Snapshot: Old Believers

The Old Believers are a people of Russian descent who practice an old form of the Russian Orthodox faith. They broke with their mother church in 1666, when its liturgy was altered to conform more closely to Greek Orthodoxy. Millions were killed in the resulting religious strife. Searching for places where they could practice their religion in peace, some Old Believers emigrated to such areas as Siberia, Turkey, Romania, the Manchurian region of China, Australia, New Zealand, Brazil, and Argentina. Many Old Believers came to the United States and Canada in the 1950s, establishing settlements in Oregon; Minnesota; Erie, Pennsylvania; Alberta, Canada; and Alaska. It is estimated that about seven hundred practicing Old Believers live in Alberta, Canada. Professor Richard Morris, of the University of Oregon, estimates that there are six to seven thousand in Oregon, fifteen hundred in Alaska, and about fifty families in Minnesota.

Old Believers set themselves apart from secular society in order to preserve their religious traditions. To do this, they have established separate communities, often in rather isolated areas. They do not reject modern technology. However, in their dress, they create a visible demonstration of their adherence to tradition and their intention to remain apart.

Dress traditions of the Old Believers grow out of their origins and history, deriving from Russian peasant dress of the seventeenth and eighteenth centuries. At baptism, up to eight days after birth, children receive a cross and a colorful handwoven belt, a *poyas*. Old Believers are expected to wear these for the rest of their lives, taking the cross off only to replace the chain or cord that holds it and removing the belt only for bathing or sleeping.

An infant is dressed in a traditional shirt called a *rubashka*. This same style may be worn by men and women of all ages. The shirt and its long sleeves, which are gathered into a band at the wrist, are cut in one, like a tunic. The rubashka has a high-standing collar and a band down the front that is embroidered in traditional designs. The shirt is belted with the poyas, and the cross is worn under the shirt. Shirts are usually made in solid, strong colors.

Their scriptures state that man is made in the image of God, and his natural appearance should not be altered. Therefore, men allow facial hair to grow and do not trim their beards. Hair is usually cut short in back and at the sides, although hair at the temples is allowed to grow longer.

Biblical text also admonishes women not to cut their hair. Unmarried girls wear hair uncut in a single braid. Married women make two braids and pin them up under a *shashmura* (cap) and over it a *platok* (kerchief or scarf). Today, in public, younger women tend to wear only the cap, although the scarf is worn for church. Elderly women, who rarely leave the community, still wear scarves over the cap. Fabric shops operated by community members sell caps decorated with sequin and bead trimmings that are ready made by skilled seamstresses.

Customary dress for men and boys generally consists of long trousers worn with the rubashka. For church, some men wear *kaftany* (long black coats similar to a priest's cassock). Outside their settlements men often wear ordinary work clothes.

Tradition required women to keep their arms covered above the wrist. Legs were not shown above the calf outside the home, and all parts of the body were to be covered. Those describing Old Believer adult women's garments speak of a shirtlike blouse, a longer version of the rubashka, under a full-length jumper that is made with wide straps attached to a horizontal band to which the body of the garment is gathered or pleated. This garment, called a *sarafan* or *sarafany,* is belted at the waist. The *talichka* is not Russian in origin. Adopted during the time in China, it is made with a wide, collarless yoke ending above the bust and is sleeveless. The rest of the dress eases in gathers or pleats to fit the yoke. Like the sarafan, it is worn over a long-sleeved blouse and belted. A collection of Old Believer dresses shown on the Internet includes traditional and modified sarafans, the latter with one shoulder strap and with sleeves and neckpieces sewn into place. This union of blouse and jumper is apparently common. An apron may be worn over the dress.

For church, women wear a one-piece sarafan of subdued color; the blouselike section is white. For daily wear and festivities, women's dresses are made of colorful fabrics. Often fabrics are printed or decorated with sequins, beads, and embroideries. The preferred fabric appears to be lightweight polyester. Community proprietors of fabric stores report that fashions in fabrics vary from year to year and season to season. At Easter, custom restricts activities for eight days and prohibits any kind of work. This allows time for visiting, and women often make a new dress for each day.

Shoes, cold-weather outerwear, and children's undergarments do not differ from those of secular neighbors. These can be ordered from catalogs or purchased in local stores.

Seeing Old Believers on the streets of Homer, Alaska, in the summer of 2006, one concludes that strict adherence to traditional practices is not required of all ages. Makeup, unacceptable for both men and women, is commonly seen on young girls. Necklines may be low cut; sleeves can be short, above the elbow. Dresses follow body lines. Young women and girls wear fashionable, hooded ready-to-wear sweaters in colors that exactly match dresses. Skirts, however, are invariably long.

Communities vary from very conservative to fairly liberal in their interpretation of customs. The more liberal settlements permit minor variations in sleeves and necklines; otherwise requirements are fairly consistent. In 2006, one more liberal community allowed girls participating in basketball at school to wear shorts instead of long skirts.

In spite of such concessions, Old Believers' dress maintains enough differences from fashionable dress to set adherents to this faith apart. The purpose of dress is not to practice an ascetic or plain lifestyle. Clothing of both men and women allows for a great deal of ornamentation and attention to aesthetics.

Rather, as researcher Timothy Gall has commented, Old Believer dress is used "to create boundaries and insure the survival of the culture."

REFERENCES AND FURTHER READING

Dolitsky, Alexander B. *Old Russia in Modern America.* Juneau, AK: Alaska-Siberia Research Center, 1998.

Gall, Timothy L. *Worldmark Encyclopedia of Culture and Daily Life.* Vol. 2. Farmington Hills, MI: Thomson Gale, 1998.

Gay, Joel. "Old Believers in a Time of Change." *Alaska Magazine* 54, no. 10 (1988): 22.

Maginnis, Tara. "Old Believer" Dresses. http://www.costumes.org/classes/uafcostumeshop/pages/costumehistcollect/oldbeliever.htm (accessed 27 June 2008).

Rearden, Jim. "Nikolaevsk—A Bit of Old Russia Takes Root in Alaska." *National Geographic* 142, no. 3 (1972): 401.

Voltz, Matt. "Wandering Old Believers Find a Home in Alaska." *Moscow Times* 6, no. 31 (20 July 2004). http://www.apostle1.com/07-22-2004-wandering_old_believers_find_a_home1.htm (accessed 27 June 2008).

Wigowsky, Paul. "Collection of Old Believer History and Tradition: Material Culture." http://www.geocities.com/Athens/Agora/2827/collection.html (accessed 27 June 2008).

Phyllis G. Tortora

Utopian and Intentional Communities

The category of social groups that fit under the rubric of "utopian and intentional communities" contains countless ideologies and represents several different kinds of social movements. *Intentional communities* are social groups that are consciously formed with the intent of creating a new social order and worldview and are, to some extent, separated from the wider society in which they are found. Some intentional communities have a social reform focus; others form around economic issues, and still others are religious in nature. Some intentional communities practice complete communal ownership of all possessions; others condemn personal ownership and instead encourage shared economic endeavors and community-wide interests. Some communities have loose social structures; some represent extreme cases of social rigidity. For these reasons, recent scholarship in communal studies has adopted the more inclusive term *intentional community* over other previously used descriptors such as *collective, cooperative,* or *communal* in order to describe these social groups. In this way, the emphasis is placed more on the motivation of communitarianism instead of on the specific form of the community.

Dress is an important aspect of life in intentional communities. Not only does dress set community members apart from those in the outside world, but it also functions to create solidarity among members within the group. Dress, as is the case with all material culture in intentional communities, functions not just to reflect ideology but also to reinforce central beliefs and tenets within the society. As such, these dress norms cannot be understood outside of their social context in these intentional communities.

Despite the almost countless variety of intentional communities (space permits discussion of only a few of the more notable groups), several common characteristics and patterns are represented in all of them to some degree or another. The founding of intentional communities tends to follow cyclical patterns coinciding with periods of intense social change, and as revitalization movements they constitute an important form of cultural critique. Through the process of creating their social structure and community, intentional community members are (directly or indirectly) enumerating what they find wrong with the larger society. Thus, the ideologies and structures of these communities are interesting indicators of how people perceive and experience social change. For example, many of the intentional communities that reacted to industrialism emphasized the value of face-to-face societies and tried actively to eliminate notions of individualism, social class, and inequality. It can be argued that these ideals point directly to aspects of the changing larger social context. While these groups rarely (if ever) cause fundamental social change on a large scale, their ideals are good indicators of how large-scale social change is perceived by members of society.

Furthermore, the ideologies of intentional communities often lead them to restructure fundamental social relations, such as class, family, and gender, and community members deliberately incorporate cultural critique and social reform into the planning and organization of their societies. Because of this, intentional communities are ideal settings in which to investigate questions pertaining to the interaction between material culture and human behavior.

INTENTIONAL COMMUNITIES AND MATERIAL CULTURE

In our daily lives we are surrounded by objects and arrangements of material things—from small and seemingly unimportant objects such as paperclips to larger objects such as buildings and landscapes. Regardless of their size, material objects communicate, situate, and condition human interaction. In many of these cases, material culture does not merely reflect our ideas; it also shapes the ways in which we experience and interpret the world.

The architects of intentional communities understand this and use material culture to reinforce their mutual knowledge in incredibly explicit ways. Intentional communities use material culture to set themselves apart from the outside world (through dress, uses of technology, and industrial endeavors), to reflect ideology and social structure (through landscape designs, subsistence practices, settlement patterning, architectural forms), and to reinforce ideology and social relations within the group. Material culture serves as an active medium to both reflect and reinforce social ideals, and community members are keenly aware of the symbolic meanings represented in artifacts. In this way, material culture can be seen as simultaneously constituted and constitutive.

Thus, material culture becomes a physical manifestation of mutual knowledge—community members all know what the symbols are about, and they have chosen to literally live within those symbol systems, both socially and physically. They begin by delineating the significant symbols, the ideologies, and the beliefs that they see as important enough to structure life around. In order for these ideologies to become worldviews, their symbols and structures must become routinized, with a more mundane, unmarked existence.

Material culture studies often focus on attempting to find significant meanings in seemingly mundane objects. Somewhat ironically, the architects of intentional communities are doing the opposite—trying to move from the significant to the mundane by imbuing everyday objects (dress, architecture, landscape, food) with more sacred meaning. Through the ritualizing of daily practice and objects, they hope to imbed their ideology in their material culture, to make it everyday and taken for granted.

INTENTIONAL COMMUNITIES AND DRESS

Dress is one of the most direct ways that members of intentional communities express their ideology through material culture. Standards in dress within the community serve to signal separateness from the wider society to both members and the outside world. At the same time, subtle differences in dress (often so subtle as to be effectively imperceptible to outsiders) communicate degrees of conformity, dissent, and personal expression to fellow community members.

The methods by which intentional communities establish dress norms are varied. Some intentional communities formally designed the dress of their members, putting much thought into imbuing the styles and dress with symbols of their ideology. Other dress norms were more informally established, evolving in the early years of the community. It is worth noting that the formal or informal establishment of such norms does not correlate with how strictly the dress codes were enforced: The Oneida Perfectionists formally designed their clothing styles but did not force members to comply, while on the other hand, the Hutterites' clothing norms were informally established but are very strictly enforced within their colonies.

Many of the clothing norms were intended as part of a wider agenda of social reform. Examples include the emphasis on gender roles and class structure. Numerous nineteenth-century intentional communities focused on reforming the status of women and, therefore, designed clothing that was more practical and comfortable than that found in the wider society, often doing away with items such as the corset. Communal groups of various kinds emphasized the equality of members, both economically and socially. This often led to discouraging decorative dress, jewelry, and other markers of class or economic status. Still other intentional communities emphasized moral reforms, leading many groups to downplay or disguise any indication of sexuality, particularly among women's attire (this is commonly noted for both Amana and the Shakers).

The establishment of dress norms often also has practical as well as symbolic dimensions. For example, many intentional communities were designed to be economically communal as well as communal in labor, centralizing many community tasks. Frequently this meant a few individuals did all of the clothing production for the entire group, thereby standardizing styles and designs. In addition, many intentional communities ordered their fabric and other materials in bulk for economic considerations. When the clothing for the entire group was produced by the same tailors out of the same bolt and was combined with other similar materials, uniformity was invariably the result, even if it was not intended. Furthermore, some intentional communities' dress norms are produced by what some scholars have termed *fossilization*. In this process, the intentional community dresses no differently than the surrounding society at its creation. Due to the insular nature of intentional communities, clothing styles within the group do not reflect the rapidly changing fashions of the outside world. Instead, the clothing styles within the intentional community become traditional and do not perceptively change. In this way, they become a reflection of the place and time that the community was founded—in the case of New Harmony, reflecting their origins on the banks of the Rhine in Germany many years before.

The following case studies illustrate many of these processes and themes, as well as the variation found in North American intentional communities. Each begins with a brief overview of the community's ideology and history. This is followed by a discussion of how material culture in general was used to both reflect and reinforce the community's social ideals, with a specific discussion of dress norms.

THE ONEIDA PERFECTIONISTS

Founded in 1848 by John Humphrey Noyes in upstate New York, the Oneida Perfectionists were one of the most successful of the numerous nineteenth-century intentional communities, living communally until 1881. Noyes and his followers believed that the millennium prophesied in the Book of Revelation had already begun. Because sin had been abolished in the millennial kingdom, Noyes and his followers believed that nineteenth-century Christians were saints and perfect beings and, therefore, life on earth could and should mirror life in heaven. This included the abolishment of marriage between individuals. Noyes called for the creation of an enlarged communal family and considered every man to be the husband of every woman and every woman to be the wife of every man, thereby instituting their famous system of complex marriage. In addition to an emphasis on the communal family, individuals were also encouraged to perfect themselves, relying partly on the system of mutual criticism. And it is these two ideas, perfectionism and the emphasis of the community over the individual, that became defining factors in their social and material world.

At Oneida ideas of perfectionism were not only applied to people. The constant planning and improvement of the built environment at Oneida reflected their belief that internal and external perfection should mirror one another. It was not just that the external world should be a reflection of their internal perfection and beauty; their physical world was tangible evidence of that inner perfection. And there are numerous examples of buildings being constantly moved, modified, and reassigned. Over many years and several additions, they eventually completed the Oneida Mansion House, a ninety-five-thousand-square-foot (roughly thirty-two-thousand-square-meter) building designed to be the physical embodiment of their social structure. All adults had individual rooms opening onto a series of communal parlors, ate meals in a large communal dining room, and held community-wide meetings in the Big Hall, designed especially for such community gatherings and entertainment. The children of the Oneida Perfectionists were raised communally and thus had their own wing of the Mansion House. All wings of the building were connected by a series of hallways that encouraged interaction among members and surrounded a quadrangle where members could gather to work or play.

Dress norms at Oneida are best known for intentionally reforming women's dress. Incorporating perhaps some aspects of the women's rights movement of the day, long skirts or dresses were replaced by shorter knee-length ones resembling smocks. These were worn over pantlets or pantaloons. *Pantlets* were similar to bloomers but did not use as much fabric and were not gathered at the ankle. Community members noted that this form of dress was much more conducive to physical work than the long and heavy women's fashions of the outside world. Additionally, many community women wore their hair in short boblike cuts, again citing the efficiency of this style over contemporary styles in the wider society. As part of their ideal of perfectionism, individuals were very much discouraged from becoming too attached to material objects or to show superiority over other community members. As a result, decorative elements of dress, such as jewelry, brooches, and other accessories like watches, were not under private ownership. For example, all watches in the community were inventoried every year and assigned temporarily to

Amana Community kitchen, ca. 1907. Amana women and girls wore a small black cap that covered the back of their heads and tied under their chins with a black ribbon. Women also wore a black modesty scarf over the upper part or bodice of the garment. It was worn pinned up close to the chin, and its triangular point was covered at the waist by a large black apron. The dress style dates from early nineteenth-century Germany, from whence the community originated, and intentionally hides the feminine form. Stereo card. Courtesy New York Public Library.

individuals, signifying their practical use as more acceptable than their decorative use. Many of these dress practices were seen as peculiar and even scandalous by the outside world—particularly the dress and hairstyles of the women of Oneida. Many community members regularly left Oneida on community business (selling community-produced items such as silk thread, lunchboxes, animal traps, chains, and many other products). Recognizing how their clothing practices were received in the outside world, these members could check out clothing for the outside world from the community stores and return it for another's use upon their return.

THE THEOSOPHICAL SOCIETY

Founded in 1875 by Madame Helene Petrovna Blavatsky, a Russian seeress, and Henry Olcott, a U.S. attorney, the Theosophical Society combined Eastern and Western philosophy and religious ideas with strong influences from spiritualism and the occult to form an awareness movement. *Theosophy* argued that what this group called a "universal brotherhood of man" could be achieved by increasing one's awareness of the relationship between humans and the universe. They believed that universal truths could be found in the various world religions, including Hinduism, Buddhism, Christianity, and Judaism. This movement spread throughout the world, and many societies were established in England, India, the United States, and elsewhere.

Following the death of Madame Blavatsky in 1891, there was a short period when the society had no formal leader. Eventually, Madame Katherine Tingley became the head of the organization. Born in Massachusetts, Tingley had always been involved in philanthropic activities. This, combined with her abiding interest in spiritualism, brought her to the Theosophists, and she became a member in 1892 and its leader in 1896. The following year she purchased property in Point Loma, California, and established the U.S. headquarters of the society and the Theosophical School for the Revival of the Lost Mysteries of Antiquity, also known as the Raja Yoga School. The school and commune (about five hundred individuals) were under the directorship of Madame Tingley until her death in 1929. The school continued to exist until 1942 but was in a state of decline throughout the 1930s.

Tingley criticized U.S. society for its competitive focus and emphasis on money as an indicator of success. These criticisms were not uncommon in late-nineteenth- and early-twentieth-century intentional communities, but Tingley did not introduce many aspects of more traditional communes in the community's organization. For example, community members were not required to relinquish private property, and differences existed between the wealthy and poor members. Generally a fee of US$500 was required up front in addition to monthly payments to cover room and board, with scale adjustments according to the individual member's finances. The community provided for all basic needs, including food, clothing, shelter, education, and medical care.

While she held out very little hope of reforming her own generation, she believed that the ills of society—poverty, crime, disconnectedness—could be removed from the next generation through education. Because of this, Tingley stressed these reforms most in the school of Raja Yoga. Incorporating many central Theosophical tenets into the curriculum, Tingley believed that children should be taught a balance of physical health, mental vigor, and moral purity. These included emphasizing the ideals of altruism, self-reliance, and the rejection of worldly pleasures such as success, money, and selfish aggrandizement. Students' coursework encompassed these values, and classes were available in literature, ancient and modern languages, philosophy, mathematics, fine arts, and horticulture. Madame Tingley argued that parents were not capable of adequately raising their own children, and while they could visit for a few hours on Sundays, the children lived apart from their parents in dormitories segregated by sex. Their daily routine was quite structured and strict. Students were up by five in the morning and had physical training before breakfast. This was followed by house chores and formal classroom instruction. After lunch they had some playtime, then garden work, more lecture, dinner, and finally music lessons. In keeping with Theosophist views on physical health and moral purity, all meals were strictly vegetarian, although milk, eggs, and butter were served on rare occasions.

As self-sufficiency was a central ideal of the community, much of the land was devoted to raising food. Hills planted with oats, barley, groves of citrus, avocado, and other fruit trees, as well as numerous vegetable gardens, provided much of the community's food. The settlement consisted of living quarters, a kitchen and dining room, a bakery, carpentry shop, stables, machine shop, print shop, and buildings housing textile and clothing production. Other structures included a temple; the Raja Yoga Academy, where students were educated; and the first open-air Greek theater in the United States. Reminiscent of the Theosophical philosophy in general, many of the buildings blended Eastern, Moorish, and ancient Egyptian architectural styles, causing several visitors to remark that it was much like having some of India in Point Loma.

Dress norms at the community are an example of practical considerations to some extent outweighing symbolic ones. Dress tended to be unintentionally uniform due to the fact that most clothing was produced at the community following simple designs. Women wore long, dark-colored dresses with plain bodices; men wore dark pants and jackets buttoned high over collarless white shirts. Young boys' dress resembled the men's clothing in miniature, and young girls wore knee-length dresses. The central importance of educating children was reinforced in the practice of children changing into special school clothing before both their classroom sessions during the day.

THE AMANA COLONIES

At the beginning of the eighteenth century, a new form of Protestantism arose called *Pietism*. Philip Jakob Spener, one of the most famous early Pietists, argued that the proper way to worship God was not through debate over theological questions, as was the practice in many Protestant sects at the time. Spener believed that simple, direct, and loving communion was necessary for both the individual and within the congregation. The model for this way of life was to be found in scripture, and true Christians must follow these tenets and attain true piety in order to attain salvation. Still other, more radical Pietists asserted that the church had become too hierarchical to ever reform in this way. Instead, they advocated that a truly Christian life could be realized only if individuals separated from the official church and worshiped in small congregations. This separatism, combined with the practice of *inspirationalism* (the belief that any individual could be divinely inspired), made the followers of this form of Pietism suffer much persecution. After several decades, the Inspirationalists decided to leave Germany and immigrate to the United States in 1842. They purchased a five-thousand-acre (approximately 2,023-hectare) tract of land near Buffalo, New York, and began arriving in 1843. The Community of True Inspiration named their new settlement Ebenezer.

Initial building and construction of Ebenezer required collective work and resources, and this pattern of communalism continued for both biblical (following several verses in Acts) and economic reasons. All land and buildings were held in common. Individual families were given living quarters, and resources were

communal. This communitarianism made an impressive number of buildings and economic endeavors possible. Soon six villages were established, including two woolen mills, a calico-print mill, two gristmills, and an oil mill, all in operation by 1855. Nearly all of Ebenezer's material needs were met through the presence of numerous other trades, including carpenters, masons, blacksmiths, soap makers, butchers, bakers, and shoemakers. Others worked in the community farms, providing much of their food. Community-produced goods were sold in both Buffalo and New York City, providing income in order for the community to purchase the items they did not manufacture themselves.

Even though the Community of True Inspiration prospered in New York, it became necessary for them to move. As more migrants arrived from Europe, their numbers passed a thousand, and the need for more land arose. Unfortunately, there was little affordable land nearby. In addition, many were increasingly worried by the close proximity of Buffalo, an expanding city that threatened to corrupt their way of life. They found an area of eastern Iowa suitable for their purposes, and in 1855, they purchased twenty-six thousand acres (almost 10,522 hectares). It took nine years for all of the villages to relocate to Amana. By the end of the nineteenth century, almost eighteen hundred people lived in the seven Amana villages.

The villages in Amana were designed in the same fashion as the ones in Ebenezer. Each village had its own trade shops, school, bakery, general store, butcher, community kitchens, and church, and each was supplied by its own farms. Two woolen mills and a calico-print mill produced goods for both the Amana colonies and for sale to the outside. In addition, several flour mills and sawmills also provided the villages with essential materials. This economy based on manufacturing and agriculture provided for all the Amana colonies' needs. This continued until 1932, when a majority of Amana's residents were no longer satisfied with communalism and voted to incorporate their holdings in a profit-sharing corporation instead.

One of the main structuring principles of Amana society was based on gender. Both boys and girls began working in the Amana colonies at the age of fourteen. Generally boys were assigned to the work on the farms, in the factories, or doing craft work (often following in their father's vocations). A small number of young men traveled to the outside world in order to be trained in professions such as medicine, dentistry, or education. Girls were assigned to work in teams at the community kitchens cooking and serving meals to as many as forty colony members, who ate at separate men's and women's tables. These types of divisions could also be found in other community activities such as church services. Even in the early twenty-first century, men and women still enter and exit through separate doors and sit on opposite sides of the room. One nineteenth-century visitor observed that boys were only allowed to play with boys, and girls were only allowed to play with girls. Such separations as these were seen as part of living a proper Pietist life among the Community of True Inspirationalists.

The dress norms among the Amana reflect these Pietist beliefs as well and is often described by outsiders as being somber and very plain. Many of the dress styles at Amana are a very apt example of fossilization and harken back to the styles and designs of the early-nineteenth-century Germany they left behind. Initially, girls' everyday dresses were short gowns mostly made from black and gray fabrics produced in the colonies. All women and girls wore a small black cap that covered the back of their heads and tied under their chins with a black ribbon. All women also wore a black modesty scarf over the upper part or bodice of the garment. It was worn pinned up close to the chin, and its triangular point was covered at the waist by a large black apron. This form of dress intentionally hid the feminine form, and other decorative elements were not encouraged. In addition, women and girls tied their hair back in a severe fashion and contained it under their caps. Men wore sober suits with little in the form of embellishment. After the turn of the twentieth century, as more and more members became dissatisfied with this way of life, breaking the society's clothing norms was a common way to express this dissatisfaction, particularly among young people. Examples include women bobbing their hair or wearing a piece of red clothing—a forbidden color.

DIVERSITY AMONG INTENTIONAL COMMUNITIES

North America has been home to several hundred intentional communities, both religious and secular. The life span of these communities has varied from several years to many decades and even centuries. The part that dress has played in these communities differs sharply. The late-twentieth-century secular cohousing movement, which originated in Scandinavia, has led to the establishment of many communities in Canada and the United States. Cohousing focuses on developing housing that balances personal privacy and community. Dress plays no part in this type of intentional community.

Transcendentalism is usually thought of as a philosophical movement that gained adherents in New England in the nineteenth century. Several intentional communities were established by individuals prominent in this movement. Dress concerns were especially important at one of these, Fruitlands, in the town of Harvard, Massachusetts. This community lasted only two or three years. The residents of Fruitlands espoused vegetarianism; they were also committed abolitionists. Dress restrictions that they adopted grew out of these beliefs. As a result of their concern for (and refusal to kill) animals, using leather was forbidden. Shoes were made, instead, of canvas. Wool was rejected because it was taken by force from sheep, and cotton was not allowed because it was harvested by slave labor. Linen fabrics were used for their clothing.

Dress within intentional communities, even when there are no formal or informal rules about dress, reflects the philosophical foundation of the community. Cohousing communities have no need to set themselves apart from those who do not choose to live in cohousing communities. Their sole focus is housing—other elements of the material culture, such as dress, are irrelevant. Religious communities are more likely to use dress as a means of making their choice to live apart from the outside world clear to members and nonmembers alike. At establishments such as Fruitlands, dress rules were directly related to the deeply held beliefs that led to the establishment of the community. The differing choices made about dress in these communities are a clear reflection of the wide range of reasons that inspire the founding of intentional communities.

References and Further Reading

Andelson, Jonathan G. "The Community of True Inspiration from Germany to the Amana Colonies." In *America's Communal Utopias*, edited by Donald E. Pitzer, 181–203. Chapel Hill: University of North Carolina Press, 1997.

Barthel, Diane L. *Amana: From Pietist Sect to American Community*. Lincoln: University of Nebraska Press, 1984.

Fischer, Gayle. "Dressing to Please God: Pants-Wearing Women in Mid-Nineteenth-Century Religious Communities." *Communal Societies* 15, no. 1 (1995): 55–74.

Foster, Lawrence. "Free Love and Community: John Humphrey Noyes and the Oneida Perfectionists." In *America's Communal Utopias*, edited by Donald E. Pitzer, 253–288. Chapel Hill: University of North Carolina Press, 1997.

Gordon, Beverly. "Dress in American Communal Societies." *Communal Societies* 5, no. 1 (1985): 122–136.

Ingoldsby, Bron B. "Group Conformity and the Amplification of Deviance: A Comparison of Hutterite and Mormon Dress Codes." *Communal Societies* 22, no. 1 (2002): 87–97.

Melton, J. Gordon. "The Theosophical Communities and Their Ideal of Universal Brotherhood." In *America's Communal Utopias*, edited by Donald E. Pitzer, 396–418. Chapel Hill: University of North Carolina Press, 1997.

Nordhoff, Charles. *The Communities of the United States: From Personal Visit and Observation*. New York: Dover Publications, 1966. (Originally published in 1875.)

Heather Van Wormer

See also Religion and Dress; Snapshot: Amish, Mennonites, Hutterites, and Brethren; Snapshot: Quakers and Shakers; Snapshot: Old Believers.

Gay, Lesbian, Bisexual, and Transgendered Persons

Reliable information about dress in the lesbian, gay, bisexual, or transgendered (LGBT) community has become available only recently. For many years negative attitudes held by much of the non-LGBT population resulted in beliefs and stereotypes that were often superficial and inaccurate. Research into the dress of members of the LGBT community is now providing a more detailed and nuanced view of the subject. When a person "comes out" or acknowledges an LGBT identity, it is often a mixed blessing; the relief of finally knowing oneself is often met with resistance from society and culture. Some people may hide their sexual orientation, whereas others proclaim it, often through dress. The process of coming out is usually continual, for sexual orientation is not necessarily visible to others, and dress provides a (coded) visual medium for expression of the self when words may be redundant or secrecy necessary.

Many scholars have presented models of coming out. While the models vary in the number of phases one goes through in the formation of a gay identity, they all do proffer a similar succession of steps. At first, one questions his or her sexual orientation, noting that something is "different" about oneself in comparing oneself to others. This is then followed by a series of stages in which the person adopts the label of "gay" on a trial basis and (possibly) informs a few people of the secret identity. This is followed by a permanent acceptance of the label and telling more people of the identity, followed by incorporating the sexual orientation within the greater scope of his or her sense of self. It is during the stages of acceptance and announcing one's gay identity that a person may adopt clothing that is associated with gay people.

Using dress to identify one's self as LGBT can be viewed as a form of community development. Social psychologists H. Tajfel and J. C. Turner's *social identity theory* posits that groups of people want to distance themselves from other groups in order to show superiority. When applied to the coming-out process, the theory explains the phenomenon of dressing different from the accepted norm of straight or heterosexual society; upon realizing their identity is different from the status quo, LGBT people strive to distance themselves from straight people to show their identity and freedom from cultural norms to which straight people are likely to adhere. However, in accord with many coming-out models, eventually dress passes into one of personal and not group identification.

Yet not all LGBT people will choose to identify their sexual orientation via dress. Depending on the social and cultural climate in which one lives and one's acceptance of one's sexual orientation, the dress of LGBT people varies along a continuum from assimilating within the dominant heterosexual society (i.e., to pass as heterosexual) to radically displaying their sexual orientation through aesthetic or cultural affectations.

SEMIOTICS

The history of LGBT persons, in the industrialized world at least, has been one of oppression. Historically, LGBT persons have been persecuted and prosecuted for their same-sex attraction. For example, in Edwardian England, "the love that dare not speak its name" was punishable by imprisonment and hard labor; under the Nazi regime in Europe, gay men were confined to concentration camps and identified by an inverted pink triangle (rosawinkle) attached to their clothing; in the United States, homosexual behavior was classified as a mental illness until 1973, when it was removed from the *Diagnostic and Statistical Manual of Mental Disorders*. Though these examples are of an extreme nature, they show the cultural conditions in which LGBT persons have likely been raised and live. Even today, LGBT people are likely to encounter discrimination from family, work, and landlords or are prohibited by law from adopting children, marrying, and serving in the military. Given this climate, many LGBT people chose to remain incognito, yet they have found avenues to communicate their identity to similar others through semiotics.

Semiotics are coded sign systems in which a sender and receiver both understand the message embedded within a seemingly innocuous artifact or gesture. Gay men in Edwardian England used a green carnation in their lapel or a red tie as a way to communicate their sexual identity to other men. In the 1980s, men communicated their gay identity by an earring in their right ear and later in both ears. Once this communication became public knowledge, the rhyme "left is right and right is wrong" was used by straight men to remember which ear was socially acceptable for jewelry. Additionally, wedding bands worn by same-sex couples were often on the right hand rather than the left hand, symbolic of one's identity but also implying a difference regarding one's attraction.

Other symbols were also used to self-identify as LGBT. The inverted triangle is a popular and easily recognized symbol. In the 1970s, the LGBT community in the United States and Germany began using the rosawinkle of Nazi Germany in order to remind people that oppression and discrimination of LGBT people still persisted. In the 1980s, lesbians began using the inverted black triangle to symbolize their own sexual orientation (the black triangle was used in Nazi Germany to identify people who were antisocial; although no hard evidence exists that demonstrates lesbians were routinely identified as such, it appears this is an instance where rumor and legend were the basis for the semiotic). Though it is curious for LGBT people to use the inverted triangle, a symbol so steeped in their own violent history, one could

The butch aesthetic. In the United States in the 1950s this was characterized by leather jackets, pinky rings, and short hair combed back. Image Copyright Katherine Welles, 2007. Used under license from Shutterstock.com.

Variations on these symbols abound, with subtle shifts in cultural meanings, but all of them demonstrate the willingness on the part of the wearer to communicate his or her sexual orientation to oneself or to others. Whether worn on T-shirts or tattooed to one's body, they no doubt speak to one's identity. Overall, whether subtle or overt, semiotics has played an important part in the history of LGBT people and their dress. In a society where everyone is assumed straight, visual codes have helped LGBT people socialize and form networks with other LGBT people while at the same time reinforcing awareness.

AESTHETICS OF GAY MEN

To say that all gay men hold one specific aesthetic above all others would be incorrect; but it does appear that gay men gravitate to specific aesthetic styles. Gay men prefer to interact and date other gay men who are dressed in similar fashion to themselves. This implies that not only do gay men like what they see in the mirror but that they are attracted to their own aesthetic as well. Additionally, it means that in order to interact with a specific group of gay men, one must meet certain appearance expectations of that group. For example, in the novel by Armistead Maupin (and subsequent PBS miniseries) *Tales of the City*, which chronicles and captures the life of fictionalized people in 1970s San Francisco, gay character Michael explains to a friend why he is dressed in penny loafers: "It was best to dress like the people you wanted to pick you up" (p. 113). Research into this notion of dressing like those you want to meet has demonstrated that gay men have preferences for similar clothing and fragrance styles that are different from the preferences espoused by straight men. However, it should be noted not all gay men are attracted to their own image. Just as in the straight community, often opposites attract.

One of the earliest identifiable gay male subcultures was the leather subculture. Beginning in the 1960s, members of the leather subculture displayed their nonstereotypical appearance through a muscular physique and leather apparel, including jackets, chaps, caps, and harnesses. As a textile-like material, leather is tough and durable, a good analogy for men wanting to display strength in the face of adversity. Leathermen also developed a sexual code using a handkerchief hanging from the back pocket of their pants, with the color and location indicative of one's sexual interest. "Castro clones" of the 1970s created a style for gay men by using working-class dress—jeans, plaid shirts, boots, and mustaches—to create an overly emphasized masculine aesthetic. (The Castro District of San Francisco was, and still is, an LGBT neighborhood.) By the early 1980s, AIDS had become closely associated with gay men in general, and the wasting away of the body had become an outward signifier (if not entirely accurate) of one's HIV status. Though there had always been overweight gay men, it was during this time that they became more valued and recognized: this may have been a causative factor in the formation of the bear subculture, whose members rejoice in the eroticization of a natural physique, bulky and hirsute. However, these subcultures were not simply an imitation of straight men in order to pass as straight; rather, they were perfecting the male form (for other men) through what social scientist M. P. Levine has called "parody and emulation" or camp and irony. Members of the leather community sported a hanky in the back pocket of their pants indicating their sexual desires for other men; bears celebrated the ideal, natural, male form through bear contests;

argue that the philosophy behind it is a form of empowerment and that one should never forget the past. The rainbow flag was introduced as part of the annual Gay Pride Parade in San Francisco in 1978. Designed by Gilbert Baker, it is a flag of six rows of colors (originally designed with more colors but reduced for economical reasons). Though it was intended to represent all aspects of sexual orientation, a flag to represent bisexual people had also been designed by Michael Page. This flag contains three horizontal stripes: the top stripe is pink (symbolizing same-sex attraction), the bottom is blue (representing opposite-sex attraction), and in the middle is a blend of the two to create purple (representing attraction to both sexes). Other variations of the rainbow flag were developed to identify specific gay subcultures: The leather subculture is identified by a flag, first used in 1989, of nine horizontal stripes alternating between blue and black with a white stripe in the middle, whereas the bear subculture is identified by a flag first used in the 1990s that contains seven stripes changing in color from brown to black and has a bear paw print in the upper left corner.

Other symbols, including the Greek letter lambda, the labrys (a double-bladed axe), or two male or female signs linked, are also used to identify one's sexual orientation. Some of these symbols are more subtle than the widely known flag and triangle, so they may appeal to LGBT people who cannot or do not want their sexual orientation known to the mass majority but still want a way of self-affirmation within the limits of their environment.

clones paid attention to achieving the flawless masculine form. Even today, myriad other gay subcultures exist, such as ones that center on gym-sculpted bodies, uniforms, or Levi's jeans.

The body plays an important role in personal and cultural identity for many gay men. The shape of the body often allows for introduction or exclusion from subcultures, where identity and affiliation are equated to appearance. Gay men report being more interested in their appearance (which includes the shape of the body) than straight men and are more concerned with their weight; they are more fearful of being overweight and have lower ideal weights than straight men. Other research reported by body image researchers M. A. Morrison, T. G. Morrison, and C. Sager found "a small, but real, difference between heterosexual and gay men in terms of body satisfaction."

Lower body satisfaction among gay men may be a reason why gay men work out for appearance reasons, whereas straight men seem to be more likely to work out for health reasons. Unlike straight women who desire to lose weight, gay men may desire to lose weight while also gaining muscle mass. Workout regimes are often coupled with eating habits that can be dangerous when taken to the extreme. The result may be painful and often deadly behavior patterns, such as anorexia, bulimia, and chronic dieting. When research showed that, compared to straight men, gay men are more likely to develop an eating disorder, the belief that gay men are more appearance conscious than straight men was reinforced.

Researchers have looked for explanations of behavior related to appearance-related eating and workout regimens and have concluded that one explanation may be *internalized* homophobia, which is a form of self-hatred directed toward one's own sexual orientation. Studies showed that men with high internalized homophobia have lower body satisfaction than men with low internalized homophobia. Such men may engage in body building in order to look masculine. Research has also linked eating disorders with internalized homophobia. The resulting conclusion was that a negative view of one's body coupled with internalized homophobia can lead to eating disorders in attempts to create an idealized figure.

Another possible explanation for body dissatisfaction among gay men is exposure to media in which male models are routinely muscular and in various stages of undress. These images have increased in muscularity and stages of undress in the past few decades. Advertising for men's underwear typically had focused on the product alone, sans any model, or else the model was of average physique. However, Calvin Klein's explosive campaign in the early 1990s featuring actor/singer Mark Wahlberg changed the landscape and began the craze for ever more muscular models in advertising. Gay men may internalize these idealized images and strive to assimilate the bodies they see on television, in magazines, and in advertisements, resulting in increased body dissatisfaction. However, it should be noted that this desire for a thin, toned body is not indicative of all gay men. Bears, a subculture of gay men whose body type is typically overweight, revere their excess poundage, and some gay men who are of average physique do not strive to achieve a hypermuscular body due to self-esteem, lack of interest, or general contentment with their body. Thus, cultural affiliation and personal psychology play a role in satisfaction with body shape.

Fragrance use is an important part of dress, in general, and gay and straight men differ on fragrance preferences and usage.

A transsexual on Bourbon Street, Mardi Gras Day, New Orleans, Louisiana, 2007. Image Copyright Brian Nolan, 2007. Used under license from Shutterstock.com.

Fragrances are grouped by notes, such as floral, citrus, woody/green, or Oriental. When surveyed, gay men prefer floral and Oriental scents, while straight men prefer woody/green scents. Floral scents are made from, or made to mimic, flowers, and Oriental scents are spicy and exotic, whereas woody/green scents are earthy and musky (e.g., patchouli). One possible explanation for this is that gay men may feel freer to cross gender boundaries. Gay men may not be held to the same social expectations as are straight men and are thus permitted more freedom to express an identity that is not strictly traditionally masculine. Thus, it may not be that gay men prefer feminine scents due simply to their sexual orientation but that they feel more comfortable in admitting their preferences for scents typically considered feminine.

Additionally, the results of research revealed that gay men owned more bottles of fragrances than straight men (five compared to four) and that many gay men used fragrance on a daily basis, whereas straight men used cologne less frequently. This could possibly be due to a higher interest in self-presentation among gay men. Men who frequently use fragrances have been reported as being concerned with their body image and are more social, findings that align with research that reports gay men are more attuned to their personal aesthetic. Straight men may use fragrances less frequently because they view colognes as something reserved for special occasions, such as holidays and celebrations; thus, gay men may view every day as an opportunity to present themselves in the best way they know how.

It should be noted, however, that this research does not apply to all gay men. Fragrances have come in and out of fashion through history, with the practice either embraced or shunned. For example, in the 1970s, men's fragrance was an important part of self-presentation for both gay and straight men. And in the early twenty-first century, *metrosexual* men (straight men who take an interest in personal aesthetics) embraced the use of fragrances. Likewise, not all gay men are as enamored of fragrances as readers of the previous research would assume. Some gay subcultures, such as the leather and bear subcultures, shun the use of fragrances because their aesthetics are based on historic notions of manliness.

AESTHETICS OF LESBIANS

Lesbian aesthetics have historically been divided into butch and femme styles. *Butch* styles are closely associated with the stereotype of lesbians (masculine), whereas *femme* styles are associated with the stereotype of straight women (feminine). Here, too, research leads to the following conclusions. For butch lesbians, the aesthetic was cultural as well as a way to identify other lesbians and to separate oneself from the dominant culture (as well as being related to class structure). In the 1950s, the aesthetic mode was split; butch lesbians (who were usually working class) wore leather jackets, pinky rings, and short hair combed back, whereas femme lesbians (who were middle-class women passing as straight) adopted makeup, dresses, skirts, and blouses. These looks were strictly enforced at this time, with a woman not adhering to the either/or dichotomy finding herself an outcast and called "kiki." It has been argued that this method was intended to protect the lesbian community from arrest; the popular thought at the time was that a woman who did not look either butch or femme was most likely an undercover officer who did not know the dress codes. By the 1970s, the androgynous look—jeans, T-shirts or flannel shirts, boots, long hair—gained popularity, but over the next two decades, there was more inclusion of different ethnicities and cultures in the aesthetic, including a return to the butch/femme dichotomy.

While it has been argued that femme women wanted to pass as straight, some lesbian women find the aesthetic attractive and actively cultivate the look within themselves or seek it in others.

Butch aesthetics encompassed a variety of masculine styles on a continuum from androgynous to hypermasculine. The butch aesthetic may be a function of acceptance of one's sexual orientation. Some researchers argue that all women, regardless of their sexual orientation, experience pressure to dress in a feminine manner and state that there is pressure to look "lesbian" after first coming out. The butch aesthetic is a way for lesbians to stand out from the dominant (feminine) female crowd by creating a radical departure from the expected appearance of women, with an intentional motive to display the self as sexually unavailable to men. However, after incorporating one's sexual orientation into one's complete identity, lesbians select a style more representative of their composite identity.

One particular style that tends to lend itself to controversy is the sadomasochist (S/M) style. Akin to the leather aesthetic of gay men, the S/M lesbian wears uniforms of leather or rubber garments with breasts barely covered or entirely revealed. For some women, this style is sexually exciting; S/M and leather tend to convey power and authority and may be used as a form of wish-fulfillment for people who are marginalized or feel powerless in society. For others, it is a radical statement meant to provoke and question social dress codes: Why cannot a woman go shirtless as a man? What gives men the privilege and not women?

Popular thought argues that lesbians are free from the beauty constraints that straight women face because their bodies are not intended to please men and, therefore, they are happier with their bodies than straight women. Research has not yet answered this question conclusively. All that can be said is that the effects of gender may be more salient for some lesbians. Women who rate their appearance as feminine have lower body satisfaction when compared to women who rate their appearance as androgynous or masculine. Feminine women may be comparing themselves to the hyperfeminine image portrayed in the media, and androgynous or masculine women may not.

Interestingly, it has been noted that the butch aesthetic (which typically includes an overweight body) was originally intended to free women from the chains of heterosexual expectations of women. However, it evolved into rigid expectations of lesbian appearance, where even if lesbians are dissatisfied with their bodies, they learn not to voice their concerns. It is interesting to notice that this is similar to the socialization of men who are taught not to complain about their bodies because it is considered feminine to do so.

GENDER IDENTITY: TRANSSEXUAL

A *transsexual* is a person who believes he or she was born as the incorrect sex. Physically, a transsexual may be a man who identifies as a woman or vice versa. Transsexuals seek to change their physical bodies to match gender identity and can accomplish this via dress, hormone treatment, cosmetic surgery, and sex-reassignment surgery. Transsexuals dress as the gender with which they identify, though this may result in issues with the body, such as body hair distribution and body proportion. The majority of transsexuals tend to be male-to-female (MTF).

Often, transsexuals employ a creative bevy of methods to disguise features that are inherent to the sex into which they were born. For example, scarves are often used to cover Adam's apples of MTF transsexuals, while breasts are bound down with gauze among female-to-male (FTM) transsexuals. Hormone therapy or cosmetic surgery is used to transform the silhouette of the body, the shape of the face, and the sound of the voice. Sex-reassignment surgery (where the genitalia are transformed into that of the desired sex) is performed after the patient has undergone a series of psychological evaluations and has lived as the gender with which they identify for a period of time. Hormone and surgical practices help transsexuals confirm their identity and feel authentic, underscoring the notion that having the body that aligns with one's identity fosters feelings of validity. Additionally, the embodiment of gender via body changes is more rigorous for MTF than FTM and may include retraining the body to conform to societal standards of the new gender.

If MTF transsexuals see themselves as women, then it is easy to assume that they would have a body image poorer than that of men because women generally do have a poorer body image than men. However, postoperative MTF transsexuals have a body image similar to that of men, but they feel just as feminine as women. This does not mean that eating disorders relating to appearance are nonexistent. They do exist and there have been some reports of cases of anorexia and bulimia. Though low, eating disorders in MTF transsexuals may be a way for them to meet the social expectation of a thin, female body.

GENDER IDENTITY: DRAG

Drag is a term associated with gender performance, whether applied to a man dressing as a woman (drag queen) or a woman dressing as a man (drag king). However, the aesthetics, which revolve around the concept of camp and exaggeration of features, also allow for a woman to dress as a faux drag queen or a man as a faux drag king. Drag is usually associated with the LGBT community, though it is not exclusive to this community.

Drag queen, 2007. Drag, the art of dressing as the opposite gender, is associated with performance. For a drag queen, a powdered face becomes the canvas on which to apply large, colorful lips, extreme eyebrows, and perhaps a mole or two. Hair or more frequently wigs are styled to enhance a large personality, padded breasts are added, and clothing is glamorous. Image Copyright Sophie Louise Asselin, 2007. Used under license from Shutterstock.com.

Drag performers are not trying to pass as another gender, as a transsexual desires to be accepted as a woman or a man. Rather, drag performers are the embodiment of robust gender. Literary theorist Susan Sontag defined *camp* as an esoteric sensibility of pretense and unnatural exaggeration/expression. With this definition, drag is camp, or campy, meaning that what is expressed via drag is not meant to be taken seriously but is meant to entertain, provoke, and perhaps question conventional wisdom. For drag queens and faux drag queens, a powdered face becomes the canvas on which to apply large, colorful lips; extreme eyebrows; and perhaps a mole or two. Hair, or more frequently wigs, are styled to enhance a large personality; padded breasts are added; unwanted hair is removed, and clothing is, if nothing else, at least glamorous. For drag kings and faux drag kings, breasts are bound, padding is used to present a more masculine appearance, and faux facial hair is attached or mimicked with makeup. Drag performers may create unique personas, sometimes with creative names such as Syphilis Diller or Bertha Nation, or they may imitate celebrities who themselves were larger than life, such as Bette Davis or Joan Crawford.

Additionally, dress scholar J. Jacob has identified a subgroup within the drag community that is aesthetically different from traditional drag queens and termed them *radical drag queens*. Radical drag queens do not impersonate female identity as traditional drag queens but rather take it to a ridiculous extreme. Additionally, radical drag queens may eliminate the illusion of femaleness by revealing the male body and revealing the tricks of the trade that traditional drag queens use to create their persona (e.g., shape-enhancing garments).

CONCLUSION

While the popular notion is that gay men are effeminate and lesbians are masculine, the truth reveals a rich landscape of LGBT style and identity. Historically, LGBT people have created or found subcultures within the LGBT community where their interests are shared by others and, by virtue of necessity or identity, used dress and appearance as a means of identification. Some embrace the stereotype; some reject it. Some use dress for political purposes; some, in order to establish identity; others, for pure shock value.

Perhaps the best example of the notion of gay aesthetics is found in LGBT dolls. With an audience that is not necessarily children, the dolls have become favorites among the LGBT community. Billy is manufactured by Totem and was introduced in the 1990s as the first "out" gay doll. Billy and his friends come in a variety of clothing styles and uniforms. Whether dressed as a sailor, cowboy, delivery person, or in casual wear, underneath the clothing is a muscular physique. Likewise, Bobbie, produced by Dykedolls, comes in a variety of styles including Diesel Dyke, Rockabilly, and Southern California Skater, though all styles have the same physique. While these dolls are an adventure in camp, they are underscored by the popular notion of what gay people look like.

References and Further Reading

Atkins, D. *Looking Queer: Body Image and Identity in Lesbian, Bisexual, Gay and Transgender Communities.* New York: Haworth, 1998.

Faderman, L. *Odd Girls and Twilight Lovers: A History of Lesbian Life in Twentieth-Century America.* New York: Columbia University Press, 1991.

Hepp, U., and G. Milos. "Gender Identity Disorder and Eating Disorders." *International Journal of Eating Disorders* 32 (2002): 473–478.

Jacob, J. "Classifying Radical Drag Queen Appearances: The Importance of Shared Aesthetic Codes." In *ITAA Proceedings #60*. (Abstract obtained from http://www.itaaonline.org/downloads/P2003-ResJacobJ-Classifying-Res051.pdf, 2003, accessed 19 July 2008.)

Levine, M. P. *Gay Macho: The Life and Death of the Homosexual Clone.* New York: New York University Press, 1998.

Morrison, M. A., T. G. Morrison, and C. Sager. "Does Body Satisfaction Differ between Gay Men and Lesbian Women and Heterosexual Men and Women? A Meta-Analytic Review." *Body Image* 1 (1994): 127–138.

Pope, H. G., Jr., K. A. Phillips, and R. Olivardia. *The Adonis Complex: The Secret Crisis of Male Body Obsession.* New York: The Free Press, 2000.

Reilly, A., and N. A. Rudd. "Is Internalized Homonegativity Related to Body Image?" *Family and Consumer Sciences Research Journal* 35, no. 1 (2006): 58–73.

Rothblum, E. D. "Lesbians and Physical Appearance: Which Model Applies?" In *Psychological Perspectives on Lesbian and Gay Issues*, vol. 1, edited by B. Greene and G. M. Herek, 84–97. Newberry Park, CA: Sage, 1994.

Rudd, N. A. "Appearance and Self-Presentation Research in Gay Consumer Cultures: Issues and Impact." *Journal of Homosexuality* 31, no. 1–2 (1996): 109–134.

Shrock, D., L. Reid, and E. M. Boyd. "Transsexuals Embodiment of Womanhood." *Gender & Society* 19, no. 3 (2005): 317–335.

Tajfel, H., and J. C. Turner. "An Integrative Theory of Intergroup Conflict." In *The Social Psychology of Intergroup Relations*, edited by E. G. Austin and S. Worchel, 33–47. Monterey, CA: Brooks-Cole, 1986.

Wolfradt, U., and K. Neumann. "Depersonalization, Self-Esteem and Body Image in Male-to-Female Transsexuals Compared to Male and Female Controls." *Archives of Sexual Behavior* 30, no. 3 (2001): 301–310.

Andrew Reilly

Antebellum African Americans

Dress figures prominently in the recollections of Africans enslaved in the United States. These remembrances include the published memoirs of people who escaped the South before emancipation and the narrations of approximately two thousand formerly enslaved people collected in the 1930s under the auspices of the U.S. government. They described in detail the clothing given them by owners and other means by which they acquired it. They described everyday wear, dress for special events such as harvest festivals and dances, and dress for religious occasions. According to the accounts, antebellum African American dress preferences became a powerful means to define themselves as individuals and as part of a larger community.

PUNISHMENT AND ESCAPE

The physical and mental punishments meted out by white owners and overseers always concerned the enslaved body, legally viewed as another piece of livestock. The most brutal punishments described by those who endured or bore witness to them included brutal trappings: chains, manacles, and metal bands around their necks with constantly ringing bells mounted above the head. They endured brands burned into the flesh, having body parts severed, and the scars from severe whippings, the most consistent punishment. In an age when both African Americans and European Americans viewed nudity as immoral, whites subjected the enslaved to stripping before whippings. Enslaved males and females underwent beatings, but the owners' intentional humiliation was the lashing of females, their clothing removed before an audience of leering whites and appalled African Americans. Other punishments did not entail physical brutality but were calculated to be devastating humiliations. Chopping off enslaved women's hair achieved this end. Another psychological punishment forced both men and women to publicly wear dress of the opposite sex.

African Americans did not take the horrific torment of their enslavement without subtle forms of rebellion. Daily revolts involved slowing down in performance of their labor, breaking tools, or even pilfering needed items such as food or clothes. Escaping from bondage became the ultimate form of rebellion, but because of the Southern white community's commitment to slavocracy, most runaways failed. When an attempted escape became known, hound dogs tracked the person after being given a piece of the escapee's clothing to smell. Punishment was extremely harsh for those who fled and were caught. Nevertheless, with careful planning and creative cunning, thousands did manage to escape. Success hinged on clever disguises: dressing in costume, cross-dressing, and dressing to pass as white. Outlandish costumes deflected from recognition based on the usual outfit. Both men and women disguised themselves by dressing in clothes of the opposite sex, an ironic twist to the humiliating punishment. Because of the widespread rape of enslaved women by white men, those children born of such unions might have lighter skin color and could pass for a European American during escape and even might continue to pass in Northern states.

ACQUIRING DRESS

For those who remained in captivity, attention to bodily adornment became fundamental—the visual way of defining oneself in the face of overwhelming odds. As children, the clothing offered no definition of sex; young boys and girls wore only a loose, singleton shirt until age twelve or older. But as in all societies, as young adults they dressed to ensure they were seen to sexual advantage. Acquisition of articles of dress beyond the meager and inferior quality doled out by owners became an obsession for many at this age, and narrators recounted ways to achieve this.

Enslaved seamstresses had access to leftover fabric, sometimes of good quality and of brighter dyes. Narrators recalled childhoods in which their mothers sewed outfits for special events. For daughters, the women stiffened petticoats with starches made of flour or cornstarch and entwined grape vines into hoop skirts. Another way of acquiring more flattering dress occurred in urban areas, where owners hired out their enslaved men and women, who were allowed to keep part of the money and often purchased dress items with these earnings. Still others acquired articles of dress by trading craft items or garden crops. Domestic servants might receive special clothing as hand-me-downs from whites, and they even related "borrowing" from an owner's wardrobe on occasion. Owners gave gifts of clothing or small amounts of money to especially hard-working laborers, sometimes as a contest prize during harvest. Items of clothing and money were given especially at Christmas. Again, people who received money at these events often used it to purchase dress items.

DAILY WEAR

Until the last quarter of the nineteenth century, people in the United States wore handmade clothing—rarely commercially manufactured garments. Wool and flax for linen were cultivated, but cotton was the important textile. Enslaved labor produced cotton through all stages of production, from planting, harvesting, and ginning to spinning, weaving, and sewing it into clothing. Even small children worked the fields, and men recalled that as young boys they spun and measured the yarns into hanks for weaving.

In households where African American women labored as weavers and seamstresses, they produced rough clothing for other enslaved people as well as finer pieces of apparel for their owners. In their narratives, these women recount an expertise in utilizing natural dyes and skill in producing a variety of fabrics and textile patterns. What owners allocated enslaved people to

contemporary European fashion but further enriched it to meet their own aesthetic senses. In other words, they took from one culture's dress fashions and put their own stylistic stamps on them. Differences included wearing brighter colors and arranging items of dress in flamboyant ways. Individualism became most evident when dressing for special events.

Special occasions for the enslaved population included the owners allowing holiday celebrations at Christmas and during such events as corn shuckings. More important, the enslaved themselves made their own good times, whether clandestine or not. Descriptions of dances and musical events demonstrate these were the paramount community entertainments, and descriptions usually include the special efforts that went into the dress worn for these dance parties. Enslaved people saved "Sunday clothes" for church attendance and also for dances.

African religions are monotheistic, and nearly all captive Africans converted to Christianity, albeit incorporating older spiritual beliefs and practices into their newer religion. Southern owners usually required the enslaved to attend white churches rather than allowing them to hold religious services of their own. To prepare for attending the white services, the formerly enslaved recalled having a once-a-week bath on Saturday night. Girls and women describe putting strings in their hair on Saturday night to have it ready for Sunday, the one day of the week they did not work. On Sunday morning, they dressed in clothes saved for special occasions. This, again, outwardly appeared as another show of the owner's prestige. Yet descriptions, particularly by whites, demonstrate the African Americans' ability to change the prescribed dress to their own stylistic tastes—styles that flaunted contemporary Euro–North American sensibilities of appropriate wear. Very often, girls wore ribbons and combs in their hair, and women wore elaborately wrapped cloths around their heads. Men described wearing ties and ascots and donning rakish hats only on Sundays. If they owned shoes, they slung them over their shoulders when walking to church to avoid getting them dusty and only put the shoes on when going within the church.

When permitted to hold funerals for someone in the enslaved community, African Americans spared no expense in holding elaborate ceremonies, and they embellished their regalia and that of the deceased with particular customs, some carried over from West Africa. As on the homeland continent, they washed and dressed the deceased in elaborate clothing, often including shoes and white gloves. The Euro–North American tradition is black dress for mourning, but enslaved people attending funerals in some communities donned special dress incorporating the color white. Women wore white veils, headwraps, aprons, gloves, and shirtwaists. Men belonging to a fraternal organization also wore white gloves and a white, embroidered apron over a black jacket and trousers.

Marriages, although not legally binding during the period of enslavement, did take place. At such a time, both the man and woman attempted to dress conspicuously. Sometimes the white mistress gave or loaned a dress or a piece of jewelry to the bride.

JEWELRY

Enslaved girls recalled making items of jewelry from such natural materials as seashells, chestnuts, and the round, hard, yellow berries from the chinaberry tree. Blacksmiths made simple rings, bracelets, and earrings from bits of metal. Of interest are

Portrait of an African American woman in a headwrap, United States, 1897. The headwrap originated in West Africa. In antebellum America, Southern whites viewed the headwrap as a symbol of slavery. African American women, however, endowed it with their own meanings by wrapping their heads with colorful, elaborately tied textiles. Library of Congress Prints and Photographs Division, LC-USZC2-6125.

wear related to the seasons and particular work stations. In the colder seasons, people were issued heavier clothing and their annual footwear. If they wore undergarments at all, and many said they never did, it was usually during the winter. Field hands wore fewer, more formless clothes of lesser-grade materials than domestic servants. The exceptions were African American men who acted as overseers and wore well-made leather boots, a symbol of their station.

Early photographs show house servants and coach drivers working for well-to-do families in finer, complete ensembles of European style. Owners in close contact with servants demanded clean hair and bodies and a neat overall appearance. Owners obviously insisted that servants seen in more public arenas wear these finer outfits to boost the whites' own self-esteem. Although better dressed, carriage drivers and house servants essentially wore uniforms. Field workers, although in more frugal and less formal attire, nevertheless were not beholden to owners' tastes and therefore had opportunities to individualize their dress.

SPECIAL EVENTS

Regardless of the type of clothing items given to people, when circumstances arose, enslaved African American dress included the archaeological finds of West African objects in the context of known slave sites in the United States. Blue glass beads are found most often, and wearing blue beads to offset harm from the evil eye has a long tradition in the Middle East, the Balkans, and over most of the African continent. Cowrie shells also have been uncovered at slave sites. Cowrie shells, from the Indian and Atlantic Oceans, likewise have a history in Africa as trade tender and were worn as jewelry or as decoration attached to clothing. A very interesting discovery is the beads found around the waists of the remains of a woman and an infant girl interred in an eighteenth-century Manhattan cemetery for free and enslaved Africans. Young girls and women in several West African nations continue to wear waist beads where they are believed to especially enhance the female figure.

As they did in Africa, the enslaved wore jewelry not only for beautification but also for protecting the body. From South Carolina and Georgia came descriptions of both men and women wearing a single earring to protect the eyes, and parents often made protective amulets of various items such as mole's feet, hard berries, nuts, and coins to guard the children who wore them. Adults also wore strings of coins or tucked them in shoes for protection.

HEADWEAR

For field work, the enslaved crafted straw hats, and women wore cloth sun bonnets. While of lesser quality, they wore the same types of head coverings as did Southern whites, with one exception. As with certain items of jewelry known to be of African origin, one other article of dress was definitely a holdover from their ancestral homeland: the woman's headwrap. In many West African communities, a woman keeps her hair covered in a turban-style cloth in public, exposing it only for her husband, for whom she prepares an elaborate hairstyle. The earliest West African account of the woman's headwrap came in 1657, from a European traveler who described a woman of Cape Verde (off the coast of present-day Senegal) wearing one.

Both men and women enslaved in the South tied simple head cloths around their head to keep off sweat and dirt because inadequate bathing facilities made it difficult to keep hair clean and groomed. But this type of cloth covering soon became a form of class identification only for an enslaved female. Indeed, a 1786 sumptuary law in Louisiana (then a Spanish colony) required females of color to bind their hair in a kerchief. In 1849 Savannah, Georgia, a journalist bemoaned that turbans and head handkerchiefs were what peasants wore but the city's "colored population" was fast discarding them.

Southern whites associated the headwrap as a symbol of slavery. African American women, however, flaunted the racial and class distinction and endowed it with their own meanings by wrapping their heads with enormous, colorful, elaborately tied textiles. They took an item of dress from their homeland and transformed its meaning by crowning themselves, making the headwrap the ultimate symbol of resistance to loss of personal and communal identity during the period of enslavement in the United States. Dress being the most straightforward and immediate way to publicly define oneself, it is evident African Americans went to extremes to achieve this in their own styles.

References and Further Reading

Douglass, Frederick. *Narrative of the Life of Frederick Douglass: An American Slave*. New York: Signet, 1968. (Originally published 1845.)

Foster, Helen Bradley. *"New Raiments of Self": African American Clothing in the Antebellum South*. Oxford: Berg, 1997.

Rawick, George P., gen. ed. *The American Slave: A Composite Autobiography*. Westport, CT: Greenwood, 1972, 1977, 1979.

White, Shane, and Graham White. *Stylin': African American Expressive Culture from Its Beginnings to the Zoot Suit*. Ithaca, NY: Cornell University Press, 1998.

Helen Bradley Foster

See also African American; volume 1, Africa: Jewelry; Head-dresses and Hairdos; Beads and Beadwork; volume 2, Latin America and the Caribbean: Caribbean Headwear; Nineteenth-Century Afro-Brazilian Women's Dress.

Immigrants Encounter North American Dress

Immigrants are defined as people who leave their country of origin to come to a new country with the intention of living there permanently. Immigrants face many challenges when settling in a new place. They arrive with cultural beliefs and practices that are different from those of their adopted country. Immigrants may elect either to reject the old and adapt their beliefs to their new culture, to preserve their "old country" culture in the new country, or to blend some aspects of their cultural heritage into their lives as immigrants. The process by which one group takes on the cultural traits of a larger group is called *assimilation*. A related concept is *acculturation*, which is a change in the cultural behavior and thinking of an individual or group through contact with another culture.

Shifting identity is at the core of the immigrant experience. Some aspects of identity, such as sex and race, are assigned at birth. Other aspects, such as language, religion, and political beliefs, are acquired through social interaction. Appearance is a vital component of identity. Dress and appearance are the first aspects about an individual or group that a stranger responds to—even before speech. Dress and appearance are understood to carry meaning. The meaning of an identity is negotiated and altered and can differ in specific contexts. In this way, new meanings are negotiated. Sociologists refer to this phenomenon as *symbolic interaction*.

MISTAKEN IDENTITY

Gary Shteyngart, a Russian-born U.S. citizen, provides an example of how symbolic interaction operates when he reports on his experience after a visit to St. Petersburg in 1999. He landed at New York's John F. Kennedy airport and headed for the line designated for U.S. citizens at passport control. An Immigration and Naturalization Service (INS) worker, observing his shaggy hair and "retro 1970s coat with outrageous fake fur collar," insisted that he go to the visitor's line. Gary liked to think of his sartorial choices as "Immigrant Chic," but next to the "clean-cut young men and women in Gore-Tex" in the U.S. citizens' line, he looked out of place to the INS worker. He does not say whether he modified his appearance to avoid mistaken national identity the next time he traveled.

All North Americans, except North American Indians, are either immigrants or descendants of immigrants. Even North American Indians are believed to have migrated to the continent from Asia across the Bering Strait some thirty-five thousand years ago. More recent immigrants who came to North America after 1600 might be categorized into three groups:

Immigrants who came voluntarily. This category consists primarily of those in search of the "American dream." It also includes refugees from war-torn countries who seek a better life in a democratic system of government, such as the Cambodians who escaped the regime of the Khmer Rouge leader Pol Pot. These immigrants quickly adapted their appearance in order to fit in and be accepted. However, they typically do not abandon their cultural heritage completely. Often they celebrate the holidays of their country of origin by wearing traditional dress.

Immigrants in search of religious freedom. Some of these groups, such as the Amish and Mennonites, settled in rural areas and continue to live a separate existence from mainstream North Americans. Other times they moved into certain neighborhoods of cities, for example, the Orthodox Jews of Brooklyn, New York. For this category of immigrants, it was and still is important to demonstrate affiliation with a religious community through appearance.

Immigrants who were brought to North America or were moved internally through force. These could be called "involuntary immigrants." Despite limited resources, dress and appearance helped to preserve cultural identity. Africans who arrived on slave ships and lived on their masters' plantations are one example. Another example is the Acadians, the French-speaking peasants who originally settled in Nova Scotia and New Brunswick but were expelled to Louisiana when France ceded these provinces to England.

In order to examine the role of dress and appearance among North American immigrants as it relates to identity, one must focus on what happened when immigrants encountered North American dress, from the arrival of the first immigrants to the present time. The breadth and depth of the immigrant experience as it affects dress is related to the history of North American immigration.

COLONISTS AND IMMIGRANTS (1607 TO 1776)

The first nonnative people to set foot on North American soil were European explorers searching for new trade routes in the late 1400s. Some decades later, immigrants began to establish colonies in coastal areas or along inland waterways. The Spanish founded St. Augustine, the first European city in North America, on the Atlantic coast of Florida in 1565. The British began their first permanent colony in Jamestown, Virginia, in 1607, followed by the Plymouth colony in Massachusetts in 1620. The Dutch laid claim to New York in 1609, quickly settling the Hudson River valley and New Jersey. The French founded a settlement on the St. Lawrence River in Quebec in 1608 and the city of Montreal in 1641. These fledgling settlements opened North America to European immigrants seeking a better life. Emigration to the New World was a convenient solution to Europe's problems of overpopulation, unemployment, and religious dissidence. Soon immigrants arrived from other countries, most notably Sweden, Scotland, and Germany.

In each settlement, the colonists encountered indigenous peoples clad in skins and furs who decorated themselves with body paint, feathers, and ornaments of shell and bone. North American Indians did not tailor skins and furs to fit the torso; instead, they wrapped or draped skins around the body. They employed off-loom techniques to make body coverings and supplements. They did not know how to weave on floor looms or to knit with needles. Instead, they twined and plaited. Most of their attire did not demand detailed production. One exception was belts and jewelry made of *wampum*, which were beads drilled from clamshells. European observers commented favorably on wampum; one European observer, John Josselyn, described it as "cunningly" made. But the Europeans had negative reactions to the amount of exposed flesh on both men and women. The French explorer Samuel de Champlain wrote: "Their robes are made of grasses and hemp, scarcely covering the body, and coming down only to their thighs. They have only their sexual parts concealed … all the rest of the body being naked. Whenever the women came to see us, they wore robes which were open in the front." While intrigued with the exotic appearance of the natives they met, the Europeans concluded that the native form of dress was "savage," "uncivilized," and "barbarous."

Europeans, on the other hand, wore clothes tailored to fit the body and ornaments of precious stones and metals. They followed the dictates of fashion, changing their appearance over time. They made their clothes from fabrics of wool, silk, linen, or cotton. Their fashionable clothes required many production steps, including fiber processing, yarn spinning, weaving or knitting fabrics, dyeing and finishing cloth, and cutting and sewing into garments. Sometimes the fabrics were embellished with lace, embroidery, or threads containing gold or silver. Leather products were well tanned and crafted into boots, shoes, and gloves. Furs were made into muffs, hats, and trimmings for coats. One of the key features of European styles was that they covered the body. Very little skin was exposed. Women, especially those who were married, covered their hair. Men sported beards. Europeans felt strongly about how people of various social strata should dress and even attempted to regulate what people wore through *sumptuary laws*, a set of rules that they transplanted to the North American colonies in the seventeenth century.

A clash of ideologies about dress and appearance ensued between colonizers and colonized. The European settlers thought that the natives' appearance signified "heathen" beliefs and sought to correct it. In an effort to convert North American Indians to Christianity, colonial authorities offered them European-style tailored clothing. The natives did not particularly like the tailored coats and doublets, which they considered too confining, or the cobbled shoes, which made too much noise in the forest. They found European men's beards contrary to their preferences for smooth-skinned faces. However, the Europeans prevailed and imposed their ideas about "civilized" dress and appearance on the native population. This ideological clash repeated itself as settlement continued westward in the eighteenth and nineteenth centuries. As Euro–North American pioneers displaced North American Indians from ancestral lands, indigenous dress gradually faded from view.

Thus, it was established that dress and appearance on the North American continent followed the fashions initiated in the capitals of Europe. At first, Dutch, French, and British ships brought ready-made clothing and supplies to the colonists. Soon immigrants trained as tailors, seamstresses, and shoemakers set up shop in the larger communities. Farmers began raising sheep for wool and cultivating flax for fiber, but their efforts satisfied only a fraction of the colonists' needs. The colonists continued to be highly dependent on imports into the eighteenth century, which suited Europe just fine. Trading with the North American colonies was big business for British manufacturers, who eventually squeezed out the Dutch and French competition. The North American colonies were thought of as "twigs belonging to the main tree," as one colonial governor quoted by W.R. Bagnall, a nineteenth-century textile historian, put it. North America was just one more market for British goods, which included textiles manufactured in Britain as well as fabrics imported from British trading partners in the East, such as silks from China and fine cottons from India. North American Indians were an important part of the North American colonial market, trading for fabrics of all sorts, especially coarse woolens, as well as ready-made clothes.

Conflicts erupted between the British and the French for control of North America in the 1750s, leading to the French and Indian War. Britain emerged as the victor, with the result that "New France" was ceded to Britain in 1763. France no longer sent immigrants to Canada, and many French who had settled in the area known as Acadia were expelled to the Spanish settlement of Louisiana. The eastern part of Canada then became another place to which the British could emigrate.

Consumerism increased as the eighteenth century progressed. North Americans kept up avid correspondence with relatives in Britain regarding the latest London fashions. Observers quoted in C.B. Kidwell and M.C. Christman's *Suiting Everyone: The*

Seal of the Massachusetts Bay Colony, ca. 1675. The figure, barefoot and with long hair, wears a leafy covering around his midsection. He says, "Come over and help us," implying that nearly naked North American Indians needed English immigrants to "civilize" them by dressing them in European-style clothing. Courtesy of the Massachusetts Archives.

Democratization of Clothing in America noted, "There is no fashion in London but in three or four months it is to be seen at Boston." Merchants advertised a wide variety of imported fabrics, which were then made into fashionable garments by local specialists. Conversely, some prominent businessmen ordered suits of clothes by mail from London tailors, who had their measurements on file. Most women could sew shirts, shifts, and baby clothes for their families. Few clothing items survive from the seventeenth and eighteenth centuries in the United States and Canada, but those that do reflect European styling. A few items from North American Indian attire were adapted for colonial wardrobes because of their functionality, namely moccasins and leather hunting shirts. Moccasins, leather stockings, and fringed leather shirts became popular in frontier regions for trapping and hunting. Later, in Victorian North America, moccasins were adopted for indoor wear as house slippers. Moccasins continue to be popular today.

Immigrants to rural Quebec adapted aspects of Indian material culture, too. In response to severe winters, French settlers crafted outerwear out of Hudson's Bay Company point blankets intended for the First Nations trade. They made hooded coats out of the warm wool blankets or their own homespun woolens and tied them with colorful sashes. On their feet they wore *bottes sauvage*, footwear cut like moccasins out of the skins of farm animals. The women, on the other hand, wore European-style cloaks, short gowns, and petticoats. On their feet they wore *sabots*, a type of wooden shoe worn in France. The blanket coat persisted into the nineteenth century, eventually becoming an icon of British Canada.

Throughout the Colonial period, trade with Africa brought blacks to North American shores. The first Africans arrived in Virginia in 1619 not as slaves but as indentured servants. Indentured servants, whether black or white, were freed after they completed the terms of their indenture, usually in five to seven years. At the conclusion of the indenture, each received a new suit of clothes, sometimes called a "freedom suit." For African slaves, however, there was no end to their bondage unless they purchased their own freedom or their masters freed them.

The nefarious triangle trade began in 1621, linking captives from Africa's West Coast to sugar cane and molasses from the West Indies to tobacco plantations and rum distilleries in the North American colonies. Slaves wore what their masters provided. The shirts worn by field hands were not unlike the loose cotton shirts and knee-length drawers of West Africa. The clothes of many slaves, particularly field slaves, were ill made, skimpy, and ragged, while house slaves were better dressed in styles that paralleled that of British Americans. H.B. Foster, who writes on culture and dress, has reported that the Southern colonies enacted slave codes meant to deter slaves from dressing above their station. By 1775, these involuntary immigrants from Africa made up about 20 percent of the population of the thirteen colonies.

The population of the British colonies was estimated to be over two million by 1770. Expansion south into the Carolinas, west to the Ohio territories, and to northern New England and Canada increased the European presence in North America. Emigration from Europe had continued. Protestant sects arrived from Germany and settled in the mid-Atlantic region, particularly the Quakers. French Huguenots, who were Protestant, fled Catholic France for freedom in Britain and in the North American colonies. Scots, Irish, and those "Scots-Irish" who came from

Ulster arrived and moved to the hinterlands of the time: New Hampshire, Virginia, and the Carolinas. Britain emptied its prisons by sending convicts and debtors to North America and Australia. While the religious sectarians often dressed in ways that identified themselves as members of specific groups, other immigrants wore styles appropriate to their social standing in the new country.

On the eve of the American War of Independence, British style and taste dominated the North American colonies and the Canadian provinces. During the period leading up to the war, North Americans sought to reduce dependence on British goods by spinning their own yarn and wearing homespun fabric. These efforts were short lived, however. After the war was over, the desire to know what was fashionable in the capitals of Europe surfaced once again. The dramatic political changes following the French Revolution also affected fashion tremendously, focusing attention on Paris as the source of the latest styles and ushering in major changes in fashion for both men and women. No longer did fashion changes emanate from the aristocracy; fashion became democratized, too. The advent of fashion periodicals at the end of the eighteenth century made it possible for people in the United States and Canada to follow European fashion more closely than ever before.

REPUBLICS AND PROVINCES (1776 TO THE 1870s)

Immigration continued at a steady pace in the nineteenth century as the United States and Canada expanded. Many Loyalists who had supported Britain during the War for Independence—about forty-two thousand in all—emigrated to Ontario, Quebec, Nova Scotia, and New Brunswick in 1783. English and Irish migration to Canadian farmland after 1815 helped populate the eastern provinces. In the United States, the majority of immigrants came from England, Ireland, Germany, and the Scandinavian countries. Ireland's potato famines contributed a particularly large influx of impoverished new arrivals.

New territories and states were annexed with great speed in the first half of the century. By 1850, most of what now constitutes the United States had been acquired, and the frontier was rapidly disappearing. Immigrants who sought a new life in farming or ranching homesteaded vast amounts of land in the West. Those who came with agricultural experience moved to the new territories and established communities, many with Old World values such as New Ulm, Minnesota, which still celebrates Oktoberfest, the German beer festival, every autumn.

Corresponding growth in manufacturing attracted immigrants for factory work. The textile industry developed in the Northern states, while cotton plantations became firmly established in the South. Both required continuing infusions of immigrant labor.

One of the offshoots of the Industrial Revolution was that it made it possible for working-class families, including immigrants, to dress reasonably well. European visitors to U.S. cities regularly commented on this fact. Factory cloth reached immigrant communities where dry goods merchants stocked a range of styles and colors. For those who lived far from town, there were peddlers who traversed the country with their wares. Immigrants started using the newly invented sewing machines and paper patterns printed in magazines as soon as they were available. The burgeoning industry in ready-to-wear clothing after the Civil

Phillis Wheatley, Negro Servant to Mr. John Wheatley, of Boston (Engraving, 1773, London). Phillis, the daughter of African slaves, dressed in styles approximating those of white servant girls because she was a house slave. This image is the frontispiece to her book, *Poems on Various Subjects, Religious and Moral*. Library of Congress, Prints and Photographs Division Digital ID: ppmsca 02947.

War found a ready market in the newest arrivals to the United States. Those same industries also provided jobs for immigrants.

The majority of the immigrants, who hailed from Northern Europe, assimilated easily into the emerging U.S. culture. The "melting pot" metaphor emerged about the same time that the United States became a country. Historian D. Wepman has quoted J. Hector St. Jean, who wrote in *Letters from an American Farmer in 1782*: "Here individuals of all nations are melted into a new race of men." He added, "He is an American who, leaving behind him all his ancient prejudices and manners, receives new ones from the new mode of life he has embraced." The melting-pot image dominated how the United States saw itself well into the twentieth century.

Northern European immigrants embraced U.S. dress, having been exposed to similar styles in their homelands. The unspoken social codes entrenched in Europe that kept people in their place did not exist in the United States, allowing them to dress as they pleased rather than according to their station in life. The United States was the land of opportunity, where anybody could be somebody. Wepman has noted these changes in the deportment of poor Irishmen, saying that they no longer had an "indolent deportment, careless manner, and slouching gait" characteristic of the old country but were soon inspired by fashion to appear tailored and respectable, even walking with a more erect posture.

For the Irish and other new U.S. citizens, clothes could indeed "make the man."

Turmoil in Central Europe caused more than two hundred thousand German Jews to immigrate to the United States between 1825 and 1875. Already having experience in the clothing trades in Europe, enterprising Jews jumpstarted the ready-to-wear apparel industry after the invention of the sewing machine in 1846. The "rag trade," as it became known, was centered in the Lower East Side of New York City, although companies opened in other cities as well. The Jews also moved into retailing. They had been the peddlers, shopkeepers, and merchants of Europe. Many began by peddling secondhand clothing, then opening stores that stocked clothing and other goods, and finally establishing manufacturing concerns. Levi's blue jeans are among the better-known contributions by Jewish immigrants to U.S. sartorial history. Levi Strauss was a Bavarian Jew who arrived in New York City in 1847. He moved west to San Francisco, where he partnered with Jacob Davis, a Jewish tailor from Latvia. The outcome was denim overalls with riveted reinforcements at the pockets and the fly, the ever-popular Levi's. Blue jeans satisfied the need for inexpensive ready-to-wear clothing and quickly found acceptance as working-class attire, an identity it held for more than a century.

Sectarian communities based on Protestant Christianity, such as the Shakers, Amish, and Mennonites, strengthened in the nineteenth-century United States. The founders of these groups, which had splintered off from various churches in Europe, had set down their U.S. roots in the previous century. "Mother" Ann Lee, for example, arrived from England in 1774 with eight followers to establish the Shakers. Their numbers grew to a peak of six thousand members in the mid-nineteenth century. Like other sectarian groups, the Shakers practiced separatism and held conservative views. Sectarian groups avoided participation in fashion—a system where rapidly changing styles require frequent (and costly) wardrobe changes. Fashion, and its attendant concern for individual identity, implies vanity and personal pride, characteristics not admired in societies based on communal ideals. Thus, the dress of sectarian groups was controlled by rules that encouraged conformity to a plain, simple appearance. They retained simple versions of bygone styles and made them customary. Sectarian dress is not immune to fashion and fabric changes, but in general, it is conservative and slow changing.

When captive Africans arrived on U.S. shores, they were issued Euro-North-American-style clothing. Plantation owners distributed sets of clothes on a seasonal basis. Male field hands wore shirts and work trousers, while women wore *short gowns* (a type of jacket); full skirts or petticoats; or loose, ankle-length dresses called *wrappers* that covered their bodies. Children were issued shirts. Some children in rural areas were reported to have gone without clothes, but Christian beliefs about decency compelled the slaveholders to provide them with some sort of body covering. The quality of the cloth differentiated slaves from other people in the United States. It was either homespun or a rough fabric called *Negro cloth* manufactured in New England mills. Shoes called *brogans* were made of cowhide on the plantations. Depending on the talent of the shoemaker, brogans could be either tolerable or downright painful to wear. Brogans created blisters if no socks were worn, and brass tacks that held the shoes together sometimes poked through to the skin. It is no wonder that many slaves preferred going barefoot in the summer or wearing rags around their feet.

Certain markers of African heritage remained. Slaves captured in Africa sometimes had permanent tribal markings on their skin. Scholars such as Foster have postulated that attention to hairstyles, headgear, and jewelry was a holdover from African culture. African American women wore headwraps, which covered their hair. These turbanlike cloths originated in sub-Saharan Africa, enjoyed widespread popularity, and continued to be worn well into the twentieth century. Men crafted hats out of various plant materials, as had their forebears. After the Civil War, the former slaves were freed. Their interest in headgear and hair, and a pride in personal appearance, continued after emancipation.

Chinese immigrants started arriving on the West Coast in midcentury after news of California's gold reached China. Most of the immigrants were men. Initially welcomed as hard workers, Chinese immigrants soon began experiencing discrimination. After mining jobs disappeared, they found work as domestic servants, agricultural workers, and factory workers. Many helped build the transcontinental railroad. Others began laundry businesses. Lack of assimilation characterized Chinese immigrants. Not only did their skin color and Asian features separate them from white North Americans, but they often retained Chinese-style clothing and footwear. Especially

noticeable was the male practice of wearing their hair in a long braided queue down the back. People in the United States regarded their appearance as peculiar and began legislating against them, preventing them from testifying in court or marrying non-Asian women. In 1876, San Francisco passed an ordinance requiring any Chinese man arrested to have his pigtail cut off. This animosity toward Chinese immigrants led to the *Chinese Exclusion Act of 1882*, which halted immigration from China. Under these hostile conditions, some of the earlier immigrants returned to China.

The backlash against Chinese immigrants forecast the rise of nativism, which protected the interests of established U.S. citizens, even though most were relatively recent immigrants themselves. The result was discrimination against certain groups who did not fit the Anglo-Saxon profile, namely, anyone who was not a white Protestant who conformed to Euro–North American expectations for appearance, which meant adhering to fashionable dress. Although all immigrants could change their clothes, shoes, and hairstyles, skin color and facial features were unalterable aspects of appearance. Nativism would come to a head in the first quarter of the twentieth century and force a change in immigration policy.

The Chinese colony, Mott Street, New York City. Drawn by W. Bengough, illustrated in *Harper's Weekly*, 1896. The new arrivals wear Chinese-style jackets, hats, and footwear. The hair is braided into a long queue. Chinese immigrants retained Chinese traditions in appearance even after living in the United States and Canada for years. Library of Congress, Prints and Photographs Division, LC-USZ62-107167.

PEAK IMMIGRATION FROM EUROPE (1880 TO 1924)

The United States entered its greatest period of immigration from 1880 to 1924. Ellis Island opened in New York's harbor as a receiving station in 1892. More than twelve million people passed through its gates before it closed in 1954. By the late nineteenth century, the pattern of immigration to the New World shifted from Northern Europe to Eastern and Southern Europe. Italians, Armenians, Greeks, German and Eastern European Jews, and Ukrainians arrived in record numbers.

Ellis Island and the Statue of Liberty are enduring symbols of freedom and opportunity in the United States. After the excitement of seeing the statue in the harbor, people dressed up in their best clothing to meet the immigration officials. This action helped mark the transition to a new life and made them look respectable to the officials, who denied admission to 2 percent of new arrivals based on very rapid judgments about physical and mental health. Scared, homesick women were advised not to cry so that their eyes would not appear reddened.

Augustus F. Sherman, who served as a registry clerk at Ellis Island, captured the appearance of hundreds of these immigrants as they waited. He focused on "types" that showed the variety of people who passed through the gates rather than on named individuals. His photographs, taken between 1905 and 1925, range from Scottish boys in kilts to Dutch toddlers in wooden shoes, from well-dressed Northern Europeans to Southern and Eastern Europeans in their national dress. Others, who did not have any good clothes to don for arrival, wore everyday shawls and head scarves and carried their belongings in makeshift rucksacks. One official remarked that Ellis Island resembled a "World Congress of Costumes." Many shed these clothes as soon as they passed the barriers at Battery Park, donning U.S. styles brought by the relatives who came to greet them so they would not look like greenhorns. The place often looked like "a sea of clothing."

During this great migration, the differences between the cultures of the newcomers and the already established U.S. residents were pronounced. As a result, the push for assimilation was stronger than ever. The ethos of this time period is reflected in the 1909 Israel Zangwill play *The Melting Pot*, in which the United States is portrayed as a nation that blended all newcomers into one nationality. Most immigrants tried to achieve the ideal by working hard, learning English, and dressing like other people in the United States. Dress became a key symbol of assimilation.

The case of Jewish immigrants, who were pouring into New York City because of religious persecution in Eastern Europe, exemplifies the complexities of assimilation. In the old country, Jewish women dressed in woolen skirts and shawls and wore heavy shoes. Married women shaved their heads and wore wigs as a symbol of piety and fidelity. These wigs, termed *sheitel*, were deeply ingrained in the values of Jewish women. However, wigs made them look very un-American. Their husbands and children became embarrassed by their old-fashioned appearance. Historian B. Schreier has reported on one fictional story about New York ghetto life, in which a Jewish man greets his newly arrived wife, whom he has not seen for three years, with the words "They don't wear wigs here." She, on the other hand, had donned her wig for the big occasion. Daughters of Jewish immigrants, much to the annoyance of their mothers, desired delicate leather heels, large feather- or flower-trimmed hats, and silk shirtwaists. For

many young immigrant women, the ideal was the Gibson Girl, with her white shirtwaist, black skirt, and upswept hairdo. This is what many immigrants, many of whom worked in apparel factories, chose as their "working girl" uniform.

Children in immigrant families in urban settings were in a particularly challenging position, straddling two worlds: the foreign world at home in crowded tenements and the U.S. world at school. Other children ridiculed them for the clothes they wore, the food they ate, and their lack of language skills. Ethnic communities sometimes solved these problems by opening their own parochial schools. Roman Catholics and Jews were especially prone to this tactic. By the time children were older, they sometimes rejected their parents as too foreign or old-fashioned.

The United States also received immigrants along its southern borders, especially from Mexico, and at Angel Island in San Francisco, where Chinese, Koreans, Filipinos, and Japanese entered. U.S. observers often fused Asian immigrants into a single category, yet assimilation differed between nationalities. Photographs from the Angel Island Immigration Station show Japanese immigrants wearing Japanese dress, but historian A. Sueyoshi has reported that soon afterward even the children donned Western styles. This reflected their desire to become Americanized. The Chinese, however, tended to retain aspects of their native dress. Chinese men wore cotton jackets with side closings, Chinese-style shoes, and long queues, with trousers and homburg hats. Chinese women dressed in side-closing jackets with trousers and wore their hair in neat buns. These were blends of Chinese and American styles. Regardless of national origin and despite what they wore, Asians faced discrimination because of race.

Debate about the differences between the descendants of previous waves of immigrants and the newcomers intensified as immigration increased. Physical appearance became part of the debate. Sociologist Edward Ross's attitude demonstrated the shift in mood against wholesale immigration, particularly from Eastern and Southern Europe. Writing in 1914, he argued that the new immigrants would pollute the dominant Anglo-Saxon stock, stating: "Now we confront the melancholy spectacle of this pioneer breed being swamped and submerged by an overwhelming tide of latecomers from the old-world hive" (p. 282). He went so far as to claim that the frequency of good-looking people in the United States would decrease: "It is unthinkable that so many persons with crooked faces, coarse mouths, bad noses, heavy jaws, and low foreheads can mingle their heredity with ours without making personal beauty yet more rare among us than it actually is" (p. 287). By the early 1920s, antiforeigner sentiments rose to new heights as the labor market became saturated. The door on unrestricted immigration was closing.

It is worth pointing out that not all immigrants stayed in the places to which they migrated. Many immigrants stayed long enough to earn decent money and then go back home. French Canadians, who went to New England in search of factory work, often went back and forth to Quebec. This practice did not encourage assimilation. The French Canadian enclaves in the United States were closed communities. French Catholic churches helped preserve ethnic identity by operating their own schools where French was the language of instruction. Older French Canadians from rural Quebec sometimes wore habitant dress, the homespun country outfits discussed earlier, but those who worked in New England's mills dressed in styles similar to those worn by others of the working class.

FROM MELTING POT TO SALAD BOWL
(1924 TO THE PRESENT)

The *U.S. National Origins Quota Act*, instituted in 1924, reduced the flow of immigrants into the United States. Policies favored Europeans from England, Ireland, and other Northern European countries who could immerse themselves into the melting pot with ease.

One of these immigrants was Lilly Daché, who arrived from France in 1924. Daché had apprenticed with leading Parisian milliners Caroline Reboux and J. Suzanne Talbot. Paris was the undisputed fashion capital of the world at that time, and at a welcoming party hosted by her cousin, she fielded questions about hem lengths and hats in Paris. She opened a hat shop and eventually became New York's best-known milliner during the 1930s and 1940s. Other foreign-born immigrants contributed to the U.S. fashion industry by designing attractive, wearable styles. Pauline Trigère, who was born and trained in France, arrived in 1937 and grew a business strong in coats, dresses, and hats by the 1950s and 1960s. Oleg Cassini, born to Russian parents in France, emigrated in 1936; in 1961, he became the official designer to First Lady Jacqueline Kennedy, who inspired millions of U.S. women to copy her style. Rudi Gernreich, of Austrian heritage, fled the Nazis in 1938 and settled in California, where he became famous in the 1960s for his unisex and futuristic designs. Oscar de la Renta, born in the Dominican Republic, trained and worked in European fashion houses before settling in New York in 1963. Since then, his reputation has steadily grown, and today he is one of the most highly regarded designers in the business.

Immigration slowed to a trickle during the Depression of the 1930s, but a larger threat was looming on the horizon: the racism of Nazi Germany. Refugees arriving in the mid-1930s had experience in the needle trades, as noted previously, and advanced quickly in the U.S. fashion industry. After the war ended, emergency relief legislation granted preference to displaced persons. Soon survivors of concentration camps and refugees from the new Soviet-bloc countries arrived. Although these new immigrants landed without resources, they were accustomed to wearing Western-style clothing and assimilated quickly. Sometimes they celebrated their lost homelands by wearing folk dress on special holidays. The Hungarians who settled in Canada, for example, remain proud of their heritage, keeping ethnic dress traditions alive through folk dance and musical ensembles.

Liberalization of U.S. immigration laws occurred in 1965. Immigration patterns once again shifted, this time to newcomers from Latin America, the Caribbean, and Asia. Illegal immigration from Mexico, where underemployment was a problem, became a political issue. Refugees from Southeast Asia who had assisted the United States during the Vietnam War marked the 1970s. By 1985, more than seven hundred thousand Vietnamese, Cambodians, and Laotians had arrived.

The Hmong from Laos came with very little because they had been living in refugee camps. A. Lynch, a scholar who studies dress, has reported that they were given U.S. clothes upon arrival, gradually replacing them with newer clothes as finances allowed. They reserved their Hmong dress for special events, such as the Hmong American New Year. Young people dressed in Hmong outfits not necessarily linked to their region of origin. The events themselves blended U.S.-style music with traditional Hmong rituals, not unlike the blending of regional differences in clothing.

Greek woman, Ellis Island, New York City, 1909, on arrival to the United States. Like most immigrants photographed at the Ellis Island receiving post, she is dressed in her best clothing. She also displays a finely embroidered towel, perhaps her own handiwork. The photograph is by Augustus F. Sherman, who served as a registry clerk at Ellis Island and captured the appearance of hundreds of immigrants at this time. Courtesy New York Public Library.

The social upheaval of the 1960s eventually brought more tolerant views of cultural difference. As a result, the melting-pot analogy fell out of favor. Instead, the salad bowl became the preferred metaphor. Immigrants no longer felt that they had to submerse their identities, including appearance, into a homogeneous Anglo-American culture. The changing times allowed ethnic groups to retain their distinctiveness within the larger culture. A number of factors influenced this change: the civil rights movement, the North American Indian movement, antiwar demonstrations, and other antiestablishment attitudes.

In the 1970s, a wave of nostalgia swept over the nation as the United States prepared to celebrate its bicentennial. Alex Haley's *Roots*, published in 1976, became a popular television series that traced his own ancestry back through seven generations to Africa. African Americans began incorporating styles of dress and types of fabric from Africa into their daily wardrobes such as *dashikis*, mudcloth, tie-dye, and kente cloth. The Afro, a distinct hairstyle that celebrated the unique qualities of black hair instead of trying to repress it through straighteners and coloring agents, became popular. Other groups began to don signifiers of their cultural heritage as well. By the 1990s, multiculturalism had become the byword and tolerance the directive. This is clearly evident in dress. It is not uncommon these days to see veiled women from Islamic countries, Rastafarians in dreadlocks, and graduation gowns accented with kente-cloth stoles.

In this era of globalized dress and multicultural awareness, some immigrants still experience problems because of difference in dress and appearance. For instance, in the days following the attacks of 11 September 2001, men wearing turbans were targets of hate crimes, and women in veils invited stares. Conformity to U.S. values is still the norm.

Snapshot: Dress of Norwegian Americans

Norwegian emigration to the New World began in 1825 when the ship *Restauration* sailed from the port of Stavanger with about fifty Norwegians aboard. Over the next century, more than a million Norwegians left their homeland for North America. While early emigrants sought to escape religious persecution, most came for economic reasons. Norway, with its deep fjords and mountains, had limited arable land, forests, and fishing grounds to support a nation of farmers, loggers, and fisherman. Additionally, inheritance laws granted only first-born sons the rights to their parents' farms. Thus, when Ole Rynning's book *A True Account of America for the Information and Help of Peasant and Commoner* appeared in 1838, it convinced many to pack their trunks and book passage. Between 1861 and 1890, one-fifth of the population of Norway left for the New World.

Many Norwegians headed west to Wisconsin, Illinois, Minnesota, Iowa, and the Dakotas, where they homesteaded or purchased inexpensive farmland. Early arrivals retained cultural traits such as language, foodways, and furniture styles. This was not the case with dress, however. People contemplating emigration were advised to sell their rural Norwegian dress because it would not be needed in the New World. L. Gilbertson, a researcher who studies quilts, quotes one observer, writing in 1855: "A newcomer can be immediately detected by their garb, and since newcomers are regarded with little esteem, all of them proceed at once to buy clothes of an American cut." Some people did wear their homespun clothes until they could afford to purchase U.S. styles. A few continued to weave Norwegian-style wool and linen fabrics after finding that local calico fabrics, made into clothes like those of their "Yankee" neighbors, wore out too quickly.

Norwegians had been accustomed to dressing up for birthdays, weddings, confirmations, and holidays, especially Christmas. In rural Norway, this had meant wearing regional folk dress. Because most emigrants did not bring their native attire with them, they resorted to wearing their everyday U.S. clothes for special occasions at first.

Part of the rapid assimilation process was on account of the young women who worked in Yankee homes as domestic servants. Norwegians girls were in high demand as maids because

Women in Madison, Wisconsin, wearing "national" costumes on Syttende Mai, 17 May, Norwegian Constitution Day, 1910s. Photograph courtesy of Vesterheim Norwegian-American Museum, Decorah, Iowa.

they were clean and worked hard. They immediately developed a hankering for the fashionable things they saw around them, much to the chagrin of the young Norwegian men who wanted to court them but feared their independent tendencies. P. Williams, who writes on immigrant dress, quotes a bachelor who wrote home saying that the Norwegian peasant and serving girls were virtually unrecognizable as they "trip about, their backs arched, with their parasols and their fans and their heads all enveloped in veils."

Conservative Lutheran doctrine encouraged plain, functional dress. Simple, dark clothes and undecorated bonnets characterized the clothing of some immigrants. Fashionable attire was seen as evidence of sinfulness, vanity, and wastefulness. Yet Norwegian-language magazines provided patterns for clothing and fancywork, including patchwork quilts. These frictions within one immigrant group reveal the ambiguity toward fashion in nineteenth-century America.

Bridal wear exemplified the complex issues associated with acculturation. In Norway, weddings had been multiday affairs, with brides dressed in traditional ensembles composed of a handwoven skirt, decorated jacket, sash, silver jewelry, and wedding crown. Each region had its own distinctive version. Having been advised not to bring these bridal outfits to the United States, most Norwegian American girls married in U.S.-style dresses that they could continue to wear for special events. According to both documentary sources and surviving material culture, these wedding dresses were often a serviceable midtoned color. Green was especially popular for wedding dresses. White was too impractical for all but the wealthiest brides in the Midwestern United States. In Stevens Point, Wisconsin, Williams has reported that the first all-white wedding dress was worn by the daughter of Norwegian immigrants who married a successful Norwegian-born businessman in 1883. The whole town turned out to see this fashion-forward daughter of Norway in her white dress. Certain details of wedding attire expressed ties to the homeland, however. Instead of veils, many brides wore floral crowns or wreaths. Silver jewelry, particularly brooches, had been used in the old country to ward off harmful spirits. Norwegian Americans continued to wear their silver jewelry although without necessarily believing the associated mythology.

At the same time that many Norwegians pondered emigration to better their lives, nationalism and romanticism rose in Norway. Sweden governed Norway until its independence in 1905. In the latter part of the nineteenth century, the dress of the Hardanger region came to represent the national dress of a united Norway. Intellectuals influenced by romanticism praised the traditions of folk culture, especially songs, dances, and regional dress. In 1903, the book *Norwegian Folk Dress*, by noted folklorist Hulda Garborg, appeared in print; it described costumes of the various regions of the country and included patterns to reproduce them. Norwegians began making and wearing regional dress for celebratory occasions. This was called the *bunad* (clothing) movement. These developments in Norway affected Norwegian Americans, who took to wearing national and regional costumes for festive attire, thereby showing solidarity with the homeland. When white-cotton lingerie dresses became popular in the United States after 1900 for summer clothing, Norwegian immigrants crafted them with intricate cutwork characteristic of the Hardanger region. Norwegian-inspired outfits were especially popular at public celebrations and community festivals. Female members of Norwegian American organizations, such as the Sons of Norway, founded in 1895, wore such dresses to their functions. Today, they may be viewed at the Vesterheim Norwegian-American museum in Decorah, Iowa.

In the last quarter of the twentieth century, it became common for U.S. residents of all ethnic backgrounds to display their cultural heritage through dress. For a Norwegian American, this might mean an act as simple as that of pinning a silver brooch to a lapel. More recently, in the age of Internet shopping, Norwegian Americans are able to buy T-shirts that proclaim "Norwegian Princess," classic bunad outfits for "young Vikings," and traditional sweaters from Oslo with a simple click of a button.

REFERENCES AND FURTHER READING

Colburn, C. H. "Norwegian Folk Dress in America." In *Norwegian Folk Art: The Migration of a Tradition*, edited by M. Nelson, 157–169. New York: Abbeville Press, 1995.

Gilbertson, L. "Patterns of the New World: Quiltmaking among Norwegian Americans." *Uncoverings* 27 (2006): 157–186.

Williams, P. "From Folk to Fashion: Dress Adaptations of Norwegian Immigrant Women in the Midwest." In *Dress in American Culture*, edited by P. A. Cunningham and S. V. Lab, 95–108. Bowling Green, OH: Bowling Green State University Popular Press, 1993.

References and Further Reading

Aperture Foundation. *Augustus F. Sherman: Ellis Island Portraits, 1905–1920*. New York: Aperture, 2005.

Bagnall, W. R. *The Textile Industries of the United States*. Vol. 1, *1639–1810*. Cambridge, MA: Riverside Press, 1893.

Beaudoin-Ross, J. "A la Canadienne: Some Aspects of 19th Century Habitant Dress." *Dress* 6 (1980): 71–80.

Beaudoin-Ross, J. "'A la Canadienne' Once More: Some Insights into Quebec Rural Female Dress." *Dress* 7 (1981): 69–81.

Champlain, S. *Voyages of Samuel de Champlain 1604–1618*. Edited by W. L. Grant. New York: Charles Scribner's Sons, 1907.

Foster, H. B. *"New Raiments of Self": African American Clothing in the Antebellum South*. Oxford: Berg, 1997.

Kidwell, C. B., and M. C. Christman. *Suiting Everyone: The Democratization of Clothing in America*. Washington, DC: Smithsonian Institution Press, 1974.

Knoll, T. *Becoming Americans: Asian Sojourners, Immigrants, and Refugees in the Western United States*. Portland, OR: Coast to Coast Books, 1982.

Lindholdt, P.J., ed. *John Josselyn, Colonial Traveler*. Hanover, NH: University Press of New England, 1988.

Lynch, A. "Hmong American New Year's Dress: The Display of Ethnicity." In *Dress and Ethnicity*, edited by J. Eicher, 255–267. Oxford: Berg, 1995.

Roach-Higgins, M.E., J.B. Eicher, and K.K.P. Johnson, eds. *Dress and Identity*. New York: Fairchild, 1995.

Ross, E.A. *The Old World in the New*. New York: The Century Co., 1914.

Schreier, B. "Becoming American: Jewish Women Immigrants 1880–1920." *History Today* 44, no. 3 (March 1994): 25–31.

Seller, M. *To Seek America: A History of Ethnic Life in the United States*. Englewood, NJ: Jerome S. Ozer, 1977.

Shteyngart, G. "The New Two-Way Street." In *Reinventing the Melting Pot: The New Immigrants and What It Means to Be American*, edited by T. Jacoby, 285–292. New York: Basic Books, 2004.

Sueyoshi, A. "Mindful Masquerades: Que(e)rying Japanese Immigrant Dress in Turn-of-the-Century San Francisco." *Frontiers: A Journal of Women Studies* 26, no. 3 (2005): 67–100.

Welters, L. "From Moccasins to Frock Coats and Back Again." In *Dress in American Culture*, edited by P.A. Cunningham and S.V. Lab, 6–41. Bowling Green, OH: Bowling Green State University Popular Press, 1993.

Wepman, D. *Immigration: From the Founding of Virginia to the Closing of Ellis Island*. New York: Facts on File, Inc., 2002.

Yeshiva University Museum. *A Perfect Fit: The Garment Industry and American Jewry*. New York: Author, 2005.

Linda Welters

See also Religion and Dress; Antebellum African Americans; American Immigrants of West European Origin; African American; Caribbean Islanders; Asian American; Hispanic and Latino American; Dress in Hawai'i since 1898; Middle Eastern.

Snapshot: Acadians

The Louisiana Acadians were originally French peasants who immigrated in the early 1600s to Acadie, the modern Canadian provinces of Nova Scotia and New Brunswick. In 1755, Acadie was surrendered by the French to the British, who subsequently expelled all Acadians who would not submit to the British Crown. Following the ensuing exodus, many Acadians were welcomed by the Spanish governor of Louisiana and settled there, where they adapted to their new home and became productive. In examining their history and culture, historian G. R. Conrad has concluded that the Acadian exiles sought to preserve their cultural identity by seeking out isolated areas for resettlement. The Acadians maintained their archaic French language and culture into the twentieth century, when factors such as compulsory education, mass communication, the oil boom, and World War II helped to break down the walls of their cultural identity. Traditional Acadian values include ownership of land, family unity, a form of religiosity, independence, self-reliance, a powerful egalitarianism, and a determination to be left alone. These values were reflected in the conservative nature of Acadian dress in eighteenth- and nineteenth-century Louisiana.

The French immigrants to Acadie brought their simple dress and methods of production with them when they traveled to the New World. After the Acadians settled in Louisiana, they adapted the tools, techniques, and weaving patterns they had used for wool and linen in France and Canada to the brown and white cottons found in the South. The production and use of handwoven textiles in clothing and for household textiles among Louisiana Acadians continued into the twentieth century (which is later than among most other subcultures in the United States). *Cotonnade* is the term used for homespun cotton fabrics by the Acadians. It is generally used to designate "clothing weight" fabrics rather than the heavier "blanket weight" textiles that they also produced. Cotonnade is noted for its durability, as indicated by the expression *il n'y a pas fin de cotonnade,* or "there is no end to cotonnade."

No depictions and few descriptions of the dress of Acadians in Louisiana exist from the early period. Museum curator

Four women in traditional Acadian dress, Louisiana, ca. 1955. Acadians were originally French peasants who settled in Louisiana. They adapted the weaving techniques they had used for wool and linen in France to the brown and white cottons found in the South. Getty Images.

V. Glasgow quotes Francisco Bouligny, a Spanish officer of 1776, who indicated that the Acadians produced cotton successfully and made "textures with which they clothe themselves and which they sell to their neighbors." C.C. Robin, a French visitor to Louisiana, wrote in 1807 that Acadian women "spin the cotton into thread of which they make coarse muslin shirts, fine cloth, mosquito nets, and multi-colored striped cotton cloth so agreeable to the eye, resembling very much our 'siamoises,' out of which they make skirts and blouses, and for men pants and jackets." He also described the "Sunday best" dress that was worn to the *bals de maison* or house dances held on Saturday nights. "The Carmagnolle [jacket] is the usual garment. Clean clothes are a great luxury for them. The women wear a simple cotton dress and often in the summer they wear only a skirt. They go to the dances barefoot, as they go to the fields, and even the men only wear shoes when they are dressed formally."

Researcher Sonya LaComb investigated the dress of early Louisiana Acadians by examining Louisiana succession records from 1765 to 1830. The common dress at that time for the Acadian female was a bonnet, a shirt or *casaquin* (buttoned jacket), a skirt, an apron, and shoes, while the Acadian male wore a hat, a shirt with or without a vest or waistcoat, pants, and shoes. Wool continued to be used in dress after resettlement in Louisiana, but its use seems to have been replaced by cotton during the early 1800s.

A sketchy picture of rural Acadian dress during the Victorian period is provided in published descriptions and illustrations by visitors to southern Louisiana. Among the aspects of dress that were noted in the 1880s as setting the Acadians apart from other Louisianians are the enormous size and limpness of the Acadian sun bonnets; the broad-brimmed palmetto hats; the use of handspun and handwoven cloth for personal wear; and men, women, and children going barefoot except for the most formal occasions. When shoes were worn throughout the nineteenth century, they were often homemade leather boots or moccasins. It was noted in the 1890s that the latest fashions had not arrived in the Acadian parishes of Louisiana and that one could study anew those styles that had long passed away in the United States. By the early twentieth century, most Acadians preferred to buy readily available commercial products rather than to continue to use their previously homemade objects and dress.

Very few intact handwoven Acadian garments have survived because most Acadians did not have large wardrobes; thus, what clothes they had were simply worn out and used up. One of the few extant pairs of Acadian men's pants illustrates how garments were repaired and patched to prolong their useful life. The pants are made of cotonnade, and most of the patches are less faded pieces of the original garment fabric; three repairs were made from commercial fabrics. A man's shirt from the same era is also of cotonnade and is faded but in otherwise good condition. The shoulder-yoke lining is made from a different handwoven fabric from the rest of the shirt. Even though few handwoven Acadian garments exist today, quilts were often made from scraps of cotonnade, either from worn clothing or pieces left over from cutting out new garments. These quilts are rare, but they are more likely to have been preserved than the garments themselves and serve as a valuable source of information on fabrics used in the construction of early Acadian garments.

The Acadians successfully adapted to their new environment in Louisiana while preserving their cultural heritage for over two hundred years. The Acadian weaving tradition is still as alive as their language, music, customs, and cuisine; however, by the mid-twentieth century, it was no longer possible to identify a rural Acadian simply by the way he or she dressed.

REFERENCES AND FURTHER READING

Conrad, G.R. "The Cajuns: Essays on Their History and Culture." In *The Acadians: Myths and Realities*, edited by G.R. Conrad, 1–14. Lafayette: Center for Louisiana Studies, 1983.

Dormon, J.H. "The Cajuns: Ethnogenesis and the Shaping of a Group Consciousness." In *The Cajuns: Essays on Their History and Culture*, edited by G.R. Conrad, 233–251. Lafayette: Center for Louisiana Studies, 1983.

Glasgow, V. "Textiles of the Louisiana Acadians." *Antiques, The Magazine* (August 1981): 338–347.

Kuttruff, J.T. "Three Louisiana Acadian Cotonnade Quilts: Adding Pieces to a Puzzle." *Uncoverings* 20 (1999): 63–86.

LaComb, Sonya. "A Study of Early Acadian Dress in Louisiana." Master's thesis, Louisiana State University, 1996.

Robin, C.C. *Voyage to Louisiana*. Translated by S.O. Landry Jr. New Orleans: Pelican, 1966. (Originally published 1807.)

Jenna Tedrick Kuttruff

American Immigrants of West European Origin

- Sociocultural Factors Influencing Dress
- Dress on Departure from the Homeland
- Arrival into the New World
- From Family to Individuality
- Body Image
- Snapshot: Aprons

The dress of North American immigrants from Western Europe is a reflection of the evolution of their sociocultural experience as they went from their homelands to the New World. Immigration has existed from the early times of settlement in North America to the present. Western Europe (defined in 1890 as Italy, Spain, France, Great Britain, Norway, Sweden, Denmark, Germany, Netherlands, Austria-Hungary, Switzerland, France, and Luxembourg) provided the largest number of immigrants to the United States and Canada from the start of colonization until the first half of the twentieth century. European immigrants who arrived after the first third of the twentieth century were already dressing very much as did citizens of the United States and Canada. It is the earlier immigrants whose dress contrasted with mainstream U.S. fashion.

Many who emigrated to the United States during the late eighteenth and early nineteenth centuries were upper-class intellectuals fleeing their home countries because of political differences, religious persecution, or lack of economic opportunities. One objective of the newcomers was to use dress to adapt to the dominant culture as rapidly as possible. Irish historians believe, from an analysis of Colonial and post-Revolutionary names and records, that approximately one-third or more of the U.S. population in 1776 was Irish. Yet due to the similarity in physical appearance, dress, and language to the dominant English population, these early Irish immigrants are rarely noted. As long as new immigrants appeared each year, older immigrants were allowed the opportunity to move up the social ladder.

Immigration to the United States can be divided into three waves. The first (84,066 people from 1820 to 1840) was 70 percent English, Irish, and German immigrants. The remaining 30 percent were from the rest of Europe, Asia, and the Middle East. The second wave (1840 to 1929) was made up of large numbers of Irish, who were poorer and less able to fit into U.S. culture due to their economic and social differences, and French, Italian, German, and Spanish immigrants leaving Europe due to famine, lack of jobs, and religious persecution. In the late nineteenth century, immigrant groups that settled in the cities were from Italy and Spain, southern Western European countries whose people differed in language, religion, and physical appearance from U.S. norms. U.S. legislation in 1921 and 1924 attempted to restrict immigration from countries such as Italy. The third wave (1924 to 1965) was based on an immigration policy that favored keeping families together, selecting individuals with desired job skills, and aiding refugees.

Canadian immigration patterns differed somewhat from those south of the border. The French were a major force within the population as a result of the Canadian territories being held by France prior to their being ceded to the British. As with the United States, immigration to British Canada was largely Anglophone (English speaking). It was not until the Canadians wanted to populate the western regions of the country to protect them from being absorbed by the United States that larger numbers of Europeans from countries other than Britain and France emigrated. Among these were more Eastern Europeans.

SOCIOCULTURAL FACTORS INFLUENCING DRESS

When immigrants left the home country and came to the United States and Canada, the change from being primarily members of an individual community to becoming part of a larger overall society was visually reflected and viewed in the changes in their dress. Scholars have examined these changes and identified certain patterns. One German scholar, Ferdinand Tonnies, speaks of sociocultural factors using German terms translated as "community" (*Gemeinschaft*) and "society" (*Gesellschaft*). In the immigrant it is possible to see a change in emphasis from family life and kinship as major influences to individuality and movement from neighborhood to city. Looking at these two changes as opposite forces with gradations in between, the meanings behind what are worn are better understood. An immigrant often arrived with a total outfit planned to reflect their home. Pictures from Ellis Island show immigrants arriving in their national or regional dress. Yet, upon arrival, many immigrants quickly learned that to become "American" is more important. Thus, immigrants experienced the wearing of the home country's dress as the community influence in their experience of coming to North America, but they soon responded to the change and pull of the pressure to take on the appearance of the larger society.

When the immigrants arrived in the United States, they lived in ethnic communities or neighborhoods. Often individual enclaves were established, such as the Irish District or Village, Little Italy, Portuguese Seaport, and French Quarter. Within these neighborhoods the questions are how much the appearance of each group is distinct and how much symbols of dress are shared.

The strength and focus of these neighborhoods were stronger than what had existed in the home country. In the home country, the focus was often the family, but once in the United States or Canada, the community gained importance and became the ethnic identity with which the new resident associated. This change was stimulated by the rise of industrialization and the availability of inexpensive, ready-to-wear apparel. The wearing of homemade garments was seen as old-fashioned and was at times ridiculed. The predominant styles of the late nineteenth century were the

Immigrant woman selling pretzels in New York City, ca. 1896. She wears a simple unfashionable blouse and skirt that may have been what she wore when she arrived in the United States. The head scarf that she wears was commonly worn by European peasant women. Her customer's dress would indicate that he is impoverished. Photograph by Elizabeth Alice Austen. Library of Congress Prints and Photographs Division, LC-USZ62-76960.

shirtwaist dress, blouse, and dark skirt that fit a variety of body shapes and sizes even though they were mass produced.

As the ethnic neighborhood became overcrowded and upward mobility continued, the aspiration to become more American/Canadian and drop traditional ethnic dress tended to encourage more conformity with North American norms.

Immigrants also brought change to the North American ideal of proper dress because they brought high standards of craftsmanship from their native country, as seen in the detail work of the Italian cobbler, the Spanish shoemaker, and the French seamstress.

DRESS ON DEPARTURE FROM THE HOMELAND

The clothing worn as the immigrants left their homes varied based on social class and economic status. An illustration of a family emigrating from Ireland in 1866 shows that their dress was typical of the dress of a proper Irish family: a woman with a fitted black-serge skirt, matching jacket, and plaid blanket draped under the arm and another woman in a cape, closely fitted bonnet, and full skirt. By contrast, the dress of destitute peasants who emigrated was often ill fitting, dirty, and threadbare even before their journey began.

The destination for early immigrants was, initially, the major cities: Boston, Chicago, Montreal, New York, Philadelphia, and Toronto. One family may have been split, with relatives going to different destinations based on ships boarded and immigration policy. It is common to find immigration records with brothers and sisters going to multiple cities in one country or multiple countries. For example, in one family, one brother went to Canada; a sister, to Boston; and another brother, to Australia.

The trip to the New World was one of hardship for the immigrant, particularly in the nineteenth and early twentieth centuries. Personal accounts from Ellis Island talk of the time it often took to reach North America. Leaving one's home village and traveling by wagon or foot to get to the large urban centers to board a shipping vessel about to depart was often the first experience that many had of being outside their province or village area. The dress they wore was practical for the dusty road and long trip. While drawings at the docks depict people in their very best dress, personal accounts state that these clothes were often put away quickly once aboard ship until disembarking in the United States or Canada.

During the voyage, conditions on the ships were cramped and lacking in sanitation, and many passengers were ill and seasick. One set of photographs in the Ellis Island collection titled "Immigrants aboard a ship heading for the port of New York, circa 1892" and photographs in the Library of Congress Picture Collection show many arriving with ill-fitting, well-worn clothing. The immigrants changed into their best outfit possible prior to

Emigrants leaving Queenstown for New York, ca. 1874. Upon arrival in the United States many immigrants quickly learned that to become "American" necessitated the wearing of the new country's dress. Library of Congress, Prints and Photographs Division, LC-USZ62-105528.

leaving the ship and passing through immigration. Foremost on their mind was a neat, clean, and healthy appearance. Prior to departure, immigrants cleaned themselves with the small amount of water available, and if an alternate outfit was available, they changed into their best clothing, often folk dress, which is shown in some depictions. Worn clothing from the home country often was left aboard ship or, among the very poor, taken to be remade into garments for children.

ARRIVAL INTO THE NEW WORLD

Photos of immigrants arriving in North America with better clothing often reflected those wealthy enough to have purchased first-class tickets on the ship or those who stored an outfit and changed just prior to departing the ship. The use of a head scarf is seen in many immigrant pictures, often reflecting the region in which the wearer originated. French and Italian immigrant photographs show women with head scarves tied in different ways and made of different fabric based on the province or village from which they had emigrated.

The garments they had been wearing on arrival were often unacceptable to the immigrant, and one of their first purchases in North America frequently was new clothing, a new body covering. Historian Oscar Handlin, in *Uprooted*, has stated that due to economics and practicality, the items purchased were often of lesser-quality fabric, poorer-quality lace trim, and subdued in color. A partly autobiographical social and religious study of late-nineteenth-century Italian immigrants adjusting to life in the United States written by Antonio Mangano tells the story of Tommaso, whose parents immigrate first and later send for the young boy. When he arrives, he is disheveled, dirty, and tattered. The first task of his parents is to find a shop "where Tommaso could be provided with a new suit of clothing." The description

continues: "Arrayed in his cheap new suit, Tommaso felt quite American already and he strutted proudly along with his parents." The change to U.S. clothing communicates the desire for Tommaso to look and be American as quickly as possible prior to being seen in the neighborhood.

The neighborhoods and cities became more crowded, and the ethnic groups began to bump into each other. The breadwinners of the family met at work, and the children met other ethnic groups at school. Thus, the neighborhood became less important and city life more important.

FROM FAMILY TO INDIVIDUALITY

The continuum of change from family influences to greater emphasis on individuality occurred upon arrival into the New World. The family established the proper mores or beliefs about appropriate dress, decorum, and behavior that represents the family, and it was the responsibility of each family member to abide by those expectations. Appearance influences the family's status in the community and the binding of the individual to the family group. "Family," in the home country, meant relatives with common blood. However, once in the United States and Canada, the concept of family was expanded to include friends from the same village and other people from the same country.

The push and pull between the smaller community and the larger society was made evident in the purchase of clothing, the role of the family, and the relationship between mothers and daughters. The purchase of clothing within the family was arranged based on economics and the role of each family member. The adult male breadwinner(s) were the first to be outfitted. Economic factors dictated that they be neat, clean, and dressed in the fashion of the day. The working young adults experimented with dress and appearance, often to the chagrin of their parents.

A number of the examples that follow are drawn from the experiences of Italian immigrant families. These examples illustrate experiences not unlike those of other immigrant groups from Western Europe and, therefore, serve as useful parallels. In the first-generation immigrant Italian or Irish household, the woman was the last to buy a new outfit of clothes. The advancement of husband and family was the focus of apparel spending. The majority of the Irish immigrants after 1840 and of Italian immigrants after 1860 were of rural peasant or rural poor background, and the women led hard and frugal lives. Practicality was the focus of each purchase, as seen in the choice of subdued colors, good cloth, and a silhouette that would last. The resourceful woman was admired in the family and community. During her early days of residence in the new country, a woman's status was not judged by the latest fashions but by the appearance of herself and her family. Proper dress was conservative, attractive, versatile, and long lasting. In the Italian family, the practical objective meant that adherence to fashion changes was minimal.

Women's role in the family was one of caring. Photographs showing women and children often reflect the image of Madonna and child. Immigrants frequently maintained the style of dress that they wore in the home country. Their continued use of the same fabrics, silhouette shapes, hairstyles, and accessories often made them look "old country." The floral shift dress seen from

Italian immigrants arriving at Ellis Island, ca. 1860. Many Italian immigrants were of rural peasant or rural poor background. Clothes were of subdued colors and good cloth, designed to last. Library of Congress, Prints and Photographs Division, LC-USZ62-26617.

1930 until 1980 and sturdy black shoes represented a woman who was working in her home. Photographs taken by Judy Flynn on the streets of Boston show women in these outfits as they lean out their windows to look at the street activities or shop in outdoor markets close to their homes.

Visitors from Italy observed these immigrants and often commented that Italians had not worn outfits like those of Italian Americans in years. The maintenance of the old look was a personal identification with their ethnic group.

As international travel became easier, certain members of the family might go back and forth to the home country "like birds of passage." For many, the journey was to see relatives unable or unwilling to emigrate and to have additional relatives return with them. What they also brought back were additional pieces of cloth, jewelry, shoes, leather products, and table linens.

Writer Maria Lurino has described the pull and tug of "good taste and bad taste" in dress in her life and compared this competition to the designs of Giorgio Armani and Gianni Versace. Armani is known for classic, subdued good taste and Versace, for his outrageous designs that push the envelope of good design with bright colors and faux items. The hidden meaning behind the competition of Armani, of northern Italy, and Versace, from the south of Italy, is a reflection of the competition between those two national regions. Dress was one's pride but also one's embarrassment if you chose incorrectly in trying to meet U.S. standards. As each successive generation came, their concept of acceptable dress changed and challenged the old rules. First-generation immigrants thought they had become Americanized with their new outfits, but the outsider could read the symbols of the home country. The jewelry worn, the hairstyle selected, and the sweater or jacket carried with the outfit or the shoes that went with it all revealed the old styles and, hence, the wearer's ethnic group.

Vivid colors and prints often identified those from southern Italy, who were often called *gavone*; pronounced "gah vone," this southern Italian variant of the word *cafone* was used as both noun and adjective to mean "lower class." The word *cafone* is used by northern, upper-class Italians to "mock poor southerners" as part of the old-country class struggle. To Lurino, the southern Italian "gavone outfits combined a sexiness and tackiness" that was excessive in color, trim, and design. The second generation often rejected the old symbols, the religious jewelry, the heavy sweaters, and the flowered dresses, knowing that rejection allowed them to assimilate. Often in their youth they wore what they believed would help them obtain jobs, move to a higher social class, and become accepted by other ethnic groups.

The conflict between generations over dress may grow out of expectations about family life that were carried to the new country from the old. Another example from Italian families may serve to illustrate. The mother's closeness to and control over her daughter is expected to continue throughout life. The mother is in charge of the children and watches over their appearance for modesty, appropriateness, sensible purchases, and clothing care. During the teenage years, this was often tumultuous, as each generation went more toward U.S. ways. If the teen was wearing what the father thought was inappropriate, it was the mother's duty to take control. The father rarely spoke directly to the daughter in these matters. As the years went by and the daughter became an adult, she would often be expected to visit the family or call daily. Older daughters commented on how demanding and time-consuming this was as they raised their own families. As the mother aged, the daughter was expected to take care of the mother's needs, including shopping for clothing and food.

BODY IMAGE

The cultural weight assigned to food as nourishment, as comfort, and as fulfillment of a good wife and mother's duties is often seen as a contributing factor to the stereotype of the overweight Italian. Photographs of immigrant Italian American women in Boston in the 1970s show them with heavy trunks and strong arms and legs, characteristics probably developed as a result of their carrying groceries, walking around the city, and walking up several flights of stairs.

Some strong, sturdy women with heavy trunks wore dark black stockings with black, half-inch- (one-centimeter-) heel laced or slip-on shoes. Their arms were strong from carrying heavy paper bags full of groceries from market to home; later, they might have stopped by the park to talk to friends. Two distinct outfits were worn most frequently. Women often wore black dresses for going to the market. The black might have represented northern Italian formality or a woman grieving. In

Mother and daughter on Salem Street, North End Boston, 1978. When Italian American women shopped in their own neighborhoods, they wore the dress typical of the neighborhood. In 1978 that was the printed, patterned, or floral, unfitted sheath. When leaving the neighborhood they made sure they were dressed in more current styles. Courtesy of Judy Zaccagnini Flynn.

southern Italy, women in mourning wore black from head to foot. The other was likely to be a shift housedress with floral print and large pockets. This style might have represented casualness or perhaps was chosen by southern Italian women for its colorful design. Individuals often carried what might have been a handkerchief or a cloth to wipe perspiration from their brow during a hot summer day. Hair was pulled tight in front, then toward the back with a bun.

The following is a description of one woman seen in the 1970s sitting on a cement bench in an outdoor Boston park, a gathering place for the local elderly and children as well as for tourists following the Freedom Trail. She was elderly and wore a floral sheath housedress with a turquoise-blue strip down the center front of the dress. (The sheath dress is flattering to a woman under five feet in stature.) Her body type was solid, thick through the center with strong upper arms, a wide midsection, and heavy thighs. Her legs were short and sturdy and projected out from below the dress. Her nylon stockings were rolled down to her ankles, and she was wearing black flip-flops. Air conditioning was rare in Boston's North End during the 1970s. Her outfit was completed by wearing multiple gold bracelets, gold hoop earrings, and a gold pendant on a chain around her neck. She was holding her glasses in her hand. She had been carrying her sweater, which she had placed next to her. She had laid a newspaper on the cement bench to keep her outfit clean. She told the interviewer that she had spent the morning making sauce for pasta and had come out during the middle of the day to escape the heat in her apartment, to become part of the neighborhood, and to see what was happening. In interviews, other women stated that housedresses were for the home or for running out for a quick errand at the neighborhood store or outdoor market, viewed as one's backyard in the city.

Other women seen dressed in floral shift dresses over the same time period might have been sweeping the sidewalk, washing the inside hall floors, and shopping in the local outdoor market and mom-and-pop stores. Tracking their locations, it would become clear that the women in floral shift dresses were shopping close to their homes. Thus, they were in their private space or neighborhood. Those dressed in solid dresses and more matching outfits lived farther from the shopping areas and were presenting themselves in public spaces. These women were choosing to make their public presentation out of the neighborhood according to the expectations of the larger U.S. society, while conforming to the ethnic neighborhood practices in private.

Although these examples of the ways that dress reflects changes in immigrants' sociocultural experience as they went from their homelands in Western Europe to the New World are drawn from specific countries and even subcultures within those countries, the experiences would be similar for people from other European countries; obviously, there are differences between the dress of affluent and comfortable followers of Western fashion and that found in various subcultures based on region, religion, or socioeconomic status. For the well-off European immigrant, dress in Europe and dress in the United States and Canada is and was virtually indistinguishable. For those whose dress is clearly different, the change from neighborhood dress or folk dress to contemporary city dress, and the transition from focus on the family and ethnic group to one driven by individuality, may be slowed but is rarely halted.

Snapshot: Aprons

The focus of the family also revolves around the importance of food. The Italian sauce is made early in the morning to allow it to simmer throughout the day, and in the summer, it allows the mother to get out of the kitchen during the mid-day heat. Dress is associated with cooking the sauce (also called "gravy"). A proper *apron* (a garment worn around the waist to protect one's outfit from getting dirty) was often worn over the skirt or dress. Several types of aprons appear in early photographs and are discussed in oral histories. The first, a rectangular piece of cloth, may be wrapped around one's waist to protect the skirt and later removed and placed over the shoulder, as was seen in Europe. The second is a rectangular cloth gathered at the waist and held together by a sewn band with ties. Often this apron was sewn by young girls in school throughout the country in the nineteenth and until the mid-twentieth century. Examples have been preserved in the Framingham State College Costume and Textile Collection in Massachusetts. A third type adds a bodice rectangle or bib with a strap to go around the neck to protect the top of one's dress.

As late as 1980, wearing aprons in Irish and Italian families was part of cooking a meal. In the twenty-first century, aprons are expected for holiday meals when women bond in the kitchen during meal preparation. Today's aprons are more ornamental than practical.

REFERENCES AND FURTHER READING

Flynn, Judith Zaccagnini. "Dress of Older Italian-American Women: Documentation of Dress and the Influence of Socio-Cultural Factors." Ph.D. dissertation, Ohio State University, 1979.

Oaks, Alma, and Hill Margot Hamilton. *Rural Costume: Its Origin and Development in Western Europe and the British Isles*. London: B. T. Batsford, 1970.

Severson, Kim. "A Grandchild of Italy Cracks the Spaghetti Code." *The New York Times*. http://www.nytimes.com/2007/02/21/dining/212srex.html?em&ex=1172379600&en=b0c807ac81964199&ei=5087%0A (21 February 2007).

Sichel, Kim, ed. *Street Portraits 1946–1976: The Photographs of Jules Aarons*. Lunenberg, VT: The Stinehour Press, 2002.

See also Snapshot: Traditional Identity and Gender in Jewish Dress

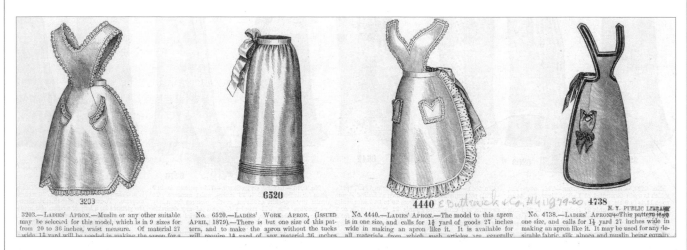

Ladies' aprons, United States, 1879–1880. As late as 1980 wearing aprons in Irish and Italian immigrant families was part of cooking a meal. Courtesy New York Public Library.

References and Further Reading

American Immigration Law Foundation. "American Policy Reports: Providing Factual Information about Immigration. A Short History of U.S. Immigration Policy, 1999." http://www.ailf.org/pubed/pe_index.asp (accessed January 2007).

Austen, Alice. *Street Views of New York City*. 69 photographic prints, New York Public Library Division: Humanities and Social Sciences Library / Photography Collection, Miriam and Ira D. Wallach Division of Art, Prints and Photographs Description. Created 1896.

Clancy, Mary, John F. Cunningham, and Alf MacLochlainn, eds. *Emigrant Experience*. Galway, Ire: Galway Labour History Group, 1991.

Flynn, Judith Zaccagnini. "Dress of Older Italian-American Women: Documentation of Dress and the Influence of Socio-Cultural Factors." Ph.D. dissertation, Ohio State University, 1979.

Handlin, Oscar. *Uprooted: The Epic Story of the Great Migrations That Made the American People*. Boston, MA: Little Brown, 1951.

Hine, Lewis Wickes. Photographer 1874–1940, New York Public Library Division Unit I, Immigration. (2), Life and labor in America with emphasis upon racial contributions: Humanities and Social Sciences Library / Photography Collection, Miriam and Ira D. Wallach Division of Art, Prints and Photographs 431 photographic prints.

Lurino, Maria. *Were You Always an Italian? Ancestors and Other Icons of Italian America*. New York: W. W. Norton, 2000.

Mangano, Antonio. *Sons of Italy: A Social and Religious Study of the Italians in America*. New York: Missionary Education Movement of the United States and Canada, 1917.

Nelli, Humbert. "Italians in Urban America: A Study in Ethnic Adjustment." *International Migration Review* 1 (Summer 1967): 38–55.

Ontario Photographic Collections. Archives of Ontario. Sir Henry Smith (photographs of Kingston, ca. 1870), M. O. Hammond (amateur photographer, 1888–1934). http://ao.minisisinc.com/scripts/mwimain.dll/406/2/6?RECLIST (accessed 10 March 2007).

Riis, Jacob. *How the Other Half Lives: Studies among the Tenements of New York*. New York: Dover, 1971. (Originally published 1890.)

Rumbaunt, Ruben G., and Alejandro Portes. *Ethnicities: Children of Immigrants in America*. Berkley: University of California Press, 2001.

Tonnies, Ferdinand. *Fundamental Concepts of Sociology: Gemeinschaft and Gesellschaft*. English translation and supplement by Charles P. Loomis. New York: American Book Company, 1940. (Originally published 1890.)

Williams, Phyllis H. *South Italian Folkways in Europe and America: A Handbook for Social Workers, Visiting Nurses, School Teachers, and Physicians*. New York: Russell & Russell, 1938.

Judy Zaccagnini Flynn

African American

Inarguably, the dress practices of many African Americans differ from those of the dominant culture. African American dress practices are both complex and diverse and are rooted in a cultural aesthetic that can be called neither African nor American. The forced symbiosis of African and American culture produced a group of people the civil rights leader W.E.B. DuBois characterized as having a "double consciousness"—a sense of being neither fully American nor fully African. The competing systems of reality, one grounded in European philosophical conceptions of the world while another negated African conceptions as "the other" and denied the African concept of self, forced tensions of "twoness," which continue to define how African Americans negotiate their multiple realities and define themselves. These tensions produced a form of cultural materialism manifest in dress which continues to be seen, especially where groups of African Americans congregate. These characteristics of dress, evident even during the years of African enslavement in the Americas, constitute an African American aesthetic of dress.

Dress practices of African Americans have been viewed as both deviant and culturally deficient. Historical writings during the period of African enslavement in the Americas are replete with descriptions of white Americans ridiculing the dress of enslaved Africans, and later, emancipated African Americans, as strange, presumptuous, and unsuccessful attempts to imitate white U.S. ways. Following the period of African enslavement in the United States, African American dress practices, which often included unusual adornment of the head and the use of colors, patterns, and garment parts that lacked congruence with white U.S. aesthetic sensibilities, were continuously mocked as pretentious and of poor taste. Exaggerated forms of African American dress served as the basis for framing media stereotypes, such as the contented slave, the wretched freedman, the comic darky, the black brute, the tragic mulatto, the local-color clown, and the exotic primitive. Sociologists, psychologists, and cultural critics contend that variations on these themes continue even in the early twenty-first century in media depictions of African Americans. Because media stereotypes are formed through manipulations of symbol systems depicting the dressed body, these stereotypes function to anchor the African American socially and culturally as the "other." Stereotypes, exemplified by exaggeration

and omission, served to perpetuate notions of difference and deficiency. While historically African American dress violated conventional Euro–North American appearance norms, these supposed aberrations have recently been shown to be signs of an African American aesthetic of dress—a blending of material culture, a manifestation of the fashioning of an identity under the pressure of double consciousness.

The complexity of African American dress practices reflects blacks' connection to both African and U.S. cultures, the attempts toward assimilation into U.S. culture by adapting/adopting beauty techniques that reflect Euro–North American standards of beauty and the struggle to define the self and to overcome the stigma of blackness being associated with inferiority. The darkness of the skin of African Americans automatically establishes binary opposition between black and white, which renders attempts to approximate Euro–North American standards of beauty impossible. The range of skin colors allowed for differences in the degree of hostility that African Americans received from whites during the period of enslavement and continues to impact opportunity in the early twenty-first century. Since slavery, skin color and other physical features (e.g., thick lips, flat nose, nappy hair) have served as a basis for discrimination where lighter-skinned African Americans receive advantages over darker-skinned African Americans. Added to the complexity is the role of hair texture where one may approximate the Euro–North American beauty norms on the one hand or ethnic authenticity on the other. Thus, it is apparent that the closer one is able to approximate conventional U.S. beauty standards, the better off one might be. Such complexity does not allow for essentialism in the discussion of African American dress practices.

Although purveyors of popular culture persist in presenting something called "dressing black" as representative of African American dress practices, the diversity in their dress is as great as that found among people of the dominant culture. Yet there is an African American aesthetic of dress, although practices related to the aesthetic may be influenced by such factors as age, gender, lifestyle, social status, economics, education, occupation, and degree of acculturation. In addition, individuals may make rational choices to abandon forms of dress representative of the aesthetic in favor of conventional dress, understanding that one might benefit from dress that signifies acculturation. Dress practices also change as the sense of self develops and may be guided by instrumental or aesthetic inclinations, or driven by cultural politics. As is the case in all cultures, dress may be viewed as both product and process. However, unlike some cultures, it is not feasible to separate dress as product from dress as process when viewed in the context of African American dress practices.

THE AESTHETIC OF DRESS

African Americans often make choices of styles, colors, and patterns in dress, and other forms of adornment that clearly bespeak a cultural aesthetic. This dress is characterized by its expressiveness, which includes the dressed body along with all of its expressive features—speech, movement, voice pitch and intonations, as well as facial expression. These aesthetic orientations are different from those of the dominant culture and encompass various values and attitudes. They vary in practice from one developmental state to another as well as from one context to another. Elements of the aesthetic can be seen and articulated by African Americans of various ages and social and economic statuses as well as of various levels of education, although they do not necessarily represent the preferences of the individual who articulates them. In addition, elements of the aesthetic are most pronounced where African Americans congregate or are found to be the majority population, such as African American churches, organizations, or institutions and certain geographic locations.

The aesthetic of dress referred to as African American has its roots in West African cultures and metaphysical beliefs with distinctive elements. The elements are also found in descriptions of dress of enslaved Africans and in West African dress during the enslaving years. This aesthetic of dress is neither African nor American but is shaped by the unique experiences of descendents of Africans caught between a double consciousness and surviving for five hundred years as a disenfranchised people in a Eurocentric culture. With improvisation as the benchmark, the patterns of personal dress encompassed the utilization of African aesthetic forms and Euro–North American impressions and materials. The aesthetic consists of four elements: the affinity for high-affect or "loud" colors, style or individual expression, improvisations and exotic features, and the tendency to dress up. While, for the purpose of clarity, these elements are discussed separately, apparel choices are not made based on the selection of isolated elements; instead, the elements discussed have tended to be historically dominant in dress practices.

The affinity for loud or high-affect colors. This element consists of the common and historic use of *high-affect colors*—colors with high intensities that are often used together, sometimes in equal amounts, resulting in the exaggeration of intensity. These colors are commonly referred to as bold, vibrant, or loud and have been used historically in negative stereotypes of African Americans. At the same time, the use of such color combinations has served as inspiration for couture fashion and also figures largely in fashion media's characterization of exotic fashion. In the global environment of the early twenty-first century, bold, vibrant, high-affect colors are seen in mass fashion and are influencing popular fashion worldwide.

The element of "style" or individual expression. The aesthetic element of style has probably received more attention in scholarly and popular culture literature than any other. *Style* includes objects of dress as well as how these objects are personalized through the injection of energy and attitude into a visible discourse. One may wear a garment that, viewed apart from the wearer, may be considered as conservative, but the wearer may transform the garment by injecting into it the element of style. Style includes acting and redefining the self in relation to others and the environment. It includes all components of dress and its public display, resulting in a unique body language that contributes immensely to a culture's discourse. In the context of the aesthetic of dress in the African American community, style is most often simply the display of the unique characteristics of the individual—a free expression of one's essence. It is when numerous individuals bring together in one setting this free expression of one's essence that the aesthetic is most pronounced.

Improvisations and exotic features. Novel, unusual effects are expressed in a variety of ways, including garments of fabrics with multiple rhythms that result from color, form, line, and texture,

and their varied and myriad combinations. In addition, the creative mixing of uncommon materials and unusual combinations in garment parts, as well as accessories, contribute to its exotic nature. Various forms of head dress, including hats and hairstyles, as well as the grooming of hands and nails contribute to the exoticism. When energy and emotion are injected into this heady blend, one fashions a style of one's own, making it visually impossible for the wearer to go unnoticed or the viewer to be unresponsive—a reaction is demanded. The use of exotic features is not relegated to formal occasions or nightlife. Such features may well be a part of the ordinary African American's way of expressing dress preference.

The tendency to dress up. Dressing up refers to the tradition of giving special consideration to dressing for any occasion deemed important, whether sacred or secular. Dress is used among many African Americans to signify that which is important, set apart, or reverenced. Many African Americans place great importance on the use of dress to display status, either acquired or desired, and give special attention to dress even when resources are limited. Dressing up for important occasions requires that some objects be set aside as special and reserved for occasions of importance. Numerous descriptions of dressing up for important occasions are found in slave narratives, among which church dress is most frequently mentioned. While dressing up for church, a sacred occasion, is common practice, it is also common for African Americans to dress up for house parties, sports events such as football games, or any gathering deemed important.

For centuries, media descriptions of dress practices of African Americans have been based on the comparison of the aesthetic against a Eurocentric milieu in which African Americans have been ridiculed, and often viewed as subversive, by members of the dominant culture because of differences in aesthetic sensibilities. Only in the last few decades have African Americans' dress practices been linked to a meaningful cultural heritage and, even

A group of young African American men dressed for church, ca. 1900. Library of Congress, Prints and Photographs Division, LC-USZ62-124854.

more recently, organized with distinctive elements and presented as a cultural aesthetic. However meaningful an African American aesthetic of dress might be, without knowledge of its historical grounding and the acknowledgment of African Americans as an ethnic group with a culture and a history, dress practices that deviate from conventional norms will continue to be viewed as deviant and deficient, if not pathological.

CHURCH DRESS

Historical documents such as journals of slave owners and slave narratives are prime sources for documenting the importance of church dress and for noting the elements of the African American aesthetic of dress even during the years of African enslavement in the United States. As the African American church served as the primary cultural and social institution in the African American community following slavery and until the later part of the twentieth century, it is no surprise the church would be the most likely place to observe dress as material culture. Although not homogeneous entities, African American churches are usually identified with the socioeconomic background of their members. Characterized by a plurality of views, African American churches still accept a broad range of responsibilities for African Americans. In addition to providing the opportunity for communicants to express their religious life through differentiation in ritual, the church ministers to various classes within the African American population. As the repository for cultural memory and the cultural and spiritual link to African American heritage, the church has maintained a voluntary form of isolation; thus, cultural forms and traditions have to a large extent been maintained. One would expect then that dress in the African American church would reflect this influence.

Perhaps the coming together of two significant cultural factors—the historical role of the African American church in the social, cultural, educational, and political life of a people and the importance of dress as a marker for that which is reverenced— naturally lead to dressing up for Sunday worship. The tradition of wearing one's newest and finest to church as a sign of showing reverence to God and to God's house has been maintained. In the early twenty-first century, the African American church is the most likely place in which to see the African American aesthetic of dress manifested in its fullness. On any given occasion dress may range from extremely conservative to exotic. Garments of bold colors and multiple rhythms may be seen next to conservative dress customized according to personal taste, or pastel ensembles with matching head dress and shoes. One may also see dress produced in Africa, primarily for Africans, worn proudly by African Americans, alongside hip-hop dress and the very latest fashion—all deemed acceptable. In addition, one may see clothes by leading fashion designers personalized and made a part of one's expressive nature.

Both males and females place emphasis on dressing up for church. It is in the church that men are most free to indulge their creative and aesthetic appetites in satisfying the cultural urge to don high-affect colors and soft lines in wearing apparel without negative consequences. A panoramic view on a typical Sunday might show a variety of colors, if not a kaleidoscope, in the dress of men. Males in the congregation might be seen in suits with softer lines and construction techniques and considerably more fullness than is the norm for the conservatively dressed male. Their suits might be seen in almost any fashion color, with matching socks, shoes, and hats. Long coats of leather, fur, or fine wool may be worn in winter as well as elaborate jewelry, coordinated walking canes, and other accessories. In addition, some men also choose to wear cultural dress often made of elaborate fabrics and soft, flowing lines. Understanding that the dominant culture considers that the well-dressed man wears somber colors and well-tailored, conservative suits, some African American men have considerable diversity in their wardrobe in order to satisfy both personal taste and professional demands; thus, choices are made based upon the context in which they expect to appear.

Not all African Americans who place importance on dressing up for church, however, subscribe to the wearing of exotic head dress, high-affect colors and pattern in apparel, or to distinctively cultural influences in dress; some instead choose the finest of conventional fashion that they can afford. In addition, the lifestyle trend of more casual dress is also found in some churches, and casual dress in general is growing in acceptance. Even in dress in the African American church, tensions of double consciousness are evident—one dresses up to show reverence to God, but one dresses up also because there are very few occasions on which some African Americans can demonstrate that racism and classism do not matter.

In most churches, the pastor is expected to be well dressed and is often provided gifts of clothing in order to satisfy that expectation. In other instances, dress of the pastor reflects the status and hierarchy of the position. Many pastors are models of the latest trends in dress and serve as fashion leaders, especially for African American males. In addition, traditional robes worn by some preachers are modified by using panels of fabric with African motifs or narrow strip palliums made of kente cloth. Thus, through dress, the preacher models symbolically the notion of both spiritual and cultural leader.

African American churches, no doubt, played the primary role in preserving the historical significance of African modalities in dress, as the church assumed the role of curator of cultural memory for African Americans. It is not surprising to find profound expression of culture in the dress of African Americans, nor to find, perhaps, its greatest expression in the African American church. The practice of dressing up for church is as old as the African American church itself. This phenomenon is prominent in slave narratives, where distinction was made between Sunday clothes and work clothes. And when clothes were not different, special care was given to them for wearing to church on Sunday. The African American church remains a place in which to freely express in multiple ways the African side of the double consciousness, if not to reconcile it.

HEAD DRESS

African Americans devote an inordinate amount of time to head dress as it is of great importance. Hair is generally the first aspect one notices of an individual's appearance and is believed by some to be the most reliable indicator of racial heritage. A primary element in the formation of first impressions, it is also a highly symbolic part of the body used in negotiating one's place in the world. Historians have noted that even under slavery, African Americans devoted special attention to hair care and appearance. Such importance remains that for many African Americans the latest fashion is secondary to head dress; one may have the best attire, but if the head is not dressed properly, little else matters. Time and resources are given to adorning the head with hairstyles ranging from the fashionable styles of the dominant culture to the decidedly African American hairstyles rooted in West African artistry and culture. Even poor women go to beauty salons on a regular basis to have their hair done. When the use of a beautician is not feasible, African American women may dress their own hair or that of family and friends from their own home.

Substantial resources are spent on hair-care products to make the hair more malleable and to improve its texture and length. The importance of hair length and texture is seen in the manner in which resources are used to enhance these characteristics. Hair length is extended through the addition of human or synthetic hair and through the removal of the natural curl from hair. Human or synthetic hair may be woven into existing hair or added into braids to extend the length for both adults and children. Such hair treatments may be quite costly, and one may spend eight or more hours sitting while hair extensions are connected or the hair is being meticulously braided.

Hot combs and curling irons are used to remove the natural curl from hair, which may serve to lengthen it and replace its natural curl with smoother curls or waves, or it can be wrapped to maintain smoothness and accentuate a desired length approximating the fashionable beauty standards of the dominant culture. Chemicals may be used to permanently remove the natural curl, leaving the hair smooth and allowing for considerable latitude in acceptable hairstyles. The malleable quality of the hair, resulting from such treatments, along with the prevailing aesthetic, provides the impetus for a unique creativity in head dress.

The use of heat, chemicals, and other implements to lengthen and change the texture of hair were designed to make African Americans more European in appearance. The use of chemicals and various means of straightening or "processing" hair for both males and females, including dyes and bleaches, close cuts and stocking caps to smooth the hair and create waves, as well as pomades and other implements, are all means by which African Americans create looks approximating current fashion in head dress. Combined with lighter skin, some African Americans, especially in the entertainment business, have been successful in obtaining crossover approval for their looks. Some African Americans consider the use of products in this manner an attempt to obtain the dominant culture's standards of beauty in head dress and this is viewed as evidence of self-hatred or forms of self-degradation.

During the 1960s and 1970s, African Americans became vocal in protest against the dominant culture's definition of beauty and established beauty norms. As black became beautiful, the natural Afro became a crown of glory for both males and females, and status in the African American community was marked by how "black" one could present oneself. Most often measured by the size of the Afro, a focus was placed on African American cultural heritage and control over self-definition and the definition of beauty. As more African Americans became educated about their cultural heritage and embraced their own ethnicity, more and more emphasis was placed on the beauty of natural hair. As a result, many African Americans chose to not remove the natural curl but to manage it in ways that spoke to their own identity and aesthetic sensibilities. In the early twenty-first century, many are choosing short cuts, braids, cornrows, coils, twists, and dreadlocks. Motives for wearing such head dress range from personal aesthetic preferences to control over self-definition, group identity, black identity development, or to make political statements

about who has control over the body. While embraced by many, many other African Americans cannot break ties with head dress that mimics that of the dominant culture.

Hairstyles may also be manipulated for cultural and political reasons. Instead of duplicating the look of white people's hair, some suggest that straightening elements tend to emphasize differences rather than similarities, almost as a parody, causing an element of surprise and forcing one to take notice. African-style braids, close-cut natural styles, coils, twist, and dreadlocks worn by women may either challenge gender conventions or be given political interpretations with negative consequences. Worn by the African American male to express ethnic pride, personal identity, or as acts of self-determination, braided hair and long dreadlocks add to the existing tensions of the "dangerous black male," as such forms of head dress deviate substantially from the norm. In addition, such head dress is often feared and vilified by both African Americans and members of the dominant culture, establishing boundaries that block opportunities one otherwise might have. Thus, African Americans may pay rather high prices for expressing aesthetic preferences, exercising control over how the body is dressed, expressing ethnic pride, or making a political statement through head dress.

In addition to the use of creative and distinctive hairstyles, both males and females adorn the head with hats and headwraps, often of the latest fashion. Hats and headwraps of various kinds are sometimes donned in creative fashion, often in opposition to conventional use. For example, a male may wear the baseball cap turned backward, with the bib over the neck instead of the forehead, or a hat might be tilted to the side in a manner unique to the wearer. *Doo rags*, cloths tied around the head that were previously worn in the privacy of the home to manage a desired hairstyle, may be worn as casual streetwear or exposed under caps as a part of head dress. On any given Sunday, women may be seen in hats of unique shapes made of straw or various fabrics and adorned with geometric designs, beaded jewelry, faux flowers, and such, crowning the head with millinery splendor even in periods in which hats are not considered fashionable. In addition, the head may be wrapped in the tradition of African head dress, which may or may not be coordinated with other items of apparel.

Commercial beauty products for both the hair and face became available to African Americans in the late 1800s. While early products were manufactured by whites, by the early 1900s, African American entrepreneurs started to own their own businesses and market their own cosmetics. Advertisements for many of these products implied that the natural Negroid features should be masked to resemble those of whites. Included among these products were creams with claims of lightening the skin. African Americans differed in their beliefs and values about the use of such products. In addition, early cosmetics were associated with women of questionable morals.

By the mid-1920s, cosmetics had become accepted as an essential part of everyday life. Instead of masking black features, the use of cosmetics tended to distinguish the wearer from the natural look of the previous generation, becoming associated with progress and personal liberation. The demand for cosmetic products was met with great enthusiasm as African Americans engaged in public discussion of beauty and appearance and began to hold their own black beauty contests and fashion parades. This led to the display of black female bodies representing a variety of

In the 1970s, many African American men and women adopted the natural hairstyle called the Afro. Leo Vals/Hulton Archive/Getty Images.

beauty. As African Americans began to take control of their definition of beauty, the notion of what constitutes beauty broadened in scope, including all skin colors, shapes, textures, and styles of hair. Yet, African Americans are cognizant of the continuing significance of skin color and its relationship to opportunity.

The importance of head dress among African Americans can be traced to African roots. The grooming and embellishing of the head has been observed in both males and females, young and old, since the period of African enslavement in the Americas. The high regard for the human head is most noticeable in African art, where the head is greatly exaggerated in size in relation to the rest of the body, often featuring ornate hairstyles. Although differences in the intensity of the drive exist, this emphasis on the head is seen in many forms among African Americans in the early twenty first century. One might conclude that the natural inclination for preoccupation with hair and head dress is one of many links to a West African cultural heritage.

DRESS AND IDENTITY

Dress preferences of African Americans are influenced by numerous factors, including the extent to which one defines the self as African or American. Persons viewing themselves as Africans in America will use the dressed body to display notions of symbolic significance in ways different from the person who sees the self as an American who happens to be of African descent. One's identity as African, American, or African American is likely to evolve over time, and dress practices change as the definition of the self evolves.

African Americans, like those of all ethnicities, use dress as a means of establishing both individual and group identities. In addition to defining the self as an individual or as a member of a group, dress is a critical element in linking one to one's heritage. The lack of knowledge of a meaningful cultural heritage prevents the authentic use of dress in serving as that link in a significant way. Only recently have African American dress practices been linked to an important aesthetic with cultural and historical roots. Anchoring African American dress practices in an aesthetic rooted in West African cultures allows for the linking of dress practices, long considered as deviant, to a meaningful cultural heritage.

Because of a lack of knowledge of, and in some cases a lack of acceptance of, an African American aesthetic of dress, many Americans, some of African descent, have mistaken the hedonism and materialism of hip-hop dress as being emblematic or paradigmatic African American dress. Body piercing and baggy clothing are a reflection of class and age differences, as well as intracultural conflict, but they are not representative of dress of African Americans in general. Dress emanating from a hip-hop culture may be used by African American youth to express identity, revolt against convention and authority, or to control self-definition, but the notion that such dress represents African American dress and identity is a misguided one. Indeed, it is the expression of a lack of sense of self, thus forming an identity based on ignorance and mistakenly calling it "African American."

As with any ethnic group, African Americans have numerous identities, and these identities continue to evolve. Numerous efforts have been made by researchers to define these identities, especially ethnic identity, often in terms of the cultural nomenclatures—Negro, black, African, African American, and so forth. Acknowledging the diversity of African American experiences and thus the complexity of individual and group identity, psychologist William E. Cross isolated five stages of black identity development ranging from the extreme of black self-hatred and low racial awareness on one end of the spectrum to sustained confidence in, and commitment to, one's personal standards of blackness. Van Dyk Lewis, an African American scholar, used Cross's stages in black identity development in describing the diversity of dress practices of African Americans. Cross's stages of black identity development prove a useful schema for explaining how dress practices of African Americans have evolved. His five stages are (1) pre-encounter, which depicts the identity to be changed; (2) encounter, which isolates the point at which the person feels compelled to change; (3) immersion-emersion, which describes the vortex of identity change; and (4) and (5), internalization and internalization-commitment, which describe the habituation and internalization of the new identity. Of particular importance in understanding black identity development is that the stages represent attitudes or perspectives that transcend social-class boundaries, geographic locations, income, or even skin color. The particular attitudes, perspectives, and cultural frame of reference come from a variety of experiences and circumstances, "including instances of success and oppression" (Cross 1991, p. 198).

The pre-encounter stage is characterized by low-salience, race-neutral, or antiblack attitudes. Often ignorant of African American history and experiences, persons in this stage tend to be socialized to favor the Eurocentric cultural perspective, negating the value of black art forms. Lewis's analysis notes that clothing worn in the pre-encounter stage often reflects Hollywood or popular culture images. Obviously influenced by multiple forms of media, many in the pre-encounter stage are likely to define appropriate dress through the lenses of the dominant culture. These persons may strive to attain European standards of beauty or measure themselves against standards impossible to attain, often leading to, or perpetuating, low self-esteem.

Other persons in the pre-encounter stage may have very low (or no) salience for African American cultural heritage in that they have received little or no education concerning their history and cultural roots and have never acquired beliefs and practices of the dominant culture. Such persons' lives may be characterized by isolation from the dominant culture's influence and may be considered marginal in terms of acculturation. It is conceivable, however, that the elements of the African American aesthetic of

dress might be more pronounced among such persons in that the isolation and insulation might have served to preserve their African orientations even though they may be unaware of the basis of their aesthetic preferences.

In the encounter stage, a person's current identity is shattered by an experience or realization that confronts the relevance of and creates anxiety regarding one's worldview, leading to a knowledge that change is needed. Dress in this stage is often used to express one's ethnicity and identifies the individual with the group. However, using dress to identify the ethnic self may be mostly influenced by external situations rather than internalized beliefs and values about one's identity. The encounter that leads to seeking ethnic forms of dress may not be personal but of a nature that forces one to confront views about the ethnic group to which one belongs. Depending on the nature of the encounter, dress used to express group identity may be relegated to periods in which African Americans focus on their history or significant current events. Without historical and cultural grounding, one might seek representations of black identity that could simply be romanticized media constructs.

The immersion-emersion stage "addresses the most sensational aspect of Black identity development." The person immerses him- or herself in the world of blackness, uprooting the old self and moving through a transformative process sometimes approximating a spiritual experience. Ultimately, one emerges to a new identity. Dress in this stage is used to define the self as ethnic, expressing pride in the ethnic self and one's heritage. Individuals are also able to manipulate dress codes to demonstrate knowledge of dress expectations by the dominant culture while appropriating signs that signify and symbolize one's ethnicity. This is also the stage in which individuals use dress to construct identities that clearly establish cultural boundaries and the context for self/other relationships. More important than conforming to the dominant culture's ideals of fashion and dress is control over the definition of self. Dress in this stage is also used as a catalyst in stimulating conversation about African American culture and heritage. Used proactively, these conversations are purposeful, with the aim of correcting the prescribed ignorance resulting from an educational system lacking in African American historical and cultural content. It is possible that at this stage there is an emergence of the two selves or at least the ability to reconcile the double consciousness, making choices about dress practices armed with culturally relevant knowledge of the two worlds in which one resides. Thus, dress is used to validate the two selves. According to Van Dyk Lewis, from an interview with Metta Winter, at the end of this stage, individuals use dress to present themselves according to the roles they have as contributing members of society.

At the internalization stage, the black identity is taken within and habituated, and blackness becomes a "backdrop for life's transitions." High salience is given to blackness, but the identity is manifested by a calm naturalness. This inner confidence in oneself leaves room for many saliencies, such as biculturalism or multiculturalism. The internalization-commitment stage differs from the internalization stage only in its enduring capacity for sustained interest in black affairs. In these stages, fashion is less critical as a marker for how African Americans think of themselves and their place in society. There is a level of flexibility in choices and images wherein the emblematic use of fashion is much less important. Instead of abandoning the dress of the dominant culture, choices may be made in terms of expediency, suggesting bicultural or multicultural competence. At these stages, one may embrace elements of the dominant culture and that of one's own, having reconciled the tension between the two selves.

Whether tied to a stage of black identity or not, African Americans do use dress to express ethnic identity. The implication is that as one develops one's own self-identity as black, dress changes to accompany such development. That is, as the black self emerges, dress serves as a symbol system communicating information about the emerging self.

Using dress to establish an identity linked to ethnicity stands in opposition to the norm of acculturation. Because of the negative stereotypes associated with the African American "race," acculturation is viewed as key to acceptance by the dominant culture. This notion has led to efforts by many to adopt beauty standards of the dominant culture as one indicator of acculturation. The use of dress for ethnic identity poses problems for African Americans desiring to benefit from the advantages that might be gained through acculturation. Such behavior carries the risk of being perceived as deviant where fairly well-defined rules concerning appropriate dress exist. For example, when wearing the natural curl in the hair, whether as a symbol representing an African heritage or simply one's preference, one might elicit perceptions ranging from eccentric to adversarial, with the potential to negatively impact career goals and other aspirations. Understanding

Omarion Grandberry at the 2006 TNT Black Movie Awards. Interest in African-inspired hairstyles for men and women can be seen in the widespread adoption of cornrow braids. Jesse Grant/WireImage.

this African Americans have become adept at reframing codes to manage impressions through dress in order to exercise some degree of control over self-definition and the situation. Thus, dress serves political functions.

DRESS AND CULTURAL POLITICS

For African Americans, dress is an instrument used for many purposes, among which cultural politics prevail. Placed in a cultural and historical context, dress has been an instrument used to define or redefine the self in an attempt to influence, control, manipulate, or shape interaction situations. Cultural critics have noted that the African American body has long been a site for contestation. For centuries, African Americans have engaged in reframing codes of domination and subordination, defined by the dominant culture, as they sought to maintain control of their bodies. Understanding that codes, even of dress, are manipulated via established visual symbols to link economic, political, and cultural resources with opportunities and social respect, the reframing of such codes continues in order to exercise control over interactions and relationships. On an individual level, when one engages in impression management through dress for the express purpose of controlling interaction, the act is political.

African Americans use dress to create meaning and to position themselves in society, albeit that such meaning is often counter to that of the dominant culture. When codes are reframed for the purpose of self-definition that are not understood outside of the group controlling the meaning, the potential for communicating unintended messages is heightened. For example, if one is in the encounter stage of black identity development and uses ethnic dress to express the emerging self, one's appearance may be seen as deviant or at least interpreted in ways unintended. When the message in the presentation is misunderstood or considered as deviant, the propensity exists to intimidate or dominate (i.e., influence) the interaction. Thus, African American ethnic dress may serve as a political instrument.

Style, an element of the African American aesthetic of dress, has been described in terms of its use in encoding, often strategically, certain messages about the wearer and as a tool for usurping unauthorized power. Often objectified as the "other," some African Americans have channeled their creative talents and energies into the construction and use of particular expressive and conspicuous styles of nonverbal behaviors through dress, demeanor, gestures, walk, stances, and handshake in order to control self-definition and the situation. When style is used as a tool of persuasion among peers, its level of affect and dynamism may be heightened through the injection of attitude, rhythmic strides, and speech. These behaviors are used to actively construct the self, keeping individuals and groups off guard about one's intentions. Therefore, style may not be innocent but purposeful. These behaviors represent a deployment of power to define or control the situation.

In this manner, style is used to put into question notions of normative dress and, thus, to engage in overt acts of resistance. For example, the dreadlock hairstyle worn by both African American men and women is not, and is unlikely to become, normalized. However, it is not uncommon for professional men and women to be found wearing such head dress. Clearly the choice of head dress is a conscious one and makes a statement about how one chooses to define the self. Most often this decision is made after one has attained a desired level of professional status, understanding that prior to attaining such, the head dress might well be interpreted as pathological, with such an interpretation being used to prevent professional upward mobility. This suggests also that the wearing of normative dress by African Americans may simply be instrumental in that it is deemed a necessity until one reaches one's goals and has achieved a desired status, at which time one wears what one chooses, be it ethnic or some other preference.

Often dress practices do not represent personal aesthetic choice but become objects of protest, making political statements about the relationship of the wearer to the cause of African Americans. This was the case with the large Afro of the 1960s and 1970s, although it was soon used by the fashion system to create attention and thereafter became trivialized. Similarly, braids, cornrows, dreadlocks, and other ethnic hairstyles are being adopted by the fashion system as exotic head dress, removing them from their original content and meaning. The use of hair and other forms of dress as political statements in the early twenty-first century varies from that of the 1960s and 1970s in that during the civil rights era, there was a greater degree of unity in form than that seen today among African Americans.

SOCIAL STATUS

Dress in the United States serves as a form of cultural capital, used in establishing social distance both within the African American community as well as between African Americans and the larger U.S. society. In serving as instruments of acculturation, African American religious, educational, and social institutions sought historically to equip their members with skills, knowledge, and attitudes that provided advantages in attaining higher economic and social positions. Thus, African Americans were not only taught how to mimic the dress of the dominant culture but to use dress as cultural capital. Emphasis was placed on "appropriate" dress, including gait, posture, and stance, requiring the abandonment of one's own cultural aesthetic, at least in situations in which appearance was likely to impact opportunity.

Since the 1920s, when black beauty contests and fashion parades began, dress and appearance, including skin color, have been used to differentiate the middle-class African American from the working-class African American. According to Australian historians Shane White and Graham White, the African American middle class used the fashion show to establish itself as the authority on what respectable blacks should wear and, thus, to differentiate itself from ordinary, working-class African Americans. In addition, the Sunday parade—an opportunity for public display of one's finest attire after church—and the fashion show were used to establish social difference.

In addition to appropriate attire, the target for reform was hair, because the treatment of hair served as an indicator of one's level of acculturation. Dress has been and continues to be a medium to express one's level of acculturation, not only for economic gain but also for personal reasons. In the early twenty-first century some African Americans reject anything that is too "black"— naturally curled hair, braids, coils, dreadlocks, and so forth—and strive to approximate beauty norms of the dominant culture, believing that all things "white" are right and, thus, negating their own cultural aesthetic as "less than." Colorism—the ascribing of value and privilege based on lightness of skin color—has persisted since slavery. During slavery, light skin color was highly correlated with free blacks and, later, the educated, social, and economic elite of African Americans. Recently, the opposite phenomenon is evident in that many young African Americans are rejecting anything they believe to be "white," opting instead to dress in ways that set them at variance with the dominant culture as they seek to establish their own definition of self.

Class differences were and continue to be encoded through skin color and dress, including the level of expressiveness displayed by the wearer. So pervasive and important are they in improving one's status that these factors, among others, have led to complex and continuing issues of colorism and classism among African Americans. Skin color was and continues to be a prime factor in social positioning and racial categorization, placing light-skinned people over dark-skinned ones as well as serving as a shortcut to placing persons in moral and ethical categories. Because of the primacy of skin color, dress and language may simply be modifiers that suggest other characteristics, such as "gangbanger" or "brainy overachiever." Skin color impacts treatment or interpersonal interaction and opportunity at every level—from treatment in the nursery/kindergarten schoolyard to corporate America and in all forms of media and entertainment. During the enslaving years, the majority of freed slaves were light skinned. Even today, one can observe a correlation between skin color and opportunity in almost every area for African Americans.

VALUING CULTURAL FORM

Through the years, African Americans have had difficulty finding apparel from commercial sources that tapped the African side of their aesthetic sensibilities while providing proper fit. As body types differ among races and cultures, mass-produced fashion has generally not been designed to fit the typical African American male or female body types. In recent decades, companies began to target the African American consumer, offering apparel with African design influences but with mixed results. In many instances, African Americans desiring to express their ethnicity through dress tend to reject such offerings, seeking instead products believed to be authentic. Mass-produced products with African influences are often viewed with disdain as the commercialization of cultural forms. The commercialization of cultural aesthetic elements is seen by some as negating or devaluing cultural symbols and relegating a culture's philosophical orientation to that of a fad. This phenomenon reflects the ambivalence of the double consciousness in its desire to satisfy both sides of the self. There is the desire for fashionable apparel, properly proportioned and constructed to fit the body while reflecting one's ethnicity. At the same time, there is the tendency to reject products produced and marketed through the very capitalist system designed to satisfy the U.S. consumer's taste. These individuals place great symbolic significance on presenting the African side of the self.

TRANSFORMATION

Discussion of dress practices of African Americans focuses on the external body. However, the external/internal dichotomy is an artificial one for African Americans in that little, if any, distinction is made between the body and the self: Each is representative of the other. Because the physical features of African Americans

Clothing made from traditional African fabrics, such as the kente cloth worn by blues musician Taj Majal (right) and the dress and headwrap worn by the woman on the left, reflects African American interest in African clothing and textiles during the 1970s. Max B. Miller/Fotos International/Getty Images.

place them as the "other" in the context of the dominant culture's hegemony, African Americans find themselves as represented in the body, both stigmatized and marginalized. Not being indifferent to their bodies, African Americans have developed feelings of love or hate for their bodies, and such feelings may be manifested in dress practices. Understanding that the body is political and central to both identity and survival, African Americans have sought to find ways to reconcile the conflict between the body as the self and the stigmatized body.

Dress is used in various ways to respond to the stigmatized and marginalized self. Historically, the prime response was to seek acceptance through acculturation. Some, however, use dress as a base for resistance, as seen in African American youth culture's choice of dress that sets them at variance with dress norms of the dominant culture, or as in the use of dress in political acts of resistance, such as that of African Americans during the civil rights era.

The aesthetic element of style has functioned historically as a means of rejecting dominant myths of beauty and as a transforming element that moves the object of convention (e.g., fashion) to one of culture. As in the case when dress for enslaved Africans was prescribed, and with conventional dress as the current standard, style is used to place the dressed body and the self in a cultural context, redefining beauty. Unlike the aesthetic object of Western cultures, technical excellence in objects of dress is insufficient in and of itself to express beauty. Objects of dress as purchased are incomplete but have the potential to become beautiful. According to sociologist Clovis E. Semmes, "One must inject beauty, heightened emotion or feeling, and idiosyncratic expression into a product or action." The injecting of idiosyncratic expression into objects of dress serves as a customizing agent that alters the intended meaning of the object. Through customizing, objects of convention are transformed and become objects of culture. Style, then, becomes a way of rejecting dominant myths, controlling the

expressive shaping of one's immediate and everyday life, as well as redefining the self and the body.

Just as the self and the body are not separate entities, the body and dress are often considered as inseparable. In the African world, all things are related, and African Americans tend to merge dress and one's being. There tends to be a lack of distinction between the spiritual and the material. In addition, everything is functionally connected. Dress is often a critical link between the self and the spirit realm as well as between the self and the collective community. There is no distinction between the spiritual and the physical or between mind, body, and soul as posited by European philosophers. It is this notion of connectedness that probably explains dressing up. Dress serves as a concrete manifestation of the link of the individual to the collective community and to the spirit realm.

While dress practices of African Americans reflect their connection to both African and American cultures, the complexity of such practices results from a blending of material culture, the fashioning of an identity under the pressure of double consciousness, and the need to reconcile the conflict resulting from the stigmatized and marginalized self. The struggle is as DuBois described: "two souls, two thoughts, two unreconciled strivings; two warring ideals in one dark body."

References and Further Reading

Allen, Richard L. *The Concept of Self: A Study of Black Identity and Self-Esteem.* Detroit, MI: Wayne State University Press, 2001.

Brown, Sterling A. "Negro Characters as Seen by White Authors." In *Dark Symphony: Negro Literature in America*, edited by J. A. Emanuel and T. L. Gross, 139–171. New York: The Free Press, 1968.

Cross, William E. *Shades of Black: Diversity in African-American Identity.* Philadelphia: Temple University Press, 1991.

DuBois, W.E.B. *The Souls of Black Folk.* New York: The New American Library, 1903.

Dyson, Michael E. *Is Bill Cosby Right?: or Has the Black Middle Class Lost Its Mind?* New York: Basic Civitas Books, 2005.

Featherston, Elena, ed. *Skin Deep: Women Writing on Color, Culture and Identity.* Freedom, CA: The Crossing Press, 1994.

Foster, Helen B. *New Raiments of Self: African American Clothing in the Antebellum South.* Oxford: Berg, 1997.

Jacobs-Huey, Lanita. *From the Kitchen to the Parlor: Language and Becoming in African American Women's Hair Care.* Oxford: Oxford University Press, 2006.

Lewis, Amanda E. *Race in the Schoolyard: Negotiating the Color Line in Classrooms and Communities.* New Brunswick, NJ: Rutgers University Press, 2003.

Majors, Richard R., and Janet M. Billson. *Cool Pose: The Dilemma of Black Manhood in America.* New York: Simon & Schuster, 1992.

Mercer, F. "Black Hair Style Politics." *New Formations* 3 (1997): 33–54.

O'Neal, Gwendolyn S. "African American Aesthetic of Dress: Symmetry through Diversity." In *Aesthetics of Textiles and Clothing: Advancing Multidisciplinary Perspectives,* edited by Marilyn R. DeLong and Ann M. Fiore, 212–223. ITAA Special Publication #7. Monument, CO: ITAA, 1994.

O'Neal, Gwendolyn S. "African-American Aesthetic of Dress: Current Manifestations." *Clothing and Textiles Research Journal* 16, no. 4 (1998): 167–175.

O'Neal, Gwendolyn S. "African-American Women's Professional Dress as Expression of Ethnicity." *Journal of Family and Consumer Sciences* 90, no. 1 (1998): 28–33.

O'Neal, Gwendolyn S. "The African American Church, Its Sacred Cosmos and Dress." In *Religion, Dress and the Body,* edited by Linda B. Arthur, 117–134. Oxford: Berg, 1999.

O'Neal, Gwendolyn S. "The Power of Style: On Rejection of the Accepted." In *Appearance and Power,* edited by Kim K. P. Johnson and Sharron J. Lennon, 127–139. Oxford: Berg, 1999.

Pasteur, Alfred B., and Ivory L. Toldson. *Roots of Soul: The Psychology of Black Expressiveness.* Garden City, NY: Anchor Press/Doubleday, 1982.

Rooks, Noliwe M. *Hair Raising: Beauty, Culture, and African American Women.* New Brunswick, NJ: Rutgers University Press, 1996.

Semmes, C. E. *Cultural Hegemony and African American Development.* London: Praeger, 1992.

White, Shane, and Graham White. *Stylin': African American Expressive Culture from Its Beginnings to the Zoot Suit.* Ithaca, NY: Cornell University Press, 1998.

Winter, Metta. "Interpreting the Influence of Diverse Cultures on Fashion." *Human Ecology* 32, no. 1 (2004): 17–19.

Gwendolyn S. O'Neal

Caribbean Islanders

Caribbean immigrants have contributed greatly to the multi-cultural and multilingual diversity of the United States and Canada for a number of years. Often grouped either with other Hispanics or with African Americans, Caribbean people are actually part of a complex mosaic of cultures, languages, and dress practices. The Caribbean, named after its main pre-Columbian inhabitants, the Carib, has been shaped by the encounter of several cultures, including native groups such as the Puerto Rican Taínos, European conquistadors, black Africans brought as slaves during the Colonial period, and immigrants from Asia and other Latin American countries. A number of languages are spoken, including Spanish, English, French, and Dutch. Caribbean islanders have migrated to North America to escape harsh economic conditions or oppressive governments in their home countries, but they have been zealous about keeping alive their languages, cultural traditions, and dress practices. As immigrants get acculturated to the host country, they adopt mainstream clothing styles. Caribbean islanders, however, continue using dress elements closely associated to some of their home country traditions. Among such traditions are those associated with the Catholic Church, such as the *quinceañera*—the celebration of a young woman's fifteenth birthday—as well as those associated with religious practices of African origin, such as Santería and Vodou. Dress associated with carnival festivities, folkloric dances, and popular music has also been exported from the Caribbean to North America. The increased presence of Caribbean people in the North American media, entertainment, and fashion worlds at the end of the twentieth century has augmented awareness of their cultural and sartorial contributions from decades past.

From the arrival of Christopher Columbus in 1492 to the late twentieth century, the history of the Caribbean has been marked by periods of colonization by foreign powers and domination by oppressive dictatorships. Caribbean islanders have moved to North America and the rest of the world for many reasons: to pursue college degrees or search for job opportunities as skilled laborers in industries including apparel and textile manufacturing. The United States and Canada have received larger quantities of immigrants from Cuba, Puerto Rico, Jamaica, and the island of Hispaniola, which is comprised of the Dominican Republic to the east and Haiti to the west. Minor immigration from the Lesser Antilles has also occurred, particularly from the Bahamas, Trinidad and Tobago, Aruba, and Barbados.

Among the first influential Caribbean immigrants were Haitians Jean-Baptiste Pointe DuSable, founder of Chicago, and painter John James Audubon. Haitian immigrants arrived during the nineteenth and twentieth centuries searching for better economic prospects. After the 1960s, however, the number of arrivals

increased due to the violent dictatorship of François Duvalier. A small Puerto Rican colony existed in New York in the nineteenth century, but more Puerto Ricans arrived after the Spanish-American War turned Puerto Rico into a U.S. commonwealth. Puerto Ricans were granted U.S. citizenship in 1917 and were later recruited to replace U.S. farm workers fighting in World War II. Cubans migrated to the United States during the nineteenth century to join the tobacco industry in Tampa but also to develop enterprises in New York. Cuban immigration intensified after the 1958 revolution, which established a communist regime led by Fidel Castro. Similarly, Dominican migration increased heavily since the 1960s due to political instability, civil war, and a military invasion from the United States that ended in the establishment of a right-wing government. Jamaicans and Trinidadians began migrating to North America after both countries gained independence from Britain in 1962.

Although some Caribbean islanders migrate to farming areas, the majority live in large cities. Most Puerto Ricans concentrate in New York and Orlando, while many Cubans remain in South

Woman on parade at the Toronto Caribana, ca. 2007. Caribbean heritage is celebrated with parades in a number of cities in North America. Copyright A.C. GobinImage, 2007. Used under license from Shutterstock.com.

Florida. Sizeable Haitian communities are found in Chicago and Toronto, while other Caribbean islanders have moved to Los Angeles and Washington, D.C. Once settled, Caribbean islanders have created communities with a strong Caribbean identity. They have opened businesses to sell products, including clothing and accessories, from their homeland. Perfume stores, barber shops, and beauty salons were also established to provide service within the community. Hometown associations and national clubs engage in social service projects and organize activities to maintain cultural traditions. Caribbean heritage is celebrated with parades in a number of cities and include the well-known Puerto Rican Day Parade in New York and the Caribana festival in Toronto.

APPEARANCE, CLOTHING, AND ASSIMILATION

Physical appearance of Caribbean islanders varies greatly due to the vast racial and ethnic mix in the islands. Differences are particularly evident in skin colors. Some Caribbean people identify themselves as white, while others can claim full African ancestry. Discrimination based on color exists among immigrants as a reflection of similar attitudes in their home countries. Puerto Ricans, for example, often use the phrase *mejorar la raza* (to improve one's race) when they wittily refer to anyone marrying a person of lighter color. They also make a clear distinction between *pelo malo* (bad hair), referring to thick and curly hair, and *pelo bueno* (good hair), describing thin and straight hair. Caribbean islanders use clothing as a code to either distinguish themselves from other immigrants and people of color or as a way to merge with other subcultures or the mainstream. Black Caribbean islanders often adopt urban wear and hip-hop fashion in order to blend with other African Americans. Some Haitian immigrants, however, criticize this "undercover" practice and insist on the importance of, as linguist Flore Zéphir notes, "looking Haitian" as a way to assert identity. Assimilation of mainstream clothing practices is partly defined by the amount of time immigrants have spent in North America. New arrivals normally go through a process of adjustment, initially retaining—at times zealously—their cultural identity, including clothing practices. As the acculturation process continues, immigrants adjust their behavior to the host country's social norms, becoming more likely to incorporate clothing elements from the mainstream. Second- and third-generation immigrants are often fully absorbed into mainstream fashion; their clothing varies mostly due to age, gender, or subculture membership. Occasionally, children born of immigrant parents make an effort to reconnect with their parents' culture and may adopt clothing styles or use imagery to reaffirm this identity; wearing the colors of a national flag is probably the most common practice for those seeking to reconnect. Differences in dress practices of new arrivals can also be marked by their social and geographical origin. Immigrants from the upper classes and urban areas are more likely to dress according to the internationalized Western style than individuals from lower socioeconomic classes and peasants from rural sectors.

Caribbean females favor bright shades and a close fit, particularly for clothing used during daytime and informal evening occasions. Black is the dominant color for formal events, but women's gowns are often richly embellished with metallic thread, beads, and sequins. For business wear and formal daytime occasions, both women and men gravitate toward tailored styles. Low- and middle-class immigrants, often employed in fields such

as farming and construction, require the use of economical and durable clothing that can be easily replaced. Farmworkers often lack proper attire and accessories to protect themselves from the dangers presented by pesticides, green tobacco, and other dangerous crops. Haitian and Jamaican female immigrants wear solid slip cotton dresses at home and while working in farming fields.

Caribbean immigrants often live in close quarters with their extended family. Distant relatives usually move to the same city; furthermore, it is not uncommon to find large communities from one hometown settled in a North American city. Due to a culture of respect for elders, their opinion on matters of appearance is usually respected and followed by younger people. Nonetheless, young members of subcultures, including punk, goth, and Rastafarian, adopt fashion styles associated with those groups, including body piercing and tattoos. Other youths wear braids, doo rags, oversized clothes, and similar trends linked to urban African American fashion. Some Caribbean men, particularly Puerto Rican and Dominican, embraced the *metrosexual* trend of the early 2000s by paying increased attention to their grooming. Attractive men with a playboy-like attitude are known as *papichulos*. Males, usually considered the main authority figures in a family unit, have a strong opinion on the way females in the household dress. Women—normally expected to take care of household chores—are usually responsible for the selection and care of clothing. Many women, often from older generations, continue practicing crafts such as crochet, embroidery, and lacemaking while also sewing or mending clothes worn by their family. Some females are actually self-employed seamstresses, itinerant beauticians, or hairdressers.

Older Cubans and Puerto Ricans living in North America occasionally use garments and accessories tied to their Spanish roots; among them are elegant shawls and long skirts for women as well as linen shirts, tailored pleated pants, and straw hats for men. The *guayabera*, considered a Cuban national symbol, remains a staple for many older upper-class men. This lightweight, pastel-colored cotton dress shirt has vertical embroidered or tucked rows on the front and back and four symmetrical pockets adorning the front. It is usually worn untucked, making the straight hem with side vents an important component. The garment was originally associated with Cuban *hacendados* (landowners) but became fashionable among young Caribbean men after it was adopted by successful Cuban Americans. It is often worn for special occasions and used as inspiration by several fashion designers. Items of African origin, such as head scarves and headdresses, traditionally used in the Caribbean are also brought by immigrants to North America. Girls typically have their ears pierced at a young age, and most women wear nail polish and elaborate makeup for special occasions. Catholics often wear neck chains with crucifixes or medallions containing images of the Virgin Mary or other saints, as well as rosaries and *escapularios* (fabric pieces with images worn for protection). Cubans sometimes wear a pendant containing a small coin from the island. Necklaces and beaded jewelry items featuring flags from the different Caribbean countries are also popular.

DRESS AND CULTURE

Caribbean islanders living in North America continue celebrating traditions associated with the Catholic Church. Puerto Ricans, for instance, celebrate *Día de Reyes* (King's Day or

Epiphany) on 6 January by exchanging gifts. Cubans hold processions in Miami and New Jersey during the *Día de la Virgen de la Caridad del Cobre*, a day commemorating an apparition of the Virgin Mary in Cuba. A tradition kept zealously alive in Caribbean countries colonized by Spain is the quinceañera, celebrated on a woman's fifteenth birthday. For this event, the young woman usually wears an elaborate floor-length gown in light color, most often white. The dresses often feature fitted bodices with short puffed or leg-of-mutton sleeves and full skirts with bead embroidery, lace, or sequin embellishments. Fifteen boys and fifteen girls chosen as the quinceañera's entourage are dressed in formal attire. Wedding dresses, in most cases, follow the same traditions used in North America, with fancy white gowns for the bride, tuxedos for the groom, and formal elegant apparel for the guests. Dressing up for Sunday church remains important for many groups.

In the 1500s, African slaves brought with them traditions, music, clothing, and religious practices that have become an integral part of Caribbean culture, particularly in Haiti, Jamaica, and some of the Lesser Antilles. New religious practices arose from the syncretism of Catholic and African traditions. After the slaves were forced to convert to Christianity, Santería allowed them to attribute characteristics of their Yoruba *orishas* (manifestations of God) to Catholic Church saints. Santería was brought to Florida by some of the Cuban settlers in the 1960s and spread to other regions. In 1993, the U.S. government accorded it status as a recognized religion. *Botánica* stores found in major North American cities offer medical herbs, talismans, and other Santería paraphernalia. Once ordained, Santería priests, or *santeros*, dress mostly in white, particularly during rituals such as the festive *bembé* or the *toque de santo* honoring the orishas. Haitian immigrants have carried with them Vodou practices, fundamental in the creation of the Creole identity. The word is used to describe a number of complex rituals mostly of African origin. Vodou songs and dances present a magical opportunity for spirits to possess one or more of the participants, who normally wear white outfits. In some rituals the vodouists actually dress in costumes representing a specific spirit. Zaka, for instance, is related to agriculture and is represented by blue jeans, a large hat, and accessories including a machete and a peasant bag. Guédés, or spirits of the dead, require possessed individuals to wear dark or purple garments. Also important is the Vodou flag, or *drapo*, created with thousands of sequins over a solid fabric panel. Clothing associated with the Rastafarian movement has been successfully exported from Jamaica to the rest of the world, including the United States and Canada. The dreadlocks, hats, and colors (green, yellow, and red) of rasta style have been used in North America since reggae music became widely known in the 1980s.

Carnival traditions were brought by the Europeans to the Caribbean, where they absorbed elements from African music and dance. Carnival is celebrated in several islands, including Trinidad and Tobago, Jamaica, and Barbados, but it has also been successfully introduced to many U.S. and Canadian cities. During Carnival, women promenade and dance wearing colorful bikini-style costumes highly embellished with metallic pieces, feathers, bright paper, sequins, beads, ribbons, shells, glitter, and mirror decorations. More elaborate costumes are created with wire frames, foam, and large amounts of fabric. Most men, participating as musicians in the parade's steel bands, wear

Man wearing a *guayabera* shirt. This lightweight cotton dress shirt has vertical embroidered or tucked rows on the front and back and four symmetrical pockets on the front. The guayabera is considered a Cuban national symbol and remains a staple for many older upper-class men. Sophia Vourdoukis/Getty Images.

white pants or Bermuda shorts and colorfully printed woven shirts. Cities with large Caribbean carnival celebrations include Toronto, Montreal, Miami, Boston, Detroit, Los Angeles, and New York. Caribana, the Toronto carnival, is actually the largest street celebration in Canada. Caribbean islanders also showcase cultural and dress elements from their country of origin with celebrations such as the Puerto Rican Day Parade in New York City, the Cuban Day Parade in New Jersey, and the Haitian Kompa festival in Miami. Folkloric attire is used during these parades along with garments and accessories incorporating home country flags and other national symbols. Parades also offer an opportunity for political dissidence. The Taíno Nation group often dresses in loincloths and native body painting to create awareness of native groups in Puerto Rico. Groups are also organized to perform traditional dances such as the Puerto Rican *bomba* and *plena*, the Haitian *tajona*, and the *junkanoo*, popular on several islands. Garments used in these dances are either constructed by experienced immigrant seamstresses familiar with the original costumes or brought by immigrants after a visit to their home country.

ENTERTAINMENT, MEDIA, AND FASHION

Portrayals of Caribbean islanders in the U.S. media have often been negative. In 1961, the movie *West Side Story* presented Puerto Ricans as gang members, while in the 1980s, Haitians were characterized as carriers of AIDS by the news media. Caribbean men are also portrayed as lazy and unemployed or as criminals and drug traffickers. Hollywood movies helped create the stereotype of the Latin Lover by exploiting the good looks of actors such as the Cuban dancer César Romero and Cuban American Andy Garcia. Along with other Latinas, Caribbean women are often stereotyped in categories such as the quiet, dignified maid; the exotic temptress; or the proper, passive *señorita*. In the last decades of the twentieth century, Caribbean islanders gained prominence as movie actors, musicians, and television personalities. Their presence in the mainstream offered more positive images of the community and strongly influenced clothing choices of other immigrants. Cuban-born Cristina Saralegui has hosted her own television show in Miami since 1989, with a large following and name recognition beyond the United States. Saralegui created Casa Cristina, a popular line of home furnishings, and is admired for her elegant but simple fashion style. Another Cuban, Daisy Fuentes, became famous as the face for MTV International and later as a model for Revlon and Pantene. Fuentes collaborated with the retail store Kohl's in the creation of her own clothing line. A more outlandish style is offered by Puerto Rican astrologer Walter Mercado, who appears daily on television wearing bright colorful tunics and large, conspicuous jewelry.

Telenovelas, soap operas produced in several Latin American countries, offer a glimpse of fashion styles used by upper classes. Since the mid-1990s, many telenovelas have been produced in Miami with multinational casts including Caribbean actors. Fashion in the shows reflects the style of middle- and upper-class Caribbean groups in Florida. In the 1970s, the television sitcom *Popa en Nueva York* depicted the life and struggles of Puerto Rican immigrants in New York. In the same decade, Iris Chacon became a household name as the *bomba de América* (America's bombshell). The Puerto Rican *vedette* was famous for singing and dancing while wearing skimpy clothes (*vedette* is a French term used in Spanish-speaking countries to refer to female stars of variety shows). With *I Love Lucy* (1951–1957), the U.S. public was introduced to the multiracial and multicultural couple formed by Cuban-born Desi Arnaz and his real-life wife, Lucille Ball. In 1937, Arnaz, while enjoying a successful career as a singer, actually led the first-ever conga line, helping start a craze for Caribbean dance music. Rhythms such as cha-cha, mambo, and rumba and the exotic dress associated with them came to prominence in the 1950s. Caribbean women were presented in the media wearing larger-than-life, colorful flounced skirts; midriff-revealing tops; ruffled blouses; and exuberant headdresses that had little to do with the original clothing used in the dances. Miami and New York actually became the cradle of some of the most famous Cuban and Puerto Rican music produced in the early part of the twentieth century. Several songs composed by Caribbean islanders told the stories and struggles of Caribbean immigrants in the United States.

After the 1970s, fashion styles of Caribbean islanders were heavily influenced by the popularity of salsa and merengue music. Salsa developed mostly in New York, Puerto Rico, and Cuba out of the combination of several tropical rhythms, while merengue was created in the Dominican Republic. Both rhythms, however, found a fertile ground in North American cities such as New York and Miami, where some of the most successful records were produced. Women usually wore fitted short dresses with bright shades dominant in the 1980s and matte solids, predominantly black, in the 1990s. Great attention was paid to matching shoes, accessories, and makeup. Men wore well-ironed pleated pants and fitted shirts in a variety of styles. Popular tropical music stars, such as Celia Cruz and Tito Puente, were well known among the Caribbean community in North America. Cruz lived most of her life in New Jersey and was a fashion icon for decades. Her style was celebrated in 2005 by the Smithsonian Institution with an exhibit called ¡Azúcar! (Sugar!), which incorporated some of the vibrant costumes worn by the singer during her career. Also influential was Juan Luis Guerra, who popularized the Dominican, guitar-based romantic *bachata*. Guerra wore colorfully printed short-sleeved shirts. Similar shirts were worn by the members of Boukman Eksperyans, a Haitian *rara* band. Trinidadians continue enjoying *soca* and *calypso* music, two genres that required comfortable clothing for the fast and elaborate dance steps. Calypso music, often used by West Indians to manifest social and political concerns, was highly popular in the 1950s, when Harry Belafonte's 1956 LP *Calypso* sold a million copies worldwide.

Pop musicians also introduced U.S. and Canadian audiences to Caribbean fashion. After gaining popularity with mainstream English-language music in the late 1980s, Gloria Estefan promoted her 1990s Latin rhythm albums wearing wide flounced skirts and loose tops reminiscent of midcentury Cuban apparel. Cuban singer Willie Chirino satirized 1980s consumerism in his 1982 song "Los Diseñadores" (The Designers). In the 1980s, teenagers imitated the fitted sleeveless tops and headbands seen in Puerto Rican boy bands Menudo and Los Chicos. Ricky Martin, a former member of Menudo, gained worldwide acclaim as a solo artist in the late 1990s. Martin dressed in comfortable black pants and fitted black shirts for his shows, making that look popular among Caribbean islanders. Also known for wearing elegant Armani suits, Martin sported neat hairstyling that was often imitated by Caribbean men. Nuyorican (that is, Puerto Rican New Yorker) Jennifer Lopez became a fashion icon after wearing a celebrated, revealing blue/green chiffon Versace gown to the 2000 Grammy awards. Lopez, considered a trendsetter thereafter, launched JLo and Sweetface, her own lines of clothing design, in 2005. A great deal of discussion in popular media and academic research has centered on the voluptuousness of Lopez's derriere, described by Negrón-Muntaner as the great Hispanic avenger of "Anglo analphobia." Lopez's flaunting of her curves has inspired other Caribbean women immigrants not only to embrace but also to flaunt a body shape different from the gaunt look promoted by U.S. and Canadian mainstream fashion outlets.

Urban fashion connected to hip-hop and rap music has strongly influenced clothing choices of Caribbean islanders in North America, particularly those of African descent. In the 1980s, the younger generations of immigrants adopted trends such as oversized T-shirts, Kangol hats, baggy pants, and exuberant jewelry, following the lead of early urban Puerto Rican artists

Cuban-born singer Celia Cruz, ca. 1970. She was a fashion icon throughout her musical career. Michael Ochs Archives/Getty Images.

such as Rock Steady Crew and Brenda K. Starr. At the height of the break-dancing craze, many Caribbean "fly-boys" and "b-girls" sported colorful, padded track suits and fitted tops. Reggae fans wore natural-fiber garments, khaki combat outfits, and beaded necklaces bearing the colors of the Jamaican flag (red, green, and yellow). The most distinctive dress element adopted by reggae fans and Rastafarians is the use of dreadlocks, a practice based on a biblical passage discouraging hair trimming. Another cultural and fashion icon of the 1990s was Haitian musician Wyclef Jean of The Fugees, a group named after Caribbean refugee migrant camps in the United States. Dancehall music, also known as *ragga*, is widely popular among West Indian immigrants. Influential dancehall performers include Shaggy, Bounty Killa, Sizzla, and Sean Paul. In Jamaica, Steeve O. Buckridge (a historian who is a native of Jamaica) has reported that dancehall fashion has been read as a form of resistance to norms of dress and sexuality, and it has been heavily criticized by the upper classes and censored by the government. Dancehall fashion has been exported to North America. Women wear risqué, revealing clothes made of inexpensive materials that often resemble lingerie. Other elements of dancehall fashion include slashed garments, mesh tops, bondage straps, animal prints, and brightly dyed hair. By the early 2000s, Puerto Rican *reggaeton* had become a worldwide sensation. Influenced by rap and dancehall, it came to prominence with artists such as Don Chezina and Don Omar. Omar partnered with soccer clothing and accessory company Umbro to create a line of urban clothing and sports shoes distributed by Foot Locker exclusively in the United States.

CONCLUSION

Caribbean islanders represent a heterogeneous multiracial group. Dress has been an important tool to communicate identity in North America, where they are often grouped with other minorities. National identity, expressed through accessories and the display of national flag colors, is nearly an obsession for many. Caribbean immigrants of Hispanic origin are part of the Latin minority, the largest in the United States at the start of the twenty-first century. The increased purchasing power of Latinos has motivated many retailers to advertise on Spanish television and in magazines targeted to Hispanics including *Latina*, *People en Español*, and *Latina Style*. Influential fashion designers from the Caribbean include Dominican Oscar de la Renta, who contributes greatly to charities and development of the island; Rafael Jiménez, a Dominican from Washington Heights, New York, who produced T-shirts with Latino inspiration in 1995 and created República Trading Co. in 2003; and Narciso Rodríguez, a successful New York designer of Cuban origin. The Perry Ellis house launched two men's sportswear lines with Caribbean inspiration in 2004; tropical-inspired Cubavera is sold at department stores, while Havanera Co. is manufactured for JCPenney. Caribbean islander immigrants have contributed greatly to the diversification of language, popular culture, and dress in North America. Increased visibility of Caribbean culture and acknowledgment of their contributions should, in turn, improve mainstream awareness of Caribbean multiculturalism.

References and Further Reading

Adjaye, Joseph K. "Mediated Lives: Memory and Construction of History in the Caribbean Diaspora." *Journal of Caribbean Studies* 19, no. 3 (2005): 207–232.

Bakare-Yusuf, Bibi. "Fabricating Identities: Survival and the Imagination in Jamaican Dancehall Culture." *Fashion Theory* 10, no. 4 (2006): 461–484.

Buckridge, Steeve O. *The Language of Dress: Resistance and Accommodation in Jamaica, 1760–1890.* Kingston, Jamaica: University of the West Indies Press, 2004.

Grasmuck, Sherri, and Ramón Grosfoguel. "Geopolitics, Economic Niches, and Gendered Social Capital among Recent Caribbean Immigrants in New York City." *Sociological Perspectives* 40, no. 3 (1997): 339–363.

Laguerre, Michel S. *Voodoo Heritage.* Beverly Hills, CA: Sage Publications, 1980.

Manning, Frank E. "Overseas Caribbean Carnivals: The Art and Politics of a Transnational Celebration." In *Caribbean Popular Culture*, edited by John A. Lent, 20–36. Bowling Green, OH: Bowling Green State University Popular Press, 1990.

Miller, Marilyn. "Guayaberismo and the Essence of Cool." In *The Latin American Fashion Reader*, edited by Regina A. Root, 213–231. Oxford: Berg, 2005.

Negrón-Muntaner, Frances. *Boricua Pop: Puerto Ricans and the Latinization of American Culture*. New York: New York University Press, 2004.

Rivera, Raquel Z. *New York Ricans from the Hip Hop Zone*. New York: Palgrave Macmillan, 2003.

Scher, Philip W. *Carnival and the Formation of a Caribbean Transnation*. Gainesville: University Press of Florida, 2003.

Zéphir, Flore. *Trends in Ethnic Identification among Second-Generation Haitian Immigrants in New York City*. Westport, CT: Bergin and Garvey, 2001.

José Blanco F.

See also Hispanic and Latino American; volume 2, Latin America and the Caribbean: Overview of the Caribbean; Vodou Ritual Garments in Haiti; Creolized Costumes for Rara, Haiti; Jamaica in the Nineteenth Century to the Present; Dress and Dance in Puerto Rico; Trinidad in the Nineteenth Century; Cuba; Caribbean Headwear.

Asian American

The United States and Canada both have experienced influxes of immigrants for a long time, and the presence of Asian immigrants is felt in both countries. Both countries represent mass societies that are characterized by mass production, mass distribution, mass consumption, and mass communication. Therefore, the way that Asian immigrants dress in both countries is similar. During the 2000–2010 U.S. census, *Asian Americans* were formally defined as people with origins in the Far East, the Indian subcontinent, and Southeast Asia. The 2000 U.S. Census listed 12.3 million people as Asian Americans. Of the twenty-five groups listed in the document, the top five ranked groups were Chinese, Filipinos, Asian Indians, Vietnamese, and Koreans.

Asian Americans have a sizable presence in both the United States and Canada. In 2004, they represented 33 percent of all immigrants in the United States and 50 percent in Canada. Among Asian American immigrants in Canada and the United States, the six largest groups of immigrants had come from the following countries: China, India, Japan, the Philippines, South Korea, and Vietnam. Even though previous studies show that immigrants acculturate over time and are assimilated to the new cultural values, their ethnic identity continues to be important for selected parts of their everyday life. Some examples include birth, initiation, and marriage and death rituals. In contrast, people from the culture of adoption by immigrants use stereotypes that Allan Canfield, professor of speech communication, has said trigger subtle "demeaning characterizations." Of these, the color barrier is used the most. Visible cues such as race and apparel reinforce these stereotypes more than any other attributes because they represent the visible self of individuals and their collective identities.

Canfield has also described ethnic identity as a social construction used by people to give meaning to the role-taking in their lives. This identity allows association between and among people based on their shared worldviews, social practices, and commonality of past experiences and helps to provide a sense of community.

When immigrants make a move from agrarian or urban industrial societies to mass societies, they enter a completely urbanized world. Such a world leads to a depersonalization of human interactions due to decreased importance of family systems, increase in the number of social roles, deeper association with professional accomplishments, and an increased sense of social equality. Social equality, from one perspective, offers an increased sense of belongingness. However, on the other hand, it also decreases the sense of individuality that could be important to enhance the self-esteem of individuals in transition. During this transition to life in a mass society, clothing becomes important. In the earlier stages of immigration, immigrants are more tied to their native countries' norms of dressing.

ACCULTURATION AND ASSIMILATION

The transitional phase shows more use of ethnic versus mainstream clothing. This trend changes over time as immigrants establish a comfort zone with the country of adoption. Maximum changes occur in the clothing of everyday wear, and the least amount of changes take place in ritual clothing for events such as marriage and death. Both acculturation and assimilation become potential possibilities for the immigrants. Acculturation requires partial acceptance of activities of the new culture and can be one-way. However, assimilation requires acceptance of most of the practices of the newly adopted culture, and mutual acceptance becomes a necessary element. Assimilation requires more tolerance on both ends than acculturation. According to dress scholar Usha Chowdhary (2006), *acculturation* refers to "the process of changing a culture or individual when an individual comes in contact with a culture different from their own culture." *Assimilation* refers to "the adoption of [the] majority culture by minorities or the adoption of an exotic culture" (p. 201).

As used here, *ethnic minority* is defined as a group of individuals who were born in an Asian country but have now settled in the United States or Canada. *Dress* is defined as any items of apparel and accessories worn by people from head to foot, exclusively or inclusively. Clothing serves as a bridge between the individual and the environment. Along with accessories used to complete the look, it serves as a visible self that conveys several personal attributes and situational attributes of the wearer without speaking even a single word. Dress can include body modifications, body supplements, enclosures for the body, attachments to the body, attachments to other elements of dress, and handheld objects.

An area of particular importance for immigrants is the sustaining status of ceremonial dress. Ceremonial dress has a sustaining function; it has the potential to attain classic status because it serves as a bridge to connect past with present and present with future. Fads and fashion changes are seen more in body modifications, attachments, and enclosures that may reflect technological advancements and the resulting information explosion.

The scholarly literature, general observation, and interviews with those from ethnic minorities make it evident that the dress of immigrants from China, India, Japan, Korea, Malaysia, and Taiwan living in the United States and Canada was Westernized for everyday and work wear. (This selection of countries is intended to be representative rather than inclusive.) However, they

A newly married Korean American couple wear Korean dress or *hanbok* consisting for women of a two-part garment: the *chogori* or blouse and the *chima* or skirt. Men's hanbok is comprised of a short jacket and trousers called *baji*. His shirt is called a *jeogori*. United States, ca. 2000. Dae Seung Seo/Getty Images.

continued to wear native dress for cultural events that highlight their heritage rituals, such as marriage and death, international fashion shows, social events, visits to tourist attractions, and educational settings.

ETHNIC MINORITIES AND BODY MODIFICATIONS

Body modifications enhance appearance. Women in all of the aforementioned ethnicities used body modifications more than men. Body building, exercising, health, and fitness were important to all six groups of immigrants. Access to these facilities is reportedly easier in the United States and Canada than in the immigrants' countries of origin. Gyms were reported to be less crowded in the adopted countries. The older generation colored hair to conceal the gray and look younger. However, younger generations color hair to manage appearance and be fashionable. Older generations do not appreciate having hair colors that deviate too much from the natural palette. Women wear makeup to beautify themselves more than do men and use piercing, plastic surgery, and waxing more than men.

Scarification, tattooing, tanning, and piercing at places other than the ears were not considered a norm. In India, piercing of the nose was considered more acceptable than for other ethnic minorities. Piercing of the eyebrows, lip, navel, and so forth is also done by teenage immigrant girls (and ear piercing, by immigrant teenage boys) in the United States and Canada more so than in their countries of origin. Orthodontic procedures were seen as acceptable for improving the bite as well as appearance.

Indian women continue to wear henna on special ceremonial occasions. Younger generations wear tattoos just like their peers in the adopted countries. Older generations of all of the ethnic minorities do not necessarily accept the body modifications used by the youth. Western fashion culture among the young has appropriated Indian *mehndi* tattoos (a type of henna), nose piercing, and the bindi (a small red dot applied in the middle of the forehead).

Colognes and perfumes were used by all ethnic minorities. Deodorant use varied. Shaving is used as means of body modification by both men and women.

Women went to hairdressers in Malaysia more often than in the United States and Canada because it is cheaper to do so there. In most of the Asian countries, people dress up more formally when going to any public place than they do in the United States and Canada. The lifestyles of ethnic minorities have become more casual since emigrating.

SPECIAL PROPERTIES OF DRESS

The materials from which items of dress are made may be important in establishing a connection to the culture from which an individual has emigrated. Often the connection can be in color, in pattern, or the type of fabric seen in a garment or applied to the body. The Indian subcontinent is particularly rich in examples of these connections. These colors and patterns have been shared with others in the new country of residence and have become part of fashionable as well as traditional dress.

Henna, a reddish-brown coloring agent that comes from the leaves of an Asian or African shrub (*Lawsonia inermis*), is utilized as a cosmetic dye and for coloring materials such as leather. In summer, it is used on the feet for a cooling effect, and during ceremonies it is placed on hands and feet for auspicious reasons. Some women use it as organic hair dye, a use not only among women from India but in the general population as well. Another color with a name derived from languages spoken on the Indian subcontinent is *khaki*. The word from which the name derives means "ash," and this olive-brown or yellowish-brown color is similar to the color of ashes. Originally khaki fabric was used for making uniforms, and the color of that fabric is now an English word.

Some ornamental patterns originated and are still used in traditional fabrics from this geographic region. *Patola* is an East Indian silk fabric used as a wedding garment by native women. Lengthwise and crosswise yarns are tie-dyed before the fabric is woven. The motifs created include conventionalized plants, elephants, human figures, birds, flowers, and geometric designs. Another pattern, now called *paisley* in English after the Scottish town that began copying the design, is a stylized pine cone–shaped motif that was used on shawls and the wrapped woman's outer garment called the *sari*, which is now commonly seen in fashionable Western dress as well. Checked or plaid cotton madras from the city of Madras (now Chennai) is another contribution from India to fashion, as was calico, an early import from the city of Calicut in India. Other contributions include cashmere fibers taken from the fleece of cashmere goats and made into a high-status, luxury fabric of exceptional softness. Tie-dyed bandanna fabrics (*bandanna* in Hindi means "to tie") are used in fabrics made into scarves, saris, dresses, and kerchiefs.

BODY SUPPLEMENTS THAT ENCLOSE

The ways in which items of dress are constructed varies considerably from one part of the world to another. Examples of body supplements used in Asian dress that enclose the body include anklets, bracelets, necklaces, rings, and wraparound or suspended apparel, such as the sari, poncho, kimono, and so forth. Body enclosures are frequently the most visible part of an individual's dress. An observer who is not part of the culture of the person wearing traditional dress is likely to decide on the nationality of a stranger based on the most visible elements of dress, which are often the body enclosures.

The *kimono* is considered to be the Japanese national dress. A T-shaped full-length garment pulled in at the waist with a sash called an *obi* that ties at the back, the kimono is symbolic of beauty and is worn by both men and women in Japan. It is a combination garment with graceful lines and flowing prints for harmonious effect. A black kimono is worn for mourning. A colored *furisode* (women's kimono with full sleeves) is worn for formal occasions. *Haori* is the term used for a lightweight jacket that is considered essential for wear with the ceremonial kimono. The *nagajuban* is a full-length under-kimono.

Men wear more subdued colors in kimonos than do Japanese women. The kimono and obi emphasize beauty and straight lines. It is not, however, the only Japanese garment. Others include the *michiyuki*, a three-quarter-length coat with a square neckline, and the *happi coat*, a casual garment worn by Japanese workers that has been adopted by fashion designers around the world for beachwear and for sleepwear.

Korean women wear cotton or hemp *hanbok* (a general term meaning "Korean dress") for everyday wear and silken hanbok for formal wear. This garment consists of two parts: a *chogori*, which is a short blouse that is tied in front, and a *chima*, a long, full-wrapped skirt. Garments are very detailed and bright. Young girls wear a miniature version. A man's hanbok consists of a short jacket and trousers that are called *baji*. The shirt worn with baji is called *jeogori*. A long coat called *durumagi* is worn by men with the hanbok. This apparel is worn only for special occasions both in Korea and the United States and Canada.

Indian women wear the sari as a national costume. The sari is a rectangle of cloth five and a half to nine yards long (5 to 8 meters) and forty-five to fifty-four inches (114 to 137 centimeters) wide that is worn in draped form, pleated around the waist, and with one end free so it can be thrown over the shoulder or pulled over the head. The sari is worn with or without a long-paneled skirted petticoat and with a short blouse, the *choli*. Saris are worn by women in India, Bangladesh, and Pakistan. Another outfit commonly worn by women consists of the *salvar*, trousers with quilted bottoms and drawstring waist, and over this a *kameez*, a tunic dress with side slits, plus the *dupatta*, a scarf. A voluminous skirt called the *ghaghra* and the choli and *chunri* (a long scarf) are commonly worn in the northwestern and central parts of India. Jackets are worn by both men and women. Anklets made from silver and gold and a wrapped strand of sacred thread worn by Hindus known as *yagyopaveet* are more likely to be used in India than other countries. Other garments and accessories include earrings, *kamarband* (waistband), scarf, wraps, and the wristwatch. In fashion shows of Indian-influenced dress held in India, the United States, and Paris, styles reflect a blend of East and West. Examples of these combinations include Western styles made with Indian textiles, Indian styles made with Western textiles, and Western dress with sari- or dupatta-like effects created by designers such as Versace and Mary McFadden and a salvar-kameez look by Issey Miyake.

Batik sarongs are worn by women in Bali. *Batik* textiles are made through a process in which wax is printed onto fabrics in

Formal dress, as worn in a family's country of origin, will often be worn on formal occasions, such as a marriage, in the family's country of adoption. In a Hindu wedding, the bride wears a *sari* of red, or shades of red, along with exquisite jewelry. The groom wears either a European-style suit or traditional *achkan* and tight-fitting pants called *churridar pajamas*. Photosindia/Getty Images.

selected areas so that the area will not absorb dyestuffs. By repeating this process many times, very complex and beautiful patterns can be created. Batiks are used for ceremonial and cultural events as well as purchased as souvenirs by those living in the United States.

In Vietnam, men wear brown shirts and white pants and wrap a cloth around their head, with plain sandals worn on the feet. For formal wear they wear long black or brown tunics in cotton or silk with side slits and a turban. Young women wear light brown short shirts with long black skirts and a black turban that has its peak in the front. For formal occasions, they wear a three-piece, layered long gown with side slits called *ao dai*. The outer brown or light brown silk garment is called *au tu than* and has four slits that are equally distributed. The second-layer gown is light yellow, and the third and undermost layer is pink. It is worn over a red brassiere. Buttons are fastened on the side, and the chest is left open to give it a collared look. The side slits serve as free-floating panels and reveal the pink silk trousers that are worn underneath. The formal dress is worn with a conical hat made from straw and called *non bait ho*. In the Western world the immigrants use these only for special occasions.

There are certain legal restrictions in Malaysia for women with regard to dress. They are not allowed to wear miniskirts, see-through blouses, and tight-fitting trousers. The law requires them to wear ankle-length dresses and cover their heads. Malaysian women wear baju kurong and a sarong and scarf. The *baju kurong* is a long tunic-type dress with full sleeves that comes in several colors, fabrics, and styles. It is worn with a wraparound sarong. Necklines are either round or round with a V-center.

ETHNIC MINORITIES AND BODY ATTACHMENTS

Body attachment refers to an accessory added to the body for functional or aesthetic reasons. Some examples include barrettes and combs that may be worn for aesthetic or religious reasons; contact lenses or eyeglasses; flowers as hair decorations; fake attachments such as beards, mustaches, or fingernails; hair fasteners; jewelry that attaches, such as earrings, lip rings, nose rings, and the like; and sunglasses. In addition to the batik sarongs, women in Bali also wear seashell jewelry, costume jewelry made of pearls and beads, fashion belts to hold sarongs, and beaded necklaces, chokers, earrings and bracelets. All these items are seen in the tourist places all over the country of origin and also in the United States because their availability and use cuts across several geographic regions.

Men in most of the Asian countries are more Westernized than are women. In most of the Asian countries, men wear pants and shirts for everyday wear and two- or three-piece suits for formal occasions. For rituals, Indian men may wear *dhoti* (a draped lower torso garment) and kurta (a paneled shirt with round neckline or band collar) or *churridar pajamas* (tight-fitting bias-cut pants with bangle-like folds on legs and drawstring waistline) and *achkan* (a long silk coat with side slits and band collar) with *khussas*, which are embroidered footwear with pointed fronts. In the early twenty-first century, they wear a long scarf around their neck rather than the turban that was used traditionally. Likewise, Japanese men may wear kimonos. However, those living in the United States and Canada wear Western-style casual wear more so than they did in their country of origin.

ETHNIC MINORITIES AND ITEMS ATTACHED TO BODY ENCLOSURES

Dress that encloses the body may have distinctive items attached. For example, in Malaysia, women tie their sarongs with belts. Indian kurtas (paneled shirts with round necks or high-neck collars) for men are adorned with fancy buttons, a style seen in dress for celebrating special rituals. Some women use silver or gold waistbands and key chains. Invariably, people use scarves, handkerchiefs, waistbands, belts, and fancy cords as attachments to body enclosures. Wraparound gowns with shawl collars and various other necklines are tied with belts or cord variations made of the same fabric. Studs or buttons used for shirts with French cuffs are also examples for this category of dress. Other examples include the bride's veil, the scarf worn with the salvar-kameez outfit of India and Pakistan, and pins or brooches used to hold saris or scarves in place. Men living in the United States and Canada invariably use neckties for formal occasions irrespective of their ethnicity.

ETHNIC MINORITIES AND HANDHELD OBJECTS

In most countries, women carry purses, and men carry wallets and briefcases. Women's purses can be the type that hangs from the wrist or is clutched in the hand. The materials from which purses are made can range from leather to natural and synthetic textiles in woven or crocheted forms. Women from Japan carry a fan and colorful parasol. Invariably, people from all ethnicities carry walking sticks in old age and many wear sunglasses and eyeglasses (unless they have had eye surgeries done or wear contact lenses) for everyday use. Umbrellas are need-driven accessories and are used by people of all ethnicities. Handkerchiefs used in Malaysia have been replaced by paper tissues in the United States and Canada.

CHILDREN'S DRESS

Children of immigrant families who were born in the United States or Canada often wear ethnic dress when they participate in ceremonial events. On holidays such as Chinese New Year, children in ethnic dress may participate in public festivals. Sometimes children take ethnic dancing or music lessons and may wear traditional dress for performances. For school and everyday dress, children tend to conform to the styles of their peers unless there is some religious or cultural restriction their families insist that they observe.

One area of children's dress that Westerners have noted when traveling in China is a style of pants for children in which the crotch area is cut with a wide opening. Young children who are not yet toilet trained are dressed in these garments as a convenience, allowing them to relieve themselves as necessary. The style prevents soiling of garments and makes it easier for caregivers to train children. Current reports indicate that disposable diapers are replacing these garments to some degree in China. Immigrants generally do not continue the practice, although a few U.S. Web sites do advertise open-crotch pants for infants and toddlers that appear to be marketed to parents of any ethnicity.

ETHNIC MINORITIES AND CEREMONIAL DRESS

Most of the immigrants that have settled in the United States and Canada continue to wear their traditional costumes for ceremonial occasions. Frequency of their use for other occasions may be related to the number of years since immigration. The rituals in which traditional attire is most used are weddings, funerals, and christenings or other ceremonies for infants.

In India, Hindu weddings are performed by a priest in front of a fire. An auspicious time and date are selected for the wedding. The procession of the groom to the bride's place of residence includes his ride on a female horse, dance, music, and sometimes fireworks. At the bride's home both families meet, and the groom's family is greeted with floral garlands, cash, and religious hymns by the priest. The bride and groom have photographs taken with the family. Guests and hosts eat, and the groom and the bride exchange garlands and go to the *mandap*, a decorated canopy area, where the wedding ceremony is performed. Marriage takes place by going around the fire seven times. It is believed that fire purifies the environment as well as people's minds. This step is followed by sending the bride off to the groom's home. The bride wears a sari of red or shades of red along with exquisite jewelry. The groom wears either a veiled turban with an English suit or traditional achkan and churridar pajamas. Hindu immigrants from India in the United States and Canada follow much the same process. If marriage takes place between a Hindu and a Christian, both ceremonies are performed.

A Sikh wedding is similar except that the marriage takes place in front of the holy *Granth Sahib*, the sacred text of Sikhism, and the bride and groom make four rounds around the area where it is placed. Sikh men wear a turban and carry a sword. For a Christian wedding in India, the bride wears a brocade sari or white gown that is long and loose with a veil. A Muslim wedding starts with mehndi (an application of henna) and takes place at the groom's home. It is conducted by the *maulvi* (priest) in the presence of family and friends.

For funerals, Indian mourners are expected to wear white. Traditionally, a widow wore only white after the death of her husband. Those living in the United States and Canada do not follow the color rule strictly. Even in India, widows wear light or pastel colors along with white these days. In Malaysia, black is worn by the immediate family. Grandchildren wear dark blue.

Newborn children in northern India are first clothed with a garment made by an elderly person of the family. This signifies long life. A black dot is placed behind the ear or at what is considered a hideous place (a part of the body that is not visible in public) to ward off evil spirits.

In Japan, a black kimono with a crest is worn for ceremonial occasions. Brides wear a white kimono and a white headdress for the ceremony. For the reception, the headdress is removed and an elaborate brocaded kimono is placed over the white one.

The *cheongsam* is worn by the women from mainland China as well as Taiwan for formal occasions. In Hong Kong, the same dress is called a *sheath*. It is tight fitting with a high-standing mandarin collar. Men wear a silk jacket with silk trousers and *kung fu boots*, which are made from cloth with hard soles at the bottom. Women's slippers sport red and pink flowers with leaves and stems. People from China, Taiwan, and Hong Kong get married in both Western as well as their native traditional dress even when they live in the United States.

Vietnamese brides wear an outer robe, the *ao choang*, over an ao dai. This long tunic with slits from the waist to the floor can be made with a mandarin or high-standing collar or wide, lower boat neck. It is placed over fitted trousers. Preferred colors for

Actress Eva Longoria wearing a dress designed by Indian-born designer Naeem Khan for the Screen Actors Guild Awards, Los Angeles, 2008. Frederick M. Brown/Getty Images.

weddings are red and yellow. The groom wears a blue ao dai. On her head the bride may wear a conical hat made of leaves (the *non la*).

In sum, red and white, with some variations, are used as the color of women's wedding attire, and white, black, or blue are used for mourning purposes. Children's christening outfits, if used, have been reported to be white.

ETHNIC DESIGNERS

Some designers who were born in Asian countries have studied in the United States or Europe and create fashions for people both in their home country and in North America. They blend Eastern and Western styles to offer innovative and tradition-driven styles. Examples include Issey Miyake, from Japan, who is known for his pleating techniques; Doo Ri Chung, from South Korea, who also worked with Geoffrey Beene; and Manish Malhotra, from India, for his Bollywood styles. Zang Toi, from Malaysia, is known for his sarongs, suits, and regal Hollywood-style dresses; Anna Sui, for her formal wear, shoes, and fragrance; and Vera Wang, from China, for bridal costumes.

Fashion designer Melwani commented on the influence of Indian fashion on mainstream North America through long skirts, *kurti* (a shorter version of the kurta), and Indian footwear called *jutthi*. U.S. designer Bill Blass was influenced by Indian embroidery and embellishments. Influences from Indian fashions, due to an increasing population of immigrants from the Indian subcontinent in Canada and the United States, are seen sometimes through silhouette and other times with color. Among well-known designers of Indian heritage are Naeem Khan, who has sold clothes to Bergdorf Goodman and Neiman Marcus; Raman Kapadia, who designs men's clothing; and Alia Khan, who uses Indian cut, color, and crafts. She designed a dress for Phylicia Rashad, a Hollywood celebrity, to wear at a fashion week opening.

Other designers of Asian heritage that have been noted by fashion commentators include Mary Ping, described as bringing elegance and wit in her styles; and Maki Doherty-Ryoke, who was born in Japan. She designs for children, drawing inspiration from story books. Jean Yu is known for her signature collection of silk lingerie and sensual dresses.

PRACTICES IN THE NEW COUNTRY

When a comparison is made between practices in the country of origin and the United States and Canada, certain differences that Asian immigrants confront are clear. In the country of origin, dress is generally more formal when an individual appears in public than in the country of adoption. Revealing clothes are generally not worn in the more conservative country of origin, whereas it is up to the individual whether or not to wear more revealing clothes in the United States and Canada. Use of clothing to demonstrate status is more likely in the country of origin, while in the country of adoption, comfort in clothing is more important.

Expectations about how individuals of a specific age, gender, class, or occupation should dress are generally more highly developed in the country of origin and less certain in the new country. For the young, certain fashion influences and practices, such as the wearing of fashion tattoos or multiple piercings, that would not be tolerated in the country of origin are acceptable in the new environment. The country of adoption is less likely to require uniforms as dress for school, except for parochial schools.

Other changes that are noted have to do with the economy, the climate, and customary practices. Services, such as beauty parlors, tend to be more expensive in the United States and Canada. Some regions in the United States and Canada have much colder climates than the countries of origin. Customs relating to birth, marriage, and death may be markedly different in the country of adoption, and it is in these kinds of areas that practices relating to dress are most likely to be continued.

Dress of ethnic minorities in the United States and Canada reflects the blend of Eastern and Western cultures and clothing. It is a function of practicing prescribed rituals, acculturating with the adopted country, assimilating the mainstream culture, and introducing new practices in the clothing habits of the people now living in the United States and Canada. The concepts of acculturation and assimilation are reflected through their dress and appearance. Ethnic diversity in the United States and Canada enriches the fabric of society.

A majority of the ethnic minorities residing in the United States and Canada wear gender-, occasion-, and function-appropriate jeans, T-shirts, sweatsuits, dresses, skirts, blouses, skirted suits and pantsuits, sweaters, two-piece suits, combination suits with sports coats, lingerie and pajamas, and work wear like those of the mainstream population that have been accepted through acculturation and assimilation processes. However, for ceremonial occasions of ethnic origin and importance, they wear ethnic dress in ethnic colors with ethnic accessories because rituals result from deep-rooted values that do not diminish very quickly. Intermarriages across religious and geographic boundaries make it even more feasible to blend cultures and reflect this blending through dress and appearance because dress can be the visible manifestation of internal strengths and inclinations. Dress serves as a bridge between an individual and his or her environment, and ethnic minorities are no exception.

References and Further Reading

Abrol, Usha. "Adaptation of JAS Modern Pattern of Basic Blouse for 85 Centimeters Bust to Different Styles of Jackets." Master's thesis, Maharaja Sayajirao University, 1974.

Asia Pacific Foundation of Canada. "Proportion of Asian immigrants to total immigrants in Canada and US." http://www.asiapacific.ca/data/people/immigration_dataset3_bycountry.cfm (accessed 11 November 2006).

Blair, Joane E. *Fashion Terminology*. Englewood Cliffs, NJ: Prentice Hall, 1992.

Canfield, Allan. "Body, Identity and Interaction: Interpreting Nonverbal Communication." http://canfield.etext.net/Chapter6.htm (accessed 11 November 2006).

Chowdhary, Usha. "Fashion Process as Related to Media Exposure, Social Participation, and Attitude toward Change in India." Ph.D. dissertation, Ohio State University, 1984.

Chowdhary, Usha. "India Abroad. Fashion and Beyond." *Fashion and Beyond* 1, no. 1 (2002): 10–15.

Chowdhary, Usha. *Clothing, Culture and Society*. New York: LINUS, 2006.

Davis, Marian L. *Visual Design in Dress*. Upper Saddle River, NJ: Prentice Hall, 1996.

Kaiser, Susan. *The Social Psychology of Clothing: Symbolic Appearances in Context*. New York: Fairchild, 1997.

Mehta, Rustam J. *Masterpieces of Indian Textiles*. Bombay, India: D.B. Taraporevala & Sons, 1970.

Pickens, Mary Brooks. *The Language of Fashion*. New York: Funk and Wagnalls, 1939.

Yamanaka, Norio. *The Book of Kimono*. Tokyo: Kodansha International, 1982.

Usha Chowdhary

Hispanic and Latino American

The heritage of Latinos living in the United States and Canada is a mixture of Spanish, Portuguese, European, native, African, Asian, and other ancestry. Dress needs vary widely and are influenced in part by socioeconomic status, age, income, education, immigration status, faith, popular culture, and gender. Family values and faith play a significant role in Hispanic families and influence dress purchases, particularly for special-occasion wear. Latinos also tend to be brand conscious. Although Latinos are a sizable cultural group and difficult to identify via their dress characteristics, one garment, the *guayabera*, is a marker that identifies Latino ethnicity more than any other garment.

THE U.S. AND CANADIAN POPULATION

The terms *Hispanic* and *Latino* apply to a heterogeneous group of peoples in the United States and Canada that identify their heritage as Mexican, Puerto Rican, Cuban, Dominican, Central or South American, or other. *Hispanic* and *Latino* are expressions that are often used interchangeably; however, each term has significantly different meanings. *Hispanic* is a term applied by the U.S. government in the 1970s to persons of Latin American heritage assuming common Spanish-speaking ancestry. The purpose was to adopt a panethnic label as a tool to measure social characteristics of the U.S. population and its progress toward remedying society's disadvantaging of racial minorities. The drawback with the usage of *Hispanic* is that it excludes peoples with indigenous or African roots. *Latino* refers to a diaspora of people that includes all people with Spanish, Latin American, indigenous, or African roots who have immigrated to the United States or Canada. Consequently, the term appeals to a wide range of individuals. In this article, *Hispanic* and *Latino* are used interchangeably.

DEMOGRAPHICS OF NORTH AMERICAN LATINOS

Hispanic appearance at the beginning of the twenty-first century in the United States and Canada is marked by the confluence of Latin American and North American cultures. People from Latin American and Caribbean countries live and work side by side, yet they seek to express their individual identities through appearance while expressing their personal ethnic identities. Choices about dress can be influenced or constrained by factors such as ethnic group membership, income and economic level, religion, and education. Therefore, it is useful to answer the questions: Who are these people? What are their origins? And where do they live?

The population of U.S. Hispanics in 2000 officially numbered 35.3 million, with individuals of Mexican heritage accounting for 59 percent (20.6 million); Puerto Ricans, 10 percent (3.4 million); Central Americans, 5 percent (1.7 million); Cubans, 4 percent (1.2 million); South Americans, 4 percent (1.4 million); Dominicans, 2 percent (0.8 million); and other Hispanics or Latinos, 18 percent (6.2 million). Although official government data indicate that 12.5 percent of the U.S. population self-identifies as Hispanic or Latino, demographers estimate the population to be sizably larger. A more recent estimate by the Pew Hispanic Center reports that Hispanics comprise 14.9 percent (44.7 million) of the U.S. population (approximately 300 million) in 2006. Pew attributes these significant population increases to immigration from Latin America and high Latino fertility rates.

The status of Latinos in Canada, on the other hand, is significantly different from that in the United States. While a relatively small population resides in Canada, immigration to Canada is a fairly recent phenomenon, beginning in the 1960s. Since the turn of the twenty-first century, a new initiative to accurately identify the growing Hispanic population has begun. In the 2001 census, the Canadian Hispanic Congress included cultural characteristics, such as ethnic origin (for example, Spanish or Peruvian), mother tongue (Spanish as mother tongue), and place of birth (that of respondent and parents) as ethnic identifiers to capture uncounted Hispanics. If a respondent indicated at least one ethno-identifier, they were included in the new Hispanic count. Applying such methods resulted in 520,260 (1.8%) Hispanics identified in the 2001 Canadian census as a part of the total Canadian population of 29,639,030.

Religion plays an important role in the lives of U.S. Latinos. Sixty-seven percent identify themselves as Catholic, and 20 percent identify themselves with one of several forms of Protestantism. Within these two significant Christian groups, 40 percent describe themselves as "born again" or "charismatics." Characteristics by religious group also vary. For example, of Latino Catholics, 55 percent speak Spanish as their first language, 68 percent are foreign born, 42 percent did not graduate from high school, and 46 percent have households with less than US$30,000 in income per year. Among evangelicals (born-again Christians), 63 percent either speak Spanish as their primary language or are bilingual, 55 percent indicate they are foreign born, 64 percent have obtained a high school diploma, and 39 percent have household incomes of less than US$30,000 annually. Mainline Protestants are only 5 percent of all Hispanics in the United States, yet 65 percent of them were born there. English is declared as mainline Protestant Hispanics' primary language (45%), and 68 percent of them earned a high school diploma; 25 percent have household incomes of less than US$30,000 annually.

When considering household income for all U.S. Latinos, regardless of religious beliefs, 39 percent report households of less than US$30,000 annually, 19 percent declare households with incomes from US$30,000 to US$49,000 annually, and 17 percent note households with US$50,000 or more annually.

In 2007, education among U.S. Latinos varied greatly. A sizable minority held a high school diploma (47%), but a large percentage of Latinos (39%) had not obtained the goal of a high school degree. For only a small percentage of Hispanic Americans (10%) was the American dream of a college education realized.

GEOGRAPHIC LOCATION

Settlement patterns for U.S. Latinos have largely concentrated in ten states in the beginning of the twenty-first century, including Arizona, California, Colorado, Florida, Illinois, New Jersey, New Mexico, New York, Texas, and Washington State. While one of every two Latinos resided in either California or Texas at the turn of the twenty-first century, exponentially high population growth is noted in the southern states and the Midwest owing to employment opportunities in the meat-processing industry and the many low-wage jobs available there and in Nevada owing to the gaming industry.

Canadian Latinos reside mainly in the eastern hubs of Toronto and Montreal, accounting for approximately half of all Canada's Hispanics. Unlike the Latinos in the United States, Canadian Hispanics are largely immigrants who have been arriving in the last twenty years of the twentieth century. The major countries of origin are, in order of magnitude, El Salvador, Mexico, Chile, Peru, Colombia, Guatemala, Argentina, Spain, and Nicaragua.

THE GUAYABERA: THE QUINTESSENTIAL ETHNIC MARKER AND ITS CUBAN ORIGINS

More than any other item of dress, the guayabera represents Latin American and Caribbean identity in the United States and Canada. A *guayabera* is an upper-body enclosure that buttons down the center front, has a collar, may have long or short sleeves with multiple front pockets, and is worn untucked with parallel, vertical front embellishment, usually pleats or embroidery. Its origin is contested, but it is believed to have originated in Cuba when a wealthy landowner asked his wife to sew a multipocketed shirt from lightweight fabric. Local peasants appropriated the style, calling it a *yayabera*, after the local river. The name was changed to *guayabera* for the guava trees under which the workers rested from the midday sun. These peasant farmers wore the guayabera for dressing up, going to church, or meeting with friends.

Oral traditions place the guayabera in Cuba as early as the eighteenth century. However, there is little documentation as to how the guayabera spread from Cuba through the Caribbean to other parts of Latin America to subsequently influence sartorial expression.

In the twentieth century, the guayabera has embodied informality, political movements, national identity, mediator roles, and fashion. So entrenched was the guayabera in early-twentieth-century Cuban culture that it became the subject of a quartet of speakers for the Ladies Lyceum Lawn Tennis Club of Havana, whose talks were later published in a book titled *El uso y abuso de la guayabera* (The Use and Abuse of the Guayabera). These speakers warned that Cubans were opting for comfort over good taste and counseled against a single style of clothing for all social events. A second speaker erroneously stated that in order for guayaberas to influence fashion, they required sustained and far-reaching economic demand that did not exist; in fact, the demand in Cuba and beyond for the guayabera was high. The third speaker of the quartet drew parallels between wearing the guayabera and the representation of savagery or the decline of civilized society. The final speaker made the connection between the guayabera and Cuba's landed class, who were the first wearers of guayaberas, and concluded that the guayabera was the only garment that represented the traditions and culture of the Cuban people; however, she also predicted that the guayabera would eventually go out of style.

These debates created great interest and dialogue among Cuban intellectuals and writers. In a survey conducted in greater Havana in 1948, an overwhelming majority of men interviewed wore guayaberas, citing their coolness and comfortable features. Men from a broad range of professions and classes responded similarly, that they wore guayaberas not for fashion but for practical reasons. Through the 1950s, the guayabera continued to be the subject of social discussion and was ultimately adopted as everyday government wear for the Castro regime. It was symbolic of socialist politics because of its humble beginnings.

The guayabera has served the role of both political icon and mediator. During the Castro administration, the guayabera symbolized the spirit of socialism. Thirty years later, Fidel Castro donned a guayabera over his military uniform in 1994 when attending the Fourth Annual Ibero-American Summit in Cartagena, Colombia, emphasizing a link between the Cuban garment and Latin American liberation struggles. Again in 2002, Castro donned the guayabera when meeting with former U.S. president Jimmy Carter, the first time a U.S. president had visited the island since the revolution. Both wore the shirt perhaps as a symbol to mediate prior antagonisms between the two nations.

THE GUAYABERA IN MEXICO AND THE UNITED STATES

The guayabera is closely associated with the Yucatán area of Mexico. Also called a "Mexican wedding shirt," the Mexican guayabera was made from both linen and cotton in the 1930s and 1940s, with embellished buttons. Later innovations included fine pleating, embroidered motifs in parallel lines down the front of the shirt, and the introduction of a female version of counted thread known as the *guayahuipil*. Mexican president Luis Echeverría (1970–1976) is credited with influencing the adoption of the guayabera across Latin America by his regular wearing of guayaberas for government and international occasions and by offering the garment as gifts. The 1970s were peak years, when over two hundred Yucatec producers plied their trade. One producer, Pedro Cab, was well known for his fine Mexican guayaberas, and his company, now in the hands of a new generation, continues to produce traditional guayaberas for local and international consumption in the early twenty-first century. Although guayabera manufacturers in the Yucatán peninsula of Mexico endure, the majority of manufacturing has been globalized and moved to countries such as China and Taiwan. The intended market of Yucatán-produced guayaberas has shifted as well. Rather than Yucatec purchasers, these guayaberas are most likely to have been bought by international tourists or visitors from outside of the peninsular area of Mexico.

In the United States, a guayabera was introduced in 1936 by retailer John Wanamaker's, capitalizing on U.S.–Cuba tourism and the increasing number of Cubans living in Florida. Wanamaker's made guayaberas of lightweight linen in light colors, dark brown, dark blue, and yellow. Later, the line was expanded to include matching linen pants and shirts from alternative fabrics and patterns. In the 1960s and 1970s, new styles included polyester and cotton blends, buttoned pockets, and back panels.

PRODUCING AND MARKETING THE GUAYABERA

Since the introduction of the guayabera in Latin America and the United States in the early twentieth century, the garment has been appropriated by both people of Latin American ancestry and non-Hispanics. For generations of Latinos, the guayabera has reflected their ethnic heritage and masculinity and increasingly is available for women and children, too. Production of the guayabera is undertaken by both small- and large-scale producers. In the United States, Ramón Puig is a legend in Miami for producing and selling high-quality guayaberas to celebrities, politicians, and anyone who can afford the often US$100-plus price tag that his custom-made, or couture, guayaberas demand. Puig, who arrived in Miami in the late 1960s, immediately established his store, La Casa de las Guayaberas (The House of Guayaberas), to cater to the Cuban exile population.

Another Miami company, Guayaberas Etc., is a family-owned business that sells guayaberas through its retail stores in the greater Miami area and via the Internet. The company sources its guayaberas from the United States, Mexico, Panama, El Salvador, and China. Depending upon the cost, design details, and delivery time, a specific factory is selected for production. This company sells guayaberas for both wholesale and retail, along with their many lines of apparel. Guayaberas Etc. has the distinction of having been selected as the supplier for the first official Miami guayabera with a city seal in 2006. City employees and officials wear the guayabera to public functions, and officials make gifts of the garment as well.

For their two online stores, Guayabera Etc. carries a full line of guayaberas for men and guayabera-styled clothing for women and children. The company launched its first Web site in 2000, and each year sales have increased approximately 20 percent. However, Miguel Gimenez, the company's vice president of sales, notes that Internet sales are largely to non-Hispanic consumers.

Across the United States, guayaberas are sold at specialty retailers, traditional department stores like JCPenney, and at discount retailers, such as Wal-Mart. Companies that in the past sold guayaberas almost exclusively, such as Supreme International in the 1960s and Haband of Paterson beginning in the 1920s, have become business giants Perry Ellis International (PEI) and Golden Gate Capital, respectively. However, these firms, such as PEI, have not moved completely away from their origins. Rather, PEI has developed brands, such as Cubavera, drawing influence from their "signature shirts" and Latin culture to market to

fashion-conscious, contemporary Hispanic consumers, or Havanera, sold at JCPenney, that includes traditional guayaberas and guayabera-inspired styles targeting both Hispanic and non-Hispanic men ages thirty and older.

Guayabera influence on turn-of-the-twenty-first-century fashion runways is evident in the prêt-à-porter line of Donna Karan and as inspiration for upscale styles for women and men by Dominican designer Arcadio Diaz. Increasingly, fashionistas are reinventing guayaberas for nights out on the town or as trendy casual wear for men and women alike.

Subcultural groups are increasingly negotiating their identities by appropriating the guayaberas as well. Latina butch lesbians, women who favor a masculine style in clothing, hair, and physical presence, also have appropriated the guayabera in the late twentieth century as a marker of their Latin American identity and masculinity. The guayabera is being interpreted and included in queer-women-of-color fashion lines in global cities such as San Francisco, Los Angeles, and New York and as a part of the contemporary globalized marketplace.

New technology has influenced Hispanic generations, with Internet-only retailers selling guayaberas and traditionally styled shirts directly to consumers beginning in the late twentieth century. Vintage guayaberas are also commonly sold over the Internet

Woman wearing a huipil shirt: a square-shaped, embroidered woman's top worn by indigenous women in southern Mexico and Guatemala. Historically, huipiles indicated the geographic origins of the wearer. Courtesy of Josephine Moreno.

via eBay or through ever-growing and savvy Internet marketers. Moreover, marketers predict that the guayabera is poised to go mainstream in the twenty-first century.

Latino Americans in the United States and Canada have many purchasing options when it comes to their appearance. The range of retailing choices is vast and includes chain and individually owned specialty stores; discount and nondiscount department stores such as Target, JCPenney, and Dillards; off-price discount stores such as TJMaxx, Kohl's, and Ross; warehouse clubs such as Costco; catalogs and Internet retailers such as Lands' End; factory outlets; and secondhand stores. Moreover, all consumers, including Latinos, shop at a combination of stores to meet their appearance needs. As evinced by the availability of the guayabera, a single key style is available at many price ranges and quality levels and at a wide range of retail choices, from Wal-Mart to Macy's.

INFLUENCE OF LATINA AND LATINO CELEBRITIES

In the late twentieth and early twenty-first centuries, an increasing number of Latino celebrities and sports figures have become visible role models and are influencing popular culture across the United States and Canada. These individuals grace the cover of magazines, appear on talk shows, are the focus of entertainment television, and are emulated for their personal styles. Both Latina and Latino celebrities are expanding their power in Hollywood and in the business world. They are lending their names and influence to apparel brands and fashion goods in growing numbers. With U.S. Hispanic consumers spending 3 percent more in 2006 over the previous year in clothing purchases, retailers are lining up Latina celebrity brands to attract Hispanic customers to their stores.

Well-known contemporary Hispanic actors include Antonio Banderas, Gael Garcia Bernard, Penelope Cruz, Eva Longoria, Jennifer Lopez, Benicio del Toro, and Jimmy Smits. A prime example of the growing influence of Latina power in Hollywood is actor Salma Hayek, who is also an executive producer of the hit series *Ugly Betty*. Hayek has brought attention to the value of Latina characters in mainstream television. In April 2007, she signed with Metro-Goldwyn-Mayer Incorporated to produce two to four Latin-themed movies each year following on the heels of *Wife of My Brother*, a moderately successful Latin-based drama released in 2005 by Canada's Lions Gate Entertainment Corporation.

Singers such as Christina Aguilera, Marc Anthony, Gloria Estefan, Ricky Martin, Paulina Rubia, the late Selena, Shakira, and Thalía have had a significant influence on Latinos and their consuming habits. Increasingly, celebrities make conscious decisions to sell their brands to an admiring public. With U.S. Hispanics spending US$6.6 billion on apparel in 2004, Latino celebrity endorsements are embraced by retailers. For example, both Thalía and the multitalented Jennifer Lopez have their own clothing lines. The Thalía Sodi collection, offered exclusively by Kmart, is inspired by the singer's culture and personal style and appeals to both Latinas and non-Latinas ranging in age from the teens through the late thirties; the line is also offered in plus sizes.

Latina personalities, those both moderately well known and those with single-name recognition, such as talk show host Christina, are lending their names to apparel and household items at all price levels, knowing that brand recognition increases sales. Daisy Fuentes's lines, sold exclusively at Kohl's, are moderately priced and target consumers from the ages of twenty-five to fifty-five. Kohl's hopes to attract a growing number of Latina consumers with the Fuentes line and would also like to expand into markets with larger concentrations of Hispanic consumers. Christina's (last name: Saralegui) apparel line will target women thirty years of age and older and will be sold in department stores.

Sport figures, such as boxer Oscar de la Hoya, major league ballplayer Alex Rodriguez, or Olympic speed skater Jennifer Rodriguez, represent the growing presence of Latinos in U.S. sports. While each has varying recognition with the general population, some, such as de la Hoya, have branded their name to benefit from their celebrity status. In 2004, Mexican American de la Hoya and Mervyn's announced a collaboration to offer Oscar de la Hoya active wear within the California-based retailer's stores.

At the turn of the twenty-first century, Hispanic Americans in the United States and Canada have a vast assortment of dress options to draw from. Specifically, retailing is sophisticated because fashion is available at all price levels. Moreover, Latino consumers tend neither to shop at only one retailer nor to purchase from one category of retailer; Latino consumers do not differentiate themselves from Anglo-Americans in many cases. Both high-end, trend-setting Latinos and middle-market Latinos are brand conscious. Perry Ellis, Kenneth Cole, Armani, Gucci, and Polo tend to be desirable name brands, for example. For mass-market and chain store retailers, Latinos are inclined to be more value oriented than brand oriented; however, these retailers also carry items for Latinos who desire branded apparel and accessories to wear. As an example, in 2007, clothing by Danskin, Hanes, Faded Glory, Wrangler, and Lee was a part of the assortment offered by Wal-Mart in a town with a significant Hispanic population to reach out to brand-conscious consumers.

WESTERN WEAR AMONG LATINOS

Among working-class male Latinos in the United States, a trend in Western-style dress has emerged since the 1990s. These young Latino consumers are increasingly construction and warehouse workers rather than agriculturalists as formerly. Moreover they are largely first-generation immigrants to the United States.

Worn largely by young men in their twenties and thirties, Western-styled clothing and accessories are offered by a variety of retailers, such as small specialty stores that focus their assortments and discount department stores that offer their customers value-priced dress. One company has sustained itself through many trends. A precursor to the modern Western trend, Rudel Western Boot Company is a unique producer of Western boots that began its operations in Mexico in 1910 and now creates boots of smooth leathers, hides, and exotic skins, such as ostrich, alligator, and caiman.

The Western styles that young Latino men prefer include bifurcated body enclosures on the lower torso, such as branded jeans, including Wrangler, Lee, or Levi's for casual wear. This pre-shaped body enclosure is worn close to the lower torso, with pant legs that flare below the knee to allow room for the boots that are worn with it. Dress pants, another form of body enclosure, are often constructed of polyester for easy care. Shirts are Western-styled, with pointed front and back yokes; may have snap closures down the center front; and are either long or short sleeved.

Common shirt brands are Wrangler, Whitehorse, and Resistol, and the fabrics can be either plaid or solid. Either leather work boots or dress boots complete the ensemble selected from brands such as Durango, Justin, Tony Lama, Rocky, and Rudel. The Western look carries over into tuxedos and suits for more formal occasions. A Western-styled hat may be worn. The addition of a Western-styled belt and belt buckle completes the look.

CHOLO STYLE

Cholos are contemporary Mexican American urban youth who may be gang members, car club members, or persons influenced by the cholo lifestyle that emerged in the latter half of the twentieth century. Specifically, cholos are recognized by their unique appearance, speech, and mannerisms. Although cultural and dress markers are singular to each group, khaki pants, denim, white T-shirts, plaid long-sleeved shirts (called Pendletons), and bandannas are commonly worn by males. *Cholas*, or female members, are associated with khaki pants, T-shirts or tank tops, plaid long-sleeved shirts, flat black shoes, heavy makeup, and long hair. Both male and female gang membership may be evident through tattoos and temporary body manipulations, such as hand gestures that are unique to a group.

Cholo style has its origins in the zoot suit–wearing pachucos of the 1940s. However, the origin of the zoot suit has been challenged. One version is that the zoot suit has its beginnings in Gainesville, Georgia, when a black bus worker, Clyde Duncan, was inspired to imitate Rhett Butler, a character in the movie *Gone With the Wind*. Alternatively, the zoot suit is reported to have its roots in jazz culture, inspired by the musicians' appearance themselves. Others claim that the zoot suit's heritage is aligned with Mexican American working-class youth or that it's derived from British military costume.

Pachucos and pachucas are a subcultural group that emerged in the United States in the 1930s and 1940s and whose culture has yet to be fully understood, although their unique dress and language, Caló, is readily acknowledged. The well-known zoot suit was not unique to pachucos, however. It was also the sartorial expression of other ethnic and youth groups in the United States and abroad.

SPECIAL-OCCASION WEAR

Mariachis are musicians who perform a particular style of Mexican folk music. Their dress, called *traje de charro* (cowboy outfit), is particularly distinctive and is drawn from the dress of Mexican cowboys and gentlemen ranchers. Now popular in the United States and Canada, mariachis are hired to play at masses, weddings, funerals, and special events, and they appear at mariachi festivals and conferences. A full mariachi group is a significant ensemble consisting of approximately eight to twelve members that can include three to six violins, a round-backed guitar called a *vihuela*, a deep-voiced guitar called a *guitarrón*, a European guitar, and two trumpets.

The whole group is outfitted similarly, depending upon the formality of the occasion. They wear a close-fitting jacket with long sleeves that meets at the center front. This jacket is solid colored (often black, gray, green, white, or tan) and worn over a long-sleeved, white collared shirt. The jacket could have welt pockets, a lapel or shawl collar, and extensive embellishment.

A matching vest is sometimes worn. Men wear a fitted body enclosure covering the lower torso that zippers in the center front. These close-fitting pants taper to the ankles but are worn long over shoes or short boots. Accessories include bow ties, a belt and belt buckle, boots, and a sombrero. The bow tie is usually made of woven satin fabric that is solid colored and can be embroidered or embellished. Sometimes the bow tie is constructed of patterned fabric. The *sombrero* is a significant component of the overall dress because of its size and placement, perched on the top of the musicians' head as they play their instrument. Sombreros can be made of straw, palm fibers, or velvet and embellished with suede, thread, soutache braid, or metal trim. As a body supplement, it visually coordinates with the individual's outfit in color and decoration and also marks the individual as a member of an ethnic group. The jacket and pants are trimmed with embroidery or shiny metal buttons and chain embellishment called *gala*, particularly down the outside length of each side of the pants and at the front of the jacket.

Increasingly, women have become members of mariachi groups. All-female mariachi groups have been common since the 1990s; consequently, the typical male mariachi uniform called for new colors and variations. Women's mariachi colors include bright pink, medium blue, purple, medium red, light gray, off-white, and white. Rather than pants and belts with buckles, women wear floor-length skirts and sometimes sashes at the waist. Closed-toed shoes or boots are the same color as the skirt. The embellishment on the jacket, vest, skirt, and sombrero of a female mariachi is similar to that of a male mariachi band member but can be more extensive. Their fabric bow is softer and larger than the bow tie worn by men. Female mariachi group members wear their hair styled away from their faces, with or without bangs, with fabric bows that hold their hair in ponytails or as an accent worn on a low hair bun to accommodate the wearing of a sombrero. They often will wear long gold-toned or silver earrings.

A *quinceañera* is another event at which special-occasion dress is worn in Latino culture. These celebrations are coming-of-age events for Latinas in their fifteenth year that differ from North American cotillions or debutante balls. Quinceañeras are rites of passage that signal the passage of a girl from childhood to young adulthood in Latino culture; that is, they are a public affirmation by family and friends that she is no longer an adolescent but a young woman. The planning leading up to the celebration can be extensive. The tradition continues to be embraced at the opening of the twenty-first century, in particular for first-generation families.

The celebration begins with a mass but is differentiated from the sacraments within Roman Catholicism. The honoree is dressed in a gown that, depending upon custom or personal choice, is often pink, pastel, or white in color. She can be attended by a court whose number historically reflects a total of fifteen years, but today the court varies widely in both number and gender. The honoree's parents, godparents, and family are usually in attendance at the mass. The honoree's dress ensemble includes a tiara or headpiece and gloves, and she may carry a bouquet of artificial or real flowers, a Bible, and a rosary. The young woman will wear a *medalla*, or medal, usually of gold and with a religious theme, that is presented before the mass and can be symbolic of the Virgen of Guadalupe. Body supplements, such as earrings and a ring, may complete the outfit. The dress elements are personal choices and vary tremendously from one individual to another depending upon personal choice, traditions, social class, and faith.

If present, the honoree's female attendants are dressed in similar attire, while the male attendants are dressed in tuxedos or suits. Dress plays a pivotal role in the festivities, particularly at the first dance of the party that follows the mass. The dance, often a waltz, is reserved for the honoree and her father or an individual designated by the honoree. The dance can be very traditional: For example, an honoree's father actually changes the shoes of his daughter prior to the waltz from flats to heels, symbolizing the actual movement from one life stage to another, that is, from childhood to young womanhood.

Dress choices and details of quinceañera celebrations are organic and fluid in nature. Contemporary lifestyles increasingly influence the nature of the quinceañera for Latinas in the United States and Canada today. In fact, a recent development is for young Latinos to observe their fifteenth-year celebrations, called *quinceros*. Increased autonomy among young women permits a wider degree of choice than perhaps existed in past celebrations. Besides an expression of gender, a quinceañera is a familial and individual expression of race, ethnicity, faith, and sexual and social class desires.

RELIGION AND DRESS

Religious beliefs play out in the importance of ceremony and appearance. Consequently, dress worn for baptism, first communion, confirmation, and weddings, for example, are notable in Hispanic cultures.

First communion is significant for many Latino American families because two-thirds of U.S. Hispanics are practicing Roman Catholics. The sacrament of first communion can be received as young as seven or eight years old, but often for immigrant families, communicants can be in their early teens. Also referred to as First Holy Communion, it is considered one of the most sacred and important occasions in a Roman Catholic's life. Accordingly, the symbolism of the child's appearance can be quite important. However, in some churches recognition of the high cost to outfit a child has grown, and church officials have encouraged parents to dress communicants in their Sunday best if new outfits are not affordable.

First communion day is usually a festive occasion for Hispanic families to gather and celebrate their religious values. A young girl usually wears a long dress that has a back zipper and is mid-calf or ankle length; white in color, symbolic of purity; with long or short white gloves. The dress can be sleeveless or might have short sleeves. Significant to the wearer is the shape, volume, and sound made when the dress is worn, because first communion dresses are usually long dresses made of organdy, damask, organza, or taffeta—fabrics that rustle when they move. The most elaborate first communion dresses resemble miniature wedding dresses, with underpinnings that have structure holding the fabric away from the body. The communicant wears a white tulle veil, perhaps with a headdress or tiara. This may also be the first time she wears a necklace with a cross and carries a rosary. Her hair is often formally arranged. On her feet she wears white dress shoes, perhaps with a slight heel, or flats worn with white hose or white socks.

Boys receiving first communion wear white suits or are simply encouraged to dress in their best clothing because new outfits can be very expensive. The suit may consist of a body enclosure that opens in the center front over a shirt; a bifurcated body enclosure over the lower torso has a zipper with waistband and pockets. He may or may not wear a vest. For accessories he may wear a belt and around his neck a cross or a saint's medal. Communicants usually dress monochromatically. Boys complete their ensembles with matching dress shoes and socks and hair that is carefully coiffed.

TRADITIONAL DRESS

A growing trend among Latina intellectuals in the United States is the wearing of indigenous or traditional dress elements. In particular the Maya *huipil*, a square-shaped woman's top worn by indigenous women in southern Mexico and Guatemala, is increasingly appropriated. The huipil continues to be a significant ethnic marker in Latin America in the early twenty-first century. Huipiles are constructed of hand- or machine-loomed yardage and can be heavily embellished with embroidery, lace, or hand-stitching on the neck and armhole edges. Historically, huipiles indicated the geographic origins of the wearer. However, contemporary native women commonly wear huipiles from villages other than their own. The sale of huipiles, particularly during periods of civil strife, has been common, especially in Guatemala during the last quarter of the twentieth century. Consequently, the garment has been sold to tourists and made available in the global marketplace.

For these Latina intellectuals, wearing huipiles provides identification as an ethnic person, psychological protection, and as a means of defining oneself as different from others. Sometimes, an individual actually has indigenous heritage; consequently, wearing traditional dress elements, such as a huipil, is a normal component of her dress repertoire because traditional dress is integral to her identity. For these individuals, if it is acceptable in the workplace, wearing traditional clothing to work is emotionally comforting while providing a nonverbal sense of security and ethnic identity.

At the commencement of the twenty-first century, Hispanics in the United States and Canada are a challenging group to describe in terms of their dress characteristics. As a heterogeneous group in both countries, it is not possible to generalize across such a large and diverse population. Only one garment, the guayabera, stands out as a panethnic identifier for many Latinos. Latina and Latino celebrities are growing in influence and set the stage for not only fashion and a Latina aesthetic but also for artistic choices in music, television, and popular culture.

For Hispanics, faith and family values consistently emerge across groups. Brand consciousness, at all price levels, are opportunities not only for marketers but also for scholars to do research. In fact, the time is ripe to endeavor to understand all aspects of Latino cultures through the further study of Latinos and their needs multidimensionally. For example, little is known about the contemporary dress habits of working-class, middle-aged Hispanic women, yet they are active consumers of apparel, makeup, and accessories. These individuals are also influential as dress purchasers for their children and extended family members. Certainly, it is the unique combination of factors that might include education, household income, immigrant status, personal values, faith, gender, and sexual orientation that influence Latinos in their personal and family dress decisions. With the already sizable numbers of Hispanic peoples in both the United States and Canada, it would be fruitful to understand the characteristics that shape this growing and influential population.

Snapshot: Jennifer Lopez

Dancer, singer, and actress Jennifer Lopez gained initial exposure on the comedy show *In Living Color* in 1991 as a "fly girl" dancer. Following small movie roles, her first significant break was opposite Wesley Snipes in *Money Train* in 1995. In 1997, the U.S. Latino population was dazzled when Lopez played the recently deceased songstress Selena, for which role she received a Golden Globe nomination for best actress in a musical or comedy in 1998. Since, Lopez's acting options have grown, and she is the highest-paid Latina actress in Hollywood, earning over US$1 million per film.

Lopez's superstardom facilitates the marketing of her lines of apparel, accessories, footwear, and perfumes said to be worth US$350 million. Glow is the first fragrance offered by Jennifer Lopez appealing to a young consumer, but it has been joined by a family of fragrances that includes Still Jennifer Lopez and Miami Glow by J.Lo, all three of which are manufactured by Coty. The fragrance Still is designed to appeal to older consumers, and Miami Glow draws inspiration from that city's tropical environment and night life.

Lopez's first apparel line, JLo, is licensed by Warnaco and can be found in Macy's department stores. JLo targets young Latinas and includes jeans, T-shirts, lingerie, and accessories. In 2005, Lopez teamed with Tommy Hilfiger's brother Alan to begin a new brand, Sweetface Fashion, which includes high-end sportswear, dresses, swimwear, career wear, jackets, coats, vests, and parkas, as well as children's wear, and is found in designer boutiques and novelty retailers such as Neiman Marcus.

As a fashion icon, every aspect of Lopez's personal style is closely followed whenever she is in the public eye. Lopez, a Latina of Puerto Rican heritage, fuses her artistic endeavors of music, acting, and fashion while drawing on her linguistic ability to move back and forth between Spanish and English. In part, her comfort in navigating both cultures allows her to reach Spanish- and English-speaking Latino consumers.

Jennifer Lopez also has signaled to the fashion industry the existence of an optional beauty form besides the waif look, one based upon a Latina aesthetic personified by Lopez's posterior. Lopez has brought attention to the form of women of color, one associated not only with Latinas but with African American women as well. One has only to look at the shape of the Glow perfume bottle, small on top and voluptuous on the bottom, to understand how Lopez, in part intentionally, promotes this Latina ethnic aesthetic.

Latina actress and fashion icon Jennifer Lopez at the "Superheroes: Fashion and Fantasy" Costume Institute Gala, New York City, 2008. Lopez, a Latina of Puerto Rican heritage, has created her own apparel lines and has done much to promote a Latina aesthetic. WireImage.

Snapshot: The Hispanic and Latino Zoot Suit

The term *zoot* emerged in the late 1930s within jazz vernacular meaning "worn" or "performed in an extravagant style." The draped style worn by black youth at first was called "drapes." It consisted of a jacket with heavily padded shoulders worn long over pants that were multipleated at the top and tapered sharply at the ankles. The zoot suit caught on with other urban youth, particularly young second-generation Mexican Americans, largely pachucos, in Los Angeles. The masculine version consisted of a broad-shouldered coat worn long, fitted at the waist and flared in a "fingertip" style. Under the coat was a long-sleeved shirt, worn open at the neck. The pachucos' pants were very baggy, achieved by pleats with a high waistline. Pachucos preferred narrow belts or suspenders. A watch chain hung low, perhaps below the knees of the wearer. Males combed their hair in a ducktail style or might wear a broad-brimmed hat with a flat crown. Thick, double-soled shoes completed the ensemble.

Female zooters also existed. Pachucas daring enough to adopt the full zoot suit wore all-black ensembles of drape jackets; short, tight skirts; heavy makeup; and teased pompadour hair styles of the 1940s. The most daring pachucas chose to cross-dress, wearing the complete men's zoot suit, including pants.

By the early 1940s, young Mexican Americans had adopted the zoot suit as their own ethnic symbol. Simultaneously, the U.S. war effort demanded the enlistment of millions of civilians and the entrance of large numbers of women into the workforce for the first time. These second-generation Mexican American youth found themselves neither included nor excluded, and some believe that the separation of families led to the erosion of parental control and authority. These young men are said to have been drawn to the streets and vulnerable to the effects of war, particularly in the Los Angeles area.

Leading up to the Zoot Suit Riots, a prior incident linked zoot suits to Mexican American youth, namely the Sleepy Lagoon incident that took place in August 1942. It involved an alleged gang altercation that resulted in a death at a local swimming hole in Los Angeles. What was significant was the role of the zoot suit as an ethnic identifier. Twenty-one Mexican American youths were singled out, along with one young white man, who were tried and convicted together for the murder. A few women who were alleged to be involved in the Sleepy Lagoon incident were also put on trial and sent to reform school. In 1944, the men were released upon appeal; however, in the eyes of the U.S. public not only were the zoot suit–wearing Mexican American youth guilty but all Mexican American youth were assumed to be gang members and a problem for law-abiding citizens as well.

The Zoot Suit Riots took place in June 1943 and were largely an outgrowth of social change. Social mobility among millions of civilians and service personnel throughout the country intensified vagrancy, particularly in military towns along the

Two men wearing zoot suits, Michigan, ca. 1940. Gordon Coster/Time & Life Pictures/Getty Images.

West Coast. Cities such as Los Angeles, Detroit, and Pittsburgh experienced the worst of the rioting. The clashes were largely between young, white U.S. servicemen and African American or Mexican American youth.

The riots certainly had racial overtones, but the larger issues were patriotism and attitudes toward the war. At the time of the Zoot Suit Riots the United States had been involved in World War II for one and a half years. A year previously, in 1942, the War Production Board had passed rationing acts that restricted the use of fabric in the production of clothing. The regulation basically restricted the production of the zoot suit style; however, the demand for zoot suits, which were quite popular at the time, continued, and manufacturing in garment centers, such as Los Angeles and New York, persisted.

Consequently, when zoot suit–wearing pachucos appeared on the streets, they were thought to be publicly mocking rationing regulations and appeared in sharp contrast to young U.S. servicemen's military uniforms. The first riots reported occurred the first weekend in June 1943, when a group of sixty "zooters" were arrested after fights broke out between themselves and servicemen on leave. The Mexican American youth had reportedly been grabbed by servicemen from bars, theaters, and the streets and stripped of their zoot suits, beaten, and shorn of their hair. Little was done by law enforcement to stop the violence or to mediate the one-sided attacks. The press was also one-sided in its handling of the Zoot Suit Riots. From the beginning, the press did not discourage the attacks and at times actually promoted the hate-mongering, as was evident in some of the newspapers of the day.

The basis of the attacks was the symbolic dress that identified the wearer as a zoot suiter, and it was the target of servicemen. In Los Angeles, Mexican American youth were hunted by servicemen as the riots escalated in the second week. Both sides sought vengeance, and arrests of both groups increased. The press attempted to subdue the riots with editorials and allay the racial undertones the riots had elicited. Much of the press reports focused more on sensational items, such as the race and ethnicities of the zoot-suited youths, their avoidance of military duty, and the ignoring of rationing acts, than on solutions. However, little was said of the military servicemen who were arrested for inciting riots, of the white Americans who wore zoot suits, or the opinions of Mexican American servicemen stationed in southern California at the time. Contemporary press of the time suppressed alternative views and missed the opportunity to provide objective, balanced coverage of the events. As the Zoot Suit Riots died down in Los Angeles, occurrences flared up in other U.S. cities such as Detroit, New York, and Philadelphia that were thought to contribute to future race and political movements in the United States in the 1950s and 1960s.

References and Further Reading

Cosgrove, Stuart. "The Zoot Suit and Style Warfare." *History Workshop Journal* 18 (Autumn 1984): 77–91.

Davalos, Karen Mary. "Quinceañeras." In *Encyclopedia of Latinos and Latinas in the United States*, vol. 3, edited by Suzanne Oboler and Deena J. Gonzalez, 531–533. Oxford: Oxford University Press, 2005.

Guzmán, Betsy. "The Hispanic Population. Census 2001 Brief." http:www.census.govprod/2001pubs/c2kbr01-3.pdf (accessed 15 February 2007).

Hinojosa, Francisco G. "Notes on the Pachuco: Stereotypes, History, and Dialect." *Atisbos: Journal of Chicano Research* (Summer 1975): 53–65.

Hurtado, Aída. "Fashion." In *Encyclopedia of Latinos and Latinas in the United States*, vol. 2, edited by Suzanne Oboler and Deena J. Gonzalez, 110–114. Oxford: Oxford University Press, 2005.

Macias, Anthony. "Zoot Suit." In *Encyclopedia of Latinos and Latinas in the United States*, vol. 4, edited by Suzanne Oboler and Deena J. Gonzalez, 368–370. Oxford: Oxford University Press, 2005.

Miller, Marilyn. "Guayaberismo and the Essence of Cool." In *The Latin American Fashion Reader*, edited by Regina Root, 213–231. Oxford: Berg, 2005.

Pew Hispanic Center. "Changing Faiths: Latinos and the Transformation of American Religion." 2007. http://pewhispanic.org/reports/report.php?ReportID=75 (accessed 28 April 2007).

Ramirez, Catherine S. "Pachucos and Pachucas." In *Encyclopedia of Latinos and Latinas in the United States*, vol. 3, edited by Suzanne Oboler and Deena J. Gonzalez, 315–316. Oxford: Oxford University Press, 2005.

Ramirez, Catherine S. "Saying 'Nothin' ': Pachucas and the Languages of Resistance." *Frontiers: Journal of Women Studies* 27, no. 3 (Winter 2007): 1–33.

Rodríguez, Russell. "Mariachi Music." In *Encyclopedia of Latinos and Latinas in the United States*, vol. 3, edited by Suzanne Oboler and Deena J. Gonzalez, 60–61. Oxford: Oxford University Press, 2005.

Statistics Canada 2001. "Profile of the Hispanic Community in Canada." http:www.statcan.ca (accessed 20 April 2007).

Torres-Saillant, Silvio. "Latino." In *Encyclopedia of Latinos and Latinas in the United States*, vol. 2, edited by Suzanne Oboler and Deena J. Gonzalez, 507–510. Oxford: Oxford University Press, 2005.

Vargas, Deborah R. "Styling Papi: Guayaberas, Latina Butches, and the Politics of Citizenship." Paper delivered at the National Association for Chicano and Chicana Studies meeting, San Jose, CA, 4–7 April 2007.

Josephine M. Moreno

Dress in Hawai'i since 1898

The Hawaiian monarchy was overthrown in 1893 after decades of conflict between the indigenous population and U.S. businessmen. The United States had established a presence there by 1820, and by 1893, it controlled Hawai'i's economy, which was based on sugar and pineapple plantations. Hawai'i became a territory of the United States in 1898. The population of native Hawaiians had been significantly reduced due to the introduction of foreign diseases in the 1800s, so the plantations imported laborers from Japan, China, Korea, Portugal, and the Philippines. Intermarriage between the indigenous Hawaiians and the immigrants led to the extraordinary ethnic diversity seen in Hawai'i today. As a consequence, no one ethnic group is in the majority.

Hawaiian dress has consistently included body adornment worn by both men and women. Forms of adornment in Hawai'i include hats made of *lauhala* (leaves of the hala or pandanus tree), floral leis worn around the neck or head, shell leis, and the use of tattoos using traditional designs, which are worn more often by men than women. All of these have been consistently worn in the past hundred years, with the exception of tattoos. Tattoos had been worn by both men and women in precontact times. The missionaries tried to eliminate their use, but men continued to wear them. Now that women are no longer prohibited from wearing them, the use of tattoos has increased for women.

By the end of the nineteenth century there were four types of clothing in Hawai'i. Most people owned a mix of clothing types, depending on ethnicity and length of time spent in the Hawaiian islands. The four types were

1. *Western dress*—Garments imported into Hawai'i, generally from the United States.
2. *Asian dress*—These garments were generally made at home by female immigrants on the plantation but worn after work. Japanese immigrants wore *kimonos* with *obi* (waist sashes) and *geta* (wooden sandals), and Chinese wore *cheongsam* (dresses) and *sam fu* (jacket and trousers). Chinese men wore their hair in a queue (long braid).
3. *Plantation work clothing*—This developed as a hybrid garment style from clothing that immigrants brought to Hawai'i from other countries, particularly heavy cotton work clothing from Japan and China.
4. *Hawaiian dress*—The styles that are now considered traditional Hawaiian clothing, which originated in 1820 when missionary wives began making garments for Hawaiian women.

One characteristic that defines Hawaiian clothing is comfort and looseness, which are needed in tropical environments. Hawaiian dresses do not have waistlines. The original Hawaiian dresses were the *holokū* and *mu'umu'u*, worn with flower leis and long hair. The holokū was a long, loose gown with long sleeves and a yoke above the bust worn before 1898. Due to the influence of European fashion on the Hawaiian monarchy, design details such as trims, ruching, and a train were added to the holokū. The mu'umu'u that had been introduced by missionary wives as a knee-length chemise to be worn under the holokū was worn by Hawaiian women in another way. They chose to wear it as a nightgown or swim dress until the late 1930s, when Hawaiian prints were introduced. In 1949, a fourth dress type, the *holomu'u*, was developed. As men assimilated into Western society, they wore Western clothing. In the 1930s, Western shirts began to be replaced by the Aloha shirt, which, when worn with long trousers, became typical dress for men in Hawai'i. Both men and women wore leis around the head and neck, and occasionally women wore Ni'ihau shell leis that were made from shells gathered on the island of Ni'hau.

1898 TO 1920

In Hawai'i at the turn of the century, a mix of garment types was worn by the multiethnic population. Whites wore Western-styled clothing, as did some of those born in Hawai'i. Most of the laborers spent their days in plantation clothing and evenings in clothing from their home countries. Kimonos and *yukata* from Japan mixed with cheongsam from China. (Kimonos were generally made of silk and were worn for important occasions, while yukata were cotton kimonos worn for casual dress.) Hawaiian dress was worn by most of the female Hawaiian population. Clothing was made by women at home, or occasionally made in small tailor shops, using fabrics imported from Japan and China. For women, the short-trained holokū was the standard dress outside the home. The silhouette of the gown became less full over time, and by 1900 it skimmed over the body.

The mu'umu'u was occasionally worn underneath the holoku as an undergarment, or more often, as a housedress or for swimming. The mu'umu'u was not considered appropriate to wear outside the home until the late 1930s, when women began making the mu'umu'u from Hawaiian-print cottons. It was a loose, knee-length or longer garment, with short sleeves and made from calico or a solid-colored cotton.

At the turn of the century, holokū were primarily made in white cottons such as muslin, batiste, and dimity. Trains lengthened, and the use of lace, eyelets, pin tucks, and ruffles at the sleeves, yokes, and hems increased significantly. The holokū was usually made in white cottons, and in the early years it was considered to be Hawai'i's version of the European tea gown. Many Hawaiian women visually showed their allegiance to the Hawaiian monarchy and its last regent, Queen Lilioukalani, as they dressed in black holokū to represent mourning after her overthrow.

Hawaiian style contrasted with Western fashion, which was increasingly worn in Hawai'i by whites and the multiethnic residents of Hawai'i as assimilation was taking place. The 1920s ushered in some changes for holokū design, which led to a more

An Hawaiian couple making *poi*, ca. 1910. The woman is wearing a traditional form of dress, while the man is wearing "Western" trousers. Library of Congress, Prints and Photographs Division, LC-USZ62-24005.

casual style and the ascendance of the mu'umu'u. While the loose, white, long-sleeved, lingerie-style holokū remained a favorite, there were dramatic changes in that yokes were eliminated and the gown became more closely fitted to the body. The result was a simple tubular style. Necklines were lowered, trains lengthened, and sleeves were shortened or eliminated altogether.

For men, Western-styled garments and plantation clothes were commonly worn. A unique garment that became important for men in Hawai'i was the *palaka jacket*. This was a common garment worn by the majority of the population who worked on the plantations. These jackets were made of a heavy cotton plaid in navy blue and white. Over time the jacket evolved into a short-sleeved palaka shirt that became symbolic of plantation workers. This was the first form of Hawaiian shirts worn for casual dress; it was quickly followed by shirts made of lightweight cotton, Japanese yukata cloth, and kabe crepe shirts (kabe crepe is a form of crepe made of silk or rayon, with a pebbly texture). By the end of the 1920s, a middle class had emerged. Most of these men had adopted Western clothing, and Asian clothing was becoming more rare in Hawai'i.

THE 1930s TO 1942

Hawai'i's multiethnic population began to set aside the occasional use of Asian dress in favor of Western dress. Nonetheless, Asian fabrics and textile designs continued to be favored. For both men and women, cotton broadcloth shirts with Asian motifs were common. These were pullover shirts with short sleeves and a V-shaped opening with three buttons in front. These shirts, and others made in Japanese cotton and kabe crepe fabrics, were originally produced in bright colors, with Japanese designs that were

intended to be used for girl's kimonos. The kabe crepe shirts were far and away the most colorful. There is no definitive conclusion as to what led to the development of these proto-Hawaiian shirts. One explanation was that they were first made by Japanese mothers out of silk and crepe kimono fabric scraps for their school-age children. However, most of the anecdotal information suggests that these proto-Hawaiian shirts originated when boys from an upper-class private school asked tailors to make custom shirts for them from bright kimono fabric to wear for special activities. Yet another common explanation has been that families had matching shirts made of bright kimono fabrics for special events. Unlike Western shirts that were tucked in, these were worn loose over trousers.

As Japanese immigrants and their children acculturated into Hawaiian society, kimonos began to disappear. As political tensions escalated between Americans and Japanese, people in Hawai'i who were of Japanese origin were caught in the middle. Abandoning the kimono and its visual symbolism was a logical response.

By the mid-1930s, Hawaiian textile prints developed. With the beauty of the tropics all around them, designers began creating tropical-print textiles using block printing. Ellery Chun trademarked the Aloha shirt in 1936. He wanted to produce an expressly Hawaiian shirt and commissioned artists to create Hawaiian designs of local flowers and fish. Small tailor shops began producing Aloha shirts, and then factories developed in the late 1930s to manufacture them. The Hawaiian sportswear industry grew as many small companies entered the business. The number and breadth of textile designs increased dramatically. The most popular designs featured Hawaiian flowers on a blue or black background.

A 1940s reproduction of an 1890 *holokū* (traditional Hawaiian dress). Photograph by Linda Boynton Arthur. Courtesy of the University of Hawai'i's CTAHR Historic Costume Collection.

While lauhala hats had been worn for some time, during the prewar years they became an even more important part of Hawaiian dress and featured high crowns and flat or rolled rims. Some were designed to be worn with fashionable Hawaiian dress and were trimmed with *kapa* (bark cloth), Hawaiian woodroses, shells, and other items from the local environment.

THE WAR YEARS (1942 TO 1945)

What are recognized around the world as Hawaiian shirts (more correctly named Aloha shirts)—characterized by brightly patterned rayons with Hawaiian motifs—were created after World War II. Hawaiian motifs did not appear on the early Aloha shirts until fabric began to be designed locally. Hawai'i had been dependent on textile imports from Japan before the war, but imports ceased during World War II. With no other options for fabrics, local production of block-printed textiles began. During this time, textile artists in Hawai'i flourished. Their designs for Aloha shirts focused on the tropical flora, fish, and Hawaiian historical motifs.

Hawaiian prints were adopted for use on both holokū and mu'umu'u; after putting bright prints on the mu'umu'u, it was no longer used only as a nightgown. Freed from the confines of the home, the mu'umu'u was now considered appropriate to wear in public. While the mu'umu'u was always loose and casual and could be worn either short or long, the holokū became formal during the war years and was generally more fitted. Hawaiian print designs grew more daring and incorporated such uniquely Pacific patterns as palm trees, hula girls, Diamond Head, the Aloha Tower, surfers, and pineapples. School children waged contests to see who could find the most outrageous outfit, and soon entire families were wearing the shirts, often in matching prints. At the same time, a large percentage of the Aloha shirts produced in Hawai'i were being exported to eager buyers in the mainland United States, Australia, and Europe. They became the ultimate picture postcards. The brightly patterned Aloha shirt became famous throughout the nation as servicemen stationed in the islands during the war brought them home and as tourism increased after the war.

POST–WORLD WAR II YEARS (1945 TO 1955)

After World War II, although most of the clothing in Hawai'i had become Western styled, the production of aloha attire increased dramatically. Although Aloha shirts were a dominant trend in Hawai'i at this time, the ones made of kabe crepe went out of fashion. The late 1940s and 1950s are considered the height of the Aloha shirt industry, for during those decades the fabric designs were very bold and vibrant, with brilliant colors used on a smooth rayon fabric. The textile designs from this era were the finest artwork produced in Hawaiian textiles. These shirts were nicknamed "silkies" for their smooth feel against the skin. Long sleeves and three-quarter-length sleeves characterized a new style introduced as dress shirts.

This time period was also the heyday of Hawaiian tourism, much of which came from the United States. Hawaiian fabrics were used extensively in island apparel both for sale to tourists and to the native-born population. The holokū continued to be a popular gown for the numerous social functions of the late 1940s and 1950s, but the long train was cumbersome for dancing. Thus, in 1947, the holomu'u was created; though primarily designed for entertainers, it soon was adopted by younger women from all occupations. Like the mu'umu'u, it had no train, but it kept the close fit of the holokū.

Although Western dress was still dominant in Hawai'i, aloha attire had become increasingly important and was worn for a variety of occasions throughout the islands. In 1947, the Honolulu City Council recognized the importance of aloha attire when it allowed Aloha shirts to be worn to work in Honolulu, but only during the annual celebration of Hawaiian heritage known as Aloha Week.

THE LATE 1950s TO STATEHOOD IN 1959

Beginning after World War II but especially after Hawai'i became a state in 1959, interest in the islands sparked dramatic growth of the local fashion industry, which increased sales by 30 percent per year until 1961. In 1954, some local businesses began to encourage broader use of Aloha shirts. Bank, newspaper, and phone company employees were directed to wear Aloha shirts throughout the humid summer.

The 1950s reflected a constant push toward Westernization in Hawai'i; after half a century as a U.S. territory, Hawai'i left the decade by becoming a state in 1959. Textile design in this period followed trends on the mainland United States and shifted toward abstract design done on fine cottons. The rayon silkies of the post–World War II period that are so highly prized in the early twenty-first century had gone out of style by the end of the 1950s.

For Hawaiian women's dress, the loose, brightly patterned and often short mu'umu'u became associated with casual day wear and the holokū, with formal evening wear. The fitted holokū became the dominant style for special events in Hawai'i.

Hawaiian prints and extremely long trains were popular on holokū of the 1950s. Long sleeves and yokes, which had formerly characterized traditional holokū, became less common. Modesty became less of a concern, as women's shoulders and chests were bared for the first time since the missionaries' campaign to completely cover Hawaiian women's bodies. Backs were also exposed in the 1950s.

THE 1960s THROUGH 1975

After Hawai'i became a U.S. state, the U.S. mainland developed a fascination with Hawai'i and its material culture. President Kennedy vowed to support the U.S. fashion industry, and Jackie Kennedy wore an elegant velvet mu'umu'u by Hawaiian designer Bete. All over the United States, women wore mu'umu'u during the 1960s.

Aloha attire became commonly worn for work as well as leisure activities during this period. "Aloha Friday" was established in 1965; people began wearing aloha attire to work on Fridays. At the same time, surfers and tourists, who primarily came from the mainland United States, took Aloha shirts home, where they became a fad among young men and led to a more casual style of dress overall. California fashion companies began producing Hawaiian shirts to meet the demand. Eventually, those young men ended up in positions of power in California, and they led the adoption of "business casual" dress for work. As a consequence, "casual Fridays" began, an offshoot of Hawai'i's Aloha Fridays.

The poststatehood boom especially benefited the fashion industry, as sales nearly doubled between 1959 and 1969. Surfwear began when the fashion industry began producing a variety of swimshorts and specialized windbreakers to meet surfer's demands. The latter were called *Kona jackets*; they were made of Hawaiian prints covered with opaque nylon, which led to a faded appearance that surfers preferred. Similarly, the faded look of well-used shirts worn by surfers led to a new style of Aloha shirt favored by local men. The *reverse-print shirt* simply uses the back side of the print on the front so that the shirt looks faded. While tourists favored the bright, bold Aloha shirts, reverse prints were embraced by men in Hawai'i, particularly for wearing to work.

As assimilation continued, there was a reciprocal influence between Western fashions and aloha attire. The lines of the slender-fitting sheath of Western fashion in the late 1950s were incorporated into the Hawaiian holokū and the mu'umu'u. Like Western-styled dresses for young women, mu'umu'u were worn short and were simply designed with bold Hawaiian prints. Because holokū were now considered formal evening garments, dress fabrics such as lace, velvet, satin, and silk were used because Hawaiian prints were considered too casual.

The 1970s were characterized by casual styles in the Western world. This trend had an impact on Hawaiian apparel. Styles became more informal, shorts became acceptable as everyday wear, and cotton Aloha shirts once again were fashionable, along with

A rayon Aloha shirt from the 1950s, known as a *silky*. This kind of Hawaiian shirt was made famous in the 1950s film *From Here to Eternity*. Photograph by Linda Boynton Arthur. Courtesy of the University of Hawai'i's CTAHR Historic Costume Collection.

polyester. In spite of how warm polyester was to wear, most of the Aloha shirts of this time were made of this synthetic fabric, as were many shirts produced in the United States in this time. While design lines and styles followed Western fashion, the fabrics were uniquely Hawaiian, and prints of the type traditionally found on tapa cloth as well as tropical motifs in very bold color combinations were favored. The holokū was not fitted as closely as it had been in the previous decade, but full skirts returned to holokū design. Lower necklines and minimal sleeves again were common elements of mu'umu'u and holokū design in the mid-1970s.

THE HAWAIIAN RENAISSANCE TO 2000

The trend toward assimilation and Americanization that began after statehood slowed down, and by 1975 a new era came, one that focused on Hawaiian history. This period has been referred to as the Hawaiian Renaissance. Hawaiians came together to build the Hokule'a, a reproduction of a Polynesian double-hulled sailing canoe. It sailed throughout the southern Polynesian Islands, relying solely on the navigation methods used prior to Western contact, to retrace the early migration routes of Polynesia. This was a goodwill tour intended to reunite the Polynesian peoples, and the impact was that it brought Hawaiians together to explore their roots.

During the late 1970s, traditional Hawaiian cultural forms took a dominant position again. Lauhala hat–making had nearly died out, but it returned, and people began wearing hats with aloha attire and leis again. (Leis never went out of style.) Aloha attire from the golden years (from the late 1930s to mid-1950s) was fashionable again, too. It was not the manufacturers but rather surfers who began this fashion renaissance. They sought out vintage Aloha shirts from the territorial era, and serious collections began. Fashionable Honolulu men's stores began to stock real "antique" shirts, and when vintage shirts ran out, manufacturers then jumped on the bandwagon and began to reproduce famous Hawaiian prints on rayon and cottons once again.

Since the 1980s, the holokū has consistently reflected Hawai'i's past rather than contemporary Western or Hawaiian fashion. Design details from the turn of the century such as white fabrics, from simple cottons to lace, were commonly seen in 1980s holomu'u and holokū.

As the end of the century approached, Hawai'i became more retrospective as the state prepared for the centennial anniversary of the overthrow of the Hawaiian monarchy. Focus on Hawaiian culture led to a resurgence of turn-of-the-century designs for both holomu'u and holokū. Long sleeves and ruffles returned. Turn-of-the-century styles, with pin tucks, ruffles, high necklines, and leg-of-mutton sleeves, became favorites for both brides and flower girls.

Although casual Western dress was the most commonly worn garment type in Hawai'i by the end of the century, aloha attire was still very prominent. It was an acceptable form of dress for nearly every occasion. As a matter of fact, invitations to social gatherings of all kinds, and even funerals, would specify that the appropriate dress was aloha attire. Collectors of Aloha shirts in the United States, Japan, and Hawai'i became passionate about the shirts of the golden years and drove prices of these collectibles over the US$5,000 mark.

For Hawai'i's men who worked in white-collar jobs at the end of the century, dress shirts were irrelevant. Aloha shirts were still the choice of Hawai'i's males, and sales of the shirts were still big business. Many men wore nothing but Aloha shirts and trousers to work. Reverse-print shirts with small repeating designs were the favorite styles of Aloha shirts for Hawai'i's middle- and upper-middle-class men.

Aloha attire continued to be important for women in Hawai'i through the 1990s and to the end of the century. Mu'umu'u and holomu'u make up a large portion of the aloha attire produced in Hawai'i and offshore. They are worn by women of all ages, classes, and occupations. Hula dancers wear holomu'u regularly, but sometimes they wear holokū for specific dances. As for formal wear, holokū continue to be worn for weddings and graduations, while men continue to wear white trousers, white shirts, and red cummerbunds as had been the case throughout recent Hawaiian history. Most notably, these formal garments can be seen at Hawaiian civic affairs, such as the Holokū Ball, and for Hawaiian rituals.

While the style of the holokū has changed somewhat over time, the function of the garment as an expression of Hawaiian ethnicity has not. Similarly, the mu'umu'u has changed from an undergarment to an outergarment but remains an expression of

A cotton sateen *holomu'u*: a Hawaiian flowered dress without a train. Photograph by Linda Boynton Arthur. Courtesy of the University of Hawai'i's CTAHR Historic Costume Collection.

Hawaiian culture. Hawaiian textile artists interpret their love of the land and its culture in fabrics that, in apparel, become a most visual expression of Hawaiian values. Reverence for Hawaiian culture continues to be expressed visually in the uniquely Hawaiian garments: the holokū, mu'umu'u, Aloha shirt, and holomu'u. As long as these garments are associated with Hawaiian tradition and culture, they will continue to be worn as a symbol of the wearer's commitment to them.

The Aloha shirt has ventured way beyond the Hawaiian islands in that these prints have influenced textile design on the mainland United States and in Europe; their bright, colorful, and entertaining prints are enjoyed by people all over the world. Hawaiian prints have been copied by apparel firms in the United States and Europe for many years, and the new century was ushered in with a men's couture line by Prada that was inspired by prints from Hawai'i.

Wearing aloha attire separates the wearers from the larger U.S. society. It highlights the blending of Hawaiian and mainland U.S. culture, showing that Hawai'i celebrates its cultural uniqueness within the larger sociopolitical U.S. reality. While individual ethnicities are valued, the overriding corporate goal in Hawaiian society is to achieve ethnic harmony. The group wearing of aloha attire is a mechanism that suppresses individual ethnic differences, if only for a moment, in favor of a pan-Hawaiian ethnicity.

References and Further Reading

Adams, Wanda. "Holoku History." *Honolulu Advertiser*, 14 March 1990, B1.

Arthur, L. B. "Hawaiian Women and Dress: The Holoku as an Expression of Ethnicity." *Fashion Theory* 2, no. 3 (1998): 269–286.

Arthur, L. B. *Aloha Attire: Hawaiian Dress in the Twentieth Century.* Atglen, PA: Schiffer Books, 2000.

Arthur, L. B. "Visual Communication of Status in Hawai'i via Clothing Changes in the Post-Contact Period." *Pacific and Asian Communication Association E-Journal* 1 (2000): 1–15.

Arthur, L. B. "The Aloha Shirt and Ethnicity in Hawaii." *Textile: The Journal of Cloth and Culture* 4, no. 1 (2006): 10–34.

Brown, D., and L. B. Arthur. *The Art of the Aloha Shirt.* Honolulu: Island Heritage Publishers, 2003.

Fundaburke, Emma. *The Garment Manufacturing Industry of Hawai'i.* Honolulu: Economic Research Center, 1965.

Goodwin, Richard. "Those Elegant Years." *Paradise of the Pacific* 74 (1962): 106–123.

Hope, D., and G. Tozian. *The Aloha Shirt: Spirit of the Islands.* Portland, OR: Beyond Words Publishing, 2000.

Morgado, M. "From Kitsch to Chic; The Transformation of Hawaiian Shirt Aesthetics." *Clothing and Textiles Research Journal* 21, no. 2, 2003: 75–88.

Norwich, W. "A Shore Thing." *Men's Fashions of the Times Magazine*, New York Times Fashion Supplement, 9 March 2003, 48–50.

Linda Boynton Arthur

See also volume 7, Australia, New Zealand, and the Pacific Islands: Hawaiian Dress prior to 1898.

Middle Eastern

The dress and fashion of Middle Eastern immigrants emphasize copying, retooling, and reinterpreting traditions and developing new identities in the United States and Canada. These changes are generally influenced by their immigration background, dress design, and values of traditional and nontraditional immigrants. They also include religious values and customs as well as types, significance, and appropriateness of dress fit and design.

MIDDLE EASTERN IMMIGRANTS IN NORTH AMERICA

The Middle East is situated between Europe, Africa, and Asia. Geographical terminology can be somewhat confusing. In North America, the region is commonly called the *Middle East*. However, more correctly, such a region might be said to correspond to Southwest Asia and parts of North Africa and Central Asia. Furthermore, in North America, *Middle Easterner* is generally thought to refer to Arabs; however, Middle Eastern people are not only Arabs but also people from non-Arab nations, such as Turks, Persians, and Pakistanis. The area is considered to consist of the following countries: Armenia, Azerbaijan, Bahrain, Egypt, Georgia, Iran, Iraq, Israel, Jordan, Kuwait, Lebanon, Oman, Palestine, Qatar, Saudi Arabia, Syria, Turkey, Turkmenistan, United Arab Emirates, and Yemen. Because of some similarity in culture and religion, residents of Afghanistan and Pakistan are considered Middle Easterners by some Westerners. Because of the variety of the climates of Middle Eastern countries, this region has experienced the production of all kinds of fibers and textiles; clothes are constructed in all forms of fittings—draped, semifitted, fitted, and distorted. Middle Easterners feel at home in North America because they can find here the exact climates they were raised in.

Middle Easterners have immigrated to the United States and Canada for political, religious, social, and economic reasons. The earliest arrivals came between 1880 and 1914 from the rural areas of present-day Lebanon, Syria, Jordan, Palestine, and Israel. Neither Canada nor the United States was eager to accept non-Christian, non-European immigrants, and it was only after World War II that they were accepted more readily. After the Islamic Revolution in Iran in 1979, many Iranians—including Jews,

Christians, Muslims, and other Middle Eastern religious minorities—relocated in the Western world, especially North America. Since 11 September 2001, many Middle Eastern communities have fallen under suspicion of being associated with terrorism aimed against the Western world, and this dynamic has resulted in negative stereotypes toward people wearing what is believed to be Middle Eastern dress.

For first-generation immigrants, the most difficult challenges are to communicate within and understand their new culture while at the same time remaining attached to their own ethnicity and cultural norms. Often something that reminds them of their original homeland is used as either a home decoration or as a clothing accessory.

Most Middle Eastern immigrants in North America practice Judaism, Christianity, or Islam or some smaller religion, such as Zoroastrianism. Each of these affiliations is composed of many different sects. Some immigrants become members of nontraditional religious groups or meld in with other religious groups.

For people from the Middle East, education is a high priority. Families are very serious about their children's education. Many Middle Eastern foreign students have come to North America for higher education and stayed, gradually becoming citizens. Census data indicates that compared to other ethnic groups in the United States, Middle Eastern immigrants are relatively economically successful.

TRADITIONAL AND NONTRADITIONAL GROUPS

Dress design and its significance differs, with some immigrants maintaining traditional, conservative values and the others, nontraditional, liberal attitudes that accept change.

Dress, to most Middle Easterners, is not just trendy clothes to cover the body; rather, it deals with inner image more than the outer. Dress represents a fashion that honors the self and values of the wearer. Like a religious conviction, dress identifies the spirit, attitude, and culture of the clan in the Middle East. When the early Middle Eastern immigrants arrived in North America, they looked exotic and alien in the eye of Westerners. The older generation did not want to lose their identity and cultural honor by converting to Western philosophy and fashion.

The conservatives are those who observe their religious rules and conventional customs and follow the strict fashion dictates of their ethnicity, such as Orthodox Jews or traditional Muslims. For this group, religious rules and customs mandate certain fashions. This group does not desire to change or reform its traditions; thus, its members retain their own fashion and ethnicity. For example, the Hasidic rabbi wears a black frock coat, a round black hat, and curled sideburns; Jewish men wear the *kippah*, a small cap, to distinguish themselves as believers in Judaism. For the same reason, traditional Muslim men wear beards because *Shari'ah*, Muslim law, demands it. They believe that men's features should be naturally distinctive from women's, and Shari'ah also defines the fashion for women. Traditional Muslim women cover their hair and wear no form-fitting clothing in public.

The second group is composed of liberal Middle Easterners. The fashion of this immigrant group goes through three phases: culturation, acculturation, and in some cases deculturation.

Modern Muslim woman in the United States, wearing a head scarf with a Western jacket. Many immigrants became subject to modernization pressures relating to dress. Although they might accept the fashions of their new society, they would, however, still wear clothes in a way that linked them to their religious and cultural background. Photograph by Dr Mary H. Farahnakian.

In the first phase, the culturation period, the choice of fashion is ruled by cultural background. At their arrival, these immigrants come with the best dress they can provide for their journey. Their clothes are either sent to them by relatives from the West, or they are especially made or selected for their trip. In any case, the fashion of putting their clothes on or mixing and matching them as an ensemble indicates their ethnicity. For example, traditional Muslim men could wear a long garment (*thobe*) with pants—sometimes contrasting colors or unmatched fabrics with a headdress—or wear a regular conservative men's suit. They are generally not supposed to be cleanshaven. Muslim men usually wear silver jewelry; however, if they wear gold jewelry, they have to remove it at the time of prayer. Traditional Muslim women prefer mostly semifitted garments and cover their hair with some sort of head covering. Their religion allows them to wear any type of jewelry of expensive gold or gems. Middle Eastern immigrants often used complex textile designs and textured materials, all foreign to the eyes of Westerners.

The second phase is the acculturation or enculturation period. Because many immigrants moved to the nation's largest cities, they became subject to modernization pressures and a mixture of Eastern and Western ideas. Thus, they gradually accepted the fashions of their new society. However, they still chose clothing that somehow linked them to their ethnicity and cultural background, preferring dress of multicolored fabric and textured materials that is less tailored in fit. They often wore ethnic jewelry with Western clothes in order to satisfy their ethnic tastes.

In the third phase, these Middle Eastern immigrants gradually became permanent residents or naturalized citizens of the United States or Canada, and they are referred to as "Middle Eastern Americans" by the North American media. These new U.S. citizens seek to compromise their styles with common Western trends in order to look American. The new generations of this Middle Eastern group have melted into the pot of Western culture. The only visible distinction of their ethnicity is physical characteristics—the ethnic features and body structure, skin and hair color, and so forth. It is from this group that a new generation evolves and moves to a different level: *deculturation*, a term used to describe this particular group of fashion rebels who reject both cultures—their ancestral ethnicity as well as the style of their adopted Western culture. Instead, they create their own radical style, which does not fit into any of the previous trends. This deculturation generation deforms ethnic ideas; for instance, they use odd-shaped, uneven, and overlayered garments; contrasted and bold-colored textiles; unusual textured materials; and excessive use of jewelry and makeup, among other things. This group has created a revolutionary style based on dissimilation and formation of their own fashion as an overstatement of their style. Although Middle Eastern immigrants came with different styles from their original countries, the liberal groups adapted to Western styles quickly. However, on special occasions or for ceremonies, they may still use their original dress.

TYPES AND SIGNIFICANCE
OF DRESS FIT AND DESIGN

It is difficult to give specific patterns for Middle Eastern immigrants' dress design and preferences because they have come from different cultures at different times. These factors place them in different stages of their identities. Researcher Philip Kayal has described the clothing and the lifestyle of the second, third, and fourth generations as "typically upper-middle-class American and fashionably New York."

The first-generation (and more recent) immigrants still share some common cultural ideas in their dress design and selection of texture, surface design, color, proportion, structure, sound, jewelry, and cosmetics in their attires. They are religiously and culturally diverse in their dress fit, pattern, and silhouette. The patterns of their clothing either follow the traditional style or liberal Western trends. The Middle Eastern Christians' dress is more similar to that of Westerners. Middle Eastern traditional Muslim and Jewish dress of those who reside in North America shows greater diversity. It is commonly semifitted, less tailored, and simple in lines of pattern. A conservative Muslim man's dress, which is worn by a sheikh or imam of a mosque, consists of the long shirt or thobe and the trousers or *shalwar* (*sirwal*). The thobe is either knee or ankle length, has long sleeves, may be with or without collar, and has a buttoned-up slit to the chest in the front for going over the head. It is usually made of white cotton. It is loose so as to conceal body shape. The shalwar are usually semifitted and held to the body with a drawstring or elastic on top. They are tapered at the ankles. The circumference of the cuff is normally fourteen to eighteen inches (thirty-five to forty-five centimeters). In summer, at times, men use a shorter version of the shalwar, which is used as underwear. These trousers are also made of cotton; however, more fashionable men in this group use the regular men's trousers from department stores. They also wear a white prayer cap that fits tightly on the scalp. Conservative Muslim dress for Middle Eastern immigrant women consists of a veil and a long gown (or shorter gown to the knee) with long trousers. Muslim women are supposed to wear semifitted clothing so that the shape of their bodies is concealed, and their hair is covered by the veil. Middle Eastern traditional female dress could be adapted and purchased from regular department stores throughout North America. However, many Middle Eastern clothing and accessories stores in North America use standard sizes—small, medium, and large, or one size fits all.

TEXTURE, FABRIC SURFACE DESIGN, AND COLOR

Middle Eastern immigrants grow up in their home countries surrounded by artistic and unique designs in architecture, painting, engraving, statuary, mirror mosaic, and textiles as well as the natural beauty of their homelands. From early history, Middle Easterners were known for their variety of textured weavings and needlework, including silver- and gold-thread embroideries. Their use of a three-dimensioned textile—applying coins, mirror-work embroidery, beaded embroideries, couching, and appliqué with metallic cords, tassels, and fringe—makes their work unique. Many fashion designers after the 1970s, such as Mary McFadden in New York, have been inspired by their rich and creative textiles. Middle Eastern immigrants are interested in natural fibers for their clothing; however, for economic reasons, they have adapted their tastes to synthetic fabrics. The shine in fabric—either with metallic thread or satin weave—is also favored. In shopping, they are attracted to clothing and textiles that remind them of their cultural heritage. The fabrics are made from natural fibers or are textured or in other ways correspond to Middle Eastern tastes. The eye-catcher for them is textiles that are shiny or printed with Middle Eastern design motifs, paisleys, stripes, and so forth; or textiles with borders or that have been embroidered by hand or machine. In general, Middle Eastern textiles feature interesting surface designs bearing all these characteristics.

Middle Eastern immigrants believe in an imperative color affinity, which they follow in many aspects of their lives, including their manner of dress. They have brought this color attraction with them, and it is still symbolically strong in their everyday lives. Selecting the right color for the right occasion is very important. The ideas and the meanings of using certain colors can be divided into those that have a universal meaning among Middle Easterners and those whose meaning varies noticeably from country to country or culture to culture. For instance, white has universal meanings among Middle Easterners, symbolizing heaven, creation and resurrection, purity, and divinity. White is commonly used in the ecclesiastical clothing of all major Middle Eastern religions: Judaism, Christianity, and Islam. White is used for the Jewish *tallit* (the prayer shawl), the Christian *alb tunic* (the ecclesiastical garment), and the Muslim *kaffan* or shroud (the cloth that wraps around the deceased's body as burial clothing).

Black, another universal color, has a shared meaning among Middle Easterners, symbolizing mysticism and spirituality, as well as dignity and power; it is also the color of death and is worn for funerals. Black is the original color of Islam's first flag. It is also used as a symbol of holiness in the clerical or religious headwear of men in Judaism, Christianity, and Islam. Black is a primary color in Middle Eastern immigrant wardrobes, used in religious ceremonies as well as in cultural festivities and on formal occasions.

Blue is another universal color for Middle Eastern immigrants. It stands for trust and tolerance, divinity and calmness. In nature, blue is the color of water and sky. In Judaism, a blue thread is woven between the two tassels, *tzitzit*, and also woven in stripes of the *tallit* to empower the wearer with tolerance and patience.

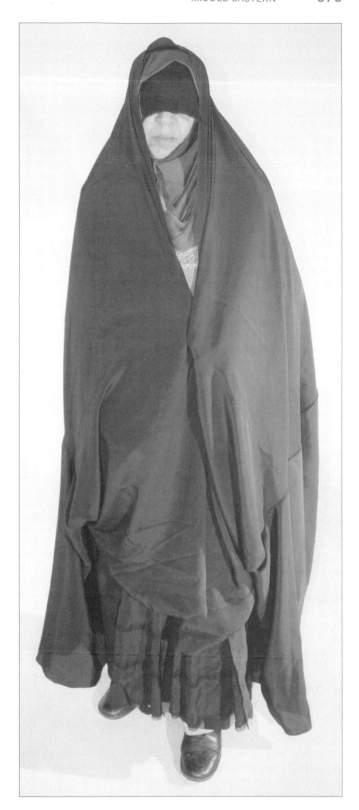

Woman wearing an *abaya*: a full-length dress with head covering. This attire would be considered suitable for public appearance by a conservative Muslim immigrant woman living in the United States in the twenty-first century. Photograph by Dr Mary H. Farahnakian.

Among the second group of colors, red has meanings that are more culturally specific rather than universal. For instance, in Christianity red means power, dignity, and remission of sin and symbolizes the sacred blood of Christ. In Hebrew the word for red is *adom*, which translates as *earth* or *adam* or *man*, and *blood*. In Judaism, *Kabbalah*, the red-string bracelet, symbolizes the connection between man and his creator. In Islam, red represents blood, command, evil, and anger. The color red is used in almost all the Islamic countries' flags. Red also represents happiness and purity. The Pakistani bride wears a red wedding dress to signify her purity and happiness.

Yellow likewise suggests different meanings for the different groups of Middle Eastern immigrants. It symbolizes the sun, gold, royalty, and grace and means "eternal" to Egyptian and Coptic Christians, whereas yellow signifies weakness, withering, childishness, caution, and even dislike among some other Middle Eastern groups, such as Persians, Palestinians, Afghans, and some Arabian cultures. Among the secondary colors, green is one of the important colors in the Islamic world. It represents the second color of Islam, after black; it means rebirth, nature, fertility, and strength. Either green or black is the color of Islam in formal Islamic attire or carries some cultural significance. Most Islamic countries have the color green in their national flags.

For Middle Eastern immigrants, wearing the appropriate color is important. For instance, in a formal funeral ceremony, it is

ill-mannered or disrespectful—to the deceased and to the memorial service—for the adult to wear red. Nevertheless, the younger Middle Eastern generation wears the most trendy clothing styles but still adhere to the appropriate colors.

On some other occasions as well, Middle Eastern immigrants, in respect for their cultural heritage, wear their traditional color for their special occasions. For example, the traditional Afghani bride wears green, which symbolizes Islamic religion and is also the sign of purity and fertility; while the groom wears white. The Indian bride wears red, and the groom wears white, both colors symbolizing purity for different genders. The Palestinian bride wears black, symbolizing divinity. After the ceremony, the brides and grooms change to Western-style wedding attire (white dress and black suit) for the reception.

Colors for nonceremonial occasions and daily wear are dependent on a number of factors: age group, patriotism, the special occasion, and relative degree of formality. The older generation of Middle Eastern immigrants, more comfortable when not noticed in the community, prefers muted and darker colors. Middle Easterners do use favorite patriotic colors for national or cultural events, such as national clothing with national colors. The best

Jewelry is an important accessory for Middle Eastern immigrant women in the United States. Traditional jewelry is sometimes worn with Western clothes. Photograph by Dr Mary H. Farahnakian.

and most colorful dress is worn for special cultural gatherings. For formal occasions it is very common to wear a black evening gown; in fact, eight out of ten women wear beaded black evening gowns for wedding receptions, parties, birthdays, concerts, and so forth. For daily wear, they prefer mixing and matching contrasting colors, but the predominant color is likely black. Middle Eastern men prefer the black suit and white shirt. Color choices for the older male generation are more conservative, preferably black or a subdued suit with a white shirt; however, the younger generation can be as trendy as Western young men. In general, black is one of the most favored colors among Middle Eastern immigrants of both genders, because it complements their dark skin tone and black hair. Shiny colors, also very popular among Middle Easterners, come in a textile surface design, used as a solid or accent in clothing.

DRESS ACCESSORIES AND COSMETICS

Most Middle Eastern immigrant women can be distinguished by their vivid use of makeup and the accessories they wear. Women own expensive jewelry, especially gold. Traditionally women receive gold jewelry from their close relatives on special occasions, such as weddings or giving birth to a child. Women are proud of their jewelry and use much of it to blend in with their attire. They do not mind if the jewelry makes noises and jingles as they move, because the sound has its own charm and attraction. In both Hebrew and Muslim traditions, some different types of amulets are believed to have supernatural protective power. The *hamsa* (*hamesh*), a stylized hand, protects against envy or the evil eye. Sometimes pieces of jewelry such as coins, jeweled buttons, or other objects are sewn to the garments as closures or embellishments. Jewelry may be used to join and shape the other pieces of accessories, such as scarf pins, scarf rings, *hijab* (veil) clips, and pins. Liberal Middle Eastern immigrant men wear multiple rings, necklaces, bracelets, watches, and so forth; however, according to Shari'ah, it is recommended that Muslim men not wear gold jewelry, especially during prayer. Conservative Muslim men wear silver or white-gold jewelry instead. Usually, the jewelry that the conservatives choose have symbolic values in their beliefs. One of the most common hand accessories for men is the rosary, or *tasbeeh*, which is sometimes made of semiprecious gems. Clothing accessories are widely accepted among Middle Eastern immigrants; for instance, Muslim women wear a veil as part of hijab, or Jewish women wear a wig as a form of modesty. There are other commonly worn items of dress, such as caps, scarves, gloves, false sleeves or arm covers, and shawls.

Muslim men have limited clothing accessories. These include different headdresses such as the *fez* or the Islamic head scarf known variously as the *shimagh, kuffie,* or *kaffiyeh* that is made in a black-and-white or black-and-red checked weave of cotton, wool, or silk. Black heavy cording, the *eqal,* holds the shimagh in place. The *kufi* is a white prayer cap, and a loose cloak, the *aba,* which is worn over the thobe, is an overall coat or cape for men.

Middle Eastern women love vivid makeup and use perfume. It is still common to use rosewater as a perfume and to put perfume on clothes, because it lingers on the wardrobe. In the early twenty-first century, although immigrants spend money on expensive designer cosmetics, they still import and use some ethnic cosmetic products such as *kohl* or *sormeh,* the black eyeliner; henna for skin and hair coloring; oiled perfume; and hair- and skin-care products called *seddr* and *katira.* In Middle Eastern culture, beauty marks or small tattoos are still used for beautification; likewise, ear and nose piercing are cultural customs and are still used by some Middle Eastern immigrants of both genders. Middle Eastern immigrants care about their personal hygiene, according to their religious law.

BLENDING IN OR STANDING OUT

Negative public perceptions after the 11 September event have discouraged many Middle Easterners from being known as Muslim and also from being recognized by their ethnicity, so they act as if they are not from the Middle East. For example, Iranians call themselves *Persians;* they wear a necklace of Farvahar, symbol of the Zoroasterian God, or a big cross, the symbol of Christianity. Middle Eastern names have been changed legally to common Western names.

Fearful of revealing their identity, many have also changed their Middle Eastern Muslim appearance, such as men sporting much less facial hair—modest beards and mustaches—or girls and women adopting fashionable Western clothing design, fabrics, and colors. On the other hand, many North Americans of Middle Eastern heritage use their religious clothing as a political statement. Although they are cautious not to be misjudged as terrorists, they support their beliefs by using some related clothing, such as veils for women and the Palestinian scarf, the kaffiyeh, as symbols of religious freedom in North America.

Although people from the Middle East have some common values and similarities, when they are brought under scrutiny as a group, they are, in fact, revealed to be quite diverse in religion, culture, politics, and ethnicity. For the same reason, it is very difficult to give a certain image or description of appearance for the North American people from the Middle East. In general, religious and secular rules require modesty, simplicity, and grace for both genders; however, the North American–born mostly mix with the larger society of the country in which they live.

CEREMONIAL DRESS

Middle Eastern culture holds many unique traditions that require different attires. Middle Eastern immigrants, like those of other cultures, struggle to hold tight to their traditions, wishing to feel at home in the Western world. The performance of any kind of ceremonial occasions reflects a diversity of Middle Eastern ethnicities. One of the most common occasions in which dress becomes important is the wedding ceremony, which usually consists of two parts: the ritual services and the reception. However, the adoption of many Western materials as replacements is common. For example, in place of a traditional green silk Afghani wedding dress, unless a dress is custom-made, a dress of a similar style, color, and texture may be purchased from a Western department store; it is embellished to the taste of the bride's family and becomes a compromise of Western style and a traditional style. Each of the Middle Eastern cultures and religions has its own way of performing the ritual and cultural services of wedding ceremonies. In general, the wedding ceremony is a major phenomenon: huge, elaborate, and colorful, an unforgettable experience and a significant event for Middle Eastern families living in North America.

Commonly, in Middle Eastern culture, the male is a dominant character; therefore, the groom is not only responsible for the wedding ring—he also chooses and pays for the wedding dress, along with all the necessary accessories for the bridal attire. The groom will bring the wedding dress to the bride on the wedding day. The details of this ceremony—the wedding dress delivery and so on—are performed differently by the various Middle Eastern groups, and each group determines how seriously they follow traditions. Usually, all expenses for the ceremony and the reception are paid by the groom; the bride's family pays for the bedding, furniture, and other household accommodations. The modern bride usually chooses the common white bridal dress for the reception; however, for the religious, ceremonial part, the brides might use an ethnic, traditional bridal dress. For example, as previously mentioned, Afghani brides wear a green wedding dress, which might be elaborated with trims and embellishments; Pakistani brides wear traditional red wedding dresses; and Palestinian brides wear a black wedding dress with colorful embroideries and flourishes of gold and silver trimmings. Nonetheless, in recent days, both parties decide how they want to arrange their wedding.

Religion has influenced the choice of people's attire throughout history. In this section, the different sects of a religion are grouped together and are discussed by their major clothing styles. In Middle Eastern culture, religious values for men, women, and children are significant. When Middle Easterners—Christians, Jews, and Muslims—arrived in North America, the Christians fit most easily into the Western culture, but Orthodox Jews and traditional Muslims were obviously identified by their religious ethnicity and by their dress ensembles. Before World War I, Arabs living under the Ottoman Empire were isolated from the West, not only in terms of distance but also culturally. Because of these differences, even their everyday clothing, such as a prayer cap and hijab, identified them with their religious beliefs. However, some religious clothing and accessories that Middle Eastern immigrants use for religious services might be adopted and inspired by other clerical costumes. For instance, according to a major work on Jewish dress by historian Alfred Rubens, the Jewish rabbinical robes are inspired by the black Geneva gown—adapted to a black silk or polyester frock coat, the *bekishe*—and the white bands of the Calvinist or Reformed Church, while the round black hat, the kippah or *kippot*, was adopted in Austria and Germany during the nineteenth century from similar headgear worn by Greek Orthodox clergy.

Traditional Muslim clerical attire is categorized in four clothing groups. The first is *body wear*: the aforementioned inner garment or thobe; the main garment, *rada* or *radae*, an ankle-length, long-sleeved coat made of a subdued-colored wool, linen, or cotton, tailored with a high collar and buttoned in front with slits at either side; and the external cloak (aba), usually made of black or dark-colored wool for winter and black or white sheer linen for summer wear. The second is *headwear*: the *kufi*, or prayer cap; the Islamic turban, *amameh* or *amaama*, a long, narrow scarf that wraps in several layers around the head and over the scalp cap, usually made of black, white, or green for clerical wear and in other colors for informal wear. Black and green define the wearer as a descendant of the prophet Mohammed; white represents that wearers are not descendents of the Prophet but have graduated from an Islamic clerical school. The *kaffiyeh*, the Islamic scarf for men (which is named and pronounced variously, including *kufiya*, *chifiya*, or *topee*), is also used as headgear at prayer. Women similarly use a veil for prayer and when in the presence of males other than their husband, father, brothers, and uncles. The third is *footwear*: The regular conservative male shoe is commonly worn. The fourth is *accessories*:

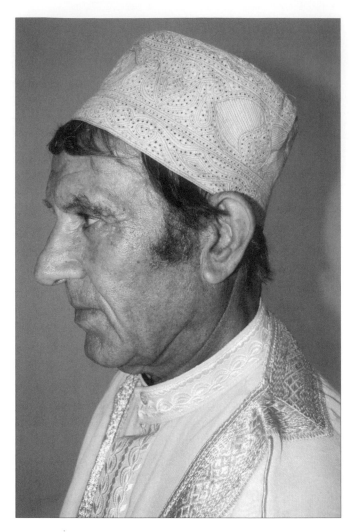

The *kufi* (Muslim prayer cap). As Middle Eastern immigrants settled in North America, they remained loyal to their original identity by holding on to their faith and culture. Photograph by Dr Mary H. Farahnakian.

According to Muslim religious law, men are not supposed to wear gold while praying; tasbeeh are used as hand accessories; the head scarf, *gutra kaffiyeh* or *shemagh*, is the symbol of resistance; and the igal, the black band, holds the scarf on the head.

As Middle Eastern immigrants have settled in North America, they have remained loyal to their original identity by holding on to their faith and culture. Depending on what they believed, they wore small souvenirs or religious symbols from their homelands. These signs and symbols—applied conspicuously or inconspicuously—were significant and meaningful to wearers. Sometimes these emblems, such as the Christian cross, Hebrew *Megan* or Star of David, and Muslim Allah motif, serve as a spiritual influence and represent religious beliefs.

For example, the *kohan*, the Jewish high priest, wears a long white robe with a white shawl and the Breastplate of Judgment, the ornament that hangs on his chest and represents the twelve tribes of Israel. A Catholic high priest wears fully symbolic attire, such as his robe or headdress, all representing his ordination to leadership. Likewise, the Muslim imam distinguishes himself with the attire of a Muslim clerical robe, *rada*, an *aba*, and a *turban*. The religious attire, interpreted as being divinely ordained, offers the religious leaders spiritual authority to guide.

FASHION AND THE MEDIA

The new technologies of the media are novel phenomena in human history. People around the globe have been touched by the magical world of electronic media. No longer limited to broadcasting TV programs with imperfect reception, the new multimedia technology offers hundreds of brilliant channels, almost unlimited digital videos, digital cell phones, DVDs, and Internet programs. Fashion shows, which used to be limited to twice or three times yearly, are now on the runway of the fashion channel twenty-four hours daily.

North Americans of Middle Eastern heritage have been touched by the magic wand of technology, which brings them to the cutting edge of trends and fashion. One of the most significant changes has been the introduction of trends in dress through multimedia and improvement in North America satellite television, so that what is shown is influential in not only North America but throughout the world. Because of this closeness between fashion and the media, contemporary trends will most likely be a major influence on the dress of the younger generations of Middle Eastern North Americans.

References and Further Readings

Alterman, Jon B. "It Comes of Age in the Middle East." *Foreign Service Journal* (December 2005): 36–42.

Boosahda, Elizabeth. *Arab-American Faces and Voices: The Origins of an Immigrant Community.* Austin: University of Texas Press, 2003.

Cohen, Yinon, and Andrea Tyree. "Palestinian and Jewish Israeli Born Immigrants in the United States." *International Migration Review* 28, no. 2 (Summer 1994): 243–255.

Haddad, Yvonne Yazbeck. "Inventing and Re-Inventing Arab American Identity." In *A Community of Many Worlds*, edited by Kathleen Benson and Philip M. Kayal, 109–123. New York: Syracuse University Press, 2002.

Kayal, Philip M. "Who Are We? Who Am I?" In *A Community of Many Worlds*, edited by Kathleen Benson and Philip M. Kayal, 90–106. New York: Syracuse University Press, 2002.

Kopp, Hollie. "Dress and Diversity: Muslim Women and Islamic Dress in an Immigrant/Minority Context." *The Muslim World* (Spring 2002): 59–79.

Lindisfarne-Tapper, Nancy, and Bruce Ingham, eds. *Language of Dress in the Middle East.* Surrey, UK: Curzon, 1997.

Marvasti, Amir, and Karyn D. McKinney. *Middle Eastern Lives in America.* Lanham, MD: Rowman & Littlefield, 2004.

Rubens, Alfred. *A History of Jewish Costume.* London: Vallentine, Mitchell, 1967.

Waugh, Earle H., Sharon McIrvin Abu-Laban, and Regula Burckhardt Qureshi, eds. *Muslim Families in North America.* Edmonton: University of Alberta Press, 1991.

Mary H. Farahnakian

See also Snapshot: Identity and Gender in Traditional Jewish Dress; Asian American.

Index

Italic numbers denote reference to illustrations.